# CHILD AND ADOLESCENT DEVELOPMENT

## A CHRONOLOGICAL APPROACH

# THE DEVELOPMENTAL STORY

## Accessible and Engaging: Tying Theory and Practice Together

**INFANCY (AGES 0–2) PART THREE**

### PHYSICAL DEVELOPMENT 5

**1** Each chapter begins with an engaging vignette and
**2** a reminder of the recurring five **"Key Themes"** or big-picture questions that developmental psychologists seek to answer.

**2** **KEY THEMES in Physical Development**

**NATURE & NURTURE** How do nature and nurture interact in physical development in infancy?

**SOCIOCULTURAL INFLUENCE** How does the sociocultural context influence physical development in infancy?

**CONTINUITY/DISCONTINUITY** Is physical development during infancy continuous or discontinuous?

**INTERACTION AMONG DOMAINS** How does physical development during infancy interact with other domains of development?

**RISK/RESILIENCE** What factors promote risk or resilience in physical development during infancy?

**3** **Research Applied to Parenting/Education, Atypical Development,** and **Controversy: Thinking It Over** features bring the study of child development to life and encourage students to think critically about the everyday applications of research.

**1** **M**arc knew he had to dress the baby quickly. It had been a hectic morning. His wife's car hadn't started, and they had to arrange for her to get a ride to work. Now he and their three-month-old daughter, Abbie, had to step up the pace to get to daycare. Marc hastily pulled out a sweatshirt and pants from the baby's dresser, grateful that Abbie was in a good mood and didn't seem to mind the rapid tempo of the morning's routine. "Here you go, honey. Let's get these pants on you. Here are your pants from Aunt Rose. Bloooie pants!" Abbie responded with a gleeful smile and a few kicks. But as he lifted the waistband over Abbie's diaper, he could see that he had a problem. Worn only once before, these pants now barely covered the middle of Abbie's little calf. "Well, little girl, you sure look funny like that. We're going to have to start all over again." Looking at the picture of a younger, newborn Abbie that stood on the dresser, he couldn't help but notice the remarkable changes that his daughter had gone through in only three short months.

149

---

**4** ### CONTEXTS OF DEVELOPMENT 16

**4** **Contexts of Development** chapters discuss development issues in the broader context of family, peers, and the community at large.

# Student-Centered Approach

**A range of study and review tools are available in every chapter.**

*Emotional Expression in Infancy* Even infants only a few days or weeks old are capable of producing the facial expressions associated with several emotions, including interest, distress, disgust, joy, sadness, anger, and surprise (Field et al., 1982; Izard, 1978; Izard et al., 1995). By seven months of age, the infant has added expressions of fear to his repertoire (Izard et al., 1980). The fact that these discrete facial expressions appear so early in infancy, before much learning can have taken place, provides strong support for the idea that emotional expressions are to some extent biologically determined. These emotions are often called **basic (or primary) emotions**.

Although even the earliest displays of basic emotions are usually readily recognized by adults, their form and the conditions that elicit them may change over the first few months. Two important emotional expressions in infancy, smiling and crying, demonstrate these changes. The smile is one of the most captivating and irresistible infant behaviors. In the newborn this behavior occurs primarily during the state of REM sleep, when dreaming is thought to occur, in bursts of several smiles in succession (Emde & Koenig, 1969). The mouth stretches sideways and up, producing a simple

**KEY THEME**
NATURE & NURTURE

**5 basic (primary) emotion** Emotion, such as joy, sadness, or surprise, that appears early in infancy and seems to have a biological foundation.

## 5 Marginal Glossary
Key terms are defined on appropriate pages within the chapter.

---

490   PART FIVE ■ CHAPTER 13 Contexts o

## 6 CHAPTER RECAP

### Summary of Developmental Themes

**SOCIOCULTURAL INFLUENCE**

**How do sociocultural factors influence the contexts of development in middle childhood?**
Culture has been shown to influence parenting demands, especially in the degree to which children are expected to be compliant and helpful in order to help the family survive.

**RISK/RESILIENCE**

**What contextual factors promote risk or resilience in middle childhood?**
Divorce and single parenthood can put children at risk, but the practice of effective parenting overrides the effects

that these variations in family structure might have. Children can be at risk for negative developmental outcomes if they experience poor peer relationships. However, research has identified several ways in which success with peers can be promoted. For example, fostering prosocial behaviors, good social skills, and effective social-information processing can help children in their interactions with peers. Certain characteristics of schools can promote or discourage academic achievement. Children thrive when they experience smooth transitions to school, have small classes, and interact with teachers who encourage autonomy and initiative.

### Chapter Review

**THE FAMILY IN MIDDLE CHILDHOOD**

**In what ways do parenting strategies vary across different cultural groups?**
Cultures vary in the degree to which children must contribute to the family's subsistence, do chores, and obey their parents. In some cultures, parents demand a very high degree of compliance, whereas in others, the emphasis in parent-child interactions is sociability.

Assistance with sources of stress, such as help with child care and counseling, can be helpful in alleviating some of the stresses that single parents face.

**What does the research indicate about the impact of having gay or lesbian parents?**

### KEY TERMS AND CONCEPTS

collaborative learning (p. 477)

cooperative learning (p. 477)

cultural compatibility hypothesis (p. 478)

sociometric nomination (p. 459)

sociometric rating scale (p. 459)

## 6 Chapter Recap
Appearing at the end of each chapter, the Chapter Recap includes:

- a **Summary of Developmental Themes**
- a general **Chapter Review**
- a **Key Terms and Concepts** list reinforcing important takeaways from the chapter.

---

## 7 PATHWAYS: CONNECTING THE STORY OF DEVELOPMENT

| | INFANCY (0–2 YEARS) | EARLY CHILDHOOD (2–6 YEARS) |
|---|---|---|
| **Physical Development** | • Evidences rapid gains in height and weight, with faster rates of growth in the head region and regions nearer the center of the body<br>• Shows period of rapid brain development, including formation and pruning of synapses<br>• Shows basic learning capabilities in the form of habituation, operant and classical conditioning, and imitation<br>• Shows improvements in visual accommodation, saccadic movements, acuity, and vergence<br>• Attracted first to external features of objects and to movement, and later to internal features of objects<br>• Localizes sounds<br>• Recognizes melodic rhythms and other features of music<br>• Shows sensitivity to smells, tastes, and tactile stimuli | • Shows advances in gross motor skills such as running, jumping, and skipping<br>• Evidences slower but regular increases in size<br>• Shows evidence of implicit learning |
| **Cognitive/ Language Development** | • Attends to increasingly complex patterns including those with facelike organization<br>• Responsive to biological motion<br>• Shows signs of depth perception<br>• Shows intermodal perception<br>• Develops *means-ends* behavior<br>• Attains the *object concept*<br>• Shows sensitivity to changes in number<br>• Relies on egocentric and landmark cues to locate objects<br>• Classifies objects according to physical similarities, as well as thematic and simple taxonomic relations<br>• Distinguishes between animate and inanimate objects<br>• Shows recognition memory for simple stimuli | • Shows gains in ability to make perceptual discriminations<br>• Can classify according to basic-level concepts<br>• Understands the meaning of simple number terms, and eventually the basic principles of counting<br>• Displays good intuitions about mathematical operations such as addition and forming fractions<br>• Uses landmark cues to negotiate spatial environments<br>• Uses geometric cues to aid spatial location<br>• Begins to be able to read maps<br>• Realizes that others can have different visual perspectives<br>• Develops a *theory of mind*<br>• Shows elementary planning activities<br>• Displays knowledge of scripts |

## 7 Pathways: The Development Story
Appearing at the end of the infancy, early childhood, middle childhood, and adolescence chapters, this chart provides an at-a-glance summary of the physical, cognitive, and socioemotional milestones across development.

# Learning and Teaching Resources

## FOR STUDENTS

### Student Study Guide
This print guide includes many resources for practice and review including learning objectives, chapter reviews, key terms, and multiple-choice questions.

### Online Study Center
The textbook website includes study aids such as ace quizzes, interactive flashcards, tutorials, and animations. Additionally, it offers critical thinking practice through the **What Do You Think?** and **See for Yourself** features.

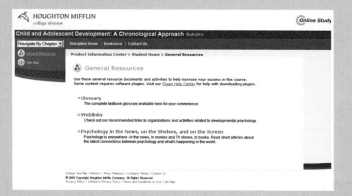

### Student CD-ROM
For self-study and practice, this CD-ROM offers video clips, overviews, animations, quizzing, and glossary terms.

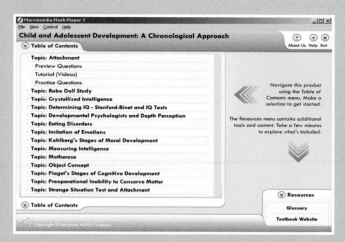

## FOR INSTRUCTORS

### Online Teaching Center
This instructor website offers many tools including PowerPoint presentations, Classroom Response Systems (clickers), art and tables from the textbook, and a downloadable *Instructor's Resource Manual.*

### Blackboard®/WebCT®
These courses allow instructors to utilize, customize, and administer all instructor resources developed specifically for this text.

### HM Testing
HM Testing (powered by Diploma) is a flexible test-editing program with a comprehensive grade-book function for easy administration and tracking. The test bank includes over 1,600 multiple-choice questions and 80 essay questions keyed to learning objectives.

### Child Development Psych in Film
Contains twelve clips from Universal Studio films illustrating concepts in developmental psychology such as cognitive development, moral reasoning, parenting styles, and adolescent development. Clips from films like *Parenthood, Snow Falling on Cedars, Sixteen Candles,* and many others are combined with commentary and discussion questions.

# CHILD AND ADOLESCENT DEVELOPMENT

## A CHRONOLOGICAL APPROACH

### DANUTA BUKATKO

COLLEGE OF THE HOLY CROSS

HOUGHTON MIFFLIN COMPANY    BOSTON   NEW YORK

*For my mother, Valentina,*
*who believes that all children should have the chance to shine brightly*

*Executive Publisher:* George Hoffman
*Sponsoring Editor:* Jane Potter
*Marketing Manager:* Amy Whitaker
*Marketing Assistant:* Samantha Abrams
*Senior Development Editor:* Rita Lombard
*Editorial Associate:* Henry Cheek
*Senior Project Editor:* Aileen Mason
*Editorial Assistant:* Andrew Laskey
*Senior Art and Design Coordinator:* Jill Haber Atkins
*Cover Design Director:* Tony Saizon
*Senior Photo Editor:* Jannifer Meyer Dare
*Composition Buyer:* Chuck Dutton
*New Title Project Manager:* James Lonergan

Cover image: Nease Studio/Fullerton, CA

Printed in the U.S.A.

Library of Congress Control Number: 2003109905

Instructor's exam copy:
ISBN-10: 0-618-83395-1
ISBN-13: 978-0-618-83395-5

For orders, use student text ISBNs:
ISBN-10: 0-618-34920-0
ISBN-13: 978-0-618-34920-3

1 2 3 4 5 6 7 8 9-DOW-11 10 09 08 07

# Brief Contents

# FEATURES

# CONTENTS

## 13 CONTEXTS OF DEVELOPMENT .............................................448

## 14 PHYSICAL AND COGNITIVE DEVELOPMENT ...........................495

# PREFACE

Most of us who teach a course in child development know that we tend to fall into one of two camps: those who teach the course from a topical perspective, treating each content area in development as a discrete entity, and those who teach a chronologically-based course, following children's growth from one age to the next. There are a lot of reasons for taking one approach versus the other, some of which may be driven by the particular teaching philosophies of the instructor, and some of which may be motivated by the needs of the students enrolled in our courses. I myself had always been a "topical" person, believing that describing language, or cognitive, or emotional development was better done in one focused stream, unbroken by interruptions about other developments also taking place at a given age. What I learned from writing this book is that there is distinct and genuine value in telling the story of development chronologically. The various content areas of development—the biological, cognitive, and socioemotional spheres—do, after all, interact with each other during each phase of the child's growth. What better way to appreciate that fact than to consider them together in the context of a particular chronological time period? Perhaps even more important, considering child development from a chronological perspective exposes the possibility that certain developmental tasks might be more important at some times than others. Indeed, the challenges mastered by the toddler are very much different from those faced by a preadolescent. Such potentially significant concepts might be overlooked if one's focus is solely on a topic rather than a developmental time period.

Regardless of which tactic the instructor takes—topical or chronological—many of the issues in teaching are similar. How do we get our students to learn so much material? How can we help them to make sense of the vast storehouse of information that keeps accumulating in our journals and books? Are there some themes or concepts that seem especially important for our students to appreciate above all others, and most important, to remember once they leave our courses? These were the very questions that motivated the first topical child development book Marvin Daehler and I co-authored almost twenty years ago, and they remained the issues that concerned me when I began this chronological text. Our answer to these dilemmas for the topical text was to organize the book around a set of fundamental themes or recurring questions. I believe that using a small set of organizing themes helps to frame the "big picture" for a chronological text as well.

There are several other considerations that are also important to me as an author. As a teacher, I have always been committed to helping students think scientifically about developmental psychology. Part of that process means that students should reflect on how the theories and data that comprise the field of developmental psychology challenge or affirm any intuitions they may have about children. It also means that students need to develop a critical stance toward what they read. Throughout their learning, students should also appreciate the historically important knowledge base upon which contemporary developmental psychology has been built. My commitments to these principles are reflected here in several ways: relying heavily on theories and empirical studies in telling the story of child development, encouraging students to think about competing ideas, and attempting to provide a balance of classic studies in developmental psychology with recent findings from the research literature.

Finally, I am deeply committed to the idea that knowledge gained from science can have important implications for the way we parent, teach, and create social policy pertaining to children. My students seem to insist on this principle, and judging from various movements to link research to practice among researchers, there is growing momentum to do precisely this in the field of psychology. I sincerely hope readers will find that this textbook helps them in their work with children, whatever form that may take.

## ■ A CHRONOLOGICAL APPROACH

Childhood is divided in this textbook into four major periods: infancy (birth to 2 years), early childhood (2 to 6 years), middle childhood (6 to 11 years), and adolescence (12 to 18 years). These seemed to be the natural ways in which to partition the first eighteen years of life given children's major accomplishments and the circumstances in which they develop. Within each time frame, the child's attainments in the physical, cognitive, and socioemotional domains are discussed along with the forces that seem to be responsible for them. In addition, for each time frame beyond infancy, I have included a chapter on the context of development in recognition of the fact that as they mature, children find themselves in different social, cultural, and educational situations, and are thus subject to new and powerful influences.

## ■ KEY THEMES

The following five themes are highlighted throughout the discussion of child development:

### Nature & Nurture

• How do nature and nurture interact in development?

### Sociocultural Influence

• How does the sociocultural context influence development?

### Continuity/Discontinuity

- Is development continuous or discontinuous?

### Interaction Among Domains

- How do the various domains of development interact?

### Risk/Resilience

- What factors promote risk or resilience in development?

By drawing out these themes, I hope that readers are stimulated to think about the process of development, or why development proceeds as it does. These **Key Themes** are designed to help students discern the importance and interrelatedness of various facts, and as vehicles for instructors to encourage critical analysis among students. In addition, some of the themes—**Risk/Resilience**, in particular—may help students to appreciate the ramifications of theory and research for applied issues such as parenting practices, education, and social policy for children.

Within each chapter, some or all of the five developmental themes serve to organize and provide coherence for the material. The themes are highlighted for students in several ways.

1. The themes most immediately relevant to a chapter are listed at its start.

2. Indicators in the margins of the chapter point to discussions of each key theme.

3. Each chapter closes with a brief synopsis of how the key themes are illustrated in the domain explored by the chapter.

Students and instructors may, of course, find additional instances of the five themes. They may also locate new and additional themes. This process is certainly in keeping with the goal of setting in motion a search on the part of readers for integration and coherence in the vast material that constitutes the scientific study of child development.

### ■ FEATURES AND STUDY TOOLS

The chapter outlines, **For Your Review** lists (bulleted recaps at the end of major sections), margin and end-of-text glossaries, and **Chapter Recap** (including a **Summary of Developmental Themes,** a general **Chapter Review,** and a **Key Terms and Concepts** list) all serve to underscore important themes, terms, and concepts. I hope that students will actively utilize these aids to reinforce what they have learned in the chapter body. In addition, several strategies are intended to make the material in this text more accessible to students: vignettes to open the chapter, the Research Applied to Parenting/Education feature, the liberal use of examples throughout the text, and an extensive program of illustrations accompanied by instructive captions.

## Research Applied to Parenting/Education

Designed to identify some of the implications of research that extend beyond the laboratory, this feature is intended to help students think about questions and concerns that typically affect parents and teachers in their interactions with children. The **Research Applied to Parenting/Education** feature addresses such topics as the steps parents might take to reduce the risk of sudden infant death syndrome and the strategies teachers might follow to promote gender equity in the classroom. Each topic covered in this feature is introduced with a continuation of the chapter-opening vignette and is followed by a set of points that, based on our current knowledge, leads to positive consequences for children and their development. These points, of course, should not be considered the final word on the subject, but they will help readers to understand how research has led to practical benefits for children, parents, and teachers. For a complete list of topics covered in this feature, see page viii.

## Atypical Development

By including an **Atypical Development** feature within each chapter, I hope to emphasize that the same processes that help to explain normal development can also help us understand development that is different from the norm. The reverse applies as well: that understanding atypical development can illuminate the factors that guide more typical child development. Thus, such topics as attention deficit hyperactivity disorder, autism, and language impairment are included in this feature. A complete list of topics appears on page viii.

## Controversy: Thinking It Over

**Controversy: Thinking It Over** boxes continue to serve as the foundation for debate and extended discussion in the classroom. They are organized in a three-question framework to better promote critical thinking and a deeper appreciation of all sides of a theoretical debate:

1. What Is the Controversy?

2. What Are the Opposing Arguments?

3. What Answers Exist/What Questions Remain?

A complete list of topics appears on page viii.

## Pathways Charts

Appearing at the end of the infancy, early childhood, middle childhood, and adolescence chapters, these charts provide an at-a-glance summary of the physical, cognitive, and socio-emotional milestones across development. The adolescence **Pathways** collects all the charts in one place, providing a complete and convenient reference and review tool.

## ■ TEACHING AND LEARNING SUPPORT PACKAGE

Many useful materials have been developed to support the study of *Child and Adolescent Development* and enhance the teaching and learning experience.

# For the Instructor

### Instructor's Resource Manual

The *Instructor's Resource Manual*, written by Lora Harpster, Salt Lake Community College, contains a complete set of chapter outlines and learning objectives, as well as lecture topics, classroom exercises, demonstrations, and handouts. It also features recommended readings, videos, and Internet sites.

### Test Bank

The *Test Bank*, written by Ashley E. Murphy, University of Minnesota, includes over 1,600 multiple-choice items. Each is accompanied by a key that provides the learning objective, the text page number on which the answer can be found, type of question (Fact, Concept, or Application), and correct answer. To encourage students to think critically, we include a set of essay questions in each chapter (over 80 in the entire test bank).

### HM Testing CD-ROM

*HM Testing* (powered by Diploma) is a flexible testing program that allows instructors to create, edit, customize, and deliver multiple types of tests via print, network server, or the web on either Macintosh or Windows platforms. The test bank contains over 1,600 multiple-choice and 80 essay questions. The test bank Word files are also included on the CD-ROM for easy reference.

### PowerPoint Presentations

A comprehensive set of *PowerPoint Presentations* accompanies this text and consists of lecture sequences, tables, and figures from the main text. The slides are available on the *Online Teaching Center*.

### Classroom Response System

*Classroom Response System (CRS)* content, available on the *Online Teaching Center*, allows instructors to perform "on-the-spot" assessments, deliver quick quizzes, gauge students' understanding of a particular question or concept, conduct anonymous polling for class discussion purposes, and take their class roster easily. Students receive immediate feedback on how well they understand concepts covered in the text and where they need to improve. Answer slides provide the correct answer and explanation of why the answer is correct.

### Online Teaching Center

The *Online Teaching Center* is a comprehensive gallery of online resources that provides one central place to access all teaching preparation tools. It includes the complete *Instructor's Resource Manual, PowerPoint Presentations*, CRS content, video guides, downloadable PDFs of the overhead transparencies, and selected art from the textbook. It can be found by following the links at **college. hmco.com/pic/bukatkoCAD1e.**

### Content for Course Management Software

*Blackboard* and *WebCT* course cartridges are available, allowing instructors to use text-specific material to create an online course on their own campus course management system. The cartridges feature all of the content described on the *Online Teaching* and *Study Centers* as well as *HM Testing*.

### Developmental Psych in Film DVD

This DVD contains twelve clips from Universal Studio films, illustrating concepts in developmental psychology such as cognitive development, moral reasoning, parenting styles, and adolescent development. Clips from films such as *Parenthood, Snow Falling on Cedars, Sixteen Candles*, and many others are combined with commentary and discussion questions to help bring developmental psychology alive for students and demonstrate its relevance to contemporary life and culture. Teaching tips are correlated to specific text chapters and concepts on the *Online Teaching Center*.

### Lecture Starter Video and Guide

The *Lecture Starter Video* contains a series of high-interest, concise segments that instructors can use to begin a class meeting or change to a new topic. The accompanying guide briefly describes each segment, indicates concepts that can be addressed using each segment, and offers suggestions on how to use each segment.

### Online Teaching Tools

Links to useful and practical information on online teaching tools can be found on the *Child and Adolescent Development* website, including a link to useful print resources such as *Teaching Online: A Practical Guide* (0-618-00042-9).

# For the Student

### Student CD-ROM

This brand new CD-ROM comes packaged with the textbook and contains videos and animations illustrating key concepts and classic and contemporary studies in child development (such as eating disorders and the Bobo doll study). It also offers supportive pedagogy that helps students test their comprehension of these key concepts.

### Study Guide

The *Study Guide*, written by Karen L. Yanowitz, Arkansas State University, contains the same set of learning objectives that appear in the *Instructor's Resource Manual* and the *Test Bank*. Each chapter also contains a detailed study outline, a key terms section, and a self-quiz consisting of thirty multiple-choice questions. An answer key tells students not only which response is correct but also why each of the other choices is incorrect.

## Online Study Center

The student website contains study aids such as self-tests (Ace Quizzes), flashcards, chapter outlines, learning objectives, and **See For Yourself** and **What Do You Think?** activities. All web resources are keyed to the textbook and can be found by following the links at **college.hmco.com/pic/bukatkoCAD1e.**

## Child Development in Context: Voices and Perspectives

The innovative reader *Child Development in Context: Voices and Perspectives*, by David N. Sattler, Geoffrey P. Kramer, Virginia Shabatay, and Douglas A. Bernstein, features personal narratives taken from popular and literary authors covering concepts, issues, and topics related to child development. Concept guides, critical-thinking questions, and research questions promote analysis of the articles. Featured authors include Brian Hall, Anne Lamott, Frank McCourt, Annie Dillard, Russell Baker, Richard Rodriguez, and Nora Ephron.

## ■ ACKNOWLEDGMENTS

My students at Holy Cross continue to serve as the primary inspiration for my work on this text. They often come to courses on child development with a genuine concern for the well-being of children. Many have jobs or do volunteer work with children, and often they plan on careers in pediatrics, child psychology, social work, speech and language pathology, education, or other fields involving children. Their need to know about how to make a difference with children continues to underlie my motivation as a teacher and an author.

I would also like to thank Holy Cross for providing the resources and the time to work on a project such as this one. A sabbatical leave, a dedicated staff, and technical assistance are just a few of the practical things Holy Cross was able to offer by way of support and I am very grateful.

I want to especially acknowledge the contributions of Marvin Daehler at the University of Massachusetts to the content of this text. Marv wrote the earlier versions of some of the chapters that appear in this book, and although I take full responsibility for any shortcomings that may be reflected here, Marv deserves thanks for providing a solid base upon which I was able to build.

I appreciate the insightful comments and criticisms provided by the reviewers of this text. Their classroom experiences have provided a broader perspective than my own, and this book becomes stronger because of their valued input. I would like to express thanks to the following reviewers:

Kristine Anthis, *Southern Connecticut State University*

Kate Byerwalter, *Grand Rapids Community College*

Donna Gray, *Irvine Valley College*

June Millovich, *Saddleback College*

John Prange, *Irvine Valley College*

Penny Skemp, *Mira Costa College*

Dennis Thompson, *Georgia State University*

Laura Walker, *Brigham Young University*

Several members of the Houghton Mifflin team deserve my sincerest thanks. I use the word "team" because this project has truly been a cooperative effort. Jane Potter, sponsoring editor, has shown exceptional enthusiasm and support for this project, as well as an array of fresh ideas about how to deliver an appealing and high quality text. Rita Lombard, senior development editor, has continued to be a friend and coach *par excellence,* infusing this project with her expert and insightful guidance. Her creativity is especially evident in many places in this book from the design elements to the special features. Aileen Mason, senior project editor, has overseen the production of this text with the greatest of patience as well as all of the attention to details that is required by a project of this scope. Ann Schroeder and Maria Sas did an outstanding job of capturing visually the concepts being conveyed in the photos and artwork. Thanks go to Henry Rachlin, designer, who gave this text a wonderful vibrant look; and to Sue Gleason, Lisa Goodman, and Sandra Cannon for their comprehensive copyediting, proofreading, and indexing; and to Lynne Blaszak, senior media producer, Dustin Brandt associate media producer, and Carolyn Nichols, senior editor, for their creative input into the technology resources accompanying the text. Special thanks to Amy Whitaker, marketing manager, and Sam Abrams, marketing assistant, who have provided unfailing support in their efforts to promote the text. I appreciate very much all of their outstanding contributions.

Lastly, I would like to thank my husband and son, Don and Nick, for their patience, encouragement, and unconditional support.

*Danuta Bukatko*

# THEMES AND THEORIES

1

**A**ndrew had spent an enormous amount of time carefully aligning the beams, braces, and other equipment at just the right locations on his building project. It looked great! He was fascinated by how he could make the crane swing up and down, and how it would lift and drop the small metal pieces with the magnet. But six-year-old Andrew was so absorbed in his play that he failed to notice his one-year-old sister, Heather, rapidly crawling toward these shiny, eye-catching objects. Benjamin, at fourteen, was the oldest child in the family and had been placed in charge of watching both Andrew and Heather as their parents prepared dinner in the kitchen. Unfortunately, he had also become distracted by the challenging new computer game he had just borrowed from his friend.

As she crawled within reach of Andrew's construction set, Heather grabbed the truck on which the crane was mounted and pulled it sharply, pitching beams, equipment, and everything else into a chaotic heap. For one brief instant, Andrew froze in horror as he observed the devastation his little sister had just wrought.

1

Then came the almost reflexive, inevitable shriek at the top of his lungs: "HEATHER! GET OUTTA HERE!" as he simultaneously swung his arm in Heather's direction in an uncontrollable burst of emotion. Andrew's shout was more than enough to produce a wail from Heather, but the sting across her back from Andrew's hand didn't help, either. Benjamin, startled by the uproar, anticipated the melee about to begin and raced to the kitchen, knowing full well that his mother and father were the only ones who would be able to reinstate tranquility after this unfortunate exchange between his little brother and sister.

A lthough the specifics may be very different, this type of exchange between siblings is probably not uncommon in families and households around the world. And it serves to introduce some of the issues central to this book. For example, consider the developmental differences displayed by Heather, Andrew, and Benjamin during this interaction. Heather, only one year of age, does not move about or handle objects in the same way as her older siblings. Perhaps even more important, Heather seems to have very little appreciation for the consequences her impulsive reach might have on both Andrew and the construction set. Her six-year-old brother displays far greater physical dexterity and more sophisticated planning and thinking about the toys that are part of his play. Andrew also has excellent verbal skills with which to express his thoughts and emotions, although he still has some difficulty regulating the latter. Yet Andrew's reasoning about his world pales in comparison with that of his older brother, Benjamin, who is captivated by a complex computer game. Moreover, at the age of fourteen, Benjamin has been given increased responsibility, such as looking after both younger siblings. Although he is not always as careful and conscientious in this task as his mother and father might like, his parents feel reasonably assured that, if things are not going well, Benjamin knows where to seek assistance.

Children undergo enormous changes in motor, cognitive, social, and emotional capabilities as they progress from birth through adolescence. Our goal in this book is to describe and try to explain those changes.

How did these enormous developmental differences come about? That is a primary question addressed in this book. But there are other matters of interest in the sequence of events described here. How should their parents now deal with the conflict in order to bring about peace between Heather and Andrew? How would you? How should his parents respond to the angry outburst from Andrew? How might they have encouraged Benjamin to take his baby-sitting responsibilities more seriously?

When we think about trying to understand how children develop and become competent individuals in interactions with one another and their physical environment, common sense seems like the place to start. For generations, common sense provided the parenting wisdom by which caregivers understood and reared children. For example, when Heather, Andrew, and Benjamin could not get along with one another, their parents often spanked the child whom they thought might be at fault. They followed a commonly accepted approach to dealing with conflict, a method that seems to be shared in many cultures. As an illustration, among the proverbs expressed by the Ovambo of southwest Africa is the saying, "A cranky child has not been spanked," and Korean parents may say, "Treat the child you love with the rod; treat the child you hate with another cake." Proverbs like these, which promote physical discipline for children, can be found in many cultures around the world (for instance, see Palacios, 1996).

Although common sense is extremely important in child rearing, in some circumstances it may yield unexpected and perhaps even undesirable consequences. For example, is physical punishment the best way to prevent unacceptable behaviors in children? Caregivers in many societies believe spanking is an effective method of dealing with angry outbursts like that displayed by Andrew. However, researchers have found that the children of parents who routinely resort to physical punishment often initiate more aggressive acts than do the children of parents who rely on alternative methods of disciplining undesirable conduct (Bandura & Walters, 1959; Dodge, Pettit, & Bates, 1994). This relationship has been observed in Native American (McCord, 1977) and British working-class homes (Farrington, 1991), as well as in families in the United States, Australia, Finland, Poland, and Israel (Eron, Huesmann, & Zelli, 1991). In other words, under some circumstances, physical punishment appears to encourage rather than discourage aggressive actions and may escalate into increasingly coercive interactions between parent and child. Thus the commonsense practice of disciplining by physical punishment, a practice supported by various cultural proverbs and recommendations, may need to be examined more closely. This is precisely the point at which the need for the scientific study of children and their development enters.

## WHAT IS DEVELOPMENT?

**D**evelopment, as we use the term, means all the physical and psychological changes a human being undergoes in a lifetime, from the moment of conception until death. The study of human development is, above all, the study of change (Overton, 2006). From the very moment of birth, changes are swift and impressive. Within a few short months, the newborn who looked so helpless (we will see that the true state of affairs is otherwise) comes to control his or her own body, to locomote, and to master simple tasks, such as self-feeding. In the years that follow, the child begins to understand and speak a language, engages in more and more complex thinking, displays a distinct personality, and develops the skills necessary to interact with other people as part of a social network. The range and complexity of every young person's achievements in the first two decades of life can only be called extraordinary.

One of the goals of this book is to give you an overview of the most significant changes in behavior and thinking processes that occur in this time span. In the pages

**development** Physical and psychological changes in the individual over a lifetime.

that follow, we *describe* the growing child's accomplishments in many domains of development. For example, we detail the basic physical and mental capabilities in infants and children and examine the social and emotional skills children acquire as they reach out to form relationships with their family members, peers, and others. We tell this story from a chronological perspective, starting with the amazing capabilities and achievements of *infancy* (from birth to two years), and moving through the important developmental accomplishments of *early childhood* (about two to six years), *middle childhood* (about six to eleven years), and *adolescence* (about twelve to eighteen years).

A second important goal is to help you appreciate just why children develop in the specific ways they do. In other words, we also try to *explain* developmental outcomes in children. How do the genetic blueprints inherited from parents shape the growing child? What is the role of the environment? How does the society or culture in which the child lives influence development? Does the child play a passive or an active role in his or her own development? We are repeatedly concerned with some other questions about development. Do the changes that take place occur gradually or suddenly? Do all children follow a common developmental pathway, and if not, what factors explain these individual differences? And how do the many facets of development influence one another? As you may imagine, although we often seek simple answers to these questions, they are neither simple nor always obvious (Horowitz, 2000).

**Developmental psychology** is the discipline concerned with the scientific study of changes in human behaviors and mental activities as they occur over a lifetime. *Developmental psychologists* rely on research to learn about growth and change in children. This approach has its limitations: researchers have not studied every important aspect of child development, and sometimes studies do not point to clear, unambiguous answers about the nature of development. Indeed, psychologists often disagree on the conclusions they draw from a given set of data. Nonetheless, scientific fact-finding has the advantage of being verifiable and is also more objective and systematic than personal interpretations of children's behavior. As you read about development in the chapters that follow, the controversies as well as the unequivocal conclusions, try to use them to sharpen your own skills of critical analysis.

An essential ingredient of the scientific process is the construction of a **theory**, a set of ideas or propositions that helps to organize or explain observable phenomena. More than a personal opinion or casual hypothesis, a scientific theory is firmly grounded in the information collected by researchers. For many students, theories seem far less interesting than the vast assortment of intellectual, linguistic, social, physical, and other behaviors and capabilities that undergo change with time. However, by describing children's accomplishments in a systematic, integrated way, theories *organize* or make sense of the enormous amount of information researchers have gleaned. Theories of development also help to *explain* our observations. Is your neighbor's little boy shy because he inherited this trait, or did his social experiences encourage him to become this way? Did your niece's precocious mathematical skills develop from her experience with her home computer, or does she just have a natural flair for numbers? Was Andrew's angry reaction to his baby sister a biological response or something he had learned? Psychologists are interested in understanding the factors that contribute to the emergence of behavioral skills and capacities, and their theories are ways of articulating ideas about what causes various behaviors to develop in individual children.

A good theory goes beyond description and explanation, however. It leads to *predictions* about behavior, predictions that are clear and easily tested. If shyness results from social experiences, for example, the withdrawn four-year-old should profit from a training program that teaches social skills. If, on the other hand, shyness is a stable, unchangeable personality trait, even extensive training in sociability may have very little impact. Explaining and predicting behavior are not only gratifying but also essential for translating ideas into applications—creating meaningful

**developmental psychology** Systematic and scientific study of changes in human behaviors and mental activities over time.

**theory** Set of ideas or propositions that helps to organize or explain observable phenomena.

**social policy** Programs and plans established by local, regional, or national public and private organizations and agencies designed to achieve a particular social purpose or goal.

programs and ways to assist parents, teachers, and others who work to enhance and promote the development of children. For example, when a theory proposes that adults are an important source of imitative learning and that parents who display aggressive behavior provide a model for responding to a frustrating situation, we can begin to understand why common proverbs like "Spare the rod and spoil the child" sometimes need to be reevaluated.

The knowledge that developmental psychologists acquire through their research can also address many concerns about social policy. **Social policies** are programs and plans established by local, regional, or national organizations and agencies. These are often government programs, but businesses, private foundations, and other groups attempt to implement social policies that are designed to achieve a particular purpose with respect to the members of a society as well. The goals of many of these policies are geared toward alleviating social problems. Social policies may, for example, be concerned with increasing the effectiveness of education for children, improving their health, reducing teenage pregnancy, eliminating child abuse, reducing low birth weight and infant deaths, preventing young people from smoking cigarettes, encouraging parents to enforce the use of seat belts, promoting self-esteem, and a host of other goals. Research can help identify social problems that limit or interfere with children's development and can assist policymakers in establishing programs to reduce or eliminate the factors that hinder psychological health and competence in children. At the same time, research may shed further light on the mechanisms and processes that underlie behavior. You will have the opportunity to consider many social policies that bear on children in the chapters that follow.

In this chapter, our discussion focuses on several broad theories, and some of their historical antecedents, which have influenced explanations of children's behavior. No single theory is sufficient to provide a full explanation of all behavior. Some theories strive to make sense of intellectual and cognitive development; others focus on social, emotional, personality, or some other aspect of development. Theories also vary in the extent to which they present formalized, testable ideas. Thus some are more useful than others in providing explanations for behavior that can be rigorously evaluated. And they often disagree in their answers to the fundamental questions of development. Before we examine specific theories, let's consider a cluster of basic questions that all theories of development must address.

## F O R ◆ Y O U R ◆ R E V I E W

◆ What is development?

◆ What is developmental psychology?

◆ What role do theories play in the scientific process?

◆ What role does developmental psychology play in the formation of social policy?

## FIVE MAJOR THEMES IN DEVELOPMENTAL PSYCHOLOGY

As you read about different aspects of child development—language acquisition, peer relationships, motor skills, emergence of self-worth, and many others—you will find that certain questions about development surface again and again. We call these questions *themes in development*. Various theories provide different answers to these questions. Good theories, grounded in careful research, help us to think about and understand these major themes. What are these key questions?

## HOW DO NATURE AND NURTURE INTERACT IN DEVELOPMENT?

We have all heard expressions like "He inherited a good set of genes" or "She had a great upbringing" to explain some trait or behavior. These explanations offer two very different answers to a basic question that has, since the beginnings of psychology, fueled a controversy among theorists, which continues to rage even today. Dubbed the **nature-nurture debate**, the dispute centers on whether the child's development is the result of genetic endowment or environmental influences.

Do children typically crawl at nine months and walk at twelve months of age as part of some inborn, unfolding program or because they have learned these motor responses? Do they readily acquire language because their environment demands it or because they are genetically predisposed to do so? Are boys more aggressive than girls because of cultural conditioning or biological factors? In some areas, such as the development of intelligence and the emergence of gender roles, the debate over nature versus nurture has been particularly heated.

Why all the uproar about such a question? One reason is that the answer has major implications for children's developmental outcomes, for parenting practices, for the organization of schooling, and for other practical applications concerning research. If, for example, experiments support the view that intelligence is guided largely by heredity, providing children with rich learning experiences may have minimal impact on their eventual levels of intellectual skill. If, on the other hand, research and theory more convincingly show that intellectual development is shaped primarily by environmental events, it becomes vital to provide children with experiences designed to optimize their intellectual growth. Answers to this type of question are likely to have an impact on social policy by affecting how funds are allocated to health, educational, and many other programs.

Psychologists now recognize that both nature and nurture are essential to all aspects of behavior and that these two forces combine to mold what the child becomes. Thus the controversy has shifted away from identifying *which* of these two factors is critical in any given situation. Instead, the question is *how* heredity and environment *interact* to fashion the behaviors we see in children and eventually in adults.

There is an important implication in this idea that nature and nurture are intimately interwoven: *children are active players in the process of development.* That active role may be evident at two different levels. The first begins with certain attributes and qualities that children possess and exhibit, perhaps because of inborn qualities of personality or behavioral style. By virtue of being placid or active, fearful or curious, children elicit reactions from others. Thus children are not simply passive recipients of the environment or blank slates on which it writes. Their own capacities and efforts to become immersed in, to get "mixed up" with, their physical and social world often modify what happens to them and can affect their development in profound ways. A second, perhaps more fundamental, way in which children contribute to their own development is through actively constructing and organizing ways of thinking, feeling, and communicating to assist them in making sense of their world. Children formulate these conceptualizations to help them respond to and understand the rich array of physical and social events they experience.

## HOW DOES THE SOCIOCULTURAL CONTEXT INFLUENCE DEVELOPMENT?

Development is influenced by more than just the immediate environment of the family. Children grow up within a larger social community: the *sociocultural context.* The sociocultural context includes unique customs, values, and beliefs about the proper way to rear children and the ultimate goals for their development. Think back to your family and the cultural standards and values that determined how you were reared. Were you allowed to be assertive and speak your mind, or were you

**nature-nurture debate**  Ongoing theoretical controversy over whether development is the result of the child's genetic endowment or environmental influences.

Children grow up in many different cultures and social settings. This Malaysian American family, celebrating the Chinese New Year at their home in San Francisco, has adopted some customs and values from American culture, yet maintained many traditions and practices brought with them from their native country. Various sociocultural contexts provide the backdrop in which specific parenting practices are carried out. Researchers must consider these different kinds of experiences to fully understand development.

expected to be compliant toward adults and never challenge them? Were you encouraged to fend for yourself, or were caregivers, relatives, and even cultural institutions, such as the school, church, or some other agency, expected to assist with your needs throughout childhood, adolescence, and perhaps even into your early adult years? How was your development affected by your family's economic status and educational attainments? by your gender and ethnic identity?

Sociocultural factors affect everything from the kinds of child-rearing practices parents engage in to the level of health care and education children receive; they affect, for example, children's physical well-being, social standing, sense of self-esteem, "personality," and emotional expressiveness. As you explore the various domains of development, you will come to appreciate that many developmental outcomes are heavily influenced by the sociocultural context.

## IS DEVELOPMENT CONTINUOUS OR DISCONTINUOUS?

Everyone agrees that children's behaviors and abilities change, sometimes in dramatic ways. However, there is less consensus on how best to explain these changes. On the one hand, development can be viewed as a *continuous* process in which new attainments in thinking, language, and social behavior are characterized by gradual, steady, small, *quantitative* advances. For example, substantial progress in reasoning or problem solving may stem from the ability to remember more and more pieces of information. Or, as neural coordination and muscle strength gradually increase, the infant may advance from crawling to walking—a progression that, by anyone's account, has substantial consequences for both child and caregiver. Thus, even though at two given points in time the child's ability to think or locomote may look very different, the transformation may arise from gradual, quantitative improvements in the speed, efficiency, or strength with which mental or physical processes are carried out, rather than from a dramatic reorganization of some underlying capacity.

Alternatively, some theories see development as *discontinuous*. They explain development in terms of the child's progress through a series of **stages**, or periods during which innovative developmental accomplishments abruptly surface, presumably because some fundamental reorganizations in thinking or other capacities underlying behavior have taken place. In this view, development undergoes rapid transitions as one stage ends and a new one begins, followed by relatively stable periods during which the child's behaviors and abilities change very little (see Figure 1.1). Abrupt or

**stage** Developmental period during which the organization of thought and behavior is qualitatively different from that of an earlier or later period.

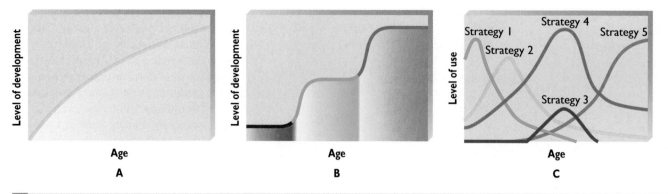

## △ FIGURE 1.1

### Development as a Continuous Versus a Discontinuous Process

Children display many changes in their abilities and behaviors throughout development. According to some, the best way to explain these changes is in terms of the gradual acquisition of the structures and processes that underlie growth (A). Others believe that development undergoes a series of stagelike transformations during which underlying structures and processes exhibit rapid reorganization followed by a period of relative stability (B). However, other approaches suggest that, at any given time, children may exhibit multiple ways of demonstrating some ability or capacity, as is evident in the "overlapping waves" (Siegler, 1998) depiction of development (C). According to this view, the ability or capacity displayed by children will depend on a variety of situational and developmental factors.

rapid changes resulting in a dramatic reorganization in how children perceive, think, feel, or behave are interpreted as *qualitative* advances in development. From this perspective, children establish new ways of thinking—for instance, during the early school years—that change problem solving, moral judgment, interactions with peers, and other activities. In adolescence they move to yet another level of thinking that influences these various domains of behavior in still different ways.

When we try to discern if development is continuous or discontinuous, it is important to remember that there is considerable variability in individual children's skills that can complicate how we decide between these two points of view. Many ways of behaving and thinking are available to children at any given time. Which one will be expressed depends on a variety of circumstances. Robert Siegler (1996, 1998) has suggested that different strategies or ways of responding can best be described as "overlapping waves," because they often coexist in the child's repertoire. Some methods of responding may be exhibited more frequently at younger ages and others at older ages. Although some strategies may be lost as the child gains more experience and as others are freshly formulated, at any particular time children are likely to be able to use several competing approaches for responding to a situation. For example, when young children demonstrate the ability to add two numbers, say 4 plus 3, they may do so using several different strategies, such as counting from 1, counting beginning with the larger of the pair of numbers, comparing the problem to another whose answer is already known, or directly retrieving the information from memory. Which specific strategy is employed will depend on how much experience the child has had with the problem, how familiar he or she is with each of the numbers, how quickly the answer must be determined, and how much effort is required to carry out the strategy, among other things. Thus to conclude that a child has moved into a stage or phase in which he or she is able to carry out addition profoundly underestimates the variety of competencies he or she can draw on to demonstrate that capacity.

Few, if any, aspects of human growth appear to mimic the dramatic transformations found in the life cycle of an insect as it changes from egg to larva to pupa and finally to adult—periods in which a stable physical organization is followed by rapid reorganization and emergence of a new point in the life cycle. Yet, over the months and years, children do become quite different. Whether these changes are best understood as quantitative or qualitative advances are points of frequent disagreement among theories of development.

An important developmental theme is that the various domains of development interact with each other. For example, children who interact with each other as they work at a computer are not only enhancing their social skills, but also advancing their thinking abilities.

## HOW DO THE VARIOUS DOMAINS OF DEVELOPMENT INTERACT?

Many times the child's development in one domain will have a direct bearing on her attainments in other domains. Consider just one example: how a child's physical growth might influence her social and emotional development. A child who has become taller than her peers may experience very different interactions with adults and peers than a child who is small for his age. The taller child might be given more responsibilities by a teacher or be asked by peers to lead the group more frequently. These opportunities may instill a sense of worth and offer occasions to practice social skills that are less frequently available to the smaller child. As these social skills are exercised and become more refined and advanced, the taller child may receive still more opportunities that promote social and even cognitive development. Our ultimate aim is to understand the child as a whole individual, not just as someone who undergoes, for example, physical, perceptual, emotional, cognitive, or social development. To do so, we must keep in mind that no single component of development unfolds in isolation from the rest.

## WHAT FACTORS PROMOTE RISK OR RESILIENCE IN DEVELOPMENT?

Human development may proceed along many different paths and at quite different rates from one individual to another. One especially important reason that differences emerge is that individual children are exposed to various kinds and levels of benefits and risks during their development. For example, *risk* may be a consequence of genetic or biological complications, as well as rearing or cultural events, that promote development in less than optimal ways. An accidental head injury; exposure to a disease, such as AIDS; being reared by an abusive parent; experiencing parents' divorce; attending an unstimulating daycare center; or exposure to the devastating consequences of war are just a few of the many factors that can affect the course of development and may limit healthy progress. Individual children, because of their genetic or biological makeup, or because of other resources available in their environment, respond to these risks in different ways. *Resilient* children, those who seem able to most effectively resist the negative consequences of risk, tend to have a constellation of individual qualities that include a relatively relaxed, self-confident character that permits them to adapt and to respond intelligently in difficult situations and circumstances. In addition, they are likely to have the benefits of a close, encouraging relationship with at least one member of their family and with others beyond the family, such as a teacher or close

▷ **FIGURE 1.2**

**Five Major Themes in Developmental Psychology**

Throughout this book, we repeatedly consider these themes and the ways developmental psychologists attempt to answer these questions. Charts like this one will appear in every chapter.

## Key Themes in Development

■ **Nature & Nurture**
How do nature and nurture interact in development?

■ **Sociocultural Influence**
How does the sociocultural context influence development?

■ **Continuity/Discontinuity**
Is development continuous or discontinuous?

■ **Interaction Among Domains**
How do the various domains of development interact?

■ **Risk/Resilience**
What factors promote risk or resilience in development?

friend, through their membership in some supportive agency or organization, such as a club or church (Luthar, Cicchetti, & Becker, 2000; Masten & Coatsworth, 1998; Runyan et al., 1998; Rutter, 1990; Werner, 1995).

Several points about risk and resilience are important to note. First, most researchers recognize that, when children are said to be at risk, it is usually not because of a single factor, such as poverty, exposure to disease, or attendance at a school with few resources. Rather, risk factors tend to occur in clusters. Thus understanding child development requires an awareness of the many layers of influence that have an impact on children's lives, from family settings, to neighborhoods, to the larger society (Sameroff, 2005). Second, some researchers feel that the term *resilience* should be restricted to instances in which children are able to overcome some adversity, and that other terms (such as *promotive factors* or *assets*) are more appropriate when we are describing positive factors in development, regardless of risk (Wright & Masten, 2005). Finally, a discussion of risk and resilience usually has strong implications for interventions that might improve the lives of children who experience hardship. Thus these topics are of special interest to developmental psychologists involved in education, clinical issues, and other applied fields.

In the discussions that follow concerning various historical contributions to developmental psychology and the major theoretical approaches still important in the field today, it will be apparent that answers pertaining to the themes often differ. These five developmental themes, summarized in Figure 1.2, will have an important influence on our discussion of developmental psychology throughout this book. Perhaps one of the best ways to review them is to take a few minutes to consider your stand on each of the themes.

## F O R ◆ Y O U R ◆ R E V I E W

◆ Can you think of ways that nature and nurture might interact in the process of child development? Can you think of examples of how children play active roles in their own development?

◆ How and to what extent do you feel that society's concerns, values, and resources affect an individual's development?

◆ Do you find it easier to understand development in terms of continuous or discontinuous, stagelike change?

◆ To what extent do you think advances or difficulties in one domain affect the child's development in other domains?

◆ Can you think of examples of factors that might put children's development at risk?

# THE STUDY OF THE CHILD: HISTORICAL PERSPECTIVES

H uman development became a focus of serious study comparatively late in the history of science, having its origins only a little over one hundred years ago. Despite its relatively short history, however, developmental psychology has grown at an astonishing rate in the last several decades and is a thriving modern-day field of study. Each year hundreds of books and thousands of articles about children's growth are published for professionals interested in specific theoretical issues and for parents or teachers. Scientists and laypersons, however, have not always had such a focused and conscious desire to understand the process of child development. In fact, societal attitudes toward childhood as a concept have shifted considerably over the last several centuries.

## THE CONCEPT OF CHILDHOOD

Contemporary society views childhood as a separate, distinct, and unique period, a special time when individuals are to be protected, nurtured, loved, and kept free of most adult responsibilities and obligations. Child labor laws try to ensure that children are not abused in the work world, and the institution of public education signals a willingness to devote significant resources to their academic training. But childhood was not always viewed in this way (Borstelmann, 1983).

***Children in Medieval and Renaissance Times*** From the Middle Ages through premodern times, European society's attitudes toward children differed strikingly from those of our contemporary society. Although their basic needs to be fed and clothed were tended to, children were not coddled or protected in the same way infants in our society are. As soon as they were physically able, usually at age seven or so, children were incorporated into the adult world of work; they harvested grain, learned craft skills, and otherwise contributed to the local economy. In medieval times, Western European children did not have special clothes, toys, or games. Once they were old enough to shed swaddling clothes, they wore adult fashions and pursued adult pastimes, such as archery, chess, and even gambling (Ariès, 1962).

In certain respects, however, premodern European society regarded children as vulnerable, fragile, and unable to assume the full responsibilities of adulthood. Medical writings alluded to the special illnesses of young children, and laws prohibited marriages of children under age twelve (Kroll, 1977). Religious movements of this era proclaimed the innocence of children and urged that they be educated. Children's souls, as well as adults', must be saved, said clerics, and they held that parents were morally responsible for their children's spiritual well-being. Parents recognized that children were also a financial responsibility and helped them set up their own households as they approached adulthood and marriage (Pollock, 1983; Shahar, 1990). Thus, even though medieval children were incorporated quickly into the adult world, they were recognized both as different from adults and as possessing special needs.

A noticeable shift in attitudes toward children occurred in Europe during the sixteenth century. In 1545 English physician and lawyer Thomas Phayre published the first book on pediatrics. In addition, the advent of the printing press during that century made possible the wide distribution of other manuals on the care of infants and children. The first grammar schools were established to educate upper-class boys in economics and politics. Upper-class girls attended convent schools or received private instruction intended to cultivate modesty

In many regions of the world, children spend much of their time engaged in physical labor. This girl, helping to harvest rice in Cambodia, very likely had little opportunity to learn to read or write. Historically, and in some cultures yet today, attitudes about childhood differ greatly from those held in recent times in most Western societies.

In premodern Europe, children often dressed like adults and participated in many adult activities. At the same time, though, children were seen as fragile and in need of protection.

and obedience, as well as other skills thought to be useful in their future roles as wives and mothers (Shahar, 1990).

Probably one of the most significant social changes occurred as a result of the transition from agrarian to trade-based economies in the sixteenth and seventeenth centuries, and the subsequent growth of industrialization in the eighteenth century. As people relocated from farms to towns and as the production of goods shifted outside the home, the primary role of the family in Western society changed from ensuring economic survival to the nurturing of children (Hareven, 1985). Closeness and emotional attachment increasingly became the hallmarks of parent-child relations.

**The Age of Enlightenment** The impact of these sweeping social changes was consolidated by the writings of several key thinkers who shaped the popular understanding of childhood. In the seventeenth and eighteenth centuries, two philosophers proposed important but distinctly different ideas about the nature and education of children. In his famous treatise *An Essay Concerning Human Understanding* (1961), originally published in 1690, the British philosopher John Locke (1632–1704) described his views on the acquisition of human knowledge. Virtually no information is inborn, according to Locke. The newborn's mind is a *tabula rasa*, literally a "blank slate," on which perceptual experiences are imprinted. Locke's philosophy of **empiricism**, the idea that environmental experiences shape the individual, foreshadowed the modern-day psychological school of behaviorism. Locke believed that rewards and punishments from others, imitation, and the associations the child forms between stimuli are key elements in the formation of the mind.

In a second work, *Some Thoughts Concerning Education* (1693/1964), Locke expounded further on his philosophy of training children:

> The great mistake I have observed in people's breeding their children … is that the mind has not been made obedient to discipline and pliant to reason when it was most tender, most easy to be bowed. … He that is not used to submit his will to the reason of others when he is young, will scarce hearken to submit to his own reason when he is of an age to make use of it.

Locke further argued in support of the importance of early experiences and proper training but also that child rearing and education should proceed through the use of reason rather than harsh discipline. In his view, parents must find a balance between being overly indulgent and overly restrictive as they manage their child's behavior. As we will see, many of these same themes resound in contemporary research on good parenting and represent a contrast to the strict disciplinary stance of Western society before the eighteenth century.

The second influential philosopher of the Enlightenment was Jean Jacques Rousseau (1712–1778), a French thinker who embraced the ideal of the child as a "noble savage." According to Rousseau, children are born with a propensity to act on impulses, but not necessarily with the aim of wrongdoing. They require the gentle guidance of adult authority to bring their natural instincts and tendencies in line with the social order. In *Émile* (1762/1895), Rousseau set forth these beliefs about child rearing:

> Never command him to do anything whatever, not the least thing in the world. Never allow him even to imagine that you assume to have any authority over him. Let him know merely that he is weak and that you are strong; that by virtue of his condition and your own he is necessarily at your mercy.

**empiricism** Theory that environmental experiences shape the individual; more specifically, that all knowledge is derived from sensory experiences.

... Do not give your scholar any sort of verbal lesson, for he is to be taught only by experience. Inflict on him no species of punishment, for he does not know what it is to be in fault.

Rousseau emphasized the dynamic relationship between the curious and energetic child and the demands of his or her social environment as represented by adults. Adults should not stifle the child's natural development and spirit through domination. Contemporary theories that acknowledge the active role of the child in the process of development have distinct roots in Rousseau's writings.

Rousseau also advanced some radical ideas about education. Children, he held, should not be forced to learn by rote the vast amounts of information that adults perceive as important. Instead, teachers should capitalize on the natural curiosity of children and allow them to discover on their own the myriad facts and phenomena that make up the world. Rousseau's ideas on the nature of education would be incorporated in the twentieth-century writings of Jean Piaget.

Both Locke and Rousseau emphasized the notion of the child as a developing, as opposed to a static, being. Both challenged the supposition that children are merely passive subjects of adult authority, and both advanced the idea that children should be treated with reason and respect. Having been elevated by the efforts of these worthy thinkers to an object of intellectual interest, the child was now ready to become the subject of scientific study.

## THE ORIGINS OF DEVELOPMENTAL PSYCHOLOGY

By the mid- to late 1800s, scholars in the natural sciences, especially biology, saw in the study of children an opportunity to support their emerging theories about the origins of human beings and their behaviors. Charles Darwin, for example, hypothesized that the similarities between the behaviors of humans and those of other species were the result of common evolutionary ancestors. Similarly, Wilhelm Preyer, another biologist, was initially interested in the physiology of embryological development but soon extended his investigations to behavioral development after birth. In the United States and Europe, key researchers who participated in the birth of psychology as an academic discipline also began to show an interest in studying children. By the beginning of the twentieth century, developmental psychology was established as a legitimate area of psychological inquiry.

**The Baby Biographers: Charles Darwin and Wilhelm Preyer** One of the first records of the close scrutiny of a child for the purpose of scientific understanding comes from the writings of Charles Darwin. Eager to uncover important clues about the origins of the human species, Darwin undertook to record in great detail his infant son's behaviors during the first three years of life. Darwin documented the presence of early reflexes, such as sucking, as well as the emergence of voluntary motor movements, language, and emotions, such as fear, anger, and affection. When he saw similarities, he linked the behaviors of the young child to those of other species, such as when, for example, he concluded that the infant's comprehension of simple words was not unlike the ability of "lower animals" to understand words spoken by humans (Darwin, 1877).

In 1882 the German biologist Wilhelm Preyer published *The Mind of the Child* (1882/1888–1889), a work that described in great detail the development of his son Axel during the first three years of life. Preyer wrote meticulously of his son's sensory development, motor accomplishments, language production, and memory, even noting indications of an emerging concept of self. Although Preyer followed in the footsteps of several previous "baby biographers," including Darwin, he was the first to insist that observations of children be conducted systematically, recorded immediately and unobtrusively, and repeated several times each day. By advocating the application of scientific techniques to the study of children, the baby biographers,

Preyer in particular, set in motion the beginnings of the child development movement in the United States.

### G. Stanley Hall: The Founder of Modern Child Psychology

The psychologist perhaps most responsible for launching the new discipline of child study in the United States was G. Stanley Hall, who, in 1878, became the first American to obtain a Ph.D. in psychology. Hall is also known for founding the first psychological journal in the United States in 1887 and, in 1891, the first journal of developmental psychology, *Pedagogical Seminary* (now called the *The Journal of Genetic Psychology*). In addition, he founded and served as the first president of the American Psychological Association (APA).

As the first American to study in Europe with the pioneer psychologist Wilhelm Wundt, G. Stanley Hall returned to the United States in 1880 with an interest in studying the "content of children's minds." Adopting the questionnaire method he had learned about in Germany, he had teachers ask about 200 kindergarten-age children questions like "Have you ever seen a cow?" or "What are bricks made of?" The percentages of children who gave particular answers were tabulated, and comparisons were made between the responses of boys and girls, city children and country children, and children of different ethnic backgrounds (Hall, 1891). For the first time, researchers were collecting data to compare groups of children, in contrast to previous approaches that had emphasized the detailed examination of individual children.

### Alfred Binet: The Study of Individual Differences

The French psychologist Alfred Binet is known primarily as the developer of the first formal assessment scale of intelligence. Binet was a pioneer in the study of **individual differences**, those unique characteristics that distinguish one person from others in the larger group.

Binet's original interest lay in the general features of children's thinking, including memory and reasoning about numbers. To that end, he closely scrutinized the behaviors of his two daughters as they progressed from toddlerhood to the teenage years. He noted, in particular, how one daughter, Madeleine, was serious and reflective as she tried to solve problems, whereas the other daughter, Alice, was more impulsive and temperamental (Fancher, 1998). His studies of children's thinking had two significant outcomes: first, they demonstrated that a description of individual differences contributed to the understanding of human development, and second, they provided the basis for more formal tests of children's mental abilities (Cairns & Cairns, 2006). In response to a request from the Ministry of Public Instruction in Paris for a tool to screen for students with learning problems, Binet and another colleague, Theodore Simon, developed a series of tasks to systematically measure motor skills, vocabulary, problem solving, and a wide range of other higher-order thought processes (Binet & Simon, 1905). This instrument could identify patterns in mental capabilities that were unique to each child.

The idea of mental testing caught on very quickly in the United States, especially among clinicians, school psychologists, and other professionals concerned with the practical side of dealing with children. For the first time, it was legitimate, even important, to consider variation in mental abilities from person to person.

### James Mark Baldwin: Developmental Theorist

Considered the founder of academic psychology in Canada (Hoff, 1992), James Mark Baldwin established a laboratory at the University of Toronto devoted to the systematic study of movement patterns, handedness, and color vision in infants (Cairns, 1992). Soon, however, his interests shifted away from gathering empirical data. He became one of the most important developmental theorists of the early twentieth century.

One of Baldwin's most important propositions was that development is a dynamic and hierarchical process, such that "every genetic change ushers in a real

G. Stanley Hall is considered to be the founder of modern child psychology.

**individual differences** Unique characteristics that distinguish a person from other members of a larger group.

advance, a progression on the part of nature to a higher mode of reality" (Baldwin, 1930, p. 86). Baldwin applied these ideas to the domain of cognitive development by suggesting that mental advances occur in a stagelike sequence in which the earliest thought is prelogical but gives way to logical and eventually hyperlogical or formal reasoning—ideas that today are often linked to Piaget.

Baldwin is also recognized for his unique perspective on social development and the formation of personality. Instead of characterizing the child as a passive recipient of the behaviors and beliefs endorsed by the larger society, he described the child's emerging self as a product of continual reciprocal interactions between the child and others. The proposition that development results from a mutual dynamic between the child and others took a long time to catch on among psychologists, but this idea, so popular today, is actually almost a century old (Cairns & Ornstein, 1979).

By the start of the 1900s, the foundations of developmental psychology as a scientifically based discipline were firmly established. Psychologists were well poised to begin the study of differences among groups of children, individual differences among children, and the hypotheses generated by emerging theories of development.

**Sigmund Freud: The Importance of Early Experience**    During the early decades of the twentieth century, Sigmund Freud's theory also became extremely influential, particularly with respect to explaining emotional and personality development. Freud proposed in his psychosexual theory of development that many aspects of the individual's personality originate in an early and broad form of childhood sexuality. The fuel that powers human behavior, according to Freud, is a set of biological instincts. The psychological tension induced by these instincts, called *libido* or *libidinal energy*, gradually builds and requires eventual discharge. Under many circumstances, this energy is reduced as rapidly as possible. Sometimes, however, tensions like those associated with hunger or pain in infants cannot be eliminated immediately. Because of these delays, mental structures and behavioral responses eventually organize into more satisfactory ways of decreasing tension. For example, behavioral acts might include calling out to the caregiver as a signal to be fed or eventually learning to feed oneself, responses that normally lead to a reduction in libidinal urges by effective, rational, and socially acceptable means.

The locus of tension and the optimal ways to reduce needs change with age. Freud identified five stages of psychosexual development, periods during which libidinal energy is usually associated with a specific area of the body. During the *oral stage*, lasting until about one year of age, libidinal energy is focused around the mouth and is reduced through sucking, chewing, eating, and biting. Throughout the subsequent *anal stage*, from about one to three years of age, this energy is centered on the anal region and is lessened by satisfactorily expelling body wastes. The *phallic stage*, typically bridging the period between three and five years of age, is characterized as a time of desire for the opposite-sex parent and of other forms of immature gratification surrounding the genitals. A relatively long *latency* period lasts from about five years of age to adolescence and is a time in which libidinal energy is submerged or expressed, for example, through a more culturally acceptable focus on the acquisition of social or intellectual skills. During the final stage, the *genital stage*, which occurs in adolescence and continues throughout adulthood, mature forms of genital satisfaction are theorized to be an important source of tension reduction.

Freud believed that the individual's progression through these stages is greatly influenced by maturation. However, the environment also plays a critical role. Lack of opportunity to meet needs adequately or to express them during a stage could lead to negative consequences in the way the child relates to others and to feelings of low self-worth. For example, the infant whose sucking efforts are not gratified may become *fixated*; that is, preoccupied with actions associated with the mouth for the rest of his or her life. A child whose toilet training is too lax may become messy, disorderly, or wasteful, whereas one whose toilet training is too strict may display a possessive, retentive (frugal and stingy) personality or show an excessive concern with cleanliness and orderliness in later adulthood.

Freud's view of development has been criticized extensively for its overemphasis on libidinal gratification, as well as for its cultural and gender limitations. So, too, has his method for arriving at his theory: asking adults to reflect on their earliest experiences. As a consequence, his contributions have often been discounted. Nevertheless, for Freud, as for many developmental psychologists today, events that occur during the earliest years of development and that involve interactions with the family were of paramount importance in understanding and explaining behavior throughout the later years of an individual's life.

## THE CONTINUED GROWTH OF DEVELOPMENTAL PSYCHOLOGY IN THE TWENTIETH CENTURY

From the beginning of the twentieth century to the mid-1940s, psychologists interested in development increasingly concentrated their efforts on gathering descriptive information about children. At what ages do most children achieve the milestones of motor development, such as sitting, crawling, and walking? When do children develop emotions, such as fear and anger? What are children's beliefs about punishment, friendship, and morality? It was during this era of intensive fact gathering that many *norms* of development—that is, the ages at which most children are able to accomplish a given developmental task—were established. For example, Arnold Gesell established the norms of motor development for the first five years of life, guidelines that are still useful to psychologists, pediatricians, and other professionals who work with children in diagnosing developmental problems or delays (Gesell & Thompson, 1934, 1938).

Over the years, questions about norms gave way to research on the variables that might be related to specific aspects of development or cause it to occur in the way it does. For example, is maturation or experience responsible for the sequence of motor behaviors most children display? Even almost seventy years ago, researchers found that the answer was not simple. Myrtle McGraw (1935, 1939), in her classic studies of the twins Johnny and Jimmy, reported that training Johnny (but not Jimmy) to reach for objects, crawl, and swim during infancy accelerated motor development, but only when he was already showing signs of physiological maturity. Similarly, does the predictable sequence of language development occur because of biological influences or learning? What factors lead to the emergence of emotional ties children form with caregivers? Researchers today continue to ask questions like these, recognizing more and more the complexities of the influences on child development.

The first half of the twentieth century also saw the founding of a number of major institutes or research centers that attracted bright young scholars who dedicated their lives to the scientific study of children. A further sign of the professionalization of the discipline was the formation of the Society for Research in Child Development (SRCD) in 1933 for scientists who wished to share their growing knowledge of child behavior and development. Today the membership of this society numbers about 5,000 (SRCD, 2002) and includes developmental researchers, practitioners, and professionals working in such settings as colleges, universities, research institutes, and hospitals.

Scholars now approach child development from an assortment of disciplines, including anthropology, sociology, education, medicine, biology, and several subareas of psychology (such as neuropsychology, comparative psychology, and clinical psychology), as well as the specialized area of developmental psychology. Each discipline has its own biases, as defined by the questions each asks about development and the methodological approaches it employs to answer those questions.

In her classic studies of a pair of twins, Myrtle McGraw found that both maturation and experience contributed to motor skill development.

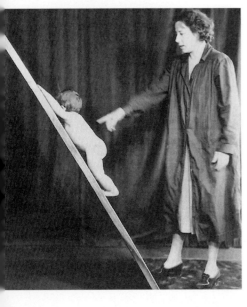

Nonetheless, our pooled knowledge gives us a better understanding of development than we might expect from a field that officially began only a century ago.

F ● O ● R ● Y ● O ● U ● R ● R ● E ● V ● I ● E ● W

● How have views of childhood changed from medieval and Renaissance times to today?

● What were John Locke's and Jean Jacques Rousseau's views of childhood?

● How did Charles Darwin, Wilhelm Preyer, G. Stanley Hall, Alfred Binet, and James Mark Baldwin contribute to developmental psychology?

● What was Sigmund Freud's psychosexual theory of development?

● What emphases emerged in research on children during the first half of the twentieth century?

## THEORIES OF DEVELOPMENT

A number of major theories influence our understanding of development today. We introduce them and briefly highlight some of the major concepts and principles associated with each in the sections that follow. However, their contributions will be a major part of our discussion in later chapters as well. In considering these theories in this first chapter, we focus in particular on where each stands with respect to the major themes in developmental psychology.

### LEARNING THEORY APPROACHES

Learning theorists study how principles of learning cause the individual to change and develop. **Learning,** the relatively permanent change in behavior that results from experience, undoubtedly contributes to why the infant smiles as her mother approaches, the three-year-old says a polite "Thank you" on receiving his grandmother's present, the five-year-old displays newfound skill in tying her shoes, and the adolescent expresses a clear preference about the most fashionable item of clothing to wear.

In the extreme view, some learning theorists believe, as John B. Watson did, that learning mechanisms can be exploited to create virtually any type of person.

> Give me a dozen healthy infants, well-formed, and my own specified world to bring them up in and I'll guarantee to take any one at random and train him to become any type of specialist I might select—doctor, lawyer, artist, merchant-chief, and yes, even beggar-man and thief, regardless of his talents, penchants, tendencies, abilities, vocations, and race of his ancestors. (Watson, 1930, p. 104)

Although present-day supporters of learning theory seldom take such a radical position, they are in agreement that basic principles of learning can have a powerful influence on child development (Bijou, 1989; Gewirtz & Peláez-Nogueras, 1992; Schlinger, 1992).

**Behavior Analysis** **Behavior analysis** is a theoretical account of development that relies on several basic principles of learning to explain developmental changes in behavior. Behavior analysis sprang from the radical learning position introduced by John B. Watson and was extended in more recent years by B. F. Skinner (1953, 1974) and others. Nearly a century ago, the Russian physiologist Ivan Pavlov observed that dogs would often begin to salivate at the sound of a bell or some other arbitrary stimulus when the stimulus had previously been accompanied by food. In this type of learning, called *classical conditioning,* a neutral stimulus begins to elicit a response

**learning**  Relatively permanent change in behavior as a result of such experiences as exploration, observation, and practice.

**behavior analysis**  Learning theory perspective that explains the development of behavior according to the principles of classical and operant conditioning.

after being repeatedly paired with another stimulus that already elicits that response. We learn certain behaviors and emotions as a result of classical conditioning. For example, children and adults may become anxious on entering a dental office because of its association with previous painful treatments performed by the dentist.

To understand a second basic principle of learning, consider two babies who smile as their caregivers approach. With one baby, the caregiver stops, says "Hi, baby!" and briefly rocks the cradle. With the other baby, the caregiver walks on past, preoccupied. Which baby is more likely to repeat his smiling response when the caregiver nears again? If you reasoned that the first is more likely than the second because the behavior was followed by a positive event (attention or approval), which often increases the frequency of a behavior, you know something about the principle of operant conditioning. *Operant conditioning* (also called *instrumental conditioning*) refers to the process by which the frequency of a behavior changes depending on response consequences in the form of a desirable or undesirable outcome. Behavior analysts have used this principle to account for the emergence of such straightforward behaviors as the one-year-old's waving good-bye to far more sophisticated skills involving memory, language, social interaction, and complex problem solving.

Operant and classical conditioning have been shown to have enormous potential to change behavior. *Behavior modification*, sometimes called *applied behavior analysis*, involves the systematic application of operant conditioning to modify human activity. To illustrate, Jason Stricker and his colleagues (Stricker et al., 2001) investigated whether thumb sucking could be reduced in children who engaged in such activity at an age when it is no longer considered appropriate. They identified a seven-year-old child with attention deficit hyperactivity disorder (ADHD) who often sucked his thumb while watching television and in other situations. Would consistent feedback to the child help him become aware of this activity and reduce this behavior? To test this possibility, the researchers attached two small transmitters to the child, one to his wrist and a second to his shirt, just below his mouth. When the child raised his hand to his mouth to engage in thumb sucking, bringing the wrist and shirt transmitter close to each other, the transmitters triggered a nearby device that began to produce a beeping tone. The researchers recorded the percentage of time the child engaged in thumb sucking during ten-minute sessions of television viewing over a number of weeks. During a baseline period, the child did not wear the transmitters. In other sessions, he wore transmitters that were either

Social learning theory emphasizes the important role that observation of another person plays in learning. This young boy is acquiring new behaviors by watching his mother and imitating what she does. Social learning provides a mechanism by which many desirable social customs and actions become part of the child's repertoire.

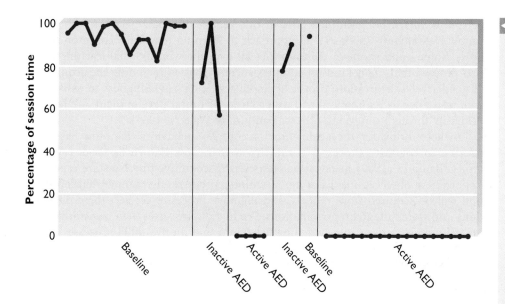

◁ **FIGURE 1.3**

**A Behavioral Approach to Reducing Thumb Sucking in Children**

The seven-year-old child observed in this study often sucked his thumb. During the baseline period sessions in which he was simply observed watching television, he engaged in this activity a high percentage of the time. Next, a set of transmitters, called an "awareness enhancement device" (AED), was attached to the child. When the device did not activate a beeping tone (Inactive AED), he continued to display such behavior frequently. However, when the tone was activated whenever the child sucked his thumb (Active AED), the practice ceased. As predicted by behavorial theories, response consequences can have a powerful effect on behavior.

*Source:* Stricker et al. (2001).

activated or not activated to provide feedback. The findings of this experiment are shown in Figure 1.3. The results clearly demonstrate the elimination of the thumb sucking when the transmitters produced feedback about the activity. The feedback may have helped the child become aware of his thumb sucking; in addition, the sound may have been annoying enough to yield the change in his behavior.

Applied behavior analysis has become a powerful approach used by teachers, therapists, and caregivers to bring about changes in behavior ranging from the elimination of temper tantrums and other disruptive responses to encouraging healthy diets and safe driving habits. Even some of its detractors have suggested that behavior analysis may have done more to benefit human welfare than any other psychological theory (Hebb, 1980). For this reason alone, learning theory has appealed to many in their efforts to understand development. Yet behavior analysis has drawn extensive criticism. Its critics, including some learning theorists, remain unconvinced that a behavior can be understood without taking into account the child's feelings and reasons for engaging in that behavior. In other words, mental, emotional, and motivational factors also play a prominent role in how a child interprets and responds to stimulation. Among various learning perspectives, social learning theory attempts to incorporate these factors into its explanation of behavior and development.

***Social Learning Theory*** **Social learning theory** emphasizes the importance of learning through observation and imitation of the behaviors displayed by others. Social learning theorists start with the assumption that whether an individual will be friendly, outgoing, confident, and honest rather than shy and perhaps hostile and untrustworthy depends largely on the socialization practices of parents and caregivers throughout that person's childhood. Although operant and classical conditioning play a substantial role, social learning theorists underscore **observational learning**, the acquisition of behaviors from listening to and watching other people, as a particularly important means of acquiring new behaviors. The two-year-old who stands before a mirror pretending to shave in imitation of his father is displaying observational learning. Similarly, you may have witnessed the embarrassment of a parent whose three-year-old has uttered a profanity, a behavior probably acquired by the same process.

According to Albert Bandura, psychology's best-known spokesperson for social learning, a society could never effectively convey complex language, social and moral customs, or other achievements to its younger members without relying extensively on observational learning. Bandura (1965) notes that significant learning occurs, often completely without error, through the act of watching and imitating another

**social learning theory** Theoretical approach emphasizing the importance of learning through observation and imitation of behaviors modeled by others.

**observational learning** Learning that takes place by simply observing another person's behavior.

person, a *model*. For example, girls in one region of Guatemala learn to weave simply by watching an expert, an approach to learning new skills common to the fields, homes, and shops of communities all over the world. Social learning theorists propose that many kinds of complex social activities, including the acquisition of gender roles, aggression, prosocial responses (such as willingness to assist others), resistance to temptation, and other facets of moral development, are learned primarily through observing others (Bandura & Walters, 1963).

In accounting for the acquisition of complex behaviors, Bandura has often referred to cognitive processes within his theory, now known as *social cognitive theory*. Bandura (1989) believes that four sets of cognitive processes are especially important in observational learning. Attentional processes determine what information will be acquired from models, and memory processes convert these observations into stored mental representations. Production processes then transform these mental representations into matching behaviors, and motivational processes define which behaviors are likely to be performed. As each of these processes becomes more sophisticated, observational and other forms of learning become increasingly refined and proficient, and the child becomes more effective in regulating his or her own behavior (Grusec, 1992).

***Learning Theory and Themes in Development*** What stance do behavior analysts and social cognitive theorists take on the five major developmental themes we introduced at the beginning of this chapter? Keep in mind that, as our discussions of behavior analysis and social cognitive theory suggest, not all learning theorists share the same views about the prime determinants of development.

- *Nature & Nurture* Behavior analysts believe that biological and genetic factors may limit the kinds of responses that can be performed and help to define which events are reinforcing or punishing. But ultimately it is the environment that controls behavior. For behaviorists, a child's functioning is the outcome of a history of behaviors and their associated consequences. In social cognitive theory, biological factors and the environment are believed to play a mutual, interactive role in contributing to development (Bandura, 1989). In keeping with their strong experiential emphasis, behaviorists believe the child's role in development is passive. Skinner claimed that "a person does not act upon the world, the world acts upon him" (1971, p. 211). According to Skinner, psychologists should abolish references to unobservable mental or cognitive constructs, such as motives, goals, needs, or thoughts, in their explanations of behavior. Bandura's social cognitive theory differs from behavior analysis by embracing mental and motivational constructs and processes for interpreting and understanding others as well as the self. Social cognitive theory therefore confers a much more active status on the child than does behavior analysis.

- *Sociocultural Influence* Behaviorists believe that, although societies differ in the responses viewed as desirable or unacceptable, the mechanisms of learning are universal for individuals in all cultures. Rewards and punishments delivered in the immediate environment are the key to understanding development. Social learning theorists give sociocultural context more emphasis than behaviorists do by pointing out, for example, that advances in communication technology (such as television) expand the opportunity for children and adults to acquire many novel skills and patterns of behavior through observational learning.

- *Continuity/Discontinuity* Both behavior analysts and social learning theorists consider development to be continuous rather than stagelike. Any departure from this pattern would stem from abrupt shifts in environmental circumstances, such as when the child enters school or the adolescent enters the work environment.

- *Interaction Among Domains* Whereas behavior analysts explain development in all domains in terms of the basic principles of learning, social cognitive theorists stress that learning is linked to the child's physical, cognitive, and social development. Thus this latter perspective acknowledges the interaction among different domains of development by recognizing that the child's learning is a consequence of what he or she feels, believes, and thinks.

● *Risk/Resilience* The general principles of learning apply to all individuals, whatever their situation, and can account for both risk and recovery from risk. It is important to analyze the unique kinds of experiences each person receives; for example, the specific models to which she or he is exposed or the particular behaviors rewarded by others in the environment.

## PIAGET'S COGNITIVE-DEVELOPMENTAL THEORY

According to **cognitive-developmental theory**, behavior reflects the emergence of various cognitive *structures*, organized units or patterns of thinking, that influence how the child interprets experience. Cognitive-developmental theories tend to share the fundamental assumption that normal children display common intellectual, emotional, and social capacities despite widely varying experiences. Most three- and four-year-olds around the world, for example, believe that a gallon of water, when poured from one container to another of a different shape, changes in amount, an error children rarely make once they reach seven or eight years of age. Cognitive-developmental theorists explain this profound change in reasoning in terms of children's acquiring new ways of understanding their world.

The most extensive and best-known cognitive-developmental theory was put forward by Jean Piaget. His vigorous defense of physical and mental *action* as the basis for cognitive development (Beilin & Fireman, 1999) and his belief that intellectual capacities undergo *qualitative* reorganization at different stages of development have had a monumental impact, not only on developmental psychologists, but also on educators and other professionals working with children.

Jean Piaget's keen observations and insights concerning the behavior of children laid the groundwork for his theory of cognitive development. Piaget's ideas about how thinking develops have influenced psychologists, educators, and many others in their attempts to understand children.

***Piaget's Theory*** Piaget's vision of human development was based on two overriding assumptions about intelligence: (1) it is a form of biological adaptation, and (2) it becomes organized as the individual interacts with the external world (Piaget, 1971). **Adaptation** is a tendency to adjust or become more attuned to the conditions imposed by the environment. **Organization** refers to a tendency for intellectual structures and processes to become more systematic and coherent. Just as arms, eyes, lungs, heart, and other physical structures assemble and take shape to carry out biological functions, so do mental structures array themselves in ever more powerful patterns to support more complex thought. These changes, however, depend on the opportunity to look and touch, handle and play with, and construct and order the rich assortment of experiences stemming from action on the environment. From the abundant encounters provided in commonplace physical and social experiences, the child confronts unexpected and puzzling outcomes that ultimately lead to reorganizations in thought.

The basic mental structure in Piaget's theory is a **scheme**, a coordinated and systematic pattern of action or way of reasoning. A scheme is a kind of template for acting or thinking applied to similar classes of objects or situations. The infant who sucks at her mother's breast, at her favorite pacifier, and at her thumb is exercising a scheme of sucking. The six-year-old who realizes that his eight Matchbox cars can be stored in an equal number of boxes regardless of how they are scattered about the floor is also exercising a scheme, this time one concerned with number. The infant's schemes are limited to patterns of action applied to objects: sucking, grasping, shaking, and so forth. The older child's schemes will often involve mental processes and be far more complex as he or she reasons about such things as classes of objects, number, or spatial relations and, by adolescence, the meaning of life and the origins of the universe. For Piaget, earlier schemes set the stage for constructing new and more sophisticated schemes.

Piaget believed that schemes change through two complementary processes. The first, **assimilation**, refers to the process of interpreting an experience in terms

**cognitive-developmental theory** Theoretical orientation, most frequently associated with Piaget, emphasizing the active construction of psychological structures to interpret experience.

**adaptation** In Piagetian theory, the inborn tendency to adjust or become more attuned to conditions imposed by the environment; takes place through assimilation and accommodation.

**organization** In Piagetian theory, the inborn tendency for structures and processes to become more systematic and coherent.

**scheme** In Piagetian theory, the mental structure underlying a coordinated and systematic pattern of behaviors or thinking applied across similar objects or situations.

**assimilation** In Piagetian theory, a component of adaptation; process of interpreting an experience in terms of current ways (schemes) of understanding things.

of current ways of understanding things. The second, **accommodation**, refers to the modifications in behavior and thinking that take place when the old ways of understanding, the old schemes, no longer fit. To illustrate these two processes, consider the infant's first experience with sucking a pacifier. Upon feeling it in the mouth, the infant engages the already formed scheme for sucking on the mother's breast. In other words, this new experience is *assimilated* into the pre-existing scheme. But the shape and taste of the pacifier are not the same as the mother's breast. The child's scheme must *accommodate* to this new encounter. In a similar manner throughout development, the child's intellectual capacities become reshaped and reorganized as the child attempts to adjust—that is, accommodate—to new experiences.

For Piaget, assimilation and accommodation are complementary aspects of all psychological activity, processes engaged in a constant tug of war in the never-ending goal of acquiring understanding (Valsiner, 2006). Fortunately, adaptation in the form of newer and more complex schemes is the result of this continuous dynamic. The outcome of adaptation is a more effective fitting together of the many pieces of knowledge that make up the child's understanding. The process by which assimilation and accommodation bring about more organized and powerful schemes for thinking is called **equilibration**. Each new experience can cause imbalance, which can be corrected only by modification of the child's schemes. In trying to make sense of his or her world, the child develops more adaptive ways of thinking.

During some periods of development, schemes may undergo rapid and substantial modification and reorganization. The more effective levels of knowledge that emerge from these restructurings are the basis for different stages in Piaget's theory of development. Piaget proposed that development proceeds through four stages: *sensorimotor, preoperational, concrete,* and *formal.* Much more will be said about each of these stages as we progress through this book; however, Table 1.1 briefly identifies them. Each higher stage is defined by the appearance of a qualitatively different level of thinking, an increasingly more sophisticated form of knowledge through which the child displays greater intellectual balance for responding to the environment. However, each new stage does not suddenly appear full-blown; it arises from the integration and incorporation of earlier ways of thinking.

Piaget's wide range of observations, his frequently surprising findings about what infants and children can and cannot do, and his theoretical explanations and

**Table 1.1  Piaget's Stages of Cognitive Development**

| Stage | Emerging Cognitive Structure (schemes) | Typical Achievements and Behaviors |
|---|---|---|
| **Sensorimotor (birth until 1½–2 years)** | Sensory and motor actions, initially reflexes, quickly differentiate by means of accommodation and co-ordinate to form adaptive ways of acting on the environment. | Infants suck, grasp, look, reach, and so forth, responses that become organized into complex activities such as hand-eye coordination, knowledge of space and objects and eventually rudimentary symbols designed to solve problems and understand the physical world. |
| **Preoperational (1½–7 years)** | Symbols stand for or represent objects and events, but communication and thought remain relatively inflexible. | Children begin to acquire language and mental representations, but thought remains unidimensional and oriented around the self. |
| **Concrete Operational (7–11 years)** | Cognitive operations permit logical reasoning about concrete objects, events, and relationships. | Children are no longer fooled by appearance, and they can reason more systematically with respect to classes, number and other characteristics of their physical and social world. |
| **Formal Operational (11 years and above)** | Operations can be performed on operations. Thought becomes abstract, and all possible outcomes can be considered. | Adolescents and adults are able to reason about hypothetical outcomes. Abstract issues (e.g., religion, morality, alternative lifestyles) are systematically evaluated. |

assumptions have sparked a wealth of research on cognitive, social, and moral development. Many researchers applaud his innovative conceptualizations concerning development. For example, Piaget vigorously embraced the notion of children as active participants in their own development, a viewpoint that others have widely adopted (Siegler & Ellis, 1996). However, the central concept of qualitative differences in thinking between children and adults, and particularly of stagelike transformations, has been less favorably received (Fischer & Bidell, 2006; Thelen & Smith, 1994). We will say more about these issues in the chapters to come.

***Piaget's Theory and Themes in Development***  How does Piaget's theory address the five major themes of development?

- *Nature & Nurture*  Piaget theorized that a number of biologically based factors contribute to cognitive development. Among them is maturation, the gradual unfolding over time of genetic programs for development. Another factor is the child's inherent tendency to act, physically or mentally, on the environment. Nevertheless, for Piaget, development is clearly the product of the interaction of these factors with experience. In Piaget's theory, knowledge is *constructed*; that is, created and formed by the continuous revision and reorganization of intellectual structures in conjunction with experience. Piaget's constructivist model depicts a mind actively engaged in knowing and understanding its environment.

- *Sociocultural Influence*  For Piaget, children develop in much the same way in all cultures around the world because of their similar biological makeup and the common physical and social world to which all humans must adapt. Different cultural or educational opportunities, however, can affect the speed and ultimate level of achievement in cognitive development.

- *Continuity/Discontinuity*  Although recognizing continuous changes, Piaget's theory focuses on the ways schemes undergo reorganization and change to form distinctive stages in development. In his later writings and conversations, Piaget began to downplay the importance of stages (Piaget, 1971; Vuyk, 1981). He believed that an overemphasis on stages had led to too much concern with describing periods of intellectual stability or equilibrium when, in fact, cognition is always undergoing development. Cognitive development, he eventually concluded, is more like a spiral in which change constantly occurs, although sometimes at faster rates than at other times (Beilin, 1989).

- *Interaction Among Domains*  Piaget's theory has implications for many domains of development. For example, his ideas about cognitive development have been used to explain changes in communication, moral thinking, and aspects of *social cognition*, such as how children understand the thoughts, intentions, feelings, and views of others. Nevertheless, Piaget has been criticized for paying relatively little attention to how social and emotional domains influence cognitive development.

- *Risk/Resilience*  Piaget placed very little emphasis on individual differences in development. His goal was to identify the principles that applied to cognitive and other aspects of development in all children. However, in his emphasis on providing children with environmental experiences that match their biological readiness to learn, Piaget does suggest some factors that might put children at risk.

## INFORMATION-PROCESSING APPROACHES

Computer information processing as a metaphor for human thinking has generated so many models and theories that it is difficult to single out any one approach as a prototype (Klahr & MacWhinney, 1998). However, one common thread evident in any **information-processing** point of view is the notion that humans, like computers, have a *limited capacity* for taking in and operating on the vast amount of

**accommodation**  In Piagetian theory, a component of adaptation; process of modification in thinking (schemes) that takes place when old ways of understanding something no longer fit.

**equilibration**  In Piagetian theory, an innate self-regulatory process that, through accommodation and assimilation, results in more organized and powerful schemes for adapting to the environment. information processing  Theoretical approach that views humans as having a limited ability to process information, much like computers.

**information processing**  Theoretical approach that views humans as having a limited ability to process information, much like computers.

information available to them. Thus changes in cognitive structures (for example, short- and long-term memory) and processes (for instance, strategies, rules, and plans associated with attending, remembering, and decision making) are an essential component in explaining how older children might process information more fully and effectively than younger children.

What sets an information-processing theory apart from many other theories is its detailed effort to explain exactly how the child comes to identify the letters of the alphabet, remember the multiplication tables, recall the main ideas of a story, give a classmate directions to his or her home, or decide whether it is safe to cross the street. For example, how does a six-year-old solve addition problems? She may have practiced this activity over and over, and learned the answer to each particular problem by rote over many months of exposure to them. Or she may rely on some kind of strategy that permits her to consistently arrive at the correct answer. For example, she could start with the first number of the addition problem and then add one unit the number of times indicated by the second number. Thus, for the problem 3 + 5, she may begin at 3 and add 1 to it the necessary five times to arrive at the correct answer.

How could we tell whether one child was engaging in the first procedure, retrieving information from long-term rote memory, and another child, the second procedure of utilizing a rule to determine the answer? One clue could come from the length of time it takes to solve various addition problems. If a child is using the first technique, she can be expected to solve each problem in about the same length of time. If she uses the second technique, however, she will likely take somewhat longer to answer a problem in which the second number is very large than when it is very small. We may also see the child producing other observable behaviors, such as holding up three fingers to begin with and counting off additional fingers to arrive at the correct answer.

As this example illustrates, information-processing theorists frequently attempt to describe the rules, strategies, and procedures that children employ to complete a task and that help them to remember, make inferences, and solve problems. Why has this approach become popular in developmental psychology? One reason is disenchantment with learning, Piagetian, and other perspectives for explaining behavior. For instance, although learning theories attempt to identify which abilities are learned, they have offered few insights into how the child's mind changes with age in learning these abilities. Piaget's cognitive-developmental theory is concerned with this issue, but his explanations have been difficult to translate into ideas about how the mind actually functions. Moreover, the information-processing approach can be extended to account for development in many other domains, including language acquisition, peer relationships, and even social and personality development. Not surprisingly, given their breadth of application, information-processing approaches are discussed further in a number of the chapters that follow.

**Information-Processing Approaches and Themes in Development**   Because of the wide variety of information-processing models theorized to account for changes in cognitive development, we can draw only broad conclusions concerning their positions on the various themes in development.

- *Nature & Nurture* Information-processing models have said little about nature and nurture. Some basic capacities to perceive and process information are assumed at or before birth, and the system may be attuned to respond in certain ways, for example, to language and other kinds of information. The environment has an obvious impact on development because it provides input for processing by the mind. The implicit assumption in most models is that basic cognitive structures and processes interact with experience to produce changes in the system. Children, of course, react to the environment, but they also initiate and construct strategies and procedures that assist in processing information more effectively. From this perspective, children take an increasingly active role in controlling their own learning and development.

- *Sociocultural Influence* As in the case of learning theory, the sociocultural context of development has been largely ignored by information-processing theorists. This is probably because researchers have typically focused on identifying how the mind operates on specific problems rather than on how the mind is affected by the kinds of problems a culture presents to it.

- *Continuity/Discontinuity* In most information-processing models, cognitive development is theorized to undergo quantitative rather than qualitative changes. For example, children retain increasing numbers of items in both short-term and long-term memory, and interpret information and apply various strategies more efficiently and effectively with development. Similarly, the acquisition of new strategies for storing and retrieving information, new rules for problem solving, and new ways of thinking about and processing information are interpreted as shifts in ability that come about because of relatively small, continuous improvements in the capacity to process information.

- *Interaction Among Domains* A notable limitation of many information-processing models is their failure to consider emotional, motivational, and other domains of behavior. How social factors, such as instructions, modeling, and the cultural context of learning, lead to developmental changes in processing information is also rarely spelled out (Klahr, 1989). However, as already noted, information-processing approaches have been extended to other domains of development, including language and social and personality development.

- *Risk/Resilience* Many information-processing theories pay little heed to the factors that might result in risks in development. However, their potential to explain such differences in terms of variations in rules, strategies, and other procedures for processing information is considerable.

## ERIKSON'S PSYCHOSOCIAL APPROACH

For the most part, the theoretical models we have examined so far have been concerned with learning and cognitive development. With *psychosocial* models, we shift to a substantially greater focus on emotions and personality. At one time, Freud's theory of personality was extremely influential in explaining emotional and personality development. However, Erik Erikson's theory has gained far greater attention in recent years. Like Freud, Erikson theorized that personality development progresses through stages. During each stage, the child must resolve conflicts between needs or feelings and external obstacles that are unique to that particular time in the life span. The satisfactory resolution of these conflicts leads to a healthy personality and a productive lifestyle. But, in contrast to Freud, Erikson included several additional stages during adulthood, and he gave socialization and society far greater importance in his theory.

**Psychosocial Theory** In his classic work *Childhood and Society* (1950), Erikson outlined eight stages of development, as summarized in Table 1.2. During the first stage, Erikson theorized that *incorporation*, or taking in, is the primary mode for acting adaptively toward the world. In Erikson's view, this mode of activity extends beyond the mouth and includes other senses, such as looking and hearing, and motor systems, such as reaching and grasping, systems designed to expand the infant's resources for absorbing and responding to reality. Each subsequent stage identified another important mode for adapting to the environment.

Society, according to Erikson, plays a critical role in shaping and forming reality for the child. Communities create their own demands and set their own criteria for socializing the child. In one society, an infant may be permitted to

Erik Erikson outlined eight stages of personality development. His psychosocial theory emphasized that at each stage, individuals must successfully adapt to new forms of demands placed on them by society. He also stressed that cultures frequently differ in how they help individuals negotiate those demands.

**Table 1.2** **Erikson's Stages of Psychosocial Development**

| Stage | Adaptive Mode | Significant Events and Outcomes |
|---|---|---|
| **Basic Trust Versus Mistrust (birth to 1 year)** | Incorporation—to take in (and give in return) | Babies must find consistency, predictability, and reliability in their caregivers' behaviors to gain a sense of trust and hope. |
| **Autonomy Versus Shame and Doubt (1–3 years)** | Control—to hold on and to let go | The child begins to explore and make choices in order to understand what is manageable and socially acceptable. |
| **Initiative Versus Guilt (3–6 years)** | Intrusion—to go after | The child begins to make plans, set goals, and persist in both physical and social exchanges to gain a sense of purpose and remain enthusiastic even in the face of inevitable frustration. |
| **Industry Versus Inferiority (6 years to puberty)** | Construction—to build things and relationships | The child acquires skills and performs "work" in the form of becoming educated and supporting the family in order to feel competent and attain a sense of achievement. |
| **Identity Versus Identity Confusion (puberty to adulthood)** | Integration—to be oneself (or not be oneself) | The adolescent attempts to discover his or her identity and place in society by trying out many roles in order to answer the question, "Who am I?" |
| **Intimacy Versus Isolation (young adulthood)** | Solidarity—to lose and find oneself in another | Having achieved a sense of identity, the young adult can now share himself or herself with another to avoid a sense of isolation, self-absorption, and the absence of love. |
| **Generativity Versus Stagnation (middle adulthood)** | Productivity—to make and to take care of | The adult produces things and ideas through work and creates and cares for the next generation to gain a sense of fulfillment and caring. |
| **Integrity Versus Despair (old age)** | Acceptance—to be (by having been) and to face not being | The older adult reviews and evaluates his or her life and accepts its worth, even if he or she not reached all goals, to achieve a sense of wisdom. |

**psychosocial theory of development** Erikson's theory that personality develops through eight stages of adaptive functioning to meet the demands framed by society.

**identity** In Eriksonian psychosocial theory, the acceptance of both self and society, a concept that must be achieved at every stage but is especially important during adolescence.

breast-feed whenever hungry over a period of several years, whereas infants in another society may be nursed or bottle-fed on a rigid schedule and weaned within the first year of life. In another example, the timing and severity of toilet training, as well as the means by which caregivers initiate it, may differ vastly from one society to another. Cultures differ in the requirements imposed on the child, yet each child must adapt to his own culture's regulations. Thus Erikson's **psychosocial theory of development** highlights the child's composite need to initiate adaptive modes of functioning while meeting the variety of demands framed by the society in which she lives.

Erikson theorized that the individual confronts a specific crisis as society imposes new demands in each stage. The resolution of each crisis may or may not be successful, but triumphs at earlier stages lay the groundwork for the negotiation of later stages. Moreover, each society has evolved ways to help individuals meet their needs. Caregiving practices, educational programs, social organizations, occupational training, and moral and ethical support are examples of cultural systems established to foster healthy, productive psychosocial development.

A common theme underlying the various features of Erikson's theory is the search for **identity**, or the acceptance of both self and one's society. At each stage, this search is manifested in a specific way. The need to develop a feeling of trust for a caregiver, acquire a sense of autonomy, initiate exchanges with the world, and learn and become competent in school and other settings are examples of how the infant and child discovers who and what she or he is and will become. During adolescence, the individual confronts the issue of identity directly. But the answer to "Who am I?" is elaborated and made clearer as the individual progresses through each psychosocial stage.

In summary, Erikson's views of personality development highlighted the practices society uses to encourage and promote healthy social and personality development. However, he painted development with a broad brush; consequently, his theory is frequently criticized for its vagueness. Still, just as Piaget identified meaningful issues in cognitive development, Erikson—regardless of the precision of his specific formulations—had a flair for targeting crucial issues in social and personality development.

***Psychosocial Theory and Themes in Development***   Our discussion of Erikson's theory has already focused on a number of themes in development, but let's consider them once more.

- *Nature & Nurture* A biological contribution to behavior, extended from Freud's theory, is evident in Erikson's positions. Yet psychosocial theory must be considered interactionist, given the momentous role the presence and absence of appropriate socializing experiences play in resolving conflicts that arise at every stage. At the same time, in Erikson's theory, the emphasis on establishing an identity for self within society suggests an active role for the child in development.

- *Sociocultural Influence* The broader sociocultural context in which caregivers encourage children to master, explore, and engage in their physical and social environments, especially during the early years of life, plays a critical role in Erikson's theory of development. For Erikson, the sociocultural context is a key factor in understanding an individual's personality and social relationships.

- *Continuity/Discontinuity* Erikson identified eight stages in personality development. The successful negotiation of earlier stages lays the groundwork for continued psychological growth. The individual unable to work through a crisis at one time, however, may still effectively resolve it at a later stage.

- *Interaction Among Domains* Erikson links social, emotional, and cognitive development together in the individual's efforts to achieve identity. For example, a sense of trust emerges from taking in through the senses as well as the motor system; a sense of industry reflects intellectual competence as well as the ability to interact effectively with others; and discovering one's identity requires the integration of all of one's psychological skills and competencies.

- *Risk/Resilience* The psychosocial stages are common to every individual in every culture. However, the success with which each stage is negotiated can vary dramatically from one individual to another and from one society to another. Although not specifically focused on risk factors in development, Erikson's theory offers many insights into how and why risks and resilience might come about.

## CONTEXTUAL APPROACHES

Psychologists have long recognized that children live in vastly different circumstances and that these differences can have a dramatic influence on development. Some children grow up in households with a single parent, others with two parents, and still others with grandparents and perhaps aunts and uncles; children in foster care, on the other hand, may be shuffled frequently from one family to another. In addition, siblings within the same family may receive quite different experiences as a function of being the eldest or youngest, or of being singled out for certain kinds of treatment and expectations by family members. Number of siblings, economic

Contextual approaches to development give recognition to the dramatic impact that broad sociocultural factors can have on children's lives. These children in Ethiopia attend an overcrowded school with few educational resources, a setting far different from classrooms in most Western countries. Schooling and work, family structure, economic resources, and many other social contexts vary tremendously for children living in different cultures. Researchers need to consider these types of broad factors affecting children's lives in order to fully understand development.

resources, space and privacy, independence, and emotional atmosphere are among the vast assortment of factors that vary in the immediate surroundings of children.

Differences in the contexts of development extend far beyond a child's immediate family, however. Physical surroundings, access to schools, job opportunities, technological innovations, natural disasters, political systems, and war, as well as the cultural dictates of the community, influence the way children are reared. Some of these circumstances will be more supportive of development than others. Apart from the physical and sociocultural contexts in which each child lives is still another factor: the innate and species-specific predispositions, the biological context that equips the child to learn and develop.

Developmental theories usually focus on immediate experience, defined narrowly in terms of contemporary circumstances and recent events, and how it affects development. Yet culture, the historical legacy of earlier generations of a given social group, as well as the evolutionary pressures that have shaped humans to exist in their natural environment, are also major factors affecting growth. Put another way, the transformation from infant to child to adult takes place within a complex, multidirectional system of influences (Gottlieb, Wahlsten, & Lickliter, 2006). **Contextual models**, sometimes called *systems views*, are concerned with understanding this broad range of biological, physical, and sociocultural settings, and how they affect development.

***Ecological Systems Theory***    The most extensive description of the context in which development proceeds has been put forth in the **ecological systems theory** proposed by Urie Bronfenbrenner (1989, 1995). Ecological theories in general stress the need to understand development in terms of the everyday environment in which children are reared, a concern that is seldom the focus of many other theories. Commenting on the state of developmental psychology several decades ago, Bronfenbrenner claimed that "much of contemporary developmental psychology is the science of the strange behavior of children in strange situations with strange adults for the briefest possible periods of time" (Bronfenbrenner, 1977, p. 513). Development, Bronfenbrenner believes, must be studied not only in the laboratory, as it had been, but also in the homes, schools, neighborhoods, and communities in which it takes place.

One of Bronfenbrenner's major theoretical contributions has been his comprehensive portrait of the environment—the ecological forces and systems that exist at several different but interrelated levels—and the bidirectional and reciprocal

**contextual models**   Theories of development that are concerned with the effects of a broad range of biological, physical, and sociocultural settings on the process of development.

**ecological systems theory**   Bronfenbrenner's theory that development is influenced by experiences arising from broader social and cultural systems as well as a child's immediate surroundings.

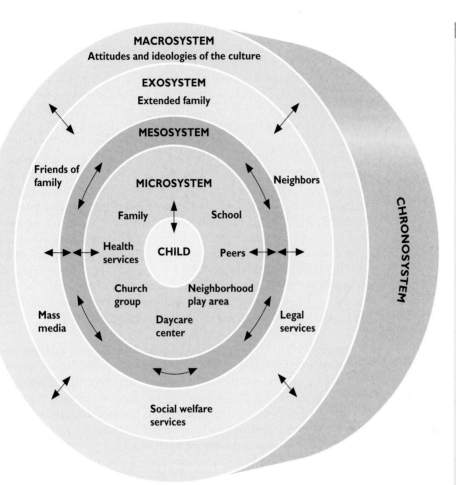

MACROSYSTEM
Attitudes and ideologies of the culture

EXOSYSTEM
Extended family

MESOSYSTEM

Friends of family

MICROSYSTEM

Neighbors

Family    School

Health services    CHILD    Peers

Church group    Neighborhood play area

Mass media    Daycare center    Legal services

Social welfare services

CHRONOSYSTEM

**FIGURE 1.4**
**Bronfenbrenner's Ecological Model**

At the core of Bronfenbrenner's ecological model is the child's biological and psychological makeup, based on individual genetic and developmental history. This makeup continues to be affected and modified by the child's immediate physical and social environment (microsystem), as well as interactions among the systems within this environment (mesosystem). Other broader social, political, and economic conditions (exosystem) influence the structure and availability of microsystems and the manner in which they affect the child. Social, political, and economic conditions are themselves influenced by the general beliefs and attitudes (macrosystem) shared by members of the society, and all of these systems are affected by changes that occur over time (chronosystem).

*Source:* Adapted from Garabino (1982).

relationships that exist among them. These levels are shown in Figure 1.4. At the center is the child's biological and psychological makeup, including her cognitive capacities and socioemotional and motivational propensities (such as temperament and personality) for responding to and acting on the environment. Settings with the most immediate and direct impact on an individual's biological and psychological qualities make up the **microsystem**. These settings include the home and members of the household, social and educational circumstances (including classmates, teachers, and classroom resources), and neighborhoods (including physical layout, friends, and acquaintances).

The **mesosystem** includes the many interrelationships among the various settings within the microsystem. For example, opportunities and expectations within the family, such as access to books and learning to read or an emphasis on acquiring basic academic and socialization skills, may critically influence the child's experiences and success in another microsystem, the school. As another example, a child of divorced parents living in separate neighborhoods may undergo frequent moves between the two homes. Such a living arrangement may have repercussions for the range and kinds of friendships the child can establish with peers.

Social, economic, political, religious, and other settings can affect development either directly or indirectly through their impact on those who care for the child. These wider contexts make up the **exosystem**. In many countries today, for example, the child seldom is part of either parent's work environment. Nevertheless, the parent who encounters a difficult problem at work may bring frustrations home and express them through angry exchanges with members of the family. Urban renewal planned at city hall may have dramatic consequences for children and their interactions with peers, hopefully for the better, but perhaps not always with that effect. Skirmishes between rival villages or countries may bring poverty if the family breadwinner is killed in fighting.

**microsystem** In Bronfenbrenner's ecological systems theory, the immediate environment provided in such settings as the home, school, workplace, and neighborhood.

**mesosystem** In Bronfenbrenner's ecological systems theory, the environment provided by the interrelationships among the various settings of the microsystem.

**exosystem** In Bronfenbrenner's ecological systems theory, environmental settings that indirectly affect the child by influencing the various microsystems forming the child's immediate environment.

The broadest context is the **macrosystem.** The macrosystem includes the spiritual and religious values, legal and political practices, and ceremonies and customs shared by a cultural group. Cultural beliefs about child rearing, the role of schools and family in education, the importance of maintaining kinship affiliations, tolerance for different lifestyles, and the ethical and moral conventions of a society affect the child both directly (through the socialization practices of the caregivers) and indirectly (through the cultural norms and strictures defining acceptable and desirable behavior).

These four systems do not remain constant over time. Historical events like famines, wars, or other natural disasters can disrupt and devastate conventional microsystems, such as schools and neighborhoods, as well as the social, economic, political, and religious framework of a community provided by the exosystem. The arrival of a new family member, the separation of parents, the move to a new home, and the loss of a peer are examples of other changes a child may experience at different times. The **chronosystem** is Bronfenbrenner's (1995) term for this temporal dimension of influence. Change is always taking place, and these time-linked shifts and transitions may have greater or lesser impact depending on when they occur during the child's development. Thus temporal events, too, have far-reaching consequences for each individual's psychological development.

***Vygotsky's Sociohistorical Theory***   Bronfenbrenner's ecological systems theory highlights the many different contexts in which development proceeds. Lev Vygotsky's sociohistorical theory blends these different levels into one overarching concept: culture. What is culture? It is, of course, the many facets of the environment that humans have created and continue to produce, including such physical artifacts as tools and furnishings. But, even more important, culture includes language and the practices, values, and beliefs accumulated and communicated from one generation to the next through that language system. Culture, in other words, is the human-generated, historical accumulation of one's surroundings, and it has an enormous influence on the way children are reared. Vygotsky's **sociohistorical theory** emphasizes the unique collective wisdom compiled by a culture and transmitted to the child through ongoing, daily interactions with the more knowledgeable members of that society.

A central tenet of Vygotsky's sociohistorical theory is that, as children become exposed to and participate in their community, they begin to internalize and adopt, often with the guidance of a skilled partner, such as a parent or teacher, the culturally based, more mature and effective methods of thinking about and solving problems (Wertsch, 1985; Wertsch & Tulviste, 1992). For example, in sitting down with and reading to the child, the caregiver demonstrates how important this activity is, so that eventually the child comes to value it in her own behavior. Vygotsky believed that language is an especially important tool in this dialogue, because it, too, is internalized by the child to affect thinking and problem solving.

One quality that permeates both ecological systems theory and sociohistorical views of development is the seamless alloy that embodies development as the child is affected by and, in turn, actively influences his or her surroundings (Sameroff, 1994). Development is dynamic, a never-ending *transaction* involving continuing, reciprocal exchanges: people and settings transform the child, who in turn affects the people and settings surrounding him, which further reshape the child in an endless progression.

Lev Vygotsky's sociohistorical theory emphasizes that the cultural experiences to which children are exposed become an indispensable part of their development. This Maya Indian father in Guatemala is teaching his young child how to make bricks. In doing so, the parent is transmitting important information to his offspring. By becoming aware of how communities transmit knowledge to their young members, we can begin to appreciate how culture influences attitudes, beliefs, and values, as well as cognitive development.

Consider the baby born with low birth weight. Such an infant often displays a sharp, shrill cry and has difficulty nursing. Because of these factors and the baby's fragile appearance, a mother who might otherwise feel confident may become anxious and uncertain about her caregiving abilities. Her apprehensions may translate into inconsistent behaviors, to which the baby, in turn, responds with irregular patterns of feeding and sleeping. These difficulties further reduce the mother's confidence in her abilities and enjoyment of her baby, leading to fewer social interactions and less positive stimulation for the infant. As a consequence, achievements in other areas of development, such as language acquisition, may be delayed. But what factor, precisely, caused these delays? To answer this question, we might point to the child's low birth weight or the mother's avoidance of her infant. However, these explanations fall far short of capturing the many complex elements that contributed to the mother's behaviors and the child's development. The importance of these complex transactions becomes especially apparent when psychologists and others attempt to modify the course of development. The mother who has avoided her low-birth-weight infant because of a widening gulf of anxious reactions brought about by disappointments and unhappy exchanges will need more than simply to be told to start talking to her child to encourage his language development. She may need to gain a greater understanding of the typical problems such babies face, receive support and reinforcement for her efforts to initiate confident caregiving skills, and acquire richer insights into how development is affected by experiences, only some of which she can control.

***Dynamic Systems Theory***   It should be evident by now that contextual theories champion the importance of many interacting events to account for development. **Dynamic systems theory** captures this idea and at the same time stresses the emergence over time of more advanced, complex behaviors from these many interactions (Lewis, 2000). Of particular interest in this theoretical orientation is the notion that development reflects more than an accumulation of past events; it is, instead, the product of reorganizations that arise from the interactions of various levels of the system that could not be observed or expected from each component level by itself. One outcome of this reorganization is a stable, more adaptive way of responding (Novak, 1996; Thelen & Smith, 1994, 2006). When the right combinations of elements are present, new, sometimes unexpected, capacities emerge.

One of the more important implications of dynamic systems theory is that development is not controlled or regulated by any one particular factor, for example, by the brain, the genes, child-rearing practices, or any other specific influence. Instead, these various components are parts of a process that induces more organized and advanced behaviors or ways of thinking. Perhaps one of the best examples illustrating a dynamic systems view is learning to walk. As Thelen and Smith indicate, "Learning to walk is less a prescribed, logically inevitable process than a confluence of available states within particular contextual opportunities" (1994, p. 72). In more concrete terms, learning to walk results from a necessary combination of inherited human anatomical and neural systems, opportunities to exercise muscles, the desire to move around more effectively, the availability of acceptable surfaces and other supportive physical environments, and parenting that fosters exploration and sensorimotor development. Walking begins when the right blend of these comes together (see Figure 1.5). So, too, do new accomplishments in perception, language, cognition, and social behavior.

***Ethological Theory***   Development is influenced by yet one more broad context: the biological history and constraints that have been a part of human evolution. In the nineteenth century, Darwin and other biologists concluded that adaptive traits—those that improved the likelihood of survival and thus ensured a greater number of offspring for further reproduction—were more likely to be found in succeeding generations of a species. Darwin hypothesized that, through *evolution*, the descent of living species from earlier species of animals, humans inherited biological traits

**macrosystem**   In Bronfenbrenner's ecological systems theory, major historical events and the broad values, practices, and customs shared by a culture.

**chronosystem**   In Bronfenbrenner's ecological systems theory, the constantly changing temporal component of the environment that can influence development.

**sociohistorical theory**   Vygotsky's developmental theory emphasizing the importance of cultural tools, symbols, and ways of thinking that the child acquires from more knowledgeable members of the community.

**dynamic systems theory**   Theoretical orientation that explains development as the emerging organization arising from the interaction of many different processes.

▶ **FIGURE 1.5**

**A Dynamic Systems Model of Walking**

According to dynamic systems theory, development arises from the interactions of several systems, each of which displays variability but which, under the right conditions, result in new, more organized patterns of behavior. For example, walking may emerge when the child's physical development, muscle strength, environment, motivation, and encouragement from parents all come together.

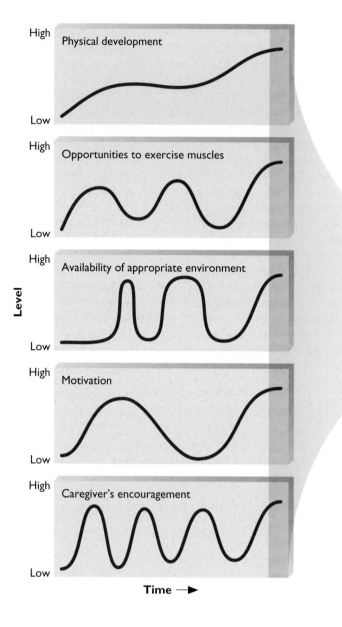

and capacities that improved their rate of survival. **Ethology** is the discipline specifically concerned with understanding how adaptive behaviors evolved and what functions they still serve for the continuation of the species.

Ethological theory surfaced in the 1930s when European zoologists, such as Konrad Lorenz (1963/1966) and Nikolaas Tinbergen (1951), investigated aggressive actions and the courtship and mating rituals of such species as the mallard duck and stickleback fish. Their observations led to explanations that took into account the *mutual* interchange between the inherited, biological bases of behavior and the environment in which that behavior was exhibited (Hinde, 1989). Ethological studies propose answers to questions like the following: Why do babies cry or smile? Why might the ten-year-old fight or be friendly? Ethologists point out the adaptive value of such activities for the individual in the specific environment in which he or she is growing up.

Ethological theory proposes that human infants, as well as the offspring of other species of animals, begin life with a set of innate, *species-specific* behaviors common to all members. In human babies, these include reflexes, such as sucking and grasping, and may also include more complex activities, such as babbling, smiling, and orienting to interesting sensory events—behaviors exhibited by normal infants around the world. These species-specific behaviors help infants meet their needs

**ethology**  Theoretical orientation and discipline concerned with the evolutionary origins of behavior and its adaptive and survival value in animals, including humans.

either directly, as in the case of sucking as a means of ingesting food, or indirectly, as in the case of smiling, a behavior that attracts caregivers and encourages them to provide support.

Besides innate behaviors, the young of many species are predisposed to certain kinds of learning that are not easily reversed, learning that may occur only during limited *sensitive* or *critical* periods in development. A **sensitive period** occurs when an organism is highly responsive or vulnerable to specific kinds of environmental stimulation. One of the best-known examples is found in various species of birds, including geese. Usually, shortly after hatching, the gosling begins to follow and prefers being near a particular object. Normally, that stimulus will be another goose, its mother. In displaying this tendency, the gosling not only learns about its species more generally but also increases the likelihood of being fed and protected. This form of learning that takes place during a brief interval early in life and is difficult to modify once established is known as **imprinting**.

Do other animals show imprinting? Mammals, such as horses and sheep, do. What about human infants? John Bowlby's (1969) theory of attachment suggests that they do, at least to some degree. Bowlby noted that the crying, babbling, and smiling behaviors of young infants signal needs and elicit supportive and protective responses from adults. These behaviors, along with following and talking in older infants, become organized and integrated with social and emotional reactions of caregivers to form the basis for attachment, a mutual system of physical, social, and emotional stimulation and support between caregiver and young. Many experts believe that the failure to form this strong emotional bond with a caregiver in infancy is linked to serious emotional and other problems that occur later in childhood, an issue that will be discussed more fully in later chapters.

***Contextual Theories and Themes in Development***    Contextual models generally agree on many of the themes in development, and where differences exist, they are most often found in ethological theories.

- *Nature & Nurture*  Contextual theories differ widely in their emphasis on nature and nurture, but all recognize the importance of both to development. For ethologists, however, behaviors are closely linked to nature because they have helped, or continue to help, humans survive. Contextual models, even those having an ethological focus, tend to view the child as actively engaged with the environment. In calling for their caregivers, exploring and playing, and seeking out playmates, infants and children elicit reactions from the adults and peers around them. Both individual and environment change in highly interdependent ways, and the relationship between the two is *bidirectional*, each influencing the other (Bell, 1968).

- *Sociocultural Influence*  Perhaps more than any other theoretical orientation, contextual theories are concerned with the ways broad sociocultural patterns affect development. Contextual approaches often search for evidence of how the larger social systems and settings in which children are reared affect their behavior and shape their minds.

- *Continuity/Discontinuity*  Most contextual models place little emphasis on qualitative changes in development. Instead, such models describe the continuous ebb and flow of interactions that transpire throughout development to produce incremental change. However, ethologists often emphasize that particular periods in development are critical for establishing certain competencies. For example, infancy is considered a crucial time for forming emotional ties with caregivers.

- *Interaction Among Domains*  Not surprisingly, most contextual models are typically concerned with the entire fabric of human growth and claim substantial interactions among cognitive, linguistic, social, and other domains. Ethological theorists especially focus on the interrelationship between biological and other aspects of development.

Konrad Lorenz, an ethologist, is being followed by young geese that have imprinted to him. Imprinting in young animals typically occurs to other members of the same species who, under normal circumstances, are present shortly after hatching or the birth of an animal. One question posed by ethologists is whether human infants also show some form of imprinting.

**sensitive period**  Brief period during which specific kinds of experiences have significant positive or negative consequences for development and behavior; also called *critical period*.

**imprinting**  Form of learning, difficult to reverse, during a sensitive period in development in which an organism tends to stay near a particular stimulus.

• *Risk/Resilience* Aside from ethological theories, contextual perspectives focus on the unique configuration of circumstances that foster cognitive, linguistic, social, and personality development. Given the immense number of factors potentially affecting the child, individual differences are often an important aspect to be explained by such theories, including factors that promote risk and resilience. In their emphasis on the multiple layers of influences on child development and on the transactions that occur between child and caregiver, contextual theories capture the complexities involved in any discussion of risk and resilience.

## F O R ◆ Y O U R ◆ R E V I E W

◆ What is learning? What are some of its basic mechanisms? How do behavior analysis and social learning theory differ in explaining what takes place during learning?

◆ What are the primary factors underlying change in Piaget's theory of cognitive development? How do schemes, assimilation, accommodation, and equilibration help to explain the increasingly adaptive and organized nature of cognition?

◆ What characteristics distinguish information-processing approaches from other theories of development?

◆ What is the focus of Erikson's theory of psychosocial development?

◆ What common assumptions underlie various contextual approaches to development—for example, Bronfenbrenner's ecological systems theory, Vygotsky's sociohistorical theory, dynamic systems theory, and ethological theory? How do they differ?

## WHAT DEVELOPS?

All theories of development, of course, are ultimately concerned with the simple question: What develops? As you have seen in this chapter, the answers differ. For learning theorists, what develops is a set of responses. For Piaget, it is a set of cognitive structures. For information-processing enthusiasts, it is mental structures and strategies for responding. For psychosocial theorists, it is identity. For most contextual theorists, it is a pattern of mutually supportive individual and cultural relationships. For ethologists, it is adaptive behaviors.

Theories, by giving us models for observing and interpreting behavior, have had an enormous influence on the way we view children and their development. Why so many different theories? The reason is that each brings an important perspective to our understanding of development. Some remind us of the importance of emotions, others of cognitive structures. Some keep us honest about the role of our biological nature; others perform the same service for the culture in which we are born and reared. Various theories enrich and broaden our understanding of development. We will frequently draw on their contributions for interpreting the many behaviors of children. We hope that you will, too.

As we have introduced developmental theories, we have also discussed their positions on five major themes of development. Table 1.3 summarizes these positions for the major theories introduced in this chapter. As you read further, you may find yourself revising your own stand on the five themes. We trace their presence throughout the remainder of this book with marginal cues placed beside important research and discussions that bear on each theme. Beginning with the chapter titled "Genetics and Heredity," we also open each chapter with a list of the most relevant themes discussed in it and conclude by summarizing how the themes have applied to the developmental domain under discussion.

**Table 1.3    The Main Developmental Theories and Where They Stand on the Five Themes of Development**

| Theme | Learning Theory Approaches | Piaget's Theory | Information-Processing Approaches | Erikson's Psychosocial Theory | Contextual Approaches |
|---|---|---|---|---|---|
| **How do nature and nurture interact in development?** | Emphasis on the role of the environment. | Emphasis on interaction of nature and nurture. Maturation sets limits on how rapidly development proceeds, but experience is necessary for the formation of cognitive structures. | Structures and processes presumably have an inherent emphasis, but experience is likely to be important for their operation. | Stress on an interactional position that recognizes societal demands as well as the child's biological makeup. | Major emphasis on the interaction of biological structures and environmental experiences. |
| **How does the sociocultural context influence development?** | Sociocultural factors determine which behaviors are reinforced, punished, or available from models, but the principles of learning are considered to be universal. | Cognitive structures underlying thought are universal. | Rules, strategies, and procedures acquired to perform tasks might differ from one culture to another, but these differences have received little attention. | Sociocultural context is a major component. | Culture is a critical determinant of behavior, although ethological principles are presumed to apply in all cultures. |
| **Is development continuous or discontinuous?** | Continuous. Development consists of the acquisition of a greater number of learned responses. | Discontinuous. Development proceeds in four qualitatively different stages. | Usually continuous. Development consists of the acquisition of more effective structures and processes for performing tasks. | Discontinuous. Development proceeds through eight stages. | Continuous. Development involves transactions between the child and the environment. |
| **How do the various domains of development interact?** | Universal learning processes work in many domains, but learning itself is highly situational. | Cognitive development has implications for social and moral development. | Usually concerned only with cognition, but have also been used to understand social and emotional relationship. | Failure to progress through stages may disrupt progress in many domains besides personality development. | Because of the strong interdependence between child and environment, all aspects of development are closely related. |
| **What factors promote risk or resilience in development?** | Risk and resilience can be understood in terms of reinforcements, punishments, and the types of models to which the child is exposed. | Does not place an emphasis on risk and resilience, but suggests that risks can occur if environmental experiences matching the child's biological readiness are not supplied. | Little explicit consideration of risk and resilience, although the potential is there. | Not specifically focused on risk and resilience, but failure to negotiate the stages can result in risk. | Focus on multiple factors that influence development as well as on role of child-caregiver transactions provides excellent starting point for examining risk and resilience. |

# CHAPTER RECAP

## Summary of Developmental Themes

### NATURE & NURTURE

**What roles do nature and nurture play in development?**

This issue is concerned with how genetic and experiential variables interact to influence behavior. One implication of this interaction is that children play an active role in the process of development.

### SOCIOCULTURAL INFLUENCE

**How does the sociocultural context influence development?**

Children grow up in a social environment and cultural community that can have a tremendous impact on the behaviors that are displayed.

### CONTINUITY/DISCONTINUITY

**Is development continuous or discontinuous?**

Changes in behavior may stem from quantitative, incremental developmental advances or qualitative reorganization.

Children's behavior also may be influenced by multiple strategies or ways of responding.

### INTERACTION AMONG DOMAINS

**How do the various domains of development interact?**

Developmental psychologists are concerned with the "whole" child; thus they are interested in how skills and capacities acquired in some area affect other aspects of behavior.

### RISK/RESILIENCE

**What factors promote risk or resilience in development?**

Certain biological or environmental factors may be associated with a course of development that is less than optimal. Other factors may protect the child from the impact of these risks. Developmental psychologists are interested in identifying the complexities of risk and resilience so that appropriate interventions can be designed.

## Chapter Review

### WHAT IS DEVELOPMENT?

**What is development?**

*Development* refers to all of the physical and psychological changes a human being undergoes from conception until death.

**What is developmental psychology?**

*Developmental psychology* is the discipline concerned with the scientific study of changes in human behaviors and mental processes over a lifetime.

**What role do theories play in the scientific process?**

*Theories* serve to organize information gathered by researchers, explain observations, and predict behaviors that should occur in future observations.

**What role does developmental psychology play in the formation of social policy?**

The information gathered in research should be helpful in suggesting specific actions for *social policy*, plans by government or private agencies to alleviate social problems.

### THE STUDY OF THE CHILD: HISTORICAL PERSPECTIVES

**How have views of childhood changed from medieval and Renaissance times to today?**

In medieval and premodern times, although recognized as vulnerable, children quickly became a part of adult society. By the seventeenth and eighteenth centuries, children were viewed as worthy of special attention in terms of parenting and education. By the beginning of the twentieth century, children became the objects of scientific study.

**What were John Locke's and Jean Jacques Rousseau's views of childhood?**

Philosophers, such as John Locke, emphasized *empiricism*, the view that experience shapes the development of the individual, whereas others, such as Jean Jacques Rousseau, wrote about the curious and active nature of the child.

**How did Charles Darwin, Wilhelm Preyer, G. Stanley Hall, Alfred Binet, and James Mark Baldwin contribute to developmental psychology?**

Baby biographers, such as Charles Darwin and Wilhelm Preyer, carried out the first systematic observations of individual children. G. Stanley Hall introduced the questionnaire method for studying large groups of children. Alfred Binet initiated the movement to study *individual differences* in children's behavior and abilities. Theorist James Mark Baldwin viewed the child as a participant in his or her own cognitive and social development.

### What was Sigmund Freud's psychosexual theory of development?

Freud emphasized the importance of early experience on development and posited a series of psychosexual stages that children must successfully negotiate in order to demonstrate normal personality development.

### What emphases emerged in research on children during the first half of the twentieth century?

For much of the first half of the twentieth century, work was carried out on gathering descriptive information about children. Arnold Gesell and others focused on establishing norms of behavior. Subsequently, research began to be initiated to investigate the variables that might cause development.

## THEORIES OF DEVELOPMENT

### What is learning? What are some of its basic mechanisms? How do behavior analysis and social learning theory differ in explaining what takes place during learning?

*Learning* is the permanent change in behavior that results from experience. *Behavior analysis* relies on two basic forms of learning, classical and operant conditioning, to bring about behavioral change. *Social learning theory*, as outlined by Albert Bandura, adds *observational learning* as an important mechanism by which behavior is continuously modified and changed.

### What are the primary factors underlying change in Piaget's theory of cognitive development? How do schemes, assimilation, accommodation, and equilibration help to explain the increasingly adaptive and organized nature of cognition?

Jean Piaget's *cognitive-developmental theory* highlights the child's construction of *schemes* or patterns of acting on and thinking about the world. Through *assimilation* and *accommodation*, a child's schemes actively adapt to the demands of the environment by becoming more organized, conceptual, and logical. These regulatory processes

of *adaptation* and *organization* result in *equilibrium*. Cognitive development progresses through a series of qualitatively different stages according to Piaget's theory.

### What characteristics distinguish information-processing approaches from other theories of development?

*Information-processing models* use the computer as a metaphor in accounting for cognitive development. Developmental differences in cognitive structures and processes, such as rules, strategies, and procedures, account for changes in attention, memory, thinking, and problem solving.

### What is the focus of Erikson's theory of psychosocial development?

Erikson's *psychosocial theory of development* focuses on the sociocultural context in which behavioral needs are met. Personality development proceeds through a series of stages in which self and societal demands are resolved to construct one's *identity*. Individuals who successfully negotiate these demands become contributing members of society.

### What common assumptions underlie various contextual approaches to development—for example, Bronfenbrenner's ecological systems theory, Vygotsky's sociohistorical theory, dynamic systems theory, and ethological theory? How do they differ?

*Contextual models* view human development from a broader framework involving multiple, bidirectionally interacting levels of influence. *Ecological systems theory* looks beyond the immediate experiences of family, peers, and friends, and considers the broader sociocultural contexts in which development proceeds. In particular, processes within the *microsystem*, *mesosystem*, *exosystem*, *macrosystem*, and *chronosystem* are considered. Vygotsky's *sociohistorical theory* views culture as the historical legacy of a community and emphasizes the social interactions by which this heritage is transferred from others and adopted by the child to become part of his or her way of thinking. *Dynamic systems theory* proposes that new, complex, and sometimes qualitatively different behaviors arise from the interaction of events at many different levels in the system. *Ethology* pays special attention to the biological, evolutionary heritage each individual brings to the world as the basis for species-specific behaviors found to be adaptive in interacting with the environment. Ethologists pay special attention to experiences that occur within *sensitive periods* in development and to mechanisms of learning like *imprinting*.

## KEY TERMS AND CONCEPTS

accommodation (p. 23)

adaptation (p. 20)

assimilation (p. 20)

behavior analysis (p. 17)

chronosystem (p. 31)

cognitive-developmental theory (p. 20)

contextual models (p. 28)

development (p. 3)

developmental psychology (p. 4)

dynamic systems theory (p. 31)

ecological systems theory (p. 28)

empiricism (p. 12)

equilibration (p. 23)

ethology (p. 32)

exosystem (p. 29)

identity (p. 26)

imprinting (p. 33)

individual differences (p. 14)

information processing (p. 23)

learning (p. 17)

macrosystem (p. 31)

mesosystem (p. 29)

microsystem (p. 29)

nature-nurture debate (p. 6)

observational learning (p. 19)

organization (p. 20)

psychosocial theory of development (p. 26)

scheme (p. 20)

sensitive period (p. 33)

social learning theory (p. 19)

social policy (p. 4)

sociohistorical theory (p. 31)

stage (p. 7)

theory (p. 4)

# Studying Child Development

To me, research is discovery: an odyssey of surprises, confirmations, and unexpected twists and turns that contribute to the excitement of a research career. ... The excitement of a research career is that the story told by the data is always more interesting than the one you expect to confirm. In this sense, human behavior is far more interesting and provocative than even the most thoughtful theories allow, and this means that the scientist must be instructed by the lessons revealed by unexpected research findings—while maintaining humility about her or his capacity to predict the next turn in the road. (Thompson, 1996, p. 69)

hese words, written by developmental researcher Ross Thompson, reveal the genuine enthusiasm of the scientist for the task of systematically observing and making sense of human behavior. Like investigators in many disciplines, developmental psychologists are firmly committed to the idea that theories and hypotheses, such as those described in the chapter titled "Themes and Theories," should be thoroughly and systematically tested using sound principles of science. But, as Thompson suggests, researchers must be prepared to modify or even cast off theories if their observations suggest other truths. At first glance, this outcome may seem discouraging. But, as many researchers can attest, great rewards lie in the simple notion of discovering something new.

Part of the reason that researchers get drawn into the enterprise of developmental psychology is that they are captivated by and want to understand the fascinating, complex, and oftentimes surprising array of behaviors children display. Moreover, there is the sheer fun of being a "child watcher." As even the most casual of observers can confirm, children are simply delightful subjects of study. Research can also make a real difference in the lives of children. For example, newborn nurseries for premature infants now contain rocking chairs so that parents and nurses can rock and stimulate babies previously confined to isolettes. Bilingual education programs capitalize on the ease with which young children master the complexities of language. Clinical interventions help shy children master the social skills that help them to establish positive peer relationships. The benefits of each of these approaches have been revealed through the systematic study of the child.

Collecting data about children, then, is an essential and rewarding aspect of scientific developmental psychology, and being well grounded in research techniques is important for students of the discipline. With this principle in mind, we devote this chapter to methodological issues in developmental psychology. We hope that, by alerting you to important issues in the research process, we will better equip you to think critically about the findings of the numerous studies you will encounter in subsequent chapters.

## RESEARCH METHODS IN DEVELOPMENTAL PSYCHOLOGY

ike their colleagues in all the sciences, researchers in child development seek to gather data that are objective, measurable, and capable of being replicated in controlled studies by other researchers. Their studies, in other words, are based on the **scientific method**. Frequently they initiate research to evaluate the predictions of a specific theory (for instance, is cognitive development stagelike, as Piaget suggests?). The scientific method dictates that theories must be revised or elaborated as new observations confirm or refute them. The process of scientific fact-finding involves a constant cycle of theorizing, empirical testing of the resulting hypotheses, and revision (or even outright rejection) of theories as new data come in. Alternatively, investigators may formulate a research question to determine an application of theory to a real-world situation (for instance, can early intervention programs for preschoolers boost IQ scores?). Regardless of the motivation, the general principles of good science are as important to research in child development as they are to any other research arena. Although many of the methods child development researchers use are the very same techniques psychologists routinely employ in other specialized areas, some methodological approaches are particularly useful in studying changes in behavior or mental processes that occur over time.

### MEASURING ATTRIBUTES AND BEHAVIORS

All researchers are interested in identifying relationships among **variables**, those factors in a given situation that have no fixed or constant value. In child development studies, the variables are individual attributes, experiences, or behaviors that differ from one time to the next or from one person to another. Ultimately, researchers

**scientific method** Use of objective, measurable, and repeatable techniques to gather information.

**variable** Factor having no fixed or constant value in a given situation.

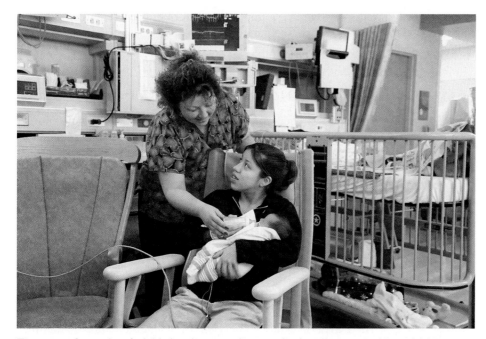

The scientific study of child development has resulted in changes in how children are treated in real-life settings. For example, because of research on the kinds of experiences that benefit premature infants, caregivers are now encouraged to touch and sensitively interact with their preterm babies.

are interested in determining the causal relationships among variables; that is, they wish to identify those variables directly responsible for the occurrence of other variables. Does watching television cause children to behave aggressively? Do withdrawn children have academic problems once they enroll in school? Does the way a parent interacts with a toddler raise or lower the child's later intelligence? In posing each of these questions, researchers are hypothesizing that some attribute or experience of the child is causally related to another attribute or behavior.

The first problem the researcher faces is that of **operationally defining**, or specifying in measurable terms, the variables under study. Take the case of aggression. This term can be defined as parental ratings of a child's physical hostility, the child's own reports of his or her level of violent behavior, or the number of hits and kicks recorded by an observer of the child's behavior. The key point is that variables must be defined in terms of precise measurement procedures that other researchers can use if they wish to repeat the study.

The measurement of variables must also be valid and reliable. **Validity** refers to how well an assessment procedure actually measures the variable under study. Parental reports of physical violence, for example, or even the child's own self-reports may not be the best indicators of aggression. Parents may not want a researcher to know about their child's misbehavior, or they may lack complete knowledge of how their child behaves outside the home. Children's own reports may not be very accurate because the children may wish to present themselves to adults in a certain way. If a trained observer records the number of hits or kicks the child displays during a school day, the resulting measurement of aggression is likely to be valid.

**Reliability** is the degree to which the same results will be obtained consistently if the measure is administered repeatedly or if several observers are viewing the same behavior episodes. In the first case, suppose a child takes an intelligence test one time, then two weeks later takes the test again. If the test has high *test-retest reliability*, she should obtain similar scores on the two testing occasions. In the second case, two or more observers viewing a child's behavior should agree about what they are seeing (for example, did the child smile in the presence of a stranger?); if they do agree, the test has high *inter-rater reliability*. Both types of reliability are calculated mathematically and are usually reported by researchers in their published

**operational definition** Specification of variables in terms of measurable properties.

**validity** Degree to which an assessment procedure actually measures the variable under consideration.

**reliability** Degree to which a measure will yield the same results if administered repeatedly.

reports of experiments; both are very important factors in good scientific research. Measurements of behavior that fluctuate dramatically from one observation time to another or from one observer to another are virtually useless as data.

## METHODS OF COLLECTING DATA

What is the best way for researchers in developmental psychology to gather information about children? Should they simply watch children as they go about their routines in natural settings? Should children be brought into the researcher's laboratory to be observed? Should the researcher ask the child questions about the topic under study? Each approach offers advantages and disadvantages, and the choice of research tactic will often depend on the nature of the investigator's questions. If we are interested in exploring children's spontaneous tendencies to behave aggressively as they play (for instance, do boys play more aggressively than girls?), we will probably find a *naturalistic approach* most appropriate. If we want to see whether children's behavior is influenced by the presence of an aggressive model, we might use a *structured observation* to systematically expose some children to this manipulation in a laboratory setting. If we want to examine how children understand aggression, its antecedents, and its consequences, we might adopt another strategy, such as a *structured interview* or a *questionnaire*. Sometimes researchers combine two or more of these data collection methods within a study or series of studies.

***Naturalistic Observation***   Researchers have no better way to see how children really behave than to observe them in natural settings: in their home, on the playground, at school, and in other places that are part of their everyday life. After all, the ultimate goal of developmental psychology is to describe and explain changes in behavior that actually occur. **Naturalistic observations** do not involve the manipulation of variables; researchers simply observe and record behaviors of interest from the natural series of events that unfolds in a real-world setting.

A study by Herbert Ginsburg and his colleagues (Ginsburg, Pappas, & Seo, 2001), for example, used naturalistic observations to assess the degree to which preschool-age children used mathematical concepts in their spontaneous free-play activities.

**naturalistic observation**   Study in which observations of naturally occurring behavior are made in real-life settings.

In naturalistic observations, researchers observe and record children's behaviors in real-life settings such as playgrounds, schools, or homes.

The study was conducted in four daycare centers that enrolled children from different ethnic and social class backgrounds. Each of the eighty children in the study was videotaped for fifteen minutes during free-play time. Then raters coded the videotapes for the presence of six types of mathematical activities: classification, dynamics (or transformation of objects), enumeration, magnitude comparison, spatial relations, and pattern and shape exploration. The results showed that children spent almost half of the observation period engaged in some form of mathematical activity. Furthermore, there were no gender or social class differences in the tendency to use mathematical concepts in free play.

Several methodological issues are especially relevant to naturalistic observations. First, as researchers code the stream of activities they observe, they need to use clear operational definitions of the behaviors of interest. Ginsburg and his colleagues did so by specifying the elements that constituted each particular form of mathematical activity. For example, enumeration was defined as counting, use of one-to-one correspondence, estimation of quantity, or any statement of number words. Second, researchers must be aware that children (and others) might react to the presence of an observer by behaving in atypical or "unnatural" ways. To reduce such **participant reactivity**, children in this study were acclimated to the video camera and cordless microphone they wore before the recordings began. Finally, to minimize the effects of **observer bias**, the possibility that the researcher would interpret ongoing events to be consistent with his or her prior hypotheses, pairs of independent observers coded thirty of the eighty children to ensure the reliability of the findings. Researchers usually require that at least one of the observers is unfamiliar with the purposes of the study.

An important advantage of naturalistic observations is that researchers can see the events and behaviors that precede the target behaviors they are recording; they can also note the consequences of those same target behaviors. In this way, they may be able to discern important relationships in sequences of events. Moreover, naturalistic observations give researchers powerful insights into which variables are important to study in the first place, insights they may not derive solely by observing children in the laboratory. For example, a laboratory study might not reveal the high level of unguided engagement preschoolers have with mathematical concepts. Often the trends or phenomena identified in such preliminary studies become the focus of more intensive, controlled laboratory experiments. Naturalistic observations also have the distinct advantage of examining real-life behaviors as opposed to behaviors that may emerge only in response to some contrived laboratory manipulation.

Some cautions regarding this method are in order, however. A wide range of variables may influence the behaviors under observation, and it is not always possible to control them. Cause-and-effect relationships, therefore, cannot be deduced. Do preschoolers evidence mathematical thinking because they are in a "school" environment or because certain kinds of toys or materials are available to them? Or do none of these environmental circumstances matter? Answering questions like these requires the systematic manipulation of variables, a tactic that is part of other research approaches.

*Structured Observation*    Researchers cannot always depend on a child to display behaviors of scientific interest to them during observation. Researchers who observe a child in the home, school, or other natural setting may simply not be present when vocalization, sharing, aggression, or other behaviors that they wish to study occur. Therefore, developmental psychologists may choose to observe behaviors in a more structured setting, usually the laboratory, in which they devise situations to elicit behaviors of interest to them. **Structured observations** are the record of specific behaviors the child displays in a situation that the experimenter constructs. Structured observations, like naturalistic observations, are a way to collect data by looking at and recording the child's behaviors, but this form of looking takes place under highly controlled conditions.

**participant reactivity**  Tendency of individuals who know they are under observation to alter natural behavior.

**observer bias**  Tendency of researchers to interpret ongoing events as being consistent with their research hypotheses.

**structured observation**  Study in which behaviors are recorded as they occur within a situation constructed by the experimenter, usually in the laboratory.

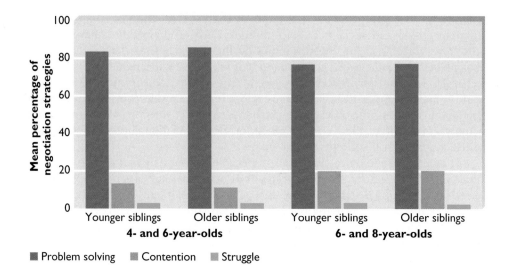

▲ **FIGURE 2.1**

**A Structured Observation**

What happens when siblings are instructed to divide up desirable toys? Ram and Ross (2001) structured a laboratory task in which children had to decide which of six toys each sibling would get. Their negotiation strategies were coded as problem solving (attempts to satisfy each child in the pair), contention (attempts to satisfy one's own desire), and struggle (withdrawing from the negotiation or using an aggressive strategy). The results show that the predominant strategy used by both older and younger children was problem solving.

*Source:* Adapted from Ram & Ross (2001).

A study of the ways in which siblings resolve potential conflicts illustrates how structured observations are typically conducted (Ram & Ross, 2001). Pairs of siblings ages four and six years and six and eight years, respectively, were brought to a laboratory. First, each child was escorted to a private room and asked to rate the quality of his or her relationship with the sibling. Each child was also asked to indicate how much he or she liked six toys that the siblings could later take home. Next, the siblings were reunited and instructed to divide up the toys between themselves. The researchers were interested in the types of negotiation strategies these children used. A portion of the results is shown in Figure 2.1. As the graph shows, the most prevalent strategy was "problem solving," attempting to achieve a solution that satisfied both children. Least frequent was a class of behaviors the researchers called "struggle," the display of some form of overt conflict.

Although these researchers could have attempted to conduct their study of sibling interactions through naturalistic observations in the children's homes, they might have had to wait a long time for the targeted interactions to take place spontaneously. Furthermore, by conducting this study in a laboratory, the researchers were able to keep tight control over the instructions the children received and the specific toys they had to divide between themselves.

At the same time, structured observations may have limitations, especially if they are conducted in a laboratory setting. Children may not react in the same ways in the research room as they do in real life. They may be reticent to display negative behaviors, such as lack of cooperation with a brother or sister, in front of the researcher, or they may show heightened distress or shyness because of the unfamiliar setting. One solution to this problem is to confirm the results of laboratory studies by conducting similar studies in children's natural environments.

Structured observations can focus on a variety of types of behaviors. Like many structured observations, the study by Ram and Ross focused on children's overt actions, in this case their physical and verbal behaviors. Researchers often record other behaviors, such as the number of errors children make in a problem-solving task, the kinds of memory strategies they display, or the amount of time they take to learn a specified task. When structured observations are conducted in the laboratory, it is also possible for researchers to obtain *physiological measures*, the shifts in heart rate, brain wave activity, or respiration rate that can indicate the child's reaction to changes in stimuli. Physiological measures are especially useful in examining the behavior of infants, because the range of overt responses that very young children usually display is more limited than that of older children.

**The Interview and the Questionnaire**    Sometimes the best way to glean information about what children know or how they behave is not simply to observe them but to ask them directly. Researchers have found that talking with children about their conceptions of friendship, gender roles, problem-solving skills—in fact, almost anything in the child's world—has yielded a wealth of material for analysis.

Many investigators use the technique of **structured interviews**, studies in which each participant is asked the same sequence of questions. For example, the goal of study conducted by Mary Levitt and her colleagues (Levitt, Guacci-Franco, & Levitt, 1993) was to explore the sources of social support for seven-, ten-, and fourteen-year-old children from different ethnic backgrounds. More than 300 African American, Anglo American, and Hispanic American children were interviewed about the people most important in their life. Each child was questioned by an interviewer of the same cultural background as the child, to maximize the child's comfort with the session and the accuracy of his or her responses. Examples of the standard questions employed in this study include "Are there people who make you feel better when something bothers you or you are not sure about something?" and "Are there people who like to be with you and do fun things with you?" The results showed that, for all children, regardless of ethnic background, the family was an important source of social support. Moreover, members of the extended family (such as grandparents, aunts, and uncles) played an increasing role during middle childhood, whereas peers assumed a significant support role during adolescence.

Structured interviews provide a useful way to obtain information on what children know, how they feel, and how they interpret their world.

**structured interview**    Standardized set of questions administered orally to participants.

Another "asking" technique that researchers use with children is to obtain written responses to a standard set of items in a **questionnaire**. Because questionnaires can be administered to large numbers of children at the same time, researchers can use this method to obtain a large set of data very quickly. Questionnaires can also be scored quickly, particularly if the items ask participants to pick from a set of multiple-choice items or to rate items on a numerical scale. Children, however, may have difficulty understanding the items and may not be able to answer accurately without guidance from an adult. Under those conditions, oral interviews with individual children may provide more reliable and valid information about how children think and feel.

Researchers who use interviews and questionnaires to collect data from children must be careful, though. Sometimes young respondents, like their adult counterparts, will try to present themselves in the most favorable light or answer questions in the way they think the researcher expects them to. In the study of children's sources of social support, for example, participants may have said that they talked with their parents when they had problems because they knew this was the expected response. To prompt participants to answer as honestly as possible, researchers try not to react positively or negatively as the participant responds and also try to explain, before the start of the interview or questionnaire, the importance of answering truthfully.

Another way to collect data by interview is the **clinical method**, a flexible, open-ended technique in which the investigator may modify the questions in reaction to the child's response. A notable example was Jean Piaget's use of the clinical method to explore age-related changes in children's thinking capabilities. Consider the following segment, in which Piaget (1929) questions a six-year-old boy about the sun:

PIAGET: *How did the sun begin?*

CHILD: *It was when life began.*

PIAGET: *Has there always been a sun?*

CHILD: *No.*

PIAGET: *How did it begin?*

CHILD: *Because it knew that life had begun.*

PIAGET: *What is it made of?*

CHILD: *Of fire …*

PIAGET: *Where did the fire come from?*

CHILD: *From the sky.*

PIAGET: *How was the fire made in the sky?*

CHILD: *It was lighted with a match.* (p. 258)

Note how Piaget follows the child's line of thinking with each question he asks. The format of the interview changes with an older boy, age nine years.

PIAGET: *How did the sun start?*

CHILD: *With heat.*

PIAGET: *What heat?*

CHILD: *From the fire.*

PIAGET: *Where is the fire?*

CHILD: *In heaven.*

**questionnaire**  Set of standardized questions administered to participants in written form.

**clinical method**  Flexible, open-ended interview method in which questions are modified in reaction to the child's responses.

PIAGET: *How did it start?*

CHILD: *God lit it with wood and coal.*

PIAGET: *Where did he get the wood and coal?*

CHILD: *He made it.* (p. 265)

Piaget gained some enormous insights into the thinking processes of children by using the probing, interactive questions typical of the clinical method. Having the flexibility to follow the child's train of thought rather than sticking to a rigid protocol of predetermined questions allows the researcher to gather fresh insights. The weakness of this approach, however, lies precisely in this flexibility. Because the questions asked of different participants are likely to vary, systematic comparisons of their answers are difficult to make. Moreover, the researcher may be tied to a theoretical orientation that biases the formulation of questions and the interpretation of answers. Nonetheless, the clinical method can be a valuable research tool, particularly in exploring the way children think and reason.

**The Meta-Analytic Study** Sometimes researchers do not actually collect empirical data themselves but instead make a statistical analysis of a body of previously published research on a specific topic that allows them to draw some general conclusions. Instead of looking or asking, they "crunch" data; that is, they combine the results of numerous studies to assess whether the central variable common to all has an important effect. This technique, called **meta-analysis**, is particularly useful when the results of studies in the same area are inconsistent or conflict with one another.

A good example of meta-analysis is a study conducted by Janet Hyde and her colleagues to assess the existence of sex differences in children's mathematical skills (Hyde, Fennema, & Lamon, 1990). Many researchers have concluded that boys perform better than girls on tests of mathematical skill, particularly after age twelve or thirteen (Halpern, 1986; Maccoby & Jacklin, 1974). Such observations have spawned numerous debates about the origins of this sex difference. Is mathematical skill biologically given, or is it learned through experiences in the environment? The answer to this question has important educational implications for male and female students. Hyde and her colleagues collected one hundred studies conducted from 1967 through 1987 that examined the question of sex differences in mathematics performance. (This body of studies represented the participation of more than 3 million participants!) For each study, a statistical measure representing *effect size* was computed, a mathematical way of expressing the size of the difference in male and female scores. Hyde and her colleagues (1990) found that the average difference between males and females across all studies was small, leading the researchers to conclude that sex differences in mathematical ability are not large enough to be of great scientific significance.

Conducting a meta-analysis requires the careful transcription of hundreds of statistical figures, a powerful computer, and a good deal of computational skill. Because the researcher taking this approach did not design the original studies, she or he cannot always be sure that the central variables have been defined in identical ways across studies. Moreover, studies that do not present their data in the form necessary for analysis may have to be eliminated from the pool; potentially valuable information may thus be lost. Despite these difficulties, the meta-analytic approach allows researchers to draw conclusions based on a large corpus of research, not just individual studies, and thereby to profit from an accumulated body of knowledge. This technique has recently become increasingly popular in developmental research and has provoked the reevaluation of more than one traditional notion about children.

From our discussion it should be clear that there is no single right way to study children. Researchers must consider their overall goals and their available resources

**meta-analysis** Statistical examination of a body of research studies to assess the effect of the common central variable.

**Table 2.1** **Advantages and Disadvantages of Information-Gathering Approaches**

| Approach | Description | Advantages | Disadvantages |
| --- | --- | --- | --- |
| **Naturalistic Observations** | Observations of behaviors as they occur in children's real-life environments. | Can note antecedents and consequences of behaviors; see real-life behaviors. | Possibility of participant reactivity and observer bias; less control over variables; cause-and-effect relationships difficult to establish. |
| **Structured Observations** | Observations of behaviors in situations constructed by the experimenter. | More control over conditions that elicit behaviors. | Children may not react as they would in real life. |
| **Interviews and Questionnaires** | Asking children (or parents) about what they know or how they behave. | Quick way to assess children's knowledge or reports of their behaviors. | Children may not always respond truthfully or accurately: systematic comparisons of responses may be difficult; theoretical orientation of researcher may bias questions and interpretations of answers. |
| **Meta-Analytic Studies** | Statistical analysis of other researcher's findings to look for the size of a variable's effects. | Pools a large body of research findings to sort out conflicting findings; no participants are observed. | Requires careful mathematical computation; variables may not have been defined identically across all studies. |

as they make decisions about how to construct a research study. Table 2.1 summarizes the advantages and disadvantages of the four general types of data collection just described.

## RESEARCH DESIGNS

Besides formulating their hypotheses, identifying the variables, and choosing a method of gathering information about children, investigators must select the research design they will use as part of their study. The *research design* is the overall conceptual approach that defines whether the variables will be manipulated, how many children will be studied, and the precise sequence of events as the study proceeds. Research designs may be fairly complex, and an investigator might choose more than one design for each part of a large study. Generally, however, researchers select from one of three study types: correlational designs, experimental designs, and case studies or single-case designs.

*The Correlational Design*   Studies in which the researcher looks for systematic relationships among variables use the correlational design and are called **correlational studies**. Instead of manipulating the variables, in this design the investigator obtains measures of two or more characteristics of the participants and sees whether changes in one variable are accompanied by changes in the other. Some variables show a **positive correlation**; that is, as the values of one variable change, scores on the other variable change in the same direction. For example, if a positive correlation exists between children's television viewing and their aggression, as the number of hours of TV viewing increases, the number of aggressive acts committed increases as well. A **negative correlation** indicates that, as scores on one variable change, scores on the other variable change in the opposite direction. Thus, using our example, a negative relationship exists if aggression decreases as TV viewing increases.

The statistic used to describe the strength of a relationship between two variables is called the **correlation coefficient**, or *r*. Correlation coefficients may range from +1.00 (perfectly positively correlated) to −1.00 (perfectly negatively correlated).

**correlational study**   Study that assesses whether changes in one variable are accompanied by systematic changes in another variable.

**positive correlation**   Relationship in which changes in one variable are accompanied by systematic changes in another variable in the same direction.

**negative correlation**   Relationship in which changes in one variable are accompanied by systematic changes in another variable in the opposite direction.

**correlation coefficient (r)**   Statistical measure, ranging from +1.00 to −1.00, that summarizes the strength and direction of the relationship between two variables; does not provide information about causation.

As the correlation coefficient approaches 0.00 (which signifies no relationship), the relationship between the two variables becomes weaker. A rule of thumb is that correlations of .70 or higher usually signify strong relationships, whereas those below .20 represent weak relationships. In most cases, values falling in between indicate a moderate relationship between two variables.

We can use a portion of a study conducted by Carol MacKinnon-Lewis and her colleagues (MacKinnon-Lewis et al., 1994) to illustrate the key features of correlational research. One objective of these investigators was to see if relationships existed between boys' aggressive behaviors and several family variables, such as the number of negative life events the child had experienced. The latter included experiences such as a parent leaving home or a divorce between parents. The investigators found a statistically significant correlation of $r = .40$ between the number of negative life events reported by boys and the number of fights they started with peers. Thus, the more stress the boys experienced within the family, the more fights they initiated in school. In contrast, the number of negative life events experienced by boys correlated $r = .04$ with the mothers' tendency to judge their sons as having hostile intentions in interactions with others, suggesting no relationship between those two variables.

Because researchers do not actively manipulate the variables in correlational studies, they must be cautious about making statements about cause and effect when strong relationships are found. In the previous study, for example, do negative life events cause boys to be aggressive? Or does their aggression contribute to stress and negative events within the family? Still another possibility is that some third factor not measured by the researchers influences both variables. Perhaps, for example, the child's father is aggressive, and that factor influences both the son's aggression and the number of negative life events in the family.

Despite these limitations on interpretation, correlational studies are often a useful first step in exploring which variables might be causally related to one another. In addition, in many instances experimenters are unable to manipulate the variables that are the suspected causes of certain behavior. In the preceding study, for example, it would be impossible to systematically vary the number of negative life events experienced by boys. In such cases, correlational studies represent the only approach available to understanding the influences on child development.

***The Experimental Design***   The **experimental design** involves the manipulation of one or more **independent variables**—the variables that are manipulated or controlled by the investigator, often because they are the suspected cause of a behavior—to observe the effects on the **dependent variable**, the suspected outcome. One major goal of this type of study is to control for as many factors as possible that can influence the outcome, aside from the independent variables. Experimental studies are frequently conducted in laboratory situations, in which it is possible to ensure that all participants are exposed to the same environmental conditions and the same task instructions. In addition, **random assignment** of participants to different treatment groups (in which one group is usually a *control group* that receives no treatment) helps to avoid any systematic variation aside from that precipitated by the independent variables. As a consequence, one distinct advantage of the experimental study design is that cause-and-effect relationships among variables can be identified.

To illustrate the experimental design, consider the following questions: Do adolescents engage in more risk-taking behaviors when they are with a group of peers than when they are alone? Moreover, in risk-taking situations, are adolescents more influenced by being with their peers than are older individuals? In one portion of a study reported by Margo Gardner and Laurence Steinberg (Gardner & Steinberg, 2005), adolescents (ages thirteen to sixteen), young adults (ages eighteen to twenty-two), and older adults (over age twenty-four) were asked to play a computer game of "Chicken." The game required participants to "drive" a car as close to an abruptly appearing wall without crashing, with the appearance of the wall signaled by a

**experimental design**   Research method in which one or more independent variables are manipulated to determine the effect on other, dependent variables.

**independent variable**   Variable manipulated by the experimenter; the suspected cause.

**dependent variable**   Behavior that is measured; suspected effect of an experimental manipulation.

**random assignment**   Use of principles of chance to assign participants to treatment and control groups; avoids systematic bias.

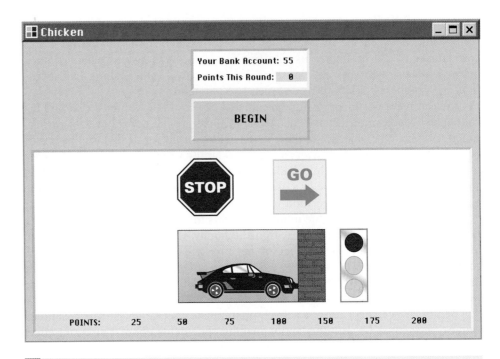

▲ **FIGURE 2.2**

**Assessing Adolescents' Risk Taking**

To assess the influence of peers' presence on adolescents' risk-taking behaviors, Gardner and Steinberg (2005) asked participants to play a computer driving game. The goal of the game was to drive the car as close to a wall as possible without crashing, in order to obtain points. Yellow and red lights flashed on the screen before the wall appeared. Here, the car crashed because the driver kept the car moving when the red light appeared.

*Source:* Gardner & Steinberg (2005).

yellow and then a red warning light (see Figure 2.2). Although points could be won by driving after the yellow light signal appeared, the risk of crashing into the wall was also greater. In this experiment, there were two independent variables—age of the participants and the test situation—whether the game was played alone or in the presence of two familiar peers. The dependent variable was the number of risk-taking behaviors displayed during the computer game. Risk taking was defined as the length of time participants moved the cars after the yellow warning light flashed on the screen. It also included the number of times a car was restarted and moved after the yellow light appeared.

On the surface, it may seem that the design of this study was relatively straightforward. However, individuals could vary their risk taking while playing "Chicken" for any number of reasons, such as the speed of car or the predictability of the warning signals and the appearance of the wall. Therefore, it was important for the researchers to control for as many variables as possible, such that only the independent variable changed across conditions. Under such circumstances, the experimenter can be more confident that the independent variable is causing changes in the dependent variable. The experimenters took steps to address these issues. The speed of the car was kept constant across all experimental conditions, for example, and the warning signals and wall were presented at varied, predetermined times across the fifteen trials for each participant. The results of this experiment, shown in Figure 2.3, indicated that adolescents displayed significantly more risky behaviors when they were with their peers than when they were alone. In addition, the effect of the peer group on risky driving was much greater for the adolescents than for the other two age groups.

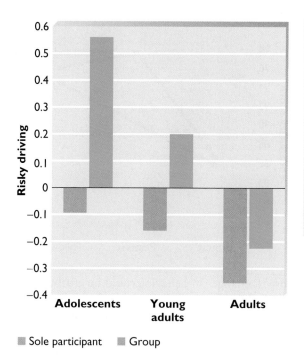

**FIGURE 2.3**

**An Experimental Study**

This graph shows the results of an experiment assessing adolescents', young adults', and adults' risk-taking behaviors in the computer driving game. The independent variables were the participants' age and the context of the game, playing alone or with two other peers present. The dependent variable was the amount of risk taking (a higher score represents greater risk taking). The results show that adolescents are more likely to take risks in the presence of peers than when they are alone and that the effect of peers is magnified for this age group compared with the others.

*Source:* Gardner & Steinberg (2005).

■ Sole participant   ■ Group

The experimental approach has been the traditional design choice for many developmental psychologists because of the "clean" answers it provides about the causes of developmental phenomena. Yet it has also been criticized for providing a narrow portrait of child development. Development in the real world is likely to be caused by many variables; few changes are likely to be the result of a single or even a few independent variables. In that sense, experimental studies typically fail to capture the complexities of age-related changes. Moreover, we have already mentioned that children may not react normally when they are brought into the laboratory setting, where most experiments are conducted. Children may "clam up" because they are shy about being in unfamiliar surroundings with strangers and mechanical equipment. Or they may rush through the experimental task just to get it over with.

In recognition of these problems, many researchers have tried to achieve a more homelike feeling in their laboratories, with comfortable couches, chairs, tables, and rugs instead of sterile, bare-walled rooms filled with equipment. Another tactic has been to conduct **field experiments**, in which the experimental manipulations are actually carried out in a natural setting, such as the child's home or school. In one such field experiment, Grover Whitehurst and his colleagues (Whitehurst et al., 1994) randomly assigned children attending preschool to one of three experimental conditions, to see if the type of reading experiences they had influenced their language skills. For six weeks, a ten-minute period was allocated each day to one of the following conditions: (1) school reading, in which the teacher read a book and concurrently asked children numerous questions about the story and promoted discussion; (2) school plus home reading, in which teachers read to children in the same special manner, but parents were also trained to read to children at home using an active discussion approach; and (3) control, in which children engaged in ten minutes of teacher-supervised play. The groups were formed such that no more than five children participated in each at any single time. The results, displayed in Figure 2.4, showed that, at the end of six weeks, children in both reading groups scored significantly higher on a test of vocabulary compared with the control group and that the school-plus-home reading group scored higher than the school reading group. In the follow-up phase six months later, both reading groups continued to show advantages over the control group in language skills. Because the only known variation in the children's experiences was systematically introduced by the researchers in their manipulation of the independent variable (the type of reading

**field experiment**  Study in which the experimental manipulations are carried out in a natural setting.

▶ **FIGURE 2.4**

**A Field Experiment**

The data from Whitehurst et al.'s (1994) field study show that children who had special reading experiences at school and at school plus home received higher scores on a test of vocabulary on a posttest (six weeks after the program began) and a follow-up test (six months later) compared with the control group. A field experiment employs many of the features of an experiment but is conducted in a natural setting.

*Source:* Adapted from Whitehurst et al. (1994).

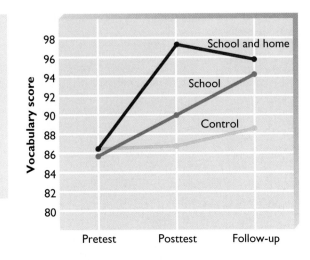

group to which children were exposed), changes in behavior could be attributed to type of reading program. In addition, the natural setting of this field experiment minimized the problems associated with bringing children into the artificial surroundings of a laboratory.

In some instances, it is not possible for the researcher to randomly assign participants to treatment groups, because of logistical or ethical difficulties. In these cases, the researcher may take advantage of the natural separation of participants into different groups. **Quasi-experiments** are studies in which researchers investigate the effects of independent variables that they do not manipulate themselves but that occur as a result of children's natural experiences. Suppose a researcher wanted to investigate the effects of a longer school year on children's academic skills. One way to make sure that it is the length of the school year that influences performance, rather than the initial characteristics of the children, is to randomly assign children to two groups, one with a longer school year and one with a regular school year. That way, children with greater and lesser abilities, for example, would be equally likely to appear in both groups. However, it would be unethical, and also logistically very difficult, to assign children to different schools in this way. Julie Frazier and Frederick Morrison (1998) learned of one elementary school that was extending its school year from 180 to 210 days and took the opportunity to assess the impact on the achievement of kindergartners in mathematics, reading, general knowledge, and vocabulary. The researchers found that children with additional time in school during the year showed greater gains in achievement, especially in mathematics, compared with students who attended a school with a regular 180-day calendar.

The results of quasi-experimental designs must be interpreted with caution. The children who experienced an extended school year may have differed in systematic ways from children who had a regular academic year, ways that could have accounted for their better performance. For example, the former group may have had parents who were very concerned with academic achievement and spent more time teaching them at home. The investigators took great care to try to make the two groups equivalent at the outset of the study by matching them on intelligence test scores, medical history, parents' occupations, parents' expectations about school, and several other dimensions. Could other competing explanations for the outcomes be ruled out? Because the schools were in the same district, their curricula were equivalent. Most revealing, though, was the pattern of exactly at what time gains in achievement were made. Through the winter, when the two school programs still had an equivalent number of days, the students in both groups showed similar patterns of growth in achievement. However, it was during the summer, after the extended days occurred, that student achievement patterns diverged. Thus researchers who conduct quasi-experimental studies must be very concerned with ruling out alternative explanations for their findings. Despite these methodological difficulties, quasi-experimental studies offer a way to address important questions about

**quasi-experiment** Study in which researchers investigate the effects of independent variables that they do not manipulate themselves but that occur as a result of participants' natural experiences.

the complex influences on child development, questions that often have powerful real-world implications.

***Case Studies and the Single-Case Design***   Some notable discoveries about developmental processes have come from the in-depth examination of a single child or just a few children. At times, psychologists make an intensive description of an individual child, much as the baby biographers did. Freud and Piaget both relied heavily on such **case studies** of individuals to formulate their broad theories of personality and cognitive development, respectively. Case studies can be particularly revealing when researchers discover a child with an unusual ability or disability, or an uncommon past history. The details of a child's background, cognitive skills, or behaviors can, in some cases, provide important insights about the process of development or even a critical test of a theory. For example, researchers (Fletcher-Flinn & Thompson, 2000) reported the case of a three-and-a-half-year-old child who was able to read at the level of an eight-and-a-half-year-old. Did this precocious reader focus on the sounds made by each letter in a word, a process that many reading specialists say is essential to skilled reading? Extensive tests and observations indicated that this child had little awareness of the correspondence between individual letters and their sounds, a finding that suggests that successful reading may not depend on phonics skills for all children. Although case studies can provide a rich picture of a given aspect of development, they must also be interpreted with caution. The observations reported in case studies can be subjective in nature and thus vulnerable to the phenomenon of observer bias that was discussed earlier in this chapter.

In other instances, researchers introduce experimental treatments to one or a few children and note any changes in their behavior over time. The emphasis is on the systematic collection of data, rather than on providing a detailed narrative, as is often done in case studies. Frequently the purpose of these **single-case designs** is to evaluate a clinical treatment for a problem behavior or an educational program designed to increase or decrease specific activities in the child.

Suppose we wish to evaluate the effectiveness of a treatment for stuttering in children. One team of researchers selected four boys, ages ten to eleven years, who had difficulty with stuttering (Gagnon & Ladouceur, 1992). Their first step was to record the percentage of stuttered syllables each boy spoke during the baseline period prior to the start of the treatment. Next, the treatment began. During two one-hour sessions per week, each boy received instruction on how to recognize stuttering and how to regulate breathing during stuttering. Special speaking exercises and parent information sessions were also introduced. Finally, the participants' speech was assessed at one month and six months following the end of treatment. Figure 2.5 shows the decline in percentage of stuttered syllables among the children from baseline through follow-up periods. Was the treatment effective? The fact that all four participants showed similar declines in stuttering and that the stuttering remained low during follow-up several months later suggests that it was.

Single-case designs do not require large groups of children or the random assignment of participants to groups. Each participant essentially serves as his or her own control by experiencing all conditions in the experiment over a period of time. As with any study involving only one or a few individuals, however, researchers' ability to generalize to a larger group of children may be limited. Perhaps the child or children they selected for the study were particularly responsive to the treatment, a treatment that might not work as well for other children. In addition, the researcher must be aware of any other circumstances concurrent with the treatment that may have actually produced the behavior changes. For example, did the children in the stuttering study mature neurologically, and did that maturation cause the reduction in speech problems? The fact that the treatment started at different times for each of the four children and was immediately followed by a decrease in stuttering suggests that the treatment and not some other factor caused the changes.

**case study**   In-depth description of psychological characteristics and behaviors of an individual, often in the form of a narrative.

**single-case design**   Study that follows only one or a few participants over a period of time, with an emphasis on systematic collection of data.

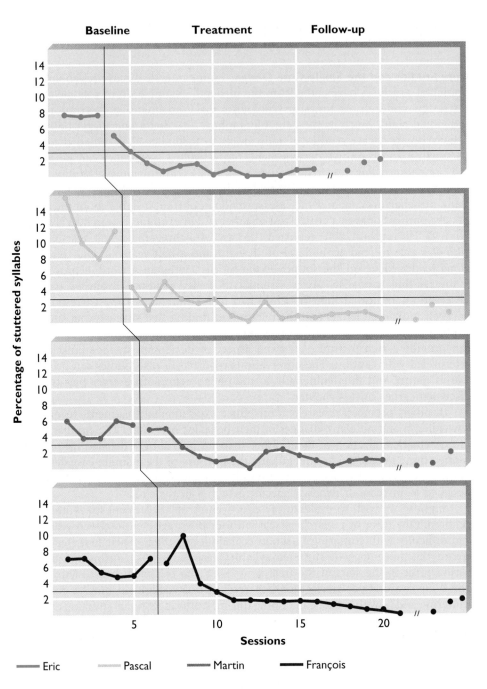

■ **FIGURE 2.5**
**A Single-Case Design**

In this example of a single-case design, four boys with stuttering problems were observed during a baseline period. Next, a program to treat their speech problems was begun. The graph shows that the percentage of stuttered syllables declined dramatically following the onset of treatment and remained low during the follow-up period. Because the four children showed similar patterns of behavior change, and because the behavior change was maintained long after the treatment ended, the researchers concluded that their treatment was effective.

*Source:* Gagnon & Ladouceur (1992).

Table 2.2 presents an overview of the strengths and weaknesses of case studies and single-case designs, as well as other research designs that we have examined briefly here.

F O R ● Y O U R ● R E V I E W

◆ What issues must researchers pay attention to when they measure attributes and behaviors?

◆ What four information-gathering techniques do developmental researchers generally have available to them? What are the advantages and disadvantages of each technique?

◆ What are the different research designs that researchers might employ to study child development? What are the strengths and weaknesses of each design?

**Table 2.2 Strengths and Weaknesses of Research Designs**

| Design | Description | Strengths | Weaknesses |
|---|---|---|---|
| Correlational Design | Researcher sees if changes in one variable are accompanied by systematic changes in another variable. | Useful when conditions do not permit the manipulation of variables. | Cannot determine cause-and-effect relationships. |
| Experimental Design | Researcher manipulates one or more independent variables to observe the effects on the dependent variable(s). | Can isolate cause-and-effect relationships. | May not yield information about real-life behaviors. |
| Field Experiment | Experiment conducted in a real-life, naturalistic setting. | Can isolate cause-and-effect relationships; behaviors are observed in natural settings. | Less control over treatment conditions. |
| Quasi-Experiment | Assignment of participants to groups is determined by their natural experiences. | Takes advantage of natural separation of children into groups. | Factors other than independent variables may be causing results. |
| Case Study/Single-Case Design | In-depth observation of one or a few children over a period of time. | Does not require large pool of participants. | Can be vulnerable to observer bias; ability to generalize to the larger population may be limited. |

# SPECIAL ISSUES IN DEVELOPMENTAL RESEARCH

B ecause of the nature of the questions that developmental researchers ask, certain research strategies take on special significance. How does some aspect of development change with age? How do individual children display transitions in how they think or behave? How do nature and nurture interact to result in a specific developmental outcome? To answer questions like these, researchers turn to an array of strategies that are especially useful when questions about child development are involved.

## STRATEGIES FOR ASSESSING DEVELOPMENTAL CHANGE

The developmental researcher faces a problem unique to this field: how to record the changes in behavior that occur over time. For the most part, the investigator has two choices: to observe individual children repeatedly over time or to select children of different ages to participate in one study at a given time. Each approach has its strengths and limitations, and each has contributed substantially to our understanding of child development.

***The Longitudinal Study*** **Longitudinal studies** assess the same sample of participants repeatedly at various points in time, usually over a span of years. This approach has the longest historical tradition in developmental psychology. The early baby biographies were in essence longitudinal observations, and several major longitudinal projects that were initiated in the early 1900s continued for decades. One of the most famous is Lewis Terman's study of intellectually gifted children, begun in 1921 (Terman, 1925; Terman & Oden, 1959).

Terman identified 952 children aged two to fourteen years who had scored 140 or above on a standardized test of intelligence. He was interested in answering several questions about these exceptionally bright children. Would they become extraordinarily successful later in life? Did they possess any specific cluster of common personality traits? Did they adapt well socially? The sample was followed until most participants reached sixty years of age, and a wealth of information was collected over this long span of time. One finding was that many individuals in this sample had highly successful careers in science, academics, business, and other professions. In addition,

**longitudinal study** Research in which the same participants are repeatedly tested over a period of time, usually years.

Longitudinal studies assess the same individuals over a span of years, sometimes ranging from infancy through adolescence. This strategy for assessing developmental change allows researchers to identify the stability of many human characteristics.

contrary to many popular stereotypes, high intelligence was associated with greater physical and mental health and adaptive social functioning later in life.

Longitudinal research is costly and requires a substantial research effort. Participants followed over a period of years often move or become unavailable for other reasons; just keeping track of them requires constant and careful recordkeeping. In addition, one might raise questions about the characteristics of the people who remain in the study: perhaps they are less mobile, or perhaps those who agree to participate in a thirty-year study have unique qualities that can affect the interpretation of the project's results (for instance, they may be less energetic or be more curious about themselves and more introspective). Another difficulty lies in the fact that participants who are tested repeatedly often get better at the tests, not because of any changes in their abilities, but because the tests become more familiar over time. Participants who take a test of spatial skill again and again may improve due to practice with the test and not as a result of any developmental change in their abilities. If the researcher attempts to avert this outcome by designing a different version of the same test, the problem then becomes whether the two tests are similar enough!

One of the biggest methodological drawbacks of longitudinal research is the possibility of an **age-history confound**. Suppose a researcher began a twenty-year longitudinal study in 1970 and found that individuals' gender-role beliefs became less stereotyped as the years progressed; that is, participants were less likely to believe that females are dependent, passive, and emotional, and that males are independent, aggressive, and logical. Are these shifts in attitude associated with development? Or did some historical factor, such as the women's movement, bring about the changes in beliefs? Because participants age as cultural and historical events occur, it is often difficult to decide which factor has affected the results of a longitudinal study. Moreover, consider a twenty-year longitudinal study begun in the 1940s versus a similar study begun in the 1990s. Many of the factors that are likely to influence children's development today—television, daycare, and computers, to name a few—probably would not have been included in studies begun five decades ago.

**age-history confound**   In longitudinal studies, the co-occurrence of historical factors with changes in age; affects the ability to interpret results.

## CROSS-CULTURAL STUDIES OF DEVELOPMENT

Some of the most fundamental questions about the nature of development concern the universality of the various features of psychological growth. Do all children learn language in the same way, regardless of the specific language they acquire? Does children's thinking develop in a universal sequence? Are certain emotions common to all children regardless of attitudes about the appropriateness of crying, smiling, or feeling angry in the larger social group in which they live?

If psychological development does display universal features, this circumstance has far-reaching implications. It could imply, on the one hand, that a child's behavior is largely shaped by biological factors and, more specifically, by the genes that govern the unfolding of some human behaviors. Variations in aspects of psychological development across cultures, on the other hand, imply that the differences in the child's experiences weigh heavily in bringing about those behaviors. **Cross-cultural studies**, which compare children from different cultural groups on one or more behaviors or patterns of abilities, can be extremely useful in answering questions like these.

Take, for example, the development of play. One hypothesis put forward by Piaget is that there is a general progression in early childhood from *exploratory play*, in which the toddler throws, manipulates, and otherwise learns about the functions of objects, to *symbolic play*, in which he or she pretends with objects—for example, sipping from an empty cup or using a block as a telephone. Marc Bornstein and his colleagues (1999) recorded and coded the naturally occurring play behaviors of twenty-month-old children and their mothers in two countries, the United States and Argentina. Mother-child pairs were provided with the same set of eight toys and were told to play as they normally would for ten minutes. These researchers found that, despite being the same age, children in the United States engaged in more exploratory play with their mothers, whereas Argentine children engaged in more symbolic play. Moreover, mothers' play behaviors were strongly related to children's patterns of play. Thus there were clear cultural differences, perhaps linked to the different social goals in the two groups. Exploratory play patterns, which involve manipulating and combining objects, are consistent with the emphasis on individual achievement, independence, and self-reliance in the United States. On the other hand, symbolic play patterns among Argentine mothers and their children often included social behaviors, such as feeding or putting a doll to sleep. These social behaviors are compatible with the orientation of Argentine society toward the larger, collective group. Thus the transition from one form of play to another may be less influenced by universal processes, as suggested by Piaget, than by culture-specific experiences.

Cross-cultural studies can present unique challenges to the researcher. If children from two cultural backgrounds are being compared, the researcher must make sure the tasks are well understood and have equivalent forms despite differences in language or in the kinds of activities the children are used to doing. For example, children in some cultures may never have seen a photograph or a two-dimensional drawing. Asking these children to categorize objects in pictorial form may put them at an unfair disadvantage if they are to be compared with children who have extensive experience with two-dimensional representations. Moreover, if the researcher is an outsider to the cultural group being observed, he or she may provoke atypical reactions from the individuals under study. Parent-child interactions, peer play, and many other behaviors may not occur as they would in the natural course of events, because of the presence of an outside observer. Cross-cultural researchers must thus pay special attention to the possibility of *participant reactivity*.

Cross-cultural studies allow researchers to explore the extent to which children's behaviors are universal or specific to a given culture. For example, are the emotions expressed by these Thai girls interpreted in common ways across cultures?

**cross-cultural study** Study that compares individuals in different cultural contexts.

For some researchers, cross-cultural studies play a different sort of role, in that they provide a way of understanding human development as it is shaped and formed by the unique contexts in which it occurs. From this perspective, a researcher may try to avoid imposing the values and concepts of his or her own culture on another, trying instead to discover the particular beliefs, values, and modes of thinking in the group under study. The goal is not to compare cultures in order to document similarities and differences; rather, it is to study cultures in an in-depth fashion in order to describe behaviors and underlying meaning systems *within* that culture (Miller, 1999; Saarni, 1998; Shweder et al., 2006; Super & Harkness, 1997). A research approach that is often used to achieve these goals is **ethnography**, a set of methods that includes observations of behaviors within the natural environment and interviews with individuals about values and practices within the culture. Ethnographers often live within a particular culture as *participant-observers*, immersing themselves over an extended period of time in the daily routines and practices of a culture (Weisner, 1996). Using these methods, researchers have obtained rich descriptions of what it means to be a child in cultures as diverse as the Gusii tribe of western Kenya (LeVine et al., 1994), Samoa (Ochs, 1988), and the poor neighborhoods of Brazil (Scheper-Hughes, 1992).

The cross-cultural approach has benefits in terms of understanding human development as it occurs not only in other countries but also in our own society, in which cultural diversity is increasingly becoming a characteristic of the population. Consider some statistics. In Canada, approximately 16 percent of children age fourteen years and under come from non-Caucasian background cultures (Statistics Canada, 2005). In the United States, over 40 percent of children under age eighteen are African American, Hispanic, Native American, or Asian (U.S. Bureau of the Census, 2005). By the year 2010, the majority of children under eighteen will have these ethnic heritages in several states, including Hawaii, California, Texas, New York, and New Mexico (McLoyd, 1998). Thus, in order to capture the elements of human development in the broadest and most meaningful sense, researchers will have to study concepts that are relevant and indigenous to these cultures. Individual autonomy and competition may be valued goals of socialization in middle-class Caucasian culture, for example, but they have less relevance in African American or Native American cultures (McLoyd, 1998). Cross-cultural studies can provide important insights into almost all aspects of child development. For this reason, we draw on available cross-cultural work as we discuss each aspect of the growth of children.

F O R ◆ Y O U R ◆ R E V I E W

◆ What four research tactics allow researchers to address questions about developmental change? What are the strengths and weaknesses of each tactic?

◆ What functions do different types of cross-cultural studies serve in developmental research?

## ETHICAL ISSUES IN DEVELOPMENTAL RESEARCH

All psychologists are bound by professional ethics to treat the participants under study humanely and fairly. In general, researchers try to minimize the risk of any physical or emotional harm that might come to participants from taking part in research and to maximize the benefits that will accrue from the findings of their work. The American Psychological Association has drawn up the following specific guidelines for the use of human participants. First, participants must give **informed consent** before participating in a research project; that is, they must be told the purposes of the study and be informed of

**ethnography** Set of methods, including observations and interviews, used by researchers to describe the behaviors and underlying meaning systems within a given culture.

**informed consent** Participant's formal acknowledgment that he or she understands the purposes, procedures, and risks of a study, and agrees to participate in it.

any potential risks to their well-being, and then they must formally agree to participate. Second, participants have the right to decline to participate or to stop participation, even in the middle of the experiment. Third, if participants cannot be told the true purpose of the experiment (sometimes knowing the experimenter's objective will influence how participants behave), they must be *debriefed* at the conclusion of the study. When participants are **debriefed**, they are told the true objective of the study and the reasons for any deception on the part of the experimenter. Finally, data collected from participants must be kept confidential. Names of participants must not be revealed, and care must be taken to protect their anonymity. To ensure that experimenters comply with these guidelines, virtually all research institutions in the United States are required to have review boards that evaluate any potential risks to participants and the researchers' compliance with ethical practice.

The same ethical guidelines apply to using children as participants in research, but frequently the implementation of these guidelines becomes a difficult matter. Who provides informed consent in the case of an infant or a young toddler, for example? (The parents do.) Is it proper to deceive children about the purposes of a study if they cannot understand the debriefing? (In general, it is a good idea to avoid any kind of deception with children, such as telling them you are interested in how quickly they learn a game when you are really interested in whether they will be altruistic with their play partner.) Are some subjects of study taboo, such as asking children about their concepts of death, suicide, or other frightening topics that might affect them emotionally? (Such studies, if conducted, must be planned very carefully and conducted only by trained professionals.) What about cases in which treatments are suspected to have beneficial outcomes for children? Can the control group properly have the treatment withheld? For example, if we suspect that children's participation in an early intervention preschool program will have real benefits for them, should children in the control group be kept out of it? (One solution to this thorny problem is to offer the control group the beneficial treatment as soon as possible after the conclusion of the study, although this is not always a satisfactory compromise. The control group still has to wait for a beneficial treatment or intervention.)

Many researchers assume that children's vulnerability to risk as they participate in psychological experiments decreases as they grow older. Because infants and young children have more limited cognitive skills and emotional coping strategies, they are viewed as less able to protect themselves and to understand their rights during participation in research. This assumption certainly has some logical basis and, in fact, is confirmed by research showing that second-graders have difficulty understanding the concept of confidentiality, as well as the contents of a debriefing statement (Hurley & Underwood, 2002). Some types of research, however, may actually pose a greater threat to older children. As Ross Thompson (1990) has pointed out, older children are developing a self-concept and a more elaborate understanding of the ways others evaluate them. Older children may thus be more susceptible to psychological harm than younger children when the researcher compares their performance with that of others or when they think teachers or parents may learn about their performance. In addition, older children may be more sensitive to research results that reflect negatively on their family or sociocultural group. These situations require awareness on the part of the researcher of the subtle ways children can be adversely affected by the research enterprise.

Table 2.4 sets forth the ethical guidelines on using children as participants in research established by the Society for Research in Child Development (1996). Probably the overriding guiding principle is that children should not be subjected to any physical or mental harm and should be treated with all possible respect. In fact, because children are frequently unable to voice their concerns and have less power than adults do, developmental researchers must be especially sensitive to their comfort and well-being.

**debriefing** Providing research participants with a statement of the true goals of a study after initially deceiving them or omitting information about its purposes.

## Should Researchers Reveal Information They Learn About Participants in Their Studies?

Researchers often study issues that are sensitive but that can have important consequences for the well-being of children. For example, a researcher might be interested in finding out the factors that predict the emergence of eating disorders in adolescents or the consequences of parental drug abuse for the child. However, research that can be very illuminating about the nature of childhood problems often raises difficult ethical dilemmas (Fisher, 1994).

### What Is the Controversy?

Suppose the researcher discovers that a particular child has a serious eating disorder or that a young child has ingested harmful illegal drugs kept by the parents in the home. What are the ethical obligations of the researcher in such situations? Should the concerns about the welfare of individual children override any potential benefits of the research for children in general? Furthermore, should the identities of children with serious problems be revealed to parents, school personnel, or others responsible for their well-being, at the risk of violating children's trust that data will be kept confidential?

### What Are the Opposing Arguments?

Ethical guidelines state that researchers who discover that a child is at risk must take steps to make sure that the child obtains appropriate assistance. Such action is based on the concept of "jeopardy" outlined by the Society for Research in Child Development and referred to in Table 2.4. The idea is that ethical concerns about the welfare of particular children should be a primary concern and override any potential benefits of the research for children in general. Also implicit in the concept of jeopardy is the notion that, in some circumstances, confidentiality must be broken to protect the best interests of the child.

However, as a consequence of such actions, the child may drop out of the study in order to receive some form of treatment or intervention. If several children in the study drop out, the opportunity to complete the research project could be lost, along with the potential benefits of the results of the study for a

### Table 2.4  Ethical Guidelines in Conducting Research with Children

- *Nonharmful procedures.* The investigator may not use any procedures that could impose physical or psychological harm on the child. In addition, the investigator should use the least stressful research operation whenever possible. If the investigator is in doubt about the possible harmful effects of the research, he or she should consult with others. If the child will be unavoidably exposed to stress in research that might provide some diagnostic or therapeutic benefits to the child, the study should be reviewed by an institutional review board.

- *Informed consent.* The investigator should inform the child of all features of the research that might affect his or her willingness to participate and should answer all questions in a way the child can comprehend. The child has the right to discontinue participation at any time.

- *Parental consent.* Informed consent should be obtained in writing from the child's parents or from other adults who have responsibility for the child. The adult has the right to know all features of the research that might affect the child's willingness to participate and can refuse consent.

- *Deception.* If the research necessitates concealment or deception about the nature of the study, the investigator should make sure the child understands the reasons for the deception after the study is concluded.

- *Confidentiality.* All information about participants in research must be kept confidential.

- *Jeopardy.* If, during research, the investigator learns of information concerning a jeopardy to the child's well-being, the investigator must discuss the information with the parents or guardians and experts to arrange for assistance to the child.

- *Informing participants.* The investigator should clarify any misconceptions that may have arisen on the part of the child during the study. The investigator should also report general findings to participants in terms they can understand.

*Source:* Adapted from the ethical standards set by the Society for Research in Child Development (1996).

larger group of children (Beauchamp et al., 1982). Some researchers believe that the benefits of a well-conducted study can override the obligation to help a particular child for whom a problem has been revealed.

### What Answers Exist? What Questions Remain?

In some cases, researchers may have a legal obligation to enforce the principle of jeopardy. A federal law, the Child Abuse Prevention and Treatment Act enacted in 1974, resulted in the creation of mandatory reporting procedures for suspected cases of child abuse and neglect in every state. In many states, researchers are included among individuals who are required to report. Thus a researcher who discovers that a child has been abused or neglected, as in the preceding example of a child who has ingested parents' illegal drugs, may be required by law to report the case to the proper authorities. The fact that the child might drop out of the study or that confidentiality is broken is simply a necessary consequence.

In other cases, the issue may be more difficult to resolve. Research can be of help, though, in supplying information on how children themselves feel when such ethical dilemmas arise. Celia Fisher and her colleagues (Fisher et al., 1996) asked adolescents to judge what researchers should do if they discover that a child has a substance abuse problem, has been physically or sexually abused, displays a life-threatening behavior, or engages in delinquent behaviors. Most adolescents favored reporting instances of child abuse or threats of suicide to a responsible adult. For less severe problems, such as cigarette smoking and nonviolent delinquent acts, adolescents were more inclined to say that the researcher should do nothing. In cases like the latter, rather than reporting children to parents or authorities, researchers might decide to urge children to seek assistance on their own.

Other questions remain. Does the age of the child matter in such ethical decisions? Should these decisions be handled differently with adolescents than with younger children? How can research help us to address questions such as these?

## F O R ◆ Y O U R ◆ R E V I E W

◆ What ethical guidelines apply to the participation of children in research?

◆ What ethical concepts should guide researchers who discover that children in their research projects may be experiencing some form of risk in their lives?

# CHAPTER RECAP

## Chapter Review

### RESEARCH METHODS IN DEVELOPMENTAL PSYCHOLOGY

#### What issues must researchers pay attention to when they measure attributes and behaviors?

Like other scientists, developmental psychologists are concerned with using sound methodologies to glean information about children. The *scientific method* is used not only to test theories but also to gather information that can have applications in the lives of children. Researchers need to be concerned with *operationally defining* the *variables* in the study. That is, the variables must be specified in measurable terms. Variables must be *valid*; that is, they must actually measure the concept under consideration. Variables must also be *reliable*; that is, obtained consistently from one time to another or from one observer to another.

#### What four information-gathering techniques do developmental researchers generally have available to them? What are the advantages and disadvantages of each technique?

*Naturalistic observations* involve the systematic recording of behaviors as they occur in children's everyday environments.

Two special concerns in this approach are *participant reactivity*, the chance that children will react to the presence of an observer by behaving in atypical ways, and *observer bias*, the possibility that the researcher will interpret observations to be consistent with his or her hypotheses.

*Structured observations*, usually conducted in the laboratory, allow the experimenter more control over situations that accompany children's behaviors. Researchers can measure children's overt behaviors or obtain physiological measures, such as heart rate or brain wave activity. One limitation of this approach is that children may not act as they would in a natural context.

Researchers can employ *structured interviews* or *questionnaires* if they are interested in children's own reports of what they know or how they behave. Alternatively, they can use a more open-ended technique, the *clinical method*. Researchers need to be aware that children may not always answer questions truthfully and that systematic comparisons and unbiased interpretations by the researcher may be difficult to obtain, especially with the clinical method.

*Meta-analysis* permits investigators to analyze the results of a large body of published research to draw general conclusions about behavior.

## What are the different research designs that researchers might employ to study child development? What are the strengths and weaknesses of each design?

In *correlational studies*, the investigator attempts to see whether changes in one variable are accompanied by changes in another variable. Researchers may observe a *positive correlation*, in which increases in one variable are accompanied by increases in another, or a *negative correlation*, in which increases in one variable are accompanied by decreases in the other. The statistic used to assess the degree of relationship is the *correlation coefficient* ($r$). One caution about this design is that cause-and-effect conclusions cannot be drawn.

In the *experimental design*, the researcher manipulates one or more *independent variables* to see if they have an effect on the *dependent variable*. *Random assignment* of participants to different treatment groups helps ensure that only the independent variable varies from one group to the other. Therefore, cause-and-effect relationships among variables can be identified. Variations on this technique are *field experiments*, in which the experimental manipulations are carried out in a natural setting, and *quasi-experiments*, in which the assignment of participants to experimental groups is determined by the participants' natural experiences. Because of this circumstance, researchers conducting quasi-experiments must be concerned with ruling out alternative explanations for their findings.

In *case studies* or the *single-case design*, the researcher intensively studies one or a few individuals over a period of time. The former usually involves a detailed narrative description, whereas the latter involves the systematic collection of data. The ability to generalize to a larger population may be limited with these approaches.

## SPECIAL ISSUES IN DEVELOPMENTAL RESEARCH

### What four research tactics allow researchers to address questions about developmental change? What are the strengths and weaknesses of each approach?

*Longitudinal studies* test the same participants repeatedly over an extended period of time. This approach requires a significant investment of time, may involve attrition of participants, and could be vulnerable to the *age-history confound*. It is the only method that allows researchers to examine the stability of traits.

*Cross-sectional studies* examine participants of different ages at the same time. Although this approach requires less time and fewer resources than the longitudinal approach, it is vulnerable to *cohort effects*.

*Sequential studies* examine children of two or more ages over a period of time, usually shorter than that used in longitudinal studies. This approach combines the advantages of the cross-sectional and longitudinal approaches but is also vulnerable to the problems associated with each.

*Microgenetic studies* require the close observation of children as they perform some task, in order to identify the specific processes that change with development. They require careful planning and the selection of tasks that will reveal developmental change, as well as intensive efforts at observation.

### What functions do different types of cross-cultural studies serve in developmental research?

*Cross-cultural studies*, which compare individuals from different cultural groups, can be especially helpful in answering questions about universals in development. Researchers must make sure that tasks are comparable across cultural groups, however.

An important methodological tool, especially for those who wish to learn about the meaning systems within a culture, is *ethnography*, the use of observations and interviews by a researcher who acts as a participant-observer.

## ETHICAL ISSUES IN DEVELOPMENTAL RESEARCH

### What ethical guidelines apply to the participation of children in research?

Participants in research must be asked to provide *informed consent*, given the chance to decline participation, be *debriefed* if there has been any deception, and receive assurance that their data will be kept confidential.

### What ethical concepts should guide researchers who discover that children in their research projects may be experiencing some form of risk in their lives?

Researchers should always be most concerned with the welfare of the child. In some cases, this concern may mean that confidentiality may have to be broken or that the child will have to drop out of the study to receive an intervention.

## KEY TERMS AND CONCEPTS

age-history confound (p. 56)

case study (p. 53)

clinical method (p. 46)

cohort effect (p. 57)

correlation coefficient (*r*) (p. 48)

correlational study (p. 48)

cross-cultural study (p. 61)

cross-sectional study (p. 57)

debriefing (p. 63)

dependent variable (p. 49)

ethnography (p. 62)

experimental design (p. 49)

field experiment (p. 51)

independent variable (p. 49)

informed consent (p. 62)

longitudinal study (p. 55)

meta-analysis (p. 47)

microgenetic study (p. 59)

naturalistic observation (p. 42)

negative correlation (p. 48)

observer bias (p. 43)

operational definition (p. 41)

participant reactivity (p. 43)

positive correlation (p. 48)

quasi-experiment (p. 52)

questionnaire (p. 46)

random assignment (p. 49)

reliability (p. 41)

scientific method (p. 40)

sequential study (p. 58)

single-case design (p. 53)

structured interview (p. 45)

structured observation (p. 43)

validity (p. 41)

variable (p. 40)

# GENETICS AND HEREDITY

3

Michelle and Derek flopped down on the couch after a long evening of teacher conferences. They had coordinated the night so that Michelle visited all of Alison's fourth-grade teachers and Derek saw Keesha's sixth-grade teachers. Now they were ready to compare notes. "Keesha's doing just great," Derek reported. "Her teachers all say she's conscientious, responsible, and very meticulous about her work. No complaints whatsoever. In fact, she seems to be a real star in math and science. How's Alison doing?" Michelle looked at him and smiled, knowing that what she was about to say would not be a surprise to her husband. Since their daughters had been toddlers, both parents had noticed just how different their two little girls were. Keesha was so absorbed and focused on whatever she was doing and always cautious about trying new things. Alison, on the other hand, was a real free and creative spirit, willing to try anything and concerned less with the details of a task than with getting it done as quickly as possible. Michelle responded, "Well, Alison's going to have to get extra help in math, but her teacher says her poems

# KEY THEMES in Genetics and Heredity

**NATURE & NURTURE**  How do nature and nurture interact in development?    **RISK/RESILIENCE**  What factors promote risk or resilience in development?

and stories are very creative. In fact, she's putting one of her poems up in the showcase by the school office. She's just got to buckle down and make sure she gets all of her homework done, though. Especially in math." Michelle and Derek prided themselves on being accepting of their girls' individual strengths and weaknesses—setting high expectations but respecting their individuality, too. But for both parents it was still a puzzle: how could two children growing up in the same house with the same family be so different?

P arents of more than one child are aware of similarities among them. However, they often take particular notice of the differences; for example, by pointing out how one child "takes after" perhaps his mother and another after her father. What are the mechanisms by which such resemblances and differences come about? Although we may grant the contribution of nature to eye color, gender, height, and many other physical traits, heredity's role in other characteristics, such as whether we are contented or quick-tempered, prone to alcoholism, likely to suffer depression, bright and quick-witted, active or more sedentary, is far less certain. Is Alison more impulsive and Keesha more cautious because these qualities developed as a result of their different genetic endowments or because their parents and others encouraged them to develop in these ways? Or did their individuality come about for more complex reasons—perhaps because Keesha and Alison actively pursued different paths of responding to their daily experiences as a result of their unique genetic makeup?

In this chapter, we examine hereditary contributions to development. Major advances in our understanding of the basic biological units of inheritance and their effects on behavior help us to better appreciate the mutual, interactive relationship between nature and nurture. Experiences mold, modify, and enhance biological predispositions, and in a similar manner, genetic endowment influences, perhaps even actively promotes, selection and preference for certain kinds of environments. Our goal is to understand just how such complex interactions evolve.

We begin with a brief overview of the principles of heredity. The blueprint for development is replicated in nearly every cell of our body. This blueprint includes genetic instructions that distinguish us from other species of plants and animals. Regardless of the language we speak, the work we do, the color of our skin, or how friendly we are, we share a genetic underpinning that makes each of us a human being. This biological inheritance also contributes to our individuality. With the exception of identical twins, each of us begins with a different set of genetic instructions. But even for identical twins, in whom genetic makeup is the same, the influence of distinctive experiences ensures that each of us is a unique individual, different from everyone else.

In this chapter, we also examine several examples of hereditary variations that pose problems for development. As researchers learn more about the ways in which genetic influences occur, we can design environments to help minimize the restrictions imposed by certain hereditary conditions. We consider, too, how genetic counseling assists parents in deciding whether to have children or how to prepare for a child who is likely to experience developmental problems.

Most psychological development, of course, cannot be linked to simple genetic instructions. Intelligence, temperament, and personality, along with susceptibility to various diseases and conditions, are the outcome of complex interactions between genetic and environmental events. In the final section of this chapter, we consider research involving identical and fraternal twins, siblings, adopted children, and other family relationships to help us understand the complex tapestry that genetic and environmental factors weave for cognitive, social-emotional, and personality development (Gottlieb, Wahlsten, & Lickliter, 2006; Rutter, 2002).

# PRINCIPLES OF HEREDITARY TRANSMISSION

**KEY THEME**
**NATURE & NURTURE**

Whether we have freckles, blond hair, or a certain type of personality can be influenced by genetic factors, but none of these characteristics is bestowed directly on us at conception. We must make a distinction between what our genetic makeup consists of and the kind of individual we eventually become. In other words, we must distinguish between the **genotype**, a person's constant, inherited genetic endowment, and the **phenotype**, his or her observable, measurable features, characteristics, and behaviors. A given phenotype is the product of complex interactions involving the genotype and the many events that are part of an individual's experience.

Modern theories of the genotype can be traced to a series of experiments reported in 1866 by Gregor Mendel, an Austrian monk. From his observations of the characteristics of successive generations of peas, Mendel theorized that hereditary characteristics are determined by pairs of particles called *factors* (later termed **genes**, the specialized sequences of molecules that form the genotype). He also proposed that the information provided by the two members of a pair of genes is not always identical. These different forms of a gene are today known as **alleles**. Sometimes many possible alternative versions exist for a particular gene.

Mendel also outlined the basic principle by which genes are transferred from one generation to another. He concluded that offspring randomly receive one member of every pair of genes from the mother and one from the father. This is possible because the parents' **gametes**, or sex cells (egg and sperm), carry only one member of each pair of genes. Thus, when egg and sperm combine during fertilization, a new pair of genes, one member of the pair inherited from each parent, is reestablished in the offspring. That individual, in turn, may transmit either member of this new pair to subsequent children. Thus genetic information is passed on from one generation to the next.

At about the same time Mendel's research was published, biologists discovered **chromosomes**, long, threadlike structures in the nucleus of nearly every cell in the body. In the early 1900s, several researchers independently hypothesized that genes are located on chromosomes. Yet another major breakthrough occurred in 1953 when James Watson and Francis Crick deciphered the structure of chromosomes and, in so doing, proposed a powerfully elegant way by which genes are duplicated during cell division. By 1956, researchers had documented the existence of forty-six chromosomes in normal human body cells. Today, some fifty years after Watson and Crick's monumental discovery, the mapping of the sequence of the **human genome**—the nearly 3 billion chemical base pairs that make up every human's biological inheritance—is complete (National Human Genome Research Institute, 2003).

## THE BUILDING BLOCKS OF HEREDITY

How could hereditary factors play a part in the differences displayed by Keesha and Alison or in a child's remarkable musical ability or in yet another's mental retardation? To understand the genotype and its effects on appearance, behavior, personality, or intellectual ability, we must consider genetic mechanisms at many different levels.

To begin with, every living organism is composed of cells—in the case of mature humans, trillions of cells. As Figure 3.1 indicates, within the nucleus of nearly all cells are the chromosomes that carry genetic information critical to the cells' functioning. Genes, regions within the strands of chromosomes, determine the production of specific proteins in the cell. The genes, in turn, are made up of various arrangements of four different chemical building blocks called **nucleotides**, which contain one of four nitrogen-based molecules (*adenine, thymine, cytosine*, or *guanine*). The nucleotides pair together in one of only two ways to form the rungs of a remarkably long, spiral staircaselike structure called **DNA**, or **deoxyribonucleic acid** (see Figure 3.1). An average of about 1,000 nucleotide pairs makes up each gene, although some genes have substantially more pairings (National Research

**genotype** Total genetic endowment inherited by an individual.

**phenotype** Observable and measurable characteristics and traits of an individual; a product of the interaction of the genotype with the environment.

**gene** Large segment of nucleotides within a chromosome that codes for the production of proteins and enzymes. These proteins and enzymes underlie traits and characteristics inherited from one generation to the next.

**allele** Alternate form of a specific gene; provides a genetic basis for many individual differences.

**gamete** Sperm cell in males, egg cell in females, normally containing only twenty-three chromosomes.

**chromosome** Threadlike structure of DNA, located in the nucleus of cells, which forms a collection of genes. A human body cell normally contains forty-six chromosomes.

**human genome** Entire inventory of nucleotide base pairs that compose the genes and chromosomes of humans.

**nucleotide** Repeating basic building block of DNA consisting of nitrogen-based molecules of adenine, thymine, cytosine, and guanine.

**deoxyribonucleic acid (DNA)** Long, spiral staircaselike sequence of molecules created by nucleotides identified with the blueprint for genetic inheritance.

1. The **human body** has about 10 trillion cells. Proteins determine the structure and function of each cell.

2. Most **cells** contain a nucleus. Located within the nucleus are forty-six chromosomes that carry the instructions that signal the cell to manufacture various proteins.

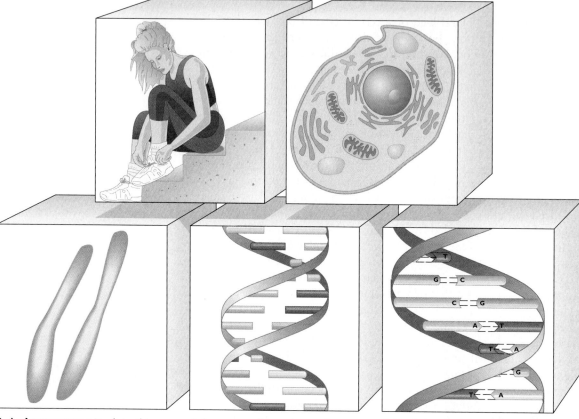

3. A **chromosome** is a long thin strand of DNA organized as a coiled double helix. A full set of forty-six chromosomes in humans is believed to contain somewhere between 26,000 and 38,000 genes, far fewer than had been believed before the human genome was mapped.

4. A **gene** can be made up of thousands of nucleotide pairs. Each gene typically has information designed to specify the production of one or more particular proteins.

5. **Nucleotides**, composed of four different kinds of chemical building blocks—adenine (A), thymine (T), cytosine (C), and guanine (G)—are the smallest genetic unit and are paired in specific combinations. Nearly 3 billion pairs of nucleotides make up the total complement of DNA in humans.

▲  **FIGURE 3.1**

**The Building Blocks of Heredity**

Hereditary contributions to development can be observed at many levels. This figure depicts five major levels. Nearly every cell in the human body carries the genetic blueprint for development in the chromosomes. Specific regions on each chromosome, the genes, regulate protein production. Looked at in even more detail, the human genome consists of chemical molecules that are the building blocks for the genes. Each of these different levels of the individual's biological makeup can offer insights into the mechanisms by which the genotype affects the phenotype, the observable expression of traits and behaviors.

*Source:* Adapted from Isensee (1986).

Council, 1988). Genes differ from one another in number and sequence of nucleotide pairings, and in their location on the chemical spiral staircases, or chains of DNA, that we call the chromosomes.

Just as Mendel theorized, hereditary attributes are, in most cases, influenced by pairs of genes or, more specifically, the two allelic forms of the pair. One member of the pair is located on a chromosome inherited from the mother; the other, on a similar, or *homologous,* chromosome acquired from the father. Figure 3.2 shows a

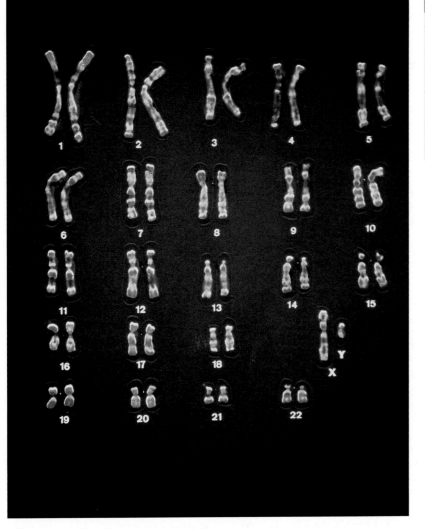

◁ **FIGURE 3.2**

**Chromosomes in the Normal Human Male**

This karyotype depicts the twenty-two homologous pairs of autosomes and the two sex chromosomes in the normal human male. In females, the twenty-third pair of chromosomes consists of an XX pair instead of an XY pair.

**karyotype**, or photomicrograph of the forty-six chromosomes that humans (in this case, a male) normally possess.

As can be seen in Figure 3.2, the homologous sets of chromosomes that are not genetically involved in the determination of sex, called **autosomes**, can be arranged in pairs and numbered from 1 to 22 on the basis of their size. The remaining two chromosomes specify the genetic sex of an individual and differ for males and females. In females this pair consists of **X chromosomes**; both are relatively large and similar in size. The normal male has one X chromosome and a much smaller **Y chromosome**. The Y chromosome is believed to carry only a few dozen genes, in sharp contrast to the 2,000 to 3,000 genes estimated to be on the X chromosome (Jegalian & Lahn, 2001).

## CELL DIVISION AND CHROMOSOME DUPLICATION

Each of us began life as a single cell created when a sperm cell, normally containing twenty-three chromosomes, from the father united with an ovum (egg), normally containing an additional twenty-three chromosomes, from the mother. The developmental processes started by this fertilized egg cell, called a **zygote**, are more fully described in the chapter titled "The Prenatal Period and Birth." Remarkably, however, nearly every one of the millions of different cells in the newborn, whether specialized for bone or skin, heart or brain, or in some other way, contains the same genetic blueprint established in the initial zygote.

**karyotype**  Pictorial representation of an individual's chromosomes.

**autosome**  One of twenty-two pairs of homologous chromosomes. The two members of each pair are similar in size, shape, and genetic function. The two sex chromosomes are excluded from this class.

**X chromosome**  Larger of the two sex chromosomes associated with genetic determination of sex. Normally females have two X chromosomes and males, only one.

**Y chromosome**  Smaller of the two sex chromosomes associated with genetic determination of sex. Normally males have one Y chromosome and females, none.

**zygote**  Fertilized egg cell.

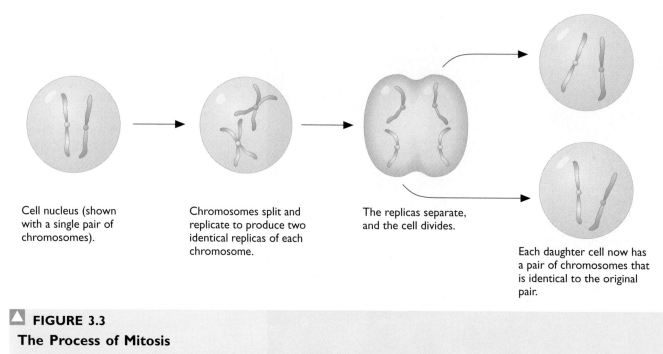

Cell nucleus (shown with a single pair of chromosomes).

Chromosomes split and replicate to produce two identical replicas of each chromosome.

The replicas separate, and the cell divides.

Each daughter cell now has a pair of chromosomes that is identical to the original pair.

▲ **FIGURE 3.3**

**The Process of Mitosis**

The process of mitotic cell division generates nearly all the cells of the body except the gametes. During mitosis, each chromosome replicates to form two chromosomes with identical genetic blueprints. As the cell divides, one member of each identical pair becomes a member of each daughter cell. In this manner, complete genetic endowment is replicated in nearly every cell of the body.

How does this extraordinary duplication of DNA from one cell to another and from one generation to the next take place? Most cells divide through the process called **mitosis**. During mitosis, genetic material in the nucleus of the cell is reproduced such that a full complement of DNA becomes available to each new cell. Even before cell division occurs, the chemical bonds linking the nucleotides that form the rungs of the DNA ladder weaken. The pairs of nucleotides separate as though they were being unzipped from each other. At the same time, additional nucleotides are manufactured in the cell and attach to the separated nucleotides. Because each nucleotide can combine with only one other type, the two newly formed strands of DNA are rebuilt exactly as in their original sequence. The two newly formed copies of DNA eventually separate completely, so that one becomes a member of each of the two new daughter cells, as depicted in Figure 3.3.

The process of cell division associated with the gametes (the sex cells) is called **meiosis**. Meiosis, which results in twenty-three chromosomes in the egg and sperm cells, actually involves *two* successive generations of cell divisions. In the first stage, each of the forty-six chromosomes begins to replicate in much the same way as mitosis begins. However, before the identical replicas split apart, the cell divides, so that each daughter cell receives only one chromosome from each of the twenty-three pairs, as pictured in Figure 3.4. In the second stage, the replicas of the twenty-three chromosomes completely separate, and the cell divides once more, each cell again receiving one of the replicas. Thus, from these two successive divisions, four cells are produced, each with twenty-three chromosomes.

Random segregation of the twenty-three homologous chromosome pairs in the first stage of meiosis yields more than 8 million possible combinations of gametes with one or more different sets of chromosomes. Along with an equivalent number of possible unique arrangements from a mate, mother and father together have a gene pool of about 64 trillion different combinations from which their offspring may derive. But the potential for genetic variability is actually far greater because of the phenomenon known as **crossing over**, a key part of the first stage of meiosis. Before homologous chromosome pairs separate in the first cell division, they

**mitosis**   Process of cell division that takes place in most cells of the human body and results in a full complement of identical material in the forty-six chromosomes in each cell.

**meiosis**   Process of cell division that forms the gametes; normally results in twenty-three chromosomes in each human egg and sperm cell rather than the full complement of forty-six.

**crossing over**   Process during the first stage of meiosis when genetic material is exchanged between autosomes.

Cell with forty-six chromosomes (only one pair of homologous chromosomes is shown here). Each member of the pair has begun to replicate similar to mitotic cell division.

First meiotic cell division begins but does not proceed as in mitosis. Instead of the replicated chromosome splitting apart, one member of each homologous pair becomes a part of the first-generation daughter cell.

The second meiotic division proceeds after the first is completed; now the replicated chromosome acquired in the first-generation daughter cell splits apart.

Each of the four gametes produced by the two-step process now has acquired one member of the pair of homologous chromosomes.

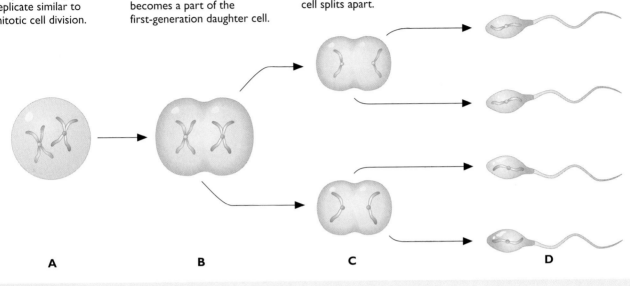

A          B          C          D

## ◢ FIGURE 3.4

### The Process of Meiosis for Sperm Cells

As meiosis begins (A), DNA replicates as in mitotic cell division. However, before the replicated arms split apart, one member of each pair of homologous chromosomes moves to become part of each first-generation daughter cell (B). Once the first generation of daughter cells is established, DNA replicas split as part of the second meiotic division (C). This one replica of one member pair of homologous chromosomes is contributed to each second-generation daughter cell (D). From these two successive divisions, four cells, each with twenty-three chromosomes, are produced.

mysteriously align, and segments of DNA transfer, or cross over, from one member to the other member of the pair, as shown in Figure 3.5. The genetic variability ensured by crossing over makes it virtually impossible for two individuals to have the same genetic makeup, even siblings, unless the two are identical twins.

## GENE EXPRESSION

We have briefly described key structures of inheritance—nucleotides, genes, and chromosomes—and the way these are replicated in cells of the body, including gametes. But how does the genotype affect the phenotype? In other words, how does the underlying genetic blueprint promote the appearance of blue eyes, baldness, and dark skin or such complex traits as shyness, schizophrenia, and intelligent problem solving? The answer begins with the alleles, the specific form a particular gene may take.

We have already learned that each of us typically inherits two genes that code for a particular protein in the cell, one from our mother and the other from our father. These may be identical—that is, have the same allelic form—or they may differ. When both have the same allelic form, a person's genotype is said to be **homozygous** for whatever characteristic that gene affects. For example, three different alleles exist for the gene that governs blood type: A, B, and O. When both inherited alleles are A, both B, or both O, a person has a homozygous genotype for blood type. But, if an individual inherits two different alleles of the gene for blood type, let's say A and B, that person's genotype is **heterozygous**.

The consequences of a homozygous genotype are usually straightforward: the child's phenotype will be influenced by whatever characteristics are specified by that

**homozygous** Genotype in which two alleles of a gene are identical, thus having the same effects on a trait.

**heterozygous** Genotype in which two alleles of a gene are different. The effects on a trait will depend on how the two alleles interact.

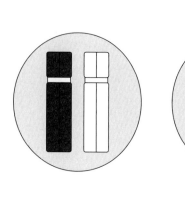

Alignment of homologous chromosomes, each a pair of sister chromatids

**A**

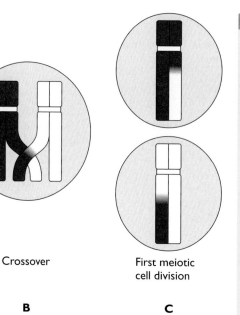

Crossover

**B**

First meiotic cell division

**C**

◀ **FIGURE 3.5**

**Crossing Over: The Exchange of Genetic Material Between Chromosomes**

In the process known as crossing over, genetic material is exchanged between homologous pairs of chromosomes during the first stage of meiotic cell division. (A) Initially, autosomes that have begun DNA replication align with each other. (B) Genetic material between homologous chromosomes is exchanged. (C) One member of each homologous pair of chromosomes randomly segregates or relocates to two different regions of the parent cell, and the first generation of cell division in meiosis takes place.

**dominant allele**   Allele whose characteristics are reflected in the phenotype even when part of a heterozygous genotype. Its genetic characteristics tend to mask the characteristics of other alleles.

**recessive allele**   Allele whose characteristics do not tend to be expressed when part of a heterozygous genotype. Its genetic characteristics tend to be masked by other alleles.

**codominance**   Condition in which individual, unblended characteristics of two alleles are reflected in the phenotype.

**polygenic**   Phenotypic characteristic influenced by two or more genes.

**genomic imprinting**   Instances of genetic transmission in which the expression of a gene is determined by whether the particular allelic form has been inherited from the mother or the father.

particular allelic form. But the effects of a heterozygous genotype depend on how the alleles influence each other. When a child's phenotype shows the effects of only one of the two allelic forms, the one whose characteristics are observed is **dominant**; the allelic form whose influence is not evident in the phenotype is **recessive**. For example, a person who inherits both an A and an O allele for blood type will be classified as having Type A; the allele for Type A is dominant, and the allele for Type O is recessive.

*Cystic fibrosis,* the most common autosomal recessive disorder in Western Europe (McGinness & Kaback, 2002) and a leading cause of childhood death among Caucasian children, provides another example of a dominant-recessive relationship between alleles. The shortened lifespan typically stems from a thickening of the mucus lining the respiratory tract, which interferes with breathing. Most Caucasian children inherit a gene pair that does not include the allelic form that codes for cystic fibrosis; they have a homozygous genotype that contributes to normal development. About one in twenty-five people of Caucasian ancestry, however, has a heterozygous genotype in which one gene is normal and the other carries the genetic information that results in cystic fibrosis. The normal allele is *dominant.* Thus someone who is heterozygous for this condition can lead an ordinary, productive life. But a child of a mother and father each of whom has a heterozygous genotype might inherit two alleles coding for cystic fibrosis (see Figure 3.6). In the latter condition, the two recessive alleles are no longer masked by a normal gene; this child (about 1 in every 2,500 Caucasian children) will suffer from cystic fibrosis. Medical researchers today are actively investigating the potential for *gene therapy,* the replacement of the gene that codes for a disorder, to reduce and even eliminate the devastating consequences of cystic fibrosis and other inherited diseases (Human Genome Project Information, 2006).

In some circumstances, the child's phenotype will reflect the influence of *both* allelic forms if they differ. When the characteristics of both alleles are observed, they exhibit **codominance**. For example, a child with Type AB blood has inherited a gene for Type A blood from one parent and another gene for Type B blood from the other parent.

Table 3.1 summarizes a number of traits and characteristics associated with dominant-recessive patterns. But we must be cautious when drawing inferences about these relationships. Many traits are **polygenic**; that is, determined by several genes, sometimes located on different sets of chromosomes. For example, eye color, although largely governed by the dominant-recessive relationship between allelic forms of a single gene, is affected by other genes as well.

**Father's genotype (Ff)**
**Meiosis**

|  | **F sperm** | **f sperm** |
|---|---|---|
| **F ovum** | FF zygote (homozygous) phenotype–normal | Ff zygote (heterozygous) phenotype–normal |
| **f ovum** | fF zygote (heterozygous) phenotype–normal | ff zygote (homozygous) phenotype–cystic fibrosis |

Mother's genotype (Ff) Meiosis

◁ **FIGURE 3.6**
## The Pattern of Inheritance for Cystic Fibrosis

The inheritance of cystic fibrosis is one of many traits that are influenced by a single pair of genes. In this figure, F symbolizes a normal allele and f represents the allele for cystic fibrosis. When parents with heterozygous genotype for this disease have children, their offspring may inherit a homozygous genotype with normal alleles (FF), a heterozygous genotype with one normal and one abnormal allele (Ff or fF), or a homozygous genotype with two abnormal alleles (ff). Because the normal allele dominates, children with a heterozygous genotype will not exhibit cystic fibrosis. When both alleles carry genetic information for the disease, however, cystic fibrosis will occur.

# GENE FUNCTIONING AND REGULATION OF DEVELOPMENT

How do genes influence the development of a phenotype? A major new field of study called *proteomics* has emerged to attempt to answer precisely that question (Ezzell, 2000). We can give only a brief glimpse into this rapidly evolving area. Although exceptions exist, genetic information is typically conveyed from the DNA in the cell's nucleus to the organic and inorganic substances in other parts of the cell. This process is performed by *messenger ribonucleic acid*, or *mRNA*, a molecule somewhat similar to DNA; mRNA replicates some segment of the DNA. This copy is transported outside the nucleus of the cell, where it can then initiate a series of events that produce proteins to give the cell its unique ability to function. It is important to remember that the genes do not directly cause appearance, behavior, or any other phenotypic expression. Instead, our appearance and behavior are, in part, the end result of an extensive chain of biochemical processes started by the instructions provided by the DNA.

Many mysteries remain concerning exactly how genes influence development. For example, humans are believed to have between 20,000 and 25,000 *structural genes* that code for the production of proteins that govern the physiological functions of a cell (Ensembl Human, 2006; International Human Genome Sequencing Consortium, 2004). Yet structural genes account for only 1 to 2 percent of the nearly 3 billion base pairs estimated to make up the human genome (Pennisi, 2001). Some of the remaining DNA consists of other types of genes that start and stop or modify the functioning of structural genes. But large stretches of DNA are made up of repeat sequences of base pairs or of other patterns that seem to have simply replicated themselves, and their functions, if any, remain unknown.

Other new discoveries are continuing to be made about genes and how they influence development. For example, sometimes it matters whether a particular gene has been inherited from the mother or the father. This phenomenon, called **genomic imprinting**, is best illustrated by the *Prader-Willi* and *Angelman syndromes*, estimated to affect about 1 in 10,000 persons. Individuals with Prader-Willi syndrome display, among other physical and behavioral characteristics, short stature, obesity, and mild to moderate mental retardation. In contrast, individuals with Angelman syndrome display marionettelike disturbances in gait, epilepsy, and more severe learning difficulties, including minimal or no speech. Prader-Willi syndrome stems from the absence of a particular gene or set of genes on chromosome 15 inherited from the father and the inability of the mother's genetic material on the homologous chromosome to compensate for this loss. In contrast, Angelman syndrome arises from the absence of that same gene or set of genes inherited from

⊶ **KEY THEME**
**NATURE & NURTURE**
**RISK/RESILIENCE**

**TABLE 3.1** Alleles of Genes That Display a Dominant and Recessive Pattern of Phenotypic Expression

| Dominant Traits | Recessive Traits |
| --- | --- |
| Brown eyes | Gray, green, blue, hazel eyes |
| Curly hair | Straight hair |
| Normal hair growth | Baldness |
| Dark hair | Light or blond hair |
| Nonred hair (blond, brunette) | Red hair |
| Normal skin coloring | Albinism (lack of pigment) |
| Immunity to poison ivy | Susceptibility to poison ivy |
| Normal skin | Xeroderma pigmentosum (heavy freckling and skin cancers) |
| Thick lips | Thin lips |
| Roman nose | Straight nose |
| Earlobe free | Earlobe attached |
| Cheek dimples | No dimples |
| Extra, fused, or short digits | Normal digits |
| Second toe longer than big toe | Big toe longer than second toe |
| Double-jointedness | Normal joints |
| Normal color vision | Red-green colorblindness |
| Farsightedness | Normal vision |
| Normal vision | Congenital eye cataracts |
| Retinoblastoma (cancer of the eye) | Normal eye development |
| Normal hearing | Congenital deafness |
| Type A blood | Type O blood |
| Type B Blood | Type O blood |
| Rh-positive blood | Rh-negative blood |
| Normal blood clotting | Hemophilia |
| Normal metabolism | Phenylketonuria |
| Normal blood cells | Sickle cell anemia |
| Familial hypercholesterolemia (error of fat metabolism) | Normal cholesterol level at birth |
| Wilms tumor (cancer of the kidney) | Normal kidney |
| Huntington's disease | Normal brain and body maturation |
| Normal respiratory and gastrointestinal functioning | Cystic fibrosis |
| Normal neural and physical development | Tay-Sachs disease |

the mother and the inability of the father's genetic material to compensate for the loss (Everman & Cassidy, 2000; Lombroso, 2000). Susceptibility to certain cancers, growth disorders, and some types of diabetes are also known to occur as a result of genomic imprinting.

Substantial progress in understanding genetic influences has been made in recent years. However, important questions still exist concerning the effects of the human genome on a wide range of complex human behaviors of interest to psychologists. In the section that follows, we highlight additional examples of several specific gene mutations and chromosomal disturbances that can have profound repercussions for development. Keep in mind that serious consequences associated with gene and chromosomal deviations affect a relatively small number of individuals. Nevertheless, the consequences often reverberate and extend well beyond those individuals, to their family and others within the community.

+ What roles do genotype and the environment play in determining a phenotype?

+ What is the human genome? How do the nucleus of the cell, chromosomes and DNA, genes, and nucleotides play a role in genetic influences on development?

+ How many autosomes exist in the human karyotype? Of what importance are the X and Y chromosomes?

+ What is the difference between mitosis and meiosis, and what is the impact of the phenomenon of crossing over?

+ How do homozygous and heterozygous genes and the presence of dominant, recessive, and codominant allelic forms account for the inheritance patterns associated with various phenotypes? What are polygenic traits?

+ How do genes regulate the development of the phenotype? What is genomic imprinting?

## GENE AND CHROMOSOMAL ABNORMALITIES

Changes in the structure of genes, or **mutations**, introduce genetic diversity among individuals. Mutations occur surprisingly often; perhaps as many as half of all human conceptions occur with some kind of genetic or chromosomal change (Plomin et al., 2001). Most mutations are lethal, resulting in loss of the zygote through spontaneous abortion very soon after conception, often before a woman even knows she is pregnant. A small number of other mutations will have little impact on development. However, some can have enduring, often negative, consequences for an individual and his or her quality of life, consequences that may be passed on from one generation to the next. In fact, more than 5 percent of all diseases observed in individuals before the age of twenty-five are at least in part the result of some type of genetic or chromosomal anomaly (Rimoin et al., 2002). Moreover, birth defects and genetically based diseases contribute to a disproportionately high number of hospitalizations and medical expenses in the United States (Yoon et al., 1997). Globally, almost 8 million children are born with genetically linked birth defects (Christianson, Howson, & Modell, 2006). We consider here the consequences of just a few of the more than 1,400 gene and chromosome anomalies that have been identified as influencing physical and behavorial development (Peltonen & McKusick, 2001).

### GENE VARIATIONS

An estimated 100,000 infants are born each year in the United States alone with some kind of problem caused by a single dominant or recessive gene. For about 20,000 of these babies, the problem is significant (Knowles, 1985). Table 3.2 lists a few of the more serious of these. In many cases, the effects are evident at birth (*congenital*), but the consequences of some are not observed until childhood or even late adulthood. We will discuss several dominant and recessive disorders to illustrate their effects on development, the interventions and treatments available for them, and the insights they provide concerning the genotype's contribution to intellectual and behavioral capacities.

KEY THEME
**RISK/RESILIENCE**

**mutation** Sudden change in molecular structure of a gene; may occur spontaneously or be caused by an environmental event such as radiation.

**TABLE 3.2  Some Inherited Gene Syndromes**

| Syndrome | Estimated Frequency (live births in U.S.) | Gene Located on Chromosome | Phenotype, Treatment, and Prognosis |
|---|---|---|---|
| **Autosomal Recessive Syndromes** | | | |
| *Huntington's Disease* | 1 in 10,000–20,000 | 4 | Personality changes, depression, gradual loss of motor control and memory caused by massive neuronal cell death that often begins in mid-adulthood. Thus affected individuals may transmit the disease to another generation of offspring before becoming aware of the disease. In some individuals, symptoms may begin earlier and be more severe if the dominant gene is transmitted by the father, another example of genomic imprinting. |
| *Marfan Syndrome* | 1 in 10,000–20,000 | 15 | Tall, lean, long limbed, with gaunt face (some believe Abraham Lincoln had syndrome). Frequent eye and heart defects. Cardiac failure in young adulthood common. Suicide second most common cause of death. Associated with increased paternal age. |
| *Neurofibromatosis Type 1* | 1 in 3,500 | 17 | Symptoms range from a few pale brown spots on skin to severe tumors affecting peripheral nervous system and distorting appearance. Minimal intellectual deficits in about 40% of cases. Other forms of neurofibromatosis are associated with genes located on other chromosomes. |
| *Williams Syndrome* | 1 in 10,000 | 7 | See text. |
| **Autosomal Recessive Syndromes** | | | |
| *Albinism* | 1 in 10,000–20,000. Several forms. Most common occurs in about 1 in 15,000 African Americans, 1 in 40,000 Caucasians, but much more frequently among some Native American tribes (1 in 200 among Hopi and Navajo, 1 in 132 among San Blas Indians of Panama). | 11 (also 15) | Affected individuals lack pigment *melanin*. Extreme sensitivity to sunlight and visual problems. |
| *Cystic Fibrosis* | Most common genetic disease in Caucasian populations in U.S., especially those of Northern European descent, affecting about 1 in 2,500. Less common among African American and Asian American populations. | 7 | Respiratory tract becomes clogged with mucus; lungs likely to become infected. Death often in young adulthood, but individuals may have children. Prognosis for females poorer than for males. Pulmonary therapy to remove mucus accumulation in lungs helps delay effects. |

**TABLE 3.2**  **Some Inherited Gene Syndromes** (continued)

| Syndrome | Estimated Frequency (live births in U.S.) | Gene Located on Chromosome | Phenotype, Treatment, and Prognosis |
|---|---|---|---|
| **Autosomal Recessive Syndromes** | | | |
| *Galactosemia* | 1 in 60,000 | 9 | Mental retardation, cataracts, cirrhosis of the liver caused by accumulation of galactose in body tissues because of absence of enzyme to convert this sugar to glucose. Heterozygous individuals have half the normal enzyme activity, enough for normal development. Galactose-free diet is only treatment, although many still display learning and behavioral problems. |
| *Gaucher Disease* | 1 in 600 Ashkenazic Jews. Others, rarer forms found in all populations. | 1 | Enlarged spleen contributing to pain, cardiac failure, and failure to thrive. Frequent bone fractures, bruising, and bleeding. Limited treatment available. |
| *Phenylketonuria* | 1 in 15,000. Somewhat higher rate of incidence in Caucasian than in Asian or African American populations. | 12 | See text. |
| *Sickle Cell Disease* | 1 in 400 African Americans. Also frequently found in malaria-prone regions of world. | 11 | See text. |
| *Tay-Sachs Disease* | 1 in 3,600 Ashkenazic Jews. Very rare in other populations. | 15 | Signs of mental retardation, blindness, deafness, and paralysis begin 1 to 6 months after birth. No treatment available. Death normally occurs by 3 or 4 years of age. |
| *ß–Thalassemia (Cooley's anemia)* | 1 in 800–3,600 in populations of Greek and Italian descent. Much less frequent in other populations. | 11 | Severe anemia beginning within 2 to 3 months of birth, stunted growth, increased susceptibility to infections. Death usually occurs in 20s or 30s. |
| **Sex-Linked Syndromes** | | | |
| *Colorblindness (red-green)* | About 1 in 100 males of Caucasian descent see no red or green. About 1 in 15 Caucasian males experience some decrease in sensitivity to red or green colors. | X | If completely red-green colorblind, lack either green-sensitive or red-sensitive pigment for distinguishing these colors and see them as yellow. If decreased sensitivity to red or greens, reds are perceived as reddish browns, bright greens as tan, and olive greens as brown. |
| *Duchenne Muscular Dystrophy* | 1 in 3,500 males. Most common of many different forms of muscular dystrophy. Several forms, including Duchenne, are X linked. | X | Progressive muscle weakness and muscle fiber loss. Mental retardation in about $1/3$ of cases. No cure, and few live long enough to reproduce. Responsible gene located on short arm of X chromosome; appears to be massive in number of nucleotide pairs. |

(continued)

**TABLE 3.2**   **Some Inherited Gene Syndromes** *(continued)*

| Syndrome | Estimated Frequency (live births in U.S.) | Gene Located on Chromosome | Phenotype, Treatment, and Prognosis |
|---|---|---|---|
| **Sex-Linked Syndromes** | | | |
| *Fragile X Syndrome* | 1 in 4,000 males; 1 in 8,000 females. | X | See text. |
| *Hemophilia A* | 1 in 10,000 Caucasian male births for the most common form. | X | Failure of blood to clot. Several different forms; not all are sex linked. Queen Victoria of England was carrier for the most common form. Potential for bleeding to death, but administration of clot-inducing drugs and blood transfusions reduces hazard. |

*Sources:* Adapted from Beaudet et al. (2001), Committee on Genetics (1996), Laskari, Smith, & Graham (1999), McKusick & Amberger (2002), Scriver et al. (2001).

The smiling face of this girl with Williams syndrome epitomizes one of the behavioral characteristics common to such children, a strong orientation to initiating and maintaining social relationships. Their unusual pattern of strengths and weaknesses in various areas of cognition and language as well as their inquisitiveness about other people are of considerable interest to those who study child development. Such observations support the view that some aspects of development may be domain specific rather than more broadly determined by intelligence or personality.

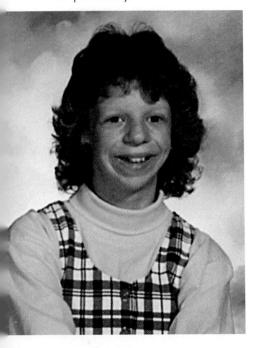

***Williams Syndrome: Discordances in Language, Cognition, and Social Behavior***   About 1 in 10,000 children is born with **Williams syndrome,** caused by the deletion of a small number of genes on chromosome 7. The syndrome is autosomal dominant, although most occurrences are the result of a mutation. Children with Williams syndrome possess a distinctive set of facial features, including a short, upturned nose and full lips. They also display curvatures of the knee and hip that produce an unusual postural appearance and gait, and they often have heart and kidney abnormalities.

Individuals with Williams syndrome are typically mildly to moderately retarded. Perhaps most puzzling, however, is their strikingly uneven profile of cognitive and social strengths and weaknesses. For example, as young children they seem especially preoccupied with the faces of adults and show relatively few social inhibitions, even among strangers (Mervis, 2003). When young, they are also extremely sensitive to certain sounds, such as those made by a drill or vacuum cleaner, or the loud noises produced by fireworks or the bursting of a balloon. Their ability to acquire language is initially slow and may never reach a high level of grammatical complexity. However, children with Williams syndrome accumulate a surprisingly large vocabulary that permits them to engage in relatively sophisticated, although somewhat stereotyped, verbal interactions (Moldavsky, Lev, & Lerman-Sagie, 2001) Complementing these verbal abilities tend to be some rather uncommon abilities with respect to creating and imitating music (Levitin & Bellugi, 1998). For example, some, after having heard a musical selection only once and regardless of the language in which it may have been sung, are able to reproduce the piece with extraordinary skill. Despite these strengths, children with Williams syndrome show poor visual and spatial abilities, poor planning and problem solving, and little competence in acquiring numerical skills.

Individuals with Williams syndrome have become of special interest to developmental, cognitive, and social psychologists because of their unusual, and quite uneven, profile of intellectual and behavioral strengths and weaknesses. As is shown later in this text, many cognitive abilities may be modular; that is, they may undergo relatively specific patterns of development that are distinct from other abilities. In addition, when we discuss the nature of intelligence in later chapters, you will see that extensive debate occurs about whether it is best to view intelligence as a general capacity or as a set of more specific abilities. The observations of children with Williams syndrome are relevant to both of these issues. They show, in particular, that genes may have highly targeted consequences for intellectual, social, and other developmental capacities.

*Sickle Cell Disease: A Problem Arising out of Adaptive Circumstance* **Sickle cell disease** is a genetic disorder whose incidence is extremely high in many regions of West Africa and around the Mediterranean basin. Sickle cell disease is also found in about 1 out of every 400 African Americans (Ashley-Koch, Yang, & Olney, 2000) and in high numbers of Greek Americans and others whose ancestors came from regions in which malaria commonly occurs. The defect introduces a change in a single amino acid in hemoglobin, the molecule that permits the red blood cells to carry oxygen. As a result, red blood cells become crescent shaped rather than round.

Sickle-shaped cells are ineffective in transporting oxygen; they also survive for a much shorter duration than normal red blood cells, and the bone marrow has difficulty replacing them. The consequences are often anemia, jaundice, low resistance to infection, and susceptibility to stroke, severe pain, and damage to various organs when the distorted cells block small blood vessels. Blood transfusions can help to alleviate the more serious problems, and research in both Europe and the United States raises the possibility that bone marrow transplants can provide a cure (Davis & Roberts, 1996). Despite their physical limitations, elementary school children with sickle cell disease appear quite similar to unaffected peers in terms of emotional well-being and view themselves no differently in terms of social satisfaction, competencies, and feelings of depression. Still, children with sickle cell disease, especially girls, tend to be somewhat less popular in the classroom and boys somewhat less aggressive, perhaps because of their more limited energy and slower physical development (Noll et al., 1996).

About one in every twelve African Americans is a carrier of the sickle cell gene. These individuals, who possess a heterozygous genotype, have the **sickle cell trait**. They manufacture a relatively small proportion of cells with abnormal hemoglobin. Few of these individuals show symptoms of sickle cell disease; most live normal lives. But insufficient oxygen, which may occur in high-altitude regions, when flying in unpressurized airplane cabins, or after strenuous exercise, can trigger sickling of red blood cells in those who have the trait. Nevertheless, carriers of the sickle cell gene are more resistant to malaria than are individuals who have normal

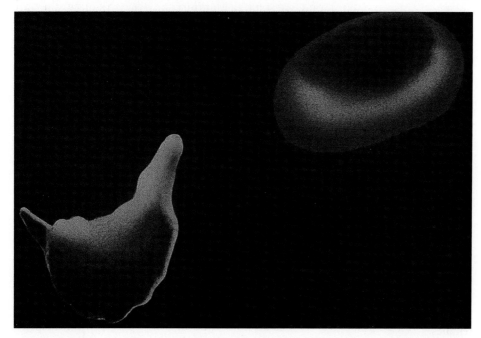

Individuals who suffer from sickle cell anemia, a genetically inherited disorder, have a large proportion of crescent-shaped red blood cells like the one shown at the bottom left. A normal red blood cell (upper right) is round and doughnut-shaped. Sickle-shaped cells are ineffective in transporting oxygen and may cause damage to various organs and pain by blocking small blood vessels.

**Williams syndrome** Dominant genetic disorder involving the deletion of a set of genes, which results in affected individuals' typically having a strong social orientation, good musical ability, and some unusual linguistic capabilities; accompanied by mental retardation and severe deficits in numerical and spatial ability.

**sickle cell disease** Genetic blood disorder common in regions of Africa and other areas where malaria is found and among descendants of the people of these regions. Abnormal blood cells carry insufficient oxygen.

**sickle cell trait** Symptoms shown by those possessing a heterozygous genotype for sickle cell anemia.

hemoglobin—an adaptive feature that accounts for the high incidence and persistence of the trait in regions where malaria is present.

***Phenylketonuria: A Genetic Problem Modifiable by Diet*** Phenylketonuria (**PKU**), a recessive metabolic disorder, provides a good illustration of how changing the child's environment—in this case, diet—can reduce a disorder's more harmful consequences. An infant with PKU appears normal at birth. However, retardation sets in soon thereafter and becomes severe by four years of age if the condition is untreated. The child may also have convulsions, hyperactivity, and other behavioral problems. In this condition, *phenylalanine*, an amino acid in milk and high-protein foods, such as meat, cannot be metabolized normally by the liver. As a result, phenylalanine and other metabolic products accumulate in the blood, and the nervous system becomes deprived of needed nutrients. Fortunately, screening using blood samples collected a day or two after birth can detect elevated levels of phenylalanine. An infant identified as having PKU can then be placed on a diet low in phenylalanine to prevent its more serious effects. Experts agree that the diet must be started relatively early, within the first few weeks after birth, and continued at least through adolescence, to ensure nearly normal mental development (Phenylketonuria, 2000). Here, then, is an excellent example illustrating that genes, by themselves, do not necessarily cause particular developmental outcomes; environmental factors interact with the genotype to yield a specific phenotype.

Even though the more serious consequences of phenylketonuria can be prevented, a completely normal prognosis for these children cannot be guaranteed. The diet is difficult to maintain; it requires a careful balance between excessive phenylalanine to prevent neural damage and sufficient nutrients. Weekly blood tests may be necessary to keep metabolite concentrations within an acceptable range, a regimen for which child, parents, and testing centers may be ill prepared. The bland and unappetizing diet can be a source of conflict between child and caregiver as well, creating management problems within households attempting to lead relatively normal lives (Phenylketonuria, 2000).

Even under optimal conditions, children with PKU may show some growth and intellectual deficiencies. For example, these children seem to have difficulty in planning and problem-solving tasks in which working memory or sustained attention is required to inhibit well-learned, simpler reactions in order to master new, more complex responses (Diamond et al., 1997; Ris et al., 1994). Moreover, individuals with PKU who successfully reach adulthood still need to be concerned about their diet. For example, children born to mothers who continue to display elevated levels of phenylalanine during pregnancy show increased risk for heart defects and mental retardation (Platt et al., 2000; Rouse et al., 2000). If a mother returns to a low-phenylalanine diet before or early in her pregnancy, the risks can be reduced substantially. Although dietary modifications are helpful, it remains unclear whether this intervention completely eliminates some negative consequences of PKU.

***Sex-Linked Syndromes*** As already indicated, only a few dozen genes may be located on the Y chromosome, whereas the X chromosome carries many. This imbalance has substantial implications for a number of phenotypes said to be *sex linked* because the gene associated with them is carried only on the X chromosome. Hemophilia, red-green colorblindness, and Duchenne muscular dystrophy (see Table 3.2) are sex linked because they are inherited via specific genes on the X chromosome. Thus they occur much more frequently in males than in females.

As with genes for autosomes, those that are sex linked often have a dominant-recessive relationship. Females, who inherit two genes for sex-linked traits, one on each X chromosome, are much less likely to display the deleterious effects associated with an abnormal recessive gene than are males, who, if they inherit the damaging allele, have no second, normal allele to mask its effects. Hemophilia, a condition in

**phenylketonuria (PKU)** Recessive genetic disorder in which phenylalanine, an amino acid, fails to be metabolized. Unless dietary changes are made to reduce intake of phenylalanine, severe mental retardation occurs.

which blood does not clot normally, is a good example because it is nearly always associated with a defective gene on the X chromosome. Because the allele for hemophilia is recessive, daughters who inherit it typically do not exhibit hemophilia; the condition is averted by an ordinary gene on the second X chromosome that promotes normal blood clotting. A female can, however, be a carrier. If she possesses a heterozygous genotype for hemophilia, the X chromosome with the abnormal allele has a fifty-fifty chance of being transmitted to either her son or her daughter. When a son inherits the abnormal allele, he will exhibit hemophilia because the Y chromosome does not contain genetic information to counter the allele's effects. If a daughter inherits the abnormal allele, she will be a carrier who may then transmit it to her sons and daughters, as has occurred in several interrelated royal families of Europe.

***Fragile X Syndrome: A Sex-Linked Contributor to Mental Retardation*** Geneticists have identified a structural irregularity that consists of a pinched or constricted site near the end of the long arm of the X chromosome in some individuals (see Figure 3.7). This anomaly, termed **fragile X syndrome**, may be the most frequently inherited source of mental retardation associated with a specific gene (Moldavsky et al., 2001). Males with fragile X syndrome commonly have a long, narrow face; large or prominent ears; and large testes. Cardiac defects and relaxed ligaments (permitting, for example, hyperextension of finger joints) are also frequent components of the disorder. Behavioral attributes include poor eye contact and limited responsiveness to external stimulation, as well as hand flapping, hand biting, and other unusual mannerisms, such as mimicry. Females who possess a heterozygous genotype often show, to a much lesser extent, some of the physical characteristics of the disorder. Many of these women display a normal or nearly normal level of intelligence, although, as with other sex-linked gene disorders, they are carriers for the syndrome.

▼ **FIGURE 3.7**

## Chromosome Illustrating Fragile X Syndrome

Fragile X syndrome is one of the most frequently occurring genetic causes of mental retardation. This photo micrograph illustrates the pinched or constricted portion of one of the pair of X chromosomes in a heterozygous female and the X chromosomes in an affected male.

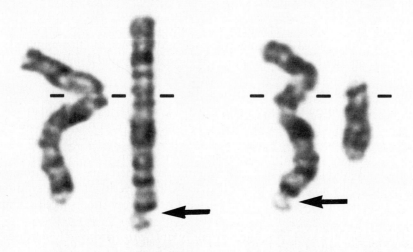

X   fra(X)      fra(X)   Y

**fragile X syndrome** Disorder associated with a pinched region of the X chromosome; a leading genetic cause of mental retardation in males.

An unusual feature of fragile X syndrome is that its severity seems to increase as the abnormal gene is passed on from one generation to the next, a phenomenon termed *anticipation*. This progression begins when one set of three nucleotides, which repeats between 5 and 50 times in the normal gene, for some reason expands to 50 to 200 repetitions. Once this expansion begins, the gene seems to become unstable for subsequent offspring, so that more copies of the three nucleotides are spewed out, as though the replication process has difficulty turning off (Eliez & Reiss, 2000). The inheritance of this unchecked expansion is accompanied by a spectrum of learning difficulties ranging from mild to severe mental retardation. Thus the size of the abnormal segment of the gene, along with the severity of the disorder, appears to increase as it is passed from a grandfather, in whom the initial amplification may occur (even if he shows no evidence of the disorder), to a daughter (who may be minimally affected because she has an additional X chromosome to compensate for the disorder), to a grandson (who now displays full-blown fragile X syndrome).

## CHROMOSOME VARIATIONS

Mutations in specific genes are only one of several sources of variation in the human genome. Occasionally, whole sections of a chromosome are deleted, duplicated, or relocated to another chromosome, or an extra chromosome is transmitted to daughter cells during cell division. When this happens, normal development is often disrupted. Perhaps as many as half of all conceptions that result in spontaneous abortion include such chromosomal abnormalities (Schreck, & Silverman, 2002; Jacobs & Hassold, 1995). If the child survives, structural aberrations of the chromosomes are often associated with mental retardation and severe physical deformations.

Human embryonic growth virtually never proceeds when a complete pair or even a member of one pair of autosomes is missing. **Trisomy**, the inheritance of an extra chromosome, also very often results in the loss of the zygote or miscarriage in early pregnancy (Jacobs & Hassold, 1995). However, three copies of chromosomes 13, 18, and 21 may be observed in surviving human newborns. Of these, trisomy 21, or Down syndrome, occurs most frequently. Even with this syndrome, however, fewer than 25 percent of conceptions survive to birth (Tolmie, 2002).

***Trisomy 21 (Down Syndrome)***    Trisomy 21, or **Down syndrome**, is one of the most common genetic causes of mental retardation, arising in about 1 out of every 800 live births (Tolmie, 2002). Physically observable features include an epicanthal fold that gives an almond shape to the eye, flattened facial features, poor muscle tone, short stature, and short, broad hands, including an unusual crease of the palm. About 40 percent of infants with Down syndrome have congenital heart defects. Cataracts or other visual impairments, as well as deficiencies in the immune system, are also common. Physical development is slowed compared with normal children, as is intellectual development.

Approximately 95 percent of babies born with Down syndrome have an extra twenty-first chromosome. Nearly 90 percent of these errors originate in egg cells, and the remainder arise from errors during the production of sperm cells (Jacobs & Hassold, 1995). A small percentage of infants with Down syndrome have a segment of chromosome 21, perhaps as little as its bottom third, shifted to another chromosome (Moldavsky et al., 2001). Another small percentage has chromosomal deviations in only a portion of their body cells. The severity of Down syndrome in these latter individuals seems to be related to the proportion of cells exhibiting trisomy.

The probability of giving birth to an infant with trisomy 21 increases with the age of the mother, as is true for most other forms of trisomy (see Figure 3.8). Although mothers over thirty-five years of age give birth to only about 16 percent

**trisomy**    Inheritance of an extra chromosome.

**Down syndrome**    Disorder resulting from an extra chromosomal material on pair number twenty-one; associated with mental retardation and distinct physical features.

This 13-year-old boy with trisomy 21, or Down syndrome, has learned to read. He has made considerable progress in academic subjects as is evident from his contribution to this geography project. By being provided with an enriching environment, many with Down syndrome are able to accomplish levels of skill that permit them to engage in meaningful work and be active members of their community.

of all babies, they bear more than half of infants with Down syndrome. To explain these findings, experts have often proposed an "older egg" hypothesis. According to this view, the ova, which begin the first phases in meiosis even before the mother's own birth, change with age, either due to the passage of time or perhaps because of increased exposure to potentially hazardous biological and environmental conditions. These older egg cells, released during ovulation in the later childbearing years, are then more susceptible to chromosomal errors while undergoing the final steps of meiosis. Other researchers have proposed a

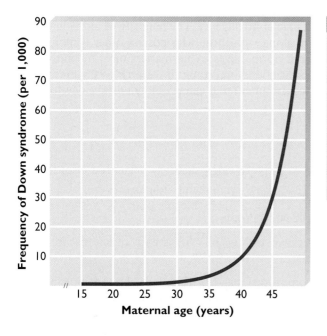

◁ **FIGURE 3.8**

**Relationship Between Maternal Age and the Incidence of Down Syndrome**

The incidence of Down syndrome increases dramatically as a function of the mother's age. One in every 1,500 babies born to a mother age twenty-one has Down syndrome. For forty-nine-year-old mothers, the incidence is much higher: one in every ten babies has Down syndrome. Several different explanations have been offered to account for these findings.

*Source:* Data from Epstein (2001).

"relaxed selection" hypothesis to account for the increased frequency of Down syndrome in older mothers. According to this view, older mothers are less likely than younger mothers to spontaneously abort a zygote with trisomy 21. Still another view is that egg cells containing the extra chromosome are unlikely to be selected during ovulation. However, as they become a proportionally larger pool of the available ova over time, the possibility that one is released during ovulation increases (Tolmie, 2002). New research suggests that the age of the father is also a factor in the incidence of Down syndrome. According to an analysis of date from 70,000 births in Denmark, fathers who were age 50 years or older were three times more likely to have a Down syndrome child than fathers age 29 years or younger (Zhu et al., 2005).

⊶ **KEY THEME**
RISK/RESILIENCE

Thanks to better medical and physical care, the majority of individuals born with Down syndrome may be expected to live more than fifty years (Tolmie, 2002). Many show considerable proficiency in reading and writing. But we still have much to discover about Down syndrome. For example, individuals with trisomy 21 who survive beyond age forty frequently develop the abnormal brain cells and show some of the same behavioral symptoms found in adults who acquire Alzheimer's disease (Janicki & Dalton, 2000). Alzheimer's disease is characterized by memory and speech disturbances, personality changes, and increasing loss of intellectual functioning, typically in individuals between fifty and seventy-five years of age. At least one form of Alzheimer's disease is thought to be inherited, and, not surprisingly, the responsible gene appears to be located on chromosome 21.

***Sex Chromosome Syndromes*** As we have already noted, males normally have an X and a Y sex chromosome, and females have two X chromosomes. However, variations in the number of sex chromosomes as a result of errors during meiosis can occur in humans. For example, an individual may inherit only a single X, an extra chromosome (XXX, XXY, XYY), and, on rare occasions, even pairs of extra chromosomes (for example, XXXX, XXYY, XXXY). Table 3.3 describes several of these variations in more detail.

⊶ **KEY THEME**
NATURE & NURTURE
RISK/RESILIENCE

When it was first discovered that some humans possess an extra sex chromosome, these individuals were typically thought to display intellectual deficits, along with an assortment of abnormal and socially unacceptable behaviors. For example, in the 1960s some researchers claimed that an extra Y chromosome contributed to more aggressive and antisocial behavior. Males with an XYY chromosomal makeup do tend to be taller than other males and display some learning difficulties, but they actually show a nearly normal range of intelligence. The majority of individuals who have this chromosomal pattern, along with those who possess other combinations of sex chromosome patterns, lead normal lives. What matters most for individuals put at risk by sex chromosome variations, according to research, is the presence of a stable and supportive family environment that can promote positive development (Bender et al., 1995).

## F O R ◆ Y O U R ◆ R E V I E W

◆ What is the basis for each of the following genetically influenced disorders?

 Williams syndrome    Sickle cell disease and sickle cell trait

 Phenylketonuria    Fragile X syndrome

◆ What phenotypes are associated with each? Why is each of interest to developmental psychologists?

◆ What variations in the chromosomal makeup of an individual are possible? What is the most common example of chromosomal trisomy? What are examples of chromosomal variation associated with the sex chromosomes?

**TABLE 3.3** **Examples of Observed Sex Chromosome Syndromes**

| Disorder | Estimated Frequency (live births in U.S.) | Phenotype | Prognosis |
|---|---|---|---|
| 45, XO (Turner syndrome) | 1 in 2,500 females (more than 90% are spontaneously aborted); 80% of cases involve the absence of the paternal X chromosome. | Short stature, usually normal psychomotor development but limited development of secondary sexual characteristics. Failure to menstruate and sterility due to underdeveloped ovaries. About 50% have webbed, short neck. Near-average range of intelligence but serious deficiencies in spatial ability and directional sense. | Increased stature and sexual development, including menstruation but not fertility, can be induced through administration of estrogen and other hormones. In vitro fertilization permits carrying of child when adult. |
| 47, XXX (Triple-X syndrome) | 1 in 1,200 females; 90% have received two copies of maternal X chromosome. | Not generally distinguishable. Some evidence of delay in speech and language development, lack of coordination, poor academic performance, and immature behavior. Sexual development usually normal. Tendency for tall stature. | Many are essentially normal, but substantial proportion have language, cognitive, and social-emotional problems. |
| 47, XXY (Klinefelter syndrome) | 1 in 600 males (increased risk among older mothers); 56% received two maternal chromosomes, 44% two paternal sex chromosomes. | Tend to be tall, beardless, with feminine body contour, high-pitched voice. Some evidence for poor auditory short-term memory and difficulty with reading. Testes underdeveloped, individuals usually sterile. | Many with normal IQ, but about 20% may have occasional mild to moderate retardation. |
| 47, XYY (XXY syndrome) | 1 in 1,000 males | Above-average height, some have learning disabilities, but near-average range of intelligence. | Most lead normal lives and have offspring with a normal number of chromosomes. Higher proportion than normal incarcerated, but crimes no more violent than those of XY men. |

*Sources:* Adapted from Beaudet et al. (2001), Jacobs & Hassold (1995), McGinniss & Kaback (2002), McKusick & Amberger (2002), Allanson & Graham (2002).

# GENETIC COUNSELING

A dvances in detecting gene and chromosomal defects, as well as in understanding the biochemical and metabolic consequences of various inherited disorders, have led to a rapidly expanding medical and guidance specialty called **genetic counseling**. Obtaining a family history to summarize the occurrence of various diseases among ancestors and other relatives is usually the first step. If warranted, *parental* **genetic screening** may be carried out. For example, chromosomal abnormalities, as well as dominant and recessive genes associated with all of the disorders listed in Tables 3.2 and 3.3 (and many more not listed in these tables), can be detected through parental screening. Thus genetic counselors can provide prospective parents with estimates of the likelihood of bearing a child with a specific problem, although parental screening, of course, does not identify new mutations that may arise in offspring. Prospective parents can then use this information to decide whether, for example, adoption or other new reproductive technologies, such as those discussed in the chapter titled "The Prenatal Period and Birth," may be a better choice than bearing their own children.

**genetic counseling** Medical and counseling specialty concerned with determining and communicating the likelihood that prospective parents will give birth to a baby with a genetic disorder.

**genetic screening** Systematic search using a variety of tests to detect developmental risk due to genetic anomalies.

There are many reasons for carrying out such tests. For example, prenatal testing is often recommended for women who are older than thirty-five because of their increased risk for Down syndrome; when a genetic disorder has been reported in the family history; if parents are members of an ethnic group at risk for a specific genetic disease; or if delayed or unusual development of the fetus occurs during pregnancy (Cuniff & Committee on Genetics, 2004). The finding of a serious inherited disorder may lead to a decision to terminate the pregnancy if religious and ethical values allow such a choice. However, prenatal screening tests, along with neonatal screening carried out shortly after birth, can serve another important purpose: that of suggesting therapy and treatment designed to prevent or minimize the more devastating consequences of some metabolic disorders (Erbe & Levy, 2002).

## PRENATAL DIAGNOSIS

Procedures now exist that can be performed prenatally to detect hundreds of genetically and environmentally induced defects in fetal development. Some of these procedures provide unequivocal answers about the presence or absence of a problem. Other, often less invasive, procedures provide estimates of increased likelihood of the presence of some defect. If they are suggestive of a developmental disability, they are followed by more conclusive diagnostic tests. One of the best-known definitive tests is **amniocentesis**, in which a small amount of amniotic fluid is withdrawn via a syringe inserted (under the guidance of an ultrasound image) in the woman's abdominal wall. Cells in the amniotic fluid are extracted and submitted to biochemical and chromosomal examination (see Figure 3.9). Amniocentesis is an especially effective

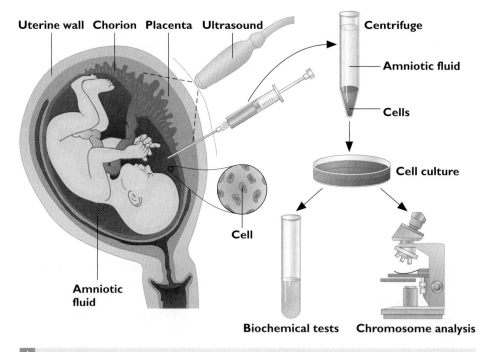

▲ **FIGURE 3.9**

### The Process of Amniocentesis

In this prenatal screening procedure, a needle is inserted into the amniotic fluid surrounding the fetus. A small amount is withdrawn, and cells shed by the fetus are separated from the fluid by centrifuge. The cells are cultured and submitted to various biochemical and other tests to determine whether chromosomal, genetic, or other developmental defects exist.

*Source:* Adapted from Knowles (1985).

**amniocentesis** Method of sampling the fluid surrounding the developing fetus through insertion of a needle; used to diagnose fetal genetic and developmental disorders.

procedure for detecting chromosomal variations, and it provides information about some metabolic problems as well. The test is usually performed between the thirteenth and eighteenth weeks of pregnancy. However, researchers are studying whether it can be safely carried out a few weeks earlier. Even when amniocentesis is performed later in pregnancy, the possibility of some increased risk exists from infections and spontaneous abortion (Elias, Simpson, & Shulman, 2002; Tongsong et al., 1998).

Another test that provides much the same information as amniocentesis but that can be carried out somewhat earlier in pregnancy (between ten and twelve weeks) is **chorionic villus sampling**. In this diagnostic procedure, a small sample of hairlike projections (*villi*) from the chorion, the outer wall of the membrane in which the fetus develops and that attaches to the woman's uterus, is removed by suction through a thin tube inserted through the vagina and cervix or, in some cases, through the abdominal wall. Information gained at this earlier time can reduce uncertainty and anxiety about the possibility of a developmental disability (Caccia et al., 1991). However, chorionic villus sampling, in contrast to amniocentesis, does not provide information about possible neural tube defects, the procedure is somewhat more difficult to carry out unless performed by skilled technicians, and some researchers report a slightly increased risk of miscarriage and limb malformations (Elias, Simpson, & Shulman, 2002; Hsieh et al., 1995).

In **fetal blood sampling**, blood is withdrawn directly from the umbilical cord of the fetus for biochemical and chromosomal examination. This particular procedure, normally carried out from about the eighteenth week of pregnancy onward, permits the detection of various chromosomal and genetic errors, and is especially useful in evaluating disorders associated with the blood. Although relatively safe, the procedure does appear to be slightly more risky than other invasive tests (Elias, Simpson, & Shulman, 2002).

Because of the possible increase in risk and their relatively high cost, amniocentesis, chorionic villus sampling, and fetal blood sampling are normally performed only when there is some reason to believe that fetal abnormalities may occur. Other, less

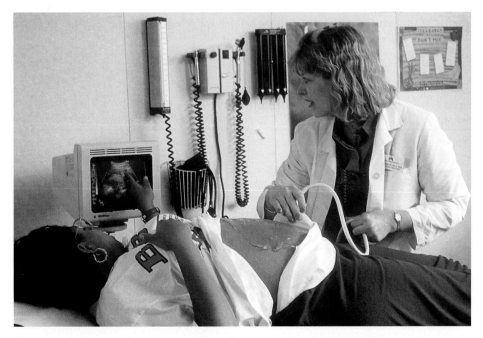

The use of ultrasound to provide a visual image of the developing fetus has become a common practice in medical facilities around the world. Prospective parents are often thrilled by this opportunity to obtain a glimpse of the fetus. The use of ultrasound can also be important for obtaining a more accurate assessment of the age of the fetus. It provides assistance in carrying out other tests to determine if development is proceeding normally and, in some case, permits surgical procedures designed to improve the likelihood of a healthy newborn.

**chorionic villus sampling** Method of sampling fetal chorionic cells; used to diagnose embryonic genetic and developmental disorders.

**fetal blood sampling** Method of withdrawing blood from the umbilical cord of the fetus; used to diagnose genetic disorders, especially those that affect the blood.

invasive procedures also exist. For example, several types of **maternal blood screening** tests, such as the *alpha fetoprotein test* and the more extensive and accurate *triple screen test,* can be carried out at around fifteen to twenty weeks of gestational age to provide evidence of increased risk for Down syndrome, neural tube defects, and certain kidney and other problems. Scientists have also begun to examine fragments of fetal DNA that circulate in the mother's blood stream for indicators of genetic problems (Kaiser, 2005). Certainly the most widespread of the noninvasive diagnostic procedures, however, is **ultrasonography**, often called *ultrasound*. Ultrasound is now used routinely in many countries to help determine whether fetal growth is proceeding normally. Sound waves, reflecting at different rates from tissues of varying density, are represented on video monitors and even printed to form a picture of the fetus. The picture can reveal such problems as microcephaly (small head size), cardiac malformations, cleft lip and palate, and other physical disabilities (Dooley, 1999; Grandjean et al., 1999). And in combination with a blood test, ultrasonography can be used to detect Down syndrome as early as 11 weeks prenatally (Malone et al., 2005).

Ultrasonography is widely used to assist in carrying out other prenatal diagnostic tests, to verify the age of the fetus (interpretation of maternal and fetal blood tests are often highly dependent on an accurate assessment of age), and to monitor lifesaving operations that may on rare occasions be performed on the fetus within the womb (Harrison, 1996). Although not universally recommended in the United States because of its limits as a diagnostic tool, ultrasound has become a popular tool for informing specialists and parents about the course of prenatal development.

## ETHICAL AND SOCIAL ISSUES

The major prenatal diagnostic tests are summarized in Table 3.4. At the same time that they offer important information, their availability also raises a number of ethical and social issues. Note, for example, that many of these tests are carried out relatively late in pregnancy, and prospective parents may have to wait several weeks longer before they learn the results. This waiting period can create enormous apprehension, especially among those who have reason to believe that a problem

**Table 3.4   Prenatal Screening Tests**

| Prenatal Test | When Usually Administered (gestational age) | Typical Waiting Period for Results | Other Comments |
|---|---|---|---|
| **Amniocentesis** | 13–18 weeks | About 2 weeks | Can be administered in weeks 11–14 but normally is not because the available supply of amniotic fluid is more limited. |
| **Chorionic Villus Sampling** | 10–12 weeks | 24–48 hours | Possibly a slightly greater risk than associated with amniocentesis, including limb deformities. |
| **Fetal Blood Sampling** | 18 weeks or later | 24–48 hours | Possibly somewhat greater risk than associated with amniocentesis. |
| **Maternal Blood Screening** | 15–20 weeks | One week | Not definitive but provides information about increased risk for Down syndrome and neural tube and some metabolic defects. |
| **Ultrasonography** | About 6 weeks and later | None | Provides picture of growing fetus. Not definitive for identifying many disorders. Little evidence of any risk. Often used to accompany other test procedures. |

may exist. Moreover, some expectant women feel almost coerced into using these technological advances to learn more about their pregnancies even when there is little to suggest a genetic problem (Henifin, 1993; Wertz & Fletcher, 1993). Some would say these tests are overused. Yet a physician who fails to at least offer prenatal diagnosis in circumstances in which it can be informative runs legal risks for incompetent obstetric practice (Wertz & Fletcher, 1998).

Prospective parents have choices regarding whether or not to have such tests performed. In many cases those about to become parents would like to know about possible problems, if for no other reason than to effectively prepare for and address them even before birth. In fact, a substantial number of expectant women who learn that the fetus carries some abnormality still elect to continue the pregnancy, especially if the problem is less severe and possibilities exist for prenatal or postnatal therapy (Pride et al., 1993). On the other hand, in some countries such tests may not be available. And, even when they are, not everyone takes advantage of them. For example, women of African American or Hispanic ethnic identity, at least in some areas of the United States, are far less likely to undergo prenatal testing than Caucasian or Asian women (Kuppermann, Gates, & Washington, 1996).

Another issue concerns access to the results of these tests. For example, might insurance companies or other health organizations drop coverage if they become aware of results that indicate expensive medical treatment in the future? And, finally, there is the issue of sex preselection.

## CONTROVERSY: THINKING IT OVER

## Should Sex Preselection Be Permitted?

At one time in medieval Germany, couples placed a hammer under their bed if they wished to conceive a boy; in Denmark they chose a pair of scissors for that location if they desired a girl (Golden, 1998). In China and India, where abortion is more widely practiced, evidence already exists that sex selection has been exercised; a disproportionate number of males have been born in these countries in recent years. As a consequence, China and India, as well as some other countries, have passed laws forbidding the use of prenatal tests solely to determine the sex of the fetus and to influence the course of pregnancy when the fetus is male or female (Wertz & Fletcher, 1998).

### What Is the Controversy?

Although many adamantly oppose the use of a procedure that leads to the selective abortion of a healthy fetus on the basis of sex, *preselection*, the effort to tilt the probability toward having either a male or a female conception, may be far less objectionable. In fact, in 1996 40 percent of individuals in the United States already supported the unrestricted availability of sex preselection if an effective procedure became available (Wertz & Fletcher, 1998).

We are, in fact, at the point at which this possibility exists. Previous efforts have focused on the timing or technique involved in procreation to increase conception of a male or female. These attempts have generally failed to provide a reliable method of conceiving a boy or a girl. However, in 1998 a new, far more effective procedure was reported, at least for promoting the conception of females (Fackelmann, 1998). This new procedure is based on the difference in the amount of DNA found in the X and Y chromosomes. With the help of a dye that attaches to the DNA and glows when exposed to the light of a laser, sperm cells carrying an X chromosome, which contain about 2.8 percent more DNA than sperm cells carrying a Y chromosome, shine more brightly. By introducing lopsided distributions of cells carrying the X chromosome into the uterus during periods when a woman might become pregnant, these specialists claim to have attained markedly higher numbers of successful pregnancies resulting in girls, a procedure that could also be expected to be successful in

**maternal blood screening** Tests performed on a woman's blood to determine whether the fetus she is carrying has an increased risk for some types of chromosomal and metabolic disorders.

**ultrasonography** Method of using sound wave reflections to obtain a representation of the developing fetus; used to estimate gestational age and detect fetal physical abnormalities.

skewing the odds toward boys. Other techniques associated with assisted reproduction (see the chapter titled "The Prenatal Period and Birth") can also be used to increase the likelihood of, or even virtually guarantee, a boy or a girl.

### What Are the Opposing Arguments?

Proponents of sex preselection claim that parents in most Western countries do not show a strong preference for having a boy or a girl first; but family balancing, having one boy and one girl, is frequently seen as the ideal family complement (Silver, 1998). Having the opportunity to rear children of both sexes is also often viewed as a desirable experience for parents. For other couples, sex preselection may serve to prevent a sex-linked genetic disease from being passed on to their offspring.

Opponents of sex preselection are concerned that, even in countries in which no strong preference exists for rearing either boys or girls, the practice supports the potential for sexual bias or increased sexism, a potential that may become more visible once a choice is available to prospective parents (Fackelmann, 1998). A second argument is that determining a conception on the basis of sex is but the first step in the emergence of a "preference mentality." This mentality can ultimately lead to preselection on the basis of other desired traits and attributes, intended to create "perfect" children and essentially treating children as a commodity (Darnovsky, 2004). Thus the potential for discrimination against those who do not meet the ethnic, cultural, or community ideal may increase substantially.

### What Answers Exist? What Questions Remain?

The American College of Obstetricians and Gynecologists (2002) currently supports the notion that sex preselection is ethical and justified in cases in which it will prevent sex-linked genetic disorders in offspring. In the United States, the public also seems to be in support of this position. Opinion is much more divided, however, with respect to sex preselection for other purposes. Recent advertisements have appeared in the United States that target some ethnic groups and emphasize, "Choose the sex of your next baby" and "Desire a son?" Declarations in favor of sex preselection for the purpose of family balancing and even for selecting the sex of a child in a first pregnancy have been made by individuals associated with organizations such as the American Society for Reproductive Medicine, established to deal with these kinds of issues (Kolata, 2001; Sachs, 2001). Perhaps to help address the controversy, psychologists need to conduct research on the following questions in order for the public to gauge whether regulations should be considered: To what extent do preferences for boys versus girls exist? What social and cultural factors promote them? Does raising offspring of both sexes in a balanced family lead to different outcomes for children? Does it result in more successful and effective parenting? Given advances in sex preselection, are we nearing a time when professionals will be recruited to help create "designer" children with respect to other traits? Could such efforts actually contribute to harmful effects by lessening genetic diversity in humans? What other kinds of psychological research might be conducted to help answer whether a need exists for regulation of sex and other kinds of trait preselection?

**behavior genetics**  Study of how characteristics and behaviors of individuals, such as intelligence and personality, are influenced by the interaction between genotype and experience.

**heritability**  Proportion of variability in the phenotype that is estimated to be accounted for by genetic influences within a known environmental range.

**identical twins**  Two individuals who originate from a single zygote (one egg fertilized by one sperm), which early in cell division separates to form two separate cell masses. Also called *monozygotic twins*.

**fraternal twins**  Siblings who share the same womb at the same time but originate from two different eggs fertilized by two different sperm cells. Also called *dizygotic twins*.

F O R ◆ Y O U R ◆ R E V I E W

◆ What are the major diagnostic tests for prenatal development? What are their limitations and their advantages?

◆ What ethical and social issues emerge from the use of prenatal diagnostic tests?

◆ What is sex preselection, and what are arguments for and against its practice?

# DEVELOPMENTAL AND BEHAVIORAL GENETICS

As our previous discussion indicates, chromosomal errors and particular genes can have drastic, often devastating, effects on physical, intellectual, and social development. Yet similarities observed among relatives—the wry sense of humor in a mother and daughter or the musical talent of a grandfather and his grandchildren—are not likely to be linked to a single, isolated gene. Might these attributes and behaviors reflect a contribution from many genes? Or are these phenotypic resemblances primarily the result of experiences shared by kin? Researchers engaged in **behavior genetics** attempt to learn to what extent the diversity of human traits, abilities, and behaviors stems from combinations of genes versus experience. Behavioral geneticists are helping to show that the entire realm of human behavior is influenced by nature and nurture in a variety of complex, sometimes surprising, ways (Plomin et al., 2001; Rutter et al., 1999a, 1999b).

⊶ **KEY THEME**

NATURE & NURTURE

## THE METHODS OF BEHAVIORAL GENETICISTS

Behavior geneticists have available to them a number of different methods. A major goal of many of these studies is to provide an estimate of the heritability of various traits and behaviors. **Heritability** refers to the extent to which the variability in a sample of individuals on some characteristic, such as shyness or assertiveness, is a result of genetic differences among those individuals. Of course, the variability that is not accounted for by the genotype must then be a result of the environmental circumstances those individuals have had the opportunity to experience. Thus, although research on heritability was initially designed to provide answers about the contribution of the genotype, it also helps to shed light on the role of experience in development (Plomin et al., 2001).

***Selective Breeding Studies***    When studying the fruit fly or the mouse, behavior geneticists can use *selective breeding* experiments to learn whether certain phenotypic expressions can be increased or decreased in offspring. Members of a species that display a specific attribute are bred to each other, usually over many generations. If the attribute is inherited, subsequent generations of offspring can be expected to display it more and more frequently or strongly. For example, after thirty generations of selective breeding in which either highly active mice were bred only to each other or mice showing only a low level of activity were bred to each other, researchers observed no overlap in terms of the amount of activity displayed by members of the two groups (DeFries, Gervais, & Thomas, 1978). Those bred for high activity were thirty times more active; they would run the equivalent of a football field during two three-minute test periods compared to the other mice, which would not even run the equivalent of a first down (Plomin et al., 2001). Selective breeding in various species of animals has revealed genetic contributions to many different attributes, including aggressiveness, emotionality, maze learning, and sex drive (Plomin et al., 2001).

***Family Resemblance Studies***    Selective breeding, of course, cannot be used to examine human behavior. Instead, behavior geneticists gain information about hereditary and environmental influences on human behavior by examining resemblances among family members. These studies investigate similarities among *identical* and *fraternal twins*, siblings, and other members of families who are genetically different from one another to varying degrees. **Identical**, or *monozygotic*, **twins** come from the same zygote: a single egg fertilized by a single sperm. A cell division early in development creates two separate embryos from this zygote, and the twins are genetically identical. **Fraternal**, or *dizygotic*, **twins** come from two different zygotes, each created from a separate egg and a separate sperm. Fraternal twins are no more genetically similar than siblings born at different times, each averaging about half of their genes in common. However, they do share some of their prenatal environment

If you were given their names, would you be able to tell these twins apart once they moved and were no longer seated side by side? Virtually everyone would have a great deal of difficulty with such an assignment unless they could constantly keep an eye on at least one of them as he moved about. Because their genetic makeup is the same, identical or monozygotic twins typically look very much alike and display very similar traits and behaviors as can be seen here. Twin studies provide important information about the contributions of heredity and environment to development.

and, by virtue of being the same age, may share other experiences to a greater extent than siblings born at different times.

If identical twins resemble each other more than fraternal twins in intelligence or shyness, one potential explanation for this similarity is their common genotype. The degree of resemblance is usually estimated from one of two statistical measures: concordance rate or correlation coefficient. The **concordance rate** is the percentage of pairs of twins in which both members display a specific attribute when one twin is identified as having it. Concordance rate is used when measuring characteristics that are either present or absent, such as schizophrenia or depression. If both members of every twin pair have a particular trait, the concordance rate will be 100 percent. If only one member of every pair of twins has some particular trait and the other does not, the concordance rate will be 0 percent. When attributes vary on a continuous scale, such that they can be measured in terms of amount or degree, resemblances are estimated from a *correlation coefficient*. This statistic helps to determine whether variables such as intelligence or shyness, which have some quantitative value, are more similar for identical than for fraternal twins or more similar among siblings than among unrelated children.

*Adoption Studies*   Identical twins may resemble each other more than fraternal twins do because identical twins share the same genotype. However, another explanation for any greater resemblance may be that identical twins share more similar experiences. One way to potentially reduce the effects of similarity in experience is to study biologically related family members who have been adopted or reared apart from each other. If an attribute is influenced by genetic factors, children should still resemble their biological siblings, parents, or other family members more than their adoptive relatives. On the other hand, if the environment is the primary determinant of an attribute, separated children can be expected to resemble their adoptive parents or other adopted siblings more closely than their biological parents or siblings.

Adoption studies, just as in the case of twin studies, pose many challenges for evaluating hereditary and environmental influences (Rutter et al., 1999a). For example, in the past, adopted children were often placed in a home similar to that of their biological parents. Under these circumstances, the relative contributions of family environment and heredity to an attribute are extremely difficult to distinguish. In addition, information on the biological family has not always been readily available in the case of adoption. Nevertheless, a number of large-scale investigations of genotype-environment effects involving twins, adopted children, siblings, half-siblings, and unrelated children in blended families are currently under way (Bouchard, 1997; Plomin, DeFries, & Fulker, 1988; Reiss et al., 2000). These and other studies are just beginning to illuminate the complex interactions and correlations that exist between heredity and experience, intricate relationships that we must consider more fully as well.

## CONCEPTUALIZING THE INTERACTION BETWEEN GENOTYPE AND ENVIRONMENT

**KEY THEME**

**NATURE & NURTURE**

How a genotype influences development depends to a great extent on the environment. Likewise, how an environment affects behavior often depends on the genotype. These conditional relationships are the basis for complex *interactions* between heredity and experience; the influence of one on the other is not constant across individuals or environmental circumstances, or even during different periods of development (Collins et al., 2000; Rutter & Silberg, 2002).

*Range of Reaction*   The interactive relationship between genotype and environment can be conceptualized in terms of the concept of **range of reaction,** the idea that, depending on environmental conditions, a broad range of phenotypes may be expressed as a function of the genotype (Turkheimer, Goldsmith, & Gottesman,

# CHAPTER RECAP

## 🗝 Summary of Developmental Themes

### NATURE & NURTURE

**How do nature and nurture interact in development?**

The phenotype, the observable behaviors and characteristics of an individual, is the product of a complex interaction between genotype and environment. Environment includes biological contexts, such as the foods we eat, but more frequently we consider it to be the experiences provided by caregivers and others. The relationship between genotype and environment is complicated by their interaction with each other and by passive, reactive, and niche-picking correlations. As a consequence, experiential factors are tightly interwoven with genotype to produce the range and variety of behaviors and characteristics an individual displays. Both genotype and environment are indispensable to development.

Researchers recognize the child's active efforts to seek out environments that support and maintain behavioral orientations and preferences influenced by hereditary factors. As the child achieves greater control over the environment, he or she has increasing opportunities to find a niche. In other words, behaviors, activities, and skills that the child displays not only are a consequence of imposed social and physical experiences, but also reflect the selective efforts of the child to discover interesting, challenging, and supportive environments. Inherited and environmentally imposed influences may be met with eager support or active resistance to determine each child's unique life history.

### RISK/RESILIENCE

**What factors promote risk or resilience in development?**

Individual differences are pervasive in intellectual, temperamental, and a host of other cognitive, social, and emotional aspects of development. Hereditary and environmental factors determine these differences. Alleles of genes contribute to the wide range of physical, cognitive, emotional, and social adaptations displayed by individuals. These individual differences are not produced solely by genes; they are also the product of a rich medley of physical, social, and cultural contexts in which each individual matures. A distinctive combination of genes and experiences promotes both the risk and the resilience we observe in human abilities and behavior.

## Chapter Review

### PRINCIPLES OF HEREDITARY TRANSMISSION

**What roles do genotype and the environment play in determining a phenotype?**

The genetic endowment inherited by an individual is the *genotype*. A *phenotype* refers to the traits and behaviors displayed by an individual. The phenotype is the result of the complex interactions between genotype and the experiences provided in the environment.

**What is the human genome? How do the nucleus of the cell, chromosomes and DNA, genes, and nucleotides play a role in genetic influences on development?**

The entire inventory of nucleotide base pairs that compose the genes and chromosomes in humans is called the *human genome*. The structures associated with the principles of heredity must be examined at several different levels. An individual's body is composed of trillions of cells. Twenty-three pairs of *chromosomes* (a total of forty-six), consisting of *deoxyribonucleic acid*, or *DNA*, are located in the nucleus of most cells in the human body. The central unit of hereditary information is the *gene*, a segment of a chromosome.

*Nucleotides* are two different sets of pairs of repeating molecules that form the biochemical building blocks for the genes and the basic structure of the chromosomes.

**How many autosomes exist in the human karyotype? Of what importance are the X and Y chromosomes?**

The human *karyotype* consists of twenty-two pairs of *autosomes*. Males and females differ in the composition of the twenty-third pair of chromsomes. In females, both members of the pair normally are X *chromosomes*. In males, one is normally an X chromosome, and the other is a Y *chromosome*.

**What is the difference between mitosis and meiosis, and what is the impact of the phenomenon of crossing over?**

Cell division in the human body takes place in two different ways. *Mitosis* is the process of cell division by which the forty-six chromosomes are duplicated in the body cells. The *gametes*, or sperm and egg cells, are formed by *meiosis*, a process of a cell division that results in twenty-three chromosomes in each of these cells. The random process by which a member of each of the twenty-three pairs of chromosomes is selected for the gametes, combined with *crossing over* during meiosis, ensures that every individual, with the exception of identical twins, has a unique hereditary blueprint. Once the gametes combine, the fertilized egg cell is called a *zygote*.

### How do homozygous and heterozygous genes and the presence of dominant, recessive, and codominant allelic forms account for the inheritance patterns associated with various phenotypes? What are polygenic traits?

Variants of genes on the twenty-three pairs of chromosomes, or *alleles*, often interact with one another to establish probabilities of inheritance for particular traits characteristics. A *dominant* allele will reflect its characteristics even when it is part of a *heterozygous genotype*, in which two alleles of a gene are different. A *recessive* allele is expressed only when it is part of a *homozygous* genotype, in which two alleles of a gene are the same. *Codominance* refers to the condition in which unblended characteristics of two alleles are reflected in the phenotype. Many human traits, however, are *polygenic*; that is, they are influenced by two or more genes.

### How do genes regulate the development of the phenotype? What is genomic imprinting?

Genetic information coded in DNA is sent by mRNA to regions outside of the cell nucleus. This process sets in motion the production of proteins that result in different cell functions. *Genomic imprinting* refers to instances of genetic transmission in which the parental source, mother or father, determines gene expression.

## GENE AND CHROMOSOMAL ABNORMALITIES

### What is the basis for each of the following genetically influenced disorders?

> Williams syndrome    Sickle cell disease and
> sickle cell trait
>
> Phenylketonuria      Fragile X syndrome

### What phenotypes are associated with each? Why is each of interest to developmental psychologists?

*Mutations*, or spontaneous changes in the molecular structures of genes, can have wide-ranging influences on development, from almost no consequence to death. Some genetic or chromosomal problems are passed from one generation to the next. *Williams syndrome* is caused by deletion of a small number of genes on chromosome 7. The phenotypic features include a short, upturned nose;

full lips; and curvature of the knee and hips. Children with Williams syndrome display uneven developmental profiles; they often have a large vocabulary, unusual skill in music, and great attention to social stimuli, but poor spatial, numerical, and problem-solving skills.

*Phenylketonuria (PKU)* results from the presence of two recessive genes for the trait. Untreated children with PKU may exhibit convulsions, severe mental retardation, and hyperactivity. Early intervention with a modified diet can prevent the symptoms from manifesting themselves.

*Sickle cell disease* results from the presence of two recessive genes that cause the red blood cells to become less efficient in transporting oxygen. The result can be anemia, jaundice, infection, and vulnerability to stroke, organ damage, and pain. An individual with *sickle cell trait* has only one of the recessive alleles but may still show symptoms under conditions of low oxygen. The presence of this allele provides protection against malaria.

*Fragile X syndrome* results from constriction in the X chromosome and is said to be sex linked. The phenotype will typically have a long, narrow face, large ears, and large testes. Fragile X is the most frequently inherited source of mental retardation associated with a single gene.

### What variations in the chromosomal makeup of an individual are possible? What is the most common example of chromosomal trisomy? What are examples of chromosomal variation associated with the sex chromosomes?

Presence of only one chromosome on the autosomes does not eventuate in human growth and development, but the presence of extra chromosomal material, or *trisomy*, can occur. The most common disorder contributing to mental retardation is trisomy 21 (Down syndrome), associated with inheritance of an extra chromosome. Variations in number of sex chromosomes also occur but do not always contribute to behavioral or other developmental problems, especially if a supportive environment is available. Some of the patterns that can occur are XO, XXX, and XYY.

## GENETIC COUNSELING

### What are the major diagnostic tests for prenatal development? What are their limitations and their advantages?

*Genetic counseling* provides prospective parents with information on the probability of having children affected by birth defects. *Genetic screening* involves the use of systematic tests on parents or fetus to locate risks due to genetics. *Amniocentesis* is effective for diagnosing chromosomal and metabolic disorders but carries some risk of infection and spontaneous abortion. *Chorionic villus sampling* can be done earlier in pregnancy but cannot diagnose neural tube defects, requires more medical skill, and is associated with a slightly elevated risk of miscarriage. *Fetal blood sampling* can detect chromosomal and genetic errors and blood disorders but carries somewhat elevated risks. *Maternal blood screening* can detect neural tube defects and Down syndrome. *Ultrasonography* can detect many physical abnormalities but cannot detect many other developmental disorders.

## What ethical and social issues emerge from the use of prenatal diagnostic tests?

Controversial ethical and social issues include whether to have the tests in the first place, decisions made once the results of the tests are known, and the opportunity to carry out sex preselection.

## What is sex preselection, and what are arguments for and against its practice?

Sex preselection refers to techniques that increase the likelihood that either a girl or a boy will be conceived. This technique allows for family balancing, may lead to a desirable parenting experience, and may prevent passing on sex-linked traits. Opponents argue that the practice may support sex bias and may lead to a "preference mentality" whereby children would be selected for other traits as well.

## DEVELOPMENTAL AND BEHAVIORAL GENETICS

## What methods do behavior geneticists use to investigate the extent to which behavior is influenced by combinations of genes and experiences? Why are identical and fraternal twins—as well as adopted children—important in work designed to evaluate the heritability of behavior?

*Behavior genetics* is a method of attempting to determine the relative contribution of heredity and environment to traits and behaviors that are often the result of combinations of genes. To determine contributions from combinations of genes, behavioral geneticists frequently engage in selective breeding with lower organisms or compare findings among various family members, such as *identical twins, fraternal twins*, siblings, and adopted children, because these groups differ in the extent to which they share a common genotype. *Heritability* refers to the extent to which the variability on some characteristic in a sample of individuals is accounted for by genetic differences among those individuals.

## How do concordance rate and correlation differ as measures in investigating genetic and environmental contributions to development?

The *concordance rate* refers to the percentage of pairs of twins who display the same characteristics. The correlation coefficient is a statistic that measures the degree of relationship between pairs of individuals of varying levels of biological relationship to one another.

## How are conceptualizations of the interaction between genotype and environment advanced by notions of range of reaction and canalization?

The concept of *range of reaction* highlights the fact that a trait or behavior influenced by a person's genotype may be unique to a particular kind of environment. The principle of *canalization* emphasizes that some traits and characteristics are highly determined by the genotype or, conversely, that some environments may have a powerful influence on how these are displayed.

## How do passive, evocative, and active niche-picking correlations between the genotype and experience differ from one another?

Correlations between genotype and environment may be *passive,* in that caregivers with specific genotypes are likely to provide environments supportive of their children's genotypes; *evocative,* in that parents, peers, and others are likely to react in ways that accommodate genetic inclinations; and *active,* in that children may attempt to find or create environments that support their individual genetic propensities; that is, engage in *niche picking.*

## To what extent are behavorial phenotypes, such as intelligence, personality and temperament, personality disorders, and other characteristics, influenced by heredity?

Intelligence, *temperament* and other personality variables, social adjustment and behavioral disorders, and other traits and characteristics often display considerable heritability, suggesting that the genotype contributes substantially to variability among children for many aspects of development.

## To what extent are shared and nonshared environments important in accounting for similarities and differences in children's behavior?

The shared environment provided by the family increases similarity among siblings, often to a limited extent. However, the nonshared environment that children within the same family experience contributes substantially to individual differences among children.

## Why might parents treat siblings differently, and how do children interpret these differential treatments?

Different inherited characteristic among children may lead parents to treat them differently. Siblings perceive differential treatment from their parents, but when the differential treatment is interpreted as equitable, even if not equal, positive relationships between siblings are fostered.

## KEY TERMS AND CONCEPTS

allele (p. 71)

amniocentesis (p. 90)

autosome (p. 73)

behavior genetics (p. 94)

canalization (p. 97)

chorionic villus sampling (p. 91)

chromosome (p. 71)

codominance (p. 76)

concordance rate (p. 97)

crossing over (p. 74)

deoxyribonucleic acid (DNA) (p. 71)

dominant allele (p. 76)

Down syndrome (p. 86)

fetal blood sampling (p. 91)

fragile X syndrome (p. 85)

fraternal twins (p. 94)

gamete (p. 71)

gene (p. 71)

genetic counseling (p. 89)

genetic screening (p. 89)

genomic imprinting (p. 76)

genotype (p. 71)

heritability (p. 94)

heterozygous (p. 75)

homozygous (p. 75)

human genome (p. 71)

identical twins (p. 94)

karyotype (p. 73)

maternal blood screening (p. 93)

meiosis (p. 74)

mitosis (p. 74)

mutation (p. 79)

niche picking (p. 98)

nucleotide (p. 71)

phenotype (p. 71)

phenylketonuria (PKU) (p. 85)

polygenic (p. 76)

range of reaction (p. 97)

recessive allele (p. 76)

sickle cell disease (p. 83)

sickle cell trait (p. 83)

temperament (p. 101)

trisomy (p. 86)

ultrasonography (p. 93)

Williams syndrome (p. 83)

X chromosome (p. 73)

Y chromosome (p. 73)

zygote (p. 73)

# THE PRENATAL PERIOD AND BIRTH

# 4

S he was expecting. It was great news. But this time her concerns outweighed the joy. Carole was already caring for two little ones, both under the age of five, and also working full time to provide income to help ends meet. Her job paid only a little more than minimum wage—never enough, even when added to her husband's paycheck. However, neither she nor her husband had gone to college. Nor did either have the kinds of skills to obtain a really high-paying job. It would be a struggle to provide for another child.

Although only four weeks into her pregnancy, Carole knew the embryo was undergoing rapid developmental changes and would continue to do so for many more weeks. She avoided alcohol as soon as she learned of her pregnancy. She had stopped smoking even before her first child was born. But was there enough money for prenatal care? Did she need to make modifications in her diet or adjustments in her work to ensure that her unborn child would have a healthy start? Would her persistent anxieties take a toll as well? She wanted the best for this new addition to the family. But she wasn't completely sure if she would be able to make that happen.

**NATURE & NURTURE**   How do nature and nurture interact during prenatal development and birth?

**SOCIOCULTURAL INFLUENCE**   How does the sociocultural context influence prenatal development and birth?

**CONTINUITY/DISCONTINUITY**   Is development before and after birth continuous or discontinuous?

**RISK/RESILIENCE**   What factors promote risk or resilience during prenatal development and birth?

Most women experience both pride and apprehension when they learn they are pregnant. Those feelings are often influenced by a multitude of social and cultural views and ideas about pregnancy. Although societies differ enormously in their specific beliefs, anthropologists report that expectant women around the world are often urged to avoid certain activities and to carry out various rituals for the sake of their unborn. In Western cultures, admonitions about pregnancy exist as well; obstetricians may advise a pregnant woman to stop smoking, avoid alcohol, and let someone else clean the cat's litterbox, and they may recommend taking supplements containing folic acid and other nutrients.

Fortunately, the mysteries surrounding this remarkable time are beginning to become clearer. Our discussion of prenatal development will open with a brief description of the amazing sequence of events taking place between conception and birth. At no other time does growth take place so rapidly or do so many physical changes occur in a matter of weeks, days, and even hours. Some cultures, such as the Chinese, tacitly acknowledge these dramatic events by pronouncing the baby one year old at birth. In the typical nine months of confinement to the womb, the fetus indeed undergoes an epic journey.

Although fetal growth proceeds in a highly protected environment, we are also discovering the ways in which drugs, diseases, and other factors affect prenatal development. We summarize our current understanding of these influences and then consider the birth process, another point at which the influences on development can be significant.

## THE STAGES OF PRENATAL DEVELOPMENT

Three major overlapping periods define the life of a human organism. **Prenatal development** is launched from the moment of conception and continues until the beginning of labor. All but the first few days of this period are spent within the confines of the womb. **The perinatal period** dawns at about the seventh month of pregnancy and extends until twenty-eight days after birth. This phase is associated with the impending birth, the social and physical setting for delivery, and the baby's first adjustments to his or her new world. Among the events included in the perinatal period are the medical and obstetrical practices associated with delivery, and the preparations and care provided by parents and others to assist in the transition from the womb to life outside. The **postnatal period** begins after birth. The child's environment now includes the broader physical and social world afforded by caregivers and others responsible for the infant's continued growth.

Prenatal development is further divided into three stages based on key biological events that take place. The **germinal period**, also known as the *period of the zygote*, encompasses the first ten to fourteen days following conception. Cell division and migration of the newly fertilized egg, culminating with its implantation in the uterine wall, characterize the germinal period. The second stage, the **embryonic period**, continues from about two to eight weeks after conception. The formation of structures and organs associated with the nervous, circulatory, respiratory, and most other systems mark the embryonic period. The final stage, the **fetal period**, lasts from about eight weeks after conception until birth. This period is distinguished by substantial physical growth, in which organs and systems are refined in preparation for functioning outside the womb.

**prenatal development**   Period in development from conception to the onset of labor.

**perinatal period**   Period beginning about the seventh month of pregnancy and continuing until about four weeks after birth.

**postnatal period**   Period in development following birth.

**germinal period**   Period lasting about ten to fourteen days following conception before the fertilized egg becomes implanted in the uterine wall. Also called *period of the zygote*.

**embryonic period**   Period of prenatal development during which major biological organs and systems form; begins about the tenth to fourteenth day after conception and ends about the eighth week after conception.

**fetal period**   Period of prenatal development, from about the eighth week after conception to birth, marked by rapid growth and preparation of body systems for functioning in the postnatal environment.

Another way to describe the period of 39 weeks that constitutes a full-term human pregnancy is in terms of three roughly equal time periods, or *trimesters*. The first trimester is the first 12 weeks, the second trimester encompasses weeks 13 to 27, and the third trimester occurs from week 28 to birth. You can see that partitioning the prenatal period in terms of trimesters does not neatly correspond to the germinal, embryonic, and fetal periods that we have just finished describing. However, this system has a long-standing tradition of use within the healthcare community.

## FERTILIZATION

Even before her own birth, Carole, like most other human females, had formed approximately 2 million primitive egg cells in her ovaries. Their numbers, however, declined with development; by puberty, perhaps only 30,000 remained. Of this abundant supply, about 400 mature and are released for potential fertilization during the childbearing years (Moore & Persaud, 2003). In contrast, male sperm production begins only at puberty, when an incredible 100 to 300 million sperm may be formed daily.

The opportunity for human conception begins about the fourteenth day after the start of the menstrual period. At this time, a capsule-like *follicle* housing a primitive egg cell in one of the ovaries begins to mature. As it matures and changes position, the follicle eventually ruptures and discharges its valuable contents from the ovary. After being expelled, the egg cell, or *ovum*, is normally carried into the Fallopian tube. This organ serves as a conduit for the egg, which moves toward the uterus at the leisurely rate of about one-sixteenth inch per hour. The Fallopian tube provides a receptive environment for fertilization if sperm are present. If unfertilized, the ovum survives only about twenty-four hours.

Sperm reach the Fallopian tube by maneuvering from the vagina through the cervix and uterus. Sperm can migrate several inches an hour with the assistance of their taillike appendages. From 300 to 500 typically negotiate the six- or more hour trip into the Fallopian tube; these usually survive about forty-eight hours.

If an ovum is present, sperm seem attracted to it, possibly because they detect its scent-like chemical cues (Spehr et al., 2003; Roberts, 1991). The egg also prepares for fertilization in the presence of sperm. Cells initially surrounding the ovum loosen their protective grip, permitting the egg to be penetrated. As soon as one sperm cell breaks through the egg's protective linings, enzymes rapidly transform its outer membrane to prevent others from invading (Moore & Persaud, 2003).

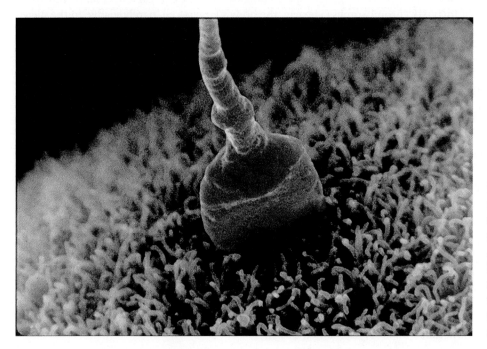

Human development begins with the penetration of the egg by a single sperm as shown here (egg and sperm are magnified greatly). Although the egg is the body's largest cell and the sperm the smallest, each contributes twenty-three chromosomes to form the hereditary basis for the development of a new living entity.

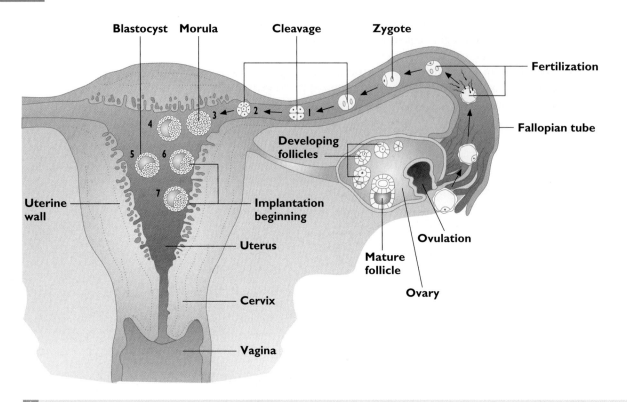

▲ **FIGURE 4.1**

**Fertilization and the Germinal Period**

During the early development of the human embryo, an egg cell is released from a maturing follicle within the ovary, and fertilization takes place in the Fallopian tube, transforming the egg cell or ovum into a zygote. Cleavage and multiplication of cells proceeds as the zygote migrates toward the uterus. Differentiation of the zygote begins within the uterus, becoming a solid sixteen-cell sphere know as the *morula,* then a differentiated set of cells known as the *blastocyst,* which prepares for implantation in the uterine wall. Once implanted, it taps a vital source of nutriments to sustain further development. (The numbers indicate days following fertilization.)

Genetic material from egg and sperm quickly mix to establish a normal complement of forty-six chromosomes. The egg, the body's largest cell, barely visible to the naked eye, weighs about 100,000 times more than the sperm, the body's smallest cell. Despite the enormous difference in size, both contribute equivalent amounts of genetic material to the zygote.

## THE GERMINAL PERIOD

After fertilization, the zygote continues to migrate down the Fallopian tube (see Figure 4.1). Within twenty-four to thirty hours after conception, the single cell divides into two cells, the first of a series of mitotic divisions called *cleavages.* At roughly twenty-hour intervals these cells divide again to form four, then eight, then sixteen cells. During the cleavages, the zygote remains about the same size; thus individual cells become smaller and smaller.

After three days, about the time the zygote is ready to enter the uterus, it has become a solid sphere of sixteen cells called a *morula.* Each cell is alike in its capacity to generate a separate, identical organism. About the fourth day after conception, however, the cells begin to segregate and carry out specific functions. One group forms a spherical outer cellular layer that eventually becomes various membranes providing nutritive support for the embryo. A second, inner group of cells organizes into a mass that will develop into the embryo. This differentiated group of cells is now called a *blastocyst* (Sadler, 2004).

father's sperm. Alternatively, with in vitro fertilization, eggs can be removed from a woman's ovaries, fertilized in a laboratory dish with the prospective father's sperm, and transferred to another woman's uterus. In this situation, the biological and social mothers may be one and the same except during the gestational period, when the surrogate mother's womb is used. Furthermore, a woman who cannot or chooses not to conceive in the traditional way might undergo in vitro fertilization and carry her own or another woman's fertilized egg during her pregnancy.

Legal, medical, and social controversies swirl around the technologies associated with assisted reproduction (Collins, 1995; Wright, 1998). For one thing, those who offer artificial insemination, apart from fertility clinics, are not always licensed, nor are they required to receive special training. Thus the competence of the practitioners, the safety of their various activities, and the frequency of this practice are unknown (Guinan, 1995). In addition, whereas adopted children are often informed of their status, children born as a result of new reproductive technologies may not know about their biological history. And, even if told, for example, that their legal and biological fathers may be two different individuals, these offspring typically are unable to obtain further information, because doctors who draw on sperm banks are not required to keep records linking donors and recipients (Guinan, 1995). In some other countries, such as England and Sweden, however, legislation has been enacted to permit individuals to obtain such information (Daniels & Taylor, 1993). Legal debates can also erupt over who is the rightful father or mother when, for example, a surrogate mother resolves to keep the child she has carried to term.

Medical concerns are linked to the use of fertility drugs because they increase the rate of multiple pregnancies to perhaps as much as 40 percent, compared with 3 percent in the general population without the use of such drugs (Centers for Disease Control and Prevention, 2005). Multiple pregnancies, especially when they involve more than two fetuses, increase risks both to the woman and to her offspring. Evidence exists, too, that single children born to mothers who receive assisted reproduction, even with various factors such as maternal age controlled, tend to be of lower birth weight and are at increased risk for birth defects (Dhont et al., 1999; Hansen et al., 2005; Tough et al., 2000). Controversies further extend to the costly medical procedures associated with assisted reproduction. The fee for assisted reproductive technologies in the United States can be $10,000 or more per treatment, and must be added to the increased costs of delivering multiple children and infants at risk (Katz, Nachtigall, & Showstack, 2002). Should insurance companies be mandated to pay expenses accompanying the repeated efforts that are often required to conceive?

The desire to have their own children is a powerful motive for many couples. This is evident from the large number of fertility clinics—perhaps as many as 400 operating in the United States alone and probably 20 or so more in Canada (Centers for Disease Control and Prevention, 2005a; Nemeth, 1997). In Western societies, about 1 in every 100 conceptions involving first-born children may be completed by means of in vitro fertilization (Van Balen, 1998). Studies conducted in Europe, the United States, and Taiwan reveal that children conceived by means of assisted reproduction show few emotional, behavioral, or other problems during their development (Hahn & DiPietro, 2001; Van Balen, 1998). For example, Susan Golombok and her colleagues (Golombok et al., 1995; Golombok, MacCallum, & Goodman, 2001; Golombok et al., 2002) have followed samples of children from the United Kingdom who were conceived by in vitro fertilization or donor insemination and who are now entering into adolescence. They found no differences between these children and children who were conceived without assistance on scales evaluating ability to function in school, peer relationships, and self-esteem. Parents, especially mothers, of these children are sometimes reported to display greater warmth and more concern than other parents, perhaps an indication of their commitment to and the value they place on their children (Hahn & DiPietro, 2001). The general conclusion from research is that the risks to children born to parents who have been assisted in their reproductive efforts are low and that their development is similar to that found in the larger population of children.

**gestational age** Age of fetus derived from onset of mother's last menstrual period.

## ENVIRONMENTAL FACTORS INFLUENCING PRENATAL DEVELOPMENT

We can readily imagine that a host of events must occur, and at the right times, for prenatal development to proceed normally. What kinds of environmental support do embryo and fetus receive in their liquid, somewhat buoyant, surroundings, and how well protected are they from intrusions that can disrupt their development?

### SUPPORT WITHIN THE WOMB

The embryo and fetus are sustained by a number of major structures, including the placenta, the umbilical cord, and the amniotic sac. The **placenta**, formed by cells from both the blastocyst and the uterine lining, produces essential hormones for the fetus. Just as important, it serves as the exchange site at which oxygen and nutrients are absorbed from the woman's circulatory system, and at which carbon dioxide and waste products are excreted from the embryo's circulatory system. The transfer takes place through a network of intermingling, blood-rich capillaries originating in the woman's and the fetus's circulatory systems. Thus blood is not normally exchanged between a woman and her fetus. Although blood cells are too large to cross the membranes separating the two systems, smaller molecules of oxygen, carbon dioxide, nutrients, and hormones can traverse the barrier. So can some chemicals, drugs, and diseases that interfere with fetal development, as we will see shortly.

The **umbilical cord** is the conduit to and from the placenta for the blood of the fetus. The fetus lives in the womb surrounded by the fluid-filled **amniotic sac**. Amniotic fluid helps to stabilize temperature, insulates the fetus from bumps and shocks, and contains substances necessary for the development of the lungs. The fluid is constantly recirculated and renewed as the fetus ingests nutrients and urinates.

### PRINCIPLES OF TERATOLOGY

Most fetuses negotiate the average thirty-eight-week period from conception to birth as healthy, vigorous newborns. Yet, as we discuss in the chapter titled "Genetics and Heredity," genetic factors can modify normal progress. So, too, can environmental factors. The study of disabilities and problems that arise from environmental influences during the prenatal period is called *teratology*. Environmental agents that cause disruptions in normal development are known as **teratogens.**

**placenta**   Support organ formed by cells from both blastocyst and uterine lining; serves as exchange site for oxygen, nutrients, and waste products.

**umbilical cord**   Conduit of blood vessels through which oxygen, nutrients, and waste products are transported between placenta and embryo.

**amniotic sac**   Fluid-filled, transparent protective membrane surrounding the fetus.

**teratogen**   Any environmental agent that can cause deviations in prenatal development. Consequences may range from behavioral problems to death.

The fact that external agents can upset the course of prenatal development in humans was first appreciated in 1941 when McAllister Gregg, an ophthalmologist, confirmed that rubella, commonly called German measles, causes visual anomalies in the fetus. During this same decade, many infants born to women exposed to the atomic bomb were reported to have birth defects. This finding, along with studies involving animals, implicated radiation as a teratogen (Warkany & Schraffenberger, 1947). The import of these early observations became more fully appreciated when researchers documented that women who had taken a presumably harmless antinausea drug called *thalidomide* frequently bore infants with severe arm and leg malformations (McBride, 1961).

The widely publicized thalidomide tragedy made it abundantly clear that environmental agents can seriously harm human embryos without adversely affecting the woman or others during postnatal development (Wilson, 1977). In fact, the embryo may be susceptible to virtually any substance if exposure to it is sufficiently concentrated (Samuels & Samuels, 1996). A number of broad generalizations have emerged from research on teratogens since the 1960s (Abel, 1989; Friedman & Hanson, 2002; Vorhees, 1986). These principles help to explain the sometimes-bewildering array of adverse consequences that specific drugs, diseases, and other agents can have on development.

KEY THEMES
NATURE & NURTURE
RISK/RESILIENCE

- *The Principle of Susceptibility:  Individuals within species, as well as species themselves, show major differences in susceptibility to different teratogens.* Thalidomide provides a good example of this principle. Scientists knew that extremely large amounts of the drug caused abnormal fetal development in rats (Cohen, 1966). However, the doses given to pregnant women in Europe and Canada, where thalidomide was available as an over-the-counter preparation to reduce morning sickness and anxiety, were considerably smaller. For reasons unknown, the embryos of humans between twenty and thirty-five days after conception are extremely sensitive to small amounts of thalidomide. More than 10,000 babies were born without limbs or with limb defects and intellectual retardation. The genotype of an individual woman and her fetus may also affect susceptibility. Some fetuses were exposed to thalidomide during this sensitive period, yet at birth these babies showed no ill effects from the drug (Kajii, Kida, & Takahashi, 1973).

- *The Principle of Critical or Sensitive Periods: The extent to which a teratogen affects the fetus depends on the stage of development during which exposure occurs.* Figure 4.3 shows that many human organs and systems are most sensitive to toxic agents during the third to eighth week after conception, when they are still being formed. However, vulnerability to teratogens exists throughout much of prenatal development. In fact, the brain continues to undergo substantial neural differentiation, migration, and growth during the second and third trimesters of pregnancy, as well as after birth. As a consequence, exposure to teratogens throughout prenatal development may have especially important behavioral consequences.

KEY THEME
CONTINUITY/DISCONTINUITY

- *The Principle of Access: The accessibility of a given teratogen to a fetus or an embryo influences the extent of its damage.* Many factors determine when and to what extent an embryo or a fetus is exposed to a teratogen. At one level, cultural and social practices may prevent a pregnant woman from using or encourage her to use drugs, prevent her from being inoculated or encourage her to be inoculated for certain diseases, or prevent her from being exposed to or encourage her to be exposed to chemicals and other toxins. For example, use of cocaine may be socially approved in one segment of a culture and avoided in another. However, even when a teratogen is present, it must still gain access to the uterine environment; for example, through a woman's inhaling, ingesting, or injecting a drug intravenously. How a woman has been exposed to the agent, the way she metabolizes it, and how it is transported to the womb influence whether a teratogen reaches a sufficient threshold to have some effect.

KEY THEME
SOCIOCULTURAL INFLUENCE

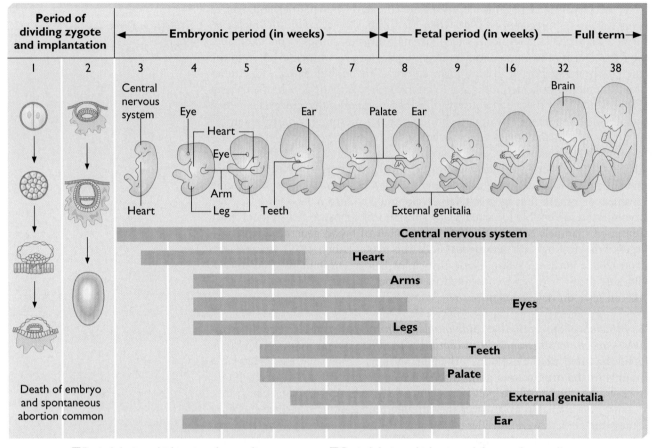

■ Period during which major abnormality occurs ■ Period during which minor defect or abnormality occurs

▲ **FIGURE 4.3**

**Sensitive Periods in Prenatal Development**

During prenatal development, organs and systems undergo periods in which they are more or less sensitive to teratogenic influences, environmental agents that can cause deviations in development. The potential for major structural defects (blue-colored sections) is usually greatest during the embryonic period, when many organs are forming. However, many regions of the body, including the central nervous system, continue to have some susceptibility to teratogens (yellow-colored sections) during the fetal period.

*Source:* Moore & Persaud (1998).

**fetal alcohol syndrome (FAS)**
Cluster of fetal abnormalities stemming from mother's consumption of alcohol; includes growth retardation, defects in facial features, and intellectual retardation.

• *The Principle of Dose-Response Relationships: The amount of exposure to or the dosage level of a given teratogen influences the extent of its damage.* The severity of a teratogen often is related to level of dosage. The more a woman smokes, for example, the greater the likelihood that her baby will be of low birth weight. The concentration of a toxic agent reaching the fetus, however, cannot always be determined from the woman's exposure to it. The severity of an illness a woman experiences—for example, rubella—does not always predict the effect of the disease on the fetus.

• *The Principle of Teratogenic Response: Teratogens do not show uniform effects on prenatal development.* Teratogens may cause death or disrupt development of specific organs and systems. They may also have behavioral consequences, impairing sensorimotor, cognitive, social, and emotional development. The principles of species and individual differences, as well as the timing, duration, and intensity of exposure to the teratogen, govern the effect a specific teratogen will have on prenatal development. Alcohol, for example, can cause congenital defects during the embryonic period but may interfere with prenatal weight gain and contribute to postnatal behavioral problems during the second and third trimesters of pregnancy (Abel, 1989). One other important implication of this principle is that very different teratogenic agents can produce a similar pattern of disabilities. Thus efforts to pinpoint why a baby was born with a given anomaly are not always successful.

- *The Principle of Interference with Specific Mechanisms: Teratogens affect prenatal development by interfering with biochemical processes that regulate the differentiation, migration, or basic functions of cells.* This principle helps to differentiate folk beliefs from scientific explanations of fetal anomalies. A woman's looking at a frightening visual stimulus, for example, has no direct consequence for the fetus. However, hormonal imbalances induced by chronic levels of stress may have an impact on development.

- *The Principle of Developmental Delay and "Sleeper Effects": Some teratogens may delay development temporarily with no long-term negative consequences; others may cause developmental problems only late in development.* Although some teratogenic effects can be observed at birth and are permanent and irreversible, others may be nullified, especially when a supportive caregiving environment is provided. However, the effects of teratogens on later development are probably substantially underestimated because many produce "sleeper effects." These are consequences that go unnoticed at birth but seed problems that become apparent in childhood and even later. For example, women treated with *diethylstilbestrol (DES)*, a hormone administered from the 1940s through the 1960s to prevent miscarriages, gave birth to daughters who showed a high rate of genital tract cancers and sons who displayed a high incidence of abnormalities of the testes when they reached adulthood.

## DRUGS AS TERATOGENS

Now that we have considered general principles involving teratogens, we can examine the effects that specific environmental agents have on the embryo or fetus. A number of substances that expectant women may use, either as medicine or as mood-altering devices, frequently become part of the intrauterine world. We focus on their consequences for both embryonic and fetal development.

***Alcohol*** Because alcohol readily crosses the placenta, its concentration in the fetus is likely to be similar to that in the woman (Teratology Society, 2005). Moreover, because it lacks some enzymes to effectively degrade alcohol, the fetus may be exposed to it for a longer period of time (Reece et al., 1995). Among pregnant women in the Western world, alcohol is more widely used than any other teratogen and, according to some experts, is the single most frequent cause of mental retardation in industrialized countries (Reece et al., 1995). Current data indicate that about 10 percent of pregnant women have consumed alcohol and 2 percent used it frequently (Centers for Disease Control and Prevention, 2004a).

Widespread recognition of the dangers of alcohol emerged in the early 1970s, when three sets of characteristics were observed in a number of babies born to alcoholic women (Jones & Smith, 1973). These included prenatal and postnatal growth retardation, microcephaly, and abnormal facial features, as well as mental retardation and other behavioral problems, such as hyperactivity and poor motor coordination, suggestive of central nervous system dysfunction. This constellation of deficits, known as **fetal alcohol syndrome (FAS)**, appears in as many as 6 percent of infants born to alcoholic mothers (Day & Richardson, 1994). *Alcohol-related neurodevelopmental disabilities (ARND)* have been identified in many other children prenatally exposed to alcohol. These children exhibit retardation or learning difficulties, along with other behavioral problems (Mattson et al., 1997; Stratton, Howe, & Battaglia, 1996). Perhaps as many as 1 in every 100 births in the United States displays FAS or ARND (Sampson et al., 1997).

Binge drinking, usually identified as five or more drinks within a short time, even if it takes place infrequently, can be especially hazardous because it exposes

This young Swedish girl, displaying features often associated with fetal alcohol syndrome, was born to a mother who was an alcoholic. Physical characteristics, including microencephaly (small head size), eyes widely set apart, and flat thin upper lip are often accompanied by delayed physical growth and mental retardation.

the fetus to highly concentrated levels of alcohol (Chasnoff, 1986; Streissguth et al., 1994). However, even limited alcohol consumption, some researchers report, is linked to an increase in spontaneous abortions and to reduced alertness, less vigorous body activity, more tremors, and slower learning in newborns compared with babies of women who do not drink (Jacobson & Jacobson, 1996; Streissguth et al., 1994). Work by Anne Streissguth and her colleagues shows that prenatal exposure to relatively moderate amounts of alcohol contributes to measurable deficits in attention and school performance, small declines in IQ, and more frequent behavioral problems in children and adolescents (Bookstein et al., 1996; Streissguth et al., 1994; Streissguth et al., 1999). For example, these children and adolescents tended to be more impulsive and had difficulty organizing their work, especially under stress. Moreover, the tendency to display neurocognitive deficits was related to the amount of prenatal alcohol exposure, an example of the dose-related principle, and was especially evident when the woman engaged in occasional binge drinking. Nevertheless, there was no clear threshold at which negative consequences began to appear. As a result, Streissguth et al. (1999) concluded that even small amounts of alcohol can be harmful.

How does alcohol produce such effects? One way is by directly modifying cell functioning. Examination of infants with fetal alcohol syndrome who died shortly after birth reveals structural changes in the brain caused by delays and errors in the way neurons migrate to form the cortex, or outer layer, of the brain (Clarren et al., 1978). Alcohol consumption has also been linked to delayed growth of the frontal cortex and to changes in the functioning of the hippocampus, which is involved in memory (Savage et al., 2002; Wass, Persutte, & Hobbins, 2001). The metabolism of alcohol also requires substantial amounts of oxygen, so less oxygen may be available for normal cell functions. These findings provide further justification for the American Academy of Pediatrics' recommendation of complete abstinence, because "there is no known safe amount of alcohol consumption during pregnancy" (American Academy of Pediatrics, 2000).

***Cigarette Smoking***    About 13 percent of women in the United States smoke during pregnancy, a percentage that has been declining in recent years. The percentage is higher among Caucasian (14 percent) and African American women (9 percent) than among Hispanic women (4 percent) (National Institute on Drug Abuse, 2003). It may also be far higher in other countries in which less effort has been directed toward publicizing the negative health consequences of smoking.

No evidence exists to indicate that smoking during pregnancy causes major congenital defects. However, nicotine and some other of the more than 2,500 chemicals found in tobacco smoke do have serious consequences for fetal and infant mortality, birth weight, and possibly postnatal development (American College of Obstetricians and Gynecologists, 1994). Spontaneous abortions, stillbirths, and neonatal deaths increase in pregnant women who smoke (Streissguth et al., 1994). The most consistent finding from studies of babies born to smokers compared with nonsmokers, however, is their smaller size (Ernst, Moolchan, & Robinson, 2001; Secker-Walker et al., 1997). The more and the longer a woman smokes during pregnancy, the lower her baby's average weight at birth, even when equated for length of gestation, because babies of women who smoke are also likely to be born a few days early (Pollard, 2000; Shah & Bracken, 2000). Every cigarette smoked on a daily basis by a mother during the last trimester of pregnancy reduces the baby's weight by about one ounce (Bernstein et al., 2005).

As with alcohol consumption, a reduction in oxygen may account for these effects. Smoking increases carbon monoxide, which displaces oxygen, in the red blood cells of both woman and fetus. Nicotine also reduces blood flow to the placenta. Moreover, a fetus's heart rate goes up when a woman smokes, a reaction that may take place to maintain adequate oxygen (Samuels & Samuels, 1996). Babies of women who use tobacco have larger placentas and more frequent placental abnormalities than babies of the same weight born to nonsmoking women (Meyer &

Tonascia, 1977; Weinberger & Weiss, 1988). Nicotine may also interfere with metabolic activity important to cell regulation and differentiation.

The long-term behavioral consequences of prenatal exposure to smoke are less well understood. Some researchers have failed to find evidence of poorer performance on cognitive, academic, or other tasks for children exposed to smoke prenatally (Ernst et al., 2001). However, other researchers have reported that infants born to smokers display poorer learning (Martin et al., 1977), a higher-pitched cry (Nugent et al., 1996), and reduced visual and auditory alertness (Franco et al., 1999). Moreover, studies carried out in the United States, the Netherlands, and New Zealand reveal a small but significant increase in behavioral problems in children and adolescents whose mothers smoked during pregnancy (Fergusson, Woodward, & Horwood, 1998; Orlebeke, Knol, & Verhulst, 1999; Weitzman, Gortmaker, & Sobel, 1992). Although efforts to control other factors potentially contributing to these observations have often been undertaken, genetic, family differences, continued passive exposure to smoke from a caregiver or others in the family, and transmission of smoking-related substances during breastfeeding cannot be eliminated as possible causal contributors to these outcomes (American Academy of Pediatrics, 2001; Becker et al., 1999; Orlebeke et al., 1999). Once the child is born, passive exposure to environmental tobacco smoke created by others in the child's household is associated with significantly increased health risks, such as sudden infant death and other respiratory problems (American Academy of Pediatrics, 1997; Brown, 2001).

**Prescription and Over-the-Counter Drugs**   Legal drugs in addition to alcohol and tobacco can be hazardous for fetal development. Some are known teratogens (see Table 4.2), but knowledge of the effects of many remains perilously limited. Aspirin, for example, has been demonstrated to impair behavioral competence in the offspring of lower animals. One well-controlled study found that aspirin may also be associated with lower IQ in early childhood (Streissguth et al., 1984). Certainly, large doses of aspirin, but also of alternative pain relievers such as acetaminophen, may increase risk to the fetus (Reece et al., 1995).

Caffeine, too, has been implicated in birth defects in animals, although studies have failed to reveal any consistent link in humans. However, babies born to mothers who consume higher amounts of caffeine tend to have lower birth weight than babies of mothers who drink less coffee (Eskenazi et al., 1999). Caffeine also has a behavioral impact on the fetus. Lawrence Devoe and his colleagues (1993) used ultrasound to record biweekly two-hour observations of fetal activity during the final ten weeks of pregnancy in ten heavy-caffeine consumers (more than 500 milligrams, or five cups of coffee, daily) and ten low-caffeine consumers (less than 200 milligrams, or two cups of coffee, daily). Fetuses exhibited considerably more arousal (defined by irregular heart rate and breathing activity, frequent body movements, and rapid eye movements) when exposed to the higher amounts of caffeine. The more highly aroused infants may have consumed more energy, a factor that could contribute to their lower birth weight. However, the long-term implications of this difference in activity remain unknown.

Perhaps an even greater concern is the number of prescription and over-the-counter drugs consumed during pregnancy. Most expectant women use at least one medication, and the average is more than three (Buitendijk & Bracken, 1991). Little is known about the effects of many of these products, and even less is known about the interactive consequences when multiple drugs are used. In addition, as new drugs are developed, their impact as potential teratogens needs to be considered. The case of Accutane, a prescription medication used to treat acne, provides a vivid example. When first introduced as a treatment, Accutane taken by pregnant women resulted in a very high rate of physical deformities in the children who were born. Between 25 and 35 percent showed such irregularities as facial deformities, heart problems, and impairment of the nervous system (Lammer et al., 1985). Because the consequences of Accutane exposure for the embryo and fetus are so severe, the U.S. Food and Drug Administration has

**Table 4.2 Prescription and Other Frequently Used Drugs and Their Effects on Prenatal Development**

| Drug | Description and Known or Suspected Effects |
|---|---|
| **Alcohol** | See text. |
| **Amniopterin** | Anticancer agent. Facial defects and a number of other congenital malformations as well as mental retardation (Hanson, 1997). |
| **Amphetamines** | Stimulants for the central nervous system, some types frequently used for weight control. Readily cross placental barrier. Fetal intrauterine growth retardation often reported but may be a result of accompanying malnutrition or multiple-drug use. Increased amounts and duration of exposure prenatally found to be correlated with aggressive behavior in 8-year-olds (Billing et al., 1994). |
| **Antibiotics (streptomycin, tetracycline)** | Streptomycin associated with hearing loss. Tetracycline associated with staining of baby's teeth if exposure occurs during second or third trimester (Friedman & Polifka, 1996). |
| **Aspirin** | Possibility of increased bleeding in both mother and infant (Hanson, 1997). See text for other complications that can arise. |
| **Barbiturates (pentobarbital, phenobarbital, secobarbital)** | Sedatives and anxiety reducers. Considerable evidence of neurobiological and behavioral complications in rats. Readily cross human placenta; concentrations in fetus may be greater than in woman. Newborns may show withdrawal symptoms (Friedman & Polifka, 1996). No consistent evidence of long-term effects in humans. |
| **Benzodiazepines (chlordiazepoxide, diazepam)** | Tranquilizers. Not shown to have teratogenic effects, although newborns may display withdrawl symptoms with diazepam (Friedman & Polifka, 1996). |
| **Caffeine** | See text. |
| **Hydantoins (Anticonvulsants)** | Treatment for epilepsy. Produce *fetal hydantoin syndrome,* including heart defects, cleft lip or palate, decreased head size, and mental retardation. Controversy continues over whether effects are entirely caused by drug or by conditions associated with the mother, including her epilepsy (Hanson, 1986). |
| **Lithium** | Treatment for bipolar disorder. Crosses placenta freely. Known to be teratogenic in premammalian animals. Strong suggestive evidence of increased cardiovascular defects in human infants. Behavioral effects unknown. Administration at time of delivery markedly reduces infant responsivy (Friedman & Polifka, 1996). |
| **Retinoids** | Antiacne medicine. Effects similar to large amounts of vitamin A. |
| **Sex Hormones (androgens, estrogens, progestins)** | Contained in birth control pills, fertility drugs, and other drugs to prevent miscarriages. Continued use of birth control pills during pregnancy associated with heart and circulatory disorders. Behavioral and personality implications suspected. Masculinization of female embryo from exposure to high doses of androgens or progestins. |
| **Thalidomide** | Reduces morning sickness and anxiety. Deformities of the limbs, depending on time of exposure, often accompanied by mental retardation (Friedman & Polifka, 1996). |
| **Tobacco** | See text. |
| **Tricyclics (imipramine, desimipramine)** | Antidepressants. Some tricyclics cross the placenta. Studies with rats reveal developmental and behavioral disturbances. Studies with humans reveal no consistent findings (Friedman & Polifka, 1996). |
| **Vitamins** | Large amounts of vitamin A known to cause major birth defects. Excessive amounts of other vitamins may also cause prenatal malformations (Reece et al., 1995). |

*Note:* This listing is not meant to be exhaustive, and other drugs may have teratogenic effects. No drug should be taken during pregnancy without consultation with a qualified physician.

recently issued a public health advisory to minimize pregnant women's exposure to this drug (Food and Drug Administration, 2005). In general, expectant women are usually advised to take *no* drugs during pregnancy, including over-the-counter remedies, or to take them only under the close supervision of their physician.

***Illegal Drugs*** The effects of illegal drugs, such as marijuana, heroin, and cocaine, on prenatal development are even more difficult to untangle than the effects of prescription and over-the-counter medications. Drug users are rarely certain of the contents or concentrations of the drugs they consume. Wide variation in frequency of use, the possibility of interactions from exposure to multiple drugs, poor nutritional status, inadequate or no prenatal care, and potential psychological and physiological differences both before and after taking such drugs compound the problem of isolating their teratogenic effects. The lifestyle of many illegal-drug users can be described as essentially chaotic (Chasnoff, 1992), so that conclusions about the impact of the drug itself are often difficult to make.

Research with animals has shown that the psychoactive ingredients associated with marijuana cross the placenta and are stored in the amniotic fluid (Harbison & Mantilla-Plata, 1972). They may also be transferred postnatally through the mother's milk (Dalterio & Bartke, 1979). Still, efforts to determine the effects of marijuana on human fetal and postnatal development reveal few consistent findings (Zuckerman & Bresnahan, 1991). As with tobacco, fetal weight and size appear to be reduced. Length of gestation may also be shorter for heavy marijuana users, a finding consistent with giving marijuana to speed labor, a practice carried out at one time in Europe.

A higher-pitched cry, visual problems, lower scores on memory and verbal tasks, and more restless sleep patterns in early childhood are reported with prenatal exposure to marijuana (Dahl et al., 1995; Fried, Watkinson, & Gray, 1998; Lester & Dreher, 1989). However, social and economic differences in the backgrounds of the children could also account for these findings. In fact, in some cultures, such as Jamaica, marijuana use correlates positively with neonatal test performance (Dreher, Nugent, & Hudgins, 1994).

⊶ **KEY THEME**

**SOCIOCULTURAL INFLUENCE**

The effects of heroin and morphine became a public concern as early as the late 1800s, when doctors reported withdrawal symptoms in newborns whose mothers used these substances (Zagon & McLaughlin, 1984). By the early 1900s, heroin and morphine were known to be transmitted through the placenta, as well as through the mother's milk. Today, an estimated 9,000 infants born in the United States each year are exposed to heroin or methadone, a pharmacologically similar product (Sprauve, 1996). Often given under regulated conditions as a heroin substitute, methadone's effects on fetal development are just as powerful as heroin's. So, too, may be the effects of a newer synthetic form of heroin, OxyContin, a prescribed painkiller that has recently achieved the status of widely sought-after street drug.

Although congenital defects have not been positively linked to heroin and methadone, stillbirths and infant deaths are more frequent, and lower birth weight is common (American College of Obstetricians and Gynecologists, 1994). About 60 to 70 percent of infants born to heroin- and methadone-addicted women also undergo withdrawal symptoms, such as diarrhea, sweating, a distinctively high-pitched cry, tremors, and irritability (Sprauve, 1996). Developmental difficulties continue to be observed in infants and children exposed to heroin and methadone. However, high-quality caregiving can play a powerful role in lessening the negative impact of prenatal exposure to heroin in children, at least for those who do not experience neurological damage (Ornoy et al., 1996).

Each year in the United States alone, more than 200,000 infants are estimated to be born to mothers who use illegal drugs (National Institute on Drug Abuse, 1995). However, probably none of these drugs has received more widespread attention than cocaine. Cocaine in its many forms—including crack, an especially potent and addictive variation—readily crosses the placenta. Once it reaches the fetus, it stays longer than in adults, because the immature organs of the fetus have difficulty breaking it down. Cocaine also can continue to influence the baby after birth through the mother's milk.

Dire effects for the fetus and subsequently for postnatal development as a result of exposure to cocaine have been widely publicized (Chavkin, 2001; Frank et al., 2001). Indeed, evidence exists that cocaine may be associated with prematurity and low birth weight (Bendersky & Lewis, 1999), as well as with attentional, motor, and some early neurobehavioral difficulties (Eyler et al., 1998; Fried et al., 1998; Singer, Arendt, et al., 1999; Stanwood & Levitt, 2001). However, these observed relationships can often be explained by other factors known to interfere with development. In fact, a detailed review of the results of a number of well-controlled studies by Deborah Frank and her colleagues concluded that exposure to cocaine for those undergoing a normal gestational period is *not* a factor that leads to poor physical growth or delayed acquisition of motor skills, lowered cognitive abilities, or behavioral, attentional, or affective disturbances in young children (Frank et al., 2001).

The primary position of Deborah Frank and her colleagues, and a common thread of agreement emerging among researchers, is that other risk factors regularly associated with the use of cocaine—such as increased exposure to tobacco and alcohol, poor nutrition, diminished parental responsiveness, abuse and neglect, social isolation of the family, and the increased stress typically accompanying poverty— play a *far more important* role in negative outcomes for development during early childhood than does cocaine itself (Bendersky & Lewis, 1999; Frank et al., 2001; Miller & Boudreaux, 1999). Thus the prognosis for children subjected to cocaine and other illegal drugs in utero should and does improve substantially when interventions are undertaken to reduce or eliminate these other risk factors (Butz et al., 2001; Field et al., 1998; Kilbride et al., 2000). In other words, although the potential for negative consequences of prenatal exposure to cocaine cannot be ruled out, intervention at other levels appears to be the key to improving the developmental outlook for children exposed to this and other drugs. So, too, may be the need to educate the public, as well as professionals, about the known consequences for development of exposure to cocaine.

### CONTROVERSY: THINKING IT OVER

## Should a Drug-Abusing Expectant Woman Be Charged with Child Abuse?

Consider the circumstances surrounding the prosecution of Cornelia Whitner of South Carolina. Her son was born with cocaine in his system. In 1992 Cornelia pled guilty to a charge of child neglect after admitting to the use of cocaine in her third trimester of pregnancy. She was sentenced to eight years in prison.

### What Is the Controversy?

Although the conviction of Cornelia Whitner has since been overturned, the issues surrounding this and similar cases deeply divide law enforcement, medical, and service agencies in the United States, Canada, and many Western European countries (Capron, 1998; Peak & Del Papa, 1993). Since the mid-1980s, more than 200 American women in thirty states have been prosecuted on charges of child abuse and neglect, delivery of drugs to a minor, or assault with a deadly weapon for allegedly harming their offspring through prenatal exposure to cocaine or other illegal drugs (Paltrow et al., 2000). Court cases with policy implications for whether a woman can or should be arrested if she exposes a fetus to illegal drugs are continuing to be debated at the highest judicial levels, including the U.S. Supreme Court (Greenhouse, 2000; Paltrow et al., 2000). Is this an effective way to reduce the likelihood of drug use and any of its accompanying risks for the fetus?

### What Are the Opposing Arguments?

Some say that a concerned society should impose criminal or other charges on a pregnant woman who uses a drug that may be dangerous to the fetus. A number of jurisdictions in the United States and provinces in Canada have implemented laws permitting a newborn to be removed from a parent on the grounds of child abuse or neglect because of drug exposure during pregnancy. In some cases, the woman has been ordered to be confined to a drug treatment facility during pregnancy. After all, anyone found to provide such illegal substances to a child would certainly expect to face criminal or other charges. Are the circumstances that much different in the case of a pregnant woman and her fetus?

Others believe the situation is vastly different and further claim that criminal charges, imprisonment, or mandatory treatment are counterproductive (Beckett, 1995; Farr, 1995). Legislation specifically targeted at pregnant drug users might actually drive prospective mothers, out of fear of being prosecuted, away from the care and treatment needed for both themselves and their fetuses. Moreover, the tendency to rely on criminal procedures could limit the resources available for the implementation of innovative, well-funded public health efforts for treating addiction and its consequences for the fetus (Chavkin, 2001).

### What Answers Exist? What Questions Remain?

At the present time, no research has been carried out on whether threats of criminal procedures or other forms of punishment dissuade a woman from using drugs during her pregnancy. If studies with this or other populations demonstrate that these kinds of actions are effective in reducing drug use, perhaps greater justification would exist for the extension of this approach to expectant women. But, given the recent findings that the negative consequences for the fetus often stem less from the illegal drugs themselves than from the myriad other factors associated with drug use, would such actions be helpful? In other words, are poor nutrition and a host of other social and economic factors, as well as the chaotic lifestyle that often accompanies drug use and over which a woman may not always have control, the primary culprits in impaired fetal development? If so, then intervention must take place at the public health level. And do your views about how to address this issue change given that alcohol and tobacco have been shown to have more serious consequences for fetal development than many illegal drugs (Bendersky & Lewis, 1999; Frank et al., 2001; Miller & Boudreaux, 1999; Streissguth et al., 1999)? If laws are introduced to protect the fetus from illegal drugs, should these laws not also be extended and applied to those who use readily available, heavily advertised, and common drugs that are known to have even more serious teratogenic effects? Research has begun to shed light on some of these issues by providing knowledge about the effects of exposure to drugs on fetal development. What other kinds of developmental research would be useful in helping to resolve these competing views? Are there alternatives that might be proposed to help solve a very complex problem: ensuring an optimal start for every child at birth?

## DISEASES AS TERATOGENS

KEY THEME

**RISK/RESILIENCE**

Somewhere between 2 and 8 percent of babies born to American women are exposed to one or more diseases or other forms of illness during pregnancy (Landry, 2004). Fortunately, most babies are unaffected. Moreover, significant progress has been made in eliminating the potentially negative fetal consequences of several diseases, such as mumps and rubella (German measles), at least in some countries. Recently, for example, the Centers for Disease Control have declared that rubella has been virtually eliminated in the United States (Centers for Disease Control and Prevention, 2005b). Unfortunately, rubella, a highly preventable illness, continues to be a major cause of fetal malformations and death worldwide, because vaccination programs are limited in some regions of the world. Other diseases, some of which are described in Table 4.3, continue to pose risks for the fetus in even the most medically advanced countries. Their impact on the fetus can be serious, sometimes devastating, even when a woman is completely unaware of illness.

***Toxoplasmosis*** Toxoplasmosis is caused by a parasite found in many mammals and birds; about 22 percent of adults in the United States have been exposed to it (Centers for Disease Control and Prevention, 2004b). However, the disease is found with greater frequency in some European countries, including France and Austria, and in tropical regions. Humans occasionally contract the disease by touching cat feces containing the parasite or, even more frequently, by eating raw or partially infected cooked meat, especially pork and lamb. Children and adults are often unaware of their exposure, because the infection may have no symptoms or cause only a minor fever or rash.

Infections early in pregnancy can have devastating consequences; fortunately, risk of transmission to the fetus at this time is lowest (Foulon et al., 1999). Growth retardation, jaundice, accumulation of fluid in the brain, and visual and central nervous system damage are the most frequent teratogenic outcomes. Some infants show no symptoms at birth; only later may mental retardation, neuromuscular abnormalities, impaired vision, and other eye problems become apparent. Research carried out in Europe indicates that early treatment with antibiotics can help reduce some of its more devastating consequences (Foulon et al., 1999).

***Cytomegalovirus*** Cytomegalovirus (CMV), a member of the herpes family of viruses, causes swelling of the salivary glands and mononucleosislike symptoms in adults. It is the single most frequent infection found in newborns today, affecting 1 to 2 of every 100 babies. As many as 10 percent of infected infants can be expected to sustain some congenital damage (Friedman & Hanson, 2002). No effective treatment exists.

**⚷ KEY THEME**

**SOCIOCULTURAL INFLUENCE**

CMV is most frequently reported in Asia, Africa, and lower socioeconomic groups, in which up to 85 percent of the population may be infected. Yet 45 to 55 percent of middle- and high-income groups in Europe and the United States are infected as well (Hagay et al., 1996). Transmission occurs through various body fluids. CMV can be passed easily between children playing together, for example, in daycare centers and in family daycare settings (Bale et al., 1999) and from child to adult through physical contact.

Fortunately, the aftermath of contracting the virus in early childhood is generally not serious. Infection can occur within the womb, during birth, and through breast-feeding with more severe consequences (Adler, 1992; Stagno & Cloud, 1994). The negative outcomes are typically greatest for the fetus if a woman contracts the disease for the first time during her pregnancy (Guerra et al., 2000). Growth retardation, jaundice, skin disorders, and small head size are common consequences. About one-third of infants showing these characteristics at birth will die in early infancy; a large percentage of those who survive will be mentally retarded. About half of infants sustaining congenital damage from CMV show no symptoms at birth, but many will subsequently display progressive loss of hearing or other, subtler defects, including minimal brain dysfunction, visual or dental abnormalities, or motor and neural problems (Pass, 1987; Landry, 2004).

***Sexually Transmitted and Other Diseases*** Several diseases identified as teratogenic are transmitted primarily through sexual contact, and the infection and its symptoms are usually concentrated in the genitourinary tract (see Table 4.3). Syphilis and certain strains of herpes simplex, for example, are virtually always contracted from infected sexual partners. On the other hand, some diseases, such as acquired immunodeficiency syndrome (AIDS) and hepatitis B, can be acquired through exposure to infected blood as well.

**Table 4.3  Diseases and Maternal Conditions That May Affect Prenatal Development**

| Disease | Physical and Behavioral Consequences for the Fetus |
| --- | --- |
| *Sexually Transmitted Diseases* | |
| **Acquired Immunodeficiency Syndrome (AIDS)** | See text. |
| **Chlamydia** | Nearly always transmitted to infant during delivery via infected birth canal. Estimated 100,000 (of 155,000 exposed in the United States) become infected. Often causes eye infection in infant and some increased risk of pneumonia. Other adverse effects suspected (McGregor & French, 1991). |
| **Gonorrhea** | If acquired prenatally, may cause premature birth (Reece et al., 1995). Most frequently contracted during delivery through infected birth canal and may then attack eyes. In the United States and many other countries, silver nitrate eye drops are administered to all newborns to prevent blindness. |
| **Hepatitis B** | Associated with premature birth, low birth weight, increased neonatal death, and liver disorders (Pass, 1987). Most frequently contracted during delivery through birth canal or postnatally. |
| **Herpes Simplex** | Of its two forms, only one is transmitted primarily through sexual activity. Both forms, however, can be transmitted to the fetus, causing severe damage to the central nervous system (Pass, 1987). Most infections occur during delivery through birth canal containing active herpes lesions. The majority of infants will die or suffer central nervous system damage (Nahmias, Keyserling & Kernick, 1983). If known to carry the virus, woman may need to be tested frequently during pregnancy to determine if the disease is in its active, contagious state because symptoms may not be present even when active. If the disease is active, cesarean delivery is used to avoid infecting the baby. |
| **Syphilis** | Damage to fetus does not begin until about 18 weeks after conception. May then cause death, mental retardation, and other congenital defects (Reece et al., 1995). Infected newborns may not show signs of disease until early childhood. |
| *Other Diseases* | |
| **Cytomegalovirus** | See text. |
| **Influenza** | Some forms linked to increased heart and central nervous system abnormalities, as well as spontaneous abortions (Reece et al., 1995). |
| **Mumps** | Increased risk of spontaneous abortion and stillbirth. |
| **Rubella** | Increased risk of spontaneous abortion and stillbirth. Growth retardation, cataracts, hearing impairment, heart defects, mental retardation also common, especially if exposure occurs in the first or second month of pregnancy. |
| **Toxoplasmosis** | See text. |
| **Varicella-zoster (chicken pox)** | Skin and muscle defects, intrauterine growth retardation, limb reduction. |
| *Other Maternal Conditions* | |
| **Diabetes** | Risk of congenital malformations and death to fetus two to three times higher than for babies born to nondiabetic women (Coustan & Felig, 1988). Excessive size at birth also common. Effects are likely to be a consequence of metabolic disturbances rather than of insulin. Rapid advances in care have helped reduce risks substantially for diabetic women. |
| **Hypertension (chronic)** | Probability of miscarriage or infant death increased. |
| **Obesity** | Increased risk of diabetes and large-for-gestational-age babies (Lu et al., 2001). |

*(continued)*

**Table 4.3    Diseases and Maternal Conditions That May Affect Prenatal Development (continued)**

| Disease | Physical and Behavioral Consequences for the Fetus |
|---|---|
| **Pregnancy-Induced Hypertension** | 5%–10% of expectant women experience significant increase in blood pressure, often accompanied by *edema* (swelling of face and extremities as a result of water retention), rapid weight gain, and protein in urine during later months of pregnancy. Condition is also known as *pre-eclampsia* (or *eclampsia,* if severe) and *toxemia.* Under severe conditions, woman may suffer seizures and coma. The fetus is at increased risk for death, brain damage, and lower birth weight. Adequate protein consumption helps minimize problems. Drugs used to treat high blood pressure may be just as hazardous to fetus as the condition itself. |
| **Rh Incompatibility** | Blood containing a certain protein is Rh positive; Rh negative if it lacks that protein. Hereditary factors determine which type the individual possesses. If fetus's blood is Rh positive, it can cause formation of antibodies in blood of woman who is Rh negative. These antibodies can cross the placental barrier to destroy red blood cells of fetus. May result in miscarriage or stillbirth, jaundice, anemia, heart defects, or mental retardation. Likelihood of birth defects increases with succeeding pregnancies because antibodies are usually not present until after birth of first Rh-positive child. A vaccine (Rhogam) can be administered to the mother within 3 days after childbirth, miscarriage, or abortion to prevent antibody formation. |

Sexually transmitted diseases (STDs) can interfere with reproduction in a number of ways. They may compromise the woman's health (AIDS, gonorrhea, hepatitis B, herpes simplex, syphilis), scar or disturb reproductive organs so that conception and normal pregnancy cannot proceed (chlamydia, gonorrhea), directly infect the fetus (AIDS, herpes simplex, syphilis), or interfere with healthy postnatal development (AIDS, hepatitis B, herpes simplex, syphilis) (Lee, 1988). In recent years, the frequency of STDs has risen rapidly in populations around the world. None, however, has had as dramatic an impact as AIDS.

Of the estimated 16,000 children having human immunodeficiency virus type 1 (HIV-1) in the United States and the more than 1.1 million children currently living with the disease worldwide, most were infected prenatally, during birth, or shortly after birth through an infected mother's breast milk (Burgess, 2001; Lindegren, Steinberg, & Byers, 2000). Prior to 1995, about 25 percent of infants born to HIV-positive women could be expected to eventually acquire AIDS. However, as can be seen in Figure 4.4, new medical treatments have reduced the transmission rate by more than one-third, at least in countries in which expensive drugs such as zidovudine are available (Lindegren et al., 2000).

Of those infants who do become infected with HIV, about 20 percent show rapid progression to AIDS and death in early childhood. However, with new advances in treatment, about two-thirds live more than five years; the average length of survival in Western countries is now greater than nine years; and about 25 percent of children do not show severe symptoms of AIDS until after ten years (Barnhart et al., 1996; Brown, Lourie, & Pao, 2000; European Collaborative Study, 2001). Children receiving medication for HIV also show substantial benefits in terms of maintaining more normal levels of cognitive functioning throughout much of their childhood (Brown et al., 2000). Thus the negative course of the disease can be slowed for cognitive and other aspects of development (Tardieu et al., 1995). Unfortunately, however, for many children around the world, limited medical services, poverty, and the absence of social support will adversely affect their development while living with the disease.

## ENVIRONMENTAL HAZARDS AS TERATOGENS

**KEY THEME**
**NATURE & NURTURE**
**RISK/RESILIENCE**

Radiation was one of the earliest confirmed teratogens, and it can cause genetic mutations as well. Radiation's effects include spontaneous abortion, small head size,

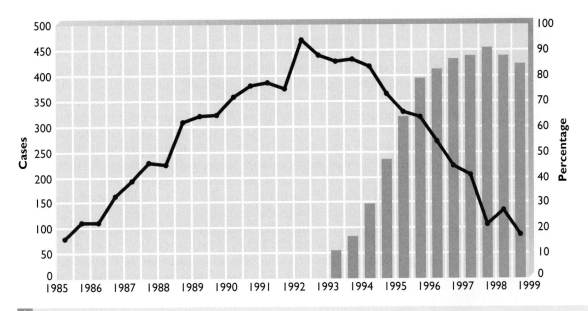

▲ **FIGURE 4.4**

### Decline in HIV/AIDS Transmitted to Offspring via HIV-Infected Women

The transmission of HIV/AIDS infection to infants and children via HIV-infected women has declined dramatically in the United States in recent years. The data from thirty-two reporting states reveal that introducing treatment with zidovudine (represented by the shaded bars as the percentage of women receiving treatment with the drug) has been as important factor in reducing the number of cases of infants and children reported with HIV/AIDS. Unfortunately, about 90% of the approximately 1.1 million children around the world with HIV/AIDS are born in sub-Saharan Africa, where this method of treatment is often too expensive or unavailable.

*Source:* Lindgren, Steinberg, & Byers (2000).

and other defects associated with the skeleton, genitals, and sensory organs. Even low doses of radiation have been linked to increased risks of cancer and neural damage; pregnant women are urged to avoid unnecessary x-rays and other circumstances in which exposure might occur.

Chemicals and other elements in the environment pose another significant source of potential risks. Known teratogens include lead, mercury, and polychlorinated biphenyls, or PCBs (a synthetic hydrocarbon once used in transformers, hydraulic fluid, and other industrial equipment), as well as many elements found in paints, dyes and coloring agents, solvents, oven cleaners, pesticides, herbicides, food additives, artificial sweeteners, and cosmetic products (Hubbs-Tait et al., 2005; Needleman & Bellinger, 1994). Careless handling and disposal of such elements and their excessive production and use are one problem. They pervade the foods we eat and the air we breathe. Mercury, for example, can occur in especially high concentrations in large predatory fish such as swordfish and tuna (Hubbs-Tait et al., 2005); the U. S. Food and Drug Administration recommends that pregnant and nursing mothers as well as young children avoid consuming these fish (U.S. Department of Health and Human Services, 2004). In addition, many women of childbearing age are exposed in the workplace to hazardous substances such as lead, formaldehyde, and carbon monoxide.

## WOMEN'S CONDITIONS AND PRENATAL DEVELOPMENT

⌐ **KEY THEME**
**RISK/RESILIENCE**

In addition to teratogens, a number of health conditions are associated with increased risk during pregnancy. Several of these conditions (diabetes, pregnancy-induced and chronic hypertension, Rh incompatibility) and their consequences for the fetus are summarized in Table 4.3. Additional factors influencing the prenatal environment include the age of the woman, her nutritional status, and her emotional state.

Teenage mothers give birth to nearly 500,000 babies in the United States each year. Many of them will be unmarried teens who have received little or no prenatal care, factors that increase the risk for delivering less healthy babies.

**Age**   The number of older mothers is on the rise in industrialized countries as women postpone pregnancy to establish careers or for other reasons. Is pregnancy riskier as women become older? As we show in the chapter titled "Genetics and Heredity," the likelihood of having a child with Down syndrome increases markedly during the later childbearing years, especially after age thirty-five. Some studies also report increased prematurity and mortality, as well as greater difficulty during labor, for women over thirty-five having their first child (Gilbert, Nesbitt, & Danielsen, 1999; Reece et al., 1995). The findings are likely due, in large part, to greater health problems (hypertension, diabetes, and others) that can accompany increased age. Despite these elevated risks, healthy women older than thirty-five routinely deliver healthy infants, just as do women between twenty and thirty-five years of age.

Teenagers, on the other hand, may be at considerably greater risk for delivering less healthy babies (McAnarney, 1987). Lack of adequate prenatal care is one reason; pregnant teenagers in the United States, particularly those who are very young and unmarried, often do not seek medical services. Another reason pregnancy at these early ages poses more problems is the complicated nutritional needs of adolescents; many teenagers are still growing themselves. Although the rate of births to teenagers has declined steadily throughout the 1990s in the United States (Hoyert et al., 2001), it is still substantially higher than in other industrialized nations and double or even triple that in most Western European countries. In any given year, about one in twenty-five teenagers is likely to bear a child; this translates into slightly over 400,000 births per year to teens (National Center for Health Statistics, 2005).

**Nutrition**   What foods are needed for the health of the woman and her fetus? The seemingly obvious but important answer is a well-balanced diet. Extreme malnutrition during prenatal development can be especially detrimental. During World War II, famines occurred in parts of Holland and in Leningrad in the former Soviet Union. When the malnutrition occurred during the first few months of pregnancy, death, premature birth, and nervous system defects were especially frequent. When famine occurred later in prenatal development, retardation in fetal growth and low birth weights were more likely (Antonov, 1947). Although not everyone agrees about the guidelines, women of normal weight for their height are typically advised to gain about twenty-five to thirty-five pounds during pregnancy.

Diets must be not only sufficient in number of calories but also balanced with respect to adequate protein, vitamins, and other nutrients. In fact, intake of many nutrients should be increased during pregnancy, as Table 4.4 indicates. Fortunately, unless deficiencies are so severe that malformations and deficits in neuron formation cannot be overcome, many cognitive problems associated with prenatal undernutrition and the lowered birth weight that often accompanies it may still be reversed when adequate nourishment and stimulation are provided following birth (Pollitt, 1996).

**◦━ KEY THEME**

**SOCIOCULTURAL INFLUENCE**

**Stress**   Cultural beliefs about potentially harmful consequences of frightening or stressful events on fetal development are pervasive, and many societies encourage a calm atmosphere for pregnant women (Samuels & Samuels, 1996). In studies in which researchers have carefully measured anxiety, family conflict, positive and negative life events, and the availability of physical and social support for the woman, stress has been linked to greater complications during both pregnancy and birth. Anxiety appears to lengthen labor, increase the need for more anesthesia during delivery, and produce more birthing complications. High stress, particularly early in pregnancy, seems to contribute to a shorter length of gestation and therefore to more frequent preterm births and more infants with lower birth weight (Glynn et al., 2001; Wadhwa et al., 1993). In addition, fatigue associated

**Table 4.4  Nutritional Need Differences Between Nonpregnant and Pregnant Women 24 Years of Age**

| Nutrient | Nonpregnant | Pregnant | Percentage Increase | Dietary Sources |
|---|---|---|---|---|
| Folic acid | 180 mcg | 400 mcg | + 122 | Leafy vegetables, liver |
| Vitamin D | 5 µg | 10 µg | + 100 | Fortified dairy products |
| Iron | 15 mg | 30 mg | + 100 | Meats, eggs, grains |
| Calcium | 800 mg | 1200 mg | + 50 | Dairy products |
| Phosphorus | 800 mg | 1200 mg | + 50 | Meats |
| Pyridoxine | 1.6 mg | 2.2 mg | + 38 | Meats, liver, enriched grains |
| Thiamin | 1.1 mg | 1.5 mg | + 36 | Enriched grains, pork |
| Zinc | 12 mg | 15 mg | + 25 | Meats, seafood, eggs |
| Riboflavin | 1.3 mg | 1.6 mg | + 23 | Meats, liver, enriched grains |
| Protein | 50 g | 60 g | + 20 | Meats, fish, poultry, dairy |
| Iodine | 150 mcg | 175 mcg | + 17 | Iodized salt, seafood |
| Vitamin C | 60 mg | 70 mg | + 17 | Citrus fruits, tomatoes |
| Energy | 2200 kcal | 2500 kcal | + 14 | Proteins, fats, carbohydrates |
| Magnesium | 280 mg | 320 mg | + 14 | Seafood, legumes, grains |
| Niacin | 15 mg | 17 mg | + 13 | Meats, nuts, legumes |
| Vitamin B-12 | 2.0 mcg | 2.2 mcg | + 10 | Animal proteins |
| Vitamin A | 800 µg | 800 µg | 0 | Dark green, yellow, or orange fruits and vegetables, liver |

*Source:* Reece et al. (1995).

with long hours at work, especially work that involves prolonged standing, increases preterm birth and health problems for a pregnant woman (Gabbe & Turner, 1997; Luke et al., 1999). Stress also may indirectly affect prenatal development by leading a woman to increase smoking, consume more alcohol, or engage in other activities known to have negative effects on the fetus (McAnarney & Stevens-Simon, 1990).

The social support a pregnant woman receives from family and friends is an important factor that can lessen the consequences of stress during pregnancy (Feldman et al., 2000). Among women who experience a variety of life changes before and during pregnancy, those with strong social and personal assistance—for example, those who can obtain a ride to work, get help when sick, or borrow needed money—have far fewer complications than women without such resources (Norbeck & Tilden, 1983). In fact, women who receive as little as twenty minutes of psychosocial support addressing their concerns and offering encouragement during regular prenatal visits have babies who weigh more than the babies of women who do not receive this benefit (Rothberg & Lits, 1991). How well a family functions during stressful times may be a more important predictor of complications during and after pregnancy than how many stressful events are actually experienced (Smilkstein et al., 1984).

After learning about the many teratogens and other factors that can affect prenatal development, we may be surprised that babies manage to be born healthy at all. But they do so every day. We should wonder, rather, at the rich complexity of prenatal development and appreciate more deeply that it proceeds normally so much of the time. Ninety to ninety-five percent of babies born in the United States are healthy and fully prepared to adapt to their new environment. Knowledge of teratogens allows prospective parents as well as others in the community to maximize the chances that all infants will be equipped to enter the world with as many resources as possible.

## F O R • Y O U R • R E V I E W

★ What kinds of supportive functions do the placenta, umbilical cord, and amniotic sac provide for the embryo and the fetus?

★ What are teratogens? What principles apply to how teratogens have their effects?

★ How do alcohol, cigarette smoke, prescription and over-the-counter drugs, and illegal drugs affect prenatal development?

★ What kinds of risks exist for the embryo and fetus exposed to rubella, toxoplasmosis, cytomegalovirus, and sexually transmitted diseases?

★ What maternal conditions affect the well-being of the fetus and embryo?

## BIRTH AND THE PERINATAL ENVIRONMENT

**KEY THEME**

**SOCIOCULTURAL INFLUENCE**

Societies vary enormously in the techniques and rituals that accompany the transition from fetus to newborn. Some interpret pregnancy and birth as natural and healthy; others, as an illness requiring medical care and attention (Newton, 1955). The !Kung, a hunting-and-gathering people living in the Kalahari Desert of Africa, build no huts or facilities for birthing. They view birth as part of the natural order of events, requiring no special intervention (Shostak, 1981). In contrast, pregnancy and childbirth in the United States and many other countries throughout much of the twentieth century has been regarded more as an illness to be managed by professionally trained medical personnel (Dye, 1986). In 1900 fewer than 5 percent of babies were born in hospitals in the United States. Today about 99 percent of all babies in the United States are born in hospitals (Declercq, 1993; Hosmer, 2001).

### PREPARING FOR CHILDBIRTH

With the shift from childbirth at home to childbirth in the hospital came an increase in the use of medication during delivery. Concerns about the impact of these medications, along with reports of unmedicated but seemingly pain-free delivery by women in other cultures, prodded professionals and expectant parents alike to reconsider how best to prepare for the birth of a baby. After observing one woman who reported a pain-free delivery, Grantley Dick-Read, a medical practitioner in Great Britain, concluded that difficult childbirth was fostered largely by the tension and anxiety in which Western civilization cloaked the event. Dick-Read (1959) proposed that women be taught methods of physical relaxation, given information about the process of childbirth, and encouraged to cultivate a cooperative relationship with their doctor to foster a more natural childbirth experience. Others, including Fernand Lamaze (1970), adopted similar ideas, adding procedures to divert thoughts from pain and encouraging breathing activities to support the labor process.

In recent years, **prepared** (or **natural**) **childbirth**, which involves practicing procedures designed to minimize pain and reduce the need for medication during delivery, has become a popular alternative for prospective mothers. Women who attend classes and adhere to the recommendations of Lamaze and other childbirth education programs (including the National Childbirth Trust in the United Kingdom) generally require fewer and lower amounts of drugs during delivery than women who have not participated in prepared childbirth. Women who attend childbirth classes may experience no less pain, but relaxation techniques and an additional element frequently promoted in these programs—the assistance of a coach or trainer, sometimes the father—seem to help counter the discomfort and lead to a more positive evaluation of childbirth (Waldenström, 1999).

**prepared (natural) childbirth**
Type of childbirth that involves practicing procedures during pregnancy and childbirth that are designed to minimize pain and reduce the need for medication during delivery.

Societies differ enormously in their approach to the birth of a baby. In the United States, most births occur in hospitals. In contrast, more than four of every five births in the Trobriand Islands (part of Papua New Guinea) take place in villages where a midwife is in charge.

## RESEARCH APPLIED TO PARENTING
### Nurturing and Caring During Labor

Carole knew the signs of the onset of labor; after all, she had already gone through two deliveries. Birthing had proceeded smoothly for her other two children despite her anxieties about the whole process, especially the first time. Maybe it helped to have her husband participate with her in childbirth classes. During those pregnancies she had learned about the various options, ranging from massage to hypnosis to traditional medication, even delivering the baby in water, an alternative the birthing center offered for those who wished to do so. One other thing had been extremely helpful: the presence of a *doula,* another woman to accompany her throughout the entire period of labor. Carole was not certain about some of the other alternatives for making the delivery easier and more comfortable. But of one thing she was very sure: she would have a doula with her throughout the birthing process this time as well.

In addition to exhilaration, most women delivering a baby go through a lot of hard work and some, perhaps considerable, discomfort. It can be a very anxious time. Human birth differs from that of other species of mammals in that it typically requires some form of assistance (Rosenberg & Trevathen, 2001). In many cultures, the help comes from friends and relatives or from midwives, just as it did in the United States many decades ago. With the relocation of childbirth to hospitals, however, women became isolated from family and friends, and a more private and impersonal procedure emerged. Perhaps with that change something very important was lost. Research has helped to identify this loss and has led to alternatives in birthing practices that may benefit both men and women as they become new parents.

1. *Include a partner or some other trusted companion in preparing for and assisting during childbirth.* Studies carried out in Botswana, Guatemala,

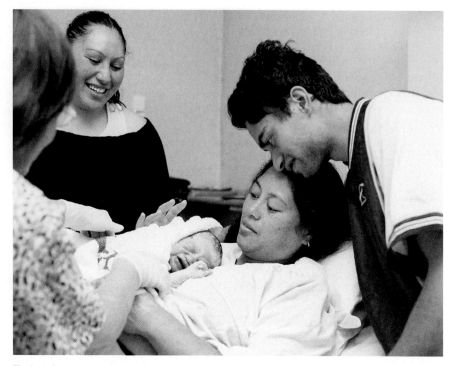

Today, fathers, and sometimes other friends and family members, are encouraged to furnish social and emotional support to women who are about to deliver a baby. When such support is provided by a trusted companion, labor is shorter, fewer drugs are required, and babies are born exhibiting less distress.

several European countries, and the United States demonstrate that having a continuously supportive companion during delivery is helpful to women and their newborns (Kayne, Greulich, & Albers, 2001; Madi et al., 1999; Scott, Berkowitz, & Klaus, 1999). For example, in the Guatamalan studies, first-time mothers were assigned a doula, a woman experienced with delivery who stayed with the mother to provide emotional support, increase her physical comfort, inform her about what was happening during labor, and advocate for her needs (Klaus & Kennell, 1982). Women given these personal attendants spent a far shorter time in labor, required drugs or forceps less frequently, and delivered babies who showed less fetal distress and difficulty breathing than women who received only routine nursing care. Sometimes fathers or other partners are actively encouraged to take on some of these functions as well and can be very effective (Cunningham, 1993), although a doula may be able to provide a more balanced and informative perspective on the sequence of unfolding events.

2. *Consider what type of practitioner might be most beneficial during childbirth.* Of course, fathers or other partners who assist in labor are not likely to be experts in the process. Midwives, nurses, or others far more experienced in childbirth, whose additional primary function is to provide personal assistance while managing labor, have received positive evaluations as well. Compared with physicians, midwives who oversee birthing produce, for example, lower rates of deliveries undergoing cesarean birth or other surgical procedures, less use of medication by the mother, and greater satisfaction with care (Butler et al., 1993; Oakley et al., 1996; Sakala, 1993). Whereas about 5 percent of births in the United States are now accompanied by midwives, this figure is nearly 75 percent in many European countries (Alan Guttmacher Institute, 1993).

3. **Explore the different alternatives available to assist in delivering a baby.** The positive outcomes achieved by midwives appear to stem from an attitude that inspires women to not just deliver babies but also draw on their own inner resources, as well as their support networks, for giving birth. For example, midwives are likely to suggest greater flexibility in positioning and moving about during labor, perhaps even soaking in a tub. Standing, squatting, or sitting in special chairs, or even hanging from a bar, are increasingly being offered as alternatives to the traditional recumbent position for delivery. These choices can increase a woman's comfort through the natural benefits of gravity and thus reduce stress for both mother and baby. In fact, in non-Western cultures, these alternative positions for childbirth are the norm (Rosenberg & Trevathen, 2001).

## LABOR AND DELIVERY

When labor begins, the wet, warm, and supportive world within the uterus undergoes a rapid transformation, and the fetus must adjust to an earthshaking series of changes. During normal birth, the fetus begins to be subjected to increasingly stronger pressure. Because the birth canal is typically smaller than the size of the head, pressure—as great as thirty pounds of force—will probably cause the head to become somewhat elongated and misshapen (Trevathen, 1987). This is possible because the cerebral plates are not yet knitted together, allowing them to slide up and over one another. At times the fetus may experience brief disruptions in oxygen as the flow of blood in the umbilical cord is temporarily obstructed. And then the infant emerges head first into a strange, new

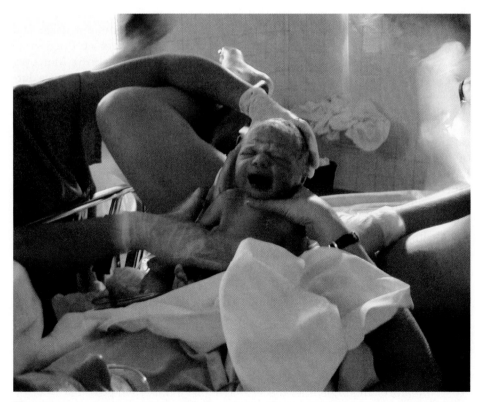

This woman, who has just given birth, now has the opportunity to see and hold her infant for the first time. In contrast to earlier practices, parents in most hospital settings today are allowed ample time to become acquainted with their newborns immediately after birth.

world, one drier, possibly colder, and often much brighter and noisier. Within minutes the new arrival must begin to take in oxygen. The baby must also soon learn to coordinate sucking, swallowing, and breathing to obtain sufficient nutrients.

Labor is a complicated, interactive process involving the fetus, the placenta, and the woman. What brings about its onset? The answer begins with the hypothalamus, pituitary, and adrenal glands of the fetus. When these become mature enough, they help to produce a cascading sequence of hormones and other events, including some in the placenta, that are especially important in initiating labor (Nathanielsz, 1996). In fact, measurement of one hormone in the placenta as early as the sixteenth to twentieth week of pregnancy can predict whether a delivery will occur somewhat before, somewhat after, or about the time of the anticipated due date (Smith, 1999).

The first of the three traditional stages of labor (see Figure 4.5) begins with brief, mild contractions perhaps ten to fifteen minutes apart. These contractions become increasingly frequent and serve to alter the shape of the cervix, preparing it for the fetus's descent and entry into the narrow birth canal. Near the end of the first stage, which on average lasts about eleven hours for firstborns and about seven hours for later-borns, dilation of the cervix proceeds rapidly to allow passage through the birth canal. The second stage consists of the continued descent and the birth of the baby. This stage usually requires a little less than an hour for firstborns and about twenty minutes for later-borns. It also normally includes several reorientations of both the head and shoulders to permit delivery through the tight-fitting passageway (Rosenberg & Trevathen, 2001). In the third stage, which lasts about fifteen minutes, the placenta is expelled. These durations are, however, averages; enormous variation exists from one woman to another.

***Medication During Childbirth*** In Western societies, births are often accompanied by some form of medication. Anesthesia blocks the transmission of pain, analgesics lessen feelings of discomfort, and sedatives help the woman to relax. All of these drugs readily pass through the placenta and enter the fetus's circulatory system. Critics of the routine use of drugs point out that babies whose mothers receive high doses during labor are less attentive and responsive to caregivers, are more irritable, and gain weight more slowly than babies exposed to small amounts or no drugs at all (Brazelton, Nugent, & Lester, 1987; Emory, Schlackman, & Fiano, 1996). Moreover, some behavioral differences may persist well beyond infancy. Heavy use of drugs during labor has been associated, for example, with an increased incidence of learning disorders among school-age children (Brackbill, McManus, & Woodward, 1985).

Developmental differences between babies born to medicated and nonmedicated women, however, are not consistent. Some experts believe the negative effects of exposure to drugs at birth have been markedly overstated and occur only when medications are used excessively (Kraemer et al., 1985). Thus women need not experience unreasonable pain or feel guilty if drugs are administered. Efforts to make the birth process gentler, such as by reducing illumination and noise or by delivering the baby under water, have also been proposed (Daniels, 1989; LeBoyer, 1975), although the advantages of these practices for either women or infants have not been documented. The use of other complementary and alternative medical procedures, such as acupuncture and various relaxation techniques, also remain unproven with respect to benefits to mother or newborn (Allaire, 2001). However, as we have already discussed, providing a network of social support does help.

***Cesarean Birth*** A *cesarean birth* is the delivery of a baby through a surgical incision in the woman's abdomen and uterus. Cesarean births are recommended, for example, when labor fails to progress normally, when the baby's head is very large, or when birth is *breech* (foot or rump first) rather than head first. Concerns about stress on the fetus that might lead to increased risk of brain damage, vaginal infections that might be transmitted to the baby, and expensive malpractice suits (should things go awry during vaginal delivery) have led to more than a fivefold increase in the frequency of cesarean sections in the past thirty years in the United States. Today slightly over 27 percent of deliveries in the United States are cesarean rather than vaginal (Centers for Disease Control and Prevention, 2005c).

**⚷ KEY THEME**

**RISK/RESILIENCE**

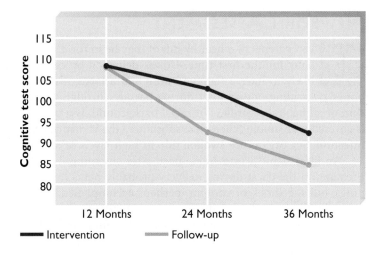

◀ **FIGURE 4.7**

**Low-Birth-Weight Children's Cognitive Development as a Function of Intervention**

In a large-scale study investigating the effects of providing home visits and educational child care for low-birth-weight infants and their families, Brooks-Gunn and her colleagues found that performance on measures of intellectual development was substantially better for those who received the intervention than for those who did not. Although some decline in scores occurred even for the group receiving intervention, it was far less than for those who did not receive the intervention. Both groups performed similarly at the youngest age (twelve months), perhaps because tests measuring cognitive skills often are not very sensitive to differences at that age.

*Source:* Brooks-Gunn et al. (1993).

Salvator, et al., 1999). Moreover, the caregivers of children born with extremely low birth weight are as enthusiastic and supportive of making every effort to provide the best medical care possible for these children as are parents of children born with normal birth weight (Streiner et al., 2001). In bringing up a low-birth-weight child, however, providing family- and child-oriented services appears to be especially important in helping to reduce stress, especially for those mothers who are less educated and may have fewer other resources available (Klebanov, Brooks-Gunn, & McCormick, 2001).

Attempts to reduce complications associated with low birth weight have proceeded on two fronts. Improved medical care in NICUs and supportive caregiving have permitted more low-birth-weight, especially extremely low-birth-weight, infants to survive and develop normally. These positive findings reflect more effective treatment (for instance, for respiratory distress) and management of the NICU (as in reductions in bright light, loud noise, and sleep interruptions), designed to reduce stress in individuals who are among the least capable of responding to stress (Als et al., 1994; Bregman, 1998). Yet, despite the increased number of survivors, the proportion of children showing neurological or cognitive problems has remained stable (Lorenz et al., 1997; O'Shea al., 1997; Piecuch, Leonard, & Cooper, 1998; Stevenson et al., 1998). Thus a second major assault on the problem has been in the form of prevention. Researchers have catalogued a long list of demographic, medical, and behavioral factors associated low birth weight; for example, inadequate prenatal care and nutrition, heavy smoking, and drug use. Because many of these factors are preventable, educational programs targeted toward pregnant women at high risk, including teenagers, have become increasingly important. These programs can reduce the incidence of low birth weight, especially when offered consistently and early in the course of pregnancy (Fangman al., 1994; Seitz & Apfel, 1994). Indeed, future progress in addressing the problems that accompany low birth weight is likely to be as closely tied to improved and more widespread programs of prevention as to new medical advances.

## FOR ◆ YOUR ◆ REVIEW

◆ What are the benefits of prepared childbirth and a supportive relationship with another individual for both parent and newborn child?

◆ What are the stages of delivery? How does medication during delivery affect the newborn?

◆ What are the benefits and disadvantages of cesarean births for mother and child? Why is this procedure often carried out?

◆ How do premature and small-for-gestational-age infants differ? What are the factors that increase the likelihood of low birth weight? What practices help children born with low birth weight?

## NEWBORN ASSESSMENT

E ven parents of a healthy infant may be in for a surprise when they see their baby for the first time. Unless delivered by cesarean section, the baby is likely to have a flattened nose and a large, distorted head from the skull bones' overriding one another during passage through the narrow birth canal. The skin of all babies, regardless of racial background, is a pale pinkish color and often is covered with an oily, cheeselike substance (the *vernix caseosa*) that protects against infection. Sex organs are swollen due to high levels of sex hormones.

An infant's most immediate need after emerging from the womb is breathing. Pressure on the chest during delivery probably helps to clear the baby's fluid-filled lungs, but the shock of cool air, perhaps accompanied by jiggling, a slap, or some other less-than-gentle activity by a birth attendant, makes the first breath more like a gasp, quickly followed by a reflexive cry. The umbilical cord may continue to pulse for several minutes after birth; in many societies the cord is not cut until after it ceases to do so (Trevathen, 1987).

The second major task the baby must accomplish upon entering the world is regulating body temperature. Babies lose body heat about four times more rapidly than adults because of their lower fat reserve and relatively large body surface (Bruck, 1962). As a consequence, newborns, although they can effectively maintain their temperature when held close to a caregiver's body, are often quickly placed under heaters.

Newborns typically weigh five and a half to ten pounds, and measure eighteen to twenty-two inches in length. Many procedures for evaluating their health have become available in recent years, but one that is routinely administered is the *Apgar Scale* (Apgar, 1953). Typically assessed at both one and five minutes after birth, the Apgar measures five vital signs: heart rate, respiratory effort, muscle tone, reflex responsivity, and color. Each vital sign is scored 0, 1, or 2 based on the criteria described in Table 4.5. In the United States, 90 percent of infants receive a total score of 7 or better; those who score lower than 4 are considered to be at risk.

**KEY THEME**
**RISK/RESILIENCE**

A more extensive measure, developed by T. Berry Brazelton (1973) and given several days after birth, is the *Neonatal Behavioral Assessment Scale (NBAS)*. The NBAS evaluates, for example, the baby's ability to interact with the tester, responsiveness to objects in the environment, reflex motor capacities, and ability to control functions such as breathing and temperature. Newborn performance on the NBAS

**Table 4.5  The Apgar Scoring System**

The Apgar Scale is used at and shortly after birth to diagnose the physical condition of a newborn. The ratings for each vital sign are added for a total score ranging from 0 to 10. An infant who scores less than 4 is considered to be at risk.

| Vital Sign | 0 | 1 | 2 |
|---|---|---|---|
| Heart rate | Absent | Slow (below 100) | Over 100 |
| Respiratory effort | Absent | Slow, irregular | Good, crying |
| Muscle tone | Flaccid | Some flexion of extremities | Active motion |
| Reflex responsivity | No response | Grimace | Vigorous cry |
| Color | Blue, pale | Body pink, extremities blue | Completely pink |

*Source:* Adapted from Apgar, 1953. From V. Apgar, "A Proposal for a New Method of Evaluation of the Newborn Infant," *Anesthesia and Analgesia: Current Researches, 32,* 260–267. Copyright © 1953. Used by permission of Lippincott Williams & Wilkins. www.anesthesia-analgesia.org

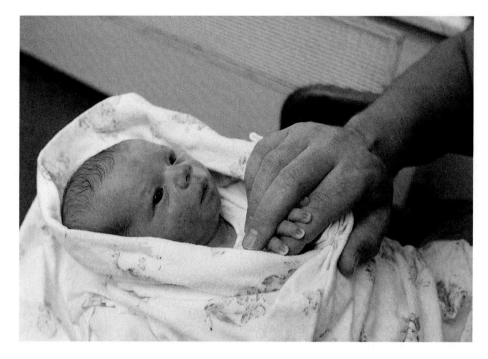

This two-day-old baby, holding her father's hand, has entered a world in which new forms of physical and social stimulation can be experienced. Although newborns and young infants spend much of their time sleeping, this infant is engaged in alert inactivity, a time in which she may be learning much about her environment.

has been used to assess neurological condition and can indicate whether certain prenatal or perinatal conditions, as well as intervention programs, have had an effect (Korner, 1987; Tronick, 1987). An NBAS score can also predict later developmental outcomes. Babies who score poorly on the scale continue to be somewhat less responsive to caregivers in the first few months after birth (Vaughn et al., 1980). In general, however, the predictive validity of the NBAS (along with other infant tests) for long-term development is only modest at best (Brazelton, Nugent, & Lester, 1987). Nevertheless, parents who observe while examiners give the NBAS or who are trained to give it themselves seem to become more responsive to and effective in interactions with their infants (Worobey, 1985).

As these last two chapters have shown, there are many events in the period from conception to birth that lay important foundations for development. By the time the infant takes its first breath and utters its first cry, many of the first steps in his or her developmental story have already been taken.

## F O R • Y O U R • R E V I E W

- What are the first tasks for the newborn following birth?

- Why are scores on the Apgar Scale and the Neonatal Behavioral Assessment Scale important?

# CHAPTER RECAP

## Summary of Developmental Themes

### NATURE & NURTURE

**How do nature and nurture interact during prenatal development and birth?**

Prenatal development is the product of complex interactions involving genetic instructions inherited from parents and the expectant woman's physical and emotional conditions, as well as exposure to drugs, diseases, hazardous chemicals, and medications before and during pregnancy and during labor. We have seen, for example, that differentiation of organs and systems in the embryo typically obeys principles established by biochemical and physiological processes. Yet these processes do not operate in a vacuum. Teratogens and various intrauterine conditions can radically alter the normal developmental path. Thus events in the life of the woman may change the immediate environment within her womb, with drastic consequences for the fetus. The reactions, attitudes, and availability of the newborn's caregivers and the stimulation they provide are other major sources of potential influence on the baby's development.

## SOCIOCULTURAL INFLUENCE

### How does the sociocultural context influence prenatal development and birth?

The immediate internal environment of the fetus and the perinatal environment provided for the newborn can be influenced dramatically by the larger social, economic, and cultural settings in which pregnancy and birth take place. The woman's actions during pregnancy are often modified or regulated by a network of expectations, advice, and resources within the culture in which she lives. An expec-tant woman in one community, for example, may have access to medical and other kinds of care that provide a more or less healthy environment for the fetus than a woman in another community may have. Industrial or government units may legislate controls on chemical pollution in one country and ignore them in another. Scientific and technological advances in prenatal testing, birthing practices, and newborn care may be available in one region of the world but not in another; even when available, however, not all parents may have the economic resources or the desire to use them.

## CONTINUITY/DISCONTINUITY

### Is development before and after birth continuous or discontinuous?

When the zygote attaches to the uterine wall and taps a new source of nourishment, its course of development changes dramatically. Once the various organs and systems are formed and become less susceptible to environmental disruptions, the fetus achieves a vastly different status. The process of birth itself is a major transition. Such spectacular changes fit with discontinuous or stagelike descriptions of development. So do the marked shifts in vulnerability to teratogens observed during prenatal development. Underlying the progressions, however, are biochemical and physiological processes governing cell proliferation, differentiation, and the emergence and functioning of biological systems, which can be seen as continuous. Many dramatic changes are essentially the product of modest accumulative modifications in the multifaceted, complex environment that promotes development.

## RISK/RESILIENCE

### What factors promote risk or resilience during prenatal development and birth?

Newborns everywhere undergo many common gestational experiences; however, differences in development arise because the fetus is not immune to the influences of the larger world. Because of exposure to teratogens and other maternal conditions, babies will differ in their physical and behavioral qualities, and their ability to cope with and adapt to their new environment. Greater knowledge of and sensitivity to those differences by caregivers, whether exhibited by a newborn with special needs, such as one with low birth weight, or by an infant who falls within the typical range for newborns, can help to ensure success for the continued development of every child.

# Chapter Review

## THE STAGES OF PRENATAL DEVELOPMENT

### What constitutes the prenatal, perinatal, and postnatal periods of development?

*Prenatal development* is the period that extends from conception to birth. The *perinatal period* extends from about the seventh month of pregnancy until twenty-eight days after birth. The *postnatal period* is the time that follows birth.

### What are the major changes that take place following conception during the germinal, embryonic, and fetal periods of prenatal development?

During the *germinal period*, about the first ten to fourteen days after conception, the zygote migrates from the Fallopian tube to the uterus, becomes multicelled, and implants itself in the uterine wall to gain access to a new source of nutrients obtained from the mother. The *embry-onic period* begins after implantation and continues until about the eighth week after conception. The embryonic period is marked by development of the placenta and other supportive structures within the uterine environment and by the differentiation of cells into tissues that form the major organs and systems of the embryo. The *fetal period*, beginning in about the eighth week after conception and lasting until birth, is marked by substantial growth and by refinement of organs and systems. By the last trimester, the ability of the fetus to survive on its own (*viability*) improves. For human infants, birth typically occurs at 274 days *gestational age*.

### When are the major organs and systems of the body established? What is the course of brain and nervous system development in the embryo and fetus?

The major body organs and systems, including the brain and nervous system, differentiate during the embryonic phase. Neurons continue to form and migrate during the fetal period. Brain activity, sensory reactions, and movement are exhibited by the fetus.

**How can various kinds of assisted reproduction help those couples who have difficulty conceiving or are concerned about the inheritance of genetic disorders in their offspring? What are some of the medical and legal issues associated with various forms of assisted reproduction?**

Among the assisted reproduction technologies are artificial insemination by donor, egg donation, fertility drugs, gamete intrafallopian transfer, in vitro fertilization, and maternal surrogacy. Some of the issues raised by these technologies include the competence of the practitioners, the fact that children born with these methods may not know about their biological heritage, and the increased risk of multiple pregnancies.

## ENVIRONMENTAL FACTORS INFLUENCING PRENATAL DEVELOPMENT

**What kinds of supportive functions do the placenta, umbilical cord, and amniotic sac provide for the embryo and the fetus?**

The *placenta* serves as the major organ for transfer of nutrients from the mother's circulatory system and for expelling waste products from the fetus. The *umbilical cord* connects the fetus to the placenta. The *amniotic sac* provides a fluid-filled, protective surrounding in which development of the fetus occurs.

**What are teratogens? What principles apply to how teratogens have their effects?**

During both embryonic and fetal development, *teratogens*, or environmental agents harmful to the organism, can disrupt development and interfere with later behavior. The effects of teratogens differ depending on the genetic susceptibility of the embryo or fetus, how the teratogen reaches the prenatal environment, its level of dosage and manner of exposure, and where it interferes with cellular activity. A teratogen's effects also differ depending on the time at which exposure occurs during prenatal development. Not all the consequences are observed immediately; they may not even be evident until well into the postnatal years.

**How do alcohol, cigarette smoke, prescription and over-the-counter drugs, and illegal drugs affect prenatal development?**

Many different drugs are able to cross the placental barrier and can have teratogenic effects. Among those known to have the greatest impact on fetal development are alcohol, which can result in *fetal alcohol syndrome (FAS)*, and cigarette smoke, which is associated with low birth weight. The effects of prescription and over-the-counter drugs on prenatal development are not always well known but can include low birth weight and lower IQ. Teratogenic effects, such as cognitive impairment, are linked to the use of illegal drugs.

However, their effects are often confounded with other factors known to have significant negative consequences for the fetus. These factors include lack of proper nutrition, poor health of the mother, absence of medical care, lack of emotional and social support, and high levels of stress.

**What kinds of risks exist for the embryo and fetus exposed to rubella, toxoplasmosis, cytomegalovirus, and sexually transmitted diseases?**

Diseases can have serious repercussions on both prenatal and postnatal development. Rubella is associated visual, auditory, and heart defects, as well as mental retardation. Toxoplasmosis can cause visual problems and intellectual impairment. Cytomegalovirus is also associated with mental retardation, as well as sensory or motor problems. Sexually transmitted diseases are associated with low birth weight, visual defects, mental retardation, and in the most serious cases, death.

**What maternal conditions affect the well-being of the fetus and embryo?**

Less positive outcomes in prenatal development are possible if the mother is either very young or in the late childbearing years; has poor nutrition, a high level of stress, or lack of social support; or suffers from certain conditions, such as diabetes, obesity, and pregnancy-induced hypertension.

## BIRTH AND THE PERINATAL ENVIRONMENT

**What are the benefits of prepared childbirth and a supportive relationship with another individual for both parent and newborn child?**

*Prepared (natural) childbirth* may reduce the need for medication during delivery and often leads women to give more positive evaluations of childbirth. The presence of someone familiar with the birth process but continuously present to provide emotional support and information to the mother, appears to have benefits for both mother and newborn.

**What are the stages of delivery? How does medication during delivery affect the newborn?**

Childbirth proceeds through three stages. In the first and longest stage, labor helps to initiate preparation of the birth canal. Passage of the fetus through the birth canal makes up the second stage. During the third stage, the placenta is delivered. Labor appears to be initiated by hormones produced by the fetus and the placenta. Newborns whose mothers receive medication during delivery may show less responsiveness, greater irritability, and slower weight gain.

**What are the benefits and disadvantages of cesarean birth for mother and child? Why is this procedure often carried out?**

Cesarean deliveries are relatively common in the United States, despite their greater expense, greater recovery time for the mother, and the risk of exposure to medication to the newborn. Babies delivered via cesarean birth may also show greater initial breathing problems. The large number of cesarean births in the United States may stem, in part, from the extensive use of *fetal monitoring devices,* which signal fetal distress during delivery. Fetal distress is linked to concerns about the long-term negative consequences of birth trauma, such as exposure to oxygen deprivation.

**How do premature and small-for-gestational-age infants differ? What are the factors that increase the likelihood of low birth weight? What practices help children born with low birth weight?**

Premature infants are born before thirty-five weeks' conceptual age. Babies who are small for gestational age are born near their due date but show growth retardation. Risk factors for low birth weight include inadequate prenatal care, poor nutrition, smoking, and drug use. Compensatory and enrichment programs for low-birth-weight infants increase early weight gains and other developmental outcomes.

## NEWBORN ASSESSMENT

**What are the first tasks for the newborn following birth?**

Respiration and maintenance of body temperature are two immediate critical goals for the newborn.

**Why are scores on the Apgar Scale and the Neonatal Behavioral Assessment Scale important?**

Tests given to the newborn shortly after birth, such as the Apgar Scale and the Neonatal Behavioral Assessment Scale, provide some indication of the baby's physiological state and ability to interact with caregivers and respond to stimulation.

## KEY TERMS AND CONCEPTS

**amniotic sac** (p. 118)

**embryonic period** (p. 110)

**fetal alcohol syndrome (FAS)** (p. 120)

**fetal monitoring device** (p. 140)

**fetal period** (p. 110)

**germinal period** (p. 110)

**gestational age** (p. 117)

**perinatal period** (p. 110)

**placenta** (p. 118)

**postnatal period** (p. 110)

**prenatal development** (p. 110)

**prepared (natural) childbirth** (p. 134)

**teratogen** (p. 118)

**umbilical cord** (p. 118)

**viability** (p. 115)

# PHYSICAL DEVELOPMENT 5

Marc knew he had to dress the baby quickly. It had been a hectic morning. His wife's car hadn't started, and they had to arrange for her to get a ride to work. Now he and their three-month-old daughter, Abbie, had to step up the pace to get to daycare. Marc hastily pulled out a sweatshirt and pants from the baby's dresser, grateful that Abbie was in a good mood and didn't seem to mind the rapid tempo of the morning's routine. "Here you go, honey. Let's get these pants on you. Here are your blue pants from Aunt Rose. Bloooie pants!" Abbie responded with a gleeful smile and a few kicks. But as he lifted the waistband over Abbie's diaper, he could see that he had a problem. Worn only once before, these pants now barely covered the middle of Abbie's little calf. "Well, little girl, you sure look funny like that. We're going to have to start all over again." Looking at the picture of a younger, newborn Abbie that stood on the dresser, he couldn't help but notice the remarkable changes that his daughter had gone through in only three short months.

**NATURE & NURTURE** How do nature and nurture interact in physical development in infancy?

**SOCIOCULTURAL INFLUENCE** How does the sociocultural context influence physical development in infancy?

**CONTINUITY/DISCONTINUITY** Is physical development during infancy continuous or discontinuous?

**INTERACTION AMONG DOMAINS** How does physical development during infancy interact with other domains of development?

**RISK/RESILIENCE** What factors promote risk or resilience in physical development during infancy?

Physical growth and advances in motor skills are among the most readily apparent signs of development in infancy. Many first-time parents are astonished at just how quickly infants outgrow their newly purchased clothes, sometimes literally overnight! And they are likely to be equally astonished that, in the course of only a few months, the young infant who could barely control his head when picked up becomes an active, mobile explorer. These transformations are accompanied by less obvious, but no less revolutionary, changes in the brain.

The growth of the body, the development of the brain, and the acquisition of physical skills affect virtually every behavior displayed by the child and are, in turn, influenced by the social, emotional, and cognitive demands made on her as growth occurs. Consider how newfound motor coordinations may, for example, dramatically awaken cognition. The six-month-old who begins to reach for and grasp objects acquires a novel and powerful means of gaining information about the world and, at the same time, a new way to control and influence her environment. By the same token, the reactions of others to changing stature and accomplishments can arouse a child's pride and promote renewed efforts, or they can lead to discouragement and apprehension. For example, when children begin to crawl, they may confront new barriers and repeated choruses of "No, don't do that." How these freshly imposed limits, inspired by burgeoning physical and mental capacities, are faced and resolved can affect many other aspects of solving problems or building relationships with others.

How do body, brain, and motor skills develop during infancy? To what extent do parenting, culture, or other environmental events influence their course? And what basic capacities does the infant possess to learn and to derive information from the senses—vision, audition, taste, touch, and smell? In this chapter we explore the basic physical capacities of the infant, as well as the rapid and important changes that take place in this sphere during the first two years.

The infant's achievements in the domain of motor development often have profound consequences for other areas of development. Consider this infant's acquisition of the ability to reach for objects. He is now equipped to explore the textures and shapes of objects, and in some cases, their tastes. By reaching, he is also able to make requests for objects, thereby gaining a stronger sense of control over events in his life.

## BODY GROWTH AND DEVELOPMENT

T here is probably no more obvious indicator of development than change in a child's physical size. We tend to use the words *grow* and *develop* interchangeably in describing the physical transformations of childhood, but they do not refer to the same processes. Strictly speaking, *growth* is the increase in size of the body or its organs, whereas *development* refers not only to changes in size but also to the orderly patterns, such as growth spurts, and the more complicated levels of functioning that often accompany increases in height and weight.

## NORMS OF GROWTH

By recording information about the height and weight of large numbers of children from diverse populations, we can determine whether a particular child's individual growth falls within the range expected for his or her chronological age and ethnic background. These **norms**, quantitative measures that provide typical values and variations in height and weight for children, have become an essential reference for attempting to answer questions about how biological and experiential factors influence growth.

*Length and Height*   The most rapid increase in body length occurs during the fourth month of prenatal development, when the fetus grows about 1.5 millimeters a day. The fetus continues to grow rapidly, albeit at a somewhat slower rate, during the remaining prenatal weeks. The newborn maintains a high rate of growth for several months following birth. In fact, if growth rate during the first six months after birth were sustained, the average ten-year-old would be about one hundred feet tall (McCall, 1979)! Girls can be expected to reach approximately half their adult height a little before two years of age and boys a little after two years of age (Fredriks et al., 2000).

Individual children, of course, may differ enormously in their growth rate, and their growth sometimes occurs in sudden spurts. One remarkable fact revealed by research is that growth of one-quarter to one-half inch can occasionally occur virtually overnight in infants and toddlers (Lampl, Veldhuis, & Johnson, 1992). Marc, in this chapter's opening vignette, may have actually been an unwitting witness to just such an event.

*Weight*   In contrast to that of height, the maximum rate of increase in weight takes place shortly after birth. In their first few days, newborns typically lose excess body fluids and shed 5 to 10 percent of their birth weight. They then usually make rapid weight gains, normally doubling their birth weight in about five months and nearly tripling it by the end of the first year (Pinyerd, 1992). To give you a sense of just how fast this process takes place, if the gains for the first six months were sustained, the average ten-year-old would weigh in at about 240,000 tons (McCall, 1979).

## PATTERNS IN BODY GROWTH

Specific organs and systems of the body often develop at rates different from that for the body as a whole. The most dramatic example is probably head size. Two months after conception, the head constitutes nearly 50 percent of total body length. By birth, however, head size represents only about 25 percent, and by adulthood only about 12 to 13 percent of total body length, as Figure 5.1 shows. The central nervous system, along with the head, undergoes an early and extremely rapid increase in weight. Other organs—for example, the muscles and the respiratory and digestive systems—follow a pattern similar to overall weight change: substantial gains during the first two years.

*Directionality of Growth*   Growth generally follows the principle of **cephalocaudal development** (*cephalocaudal* combines the Greek words for "head" and "tail"). This principle describes the tendency for systems and parts of the body near the

**norm**   Quantitative measure that provides typical values and variations in such characteristics as height and weight for children.

**cephalocaudal development**   Pattern in which organs, systems, and motor movements near the head tend to develop earlier than those near the feet.

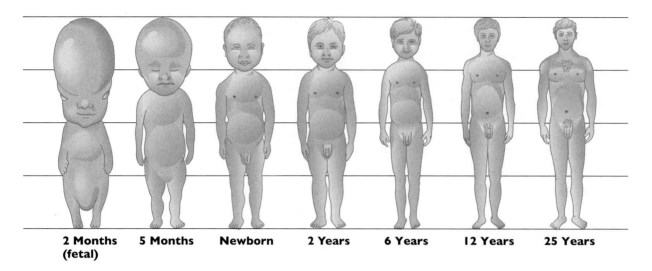

2 Months | 5 Months | Newborn | 2 Years | 6 Years | 12 Years | 25 Years
(fetal)

▲ **FIGURE 5.1**

## Changes in Body Proportions during Prenatal and Postnatal Growth

The size of the human head in proportion to the rest of the body shows striking changes over the course of prenatal to adult development. Two months after conception, the head takes up about half of the entire length of the body. By adulthood, the head makes up only about 12 to 13 percent of total body length. The head's tendency to grow more rapidly than regions of the body near the "tail" demonstrates patterns of cephalocaudal development.

*Source:* Adapted from Robbins et al. (1928).

head to mature sooner than those more distant from the head. Body growth also tends to reflect a pattern of **proximodistal development**. This principle points up the fact that regions nearer the trunk of the body tend to grow and become more differentiated earlier than those more peripheral to the body.

***Individual and Group Differences***   Children show substantial deviations from the norm in their rates of physical growth and development. Individual variations in size are already noticeable at birth; for example, boys tend to be slightly longer and heavier than girls at this time (Copper et al., 1993). Variability in growth occurs among ethnic and cultural groups as well. For example, although individual differences account for much of the variability in size, American infants of African heritage tend to weigh slightly less than American infants of European heritage at birth, even when social class, gestational age, and other factors known to affect birth weight are equated (Goldenberg et al., 1991).

### F O R ◆ Y O U R ◆ R E V I E W

◆ What are norms for growth? How do they provide information about whether physical growth is proceeding normally?

◆ What patterns of growth are observed during infancy? How do they differ for various parts of the body? How do they differ among individuals and ethnic groups?

## THE BRAIN AND NERVOUS SYSTEM

**proximodistal development**  Pattern in which organs and systems of the body near the middle tend to develop earlier than those near the periphery.

In no other time before now has the brain and its influence on the development of human behavior received more attention. Major advances in the field of *cognitive neuroscience*, the study of neural and other structures and systems of the brain associated with behavior, have produced insights and generated widespread interest among psychologists, parents, and the public about the relationship

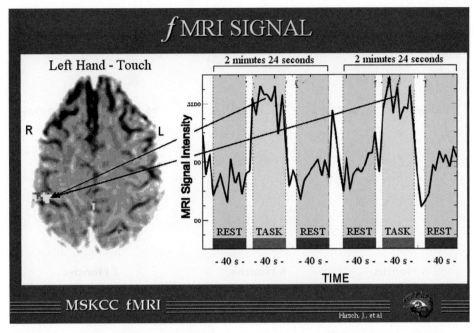

Cognitive neuroscientists employ many newer methods to understand how the brain functions as it processes information. One procedure involves functional magnetic resource imaging (fMRI). In this procedure, information about blood flow and the availability of oxygen to various regions of the brain, an indicator of neural activation, is measured. Here, while the left hand is receiving tactile stimulation, one section of the brain (the right post central gyrus) shows activation, as indicated by the bright yellow and red coloration in that region. When the hand was not being touched (rest periods), the intensity of the fMRI signal was much less. This and other emerging technologies hold great promise for learning which specific areas of the brain are involved in various kinds of cognitive processing.

between the brain and behavior. In large part, much of this enthusiasm has been spurred by the emergence of fascinating new technologies for studying the brain (Thompson & Nelson, 2001). Among these innovative procedures are *positron emission tomography* (PET scans), *functional magnetic resonance imaging* (fMRI), and the recording of *event-related potentials* (ERP). These techniques measure metabolic activity, blood flow, and electrical events, respectively, and provide clues about which areas of the brain are functioning when an individual is engaged in motor, sensory, linguistic, emotional, and other information processing. At the present time, PET scans have limited utility for studying normal infants and children because they require injection of a radioactive substance. However, fMRI (which measures cerebral blood flow) and ERP (which is a measure of electrical activity generated by the synchronous firing of neurons) are among the more widely available noninvasive procedures that hold considerable promise for investigating normal and abnormal brain development (Casey, Thomas, & McCandless, 2001; Nelson & Monk, 2001). Theoretical and practical questions about the importance of early experience and the possibility of critical periods for receiving certain kinds of stimulation have further fueled enthusiasm for studying the brain (Bruer, 1999). We summarize here a few of the major developmental changes that take place in the brain during the child's first two years.

## THE DEVELOPING BRAIN

Even before birth, brain growth is rapid. As Figure 5.2 shows, the size of the brain swiftly increases, from about 4 percent of its adult weight at five months after conception to about 25 percent at birth (Spreen, Risser, & Edgell, 1995). The *brainstem*

▷ **FIGURE 5.2**
**The Developing Human Brain**

During prenatal development, the human brain shows dramatic increases in size, and the cerebral cortex takes on a convoluted pattern to increase surface area. During the last trimester of prenatal development, the brain takes on an adult-like shape, and by birth most of the neurons have formed. The brain's weight increases most dramatically from about the fifth prenatal month until the infant is about two-and-a-half years of age. The drawings have been made to a common scale; however, the first five have been enlarged to a common size to show details.

*Source:* Adapted from Cowan (1979).

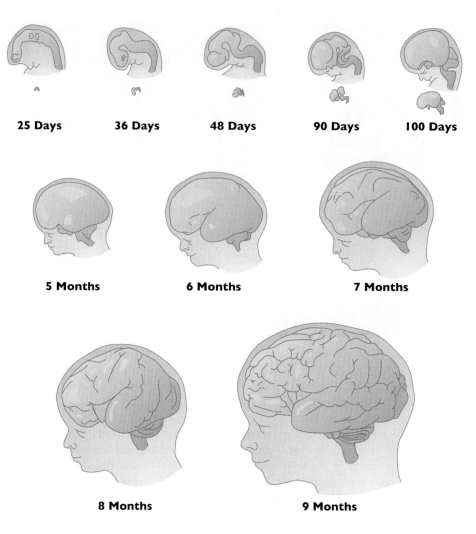

25 Days        36 Days        48 Days        90 Days        100 Days

5 Months        6 Months        7 Months

8 Months        9 Months

and *midbrain* (see Figure 5.3), which are involved in basic reflexes and sensory processing, as well as such essential biological functions as digestion, elimination, and respiration, are fairly well established at birth (Joseph, 2000). In contrast, neural changes in the *cortex*, the part of the brain most closely linked to sensation, motor responses, thinking, planning, and problem solving, continue to take place well after birth. Within the cortex, regions associated with sensory and motor functions tend to be among the earliest to mature. The frontal cortex, the region of the brain most directly involved in higher levels of cognition, tends to be among the latest.

With development, several important changes occur in **neurons**, the cells that carry electrochemical messages. These changes include *proliferation, migration,* and *differentiation.* Parts of many neurons also become surrounded by **myelin**, a sheath of fatty material that serves to insulate and speed neural impulses by about tenfold. An estimated ten times more **glial cells** (from the Greek word for "glue") than neurons also form within the brain. Glial cells establish a scaffolding for neuron migration, provide the material from which myelin develops, facilitate the transfer of nutrients to neurons, and instruct the neurons to form synapses with other neurons (Ullian et al., 2001).

**neuron**    Nerve cell within the central nervous system that is electrochemically designed to transmit messages between cells.

**myelin**    Sheath of fatty cells that insulates and speeds neural impulses by about tenfold.

**glial cell**    Brain cell that provides the material from which myelin is created, nourishes neurons, and provides a scaffolding for neuron migration.

***Neuron Proliferation***    The production of new nerve cells is known as *neuron proliferation*. Neuron production in humans begins near the end of the first month of prenatal development, shortly after the neural tube closes, and much of it, at least in the cerebral cortex, is completed by the sixth month of prenatal development. Thus, at a very early age, a finite but very large number—certainly well over 100 billion—of young neurons have formed (Nelson, 1999a; Nelson, Thomas, & de Haan, 2006).

***Neuron Migration***    Shortly after their formation, neurons move, or *migrate*, from the neural tube where they were produced to other locations. In some regions of

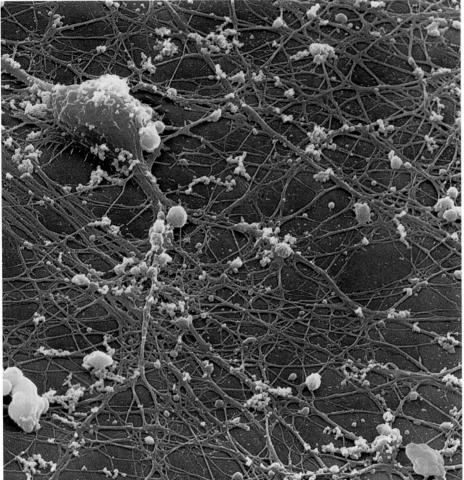

This color-enhanced photo, taken with a scanning electron microscope, shows a neuron. Neurons carry the electrochemical messages that are the basis for behavior. Even before birth, massive numbers of neurons are manufactured and migrate to various regions of the brain, where they begin to establish connections with other neurons.

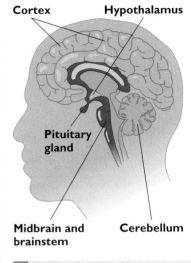

▲ **FIGURE 5.3**

**Cross-Section of the Human Brain**

Certain regions of the brain are closely associated with specific functions. The overarching cortex is essential for most of behavior and includes regions associated with processing sensory and motor information, as well as areas heavily involved in thinking, planning, and problem solving. The early-developing midbrain and brainstem are important to basic biological functioning. The cerebellum is centrally involved in coordination and control of voluntary movements. Both the hypothalamus and pituitary glands are believed to play a major role in the regulation of physical growth.

the brain this movement occurs passively, so that, as additional neurons are born, older neurons are pushed farther to the outside of that portion of the brain. This type of growth takes place, for example, in the hypothalamus, the brainstem, and the cerebellum. However, for many other regions of the brain, such as the cerebral cortex, the neurons may migrate a great distance, passing through levels of older neurons that already have reached their final destination. These regions of the brain are formed by an *inside-out* pattern of development in which layers of nerve cells nearer the outer surface are younger than layers deeper in the cortex (Nelson et al., 2006). Under these circumstances, how do neurons know where to migrate and when to stop migrating? Both neurochemical and mechanical information probably play a role. Young neurons attach to and maneuver along the surfaces of fibers of glial cells radiating to the region of their destination, detaching from their guide, as shown in Figure 5.4, at programmed locations. Both the production and the migration of large numbers of neurons in the cortex occur in waves, especially during the seventh and eleventh weeks of gestational age (Spreen et al., 1995). However, some teratogens, including mercury and alcohol, are known to interfere with the onset and path of neuron migration. In fact, developmental defects ranging from mental retardation to behavioral disorders have been linked to interference in the migratory patterns of nerve cells (Gressens, 2000).

**KEY THEME**

**RISK/RESILIENCE**

***Neuron Differentiation*** Whereas neuron proliferation and migration take place prenatally for the most part, *neuron differentiation*—the process of enlarging,

▶ **FIGURE 5.4**

**The Migration of Neurons via Glial Fiber**

Wrapping themselves around glial fibers, neurons climb in spiral fashion to a particular layer in the cortex of the brain. Because the cortex of the brain develops in an inside-out pattern, earlier waves of neurons need to progress across shorter distances, and their migration may be completed within a day. However, later waves of neurons pass through earlier layers of the cortex and migrate across a greater distance, so that their journey may require several weeks. Some teratogens can interfere with this migratory pattern and, if the disruption is severe, result in a variety of developmental defects.

*Source:* Adapted from Kunzig (1998).

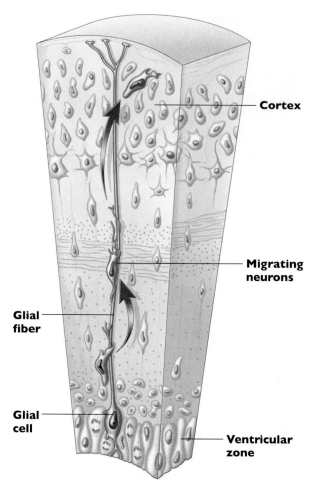

Cortex

Migrating neurons

Glial fiber

Glial cell

Ventricular zone

🔑 **KEY THEME**

**NATURE & NURTURE**

forming synapses with other neurons, and beginning to function—flourishes postnatally. Neural differentiation, along with the growth of glial cells and other tissues, including myelin, contributes to the substantial postnatal increase in the size of the brain.

Some aspects of neuron differentiation proceed without external stimulation. Experience, however, plays a major role in the selection, maintenance, and strengthening of connections among many neurons (Nelson et al., 2006). Scientists knew this even decades ago when classic work investigating the effects of vision on brain development in cats illustrated this complex relationship (Hubel & Wiesel, 1979). By the time a kitten's eyes open, neurons in the visual receptor areas of the cerebral cortex have already established some connections and can respond, for example, to sensory information from either eye or to visual patterns with a broad range of characteristics. But the neurons become far more selective and tuned to particular kinds of sensory information as the kitten experiences specific forms of visual stimulation. If the kitten is exposed only to dark-light transitions in the visual field that are horizontal, for example, neurons begin to respond only to those patterns; likewise, exposure only to dark-light transitions that are vertical produces neurons sensitive only to that orientation.

Without stimulation and the opportunity to function, neurons are unlikely to establish or maintain many connections with other neurons; their synaptic density becomes substantially reduced. For example, in the visual cortex the total number of synapses rises meteorically in the first few months after birth, but then the connections show a small decline from about eight months of age to the late preschool years, followed by a more substantial decline between about four and ten years. These dramatic changes in the visual cortex can be seen in Figure 5.5. Neurons may even die if no synapses are formed with other neurons. In fact, one theory holds that massive cell death, perhaps as great as 50 to 75 percent of neurons, occurs

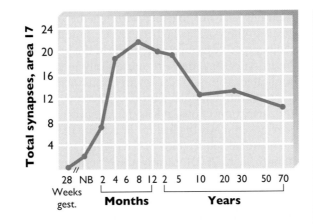

**FIGURE 5.5**

**Estimated Number of Synapses for Neurons in the Human Visual Cortex as a Function of Age**

Differentiation of the neurons in the human visual cortex proceeds rapidly shortly after birth and reaches a peak before the end of the first year. The number of synapses ($\times 10^{11}$), connections of dendrites to other neurons, then declines to about half of the original peak number over the lifespan. The rapid increment is associated with visual stimulation after birth and accompanies significant improvements in visual abilities before a year of age. The number of synapses reflects an initial overproduction; those that become functional are then likely to be maintained over the remaining years. Other regions of the cortex may show a similar pattern of rapid increase and then decline in number of synapses, although perhaps at different periods in development.

*Source:* Adapted from Huttenlocher (1994).

during normal development in the brains of some animals and perhaps in some regions of the human brain, although probably not in the cerebral cortex (Huttenlocher, 1994). Thus the typical infant is genetically equipped with the capacity for neurons to generate many synaptic connections, perhaps far more than a person will ever need. That surplus provides the opportunity for a rich variety of experiences to affect development; it also means that, if damage or destruction occurs to some synapses early in life, others may replace them.

## PLASTICITY IN BRAIN DEVELOPMENT

Because of the unspecialized nature of young neurons, the immature brain displays substantial **plasticity**, or the ability, within limits, of alternate regions of the cerebral cortex to take on specialized sensory, linguistic, and other information processing (Johnson, 2000). Infants or children who suffer damage to regions of the cerebral cortex that process speech, for example, are often able to recover because neurons in other parts of the cortex take on this function. On the other hand, although considerable plasticity is retained by some regions of the mature adult brain (Thompson & Nelson, 2001), the prognosis for recovery of language in adults after an accident or a stroke is usually much poorer because the remaining neurons in various regions of the brain have become dedicated to processing certain kinds of experiences.

William Greenough and his colleagues contend that neurons in human and other mammalian brains exhibit two different kinds of plasticity (Greenough, Black, & Wallace, 1987). Some neurons are sensitive to *experience-expectant* information. As a result of a long evolutionary process, these neurons begin to grow and differentiate rapidly at about the time they can be expected to receive the kinds of stimulation important to their functioning. In many mammals, for example, parts of the visual cortex involved in depth or pattern perception develop quite rapidly shortly before and after the eyes open or, in the case of humans, shortly before and after birth. Research with lower animals indicates that visual deprivation during these periods—being reared in the dark or without patterned light, for example—results in the permanent loss of some kinds of depth and pattern vision, losses that do not occur when equivalent lengths of deprivation occur during other periods.

Other neurons are sensitive to *experience-dependent* information. Many opportunities for learning occur at unpredictable times during development. Each person learns different and unique things, even into old age. The distinctive perceptual features forming the image of a neighbor or the attributes defining the concept of democracy are unique representations registered within an individual's neural system. Here, then, is a form of plasticity that implicates neural differentiation as a critical aspect of brain functioning throughout a person's lifetime.

How do neurons form connections with one another as a result of experiences in the environment? A now-familiar mantra among contemporary neuroscientists is

**plasticity** Capacity of immature systems, including regions of the brain and the individual neurons within those regions, to take on different functions as a result of experience.

"Neurons that fire together wire together." As the organism encounters particular events in the world, whether they are sounds, visual stimuli, or other forms of stimulation, specific groups of neurons in the brain become activated. Each time neurons fire in synchrony, they are more likely to maintain connections with one another. Implicated in this process is an amino acid called *glutamate*, which is involved in communication among neurons. When neurons fire out of synchrony, however, they lose their connections, at least in part because the receptors for glutamate are altered or removed. Thus the history of activity that neurons have with one another shapes the neuronal connections that remain versus those that are lost (Heynen et al., 2003; Penn & Shatz, 2002). Clearly, these findings from the laboratories of neuroscientists have important implications for the role of early experience in infancy.

## BRAIN LATERALIZATION

One of the brain's most obvious physical characteristics is its two mirrorlike structures, a left and a right hemisphere. By and large, sensory information and motor responses on the left side of the body in humans are processed by the right hemisphere, and those on the right side of the body are processed by the left hemisphere. In addition, in most adults the left hemisphere is especially involved in language functioning, whereas the right hemisphere is more typically engaged in processing certain types of spatial, emotional, or other nonverbal information. But these differences are by no means absolute. For example, speech is controlled primarily by the left hemisphere in about 98 percent of right-handed adults but in only about 60 percent of left-handed adults (Caplan & Gould, 2003).

Does hemispheric specialization already exist at birth, or does the brain show progressive **lateralization**, the process by which one hemisphere comes to dominate the other in terms of a particular function? Based on research on left-hemisphere damage in children, Eric Lenneberg (1967) proposed that, at least until age two, both hemispheres are capable of carrying out language functions equally well and that lateralization increases only gradually until adolescence. Other researchers, however, suggest that lateralization actually begins much earlier (Kinsbourne & Hiscock, 1983), perhaps as a consequence of exposure to fetal testosterone (Geschwind & Galaburda, 1987; McManus & Bryden, 1991). For example, some physical differences in the two hemispheres already exist at birth (Kosslyn et al., 1999). Perhaps such brain asymmetries contribute to the observation that most infants lie with the head oriented to the right rather than to the left, an orientation that later predicts hand preference (Michel, 1988). Even before three months of age, most babies more actively use and hold objects longer in the right hand than in the left (Hawn & Harris, 1983). Most dramatic is evidence from ultrasound images of fifteen-week-old fetuses: 90 percent were observed to suck their right thumb, a preference that was linked consistently to handedness at ten to twelve years of age (Hepper, Wells, & Lynch, 2005).

## F O R ⋄ Y O U R ⋄ R E V I E W

⊷ What are the major methodological procedures that have permitted advances in the study of the developing brain?

⊷ Which regions of the brain develop earliest and latest? To what functions do those regions contribute?

⊷ What developmental changes occur in neurons? How do myelin and glial cells contribute to neuronal development?

⊷ When does the plasticity of the brain decline? What is the difference between experience-expectant and experience-dependent information?

⊷ What evidence exists for brain lateralization in infancy?

**lateralization**  Process by which one hemisphere of the brain comes to dominate the other; for example, processing of language in the left hemisphere or of spatial information in the right hemisphere.

# MOTOR SKILL DEVELOPMENT

D uring postnatal development, cartilage continues to be transformed into bone, and bones elongate and increase in number to become scaffolding to support the body in new physical orientations. As the brain and nervous system mature, neural commands begin to coordinate thickened and enlarged muscles, permitting more powerful and refined motor activities. Infants begin to roll from side to back, reach for objects, and eventually crawl, stand up, and walk. Two complementary patterns are evident in the emergence of motor activity: *differentiation*, the enrichment of global and relatively diffuse actions with more refined and skilled ones, and *integration*, the increasingly coordinated actions of muscles and sensory systems. Throughout infancy, motor skills become more efficient, coordinated, deliberate, or automatic as the task requires.

For child development theorist Jean Piaget, sensorimotor activity was essential to understand, for it served as the prototype and first stage in the construction of knowledge. Contemporary child development researchers, too, recognize that the acquisition, coordination, and integration of basic motor skills are not only interesting topics of study in their own right but also can give us important insights into early cognitive and perceptual development.

## THE FIRST ACTIONS: REFLEXES

At first glance, newborns seem helpless and incompetent. Babies eat, sleep, and cry; their diapers always seem to need changing. Yet a more careful look reveals that infants enter their new world with surprisingly adept abilities, among them a set of **reflexes**, involuntary reactions to touch, light, sound, and other kinds of stimulation, some of which are exhibited even prenatally.

Reflexes are among the building blocks that soon give rise to voluntary movements and the acquisition of *developmental milestones*—significant achievements in motor skills. Along with breathing and swallowing, *primitive reflexes*, such as rooting and sucking (see Table 5.1), provide nourishment for the infant's survival. Among our evolutionary ancestors, other reflexes, such as the Moro and palmar reflexes,

Among the reflexes that babies display is the swimming reflex. When young infants are placed in water, breathing is suspended, and they engage in swimlike movements with their arms and legs.

**reflex** Involuntary reaction to touch, light, sound, and other kinds of stimulation.

**Table 5.1    Typical Reflexes Observed in Newborns and Infants**

Considerable variability exists among infants in their reflexes and the ages at which they can be elicited (Touwen, 1974). The presence or absence of any single reflex provides only one among many indicators of healthy or atypical development.

| Name of Reflex | Testing Procedure | Response | Developmental Course | Significance |
|---|---|---|---|---|
| **Primitive Reflexes** | | | | |
| *Palmar or Hand Grasp* | Place finger in hand. | Hand grasps object. | Birth to about 4 months | Absence may signal neurological defects; persistence could interfere with voluntary grasping. |
| *Rooting* | Stroke corner of mouth lightly. | Head and tongue move toward stimulus. | Birth to about 5 months | Mouth is brought to stimulus to permit sucking. |
| *Sucking* | Place finger in mouth or on lips. | Sucking begins. | Birth to about 6 months | Ensures intake of potential nutrients. |
| *Moro* | (1) Sit child up, allow head to drop about 20 degrees backward, or (2) make a loud noise, or (3) lower baby rapidly. | Baby extends arms outward, hands open; then brings hands to midline, hands clenched, spine straightened. | Birth to about 5–7 months | Absence may signal neurological defects; persistence could interfere with acquisition of sitting. |
| *Babinski* | Stroke bottom of foot. | Toes fan and then curl. | Birth to about 1 year | Absence may signal neurological defects. |
| *Asymmetric Tonic Neck Reflex* | Place baby on back, arms and legs extended, and rotate head 90 degrees. | Arm on face side extends, arm on back side of head flexes. | About 1 month to 4 months | Absence may signal neurological defects; persistence could prevent rolling over, coordination. |
| **Postural Reflexes** | | | | |
| *Stepping* | Hold baby under arms, upright, learning forward. | Makes walk-like stepping movements. | Birth to about 3 months | Absence may signal neurological defects. |
| *Labyrinthine* | (1) Place baby on back. | Extends arms and legs. | Birth to about 4 months | Absence may signal neurological defects. |
| | (2) Place baby on stomach. | Flexes arms and legs. | | |
| *Swimming* | Place baby in water. | Holds breath involuntarily; arms and legs move as if trying to swim. | Birth to about 4–6 months | Absence may signal neurological defects. |
| *Placing* | Hold baby under arms, upright, top of foot touching bottom edge of table. | Lifts foot and places on top of table. | Birth through 12 months | Absence may signal neurological defects. |
| *Landau Reaction* | Place baby on stomach, hold under chest. | Lifts head, eventually other parts of body, above chest. | Head at 2 months, other parts of body later | Absence may signal neurological defects; inadequate muscle tone for motor development. |
| *Body Righting* | Rotate hips or shoulder. | Rotates remainder of body. | 4 months to more than 12 months | Absence may signal neurological defects; difficulty in gaining postural control and walking. |

helped to protect newborns from danger. *Postural reflexes*, including stepping, swimming, and body righting (which are surprisingly similar to later voluntary movements), appear to be designed to maintain a specific orientation to the environment. If primitive or postural reflexes are absent, are too strong or too weak, display unequal strength when normally elicited from either side of the body, or continue to be exhibited beyond certain ages, a pediatrician may begin to suspect cerebral palsy or some other neurological impairment and developmental difficulties for the baby (Blasco, 1994).

## MOTOR MILESTONES

Reflexes are often viewed as fixed responses to a stimulus. However, many early motor behaviors that young infants soon produce consist of coordinated actions. For example, babies exhibit **rhythmical stereotypies**, repeated sequences of motions performed with no apparent goal. Rubbing one foot against the other, rocking back and forth, bouncing up and down, swaying side to side, striking or banging objects, mouthing and tonguing, and shaking and nodding the head are just a few of the movements that exercise bones, joints, and muscles. Stereotypies, along with early reflexes, appear to be the bits and pieces of the primitive melody of behavior that eventually are recruited and integrated into organized voluntary motor skills and activities (Thelen, 1996).

Many more organized goal-directed voluntary actions emerge during the first year, as infants gradually gain neuromotor control of their heads, arms, and legs. Some of these actions—grasping, crawling, and walking, for example—are motor milestones: once mastered, new worlds open up to the infant. Moreover, they lead caregivers to respond in different ways: childproofing the home to prevent accidents, allowing greater independence, expecting more mature behavior. Most gains in infant movement illustrate progress in coordinating (1) *postural control*, the ability to maintain an upright orientation to the environment; (2) *locomotion*, the ability to maneuver through space; and (3) *manual control*, the ability to manipulate objects (Keogh & Sugden, 1985). Table 5.2 contains a summary of the young child's major achievements in motor development.

*Postural Control*  Keeping the head upright and stable at about two to three months of age represents one of the first milestones in infant motor development. This achievement is followed by mastery of other significant postural skills, such as maintaining an upright sitting position, moving to a standing position, and standing without assistance. The milestones, built on various postural reflexes among other things, often reflect a *cephalocaudal* progression. Head control, for example, precedes control of the trunk, and command of the legs is the last to develop. The integration of postural skills is also important. For example, the ability to keep the head upright while sitting or while standing on a stable surface is one thing; the ability to do this when being carried about or during self-movement requires integration of far more information to retain motor control.

*Locomotion*  No one doubts that a monumental achievement in infancy is the ability to move about the environment. One early milestone in locomotion is the capacity to roll over. Then comes success at initiating forward motion, a skill marked by considerable variation (Adolph, Vereijken, & Denny, 1998; Freedland & Bertenthal, 1994). Some infants use arms to pull and legs to push, others use only arms or legs, and still others scoot forward while sitting. *Crawling*, locomotion with stomach touching the floor, may soon give way to *creeping*, locomotion on hands and knees—and then again it may not. The varieties of forward motion invented by babies often generate lively discussions among caregivers.

Once babies are able to pull themselves upright, they often *cruise*; that is, move by holding onto furniture or other objects to help maintain their balance while stepping sideways (Barela, Jeka, & Clark, 1999). Forward walking while holding onto

**KEY THEME**

INTERACTION AMONG DOMAINS

**rhythmical stereotypy**  Repeated sequence of movements, such as leg kicking, hand waving, or head banging, that has no apparent goal.

**Table 5.2** **Milestones of Motor Development**

This table describes the sequence of motor skill development that takes place during infancy. Children often show individual differences in the exact ages at which they display the various developmental achievements outlined here. Nonetheless, successful attainment of these milestones is often used as one indicator of healthy development.

**2 Months**
- Holds head steadily when held upright
- Lifts head up

**3 Months**
- Holds head steady while being carried
- Rolls over
- Raised head and chest

**4 Months**
- Grasps cube

**6 Months**
- Sits without support
- Stands while holding onto something

**7 Months**
- Rolls from back to stomach
- Attempts to crawl and/or creep

**8 Months**
- Achieves sitting position without help
- Pulls to standing

**9 Months**
- Walks while holding furniture (cruises)
- Demonstrates neat pincer grasp
- Bangs two objects held in hands

**10 Months**
- Walks with help
- Plays pat-a-cake

**11 Months**
- Stands alone
- Turns pages of book

**12 Months**
- Walks alone
- Drinks from cup

**14 Months**
- Builds tower using two cubes
- Scribbles

**15 Months**
- Walks sideways and backward
- Attempts to use spoon and fork

**17 Months**
- Walks up steps

**18 Months**
- Begins to run

**20 Months**
- Kicks ball forward
- Throws ball overhead

someone's hand typically follows. By about twelve months of age, about half of American babies and infants in many other countries walk alone. Skill in walking continues to be refined throughout infancy and early childhood. The infant's steps become longer and show less side-to-side motion, while the toes point more forward, refinements that are linked with opportunities to practice walking (Adolph, Vereijken, & Shrout, 2003).

Prewalking and walking skills likely depend on the growth of higher brain centers. But even before independent walking, many of the components of this ability are evident. For example, when babies six months of age are placed on a treadmill and held so they do not have to support their full weight, they display alternating stepping similar to that involved in walking (Thelen & Ulrich, 1991). Even six-week-olds produce surprisingly coordinated leg movements when lying on their backs (Thelen, Skala, & Kelso, 1987). However, even though the coordinated action pattern underlying these abilities may be available much earlier, the task constraints of maintaining upright posture, lifting the leg against gravity, moving forward, and other factors delay the onset of walking.

***Manual Control*** Generally speaking, infants show an ability to control arms and legs much sooner than areas more distant, such as fingers and toes, an example of the principle of *proximodistal development*. However, in the weeks that follow birth, infants make enormous progress in reaching. Moving the hand to the mouth appears to be among the earliest goal actions (Lew & Butterworth, 1997; Rochat, 1993). Newborns also display *prereaching* in their attempts to contact objects that catch their attention. These early efforts are neither accurate nor coordinated with grasping. Still, movements show speeding up, slowing down, and changes in direction, just as in later, more accurate reaches (Rönnqvist & von Hofsten, 1994; von Hofsten & Rönnqvist, 1993). Systematic reaching for objects begins at about three months of age. By about five to six months, infants display mature, *ballistic* reaches to rapidly and accurately retrieve an object in the visual field. In gaining mastery over this response, babies engage in a series of submovements, not always perfectly executed but often quickly corrected to meet the goal of obtaining the target (Berthier, 1996; Berthier & Robin, 1998), and will even intercept a target moving past their line of sight (Robin, Berthier, & Clifton, 1996). The ability to see their own hands is not necessary in early reaching; however, infants eventually make greater use of visual cues to help them retrieve an object (Clifton et al., 1993; McCarty et al., 2001; Robin, Berthier, & Clifton, 1996).

When first attempting to reach, very young infants typically keep their hands closed in fistlike fashion. By about four months of age, infants awkwardly pick up an object by grasping it with the palm of the hand. Over the next few months, they shift from using the inner palm to using opposing thumb and fingertips, a progression that culminates in a neat *pincer grasp* at about nine months of age.

Another important component of motor skill is increased coordination between the two hands. Very young infants often attempt to grasp objects with both hands, but once babies gain an ensemble of skills, including head control and postural balance while sitting by themselves and when leaning forward, one-handed reaches and more consistent, stable reaching become a part of their repertoire (Rochat & Goubet, 1995; Spencer et al., 2000). Increased coordination is further reflected in the appearance of complementary hand orientations, such as holding a toy dump truck in one hand while using the other hand to fill it with sand. This *functional asymmetry* emerges at about five to six months of age but becomes especially refined as the child enters the second year and begins to display self-help and advanced motor tasks requiring sophisticated use of both arms and hands.

## DETERMINANTS OF MOTOR DEVELOPMENT

Are the emergence, refinement, and integration of motor skills primarily dependent on genetic or maturational factors? Or are they the consequence of practice, cultural, or other experiential factors? Many pioneers in developmental psychology advocated a strong maturational theory to explain the orderly acquisition of motor skills. But we now recognize that these changes are better understood in terms of the confluence of both biological and experiential factors.

***Biological Contributions*** One of the strongest arguments in support of a genetic or maturational basis for the development of motor skills is their tendency to be displayed at predictable times and in similar ways in normal children. Moreover, the onset of such skills as sitting and walking shows greater concordance for identical than for fraternal twins. Greater similarity in gross motor activities, such as running, jumping, and throwing, is found in children who are more closely related biologically (Malina, 1980). Even intellectually and physically disabled babies attain major milestones in an orderly manner, although at a later age than other children. For example, blind children, who show substantial delays in acquiring postural, locomotion, and manual coordination skills, eventually acquire them nonetheless (Tröster & Brambring, 1993).

A major motor milestone that babies around a year of age typically reach is that of walking. Although this baby is not quite old enough to walk independently, infants show surprisingly coordinated leg movements well before this milestone is reached. Do you think this kind of practice might also help her to begin walking earlier? Although we typically think of the onset of walking as primarily the result of maturation, cross-cultural research suggests that, in communities in which a great deal of opportunity is provided to acquire this ability, children begin to walk at somewhat earlier ages.

**KEY THEME**
**NATURE & NURTURE**

In the Navajo culture babies are often swaddled for most of the day. Wayne Dennis's research with Hopi infants who were also cared for in this way suggests that this baby, despite the lack of opportunity to practice sitting up, crawling, and standing alone, will begin to walk about the same time as an infant who has not been swaddled.

***Experiential Contributions***   Could experiential variables also play a role in motor development? With respect to the acquisition of expert motor skill, the answer is most certainly yes. However, it may be true for attaining basic developmental milestones as well. Lack of opportunity to engage in physical activity seriously interferes with reaching developmental milestones. For example, babies who spent most of their first year in an orphanage lying in cribs and receiving few other forms of stimulation typically did not walk before age three or four (Dennis, 1960). When special programs encourage blind infants to acquire self-initiated movement, they do so at ages more comparable to their sighted peers (Fraiberg, 1977).

Several investigators in the 1930s conducted studies with sets of twins to test the role of experience in motor skill development. Typically, one twin received extensive training in, say, handling blocks, climbing stairs, or roller skating; the other twin did not (Gesell & Thompson, 1934; Hilgard, 1932; McGraw, 1935). When given a chance to acquire the skills, the untrained twin often rapidly achieved the same level of skill displayed by the trained twin. In another early study, Wayne and Marsena Dennis investigated child-rearing practices among the Hopi Indians (Dennis & Dennis, 1940). Some Hopi Indian mothers followed the tribal tradition of tightly swaddling their babies in a cradleboard; the mother would strap the board to her back for all but about an hour a day during her waking hours for the first six to twelve months of her child's life. These Hopi babies had little opportunity to practice sitting up, crawling, and walking. Other Hopi mothers reared infants without swaddling. The researchers found that swaddling had little bearing on when infants initiated walking, an observation reconfirmed in a later study of the effects of Hopi rearing customs (Harriman & Lukosius, 1982).

What can we conclude from these investigations? Perhaps that the typical range of daily activities and experiences in which infants and children are engaged is sufficient to promote normal locomotor development. But consider other findings. Infants from one to seven weeks of age, given a few minutes of daily practice with the placing and stepping reflexes, retain them and begin walking earlier than infants who receive no special training or whose legs are passively moved back and forth (Zelazo, 1983). Moreover, practice in sitting helps infants acquire these skills (Zelazo et al., 1993).

Esther Thelen and her colleagues (Thelen & Smith, 1994, 2006) have applied a far broader perspective to the role of experience in motor development. Thelen has argued that all complex motor skills require the assembling and reassembling of multiple processes involving, among other things, motivation, elements of the nervous system that regulate posture and balance, increased bone and muscle strength, and changes in body proportions. These assemblages are further constrained by the biodynamics of the human body, as well as the situational context. However, when the right improvisation of components exists, infants display mastery of motor skills or advance to new levels of competence. Neither biological nor experiential factors alone are responsible. Instead, motor development is a dynamic system; its multiple components become "tuned" into sequences of more effective, self-organized actions over time (Lockman & Thelen, 1993).

**KEY THEME**
SOCIOCULTURAL INFLUENCE

## CROSS-CULTURAL DIFFERENCES

Given the multiple processes involved, it should not be surprising to learn that ethnic and cultural differences in motor development exist as well. At birth and throughout their first year, African American babies, as well as infants among the Wolof of Senegal, the Gusii of Kenya, the Yoruba of Nigeria, the Bantu of South

Africa, and the Ganda of Uganda, typically outperform Caucasian infants on a variety of motor skills (Lester & Brazelton, 1982; Werner, 1972). Parents in a fairly prosperous rural community in Kenya made extensive efforts to teach their infants to sit or walk (Super, 1976). In fact, their language, as in some other regions of East Africa, contained distinctive words to denote the specialized training. The more caregivers promoted specific motor skills, the earlier their children tended to display them. For example, 93 percent of one group of caregivers said they taught their babies to crawl, and babies in this group began crawling at about five and a half months of age. In contrast, only 13 percent of the caregivers in a nearby group expressed support for teaching their infants to crawl, and these babies did not crawl until about eight months of age.

Many factors could contribute to the cultural differences, but one finding strongly implicates child-rearing efforts. Advanced motor development in this part of Kenya was limited to sitting, standing, and walking, skills considered culturally important. Other milestones not taught or valued, such as head control or the ability to roll over, were acquired later than they are by American infants. A similar observation comes from Jamaica. Some mothers in that country perform special stretching and massaging exercises to encourage their infants to sit and walk alone (Hopkins & Westra, 1990). Children of these mothers sit by themselves and walk earlier than other children.

We cannot be certain whether training focused on particular skills or more general experiences are responsible for cultural differences. Children in East Africa, for example, spend more time in an upright position, seated on a caregiver's lap or riding on her back, than children in the United States (Super, 1976). The activities may strengthen trunk and leg muscles to aid the earlier appearance of sitting, standing, and walking. However, gains achieved from training in one of two particular skills, such as stepping or sitting, do not appear to generalize to the other (Zelazo, 1998; Zelazo et al., 1993). And infants who become increasingly proficient in crawling up and down a slope have to relearn how to go up and down the same slope when they start to walk (Adolph, 1997).

Children of the Ache of Eastern Paraguay are significantly delayed in acquiring a host of motor skills. For example, walking is not exhibited until twenty-one to twenty-three months of age. This small band, which engages in hunting and gathering, does not encourage the acquisition of motor skills in infants. When families migrate to the forests, the women closely supervise their children younger than three years, preventing them from venturing more than a yard or so into the uncleared vegetation (Kaplan & Dove, 1987). For the Ache, keeping infants close by may be crucial for their continued survival, but it gives little opportunity for infants to practice motor skills. Because the Ache have been relatively isolated and the total population at times quite small, genetic factors cannot be ruled out as contributing to the delay, but cultural concerns and efforts to either promote or discourage the acquisition of motor skills appear to have a significant effect on their development.

## F O R · Y O U R · R E V I E W

* How do primitive and postural reflexes differ? What purpose do they serve for the infant?

* When are rhythmical stereotypies exhibited?

* What are the major milestones associated with the development of postural control, locomotion, and manual control? How do the principles of cephalocaudal and proxomodistal development apply to the emergence of the major motor milestones?

* What factors contribute to motor development? How do cultural practices influence their acquisition?

## SLEEP

I nfants display a wide variety of behavioral states: regular and irregular sleep, drowsiness, alert inactivity, alert activity, and crying. Each of these has distinctive features. Crying or distress usually begins with whimpering but swiftly shifts to full-scale cries, often accompanied by thrashing of arms and legs. During alert activity, the infant also exhibits vigorous, diffuse motor activity, but such exertions are not accompanied by signs of distress. During alert inactivity, the baby is relatively quiet, at least in terms of motor activity, but actively engages in visual scanning of the environment. In this state, the baby appears to be most responsive to sensory stimulation and may be learning a great deal. But it is sleep that is usually of greatest concern to parents, especially in the first few months when the adults in the household are often awakened by the child's cries, sometimes several times in a night. Fortunately, part of the process of physical development includes changes in sleep patterns that bring the cycles of infants and caregivers into greater alignment with one another.

### PATTERNS OF SLEEP

Babies sleep a lot. Although individual differences are great, newborns average sixteen to seventeen hours of sleep a day. Sleep and wake cycles are extremely short, and babies are easily disrupted by external stimulation. As the weeks pass, infants gradually sleep less, but for longer periods; by about three to five weeks of age, a pattern begins to emerge in which the longest sleep periods take place at night (Thompson, 1982). But naps during the day continue to be a regular occurrence all the way through the preschool years. In fact, in some cultures, such naps are never eliminated.

The development of sleep patterns differs substantially across various cultures. In most industrialized countries, parents eagerly look forward to having their infants adopt a routine that matches their own. A significant milestone is reached when the baby of three or four months finally sleeps through the night. In some cultures, such as the Kipsigi of rural Kenya, however, infants are permitted more flexibility and will not sleep through the night until much older (Super & Harkness, 1982).

Like adults, infants (even before they are born) display two distinct sleep states (Groome et al., 1997). During active or REM *(rapid eye movement)* sleep, eye movements and muscle jerks are frequent, and breathing and heart rate are irregular. During quiet sleep *(NREM)*, eye and muscle movements are few, and physiological activity is more regular. The proportion of time spent in the two states, however, shifts dramatically with development. About eight in sixteen hours of sleep is spent in REM sleep as a newborn, but only about two in seven hours of sleep as an adult.

Active or REM sleep has been linked to dreaming, but it is not clear whether young infants dream. However, REM sleep is believed to be important for normal brain activity (Roffwarg, Muzio, & Dement, 1966). *Autostimulation theory* proposes that REM sleep provides powerful stimulation to the central nervous system, which in adults is interpreted as sensory and motor activity associated with dreaming. According to this theory, stimulation during REM sleep compensates for the relatively brief number of hours each day that the infant is awake. Infants kept awake for relatively lengthy periods of time show reduced amounts of REM sleep, and premature infants, whose wakeful periods are even shorter, show more REM sleep than full-term babies (Halpern, MacLean, & Baumeister, 1995). If autostimulation theory is correct, it is a further demonstration of how important stimulation is for development, even at those times when a large amount of sleep is essential as well.

### SLEEPING ARRANGEMENTS

**KEY THEME**

SOCIOCULTURAL INFLUENCE

Where should infants sleep? The answer is actually very controversial. Historically, and in most cultures today (such as Japan), an infant and mother sleeping together—or *co-sleeping*—is the norm (Latz, Wolf, & Lozoff, 1999). In fact, Mayan mothers view putting very young children in a separate room at night as almost equivalent to child

# THE BRAIN AND NERVOUS SYSTEM

## What are the major methodological procedures that have permitted advances in the study of the developing brain?

New methodologies to investigate the brain, including positron emission tomography (PET), functional magnetic resonance imaging (fMRI), and recording of event-related potentials, have recently promoted widespread attention to the brain and its development.

## Which regions of the brain develop earliest and latest? To what functions do those regions contribute?

The brainstem and midbrain, which control essential biological functions, are fairly well established at birth. The cortex, the portion of the brain that controls thinking, planning, and voluntary responses, develops after birth. The sensory and motor regions of the cortex develop earliest; the frontal cortex develops later.

## What developmental changes occur in neurons? How do myelin and glial cells contribute to neuronal development?

The three major changes that *neurons* undergo are proliferation (production of neurons), migration (movement of neurons to their final destination), and differentiation (formation of synapses with other neurons). *Myelin* speeds neural impulses, and *glial cells* nourish and provide scaffolding for migrating neurons.

## When does the plasticity of the brain decline? What is the difference between experience-expectant and experience-dependent information?

*Plasticity* of the brain is apparent in infancy and declines toward the end of childhood, although considerable plasticity is still evident in mature adult brains. Neuron differentiation may proceed at critical or sensitive times for experience-expectant information but occurs throughout development for experience-dependent information. An important principle underlying the development of neural connections is repeated episodes of firing in synchrony.

## What evidence exists for brain lateralization in infancy?

Infants display behaviors suggestive of hemispheric specialization, or *lateralization*, at birth. They lie with head oriented in one direction, hold objects in preferred hands, and show preferences in the direction in which they turn to localize a sound.

# MOTOR SKILL DEVELOPMENT

## How do primitive and postural reflexes differ? What purpose do they serve for the infant?

*Reflexes*, involuntary responses to stimulation controlled by subcortical processes, are among the earliest motor actions displayed in newborns. Primitive reflexes (such as rooting and sucking) help to increase the likelihood of survival, whereas postural reflexes (such as stepping and swimming) help the infant to maintain a specific orientation in his or her environment.

## When are rhythmical stereotypies exhibited?

*Rhythmical stereotypies*, repeated motor actions with no apparent goal, are among the earliest organized motor behaviors displayed by infants.

## What are the major milestones associated with the development of postural control, locomotion, and manual control? How do the principles of cephalocaudal and proximodistal development apply to the emergence of the major motor milestones?

Postural control includes keeping the head upright and balanced, maintaining an upright sitting position, and standing with, and later without, assistance. Locomotor skills include rolling over, crawling or creeping, cruising, and walking. Manual control includes prereaching, ballistic reaching, and a shift from reach with hands formed in a fist to use of a pincer grasp. The cephalocaudal principle highlights the fact that regions nearer the head tend to undergo more rapid development than regions farther away from the head. The proximodistal principle is illustrated by the fact that arms and legs come under the infant's control before fingers and toes.

## What factors contribute to motor development? How do cultural practices influence their acquisition?

Genetic preadaptation may contribute to the emergence of motor skills, but research indicates that experience can be important as well. Some societies promote the acquisition of basic motor skills, such as crawling and walking, and as a consequence, such skills often appear somewhat earlier among infants and very young children in those societies.

# SLEEP

## What states do newborns display?

Newborns display regular and irregular sleep, drowsiness, alert inactivity, alert activity, and crying. Alert inactivity is the state in which the infant appears to be most able to profit from experience.

## What kinds of sleep patterns are found in newborns?

Newborns sleep for about two-thirds of the day, but in short sleep-wake cycles. A relatively large proportion of the infant's time involves REM sleep, a state that may provide him or her with stimulation even while asleep.

## Why does controversy exist concerning the sleeping arrangements for young infants?

Some cultures encourage the practice of co-sleeping. In addition, some researchers hypothesize that co-sleeping may help to prevent such problems as apnea in infants. These practices stand in contrast to the general belief in our culture that sleeping in one's own room promotes self-reliance and independence. In addition, the medical community currently advises against co-sleeping. One compromise is to have the infant sleep in a crib in the caregiver's room.

## What factors are associated with SIDS? What steps can caretakers take to reduce the likelihood of SIDS?

The risk of *sudden infant death syndrome*, or *SIDS*, is highest at age two to four months. SIDS is also associated with the colder months, poverty, low birth weight, having a cold, being a male, and being a later-born or multiple-birth child. To reduce the risk of SIDS, caregivers should place the infant to sleep on the back, provide a pacifier, eliminate exposure to cigarette smoke and co-sleeping, remove soft bedding materials, and provide adequate ventilation in the child's room.

## BASIC LEARNING PROCESSES

## What are the basic principles of habituation, classical conditioning, and operant conditioning? What does recovery from habituation tell us about the habituation process?

*Habituation* refers to the gradual decline in responding as a result of repeated exposure to an event, a basic form of learning that helps in orienting to new information in the environment. Increased attention to new information following habituation indicates *recovery from habituation (dishabituation)*. This response suggests that infants are able to distinguish between familiar and new events. *Classical conditioning* involves the pairing of a neutral stimulus with one that naturally elicits a response. The neutral stimulus then begins to elicit the response as well. *Operant conditioning* involves the delivery or removal of a reinforcing or punishing stimulus so that behaviors preceding the stimulus increase or decrease.

## What are an unconditioned stimulus, an unconditioned response, a conditioned stimulus, and a conditioned response?

The *unconditioned stimulus (UCS)* is the stimulus that elicits a reflexlike response. No training is required to obtain it. The *unconditioned response (UCR)* is the reaction that results from the presentation of the UCS. The *conditioned stimulus (CS)* is a neutral stimulus that begins to elicit a response similar to the UCS with which it has been paired. The *conditioned response (CR)* is the resulting learned response to the CS.

## How do positive reinforcement, negative reinforcement, negative punishment, and positive punishment affect behavior?

Reinforcement increases the future likelihood of a behavior through the occurrence of a reward (*positive reinforcement*) or the removal of an aversive stimulus (*negative reinforcement*). Punishment results in the decrease of a future behavior through the removal of a desired stimulus (*negative punishment*) or the application of an aversive stimulus (*positive punishment*).

## Why is imitation an important component of learning theory? What evidence exists for imitation in early infancy? What is the significance of deferred imitation?

Imitation is often the means by which infants and children learn the social and cultural behaviors that are important to their community. Research shows that newborns and young infants imitate behaviors such as tongue protrusion, mouth opening, and facial expressions of emotion. *Deferred imitation* refers to the infant's ability to reproduce a model's behavior at a later time. Its presence suggests a capacity for symbolic thinking.

## SENSORY CAPACITIES

## What is the difference between sensation and perception?

*Sensation* refers to the receipt of information by the sensory receptors (eyes, ears) and the brain. *Perception* refers to the organization and interpretation of that information.

## How are attention and other behavioral and physiological measures used to investigate infant sensory and perceptual capacities?

Researchers rely on measures of *attention*, habituation and recovery from habituation, and learning, as well as measures of heart rate and neurological activity of the brain, to study infant sensory and perceptual capacities.

**What limitations exist in infant visual accommodation, saccadic eye movements, smooth visual pursuit, vergence, and other visuomotor capacities? How quickly do these achieve adultlike ability?**

The infant's *visual accommodation* response, the ability to focus at different distances, is initially limited but improves by three months of age. *Saccades*, rapid eye movements to inspect objects, are initially slow and cover small distances. Improvements are seen in the first three to four months and throughout childhood. *Smooth visual pursuit*, maintaining fixation on a moving target, is displayed for only brief periods by newborns but become adultlike by six to eight months. *Vergence*, the ability of the eyes to rotate in opposite directions, is irregular prior to two months. *Visual acuity*, a measure of how well infants can see, improves rapidly in the first six months.

**What kinds of visual problems are found among infants? Why is the correction of these problems important in infancy or early childhood?**

Among the problems infants may display are cataracts, the clouding of the lens, and amblyopia, the failure of vision to develop in one eye. Early treatment is important because visual input may influence the kinds of neural connections that are made. If treatment is delayed, visual capacities may be permanently lost.

**What is infants' ability to perceive color?**

Color vision is limited prior to the age of three months. Initially infants detect primarily red hues but see the full range of colors in successive weeks.

**What are the basic auditory capacities of the infant? How does sound localization develop?**

Infants are sensitive to different frequencies and intensities of sound by six months of age. Their *sound localization* skills start out as reflexive but by four months of age become more deliberate and precise.

**Can newborns and very young infants discriminate smells, tastes, touch, and temperature differences? Can they feel pain?**

Newborns and young infants are responsive to different smells, including the smell of their caregivers. They can discriminate tastes such as sweet, sour, and bitter. Newborns respond to tactile stimulation and changes in temperature, and show through their behavioral responses that they feel pain.

## KEY TERMS AND CONCEPTS

**attention** (p. 174)

**cephalocaudal development** (p. 151)

**conditioned response (CR)** (p. 171)

**conditioned stimulus (CS)** (p. 171)

**deferred imitation** (p. 173)

**glial cell** (p. 154)

**habituation** (p. 169)

**lateralization** (p. 158)

**myelin** (p. 154)

**negative punishment** (p. 171)

**negative reinforcement** (p. 171)

**neuron** (p. 154)

**norm** (p. 151)

**perception** (p. 174)

**plasticity** (p. 157)

**positive punishment** (p. 171)

**positive reinforcement** (p. 171)

**proximodistal development** (p. 152)

**recovery from habituation (dishabituation)** (p. 171)

**reflex** (p. 159)

**rhythmical stereotypy** (p. 161)

**saccades** (p. 177)

**sensation** (p. 174)

**smooth visual pursuit** (p. 177)

**sound localization** (p. 180)

**sudden infant death syndrome (SIDS)** (p. 167)

**unconditioned response (UCR)** (p. 171)

**unconditioned stimulus (UCS)** (p. 171)

**vergence** (p. 177)

**visual accommodation** (p. 176)

**visual acuity** (p. 177)

# 6 PERCEPTION, COGNITION, AND LANGUAGE

The apartment had suddenly grown quiet. The three other babies and their mothers who had been helping to celebrate Chad's first birthday had departed. Only Tanya, Chad's mother, remained with him as the light faded at the end of the day. Picking up the torn gift wrappings, Tanya reflected on the events of the past year. She thought back to her first glimpse of Chad. She had counted his toes and fingers to make sure they were all there. She had wondered aloud, as she first held him, "What do you see? Do you recognize me? What do you hear? Do you like my songs? What are you thinking?" Tanya had vowed to be a good mother, to help Chad learn. She couldn't afford the colorful playland that had beckoned to him at the toy store. But she had picked up some nice secondhand toys and books at a neighbor's yard sale and looked forward to showing them to Chad when the novelty of his new birthday gifts wore off. She wasn't sure if playing with him would make him smarter. She knew, though, that she loved those moments when he seemed to be captivated by her songs and stories about the world.

**NATURE & NURTURE** How do nature and nurture interact in perception, cognition, and language development in infancy?

**SOCIOCULTURAL INFLUENCE** How does the sociocultural context influence perception, cognition, and language development in infancy?

**CONTINUITY/DISCONTINUITY** Are perception, cognition, and language development during infancy continuous or discontinuous?

**RISK/RESILIENCE** What factors promote risk or resilience in perception, cognition, and language development during infancy?

A s you saw in the last chapter, newborns are already engaging in the lifelong process of learning. Their vision, hearing, and other sensory capacities provide enormous amounts of information. But how do infants organize that information? Do they think? What can they remember? How do they embark on the extraordinary but essential process of communicating with others? And, as Tanya wondered, what part do the infant's early experiences play in later development?

These are precisely the kinds of questions psychologists have often asked. Why? Because perception, cognition, and language are fundamental processes by which children come to understand their world. *Perception*, the interpretation of sensory information from visual, auditory, and other receptors, is the vehicle by which we glean information about the world in the first place. **Cognition** refers to those thought processes and mental activities that include attention, memory, concept formation, and problem solving. Remarkably, as you will see in this chapter, there is good evidence that many elements of cognitive processing are present early in infancy. We will also consider the views of two major theorists—Piaget and Vygotsky—in their conceptualizations of cognition in infancy. Finally, we will examine the major milestones in the acquisition of language skills in infancy, a feat that marks the entrance of the child into the world of human communication. All of these processes—perception, cognition, and language—serve as the essential foundation for the more complex aspects of development to be described in the rest of the chapters that follow.

## PERCEPTION

T anya's queries about whether Chad could see or hear as she first held her son are the kinds of questions many parents pose to their newborns even as they seem to provide their own answers by vocalizing, making funny facial expressions, touching, caressing, and rocking the baby. Still, the uncertainty remains: what exactly do infants *perceive* when, for example, caregivers interact with them or when shiny new toys are given to them?

Is the world of the newborn a "great blooming, buzzing confusion" caused by a barrage of unorganized sensations, a view proposed by William James (1890) more than a century ago? If so, the young infant would not apprehend objects or meaningful events at first but would acquire the ability to do so only from learning, over a lengthy period of time, which pattern of basic sensory features is associated with a particular perceptual array (Gordon & Slater, 1998). Perhaps, then, as a result of repeated experience with distinctive sensory input, the infant comes to recognize the human face or to perceive how far away an object is located or to hear a sequence of sounds as a lullaby. According to this viewpoint, perceptual development is a *constructive* process; that is, one of imposing sense and order on the multisensory external world.

James and Eleanor Gibson and many of their students offer a strikingly different opinion of the early perceptual capacities of infants (Pick, 1992). For them, babies come into the world well equipped to respond to the structure and organization of many stimuli and readily perceive the patterns afforded by objects and other sensory events. Some theorists go even further. According to the *nativist* position, the newborn from very early on has, for example, a set of *core principles* and mechanisms to process complex visual cues signifying objects and three-dimensional

**cognition** Processes involved in thinking and mental activity, such as attention, memory, and problem solving.

space, and to interpret other sensory input (Spelke & Newport, 1998). Of course, even within this framework, experience provides ever greater opportunity to refine knowledge about which properties processed by the senses are stable and important, and which can be ignored as relatively uninformative.

## VISUAL PERCEPTION

Because newborns have limited motor skills, we are often tempted to assume that their sensory systems—their eyes, ears, nose, mouth, and skin—must be passive, too, that receptors merely await stimulation. But Eleanor and James Gibson convincingly argue that perceiving is an active process (Gibson, 1966). "We don't simply see, we look" (Gibson, 1988, p. 5). Even neonates actively mobilize sensory receptors to respond to stimulation flowing from their bustling environment, skills that become apparent when we examine their visual perceptual abilities.

**Perception of Pattern and Form**   Few questions fascinate psychologists more than when and how infants recognize patterns and other configurations of visual arrays. Are babies born with the ability to perceive objects as wholes? Some researchers think so. Others have argued the more traditional view: that this capacity is acquired only through extensive visual experience and that infants become aware of or construct perceptions of integrated, holistic, and meaningful visual figures through repeated opportunities to process contours, angles, shading, and other primary sensory features.

As we have already learned, very young infants detect contours of visual stimuli. They also respond to movement associated with contours. Does that necessarily mean that they see a unitary object or pattern? Perhaps not, but evidence suggests that, by two or three months of age, babies are likely to see the whole. Furthermore, infants now additionally inspect and analyze the components of complex stimuli, scanning a variety of their visual properties and carrying out a much more deliberate, organized search (Bronson, 1994). A good example of this developmental change is demonstrated by the **externality effect**: infants younger than about two months of age typically focus on the outer contours of a complex stimulus as if caught by this sensory feature, so that little systematic exploration of its internal characteristics takes place. However, older infants tend to scan its internal features as well (Maurer, 1983; Salapatek, 1975). We saw an illustration of the externality effect in the previous chapter's discussion of preferential looking. Babies younger than two months tend to fixate on the outer contours of the face, such as hair or the chin line; older infants much more frequently inspect internal features, such as the eyes or mouth (see Figure 5.8).

Other experiments provide further evidence that babies perceive entire forms and patterns at least within a few months after birth but continue to show improvement in form perception throughout infancy (Kellman & Arterberry, 1998). One especially convincing illustration involves subjective, or gradient-free, contours. Look at the Kanizsa figure shown in Figure 6.1. You should see a highly visible triangle appearing to stand "above" three black, disklike figures at each of its corners. But closer inspection will reveal that the brain subjectively assumes the triangular form; no contour is present to mark its edges. Infants, perhaps when as young as one or two months and certainly by three to four months, perceive subjective figures, too, a powerful demonstration that perception of form is not always based on a detectable contour (Ghim, 1990; Treiber & Wilcox, 1980).

**Perception of Faces**   Some perceptual patterns are especially significant to the infant. One is the human face. Do even newborns recognize faces, perhaps the faces of their caregivers? Based on the discussion so far, it should not be surprising to learn that, by about two months of age, infants do assign great importance to the

**externality effect**   Tendency for infants younger than two months to focus on the external features of a complex stimulus and explore the internal features less systematically.

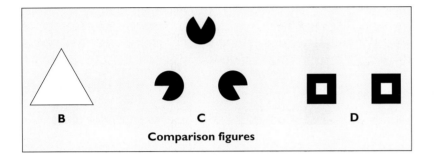

## △ FIGURE 6.1

### Infants' Subjective Perception of Form

Infants, as well as adults, perceive the subjective triangular figure (A) even though no contour is present to define it. After becoming habituated to the Kanizsa figure, babies are shown other figures, including a standard triangle formed by visible contours (B), the indented circular figures rotated to eliminate the subjective triangle (C), or a completely different array of stimuli (D). Infants show the least recovery from habituation to the traditional triangle (B), suggesting that they perceived the triangular shape produced by the Kanizsa figure.

*Source:* Adapted from Trieber & Wilcox (1980).

face, attending to it more than to other, equally complex arrays. But an even earlier, perhaps innate preference also makes evolutionary sense, because faces are a vital source of information for social and emotional relationships.

Some researchers have found evidence that newborns prefer, at least for moving configurations, a facelike image—two eyelike representations above a mouthlike feature—to other arrangements of the same components (Johnson et al., 1991). Mark Johnson and his colleagues (Johnson, 1992; M. H. Johnson et al., 2000) suggest that this inborn preference arises from a fairly primitive subcortical visual system that functions in newborns. Within about two months of age, this primitive system is supplanted by a more sophisticated cortical visual system that explores and discriminates faces from other, equally complex stimuli (Mondloch et al., 1999). The primitive system helps to ensure, however, that the infant gets off to the right start by preferring this extremely important perceptual array. Moreover, newborns display preferences for certain kinds of faces. Alan Slater and his colleagues (Slater et al., 1998) showed babies between one and six days of age pairs of female faces that had been judged by adults as attractive and unattractive. These infants gazed at the attractive faces longer than the unattractive faces. By five months of age, they also prefer looking at pictures of faces with larger eyes, just as do adults (Geldart, Maurer, & Carney, 1999).

On the other hand, infants' early preferences for faces may be simply a manifestation of their general tendency to prefer stimuli with certain kinds of configurations—in this case, stimuli with a top-heavy arrangement of features. In a series of three experiments, Viola Cassia and her colleagues recorded the looking times of

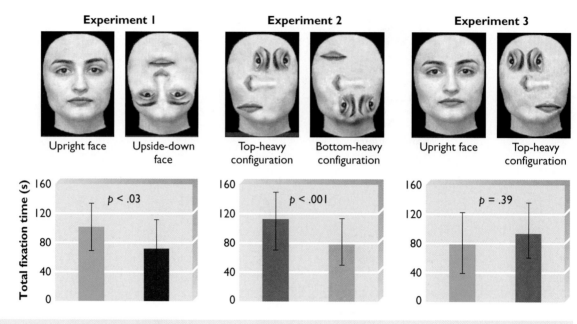

▲ **FIGURE 6.2**

**Newborn Attention to Facelike Stimuli**

Is there a newborn tendency to look at human faces? Or are there other properties of facelike stimuli that capture their attention? To answer this question, Cassia and colleagues (2004) presented newborns with pairs of stimuli that varied in a number of ways. Looking times for each of the pairs are provided along the bottom of the figure. In experiment 1, newborns looked significantly longer at the human face. In experiment 2, they preferred the top-heavy configuration on the left. In experiment 3, there was no significant preference between a correctly configured human face and a top-heavy stimulus that contained the elements of a face. The results argue against an inborn face preference and instead support the idea that infants prefer stimuli that have a greater number of features at the top.

*Source:* Cassia, Turati, & Simion (2004).

newborns as they viewed pairs of facelike stimuli (see Figure 6.2). Newborns showed consistently greater interest in stimuli for which features clustered at the top and showed no specific preference for a correctly ordered human face when it was paired with another top-heavy, but rearranged, facelike stimulus. The researchers concluded that general perceptual preferences were at work rather than a specific tendency to prefer human faces (Cassia, Turati, & Simion, 2004).

When does a baby discriminate his or her mother's face from that of another person? Perhaps within days after birth (Bushnell, Sai, & Mullin, 1989). However, as you might guess, this recognition is based on outer elements, such as hairline or head contours, rather than on a full appreciation of a mother's facial features (Pascalis et al., 1995). By six months of age, differences in brain wave patterns are evident when a baby looks at her mother's face compared with a stranger's face (de Haan & Nelson, 1997). The safest conclusion is that infants are attracted to and identify significant aspects of the human face early in their development and make rapid strides in perceiving and recognizing this important social stimulus.

***Perception of Objects*** Much of the visual environment is made up of objects and their surfaces. How does a baby perceive a rattle apart from the table on which it lies or the family dog as distinct from the floor on which it sits? James J. Gibson (1979) argued that the dynamic flow of visual information provided by kinetic cues is essential to this capacity.

Research carried out by Philip Kellman, Elizabeth Spelke, and others supports Gibson's position regarding the importance of kinetic information for perceiving objects, even in infants as young as three months of age (Kellman, 1996; Kellman & Spelke, 1983). Kellman, Spelke, and their colleagues initiated similar studies

(Balaban, Anderson, & Wisniewski, 1998). Moreover, the ability to detect satisfying musical phrasings may be important not only for appreciating music but also for the phrasing and sound rhythms that commonly underlie speech.

**Speech** Research on infants' hearing abilities has often been conducted to answer another question: How soon do babies perceive human speech? Practically right from birth, it seems. Two- to six-month-old infants show a distinct preference for human speech over nonspeech sounds by listening to it longer (Vouloumanos & Werker, 2004). And the language areas of the brain show greater activation when infants only a few days old listen to speech as opposed to nonspeech sounds (Peña et al., 2003). Most important for our understanding of language development, however, infants respond in specific ways to small acoustic variations in human speech that distinguish one word or part of a word from another.

The smallest unit of sound that affects the meaning of a word is called a **phoneme**. Phonemes are surprisingly complicated bursts of acoustic energy. For example, a difference of less than one-fiftieth of a second in the onset or transition of a frequency of sound is enough for adults to discriminate the distinctive phonemes /p/, /b/, and /t/ in the sounds *pa, ba,* and *ta.* (Linguists use slashes to identify the phonemes of a language.) Are infants able to hear the differences? Indeed they are. In fact, before six months of age babies distinguish all the important sounds in any of the hundreds of languages spoken around the world (Werker & Desjardins, 1995).

From these findings, some who study language acquisition argue that babies are born with a "speech module," an innate capacity to detect and process the subtle and complicated sounds that make up human language (Fodor, 1983). The complexity of language acquisition, according to this view, requires a specialized ability because the cognitive skills of infants and young children are so limited. An alternative view is that phoneme discrimination hinges on broader, more general auditory capacities, capacities not limited to processing speech sounds or even necessarily unique to humans but that infants are able to exploit quite early in development.

What evidence exists for either of these positions? Certain research findings contribute to the view that speech perception involves special language-oriented mechanisms. These are based on the concept of **categorical perception**, the classification of sounds as the same even when they differ on some continuous physical dimension, except when on opposite sides of a critical juncture. For example, the English consonants /b/ and /p/ in the sounds *ba* and *pa* differ only in voice onset time (VOT), the period during which the vocal chords begin to vibrate relative to the release of air by the vocal apparatus. Small changes in VOT are typically not heard as more or less like *ba* or *pa.* Instead, English speakers hear only *ba* as long as VOT continues to fall on one side of the categorical boundary and only *pa* when it falls on the other side. But if the difference in VOT crosses a critical point, the phoneme boundary, the two sounds are readily distinguishable. Infants as young as one month already demonstrate categorical perception for many different speech sounds (Aslin, 1987b; Kuhl, 1987). These findings imply that there might be something special (and innate) about how speech signals are processed.

However, many researchers remain uncertain about whether babies are born with a special sensory mode for speech (Saffran, Werker, & Werner, 2006). For one thing, categorical perception can be observed with some sounds other than those found in speech. For another, monkeys, and even chinchillas, also distinguish speech sounds categorically (Kuhl & Miller, 1978; Kuhl & Padden, 1983), a finding that further argues against a specialized innate human ability to process phonemes.

## INTERMODAL PERCEPTION

We have considered the development of seeing, hearing, and other senses in isolation from one another, but, of course, most objects and events bombard us with multiple sensory inputs. The sight of a cup provides information about how to shape the mouth to drink from it. The toddler who hears his mother's voice from

**KEY THEME**
**NATURE & NURTURE**

---

**phoneme** Smallest unit of sound that changes the meanings of words.

**categorical perception** Inability to distinguish among sounds that vary on some basic physical dimension except when those sounds lie at opposite sides of a critical juncture point on that dimension.

another room expects to see her when he walks into that room. We often perceive these experiences as integrated and coordinated, and draw perceptual inferences because of the typical relationships observed from multimodal stimulation. Sometimes, of course, we can be fooled by all these correlated experiences: a good ventriloquist really does make the dummy appear to be talking!

How does the capacity to integrate several sensory inputs, referred to as **intermodal perception**, begin, and how important is it for development? One traditional view is that input received via the various senses is initially *unimodal*; that is, the senses function separately and independently. Only after repeated multimodal experiences, this argument runs, do babies come to recognize the correlations among various sensory inputs. Thus intermodal perception involves, for example, learning that, when objects are shaken, some rattle and make a noise, but others do not; that material that feels soft can also look soft; and that a square-looking peg will not fit into a round-looking hole. According to this viewpoint, intermodal perception stems from *integration* or *enrichment* through the repeated association of sensations from two or more modalities. Alternatively, from a more Piagetian perspective, it is the outcome of constructing multisensory schemes from correlated sensory experiences (Lickliter & Bahrick, 2000).

But others have suggested that some intermodal perception is already possible at birth (Gibson, 1982; Gibson, 1979). According to this perspective, a primitive unity exists among the senses in early infancy, and with development and experience, **perceptual differentiation**, the ability to distinguish information coming through each particular sensory modality, occurs. A related aspect of this point of view is that important sensory information is often *amodal*; that is, not tied to a particular sensory modality but shared across two or more of them. Examples of amodal characteristics of sensory input are *temporal synchrony*; that is, the correlated onset and offset of stimulation that can occur between two or more sensory modalities (such as hearing someone begin and stop speaking while simultaneously seeing their lips start and stop), and tempo and rhythm, common components of both auditory and visual experience.

Some researchers believe that the ability to process amodal properties is especially important for early perceptual development (Bahrick & Lickliter, 2000; Lewkowicz, 2000). For example, Lorraine Bahrick and Robert Lickliter (2000) suggest that the redundancy of different perceptual cues that contribute to temporal synchrony attracts the infant's attention. As a consequence of this attentional bias, infants begin to learn about arbitrarily correlated properties and qualities of objects and events, such as the voice that belongs to a particular parent, the bark that signifies the family's pet dog, or the verbal label for a particular color. Some go so far as to claim that this kind of learning begins very shortly after birth (Slater et al., 1999). But regardless of how early it begins, this perspective emphasizes that intermodal properties cannot be ignored as important components in perceptual development very early in infancy.

***Sight and Sound*** To determine whether infants link visual and auditory events, Elizabeth Spelke (1976) developed a simple procedure in which four-month-olds could look at either of two films shown side by side. At the same time, the infants could hear a soundtrack coming from a speaker located between the two viewing screens. The soundtrack matched events in one of the two films; for example, an unfamiliar woman engaged in a game of peekaboo or someone playing a percussion instrument. Would infants pay more attention to the film synchronized with the soundtrack? Spelke found this to be the case, at least when the percussion sounds could be heard.

Before four months of age, infants can also infer that a sound made by one object versus multiple objects hitting a surface should match up to visual arrays containing one object versus multiple objects (Bahrick, 2002). Five-month-olds even link sounds such as an auto or a train coming or going with concordant visual progressions of approaching and retreating movement (Pickens, 1994; Walker-Andrews & Lennon, 1985).

Experience may have permitted three- to five-month-olds to learn about these relationships. However, other research suggests that newborns quickly master the

**intermodal perception** Coordination of sensory information to perceive or make inferences about the characteristics of an object.

**perceptual differentiation** Process postulated by Eleanor and James Gibson in which experience contributes to the ability to make increasingly finer perceptual discriminations and to distinguish stimulation arising from each sensory modality.

association between a sound and a visible toy. After seeing a toy presented in several different locations and making a particular sound for brief periods of time, neonates displayed increased attention if the sound originated apart from the toy or if it accompanied a different toy (Morrongiello, Fenwick, & Chance, 1998). Thus even newborns possess some kind of amodal process that guides and unifies sensory information from separate senses, such as hearing and vision (Kellman & Arterberry, 1998).

Intermodal perception in infants extends to social and linguistic information as well. For example, three-and-a-half-month-olds are likely to look at that parent, seated to one side, whose voice is coming from a speaker centered in front of the baby (Spelke & Owsley, 1979). By six months of age, babies hearing a strange male or female voice recite a nursery rhyme look longer at a face of the same sex than at a face of the opposite sex (Walker-Andrews et al., 1991). In addition, babies are able to match the maturity of a face with its voice; they look more at the face of an adult or a child, depending on who is heard talking from a central speaker (Bahrick, Netto, & Hernandez-Reif, 1998). By two months of age, babies also recognize auditory-visual correspondence in people who are speaking, attending more to facial expressions articulating vowel sounds that match than to facial expressions that do not match what they hear (Patterson & Werker, 2003).

**Sight and Touch**   By six months of age, infants who explore an object with their hands alone can also recognize it by sight alone (Pineau & Streri, 1990; Rose, Gottfried, & Bridger, 1981; Ruff & Kohler, 1978). But coordination of some visual and tactile information exists much earlier, when the mouth is used to explore objects. In one experiment, one-month-olds showed greater visual attention to a hard, rigid object or a soft, deformable object, depending on which they had been given time to suck (Gibson & Walker, 1984). Other research reveals that infants five months of age exhibit intermodal perception between proprioceptive (or internal body cues) and visual cues. Infants showed differential visual attention to point light displays (similar to those used in studying sensitivity to biological motion) depending on whether those displays mirrored the motion produced by the movement of their own hidden legs or the movement of the legs of another infant (Schmuckler & Fairhall, 2001).

Babies can even be surprised by a discrepancy between vision and touch. Emily Bushnell (1981) showed infants a solid object within a box. Its location was distorted by mirrors. When babies reached for it, they touched another object that differed in size, shape, and texture. Infants younger than nine months failed to investigate the novel object actively or to search for the one they could see, but older infants did both. Thus there is substantial evidence that infants before a year of age make inferences about their world based on intermodal perception.

F O R ◆ Y O U R ◆ R E V I E W

◆ What sound patterns do infants prefer to listen to?

◆ What arguments exist for or against the view that infants possess an innate capacity to detect phonemes?

◆ How does intermodal perception develop?

◆ What evidence exists to show that infants recognize the correlation between visual and auditory information as well as visual and tactile cues?

## Cognition

Tanya wondered aloud what one-year-old Chad was thinking. Does it even make sense to use the word *thinking* when we are describing an infant? Are we attributing too much competence to a child who is so young and who has so much growing yet to do? Perhaps infants do not think in the same ways as older children and adults, but Piaget and Vygotsky, two preeminent theorists in developmental psychology, saw the roots of complex thought in infancy. Even more compelling evidence for "thinking" in infants comes from recent studies of how they react to disappearing objects and how they behave in simple problem-solving situations.

## PIAGET'S THEORY AND INFANCY

As we saw in the chapter titled "Themes and Theories," one of the most important beliefs espoused by Piaget is that children actively construct their knowledge of the world, incorporating new information into existing knowledge structures, or *schemes*, through *assimilation*. As a result, schemes are modified or expanded through the process of *accommodation*. To Piaget, this process clearly begins in infancy. For example, the young infant may attempt to grasp a new, round squeeze toy, relying on a pre-existing scheme for grasping objects. As a consequence, that scheme becomes altered to include information about grasping round objects. The outcome is greater *equilibrium* or balance among the pieces of knowledge that make up the child's understanding. Thus what a child can understand or mentally grasp at any given point in time is heavily influenced by what the child already knows or understands. At the same time, the child's schemes are constantly transformed, as equilibrium is continually disrupted by the never-ending flow of information from the surrounding world.

**⊶ KEY THEME**
**CONTINUITY/DISCONTINUITY**

Piaget maintained that thought processes become reorganized into distinct stages at several points in development. Although the schemes in early stages lay the foundation for later knowledge structures, their reorganization is so thorough that schemes in one stage bear little resemblance to those in other stages. According to Piaget, the child progresses through the *sensorimotor, preoperational, concrete operational*, and *formal operational* stages, reflecting major transitions in thought in which early, action-based schemes evolve into symbolic, then logical, and finally abstract mental structures.

Piaget claimed that all children progress through the stages of cognitive development in an invariable sequence in which no stage is skipped. In addition, each stage contains a period of formation and a period of attainment. When the child begins a new stage, his schemes are somewhat unstable and loosely organized. By the end of the stage, his schemes are well formed and well organized. Even though Piaget provided age norms for the acquisition of each stage, he believed that, because cognitive development is the result of maturational factors working in concert with environmental experiences, some children may reach a stage more quickly or more slowly, depending on the opportunities for learning that their environment has provided. Ultimately, though, the evolution of thought shows a universal regularity, according to Piaget. The foundations for this course of cognitive growth are laid down during the sensorimotor stage.

***The Sensorimotor Stage (Birth to Two Years)*** The most striking characteristic of human thinking during the **sensorimotor stage** is its solid basis in action. Each time the child reaches for an object, sucks on a nipple, or crawls along the floor, she is obtaining varied feedback about her body and its relationship to the environment, which becomes part of her internal schemes. At first, the infant's movements are reflexive, not deliberate or planned. As the child passes through each of the six substages of the sensorimotor period, outlined in Table 6.1, her actions become increasingly goal directed and aimed at solving problems. Moreover, she is able to distinguish self from environment and learns about the properties of objects in that environment and how they are related to one another.

A significant accomplishment of the sensorimotor stage is the infant's progression toward **means-ends behavior**, the deliberate use of an action to accomplish some goal. During the early substages of sensorimotor development, the infant often

**sensorimotor stage** In Piagetian theory, the first stage of cognitive development, from birth to approximately two years of age, in which thought is based primarily on action.

**means-ends behavior** Deliberate behavior employed to attain a goal.

**Table 6.1  The Six Substages of Piaget's Sensorimotor Stage**

| Substage | Major Features | Object Concept |
|---|---|---|
| **Reflexive Activity (Birth–1 month)** | Formation and modification of early schemes based on reflexes such as sucking, looking, and grasping | No attempt to locate objects that have disappeared |
| **Primary Circular Reactions (1–4 months)** | Repetition of behaviors that produce interesting results centered on own body (e.g., Lucienne accidentally, then repeatedly, touches her quilt) | No attempt to locate objects that have disappeared |
| **Secondary Circular Reactions (4–8 months)** | Repetition of behaviors that produce interesting results in the external world (e g., Lucienne accidentally, then repeatedly, kicks the dolls in her bassinet) | Search for objects that have dropped from view or are partially hidden |
| **Coordination of Secondary Schemes (8–12 months)** | Combination of actions to achieve a goal (e.g., Lucienne pulls a doll to make her bassinet hood sway) | Search for completely hidden objects |
| **Tertiary Circular Reactions (12–18 months)** | Experimentation with different actions to achieve the same goal or observe the outcomes (e.g., Laurent drops a case of soap, then a piece of bread) | Ability to follow visible displacements of an object |
| **Invention of New Means Through Mental Combinations (18–24 months)** | Thinking through of potential solutions to problems and imitation of absent models (e.g., Jacqueline imitates her playmate's tantrum) | Ability to follow invisible displacements of an object |

initiates actions accidentally rather than purposefully. When Piaget's daughter Lucienne was almost four months old, she was observed to shake her bassinet

> by moving her legs violently (bending and unbending them, etc.), which makes the cloth dolls swing from the hood. Lucienne looks at them, smiling, and recommences at once. (Piaget, 1952b, pp. 157–158)

Lucienne repeated her kicking to make the dolls shake in what Piaget calls a *circular reaction*, the repetition of a motor act to experience the pleasure it brings. Her first kick, however, was totally accidental. Several months afterward, when Lucienne was eight months old, Piaget placed a new doll over the hood of her bassinet. This time her behavior revealed a greater degree of intentionality.

> She looks at it for a long time, touches it, then feels it by touching its feet, clothes, head, etc. She then ventures to grasp it, which makes the hood sway. She then pulls the doll while watching the effects of this movement. (Piaget, 1952b, p. 256)

Throughout the first two years, the child increasingly uses actions as a means to obtain some end or goal. He also experiments with new means to reach the same goal, as Piaget's son Laurent did when he successively dropped a soap case and then a piece of bread to investigate how objects fall.

A second aspect of sensorimotor development is the child's gradual separation of self from the external environment. Initially, the child derives pleasure from actions that center on her own body. At three months of age, Lucienne "strikes her quilt with her right hand; she scratches it while carefully watching what she is doing, then lets it go, grasps it again, etc." (Piaget, 1952b, p. 92). The circular reaction, in this case, was repeated because of the satisfying sensations it brought to Lucienne's hand. Weeks later, in the episode of the swinging dolls, Lucienne's

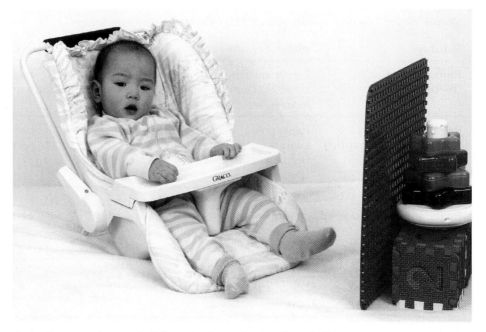

A significant attainment in infancy is the understanding of object permanence. Children under three to four months of age act as if a hidden or obstructed object no longer exists. By age eight months, though, children will remove a barrier to look for a hidden object.

kicking in the bassinet produced a gratifying result in the external environment. In general, the child becomes less centered on the self and more oriented to the external world.

The completion of the sensorimotor stage and the beginning of the next stage is signaled by the child's display of *deferred imitation*, the ability to imitate a model that is no longer present. At age sixteen months, Piaget's daughter Jacqueline was playing with a boy who suddenly had a dramatic temper tantrum. The next day, the normally well-behaved Jacqueline mimicked the little boy's behaviors with remarkable accuracy. To do so, she must have had the ability to *represent* the boy's overt behaviors in internal form and to draw on that representation hours later. This ability to represent events and objects internally marks the beginning of a major transition in thought.

***The Object Concept***   An important accomplishment of the sensorimotor stage is the attainment of the **object concept**, or *object permanence*. Infants who possess the object concept realize that objects continue to exist even though they are not within immediate sight or within reach to be acted on. Up to three months of age, the saying "Out of sight, out of mind" characterizes the child's understanding of objects. At about four months of age, he will lift a cloth from a partially covered object or show some reaction, such as surprise or puzzlement, when an object disappears. At about eight months of age, he will search for an object that has completely disappeared; for example, when it has been covered entirely by a cloth. In the last two phases of the attainment of the object concept, he will be able to follow visible and then invisible displacements of the object. In the first instance, the twelve-month-old will follow and find a toy that has been moved from under one cloth to another, as long as the movement is performed while he is watching. In the second instance, the eighteen-month-old can find an object moved from location A to location B, even if the displacement from A to B is done while he is not looking. Thus Piaget believed that the object concept emerges late in the first year of life and does not become fully elaborated until the second year.

**object concept**   Realization that objects exist even when they are not within view. Also called *object permanence*.

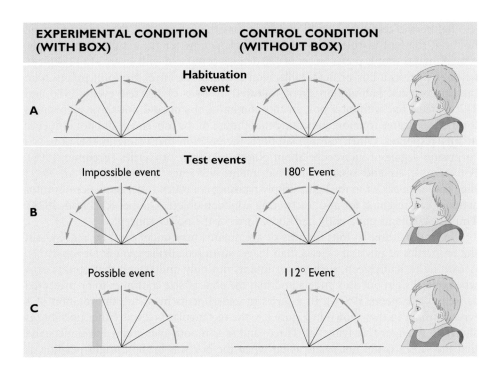

| EXPERIMENTAL CONDITION (WITH BOX) | CONTROL CONDITION (WITHOUT BOX) | |
|---|---|---|

**Habituation event**

A

**Test events**

Impossible event / 180° Event

B

Possible event / 112° Event

C

## ▲ FIGURE 6.6

### Do Infants Have an Object Concept?

In Baillargeon's experiment, infants were habituated to a screen rotating 180 degrees (A). Next, infants in the impossible-event condition saw the screen appearing to pass through the location of a box (B, on left), whereas infants in the *possible-event* condition saw the screen stop at the location of the box (C, on left). Infants in the *impossible-event* condition looked significantly longer at this event, suggesting that they were puzzled by what they saw and therefore had an object concept. The control conditions (shown at right) were included to make sure the infants were not responding to the arc of the screen's movement.

*Source:* Adapted from Baillargeon (1987a).

Not all researchers think that the object concept is a relatively late accomplishment in infancy. Renée Baillargeon (1987a) believes she has obtained evidence showing that infants as young as four months of age have a rudimentary understanding of the continuing existence of objects. She conducted a unique experiment in which infants behaved as if they understood that an object continued to exist even when it was concealed by a screen. Figure 6.6 shows the phases of this experiment. At first, infants observed a screen that rotated back and forth 180 degrees over repeated trials. As you might expect, they eventually showed habituation of fixation to this display. Next, a box was placed behind the screen. Initially, when the screen was still flat against the table, the box was visible, but as the screen rotated away from the child, it hid the box from view. In the possible-event condition, the screen stopped moving at the point where it hit the box. In the impossible-event condition, the box was surreptitiously removed and the screen passed through the space the box would have occupied. As you already know, infants in a habituation experiment should look longer at the novel event, in this case, the screen that rotated only 112 degrees. However, these infants looked significantly longer at the impossible event, apparently drawn in by the fact that the screen was moving through the space where the object should have been. Because infants are presumed to look longer at the stimulus display that goes against their internal knowledge, this procedure is often called the *violation-of-expectation* method.

Before the researcher could conclude that the infants had the object concept, however, she had to rule out alternative explanations for the results. For example, what if infants simply prefer an arc of 180 degrees compared with an arc of 112 degrees, whether there is a box or not? Baillargeon included a control group of infants who saw the original habituation event followed by each of the test events (180 and 112 degrees) but without a box. In this condition, infants did not show preferences for the 180-degree rotation, indicating that the arc of the movement did not influence infants' responses. Other research supports the position that young infants possess a surprising degree of knowledge about objects and their properties (Bremner, 1998). For example, six-and-a-half-month-old infants will reach in the dark for an object they have seen earlier in the light. Simply reaching is a much easier sequence of motor actions than reaching for and uncovering a hidden object (Goubet & Clifton, 1998). Thus these infants apparently had some form of the object concept.

In fact, by three to four months of age, infants may understand far more about the properties of physical objects than Piaget surmised (Baillargeon & DeVos, 1991). According to Baillargeon, such young infants not only understand that objects exist when out of sight but also understand that the objects' size continues to be preserved as well (Baillargeon, 1987b). In a series of experiments involving the rotation of a screen similar to that shown in Figure 6.6, the rectangular box was either upright (as shown in the figure) or lying flat. Three- and four-month-olds seemed to understand that the screen could not rotate as far when the box was in the upright position as it could when lying down. Moreover, if the object was something that could be squeezed, such as a ball of gauze the infants had previously played with, they were not surprised by the continued rotation of the screen in front of it. They did show surprise when the screen seemed to rotate past the position of a hard and rigid box. Apparently, young infants quickly move beyond simply understanding that an object exists under a cover or behind a barrier; they also develop ideas about physical properties of objects, such as their height and rigidity (Baillargeon, 1995).

Similarly, experiments by Elizabeth Spelke and her colleagues show that infants seem to appreciate the concept of *solidity*, the fact that one object cannot pass through the space occupied by another object. In one study, represented in Figure 6.7, two-and-a-half-month-old infants saw a ball roll across a ramp and behind a screen for several trials. Next they saw the ball roll as a partially visible box blocked its path. When the screen was removed, infants viewed the ball either resting in front of the box or at the end of the ramp. Infants looked significantly longer at the impossible result, the ball at the end of the ramp, suggesting to Spelke that infants recognize the concept of solidity. Some of Spelke's other experiments imply that young infants also understand the principle of *continuity*, the idea that objects move continuously in time and space (Spelke et al., 1992).

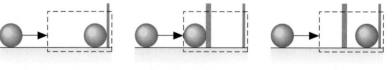

**Habituation**          **Consistent**          **Inconsistent**

◢ **FIGURE 6.7**

**Infants' Concepts of Solidity**

In an experiment conducted by Elizabeth Spelke and her colleagues, two-and-a-half-month-old infants were habituated to the scene on the left, a ball rolling across a ramp. In the test phase, infants saw events that were either consistent or inconsistent with the principle that one object cannot pass through the space occupied by another. The infants looked longer at the inconsistent event, leading Spelke and her colleagues to postulate that this early knowledge about objects is innate.

*Source:* Spelke et al. (1992).

*The Core Knowledge Hypothesis* The results of the violation-of-expectation experiments have led some contemporary researchers to formulate the **core knowledge hypothesis**, the idea that young infants possess innate knowledge concerning important fundamental properties of objects (Baillargeon, 2001; Spelke & Hespos, 2001). The implication is that even young infants possess a startling degree of competence as they encounter items and events in the world. Core knowledge becomes elaborated with experience, according to these theorists, but the infant starts out with much more capability than Piaget presumed. There are some problematic findings for those in this camp, however. For example, Neil Berthier and his colleagues (Berthier et al., 2000) had two- and three-year-olds participate in a task similar to the one shown in Figure 6.7. In this case, however, the researchers asked the children to retrieve the ball from behind one of several doors positioned in front or in back of the wall. Children under age three performed poorly; they did not open the door right in front of the wall. If infants have early knowledge of the concept of solidity and can represent hidden objects, why would children several years older fail to locate the object? At the very least, the findings suggest that a great deal of knowledge about the locations and properties of objects develops in infancy and beyond (Butler, Berthier, & Clifton, 2002; Keen & Berthier, 2004).

The contrasting point of view is that infants' performance in violation-of-expectation tasks is due not to innate core knowledge but rather to perceptual and memory processes that detect more broadly that "something is different" or "something is familiar" (Bogartz, Shinskey, & Schilling, 2000). It is wrong, say the critics, to imbue young infants with more advanced or specialized cognitive and representational skills about the properties of objects than is warranted (Haith, 1998; Smith, 1999b). Rather, it is better to assume that basic, general cognitive processes are responsible for the behaviors we observe. Knowledge about objects is built, say many of these theorists, through rapid advances in attention and memory abilities, as well as the child's experiences in the world. Experts hope that well-designed experiments that rule out competing explanations will help to resolve this controversy (Aslin, 2000; Cohen & Cashon, 2006).

Even if young infants do have some form of object concept, why do they fail to retrieve a covered object prior to eight months of age? One possibility is that infants do not yet have the skill to solve means-ends tasks; that is, to develop and execute a plan to reach for and uncover the hidden object. However, seven-month-old infants will pull down a transparent screen to reach for an object behind it; they do not make this response when the screen is opaque (Shinskey & Munakata, 2001). A means-ends deficit cannot account for such results, as, under some circumstances, we see that infants can put into action a sequence of steps in order to obtain a visible object. Yuko Munakata and her colleagues hypothesize that infants' representations of hidden objects are weaker than for visible objects and thus make search tasks more demanding (Munakata et al., 1997). As infants have more experiences in the world, however, and the neural networks that underlie representations of objects become strengthened, children become more successful in retrieving hidden objects (Munakata, 2001, 2006).

*The A-Not-B Error* A common error that occurs when the child is about seven to nine months of age is the A$\overline{\text{B}}$, or **A-not-B error**. In this task, an object is hidden in location A, found by the infant, and then, in full view of the infant, moved to location B. Piaget observed that the child would mistakenly but persistently search for the object in location A. He hypothesized that the infant's incomplete knowledge of the object concept leads to this error, in large part because the sensorimotor scheme for searching in location A still controls the child's thought. Researchers, however, have generated several alternative hypotheses about the reasons for the A-not-B error.

For one thing, memory difficulties may play a role. Eight- to twelve-month-old infants are less likely to make the A$\overline{\text{B}}$ error when they can search for the object at B immediately, as opposed to after a delay. In addition, when watching infants make the A$\overline{\text{B}}$ error, Adele Diamond noticed that, even though some infants mistakenly reached for A, they actually looked at B, the correct location of the hidden toy (see

**core knowledge hypothesis** The idea that infants possess innate knowledge of certain properties of objects.

**A-not-B error** Error that an infant makes when an object is hidden in location A, found by the infant, and then, in full view of the infant, moved to location B. Piaget observed that the child will mistakenly but persistently search for the object in location A.

▲ **FIGURE 6.8**

**Alternative Explanations for the A$\overline{B}$ Error**

A toy has been hidden first in the right well (location A), then is placed in the well on the left (location B), as shown in the first photograph. The next three photographs show that after the object is hidden, the infant reaches for location A even though he looks persistently at location B. The looking behavior suggests that he has the object concept when there are visible displacements of the object. Diamond (1991) believes that one reason infants reach for the incorrect location is because they fail to inhibit motor responses.

Figure 6.8) (Diamond, 1985). They behaved as though they knew the correct location of the toy but could not stop themselves from reaching to A. In other studies, adult monkeys, which normally perform successfully on the A$\overline{B}$ task, make mistakes identical to those of seven-to-nine-month-old human infants when lesions are made in very specific areas of their frontal cortex; these are the brain areas that control the inhibition of responses (Diamond & Goldman-Rakic, 1989). Diamond (1991) proposes that infants have the object concept well before age seven months but, due to the physical immaturity of this special cortical area, they cannot suppress their tendency to reach for location A. Lending support to this hypothesis are data showing that infants who are successful in the A$\overline{B}$ task display more powerful brain electrical activity from the same frontal region of the cortex (Bell & Fox, 1992). Moreover, when infants' responses to the A$\overline{B}$ situation are assessed using the habituation procedure rather than using the child's motor response, they look longer at an impossible event (a toy moves from A to B and is then found at A) than at a possible event (a toy moves from A to B and is found at B) (Ahmed & Ruffman, 1998). Thus infants seem to know the correct location of the transposed object but do not show this knowledge when tasks require reaching.

Another account of the A$\overline{B}$ error states that infants may not be able to efficiently update their representation of the object's location after it is moved to B; in fact, they perform better when the A and B locations are covered with distinctive shapes and colors (Bremner & Bryant, 2001). Perhaps the most comprehensive description comes from a dynamic systems perspective. In this view, the infant's errors arise from competing tendencies of different strengths: the strong memory of the object at A and a deteriorating plan to look at location B in the face of few perceptual cues (Smith et al., 1999; Spencer, Smith, & Thelen, 2001). Any of several factors can improve performance: better memory for spatial locations, stronger perceptual cues about the object's location, or heightened attention to the events in the task. As you can see, we now have several alternatives to Piaget's notion that the object concept relies on an internal, sensorimotor-based scheme, all of them emphasizing changes in the ability of infants to process information.

***Early Spatial Reasoning***   From early infancy onward, children organize the objects in their world according to relationships in space. Where does the infant find her shoes or an enticing snack? Usually she has developed a mental picture of her home and other familiar physical spaces to guide her search for missing objects or to reach a desired location. As he did for many other areas of cognitive development, Piaget set forth some of the first hypotheses about the child's concepts of space, ideas that researchers have subsequently modified or enriched.

During infancy, Piaget (1954) stated, the child's knowledge of space is based on her sensorimotor activities within that space. For example, the child searches for objects by using *egocentric* frames of reference. In other words, if a ball disappears under a couch or chair, the infant represents its location in relation to her own body ("to the left of my arm") rather than in relation to some other external object ("to the left of the door"). Only with the advent of symbolic ability at the end of the sensorimotor stage are children able to use frames of reference external to the self.

Many researchers have confirmed that infants, in the absence of environmental cues, indeed rely on the positions of their own body in space to locate objects. For example, in one study, nine-month-olds readily learned to locate an item hidden under one of two covers situated to either their left or their right. Shifted to the opposite side of the table, however, they looked in the wrong location because of their egocentric responding (Bremner & Bryant, 1977). When the investigator made the covers of the two hiding locations of distinctively different colors, infants were able to locate the hidden toy even when they were moved to a different position around the table (Bremner, 1978).

Toward the end of the first year, children quite literally reach out into the world for cues denoting spatial relationships. Infants slightly under nine months of age use landmarks denoting the physical locations of objects to find them in larger spatial environments. When playing peekaboo, for example, infants in one study were assisted in locating a face when different-colored lanterns were positioned by the correct window. These cues helped, even if their own positions were shifted (Lew, Bremner, & Lefkovitch, 2000). Thus infants are not as egocentric as Piaget claimed when other external information is available to assist them in finding objects. Moreover, it is likely that the infant's growing ability to locomote toward the end of the first year—to crawl and walk around in his environment—is connected in some way to advances in spatial reasoning (Newcombe & Huttenlocher, 2006).

## F O R • Y O U R • R E V I E W

◆ What are the infant's chief accomplishments during the sensorimotor stage according to Piaget? What is the primary basis for thought in this stage?

◆ What is the object concept? What are the stages of acquisition of this concept according to Piaget?

◆ What is the core knowledge hypothesis? What research findings support this position on infants' conceptual knowledge? What are the criticisms of this point of view?

◆ What is the A-not-B error? How does Piaget account for this error? What are some other explanations for the occurrence of this behavior in infants?

◆ What principles guide infants' spatial understanding according to Piaget? Does research support his point of view?

## CONCEPTS

Aside from learning about the properties of single objects, as in the object concept, children also quickly learn about relationships that can exist among sets of objects. Sometimes objects resemble one another perceptually; they seem to "go together" because they are the same color or shape. At other times, the relationships among objects can be more complex. The perceptual similarities may be less obvious; moreover, some sets can be embedded within others. Cocker spaniels and Great Danes, two different-looking dogs, can be classified together in the group "dogs," and both breeds fit into a larger category of "animals." In each case, we are describing children's **concepts**, the organization of information on the basis of some general or abstract principle.

As one psychologist put it, "Concepts and categories serve as the building blocks for human thought and behavior" (Medin, 1989). Concepts allow us to group isolated pieces of information on the basis of common themes or properties. The result is greater efficiency in cognitive processing. Suppose someone tells you, "A quarf is an animal." Without even seeing one, you already know many of the quarf's properties: it breathes, eats, locomotes, and so on. Because concepts are linked to one of the most powerful human capabilities—language—as well as to other aspects of cognition, understanding how different kinds of concepts develop is an important concern of developmental psychologists. Many modern-day accounts of concept development arose out of attempts to test or expand the groundbreaking ideas of Piaget about how children understand classes of objects. Today's research findings are quite clear. Already in infancy, we see progress in how children think conceptually.

***Early Classification Skills***  One of the earliest signs of classification skills in young children occurs toward the end of the first year, when children begin to group perceptually similar objects together. Susan Sugarman (1982, 1983) carefully watched the behaviors of one- to three-year-olds as they played with successive sets of stimuli that could be grouped into two classes, such as plates and square blocks, or dolls and boats. Even the youngest children displayed a spontaneous tendency to group similar-looking objects together by pointing consecutively to items that were alike. With the habituation paradigm, it has also been possible to show that three- and four-month-old infants respond to different classes of items, such as dogs versus cats or horses, on the basis of perceptual similarity (Oakes, Coppage, & Dingel, 1997; Quinn, Eimas, & Rosenkranz, 1993). But what is especially important to the emergence of more fully developed concepts is that as infants get older, they notice the *correlations* among perceptual features—that wings typically go with beaks, for example, or that long ears consistently accompany small, puffy tails (Younger, 2003).

Between ages one and three, children experience a rapid growth in classification skills. One important way in which we see changes is in terms of the bases they use for grouping objects together. For example, at fourteen months of age, infants successively touch objects that appear in common contexts, such as "kitchen things" and "bathroom things" (Mandler, Fivush, & Reznick, 1987). Two-year-olds will match items on the basis of *thematic relations*, clustering items that function together or complement one another, such as a baby bottle and a baby (Markman & Hutchinson, 1984). They will also occasionally classify items *taxonomically*, grouping objects that may not look alike on the basis of some abstract principle, such as a banana with an apple (Ross, 1980). Taxonomic classification is easier for young children when they hear that objects from the same category share the same label even though they may not look very much alike (for instance, a panther and a tabby house cat are both called "cats") or when their similarities are pointed out in some other way (Deák & Bauer, 1996; Nazzi & Gopnik, 2001).

In fact, mothers often provide varied information of this sort to their young children about objects and their membership in categories, saying such things as "That's a desk. That's a desk, too." Or they point sequentially to objects that come from the same conceptual group (Gelman et al., 1998). As children encounter new

**concepts**  Definition of a set of information on the basis of some general or abstract principle.

**Sequence of events I + I = I or 2**

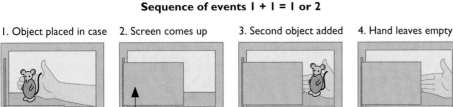

1. Object placed in case    2. Screen comes up    3. Second object added    4. Hand leaves empty

**Then either: possible outcome**      **or: impossible outcome**

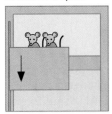

5. Screen drops....    revealing 2 objects      5. Screen drops....    revealing I object

◁ **FIGURE 6.9**

**Can Infants Add?**

This figure shows the sequence of events used in Wynn's (1992a) experiments with five-month-olds. Infants first saw a hand place a mouse doll in the display. Next, a screen rotated up to hide the doll. A hand appeared with a second doll, placing it behind the screen and leaving the display empty-handed. During the test, the screen dropped down and revealed either two dolls (possible event) or one doll (impossible event). Infants looked longer at the impossible event, suggesting they knew something about the additive properties of numbers.

*Source:* Adapted from Wynn (1992a).

instances of a category, they incorporate information about those examples into their prior knowledge about the category (Carmichael & Hayes, 2001). And, as children grow older, they become capable of using a wider range of relations to classify objects so that their exclusive reliance on shared perceptual features lessens.

***Infants' Responses to Number*** Another kind of conceptual understanding has to do with numbers. When and how do children begin to understand that some sets of objects have "more" than others? When do they begin to appreciate that "2" is different from "4" and that the objects themselves do not matter when numerical entities are being compared? Thanks to a growing body of research, we now know that infants demonstrate sensitivity to basic aspects of numerical relationships. Habituation studies show that newborns can detect differences in small numeric sets, such as two versus three (Antell & Keating, 1983), and that six-month-olds differentiate between eight and sixteen dots (Xu & Spelke, 2000). Infants even seem to understand something about additive properties of numbers. In one experiment, five-month-old infants watched as a toy was placed in a case and then was hidden by a screen. The infants watched as a second, identical toy was placed behind the screen (see Figure 6.9). When the screen was removed and only one toy remained— an impossible outcome if the infants appreciated that there should still be two toys—they showed surprise and looked longer than they did when two toys were visible (Wynn, 1992a). Other researchers have confirmed that, before age six months, babies show numerical competencies that likely serve as the foundation for more complex reasoning about quantities (Canfield & Smith, 1996; Simon, Hespos, & Rochat, 1995).

But what exactly is the nature of those competencies? The preceding findings raise several interesting questions about the processes that underlie infants' behaviors. First, is sensitivity to number another example of innate core knowledge? To some researchers, the answer is yes, especially because infants only five months old appear to be sensitive to addition and subtraction events (Wynn, 1998). Others disagree and point out that the infants in these experiments might be responding on the basis of changes in the visual display other than number. For example, when stimulus items change in number, they also change in the amount of contour, or exterior boundary length, that they contain; two mouse dolls have more total "outline" than one mouse doll. In a study in which the stimuli varied either in contour length or in number, infants responded on the basis of contour length rather than

●━ **KEY THEME**

**NATURE & NURTURE**

▷ **FIGURE 6.10**

**Infant Recognition Memory**

Fagan tested infant recognition memory by using visual stimuli in a paired-comparison procedure. For each row, one of the stimuli was presented repeatedly until habituation occurred. Then one of the other stimuli in the row was paired with the familiar stimulus to see if infants preferred the novel item. Infants only a few months old looked longer at novel items up to fourteen days after the initial familiarization.

*Source:* Adapted from Fagan (1974).

number (Clearfield & Mix, 1999). Similarly, infants respond to changes in surface area of stimuli as opposed to their number (Clearfield & Mix, 2001). Thus it may be more accurate to say that infants respond on the basis of the *amount* of things rather than the *number* of things (Mix, Huttenlocher, & Levine, 2002).

## MEMORY

Few cognitive skills are as basic as the ability to store information encountered at a given time for potential retrieval seconds, minutes, days, or even years later. It is hard to imagine how any other cognitive activity, such as problem solving or concept formation, could take place without the ability to draw on previously experienced information. How could we classify dogs, horses, and giraffes into the category "animals" without remembering the shared features of each? In one way or another, memory is a crucial element in most of our thinking. How early can we demonstrate the presence of memory? How long do the memories of young infants last? How much information are infants capable of retaining through memory? Before we begin to answer these questions, we need to consider some of the distinctions researchers have made concerning different types of memory.

One contrast is the difference between recognition and recall memory. Tasks that measure **recognition memory** require participants to indicate somehow that they have experienced a picture, word, or other stimulus before. In other words, there has to be some behavioral response to the experimenter's question "Have you encountered this item on previous trials of this experiment?" In **recall memory**, participants must reproduce previously presented stimuli. For example, they might be asked to generate a series of actions they had previously witnessed ("Can you show me how we fed the fish before?") or, among older children who can speak, to say a list of words or numbers they had heard previously. Another contrast is sometimes made between explicit and implicit memory. **Explicit memory** refers to recollection of a past event or experience, such as hearing a story being read or viewing a picture of a female face in a laboratory experiment. Explicit memory is a conscious process and can be demonstrated via either recognition or recall. **Implicit memory** refers to nonconscious recollections of how to do something behaviorally, such as learning to use a spoon to eat cereal or, among older children, learning how to ride a bike. The child may have little awareness of all of the small improvements that have taken place in those skills over time. For the most part, the research described below concerns the development of explicit memory.

***How Can We Study Infant Memory?***    A big obstacle to studying infant memory, of course, is that infants do not speak. How, then, can researchers determine anything

**recognition memory**  Ability to identify whether a stimulus has previously been encountered.

**recall memory**  Ability to reproduce stimuli that one has previously encountered.

**explicit memory**  Conscious recollection of a past event or experience.

**implicit memory**  Nonconscious recollections of how to do something behaviorally.

***Individual and Cultural Differences in Language Development*** Although children show many common trends in the way they acquire language, they also show significant individual differences in rates and types of language production. You may have heard a family member or friend report that her child said virtually nothing for two or three years and then began speaking in complete sentences. Although such dramatic variations in language milestones are not frequent, children sometimes show unique patterns in their linguistic accomplishments, patterns that still lead to the attainment of normal language by later childhood.

One example of wide individual variation is the age at which children say their first word. Some children produce their first distinguishable word as early as nine months, whereas others may not do so until sixteen months (Barrett, 1989). Similarly, some children show good pronunciation, whereas others have difficulty making certain sounds, consistently substituting *t* for *k* or *b* for *v*, for example (Smith, 1988). In addition, not all children display the vocabulary spurt (Acredolo & Goodwyn, 1990b), or they may start their spurt at different ages, as Figure 6.16 indicates. The results of a study of more than 1,800 children underscore just how variable the size of children's vocabularies can be: at sixteen months of age, some children spoke 10 or fewer words, whereas others spoke as many as 180 words (Fenson et al., 1994).

Children may also differ in the content of their one-word speech. Most one-year-olds tend to use nominals predominantly, displaying what Katherine Nelson (1973) termed a **referential style**. Other children show a different pattern: rather than naming objects, they frequently use words that have social functions, such as *hello* or *please*, thus displaying an **expressive style**. Expressive children use words to direct or comment on the behavior of other people. According to some research, referential children tend to have a larger vocabulary and show more rapid advances in language development, at least in the early stages (Bates et al., 1988; Nelson, 1973).

How do we explain these individual differences in the rates and styles with which children acquire language? There are several hypotheses. Perhaps individual differences result from differences in the neurological structures that control language or from inborn differences in temperament. For example, referential children tend to have a long attention span, smile and laugh a lot, and be easily soothed (Dixon & Shore, 1997). Children who are more advanced in language comprehension and production show a similar profile (Dixon & Smith, 2000). This style might allow them to profit from incoming information about the names of objects. Another possibility is that parents influence the rate and form of children's vocabulary development. Some parents, for example, may spend a great deal of time encouraging their infants to speak, focusing especially on labeling objects. Others may be more relaxed about letting the infant proceed at his or her own pace. Researchers have confirmed that the overall amount and variety of speech that parents produce for their infants is related to the acceleration of vocabulary growth (Hoff & Naigles, 2002; Huttenlocher et al., 1991).

Cultural differences in how children speak in the one-word stage bolster the idea that what children hear others say influences what they themselves say. Unlike American children, Korean toddlers show a "verb spurt" before a "noun spurt" (Choi, 1998; Choi & Gopnik, 1995); similarly, Mandarin-speaking toddlers utter more verbs than nouns as they and their mothers play with toys (Tardif, 1996; Tardif, Gelman, & Xu, 1999). Mothers from both Asian groups pepper their speech with many more verbs and action sequences, saying things such as "What are you doing?" and "You put the car in the garage." American mothers, in contrast, use far more nouns (for instance, "That's a ball") and ask questions that require a nominal as an answer (such as "What is it?").

Chinese mothers use more verbs and action sequences in their speech to children than American mothers. It is interesting to note that Chinese-speaking toddlers use more verbs than nouns in their early speech. Thus the form of early speech is influenced by the sociocultural context in which the child lives.

### ATYPICAL DEVELOPMENT
## Developmental Delay

We have emphasized in this text that it is not unusual to observe individual variations in the ages at which children achieve milestones in motor development, and as we have just seen, in cognitive and language development as well. When children deviate noticeably from those milestones in one or more areas, however, they are said to have a **developmental delay.** About 5 percent of children under age three years display developmental delays. The causes can be a genetic disorder, low birth weight, exposure to disease, or an environment that does not support the child's progress. Typically, the first identification is made by the child's pediatrician during regular medical checkups. The physician may recommend a developmental screening to identify the degree and specific areas of delay. Federal legislation, the Individuals with Disabilities Education Act (IDEA) Amendments of 1997, requires early identification of developmental delays as well as provision of appropriate services from educational and social systems within the community (American Academy of Pediatrics, 2001). The idea is that early diagnosis and treatment can result in better outcomes for each child.

What kinds of assessment tools are used to perform a screening? A variety of measures are available, including the Denver Developmental Screening Test, the Peabody Picture Vocabulary Test, and an assortment of questionnaires that ask parents to report their children's behaviors. Sometimes, an early childhood specialist will use an infant intelligence test. Most tests of infant intelligence are based on norms for behaviors that are expected to occur in the first year or two of life. Because the infant's accomplishments tend to be in the domains of motor, language, and socioemotional development, these areas appear most frequently on the various tests.

One widely used test is the *Bayley Scales of Infant and Toddler Development*, designed by Nancy Bayley (2005) to predict later childhood competence. The test consists of several scales. The Cognitive and Language scales assess the young child's sensory and perceptual skills, memory, learning, acquisition of the object concept, and linguistic skill. The Motor Scale measures the child's ability to control and coordinate the body, from large motor skills to finer manipulation of the hands and fingers. Table 6.2 shows some sample items from each scale. Designed for infants from one through forty-two months of age, the test yields a *developmental index* for both the mental and the motor scale. In other words, the infant's scores are compared with the scores for the standardization sample (the large sample of normal infants whose performance was assessed at the time the test was developed) and are expressed in terms of how much they deviate from the average scores of that sample. The Bayley scales also contain a Behavior Rating Scale to assess the infant's interests, emotions, and general level of activity compared with the standardization sample.

If a child has been identified as having a developmental delay, he or she is referred to a local early intervention program. Here, a multidisciplinary team—often a pediatrician, psychologist, social worker, physical therapist, occupational therapist, nutritionist, and speech and language specialist, among others—develops an *individual family service plan* to help the child achieve the most positive outcomes. Parental support and involvement are often cornerstones of successful early intervention programs. More will be said about the impact of early intervention programs on child development in upcoming chapters.

**developmental delay** The condition children are said to have when they deviate noticeably from motor, cognitive, or language milestones in one or more areas.

**Table 6.2 Sample Items from the Bayley Scales of Infant and Toddler Development**

| Age | Cognitive/Language Scales | Motor Scale |
|---|---|---|
| **2 months** | Turns head to sound<br>Plays with rattle<br>Reacts to disappearance of face | Holds head erect and steady for 15 seconds<br>Turns from side to back<br>Sits with support |
| **6 months** | Lifts cup by handle<br>Looks for fallen spoon<br>Looks at pictures in book | Sits alone for 30 seconds<br>Turns from back to stomach<br>Grasps foot with hands |
| **12 months** | Builds tower of 2 cubes<br>Turns pages of book | Walks with help<br>Throws ball<br>Grasps pencil in middle |
| **17–19 months** | Imitates crayon stroke<br>Identifies objects in photograph | Stands alone on right foot<br>Walks up stairs with help |
| **23–25 months** | Matches pictures<br>Uses pronoun(s)<br>Imitates a 2-word sentence | Laces 3 beads<br>Jumps distance of 4 inches<br>Walks on tiptoe for 4 steps |
| **38–42 months** | Names 4 colors<br>Uses past tense<br>Identifies gender | Copies circle<br>Hops twice on 1 foot<br>Walks down stairs, alternating feet |

*Source*: Bayley Scales of Infant and Toddler Development. Copyright © 2005 by The Psychological Corporation, a Harcourt Assessment Company. Reproduced by permission. All rights reserved. "Bayley Scales of Infant Development" is a registered trademark of The Psychological Corporation.

## LANGUAGE IN THE CONTEXT OF SOCIAL INTERACTIONS

Many researchers of child language hold as a central tenet that language is a social activity, one that arises from the desire to communicate with others and that is nurtured in social interactive contexts. Although these researchers acknowledge that there may be innate predispositions of the young human organism to learn language, they emphasize the role that experiences with more mature, expert speakers play in fostering linguistic skill.

*Parentese and Language Development* Children need models whose speech does not exceed their processing abilities. Many qualities of parental speech directed at children are well suited to the child's emerging receptive and productive skills, providing a *scaffolding*, or framework, from which the child can learn. Most parents present a scaled-down version of spoken language as they interact with their young offspring, a version that contains simple, well-formed sentences and is punctuated by exaggerated intonation, high pitch, and clear pauses between segments of speech (Newport, 1977). Caregivers describe concrete events taking place in the present and often refer to objects with diminutives, such as *kitty* or *doggie*. They also include repetitions of what the child has said, as well as many questions. Questions in particular serve to facilitate the occurrence of **turn taking**, the alternating vocalization by parent and child. Some questions are also used as **turnabouts**, elements of conversation that explicitly request a response

KEY THEME

NATURE & NURTURE

**turn taking** Alternating vocalization by parent and child.

**turnabout** Element of conversation that requests a response from the child.

from the child, as in "You like that, don't you?" or "What did you say?" Also, parents often follow the child's verbalization with a **recast**, repeating what the child has said but correcting any errors. **Expansions**—more elaborate verbal forms—may be added, too. Thus, when a child says, "Ball fall," his mother might reply, "Yes, the red ball [expansion] fell [recast]." Recasts and expansions provide children with cues that their verbalization needs improvement and a model for how to improve. Children, in fact, often imitate and retain their parents' recasts (Farrar, 1992; Saxton, 1997).

The following exchange between one seven-month-old, Ann, and her mother illustrates several of these concepts (Snow, 1977).

| MOTHER | ANN |
|---|---|
| Ghhhhh ghhhhh ghhhhh ghhhhh | |
| Grrrrr grrrrr grrrrr grrrrr | |
| | (protest cry) |
| Oh, you don't feel like it, do you? | |
| | aaaaa aaaaa aaaaa |
| No, I wasn't making that noise. | |
| I wasn't going aaaaa aaaaa. | |
| | aaaaa aaaaa |
| Yes, that's right. | |

Notable in the exchange is the mother's pattern of waiting for her child's vocalization to end before she begins her response, an example of turn taking. If the child had spoken actual words, a real conversation would have taken place. The mother also repeated the child's vowel-like sound but embedded it in more elaborate speech. By the time the infant reaches eighteen months, the mother's tendency to expand or explain her utterances becomes even more pronounced, as in the following brief episode (Snow, 1977):

| MOTHER | ANN |
|---|---|
| | (blowing noises) |
| That's a bit rude. | |
| | Mouth. |
| Mouth, that's right. | |
| | Face. |
| Face, yes, mouth is in your face. | |
| What else have you got in your face? | |
| | Face. (closing eyes) |
| You're making a face, aren't you? | |

According to Snow (1984), two general principles operate during caregiver-child interactions. First, parents generally interpret their infants' behaviors as attempts to communicate, even when that interpretation may not seem warranted to an objective observer. Second, children actively seek relationships among objects, events, and people in their world and the vocal behaviors of their caregivers. The result of these two tendencies is that parents are motivated to converse with their children and children have a mechanism for learning language.

Parentese may serve a number of functions in the child's growing competence with language. First, this form of speech may assist the child's acquisition of word meaning. Mothers tend to say the names for objects more loudly than other words in their speech to infants, and often they place the object label in the last position in their sentence, as in "Do you see the *rattle*?" (Messer, 1981). Mothers also tend to highlight new words by raising their pitch as they say them (Fernald & Mazzie, 1991) or moving an object as they label it (Gogate, Bahrick, & Watson, 2000). Second, the intonations of motherese may

**recast** Repetition of a child's utterance along with grammatical corrections.

**expansion** Repetition of a child's utterance along with more complex forms.

facilitate the child's acquisition of phonology and *syntax*, the rules concerning how words can be combined to express particular meanings. In one recent study, for example, researchers found that, the more exaggerated a mother's speech (by lengthening the vowels between consonants), the more likely an infant was to successfully discriminate speech sounds (Liu, Kuhl, & Tsao, 2003). Another study demonstrated that seven- to ten-month-olds oriented more frequently to motherese that contained pauses at clausal boundaries (for example, "Cinderella lived in a great big house/but it was sort of dark. …") than to motherese that was interrupted within clauses (for example, "Cinderella lived in a great big house but it was/sort of dark. …"). Infants did not show these differential preferences in response to regular adult speech (Kemler Nelson et al., 1989). Infants show a similar sensitivity to even smaller grammatical units, the phrases and even the words within a sentence, but only when sentences are spoken in motherese (Jusczyk et al., 1992; Myers et al., 1996; Nazzi et al., 2000). The prosodic features of motherese may thus assist the infant in identifying phonologically and syntactically relevant elements of language. Finally, exposure to motherese may provide lessons in conversational turn taking, one aspect of pragmatics that governs speech in interactions with others.

Are there any other effects of interactions with caregivers on child language development? Researchers have observed that, the more mothers talk with their children, the more words their children acquire (Huttenlocher et al., 1991; Olson, Bayles, & Bates, 1986). It is not just *how much* mothers talk to their children that makes a difference, however; *how* they talk also matters. When mothers use many directives to control their children's behaviors and are generally intrusive, language development is slowed. When mothers (or teachers) use questions, expansions, and conversational turn taking to elicit language from children or follow the children's vocalizations with a response, language development proceeds more rapidly (Hoff-Ginsberg, 1986; Nelson, 1973; Tamis-LeMonda, Bornstein, & Baumwell, 2001; Valdez-Menchaca & Whitehurst, 1992).

As important as motherese may seem, it is not a universal phenomenon. Although features of motherese have been observed in many languages and even among deaf mothers signing to their deaf infants (Gleason & Weintraub, 1978; Masataka, 1996), mothers in some cultures adopt a distinctly different style in talking with their infants. Consider the following two examples of maternal speech, one American and the other Japanese, as observed by Anne Fernald and Hiromi Morikawa (1993):

> AMERICAN MOTHER: *That's a car. See the car? You like it? It's got nice wheels.*
>
> JAPANESE MOTHER: *Here! It's a vroom vroom. I give it to you. Now you give it to me. Give me. Yes! Thank you.*

Whereas American mothers tend to name objects and focus on the exchange of information, Japanese mothers rarely name objects, using them instead to engage their infants in social routines. Perhaps it is not surprising, then, that American infants use substantially more nouns in their speech at nineteen months of age. Similarly, other researchers have noted that Japanese mothers ask fewer questions but use more nonsense sounds and songs than American mothers (Bornstein et al., 1992; Toda, Fogel, & Kawai, 1990). Thus mothers may have different agendas as they speak with their children, and their style of speech may subtly shape the children's utterances.

Another example of variation in the use of motherese can be found in the Kaluli society of Papua New Guinea. In this culture, talking with others is a highly valued social skill, yet few adult verbalizations are directed to infants. Infants may be called by their name, but until they pass their first year, little else is said to them. When mothers do begin to talk to their babies, their speech contains few of the elements of motherese. Turn taking, repetitions, and elaborations are absent; usually mothers simply make directive statements that require no response from the child. Nevertheless, Kaluli children become proficient users of their language within developmental norms (Schieffelin & Ochs, 1983). Joint linguistic interactions between caregiver and child thus may not be essential to the emergence of language.

Linguistic exchanges with other interaction partners—fathers, siblings, peers, and others—may uniquely influence the child's eventual level of linguistic skill. For example, when fifteen-month-olds "converse" with their father, they experience more commu-

**KEY THEME**
**RISK/RESILIENCE**

**KEY THEME**
**SOCIOCULTURAL CONTEXT**

nication breakdowns than when they talk with their mother. Fathers more often request clarification, change the topic, or do not acknowledge the child's utterance after they fail to understand what she or he said (Tomasello, Conti-Ramsden, & Ewert, 1990). Thus, in communicating with fathers, children are challenged to make adjustments to maintain the interaction. Children also learn language by overhearing it on educational television (Wright et al., 2001), in conversations between mother and older siblings (Ashima-Takane, Goodz, & Derevensky, 1996), or even between two strangers (Akhtar, Jipson, & Callanan, 2001). Children are normally exposed to a rich and varied range of linguistic stimuli from different sources in the environment; many theorists believe this fact ensures that children will learn the details of linguistic structures that may not be present in the verbalizations of a single conversation partner, such as the mother (Gleitman, Newport, & Gleitman, 1984; Wexler, 1982).

***Joint Attention and Language Development***   One of the most remarkable observations made in recent years is that young language learners are able to use subtle social cues to figure out which objects new words are labeling. Suppose an adult says, "Let's find the *gazzer*" and looks at an object, rejects it, and excitedly picks up another object without naming it. The infant assumes the second object is the *gazzer* (Tomasello, Strosberg, & Akhtar, 1996). Or suppose an adult and an infant are playing with several unfamiliar, unnamed objects; then the adult introduces a new object, saying, "Look, I see a *modi!*" without pointing to any object. Again, the infant assumes the newest object is the *modi* (Akhtar, Carpenter, & Tomasello, 1996). These studies demonstrate that infants have an impressive ability to interpret social cues in deciding how labels and objects match up. They also show that episodes of **joint attention**, those times in which child and caregiver share the same "psychological space," are important contexts for language acquisition. Many parents and infants tend to spend substantial time in these moments of mutual engagement. For example, parents of infants tend to label many objects, often in the context of joint book reading or the child's manifest interest in a particular object or person in her surroundings (Ninio & Bruner, 1978). A typical scenario goes like this: The infant turns his head, points, and maybe even coos as the family dog enters the room. The mother also turns and looks, and says "Doggie." These are precisely the conditions under which infants seem to remember the words that name objects (Masur, 1982).

Researchers have found that the amount of time infants spend in joint attention with their caregivers, whether in book reading or other contexts, is a strong predictor of their early language skills (Carpenter, Nagell, & Tomasello, 1998). According to Paul Bloom (2000), this evidence indicates that the child is actively seeking to find out what is on the minds of the adults with whom she is interacting—what their words refer to and what they are intending to communicate.

**RESEARCH APPLIED TO PARENTING**

### Reading to Children

It was only a couple of months later that Chad began to say a few different words. But after that, his vocabulary expanded rapidly, and he started stringing words together. As she prepared her son's bed, Tanya marveled at the progress Chad was making. This was her favorite time of day. Every night, just before Chad was put to bed, Tanya would pull him up in her lap and take a picture book from the shelf. At first, she just pointed to and named things in the book, often encouraging Chad to participate by asking, "What's that?" As his vocabulary increased, Tanya elaborated on his answers and asked other questions: "What does the doggie say?" "Woof-woof!" squealed Chad, enjoying the ritual perhaps every bit as much as, maybe even more than, his mother.

The research findings discussed earlier show that how and how often parents speak to children can influence language development. One context in which mothers' speech tends to be particularly lavish is during book reading. Erika Hoff-Ginsberg (1991) found that, when mothers and two-year-olds were

**joint attention**   Episodes in which the child and another individual share the same "psychological space" as they encounter experiences in the world.

reading books, mothers showed the greatest diversity in the vocabulary they used, the greatest complexity of syntax, and the highest rate of replies to their children compared with other contexts, such as mealtime or toy play. Other research has shown that the amount of time parents spent reading stories to their twenty-four-month-olds predicted the children's language ability up to two years later (Crain-Thoreson & Dale, 1992). As a result of such findings, many child development experts encourage parents to read to their young children.

Grover Whitehurst and his colleagues have developed a program called *dialogic reading* to stimulate language development in preschool children at risk for academic failure, but the general principles can be applied by any parent interested in promoting his or her child's language development. Here is some advice the researchers have developed for parents:

1. *Ask what questions (such as "What is this?") to stimulate the child to speak.* Avoid yes/no questions that require only brief answers.

2. *Follow the child's answer with a question.* Ask, for example, what shape or color an object has or what it is used for.

3. *Repeat the child's utterance in the form of a recast.* For example, follow "Cow" with "Yes, that's right, it's a cow." This gives the child feedback that she is correct.

4. *If the child does not have an answer, provide a model and ask him to repeat.* For example, say "That's a bottle. Can you say 'bottle'?"

5. *Be generous with praise and encouragement.* Make comments such as "Good talking" or "Nice job."

6. *Be responsive to the child's interests.* When the child expresses an interest in a picture or part of the story, follow her interest with encouragement to talk.

7. *Have fun.* Do not pressure the child; take turns with the child, and even make the activity a game.

Dialogic reading has been shown to increase language skills in children from different social classes when used by daycare teachers as well as parents (Arnold & Whitehurst, 1994). Of course, children learn language skills in many other contexts, such as mealtime conversations (Snow, 1993). Thus children whose parents do not read to them often are not necessarily fated to have poor language skills (Scarborough & Dobrich, 1993). Nonetheless, reading to children, even when they are as young as 8 months old, leads to desirable outcomes in language development (DeBaryshe, 1993; Karrass & Braungart-Rieker, 2005).

## F O R ◆ Y O U R ◆ R E V I E W

◆ What kinds of phonological skills and preferences have researchers observed in infants?

◆ What are some of the features of infants' early vocalizations?

◆ How do infants use gestures as communication tools?

◆ What are the important features of children's language during the one-word stage?

◆ What are some of the individual and cultural variations in language acquisition that have been observed by researchers?

◆ Which features of social interactions help to explain language in infants? What parental activities can promote infants' language skills?

# CHAPTER RECAP

## ⚷ Summary of Developmental Themes

### NATURE & NURTURE

**How do nature and nurture interact in perception, cognition, and language development in infancy?**

There are several indicators that, for humans, nature sets early predispositions to perceive, think, and develop language in certain ways. For example, young infants seem to understand the principle of solidity, the idea that one object cannot pass through the space occupied by another object. Although not everyone agrees, some researchers see a part for nature here. Infants also show an early sensitivity to phonemes and prosody in language. However, many of these abilities also seem to be nurtured within the context of interactions with caregivers.

### SOCIOCULTURAL INFLUENCE

**How does the sociocultural context influence perception, cognition, and language development in infancy?**

Piaget's theory emphasizes the universal cognitive attainments of all children, regardless of their cultural background. However, research has shown that the sociocultural context, the cornerstone of Vygotsky's theory, cannot be ignored. For example, cultures vary in the extent to which caregivers use parentese with their infants, a factor that may influence the rate of language acquisition.

### CONTINUITY/DISCONTINUITY

**Are perception, cognition, and language development during infancy continuous or discontinuous?**

Piaget stressed stagelike attainments in thinking. However, others who have empirically reevaluated his work and who have studied perception and language make claims for more continuous changes in their focus on the underlying basic processes that contribute to development.

### RISK/RESILIENCE

**What factors promote risk or resilience in perception, cognition, and language development during infancy?**

One domain in which children frequently show striking differences is in the rate at which they achieve language milestones. The type of speech they experience from caregivers has been shown to predict advances versus delays in the acquisition of language.

## Chapter Review

### PERCEPTION

**How early do infants see patterns and forms in the visual world? What is the externality effect?**

Newborns do not examine visual patterns systematically and are often attracted to external features that show high contrast (the *externality effect*) or movement. Within a few months, they engage in more systematic exploration of visual arrays. Their perception of the unity and coherence of objects is enhanced by kinetic cues and prior experience with the stimuli.

**What is the developmental course of infant perception of faces? When can an infant distinguish the faces of caregivers from the faces of others?**

Some research suggests that a preference for facelike forms shows up as early as the newborn period. Infants show a clear preference for faces over other complex forms by two months of age. According to some evidence, infants can distinguish the caregiver's face a few days after birth.

**How early and using what kinds of cues do infants perceive objects in their world?**

Infants perceive objects as entities by at least three months of age. Kinetic cues seem to provide especially important information about the integrity of objects.

**What is meant by the perception of biological motion?**

In some experiments, the only visual information provided is points of light attached to the joints of a moving organism. Infants seem to distinguish these stimuli as different and unique as compared with random motions of points of light.

**How early and using what kinds of cues do infants perceive depth? What evidence exists to indicate that its perception does not always produce appropriate responses to the dangers associated with depth?**

Depth information is provided to infants by kinetic cues, the differential flow of optic information that derives from self-induced movement or as a result of movement among arrays in the visual field. It is also provided by *stereopsis*, fusing the two images delivered by each eye into a single image. At about five to seven months of age, infants begin to process depth provided by pictorial cues. Infants also show recognition of depth cues when they are placed on an apparatus called the *visual cliff*.

### Why do developmental psychologists no longer believe the infant's visual world is simply a "blooming, buzzing confusion?"

Young infants do not respond to all visual stimuli with equal likelihood right from birth. The fact that they have preferences for some stimuli over others suggests that they are not bombarded with an array of visual information. In addition, perceptual development proceeds in an organized manner. For example, young infants tend to scan only the exteriors of stimuli and begin to explore the interiors of stimuli only as they mature.

### What sound patterns do infants prefer to listen to?

Infants show a preference for listening to human speech and to songs delivered in a child-oriented style. They also prefer musical patterns that conform to acceptable phrasing.

### What arguments exist for or against the view that infants possess an innate capacity to detect phonemes?

Young infants can detect *phonemes*, the basic unit of sound used to differentiate the meaning of words in languages. They also respond to them *categorically*. However, by the end of the first year, as a result of exposure to only a subset of these sounds, they often discriminate only those phonemes heard in their own language.

### How does intermodal perception develop?

*Intermodal perception* is the ability to integrate information arising from more than one sensory modality. One current position holds that intermodal perception is possible at birth and that *perceptual differentiation*, the ability to identify information coming from specific senses, arises with experience. Some amodal properties of stimulation, such as temporal synchrony, may be highly salient to young infants and assist in their acquiring an understanding of the correlations that exist among the various sensory properties of objects and events.

### What evidence exists to show that infants recognize the correlation between visual and auditory information as well as visual and tactile cues?

Infants will look at film sequences that correspond in tempo to sound tracks and at the face of the caregiver whose voice they hear on a speaker, indicating a recognition that certain sights go with particular sounds. Infants also show visual recognition of items they had previously put in their mouths, showing awareness of the correlation between visual and tactile cues.

## COGNITION

### What are the infant's chief accomplishments during the sensorimotor stage according to Piaget? What is the primary basis for thought in this stage?

The chief feature of the *sensorimotor stage* is that thought (*cognition*) is based on action. Children develop *means-ends behavior*, separate the self from the external environment, and attain the *object concept*. The end of this stage is signaled by the child's ability to engage in deferred imitation, a form of representation skill.

### What is the object concept? What are the stages of acquisition of this concept according to Piaget?

The *object concept* refers to the child's understanding that objects continue to exist even if they are not in view. Piaget described the following stages in the acquisition of object concept: up to three months, the infant will not search for a covered object; at about four months, the child will search for a partially covered object; at about eight months, the child will search for a completely covered object; at about twelve months, the child can follow visible displacements of the object; and at about eighteen months, the child can follow invisible displacements of an object.

### What is the core knowledge hypothesis? What research findings support this position on infants' conceptual knowledge? What are the criticisms of this point of view?

The *core knowledge hypothesis* asserts that young infants possess early knowledge about the properties of objects, such as their solidity and the fact that they move in continuous paths. Supporting experiments show that infants look longer when impossible events, such as a ball rolling through a path occupied by a box, take place. However, other studies show that much older children have difficulty predicting the specific location of a ball rolling down an obstructed track.

### What is the A-not-B error? How does Piaget account for this error? What are some other explanations for the occurrence of this behavior in infants?

The *A-not-B error* occurs when infants about seven to nine months of age see an object hidden in location A and then moved to location B. The typical response is to look for the object in location A. Piaget believes that the error occurs because infants are still guided by the sensorimotor scheme to look in location A. Others suggest that memory problems, the failure to inhibit the response to reach for location A, or the failure to update the representation of the events are responsible.

### What principles guide infants' spatial understanding according to Piaget? Does research support his point of view?

Infants respond to spatial tasks based on egocentric frames of reference, according to Piaget. They determine an object's location in relation to their own body rather than in relation to some external object. Researchers have confirmed that, in the absence of strong external cues, infants do use egocentric frames of reference. However, when strong cues, such as color cues or distinctive landmarks, are made available, infants do not respond on an egocentric basis.

### What changes have researchers observed in classification skills during infancy?

At age one year, infants classify objects on the basis of shared perceptual features. By age two, children classify on the basis of thematic relations and, to some extent, on the basis of taxonomic relations. These are all manifestations of infants' ability to understand and use *concepts*.

### What kinds of numerical competencies do infants display?

Infants age six months and younger have been shown to detect differences in number with small-size sets. They also seem to detect the addition or subtraction of items to a set of stimuli.

### What are the major features of recognition memory in infancy?

Infants are capable of recognizing stimuli after brief exposure to them and for long periods of time—even two weeks. *Recognition memory* can be disrupted in young infants, though, by changes in the context of the event. Even newborns have been shown to be capable of recognition memory. Recognition is one form of *explicit* (as opposed to *implicit*) *memory*.

### What do studies employing the elicited imitation technique tell us about recall memory in infancy?

In *elicited imitation*, children must repeat a sequence of actions to which they had previously been exposed. By two years of age, children can remember a three-part sequence for a month or more after only one viewing of it, suggesting that they are capable of *recall*.

### What major changes in the brain accompany developmental improvements in memory?

Changes in the temporal and prefrontal lobes seem to correspond to developmental improvements in memory.

### When do infants first evidence the ability to engage in problem solving and transfer?

Children show evidence of problem solving by age twelve months, when they will perform several behaviors in sequence in order to achieve a goal. Once successful in a simple problem-solving task, they can transfer the solution to other situations which have the same goal sequence.

### What are the central elements of Vygotsky's sociocultural theory as they apply to infancy?

Vygotsky stated that, in order to understand development, it is vital to understand the cultural context in which the child lives. He emphasized the concept of *scaffolding*, the temporary support for problem solving provided to the child by caregivers and teachers. For the infant, this could involve the caregiver's defining the problem, demonstrating a solution, and providing motivation to succeed. As the infant becomes more competent, this support is withdrawn.

### What is the significance of the phenomenon of intersubjectivity?

*Intersubjectivity* refers to the mutual attention and shared communication that take place between child and caregiver. These may be opportune times for children to learn language and also to develop emotionally and cognitively.

## LANGUAGE

### What kinds of phonological skills and preferences have researchers observed in infants?

Newborns show a tendency to respond to language as a unique auditory stimulus. Young infants detect phonemes and vowel sounds from a variety of languages but show a decline in this ability by the second half of the first year. Infants show an early sensitivity to the *prosody*, patterns of intonation, stress, and rhythm that mothers around the world include in their speech to young children. Children's sensitivity to rhythmic properties of language helps them to differentiate their native language from others and possibly to detect the presence of specific words in a stream of speech. The focus of language development during infancy is on mastering *phonology* and some aspects of *semantics*.

### What are some of the features of infants' early vocalizations?

Infants typically *coo* at six to eight weeks, *babble* at three to six months, and produce syllablelike *canonical babbling* at seven months.

### How do infants use gestures as communication tools?

They might use a *protodeclarative communication* to call attention to an object or a *protoimperative communication* to make a request. Sometimes children's gestures symbolize objects; later in development, gestures may accompany verbalization in order to elaborate a point.

### What are the important features of children's language during the one-word stage?

By one year of age, most children are speaking one-word utterances, usually *nominals*, or nouns. At about eighteen months or so, children may show a particularly rapid phase of growth in word acquisition called the *vocabulary spurt*.

At the earlier stages of word learning, children may restrict their use of some words to particular contexts (*underextension*) or apply them to too broad a category (*overextension*). Children comprehend word meanings much earlier than they are able to produce words. Their *receptive language* exceeds their *productive language*. Labels for verbs are harder for children to understand than labels for nouns.

## What are some of the individual and cultural variations in language acquisition that have been observed by researchers?

Some children's early speech is *referential*; it includes mostly nominals. Other children are *expressive*; they use words with social functions. Fairly substantial individual differences also occur for the rate of language acquisition. Culture, too, can have an influence on the types of words children produce in the early stages of acquisition. For example, children from some Asian cultures learn verbs before they learn nouns. Despite these variations, the patterns of language development across children are so regular that they are used as one way to assess the possibility of *developmental delay*.

## Which features of social interactions help to explain language in infants? What parental activities can promote infants' language skills?

Several characteristics of caregiver-child speech, called *motherese* or *parentese*, facilitate development. Specific techniques include *turn taking, turnabouts, recasts,* and *expansions*. The amount and content of maternal speech to children, especially in episodes of *joint attention*, predict the rate and form of children's language acquisition. Reading to children is an excellent way to promote language skills.

## KEY TERMS AND CONCEPTS

**A-not-B error** (p. 205)

**babbling** (p. 220)

**canonical babbling** (p. 220)

**categorical perception** (p. 197)

**cognition** (p. 189)

**concepts** (p. 208)

**cooing** (p. 220)

**core knowledge hypothesis** (p. 205)

**developmental delay** (p. 226)

**elicited imitation** (p. 212)

**expansion** (p. 227)

**explicit memory** (p. 210)

**expressive style** (p. 224)

**externality effect** (p. 190)

**implicit memory** (p. 210)

**intermodal perception** (p. 198)

**intersubjectivity** (p. 216)

**joint attention** (p. 230)

**means-ends behavior** (p. 200)

**motherese (parentese)** (p. 218)

**nominal** (p. 223)

**object concept** (p. 202)

**overextension** (p. 224)

**perceptual differentiation** (p. 198)

**phoneme** (p. 197)

**phonology** (p. 217)

**productive language** (p. 224)

**prosody** (p. 218)

**protodeclarative communication** (p. 220)

**protoimperative communication** (p. 220)

**recall memory** (p. 210)

**recast** (p. 227)

**receptive language** (p. 224)

**recognition memory** (p. 210)

**referential style** (p. 224)

**scaffolding** (p. 215)

**semantics** (p. 217)

**sensorimotor stage** (p. 200)

**stereopsis** (p. 194)

**turn taking** (p. 227)

**turnabout** (p. 227)

**underextension** (p. 224)

**visual cliff** (p. 194)

**vocabulary spurt** (p. 223)

# 7 SOCIAL AND EMOTIONAL DEVELOPMENT

I t's a quiet time on Sunday morning, just after a big breakfast, and Cindy admires her eight-month-old son Michael as he sits in his infant seat. He is looking at her so intently, raising his eyebrows a bit and scanning her face, gurgling contentedly. Suddenly the phone rings. Michael falls silent and opens his eyes wide. Cindy raises her eyebrows into two big arches and opens her mouth, making an exaggerated "Oohh" sound, suggesting surprise. Her baby eyes her with fascination, chortles, then smiles broadly. Cindy smiles back, chuckles, and says, "Must be Grandma calling to see how you are. Let me answer the phone, okay, honey?" She touches Michael affectionately under the chin as she gets up to reach for the phone. The baby lets out a shriek of delight and smiles again. Cindy can't help but laugh at the antics of her young son.

## What is the impact of child care on attachment?

The most recent data show that, in general, early experiences in child care do not lead to disruptions in attachment. Rather, it is important to consider the emotional climate of the home and the quality of interactions that parents and infants have when both parents work.

## What do the cases of prematurity, adoption, and abuse tell us about the concept of attachment?

Studies of premature infants, adoptees, foster children, and abused children indicate that attachments can form under less-than-optimal circumstances but that extreme deviations in caregiver-child interaction patterns can have serious negative consequences for the child, including *failure to thrive.*

## What is the relationship between early emotional experiences and the development of the brain?

There is growing evidence to suggest that early emotional experiences are linked to changes in the underlying physiology of the central nervous system. Changes in the action of cortisol and neurotransmitters have been observed in young organisms that experience prolonged early stress.

## SELF AND OTHERS

## What are the early indications of the concept of self during infancy? How do researchers measure self-recognition?

Infants recognize the movement of their own legs at three months and their own voice and face especially between fifteen and eighteen months of age. In order to get a measure of self-recognition, researchers often observe infants' reactions to a spot of rouge placed on the nose as infants look in the mirror.

## How does effectance motivation begin and develop?

Infants seem to be born with an intrinsic desire (*effectance motivation*) to gain control of their world. To the extent that an environment provides consistent feedback, children acquire an increasing sense of agency.

## What are the infant's major accomplishments in the understanding of others?

At two months of age, infants show a distinct orientation to social stimuli. At about nine months of age, infants exhibit more intentional participation in social interactions.

## How do infants typically react to other children of similar ages?

At about three months, infants react with arousal and activity to the presence of other infants. By six months, they smile at and touch other infants, and by the time they are mobile, they crawl toward and explore the faces of infant strangers.

## KEY TERMS AND CONCEPTS

ambivalent (resistant) attachment (p. 250)

attachment (p. 247)

avoidant attachment (p. 250)

basic (primary) emotion (p. 240)

disorganized/disoriented attachment (p. 250)

effectance motivation (p. 263)

emotion (p. 237)

failure to thrive (p. 260)

interactive synchrony (p. 242)

primary reinforcer (p. 248)

reunion behavior (p. 249)

secondary reinforcer (p. 248)

secure attachment (p. 250)

secure base (p. 250)

separation anxiety (p. 249)

social referencing (p. 242)

stranger anxiety (p. 249)

Strange Situation (p. 250)

temperament (p. 245)

# PATHWAYS: CONNECTING THE STORY OF DEVELOPMENT

| | INFANCY (0–2 YEARS) | EARLY CHILDHOOD | MIDDLE CHILDHOOD | ADOLESCENCE |
|---|---|---|---|---|
| **Physical Development** | • Evidences rapid gains in height and weight, with faster rates of growth in the head region and regions nearer the center of the body<br>• Shows period of rapid brain development, including formation and pruning of synapses<br>• Shows basic learning capabilities in the form of habituation, operant and classical conditioning, and imitation<br>• Shows improvements in visual accommodation, saccadic movements, acuity, and vergence<br>• Attracted first to external features of objects and to movement, and later to internal features of objects<br>• Localizes sounds<br>• Recognizes melodic rhythms and other features of music<br>• Shows sensitivity to smells, tastes, and tactile stimuli | See p. 376 | See p. 493 | See pp. 576–577 |
| **Cognitive/ Language Development** | • Attends to increasingly complex patterns including those with facelike organization<br>• Responsive to biological motion<br>• Shows signs of depth perception<br>• Shows intermodal perception<br>• Develops *means-ends behavior*<br>• Attains the *object concept*<br>• Shows sensitivity to changes in number<br>• Relies on egocentric and landmark cues to locate objects<br>• Classifies objects according to physical similarities, as well as thematic and simple taxonomic relations<br>• Distinguishes between animate and inanimate objects<br>• Shows recognition memory for simple stimuli<br>• Shows long-term recall in elicited imitation tasks<br>• Shows simple problem-solving behaviors, including transfer<br>• Discriminates among phonemes<br>• Discriminates own language from others<br>• Detects words in speech stream<br>• Produces gestures to communicate<br>• Comprehends many words<br>• Speaks in single-word utterances | | | |
| **Social/ Emotional Development** | • Displays basic emotions<br>• Imitates emotional expressions of others<br>• Recognizes others' emotions<br>• Begins to regulate own emotions through withdrawal or distraction<br>• Forms attachments<br>• Recognizes self<br>• Begins to be able to delay gratification<br>• Shows early signs of agency<br>• Shows intersubjectivity<br>• Shows early signs of empathy | | | |

# PHYSICAL, COGNITIVE, AND LANGUAGE DEVELOPMENT

# 8

J eremy! Let's play hide-and-seek!" shouted Tommy to his three-year-old brother. "See. You hide. I'll count to ten. Then I'll find you. It's fun, Jeremy. Let's try it." Tommy took pride in being a big brother; with seven years between them, he often baby-sat while his parents did chores around the house, and he especially enjoyed teaching Jeremy new things like this favorite game of his.

"Okay," smiled Jeremy. "I hide." The toddler stepped carefully over the family's Labrador retriever and plunked himself squarely behind the couch, or so he thought since he could not see his older brother. In the distance, he heard Tommy say, "Ten! Ready or not, here I come!" and held his breath. In barely a few seconds, though, Tommy was right in front of him, grinning widely. "Silly Jeremy," chuckled Tommy, "You can't let your legs stick out like that from behind the couch. I can see you!"

**NATURE & NURTURE** How do nature and nurture interact in physical, cognitive, and language development in early childhood?

**SOCIOCULTURAL INFLUENCE** How does the sociocultural context influence physical, cognitive, and language development in early childhood?

**CONTINUITY/DISCONTINUITY** Are physical, cognitive, and language development in early childhood continuous or discontinuous?

**INTERACTION AMONG DOMAINS** How do physical, cognitive, and language development in early childhood interact with other domains of development?

**RISK/RESILIENCE** What factors promote risk or resilience in physical, cognitive, and language development during early childhood?

There is no doubt about it. Young children act, think, and speak differently than older children, as the preceding scene suggests. They do not understand, for example, that other individuals may have different information about objects and events in the world than they themselves do. They may not have mastered the complexities of counting, especially when the numbers go past ten, nor do they verbalize quite like sophisticated orators. Yet at the same time, it is obvious that preschoolers are functioning in more advanced ways on many fronts when compared with infants. Sometimes when you watch three- or four-year-olds, you can almost "feel the wheels turning" in their heads, so obvious are their deliberate efforts to gain information, remember the past, or solve problems. Armed with the ability to communicate and notorious for their "why" questions, most preschoolers are literally bursting to learn about the world around them, and they are developing the requisite skills to do precisely that.

The early childhood years are marked by noticeable changes in physical size and motor capabilities. Running, trying out various tricks on the backyard climbing gym, or coloring a picture become a normal part of many young children's daily routines. Preschoolers also show tremendous advances in the breadth and detail of their general knowledge, in large part because of enhancement in cognitive skills. Another extremely important dimension of the preschool years is children's nearly complete acquisition of the complexities of language. Astonishingly, most preschoolers have mastered the bewildering variety of sounds in their native language to produce thousands of recognizable words, and they understand the meanings of those words reasonably well. They also become more proficient in using the rules of grammar of their language and become aware of the interactive and sociocultural rules of communication. The end result of the child's progress in these three areas of development is an active, delightful, and sometimes challenging being that is getting ready to take its place in human society.

## PHYSICAL DEVELOPMENT IN EARLY CHILDHOOD

In contrast to the dramatic gains in height and weight that we see during infancy, physical growth rate generally follows a slow and steady pace throughout much of early childhood. The average preschooler grows from a little under three feet tall at age two to a little under four feet tall at age six. Weight gains are smallest during childhood between ages two and three and gradually increase so that by age six, most children weigh between thirty-five and sixty pounds.

The brain, too, has passed its period of most rapid growth in size. By age four years, the size of the brain is about 80 percent of its adult weight (Spreen et al., 1984). The total volume of the brain does not change very much after about the age of five. Such a statement is a bit misleading, though, because the volume of the white matter increases throughout childhood and into adulthood largely because of continuing myelination of neurons. In contrast, the volume of gray matter, usually associated with the neurons, decreases largely as a result of pruning and perhaps cell death (Durston et al., 2001).

## DETERMINANTS OF BODY GROWTH AND DEVELOPMENT

What are the roles of nature and nurture in human physical growth? On the one hand, the contributions of nature, or heredity, are suggested by research indicating significant biological influences on physical development, as well as correlations among related family and cultural members in mature size and in the onset and pattern of physical changes. On the other hand, nurture, or environment—including diet and disease—has a bearing on physical growth as well. We take the time here to examine the determinants of physical growth because the foundation that it lays at this early time in development may have implications for cognitive and social functioning now as well as later in life.

*Genetic Factors*    A person's height is likely to be closely related to that of his or her mother and father. What is true for the family in miniature is also true for larger human populations that are genetically related. The Lese of Zaire, for example, are much taller as a group than their nearby neighbors the Efe, the pygmies of the Ituri rain forest. Even body proportions differ among groups. For example, although many individual differences and much overlap occur among people of different ethnic backgrounds, leg and arm lengths tend to be relatively greater in individuals of African descent, and even more so in Australian aborigines, than in other ethnic groups when length of the torso is equated (Eveleth & Tanner, 1990). Such similarities and differences implicate genetic factors in physical development. But genes do not control growth *directly*. Genes regulate physical development by means of neural and hormonal activity in different organs and body systems.

*Neural Control*    Many researchers believe that the brain includes a growth center, a genetically established program or template that monitors and compares expected and actual rates and levels of growth for the individual. The claim has been supported by observations of **catch-up growth**, an increase in growth rate that often occurs if some environmental factor interferes with normal increases in height during infancy or childhood. Illness or malnutrition, for example, may disrupt physical growth. However, if the duration and severity are limited and do not occur at some critical time, the child's rate of growth often accelerates once she or he recovers. The acceleration continues until height "catches up" to the level expected had no disruption occurred.

The presence of a growth center is also suggested by the converse finding: **lagging-down growth** (Prader, 1978). Some rare congenital and hormonal disorders produce unusually rapid growth. If the disorder is corrected, growth halts or slows until actual and projected height match the trajectory established before the disruption. Where might this neural control center be located? Researchers theorize that the *hypothalamus*, a small region near the base of the brain, orchestrates the genetic instructions for growth.

*Hormonal Influences*    **Hormones**, chemicals produced by various glands that are secreted directly into the bloodstream and can therefore circulate to influence cells in other locations of the body, furnish another key mechanism for converting genetic instructions into physical development. For example, hormones produced by cells in the hypothalamus, the suspected site of the growth center, trigger or inhibit production of still other hormones in the nearby *pituitary gland*, including one known as *human growth hormone (HGH)*. Infants with insufficient HGH may be nearly normal in size at birth, but their growth slows dramatically over the ensuing months and years; they typically reach an adult height of only about four to four-and-a-half feet. HGH, however, only indirectly promotes growth. It spurs the

▬ **KEY THEME**

NATURE & NURTURE

**catch-up growth**    Increase in growth rate after some factor, such as illness or poor nutrition, has disrupted the expected, normal growth rate.

**lagging-down growth**    Decrease in growth rate after some factor, such as a congenital or hormonal disorder, has accelerated the expected normal growth rate.

**hormones**    Chemicals produced by various glands which are secreted directly into the bloodstream and can therefore circulate to influence cells in other locations of the body.

production of *somatomedins,* specialized hormones manufactured by many other cells in the body that directly regulate cell division for growth (Underwood, 1991).

However, variations in amounts of hormones, as long as they fall within a reasonable range, do not account for individual differences in height. Individual differences seem to depend on the sensitivity of cells to the hormones (Tanner, 1978). For example, the pygmy Efe produce normal quantities of HGH but seem unable to use it to produce one kind of somatomedin important for growth to heights typical of other groups (Merimee, Zapf, & Froesch, 1981).

*Nutrition and Health*    For a large proportion of the world's children, adequate nutrition and exposure to diseases may be the primary determinants of whether physical growth proceeds normally or even at all. We pointed out some consequences of malnutrition for fetal development in the chapter titled "The Prenatal Period and Birth." Illness and nutritional deprivation can affect postnatal growth as well. During much of the first half of the twentieth century in Western Europe, for example, the average height gain of children at various ages increased gradually over the years, except during World Wars I and II and periods of agricultural and economic crisis, when food was far more limited. In 1984 a severe, three-month-long drought struck Kenya while researchers were engaged in a study of malnutrition in that region (McDonald et al., 1994). Food intake was cut sharply. The normal rate of weight gain among children was halved.

Severe protein-energy malnutrition can have a particularly devastating effect on growth. Children with *marasmus* fail to grow because they lack sufficient calories. Consequences include eventual loss in weight; wrinkly, aged-looking skin; an often-shrunken abdomen; and a hollow body appearance, suggesting emaciation. Another prevalent form of protein-energy malnutrition is *kwashiorkor,* or failure to develop because the diet either contains an inadequate balance of protein or includes potentially harmful toxins. Kwashiorkor typically appears in one- to three-year-old children who have been weaned, usually because of the arrival of a newborn sibling, and whose subsequent sources of protein are inadequate or contaminated.

The symptoms of kwashiorkor include lethargic behavior and apathy, wrinkled skin, and thin, wispy, slightly reddish-orange hair, but most defining is edema or swelling, especially of the stomach, giving the child a bloated appearance (Balint, 1998). Kwashiorkor leads not only to disruption in growth of the body but also to deterioration of the brain. Although some of the damage can be quickly reversed when adequate nutrition is reinstated early (Gunston et al., 1992), long-term cognitive deficits and poorer school-related performance may persist due to impaired attention and memory (Galler et al., 1990). Studies of the effects of supplementary feeding during the first few years of life, provided for nutritionally deprived families in Colombia, Guatemala, Jamaica, Taiwan, and Indonesia, indicate that both motor and mental development are enhanced (Pollitt, 1994).

As Figure 8.1 suggests, malnutrition operates at many levels to produce negative consequences for development. For example, cognitive deficits may stem from lessened motivation or curiosity and an inability to respond to or engage the environment (Brown & Pollitt, 1996). To illustrate, during the relatively brief drought in Kenya, schoolchildren became less attentive in class and less active on the playground (McDonald et al., 1994). To counter the disruption in motivation, attention, and activity level that can accompany malnutrition, some projects have been designed to encourage mothers to become more competent and effective teachers and caregivers for their young children. When nutritionally deprived children in Jamaica have been given extra play opportunities and mothers have been taught how to positively influence their children's development, children have shown substantially higher performance on developmental and intelligence tests over a fourteen-year time period compared to children not receiving the intervention (Grantham-McGregor et al., 1994). However, the scores of malnourished children, even those given this kind of intervention, continue to fall below those of children

**KEY THEME**
SOCIOCULTURAL INFLUENCE

**KEY THEME**
RISK/RESILIENCE

**KEY THEME**
INTERACTION AMONG DOMAINS

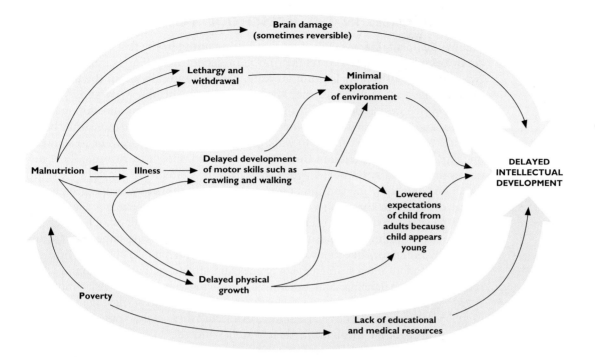

**FIGURE 8.1**

**The Many Routes by Which Malnutrition Affects Development**

Nutritional deprivation can influence development at many different levels. More frequent and severe illness, delayed growth, and slower motor skill development are among the more visible consequences. Lower intellectual development is often an outcome as well. Malnutrition can damage the brain directly. However, limited capacity to engage the environment and other repercussions from the kinds of experiences a malnourished child receives may take a further toll on intellectual development. The context in which it often persists, such as poverty and the lack of essential resources, must also be factored into a consideration of how nutritional deprivation affects development.

*Source: From Malnutrition, Poverty and Intellectual Development* by J. Larry Brown and Ernesto Pollitt. Copyright © 1996 by Scientific American. All rights reserved.

who have been adequately nourished, a finding consistently reported in studies on the long-term consequences of malnutrition (Drewett et al., 2001). Even in the United States, lower academic performance and less positive interpersonal relationships are reported among large numbers of children living in families in which inadequate amounts of nutritional food are available (Alaimo, Olson, & Frongillo, 2001).

Deficiencies in specific nutritional elements—for example, vitamins A, B complex, D, and K, as well as iron and calcium—are also linked to growth disorders affecting hundreds of thousands of children throughout the world (Balint, 1998; Hansen, 1990). Some of these disorders, especially iron-deficiency anemia, spawn lower performance on intelligence and other kinds of psychological tests. Although the problem is often assumed to be limited to low-income countries, iron-deficiency anemia is a major nutritional concern in the United States, affecting perhaps as much as 20 percent of some ethnic groups (Pollitt, 1994). More alarming is the claim that, for more than three-quarters of the children in the United States, the quality of their diet is poor or in need of improvement (Federal Interagency Forum on Child and Family Statistics, 2005).

**KEY THEME**
**RISK/RESILIENCE**

## MOTOR SKILLS IN THE PRESCHOOL YEARS

Many fundamental motor skills that the child acquired in the first two years of life continue to be modified and refined in the preschool years. For example, between two and six months after learning to walk, children typically begin to run. In the months and years that follow, they show increasingly effective body and eye-hand or eye-foot coordination, evident in their greater ability to hop and skip, or kick, dribble, and catch a ball. With increasing age, children also demonstrate better balance, reflected in the ability to walk greater distances on a beam or to stand on one foot for a longer period of time; increased speed, shown by running short distances more rapidly; improved agility, revealed, for example, in the ability to shift directions quickly while running; and greater power, shown by jumping higher or longer distances or throwing a ball farther and faster than at younger ages.

In general, activities that exercise large muscles attract the interest of toddlers and preschoolers—pulling and pushing things, stacking and nesting large objects, and eventually riding toys like kiddy cars and tricycles. As preschoolers begin to organize and display more interest in energetic games and athletic activities—jumping, hopping, running, balancing, and catching or throwing a ball—feats that emphasize speed, strength, and efficiency of performance become frequent ingredients of their everyday schedule. When first attempting to execute these skills, young children fail to prepare or follow through on their actions, and the speed or force needed to complete them in a mature way is absent. Before finally demonstrating mastery of a skill, children may also have difficulty synchronizing all of the complex movements. But, as any childhood observer can attest, gross motor skills undergo substantial improvements in the time between two and six years of age.

Fine motor skills advance, too. Older preschoolers supplement their large-muscle and athletic exercises with coloring and drawing, cutting and sculpting, and other activities that demand greater neural control and small-muscle coordination, a longer attention span, and more sophisticated planning and organization.

## IMPLICIT LEARNING

Whether it is figuring out how to pedal a tricycle or getting one's first lessons in gymnastics, many motor abilities, especially those requiring some level of skill, involve learning and practice. Implicit learning has become of increasing interest to researchers because it may help to explain the acquisition of some fundamental aspects of knowledge, not just procedural routines that accompany many motor behaviors in children, but also language and concepts. **Implicit learning** refers to knowledge that is not available to conscious reflection. It is knowledge incidentally acquired from processing structured information; the learning is unintentional. Because much of the stimulation to which we are exposed—for example, the visual-spatial environment and language—is organized by patterns and rules, learning these systematic relationships is important for adaptation to both the physical and social worlds. Essentially, as a result of the frequent covariation of specific features and attributes in experience, we implicitly become sensitive to these patterns or rules.

Research by Annie Vinter and Pierre Perruchet (2000) illustrates how the concept of implicit learning applies to a motor skills task. When we draw a figure, such as a circle, we tend to do so either clockwise or counterclockwise, depending on the position of the starting point. For example, if the starting point is above an imaginary line drawn to connect the positions of approximately eleven o'clock and five o'clock on the circle, we tend to draw it counterclockwise; if below the line, clockwise. Of course, the requirement of drawing the entire circle is the same no matter which direction is employed. In Vinter and Perruchet's study, children practiced drawing the circle but were instructed at what point to start and in which direction to draw it. Some children received far more experience drawing the circle in the direction opposite to the one they would spontaneously employ. When no longer instructed to draw the circle in a particular direction, they were much more likely to draw it in

**implicit learning** Abstract knowledge not available to conscious reflection; acquired accidentally from processing structured information.

the direction with which they had more experience. The children (as is true of adults as well) did not realize that they had drawn the circle in one direction more frequently than the other during the practice session. Nevertheless, they continued to display this behavior, a kind of implicit learning, as much as an hour after the practice session. These findings suggest that learning takes place in many contexts and situations of which we are totally unaware and by different mechanisms than those involved in, for example, classical and operant conditioning. In other words, even young children's behavior could be dramatically influenced and driven by the various kinds of regularities that they experience in their world.

F O R ◆ Y O U R ◆ R E V I E W

◆ How do genetic factors, neural control, and hormonal variations affect growth?

◆ What are catch-up and lagging-down growth?

◆ What are the consequences of poor nutrition for growth?

◆ What are the child's major achievements in motor skills in the years from two to six?

◆ What is implicit learning?

## PERCEPTION IN EARLY CHILDHOOD

R ichard Aslin and Linda Smith (1988) have noted a predicament facing anyone interested in learning about perceptual development after infancy. As research has increasingly documented sophisticated abilities in newborns and infants, interest in studying perceptual development at older ages appears to have faded. Nonetheless, researchers do find evidence of improved sensory processing during childhood (Ellemberg et al., 1999; Tschopp et al., 1999).

Perception also becomes more difficult to investigate without considering at the same time the child's developing attentional, linguistic, and cognitive skills. All of these factors may contribute to the observation that perceptual skills become more focused, organized, and confined to the meaningful and important features of the environment; in other words, perception becomes increasingly efficient with development. Eleanor Gibson (1969, 1982, 1988) has outlined an influential view of perceptual learning to account for these kinds of findings.

### PERCEPTUAL LEARNING

Eleanor Gibson's theory of perceptual learning emphasizes three changes with age: increasing specificity in perception, improved attention, and more economical and efficient acquisition of perceptual information. As we have seen earlier in this text, much of the child's first year is spent learning the sensory properties of objects, the spatial layout of her world, and the perceptual repercussions of her actions. But perceptual learning continues. For example, children acquire new kinds of visual discriminations when they learn to read. They must begin to pay attention to consistencies and variations in letters and text.

To study perceptual learning, Eleanor Gibson and her colleagues (Gibson et al., 1962) created sets of letterlike figures, such as those shown in Figure 8.2. One member of each set was designated a standard, but each set included variations of that standard. A straight line, for example, might be redrawn as a curved line, the standard rotated or reversed, a break introduced in a continuous line, or the line's perspective changed by tipping or elongating some aspect of the figure. Children four through eight years of age were shown a stack of each set of figures and asked to pick out only those identical to the standard.

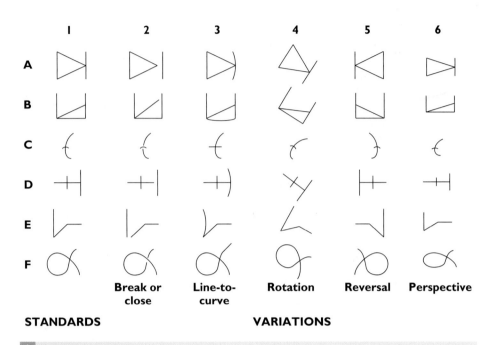

▲ **FIGURE 8.2**

**Sensitivity to Perceptual Differences**

Column 1 gives different letterlike forms used as standards in a sorting task. Columns 2 through 6 display various transformations of each standard. Four- to eight-year-olds, when shown a stack of the figures and asked to select only those identical to the standard, commit relatively few errors on variations that involve a break in the figure, presumably because the distinction is important for identifying many objects, as well as alphabetic symbols. With increasing age, errors involving rotation, reversal, and line/curve variations decrease substantially because, according to Eleanor Gibson, children who are beginning to learn to read must pay attention to these features of the stimuli. Errors involving perspective remain high at all ages, perhaps because the transformation is not important for identifying either objects or letters of the alphabet.

*Source:* Adapted from Pick (1965).

Children made many more errors for some kinds of variations than for others. Children of all ages seldom confused the standard with versions that contained breaks, perhaps because these features are important for identifying objects in the environment, as well as letters of the alphabet. However, older children did substantially better than younger children in discriminating rotations, reversals, and line-curve transformations, presumably because children who are learning to read must begin to distinguish such variations. Finally, children of all ages found it difficult to discriminate changes in perspective from the standard, a variation that can and normally should be ignored for identifying both physical objects and letters of the alphabet.

Eleanor Gibson believed the age-related improvements in performance on this activity do not come about by reinforcing children to make the discriminations. In fact, when asked to classify the letterlike forms over a series of trials, children showed steady improvement in sorting, without any feedback about their accuracy. Gibson argued that, through repeated exposure to and inspection of letters of the alphabet, children are afforded the opportunity to recognize certain critical features distinguishing such figures, an example of the powerful influence of implicit learning discussed earlier.

Still other changes are evident in perceptual development. Young children, for example, have difficulty making precise and systematic judgments about the similarity of objects based on a single dimension or attribute (Smith, 1989). Preschoolers

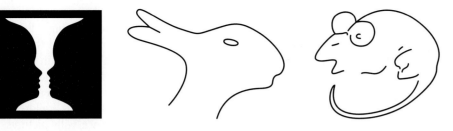

**FIGURE 8.3**

**Perceiving Ambiguous Figures**

What do you see in these ambiguous figures? If you look at each figure long enough, you will most likely see (in one or the other order) a vase and two people looking at each other, a duck and a rabbit, and a rat and an old man with glasses. In fact, your perception of the figures may often shift back and forth between the two interpretations. If you did not see both initially, you will readily detect them when told about the two possible representations. However, children less than five years of age seem unable to see more than one representation even when told about the alternative interpretation. Cognitive limitations associated with attributing multiple representations to a stimulus may be a factor in seeing both aspects of the ambiguous figures.

*Source:* Gopnick & Rosati (2001), p. 176.

might put a red rubber ball with a slightly smaller ball of pink yarn because the overall appearance of the two is similar, whereas older children are likely to lump the red rubber ball with a white foam ball on the basis of their being exactly the same size. Preschoolers also do not perceive the two distinctive interpretations that typically can be given to ambiguous figures (see Figure 8.3). Even after looking at an ambiguous figure for a long period of time, children younger than about five years of age fail to see the figures reverse, as do older children and adults (Gopnik & Rosati, 2001). Perhaps cognitive limitations in organizing perceptual information and in understanding that arrays can have multiple meanings are factors contributing to the difficulty that young children have with these kinds of perceptual tasks.

## EXPERIENCE AND PERCEPTUAL DEVELOPMENT

How do experience and inborn sensory capacities interact to determine perception? Throughout the history of psychology this has been an important question, and it continues to be so as medical and technical advances provide opportunities to compensate for some kinds of sensory disabilities. For example, blind children can perceive the existence of distant objects, presumably from changes in auditory cues they receive while moving about (Ashmead, Hill, & Talor, 1989). As a consequence, blind children are now being fitted with sonic devices to help them hear echoes to signal the direction, distance, and other qualities of objects.

The effects of these efforts with blind children are still to be demonstrated, but we can be sure of one thing from research we discussed earlier that showed evidence for sensitive periods in the development of vision: experience is extremely important for maintaining many perceptual capacities. Experience also helps to explain cross-cultural differences in perception. Environments around the world differ in their degree of "carpenteredness" (Segall, Campbell, & Herskovits, 1966). In most urban, technically advanced societies, houses are constructed according to rectilinear principles, which involve perpendicular and right-angle dimensions. Even the layouts of roads and other artifacts of the environment often follow these principles. In other environments, such as in Oceanic and many African cultures, walls and roofs may be curved, and straight lines and angular intersections may be few.

**⊶ KEY THEME**

**NATURE & NURTURE**

⊶ KEY THEME

SOCIOCULTURAL INFLUENCE

In one study, field workers administered several optical illusions, such as the Müller-Lyer and horizontal-vertical illusions, whose effects depend on straight lines that intersect, to samples of children and adults in Africa, the Philippines, and the United States (Segall et al., 1966). The researchers theorized that individuals living in a carpentered environment, who often see intersecting rectangular contours, would be more susceptible to these illusions than people living in noncarpentered environments. In fact, their results conformed to their prediction. In a related set of findings, children and adults in cultures with minimal formal education, little experience with pictures, or artworks that incorporate few depth cues were unlikely to perceive pictures or photos in three dimensions (Pick, 1987). Thus the ways in which children and adults interpret their sensory environment can be greatly affected by cultural opportunities, a finding that fits well with the conclusion that perception is influenced by experience.

F O R ● Y O U R ● R E V I E W

● What are the basic elements of Gibson's perceptual learning theory?

● What aspects of objects do children have difficulty perceiving?

● How might cross-cultural factors influence perceptual development?

## COGNITION IN EARLY CHILDHOOD

Much of our exploration of cognitive development in early childhood continues to be grounded in the foundational ideas of Jean Piaget, who outlined major advances in the thinking of children who have grown past infancy. However, contemporary research has added an abundance of fascinating details to the initial portrait Piaget painted of the emerging thinker that we find in the preschool-age child. In this section, we describe several types of conceptual knowledge, memory, and problem-solving skills that we observe in the period from two to six years of age. Because the end of early childhood signals the entrance of most children into a formal educational system, it is especially important to consider how the child's skills match the demands that will be placed on her or him as that landmark first day of school approaches.

### PIAGET'S THEORY AND EARLY CHILDHOOD

In Piaget's theory, the period of early childhood is characterized by thought that is *preoperational*. Piaget employed a classic series of problem-solving tasks to reveal the major features of children's thinking during this developmental stage.

***The Preoperational Stage (About Two to Seven Years)*** The key feature of the young child's thought in the **preoperational stage** is the *semiotic function*, the child's ability to use a symbol, an object, or a word to stand for something. The child can play with a cardboard tube as though it were a car or draw a picture to represent the balloons from her third birthday party. The semiotic function is a powerful cognitive ability because it permits the child to think about past and future events and to employ language. In fact, Piaget asserted that language would not be possible without this significant characteristic of thought; the child must possess the general cognitive ability to let one thing stand for another before she can use words to represent objects, events, and relationships. The semiotic function is also a prerequisite for imitation, imagery, fantasy play, and drawing, all of which the preschool child begins to manifest.

Despite this tremendous advance in thinking, preoperational thought has distinct limitations. One is that children in this stage are said to be **egocentric**, a term that describes the child's inability to separate his own perspective from others'. Put into words, his guiding principle might be "You see what I see, you think what I

**preoperational stage** In Piagetian theory, the second stage of development, from approximately two to seven years of age, in which thought becomes symbolic in form.

**egocentric** Term applied to the preoperational child's inability to separate his or her own perspective from those of others.

think," much like Jeremy in this chapter's opening scene, who thinks he is hiding from his older brother by crouching behind a couch. Even though his legs and feet might be sticking out for all present to see, the youngster believes he is well concealed because he himself is unable to see anyone. According to Piaget, the preschooler's egocentrism has ramifications for both his social communicative behavior and his perceptual skills. Piagetian theory predicts that children under age seven years may neither be fully attentive to the needs of a listener in a conversation nor able to appreciate the perspectives of others in perceptual tasks.

The second limitation of preoperational thought lies in the child's inability to solve problems flexibly and logically. The major tasks Piaget used to assess the status of the child's cognitive development are called the **conservation tasks**. These "thinking problems" generally require the child to observe some transformation in physical quantities that are initially equivalent and to reason about the impact of the transformation. Figure 8.4 shows several conservation tasks.

We can use the conservation of liquid quantity task to illustrate how the preoperational child thinks. The four- or five-year-old will usually quickly agree that two equal-size glasses of water contain the same amount of liquid. If the liquid from one glass is poured into a tall cylinder, however, the child will state that the cylinder now contains more than the glass does. According to Piaget, this error is the result of several limitations in preoperational thinking. One is **centration**; that is, focusing on one aspect of the problem—in this case, the height of the cylinder—to the exclusion of all other information, such as its narrower width, that could help to produce a correct solution.

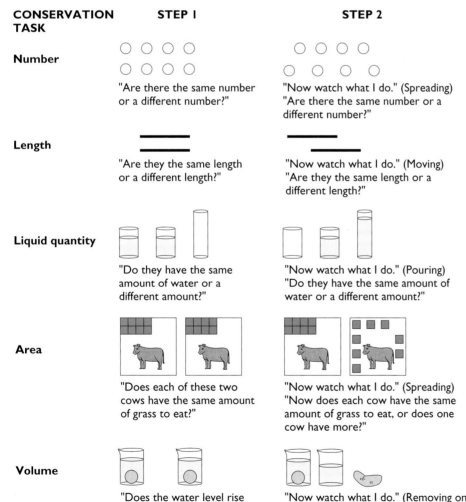

◀ **FIGURE 8.4**

**Examples of Conservation Tasks**

Depicted here are several Piagetian conservation tasks that children can solve once they reach the stage of concrete operations. Preoperational children usually say the quantities change after the transformation. Piaget believed they lack the logical thought structures necessary to reason correctly.

**conservation task** Problem that requires the child to make judgments about the equivalence of two displays; used to assess stage of cognitive development.

**centration** In Piagetian theory, tendency of the child to focus on only one aspect of a problem.

An important question concerning cognitive development is whether changes in thinking are domain-general, as Piaget claimed, or domain-specific. For example, proponents of a domain-specific view believe that children's understanding of numerical concepts advances more quickly than knowledge in other domains.

A second cognitive trait at work here is lack of **reversibility**. The preoperational child cannot mentally reverse the action of pouring from the tall cylinder to the shorter glass; if she could, she would realize that the two containers still hold the same amount of liquid that they did at the start of the problem. Third, the preoperational child tends to **focus on states** rather than on the events that occur between states. It is as though he has stored two static photographs of the two equal-size glasses, followed by static photographs of the shorter glass and the tall cylinder, rather than a video of the sequence of events. He fails to realize the connection between the two components of the conservation problem and, as a result, fails the conservation task.

### How Accurate Was Piaget About Thinking in Early Childhood?   Piaget is widely acknowledged as one of the most influential of all thinkers in the history of psychology and a founder of the study of cognitive development as we know it (Brainerd, 1996; Flavell, 1996). By introducing questions about what develops as well as how development occurs, Piaget went well beyond the descriptions of norms of behavior that had been the staple of the early years of research in developmental psychology. Moreover, once American psychologists learned of his ideas in the 1960s and early 1970s, they could no longer conceptualize development solely in terms of learning theory, which was a dominant psychological view at that time. Piaget's method of closely watching the nuances of children's behaviors and listening as they explained their reasoning provided an important and inspiring lesson for developmental psychologists: that "grand questions can actually be answered by paying attention to the small details of the daily lives of our children" (Gopnik, 1996, p. 225). At the same time, though, like all good theories, Piaget's ideas have spawned a host of debates about the fundamental nature of cognitive change. Two important issues concern the generality of cognitive growth and the precise nature of the processes that underlie advances in thinking.

Piaget maintained that, for the most part, changes in mental structures—like the shift from sensorimotor to preoperational thought—are broad, sweeping reorganizations that influence thinking in multiple domains. Development, in this view, is said to be *domain-general*. However, some theorists maintain that advances in thinking occur more rapidly in some domains than in others; that is, development is seen as *domain-specific* (Hirschfeld & Gelman, 1994). One example of domain-specific processes is children's rapid acquisition of certain concepts, such as the properties of biological entities. Children seem to acquire a vast amount of information about animals, plants, and other living things at very young ages and at a particularly rapid pace (Gelman & Williams, 1998). Moreover, this knowledge does not seem to "spill over" into other kinds of conceptual understanding. Children's acquisition of basic numerical concepts—which we already noted starts during infancy—is another candidate for domain-specific knowledge.

Many studies have confirmed Piaget's general claims about the patterns of behavior that children display at different ages. Without special training, for example, most children under age six or seven years fail conservation tasks, whereas older children perform them successfully. Yet many psychologists disagree with Piaget about the precise mechanisms that account for such patterns in the development of thinking processes. The basic challenge to Piaget's theory centers on whether cognitive development is best understood in terms of emerging symbolic, logical, and (later) hypothetical thought structures or whether some other explanation is more tenable. A case in point is the successful training of conservation by Rochel Gelman (1969). Gelman suggests that young children normally fail conservation tasks because they fail to attend to the correct portions of the problem, not because they lack mental operations like reversibility. If children's attention is directed to the salient cues, such as length or number, Gelman and others argue, they will be successful in conserving. Younger children may also be less skilled at remembering than older children, forgetting

**reversibility**   In Piagetian theory, the ability to mentally reverse or negate an action or a transformation.

**focus on states**   Preoperational child's tendency to treat two or more connected events as unrelated.

elements of problems that are essential to reaching the correct solutions. Thus cognitive development may result from a change in how information is gathered, manipulated, and stored, rather than from the alteration of cognitive structures themselves.

## CLASSIFICATION

We have already seen in Chapter 6 that infants learn about relationships that can exist among sets of objects. They use shared *perceptual* features to group items together, and by age two, can also use *thematic* and occasionally *taxonomic* relations. They will put a banana and an apple together, presumably because they belong to the higher-order conceptual group "fruit." Piaget believed that, before age seven years, children's ability to classify objects, particularly in the hierarchical manner of the latter example, is limited. Ask a young child who sees six brown beads and three white beads, all of which are wooden, "Do I have more brown beads or more wooden beads?" Chances are the four- or five-year-old will respond, "More brown beads." According to Piaget, preoperational children lack the logical thought structures to permit understanding that some classes can be subsets of others (Piaget, 1952a). Piaget was right in claiming that classification skills undergo changes with development, but the research that followed his work has revealed a far more complex portrait of this cognitive skill. Rather than showing a single kind of progression in classification skills, children evidence a range of types of conceptual skills depending on the kind of information with which they are confronted (Gelman & Kalish, 2006).

***Basic-Level Categories***   Some groupings of objects can be described as *basic level*; that is, objects go together when they look alike and can be used in similar ways, and when we can think of "average" members of the class. "Chair" is an example of a basic-level concept because virtually all chairs have seats, legs, and backs; all are used for sitting; and we can think of such a thing as a "typical" chair. In contrast, other concepts are *superordinate level*. Members of superordinate-level groups, such as "furniture," do not necessarily share many perceptual attributes, and they are broader and more general than basic-level concepts. Figure 8.5 illustrates this example of a basic-level and a superordinate-level grouping.

Eleanor Rosch and her colleagues believe that, because basic-level groups carry more information, especially perceptual information, than superordinate-level groups, they are easier for children to process. Children under age five years readily put together four pictures of different shoes or four pictures of different cars; that is, they can sort according to basic-level groupings (Rosch et al., 1976). Children in Rosch's study could not, however, proficiently sort on the basis of superordinate category by putting a shoe, shirt, sock, and pants together until they reached age eight or nine years. In fact, other research shows that the ability to sort basic-level stimuli does indeed appear early in development; it is evident as early as eighteen months of age (Gopnik & Meltzoff, 1992).

Even though Rosch's theory of basic-level categories has had widespread appeal, there are two important points of contention. First, do children really evidence knowledge and use of superordinate categories later (as opposed to early) in development? Not according to findings by Behl-Chadha (1996), which indicate that children as young as three to four months can categorize superordinate items when the habituation procedure is used. Second, do children's early categories really rely primarily on perceptual information, as the notion of basic-level concepts suggests? Jean Mandler thinks the answer is no (Mandler, 2004). Consider the items shown in Figure 8.6, which are perceptually similar but belong to two different conceptual categories. A group of seven- to eleven-month-olds was allowed to examine several items from one category, say birds, until they were familiar with them. Then two more objects, a new bird and a new plane, were presented. Infants spent more time looking at and manipulating the item from the new category—in this particular instance, planes—than the item from the familiar category, despite the striking perceptual similarities between the two groups (Mandler & McDonough, 1993). Mandler argues that, during the latter portion of the first year, infants form categories based on *meanings* rather than perceptual similarities.

## ▲ FIGURE 8.5

### Basic- and Superordinate-Level Categories

The left panel gives an example of objects that are considered a basic-level grouping. These stimuli share perceptual features, and an "average" member of the class can be conceptualized. The right panel gives an example of superordinate-level grouping. Members of such classes do not necessarily share many perceptual features, and it is more difficult to think of an "average" class member. Basic-level categories are easier for young children to employ than superordinate-level groupings.

## ▲ FIGURE 8.6

### How Do Infants Group Birds and Airplanes?

According to research by Mandler and McDonough (1993), seven- to eleven-month-old infants treated these stimuli as belonging to two separate categories, birds and planes, despite the strong perceptual similarities between them. Thus, Mandler argues, young children's categories are based on meanings rather than shared perceptual features.

*Source:* Mandler (1997).

Moreover, rather than starting with basic-level categories and progressing to superordinate categories as Rosch has postulated, Mandler and her colleagues maintain that infants begin with broad, general categories. They understand, for example, that different animals (both a dog and a bird) can drink water from a cup but that an airplane cannot. These broad categories of "animalness" become increasingly more fine-tuned and refined with experience (Mandler & McDonough, 1998, 2000), processes that presumably continue through the preschool years and perhaps beyond.

***Natural Domains*** Several developmental psychologists have asserted that some concepts or categories of objects are easier to acquire than others. Children seem to be biologically "programmed" to learn about certain conceptual domains quickly and effortlessly. In other words, some objects and events in the environment offer "privileged relationships" for the child to learn about (Gallistel et al., 1991). Among these so-called **natural domains** is knowledge about biological entities.

◄— **KEY THEME**
**NATURE & NURTURE**

Children show a dramatically early ability to classify animate versus inanimate objects. For example, a twenty-four-month-old will show obvious surprise when a chair seems to move forward on its own (Golinkoff et al., 1984), and a twelve-month-old will fuss and cry more when a robot starts to move, as opposed to a human stranger (Poulin-Dubois, Lepage, & Ferland, 1996). Three-year-olds know that living things can feel emotions but inanimate objects cannot; they say that a person can feel sad, but a doll or a rock cannot (Gelman, Spelke, & Meck, 1983). Preschoolers also begin to recognize that other processes, such as growth, illness, healing, and death, are unique to biological organisms (Backscheider, Shatz, & Gelman, 1993; Rosengren et al., 1991; Siegal, 1988).

Part of the usefulness of concepts, of course, is that they permit us to make assumptions about other category members. In other words, we go beyond the information given, perhaps even beyond the similarities of perceptual features of objects, to make conceptually based judgments or inductions about them. According to Susan Carey (1985) and Frank Keil (1989), children's inductions are largely guided by "theories" they construct about the nature of specific concepts. For the domain of biological entities, Carey found that children's theories undergo revision with development to allow more and more accurate judgments. For example, a four-year-old who is told that humans have "omenta" will say that only other animals that are very similar to humans also have "omenta." The child's theory about biology centers on what he knows about humans. In contrast, an older child would state that even animals physically dissimilar from humans have "omenta." Her theory of biology extends beyond resemblances to human beings to the broader properties that characterize living things. Theories do seem to play a role in children's categorization. When provided with theories about fictitious animals and their features, for example ("Wugs are animals that like to fight" and "Gillies are animals that like to hide in trees"), children were more successful in categorizing pictures of "wugs" and "gillies" than when they were trained to focus solely on their features ("Wugs are animals that have claws") (Krascum & Andrews, 1998).

***Individual and Cultural Variations in Classification*** Implicit in Piagetian ideas about classification is the notion that there should be many similarities in concept development among children, even those from different cultures. However, research suggests that this is not the case. For example, some three-year-olds show a clear propensity to use thematic classification, whereas others prefer taxonomic classification. Interestingly, these individual differences in classification preferences are linked to earlier unique profiles in play and language use. As one-year-olds, "thematic" children have been noted to play with objects in spatial, functional ways and, at age two, use words such as *in* and *down* more than "taxonomic" children do; that is, they have seemingly stable preferences to focus on how objects work in relation to one another (Dunham & Dunham, 1995).

**natural domain** Concept or category that children acquire especially rapidly and effortlessly.

Like this four-year-old, many preschoolers are able to count and understand at least some principles of numerical relationships, such as *cardinality*. By claiming that preoperational children do not have a conceptual understanding of number, Piaget probably underestimated children's numerical competence.

**one-to-one correspondence**
Understanding that two sets are equivalent in number if each element in one set can be mapped onto a unique element in the second set with none left over.

**cardinality** Principle that the last number in a set of counted numbers refers to the number in that set.

**ordinality** Principle that a number refers to an item's order within a set.

Cultural variations in classification occur, too. One group of researchers found that residents of rural Mexico with little formal schooling tended to group objects on the basis of their functional relations. "Chicken" and "egg" were frequently classified together because "the chicken lays eggs." On the other hand, individuals with more education relied on taxonomic classification, grouping "chicken" with "horse" because "they are animals" (Sharp, Cole, & Lave, 1979). It may be that taxonomic classification strategies are taught explicitly in schools or that education fosters the development of more abstract thought, a basic requirement for taxonomic grouping. Any full explanation of the development of classification skills will have to take into account the experiences of children within their specific sociocultural contexts.

## NUMERICAL CONCEPTS

Children as young as two years of age frequently use number terms, either to count toys, snacks, or other items or in playful ways, such as shouting, "One, two, three, jump!" as they bounce off their bed (Saxe, Guberman, & Gearhart, 1987). But do young children really understand the full significance of numbers as a tool for establishing quantitative relationships? Or are they merely repeating a series of words they have heard someone else say, without fully appreciating the conceptual underpinnings of those words?

Piaget's (1952a) position was that children under age seven years or so, before they enter the concrete operational stage, lack a full grasp of the meaning of numbers. One indication is the failure of preoperational children to succeed in the conservation of number task. In this problem, you will recall, children see two equal rows of objects—say, red and white poker chips—as was shown in Figure 8.4. Initially the rows are aligned identically, and most children will agree that they have equal numbers of chips. But when the chips in one row are spread out, the majority of children state that this row now has more chips, even though no chips have been added or taken away.

Preoperational children, Piaget maintained, fail to comprehend the **one-to-one correspondence** that still exists among items in the two rows; that is, each element in a row can be mapped onto an element in the second row, with none left over. Moreover, he believed young children have not yet attained an understanding of two important aspects of number. The first is **cardinality**, or the total number of elements in a class, as in six red poker chips. The second is **ordinality**, the order in which an item appears in the set, as in the second poker chip. According to Piaget, the child must grasp both these concepts to judge two sets of items as being equivalent.

Many contemporary researchers believe that Piaget underestimated preschool children's understanding of number concepts. For example, two-year-olds will correctly point to a picture with three items, and not a picture with one item, when asked, "Can you show me the three fish?" (Wynn, 1992b). By age four years, many children count—they say number words in sequence and, in so doing, appreciate at least some basic principles of numerical relationships. Rochel Gelman and her associates have argued that young children have knowledge of certain important fundamental principles of counting (Gelman & Gallistel, 1978; Gelman & Meck, 1983). Among these principles are (1) using the same sequence of counting words when counting different sets, (2) employing only one counting word per object, (3) using the last counting word in the set to represent the total number, (4) understanding that any set of objects can be counted, and (5) appreciating that objects can be counted in any order.

noted, for example, that performance on the false belief task is related to the child's social skills with peers (Watson et al., 1999). You will encounter several other examples of the link between theory of mind and the child's social and emotional functioning in other chapters.

## ATYPICAL DEVELOPMENT
## Childhood Autism

Childhood autism is a puzzling disorder affecting about 1 or 2 of every 1,000 children born. The disorder, more common among boys than girls, is characterized by the child's preference to be alone, poor eye contact and general lack of social skills, often the absence of meaningful language, and a preference for sameness and elaborate routines. Some autistic children show unusual skills, such as being able to recite lengthy passages from memory, put together complex jigsaw puzzles, or create intricate drawings. Often these children show a fascination with spinning objects or repeating the speech patterns of someone else. The hallmark trait, though, is the lack of contact these children have with the social world, starting at an early age. Kanner's (1943) description of one autistic boy captures the syndrome well: "He seems almost to draw into his shell and live within himself" (p. 218).

Since Leo Kanner first identified this psychopathology, numerous causes of autism have been proposed, ranging from deprived early emotional relationships with parents to defective neurological wiring in the brain (Waterhouse, Fein, & Modahl, 1996). An intriguing more recent suggestion is that autistic children, for biological reasons, lack the ability to think about mental states; that is, they lack a "theory of mind" that most children begin to develop during the preschool years. Consider how autistic children behave in the "false belief" task described earlier. Whereas most normal four-year-olds are successful, most nine-year-old autistic children fail this problem (Baron-Cohen, Tager-Flusberg, & Cohen, 1993; Peterson, Wellman, & Liu, 2005). These results suggest that autistic children cannot conceptualize the mental state of another individual. Autistic children, the argument proceeds, have severe deficits in communication and social interaction precisely because they cannot appreciate what the contents of another person's mind might be (Frith & Happé, 1999).

Not all researchers believe that the absence of a "theory of mind" explains childhood autism. Some maintain that autistic children cannot disengage their attention from a stimulus on which they are focusing, such as the hiding location in the "false belief" task (Hughes & Russell, 1993). Others suggest that problems with memory or executive control processes are responsible (Bennetto, Pennington, & Rogers, 1996; Carlson, Moses, & Hix, 1998). Moreover, even if autistic children lack a theory of mind, it may not be because of a neurological deficit. Deaf children who are not exposed to sign language for several years, for example, perform similarly to autistic children on the false belief task. Thus, as discussed earlier, the opportunity to engage in conversations from which one might glean information about the mental states of others may be a crucial factor in the development of a theory of mind (Peterson & Siegal, 1999; Woolfe, Want, & Siegal, 2002). Whatever the ultimate basis for autism, however, it seems likely that understanding basic cognitive processes will be helpful in deciphering the mechanisms underlying this perplexing childhood disorder. One outcome of this active area of research, for example, is awareness that autistic children show deficits in joint attention in the preschool years and as early as age one (Dawson et al., 2002; Leekam, Lopez, & Moore, 2000; Osterling & Dawson, 1994), a finding that can be useful in early diagnosis and treatment of this disorder.

✦ What developmental changes in visual perspective taking have been identified by researchers?

✦ What is meant by the child's "theory of mind"? What contrasting positions have been suggested as explanations for the development of a theory of mind?

✦ What is childhood autism? What are some hypotheses about its causes?

## MEMORY

Given the excellent memory skills of infants, especially in recognition and elicited imitation tasks, it should be no surprise that preschoolers, too, show superb memory in similar situations. Yet the advent of language permits something new: preschoolers can now *talk* about past events. They can talk about specific events in their lives, a form of memory called **episodic memory** (as in "What did you do at your birthday party?"). In addition, they can talk about the general knowledge they have acquired and stored, a phenomenon called **semantic memory** (as in "How many legs does a dog have?"). Interestingly, this general knowledge in turn has an impact on the ability to remember new events. For example, when preschoolers witness a logically ordered event, such as making "fun dough," they remember more details about the sequence than when the event consists of arbitrary segments, such as different activities in sand play (Fivush, Kuebli, & Clubb, 1992). In other words, knowledge about logical and causal relations among events helps memory.

*Scripts*   One way to describe the effect of a growing knowledge base on memory is in terms of scripts. **Scripts** are the organized schemes of knowledge that individuals possess about commonly encountered events. For example, by the time they are three or four years old, most children have a general schematic representation for the events that occur at dinnertime—cooking the food, setting the table, sitting down to eat—as well as for other routine events, such as going to school or attending a birthday party (Fivush, 1984; Nelson & Gruendel, 1981). When asked to remember stories based on such familiar scripts, children typically recall script-based activities, such as "eating dinner," better than other details less closely related to scripts (McCartney & Nelson, 1981). Thus scripts serve as general frameworks within which specific memories can be stored and may be one of the earliest building blocks for memory.

Conversations with parents and others probably foster the formation of scripts. When parents reminisce using rich and detailed language about past events with their children, children have better recall about the past (Reese & Fivush, 1993; Reese, Haden, & Fivush, 1993). Thus scripts are likely to be influenced by the types of social experiences the child has. Within this framework, memory is better conceptualized as something children *use* than as something they *have* (Fivush, 1997).

*Autobiographical Memory*   Think back to your childhood and try to identify your earliest memory. How old were you? It is unlikely that you will report that you were an infant or perhaps even a toddler. Most people are not able to recount memories for experiences prior to age three years (Pillemer & White, 1989; West & Bauer, 1999), a phenomenon called **infantile amnesia**. The question of why infantile amnesia occurs has intrigued psychologists for decades, especially in light of the ample evidence that infants and young children can display impressive memory capabilities.

**episodic memory**  Memory for events that took place at a specific time and place.

**semantic memory**  Memory for general concepts or facts.

**script**  Organized scheme or framework for commonly experienced events.

**infantile amnesia**  Failure to remember events from the first two to three years of one's life.

Many find that understanding the general nature of **autobiographical memories**, memories of events that have occurred in one's own life, can provide some important clues to this mystery. Between ages three and four, children begin to give fairly lengthy and cohesive descriptions of events in their past, often marking them with explicit references to time ("last Halloween" or "on my birthday") (Fivush, Haden, & Adam, 1995; Nelson & Fivush, 2004). What factors are responsible for this developmental turning point?

One explanation goes back to an idea raised by Piaget, namely, that children under age two years represent events in a qualitatively different form than older children. According to this line of thought, the verbal abilities that blossom in the two-year-old allow events to be coded in a form radically different from the action-based codes of the infant. The child's emerging verbal skills are, in fact, related to memory for personal experiences. Preverbal children who see unique events at age two do not describe them in verbal terms six months later when they are able to talk. Thus early memories seem to be encoded in a format that cannot be translated into verbal terms later on (Simcock & Hayne, 2002).

Another suggestion is that, before children can talk about past events in their life, they need to have a reasonable understanding of the self as a psychological entity (Howe & Courage, 1993, 1997). As we saw in Chapter 7, the development of the self becomes evident between the first and second years of life and shows rapid elaboration in subsequent years. The realization that the physical self has continuity in time, according to this hypothesis, lays the foundation for the emergence of autobiographical memory. Research has confirmed that the ability to recognize the self at nineteen months of age predicts the frequency with which children talk about past events when they are a few months older (Harley & Reese, 1999).

A third possibility is that children will not be able to tell their own "life story" until they understand something about the general form stories take; that is, the structure of narratives (Nelson, 1993a). Knowledge about narratives arises from social interactions, particularly the storytelling children experience with parents and the attempts parents make to talk with children about past events in their life (Reese et al., 1993). When parents talk with children about "what we did today" or "last week" or "last year," they guide the children's formation of a framework for talking about the past. They also provide children with reminders about the memory and relay the message that memories are valued as part of the cultural experience (Nelson, 1993b). It is interesting to note that Caucasian children have earlier childhood memories than Korean children do (Mullen, 1994). American children also provide more extensive, detailed descriptions of events in their past than do Korean and Chinese children (Han, Leichtman, & Wang, 1998; Wang, 2004). By the same token, Caucasian mother-child pairs talk about past events three times more often than do Korean mother-child pairs (Mullen & Yi, 1995). Moreover, Caucasian mothers who ask their children many questions about past events, elaborating on their children's comments or asking for more details ("And what did Daddy do on the boat?"), tend to have children who talk more about the past (Harley & Reese, 1999). Thus the types of social experiences children have factor into the development of autobiographical memories.

A final suggestion is that children must begin to develop a "theory of mind" before they can talk about their own past memories. Once children begin to accurately answer questions like "What does it mean to *remember*?" and "What does it mean to *know* something?" improvements in memory also seem to occur (Perner & Ruffman, 1995).

It may be that the developments just described are intertwined with and influence one another, that the ability to talk about one's past arises from the interplay of several factors, not just one (Pillemer, 1998). Talking with parents about the past may enhance the development of the self-concept, for example, as well as help the child understand what it means to "remember" (Welch-Ross, 1995).

**KEY THEME**

**INTERACTION AMONG DOMAINS**

**KEY THEME**

**SOCIOCULTURAL INFLUENCE**

**autobiographical memory**
Memory for specific events in one's own life.

## How Reliable Is Children's Eyewitness Testimony?

The research on children's memory, particularly recognition memory, suggests that their ability to remember events from the past is very impressive. But when children are called on to testify in court after they have witnessed or been victims of abuse, neglect, or other crimes, their capability to render an accurate account of past events has been called into question.

### What Is the Controversy?

Just how reliable is children's memory when they are called on to give eyewitness testimony? Children's memory for events, even those that occurred months or years in the past, is remarkably good. On the other hand, children's memory is also susceptible to suggestive or leading questions by attorneys, clinicians, and other interrogators (Bruck & Ceci, 1999, 2004). The stakes are high regarding these issues. If children have been the victims of crime, the perpetrators should be punished; but if children's memories are inaccurate in these contexts, a criminal suspect might be falsely accused.

### What Are the Opposing Arguments?

Some research indicates that children's recall of distinctive events, such as a trip to Disney World or a medical emergency, is surprisingly complete and accurate even four or five years after the event (Fivush & Schwarzmueller, 1998; Peterson & Whalen, 2001). For example, in one study of two- to thirteen-year-old children who had been treated in a hospital emergency room, even two-year-olds remembered a substantial amount about their injuries when they were interviewed five years later (Peterson & Whalen, 2001). Data like these suggest that children's memories are reliable.

On the other hand, other studies have shown that children, especially preschoolers, are likely to misreport a past event if they are asked misleading questions. In some of the original studies of "false memory" in children, Stephen Ceci and his colleagues tested children ages three through twelve years on their ability to remember the details of a story (Ceci, Ross, & Toglia, 1987). A day later, children in one of the experimental conditions were asked leading questions that distorted the original information, such as "Do you remember the story about Loren, who had a headache because she ate her cereal too fast?" In the original story, Loren had a stomachache from eating her eggs too fast. Compared with children who did not hear misleading questions, children who heard biased questions made more errors on a subsequent test that required them to select pictures depicting the original story: they chose the pictures showing a girl eating cereal and having a headache. This tendency to err was especially pronounced in children ages four and under.

### What Answers Exist? What Questions Remain?

Many factors may influence just how suggestible children are. One is exactly who is doing the questioning. For example, in Ceci's study just described, misinformation provided by an adult tended to distort memory more than misinformation provided by another child; the perceived power of the questioner may make a difference. Second, when children are asked questions repeatedly, particularly yes-no questions, they are likely to change their answers or speculate inappropriately (Poole & White, 1991, 1993). Preschoolers in particular may perceive the repeated question as a signal that their first answer was incorrect. Repeated questions, even when they are neutral, can lead to false memories because the information contained in them can be incorporated into the "gist" of the real memory (Brainerd & Mojardin, 1998). Third, supplying dolls and props for children to reenact the event can lead to elevated false reports, especially among younger children (age three) and when this form of interview occurs after a delay of several weeks (Greenhoot et al., 1999). Finally, suggestibility may be reduced when children first are reminded to consider the basis of their information, a phenomenon called *source monitoring* (Poole & Lindsay, 2002; Thierry & Spence, 2002). In one laboratory study, for example, preschoolers were first asked to answer "Did you see it on the tape?" or "Did I tell you?" before they were asked leading questions about the story. This group was less likely to be influenced by leading questions compared with a group of children who were asked the leading questions first (Giles, Gopnik, & Heyman, 2002).

An important, and perhaps obvious, consideration in this discussion is that memories—those of both children and adults—generally decline with the passage of time. The results of a recent experiment showed that the amount and accuracy of information that children spontaneously recalled about past events went down after two years, especially if they did not have an opportunity to be reminded of the original event. Under the latter conditions, up to 50 percent of the new information that children added to their memories after being prompted by an experimenter was found to be inaccurate (Pipe et al., 1999). Because extended periods of time often elapse between a criminal event and the trial, these findings are especially relevant.

Given this information, what is the best way for professionals in the criminal justice system to encourage children to give reliable eyewitness accounts based on what we know from research?

## PROBLEM-SOLVING SKILLS

Problem-solving skills become more elaborate and complex as children pass through early childhood. Although these children are not yet in school, an environment that explicitly demands more focused problem solving, many are enrolled in child care centers or preschools, which often present children with educational tasks that include elements of problem solving. Furthermore, during their play, children may encounter their own "problem situations" which require some form of resolution. Whether it is completing a simple puzzle or figuring out how to arrange blocks to make a bridge over a road, preschoolers often find themselves in circumstances in which they have to think through some options in order to achieve specific goals.

*Representation*   One of the most basic capacities required for problem solving is the ability to use symbols—images, words, numbers, pictures, maps, or other configurations that represent real objects in the world. Piaget argued that children are unable to think with symbols—that is, use representations—until near the end of the sensorimotor stage of development at about eighteen months of age. Others, however, have challenged this position and argue that representational capacities are evident much earlier in infancy. Jean Mandler (1988, 1998) has pointed out that a number of early abilities that infants display support this thesis. For example, infants begin to use gestures to stand for objects or events prior to age one year. Similarly, young infants' apparent knowledge about the physical properties of objects, described in Chapter 6, suggests that they must hold some internal representation of them.

Although infants may have basic representational capacities, toddlers and older children far more readily recognize that external symbols of real objects in the world can be used to further their problem-solving efforts. For example, Judy DeLoache (1987) asked two- and three-year-olds to search for a small toy hidden in a scale model of a room. Next, the children were brought into a life-size room that corresponded to the scale model they had just seen. Could they find the real-life toy that corresponded to the smaller replica in the previous segment of the experiment? If they saw a small Snoopy toy under a miniature couch, would they look for a large

An important cognitive skill that emerges at about age three is the understanding that a model may *represent* a real-life event. Representation is a fundamental skill necessary for problem solving.

Snoopy under the couch in the life-size room? The three-year-olds could find the hidden object on more than 70 percent of the trials. But the two-year-olds could do so on only 20 percent of the trials. Later, when both age groups were asked to locate the toy back in the scale model, they did so with few errors. Thus the search failures of two-year-olds in the life-size room were not due to memory problems. DeLoache believes that two-year-olds have difficulty with *dual representation*; that is, with understanding that a scale model can be both an object in its own right and a representation of a life-size room. By age three, however, children have the cognitive capacity, flexibility, and conceptual knowledge to appreciate that a symbol, such as a model, can "stand for" a real-life event. In other words, children gain **representational insight** (DeLoache, 2000; DeLoache & Smith, 1999).

Some factors can accelerate young children's tendency to develop representational insight. Repeated exposure to scale models, drawings, and live video photography helps children younger than three years to understand that these are symbols of real-world events (Callaghan & Rankin, 2002; DeLoache, 2004; Troseth, 2003). So do explicit explanations that scale models have been created for the purpose of standing for corresponding large-scale objects and spaces. As young children generally become more aware of the intentions of others, they are better able to grasp that people create representations for this purpose (Sharon, 2005). The great interest that contemporary researchers have in illuminating the development of representational skills is understandable given the growing presence of images and graphic symbols in contemporary culture.

***Transferring Skills***    One essential element in higher-order thinking is the ability to use what you have learned in one situation and apply it to other, similar problems. How well do children extend their existing problem-solving skills to new circumstances? This has been a long-standing question in psychology, particularly among researchers who have studied the role of generalization in learning. It has also been a question of paramount importance to educators, who assume that children will find some application in their everyday life for what they have learned in the classroom. The ability to transfer knowledge requires that children learn the original

**representational insight**    The child's ability to understand that a symbol or model can stand for a real-life event.

problem well, note the resemblance between the old and the new problem, and apply the appropriate activities to the new problem. This process is called **analogical transfer**, in that the child must notice the one-to-one correspondence that exists between the elements of one problem and those of another, and then apply the familiar skills to the novel context.

An experiment by Ann Brown and her coresearchers illustrates how this process can occur (Brown, Kane, & Echols, 1986). Three- to five-year-olds were read a story in which a magical genie had to move his jewels from one bottle across a high wall to another bottle. Several items were available to help the genie: glue, paper clips, sheets of paper, and so on. The experimenter and each child enacted the solution, rolling up the paper into a tube and using it to transport the jewels from one bottle to the other. The children were then presented with a different problem having the same general solution (a rabbit that needs to get its Easter eggs across a river can roll paper into a tube to transport them). Whether the children were able to transfer the solution to a new problem depended on whether they recalled the goal structure of the previous problem. If they remembered the major actor, his goal, and the solution to his problem, even three-year-olds could solve the new problem. Other research by Zhe Chen has shown that four- and five-year-olds can profit from viewing a series of drawings depicting a rabbit using sticks to obtain an apple from the bottom of a container. When faced with a similar problem, these children were more likely to enact the solution than children who had seen irrelevant drawings (Chen, 2003). Based on studies like these, as well as the research on infants' problem-solving capabilities that we have already encountered in Chapter 6, it seems clear that young children are capable of a very important cognitive skill—analogical transfer.

## F O R ✦ Y O U R ✦ R E V I E W

- ✦ What forms of memory are evident in preschool children?

- ✦ What role do scripts play in the memory processes of preschool-age children?

- ✦ What explanations have been offered for the emergence of autobiographical memory?

- ✦ What has research told us about the reliability of eyewitness testimony among young children?

- ✦ What kinds of changes have researchers observed in young children's ability to demonstrate representational insight?

- ✦ What factors encourage children to transfer skills from one situation to another?

## LANGUAGE IN EARLY CHILDHOOD

round the child's second birthday, a significant achievement in language production appears: the child becomes able to produce more than one word at a time to express ideas, needs, and desires. At first, two-word utterances, such as "Doggie go" and "More juice," prevail, but the child soon combines greater numbers of words in forms that loosely resemble the grammatical structure of his or her native language. When children combine words, they are stating more than just labels for familiar items; they are expressing relationships among objects and events in the world. Most impressive is that most of this process is conducted with relatively little deliberate instruction about grammar from adults. All of this represents no small feat for a two-year-old who is now mastering some of the more complex aspects of language.

**analogical transfer** Ability to employ the solution to one problem in other, similar problems.

The effective use of language includes a host of nonverbal behaviors, rules of etiquette, and even changing the content of speech according to the identity of the listener and the situation surrounding the communication. How do you ask someone for a favor? Not, the child soon learns, by saying, "Hey, you, get me that ball!" The child also learns that, if someone did not hear what she said, she can sometimes add a gesture to complete the communication. And the proper way to speak to an adult who has some authority will probably include more polite forms and fewer terms of familiarity than when speaking to a peer.

Clearly, language is a multifaceted skill with many overlapping dimensions, from understanding and uttering sounds to appreciating the sometimes subtle rules of social communication. Despite the complexities, by the time they are four or five years old, most children speak much as adults do. Their progress in mastering vocabulary, syntax, and pragmatics continues during the school years and thereafter, but they acquire the essential elements of the language system in an impressively brief period.

## SEMANTICS

The number of new words that the child learns grows rapidly from age eighteen months through the preschool years. By the time they enter school, children know more than 14,000 words (Carey, 1978). How do children learn the meanings of so many new words in such a short period of time?

Many researchers believe that certain biases operate in the child's literal "search for meaning." Consider the toddler who hears a new word, such as *eggbeater*. What does that word mean? Logically, it could refer to a host of objects or perhaps an action instead of an object. Testing the numerous hypotheses could take an inordinate amount of time. Several researchers argue that children are biased to form more restricted hypotheses about the meanings of words; if they were not, they would not learn language so rapidly and with so few errors. *Constraints* on word learning give young children an edge in figuring out the meanings of words from the vast array of possibilities.

One way that the child acquires word meanings is by a process called **fast-mapping**, in which the context in which the child hears words spoken provides the key to their meanings. Often the child's initial comprehension of a word is an incomplete guess, but a fuller understanding of its meaning follows from successive encounters with it in other contexts (Carey, 1978). Upon hearing the word *eggbeater* while watching someone unload various implements from the dishwasher, the child may think it is some kind of cooking tool; hearing the word again, as someone uses a specific object to mix a bowl of eggs, refines the meaning of the word in the child's mind. Children are often able to derive the meanings of words quickly, even when the exposure is brief, if the context in which they hear those words is meaningful (Rice & Woodsmall, 1988).

Young children also tend to assume that new words label unfamiliar objects, a phenomenon called the **mutual exclusivity bias** (Littschwager & Markman, 1994; Markman, 1987, 1990). Researchers have been able to demonstrate that children tend to treat new words as labels for new objects rather than as synonyms for words they already know. For example, Ellen Markman and Gwyn Wachtel (1988) showed three-year-olds pairs of objects; in each set, one object was familiar and the other was unfamiliar (for example, a banana and a pair of tongs). When children were told, "Show me the X" where X was a nonsense syllable, they tended to select unfamiliar objects. The mutual exclusivity bias emerges at about age three and is evident even in deaf children who use American Sign Language (Lederberg, Prezbindowski, & Spencer, 2000).

Another bias in word learning, the **shape bias**, refers to the child's assumption that a new word labels an entire object, specifically its form. Young children learning that a new object is called a *zup*, for example, apply that word to other objects

**fast-mapping**   Process through which the context in which the child hears words spoken provides the key to their meanings.

**mutual exclusivity bias**   Tendency for children to assume that unfamiliar words label new objects.

**shape bias**   The child's assumption that a new word labels an entire object, specifically its form.

similar in shape, but not in color, rigidity, or other characteristics (Graham & Poulin-Dubois, 1999; Samuelson & Smith, 2000). Children extend new words to objects that come from a similar conceptual category, too. Consider a study conducted by Ellen Markman and Jean Hutchinson (1984). Four- and five-year-olds looked at a picture as the experimenter labeled it with a nonsense syllable. For example, a cow was called a *dax*. Then two other pictures were presented: in this case, a pig and milk. When asked, "Can you find another *dax?*" most children pointed to the pig, not the milk. In contrast, when children heard no label for the cow and were simply instructed to "find another one," they tended to associate the cow with milk.

Where do constraints on word learning come from? Some researchers believe they are innate and unique to word learning (Waxman & Booth, 2000). Others suggest that they arise from growth in general knowledge about objects and their relationships to one another (Smith, 1995; Smith, 1999). It may also be that some word-learning biases, such as the "whole object bias," are more important in the early stages of semantic development, whereas others, such as the "category bias," play a larger role in later stages (Golinkoff, Mervis, & Hirsh-Pasek, 1994).

## GRAMMAR

As the child begins to combine words, she learns the principles of **grammar**, the rules pertaining to the structure of language. Grammar includes two components, *syntax* and *morphology*. **Syntax** refers to the rules that dictate how words can be combined. The order in which words are spoken conveys meaning; for example, "Eat kitty" and "Kitty eat" do not mean the same thing, even in the simplified language of the young child. A word's position in a sentence can signify whether the word is an agent or the object of an action, for example. The rules of syntax vary widely from one language to another, but within a given language they operate with consistency and regularity.

**Morphology** refers to the rules for combining the smallest meaningful units of language to form words. For example, the word *girl* has one morpheme. Adding *-s* to form *girls* makes the number of morphemes two and changes the meaning from singular to plural. Similarly, morphemes like *-ed* and *-ing* create a change in the tense of words. One of the most remarkable features of language acquisition is the child's ability to detect the rules of syntax and morphology and to use them to create meaningful utterances of his own with little direct instruction.

***Early Grammars: The Two-Word Stage***   At first, children's two-word utterances consist of combinations of nouns, verbs, and adjectives, and omit the conjunctions, prepositions, and other modifiers that give speech its familiar flow. In addition, young talkers use very few morphemes to mark tense or plurals. Because speech at this stage usually contains only the elements essential to getting the message across, it has sometimes been described as **telegraphic speech**.

In his systematic observations of the language of three children, Martin Braine (1976) noted that speech at this stage contained a unique structure which he dubbed *pivot grammar*. The speech of the children he observed contained noticeable regularities: one word often functioned in a fixed position, and other words filled in the empty slot. For example, one child said, "More car, more cookie, more juice, more read." Table 8.1 contains several other examples of a two-year-old's early word combinations.

More recent research has confirmed that children use nouns in particular in these pivot-type constructions, even when the noun is a nonsense word, such as *wug*. Thus, if a caregiver says, "Look! A wug!" children would say "More wug" or "Wug gone" (Tomasello et al., 1997). Children do not yet produce utterances according to a well-developed grammar, though; their constructions are probably based on the phrasings they hear as the adults around them speak (Tomasello & Brooks, 1999).

**grammar**   Rules pertaining to the structure of language.

**syntax**   Grammatical rules that dictate how words can be combined.

**morphology**   Rules of how to combine the smallest meaningful units of language to form words.

**telegraphic speech**   Early two-word speech that contains few modifiers, prepositions, or other connective words.

**Table 8.1   One Child's Early Grammar**

This table shows several examples of one two-year-old's two-word speech. Frequently, one word—the pivot word—is repeated, while several other words fill the other slot. The pivot word can occupy either the first or second position in the child's utterances.

| | | | |
|---|---|---|---|
| no bed | boot off | more car | airplane all gone |
| no down | light off | more cereal | Calico all gone |
| no fix | pants off | more cookie | Calico all done |
| no home | shirt off | more fish | all done milk |
| no mama | shoe off | more high | all done now |
| no more | water off | more hot | all gone juice |
| no pee | off bib | more juice | all gone outside |
| no plug | | more read | all gone pacifier |
| no water | | more sing | salt all shut |
| no wet | | more toast | |
| | | more walk | |
| | | outside more | |

*Source:* Adapted from Braine (1976).

Roger Brown (1973) also studied the regularities of child speech in the two-word stage in ten different cultures. Table 8.2 summarizes some of the results. In children's verbalizations, agents consistently precede actions, as in "Mommy come" or "Daddy sit." At the same time, inanimate objects are usually not named as agents. The child rarely says, "Wall go." To avoid making this utterance, the child must know the meaning of wall and that walls do not move. Thus the child's semantic knowledge is related to the production of highly ordered two-word utterances.

**Table 8.2   Examples of Semantic Relations in Child Syntax**

Children's word orders often reflect knowledge of semantic relationships, such as the idea that agents precede actions or that actions are followed by locations. Roger Brown believes the semantic relations shown in this table are incorporated into the syntactic constructions of children in many different cultures.

| Semantic Relation | Examples |
|---|---|
| agent + action | Mommy come; Adam write |
| action + object | eat cookie; wash hand |
| agent + object | Mommy sock; Eve lunch |
| action + location | sit chair; go park |
| entity + location | lady home; baby highchair |
| possessor + possession | my teddy; Daddy chair |
| entity + attribute | block yellow; box shiny |
| demonstrative + entity | dat book; dis doggie |

*Source:* Adapted from Brown (1973).

Many experts believe that no one syntactic system defines the structure of early language for all children (Maratsos, 1983; Tager-Flusberg, 1985). Some children speak with nouns, verbs, adjectives, and sometimes adverbs, whereas others pepper their speech with pronouns and other words such as *I, it,* and *here* (Bloom, Lightbown, & Hood, 1975). Most researchers agree, however, that individual children frequently use consistent word orders and that their understanding of at least a small set of semantic relationships is related to that word order. Moreover, numerous detailed observations of children's language indicate that they never construct "wild grammars"; some utterances, such as "Big he" or "Hot it," are simply never heard (Bloom, 1990). Such observations have distinct implications for explanations of syntactic development.

As we saw with semantics, children just starting to use more complex speech are able to comprehend more information conveyed by different grammatical structures than they are able to produce. Two-year-olds, for example, demonstrate an understanding of the difference between past, present, and future tenses, even though these distinctions do not typically appear in their own speech (Wagner, 2001). They also show that they understand the different meanings conveyed by transitive versus intransitive verbs (those with and without objects, respectively). In one study, twenty-five-month-old children saw a video of a duck bending a bunny over as both animals made arm circles. The experimenter said either, "The duck is blicking the bunny" or "The duck and the bunny are blicking," constructions that are more complex syntactically than the child's own spontaneous utterances. Then children saw two screens, one that portrayed bending and one that portrayed arm circling. When asked to "Find blicking," children who had heard the term as a transitive verb looked at bending, and those who had heard the term as an intransitive verb looked at arm circling (Naigles, 1990). What cues are children using to make this correct distinction? Two-year-olds can detect the difference between transitive and intransitive verbs when subject and object are represented by nouns and also when they are made more ambiguous in the form of pronouns, as in "She pilks her back and forth" versus "She pilks back and forth." These results suggest that information denoted by the number of arguments or relationships expressed in the sentence helps children decipher its meaning (Fisher, 2002).

***Later Syntactic Development*** At age two and a half, children's speech often exceeds two words in length and includes many more of the modifiers and connective words that enrich the quality of speech. Adjectives, pronouns, and prepositions are added to the child's repertoire (Valian, 1986). Between ages two and five, the child's speech also includes increasingly sophisticated grammatical structures. *Morphemes,* such as *-s, -ed,* and *-ing,* are added to words to signal plurals or verb tense, and more articles and conjunctions are incorporated into routine utterances. The child also comes to use negatives, questions, and passives correctly.

Several other sophisticated forms of speaking emerge after age two, one of which is the use of negatives. In her examination of language acquisition in four children, Lois Bloom (1991) found a predictable sequence in the use of negatives. Initially, children use the negative to express the *nonexistence* of objects, as in "No pocket," said as the child searches for a pocket in her mother's skirt. In the second stage, children use the negative as they *reject* objects or events. For example, one of Bloom's participants said, "No sock" as she pulled her sock off her foot. Finally, negatives are used to express *denial,* such as when the child states, "No dirty" in response to his mother's comment about his dirty sock. This sequence has also been observed cross-culturally, among Chinese children learning to speak Cantonese (Tam & Stokes, 2001). Young children form negatives not just by putting the negative marker at the beginning of an utterance but also by embedding it deep within a statement, as in "My sweetie's no gone" (de Villiers & de Villiers, 1979).

Questions, too, are formed in a fairly consistent developmental sequence, although not all children display the pattern we are about to describe (Maratsos, 1983). Children's earliest questions do not contain inverted word order but consist instead of an affirmative sentence or a declarative preceded by a *wh-* word (*who, what, why, when, where*), with a rising intonation at the end of the statement ("Mommy is tired?"). Subsequently, children form questions by inverting word order for affirmative questions ("Where will you go?") but not negative ones ("Why you can't do it?"). Finally, by age four, children form questions for both positive and negative instances as adults do (Klima & Bellugi, 1966).

One of the more difficult linguistic constructions for children to understand is the passive voice, as in "The car was hit by the truck." Children typically begin to comprehend the meaning of a passive construction by the later preschool years, but they may not use this grammatical form spontaneously and correctly until several years later. Prior to age four, children are also limited in their ability to generate sentences using subject-verb-object (the transitive) with novel verbs they have just learned, as in "He's meeking the ball" (Tomasello & Brooks, 1998). Michael Tomasello maintains that, when two- and three-year-olds do use more complex syntactic constructions, such as the passive and transitive voices, they are initially imitating what adults say. Only later in the preschool and early school years do they have a deeper appreciation for the forms that grammatical constructions can take (Brooks & Tomasello, 1999; Tomasello, 2000).

One particularly interesting phenomenon of the preschool and early school years is the child's tendency to use **overregularizations,** the application of grammatical rules to words that require exceptions to those rules. From time to time, for example, young children use words like *goed* or *runned* to express past tense, even if they previously used the correct forms, *went* and *ran*. Perhaps children make these mistakes because they forget the exception to the general rule for forming a tense (Marcus, 1996). Whatever the reason, these constructions suggest that the child is learning the general rules for forming past tense, plurals, and other grammatical forms (Marcus et al., 1992).

How exactly do children master the rules of syntax? Some clues may come from the phonology or sounds of language. Is the word *record* a noun or a verb, for example? The answer depends on which syllable is stressed; if the first, the word is a noun; if the second, it is a verb. Children may pick up cues from stress, the number of syllables in a word, or other tips from the sounds of language to help them classify words as nouns, verbs, or other grammatical categories (Kelly, 1992). Other cues about syntax may come from the meanings of words. According to the **semantic bootstrapping hypothesis,** for example, when children learn that a certain animal is called a "dog," they also notice that it is a thing (noun) and, later in development, that it is an agent (subject) or a recipient (object) of action (Pinker, 1984, 1987). Noticing that adults use certain patterns of speech and understanding their contents may help, too. For example, when young children hear adults say, "Look! The dog's hurling the chair. See? He's hurling it," the pronouns in the pattern "He's [verb]ing it!" may help children understand the unfamiliar verb *hurling* and its use with a subject and object in a transitive sentence. In other words, children's knowledge of semantics influences their mastery of grammar (Childers & Tomasello, 2001).

**⚷ KEY THEME**

**INTERACTION AMONG DOMAINS**

## PRAGMATICS

Just as important as semantic and syntactic rules are cultural requirements or customs pertaining to the proper use of speech in a social context. Is the child speaking with an elder or a peer? Is the context formal or informal? How does the speaker express politeness? Each situation suggests some unique characteristics of speech, a tone of voice, a formal or more casual syntactic structure, and the choice of specific words. In the context of playing with a best friend, saying, "Gimme that" might be perfectly appropriate; when speaking with the first-grade teacher, saying, "Could I please have that toy?" will probably produce a more favorable reaction. These examples demonstrate the child's grasp of **pragmatics,** the rules for using language effectively and appropriately according to the social context.

**overregularization** Inappropriate application of grammatical rules to words that require exceptions to those rules.

**semantic bootstrapping hypothesis** Idea that children derive information about syntax from the meaning of words.

**pragmatics** Rules for using language effectively within a social context.

***Acquiring Social Conventions in Speech***  When do children first understand that different situations call for different forms of speech? When Jean Gleason and Rivka Perlmann (1985) asked two- to five-year-olds and their parents to play "store," they observed that, at age three, some children modified their speech depending on the role they were playing. For example, one three-and-a-half-year-old boy who was the "customer" pointed to a fake milk bottle and said, "I want … I would like milk." His revision showed an understanding that an element of politeness is required of a customer. Preschoolers also have some limited understanding that different listeners are typically spoken to in different ways. In a study in which four- and five-year-olds were asked to speak to dolls portraying adults, peers, or younger children, the participants used more imperatives with dolls representing children and fewer with dolls representing adults and peers (James, 1978).

The child's facility with social forms of politeness increases with age. Researchers in one study instructed two- to six-year-olds to *ask* or *tell* another person to give them a puzzle piece. Older children were rated by adults as being more polite than the younger children, particularly when they were asking for the puzzle piece. Usually, older children included such words as *please* in their requests of another person (Bock & Hornsby, 1981).

Parents undoubtedly play a significant role in at least some aspects of the acquisition of pragmatics, especially because they deliberately train their children to speak politely. Esther Greif and Jean Gleason (1980) observed the reactions of parents and children after children had received a gift from a laboratory assistant. If the child did not say, "Thank you" spontaneously (and most of the preschoolers in the sample did not), the parent typically prompted the child with "What do you say?" or "Say thank you." Parents also serve as models for politeness routines; most parents in the study greeted the laboratory assistant upon entry and said good-bye when the assistant departed. In cultures such as Japan, in which politeness is a highly valued social behavior, children begin to show elements of polite language as early as age one year (Nakamura, 2001), probably because parents model and reinforce these verbal forms.

Incorporating social conventions into language often involves learning subtle nuances in behaviors, the correct words, vocal intonations, gestures, or facial expressions that accompany speech in different contexts. Children may get direct instruction on the use of verbal forms of politeness, but it is not yet clear exactly how they acquire the other behaviors that accompany socially skilled communication.

***Referential Communication***  A group of experiments that has been especially useful in providing information on children's awareness of themselves and others as effective communicators centers on **referential communication,** situations that require the child to either talk about a topic specified by the experimenter or evaluate the effectiveness of a message describing some sequence of events. Researchers note whether the child's message is sufficient to communicate his or her intent or, alternatively, whether the child is able to detect ambiguous or uninformative components in the messages heard.

In a classic study of referential communication, Robert Krauss and Sam Glucksberg (1969) asked four- and five-year-olds to describe a series of unfamiliar geometric forms to another child who could not see them (see Figure 8.8). The speaker had to provide the listener with enough information to duplicate an array the speaker was constructing. The results showed that children at this age often rely on personal descriptions of the stimuli (for instance, "It looks like Daddy's shirt"), messages that are not at all helpful to the listener. Thus young children's ability to understand the requirements of the listener and to adjust their speech accordingly is limited when they are describing unfamiliar items and when the interaction is not face to face.

On the other hand, observations of children in more natural interactions with one another suggest that, well before they enter school, children appreciate at least some of the requirements of the listener and can modify their speech to make their communication effective. In a study of the communication skills of preschool-age

**referential communication**  Communication in situations that require the child to describe an object to a listener or to evaluate the effectiveness of a message.

▶ **FIGURE 8.8**

**An Experiment in Referential Communication**

In Krauss and Gluckberg's (1969) study of referential communication, four- and five-year-olds had to describe a series of unfamiliar geometric forms (pasted on blocks) to other children who could not see them. In this illustration, for example, the speaker on the left must explain to the listener on the right which forms to place on the stacking peg. The results showed that children this age are generally ineffective in transmitting this type of information. Research in more naturalistic settings, however, demonstrates that preschoolers can engage in effective referential communication.

*Source:* Adapted from Krauss & Glucksberg (1969).

children, Marilyn Shatz and Rochel Gelman (1973) asked four-year-olds to describe a toy to either an adult or a two-year-old listener. When the children spoke to the younger child, they shortened their utterances, used simple constructions, repeated utterances, and employed more attention-getting devices than when they spoke to the adult. Other researchers have also observed that even two-year-olds use techniques to make sure their messages get across during the normal interactions that occur in a nursery school. Children point, seek eye contact with listeners, and use verbal attention getters, such as "Hey," to ensure that listeners hear what they have to say (Wellman & Lempers, 1977). In addition, when a listener somehow indicates that he has misunderstood or says, "What?" two- and three-year-olds attempt to make their communication more effective. They may repeat their statement or restate the utterance with a better choice of words, a change in verb form, or some other linguistic correction (Ferrier, Dunham, & Dunham, 2000; Levy, 1999; Shwe & Markman, 1997).

The mature use of language involves the ability to understand the demands of the situation, be sensitive to the needs of the listener, and employ subtle nuances in speech that are compatible with the situation. The child's failure to acquire the social skills that are part of effective communication can have broad consequences for the qualities of relationships that she or he establishes with parents, teachers, and peers, among others.

## THE LINGUISTIC PERSPECTIVE ON LANGUAGE DEVELOPMENT

When you consider the sequence of language acquisition, three points are especially noteworthy. First, language development proceeds in an orderly fashion. Although individuals may vary in the age at which they attain language milestones or in the precise form of those achievements, children do not acquire language in a haphazard fashion. Second, children learn language rapidly and with seemingly little effort. With the exception of those with some serious physical or psychological problem, all children learn to speak within only a few years, despite the diverse range of skills required. Third, children produce *generative* language; that is, they do not merely duplicate what others say, but create novel and unique expressions of their own. How do children accomplish all of this? An important theoretical perspective—the linguistic perspective—attempts to account for these remarkable achievements.

Noam Chomsky (1980, 1986) and other linguists emphasize the structures that all languages share, those syntactic regularities that the young language learner quickly identifies in the course of everyday exposure to speech, such as when the child learning English notices that nouns representing agents precede verbs and nouns representing the objects of actions follow verbs. According to Chomsky, children possess an innate system of language categories and principles, called *universal grammar*, which predisposes them to notice the general linguistic properties of any language. As children are exposed to a specific language, a process called *parameter setting* takes place; that is, "switches" for the grammatical rules that distinguish English from Japanese or Arabic from French are set. After abstracting the general rules of language, children apply them to form their own novel and creative utterances. Language learning, say most linguists, is different from other forms of learning; there are constraints on what the child will be predisposed to learn, and language learning is governed by its own set of principles. In other words, language learning is *modular*, separate and distinct from other kinds of processing. Furthermore, many linguists believe language is a uniquely human enterprise, one that is not part of the behavioral repertoire of other species.

Research evidence generally supports the idea that learning and applying rules is part of the process of learning language. Children rapidly learn syntactic rules for forming plurals, past tense, and other grammatical forms in their first five years, and can even apply them to words they have never heard before. In a famous experiment, Jean Berko (1958) demonstrated this phenomenon by presenting children with several nonsense words, such as *wug*. Children were able to state correctly that the plural form of *wug* is *wugs*, although they had never heard made-up words like these. Even seven-month-old infants show evidence of being able to learn rules that can help them to learn language. In one study, infants heard several three-word sentences from an artificial language until they showed a decline in interest in them. For example, they heard constructions that had an ABA form such as "ga ti ga" and "li na li." During the test phase, though, they showed a distinct preference for sentences with an ABB construction, such as "wo fe fe." Likewise, infants who were habituated to the ABB structure preferred sentences with the ABA structure during the test phase (Marcus et al., 1998). Moreover, linguistic theories provide a plausible explanation of the occurrence of *overregularizations*; these can be seen as the product of a language learner who has done too good a job, implementing rules even in cases in which exceptions exist. The drive to find structure in language is evident in another interesting way—in the development of *creole* languages, in which children in a particular cohort permanently embellish or expand the organization of the language they hear. Researchers have discovered a deaf community in Nicaragua in which individuals created their own version of sign language. With each new generation of children, the complexity of that language's structure has increased (Senghas & Coppola, 2001). The implication is that children do not simply pattern their speech after what they hear; rather, they use language in creative and highly organized ways.

Linguistic approaches help to explain just how children can master the complex, abstract rules that characterize all languages, given what some have called the "impoverished input"—the incomplete or ungrammatical utterances—that they typically hear (Lightfoot, 1982). They also help us understand how children learn language without explicit teaching of the rules of grammar or lists of vocabulary words. However, critics point out that linguistic approaches may reflect more closely the biases of adult theoreticians who attempt to describe the logical necessities of language achievements than the actual processes children use. Michael Tomasello (2000), for example, maintains that young children's use of language does not always reflect an appreciation of abstract principles of syntax. When children first learn how to use verbs, they use some in very restricted ways ( "cut paper," "cut it") and others in varied types of constructions ("I draw on man," "Draw it by Santa Claus"). This lack of consistency suggests that children are not using general rules about how verbs work to produce their utterances.

What about the linguists' claim that language is uniquely human? In the past several decades, numerous attempts have been made to train members of the ape family to use language, all with some apparent success (Gardner & Gardner, 1971;

Premack, 1971; Rumbaugh, Gill, & von Glasersfeld, 1973), although many early studies were criticized on methodological grounds (Terrace et al., 1979). Nevertheless, in one well-controlled study, an ape named Kanzi was raised from infancy with exposure to human speech similar to that provided to a young girl named Alia. When Kanzi was eight years old and Alia was two, they were tested on their ability to comprehend an assortment of novel sentences, such as "Take the potato outdoors." On many of the sentences, ape and child performed equally well (Savage-Rumbaugh et al., 1993). Scientists have also identified areas in the left hemisphere of the chimpanzee brain that seem to correspond to Broca's area and Wernicke's area in humans (Cantalupo & Hopkins, 2001; Gannon et al., 1998). However, compare the ages of Kanzi and Alia; it took many more years to bring the ape to the two-year-old child's level of mastery. Furthermore, although apes may be able to use visual props or sign language to form two-word communications, they rarely generate more complex grammatical structures. Perhaps most important, when observed in their natural habitat, apes do not point to or show objects to other apes. In other words, although they do use highly patterned signals to communicate with one another, they do not use signs or gestures in referential or symbolic ways (Tomasello, 1998). Perhaps their limitation is a cognitive rather than a linguistic one, so questions about the modularity of language skills in humans cannot be answered from these observations. Even so, apes are evidently limited in their ability to use language, despite intensive efforts to teach them.

## F O R • Y O U R • R E V I E W

- ♦ What are the processes by which young children acquire the meanings of words?

- ♦ What are the major grammatical accomplishments of children in the two-word stage of language acquisition?

- ♦ What syntactic accomplishments follow the two-word stage?

- ♦ What aspects of pragmatics do children acquire in the preschool years?

- ♦ How does the linguistic perspective account for language acquisition? What research findings are consistent with a linguistic perspective?

# CHAPTER RECAP

## Summary of Developmental Themes

### NATURE & NURTURE

**How do nature and nurture interact in physical, cognitive, and language development in early childhood?**

Genetic factors, brain centers that regulate growth, and hormones such as HGH are biological factors that contribute to physical growth. Nutrition is an example of an environmental factor that influences physical growth. According to Gibson, perceptual development involves perceptual *learning*—in particular, noticing consistencies and variations among stimuli in the environment. In Piaget's theory, maturation, in conjunction with experience, is responsible for the child's cognitive growth. Linguistic

theories emphasize the child's innate tendencies to process language information in particular ways. However, the child must be exposed to linguistic input to manifest these tendencies.

### SOCIOCULTURAL INFLUENCE

**How does the sociocultural context influence physical, cognitive, and language development in early childhood?**

Knowledge of and access to nutrition can have important consequences for children's physical growth. Perceptual development may be influenced by cultural factors, such as the degree of "carpenteredness" in the environment.

Elements of language acquisition, such as learning pragmatics, are also influenced by the unique cultural context in which the child is developing.

## CONTINUITY/DISCONTINUITY

**Are physical, cognitive, and language development in early childhood continuous or discontinuous?**

Piaget stressed stagelike attainments as the child progresses from sensorimotor to preoperational thought. However, changes in cognitive skills, such as memory, appear to arise from successive increments, not qualitative stagelike changes.

## INTERACTION AMONG DOMAINS

**How do physical, cognitive, and language development in early childhood interact with other domains of development?**

The child's emergent cognitive skills interact with social capabilities. For example, children's decreasing cognitive

egocentrism will affect their ability to make judgments in perspective-taking tasks, which have important social ramifications. At the same time, social experiences influence cognitive skills. For example, autobiographical memory emerges in the context of learning how to tell a narrative.

## RISK/RESILIENCE

**What factors promote risk or resilience in physical, cognitive, and language development during early childhood?**

Exposure to malnutrition poses a serious risk to children's physical and intellectual development. Deficiencies in certain vitamins, iron, and calcium are also linked to physical and cognitive risks.

# Chapter Review

## PHYSICAL DEVELOPMENT IN EARLY CHILDHOOD

**How do genetic factors, neural control, and hormonal variations affect growth?**

Genetic factors predict a person's height and body proportions. Genetic factors work primarily through neural and *hormonal* activity. The hypothalamus contains cells that may determine whether growth is proceeding according to genetic instructions. These cells trigger human growth hormone, a substance that interacts in complex ways with other hormones to influence growth.

**What are catch-up and lagging-down growth?**

*Catch-up growth* refers to the tendency for the rate of growth to increase for a period of time after disease or illness. *Lagging-down growth* is the tendency for it to decrease for a period of time after rapid gains.

**What are the consequences of poor nutrition for growth?**

Poor nutrition can result in decreased height and weight, deterioration of the brain, long-term cognitive deficits, and, ultimately, death.

**What are the child's major achievements in motor skills in the years from two to six?**

During early childhood, children show advances in gross motor skills such as running, jumping, and skipping. They also show major improvements in fine motor skills which

enable children to use scissors, hold crayons, and perform other actions requiring small muscle movements.

**What is implicit learning?**

*Implicit learning* refers to knowledge acquisition that is not always within conscious awareness. Motor skills are often acquired in this fashion.

## PERCEPTION IN EARLY CHILDHOOD

**What are the basic elements of Gibson's perceptual learning theory?**

Gibson's theory helps us to understand how, with experience, children show steady improvements in the ability to classify different stimuli that share similar features, such as certain letters of the alphabet. Reinforcement is not necessary for this form of learning to take place.

**What aspects of objects do children have difficulty perceiving?**

Children have difficulty making similarity judgments among stimuli based on just one feature. They also have difficulty seeing both interpretations in ambiguous figures.

**How might cross-cultural factors influence perceptual development?**

Environments that are highly "carpentered" may be responsible for children's being more susceptible to visual illusions like the Müller-Lyer and horizontal-vertical illusions. Also, children who live in cultures that do not emphasize formal education have difficulty perceiving depth cues in pictures and photographs.

# COGNITION IN EARLY CHILDHOOD

### What are the major characteristics of preoperational thought according to Piaget?

Children in the *preoperational stage* can think using symbols, but their thought is limited in that it is *egocentric*. Children fail *conservation tasks* because they do not yet have the logical thought structures that allow them to think about *reversibility*. They also focus on only one aspect of a problem (*centration*), and they tend to *focus on states*.

### What are some criticisms of Piaget's theory? What research evidence supports these criticisms?

Some critics maintain that cognitive development is not as general as Piaget maintained, but rather shows more rapid advances in some domains than in others. One example is children's early sensitivity to biological entities. Researchers have also proposed explanations for the behaviors Piaget observed. Some data suggest that changes in information processing—such as the ability to pay attention to the correct cues in a problem—lie behind advances in cognition.

### What developmental changes have researchers observed in children's classification, numerical reasoning, and spatial concepts in the preschool years?

Some researchers believe that children begin to classify with basic-level categories and progress to superordinate relations. Others maintain that children's early concepts are global and based on meanings, and that they become more refined with age. The learning of concepts in *natural domains* occurs at an accelerated pace. Children also seem to form theories about the meanings of concepts, ideas that become more elaborated with age.

Piaget maintained that preoperational children fail to comprehend *one-to-one correspondence, cardinality,* and *ordinality*. However, by age four, children are able to count, and they display some knowledge of important numerical principles. Preschoolers understand relations such as "bigger" and "smaller," and have basic intuitions about fractions, but have more difficulty with large number sets and numbers that are close together.

Preschoolers are able to use landmark and geometric cues to orient themselves in space. They can use simple maps to navigate a route, but map-reading skills improve over the next few years. Children learn to understand that symbols on a map refer to corresponding real-world objects, understand the scale and alignment of a map, and become able to plan an efficient route using a map.

### What developmental changes in visual *perspective taking* have been identified by researchers?

Children first recognize that their own view is not identical to that of another person (Level 1). Later in development, about age three or four years, they can determine the specifics of the other's view (Level 2).

### What is meant by the child's "theory of mind"? What contrasting positions have been suggested as explanations for the development of theory of mind?

*Theory of mind* refers to the child's awareness of his or her own mental states, as well as the mental states of others. In contrast to Piaget's claims for early childhood *realism*, children can distinguish between mental and physical phenomena in the preschool years. Some researchers feel that theory of mind is an innate, modular form of knowledge, whereas others claim it arises from the child's experiences with language.

### What is childhood autism? What are some hypotheses about its causes?

Childhood autism is a disorder in which children display a lack of contact with the social world which is manifested by communication deficits. Some researchers believe autism arises from the lack of a theory of mind. Others suggest that information-processing deficits, such as attention, memory, or executive control processes, are responsible.

### What forms of memory become evident in preschool-aged children?

Preschoolers evidence both *episodic* and *semantic* memory. In the first case, they begin to talk about specific events that took place in their life. In the second case, they evidence general knowledge about things and events in the world.

### What role do scripts play in the memory processes of preschool-aged children?

Preschoolers have clearly formed *scripts* for common events; these are organized schemes that include the repeated general elements of those events. Preschoolers show evidence of using scripts to recall the details of stories they have heard.

### What explanations have been offered for the emergence of autobiographical memory?

Few people can remember events that occurred prior to age three, a phenomenon called *infantile amnesia*. Improvements in memory for specific events in one's life, or *autobiographical memory*, are tied to the child's emerging verbal skills, a growing awareness of the self, and increasing understanding of the form of a narrative.

### What has research told us about the reliability of eyewitness testimony among young children?

Young children's memories, like adults', are vulnerable to the influence of misleading questions. In fact, children under age four years may be especially susceptible. Factors such as a powerful questioner, the use of repeated questions, and the use of props can exacerbate the distortion of memory. Encouraging source monitoring can reduce the influence of leading questions.

### What kinds of changes have researchers observed in young children's ability to demonstrate representational insight?

By age three, children attain *representational insight*, the ability to use a symbol for a real-world event.

### What factors encourage children to transfer skills from one situation to another?

*Analogical transfer*, the ability to employ the solution to one problem in other similar problems, can be encouraged by helping children to see the goal structure of the problem.

## LANGUAGE IN EARLY CHILDHOOD

### What are the processes by which young children acquire the meanings of words?

Children seem to learn the meanings of words by relying on constraints such as *fast-mapping*, the *mutual exclusivity bias*, and the *shape bias*.

### What are the major grammatical accomplishments of children in the two-word stage of language acquisition?

Two-year-olds begin to use two-word utterances, sometimes called *telegraphic speech* because it contains few modifiers, prepositions, and connective words. They also use few morphemes to mark tense or plurals. Although no single syntactic system defines the structure of language at this stage, acquisition for individual children is orderly and may rely on semantic knowledge.

### What syntactic accomplishments follow the two-word stage?

As children begin to speak more words, they learn and apply the rules of *grammar*. These rules include both *syntax* and *morphology*. Children add morphemes, modifiers, prepositions, pronouns, and connective words to their speech. They begin to use negatives, questions, and eventually the passive voice. One interesting type of error they sometimes make is called *overregularization*, the application of grammatical rules to words that are exceptions. Children also evidence *semantic bootstrapping*, using the meanings of words to help them apply the rules of syntax.

### What aspects of *pragmatics* do children acquire in the preschool years?

Children begin to show that different situations call for different forms of speech around age three. They adjust their speech, depending on the listener, and begin to use polite forms, probably because parents instruct them to. Some research indicates that preschoolers have problems with *referential communication*, but when observed in natural settings, young children evidence sensitivity to the needs of their communication partners.

### How does the linguistic perspective account for language acquisition? What research findings are consistent with a linguistic perspective?

Linguistic theorists emphasize the child's abstraction of general grammatical principles from the stream of speech. They tend to take a nativist stance and believe that language skills are modular. Data showing that children are able to learn rules, that they creolize language, and that animals are limited in their ability to learn language are consistent with linguistic theory.

## KEY TERMS AND CONCEPTS

analogical transfer (p. 295)

autobiographical memory (p. 291)

cardinality (p. 284)

catch-up growth (p. 271)

centration (p. 279)

conservation task (p. 279)

egocentric (p. 278)

episodic memory (p. 290)

fast-mapping (p. 296)

focus on states (p. 280)

grammar (p. 297)

hormones (p. 271)

implicit learning (p. 274)

infantile amnesia (p. 290)

lagging-down growth (p. 271)

morphology (p. 297)

mutual exclusivity bias (p. 296)

natural domain (p. 283)

one-to-one correspondence (p. 284)

ordinality (p. 284)

overregularization (p. 300)

perspective taking (p. 286)

pragmatics (p. 300)

preoperational stage (p. 278)

realism (p. 288)

referential communication (p. 301)

representational insight (p. 294)

reversibility (p. 280)

script (p. 290)

semantic bootstrapping hypothesis (p. 300)

semantic memory (p. 290)

shape bias (p. 296)

syntax (p. 297)

telegraphic speech (p. 297)

theory of mind (p. 288)

# 9 SOCIAL AND EMOTIONAL DEVELOPMENT

icky," the author said to her then-five-year-old son. "What do you think should be on the cover of this book? It's about children, you know."

"Well … ," he thought for a moment.

"How about a picture of a child?"

"A boy or a girl?" asked the mother.

"How about one of each?" he suggested. The mother was pleased that her son chose a girl as well as a boy. She had tried hard to teach him to think about gender in nonstereotypical ways, and his willingness to include girls seemed to indicate that her efforts were successful.

"What should they be doing?" the mother continued.

"Well, how about having the boy play with a computer?" he quickly responded.

"And the girl?" she asked.

"I think she should have a tea party or something."

**NATURE & NURTURE** How do nature and nurture interact in social and emotional development in early childhood?

**SOCIOCULTURAL INFLUENCE** How does the sociocultural context influence social and emotional development in early childhood?

**CONTINUITY/DISCONTINUITY** Are social and emotional development during early childhood continuous or discontinuous?

**INTERACTION AMONG DOMAINS** How do social and emotional development in early childhood interact with other domains of development?

**RISK/RESILIENCE** What factors promote risk or resilience in social and emotional development during early childhood?

As this brief scene suggests, preschoolers are becoming very much aware of the intricacies of their social world. Not only do they know the obvious and sometimes subtle elements of *gender stereotypes*—beliefs and expectations about the characteristics of males and females—but they are also learning about other important dimensions of human interactions. They make important strides in mastering the world of emotions, develop a more complex sense of self, and evidence the beginnings of moral awareness. Growing cognitive and language skills permit the child's self-expression—her wants, needs, and desires—in the full-blown sense of the word. Perhaps for the first time, as they experience the full force of the preschooler's growth as a social being, parents feel the need to start to guide or limit their child's behaviors. Social and emotional development occurs at a remarkably swift pace during the preschool years. In this chapter, we focus on the most significant elements of that growth.

## EMOTIONAL DEVELOPMENT IN EARLY CHILDHOOD

Anyone who has spent time with preschoolers is probably aware of the intensity and range of the emotions they express. From their infectious bursts of unbridled laughter to their sometimes distressing temper tantrums, preschoolers are for the most part the epitome of emotionally expressive beings. One of the major developmental tasks for this age group is to learn to regulate and control their emotional displays in keeping with the social norms and values of their background culture.

### EXPRESSING EMOTIONS

We have already learned that infants express such basic emotions as joy, sadness, and fear. Preschoolers build on this initial repertoire, expanding in both the number of specific emotions they communicate and the ways in which they convey them. In addition, basic emotions, such as fear, undergo developmental changes, particularly in the types of stimuli that elicit them. Whereas early expressions of fear result from physical events, such as loud noises or strange people, now fear occurs as a response to more complex psychological events, such as the possibility of failing an academic task or being rejected by peers (Morris & Kratchowill, 1983; Rutter & Garmezy, 1983). As you can see, the child's cognitive skills and social awareness are very much intertwined with emotional development.

***The Emergence of Self-Conscious Emotions*** By their second year, many children begin to show emotions that reflect a more complex understanding of the self and social relationships: shame, guilt, and envy, for example. Each of these emotions requires the child to understand the perspective of another person—that the person may be disappointed with the child, may be hurt, or may feel affection for a third party. Such emotions also require a consciousness about the self and about one's

By the time they are two years old, children start to show more complex emotions such as jealousy. As they get older, children become better able to manage their emotions when they are in front of other people.

relations to others (Campos et al., 1983; Lewis, 1989). Accordingly, emotions like envy and guilt are known as **self-conscious emotions**.

The visible signs of self-conscious emotions can be multifaceted: a child displaying shame lowers her head and eyes, collapses her body, and often has an odd smile on her face (Lewis, Alessandri, & Sullivan, 1992). Asked to dance in front of people or told that he or she has failed a task, a preschooler might show embarrassment with a smiling face, a look away, and nervous body movements (Lewis & Ramsay, 2002). The expression of self-conscious emotions changes with age. At age two years, children show discernible signs of jealousy through physical actions. The child may wedge himself between his mother and father as they are hugging or hit a sibling whom his parent just kissed (Cummings, Zahn-Waxler, & Radke-Yarrow, 1981). But as children get older, they are better able to manage their jealousy, especially in front of their parents (Miller, Volling, & McElwain, 2000).

*Talking About and Understanding Emotions*   With the advent of language, children can communicate feelings by verbalizing instead of just furrowing their brow and crying or making some other facial display. Children begin to use language to describe feeling states between eighteen and thirty-six months of age, shortly after they begin to talk. Inge Bretherton and Marjorie Beeghly (1982) asked mothers of twenty-eight-month-olds to keep a diary of their children's verbalizations that referred to psychological states. Besides being able to apply a wide range of terms to express both positive and negative feelings, these children were able to discuss the conditions that led to a specific emotion and the actions that followed as a consequence. Several children, for example, made statements similar to "Grandma mad. I wrote on wall," suggesting an understanding of the reasons for another's emotion. Another type of utterance made by several children—"I cry. Lady pick me up and hold me"—signifies an understanding that emotions may be related to subsequent actions.

From age three to four years and older, children use more varied and complex emotion words (Fabes, Eisenberg, et al., 2001). At this age, children also become more proficient in verbally describing the causes and consequences of emotions (Barden et al., 1980). They tend to agree that certain events, such as receiving a compliment, lead to happy emotions, whereas others, such as being shoved, lead to negative feelings. Furthermore, they are able to suggest ways to ameliorate another's negative emotions, such as hugging a crying sibling or sharing toys to placate an angered playmate (Fabes et al., 1988).

○━┱ KEY THEME

**INTERACTION AMONG DOMAINS**

**self-conscious emotion**   Emotion, such as guilt and envy, that appears later in childhood and requires more knowledge about the self as related to others.

By age three or four, children's understanding of emotions includes knowledge about how to soothe others' negative emotions. Preschoolers might suggest hugging or sharing a toy with a distressed child, for example.

***Sex Differences in Emotions***    According to the familiar stereotype, females are more emotionally expressive and more sensitive to the emotional states of others than are males. Do boys and girls actually differ in any facet of emotional development? It seems that for the most part the answer is yes—girls are more emotionally expressive and more attuned to emotions than are boys.

During the preschool years, there do not appear to be strong, clear-cut sex differences. Some studies find that girls tend to show more positive emotions than boys (e.g., Matias & Cohn, 1993), but other researchers report that boys are more expressive in general (Weinberg et al., 1999). Eventually, though, sex differences in emotion show up. By elementary school, girls show a greater range of emotions than do boys (Casey, 1993). Boys, in contrast, tend to express one particular emotion—anger—more often than do girls (Hubbard, 2001). Finally, to some degree, girls show a heightened sensitivity to emotions compared with boys. For example, female children and adults from widely varying cultures are better than males at identifying the positive and negative emotions displayed on faces (Brown & Dunn, 1996; Hall, 1984).

Observations of parents' behaviors suggest that many of these sex differences that appear later in childhood may be taught or modeled directly in interactions that begin in infancy but are especially apparent in the preschool years. Mothers of preschoolers mention feeling states more often and discuss a wider variety of emotions when they talk with their daughters than when conversing with their sons (Dunn, Bretherton, & Munn, 1987; Kuebli, Butler, & Fivush, 1995). Mothers are also more facially expressive when they play with their two-year-old girls than with boys, thus exposing girls to a greater range of emotions and displaying more social smiles to them (Malatesta et al., 1989). In general, parents encourage girls to maintain close emotional relationships and to show affection, whereas they instruct boys to control their emotions (Block, 1973). Thus, although biological explanations of sex differences cannot be ruled out completely, many of the emotional behaviors we see in males and females appear to be influenced by their learning histories.

**KEY THEME**

**NATURE & NURTURE**

Caregivers start to expect preschoolers to regulate their emotions. Once children become more facile with language, they start to express their feelings by speaking rather than with tantrums or by crying.

**KEY THEME**

**INTERACTION AMONG DOMAINS**

**KEY THEME**

**RISK/RESILIENCE**

## REGULATING EMOTIONS

By the preschool years, most caregivers begin to expect children to control their emotional displays. Two-year-olds continue to use the emotion regulation strategies we saw in infants, such as distraction; when they are presented with a snack or a gift but must wait to obtain it, they typically shift their attention to other objects. Normally, this strategy alleviates their distress (Grolnick, Bridges, & Connell, 1996). But when young children focus on the source of their frustration, their anger tends to increase (Gilliom et al., 2002). By age three, many children show fewer tantrums and intense negative outbursts as they increasingly rely on language to communicate their intents and desires (Kopp, 1992). Physiological maturation probably contributes, too. Researchers believe that early childhood is a time when the frontal portions of the brain, which control excitation and inhibition of emotion-linked behavior, are maturing (Fox, 1994; Schore, 1996).

One of the most important aspects of emotion regulation is what it predicts later in development. Preschoolers and elementary-age children who express a great deal of anger, hostility, and other negative emotions show poorer social competence in school and are isolated from or rejected by peers (Eisenberg et al., 1997; Fabes et al., 2002; Hubbard, 2001). Perhaps of most concern, researchers have found that the inability to regulate negative emotions is part of the behavioral profile of children with conduct problems. In one study, preschool-age children, some of whom were identified as being at risk for behavior problems, were invited to a laboratory to participate in several cognitive tasks. After each child finished the session, he or she was offered a prize that was undesirable and disappointing. The children's emotional expressions were observed in both the presence and absence of the experimenter. As Figure 9.1 indicates, boys who were at risk for conduct problems expressed more anger, speaking rudely and with obvious negative emotion, compared with low-risk boys. High-risk boys also maintained that anger for longer periods of time while in the presence of the experimenter. Low-risk boys showed anger, too, but only when they were alone. The pattern for girls differed: girls from almost all risk categories expressed fewer negative emotions. These results suggest that boys who are reported by parents and teachers to have fewer behavior problems are better able to manage their emotions when in a social setting. Boys with conduct problems, on the other hand, seem to have difficulty regulating their anger, a fact that could be a source of their generally disruptive behavior (Cole, Zahn-Waxler, & Smith, 1994). The evidence linking emotion regulation and later social development continues to mount, not only for children in the United States but also for those in other cultures, such as Indonesia and China (Eisenberg, Pidada, & Liew, 2001; Zhou et al., 2004).

Is there anything that parents can do to encourage healthy emotion regulation in their preschoolers? Researchers have reported that mothers who at least *attempt*

Even preschoolers display care and concern about others. Here a boy brushes sand from the face of his younger sister in an effort to keep her from becoming upset. These kinds of actions suggest that prosocial behavior is an early aspect of human development. Moreover, its expression very likely is greatly influenced by the socialization practices of parents and other caregivers.

communications, attempt to behave in ways consistent with those representations (Grusec & Goodnow, 1994). Nevertheless, describing changes in the child's ability to reason about moral questions has been left largely to other theorists, such as Jean Piaget and Lawrence Kohlberg, whose ideas on moral development we will encounter in later chapters.

## PROSOCIAL BEHAVIOR AND ALTRUISM

A young child consoles a friend in distress, helps her pick up the pieces of a broken toy, or shares a snack. These **prosocial behaviors**, social actions performed to benefit others and perhaps the self, have come under increasing investigation in recent years as another way to understand the development of values and moral behavior in children. Among prosocial behaviors is **altruism**, behavior carried out to help others without expectation of rewards for oneself. Acts of kindness or assistance are often discretionary but highly valued in many communities.

Several contemporary theorists believe an essential element underlying prosocial or altruistic behavior is **empathy**, a vicarious, shared emotional response involving an understanding and appreciation of the feelings of others, which includes sympathetic concern for the person in need of assistance (Eisenberg, Fabes, & Spinrad, 2006). Perhaps humans are biologically predisposed to exhibit such a trait. Even infants show signs of sensitivity to the distress of others. Two-and three-day-olds may cry when other infants cry, but not in response to other, equally loud noises (Simner, 1971). In addition to crying, ten-to fourteen-month-olds may whimper or silently attend to expressions of distress from another person. Often they respond by soothing themselves, sucking their thumb, or seeking a parent for comfort (Radke-Yarrow & Zahn-Waxler, 1984). Perhaps because the boundary between self and another individual is not yet clear at this age, consoling the self is a form of coping with another's distress, a self-focused emotional reaction more than a genuine prosocial behavior.

Between one and two years of age, empathy promotes new behaviors, typically called *sympathy*: touching or patting the distressed person as though to provide solace, seeking assistance for the person, or even giving the person something to provide comfort, such as a cookie, blanket, or teddy bear. The person's emotional

**prosocial behavior** Positive social action performed to benefit others.

**altruism** Behavior carried out to help another without expectation of reward.

**empathy** Understanding and sharing of the feelings of others.

state may also be labeled with such expressions as "Cry," "Oh-oh!" or "Hurting." Slightly older children display more varied and complex responses, including comforting and helping the troubled child, asking questions of her, punishing the agent of the child's distress, protecting the child, and asking an adult for help (Radke-Yarrow & Zahn-Waxler, 1984; Zahn-Waxler et al., 1992). Such expressions are not uncommon. In one study of toddlers playing at home with familiar peers, almost half of the children who observed distress in their peers responded with an attempt to comfort or assist them. They were especially likely to do so if they themselves had caused the distress (Demetriou & Hay, 2004)

## F O R ◆ Y O U R ◆ R E V I E W

◆ What are the signs of the development of conscience in the early childhood years?

◆ What factors are related to the development of conscience?

◆ How does social learning theory account for the development of moral behaviors?

◆ What is the evidence that children are capable of prosocial behaviors in early childhood?

## GENDER ROLES IN EARLY CHILDHOOD

Many **gender stereotypes** exist in our society; that is, most of us have beliefs and expectations about the characteristics of females and males. Boys, according to these stereotypes, are active, aggressive, independent, and interested in science. Girls, on the other hand, are passive, not aggressive, and socially oriented. At what ages and to what extent do children have knowledge of these stereotypes? Furthermore, are such common beliefs actually manifested in the everyday behaviors of children? Are any differences we might observe due to the biological makeup of males and females? What part do socialization and cognitive development play in this process? We will address these central questions as we discuss **gender-role development**, the process by which children acquire the characteristics and behaviors prescribed for males and females in their culture. Before the mid-1960s, most psychologists regarded the socialization of children into traditional masculine and feminine roles as both a natural and a desirable outcome of development. Behavioral sex differences were viewed as inevitable and were linked to comparable sex differences among nonhumans (Kohlberg, 1966; Mischel, 1966; Shaw & Darling, 1985). But changes in social values in the mid-1960s, especially those accompanying the women's movement, shifted the ways in which psychologists approached sex differences and gender-role socialization. Many of the questions that interest developmental psychologists today represent both a challenge to traditional assumptions about the nature and origins of gender roles and sex differences and a concerted effort to determine the developmental processes that underlie children's acquisition and enactment of gender roles.

### GENDER STEREOTYPES

Suppose a group of college students is asked to rate the "typical" boy or girl on a number of psychological attributes. Will they rate certain traits as more typical of males than of females, and vice versa? College students respond that characteristics like independence, aggression, and self-confidence are associated with masculinity. In general, attributes like these, which are associated with acting on the world, are classified as **instrumental**. In contrast, emotional expressiveness, kindness, and gentleness are linked with femininity. These perceived feminine characteristics are often classified as

**gender stereotype** Expectation or belief that individuals within a given culture hold about the behaviors characteristic of males and females.

**gender-role development** Process by which individuals acquire the characteristics and behaviors prescribed by their culture for their sex. Also called *sex typing*.

**instrumental characteristics** Characteristics associated with acting on the world; usually considered masculine.

**expressive**, or associated with emotions and interactions with other people. Table 9.1 shows other traits often associated with masculinity and femininity (Martin, 1995).

These gender stereotypes are not limited to our own society. Researchers asked children and adults from thirty nations in North and South America, Europe, Africa, and Asia to indicate whether certain traits are more frequently associated with men or women in their culture. The results showed many cross-cultural similarities in the stereotypes that adults attributed to males and females (Williams & Best, 1982).

**Table 9.1    Stereotypic Characteristics Attributed to Males and Females**

When college students were asked to rate a typical boy or girl on a number of personality traits, strong patterns emerged among traits that were seen as being associated with each sex. Male traits generally fall into a cluster called *instrumentality* and female traits into a cluster labeled *expressiveness*.

| | Mean Typicality Ratings by Sex of Child Target[a] | |
| Item Type | Boys | Girls |
|---|---|---|
| **Sex-typed Masculine[b]** | | |
| Self-reliant | 5.05 | 3.69 |
| Does dangerous things | 4.96 | 2.57 |
| Enjoys mechanical objects | 5.57 | 2.68 |
| Dominant | 5.36 | 3.54 |
| Enjoys rough play | 6.09 | 3.07 |
| Independent | 4.95 | 3.59 |
| Competitive | 5.70 | 4.16 |
| Noisy | 5.78 | 3.93 |
| Physically active | 6.23 | 4.80 |
| Aggressive | 5.60 | 3.41 |
| Conceited | 4.38 | 3.46 |
| **Sex-typed Feminine[c]** | | |
| Gentle | 3.21 | 5.36 |
| Neat and clean | 3.05 | 5.42 |
| Sympathetic | 3.42 | 5.33 |
| Eager to soothe hurt feelings | 3.35 | 5.33 |
| Well-mannered | 4.01 | 5.44 |
| Cries and gets upset easily | 3.20 | 4.95 |
| Easily frightened | 3.27 | 4.89 |
| Soft-spoken | 3.00 | 4.64 |
| Helpful around the house | 3.27 | 5.31 |
| Gullible | 3.74 | 4.33 |
| Reliable | 4.33 | 4.74 |
| Truthful | 4.31 | 4.91 |
| Likeable | 4.99 | 5.68 |
| **Nonsex-typed** | | |
| Adaptable | 4.90 | 4.72 |

[a]Maximum scores = 7.0
[b]Indicates the ratings for boys were significantly higher than for girls.
[c]Indicates that ratings for girls were significantly higher than for boys.

*Source:* Martin (1995).

**expressive characteristics**
Characteristics associated with emotions or relationships with people; usually considered feminine.

Children show an awareness of gender stereotypes remarkably early in development. Like this boy, many two-year-olds play with toys in a manner that is consistent with gender stereotypes.

**⚷ KEY THEME**

**SOCIOCULTURAL INFLUENCE**

Despite the many similarities in gender stereotypes across cultures, some differences occurred among nations in the specific characteristics attributed to males and females. For example, Italian adults stereotypically associated "endurance" with women, although most adults in other countries believed this is a masculine trait. Nigerian adults believed "affiliation" is neutral, whereas adults in other countries said it is a feminine characteristic. Thus we cannot say that specific characteristics are always attributed to males or to females. We can say, however, that the tendency to stereotype on the basis of sex is found in a variety of cultural settings.

Children begin to acquire gender-role stereotypes and employ them as guides for their behavior at a surprisingly early age—from about two years onward. At eighteen months of age, infants prefer to look at toys stereotypically associated with their own sex (Serbin et al., 2001). By age two, boys prefer to play with cars, balls, and trains, whereas girls prefer dolls, cooking utensils, and brush and comb sets (Campbell, Shirley, & Caygill, 2002). Preschoolers' knowledge about gender stereotypes includes personality traits, occupations, appearance qualities, and household activities that are associated with males and females (Bauer, Liebl, & Stennes, 1998; Poulin-Dubois et al., 2002). Their thinking about gender stereotypes even extends beyond these qualities to items that may serve as metaphors for masculinity and femininity; they believe, for example, that fir trees and bears are "for boys," and that maple trees and butterflies are "for girls" (Leinbach, Hort, & Fagot, 1997).

## GENDER DIFFERENCES IN BEHAVIORS

In light of such durable and pervasive stereotypes about "femaleness" and "maleness," it is logical to ask whether researchers have documented actual differences in the characteristics or behaviors of females and males. For many human traits, the data show that average differences between the sexes are smaller than the variability in performance within each sex. Nonetheless, in some domains the characteristics of females and males have been found to differ, and often these differences start to show up in the early childhood years.

**Physical Development**   Females and males physically differ in a number of ways, including the makeup of their chromosomes, their genitalia, and levels of certain hormones. Females are physically more mature at birth, whereas males show a special physical vulnerability during infancy. Compared with females, males are

The tendency of children to disapprove of cross-gender behavior is more pronounced in cultures that emphasize the importance of traditions and adherence to social norms (for example, Taiwan) as opposed to freedom to break from traditions and individualism, as in Israel (Lobel et al., 2001). This tendency also increases with age. When researchers interviewed kindergartners through sixth-graders to determine how these children would respond to hypothetical cases of cross-gender behavior in their peers, older children reported that they would respond more negatively to cross-gender behavior than did younger children. Moreover, children stated that they would respond more negatively to cross-gender behavior in their male peers than in their female peers. The degree of negativity that children exhibited was particularly surprising. Children were virtually unanimous in their assertion that they would not want to play with a cross-gender child. Children's reports of how they would respond ranged from fairly innocuous comments (such as "I'd stay away") to statements indicating that they would physically abuse cross-gender children (Carter & McCloskey, 1984).

**KEY THEME**

**SOCIOCULTURAL INFLUENCE**

# F O R ◆ Y O U R ◆ R E V I E W

◆ What are the characteristics associated with masculine and feminine stereotypes?

◆ What do cross-cultural studies reveal about the nature of gender stereotypes?

◆ What is the nature of children's knowledge about gender stereotypes during the early childhood years?

◆ What actual sex differences exist in the physical, cognitive, and social domains?

◆ What are the major ways in which biology is thought to influence gender-role development? What specific research findings support a biological perspective? What research findings challenge the idea that biology alone is responsible for role development?

◆ How does social learning theory account for gender-role development? What research findings support the social learning perspective?

◆ What are the essential features of Kohlberg's cognitive-developmental theory of role development? What specific research findings support Kohlberg's theory?

◆ What are the elements of gender schema theory? What specific research findings support gender schema theory?

◆ What are some of the ways in which parents influence children's gender-role development?

◆ What effects do nontraditional parents have on gender-role development?

◆ What do early play patterns reveal about the role of peers in gender-role development?

◆ What role do peers play in the enforcement of sex-typed behaviors?

◆ What are the consequences of cross-gender behaviors for boys and for girls?

# CHAPTER RECAP

## ⚷ Summary of Developmental Themes

### NATURE & NURTURE

**How do nature and nurture interact in social and emotional development in early childhood?**

Socialization becomes a more prominent force in explaining emotional development during early childhood, particularly in the emergence of self-conscious emotions, such as guilt and envy, and in emotion regulation. Socialization also plays a major role in shaping other aspects of the child's behaviors, including self-regulation and moral orientation. The development of gender roles is a good example of the interaction of biological and social forces.

### SOCIOCULTURAL INFLUENCE

**How does the sociocultural context influence social and emotional development in early childhood?**

Although there appear to be many commonalities in social and emotional development in early childhood, cultural variations are apparent in concepts of gender roles and in tolerance for cross-gender behaviors.

### CONTINUITY/DISCONTINUITY

**Are social and emotional development during early childhood continuous or discontinuous?**

Most of the research on the child's social and emotional development implies that development is continuous.

However, Lawrence Kohlberg's theory of gender role development describes a stagelike process. Children are hypothesized to progress through a sequence of attaining gender identity, gender stability, and gender constancy.

### INTERACTION AMONG DOMAINS

**How do social and emotional development in early childhood interact with other domains of development?**

Emotional development is closely intertwined with language and cognitive development. For example, the self-conscious emotions require the child to understand the perspectives of other people, a significant cognitive achievement. Similarly, gender-role development relies on cognitive processes. In Bandura's work, attention influences which models, male or female, children will imitate.

### RISK/RESILIENCE

**What factors promote risk or resilience in social and emotional development during early childhood?**

The child's ability to regulate his or her emotions is an important predictor of successful social development later in childhood. The child's attachment status also continues to have repercussions for social and cognitive development in early childhood.

## Chapter Review

### EMOTIONAL DEVELOPMENT IN EARLY CHILDHOOD

**What are self-conscious emotions? Give some examples.**

*Self-conscious emotions* are those that require knowledge of the self as related to others. Some examples include guilt, envy, and shame.

**What types of knowledge about emotions emerge in early childhood?**

Preschoolers begin to understand many of the situations that give rise to specific emotions and the consequences of displaying them. They also begin to understand how to ameliorate negative emotions.

**How do boys and girls differ in the expression of emotions? What factors might be responsible for these differences?**

Sex differences in emotions are more likely to show up later in childhood than in the preschool years. Girls tend to express a wider range of emotions and are better at identifying emotional expressions in others than boys. However, these sex differences may arise from socialization experiences that take place in early childhood. Mothers are more expressive with and tend to engage in more "emotion talk" with their daughters than with their sons. Parents also encourage girls to maintain emotional closeness and boys to control their emotions.

**What strategies do young children typically use to regulate their emotions? What is the significance of the ability to do so?**

Young children typically use distraction to regulate their emotions. The ability to regulate emotions is important because it predicts behavioral conduct and the quality of social relationships later in childhood.

**How can parents and caregivers promote emotion regulation among children?**

Parents who provide supportive guidance and who at least attempt to help children manage their emotions have children who are better at emotion regulation.

**What are the consequences of attachment styles for development in early childhood?**

Secure attachment in infancy is related to successful problem-solving, more symbolic play, advanced language development, social competence, more positive emotions, and the development of conscience in the early childhood years.

## SELF AND SELF-REGULATION IN EARLY CHILDHOOD

**What are the features of the self-concept during early childhood?**

Preschool-aged children typically define themselves in terms of a *categorical self*; that is, by referring to various categories that provide membership in one group or another.

**What are some signs of the preschool child's growing sense of agency?**

Preschoolers show signs of protest when caregivers attempt to help them with an activity such as dressing or feeding. They also show signs of emotion after either success or failure in a problem-solving situation.

**What is the difference between self-regulation and self-control?**

Parents expect preschoolers to begin to display *effortful control*, the ability to suppress undesirable responses. *Self-regulation* refers to the child's ability to control his or her own behaviors in accordance with the expectations of caregivers and other adults. *Self-control* refers to the ability to comply with moral and ethical expectations, especially when adults are not present.

**How does self-regulation change during early childhood?**

Regulation of the child's behaviors typically shifts from parents to children in the second year. On *delay-of-gratification tasks*, in which children are asked to wait for some period of time before attaining a highly desirable object, children become increasingly able to delay their behavior. Progress

in language development and attentional capacities seems to be related to this ability.

**What factors seem to promote children's compliance?**

Children's compliance is facilitated when parents are responsive and supportive, justify their demands, offer compromises, and focus on "do" rather than "don't."

## MORAL DEVELOPMENT IN EARLY CHILDHOOD

**What are the signs of the development of conscience in the early childhood years?**

Some signs of conscience development include the display of moral emotions, such as guilt or shame, as well as increasing willingness to comply with adult rules, even when adults are not present.

**What factors are related to the development of conscience?**

Children are increasingly able to recognize the adult emotions that give them feedback about appropriateness of their own actions. They are also better able to regulate their own behaviors. Positive and mutually responsive interactions with caregivers are also important in conscience development.

**How does social learning theory account for the development of moral behaviors?**

Social learning theory emphasizes the reinforcements that children receive from parents and other agents of socialization, as well as their observations of the behaviors of others, in explaining moral development.

**What is the evidence that children are capable of prosocial behaviors in early childhood?**

*Prosocial behaviors*, social actions performed to benefit others, include *altruism*, behavior carried out to help others without expecting a reward for one's self. Some signs of this capacity in early childhood include the following: displays of *empathy* (a vicarious, shared emotional response) for the distress of others, soothing a person in distress, and seeking assistance for that person.

## GENDER ROLES IN EARLY CHILDHOOD

**What are the characteristics associated with masculine and feminine stereotypes? What do cross-cultural studies reveal about the nature of gender stereotypes?**

*Gender stereotypes* are the expectations or beliefs that individuals within a given culture hold about the characteristics of women and men. Children learn these stereotypes as part of the process of *gender-role development*. Stereotypes of masculinity center on *instrumentality*, qualities associated with acting on the world. Stereotypes of femininity center on *expressiveness*, qualities associated with emotions and relationships. There are many cross-cultural similarities in the content of gender stereotypes but also a few notable variations.

## What is the nature of children's knowledge about gender stereotypes during the early childhood years?

Children demonstrate knowledge of gender stereotypes as early as age two. They are familiar with the personality traits, occupations, appearance qualities, and household activities associated with males and females. They are also familiar with many metaphors for masculinity and femininity.

## What actual sex differences exist in the physical, cognitive, and social domains?

Males and females differ in several physical qualities, including activity level, rate of maturity, and physical size. The most notable sex differences in cognition are in visual-spatial tasks, such that males tend to perform better than females on mental rotation and spatial perception tasks. In the social domain, males tend to be more physically aggressive than females.

## What are the major ways in which biology is thought to influence gender-role development? What specific research findings support a biological perspective? What research findings challenge the idea that biology alone is responsible for role development?

Biological theories emphasize the role of hormones, such as *androgens,* and differences in the structures of the male and female brains in explaining sex differences. Animal and human studies show that prenatal exposure to androgens is related to aggressive, rough-and-tumble behavior and more male-type play. However, hormone levels can change in response to environmental experiences, indicating that caution is in order when interpreting findings about biology and gender.

## How does social learning theory account for gender-role development? What research findings support the social learning perspective?

Social learning theory emphasizes the roles of reinforcement, imitation, and eventually self-regulation in producing sex-typed behaviors. An important factor in influencing the likelihood of imitation is the *sex typicality* of the model's behavior. Research shows that children are more likely to imitate same-sex than other-sex models and that self-regulation of sex-typed behavior increases with development.

## What are the essential features of Kohlberg's cognitive-developmental theory of role development? What specific research findings support Kohlberg's theory?

Kohlberg's theory hypothesizes that children's awareness of gender grows through successive mastery of *gender identity, gender stability,* and *gender constancy.* Cross-cultural research has confirmed this developmental progression. For example, by age two or three, most children can label themselves as male or female.

## What are the elements of gender schema theory? What specific research findings support gender schema theory?

*Gender schema theory* states that children first form cognitive representations of the same-sex/opposite-sex schema and then form more elaborate *gender schemas* for their own sex. Research has shown that children prefer neutral objects labeled for their own sex and that gender schemas can have an impact on social information processing. For example, gender-schematic children distort information about sex-atypical behaviors.

## What are some of the ways in which parents influence children's gender-role development?

Many parents express stereotypical attitudes and beliefs about their male and female children. They also treat children differently based on their biological sex, from the way they furnish their rooms to the kinds of activities and play they encourage.

## What effects do nontraditional parents have on gender-role development?

Children who have nontraditional parents show less knowledge of gender stereotypes, and girls show more independence and achievement.

## What do early play patterns reveal about the role of peers in gender-role development?

Children display more positive and negative social behaviors when they play with a peer of the same sex. Girls in mixed-sex pairs are more likely to be passive and to become upset. Thus gender-role dynamics are already apparent at age two years.

## What role do peers play in the enforcement of sex-typed behaviors?

Peers reward sex-typical play and reliably punish sex-atypical behaviors in children, especially boys.

## What are the consequences of cross-gender behaviors for boys and for girls?

Children who consistently display cross-gender behaviors are likely to be isolated from their peer groups.

## KEY TERMS AND CONCEPTS

altruism (p. 321)

androgen (p. 327)

categorical self (p. 315)

delay of gratification (p. 316)

effortful control (p. 316)

empathy (p. 321)

expressive characteristics (p. 323)

gender constancy (p. 330)

gender identity (p. 330)

gender schema (p. 331)

gender schema theory (p. 330)

gender stability (p. 330)

gender stereotype (p. 322)

gender-role development (p. 322)

instrumental characteristics (p. 322)

prosocial behavior (p. 321)

self-conscious emotion (p. 310)

self-control (p. 316)

self-regulation (p. 316)

sex typicality (p. 329)

# 10 CONTEXTS OF DEVELOPMENT

Four-year-old Joey looked at his loaded dinner plate and announced, "I'm not hungry. Can I just have dessert?" "No, you may not!" his embarrassed mother replied as she turned toward her house guest. "I can't think why he gets like this. He's stubborn as a mule." The guest wondered why no one mentioned that Joey, in full view of his mother, had eaten most of a gift box of cookies before dinner.

"I don't want this! It stinks! You stink!" Joey shouted. He pushed away his plate, got up from the table, and ran to the television, which he turned up to full volume.

"Turn that down this minute or go to your room!" his mother ordered. Joey ignored her. Spying Joey reaching for the cookie box, she warned, "Don't take that cookie!" Joey removed his hand from the box and gave his mother a mournful, pleading look. "All right, but just one!" she conceded. Joey took two and returned to the TV.

**SOCIOCULTURAL INFLUENCE** How do sociocultural factors influence the contexts of development in early childhood?

**RISK/RESILIENCE** What contextual factors promote risk or resilience in early childhood?

By the time children are two or three years old, caregivers begin to be concerned with **socialization**, the process by which children acquire the social knowledge, behaviors, and attitudes valued by the larger society. Among many other things, we start to expect children to eat their dinner before dessert, to be polite to visitors to their home, and to listen to the requests made by parents. These behaviors do not always come easily, as the above scene with Joey suggests. And guiding children to maturity on the social and cognitive fronts takes more than a mere couple of years and one or two parents. As children grow beyond infancy, the wider world—peers, teachers, neighbors, and the media—also begins to exert its influence. For the great majority of children ages two through six, though, the family is the primary context for the process of development. Parents, siblings, and others within the family unit are the people with whom the child usually spends the most time and forms the strongest emotional bonds, and they thus play an undeniable role in the child's life. Therefore, in this chapter, we examine more closely the ways in which the family has an impact on children's social and cognitive development. Because children also have increasing opportunities to spend time with peers, and because, for a significant proportion of children, a considerable amount of time is spent in some form of child care, we also take a look at the influence of these two other important contexts in the life of the young child. Finally, we provide a beginning glimpse of how the powerful force of the media impinges on the life of the preschool-aged child.

## THE FAMILY IN EARLY CHILDHOOD

In a sense, virtually every domain of development is deeply influenced by the family environment. Cognition, moral awareness, gender identity, and emotional growth are all nurtured largely within the family. However, the study of the impact of the family is no simple matter, primarily because the direction of influence within families runs along several paths. Just as parents and siblings affect the child's behavior, the child affects the reactions of other family members. Because the family experience includes fluid, constantly changing effects and outcomes for its various members, studying the influence of the family presents a special research challenge to developmental psychologists.

### STUDYING THE FAMILY

We begin by considering the question of just what we mean by "family." Is there a typical structure in contemporary families? Has the composition of the family undergone any significant shifts in recent years? Then we elaborate on the idea that families are contexts for development in which the effects are reciprocal and multifaceted. This discussion will allow you to understand the family's role in socialization in a richer and more meaningful way.

***The Demographics of the American Family*** Historians, sociologists, and anthropologists who study the family as a social unit point to the changes in its structure and functions over the last two centuries. With the industrialization of nineteenth-century America, for example, the extended family, in which secondary relatives, such as grandparents, aunts and uncles, or cousins, lived in the same household as the primary family, gave way to the nuclear family, consisting solely of parents and their offspring living in a single household. Similarly, as we saw in the chapter titled "Themes and Theories," the modern notion that families are havens for nurturing the child's growth and development was not always prevalent. As we look back in

**socialization** Process by which children acquire the social knowledge, skills, and attitudes valued by the larger society.

▶ **FIGURE 10.1**

**Demographic Changes in Family Structure**

The percentage of children living with two parents has declined since 1970, and the percentage living with a single parent (most frequently the mother) has increased dramatically. About one-fourth of American children live with a single parent. The higher rates of divorce and single-parent births have contributed to this trend.

*Source:* U.S. Bureau of the Census (2005).

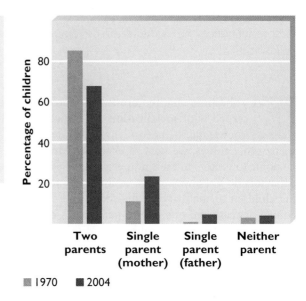

Family structures vary greatly in contemporary society. For example, today, about 28 percent of American children live with a single parent.

history, we see that the family has been a changing social structure, and all signs indicate that it will continue to take different shapes in the future to reflect larger social, economic, and historical trends.

No one family structure typifies contemporary American society. The 1950s' model of a two-parent family with two children and a nonworking mother no longer applies. For example, as Figure 10.1 shows, only 68 percent of children younger than eighteen years lived with two parents in 2004, compared with 85 percent in 1970. Today, 28 percent of American children live with only one parent (U.S. Bureau of the Census, 2005). High rates of divorce and single-parent births have contributed to this trend. Current data show that a little over 40 percent of current marriages end in divorce (compared with about 15 percent in 1960), and about 35 percent of all births are to single women (Bramlett & Mosher, 2001; Federal Interagency Forum on Child and Family Statistics, 2005). Moreover, about 2 percent of children live with their grandparents (Federal Interagency Forum on Child and Family Statistics, 2005), and a growing number live with gay or lesbian parents. Finally, more than 70 percent of married women with children younger than eighteen years work outside the home, compared with about 45 percent in 1975 (U. S. Bureau of the Census, 2005). All of these changes in family structure have distinct implications for the child's experiences within the family.

***A Systems Approach*** Many child development researchers have found it fruitful to focus on family dynamics, the interactions among all members of the group, rather than on the structure of the family per se as they study the impact of the family. An important influence on contemporary thinking about the family is **systems theory**. Its premise is that all members influence one another simultaneously and that the interactions flow in a circular, reciprocal manner. In systems theory (see Figure 10.2), the individual child's development is understood as being embedded in the complex network of multidirectional interactions among all family members (Bronfenbrenner, 1986; Cox & Paley, 2003).

Systems theory assumes that families undergo periods of stability and change. The family tends to adapt in order to maintain a state of *homeostasis*, or equilibrium. Thus, as children attain significant milestones like going to preschool, the family system must readjust to absorb the child's new routines or demands for independence. At other times, families may experience crises, such as financial hardship, moving, or divorce. In these instances, changing external circumstances require the

## Key Terms and Concepts

**authoritarian parent**
(p. 344)

**authoritative parent**
(p. 345)

**control theory** (p. 351)

**cooperative play**
(p. 358)

**instrumental
competence** (p. 345)

**interagent
consistency** (p. 347)

**intra-agent
consistency** (p. 348)

**parallel play** (p. 358)

**permissive parent**
(p. 345)

**social pretend play**
(p. 358)

**socialization** (p. 341)

**solitary play** (p. 358)

**systems theory** (p. 343)

**time-out** (p. 348)

**uninvolved parent**
(p. 347)

# PATHWAYS: CONNECTING THE STORY OF DEVELOPMENT

| INFANCY | EARLY CHILDHOOD (2–6 YEARS) | | MIDDLE CHILDHOOD | ADOLESCENCE |
|---|---|---|---|---|
| See p. 268 | **Physical Development** | • Shows advances in gross motor skills such as running, jumping, and skipping<br>• Evidences slower but regular increases in size<br>• Shows evidence of implicit learning | See p. 493 | See pp. 576–577 |
| | **Cognitive/ Language Development** | • Shows gains in ability to make perceptual discriminations<br>• Can classify according to basic-level concepts<br>• Understands the meaning of simple number terms, and eventually the basic principles of counting<br>• Displays good intuitions about mathematical operations such as addition and forming fractions<br>• Uses landmark cues to negotiate spatial environments<br>• Uses geometric cues to aid spatial location<br>• Begins to be able to read maps<br>• Realizes that others can have different visual perspectives<br>• Develops a *theory of mind*<br>• Shows elementary planning activities<br>• Displays knowledge of scripts<br>• Displays autobiographical memory<br>• By age three, attains *representational insight*<br>• Uses two- and then multiword utterances<br>• Uses morphemes, negatives, questions, and passive voice<br>• Shows rapid growth in vocabulary and use of syntax<br>• Displays overregularizations<br>• Shows growth in referential communication and other aspects of pragmatics | | |
| | **Social/ Emotional Development** | • Displays self-conscious emotions<br>• Uses language to express emotions<br>• Understands causes and consequences of emotions<br>• Shows more effective emotion regulation strategies and, eventually, a decline in tantrums<br>• Displays more complex aspects of attachment by considering motives, feelings of caregiver<br>• Shows decline in separation distress and other attachment behaviors typical of infants<br>• Has notion of categorical self<br>• Displays overt behaviors signaling independence<br>• Shows first signs of self-control<br>• Shows early signs of conscience and altruism<br>• Thinks in terms of preconventional ideas<br>• Shows awareness of own gender and gender stereotypes | | |

# PHYSICAL, COGNITIVE, AND LANGUAGE DEVELOPMENT

T omorrow's geography test is going to be really tough," Nate lamented to his friend on the way home from school. "I should have paid more attention in class and kept up with my assignments. Now I have to study so much!" Normally a good student, Nate had been preoccupied with the success of his baseball team. As pitcher, he was proud to be a contributor to that success. Now there was a price to be paid as he prepared for the next day's test, and he was decidedly anxious about it. Nate had made up one "trick" for remembering the states in the Southeast: he strung their first letters to make the phrase "True aces for-get no states" for Tennessee, Alabama, Florida, Georgia, North Carolina, and South Carolina, respectively. And it helped him to identify some of the states by tying their shapes to things he knew; for example, Florida really did look as though it had a "panhandle." But there was so much more to remember! Maybe he could just repeat the capitals of the states over and over to himself. One thing he knew for sure: next time he would not save all of his studying for the night before the test.

**NATURE & NURTURE** How do nature and nurture interact in physical, cognitive, and language development in middle childhood?

**SOCIOCULTURAL INFLUENCE** How does the sociocultural context influence physical, cognitive, and language development in middle childhood?

**CONTINUITY/DISCONTINUITY** Are cognition and language development during middle childhood continuous or discontinuous?

**INTERACTION AMONG DOMAINS** How do physical, cognitive, and language development interact with other domains in middle childhood?

Nate, as it turns out, had a pretty good understanding of his mental capabilities. He knew that paying attention in class was helpful and that certain techniques, such as rehearsal, mental imagery, and other "tricks," could help him remember information. He also knew there were limits to what he could accomplish in the few hours he had to prepare for his exam. In fact, many aspects of Nate's own thinking—attention, memory, and even the fact that he could evaluate his thought capabilities—have been topics of great interest to developmental psychologists. Middle childhood is a time, of course, when the child's cognitive skills have significant import; children must apply their thinking skills as they go to school and learn to read, do mathematics, and master an assortment of other academic subjects. Nate's involvement in baseball also reflects children's growing physical stature and mastery of complex motor skills. In this chapter, we start with a summary of physical development during the middle school years. Next, we focus on the main accomplishments in children's thinking during those all-important early school years. We will begin by revisiting Piaget's theory. Then we will survey several topics that have been studied extensively from the stance of information-processing theory, including attention, memory, and problem solving. Finally, we discuss the main features of the child's accomplishments in language use.

## PHYSICAL DEVELOPMENT IN MIDDLE CHILDHOOD

One of the most obvious differences you would notice between a six-year-old standing next to an eleven-year-old is the disparity in their physical size—about a foot on average and more than thirty pounds. Accompanying the steady pace of growth in height and weight in middle childhood are noticeable changes in motor skills, as anyone who has coached a softball team or watched children draw can testify. As we document changes in these arenas, it is important to be thinking about the implications of these skills and characteristics for the psychological functioning of the child, especially as he or she enters school, with all of the new expectations and opportunities it affords.

### MOTOR SKILLS

Motor skills during middle childhood become more efficient and better controlled, involve complex and coordinated movements, and are exhibited quickly and in a wider variety of contexts and circumstances (Keogh & Sugden, 1985). With the exception of balance, boys tend to slightly outperform girls on many gross-motor tasks by the time they enter elementary school (Gallahue, 1989). However, differences between boys and girls may become especially large for some activities as children approach the end of middle childhood and enter the adolescent years, as Figure 11.1 indicates for running speed and the distance a youngster can throw a ball.

Fine-motor coordination improves dramatically during the school years. For example, writing as a motor activity independent of drawing emerges around six years of age (Adi-Japha & Freeman, 2001). In addition, children may begin to construct models or do needlework, master the complex finger sequencing needed to play musical instruments, and produce more detailed drawings. All of these activities confirm that motor skills are undergoing significant developmental advances.

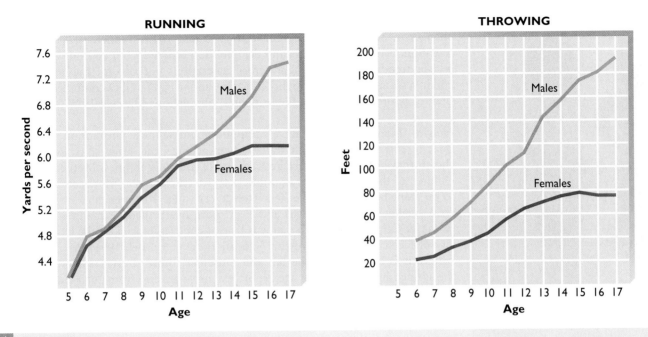

**△ FIGURE 11.1**

**Running Speed and Throwing Distance for Boys and Girls at Different Ages**

Boys tend to outperform girls on many motor skill tasks during the elementary school years, as indicated by these data on speed of running and distance throwing a ball, summarized from a number of studies carried out since 1960. The differences between girls and boys often increase substantially as children enter adolescence.

*Source:* Gallahue (1989), adapted from Haubenstricker & Seefeldt (1986).

As children grow older, differences in individual abilities often increase. Of course, to some degree, this may stem from practice—some children focus on acquiring particular competence relevant to their social and cultural milieus. The acquisition of expertise or specialized motor skills in sports, dance, crafts, hobbies, playing of musical instruments, and, in some cultures, trade- or work-related endeavors permits older children to become more effective members of their society and gain greater social status among peers and adults.

## BODY GROWTH

Children also undergo dramatic changes in physical size, a highly visible indicator of development. For parent and child alike, the ever-higher marks penciled on the bathroom wall give eloquent testimony to increasing maturity. A long-absent aunt who cries, "My, how you've grown!" may summon a grin or a blush from the wary seven-year-old, but she is confirming the social importance of this sign of change. Throughout childhood, boys and girls grow at similar rates, although individual children, of course, may differ enormously. Is physical size important to development and the way others interact with a child? If so, perhaps it is because the adult world appears to have strong preferences concerning height and weight.

**Secular Trends** Increased knowledge of nutrition and the ability to treat disease have yielded dramatic changes in patterns of growth in many societies in recent generations. These generational changes are termed **secular trends**. Children today grow faster and become taller as adults than did previous generations in most regions of the world.

Between 1880 and 1950, the average height of Western European and American children increased by nearly four inches. A slower increase or even stability in size has been found since the 1960s. Similar findings have been reported for other

**secular trend** Consistent pattern of change over generations.

Many children become sensitive to physical appearance, and weight, in particular, in the middle school years. Overweight individuals are viewed negatively in many contemporary Western cultures.

cultures, although at different times. For example, in Japan the most substantial changes in height took place between 1950 and 1970 (Tanner, 1978). Improved nutrition, better medical care, and the abolition of child labor account not only for secular trends in greater height across generations but also for the larger size of children from professional, highly educated, and urban families compared with children of poorer families and those in rural populations (Tanner, 1978).

*Height*   Many societies share a mystique about tallness, the notion that height directly correlates with such traits as competence and leadership. Research has shown that height does affect impressions of a child's abilities. Mothers of young children of the same age, for example, perceive taller boys as more competent (able to get along better with others, less likely to cry when frustrated, and so forth). They treat smaller boys as younger and in a more overprotective manner (Sandberg, Brook, & Campos, 1994). The same is true of children judged on the basis of maturity of facial features (Zebrowitz, Kendall-Tackett, & Fafel, 1991). Moreover, boys believe it is important to be tall and muscular; those substantially shorter than the average height for their age report extensive teasing from their peers; greater dissatisfaction with their skill in athletic endeavors; and increasing unhappiness as they approach adolescence (Finch, 1978).

Despite these observations, lower self-esteem and other behaviorial problems among children of short stature have not been consistently reported. And short adults typically function well within the norm socially and intellectually (Kranzler et al., 2000; Sandberg et al., 1994; Zimet et al., 1997). Until 1985, little could be done to alter the course of growth or eventual height for most children. Today, human growth hormone (HGH) can be produced synthetically. For children whose lack of growth stems from insufficient HGH, the breakthrough represented an enormously positive step toward more typical growth. However, increasing numbers of children who are genetically short or whose delay in growth is a normal part of their pattern of maturation are also being given HGH to speed up growth or increase their height, even though this practice is not officially recommended in many countries, including the United States (Cuttler et al., 1996).

Should such treatments, which tend to be motivated by perceptions and expectations about the benefits of being tall rather than by a medical condition, be encouraged? It is an expensive course of treatment and many children who are not HGH deficient gain few long-term benefits from its administration (Brook, 2000). Nor is the potential for negative side effects fully understood (Betts, 2000; Drug and Therapeutics Committee, 1995), although some pediatric endocrinologists believe it is very safe. In some countries (for instance, France, Japan, and Sweden) HGH is officially approved for use with individuals born with Turner syndrome and with children of short stature or who are simply failing to grow at normal rates (Bercu, 1996). However, attempting to alter normal physical development to conform to a cultural stereotype is a drastic action that raises many ethical issues.

*Obesity*   Most estimates of obesity today make use of a measure called the *body mass index (BMI)*. The BMI is determined by dividing the weight of a child or adult (in kilograms) by the square of his or her height (in meters). Children and adults above the 95th percentile for their age on this measure compared with a reference population (which for the United States usually has been a large sample of children and adults who were tested in this country in the 1970s) or whose BMI is above 30 are considered obese. Children between the eighty-fifth and ninety-fifth percentile or who show rapid changes in weight relative to other children their age also are considered at risk for becoming obese (Strauss, 1999; Styne, 2001). Estimates are that, today, approximately 16 percent of children are either obese or at risk for being obese (Federal Interagency Forum on Child and Family Statistics, 2005).

Being overweight has strong social-emotional consequences in most cultures. At earlier times it carried positive connotations of substance and prosperity in industrialized societies and still does in many developing countries today (Sobal & Stunkard,

1989). For example, females in some regions of the world are encouraged to increase their body fat in preparation for marriage (Brown & Konner, 1987). However, in contemporary Western cultures obesity is often viewed negatively. For example, children as young as six, when describing drawings or photographs of people who are chubby or thin, are likely to label obese figures as "lazy," "cheater," or "liar" and are unlikely to select a chubby child as a "best friend" (Kirkpatrick & Sanders, 1978; Lawson, 1980; Musher-Eizenman et al., 2004). In addition, overweight children as young as seven years old experience more negative interactions with parents and peers than do other children (Davison & Birch, 2002). Although research has revealed a mixed pattern of findings, self-esteem may suffer as well (Klesges et al., 1992; Pierce & Wardle, 1997), especially for children who feel (or are made to feel) that they are responsible for being overweight (say, because of overeating or insufficient exercise) even as early as five years of age among girls (Davison & Birch, 1999).

Genetic factors predispose some children to obesity. At least five single gene disorders are known to be related to its early onset (Farooqi & O'Rahilly, 2000). Behavioral genetics studies further suggest a relationship as a function of multiple genes, perhaps because of inherited differences in metabolic processes (Strauss, 1999). Not surprisingly, either because of a genetic component or because parents serve as models for their children's eating and exercise habits, overweight parents are more likely to have obese children (Birch & Davison, 2001). Early obesity, as well as the length of time a child continues to be overweight, increase the likelihood he or she will be obese as an adult (Strauss, 1999; Whitaker et al., 1997).

Controlling weight is complicated by heavy children's tendency to be more sensitive to external food-related cues and less responsive to internal hunger cues compared with their normal-weight peers (Ballard et al., 1980; Costanzo & Woody, 1979). Infants and children are responsive to the amount of energy provided by the foods they consume (Birch & Davison, 2001; Fomon, 1993). However, eleven-year-old obese children tend to eat faster than other children. They also fail to slow down their rate of food intake as they near the end of their meal, a pattern of responding that is at odds with what is typically observed in children of normal weight (Barkeling, Ekman, & Rössner, 1992). Obese children are also somewhat less accurate in reporting how much they eat (Maffeis et al., 1994).

Leann Birch and her colleagues (cf. Birch & Davison, 2001) believe that children can learn to become unresponsive to internal satiation cues through child-feeding practices imposed by parents. For example, some parents express concerns about

**KEY THEME**
**NATURE & NURTURE**

Parents can play an influential role in the development of childhood eating habits. When parents encourage children to finish everything on their plate or reward good behavior with sweets, children begin to rely more on external than internal cues for satiation, placing them at risk for obesity.

> **FIGURE 11.2**

### Trends in Overweight (BMI ≥ 95th Percentile): United States

These data, collected from a series of studies carried out in the United States between 1963 and 1999, reveal the marked increase that has taken place in the number of children who are considered obese. Some believe obesity has become a health epidemic in this and other countries because of the dramatic change and accompanying health risks that are associated with being overweight.

*Source:* Centers for Disease Control and Prevention (2002).

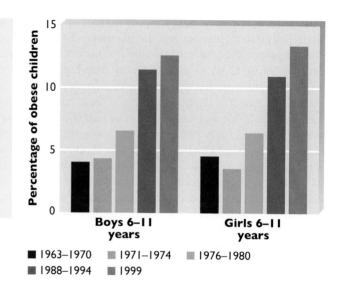

their infants' gaining sufficient weight. As a consequence, they may initiate meal-related practices designed to encourage food consumption ("clean their plates") and use certain foods, such as sweets, to reward good behavior and to calm and quiet the child. These efforts, however, could have the unintended effect of shifting the child's reliance on internal signals for hunger to external signals based on how much has been eaten and of increasing preferences for some foods that may not be so healthy. In addition, if concerns begin to emerge about weight, parents may attempt to restrict ingestion of high-calorie foods, an action that seems to have the unintended consequence of making the forbidden foods even more attractive to children.

▸ **KEY THEME**

**SOCIOCULTURAL INFLUENCE**

Recent health surveys reveal a worrisome increase in obesity among children and adolescents in the United States (see Figure 11.2). Increases have been greatest among African American, Hispanic American, and Native American children (Crawford et al., 2001). Although less information is available from other countries, increases in obesity in children also have been reported in England (Reilly & Dorosty, 1999) and are taking place in many other regions of the world if the reports of the rise of obesity for adults are any indication (Taubes, 1998).

What are the reasons for this secular trend? Researchers have advanced various hypotheses. For example, compared with a generation ago, children today spend more time in sedentary activities, such as watching television. In general, children who watch more television per day have a higher BMI (Andersen et al., 1998; Robinson, 2001); the likelihood of becoming overweight is correlated with the number of hours spent watching television, as can be seen in Figure 11.3. Perhaps an even greater influ-

> **FIGURE 11.3**

### The Relationship Between Becoming Overweight and Hours of Television Viewing per Day

The more time children spend watching television each day, the more likely they are to be overweight. Ten- to fifteen-year-olds who were reported to watch more than five hours of television each day in 1990 were greater than eight times (8× in the figure) more likely to have become overweight (BMI greater than 85th percentile) between 1986 and 1990 than children who watched less than two hours each day. These findings provide powerful arguments for the view that obesity is increasing among children because they do not spend enough time engaging in physical activity or because the advertising messages on television encourage excessive food consumption.

*Source:* Adapted from Strauss (1999). Data from Gortmaker et al. (1996).

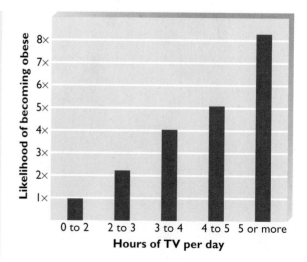

ence stems from television advertising, which rarely promotes consumption of fresh fruits and vegetables over calorie-laden snack and convenience foods; consumption of these latter foods has gone up substantially over the last twenty-five years (Jahns, Siega-Riz, & Popkin, 2001). Although culture may attach a negative label to being overweight on the one hand, television actively serves to promote it on the other.

## F O R • Y O U R • R E V I E W

* What kinds of improvements in motor skills are observed during the middle school years?

* What is a secular trend?

* What are the concerns about short stature and obesity in many cultures?

* What factors may be contributing to the increase in obesity observed in many Western nations?

## COGNITION IN MIDDLE CHILDHOOD: PIAGET'S THEORY

Recall Piaget's description of the preschooler who views much of the world from his own perspective and who lacks the thought structures to solve problems like the conservation of number or liquid tasks. As children begin the early school years, the change in their thought capabilities is dramatic, according to Piaget. Shedding his or her earlier egocentrism and beginning to reason logically, the child is well on the way to becoming a mature thinker and skilled problem solver.

## THE CONCRETE OPERATIONAL STAGE

In Piaget's theory, children are said to be in the **concrete operational stage** from approximately seven to eleven years of age. Children enter this stage when they begin to be able to solve the conservation tasks correctly. At first, the six- or seven-year-old may solve only a few of the simpler problems, such as conservation of length, number, or liquid quantity. Later, she will succeed on tasks that involve area or volume. Piaget called this extension of the same cognitive structures to solve increasingly difficult problems within a given stage *horizontal décalage*.

The reason for this shift is that the child is now capable of performing **operations**, mental actions such as *reversibility*, that allow him to reason about the events that have transpired. He can pour the liquid back from the cylinder to the glass "in his head" or think about the narrow width of the tall cylinder as compensating for its height. In other words, the child now thinks logically, although the physical components of the problem must still be present (if not externally in the world, then as images in the mind). The child's growing logical capabilities are also manifested in his ability to *seriate* objects, putting sticks of varied lengths into a systematic series arranged from shortest to longest, for example. Unlike the preoperational child who performs this task in a haphazard way, the concrete operational child starts with the shortest (or tallest) and compares each successive stick with those that are shorter and longer so that an orderly array results. The child's thought in this stage is also less egocentric, allowing him to understand that other individuals' perceptions, beliefs, and feelings may differ from his own. The concrete operational child is becoming a true "thinker," as long as there are specific objects or events to which he can apply his logic.

## CONCEPTS OF CAUSALITY

Piaget (1930, 1974) believed that, up until the early school years, ages seven or eight years, children lack a mature awareness of physical causality. Once they are verbal

⊶┮ KEY THEME
CONTINUITY/DISCONTINUITY

**concrete operational stage**  In Piagetian theory, the third stage of development, from approximately seven to eleven years of age, in which thought is logical when stimuli are physically present.

**operation**  In Piagetian theory, a mental action that allows a child to reason about events that have transpired.

and can discuss causality, they make some interesting errors. One type of error is **animism**, attributing lifelike properties to inanimate objects. In one of Piaget's examples of animism, a six-year-old boy named Vern was asked why a boat floats on water but a little stone sinks. Vern answered, "The boat is more intelligent than the stone" (Piaget, 1929, p. 223). Another child, age seven, is asked if the sun can do whatever it likes. The child responds affirmatively; asked why the sun doesn't stop giving light, the child says, "It wants it to be fine weather" (Piaget, 1929, p. 227). Animism is often accompanied by **artificialism**, the belief that people cause naturally occurring events. Piaget provides the example of a six-year-old named Hub.

PIAGET: *Has the sun always been there?*

HUB: *No, it began.*

PIAGET: *How?*

HUB: *With fire …*

PIAGET: *How did that start?*

HUB: *With a match …*

PIAGET: *Who struck it?*

HUB: *A man. (Piaget, 1929, p. 266)*

In Piaget's view, children are slow to shed their animistic and artificial beliefs; the latter may persist until age ten years or so (Piaget, 1929).

Susan Gelman and Kathleen Kremer (1991) attempted to replicate some of Piaget's studies by asking preschoolers, "Do you think people made (or make) _____?" in which the blank was filled in by an object, such as the sun, the moon, dogs, flowers, dolls, and shoes. Few of the children showed evidence of artificialism; most recognized that objects like dolls are made by humans but that the sun and moon are not. Moreover, these young children often cited natural causes for the behaviors of living things (birds fly because they have wings) and human causes for the things artificial objects do (cars go uphill because people make them do so). Why the discrepancy from Piaget's observations? Gelman and Kremer (1991) postulate that direct questions, like the ones they used, were more likely to tap children's underlying knowledge of causality than the free-ranging interview questions Piaget employed. Their findings add to the body of research we have already discussed, suggesting that Piaget may have underestimated the cognitive capabilities of young children.

## IMPLICATIONS FOR EDUCATION

Many educators have found inspiration in Piaget's distinctive ideas about child development. His theory carries some clear implications for teaching children. The first is that the individual child's current stage of development must be carefully taken into account as teachers plan lessons. For example, a seven-year-old who is in the stage of concrete operations should be given problems involving actual physical objects to observe or manipulate, rather than abstract word problems or diagrams (Flavell, 1963).

A second, related implication is that what the child already knows will determine what new information she is able to absorb. Because her current cognitive structures limit what she will be able to assimilate, it is important that the teacher be aware of the child's current state of knowledge. In addition, cognitive advances are made most optimally when new material is only slightly different from what the child already knows (Ginsburg & Opper, 1988). Thus the teacher's task is to plan lessons that are tailored to the needs of the individual child rather than to the class as a whole and to be flexible in devising instructional materials that stretch the child one step beyond what she already knows.

One of Piaget's most important statements about cognitive development is that it is the result of the *active engagement of the child*. Early sensorimotor schemes and

**animism**   Attribution of lifelike qualities to inanimate objects.

**artificialism**   Belief that naturally occurring events are caused by people.

later mental operations are all founded first on the child's physical activity and later on mental actions. Thus education, too, must be structured in such a way that it will promote the child's active participation. Instead of emphasizing rote learning, teachers following a Piagetian model provide children, for example, with experiments that allow them to discover scientific principles on their own. Children do not memorize numerical relationships, such as the multiplication tables, but discern them by manipulating sets of objects under the close guidance of the teacher. According to Piagetian thinking, active learning of this sort promotes deeper and more enduring understanding.

## F O R ◆ Y O U R ◆ R E V I E W

◆ What are the major features of thinking in the concrete operational stage?

◆ What are Piaget's ideas about concepts of causality during the middle childhood years?

◆ What are the implications of Piaget's theory for education?

## COGNITION IN MIDDLE CHILDHOOD: THE INFORMATION-PROCESSING APPROACH

Most of the child's cognitive attainments during the school years have been understood through the information-processing perspective. As we saw in the chapter titled "Themes and Theories," information-processing theorists believe that human cognition is best understood as the management of information through a system with limited space or resources. In the information-processing approach, mental processing is usually broken down into several components or levels of activity. For example, memory processes are often partitioned into *encoding, storage,* and *retrieval* phases. Information is assumed to move forward through the system, and each stage of processing takes some time (Massaro & Cowan, 1993; Palmer & Kimchi, 1986).

Many traditional information-processing models are called **multistore models**, because they posit several mental structures through which information flows, much as data pass through a computer. One example of this type of model is shown in Figure 11.4. Most multistore models distinguish between psychological structures and control processes. *Psychological structures* are analogous to the hardware of a computer. The *control processes* are mental activities that move information from one structure to another, much as software functions for the computer.

Suppose someone asks you to repeat a list of words, such as *shoe, car, truck, hat, coat, bus.* If you have paid attention to all of the words and, like an efficient computer, have "input" them into your cognitive system, processing will begin in the **sensory register**. Information is held here for a fraction of a second in a form very close to the original stimuli—in this case, the audible sounds you experienced. Next, the words may move to the memory stores. **Working memory** (sometimes called *short-term memory*) holds information for no more than a couple of minutes. Many researchers consider working memory to be a kind of work space in which various kinds of cognitive tasks can be conducted. If you were to repeat the words over and over to yourself—that is, rehearse them—you would be employing a control process to retain information in working memory. You might also use the second memory store, **long-term memory**, the repository of more enduring information, and notice that the items belong to two categories, clothing and vehicles. The *executive control* oversees this communication among the structures of the information-processing system. Finally, when you are asked to say the words aloud, your *response system* functions to help you reproduce the sounds you heard moments earlier.

Other theorists in this field have advanced a **limited-resource model** of the cognitive system that emphasizes a finite amount of available cognitive energy that

**multistore model** Name for many traditional information-processing models which posit several mental structures through which information flows.

**sensory register** Memory store that holds information for very brief periods of time in a form that closely resembles the initial input.

**working memory** Short-term memory store in which mental operations such as rehearsal and categorization take place.

**long-term memory** Memory that holds information for extended periods of time.

**limited-resource model** Information-processing model that emphasizes the allocation of finite energy within the cognitive system.

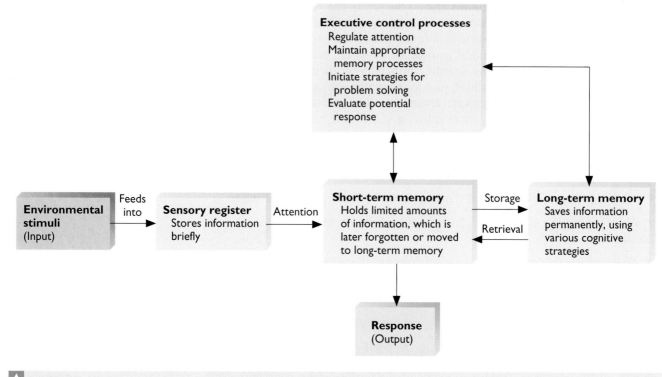

⚠ **FIGURE 11.4**

**A Schematic Model of Human Information Processing**

This highly simplified model includes several cognitive structures and processes that many information-processing theorists believe to be important in cognitive development. As the arrows indicate, information often flows in several directions between various structures. The goal of information-processing models is to identify those structures and processes that are at work when a child responds to his or her environment.

*Source:* Adapted from Atkinson & Shiffrin (1968).

can be deployed in numerous ways, but only with certain tradeoffs. Limited-resource models emphasize the allocation of energy for various cognitive activities rather than the mental structures themselves. The basic assumption is that the pool of resources available for processing, retaining, and reporting information is finite (Bjorklund & Harnishfeger, 1990). In one such model, Robbie Case proposes an inverse relationship between the amount of space available for operating on information and that available for storage (Case, 1985; Case, Kurland, & Goldberg, 1982). *Operations,* as we have seen, include processes such as identifying the stimuli and recognizing relationships among them; *storage* refers to the retention of information for use at a later time. If a substantial amount of mental effort is expended on operations, less space is available for storage or retention.

In the simple memory experiment we just examined, the effort used to identify the words and notice the categorical relationships among them will determine the space left over for storing those words. If we are proficient at recognizing words and their relationships, storage space will be available. If these tasks cost us substantial effort, however, our resources will be taxed and little will be left for the task of remembering. Robert Kail's research (1986, 1991a, 1991b) supports the idea that a central component of cognitive development is an increase in processing speed with age. As children grow older, they can mentally rotate images, name objects, or add numbers more rapidly. More resources then become available for other cognitive tasks.

How do these two general information-processing frameworks, the multistore model and the limited-resource model, account for cognitive development? Multistore models allow for two possibilities. Changes in cognition can stem from either

## SOCIOCULTURAL INFLUENCE

**How does the sociocultural context influence physical, cognitive, and language development in middle childhood?**

According to Vygotsky, cultural beliefs and values are transmitted to children through the scaffolding provided by experts. In the domain of language development, the content and structure of language often provide cues about the culture's social order and values.

## CONTINUITY/DISCONTINUITY

**Are cognition and language development during middle childhood continuous or discontinuous?**

Piaget stressed stagelike attainments as the child progresses from preoperational to concrete operational thought.

However, information-processing theorists suggest that changes in such cognitive skills as attention and memory arise from successive increments, not qualitative, stagelike changes.

## INTERACTION AMONG DOMAINS

**How do physical, cognitive, and language development interact with other domains in middle childhood?**

Social interactions with parents, teachers, and others form the basis for cognitive development within a given cultural context. For language development, we have seen that bilingualism may have an impact on such cognitive functions as analytic thinking and mental flexibility.

# Chapter Review

## PHYSICAL DEVELOPMENT IN MIDDLE CHILDHOOD

**What kinds of improvements in motor skills are observed during the middle school years?**

Children become more adept at fine-motor coordination and show more controlled, coordinated, and complex motor movements.

**What is a secular trend?**

A *secular trend* refers to a change in some aspect of development that occurs across generations. Height is an example of a secular trend, in that today's children grow faster and taller than in previous generations.

**What are the concerns about short stature and obesity in many cultures?**

Children, especially boys, prefer being tall, but little evidence exists to indicate that those who develop normally but are constitutionally small are seriously disadvantaged. Nevertheless, parents of children with short stature may request synthetic growth hormone despite lack of evidence that it provides long-term gains in height. Being overweight typically has negative connotations in today's society. Overweight children have more negative interactions with parents and peers, and may display low self-esteem.

**What factors may be contributing to the increase in obesity observed in many Western nations?**

The numbers of children who are obese have increased dramatically over the past several decades, in part because of a more sedentary lifestyle as well as increasing availability of calorie-laden convenience foods and drinks.

## COGNITION AND MIDDLE CHILDHOOD: PIAGET'S THEORY

**What are the major features of thinking in the concrete operational stage?**

The *concrete operational stage* is characterized by logical thought but only in the presence of real objects or images. Because children are capable of performing *operations*, they are successful in increasingly difficult conservation tasks, as well as seriation tasks.

**What are Piaget's ideas about concepts of causality during the middle childhood years?**

Piaget claims that children may show *animism* and *artificialism* up until even ten years of age. However, when children are asked direct questions about the causes of things, they show a more mature understanding of causality than Piaget acknowledged.

**What are the implications of Piaget's theory for education?**

Piaget's theory implied that teachers must take into account the child's current stage of development and supply activities consistent with his or her capabilities. Teachers should also be aware of the individual child's current state of knowledge, so that new material can be readily assimilated. Piagetian theory supports the active role of the child in the educational process.

## COGNITION AND MIDDLE CHILDHOOD: THE INFORMATION-PROCESSING APPROACH

### What are the major differences between multistore and limited-resource models of information processing? How do they differ in accounting for developmental changes in cognition?

*Multistore models* include such structures as the *sensory register*, *working memory*, and *long-term memory*, as well as control processes, such as rehearsal. Developmental changes are due largely to increased use of control processes to move information from one part of the system to another. *Limited-resource models* describe tradeoffs between energy used to operate on stimuli and the capacity left over for storage. Developmental change is characterized in terms of increased cognitive efficiency.

### What is selective attention? How does it change by the time a child gets to the early school years?

As children grow older, they are better able to select certain aspects of the environment to attend to. Physiological maturation and the child's increasing control over cognitive processing are responsible for these changes.

### What is ADHD? What factors may be responsible for its occurrence?

ADHD is a developmental disorder linked to problems of attention. Problems with executive control and allocating resources in working memory are thought to underlie this disorder.

### What have memory span and free recall studies told us about age changes in memory performance?

From preschool to preadolescence, children show an increase in *memory span*, the number of items that can be recalled after a brief period of time. Changes in *processing speed*, the rapidity with which cognitive activities can be carried out, contribute to this increase. Children participating in free-recall tasks typically show *primacy* and *recency effects*. The former refers to elevated recall at the beginning of the list and reflects rehearsal. The latter refers to good recall for the last few items in a list.

### What factors are primarily responsible for developmental improvements in recall memory?

As children progress through the school years, they show an increase in the deliberate production of *memory strategies* for both encoding and retrieval. Among these are *rehearsal* (repeating items), *organization* (reordering items on the basis of higher-order relationships), and *elaboration* (linking items in an image or sentence). Improvements in memory are tied to the child's increasing control over his or her cognitive processing. One aspect of cognitive control is *metamemory*, the child's understanding of memory as a process. Improvements in cognitive inhibition and reliance on the gist of an event are also part of memory development.

### What are the major ways in which children show changes in problem-solving skills as they develop?

With development, children are better able to plan the steps in problem solving. They also become more flexible in their strategy use.

### What factors encourage children to transfer skills from one situation to another?

An important factor that can influence the likelihood of transfer is making the parallels between problems more obvious to children. Similar skills should be taught in a variety of contexts, information should be presented to children in an organized fashion, and tests should assess the ability to apply already-learned information in new situations.

### What basic forms of mathematical reasoning do children display in the early school years?

Young children display good intuitions about mathematical operations such as addition and forming fractions. These understandings can form the basis for mathematical instruction.

## COGNITION AND MIDDLE CHILDHOOD: VYGOTSKY AND THE SOCIOCULTURAL CONTEXT OF LEARNING

### How do the processes of scaffolding and guided participation contribute to cognitive development according to Vygotsky?

Novice learners often get more scaffolding from experts, but as their skills improve, that support is gradually withdrawn. This process is called guided participation. Tutors often work within the child's *zone of proximal development*, the distance between what the child can do alone and what she can do with guidance.

### What do research findings tell us about the role of skilled collaborators in promoting children's cognitive advances?

Research shows that adults play a critical role in the transmission of skills, probably because they encourage children to be active and think out loud. Some communities afford children more opportunities for guided participation than others, especially when the children are routinely in the company of adults.

## LANGUAGE IN MIDDLE CHILDHOOD

### What are some examples of children's metalinguistic awareness?

Examples of *metalinguistic awareness* include the ability to create humor and showing an understanding of *metaphor*.

## What have neuropsychological studies revealed about the involvement of the brain in language acquisition?

Specific brain structures are associated with *expressive aphasia* (Broca's area) and *receptive aphasia* (Wernicke's area). Children sustaining damage to these areas show a greater ability to recover language functions than adults do. Neuropsychological studies suggest that language functions begin to become lateralized shortly after the first year and look adultlike by age seven. The predictability of language milestones and the universality of certain language structures also support the role of biology. Research on later language learners and neuropsychological evidence support a critical period for language learning, although not a strong version of it.

## In what ways does language influence cognitive processing? What are the particular effects of bilingualism on cognition?

Language has been shown to influence specific cognitive processes, such as memory and classification. Bilingual children are more flexible and analytic in certain cognitive tasks. They also perform better than monolingual children on tasks that require response inhibition.

## What are the functions of private speech for the developing child?

Children often use *private speech* and, later, *inner speech*, to direct their behavior. They tend to use private speech when tasks are difficult or goal directed.

## In what ways does language provide cues about cultural values and socialization goals?

Language can be a vehicle to transmit to children the specific values and expectations of their native culture through formal and informal versions of words, gender categories of words, and even the specific words that are included (or not included) in the language.

## KEY TERMS AND CONCEPTS

**animism** (p. 384)

**artificialism** (p. 384)

**Broca's area** (p. 403)

**concrete operational stage** (p. 383)

**elaboration** (p. 391)

**expressive aphasia** (p. 403)

**inner speech** (p. 409)

**limited-resource model** (p. 385)

**long-term memory** (p. 385)

**memory span** (p. 388)

**memory strategy** (p. 391)

**metalinguistic awareness** (p. 401)

**metamemory** (p. 392)

**metaphor** (p. 402)

**multistore model** (p. 385)

**operation** (p. 383)

**organization** (p. 391)

**primacy effect** (p. 391)

**private speech** (p. 409)

**processing speed** (p. 391)

**recency effect** (p. 391)

**receptive aphasia** (p. 403)

**rehearsal** (p. 391)

**secular trend** (p. 379)

**sensory register** (p. 385)

**Wernicke's area** (p. 403)

**working memory** (p. 385)

**zone of proximal development** (p. 399)

# 12 SOCIAL AND EMOTIONAL DEVELOPMENT

Michael had just finished his math assignment when he heard the door slam. Then he heard the loud, angry voice. "Kids today!" his grandfather fumed to no one in particular. "A couple of 'em almost ran me down on the sidewalk. Didn't bother to apologize. One even yelled, 'Get out of my way!' as she chased after her friends. Kids don't respect anybody, not even themselves—wearing those weird clothes, dying their hair every color you can think of, poking holes in their ears, even their noses! I suppose if I had stopped 'em, they'd have taken a swing at me or even worse. ..." His voice trailed off to a mutter.

Michael had heard such tirades before: how the world has changed, how children today don't know right from wrong. Michael also worried about reports on the news: the first-grader who punched his teacher, the large number of sixth-graders who felt cheating was okay. Did his grandfather have a valid point? But he also thought about the fund raiser he and his friends had held to help hurricane victims whose homes and neighborhoods had been destroyed in the

**NATURE & NURTURE** How do nature and nurture interact in social and emotional development in middle childhood?

**SOCIOCULTURAL INFLUENCE** How does the sociocultural context influence social and emotional development in middle childhood?

**CONTINUITY/DISCONTINUITY** Are social and emotional development in middle childhood continuous or discontinuous?

**INTERACTION AMONG DOMAINS** How do social and emotional development in middle childhood interact with other domains?

**RISK/RESILIENCE** What factors promote risk or resilience in social and emotional development during middle childhood?

southern part of the country. Collecting bottles and cans from the school cafeteria, as well as those brought by community members to a drop-off spot at school, they had managed to raise over $500 to send to a relief agency. It made him feel good to be able to do even such a small thing to help people in that devastated region. "Grandpa," he now said, hoping to placate his grandfather, "Don't worry. Next time you go out for a walk, I'll go with you. Now would you like me to make you a cup of hot tea?"

To instill in children a sense of satisfaction with who they are and recognition of the standards of conduct considered acceptable and ethical within their community are among the most important goals of society. We expect children and adults to take pride in their accomplishments, learn to judge right from wrong, and refrain from actions that harm family, friends, or neighbors. Broadly speaking, survival in a social community depends on helping, cooperation, and sharing, behaviors that benefit others. Children display an awareness of self and the consequences of their conduct, both good and bad, early on, but these understandings undergo noticeable changes in the middle school years.

Michael's grandfather believes his generation has witnessed a decline in a positive sense of self and in courtesy and concern for others. Although one might debate whether such a change has actually taken place, the concerns voiced by Michael's grandfather are not new. Philosophers, theologians, and scientists have argued for decades about whether human nature is good or evil and whether experience serves to channel children's inborn tendencies in either direction. In this sense, the interaction of nature and nurture remains embedded in contemporary discussions of the roots of self, moral behavior, and values. In this chapter, we look first at the continuing course of emotional development in middle childhood. We next examine self-identity, self-esteem, and self-regulation. We spend a good portion of this chapter examining several theories of moral development and how society promotes the development of prosocial values. Finally, we revisit the topic of gender-role development to highlight its main features in middle childhood.

## EMOTIONAL DEVELOPMENT IN MIDDLE CHILDHOOD

There are two main aspects to emotional development in middle childhood: continuing growth of children's knowledge about the emotions themselves and progress in the management of their own emotional states. Researchers increasingly recognize the integral role that emotions play in communication and the social interactions that children have with adults and with their peers. At the core of successful social development is the ability to make judgments about the emotions displayed by others as well as the emotions one decides to display oneself.

During middle childhood, children learn the rules that their culture prescribes for the display of emotions. In many cultures, for example, children learn that they should exhibit happiness when they receive a gift.

○┱ **KEY THEME**

**NATURE & NURTURE**

○┱ **KEY THEME**

**RISK/RESILIENCE**

○┱ **KEY THEME**

**INTERACTION AMONG DOMAINS**

**display rule** Cultural guideline concerning when, how, and to what degree to display emotions.

# KNOWLEDGE ABOUT EMOTIONS

Much of what we know about emotional development in middle childhood has to do with how children think and reason about emotions. Between about ages eight and ten, for example, many children understand the emotional behaviors prescribed by cultural rules (you are supposed to look happy when you receive a gift even if you don't like it) and the behaviors necessary to obtain certain goals (you should smile even if you don't feel well if you want your mother to allow you to go to a friend's party). In such cases, the individual masks or "fakes" an emotional state. Paul Harris and his associates (Harris et al., 1986) examined this skill in using emotional **display rules**, the cultural guidelines governing when and how to express emotions, by asking six- and ten-year-olds to listen to stories in which the central character felt either a positive or a negative emotion but had to hide it. After hearing the story, children were asked to describe verbally the facial expression of the protagonist, along with how this person really felt. Even six-year-olds could state that the emotion displayed would not match the emotion felt, although ten-year-olds provided a fuller explanation. These results suggest that, by the middle school years, children have developed a broad understanding of the social norms and expectations that surround the display of feelings.

Knowledge about emotions can have significant ramifications for the child's social development. For example, five-year-old children who are able to correctly label facial expressions of emotions are more likely to display positive social behaviors at age nine (Izard et al., 2001). Moreover, children who have substantial knowledge about the emotions have higher scores on tests of moral development, are less likely to evidence behavior problems, and are better liked by their peers (Cook, Greenberg, & Kusche, 1994; Denham et al., 1990; Dunn, Brown, & Maguire, 1995). The reason may be that children who have greater knowledge about emotions are more likely to respond appropriately to the emotional expressions of their agemates—they have greater social skills (Mostow et al., 2002).

Knowledge about emotions is probably gleaned, at least in part, from parents. Children who have greater knowledge about emotions—who can label emotional expressions on faces, describe the feelings of another person in an emotion-related situation, and talk about the causes of emotions—typically have mothers who discuss and explain emotions, often in the context of the child's expressing a negative emotion himself. In other words, these mothers are good "emotion coaches." On the other hand, when parents display more negative affect themselves or dismiss children's experiences of emotions ("You're overreacting!"), children's understanding of emotions is poorer and they are less socially competent (Denham et al., 1997; Dunn & Brown, 1994; Laible & Thompson, 2002). Parents who engage in such behaviors are probably missing opportunities to explain to their children the important elements of emotional responding. The extreme case is represented by children who are physically abused or neglected by their parents. These children have noticeable deficits in their ability to identify the emotional expressions that correspond to particular situations, such as going to the zoo and getting a balloon or losing a pet dog to disease. Physically abused children, perhaps not surprisingly, have a bias toward selecting angry expressions no matter what the context (Pollak et al., 2000).

Emotional development is closely affiliated with advances in cognition that allow children to think in more complex, abstract terms. By the time they enter school, children begin to understand that changes in thoughts may lead to changes in feelings—that thinking happier thoughts, for example, might make a sad mood go away (Weiner & Handel, 1985). In addition, they comprehend the possibility of experiencing two contrasting emotions at the same time, such as feeling happy at receiving a gift but disappointed that it cannot yet be opened (Brown & Dunn, 1996). As children approach adolescence, their concepts of emotions center increasingly on internal psychological states. In other words, whereas younger children identify their own emotional states based on the situations they are in ("I'm happy when it's my birthday"), older children refer more frequently to their mental state ("I'm happy when I feel good inside") (Harris, Olthof, & Meerum Terwogt, 1981).

## REGULATING EMOTIONS

○━ᴵ **KEY THEME**
**RISK/RESILIENCE**

In addition to becoming more adept at understanding various emotions, during the middle childhood years children generally become better able to regulate their own emotional states. Part of the process of enacting display rules—to smile even when a gift is not exactly what one wanted—depends on the capacity to control one's actions (Kieras et al., 2005). These behaviors, as well as others, such as calming down after getting angry, have important repercussions for the child's social relationships and perhaps even mental health in the United States, China, and probably many other cultures (Cicchetti, Ackerman, & Izard, 1995; Zhou et al., 2004). In fact, much of the development of emotion that we have described in this book— expressing, recognizing, and understanding emotions, as well as socialization experiences regarding emotions—culminates in the ability to regulate one's affective state (Denham, 1998).

The way children learn to manage their emotions depends, at least in part, on the kinds of experiences their parents provide (for example, do parents provide opportunities for children to become aroused or to calm down?), as well as what children learn are the consequences of their own emotional displays (what happened when I had an angry tantrum versus when I "used my words"?). When parents become distressed at their children's displays of negative emotions and punish them, children later tend to express more anger and hostility, and have more behavior problems and poorer social functioning in school (Eisenberg, Fabes, et al., 1999; Fabes, Leonard, et al., 2001). On the other hand, when parents provide supportive coaching and guidance for children's expression of emotion—by helping children talk about how they feel and suggesting ways of dealing with their emotions—children are better able to soothe themselves and moderate their negative emotions (Gottman, Katz, & Hooven, 1997). The general emotional tone of interactions with parents may play a role, too. Nancy Eisenberg and her colleagues have found that mothers who were more positive in their emotional expressivity, in contrast to mothers who generally expressed negative emotions, had children who were better able to regulate their own emotions. The children of more negative mothers, in turn, behaved more aggressively and were rated as less socially competent by parents and teachers (Eisenberg, Gershoff, et al., 2001; Eisenberg, Valiente, et al., 2003).

It is important to remember that all of these findings need to be considered within the context of the child's temperament style. Some children tend to be more impulsive and quick to react than others, qualities that are related to their greater emotional expressiveness. Other children are cautious and deliberate, and more likely to hide their feelings. Parental behaviors can both shape and be a reaction to their children's tendencies (Eisenberg, Zhou, et al., 2003), yet another manifestation of the complex ways in which developmental outcomes are influenced by dynamic, mutually influential interactions. Recent longitudinal evidence suggests, though, that the sequence of events that seems to make the most sense given the data is parental warmth, followed by children's emotion regulation, and then fewer behavior problems as rated by parents and teachers (Eisenberg et al., 2005). In terms of emotion regulation, with development, too, children probably become more aware of their own emotional styles and seek out experiences that are compatible with their needs; some children may learn that sitting alone and playing is soothing, whereas others may seek the emotional release of a fast-paced basketball game (Thompson, 1994).

New research indicates that children's increasing ability to regulate behaviors, and emotions in particular, is accompanied by distinct changes in how the brain functions. In one study, children played a computer game in which they were required

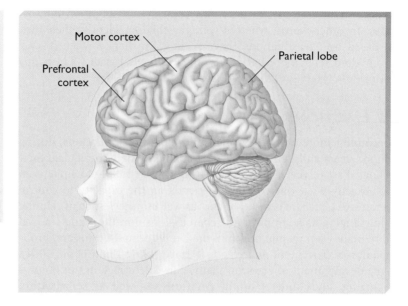

**▶ FIGURE 12.1**

**Brain Areas Associated with Inhibition**

Recent fMRI studies have shown that children display elevated activation in the prefrontal cortex and the parietal lobes when they are involved in tasks that require them to inhibit a response. Adults show less dramatic levels of activation in these brain areas.

Motor cortex

Parietal lobe

Prefrontal cortex

to press a button when certain target stimuli appeared on the screen, but not to press when a nontarget showed up. In this case, children were told, "Catch all the Pokemon except for Meowth." Brain scans (fMRI) obtained while children played this game revealed that there was pronounced activation of the prefrontal and parietal regions of the brain when responses had to be inhibited (see Figure 12.1), much more so than was observed when adults played the same game (Durston et al., 2002). Other researchers have focused on changes in electrophysiological responding of regions of the brain involved in the inhibition and control of behaviors. When children played a computer game in which they suddenly and briefly lost all of the "points" they had earned (and thus experienced a negative emotion), areas of the prefrontal cortex showed particular patterns of electrophysiological activity. For older children, those physiological responses were quicker, less dramatic, and more localized in the prefrontal regions, a pattern suggesting that development of emotion regulation corresponds to greater neural efficiency in specific regions of the brain (Lewis et al., 2006).

## CULTURAL DIFFERENCES IN EMOTIONS

**KEY THEME**

**SOCIOCULTURAL INFLUENCE**

The tendency of children to express and detect emotions varies as a function of the culture in which they are raised. American children, for example, tend to smile more than Chinese children as early as infancy (Camras et al., 1998). On the other end of the emotional spectrum, Chinese children are better able to identify fearful and sad situations than are American children, and they cry less (Borke, 1973; Camras et al., 1998). These differences may reflect the child's incorporation of particular cultural beliefs about emotions.

A study of two different cultural groups in rural Nepal further illustrates this concept. Pamela Cole and her colleagues (Cole, Bruschi, & Tamang, 2002) studied children in two small villages, each comprising a different ethnic group—one Brahmin and the other Tamang. The Brahmins subscribe to a caste system in which strict rules dictate which social groups may interact. They are very oriented to status differences and the power of authority, and they have a great deal of pride in their own ethic group. The Tamang, on the other hand, place great value on community rather than on the individuals within the group. Resources are shared, and important decisions are made by consulting all group members, in accordance with their Buddhist values of selflessness. How do school-age children in these two very different cultures express emotions? All children were asked to react to scenarios likely to lead to an emotional reaction, such as having a friend snatch away a piece of candy or watching as a parent spills tea all over homework papers. Brahmin children, although they expected to feel anger in such situations, clearly stated that anger should not be expressed, primarily because authority needed to be respected and group orderliness preserved. Tamang children, in contrast, did not express anger; rather, they reported a feeling of *thiken*, or making the mind calm, in accordance with their Buddhist beliefs. American children, also participants in this study, endorsed anger as an appropriate response. This belief is consistent with the value we place on self-assertion and independence in our culture (Cole et al., 2002).

Cultural belief systems extend even to the kinds of temperamental styles that are valued within a particular society. A good example is the dimension of shyness and inhibition. In European-heritage families, shyness is often seen as a liability; instead, children are expected to be outgoing, sociable, and eager to interact with the environment. In Chinese society, however, shyness has traditionally been a valued trait. Parents and teachers believe that shy children are well behaved, and as testimony to that belief, shy children in China assessed up until just a few years ago expressed positive views of themselves (Chen, Rubin, & Li, 1997; Chen et al., 1999). In an interesting example of how historical forces interact with culture, though, a more contemporary sample of urban Chinese children showed links between shyness and academic, social, and behavioral problems (Chen et al., 2005). Even long-standing cultural values are not immune to the influences of an increasingly global and interconnected world.

Why is it important to recognize cultural differences in the values placed on various emotions? Simply put, cultural beliefs are likely to be expressed in the socialization practices that parents and others employ as they respond to the child's emotional displays.

## F O R ◆ Y O U R ◆ R E V I E W

- What kinds of knowledge do children acquire about emotions during middle childhood?

- What factors influence children's acquisition of knowledge about emotions?

- What factors are involved in children's increasing ability to regulate emotions?

- How does culture play a role in emotional development?

## THE DEVELOPMENT OF SELF IN MIDDLE CHILDHOOD

"I know how."

"Look! See what I did!"

"I'm smart."

"I'm stronger than you!"

"I'm really good at this!"

These declarations express in no uncertain terms what children believe they can do, what they think they are like, and how they feel about their abilities. The statements reveal the school-age child's awareness of self. How does this understanding of self—as someone who is an independent, unique person, able to reflect on his or her own beliefs and characteristics—develop?

To answer this question, it will be useful to adopt a distinction first offered by William James (1892) more than a century ago. The distinction continues to be every bit as useful today (Harter, 1999). For James, there were two components of self: the "me," or *objective self*, and the "I," or *subjective self*. James's objective, or the "me" aspect of self, is often called *self-concept*. An individual's self-concept includes an understanding of his or her physical qualities, possessions and status, skills, and psychological characteristics, including personality, beliefs, and value systems. To a large extent, many of the developments we have described up to middle childhood reflect acquisitions in this objective self.

The "I," or the subjective component, is made up of several key realizations about the self: (1) I can be an agent of change and can control events in my life (sense of autonomy); (2) my experiences are unique and accessible to no one else in exactly the same way (sense of individuality); (3) my past, present, and future are continuous (sense of stability); and (4) I can reflect on—that is, think about—my self (sense of reflection, or self-consciousness). We see progress in all of these aspects of self during the period of middle childhood.

## THE CONCEPT OF SELF

When children reach about seven years of age, a new element enters their self-descriptions. Whereas younger children describe themselves in terms of typical physical characteristics and activities ("I run fast"), older children begin to make relational statements. For example, in response to the question "Who are you?" a fifth-grader might say, "I can run faster than anyone else in my class," "I'm not as pretty as my older sister," or "Other kids in my class are better than I am at math." In other words, instead of itemizing their skills, actions, or social and psychological qualities, they compare their qualities with those of others (Harter, 1999; Ruble, 1983).

As children become older, they also view self in terms of increasingly differentiated qualities (Harter & Monsour, 1992). During the elementary school years, children effectively distinguish self in terms of separate skills: academic abilities, physical appearance, behavioral conduct, social skills, and athletic competence (Cole et al., 2001; Hymel et al., 1999). As children acquire a better understanding of their strengths and limitations, their evaluation of self may be somewhat less positive than during the preschool years. Their self-concept shows some positive increases in most domains in the later elementary school years but then tends to dip again as they begin to enter the adolescent years. Moreover, gender differences exist in how favorable these different domains of self are perceived, as can be seen in Figure 12.2.

An important factor to consider in the development of the concept of self is the culture in which the child is growing up. Children in Western societies tend to use many personal references in responding to questions about things that "tell about you." They might say, "I am a very smart person" or "I like hockey." Children from China, however, tend to comment on their social networks or social interactions, saying, for example, "I like to help my mom wash dishes" or "I am in second grade," responses that are consistent with their culture's emphasis on the connections among individuals in the social group (Wang, 2004).

***Social Comparison***   During the early and middle school years, as we already indicated, children begin to reference others in describing themselves. Whether Jim

▶ **FIGURE 12.2**

**Evaluations of Self as a Function of Gender**

The different domains of self are not always evaluated equally. Females consistently give less favorable ratings (on a 4-point scale) to their appearance and to their athletic ability than do males. These data have been averaged over thirteen different studies carried out by Susan Harter with children from elementary school through high school (Harter, 1999). In addition, research cited by Harter (1999) and carried out by others in England, Ireland, Australia, and many non–English-speaking countries, including Switzerland, Italy, Holland, China, Japan, and Korea, reveals a similar pattern of findings.

*Source:* Harter (1999), p. 131.

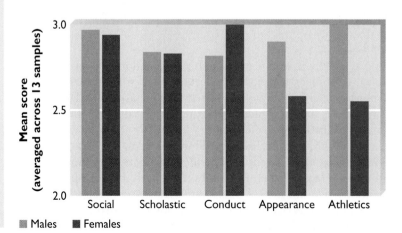

feels he is nice or can run fast, or Ellen believes she is smart or throws a ball well, depends on how Jim or Ellen thinks he or she stacks up against agemates and friends. How important is this process, called **social comparison**, the tendency of people to use others as mirrors to evaluate their own abilities, interests, and values? The answer appears to be that it becomes increasingly important as children move through the elementary school years. For example, nine-year-olds who could not actually determine their success but were told that they did better than, or not as well as, peers in a ball-throwing contest predicted future performance based on the feedback they received. If told they were successful, they expected to show continued superior ability; if told they were less successful, they expected to continue to perform more poorly than children who received no feedback. Five- and seven-year-olds, however, were unaffected by the information; they predicted that they would do equally well, regardless of how they compared with others (Ruble et al., 1980).

In fact, young children frequently are unrealistic about their skills; they claim they will do far better than they actually can (Butler, 1990; Harter, 1999). Kindergartners rate themselves more positively than older children do and tend to ignore feedback to adjust their evaluations, particularly when information about failure is given to them (Ruble, Eisenberg, & Higgins, 1994). However, by attending to the attributes and qualities of others, children may gain a more realistic means of predicting how well they can do. For example, Diane Ruble (1987) found that children in kindergarten and first grade who more frequently made social comparisons involving achievement tended to have greater knowledge of their relative standing in the classroom. Comments from classmates make a difference, too. When other children say things like "You're good at math," children acquire a sense of academic areas they are good at and those they are not (Altermatt et al., 2002).

Older school-age children engage in increasingly subtle, indirect social comparisons to determine how well they are doing, perhaps because more conspicuous forms of information gathering are perceived as inappropriate behaviors. For example, nine- or ten-year-olds are more likely than younger children to ask classmates, "What question are you on?" to assess their progress among peers (Pomerantz et al., 1995). On the other hand, the kind of educational environment in which children participate also influences this behavior. In Israel, for example, children in kibbutz schools, which place greater emphasis on cooperative activity than more traditional urban schools in that country, continue to be more likely to interpret glances among one another as efforts to increase mastery rather than as social comparisons (Butler & Ruzany, 1993).

***Self-Determination*** Children become increasingly sophisticated about how the world responds to their actions. For example, if asked, "How did you get to be the way you are?" a preschooler is likely to refer to uncontrollable factors ("I just grew. … My body just got bigger"), whereas a ten-year-old mentions her own efforts ("From getting good grades in school from studying"). Most children believe individual effort is an important aspect of achieving success and avoiding failure, even in societies that have emphasized a more collective orientation, such as Russia (Stetsenko al., 1995). For example, elementary school children in Los Angeles, Tokyo, Berlin, Moscow, and Prague are in close agreement in their views that effort in particular, rather than other factors, such as the teacher or luck or even ability, is the most important determinant of school performance (Little & Lopez, 1997). Yet, within every community, individuals can differ substantially in their sense of self-determination and control. Some children are convinced that what happens to them depends on their actions; that their choices, decisions, and abilities govern whether outcomes are good or bad, successful or unsuccessful. When asked how to find a friend, such a child might say, "Go up to someone you like and ask them to play with you." When asked how to do well on a test, the child might answer, "Study for it and you'll get smarter!" Such children have a strong **mastery orientation**, a belief that success stems from trying hard; failures,

This fifth-grade boy exhibits pride in the certificate of achievement he received as he describes his work on a project designed to save energy. Such positive feedback can play an important role in promoting continued academic effort. As he enters into and proceeds through the adolescent years, he will increasingly rely on his own standards for determining whether he has done a good job in the various activities he undertakes.

**social comparison** Process in which individuals define themselves in relation to the skills, attributes, and qualities of others; an important contributor to self-concept during middle childhood.

**mastery orientation** Belief that achievements are based on one's own efforts rather than on luck or other factors beyond one's control.

these children presume, are conditions to be overcome by working more or by investing greater effort (Dweck & Elliott, 1983).

Other children, in contrast, believe luck, fate, or other people have an inordinate influence on what happens to them. When asked why he cannot catch a ball, such a child might say, "The others throw it too fast." When asked why he got a poor grade, he might say, "The teacher doesn't like me." His explanation for a good grade might be "I was lucky." Such children often express little confidence in their ability and feel powerless to influence the future. They perceive themselves as being unable to achieve, perhaps because their efforts have not led to regular success. In place of a sense of mastery, they have a sense of **learned helplessness** (Dweck & Elliott, 1983).

These differing interpretations about success and failure are linked to another property of the belief system. To the extent that children think the characteristics they and others display are stable *entities*—that is, fixed or unchangeable qualities or traits, such as being smart, friendly, or popular—the more vulnerable they are to a helpless orientation. As a consequence, when faced with a challenging situation, the focus tends to be on evaluating how well they perform or "measure up" rather than on what steps might be taken to improve their performance or activity. In contrast, when children hold beliefs that characteristics or traits of individuals are *incremental* or malleable and can therefore be changed, their focus in challenging situations is more likely to be directed toward learning procedures and strategies reflecting resilience and increased effort (Erdley et al., 1997; Heyman & Dweck, 1998). Why might this be so? If traits are seen as enduring characteristics, little can be done to change them; thus the child places greater emphasis on determining the degree to which he or she (and others) possesses them as indicated by *performance* on the problem or task. On the other hand, if traits are seen as temporary characteristics, then the child can focus on the processes required to improve on or modify them, that is, on better ways of *learning* the task or how to solve the problem (Dweck, 1999).

◉┲ **KEY THEME**

**RISK/RESILIENCE**

Differing beliefs about the degree to which traits are fixed or modifiable and the causes of success or failure have a powerful bearing on academic achievement, participation in athletics and other physical activities, efforts to establish social relationships, self-esteem, and career aspirations (Bandura et al., 2001; Chapman, Skinner, & Baltes, 1990; Heyman & Dweck, 1998). Children who display evidence of learned helplessness in school, for example, may be caught in a vicious cycle involving self-fulfilling anticipation of failure accompanied by excuses that they have little control over what happens to them (Bandura et al., 1996). They are especially likely to expect failure on tasks found difficult in the past and may avoid them when given further opportunity to work on them (Dweck, 1991; Erdley et al., 1997). Note that high ability is not the factor that determines a mastery orientation (Dweck, 1999). Deborah Phillips (1984) reported that nearly 20 percent of fifth-graders with high ability limit their goals and persistence in school activities. In the academic realm, this pattern occurs more frequently among girls than boys, perhaps because girls are more likely than boys to view their failures in terms of such uncontrollable factors as lack of ability (Crandall, 1969; Dweck, Goetz, & Strauss, 1980; Stipek & Hoffman, 1980).

A mastery-versus-helplessness orientation can be observed in kindergartners and remains stable for up to five years (Ziegert et al., 2001). However, teachers can have an important influence on children's beliefs about their academic competence. When teachers provide a supportive, responsive learning environment, children come to believe that they have greater control over their understanding of academic materials and, as a consequence, become more actively engaged, as well as more successful in their efforts. Where learning environments are unsupportive, children are more likely to conclude that external factors are responsible for what happens, which, in turn, leads to less satisfaction and lower achievement in the classroom. Longitudinal data reveal that these differences in perceived control form a cyclic pattern of confidence and success that feeds into and magnifies individual differences in children's views of beliefs about their achievements and failures in the classroom (Skinner, Zimmer-Gembeck, & Connell, 1998).

**learned helplessness** Belief that one has little control over situations, perhaps because of lack of ability or inconsistent outcomes.

### RESEARCH APPLIED TO PARENTING

## Preventing Learned Helplessness

The rule in Michael's house was that, once homework was finished, the remaining time before bedtime was his to do with as he wished. He often played chess with his grandfather. This evening, however, his grandfather had become busy on another project. "Perhaps just as well," thought Michael as he reflected on the earlier exchange that had so angered his grandfather. Michael dialed his friend Jonathon. "Can you play some catch?" he queried when Jonathon answered the phone. "You must have finished your math already," Jonathon retorted. "I hate math, still have a lot more problems to do," he continued. But Michael quickly interjected, "You did really well on that last test." But before he could finish, Michael knew what Jonathon's reply would be: "I was lucky. The teacher asked the right questions. I wish I were good at math."

Children who gain little mastery over their environment or who face conflicting and inconsistent reactions, such as those they might receive from abusive parents, are among the most likely to display learned helplessness. But even well-intentioned parents and teachers may unwittingly help to foster a sense of helplessness. The seeds of a sense of helplessness, Carol Dweck (1999) believes, are sown in preschoolers who tend to judge their performance on tasks as "good" or "bad." When the value of self becomes contingent on feeling worthy or unworthy, young children become especially vulnerable to learned helplessness.

A study conducted by Melissa Kamins and Carol Dweck (1999) provides some experimental evidence to indicate that certain types of feedback with respect to either criticism or praise can lead to a more helpless orientation when children are subsequently confronted with similar situations involving a setback. In this study, five- and six-year-olds engaged in role-playing a series of four different stories that involved various tasks. In each of these tasks, children acted in the role of a doll, either making an error or completing the task successfully. At the end of each story the experimenter (who was engaged in role-playing as the teacher) provided one of three different types of feedback. When the task involved an error, the feedback from the "teacher" was directed either at the person ("I'm very disappointed in you"), at the outcome of the task ("That's not the right way to do it"), or at the process that contributed to the error in the task ("Maybe you can think of another way to do it"). (Special effort was made to ensure that the children understood they were role-playing and that the scenarios were "pretend" situations.) When praise for success was administered, the child heard something like "I'm very proud of you" or "That's the right way to do it" or "You must have tried really hard" for the person, outcome, and process feedback conditions, respectively.

How would children respond after role-playing in a similar but new task when a setback occurred? To answer this question the researchers asked children to evaluate how well the new problem had been completed (product rating); how performance in the task reflected such abilities as being good, bad, smart, not so smart, and so forth (self-assessment); whether they felt happy or sad (affect); and their willingness to continue in the role-playing activity or to attempt to correct the error (persistence). The results are shown in Figure 12.3. Higher scores indicate a more positive rating.

The results revealed a consistent pattern of reactions typical of helplessness when the emphasis in the feedback had been on the person (and, to a lesser extent, on the outcome) than when the feedback focused on the process of completing the task effectively. Somewhat surprisingly, this relationship held up whether the children had been exposed earlier to criticism or to praise in the role-playing activity, a finding reported by other researchers as well (Henderlong

▶ **FIGURE 12.3**

**The Consequences of Different Types of Feedback for Learned Helplessness**

When given praise or criticism for their work on a task, children may hear comments that are directed at them as a person ("good," "bad"), at the outcome ("right way to do it," "wrong way to do it"), or at the process ("really tried hard," "think of another way"). Hearing these different types of feedback influences how children subsequently respond to a setback on a similar task. Children who have heard person-oriented feedback evaluate the outcome of the new work less positively (product rating), view themselves as having fewer positive abilities (self-assessment), feel less happy with themselves (affect), and are less willing to continue the activity (persistence) than children who experience process-oriented feedback and, to a lesser extent, outcome-oriented feedback. Moreover, these kinds of responses are produced even though errors have not occurred in the previous tasks and children heard praise. The results suggest that the extent to which children express a sense of helplessness after experiencing a setback is affected by the specific form of praise or criticism they have heard in previous similar situations.

*Source:* Adapted from Kamins & Dweck (1999).

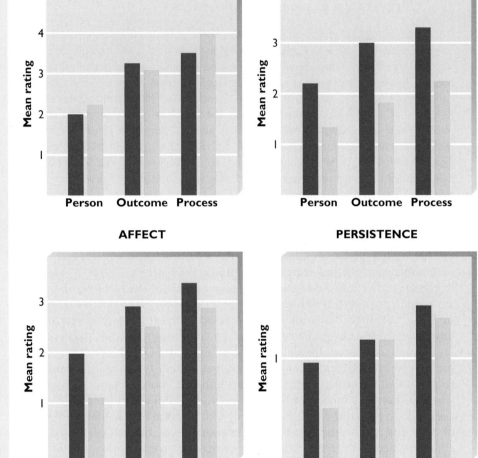

& Lepper, 2002). These findings and the research of many others suggest that parents can take several steps to reduce the likelihood that children will acquire a sense of learned helplessness.

1. *Avoid frequent criticism and punishment, especially of younger children.* The younger child who is often criticized or punished for, say, being messy or failing to finish a task may be particularly susceptible to the belief that he is "bad." In arriving at this stable view of his personality, he may have little reason to try to do better or may shun similar challenges to avoid receiving further negative evaluations. Thus it is important that parents help the younger child to avoid feelings of shame or limited self-worth when evaluating behavior (Kelley, Brownell, & Campbell, 2000).

2. *Motivate effort by identifying positive process approaches to problem solving.* As children become older and more knowledgeable, parents and teachers can promote a mastery orientation by emphasizing the various skills and procedures important to success; that is, what children can do to more effectively achieve a goal. Such feedback should help children to appreciate the malleability of traits and capacities.

3. *Attribute poor performance to factors other than ability.* When a child does perform poorly, a parent's or teacher's evaluation should focus on nonintellectual and temporary factors that may have reduced the child's performance

rather than on her intrinsic ability, thereby inspiring effort when the next opportunity arises.

4. ***View activities as opportunities to learn rather than as tests of ability.*** Parents and teachers can encourage children to approach academic tasks as opportunities to learn rather than as situations in which their performance will be evaluated in terms of competence (or lack of competence) (Dweck, 1999; Erdley et al., 1997).

Younger children must be convinced that their failures and successes are not the outcome of being "bad" or "good." Older children should be assured that shortcomings in performance on, say, academic tasks stem less from lack of ability than from insufficient effort or some other factor that can be modified. Children who have already acquired an orientation to learned helplessness can benefit from *attribution retraining*, a procedure designed to change their beliefs about the cause of their failures. This procedure emphasizes tying lack of success more directly to poor or ineffective effort than to inability. Attribution retraining has become an effective method of replacing self-limiting styles with positive approaches to success, a means of converting learned helplessness into a greater sense of mastery and agency (Dweck, 1986).

## SELF-ESTEEM

A child's description of self often includes an evaluation component. **Self-esteem** or self-worth is specifically concerned with the positive feelings of merit and the extent to which the child believes his attributes and actions are good, desired, and valued (Davis-Kean & Sandler, 2001). This aspect of self appears to be related to social affiliations, success in school, and overall mental health (Dusek, 2000; Harter, 1999; Kling et al., 1999). For example, later life satisfaction and happiness have been linked to high self-esteem (Bachman, 1970; Crandall, 1973); depression, anxiety, and poor adjustment in school and social relationships have been associated with low self-esteem (Damon, 1983; Zimmerman et al., 1997).

***Defining Self-Esteem***    How should we describe a child's self-esteem if the child takes pride in how smart she is, concludes that she is not very good at sports (but sports are unimportant anyway), and is unsure whether she is pretty enough to become a movie star? Work by Susan Harter and others (Eccles, Wigfield, et al., 1993; Harter, 1999; Marsh, Craven, & Debus, 1998) has revealed that children often give different evaluations of self when asked about academic competence, athletic skill, social acceptance, or physical appearance. Still, by about eight years of age, children can give answers to such global questions as "Do you like yourself?" and "Are you happy the way you are?" The responses to these broad inquiries, however, are not simply the sum of all the different evaluations made of one's attributes and abilities, and they can vary across situations and time (Harter, Waters, & Whitesell, 1998). What, then, are some of the factors that influence how a child arrives at a global sense of worth?

***Origins of Self-Esteem***    William James (1892) theorized that self-esteem depends on the success a person feels in areas in which she wants to succeed. Other theories emphasize that self-esteem originates in how a person thinks others see him; the *generalized other*—the combined perceived evaluations of parents, peers, and teachers influential in a person's life—helps to determine sense of worth (Cooley, 1902; Felson, 1993; Mead, 1934).

Both success in a highly regarded domain and the perceived evaluations of others do appear to affect self-esteem. Susan Harter (1987) obtained ratings of how children viewed themselves in scholastic competence, athletic competence, social acceptance, physical appearance, and behavioral conduct, as well as in terms of

**self-esteem**   One's feelings of worth; extent to which one senses that one's attributes and actions are good, desired, and valued.

global success. Children were also asked how critical it was for them to do well in each of these domains. Harter reasoned that greater discrepancies between perceived competence and the importance of a domain, especially one highly valued, would be linked to lower self-esteem. Children also rated how others (parents, peers) viewed them, felt they were important, liked them, and so on.

For children in the third to eighth grades, the more an area rated as important outstripped a child's perception of her competence, the lower was the child's sense of her overall worth. In fact, children with low self-esteem seemed to have trouble disregarding the significance of domains in which they were not skilled (Harter, 1985). In contrast, children with high self-esteem minimized the value of those fields in which they were not especially competent and gained considerable satisfaction from areas in which they were relatively successful. Are some domains more important than others for a child's overall sense of worth? The answer appears to be yes. Boys and girls of elementary and middle school age who are dissatisfied with and keenly concerned about their physical appearance tend to have lower self-esteem. Although discrepancies are also important in other domains, they correlate less highly with judgments of overall self-worth. Harter (1987, 1998) speculates that, in American culture, the relationship stems from the enormous emphasis in movies, television, and magazines on physical appearance as the key to success and acceptance. As children become older, discrepancy scores on social acceptance take on increasingly greater significance, whereas discrepancy scores on athletic competence show a decline in importance (Harter, 1987). Nevertheless, positive assessments of physical appearance continue to be an important predictor of higher self-esteem for boys and girls as they enter the adolescent years (DuBois et al., 2000; Lord, Eccles, & McCarthy, 1994).

Harter also found that the perceived social support of others was correlated with the child's sense of self-worth. As Figure 12.4 shows, elementary school children with low discrepancy *and* high social support scores showed superior levels of self-worth. Children with high discrepancy and low social support displayed the lowest levels of self-esteem. The opinions of others do matter in children's feelings of self-worth, but the need for approval from others diminishes as children grow older. Moreover, some children seem to respond more to the degree of approval they get from others, some to how much disapproval they receive, and still others to both (Rudolph, Caldwell, & Conley, 2005). Thus efforts to improve self-esteem in children may require the formation and acceptance of realistic personal goals, as well as an understanding of how the need for approval works for each individual child.

▶ **FIGURE 12.4**
**How Self-Esteem Develops**

Self-esteem reflects the combined influence of social support and the discrepancy between the child's perceived and desired competence in some ability or attribute. Harter divided elementary school children into three groups based on these two measures. Those with the highest self-esteem reported high social support and a low discrepancy between perceived and desired competence. Those with the lowest self-esteem reported low social support and a high discrepancy between perceived and desired competence. The findings suggest that parents, teachers, and others concerned with increasing self-esteem need to consider both the kind of social encouragement and positive regard they provide and the children's own beliefs about what is important.

*Source:* Adapted from Harter (1987).

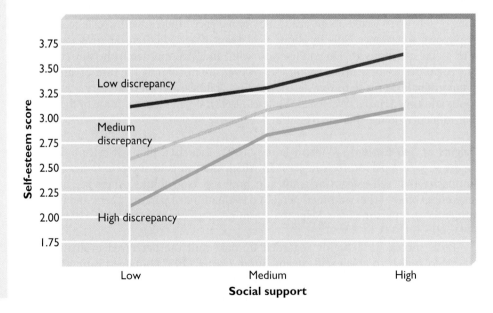

### CONTROVERSY: THINKING IT OVER

## Is Praise Always a Good Thing?

In the discussion of ways to prevent learned helplessness, one finding by Kamins and Dweck (1999) may come as a surprise to many. These researchers noted that praise directed toward children for success did not necessarily inoculate the children from reporting a greater sense of helplessness when faced with a setback in a new task. Are we to conclude that praise (such as "I am really proud of you," "You are really smart," "You are a star") is not a particularly good means of promoting effective behavior?

### What Is the Controversy?

If there is one prescription that many parents and professionals in Western societies, particularly in the United States, would offer for encouraging the development of a competent child, it would very likely be to praise generously for his or her accomplishments. As Carol Dweck (1999) points out, it is one of our most treasured assumptions. Enlightened parents attempt to (and often do) follow such a practice, and many teachers and others working with children are advised to unstintingly administer praise to promote learning. Yet in their recent examination of the effects of praise on children, Jennifer Henderlong and Mark Lepper (2002) have concluded that the research literature often paints a far different picture of its motivational consequences for children.

### What Are the Opposing Arguments?

Learning theory has long recognized the importance of reinforcement for enhancing behavior. Telling a child that he or she is good, excellent, or really smart after completing a task should be reinforcing and promote continuing efforts to engage in that behavior. Moreover, a common belief is that such praise helps to bring about and strengthen intrinsic motivation for accomplishing various goals. To top it off, praise is routinely viewed as an effective way of enhancing a child's self-esteem, another desirable goal, as our discussion of this concept has suggested.

Yet others have raised serious questions about the effectiveness of frequent praise. The concern is that praise, although a presumably positive source of feedback for a child, is nevertheless a *judgment*. As a consequence, it can lead a child to become concerned about performing well and to avoid risks (Henderlong & Lepper, 2002). In other words, the child may place greater value on receiving the praise at the expense of working autonomously or of learning from one's own mistakes. Moreover, when given indiscriminately, such as for an easy task, praise may be interpreted by the child as indicating low ability. Thus frequent praise can have the paradoxical effect of lowering motivation and of promoting a kind of *contingent self-worth*; that is, of feeling worthy only when successful (Dweck, 1999).

### What Answers Exist? What Questions Remain?

When is praise beneficial to a child? In their summary of the research literature, Henderlong and Lepper (2002) suggest a number of conditions under which some types of praise may have positive consequences for a child. These conditions include praise that is sincere and appropriate; that focuses on the type of effort, strategies, and self-corrections the child initiates in an activity rather than on his or her stable attributes (being good, smart, and so on); that encourages the child to be autonomous in his or her activity rather than serving as a way of controlling behavior; that emphasizes effectiveness in the task rather than social comparison; and that is informative in providing feedback about realistic expectations for the task.

Still, many questions remain about praise as a motivational tool. How could professionals and the public be so convinced of its unbridled value, whereas still others have now come to question its general effects on children's development? Thus controversy continues over what kind of and how frequently praise should be administered. Moreover, virtually all of the research on the consequences of praise has been completed on children in the United States (Henderlong & Lepper, 2002). However, cultures differ dramatically in the extent to which children are praised. For example, could its effects on children be very different in a collectivist society in which the emphasis is on improving oneself for the good of the group rather than on self-enhancement? Methodological limitations in the research that has been carried out on this topic present further challenges to some of the conclusions about the effects of praise. Broad acceptance of the value of praise for self-esteem and of its motivational consequences for effort remain controversial and in need of further examination. What kinds of evidence must researchers obtain to decide whether this long-cherished assumption needs to be amended?

## F O R ◆ Y O U R ◆ R E V I E W

◆ What are the primary distinctions between self as object and self as subject? What are the typical behaviors that illustrate these two characterizations of self?

◆ How does social comparison contribute to concept of self in middle childhood?

◆ What factors contribute to mastery orientation and learned helplessness? What steps can parents and teachers take to reduce learned helplessness?

◆ What factors contribute to high self-esteem?

◆ What role does praise play in self-esteem and in promoting achievement motivation?

## Moral Development in Middle Childhood

Like Michael, the child in this chapter's opening vignette, school-aged children typically have daily opportunities to make decisions that have a moral dimension to them. From choosing how to respond to a sibling who absconds with a favorite toy ("Should I hit him, or should I share?") to deciding whether to tell parents about a misbehavior at school (Should I confess, or should I hide the truth for as long as I can?"), to selecting a way to handle an irritated grandfather ("Should I talk back, or should I find a way to make him feel better?"), children's behaviors often reflect the value system that their parents, teachers, and others have tried to pass on to them. But when parents and teachers engage in "moral education," what can they expect the child to understand about these all-important lessons? And even if children understand what is right and what is wrong, how can they be encouraged to behave in ways that reflect those judgments? Some of the answers arise from a long line of theory and research on children's moral development.

### COGNITIVE-DEVELOPMENTAL THEORIES

Cognitive-developmental explanations of moral development highlight the ways children *reason* about moral problems. Should a person ever steal, even if the transgression would help another person? Are there circumstances under which lying is acceptable? The child's capacity to think through the answers to such questions depends on his ability to consider the perspectives, needs, and feelings of others. In other words, moral development is intimately connected with advances in general thinking abilities. The two most prominent cognitive-developmental theorists concerned with moral development, Jean Piaget and Lawrence Kohlberg, have suggested stage theories in which children's reasoning about moral issues is qualitatively different depending on their level of development.

➤ **KEY THEME**

**INTERACTION AMONG DOMAINS**

➤ **KEY THEME**

**CONTINUITY/DISCONTINUITY**

***Piaget's Theory***   Piaget (1932/1965) derived many of his ideas about moral development from two contexts: as children played a formal game with a shared set of rules and as they encountered moral dilemmas created to assess thinking about ethical problems. For example, Piaget observed and interviewed children playing marbles, a popular children's game. Children were asked questions about this game: What are the rules? Can new rules be invented? Where do rules come from? Have they always been the same?

Preschoolers, Piaget stated, are not guided by rules. They engage in the activity for the pure pleasure it provides, and their play is largely solitary. Thus young children may hide marbles or throw them randomly, ignoring the formal rules of the game. By about age six, however, children come to regard rules as sacred and inviolable. Rules, handed down by adults, must be respected and have always existed in the same form; people played marbles in exactly the same way over the years. By about ten years of age, children understand rules to be the result of cooperation and mutual consent among all the participants in the game. Thus rules may be modified to suit the needs of the situation if all the players agree.

The second method Piaget used to study moral development consisted of noting children's responses to moral dilemmas, stories in which a central character committed a transgression. The intentions of that character and the consequences of his or her act varied, as the following stories illustrate:

A. A little boy who is called John is in his room. He is called to dinner. He goes into the dining room. But behind the door there was a chair, and on the chair there was a tray with fifteen cups on it. John couldn't have known that there was all this behind the door. He goes in, the door knocks against the tray, bang go the fifteen cups, and they all get broken!

B. Once there was a little boy whose name was Henry. One day when his mother was out he tried to get some jam out of the cupboard. He climbed up onto a chair and stretched out his arm. But the jam was too high up and he couldn't reach it and have any. But while he was trying to get it he knocked over a cup. The cup fell down and broke. (Piaget, 1932/1965, p. 122)

Which boy is naughtier? Younger children typically choose John, the child who broke more cups. According to Piaget, children younger than about ten are in the stage of moral development called **moral realism**, or *heteronomy*. They judge the rightness or wrongness of an act by the objective visible consequences—in this case, how many cups were broken. They do not consider the boys' intentions to behave well or improperly.

In the stage of moral realism, rules are viewed as unbreakable; if the rules are violated, the child sees punishment as the inevitable consequence. The belief in **immanent justice** is reflected in such statements as "That's God punishing me," made when the child accidentally falls off a bike after lying to her mother, for example. Although the fall is unrelated to the child's transgression, she believes the causal link exists. Children in this stage also believe that a punishment need not be related to the wrongful act if it is severe enough to teach a lesson. Thus stealing a friend's toy can be punished by any means, not necessarily by returning the toy or making reparations.

From a limited ability to reason about moral issues, children progress to **moral relativism**, or *autonomy*. Now the transgressor's motives are taken into account. Thus Henry is named as the naughtier boy. In addition, the child no longer believes

**moral realism**   In Piaget's theory of moral development, the first stage of moral reasoning, in which moral judgments are made on the basis of the consequences of an act. Also called *heteronomy*.

**immanent justice**   Young child's belief that punishment will inevitably follow a transgression.

**moral relativism**   In Piaget's theory of moral development, the second stage of moral reasoning, in which moral judgments are made on the basis of the actor's intentions. Also called *autonomy*.

every violation will be punished. Punishments, however, should relate to the misdemeanor so that the individual appreciates the consequences of his act.

What precipitates the shift from moral realism to moral relativism? Piaget points to changes in the child's cognitive capabilities, especially decreasing egocentrism, as one important element. To understand another's intentions, for example, the child must be able to appreciate the point of view of that person as distinct from her own. Another important factor is the opportunity to interact with peers. Peer interactions force the child to consider the thoughts and feelings of others and eventually lead to an understanding of their intentions and motives. Parents can further promote the shift from realism to relativism, notes Piaget, by encouraging mutual respect and understanding, pointing out the consequences of the child's actions for others, and articulating their needs and feelings as parents.

***Evaluating Piaget*** How well does Piaget's theory stand up? Research confirms that reasoning about moral problems shifts as children grow older. With development, children from diverse cultures, from different social classes, and of varying intellectual abilities more fully consider intentions in judging the actions of another person. But in contrast to Piaget's claims, children younger than age ten can be sensitive to the motives behind a given act—that intentional hitting is worse than accidental hitting, for example (Zelazo, Helwig, & Lau, 1996). In addition, as early as the preschool years, children recognize that actions that produce harmful psychological consequences (such as causing embarrassment or frightening another person) are as unacceptable as behaviors that produce physical harm (Helwig, Zelazo, & Wilson, 2001).

As Piaget described, beliefs in immanent justice and arbitrary punishment decline with age (Hoffman, 1970; Lickona, 1976). Moreover, as children reach the stage of concrete operations, become less egocentric, and demonstrate improved ability to take the perspective of another person, they are more likely to recommend punishment appropriate to the moral transgression (Lee, 1971). However, the manner in which *both* parents and peers reason with younger children influences the level of reasoning the children display concerning moral conflicts later in their development (Walker, Hennig, & Krettenauer, 2000). In other words, parents and not just peers (as Piaget claimed) have a significant impact on moral reasoning.

It is clear from Piaget's work that the child's conceptualization of what is moral becomes more elaborate and complex with age, and that any attempt to understand moral development must include an explanation of the child's thought as well as behavior. Subsequent theorists, Lawrence Kohlberg in particular, have found Piaget's writings a useful springboard for their own theoretical formulations.

***Kohlberg's Theory*** Like Piaget, Kohlberg (1969, 1976) proposed a stage theory of moral development in which progress through each stage proceeds in a universal order and regression to earlier modes of thinking is rare. Kohlberg based his theory on children's responses to a set of dilemmas that put obedience to authority or the law in direct conflict with helping a person in need ("Should a man steal an overpriced drug that he cannot obtain legally in order to save his wife?").

Using an analysis of the reasoning of boys ranging in age from ten to sixteen, Kohlberg identified three general levels of moral orientation, each with two substages, to explain the varying responses of his participants (see Table 12.1). At the **preconventional level**, the child's behavior is motivated by external pressures: avoidance of punishment, attainment of rewards, and preservation of self-interests. Norms of behavior are not yet derived from internalized principles, and the child's needs and desires are primary. At the **conventional level**, conforming to the norms of the majority and maintaining the social order have become central to the child's reasoning. The child now considers the points of view of others, along with their intentions and motives. The child also feels a sense of responsibility to contribute to society and to uphold the laws and institutions that serve its members. Finally, at the **postconventional level**, the individual has developed a fuller understanding

**preconventional level** In Kohlberg's theory, the first level of moral reasoning, in which morality is motivated by the avoidance of punishments and attainment of rewards.

**conventional level** In Kohlberg's theory, the second level of moral reasoning, in which the child conforms to the norms of the majority and wishes to preserve the social order.

**postconventional level** In Kohlberg's theory, the third level of moral reasoning, in which laws are seen as the result of a social contract and individual principles of conscience may emerge.

**What is the relationship between prosocial behavior and other aspects of development?**

Children who display prosocial behaviors are more popular with peers and have stronger friendships. They are also more likely to have higher academic achievement.

## GENDER ROLES IN MIDDLE CHILDHOOD

**How do children's concepts of gender stereotypes change during middle childhood?**

During middle childhood, knowledge about gender stereotypes becomes more extensive but also more flexible. Stereotypes are often enacted by children in the types of activities in which they choose to participate.

**What changes in gender identity occur during middle childhood?**

Gender identity begins to include assessments of gender typicality during middle childhood. Children who see themselves as typical for their sex have higher self-esteem and lower incidence of internalizing disorders.

**How does sex segregation contribute to the development of gender roles?**

*Sex segregation* is a robust phenomenon that provides different socialization experiences for boys and girls. Boys' groups promote dominance and assertiveness, whereas girls' groups promote a relationship orientation and shared intimacy.

## KEY TERMS AND CONCEPTS

**conventional level** (p. 430)

**display rule** (p. 416)

**immanent justice** (p. 429)

**induction** (p. 438)

**learned helplessness** (p. 422)

**mastery orientation** (p. 421)

**moral realism** (p. 429)

**moral relativism** (p. 429)

**morality of care and responsibility** (p. 434)

**morality of justice** (p. 434)

**postconventional level** (p. 430)

**power assertion** (p. 438)

**preconventional level** (p. 430)

**self-esteem** (p. 425)

**sex segregation** (p. 443)

**social comparison** (p. 421)

**social convention** (p. 434)

# 13 CONTEXTS OF DEVELOPMENT

t was the start of the first day of school. Ms. Klein, the third-grade teacher, surveyed her new charges as they played in the schoolyard before the bell rang. It was a familiar scene: the boys played a raucous game of kickball, cheering their teammates and urging victory. The girls gathered in small groups, talking with great animation about their summer experiences and their excitement to see each other again. As always, certain children in both groups were the center of activity; they seemed to attract their peers as a pot of honey draws bees. Other children stayed on the fringes of the playground; few of their peers approached or spoke to them. Already, Ms. Klein has a sense that third grade, with all of its academic and social challenges, will be easier on some of these fresh new faces than on others.

SOCIOCULTURAL INFLUENCE How do sociocultural factors influence the contexts of development in middle childhood?

RISK/RESILIENCE What contextual factors promote risk or resilience in middle childhood?

Middle childhood brings a host of new experiences for children and, consequently, new contexts for their development. The most significant is the start of formal schooling. The child's typical day is now more highly structured, involves serious work, and requires greater independence than ever before. And with the start of school come other new opportunities for children—to make new friends, participate in athletics, or perhaps begin music or art instruction. The family still plays a pivotal role to be sure, but the sphere of influences on children's development—peers, teachers, media—is now greatly expanded. In this chapter, we take the opportunity to focus on these important new circumstances in which growth takes place.

## THE FAMILY IN MIDDLE CHILDHOOD

As we have already pointed out in this text, in today's society we see the concept of family undergoing somewhat of a transition. There are now many variations from the traditional two-parent nuclear family. Single-parent families, families in which parents have divorced, and same-sex parents are more prevalent. What are the effects of these emerging family structures on child development? Research shows that development is influenced not so much by changes in family arrangement as by the ways in which interpersonal relations take place within the family.

During middle childhood, relationships between parents and children are no longer so one-sided. Instead of playing such a large supervisory role, parents now begin to nurture greater independence, especially as children enter school. Parents and children begin to negotiate as they make decisions and solve family problems.

In this portion of the chapter, we examine variations in families, across cultures and across the different forms and structures they may take. It should become apparent that the principles of effective parenting that we described in the chapter on early childhood continue to apply during the middle childhood years. Parents who are warm and nurturant but also set clear, consistent limits for their children provide a healthy, positive context for the child's continuing growth. These principles apply regardless of who the parents are and how many of them live in the child's immediate environment.

### CROSS-CULTURAL DIFFERENCES IN PARENTING

**KEY THEME**
**SOCIOCULTURAL INFLUENCE**

Beatrice Whiting and Carolyn Pope Edwards (1988) have provided an extended analysis of variations in parenting by comparing societies as diverse as rural Kenya, Liberia, and the Philippines with urban America. Despite vast differences in economic, social, and political conditions, many similar, overarching patterns were apparent in the ways parents socialized their children. Whereas parents of infants and toddlers emphasized nurturance and, slightly later, corrections of misbehavior, when children reached school age parents became concerned with training them in the skills and social behavior valued by their cultural group.

At the same time, though, Whiting and Edwards (1988) observed notable differences. For example, mothers from rural villages in Kenya and Liberia emphasized training children to do chores responsibly and placed a high premium on obedience. From an early age, children were taught how to care for the family's fields and animals, and they assumed a major role in caring for younger siblings. Children were punished for performing tasks irresponsibly and were rarely praised. Consistent

Children's socialization experiences are influenced by cultural values and beliefs. For example, in rural Kenya, children care for the family's fields and animals, and have responsibility for younger siblings. Children growing up in such communities were found to display a high degree of compliance with mothers' requests.

with this orientation to child rearing was the family's dependence on women and children for producing food. Because women in these cultures typically had an enormous workload, they delegated some tasks to children as soon as children were physically capable of managing them; because accidents and injury to infants and the family's resources must be prevented, deviant behaviors were not tolerated in children. Children growing up in these communities were highly compliant with mothers' commands and suggestions.

An even more controlling style characterized the Tarong community in the Philippines, in which subsistence farming is the mainstay but responsibilities for producing food are more evenly distributed among the group's members. When the mother did not rely so heavily on her children to work for the family's survival and when the goals of training were thus less clear, arbitrary commands and even punishment became more common. Children were scolded frequently for being in the way of adults or for playing in inappropriate places. By middle childhood, Tarong children showed a marked decline in their tendency to seek attention from or be close to their parents.

These patterns provided a striking contrast to the "sociability" that characterized the middle-income American mothers in the sample. Interactions between mothers and children consisted of significant information exchange and warm, friendly dialogues. Mothers emphasized verbalization, educational tasks, and play, and they were liberal in their use of praise and encouragement. Because children in American society normally do not work to ensure the economic survival of the family unit, firm training and punishing were not part of these parents' styles. The emphasis on verbalization and educational activities was consistent with the high value Americans place on social interactions and schooling.

Other researchers examining parent-child relationships in Asian cultures have reaffirmed the idea that culture affects parenting styles. Japanese mothers use less physical punishment and more verbal reasoning to control their children than American mothers (Kobayashi-Winata & Power, 1989). Japanese culture emphasizes responsibilities and commitments to others, a socialization goal that is achieved more effectively through reasoning than through power-assertive techniques. Japanese children, in fact, comply with rules at home and in school more than their American counterparts do. Similarly, when Chinese parents are asked to describe their child-rearing practices, they report a greater emphasis on control and achievement in children than American parents (Chao, 1994; Lin & Fu, 1990). In Chinese society, character development and educational attainment are highly valued, and parental practices follow directly from these larger societal goals.

As Whiting and Edwards (1988) point out, parents around the world resemble one another in numerous ways because of the universal needs children have as they grow and develop. But it is also true that the specific ecology of each culture, its socialization goals, and the demands it places on the family unit can dramatically shape parenting practices and the course of the individual child's socialization.

## DIVORCE

The statistics are dramatic: the divorce rate among couples in the United States is a little under 50 percent, and estimates suggest that 40 percent of children in contemporary society will live through the divorce of their parents (Bramlett & Mosher, 2001; Cherlin, 1992; Furstenberg, 1994). Far from being an atypical event, divorce affects a significant proportion of American children. Unfortunately, the effects of divorce on children are rarely positive; the absence of one parent, the emotional and financial tension, and sometimes the continuing conflicts between parents that accompany divorce can lead to a range of psychological problems for

**KEY THEME**
**RISK/RESILIENCE**

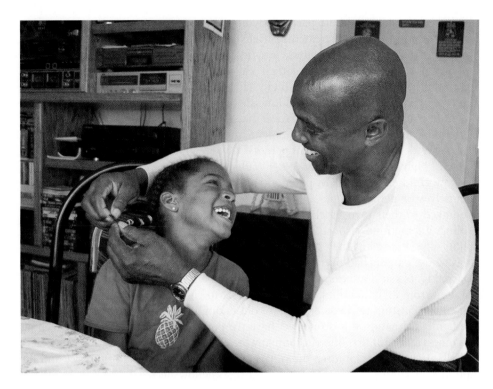

Parents around the world look similar on some dimensions because of the universal needs of children. For example, like this father, many parents across a variety of cultures express nurturance but also expect children to conform to specific cultural-linked values.

both boys and girls, at least in the period immediately following the breakup of the family. Children's ability to cope with the stresses of divorce, particularly in the long run, depends on a number of variables. Most important is the way parents manage the transition in family structure.

***Consequences of Divorce***   A major longitudinal study of the effects of divorce on parents and children, conducted by E. Mavis Hetherington and her associates, illuminated how parental separation affects children and how the nature of parent-child interactions changes (Hetherington, Cox, & Cox, 1982). The researchers compared two groups over a period of two years, a sample of forty-eight preschool-age, middle-class children whose parents divorced and another group of forty-eight middle-class children matched on several variables, such as age and sex, whose families were intact. In all the divorced families, mothers had custody of their children. During the course of the study, the researchers made several assessments of both parents and children, including parental interviews, observations of parent-child interactions in the laboratory and at home, observations and ratings of children's behavior in the home and at school, and personality tests.

The results of the study indicated that the worst period for most children was the first year after the divorce, when they exhibited many negative characteristics such as aggression, distractibility, and noncompliance. The extent of their undesirable behaviors surpassed those of children from intact families with a high level of conflict; it was particularly noticeable in boys. Two years after the divorce, many of the effects on children had diminished, especially for girls. In a six-year follow-up, however, many boys continued to show patterns of aggression and noncompliance, academic difficulties, poor relations with peers, and extremely low self-esteem (Hetherington, 1989).

A look at family interaction styles after divorce helps to account for the poor initial adjustment of children. Hetherington and her colleagues noted that, soon after they separated from their husbands, mothers tended to adopt a more authoritarian style of parenting (Hetherington et al., 1982; Hetherington & Kelly, 2002). They gave out numerous commands and prohibitions, and displayed little affection or responsiveness to their children. These mothers were undoubtedly having problems coping, in both emotional and practical terms, with their new status as single parents. At the same time, the fathers withdrew, participating little in the management of their children's behavior. Children, particularly boys, became less compliant, and mothers in turn responded with increased restrictiveness and punitiveness. Caught up in a spiral of frustration, helplessness, and feelings of incompetence, these mothers responded negatively to many of their children's behaviors, even those that were neutral or positive, and, despite their harsh threats, followed up on few of the directives they gave. The result was a negative cycle of parent-child interactions.

Other researchers have confirmed that many children show more heightened aggression, lower academic achievement, more disruptions in peer relationships, and more depression after their parents' divorce than previously (Amato, 2001; Emery, 1999b; Stolberg & Anker, 1984; Wallerstein, Corbin, & Lewis, 1988). Research on how children respond to parental conflict suggests that children either blame themselves or perceive a personal threat when their parents fight, judgments that are linked to their own psychological adjustment (Grych, Harold, & Miles, 2003). Sibling interactions also suffer. Carol MacKinnon (1989) observed elementary school–age children as they played games with their siblings in the laboratory. Siblings whose parents had been divorced for one year or longer showed more teasing, quarreling, physical attacks, and other negative behaviors toward one another than children from intact families. Children ages six to eight years seem to have the most difficulty adjusting to divorce; they are old enough to recognize the seriousness of the family's situation but do not yet have the coping skills to deal with the feelings of sadness and guilt that often accompany the change in family structure (Wallerstein & Kelly, 1980). Older children often have a better understanding of divorce and the notion that conflicts between parents must somehow be resolved (Kurdek, 1989). However, even adolescents often suffer negative psychological consequences after their parents divorce. Adolescent boys in particular were found to be more likely to use alcohol or illicit drugs after their parents separated than boys in a control group whose parents remained married (Doherty & Needle, 1991).

For some individuals, the aftermath of divorce may last well into young adulthood. According to data collected as part of a major longitudinal study in Great Britain, young adults whose parents had previously divorced reported more depression, anxiety, and other emotional problems than adults from intact families (Chase-Lansdale, Cherlin, & Kiernan, 1995). In addition, in a twenty-year follow-up of her original sample, Hetherington (1999) found that young adults whose parents had divorced were less likely to finish high school, had smaller social networks, experienced more conflicts with siblings and friends, and had more conflicts in their own marriages. The results of another longitudinal study showed that adults whose parents had divorced were more likely to experience a breakup of their own marriages (Amato, 1999).

**KEY THEME**

**RISK/RESILIENCE**

***Adjusting to Divorce***   The consequences of divorce are not always so grim for all children. In fact, most children whose parents have divorced do not look different from children in intact families when they are followed over time (Emery, 1999a). We need to remember that the psychological distress experienced by children at the time of the divorce is different from a long-term psychological disorder (Emery, Otto, & O'Donohue, 2005). E. Mavis Hetherington (1989) observed that, after six years, some of the children in her original study recovered from the family crisis and showed a healthy adaptation to their new family lifestyle, whether or not their mother remarried. These children displayed few behavior problems, high self-esteem, successful academic performance, and positive relations with peers.

What factors were associated with this favorable pattern of adjustment? For one thing, mothers of children in this group had become less authoritarian and more authoritative in their parental style, encouraging independence but also providing a warm, supportive climate for their sons and daughters. If the mother was not available, many of these children had contact with some other caring adult, such as a relative, teacher, or neighbor. In addition, several children in this category had responsibility for the care of another individual: a younger sibling, an aging grandparent, or someone with a physical or emotional problem. These relationships may have offered children an opportunity to feel needed and provided an alternative source of emotional gratification and support. In contrast, mothers of children with long-lasting adjustment problems continued to manifest coercive negative styles of interaction. Mothers and sons were especially likely to fall into this pattern. Children are also more likely to show successful adjustment to divorce when conflict between divorced parents is low, when the child does not feel "caught" between the two parents, and when the child does not feel that he or she will be abandoned (Amato & Rezac, 1994; Buchanan, Maccoby, & Dornbusch, 1991; Wolchik et al., 2002). Maintaining a close relationship with grandparents can also help (Lussier et al., 2002).

Divorce represents a difficult transition for all members of the family. Some of the effects of divorce on children may actually be due to personal attributes in parents that are passed on genetically to children. Parents and children may share biological predispositions to poor social and academic skills, and these may be the very characteristics that lead to marital problems for parents, as well as problematic postdivorce behaviors in children (O'Connor et al., 2000). However, research also suggests that a key variable in understanding the effects of divorce is the quality of relationships among all family members: the more conflict and negative emotion associated with the process and the more prolonged the maladaptive patterns of interaction, the worse the outcomes for the child. In addition, the child's overall adjustment needs to be considered in the broader context of such factors as socioeconomic status, neighborhood, and parental emotional state. These risk factors operate in a similar fashion whether the parents are divorced or not (Deater-Deckard & Dunn, 1999).

***Custody Arrangements*** After divorce, most children reside with their mother, in large part because of long-standing societal beliefs about the privileged nature of mother-child relationships. Yet when children live with their mother after a divorce, they are more likely to experience economic hardship than if they live with their father. Studies have found that income for divorced women with children declines an average of 30 percent, whereas income for fathers declines much less or even increases (Burkhauser et al., 1991; Weitzman, 1985). Children living with their mother also typically show a dramatic impairment in their relationship with their father. For example, according to one national study, more than one-third of the children in the sample did not see their father *at all* or saw him only a few times a year (Selzer, 1991).

Many states now have laws that favor joint custody of children following divorce. In most cases, this means that both parents have equal responsibility for making decisions about the child's medical care and education; that is, they have *joint legal custody*. In other cases, children reside for substantial periods of time with each parent; this arrangement refers to *joint physical custody*. A meta-analysis of studies comparing the effects of joint custody versus sole custody shows that joint custody—whether it is legal or physical—is generally associated with greater benefits for children. Children in joint custody display higher self-esteem and fewer behavioral and emotional problems than children in sole custody. An important factor related to these benefits is children's ability to spend time with each parent; also, parents of children in joint custody tend to have fewer conflicts than parents in a sole-custody situation (Bauserman, 2002). However, it may not be the custody situation per se that influences children's well-being. Rather, it may be that parents who select this custody arrangement tend to have a low conflict style to begin with (Emery, Otto, & O' Donohue, 2005). Researchers have also reported that parental participation in a wide range of activities, even such everyday ones as shopping and watching TV together, predicted children's successful adjustment better than the frequency of special trips or activities (Clarke-Stewart & Hayward, 1996).

## SINGLE-PARENT FAMILIES

**KEY THEME**
**RISK/RESILIENCE**

Slightly over one-third of American children are born to single mothers (Hamilton et al., 2005). Children growing up in single-parent families are at greater risk for a broad array of developmental problems, including poor academic achievement, behavior problems, and high-risk behaviors, such as substance abuse (Barber & Eccles,

1992; Demo & Acock, 1996; Turner, Irwin, & Millstein, 1991). It is also important to note that the poverty rate for families headed by single mothers is almost 30 percent, higher than for any other family type (DeNavas-Walt, Proctor, & Lee, 2005).

In light of these risks, it is important for research to identify the factors associated with more successful child outcomes in single-parent families. One of these is more involved parenting (Avenevoli, Sess, & Steinberg, 1999). In a study of almost 200 inner-city African American and Hispanic families, most of whom earned less than $20,000 per year, adolescent boys from mother-only families showed fewer problem behaviors when mothers used effective discipline strategies (firm but warm), allowed for the child's growing autonomy, provided a structured family environment, and facilitated the growth of relationships with other male family members (Florsheim, Tolan, & Gorman-Smith, 1998). In contrast, when parents are too punitive, children may not fare so well. In a study of 290 single-parent, poor families, most of whom were African American, children with fewer behavior problems and better school readiness had parents who were less likely to use harsh discipline (Zaslow et al., 1999).

Another factor is the involvement of mothers in religion. Among single-parent, poor African American families in the rural South, maternal religiosity was related to use of "no-nonsense" parenting (firm but warm), higher quality of mother-child relationships, and more maternal involvement in school. These latter variables, in turn, were linked to the child's overall successful development in cognitive, social, and behavioral domains (Brody & Flor, 1998).

Studies of single-parent families, as well as families that are undergoing other types of transitions, emphasize that it is important to find ways to promote healthy, positive interactions between parents and children. Effective parents are involved and nurturant, and provide firm, steady guidance to their children. When parents are stressed or distracted, or when they are unaware of the importance of parenting style, they are less likely to engage in successful interactions with their children. Assistance with child care, parent training programs, and counseling support for families experiencing stress are some of the societal programs that can be helpful.

## GAY AND LESBIAN PARENTS

Because of the legal and social controversies surrounding gay and lesbian parenting, it is difficult to obtain accurate estimates of how many children grow up in families with same-sex parents. But most experts agree that the numbers are rising and might be in the millions. Research on the impact of growing up in families in which parents are gay or lesbian is clearer, however. When children whose parents are homosexual are compared with children whose parents are heterosexual, there are virtually no identifiable differences in their academic performance, social development, peer relationships, mental health, or sexual orientation (Patterson, 2000; Wainright, Russell, & Patterson, 2004). As with most studies of the impact of the family on child development, what matters most, say the results, is the quality of the day-to-day interactions that family members have with one another.

A study by Susan Golombok and her colleagues (Golombok et al., 2003) is representative of this body of research. Samples of seven-year-old children with two lesbian parents, two heterosexual parents, or single heterosexual mothers were compared on a number of measures of social and emotional well-being, including self-esteem, peer relations, gender-role activities, and mental health. Parental warmth, emotional involvement, and conflict resolution styles were also assessed. The findings showed that, in general, lesbian mothers were not significantly different from heterosexual mothers on most dimensions of parenting. In fact, lesbian mothers spanked their children less and engaged in more imaginative play. No differences were found in the adjustment scores of children from the various groups. Most revealing was the finding that the strongest predictor of children's adjustment was not mothers' sexual orientation or the structure of the family, but rather the amount of stress parents reported. For children in all families, the greater the difficulty mothers reported in their parental roles, the more likely were children to experience adjustment problems.

## SIBLINGS

Siblings play an important but often unacknowledged role within the family. Older siblings act as teachers and role models, and can be important sources of emotional support for younger siblings. For better or worse, they instruct younger brothers and sisters on how to think and act, and in times of conflict or trouble within the family, they can buffer younger siblings from emotional distress (Jenkins, 1992). Aside from their direct impact on other children in the family, however, siblings can have effects that are more indirect (Brody, 2004). Consider what happens when an older sibling is rebellious or cooperative, successful in school or not. Parents' positive or negative experiences with an older sibling can color their expectations of the younger sibling (Whiteman & Buchanan, 2002). Moreover, older siblings who do well academically and who have good relationships with their peers give their parents confidence in their parenting skills, which in turn has an impact on their interactions with younger children in the family. Positive parenting results in better self-control and fewer behavioral problems in younger siblings (Brody et al., 2003). These kinds of findings provide vivid examples of how families function as systems with multiple layers of reciprocal influences.

How do older children interact as siblings? For one thing, children tend to fight more with their siblings than with their friends. When fifth- through eighth-graders were asked to describe conflicts with their siblings, they reported that they allowed quarrels with siblings to escalate, whereas they tried to resolve conflicts with friends. Most of the time, siblings fight about privacy and interpersonal boundaries (Raffaelli, 1989). Typically, parents do not intervene in sibling conflicts, and when they do not, those conflicts continue (Perozynski & Kramer, 1999). On the other hand, when parents discuss each child's needs (as opposed to using controlling tactics), subsequent conflicts between siblings are less likely (Kramer, Perozynski, & Chung, 1999). Siblings also express more positive behaviors with one another when their fathers, in particular, are nurturant and try to be fair to each child (Brody, Stoneman, & McCoy, 1992). Researchers have noted that the degree of conflict in sibling relationships is related to the amount of aggression a child shows in school, whereas the amount of warmth in sibling relationships is linked to emotional control and social competence in school (Garcia et al., 2000; Stormshak et al., 1996).

Whether positive or negative in character, the quality of sibling relationships initiated in early childhood tends to remain stable through middle childhood (Dunn, Slombowski, & Beardsall, 1994) and then typically changes from middle childhood through adolescence. Duane Buhrmester and Wyndol Furman (1990) administered the Sibling Relationship Questionnaire to third-, sixth-, ninth-, and twelfth-graders to assess several dimensions of sibling interactions. Older siblings reported being more dominant and nurturant toward their younger siblings, and younger siblings confirmed that they received more often than dispensed dominance and nurturance. These differences between older and younger siblings disappeared over time, however. The older children in the sample reported having more egalitarian relationships with their siblings, as well as less intense feelings of both warmth and conflict. Initial differences in power and nurturance usually disappeared when the younger sibling was twelve years old, by which time she or he had become more competent and needed less guidance and emotional support.

Although the presence of siblings may mean that the child has fewer opportunities to interact with parents, it also provides the context for developing other unique skills. Older siblings have opportunities to become nurturant and assertive, and younger siblings have more models for a range of behaviors than do only children.

F O R • Y O U R • R E V I E W

◆ In what ways do parenting strategies vary across different cultural groups?

◆ What are the effects of divorce on child development?

◆ What factors can help children adjust to the divorce of their parents?

◆ What kinds of custody arrangements are best for children?

◆ What factors are associated with successful outcomes in single-parent families?

◆ What does the research indicate about the impact of having gay or lesbian parents?

◆ What role do siblings play in the development of younger children in the family?

## PEER RELATIONSHIPS IN MIDDLE CHILDHOOD

Research evidence suggests that the ability to have successful and rewarding interactions with peers during childhood can be the harbinger of successful later adjustment and that poor peer relations are often associated with a range of developmental problems. Boys and girls who have good peer relationships enjoy school more and are less likely to experience academic difficulties, drop out of school, or commit delinquent acts in later years than agemates who relate poorly with their peers (Bagwell, Newcomb, & Bukowski, 1998; Morison & Masten, 1991; Parker & Asher, 1987). Children who are accepted by their peers are also less likely to report feeling lonely, depressed, and socially anxious than children who are rejected (Boivin & Hymel, 1997; Cassidy & Asher, 1992; Crick & Ladd, 1993). Of course, the quality of peer relations is not the only factor that predicts later developmental outcomes. But it is hard to deny that experiences with peers play a substantial role in the lives of most children. Thus, peer relationships have become an important focus of developmental research.

What do child development theorists say about the role of peers? Social learning theorists believe that peers exert a powerful influence on the child's socialization by means of modeling and reinforcement. Piaget (1932/1965) and Vygotsky (1978) have discussed the ways in which peer contacts alter the child's cognitions, which can in turn direct social behavior. Piaget contends that peer interactions prompt or even coerce the child to consider the viewpoints of others, thus broadening her social perspective-taking ability and diminishing her egocentrism. The result is a greater capacity for social exchange. Vygotsky maintains that contact with peers, especially those who are more skilled in a given domain, stretches the child's intellectual and social capacities. As a result of experiences with peers, the child internalizes new modes of thinking and social interaction and then produces them independently.

### PEER GROUP FORMATION

How do peer groups form in the first place? Undoubtedly, they coalesce on the basis of children's shared interests, backgrounds, or activities. Children associate with other members of their classroom, soccer team, or school band, for example. Other variables, such as socioeconomic status or ethnic and racial group membership, can also contribute. Youngsters often join with others of similar social class or ethnic/ racial background (Clasen & Brown, 1985; Larkin, 1979). Gender is another powerful variable; groups for the most part tend to be of the same sex throughout childhood and early adolescence.

A particularly enlightening description of how peer groups form and operate can be found in a classic experiment called the Robbers Cave study, named after the state park in Oklahoma where it took place. Muzafer Sherif and his colleagues invited twenty-two fifth-grade boys who did not know one another to participate in a summer camp program (Sherif et al., 1961). The boys were divided into two groups housed in separate parts of the state park. Initially, each group participated in its own program of typical camp activities—hiking, crafts, structured games— and was unaware of the existence of the other group. In this initial period of the experiment, each group began to develop a unique identity, and individual members performed distinct roles in relation to this group identity. One group became "tough"; the boys swore, acted rough, and ridiculed those who were "sissies." Members of the other group were polite and considerate. As group solidarity grew, members decided to name themselves, the former calling themselves the Rattlers and the latter the Eagles.

The experimenters found that, when they deliberately structured certain situations to encourage cooperation, group identities could be further strengthened. One day, for example, each group returned to the campsite only to find that the staff had not prepared dinner; only the uncooked ingredients were available. The boys quickly took over, dividing up the tasks so that some cooked, others prepared drinks, and so forth. Some boys assumed a leadership role, directing the suppertime activities, and others followed their directives. It was quite apparent that the boys had a strong sense of identity with the group and that the group had a clear structure. In other words, for both the Rattlers and the Eagles, there was strong intragroup cooperation and identity.

Another change in circumstances made the group identities even more pronounced. The camp counselors arranged for the Rattlers and Eagles to meet and organized a series of competitions for them, including games, such as baseball and tug-of-war. The effects of losing in these competitions were dramatic. The losing group became very disharmonious and conflict ridden. Members accused one another of causing the loss, and some boys who had previously enjoyed status and prestige were demoted in standing if they had contributed to the group's humiliation. After these initial conflicts, however, group identity became stronger than ever. The effects of competition on behavior *between* the groups were even more pronounced. The Rattlers and Eagles verbally antagonized each other and retaliated for a loss in the day's competition by raiding each other's campsites and stealing possessions, such as comic books and clothing. Each episode forged intragroup identity but also increased intergroup hostility.

In the last phase of this social experiment, the counselors attempted to lessen the bad feelings between the Rattlers and the Eagles by having them share meals or watch movies together. Instead of promoting harmony between the groups, however, this tactic produced continuing hostilities, punctuated with fights and verbal assaults. In contrast, when the experimenters created situations in which the two groups had to work together to achieve some common goal, antagonisms between them began to crumble. One hot day, for example, when the counselors "discovered" that the water pipeline for the campsites was broken, boys from both Rattlers and Eagles began to search together for the broken pipes. On another occasion, the food delivery truck broke down; again, the boys all worked together to restart the engine. The acrimonious behavior between the two groups diminished, and boys from the two groups actually began to form friendships with one another.

Few studies of the formation and function of peer groups match the scope of the Robbers Cave study. However, a more recent series of studies sheds further light on the factors that promote peer group identity. Rebecca Bigler and her colleagues (Bigler, Jones, & Lobliner, 1997) divided children in each of several summer school classrooms into a "blue" group and a "yellow" group. For some children, their assignment to a group was based on a biological characteristic: whether their hair color was light or dark. For others, assignment to a group was random. Teachers in both groups were instructed to emphasize group membership with verbal comments and by other overt actions, such as seating children and having them line up for recess according to their group. Children in all the groups wore T-shirts bearing the color of their group. The researchers also included a control group, in which children wore either yellow or blue T-shirts but did not experience emphasis on the groups from their teachers. At the end of four weeks, children were asked a series of questions evaluating their attitudes toward their own group (the in-group) and the other group (the out-group). Children in the experimental conditions showed a strong tendency to ascribe positive traits to *all* members of the in-group and *none* of the members of the out-group. The control group, in contrast, did not show this pattern. Thus, when adults actively use obvious perceptual categories to describe children's groups, children exhibit strong favoritism toward their own group and bias against the out-group. In-group favoritism does not operate in all circumstances, however. In a subsequent study, Bigler and her colleagues manipulated the status of the yellow and blue groups by displaying photographs of past winners of athletic and academic competitions on posters placed around the classrooms. They purposely showed more "winners" from the yellow group. Under these conditions, children in the low-status group, the blue group, did not show a bias toward their own group, whereas children in the high-status group did (Bigler, Brown, & Markell, 2001). These studies, together with the Robbers Cave study, reveal important information about the factors that influence peer group dynamics. In particular, they provide clues about the strategies that either promote or break down animosities among children's groups, findings that have implications for interventions aimed at reducing gender or racial and ethnic biases.

## PEER POPULARITY

Parents, teachers, and others who have the opportunity to observe children over time usually notice the two extreme ends of the sociability spectrum: some children seem to be at the center of many activities, from school projects to playground games, whereas others are ridiculed or ignored. Frequently the patterns of peer acceptance that become established in the early school years persist for years afterward, along with the psychological rewards or disappointments that accompany them. Research shows that, once children are rejected by peers, they are on a trajectory that often leads to lower school achievement and emotional problems. In

**KEY THEME**
RISK/RESILIENCE

Children who lack social skills may be rejected or neglected by their peers. In contrast, popular children display prosocial behaviors and a wide range of social knowledge.

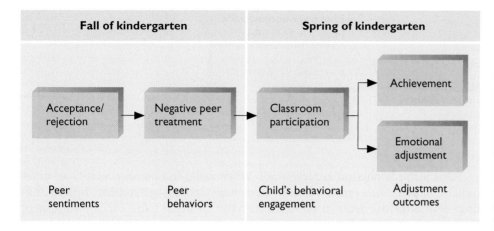

| Fall of kindergarten | | Spring of kindergarten | |
|---|---|---|---|
| Acceptance/ rejection → | Negative peer treatment → | Classroom participation → | Achievement / Emotional adjustment |
| Peer sentiments | Peer behaviors | Child's behavioral engagement | Adjustment outcomes |

**FIGURE 13.1**

**The Impact of Peer Rejection**

Peer rejection is associated with negative consequences among children, including emotional and academic problems. To study more closely the dynamics of this process, Eric Buhs and Gary Ladd (2001) monitored kindergarten children's peer status, peer interactions, classroom participation, and eventual adjustment over the school year. They found that the results of the study generally supported a model like that depicted here.

*Source:* Buhs & Ladd (2001).

one study, Gary Ladd observed children in both the fall and the spring of their kindergarten year, noting their peer status, peer interactions, classroom participation, and emotional adjustment over the school year. The data fit the model depicted in Figure 13.1. Unpopular children were subjected to more negative treatment from peers (such as exclusion from peer activities and victimization) and participated less in classroom activities, which in turn predicted lower achievement and emotional difficulties (Buhs & Ladd, 2001). Given the developmental pathway that many rejected children follow, finding ways to help them negotiate their social world, especially as they begin school, seems all the more important. Psychologists have uncovered several factors related to peer acceptance and popularity.

***Assessing Popularity***   Psychologists usually assess the quality of peer relations by administering questionnaires to children, asking about the social standing of their agemates. Peer assessments frequently consist of a **sociometric nomination** measure in which children are asked to name a specified number of peers (usually between three and five) who fit a certain criterion. For example, children might be asked to "Name three classmates you especially like (or dislike)" or "List three peers you would like to walk home from school with." The number of positive or negative nominations the child receives from other children serves as a measure of his popularity. Alternatively, children are sometimes asked to rate each peer in the class or group on a **sociometric rating scale,** a series of items like "How much do you like to be with this person at school?" The target child's average rating by the other children is the index of peer acceptance.

Peer nomination measures, in turn, are used to classify children's *peer status.* *Popular* children receive many more positive ("like") than negative ("dislike") nominations. *Rejected* children, in contrast, receive few positive but many negative nominations. *Neglected* children receive low numbers of nominations in either category; although they lack friends, they are not actively disliked (Asher & Dodge, 1986). *Controversial* children receive high numbers of both positive and negative nominations. They have a high degree of "social impact" because they are active and visible, but they are generally not preferred as social partners (Coie, Dodge, & Coppotelli, 1982). Finally, *average* children do not receive extreme scores on peer nomination measures. Figure 13.2 summarizes these categories of peer status.

***Characteristics of Popular and Unpopular Children***   What exactly is it about unpopular children that makes them so unappealing to their agemates and places them so consistently in an undesirable status? This is a particularly important question for those attempting to intervene in these children's "at-risk" circumstances. Peer popularity, as defined by sociometric measures, is related to a number of variables, some of which lie within the child's control and some of which, unfortunately, do not.

**sociometric nomination**   Peer assessment measure in which children are asked to name a specified number of peers who fit a certain criterion, such as "peers you would like to walk home with."

**sociometric rating scale**   Peer assessment measure in which children rate peers on a number of social dimensions.

▶ **FIGURE 13.2**

**Classification of Peer Status**

The number of positive and negative peer nominations received determines whether a child's peer status is classified as controversial, rejected, neglected, or popular. Average children receive less extreme scores on peer nomination measures.

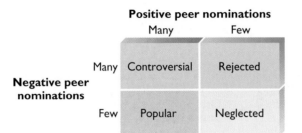

One factor is physical attractiveness. When asked to rate photographs of unfamiliar children, both preschool- and elementary school–age children believe children with attractive faces to be more friendly, intelligent, and socially competent than unattractive children (Dion & Berscheid, 1974; Langlois & Stephan, 1981). Correlations between children's ratings of peers' attractiveness and sociometric measures of peer acceptance typically range between +0.35 and +0.50, indicating a moderately strong relationship between these two variables (Cavior & Dokecki, 1973; Lerner & Lerner, 1977). Body type makes a difference, too. For example, boys with broad shoulders and large muscles are the most popular, and short, chubby boys are the least popular (Staffieri, 1967). The reasons for these stereotypic beliefs are unknown, but they can lead to self-fulfilling behaviors in children who have been labeled (Hartup, 1983). For example, a child who receives peer attention because of attractiveness may have numerous opportunities to develop the social skills that lead to even greater peer acceptance.

Another factor related to peer acceptance is the child's proficiency in motor activities. Both boys and girls who are coordinated, strong, and skilled in such activities as throwing a ball are rated as more popular by peers and as more socially competent by their teachers and parents (Hops & Finch, 1985). It may be that the value our society places on athletic prowess is reflected in children's preferences in playmates. Alternatively, motor skill may facilitate the manipulation of objects and game playing that constitute the majority of children's shared activities. Those who are talented in this arena will naturally have more peer contacts and eventually be better liked.

One of the most important factors in peer acceptance is the constellation of social behaviors displayed by popular and unpopular children. Researchers who have observed the overt activities of accepted and unaccepted peers have learned that each presents a distinct behavioral profile. In general, popular children engage in prosocial, cooperative, and normative behaviors and show a high degree of social skill. In contrast, about 50 percent of rejected children are aggressive (Bierman, Smoot, & Aumiller, 1993), and about 20 percent are highly socially withdrawn (Volling et al., 1993). Both of these types of rejected children, as well as neglected children, display socially inappropriate behaviors for which they receive little social reinforcement (Parkhurst & Asher, 1992; Pettit et al., 1996).

For example, when Gary Ladd (1983) observed third- and fourth-grade students during recess, he noted several differences in the behavioral styles of popular and rejected children. Popular children spent more time in cooperative play, social conversation, and other positive social interactions with peers than did their rejected counterparts. Rejected children, on the other hand, spent more time engaging in antagonistic behaviors, such as arguing and playing in a rough-and-tumble fashion, or playing or standing alone, at a distance from peers. According to the results of another study that examined the peer-directed behaviors of first- and third-grade boys, neglected and controversial children display still other clusters of behaviors (Coie & Dodge, 1988). Neglected boys were the least aggressive of any group observed. They tended to engage in isolated activities and had low visibility with peers. Controversial boys were intellectually, athletically, or socially talented and very active, but they were sometimes prone to anger and rule violations. The mixture of their positive and negative social behaviors thus elicited a similarly mixed reaction from their classmates. Thus children may be unpopular with their peers for a number of reasons, ranging from social withdrawal to outright aggression.

Finally, research is increasingly pointing to a link between children's ability to regulate their own emotions and the reactions they receive from peers. For example, in one study, peers reported that children they had categorized as rejected were irritable and inattentive in their behaviors. Peers saw them as complaining and getting upset when things went wrong and as being easily distracted (Pope & Bierman, 1999). In fact, rejected children do tend to express more anger, in both their facial expressions and their verbalizations, in contexts such as losing a game (Hubbard, 2001). Or they may show inappropriate happiness as they behave aggressively with their peers (Arsenio, Cooperman, & Lover, 2000). Observations of young children also show that there is a relationship between the ability to inhibit undesirable behaviors and social competence with peers. Children who are able to control their behaviors (that is, those who are attentive and follow directions) tend to express fewer negative emotions and generally have more positive interactions with their classmates (Fabes et al., 1999). This pattern of findings has been observed in varying cultures, such as Indonesia, for example (Eisenberg, Pidada, & Liew, 2001).

## ATYPICAL DEVELOPMENT
## Social Withdrawal

Some children are "loners." They have few or no friends, and they end up playing or doing their schoolwork on their own, even if surrounded by other children. Along with aggression, social withdrawal is considered by many child development experts to be one of the two most important indicators of a behavior problem (Rubin & Asendorpf, 1993). Withdrawn children are prone to express anxiety, loneliness, negative conceptions of themselves, and depression (Boivin & Hymel, 1997; Rubin, Hymel, & Mills, 1989). Moreover, lack of social contact is a feature of several clinical categories of psychopathology (Rubin & Asendorpf, 1993).

Children may have limited interactions with their peers for a number of reasons. Some children may simply prefer to play by themselves, curling up with a book or becoming involved with an interesting toy. This pattern is usually noted in the preschool and early school years, and is not necessarily an indication that the child is at risk for abnormal development. A second pattern is that of the shy child, who is nervous about being in new environments or with strangers but generally desires social interactions. This characteristic may stem from a biologically based temperament that results in the child's wariness and inhibition (Kagan, Snidman, & Arcus, 1993). If either of these patterns persists, peers may react negatively and reject the child outright (Gazelle & Ladd, 2003; Rubin, 1993). Early negative experiences like these can escalate into more severe social withdrawal, and even depression, as the childhood years progress (Gazelle & Rudolph, 2004). A third category is children who desire social interactions but, because of their inept social skills, are avoided by their peers. These children may react with aggression, which further contributes to their isolation (Rubin & Asendorpf, 1993).

Researchers are just beginning to understand some of the factors, aside from biological temperament, that may contribute to social withdrawal in children. For example, Rosemary Mills and Kenneth Rubin (1993) found that mothers of withdrawn children were highly controlling and directive when attempting to teach their children how to interact with peers. They also expressed more anger, disappointment, and guilt about their children's behaviors than mothers of aggressive and "average" children. The reactions of peers may make a difference, too. First-grade children do not seem to think about social withdrawal as a liability when asked to rate the likeability of children described in vignettes. By age ten, though, social withdrawal was viewed as an abnormal behavior

(Younger, Gentile, & Burgess, 1993). Interestingly, even in China, where adults value shyness as a personality trait, children shift from positive to negative evaluations of shy children at around age twelve (Chen, Rubin, & Li, 1995). These studies, along with the different patterns of social withdrawal described here, suggest the complex nature of this style of social functioning.

Despite these complexities, it is important that researchers continue to examine the nature of social withdrawal in childhood because of its potential lingering impact even well into adulthood. Kenneth Rubin gives one example in a letter he received from a fifty-one-year-old individual who had read about his research.

> I recall one instance in my third year of grade school and my teacher approached me after recess with the enquiry "have you no one to play with—I have noticed you standing by yourself at recess for several days now." I recalled replying and LYING—"yes I've friends." The teacher was observant and I give her credit for this, however, I wish, oh how I wish, something had been done about my isolation at the tender age of 7 or 8. It has been a long, lonely road. (Rubin & Asendorpf, 1993, p. 4)

## THE ORIGINS OF SOCIAL COMPETENCE

What factors are responsible for the skilled social behaviors of some children but not others? Researchers draw their answers from a number of perspectives, from the early attachment relationships children form with their caregivers to capabilities in processing the subtle cues that form such an integral part of social interactions.

***Attachment Relationships*** Attachment teaches children about emotional ties: how to recognize affection and how to show it. This knowledge about the central ingredients of relationships and the "internal working models" that children construct regarding relationships may assist them as they expand their social world (Hay, 1985; Sroufe, 1983). In their early relationships with caregivers, children have the opportunity to learn and practice a variety of social skills, such as turn taking, compromise, and effective communication. Once honed and refined, these abilities can later be employed with peers and other individuals in the child's life. Longitudinal studies confirm that children who have more positive relationships with peers tended to have secure attachments with their parents during infancy and toddlerhood (Booth et al., 1995; Sroufe, Egeland, & Carlson, 1999; Youngblade & Belsky, 1992). Other researchers have noted that seven- to twelve-year-olds who reported positive relationships with their mother also had positive cognitions about relationships with peers. For example, those who characterized their mother as being indifferent made similar judgments about interactions with peers (Rudolph, Hammen, & Burge, 1995).

***Parental Influences*** Parents play an influential role in the relationships their children form with peers. Broadly speaking, parents who exhibit an authoritative style—that is, are responsive, are nurturant, and provide verbal explanations—tend to have children who are popular and who display prosocial behaviors with peers. In contrast, children of authoritarian, power-assertive parents are more likely to be classified as rejected (Dekovic & Janssens, 1992; Hart et al., 1992; Pettit et al., 1996).

Parents serve as important models of social competence for their children; they may also provide explicit instruction on appropriate ways to behave in social situations. In one study, mothers of popular and unpopular preschoolers were observed as they introduced their children to a pair of peers busily playing with blocks. Mothers of unpopular children tended to disrupt the ongoing play and use their authority to incorporate their own child into the group. In contrast, mothers of popular children encouraged them to become involved in play without intervening in the activity of the host peers. Moreover, in a subsequent interview, these mothers displayed greater knowledge of how to encourage their children to make friends, resolve conflicts, and display other positive social behaviors (Finnie & Russell, 1988). Others have noted that, compared with parents of less popular children, parents of popular and socially competent children are generally less disagreeable and demanding, and express less negative affect when they play with their children (Isley et al., 1999; Putallaz, 1987). In addition, both mothers and fathers of unpopular children have been found to shift conversations to irrelevant topics, speak while someone else is talking, and ignore their children's requests. Perhaps not surprisingly, their children showed similar ineffective communication styles (Black & Logan, 1995).

Finally, parents can influence children's social competence on another level: by managing their children's social activities. Parents vary in the extent to which they create opportunities for their children to interact with peers, experiences that provide the context for the emergence of social skills. Some parents seek out play groups for their children or periodically get together with friends who have children. When parents deliberately arrange peer contacts for their children, children have a greater variety of playmates and a larger number of consistent play partners, display more prosocial behaviors at school, and have higher sociometric status (at least among boys) than when parents do not make such efforts (Ladd & Golter, 1988; Ladd & Hart, 1992).

***Social-Cognitive Development***    Children's social competence includes an array of intertwined cognitive and behavioral skills. An information-processing model of social competence formulated by Nicki Crick and Kenneth Dodge (see Figure 13.3) suggests more precisely how cognitions and behaviors are related and where problems in social functioning might occur (Crick & Dodge, 1994).

According to the model, the first step in processing social information is to focus on the correct cues. For example, suppose a boy initiates a conversation with a peer. It is more important for the child to encode the peer's facial expression ("Is that a smile or a sneer?") than to encode the color of her clothing. Second, the child must meaningfully interpret the social cues based on his past experiences. Most

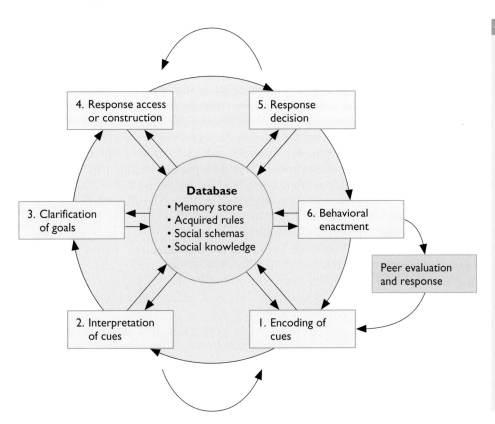

**FIGURE 13.3**

**Social Competence: An Information-Processing Model**

Crick and Dodge (1994) have proposed a six-step model of social competence based on the child's growing social information-processing skills. The process begins when the child is able to correctly encode and then interpret a social cue. Next, the child generates a set of social goals and possible responses to achieve them. Finally, the child evaluates those responses and enacts the behavior that he or she internally selected. Children low in social competence may have difficulty in any step in this model.

*Source:* Adapted from Linn et al. (1985).

children would interpret a scowl on a peer's face as a sign of hostility and a smile as a mark of friendliness. In the third step of processing, the child selects a goal for the situation, such as retaliating against an aggressor or making a friend. Fourth, the child generates one or more potential behavioral responses. If he perceives the peer as hostile, he may contemplate avoiding her or matching her hostility. If he reads her signals as friendly, he may consider smiling back or beginning to talk. Fifth, the child evaluates the potential consequences of each possible behavior. Hostility and aggression could lead to physical harm whereas avoidance might not; hence, avoidance might be preferable. Finally, the child enacts the chosen response verbally or physically, monitors the outcome of his behavior, and, if necessary, modifies it, engaging in the six-step cycle over again. This model thus includes a number of steps where things can go wrong and disrupt a smooth, mutually rewarding social interaction.

Studies of peer relations suggest that popular children are more skillful than unpopular (and, in particular, rejected) children at several steps in the model. First, they are better able to encode and decipher social information correctly. In one study, elementary school children were asked to label the emotions depicted in sets of pictures. For example, one was a series of faces depicting anger, happiness, sadness, disgust, surprise, and fear. Rejected children were less able than popular children to correctly identify the emotions represented in these stimuli (Monfries & Kafer, 1987).

Second, some rejected children tend to make incorrect attributions about the behaviors of peers. In one experiment, researchers asked children to view videotaped episodes of an actor destroying a second actor's toy with hostile, prosocial, accidental, or ambiguous intent. Both rejected and neglected children tended to attribute hostile intentions to the actor's actions, even when the acts were accidental or prosocial. Popular children were more often correct in their judgments (Dodge, Murphy, & Buchsbaum, 1984). Numerous studies have confirmed that aggressive children in particular tend to make more hostile attributions about the intentions of others than nonaggressive children (Orobio de Castro et al., 2002). The tendency to hold negative beliefs about peers is linked to two factors: prior negative experiences with parents and past low social acceptance from peers (MacKinnon-Lewis, Rabiner, & Starnes, 1999). As a result of these mistaken attributions, aggressive children often retaliate with further negative behavior. Children who exhibit this style of overattributing hostile intent are called *reactive aggressive* (Crick & Dodge, 1996).

Third, some rejected children tend to suggest inappropriate strategies to resolve social problems and have difficulty devising alternative paths to attain their social goals (Rubin & Krasnor, 1986). Researchers typically assess social problem-solving skills by presenting children with hypothetical social dilemmas and examining their proposed solutions. Researchers in one study asked kindergartners to react to a series of dilemmas in which, for example, one child takes away another's toy. Unpopular children were much more likely than popular children to recommend an aggressive solution, such as "Punch him" or "She could beat her up." A preference for aggressive solutions to problems is typical of children who are *proactive aggressive* (Crick & Dodge, 1996). In addition, when Kenneth Rubin and Linda Krasnor observed children's strategies for handling social problems in naturalistic settings, they noted that rejected children were rigid in their attempts (Rubin & Krasnor, 1986). If, for example, a rejected child failed to convince another child to give him an object, he simply repeated the same unsuccessful behavior. Popular children often tried a different approach to attaining their goal, indicating a broader and more flexible repertoire of social problem-solving skills.

Popular children thus possess social knowledge that leads to successful interactions with their peers and also behave in ways that manifest this expertise. They know what strategies are needed to make friends (ask others their names, invite them to do things) and can describe prosocial behaviors that tend to foster peer relationships (be generous, keep promises) (Wentzel & Erdley, 1993). They also recognize that the achievement of their social goals may require time and work, and adjust their behaviors according to the sometimes-subtle demands of the situation (Asher, 1983). Rejected children, on the other hand, have a more limited awareness of how to solve social problems, believing particularly in the effectiveness of aggression. Unfortunately, their antagonistic actions frequently lead to a spiral of continuing rejection. As they become disassociated from more socially skilled, popular peers, they have fewer opportunities to learn the basics of successful social interaction from them. Moreover, the child who receives consistently negative feedback from peers would probably be hard pressed to be positive, cooperative, and friendly. In this context, it is perhaps not surprising that aggression tends to remain a fairly stable trait, or may even accelerate, among rejected children during the school years (Dodge et al., 2003; Ladd & Burgess, 1999). Neglected children have their own special problems. Rubin and Krasnor (1986) believe that children in this special category do not display social cognitive deficits, but insecurities and anxieties about the consequences of their social actions. What they need is more self-confidence in their abilities to interact with and be accepted by their peers.

## RESEARCH APPLIED TO EDUCATION
### Preventing Bullying

Ms. Klein's attention was drawn to the loud shouts of a circle of boys at the back of the playground. As she approached, she saw two boys in the middle of the circle, one waving clenched fists and yelling at the other. Quickly she stepped in and broke up the fight, fortunately before anyone got hurt. She recognized the older of the two boys; he was a fourth-grader who had a reputation for being a "bully." The other child was a small, frightened-looking second-grader who was on the verge of tears. Ms. Klein knew she would have to do some talking to both of them and probably to their parents as well.

Researchers have documented many of the characteristics of children who are rejected, particularly those who are aggressive with their peers. But what about children who are the victims of aggression? About 9 percent of children are chronic targets of peer aggression, a pattern that can begin as early as kindergarten age. Being a victim is associated with poorer school adjustment, anxiety, low self-esteem, loneliness, and depression (Boulton & Underwood, 1992; Egan & Perry, 1998; Kochenderfer & Ladd, 1996; Olweus, 1993a). Given these characteristics of victims, is there anything parents and teachers can do to stop this negative cycle?

Dan Olweus has studied the problem of bullies and victims among children in grades one through nine in Norway and Sweden. He found that victims are often anxious, sensitive, and quiet children who react to bullying by crying and giving in. Often they are physically weaker than most children their age and generally have few friends. Olweus believes this pattern of passive characteristics signals to other children that they are unlikely to retaliate against aggression (Olweus, 1993a). Other researchers, including those who have studied children from varying cultures, such as China, have confirmed that chronic victims tend to be unassertive and submissive when they are with their peers (Schwartz, Chang, & Farver, 2001; Schwartz, Dodge, & Coie, 1993). A major intervention program to deal with the problems of bullying was launched in Norway over a three-year period. The program involved about 2,500 students from forty-two elementary and junior high schools, as well as their parents and teachers. Advice to the parents of chronic victims included the following:

1. *Help the child to develop self-confidence by encouraging special talents or abilities he displays.* Children who gain confidence are more likely to be assertive and refuse to tolerate the behaviors of bullies.

One way to help children who are the victims of bullies is to encourage their physical development so that they do not send cues suggesting "weakness" to potential aggressors. Building the victim's confidence by encouraging abilities and talents can also be beneficial.

2. *Encourage the child to undertake some form of physical training or to participate in sports.* By doing so, he will feel less anxiety about his body and send out signals of strength rather than weakness to potential aggressors.

3. *Help the child get to know a friendly student in the class who has similar interests or is also looking for a friend.* A relationship with another peer can help with feelings of loneliness and depression.

4. *Encourage the child's attempts to become involved with people or activities outside the family.* This suggestion is especially helpful if the family tends to attempt to protect the child every time he is attacked.

This advice was combined with several other programmatic changes involving the school, including teachers' institution of class rules against bullying, better supervision of lunch and recess, talks with the parents of bullies, and promotion of more positive classroom experiences and cooperative learning (Olweus, 1993b). The results showed a 50 percent reduction in the number of children being bullied (and in those acting as bullies as well). In addition, the incidence of other antisocial behavior, such as thefts and vandalism, was reduced, and the social climate of the classroom became more positive. A key to the program's success was the involvement of all children in the program (not just bullies and victims), greater supervision of children during the school day, and good communication between teachers and parents (Olweus, 1994, 1997). Other researchers support the idea that, to be most effective, antibullying interventions in schools should take a broad-based approach. When all of the children in a classroom are exposed to prosocial beliefs and learn skills in conflict resolution and establishing positive relationships with peers, not only does bullying decline, but so does the participation of children as bystanders who reward and perhaps even assist the bullies (Frey et al., 2005).

## FRIENDSHIP

In the middle childhood years, children are very concerned with being accepted by their peers and with avoiding the insecurity that peer rejection brings; both factors motivate friendship formation. Most friends are of the same age and sex, although

relationships with younger and older children occasionally occur as well. Cross-sex friendships are rare, however, constituting only about 5 percent of the mutual friendships reported in one study of more than 700 third- and fourth-graders (Kovacs, Parker, & Hoffman, 1996). In fact, researchers in another study found their fifth-grade participants to be openly resistant to the idea that they might have a friend of the opposite sex (Buhrmester & Furman, 1987). By the time children approach preadolescence, the time they spend with same-sex friends surpasses the time they spend with either parent.

Friendship partners may change, though, sometimes rather frequently, over the childhood years. As part of a comprehensive longitudinal study of the social development of children beginning in fourth grade, Robert and Beverly Cairns (1994) asked children to name their best friend each year through eleventh grade. Figure 13.4 shows that the friend named in fourth grade was unlikely to be named again in successive years. Friendships can shift even within a time span of a few weeks. When this same research group observed the nature of fourth- and seventh-graders' friendships, they found that children who mutually nominated each other as friends the first time they were interviewed usually did not name each other as close friends

Boys and girls differ in the patterns of their friendships and the types of activities they engage in with friends. Boys tend to have larger networks of friends, with whom they tend to participate in shared activities. Girls' networks, on the other hand, are smaller and center on affective communication and self-disclosure.

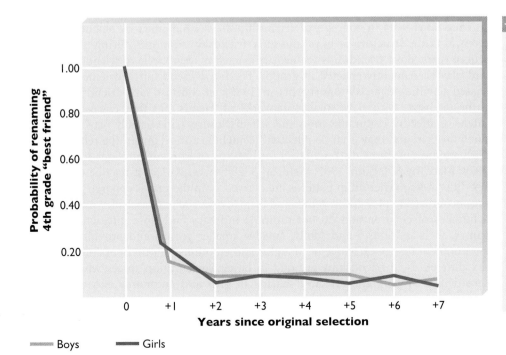

◁ **FIGURE 13.4**

**Changes in Best Friends**

In a longitudinal study of best friends, Cairns and Cairns (1994) found that children named as best friends in fourth grade were seldom renamed as best friends in successive years. Friendships may therefore be less stable than generally thought. On the other hand, other research suggests that the stability of friendships over time may depend on the specific personality characteristics of individual children.

*Source:* Cairns & Cairns (1994).

three weeks later (Cairns et al., 1995). However, the tendency for children to have new mutual friends at different points in time may depend on the characteristics of the child. In another project, children who switched friends more frequently over the four weeks of a summer camp session tended to be perceived by other children as playful, humorous, and "gossipy," but also as aggressive, unreliable, and untrustworthy; that is, they had qualities that probably both attracted and disappointed friends (Parker & Seal, 1996).

In middle childhood, friendship interactions typically include conflicts as well as cooperation (Hartup et al., 1993), and gossip becomes a predominant format for communication, as the following episode between two girls illustrates:

E: *Oh, see, um, you know that tub she gave us for the spider?*

M: *Yeah.*

E: *She acts like she owns the whole thing.*

M: *The whole spider.*

E: *I know. (Parker & Gottman, 1989, p. 114)*

Parker and Gottman (1989) believe that gossip allows children to sample the attitudes and beliefs of their agemates without taking the risk of revealing their own views. Because gossip involves the sharing of "privileged" information, it also solidifies the child's membership in the friendship circle.

During this age period, the internal psychological aspects of friendship grow in importance. When sixth-graders are asked, "How do you know that someone is your best friend?" they respond with statements such as "I can talk to her about problems" or "He'll keep a secret if you tell him." In other words, intimacy and trust, as well as loyalty, generosity, and helpfulness, become integrated into the child's understanding of friendship (Berndt, 1981). Girls in particular speak about the value they place on intimacy in friendship relations. Girls cite the importance of sharing confidences and private feelings with friends far more frequently than boys do and find that their same-sex friendships provide more support than boys' same-sex friendships do (Buhrmester & Furman, 1987; Furman & Buhrmester, 1992; Jones & Dembo, 1989). This tendency, however, may stem in part from their stereotyped knowledge that female relationships are supposed to be close (Bukowski & Kramer, 1986).

Sex differences in concepts of friendship are accompanied by heightened differences in the structure of boys' and girls' friendship networks during the middle school years. Boys' friendships are usually extensive; their circle of friends is larger, and play is frequently enacted in groups. For boys, friendship is oriented around shared activities, especially sports (Erwin, 1985). In contrast, girls' friendships tend to be intensive. Girls have smaller networks of friends, but they engage in more intensive affective communication and self-disclosure. Girls usually play with only one other girl and may even be reluctant to include a third girl in the relationship. Girls also become more distressed over the breakup of a friendship (Eder & Hallinan, 1978; Maccoby & Jacklin, 1987; Waldrop & Halverson, 1975). It may be that these sex differences in friendship patterns are derived from the games children play. Boys are encouraged to play group games and team sports, such as baseball, which involve a number of children and do not promote intimacy and close interaction. Girls' games, such as "house" and "dolls," involve smaller groups and provide an ideal environment for the exchange of thoughts and emotions. Another possibility is that sex differences in friendships are due to larger socialization forces which foster sensitivity to others and affective sharing in girls and autonomy and emotional reserve in boys (Winstead, 1986).

Some children tend to have more friends and better-quality friendships than other children. Their relationships with friends are marked by shared intimacy, caring, support, companionship, and the ability to resolve conflicts. In responding to vignettes about potential situations involving good friends (for example, watching a friend being laughed at for botching a class presentation), these children did not propose to avoid or blame the friend ("I'd stay away from my friend"; "It was his own fault") (Rose & Asher, 2004). In other vignettes in which there was a conflict with a friend (for example, the friend changes the television channel), these children refrained from using revenge as a motive for their actions (Rose & Asher, 1999). Information about the specific goals and behaviors used by children who are good friendship partners can be useful in interventions for children with fewer friends.

***Becoming Friends***    How do two previously unacquainted children form a friendship? What behaviors must occur to produce an affiliative bond between these two peers? A time-intensive investigation by John Gottman (1983) provides a fascinating glimpse into the process of friendship formation among children who initially met as strangers. Gottman's method involved tape-recording the conversations of eighteen unfamiliar dyads ages three to nine years as they played in their homes for three sessions. Even in this short time, friendships among some of the pairs began to emerge. In all cases, each member of the pair was within one year of the age of the other. Some were same-sex pairs, others opposite-sex. The behaviors of the child whose home it was (the host child) and the visiting child (the guest) were coded separately; the sequences of behaviors these children displayed—that is, how one child's behavior influenced the other's—were also analyzed.

Children who "hit it off" in the first play session showed several distinct patterns of interaction. First, they were successful in exchanging information, as in the following conversation one pair had:

A: *Hey, you know what?*

B: *No, what?*

A: *Sometime you can come to my house.*

Children who became friends made efforts to establish a common ground by finding activities they could share or by identifying similarities and differences between them.

In addition, any conflicts that occurred as they played were successfully resolved, either by one member of the dyad's explaining the reason for the disagreement or by one child's complying with the other child's demands, as long as they were not excessive or unreasonable. Alternatively, as activities escalated from simply coloring side by side ("I'm coloring mine green.") to one child's issuing a command ("Use blue. That'd be nice."), children who became friends tempered potential conflict by de-escalating the intensity of play (in this case, going back to side-by-side coloring) or using another element of play that was "safe"—namely, information exchange ("I don't have a blue crayon. Do you?"). In contrast, children who did not become friends often persisted in escalating their play until the situation was no longer amicable. Children who became friends thus modulated their interactions to preserve a positive atmosphere. Over time, other social processes also came into play; clear communication and self-disclosure (the revelation of one's feelings) were among these.

Generally speaking, children become friends with agemates who resemble themselves on a number of dimensions. Young children and their friends often share similar play styles and language skills (Dunn & Cutting, 1999; Rubin et al., 1994). Among older children, friends are similar in temperament, popularity, and the tendency to behave prosocially or aggressively (Haselager et al., 1998). By becoming friends with like-minded agemates, children select contexts in which some of their own initial tendencies—their aggression or prosocial behavior, for example—may become even more accentuated. In fact, friends become more similar to one another as their relationship continues (Newcomb, Bukowski, & Bagwell, 1999).

▶ **FIGURE 13.5**

**Friendship as a Buffer Against Loneliness**

Having even one best friend can significantly lower children's reports of loneliness. In this study, third- through sixth-graders filled out a questionnaire assessing their feelings of loneliness and social dissatisfaction partway through the school year. A high score indicated greater feelings of loneliness. Children who had a reciprocal relationship with at least one friend had significantly lower loneliness scores than children who had no such relationship.

*Source:* Renshaw & Brown (1993).

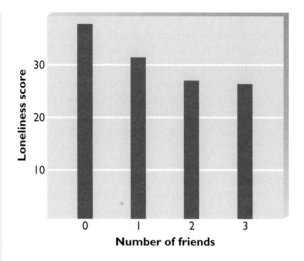

🔑 **KEY THEME**
**RISK/RESILIENCE**

**The Functions of Friendship**   By virtue of their special qualities, friendships contribute to the child's development in ways that differ from other, more transient peer interactions. Friendships involve a distinct sense of mutual reciprocity between peers and a significant affective investment from each child (Hartup & Stevens, 1999). Thus they provide a fertile ground for the child's social and emotional development.

Because friendships include the sharing of affection and emotional support, especially among older children, they may play a vital role in protecting children from anxiety and stress, particularly when there are problems in the family. For example, boys seem to adjust better to the practical and psychological consequences of divorce when they have friends (Wallerstein & Kelly, 1980). Likewise, when children come from harsh, punitive home environments, they are at risk for becoming the victims of peer aggression and for behaving aggressively and defiantly; however, this risk is diminished for children who have friends (Criss et al., 2002; Schwartz et al., 2000). Children who have close and intimate friendships have higher levels of self-esteem, experience less anxiety and depression, and are more sociable in general than those with few close friends (Buhrmester, 1990; Mannarino, 1978). Because many studies of friendship are correlational, the direction of influence is not always clear. In other words, less anxious children may be more capable of forming intimate friendships, or the reverse may be true: friendships may make them less anxious. Nonetheless, it is reasonable to hypothesize that friends provide an important source of social support for and feedback about one's competence and self-worth. In fact, as Figure 13.5 shows, having even just one "best friend" can mean less loneliness for the child (Parker & Asher, 1993; Renshaw & Brown, 1993).

F O R • Y O U R • R E V I E W

❧ What factors promote the formation of peer group identities? What factors can lessen hostilities among groups of peers?

❧ How do researchers assess children's peer status?

❧ What are some of the characteristics displayed by popular children?

❧ What are some of the influences on the development of children's social competence?

❧ What are the qualities of children's friendships during middle childhood?

❧ What factors influence the formation of children's friendships?

❧ How do friendships contribute to the child's social and emotional development?

# SCHOOL

The main aim of education is to provide children with the skills necessary to function as independent, responsible, and contributing members of society. Schools reinforce cultural practices for how to get things done (Matusov, Bell, & Rogoff, 2002). Academic accomplishment and the development of cognitive skills are the chief points of emphasis. For example, school experience cultivates rote memory, classification, and logical reasoning (Morrison, Smith, & Dow-Ehrensberger, 1995; Rogoff, 1981). One especially important goal of schooling is the development of literacy, the ability to read and write using the symbol system of the culture's language. Literacy is virtually a prerequisite for survival in most societies; more and more jobs in the professional and technical sectors require not only reading and writing skills but also the ability to communicate, reason, and apply mathematical and scientific concepts (Jackson & Hornbeck, 1989). Yet societies vary in the extent to which they stress the experience of formal schooling; rural and agrarian subcultures in some countries, for example, do not have compulsory schooling.

How well are children learning in schools? Major national surveys often conclude that academic achievement among American students is not high and compares unfavorably with that of students from other industrialized countries. The United States ranks below many countries in student performance on tests in science and mathematics, as indicated by the results of the Trends in International Mathematics and Science Study (TIMSS). This research project has included evaluations of academic performance by fourth-graders and twelfth-graders, as well as for eighth-graders whose relative level of performance is shown in Figure 13.6. Because children in many East Asian and European nations perform better than those in the United States, the findings are among those that have created concern about the adequacy of our educational system.

## STARTING SCHOOL

Few occasions in a child's life are as momentous as the first day of school. Parents typically find this a time of mixed emotions, of eager anticipation about the child's future accomplishments coupled with anxieties about whether school will provide positive and rewarding experiences for their child. Children have many major adjustments to handle, including accommodating to a teacher and a new physical environment, making new friends, and mastering new academic challenges. Success in making the initial transition to school can set the tone for later academic and socioemotional development.

School policies that prepare young children and their parents for the start of school make a difference. Providing parents with information about the kindergarten program, inviting preschoolers and their parents to visit the kindergarten classroom, or sponsoring an orientation program are all tactics associated with better academic performance and greater parental involvement by the end of the kindergarten year. These policies were especially predictive of success for children from middle- or lower-income backgrounds (Schulting, Malone, & Dodge, 2005).

In addition, children who bring to school certain entry-level skills, such as a battery of positive social behaviors (for instance, cooperativeness in their preschool play or friendliness in their interactions with peers), and who exhibit cognitive and linguistic maturity (such as ability to engage in or be ready for school-related activities as a result of preschool and family experiences) do better in kindergarten (Entwisle, 1995; Ladd, Birch, & Buhs, 1999; Ladd & Price, 1987). Gary Ladd and his colleagues (Ladd et al., 1999), testing several hundred kindergartners throughout the school year, found that positive behavioral orientations exhibited by children in the first weeks of kindergarten fostered the formation of friendships and peer acceptance, whereas antisocial behaviors resulted in children's being less liked by peers over the year and having greater conflict with teachers. Cognitive and linguistic

▶ **FIGURE 13.6**

**International Data on Mathematics and Science Achievement**

This table presents the average scores of eighth-graders for the countries included in the Trends in International Mathematics and Science Study (TIMMS). These findings typically receive considerable interest from educators and politicians, and may have policy implications for education.

*Source:* Gonzalez et al. (2004).

**MATHEMATICS**

| Nation | Average |
| --- | --- |
| Singapore | 605 |
| Korea, Republic of | 589 |
| Hong Kong SAR | 586 |
| Chinese Taipei | 585 |
| Japan | 570 |
| Belgium-Flemish | 537 |
| Netherlands | 536 |
| Estonia | 531 |
| Hungary | 529 |
| Malaysia | 508 |
| Latvia | 508 |
| Russian Federation | 508 |
| Slovak Republic | 508 |
| Australia | 505 |
| **United States** | **504** |
| Lithuania | 502 |
| Sweden | 499 |
| Scotland | 498 |
| Israel | 496 |
| New Zealand | 494 |
| Slovenia | 493 |
| Italy | 484 |
| Armenia | 478 |
| Serbia | 477 |
| Bulgaria | 476 |
| Romania | 475 |
| Norway | 461 |
| Moldovia, Republic of | 460 |
| Cyprus | 459 |
| Macedonia, Republic of | 435 |
| Lebanon | 433 |
| Jordan | 424 |
| Iran, Islamic Republic of | 411 |
| Indonesia | 411 |
| Tunisia | 410 |
| Egypt | 406 |
| Bahrain | 401 |
| Palestinian National Authority | 390 |
| Chile | 387 |
| Morocco | 387 |
| Philippines | 378 |
| Botswana | 366 |
| Saudi Arabia | 332 |
| Ghana | 276 |
| South Africa | 264 |
| Average international score | 466 |

**SCIENCE**

| Nation | Average |
| --- | --- |
| Singapore | 578 |
| Chinese Taipei | 571 |
| Korea, Republic of | 558 |
| Hong Kong | 556 |
| Estonia | 552 |
| Japan | 552 |
| Hungary | 543 |
| Netherlands | 536 |
| **United States** | **527** |
| Australia | 527 |
| Sweden | 524 |
| Slovenia | 520 |
| New Zealand | 520 |
| Lithuania | 519 |
| Slovak Republic | 517 |
| Belgium-Flemish | 516 |
| Russian Federation | 514 |
| Latvia | 512 |
| Scotland | 512 |
| Malaysia | 510 |
| Norway | 494 |
| Italy | 491 |
| Israel | 488 |
| Bulgaria | 479 |
| Jordan | 475 |
| Moldova, Republic of | 472 |
| Romania | 470 |
| Serbia | 468 |
| Armenia | 461 |
| Iran, Islamic Republic of | 453 |
| Macedonia, Republic of | 449 |
| Cyprus | 441 |
| Bahrain | 438 |
| Palestinian National Authority | 435 |
| Egypt | 421 |
| Indonesia | 420 |
| Chile | 413 |
| Tunisia | 404 |
| Saudi Arabia | 398 |
| Morocco | 396 |
| Lebanon | 393 |
| Philippines | 377 |
| Botswana | 365 |
| Ghana | 255 |
| South Africa | 244 |
| Average international score | 473 |

▨ Average is higher than the U.S. average
▨ Average is not measurably different from the U.S. average
▨ Average is lower than the U.S. average

maturity directly facilitated classroom participation and higher achievement. In addition, classroom participation, which ultimately plays an important part in contributing to achievement in kindergarten, was influenced by the relationships children established with their peers and their teachers. The negative qualities displayed by some children (lack of friends, peer rejection, poor teacher-child relationship) seemed to be increasingly detrimental for adjustment to this new environment (Ladd et al., 1999). These findings confirm that many factors working within the school, as well as the qualities that children bring to the school environment, affect their early academic success.

The presence of familiar peers in the kindergarten classroom also facilitates peer acceptance (Ladd & Price, 1987) and is related to more positive attitudes toward school and fewer anxieties at the start of the school year. In general, factors promoting continuity between the preschool and kindergarten experiences seem beneficial to the child's adjustment, suggesting that parents should consider ways to foster their children's friendships with peers who will be future classmates. These results underscore the fact that the transition to school can be a particularly crucial time and that successes in one domain, peer relations, are related to successes in another, competence in school.

One major controversy that surrounds this first school transition is the age of the child upon school entry. Most children begin kindergarten at age five or six. Some researchers claim that younger members of the classroom do not perform as well academically as older members and continue to have difficulty in the later school years (Breznitz & Teltsch, 1989; May, Kundert, & Brent, 1995). Others, however, have pointed out methodological and other problems in this research and have failed to find evidence that younger and older children in the classroom differ in any meaningful way (Alexander & Entwisle, 1988; Shepard & Smith, 1986). Frederick Morrison and his colleagues have carried out further work on this issue with Canadian schoolchildren (Morrison, Griffith, & Alberts, 1997). They found that younger children do tend to score below older children on reading and mathematics achievement tests at the end of the school year. However, the same is true even at the beginning of the school year. In fact, when measures of progress in reading and mathematics were used as the criteria, younger first-graders gained just as much as older first-graders did. Furthermore, the first-graders, whether younger or older, gained more than children who remained in kindergarten but could have been enrolled in first grade. Although additional research needs to be carried out, these findings suggest that entrance age by itself may not be an important factor in academic progress and that children should not be delayed in entering school on that basis alone.

## SCHOOL ACHIEVEMENT

Schools can vary substantially in their organization and structure. Although the one-room classroom is rarely found today, schools and classes can be large or small depending on the community, and both are likely to increase in size in the upper grades. Of course, the people involved in the child's schooling probably play the biggest role. Parents, peers, and teachers all contribute to the mix of how children experience school. What are some of the effects of these factors on children's achievement?

***Parents, Peers, and School Achievement*** Several factors aside from aspects of the school curriculum itself are associated with academic success. Not surprisingly, parents are of paramount importance. Consider, for example, a model proposed by Wendy Grolnick and her colleagues (Grolnick, Ryan, & Deci, 1991) and illustrated in Figure 13.7. According to these researchers, parental support for their children's autonomy (such as encouraging independent decision making) and involvement with their children (such as spending time talking with them about the children's problems) are related to the strength of children's "inner resources." In other words, children develop

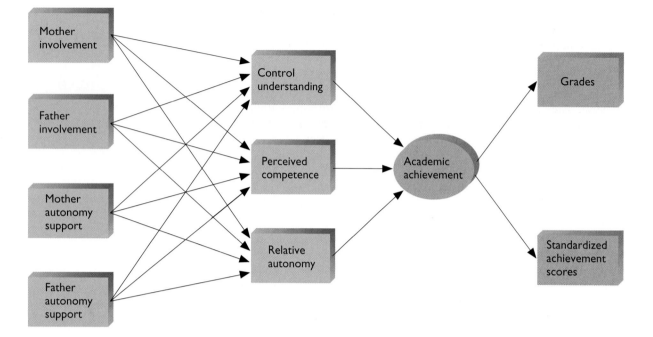

**FIGURE 13.7**

**A Model of Parental Influence on Children's Academic Achievement**

One model of children's academic achievement suggests that parental involvement and support of children's autonomy predict children's "inner resources." These resources include children's feelings of control, competence, and autonomy. These characteristics in turn predict academic achievement. Research has found support for major elements of this model.

*Source:* Grolnick, Ryan, & Deci (1991).

feelings of competence, autonomy, and control, which in turn influence academic performance. To test these ideas, the researchers measured both parental and child qualities that were components of the model, as well as children's academic success. Using sophisticated statistical techniques, they were able to show the relationships they had predicted. Other researchers add that authoritative parenting (characterized by warmth and extensive verbal explanation) and the social support that parents provide predict, at least indirectly, exactly how well children will do in school during middle childhood (DeBaryshe, Patterson, & Capaldi, 1993; Dubow et al., 1991; Steinberg et al., 1992). Frequent transitions in parenting (such as divorce and remarriage followed by another divorce) and a more discordant family climate, on the other hand, are related to less positive outcomes in school (Kurdek, Fine, & Sinclair, 1995).

An especially important way that parents can bolster their children's school-related motivations is to be involved in schooling. When parents attend open houses, parent-teacher conferences, and other school functions, and keep track of how their children are doing in school, children show higher academic motivation and, ultimately, better performance in school (Grolnick & Slowiaczek, 1994). By being involved, parents learn about how to handle the challenges their children face in school, and children receive an important message—that parents and teachers agree on objectives and standards for behavior (Hill & Taylor, 2004).

Peers make a difference, too. As early as fourth grade, children tend to sort themselves into groups that have different levels of school motivation, and children who are members of a particular group at the start of the school year become even more aligned with the group's motivation level by the end of this period (Kindermann, 1993). For example, when a student at the beginning of the school year has friends who consider themselves disruptive in school, that student will begin to demonstrate more disruptive behavior as the school year progresses (Berndt & Keefe, 1995).

*Class Size*   Many countries around the world, as well as numerous states within the United States, have invested huge amounts of money to reduce class size (Ehrenberg et al., 2001b). For example, the number of students per teacher in elementary school classrooms in the United States has fallen from 25.1 to 18.3 over the past three decades; a similar decrease, from 19.7 to 14.0, has occurred in secondary schools (Ehrenberg et al., 2001b). Although research has not always revealed a consistent benefit from such efforts, the general consensus is that children in small classes, especially in the earlier grades, show academic advances over children in large classes (Ehrenberg et al., 2001a). Perhaps the most influential of these studies was carried out in Tennessee and involved seventy-six schools. Kindergarten children and teachers were randomly assigned to classes of different sizes (thirteen to seventeen versus twenty-two to twenty-five pupils per class). By the end of first grade, children in the small classes showed marked improvement performance on standardized tests of reading and mathematics compared with children from regular-size classes. The benefits of small classes were especially pronounced for minority children (Finn & Achilles, 1990).

The long-term consequences of smaller class size have also been investigated. Children in small classes in kindergarten through third grade in the Tennessee study continued to do better than their classmates assigned to larger classes, even after entering regular-size classrooms beginning in fourth grade (Mosteller, 1995). The benefits of the smaller-class experience were exhibited by children in later grades as well. Moreover, when small class sizes were introduced to the poorest districts in the state, children in these districts moved from displaying reading and mathematics scores that were well below average to scores above average for the state.

Why do smaller classes work? For one thing, teachers probably have greater enthusiasm and higher morale when they are not burdened with large numbers of students. Teachers also have more time to spend with individual children, and students are more likely to be attentive and engaged in classroom activities, and show fewer behavioral problems in small classes (Finn & Achilles, 1990; Mosteller, 1995). But it is likely that benefits of reduced class size emerge only when teachers are trained to take advantage of the opportunities of working with smaller numbers of students (Bennett, 1998; Ehrenberg et al., 2001a, 2001b).

*Teacher Expectations*   No single factor in the school experience plays a more critical role in student achievement and self-esteem than teachers. One way that they have an influence is through the expectations they have of their students. A highly publicized study by Robert Rosenthal and Lenore Jacobson (1968) documented just how readily teachers' expectations of students' performance can affect students' actual attainments. The researchers told teachers that certain elementary school children could be expected to show sudden gains in intellectual skills during the course of the school year based on their scores on an IQ test administered at the beginning of the term. In reality, the students they designated as "rapid bloomers" were chosen randomly. An IQ test administered at the end of the school year revealed that the targeted children indeed showed significantly greater improvement than other students in the class, an outcome called the *Pygmalion effect*. The investigators explained the findings by suggesting that teachers somehow treated the targeted children differently based on their beliefs about the children's intellectual potential, thereby creating a self-fulfilling prophecy.

Differing expectations, especially when they are clearly evident to students, have consequences for achievement. Margaret Kuklinski and Rhona Weinstein (2001) looked at children in grades one through five to determine whether teacher expectations affected performance on reading achievement. As Figure 13.8 suggests, the researchers anticipated that teacher expectations about reading ability would influence not only achievement in reading at the end of the school year but also the children's own self-perceptions of their reading ability. These self-perceptions would, in turn, also influence their reading achievement. The results of the study generally supported these hypotheses, especially in classrooms in which teacher expectations

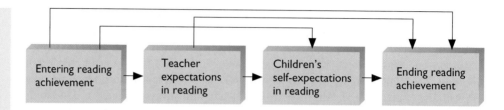

▶ **FIGURE 13.8**

**Teacher Expectancy Effects on Children's Reading Achievement**

Teacher expectancies not only may have a direct effect on reading achievement but also can influence behavior by modifying children's own expectations for themselves, as this model suggests. Margaret Kuklinsky and Rhona Weinstein (2001) obtained support for this model, especially in classrooms in which teacher expectancies could be recognized easily by children. The impact of the children's own self-perceptions pertaining to reading, as influenced by teacher expectations, was especially evident when children were in the fifth grade but far less evident in earlier grades.

*Source:* Kuklinsky & Weinstein (2001), p. 1557.

were more readily apparent to children, although children's self-perceptions tended not to become a factor until they reached the fifth grade.

Other studies have confirmed that high achievers *are* treated differently in the classroom by many teachers; they are given more opportunities to participate, given more time to answer questions, receive more praise for being correct, and receive less criticism than lower achievers (Minuchin & Shapiro, 1983). In other words, the classroom climate is most supportive for those who have already demonstrated success, whereas those who most need the teacher's attention and encouragement may actually get it least.

***Classroom Management Strategies***   Students achieve most in school when their teachers maximize the time spent in actual learning. This statement may seem obvious, but not all school time is spent in direct instruction. Effective teachers plan their lessons well, monitor the entire classroom continuously, minimize the time spent in disciplining children who misbehave, and keep transitions between activities brief and smooth (Brophy, 1986). They make sure there is little "dead time" in the classroom when students are unoccupied, and they keep the focus on instruction.

Another key ingredient in a teacher's success is active involvement in the learning process. This means that teachers remain personally involved in every phase of instruction, from the initial presentation of a new lesson to supervising the individual work of students. Involvement also refers to the teacher's enjoyment and knowledge of students. Even when students are working in groups, teachers who guide the discussion or progress of the group will foster higher levels of mastery and greater feelings of competence than those who leave students completely on their own (Brophy, 1986; Skinner & Belmont, 1993). Effective teachers also provide students with clear feedback on the quality of their performance and on what is expected of them (Rutter, 1983).

One of the most important factors in a child's school experience is teacher encouragement. This boy is receiving the kind of assistance with writing that will promote learning. Effective teachers are involved in all phases of instruction, provide clear feedback, and create a positive emotional climate in the classroom.

Creating peer-centered learning experiences can be an effective means of involving students in the educational enterprise of the school. In studies of **cooperative learning**, students work in groups rather than individually to solve academic problems. These groups may consist of, for example, four or five students, some boys and some girls, with a range of abilities and from diverse backgrounds. The teacher is usually instrumental in introducing a topic or set of materials, but then the team members work and study together on the problems, quizzing one another until they decide collectively that they understand the unit. Cooperative learning has been found to increase affiliations among students from diverse backgrounds (for instance, cross-racial friendships), improve self-esteem, and produce more favorable attitudes toward academic achievement (Slavin, 1990).

As an illustration of the effectiveness of cooperative learning, Hanna Shachar and Shlomo Sharan (1994) compared the communication and achievement skills of 197 eighth-graders assigned to cooperative learning classrooms in history and geography with those of 154 students in classrooms taught by traditional teacher-led methods. The study, carried out in Israel, included Jewish students from Western and Middle Eastern backgrounds. The classes were taught for six months. The cooperative learning groups were reconstituted several times throughout the year to give students the opportunity to work with a number of different peers. At the end of the year, a videotaped discussion of a topic in history and geography involving six-person groups revealed that those who participated in cooperative learning expressed themselves more frequently, were more likely to take a personal position and expand on the ideas brought up by another student, and were less likely to interrupt their peers than students who participated in traditional classrooms. The gains in communication skills were especially great for Middle Eastern students; those with this background who came from the traditional classroom were far less likely to express themselves than their peers from Western backgrounds. Gains in scores on achievement tests in history were also much higher among students who participated in the cooperative groups than among students in the traditional classroom.

Another form of peer-centered education is called **collaborative learning**. Here students work jointly on the same problems, often without competing with other groups but with the goal of arriving at solutions jointly, solutions that would be unlikely to arise from students working by themselves (Littleton & Häkkinen, 1999). For example, in one study, fourth-graders worked in pairs on mathematics and spatial reasoning problems, some that required rote learning and copying and some that required formal reasoning (Phelps & Damon, 1989). After six sessions of collaboration, children showed significant gains in performance on math and spatial problems compared with a control group of children who did not participate in collaborative efforts. This effect occurred for tasks that required formal reasoning but not for those that required rote learning or copying. Another interesting outcome was that the superiority of boys over girls on spatial problems at the start of the study significantly diminished. In fact, other research indicates that cooperative and collaborative learning may be especially beneficial in certain areas for students, such as, for example, girls learning math or science. These gains could come about because girls now have a chance to take on leadership roles or because cooperative or collaborative learning more closely fits their preferred style of learning and helps to maintain interest in these subjects (Eccles & Roeser, 1999; Peterson, Johnson, & Johnson, 1991).

**The Classroom Climate**   When students participate in cooperative and collaborative learning efforts, they may get the idea that the teacher and the school are promoting *autonomy,* or increased student initiative within the classroom, a perception that appears to be beneficial to student progress (Boggiano et al., 1992; Valeski & Stipek, 2001). Children who view their teachers as giving them greater responsibility within the classroom have higher self-esteem scores than those who perceive teachers as controlling and directive (Ryan & Grolnick, 1986). Moreover, teachers who

**cooperative learning**  Peer-centered learning experience in which students work together in small groups to promote the learning of each group member.

**collaborative learning**  Peer-centered learning in which students work together on academic problems with the goal of arriving at solutions that are more effective than solutions that could have been derived from individual effort alone.

display the kinds of qualities associated with good parenting—that is, who have high expectations for their students and who show caring, supportive, and nurturant qualities in contrast to an emphasis on negative feedback in their educational approach—are more effective in promoting student adjustment to the classroom and high academic performance (Linney & Seidman, 1989; Rutter, 1983; Wentzel, 2002).

Children as early as first grade are able to recognize the strength of their interpersonal relationship with a teacher. When they perceive that teachers care about them, children have more favorable attitudes toward school (Valeski & Stipek, 2001). Moreover, teacher-child relationships that begin early in the schooling process have long-term outcomes. Bridget Hamre and Robert Pianta (2001) asked kindergarten teachers in a small community to assess their personal relationships with each of their students. Nearly 200 of these students were followed through eighth grade. Those reported to have had a negative relationship with the teacher as kindergartners (for example, conflict and overdependency) continued to have difficulties with school over the next eight years. However, if children who displayed behavior problems in kindergarten were able to develop positive relationships with their kindergarten teachers, it helped to counter behavioral difficulties in the later school years, a finding that has considerable implications for the importance of a young student's relationship with his or her teacher and academic success.

## CULTURAL DIFFERENCES IN SCHOOL ACHIEVEMENT

⚷ **KEY THEME**

**SOCIOCULTURAL INFLUENCE**

The school experience is not the same for children of different racial and ethnic backgrounds. Children who attend school bring with them attitudes about school that are first nurtured within their families, as well as cultural beliefs that may be in synchrony or in conflict with the predominant belief system of the school (Gibson & Ogbu, 1991). For example, are schools a vehicle for economic and personal advancement? Cultural and ethnic groups may vary in their responses to this question. Is verbal, rational expression (which schools emphasize) the optimal means of human communication, as opposed to emotional or spiritual sharing? Again, cultures differ in the extent to which they value these skills. One of the major challenges facing educators is how to ensure the academic success of children who come from a range of cultural and ethnic backgrounds.

***School Achievement Among African American Children***    A persistent finding in past research on school achievement in the United States is that children from some minority groups—for example, African American children—score significantly lower than Caucasian children on many measures of academic performance. In the 1960s, the prevailing explanation for the school difficulties of minority children centered on the *cultural deficit hypothesis,* the notion that some deficiency in the backgrounds of minority children hindered their preparation for the academic demands of school. However, Herbert Ginsberg (1972) pointed out that, rather than being culturally deficient, minority children are *culturally different;* that is, the behaviors that minority children display help them to adapt to their specific life circumstances. For example, rather than having poor language skills, African American children display rich images and poetic forms when speaking to one another in Black English. According to the **cultural compatibility hypothesis,** school instruction produces greater improvements in learning if it is consistent with the practices of the child's own culture (Tharp, 1989).

In a study of children in the first two years of school, Karl Alexander and Doris Entwisle (1988) found that African American and Caucasian first-graders did not differ significantly on a standardized test of verbal and quantitative achievement when they were assessed at the beginning of the school year. But by the end of the year and during the second year, the scores of African American and Caucasian students began to diverge noticeably. In keeping with the cultural compatibility hypothesis, some have argued that, for many African American students, a conflict

**cultural compatibility hypothesis**   Theory that school instruction is most effective if it is consistent with the practices of the child's background culture.

exists between their background culture and the social and cognitive structure of traditional schools. For example, the spiritualism, expressiveness, and rich oral tradition characteristic of the African American heritage frequently clash with the materialism, emotional control, and emphasis on printed materials characteristic of European Americans and their schools (Boykin, 1986; Heath, 1989; Slaughter-Defoe et al., 1990). Some African American children may also perceive that academic success does not necessarily lead to occupational or economic success and therefore do not take academic performance seriously (Ogbu, 1974). Furthermore, many African American children believe they will do well in school even though past performance indicates they are likely to do otherwise. These children may need not only to overcome the hurdles imposed by racism and economic hardship but also to more fully understand what behaviors will be necessary to achieve their expectations, that is, to become motivated to master the academic materials and skills necessary to achieve their goals (Alexander, Entwisle, & Bedinger, 1994; Steinberg, 1996).

In focusing on cultural differences, however, researchers need to recognize that they may be unwittingly contributing to stereotypes. After all, many children in all cultural and ethnic groups in the United States are doing well in school. In fact, children of immigrant families in the United States, who are often poor and members of minority groups, generally do better in mathematics and English courses in high school than children of native families (Fuligni, 1997). What factors contribute to their success? Tom Luster and Harriette McAdoo (1994, 1996) have provided some answers for African American children, and the answers should not be too surprising. African American children who are high achieving, just like other children who are high achieving, experience relatively supportive home environments in which mothers display self-esteem and are members of smaller families whose incomes are above the poverty line. Luster and McAdoo (1996) followed African American children from preschool age until young adulthood. All the children lived in families with low socioeconomic status during the preschool period. Consistent with our earlier discussion emphasizing the importance of parents in promoting school success, the cognitive competence and academic motivation that these children brought to the public school setting, as well as their degree of social adjustment, predicted performance on achievement tests during the elementary school years. Children of mothers who were more involved with their children's schooling also tended to do better in the lower grades, although this relationship did not hold up during adolescence. However, parents' expectations for success in the classroom were correlated with achievement throughout the school years. These findings further confirm the important role families play in the education of African American children, just as in the education of all children (Fuligni, 1997; Steinberg, 1996).

***Achievement Among Asian Children***   Beginning in the mid-1980s, Harold Stevenson and his associates have conducted comparative research on the academic abilities of Taiwanese Chinese, Japanese, and American students. This research has been guided by an effort to understand why Asian students seem to do particularly well in the areas of mathematics and science. First- and fifth-grade students from middle- to upper-class backgrounds in all three countries were tested on a battery of specially designed cognitive tasks that assessed, among other things, spatial relations, perceptual speed, auditory and verbal memory, and vocabulary, along with reading and mathematics achievement (Stevenson, Lee, & Stigler, 1986).

Most noteworthy about the findings was that American children scored far lower in mathematics than the other two groups (see Figure 13.9). The distinctive patterns of achievement could not be explained by superior cognitive skills in any one group. The researchers found no predictive relationships between scores on the various cognitive assessments and scores on achievement tests. In fact, the children's cognitive profiles were quite similar across cultural groups by the time

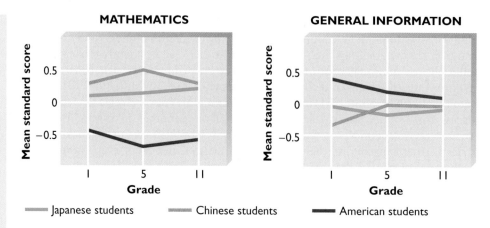

▶ **FIGURE 13.9**

**Mathematics Achievement and General Information Scores as a Function of Sociocultural Context**

Chinese and Japanese students score higher than American students on tests of mathematics achievement beginning in first grade, and their superiority in this area continues throughout high school. However, on tests of general information, children from all three cultures perform at similar levels, especially in the higher grades. The better performance on mathematics tests by East Asian children may reflect both school- and family-related cultural influences.

*Source:* Stevenson, Chen, & Lee (1993).

they reached fifth grade (Stevenson et al., 1985). When again tested in eleventh grade, American children continued to lag well behind the Chinese and Japanese in mathematics achievement, although, as Figure 13.9 shows, on age-appropriate tests of general information ("What are two things a plant needs in order to grow?" or "Why has it been possible to make smaller computers in recent years?"), the Asian children were not superior to the American children (Stevenson, Chen, & Lee, 1993).

What accounts for this pattern of findings? Stevenson's research group reported significant differences in children's school routines and parents' attitudes and beliefs among the Taiwanese Chinese, Japanese, and American groups, as well as differences between Asian American and Caucasian American families. For example, during the year, Taiwanese Chinese and Japanese children attended school about fifty more days than American children (Fuligni & Stevenson, 1995). The percentage of classroom time actually spent in academic activities also differed. For fifth-grade students, the figures were 64.5 percent of the time for American children, 91.5 percent for Taiwanese Chinese children, and 87.4 percent for Japanese children. Furthermore, American children studied language arts more than twice as long as they did mathematics, whereas the Asian children spent equal amounts of time on each subject. Thus the American children received far less instruction in mathematics than did their Taiwanese Chinese and Japanese counterparts (Stevenson, Lee, & Stigler, 1986). Moreover, the Asian teachers were far more likely to use their time in mathematics classes directly teaching the entire class, whereas American children spent more than half their time in mathematics classes working alone (Stigler, Lee, & Stevenson, 1987).

Stevenson's research group also examined attitudes and behaviors related to homework. American children devoted substantially less time to doing homework—an average of 46 minutes per day among fifth-graders, according to mothers' estimates—compared with 114 and 57 minutes for Taiwanese Chinese and Japanese children, respectively. American mothers were not dissatisfied with the small amount of homework their children received, nor were Taiwanese Chinese and Japanese mothers dissatisfied with the large amounts their children were assigned (Stevenson, Lee, & Stigler, 1986). In addition, compared with Americans, students, their peers, and their parents in the two Asian cultures seemed to expect higher standards and voiced greater concern about education, with Asian Americans surpassing their Caucasian American counterparts on these measures (Chen & Stevenson, 1995). Finally, Asian students (including Asian Americans) were more likely than American students to believe that their own effort was the best route to accomplishment (Chen & Stevenson, 1995). Indeed, effort is a central component of the socialization process in many Asian cultures; that is, the procedures by which one achieves a goal are considered extremely important (Bempechat & Drago-Severson, 1999).

These data confirm that a number of factors other than pure cognitive ability determine the child's level of achievement in school. As we have seen throughout this section, the events that transpire in the classroom, parental attitudes, and larger cultural influences are all related to patterns of academic success or failure. If we are concerned about the educational attainments of students and their overall psychological development, research on the influence of schools reveals that there are many ways to more fully engage children of all ability levels and diverse sociocultural backgrounds (Steinberg, 1996).

## GENDER ISSUES IN SCHOOL

Teachers, like peers and parents, treat children differentially according to sex, reinforce and punish sex-typed behaviors, and model sex-typical behavior for their students. Moreover, schools may foster sex typing through the teaching materials and curriculum to which children are exposed. For example, one survey of children's readers found that, although boys and girls were portrayed with almost equal frequency, girls were more often the characters in stories in need of rescue, and boys were rarely shown doing housework or displaying emotions (Purcell & Stewart, 1990).

*Teacher Attitudes and Behaviors*    Teachers, like other adults, may express stereotypical, gender-based views about the capacities of their students. They believe that female students are feminine and male students are masculine, although more experienced teachers are less likely to hold stereotyped beliefs and more likely to treat in an egalitarian fashion than are less experienced teachers (Fagot, 1978; Huston, 1983). When teachers are asked to nominate their best students or those with the most potential, they are more likely to nominate boys than girls. They are especially likely to name boys as most skilled in mathematics. When asked to think of students who excel in language or social skills, teachers are more likely to name girls (BenTsvi-Mayer, Hertz-Lazarowitz, & Safir, 1989). These patterns in teacher responses occur despite the fact that actual sex differences in many of these domains are minimal.

In addition, teachers respond differently to students on the basis of sex as opposed to behavior. Boys, for example, receive more disapproval from teachers than girls, even when boys and girls engage in similar amounts of disruptive behavior (Huston, 1983; Serbin et al., 1973). Teachers' responses may reflect a belief that boys are more likely than girls to cause trouble in the classroom unless rules are strictly enforced (Huston, 1983). On the other hand, teachers pay more attention to a girl when she sits quietly in the front of the classroom, whereas the amount of attention paid to a boy is high regardless of where he sits (Serbin et al., 1973). Within elementary school classrooms, teachers tend to call on boys more often than girls and give them more explicit feedback regarding their answers. When girls answer, they are more likely to receive a simple acceptance from the teacher ("Okay"), whereas boys tend to receive more praise, constructive criticism, or encouragement to discover the correct answer (Sadker & Sadker, 1994). Thus boys receive more explicit academic instruction and tend to dominate classroom interactions.

Teachers can influence the degree to which children pay attention to stereotypes when they highlight gender as a relevant social grouping. In one study, teachers in one set of classrooms were told to behave in ways that emphasized gender groups. For example, they used separate bulletin boards to display girls' and boys' artwork, and made frequent comments like "All the boys should be sitting down" or "Amber, you can come up for the girls." Teachers in this group made an average of 7.2 references to gender per twenty-minute time period. Compared with a control group in which teachers were instructed to refer to children as individuals rather than according to gender, children in the "gendered" classrooms showed significant increases in stereotyping over the course of four weeks (Bigler, 1995).

### RESEARCH APPLIED TO EDUCATION

## Promoting Gender Equity in the Classroom

Nicky is sitting in a circle with the other third-graders in his class, listening to Brittany read the story she wrote during Writing Workshop. The children seem captivated by her story; even the most restless among them sits quietly, eyes glued on the storyteller. When Brittany is done, Ms. Klein says, "Okay, does anyone have any questions or comments about Brittany's story? Go ahead, Brittany. You can call on someone." Hands fly up eagerly.

"Stephen," says Brittany.

"Why did you make the character live by a pond?" asks Stephen.

"Because he has a lot of animal friends that live there," she responds.

More hands churn in the air. "Nicky," she calls out next. "Wait a minute," says Ms. Klein. "Remember our rule. You have to call on a girl next."

"Reesha," Brittany calls out.

"I like how the words you picked make me think of beautiful pictures in my head," comments Reesha.

"Thank you," responds Brittany, a little shyly.

Nicky's mother, observing all of this, thinks that maybe her son feels slighted for being passed over. Later, when she asks him about this, he firmly proclaims, "All Ms. Klein is trying to do is to be fair to the boys and girls in the class. I didn't feel bad at all. I think it's the right thing to do."

Just as teacher behavior can perpetuate stereotypes, it can also change sex-typing patterns among children in classroom settings. A collection of studies suggests some specific techniques that teachers can use to reduce sex segregation, modify children's attitudes about gender, and promote girls' participation in the classroom.

1. *Use reinforcement to facilitate cooperative cross-sex play.* In one study involving preschoolers and kindergartners, teachers praised children who played in mixed-sex groups by pointing out their cooperative play to the class and complimenting the children. Cross-sex play subsequently increased (Serbin, Connor, & Iler, 1979; Serbin, Tonick, & Sternglanz, 1977).

2. *Prepare lessons that explicitly allow children to question gender stereotypes about personal qualities, occupations, and activities.* Researchers in Dublin, Ireland, had student teachers present a series of lessons to children in the first through sixth grades. The lessons encouraged children to think of counterexamples to common stereotypes—for example, instances in which women show an interest in football or in which men have been observed to be warm and gentle. Discussions were supplemented by opportunities to meet people who worked in nontraditional roles, such as a male nurse and a female veterinary surgeon. In addition, children read poetry and fairy tales, as well as worksheets, that brought up themes counter to traditional stereotypes. At the end of four months, children who had experienced the lessons had significantly lower stereotype scores than those in a control group (Gash & Morgan, 1993).

3. *Be conscious of the need to give girls a chance to participate.* One way to do this is to wait three to five seconds before calling on a student to answer a question. Girls, especially those who are shy or less confident, may need time to formulate their answers and decide that they are willing to share them with the class. Also, don't call only on students who volunteer, because these are more likely to be boys. Teachers can even have an observer record the number of times they call on boys versus girls. Myra and David Sadker (1994) found that, when teachers saw the results of such observations, and,

further, when they received training on how to be more gender equitable, girls in their elementary and secondary school classrooms became more equal partners with boys in class participation.

***Student Attitudes Toward Coursework*** For several decades, research has indicated that students, teachers, and parents alike view some academic subjects as masculine and others as feminine (Huston, 1983). As we noted earlier, mathematics has generally been seen as a masculine activity and reading as feminine (Eccles, 1983; Eccles, Wigfield, et al., 1993; Huston, 1983; Yee & Eccles, 1988). Such sex typing has not been limited to American schoolchildren. In a study of first- through fifth-grade Chinese, Japanese, and American boys and girls, the investigators found that most children believed boys are better in mathematics and girls are better at reading (Lummis & Stevenson, 1990). Moreover, boys in these three societies predicted that they would do better in mathematics in high school than girls predicted they would do, although no sex differences were found in children's predictions of their future reading skills.

Society's messages about girls' mathematical abilities may be changing, however. In a recent study including data from children in first through twelfth grades, researchers asked children to report how competent they felt in math. Although in the early grades boys clearly felt more capable in math than girls, the gender gap in beliefs declined with age, such that by twelfth grade there was virtually no difference between boys and girls. The researchers suggest that one reason for this shift may be a general societal push for girls to participate in math courses and activities (Fredricks & Eccles, 2002).

***Sex Differences in Academic Self-Evaluations*** Girls generally show greater self-criticism of their academic work than boys do. Karin Frey and Diane Ruble (1987) have studied instances of self- and peer criticism for academic work in classroom settings. Children between ages five and ten years were observed at work in academic tasks in their classrooms, and their spontaneous critical and complimentary comments about themselves and their peers were tallied. Several sex differences emerged in the nature of comments children made. Overall, both girls and boys made more self-compliments than self-criticisms, but boys made a greater number of self-congratulatory statements relative to self-criticisms than girls did. Boys complimented themselves and criticized their peers more than girls did, whereas girls criticized themselves and complimented their peers more than boys did. Girls also were more likely to attribute their failures to a lack of ability ("I'm so stupid") than boys were. If girls tend to take greater responsibility for their own failures than boys do, it is possible that there may be emotional consequences for them—for example, greater anxiety and depression.

The link between emotions and academic self-evaluations was demonstrated in a longitudinal study in which third- and sixth-graders were asked to evaluate their scholastic competence each year for a period of three years. Teachers also evaluated children's academic abilities. Boys and girls were similar in their estimates of their academic ability in grade three, but in successive years, their profiles diverged. As Figure 13.10 illustrates, starting at about fourth grade and continuing through eighth grade, boys tended to overestimate their academic abilities, and girls tended underestimate theirs. In addition, symptoms of anxiety and depression were correlated with the tendency to overestimate one's abilities (Cole et al., 1999). Thus gender differences in self-evaluations can have important connections to children's emotional well-being.

The preceding findings should be a concern in light of the findings of a cross-cultural study that found that, in settings as diverse as Japan, Germany, and Russia, girls who outperformed boys on academic measures did not see themselves as more talented than boys (Stetsenko et al., 2000). Just why talented girls tend to underplay their abilities and the repercussions of this tendency are key questions for developmental researchers.

**KEY THEME**

SOCIOCULTURAL INFLUENCE

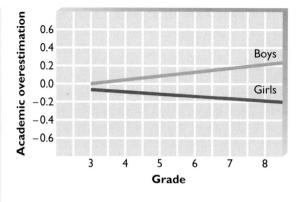

▶ **FIGURE 13.10**
### Gender Differences in Academic Self-Evaluations

In a study by Cole et al. (1999), third- and sixth-graders were asked to evaluate their scholastic competence each year for a period of three years. Teachers also evaluated children's academic abilities. The graph shows that there are sex differences in children's tendency to overestimate their academic abilities, starting at about fourth grade and continuing through eighth grade. (The y-axis shows a statistical estimate of the tendency to overestimate, such that a higher positive number indicates greater overestimation.)

*Source:* Cole et al. (1999).

## F O R • Y O U R • R E V I E W

❧ What factors help to promote a smooth transition to the start of school?

❧ How do parents and peers influence school achievement?

❧ What is the role of class size in children's school achievement?

❧ How do teacher behaviors influence school achievement?

❧ What factors seem to facilitate learning among minority-group children? What factors seem to be responsible for the unique achievement patterns of Asian children?

❧ In what ways do teachers sometimes contribute to gender-typed behaviors and attitudes among children?

❧ How do children's own attitudes contribute to gender bias in school achievement?

## MEDIA

M edia in all its forms—television, movies, radio, and magazines—has an undoubtedly enormous influence on school-age children. Perhaps there is no more visible symbol of the technological and "digital" age than the computer. Just as most adults in many countries are now likely to encounter computers in their daily experiences, so, too, are children. For example, within the United States, *100 percent* of children now have access to computers and the Internet in school (National Center for Education Statistics, 2005). Furthermore, the availability of computers in the homes of school-age children in the United States has increased dramatically within the last few years. About 65 percent of all children under age eighteen in the United States currently operate a home computer for educational and entertainment purposes, as well as for communicating with others. However, the level of home computer use drops substantially for African American, Hispanic, and poor children. Some refer to this disparity as the "digital divide." Children spend the largest proportion of time on the computer playing games, using the Internet, and working on school assignments (DeBell & Chapman, 2003). Figure 13.11 shows just how prevalent computer and Internet use are for school-age children. In this section we examine the question "What is the effect of computers on children's development?" In addition, we consider some of the research on the impact of television viewing on children, especially on their attitudes about gender and ethnicity, and on their consumer behavior.

### COMPUTERS AND CHILD DEVELOPMENT

Does experience with computers influence the ways children tackle problem solving and other cognitive tasks? Are young "keyboard junkies" who spend long hours glued

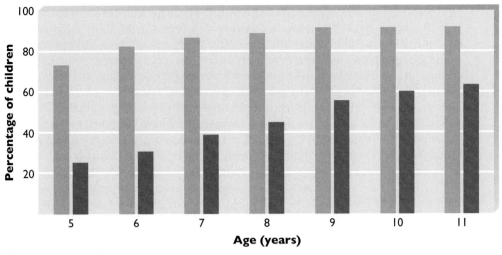

▲ **FIGURE 13.11**

**Percentage of School-Age Children Using Computers and the Internet**

As the graph shows, a high percentage of school-age children use computers, either at home or at school, even at age five years. Most young children do not use the Internet, but usage rises dramatically over the next several years.

*Source:* DeBell & Chapman (2003).

to the video screen missing other critical experiences, particularly the social interactions crucial to their socioemotional development? The pervasive presence of computers in today's world makes these questions well worth exploring. The emerging answer is clear: there is no such thing as an "effect of computers" per se on child development. What matters, rather, is the way children use them (Behrman, 2000).

***Academic Mastery and Cognition*** The first relatively widespread use of computers in education began in the 1960s, when computer-assisted instruction (CAI) was touted as a valuable, efficient educational tool. CAI programs serve primarily to supplement classroom instruction, providing highly structured tutorial information along with drill-and-practice exercises in content areas such as mathematics and reading.

Newer educational software places less emphasis on rote memorization and more on providing children with opportunities to use higher-order thinking skills as they master academic subjects. To date, the effects of these efforts have been mixed (Roschelle et al., 2000). For example, math education programs designed to encourage children to think more fully seem to have positive effects, whereas those that are oriented toward making repetitive math learning more fun seem to have no, and perhaps even detrimental, effects on learning (Wenglinsky, 1998). In general, however, the areas in which computer learning seems to have the greatest benefits are in science and mathematics (Roschelle et al., 2000). Being able to visualize and observe simulations of scientific concepts appears to encourage children to engage in levels of thinking generally more advanced than had been thought possible (Gordin & Pea, 1995; White & Fredriksen, 1998). Another factor associated with computers, which may have powerful benefits, is the opportunity to work on real-world problems that are available through the Internet. More specifically, with increased access to recently collected data from scientific research, children can engage in the very same types of activities of experimentation, design, and reflection that scientists and researchers carry out in their efforts to make contributions to understanding the environment, society, and the physical and biological world.

Other major advantages of the computer, especially with Internet access, stem from the opportunity to learn about issues and topics that simply would not be available to most children any other way. For example, with very little investment, children can explore and even design art and music, choreograph dramatic scenes, acquire information about other cultures (both existing and extinct), and communicate with other peoples. They can also find others who share similar academic interests and activities. As a consequence of these opportunities, children become more willing to take on more difficult academic problems (Roschelle et al., 2000).

Among the cognitive skills that may be enhanced are spatial representation, iconic skills, and increased ability to attend to multiple events, as is often required in action game playing associated with the computer and video games (Subrahmanyam et al., 2001). The limited research carried out on the impact of computers on these abilities suggests positive effects (Greenfield, 1998; Greenfield & Cocking, 1996).

*Social Development*   Contrary to popular opinion, the interactions a child has with the computer do not necessarily displace other activities of a more social nature, nor is computer use itself necessarily a solitary activity (Crook, 1992). In one survey of more than 500 children, those with computers at home resembled nonowners in the frequency with which they visited friends, participated in club meetings, and engaged in sports (Lieberman, 1985). Furthermore, children who work on computer projects in school tend to collaborate and share ideas more in these settings than they do in other school activities (Hawkins et al., 1982). Thus, rather than inhibiting social interactions, computer activities may actually promote them, especially when teachers encourage group problem solving as opposed to individual projects (Bergin, Ford, & Hess, 1993).

Older children do spend much of their time at the computer alone. Nevertheless, a substantial portion of children's involvement with the computer, especially after it is no longer a novelty in the home, is devoted to communicating and maintaining social relationships with others via e-mail, with instant messaging, by playing games, or in chat rooms (Subrahmanyam et al., 2000; Subrahmanyam et al., 2001). Of course, one major concern is what kinds of social interactions may be occurring during some of these on-line activities, especially with individuals with whom the young person is not acquainted.

*Gender Differences*   Ask children ranging from kindergarten age to twelfth grade to rate the word *computer* on a scale labeled M (for "male") at one end and F (for "female") at the other. Ask them also to rate how much they like the item. Researchers who have followed these and other procedures have found that children place computers toward the "male" side of the rating scale. In general, boys like computers more than girls do (Culley, 1993), and children sometimes perceive school computers as "belonging more" to boys (Cassell & Jenkins, 1998). Yet these gender differences are apparent primarily at the elementary and high school levels and are not present at younger ages; preschoolers and kindergartners are much less likely to display these stereotypes, at least with respect to interest in the computer (Bergin et al., 1993; Collis & Ollila, 1990; Krendl & Broihier, 1992). Moreover, the gender gap appears to be narrowing; girls now indicate that they use their home computer as much as boys do (DeBell & Chapman, 2003; Subrahmanyam et al., 2000). And boys and girls use the Internet about equally often, although the sites they access may differ (Clark, 2001). New computer games designed for girls have helped to reduce the disparity (Subrahmanyam & Greenfield, 1998), as has the increasing availability of websites responsive to girls' interests (Subrahmanyam et al., 2000).

## TELEVISION AND DEVELOPMENT IN MIDDLE CHILDHOOD

Children, at least in the United States, spend more time watching television than at any other activity except sleep (Roberts et al., 1999). In fact, by high school graduation, three years will, on average, have been given to watching television, usually general entertainment shows (Roberts & Foehr, 2004; Strasburger, 1993). Moreover, with the advent of cable television, DVDs, and digital games, children have more opportunities than ever to spend time in front of a television screen. We have already discussed how television can influence cognitive and language development, as well as the incidence of aggressive behaviors, in early childhood. Here, we look more closely at the relationship between TV viewing and a number of other dimensions of social development.

**Gender Stereotypes**   Television occasionally portrays males and females in nontraditional roles: fathers cook and care for their children, and women are employed in customarily masculine jobs. These programs, however, are not standard fare on commercial television. The portrayal of working women has increased over recent decades, but women are still more likely to be found in situation comedies and dramas than in action-adventure shows (Signorielli & Bacue, 1999). Consistent with stereotypes of female behavior, girls and women on television act nurturantly, passively, or emotionally. In contrast, males are more frequently the central characters of television shows, and they act forcefully, have more power and authority than women, and display reason rather than emotion (Lovdal, 1989; Signorielli & Bacue, 1999).

These stereotypical portrayals are likely to have some impact on children. When asked to write about their favorite shows, both boys and girls focus more on male than female characters and write about more masculine than feminine behaviors (Calvert et al., 2003). Children's attention to gender stereotypes very likely depends on other developmental changes children undergo. For example, boys who demonstrate gender constancy are more likely to watch male characters on television and prefer programs that contain a greater proportion of males than boys who do not display gender constancy (Luecke-Aleksa et al., 1995). In addition, gender-constant boys are more likely to watch shows created for adult entertainment, particularly sports and action shows, than their counterparts who still do not exhibit gender constancy. This difference in viewing preferences does not seem to be linked to earlier maturity in other cognitive abilities. In contrast, gender constancy in girls has relatively little effect on their television preferences or viewing habits. Perhaps this sex difference reflects the greater attractiveness of male roles on much of television and, therefore, accounts for such programs' increased interest value for gender-constant boys. Alternatively, perhaps this sex difference reflects a lessened need on the part of girls to exploit television as a basis for gender-role differentiation.

**Ethnic Attitudes**   The characters on American television are predominantly white. African Americans are occasionally shown, but Hispanic, Asian, and Native American individuals are not commonly seen (Greenberg & Brand, 1994). This portrait applies even more strongly to commercial entertainment programs for children, although in both commercial and public educational programming for children about one-fourth to more than one-third of the characters are minorities, and minorities are becoming represented in increasing numbers on American television (Calvert, 1999). Relatively little research has been carried out to determine how important the representation of ethnic minorities may be to children. However, evidence shows that African American young people tend to prefer to watch and identify with African American characters (Greenberg & Brand, 1994). The extent to which they do so has been found to be positively related to self-esteem (McDermott & Greenberg, 1984) and, in some cases, although not consistently, to positive attitudes about their own race (Graves, 1993). Findings like these point to the potential for television to influence attitudes toward the self and toward other ethnic groups.

**Consumer Behavior**   Because of their tremendous spending power, either directly or through their parents, children are the targets of a significant number of television commercials. According to some estimates, the average child sees almost 40,000 television commercials each year (Comstock & Scharrar, 2006). Of concern to many child advocates is the proliferation of television shows linked to specific toys and product endorsements for expensive items, such as athletic shoes, by popular sports figures and other celebrities, all of which put pressure on children to spend money.

Children certainly respond to the messages of commercials. For one thing, they frequently request the cereals and other foods they see advertised (Taras et al., 1989). By age five, children distinguish commercials from other programming, but they do not always recognize commercials as messages specifically intended to influence their behavior; four- and five-year-olds, for example, believe "commercials are to help and entertain you" (Kunkel, 2001; Ward, Reale, & Levinson, 1972). Young children are especially likely to confuse programs with commercials if toys or cartoon characters appear in both (Wilson & Weiss, 1992). It is usually not until children are eight years of age or older that they understand that commercials are intended to influence viewers' buying habits (Blosser & Roberts, 1985). Because young children are not able to critically evaluate the information presented to them in commercials, they may pressure their parents to purchase expensive toys and clothes, heavily sugared foods, and other products (Kunkel & Roberts, 1991).

In more recent years, controversy has swirled around the introduction of Channel One in public schools. This program consists of ten minutes of news and two minutes of commercials for products of interest to young people. If a school agrees to air these broadcasts to students, free televisions are provided. It has become a popular idea in American school systems; approximately 12,000 schools and an estimated 7 million young people have access to the program. In general, students seem to learn about current events from such programming, and it is liked by teachers and principals (Johnston, Brzezinski, & Anderman, 1994). But the commercials also are reported to be effective as well; students more positively evaluate and express greater interest in buying the products that are advertised (Brand & Greenberg, 1994). Other companies are providing school computer labs with free equipment in which the advertising is available on a small part of the screen continuously. In addition, based on information provided when the student logs on, these companies are collecting information about the age and gender of children working with the computer, as well as the kinds of Web sites they visit. Although schools are being provided with state-of-the-art computer facilities, critics worry about the potential invasion of privacy and the consequences of what could be interpreted as school-sanctioned commercialism from these kinds of arrangements.

### RESEARCH APPLIED TO PARENTING
## Encouraging Critical Skills in Television Viewing

Nicky finished his homework just before his mother came home. Fortunately, there still was enough daylight for his best friend, Aaron, to come over for a visit. As soon as he arrived, the conversation turned to the afternoon's television fare and some of the toys that were advertised on their favorite shows. "Hey, did you see that car that spins off the race track? That is really awesome!" "Yeah," Aaron replied. "I really want to get one." "Me, too. And I want that robot they showed after that," Nicky proclaimed. Nicky's mother worried when she overheard this conversation. Was this generation of kids being steered to buy more consumer goods than children in prior years? These fears were added to her growing concerns about the effects of watching all of that violence on television. Was there anything she could do to control the large impact of television on the thinking and behavior of her young son?

As we have seen, television holds enormous promise to enhance children's intellectual and social functioning. However, there is also clear evidence of potential dangers, especially when television viewing takes up much of a child's time or is directed at programs that are age inappropriate. Apart from the option not to have a television set available in the home (an alternative that relatively few parents defend), what steps might parents take to promote positive benefits from this medium? Any recommendations will, of course, depend on the maturity of the child, as well as the values caregivers wish to promote. However, developmental psychologists and others concerned about the influence of television on children generally agree with the following guidelines:

1. *Be aware of how much time is being spent watching television and what is being watched.* Parents may not always realize how much of the day their children spend in front of the television set, what they are watching, or how the program is affecting them. Continuous supervision may not be possible when parents are busy with other household duties or away at work. However, knowing what children are watching, and for how long, is the first step in understanding what they might be learning from television.

2. *Decide what is acceptable to watch.* Even young children may be attracted to programming that is frightening or inappropriate, not because they necessarily enjoy it but because the rapid pace of events or some other convention of the programming is attracting their attention. Parents have the responsibility to determine which programs are permissible and ensure that children limit their television viewing those programs. Recognize, however, that as children become older and more independent, parental monitoring will be more difficult. Older children must learn to take increasing responsibility for their own television viewing.

3. *Establish acceptable times for watching television.* Family members need to know when they can watch television. For example, can the television be on during the dinner hour? Is watching television permitted if homework, chores, or other obligations are not yet finished? How late in the evening is television viewing allowed?

4. *Watch television with children whenever possible.* When jointly watching programs with their children, parents have the opportunity to discuss such things as what is real and what is fantasy, how conflict might be resolved other than through violence, the stereotypes being portrayed, the goals of advertising, and many other issues presented through this medium that are valued or not approved within the household. In addition, by commenting on the material, parents can stimulate vocabulary development and provide different perspectives that may promote cognitive and social skills. Unfortunately, coviewing involving active discussion of television content appears to be infrequent in most families (Huston & Wright, 1998).

# F O R • Y O U R • R E V I E W

- What benefits do computers provide in the mastery of academic material?

- What has been the impact of computers on children's social development?

- How do boys and girls differ in their use of computers?

- What influence does television viewing have on children's gender role beliefs?

- How is television viewing related to children's ethnic group attitudes?

- How is television viewing related to children's consumer behavior?

# CHAPTER RECAP

## 🔑 Summary of Developmental Themes

### SOCIOCULTURAL INFLUENCE

**How do sociocultural factors influence the contexts of development in middle childhood?**

Culture has been shown to influence parenting demands, especially in the degree to which children are expected to be compliant and helpful in order to help the family survive.

### RISK/RESILIENCE

**What contextual factors promote risk or resilience in middle childhood?**

Divorce and single parenthood can put children at risk, but the practice of effective parenting overrides the effects that these variations in family structure might have. Children can be at risk for negative developmental outcomes if they experience poor peer relationships. However, research has identified several ways in which success with peers can be promoted. For example, fostering prosocial behaviors, good social skills, and effective social-information processing can help children in their interactions with peers. Certain characteristics of schools can promote or discourage academic achievement. Children thrive when they experience smooth transitions to school, have small classes, and interact with teachers who encourage autonomy and initiative.

## Chapter Review

### THE FAMILY IN MIDDLE CHILDHOOD

**In what ways do parenting strategies vary across different cultural groups?**

Cultures vary in the degree to which children must contribute to the family's subsistence, do chores, and obey their parents. In some cultures, parents demand a very high degree of compliance, whereas in others, the emphasis in parent-child interactions is sociability.

**What are the effects of divorce on child development?**

Children whose parents divorce evidence socioemotional and academic difficulties, especially boys. Many effects disappear after the first year following divorce, however.

**What factors can help children adjust to the divorce of their parents?**

More positive adjustment to divorce is associated with a shift from power-assertive to authoritative parenting, low parental conflict after separation, and the presence of sources of social support for children outside of the immediate family.

**What kinds of custody arrangements are best for children?**

Research suggests that joint custody, whether legal or physical, has the greatest benefits for children.

**What factors are associated with successful outcomes in single-parent families?**

Children do best when single parents are involved, use effective discipline strategies, and display warmth.

Assistance with sources of stress, such as help with child care and counseling, can be helpful in alleviating some of the stresses that single parents face.

**What does the research indicate about the impact of having gay or lesbian parents?**

Research shows that children growing up with same-sex parents do not differ from children with heterosexual parents on academic, social, or emotional traits. What matters most for all children is the quality of caregiver interactions that they experience.

**What role do siblings play in the development of younger children in the family?**

Older siblings act as teachers, models, and sources of social support for young children in the family. Older siblings are usually more dominant and nurturant than younger siblings, but these differences diminish as children get older.

### PEER RELATIONSHIPS IN MIDDLE CHILDHOOD

**What factors promote the formation of peer group identities? What factors can lessen hostilities among groups of peers?**

Children show especially strong identity with peer groups when their groups compete against others. Peer groups show in-group favoritism when their groups are highly defined and have high status. Intergroup hostilities can be reduced by having groups work together on some common goal.

## How do researchers assess children's peer status?

Peer status is usually measured through *sociometric nominations* or *sociometric rating scales*. Based on the outcomes, children are classified as popular, rejected, neglected, or controversial.

## What are some of the characteristics displayed by popular children?

Popular children tend to engage in prosocial behaviors. The child's peer status is also related to physical attractiveness, motor skills, and emotion regulation.

## What are some of the influences on the development of children's social competence?

Social competence has its roots in the child's earliest attachment relationships but is also influenced by parental styles of social interaction, as well as social-cognitive skills, such as the ability to perceive social cues accurately.

## What are the qualities of children's friendships during middle childhood?

During middle childhood, children begin to value friends for their psychological qualities, rather than the fact that friends share activities with them.

## What factors influence the formation of children's friendships?

Children become friends with peers who share interests, personality qualities, or other behaviors and characteristics with them. Children form friendships by keeping social interactions positive in tone and de-escalating conflicts.

## How do friendships contribute to the child's social and emotional development?

Friendships seem to protect children from anxiety and stress, and are associated with higher levels of self-esteem.

# SCHOOL

## What factors help to promote a smooth transition to the start of school?

Children who initially demonstrate competence with respect to social behaviors and cognitive/linguistic skills tend to make smoother transitions to the start of school. Entering school with familiar peers has advantages as well.

## How do parents and peers influence school achievement?

Parents who are involved with their children and who encourage their children's autonomy tend to have children with higher academic achievement. The peers with whom a child aligns himself or herself can affect school motivation.

## What is the role of class size in children's school achievement?

Smaller classes, especially during the early grades, appear to have positive consequences for children. The research shows that, for early grades, class sizes of thirteen to seventeen students are associated with greater achievement on standardized tests of reading and mathematics.

## How do teacher behaviors influence school achievement?

Teacher expectations about students' abilities can have important consequences for their school achievement. Certain classroom management styles can be influential; studies of *cooperative learning* and *collaborative learning* reveal more favorable outcomes for students. In addition, teachers have a positive impact on students when they encourage autonomy and initiative, and when they form close interpersonal relationships with their students.

## What factors seem to facilitate learning among minority-group children?

According to the *cultural compatibility hypothesis*, children's academic performance rises when educational practices incorporate elements of the child's background culture.

## What factors seem to be responsible for the unique achievement patterns of Asian children?

Children in Asian societies display higher levels of achievement in mathematics and science perhaps because of the amount of time spent learning these subjects, demands for homework, concerns of parents for successful school performance, and the central role that effort plays in many Asian cultures.

## In what ways do teachers sometimes contribute to gender-typed behaviors and attitudes among children?

Teachers may contribute to gender-role socialization through their attitudes and behaviors. For example, they may have different expectations about the academic skills of boys and girls, and often focus more attention on boys than on girls.

## How do children's own attitudes contribute to gender bias in school achievement?

Girls and boys often believe that girls are better at reading and boys are better at mathematics. In the domain of mathematics, however, girls' beliefs in their competence seem to be increasing. Girls often underestimate their academic abilities and attribute failures to lack of ability.

# MEDIA

## What benefits do computers provide in the mastery of academic material?

Computers appear to enhance the learning of science and mathematics, especially by providing opportunities to visualize concepts. Children can access real-world data on-line and learn about a wide array of topics and issues that might not normally be available to them.

### What has been the impact of computers on children's social development?

Computers can promote social involvement, especially when they are used for group projects. Even when children are on the computer alone, they are often engaged in social networking through e-mail and instant messaging.

### How do boys and girls differ in their use of computers?

Younger children do not show gender differences in their used of computers. Although the stereotype is that computers are for boys, gender differences in computer use are diminishing in contemporary society.

### What influence does television viewing have on children's gender role beliefs?

Gender stereotypes are commonly exhibited in television programming. Children show evidence of learning these stereotypes, although their attention to them appears to be dependent on an understanding of their own gender.

### How is television viewing related to children's ethnic group attitudes?

Children watch and identify with television characters that belong to their own ethnic group, and the extent to which they do so is linked to positive self-esteem.

### How is television viewing related to children's consumer behavior?

Children do not understand that commercials are intended to influence consumer behavior until about age eight. Children tend to request the products they have seen on television commercials.

## KEY TERMS AND CONCEPTS

collaborative learning (p. 477)

cooperative learning (p. 477)

cultural compatibility hypothesis (p. 478)

sociometric nomination (p. 459)

sociometric rating scale (p. 459)

# PATHWAYS: CONNECTING THE STORY OF DEVELOPMENT

| INFANCY | EARLY CHILDHOOD | MIDDLE CHILDHOOD (6–11 YEARS) | | ADOLESCENCE |
|---|---|---|---|---|
| See p. 268 | See p. 376 | | | See pp. 576–577 |
| | | **Physical Development** | • Shows more efficient and better-controlled motor skills<br>• Becomes more adept at fine-motor coordination<br>• Shows steady growth in physical size | |
| | | **Cognitive/ Language Development** | • Shows systematic and efficient attention strategies<br>• Shows logical thought on conservation tasks but only in the presence of real objects or images<br>• Develops increasing memory span<br>• Produces various kinds of memory strategies to enhance recall<br>• Shows greater control of cognitive processing<br>• Shows gains in ability to plan the steps in problem solving<br>• Becomes more flexible in strategy use<br>• Shows growth in metacognition<br>• Shows metalinguistic awareness including appreciation of humor and metaphor | |
| | | **Social/ Emotional Development** | • Shows understanding of display rules<br>• Engages in social-comparison<br>• Displays global self-esteem<br>• Shows mastery orientation<br>• Exercises self-regulation through internalized language<br>• Thinks in terms of moral realism or conventional ideas<br>• Shows greater knowledge of and greater flexibility toward gender stereotypes | |

# PHYSICAL AND COGNITIVE DEVELOPMENT

14

S he stared intently at the thirteen-year-old who had just finished her routine. Danielle couldn't believe what she had just seen. How could any girl her own age do that? Danielle's words expressed admiration and awe, but her voice was tinged with envy as she confided to her best friend, "We've been in gymnastics ever since we were five. If we tried that, we'd probably break our necks!"

Even as a toddler, Danielle had seemed captivated by leaping and tumbling. Her parents took great pride in their daughter's graceful athleticism and precocious motor skills. Danielle enrolled in ballet and gymnastics at an early age. Both activities had been fun. As Danielle became older and more skilled, she especially seemed to thrive on the competition that permeated gymnastics meets. She liked being good at what she did; she preferred being the best. Through the applause, her friend had no difficulty hearing Danielle mutter, "I'll bet I can do that. Watch me next time we're at practice." But she also knew that her body had changed. All of a sudden her legs seemed too long for the pommel horse, and her own program took more effort to carry out. She wondered silently if she really could complete a routine as challenging and remarkable as the one she was now observing.

**NATURE & NURTURE**  How do nature and nurture interact in physical and cognitive development in adolescence?

**SOCIOCULTURAL INFLUENCE**  How does the sociocultural context influence physical and cognitive development in adolescence?

**CONTINUITY/DISCONTINUITY**  Are physical and cognitive development during adolescence continuous or discontinuous?

**INTERACTION AMONG DOMAINS**  How do physical and cognitive development in adolescence interact with other domains of development?

Danielle, who is physically poised and skilled, displays a fair amount of confidence in the demands of learning a new and difficult gymnastic routine. Toward the end of childhood, many skills become highly specialized talents: youngsters like Danielle are already accomplished athletes; others her age are concert musicians. On the verge of adulthood, adolescents undergo sweeping changes on all fronts—the physical, cognitive, emotional, and social. Interpreting and orchestrating all these changes is the increasingly sophisticated and complex brain. And part and parcel of the myriad transformations that the brain directs during this developmental phase are notable advances in the way adolescents think and solve problems.

## PHYSICAL DEVELOPMENT IN ADOLESCENCE

Probably the most obvious changes that signal the transition to adolescence occur in the domain of physical development. Although parents may long ago have dropped the typical childhood practice of penciling ever-higher marks on the bathroom wall, a long-absent aunt might still cry out, "My, how you've grown!" upon seeing her thirteen-year-old niece. And by this she might be referring

Variations in height and weight are just two of the many ways that children of similar ages differ in their physical development. These middle school children joining together to socialize after school illustrate a wide variation in height. Some may not have begun their adolescent growth spurt, others may be in the middle of this developmental phase, and still others may have completed it.

not just to a conspicuous change in height, but also to numerous changes in physical characteristics that signify the emergence of adulthood. Her proclamation might just mean "You look grown up."

## PHYSICAL GROWTH

In the United States, the onset of rapid adolescent growth typically occurs between ages ten and fourteen for girls and between ages twelve and sixteen for boys (Sinclair, 1985). During this period, height increments occur at nearly double the rate in childhood. Because the growth spurt usually does not start in boys until about two years later, girls may be head and shoulders over their male peers for a brief period in early adolescence. During the approximately three years over which the growth spurt occurs, girls add about twenty-eight centimeters (eleven inches) and boys about thirty centimeters (twelve inches), or about 17 percent of their total height (Abbassi, 1998). Figure 14.1 illustrates the growth typically observed in many populations of children during their first eighteen years.

Individual differences in growth are especially evident during the adolescent years, when children are likely to show enormous variation in the timing, speed, and duration of the adolescent growth spurt. A girl who once towered over her childhood girlfriends may suddenly find at age thirteen that she is looking up to them, at least temporarily. A boy whose athletic skills were unremarkable may find himself the starting center for the middle school basketball team if he undergoes an early adolescent growth spurt.

In earlier chapters, we pointed to the fact that much physical growth during childhood follows the *cephalocaudal* and *proximodistal* principles. However, physical growth

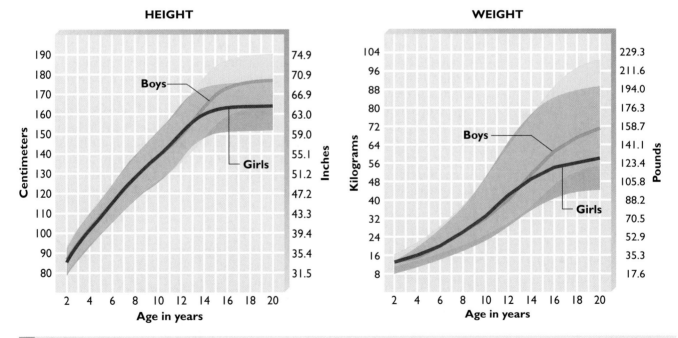

### ▲ FIGURE 14.1

### Growth in Height and Weight over the First Twenty Years

Height and, to a lesser extent, weight rapidly increase in the first two years following birth. Changes in height and weight continue at a fairly modest rate throughout childhood, followed by a brief, more rapid upturn sometime during the preadolescent or adolescent years. However, there is a wide range in height and weight among children, especially during the adolescent years. This figure (based on children in the United States) shows height and weight growth charts for boys and girls between the third and ninety-seventh percentiles.

*Source:* Centers for Disease Control and Prevention, National Center for Health Statistics (2000).

does not necessarily conform to these principles during adolescence. During the adolescent growth spurt, for example, some parts of the body undergo rapid growth in a pattern almost the reverse of the proximodistal principle. We are all familiar with the teenager who seems to be all hands and feet. Hands and feet are in fact among the first body parts to show a dramatic change during this period; they are followed by arms and legs and, last of all, the trunk (Tanner, 1978). An adolescent, in other words, is likely to outgrow his shoes first, then his trousers, and finally his jacket.

The organ systems, which have been growing at a stable rate throughout the childhood years, show a rapid increase during adolescence. However, the reproductive system follows a strikingly different pattern: only during adolescence do organs associated with reproduction begin to mature and rapidly approach their adult size. These different patterns mirror the functional importance of various systems of the body at specific points in development.

## WEIGHT

Just as we pointed to concerns about the climbing rate of obesity in younger children, so, too, do health experts express similar concerns about adolescents. As Figure 14.2 indicates, the prevalence of being overweight in this age group has climbed substantially over the last 40 years. This increase has been especially pronounced among adolescents who grow up in poor families (Miech et al., 2006). At the same time, one-third of high school students report that they do not engage in regular physical activity (National Center for Health Statistics, 2005). This factor, along with poor dietary habits, no doubt contributes to adolescent overweight.

⌐ **KEY THEME**

**SOCIOCULTURAL INFLUENCE**

In many cultures, a concern with being overweight seems to have contributed to another problem: efforts to initiate dieting, even by children who are within a normal weight range. In the United States, many young people, especially women, are dissatisfied with their weight. Concerns about becoming obese are expressed as early as age five (Feldman, Feldman, & Goodman, 1988). These concerns continue to be seen among eight-year-olds from nearly all ethnic groups (Robinson et al., 2001), and various studies report that up to half of third-grade girls have attempted to diet (Strauss, 1999). By the time they get to high school, more than 40 percent of women report that they are dieting (Centers for Disease Control, 1991), and as many as 75 percent indicate that they have attempted to lose five or more pounds at some time (Emmons, 1996). Similar percentages of girls have been found to be dieting in Australia, and the levels may be the same in many other countries (Paxton et al., 1991).

Repeated messages from fashion magazines, and sometimes from family and peers, stress the importance of slenderness for beauty and success, and undoubtedly place enormous pressure even on preteens to control weight. When girls report that

▷ **FIGURE 14.2**

**Trends in Overweight**

These data, collected from a series of studies carried out in the United States between 1963 and 1999, reveal the marked increase that has taken place in the number of children and adolescents who are considered obese. Some believe that obesity has become a health epidemic in this and other countries because of the dramatic changes and accompanying health risks that are associated with being overweight.

*Source:* Centers for Disease Control and Prevention (2002).

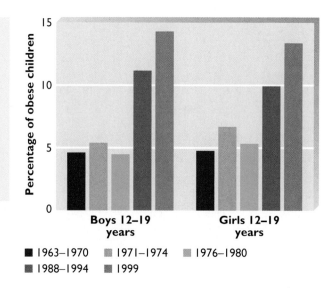

■ 1963–1970   ■ 1971–1974   ■ 1976–1980
■ 1988–1994   ■ 1999

they feel pressure from family and friends to be thin, they are also likely to express dissatisfaction with their body (Stice & Whitenton, 2002).

During the adolescent years, many girls believe it is important to have a boyfriend and to be physically attractive. Having dates, at least among Caucasian girls and African American girls whose mothers are more highly educated, is correlated with lower body fat, an indication that concern about weight has some basis in real experience (Halpern et al., 1999). Many teenage girls also tend to talk a lot with their friends about appearance—about how to look good and how to improve physical appearance. The extent to which they do so, as well as the extent to which they compare themselves with celebrities or other girls in school, predicts the degree of body dissatisfaction that they report (Jones, 2004).

## ATYPICAL DEVELOPMENT
## Dieting and Eating Disorders

The large number of girls who attempt to diet has become an almost normative, although troubling, aspect of growing up in many cultures. Sometimes, however, young people initiate more drastic steps to encourage weight loss. For example, in one study, nearly 10 percent of girls and 4 percent of boys in the sixth through eighth grades indicated that they have resorted to vomiting or use of laxatives in their efforts to remain thin (Krowchuck et al., 1998). A substantial number of teenagers, especially girls, including many who are not obese, go to great and even life-threatening lengths to reduce their weight. Anorexia nervosa and bulimia nervosa are two self-initiated forms of extreme weight control efforts, disorders that affect perhaps as many as 3 percent of women in industrialized countries at some time during their lifetime (Walsh & Devlin, 1998). *Anorexia nervosa* is a kind of self-imposed starvation. Individuals with anorexia appear to be obsessed with the fear of appearing too heavy and as a consequence become dangerously thin. As weight loss becomes severe, muscle tissue degenerates, bone marrow changes, menstrual periods are disrupted in girls, and cardiac stress and arrhythmias can occur. *Bulimia nervosa* is an eating disorder in which the individual often engages in recurrent bouts of binge eating, sometimes consuming enormous quantities of high-calorie, easily digested food. For many, binge eating alternates with self-induced vomiting, actions sometimes accompanied by use of laxatives or diuretics. Although they share with anorexics an intense concern about their body, individuals suffering from bulimia often fall within a normal weight range for their age and height.

A substantial increase in these disorders, particularly the more frequent of the two, bulimia, has been reported since the 1970s (Bryant-Waugh & Lask, 1995). Its incidence is greatest among Caucasian, middle- to upper-income young women (Harris, 1991), but both disorders appear to be increasing in males and in some cultural groups that have begun to adopt Western values. Their frequency may also be greater in certain groups, such as athletes and dancers, who are especially concerned about weight gain. Eating disorders may begin as part of the larger spectrum of anxieties that children, adolescents, and young adults experience about physical changes, especially as they approach and continue through puberty (Keel, Fulkerson, & Leon, 1997). For some individuals, an inherited, biological susceptibility, particularly in cases of anorexia nervosa, may exist (Katzman et al., 2000). Because sociocultural, psychological, and biological factors appear to interact, it should not be surprising that the treatments most effective for dealing with such disorders have been difficult to identify. However, about two-thirds of individuals who display anorexia nervosa show good recovery if treatment is begun early (Herpetz-Dahlmann et al., 2001). Because eating disorders can have serious long-term consequences, individuals experiencing one of them should be strongly encouraged to seek professional help.

# PHYSICAL MATURITY

The growth spurt of early adolescence is only one of numerous indicators of approaching physical maturity. Accompanying the growth spurt are important progressions indicating sexual maturity. We briefly consider these and the psychological issues a young person may confront during the passage from late childhood to early adulthood.

***Defining Maturity*** Because rate and final level of growth vary so greatly among individuals and for different parts of the body, researchers have turned to other criteria to define physical maturity. One reliable indicator is **skeletal maturity**, the extent to which *ossification,* the chemical transformation of cartilage into bony tissue, has been completed. The change begins prenatally about the eighth week after conception, when cartilage in the ribs and in the center of the long bones of the arms and legs is transformed. The process continues into late adolescence or early adulthood, when bones in the wrist and ankle are finally completely formed. Although skeletal maturity has become the standard for defining the end of physical growth, other, visible markers of approaching maturity appear just before and during the adolescent years. These important markers comprise a series of events associated with **puberty**, the developmental milestone reached when a young person gains the ability to reproduce.

During puberty, the *primary sexual organs*—testes and penis in males; vagina, uterus, and ovaries in females—enlarge and become capable of functioning. *Secondary sexual characteristics* that distinguish men from women, such as facial hair or breasts, also mature. Boys take on a more muscular and angular look as shoulders widen and the fat tissue of childhood is replaced with muscle. Girls' hips broaden, a change especially adaptive to bearing children. Girls also tend to retain a higher proportion of fat to muscle tissue and assume a more rounded appearance overall than boys. Like the growth spurt, the timing of each of the many events associated with puberty differs enormously from one young person to another. As a rule, however, this cluster of characteristics tends to appear somewhat earlier in girls than in boys.

Although there are numerous indicators of increasing sexual maturity, perhaps none are more significant than **menarche**, the first menstrual period in females, and **spermarche**, the occurrence of the first ejaculation of sperm in males. Menarche typically takes place between about twelve and thirteen years of age for females and spermarche between thirteen and fourteen years of age for males. However, as with other indicators of puberty, their initial appearance varies considerably from one individual to the next. For example, in the United States, the events accompanying sexual maturity begin somewhat earlier in African American girls than in Caucasian American girls (Biro et al., 2001).

What triggers these remarkable changes? The brain, including the hypothalamus and pituitary gland, and various hormones are centrally involved. *Adrenarche* initiates many of the changes taking place during early adolescence (McClintock & Herdt, 1996). Adrenarche refers to the maturation of the adrenal glands, small glands located above the kidneys. These glands release hormones important for the growth spurt and the emergence of underarm and pubic hair in girls. In addition, adrenarche may play an important role in the emergence of sexual attraction, which Martha McClintock and Gilbert Herdt (1996) argue typically occurs as early as ten years of age. In girls the hypothalamus may monitor metabolic cues associated with body size or the ratio of fat to muscle, because body mass index appears to be a good, although not the only, predictor of onset of menarche (Kaplowitz et al., 2001).

Still other *gonadotropic* (gonad-seeking) hormones released by the pituitary gland stimulate, in the case of females, the production of estrogen and progesterone by the ovaries and regulate the menstrual cycle. Estrogen promotes the development of the breasts, uterus, and vagina, as well as the broadening of the pelvis. Even family relationships, such as greater stress in the family, which can affect hormonal balances, may accelerate female development (Ellis & Garber, 2000). In the case of males, hormones contribute to the production of sperm and elevate the production of testosterone by the testes. Testosterone, in turn, promotes further growth in height, an increase in size of the penis and testes, and the appearance of secondary sexual characteristics, such as pubic and facial hair.

***Early Versus Late Maturity***    Today adult height in most industrialized societies is typically reached by about age seventeen; a century ago, it often was not achieved until about age twenty-three (Rallison, 1986). Changes in the age of menarche reveal a similar trend toward increasingly early occurrences over recent generations (see Figure 14.3).

The secular changes stem from improved socioeconomic conditions, including more adequate nutrition. Do the individual differences that are a part of this transition affect socioemotional development? The answer appears to be yes. For example, girls who are unprepared for menarche, either due to lack of information or because of its early onset, perceive the event more negatively than other girls, whose reactions are often a mixture of positive and negative feelings (Koff & Rierdan, 1995; Ruble & Brooks-Gunn, 1982). Thanks to greater communication within the family, including emotional support and assurance that menstruation is normal and healthy, girls' reactions to menarche today seem more positive (Brooks-Gunn & Ruble, 1980; Koff & Rierdan, 1995).

The limited research conducted with boys suggests that they are often uninformed, surprised, and confused about spermarche (Stein & Reiser, 1994). For many boys, sex education classes may either fail to explain what they need to know or are provided too late to prepare them. Their feelings about the event are mixed, and they seldom talk about it with others (Gaddis & Brooks-Gunn, 1985; Stein & Reiser, 1994). Nevertheless, early maturity seems to have positive aspects for boys (Alsaker, 1992; Petersen, 1988). Compared with early maturers, late-maturing boys report more negative feelings about themselves, feel more rejected, express stronger dependency and affiliative needs, and are more rebellious toward their parents (Mussen & Jones, 1957). Although late maturers want to be well liked and accepted, their efforts to obtain social approval often translate into attention-getting, compensatory, and childish behaviors disruptive to success with peers and adults (Mussen & Jones, 1958). The differences continue to be observed even into adulthood (Jones, 1965).

**KEY THEME**

**SOCIOCULTURAL INFLUENCE**

**KEY THEME**

**INTERACTION AMONG DOMAINS**

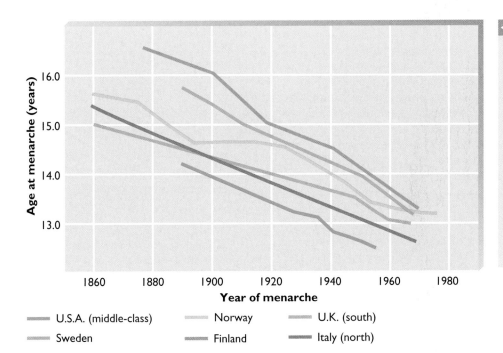

◁ **FIGURE 14.3**

**Secular Trends in the Age of Menarche**

Evidence exists for a secular trend in the decrease in age of the onset of menarche from 1845 through 1960. Although most of the data were obtained by questioning adolescents and young adults, some, especially those from earlier generations, depended on the memories of older individuals.

*Source:* Adapted from Tanner (1990).

What are girls' reactions to early and late maturity? Here the picture differs (Alsaker, 1992; Greif & Ulman, 1982; Simmons, Blyth, & McKinney, 1983). Early maturity may enhance status and prestige for girls just as for boys, but it can also be embarrassing; decrease their popularity, at least among agemates; and lead to greater social pressure and expectations from older friends, parents, and other adults to conform to more mature behavior patterns (Brooks-Gunn, 1989). In research in Sweden, girls who reached menarche early were more likely than late-maturing girls to engage in a variety of norm-breaking activities, such as staying out late, cheating on exams, pilfering, or using alcohol (Magnusson, Stattin, & Allen, 1986). Early-maturing girls preferred older and more mature friends, who may have inspired their greater independence from socially approved conventions of behavior. Indeed, among those maturing early but reporting no older friends, the frequency of norm-breaking activities was about the same as for girls who matured later.

As they grew older, early maturers with and without older friends began to look more alike in their frequency of many norm-breaking activities, and late maturers began to engage in such activities as use of alcohol as often as early maturers. Still, a few unacceptable behaviors, such as the use of drugs, remained higher throughout adolescence among early-maturing than among late-maturing girls.

As illustrated in Figure 14.4, another important component of girls' responses to early maturity appears to be whether their group of friends includes only other girls or also boys (Ge, Conger, & Elder, 1996). Early-maturing girls growing up in a rural area of the United States reported that they felt somewhat more stress than their on-time or late-maturing counterparts. They continued to report this greater stress over several years but particularly if their friends included boys. Although peer influences may be a factor in norm breaking, other changes taking place within the family, including less careful monitoring by parents, may contribute as well (Dick et al., 2000).

Some of the negative consequences of early maturity for females may also spring from the cultural ideals of beauty and maturity that exist in most Western societies. Slenderness and long legs are considered desirable traits in women. Although initially taller than their peers during the growth spurt, early-maturing girls have less opportunity to grow tall and often end up somewhat shorter, heavier, and more robust than their later-maturing peers (Biro et al., 2001). Not surprisingly, early-maturing girls are therefore initially less satisfied with their weight and appearance than are late-maturing girls (Williams & Currie, 2000). Personality disturbances, such as depression, are also more frequent among girls who mature

**KEY THEME**

SOCIOCULTURAL INFLUENCE

▶ **FIGURE 14.4**

**Psychological Distress Reported by Early-, On-Time, and Late-Maturing Girls as a Function of Sex Composition of Their Friends**

In general, early-maturing girls report somewhat greater stress than girls who mature later or on time. However, this increased stress in early maturers is especially evident when their group of friends includes boys as well as girls. Early-maturing girls undergoing greater stress may initiate friendships that include boys, which continue to heighten their concerns throughout the adolescent years.

*Source:* Ge, Conger, & Elder (1996).

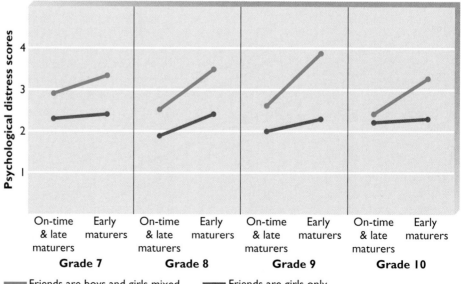

early (Ge et al., 2003; Stice, Presnell, & Bearman, 2001). In contrast, early-maturing boys more quickly assume the rugged, muscular physique stereotypically portrayed in American society as ideal for men and are more pleased by their weight and appearance than late-maturing boys (Petersen, 1988). Even if they show depressive symptoms early in puberty, boys seem to bounce back two years later, a pattern that is not found for early-maturing girls (Ge et al., 2003).

Girls who mature early and boys who mature late are also out of step with most of their classmates. Young people usually prefer friends who share interests, and interests change with increasing maturity. Late-maturing boys may find that their peers move on to other pursuits, making it more difficult to maintain positive relationships with their friends. Early-maturing girls may redirect friendships to older peers and boys. But this desire can be a problem, because it can contribute to increased behavioral and school problems, as well as greater personal unhappiness caused by pressures to conform to the interests of these older peers or boys. In other words, biological, immediate social, and broader cultural factors combine to help define the consequences of early and late maturity.

## SEXUAL BEHAVIOR

Few changes accompanying puberty are as contentious in many families as the sexuality that attends physical maturity. Anthropological research indicates that the majority of cultures are likely to permit or at least tolerate some sexual activity during the teen years. But Western societies have generally been more restrictive in its expression (Schlegel & Barry, 1991). Many mothers in the United States tend to underestimate the extent of sexual activity among their offspring; their children, in turn, tend to underestimate the degree to which their mothers disapprove of this activity (Jaccard, Dittus, & Gordon, 1998). Nevertheless, large numbers of teenagers are sexually active, and at young ages. In one study, for example, 30 percent of students entering sixth grade (averaging 11.7 years of age) in impoverished areas of one major city in the United States reported that they have engaged in sexual inter-course (Kinsman et al., 1998). Although teen sexual activity has declined from 1993 to 2003, 47 percent of ninth- through twelfth-graders still state that they have engaged in sexual intercourse (Kaiser Family Foundation, 2005).

What factors play a role in whether a teenager will engage in sexual activity? Several different family variables seem to be instrumental, according to a review by Brent Miller, Brad Benson, and Kevin Galbraith (2001). One especially important parameter is how the members of the family "connect" with one another. More specifically, when parents are warm and supportive of their children—that is, seem to be close and responsive to them—teenagers are more likely to remain sexually abstinent until they are somewhat older. Additionally, a similar outcome occurs when parents maintain relatively closer supervision and monitoring of their children's behavior, although evidence exists that there is a limit to this factor; when parents become intrusive and overcontrolling, sexual activity may be started somewhat earlier by their offspring. Not surprisingly, another important factor is the values parents hold concerning the appropriateness of sexual activity among teenagers. On the other hand, research on the extent to which parents communicate with their sons and daughters about sexual issues does not appear to be related to the timing with which sexual activity initiated. However, few studies have examined when such communications begin; information about this subject may often be initiated by parents only after they are aware that their children are sexually active.

Other contextual variables associated with the family are also related to sexual activity. In general, children in families living in neighborhoods where there is greater poverty, higher crime rates, and less stability—factors that are generally correlated with lower education and income—tend to engage in earlier onset of sexual activity. Children of single parents are more likely to initiate sexual behavior earlier, and so are children who are growing up in abusive family

⌐ **KEY THEME**
SOCIOCULTURAL INFLUENCE

environments or who have older teenage siblings who are already parents (East & Jacobson, 2001).

Aside from the moral and ethical issues that adolescent sexual behavior raises, there are important health and social consequences. Among the most frequent concerns are sexually transmitted diseases (STDs), teenage pregnancy, and the tendency of teenage parents to drop out of school. Adolescents appear to be more susceptible than adults to STDs; an estimated 3 million are infected each year by one of these diseases—a number that has spread considerable alarm among members of the medical profession (Eng & Butler, 1997; McIlhaney, 2000). In the 1980s approximately 20 percent of unmarried American women of European heritage eighteen years or younger and 40 percent of African heritage became pregnant during their adolescent years (Furstenberg, Brooks-Gunn, & Chase-Lansdale, 1989). The rate of teen pregnancy has shown some decline throughout the 1990s and early 2000s but still remains far higher in the United States than in other technologically advanced countries (Hamilton et al., 2005). Moreover, approximately 300,000 of the nearly half a million teenage women delivering their first child and 75 percent of all adolescents giving birth to a child each year will remain unmarried, a substantial increase from forty years ago, when only 15 percent who gave birth were unmarried (Allen et al., 1997; Coley & Chase-Lansdale, 1998). Only about half of these women will finish high school (Hotz, McElroy, & Sanders, 1997). Moreover, their children will often have difficulty when they begin school (Brooks-Gunn & Chase-Lansdale, 1995).

### CONTROVERSY: THINKING IT OVER

## What Should Sex Education Programs Emphasize?

Because of the risks associated with sexual activity, such as pregnancy and contracting AIDS or other STDs, many individuals working with elementary, middle school, and high school students in the United States and other countries around the world have argued that young people need to be better educated about their sexuality.

### What Is the Controversy?

Nearly everyone agrees that sex education should begin in the home at a young age, taught by parents. Moreover, parents generally wish to see instruction about sexuality provided in the schools. Most adults in the United States believe that sex education is appropriate, and when given the opportunity, only a small proportion of parents ask to have their children excused from sex education classes (Kaiser Family Foundation, 2004). In fact, sex education is either required or recommended in all states today and in most other countries in which formal education is offered. But beyond that, much less accord exists about sex education and, in particular, on what the focus of the instructional content should be, especially in the United States. Should the emphasis be on encouraging young people to abstain from sexual relationships until they are married? Or should sex education in the schools attempt to promote the acquisition of skills to handle maturely the complexities and consequences of relationships and provide clear information and access to resources that will help young people to think clearly about and be comfortable with their emerging sexuality?

### What Are the Opposing Arguments?

From the perspective of some, the only effective way for teenagers to avoid the negative outcomes associated with sexual relationships is to abstain from them. Harmful consequences, both psychological and physical, are the inevitable result of such premature activity. Moreover, to promote anything other than abstinence in sex education classes sends a mixed message that communicates a double

Sex education is part of the school curriculum in most states and in many countries. There is considerable controversy about what the content of sex education programs should be, but some recent programs show promise in lowering the rate of teen sexual activity and exposure to sexually transmitted diseases.

standard: "Avoid sexual relationships, but in case you can't, here is what you should know."

To others, however, a message that focuses only on abstinence ignores the fact that many teenagers are already engaging in sexual relationships. In fact, somewhere between 800,000 and 900,000 adolescent girls less than nineteen years of age will become pregnant each year in the United States alone, and about half of them can be expected to deliver babies (Centers for Disease Control, 2000). The number who are sexually active is substantially higher. Youths need information on the best ways to avoid pressure to initiate sexual activity and to prevent becoming infected with sexually transmitted diseases and becoming pregnant. Thus a more balanced perspective is to encourage postponing sexual involvement but, for those already involved or likely to initiate it, to emphasize engaging in it responsibly and safely.

### What Answers Exist? What Questions Remain?

Tests of the effectiveness of various sex education curricula have yielded mixed results, although some success has been reported. Knowledge of sexuality typically increases, but young people do not consistently report that they are involved in fewer sexual relationships or practice sex more responsibly or safely after exposure to many of these programs. Moreover, little evidence exists to indicate that abstinence-only programs are any more effective than other programs in reducing initiation into sexual activity or risky behaviors associated with it. Rarely have sex education programs been found to lead to an increase in sexual activity, another fear that is occasionally expressed (Grunseit et al., 1997). Nevertheless, some types of programs seem to hold considerable promise for delaying the onset of sexual activity or reducing the number of partners, unplanned pregnancies, or rate of sexually transmitted diseases (Franklin al., 1997; Grunseit et al., 1997; Kirby, 1997). One example is Teen Outreach. This program is designed to involve high schoolers in voluntary community service and encourages them to reflect on the normative tasks of adolescence, such as career goals and appropriate social relationships; only a small component of the curriculum is geared to sex education. Students participating in it, however, displayed a significant decline in pregnancy and other school-related problems compared with other students who did not participate (Allen et al., 1997). What makes this or other sex education programs more effective? At the present time, the essential ingredients are unknown. In that many young people are already sexually active before they participate in sex education classes, do programs need to be offered at earlier ages? Should the curricula include emphasis on more than the biology of reproduction? For example, could young people benefit from learning the social skills needed to respond to the many pressures they face to engage in sexual relationships? Have programs stressing abstinence, which for the most part have only recently gained widespread adoption, not been in schools long enough to prove themselves? Or are these programs too biased and narrow in their focus, often emphasizing fear instead of knowledge, extolling a simplistic solution to a complex problem that can have life-and-death consequences?

## BRAIN DEVELOPMENT

For many years, scientists believed that, by adolescence, the growth of the brain is essentially complete. However, growing evidence indicates that remodeling of the brain continues well into adulthood (Spear, 2000; Tanapat, Hastings, & Gould, 2001). For adolescents, most of the changes appear to occur in the frontal regions of the cortex. One important development is that axons in this region continue to grow and become myelinated, speeding the transmission of signals among neurons within this area of the brain as well as to other portions of the brain (Paus, 2004; Yakovlev & Lecours, 1967). Thus, not only is communication among brain cells faster, it is also more integrated among brain regions. A second change is in the number of synapses in the frontal cortex. At the start of puberty, there is an abundance of synapses in this region of the brain, but over time, synaptic density declines, probably because of synaptic pruning, the elimination of weaker synaptic connections (Huttenlocher, 1979). In some ways, this pattern of overabundance of synapses followed by a decline resembles the pattern of brain development that we saw in prenatal development and early infancy. However, it is not yet clear that the physiological processes underlying these major two waves of brain development are the same (Spear, 2003).

Studies using fMRI scans show that, in general, activity in the prefrontal cortex increases in adolescents as they perform a variety of cognitive tasks, in particular those that involve inhibition of responses. For example, if individuals are required to suppress the movement of their eyes to a visual stimulus, adolescents show greater activation of the prefrontal region than children or adults (Luna et al., 2001). In another experiment, adolescents were instructed to press a button in response to one visual target, but avoid pressing when they saw a different target. While they were performing, fMRI scans were obtained. Of special interest was how the brain responded when participants had to inhibit their responses. When scans of children at age nine were compared to their scans at age eleven, they showed an age-related decrease in activity in the prefrontal cortex. In addition, the areas that were activated were more localized rather than diffuse (Durston et al., 2006). All of this suggests that, with development, brain functioning seems to become more efficient and more specialized. As brain researcher Linda Spear (2003) puts it, "The adolescent brain is a brain in the process of becoming leaner, more efficient, and less energy consuming" (p. 66).

Researchers are intrigued by all of these changes in the brain because they seem to correspond to such behaviors as planning, higher-level reasoning, and impulse control in adolescents. If we see notable changes in thinking, social behavior, and even risk taking in the teen years, the reason may be, say some researchers, that underlying brain physiology is at least partly responsible.

**⚿ KEY THEME**

INTERACTION AMONG DOMAINS

## SLEEP

Ask any parent of a teenager—adolescents tend to be night owls. They go to bed later, often after 11:30 P.M. At the same time, because most high schools have earlier start times than elementary schools, adolescents must wake up early, typically at 6 A.M. or even earlier, in order to make it to school on time. About 26 percent of adolescents get less than 6.5 hours of sleep per night (Wolfson & Carskadon, 1998). But teens may actually need more sleep, as much as 9 hours daily compared to the typical 7 or 8 hours that we think of for adults (Carskadon, Harvey, & Duke, 1980). This means that many teenagers are not getting enough rest to be alert during the day; by some estimates, as many as 85 percent can be categorized as sleep deprived (Dahl & Lewin, 2002; Wolfson & Carskadon, 1998).

Besides needing more sleep, adolescents also experience a phase shift in sleep cycle—a biological tendency to go to bed later and wake up later in the morning—which appears to be triggered by the onset of puberty (Carskadon, Acebo, & Jenni, 2004). Several other factors add to the tendency for teens to stay up later. In contrast to the regulation of bedtimes that most parents practice with younger children, very few parents of teenagers tell them when to go to sleep. Homework, computers and the Internet, and work schedules also contribute to this pattern (Wolfson & Carskadon, 1998). Sometimes teens try to catch up by sleeping more on weekends and holidays, but this further upsets the sleep-wake rhythm when they have to awaken early on the next school day (Dahl & Lewin, 2002).

What are the consequences of insufficient sleep for adolescents? Lack of sleep is associated with lower grades in school, moodiness and depression, and lower self-esteem (Fredriksen et al., 2004; Wolfson & Carskadon, 1998). Excessive sleepiness is a special concern when teenagers drive; it is associated with the tendency to be involved in serious automobile accidents. The consequences of adolescent sleepiness are serious enough that several school districts across the United States have made changes toward later school start times for high school students. According to early reports from one of these districts, school attendance is up, and daytime sleepiness among students has declined (Wahlstrom, 2002).

## F O R ◆ Y O U R ◆ R E V I E W

◆ What patterns of physical growth are observed during adolescence?

◆ Why are dieting and eating disorders of concern? What factors lead to efforts to control weight?

◆ How is physical maturity defined?

◆ What are the developmental changes that accompany puberty?

◆ What are the social and behavioral consequences of early and late maturity for males and females?

◆ What factors are related to sexual behavior in adolescents? What are the health implications of such behavior?

◆ What are the controversies associated with sex education programs in the public schools?

◆ What major changes occur in the brain during adolescence?

◆ How do patterns of sleep change in adolescence?

## COGNITIVE DEVELOPMENT IN ADOLESCENCE

Earlier in this text, we documented the growth in children's cognitive processes from infancy through middle childhood. The range and scope of these changes might lead you to surmise that, by adolescence, cognitive development is complete. However, research shows that this supposition would be incorrect. For example, by looking at how participants perform when they are asked to locate a target in a string of letterlike stimuli or to judge how a spatial figure would look if it were rotated a few degrees, researchers have concluded that there are increases in the speed of processing information from middle childhood to adolescence (Kail & Miller, 2006). The ability to perform accurately in tasks in which memory must be used to locate a visual target improves up until age nineteen years, and the ability to suppress a behavioral response (such as looking at an intruding visual stimulus when instructed not to) improves until age fourteen years (Luna et al., 2004). Generally speaking, cognition in adolescence becomes more controlled, better coordinated, and in many instances, more subject to self-reflection.

## PIAGET'S THEORY AND ADOLESCENCE

⊶ **KEY THEME**
**CONTINUITY/DISCONTINUITY**

By the time the child reaches adolescence, she will most likely have moved to the final stage in Piaget's theory, the **formal operational stage**. Thinking in this stage is both logical and abstract. Problems like "Bill is shorter than Sam but taller than Jim. Who is tallest?" can now be solved without seeing the individuals or conjuring up concrete images of them. The adolescent can also engage in **hypothetical reasoning**; that is, she can generate potential solutions to problems in a thoroughly systematic fashion, much as a scientist approaches an experiment. According to Piaget, the development of formal operational thought represents the culmination of the reorganizations in thought that have taken place throughout each preceding stage in childhood. By adolescence, thought has become logical, flexible, and abstract, and its internal guiding structures are now highly organized.

Piaget's pendulum problem allows us to examine the thinking of the formal operational adolescent. In this task, the person is shown an object hanging from a string and asked to determine the factor that influences the frequency of oscillation, or the rate at which the pendulum swings. The length of the string, the weight of the object, the force of the push on the object, and the height from which the object is released can all be varied. How do children in earlier Piagetian stages approach this problem? Children in the preoperational and concrete operational stages typically try various manipulations in a haphazard fashion. They might compare the effect of a long string attached to a heavy weight and a short string tied to a light weight. Or they might vary the weight of the object and the force of the push, but leave out the length of the string. In contrast, formal operational children are both systematic and complete in testing the potential influences on oscillation. For example, while keeping weight constant, they observe the effects of varying length, push, and height; while keeping length the same, they investigate the effects of varying weight, push, and height; and so forth. Most adolescents, Piaget observed, could correctly determine that the length of the string was the critical factor in how fast the pendulum swings (Inhelder & Piaget, 1958).

In the social realm, achieving abstract thought means that the adolescent can think about the nature of society and his own future role in it. Idealism is common at this developmental stage because he understands more fully such concepts as justice, love, and liberty, and thinks about possibilities rather than just realities. In some ways, the adolescent may be more of a "dreamer" or a utopian than the adult because he has not yet had to confront the practical facts of living and working in the world (Inhelder & Piaget, 1958).

The contemplative nature of adolescent thought may manifest itself in two other ways, according to David Elkind (1976, 1981). First, adolescents may believe that others scrutinize and evaluate them as much as they think about themselves. This belief, called the **imaginary audience**, may cause a young girl to avoid going out because she just got braces on her teeth ("Everybody will see me!") or make a teenage boy avoid answering a question in class because he is certain all his classmates will think he is "dumb." Second, adolescents may show signs of holding a **personal fable**, the belief that they are unique, that no one can fully understand them, and

**formal operational stage** In Piagetian theory, the last stage of development, from approximately eleven to fifteen years of age, in which thought is abstract and hypothetical.

**hypothetical reasoning** Ability to systematically generate and evaluate potential solutions to a problem.

**imaginary audience** Individual's belief that others are examining and evaluating him or her.

**personal fable** Belief that one is unique and perhaps even invulnerable.

Many adolescents have the false belief that others inspect them in the same detail as they evaluate themselves, a phenomenon called the "imaginary audience."

even that they are invulnerable. A teenage boy prohibited from going to a late-night rock concert by his parents might say, "You just don't understand how important this is to me!"

You will recall that Piaget made strong claims that the sequence of development is universal. Yet not all children reach the stage of formal operations, and some do not even attain the highest levels of concrete operations. Many American adults, in fact, fail to display formal operational thought (Neimark, 1979). Members of many non-Western cultures do not display formal operational thinking, especially when they have little experience with formal schooling (Dasen, 1972; Rogoff, 1981). Other research shows that adolescents today receive higher scores on tests of formal operations than adolescents did twenty and thirty years ago (Flieller, 1999). Studies like these imply that the child's experiences in the sociocultural context may shape the nature of thought to a greater degree than Piaget acknowledged.

**⊶ KEY THEME**
**SOCIOCULTURAL INFLUENCE**

## THE DEVELOPMENT OF SCIENTIFIC THINKING

Most of us have received at least some formal training in the complex type of reasoning called *scientific thinking*. Scientific reasoning involves formulating a hypothesis, designing experiments in which one factor varies while others are held constant, and deciding on the validity of the hypothesis based on the observable evidence. We have just seen that, according to Piaget, this form of logical thought is not observed prior to the start of the formal operational stage. Contemporary research confirms that there are indeed observable developmental accomplishments in scientific reasoning; however, the foundations of this type of thinking are evident early in childhood. Even children who are just starting school show impressive knowledge about some of the basic tenets of scientific thinking.

One element of scientific thinking is the ability to distinguish between theory and evidence. Preschoolers often behave as if there is no distinction between the two. Shown a series of pictures depicting two runners in a race, younger children typically answer the questions "Who won?" and "How do you know?" with theory ("He has fast sneakers") rather than evidence ("He's holding the trophy"). By age six, though, children are likely to cite objective evidence (Kuhn & Pearsall, 2000).

A related skill is the capacity to see which conclusions are warranted by the evidence. Let us consider one example in which the child is presented with a series

Research shows that when children have the opportunity to engage in repeated scientific problem solving, they become more proficient in designing controlled experiments.

of pictures depicting the phases of the moon, along with two theories about why they occur: (1) clouds cover different portions of the moon at different times, or (2) the moon has a dark and a light side. Then the child hears the evidence: an astronaut reports that the moon is dry and has no water, that he landed on some white rock, and that he later walked on black gravel. Which theory about the moon could possibly be correct? Most first-, third-, and fifth-graders in this study chose the second theory, the one that was consistent with the evidence (Samarapungavan, 1992). Other researchers have confirmed that first-graders can go even further and correctly identify whether a specific piece of empirical evidence provides conclusive or inconclusive support for a hypothesis (Sodian, Zaitchik, & Carey, 1991).

Yet scientific thinking involves greater complexities. For example, hypotheses must be formed in the first place, and usually several hypotheses are concurrently in the mind of the scientist. Often, several variables operate at the same time. Experiments must be designed and conducted, and their outcomes coordinated with the hypotheses, to determine which variable causes the observed outcomes (Klahr & Dunbar, 1988). It is here that developmental changes are most apparent. When third-graders are asked to generate and evaluate hypotheses by running a series of experiments, they usually are not systematic in designing experiments that isolate the key variable and do not write down the outcomes of their experiments. Sixth-graders show improvements but still design a limited number of experiments, and their experiments are often difficult to interpret. In one study in which sixth-graders were asked to use a software package to test which variables played a role in the risk of earthquakes, 83 percent of the students investigated three or more variables at once (Kuhn & Dean, 2005). Adults do the best, but not because their reasoning about the relationship between theory and evidence is stronger. Rather, adults can coordinate the generation of hypotheses with the design of the set of experiments necessary to test them (Klahr, Fay, & Dunbar, 1993).

When children are encouraged to engage repeatedly in scientific problem solving, their skills improve noticeably. Deanna Kuhn and her colleagues (Kuhn, Schauble, & Garcia-Mila, 1992) asked preadolescents to identify which variables affected the speed of a model boat being towed in a tank of water: the water depth, boat size, boat weight, sail color, or sail size. The instructor gave minimal feedback to the students, but they were encouraged to make a plan about what they wished to find out, state what they found out after each experiment, and record their findings in a notebook.

to one item at a time (Oakland, 1982). Minority children may lack this basic "savvy" regarding how to take tests. Because most tests do not permit examiners to be flexible in administering them, they may underestimate minority children's skills (Miller-Jones, 1989). Moreover, minority children may score lower simply because they do not see the point of performing well or have not acquired the same drive to achieve in academic settings that is part of the majority culture (Gruen, Ottinger, & Zigler, 1970; Zigler & Butterfield, 1968). For some, IQ tests may even represent a part of the majority culture that is to be rejected outright (Ogbu, 1994). Still another factor to consider is the extent to which children are accustomed to having questions asked of them by adults. Greenfield (1997) points out that, in Asian, African, and Hispanic cultures, children are expected not to speak to adults but to listen to them and respect their authority. By answering questions posed by an adult, the child may be violating cultural norms.

Not all researchers are convinced that test bias and motivational factors play a large part in explaining the lower IQ scores of certain groups of children (Jensen, 1980). Even for the skeptics, however, these ideas have highlighted the importance of structuring test situations so that all children are given the opportunity to display their best performance.

***Stereotype Threat***    How an individual thinks about his or her abilities in relation to negative stereotypes about gender or race can affect performance on different tasks, a concept called **stereotype threat**. This phenomenon has been demonstrated among adults: African American individuals initially primed to think that an upcoming test would assess their abilities scored lower on a challenging verbal test than did Caucasian individuals. However, there was no difference in performance when the groups were given instructions that did not emphasize ability testing (Steele & Aronson, 1995). Similar findings have been reported with upper and lower elementary and middle school Asian American girls given a standardized math test. Right before taking the test, each girl colored a picture that activated stereotypes about either "girls" or "Asians." A third group colored a neutral landscape scene. Figure 14.8 shows the performance of each of the groups on the math component of the Iowa Test of Basic Skills. For the youngest and oldest age groups, activating stereotypes about girls resulted in lower math test scores, whereas activating stereotypes about ethnicity resulted in higher scores (Ambady et al., 2001). (It is unclear why upper elementary students did not fit this pattern of performance.) Results like these suggest that stereotype threat may be an important factor in interpreting racial and ethnic group differences in IQ scores.

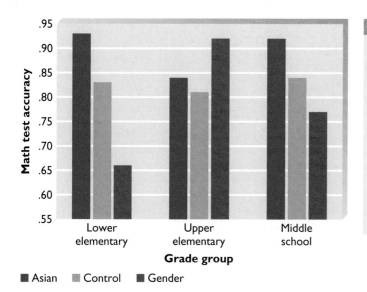

**◁ FIGURE 14.8**

**Stereotype Threat and Test Performance**

In a study of lower and upper elementary and middle school Asian American girls, Nalini Ambady and her colleagues found that activation of gender stereotypes resulted in lower math test scores but that activation of ethnic stereotypes resulted in higher scores at least for the youngest and oldest groups. These findings suggest that it is important to consider the phenomenon of stereotype threat in evaluating ethnic differences in intelligence test scores.

*Source:* Ambady et al. (2001).

## F O R • Y O U R • R E V I E W

❧ What are the main features of psychometric approaches to intelligence?

❧ What are the main features of information-processing approaches to intelligence?

❧ What are the principal ideas in Sternberg's and Gardner's theories of intelligence?

❧ What assumptions do psychologists make about the distribution of IQ scores in the population?

❧ How is giftedness defined? What are the unique ways in which gifted children process information? What are the behavioral characteristics of gifted children?

❧ What are the major features of the tests that have been used to assess intelligence in children?

❧ What kinds of developmental outcomes do IQ scores predict?

❧ What are the complexities in trying to assess the contributions of heredity to group differences in IQ?

❧ How might concepts like test bias and stereotype threat play a part in explaining group differences in IQ?

# CHAPTER RECAP

## ⚷ Summary of Developmental Themes

### NATURE & NURTURE

**How do nature and nurture interact in physical and cognitive development in adolescence?**

The processes of physical growth and physical maturity are set in motion by biological forces, but social variables like body image can lead to behaviors such as dieting and eating disorders that influence health and physical well-being among adolescents. In Piaget's theory, maturation, in conjunction with experience, is responsible for the child's entry into the stage of formal operations. Some changes in cognition, such as executive control, are linked to development of the brain in adolescence, especially in the prefrontal region. However, the child's exposure to experiences that nurture the emergence of cognitive skills—for example, the elements of scientific reasoning—is also important.

### SOCIOCULTURAL INFLUENCE

**How does the sociocultural context influence physical and cognitive development in adolescence?**

Secular trends in the age of menarche are linked to socio-historical shifts six economic conditions, especially access to good nutrition. The influence of culture is also seen in

the fact that not all children in all cultures attain formal operational thought. Finally, culture broadly influences the kinds of skills that its members value and nurture, which are believed to constitute "intelligence."

### CONTINUITY/DISCONTINUITY

**Are physical and cognitive development during adolescence continuous or discontinuous?**

Physical development and brain development show spurts of growth in adolescence. But even pubertal changes are grounded in processes undergoing continuous transformations. Small, incremental changes in the production of hormones may initiate substantive, dynamic reorganizations in complex systems of behavior. Piaget stressed stagelike attainments as the child progresses to formal operational thought. However, many descriptions of cognition in adolescence do not reveal qualitative stagelike changes.

### INTERACTION AMONG DOMAINS

**How do physical and cognitive development in adolescence interact with other domains of development?**

An adolescent's physical appearance, even the degree to which he or she matures early or late, can have dramatic influences on the responses of caregivers and peers, and can influence the child's evaluation of self. Brain development in adolescence is linked to cognitive attainments, such as speeded processing of information and greater ability to control behaviors and cognition.

# Chapter Review

## PHYSICAL DEVELOPMENT IN ADOLESCENCE

### What patterns of physical growth are observed during adolescence?

Most adolescents show a final growth spurt before or during early adolescence. Unlike the pattern observed earlier in childhood, physical growth at this time does not conform to the principles of cephaolcaudal and proximodistal development.

### Why are dieting and eating disorders of concern? What factors lead to efforts to control weight?

Of concern is the trend for an increasing number of individuals, especially girls, to engage in dieting and to display such eating disorders as anorexia and bulimia. Cultural pressures to be thin, as well as the influence of parents and peers, may contribute to these trends.

### How is physical maturity defined?

Maturity is defined not by size but by ossification of bone material, or *skeletal maturity*. This process ends in late adolescence when bones in the wrists and ankles complete their formation.

### What are the developmental changes that accompany puberty?

Puberty is defined as the period during which the individual gains the ability to reproduce. *Menarche*, or the first occurrence of menstruation, and *spermarche*, the initial occurrence of ejaculation of sperm, signal the ability to reproduce in females and males, respectively. The primary sexual organs enlarge, and secondary sexual characteristics, such as facial hair and breasts, emerge.

### What are the social and behavioral consequences of early and late maturity for males and females?

Boys seem to benefit from early maturity. They have more positive feelings about themselves and have better relationships with their parent and peers. For girls, early maturity is associated with a decline in body satisfaction, depression, and association with norm-breaking peers.

### What factors are related to sexual behavior in adolescents? What are the health implications of such behavior?

Among the factors that are related to whether youth engage in sexual behavior are the connectedness they feel with their families, the extent to which they are supervised, and the attitudes their parents hold with respect to sexual activity. Fewer resources in the family and the presence of a teenage sibling who is already a parent are also factors. Health concerns include increase in the incidence of sexually transmitted diseases and pregnancy.

### What are the controversies associated with sex education programs in the public schools?

Some programs focus on encouraging abstinence; others acknowledge that teens are sexually active and seek to promote responsible and safe sexual practices. The effectiveness of various kinds of sex education programs to reduce sexual activity among young people remains uncertain.

### What major changes occur in the brain during adolescence?

Most brain changes during adolescence occur in the frontal regions. Neurons continue to become myelinated, and after a period of overabundance of synapses, the number of synapses declines. The prefrontal cortex is more active in adolescents than in other age groups when certain kinds of cognitive tasks are performed, leading some to conclude that the brain areas that control inhibition and other regulatory behaviors are immature.

### How do patterns of sleep change in adolescence?

Adolescents tend to need more sleep than younger children and show a shift toward a later sleep-wake cycle. Because these tendencies conflict with many of the daily demands placed on adolescents by school, work, and other forces, many adolescents are sleep-deprived.

## COGNITIVE DEVELOPMENT IN ADOLESCENCE

### According to Piaget, what are the major features of thinking in the formal operational stage?

By the time children reach the *formal operational stage*, they can think abstractly and *hypothetically*, generating multiple solutions to a problem. Thought is also systematic. Adolescents in this stage may display beliefs in the *imaginary audience* and the *personal fable*.

### What changes are observed in children's scientific reasoning skills as they progress to adolescence?

Before adolescence, children display the ability to distinguish between theory and evidence and can identify which evidence supports a given hypothesis. Developmental changes are most apparent in the ability to design systematic experiments to test hypotheses. This ability can be enhanced with increased experiences in scientific problem solving, as well as with direct instruction on how to design an experiment without confounds.

## What role does the executive function play in cognitive processing? In what ways does the executive function change with development?

An important element in cognitive development is the ability to control and coordinate one's own cognitive processes, a concept called *executive function*. One element of executive function is *metacognition*, the child's awareness and knowledge of cognitive processes. This awareness, as well as the ability to regulate and monitor one's thinking, grow throughout the adolescent years. Still, adolescents may opt for risky choices in the face of promising large rewards.

## What are the main features of adolescents' decision-making behaviors?

Decisions may not always be made on the basis of rational, logical thinking but may be influenced by *judgment biases*, opinions based on vivid evidence or personal/social beliefs.

## INTELLIGENCE

## What are the main features of psychometric approaches to intelligence?

*Psychometric approaches* to intelligence emphasize individual differences in test scores. Several historically important ideas in this tradition include those of Spearman, who conceptualized a general intelligence factor called *g*, and Thurstone, who believed in seven primary mental abilities. In Cattell and Horn's view, intelligence could be seen as having two components: *fluid intelligence*, which was free of cultural influence, and *crystallized intelligence*, which referred to culturally derived skills. Fluid intelligence shows an earlier developmental decline than crystallized intelligence.

## What are the main features of information-processing approaches to intelligence?

Information-processing models focus on the mental activities of individuals as they engage in problem solving. Speed of processing and working memory capacity are two information-processing activities thought to be involved in intelligence.

## What are the principal ideas in Sternberg's and Gardner's theories of intelligence?

Sternberg's *triarchic theory* points to (1) the ability to adapt to the environment; (2) the ability to encode, combine, and compare stimuli; and (3) the ability to deal with novelty and to automatize as components of intelligence. Gardner's theory of multiple intelligences states that individuals can differ in discrete skill areas, such as language, music, mathematics, spatial perception, physical activities, personal awareness, social interaction, and nature.

## What assumptions do psychologists make about the distribution of IQ scores in the population?

*IQ scores* are normally distributed in the population. The mean IQ is 100 and the standard deviation is 15. Individuals who fall beyond two standard deviations from the mean are considered to be exceptional.

## How is giftedness defined? What are the unique ways in which gifted children process information? What are the behavioral characteristics of gifted children?

A child who obtains an IQ score greater than 130 is generally regarded as gifted. Gifted children are good planners and show skill in dealing with novelty. They are also efficient and fast in processing information. Gifted children tend to take advantage of educational opportunities, have good relationships with peers, and are generally well adjusted.

## What are the major features of the tests that have been used to assess intelligence in children?

IQ tests are designed by being administered to large groups of individuals to assess norms of performance and to establish the validity and reliability of the test. School-age children are most frequently tested with the Stanford-Binet Intelligence Scales or the Wechsler Intelligence Scale for Children–III (WISC-III). These tests are based on the psychometric model and assess a range of verbal, visual-spatial, quantitative, and problem-solving skills.

## What kinds of developmental outcomes do IQ scores predict?

IQ scores generally predict academic success but are not necessarily related to other measures of life satisfaction.

## What are the complexities in trying to assess the contributions of heredity to group differences in IQ?

Social class and racial differences in IQ scores illustrate the difficulty of drawing simple conclusions about the sources of intelligence. One problem is that estimates of heritability do not necessarily explain between-group differences in scores. Cross-fostering studies of children who were raised in environments that differed from those of their biological parents indicate that IQ scores rise in enriched environments but that scores are still more strongly related to educational levels of biological parents than to IQ levels of adoptive parents.

## How might concepts like test bias and stereotype threat play a part in explaining group differences in IQ?

*Test bias*, the idea that the content of IQ tests may not be fair to children from different cultural backgrounds, can help to explain group differences in IQ scores. Other factors in the testing situation may also interfere with children's optimal performance. *Stereotype threat*, the negative psychological impact of being sensitized to a stereotype about gender or ethnicity, has been linked to diminished performance on standardized tests.

## KEY TERMS AND CONCEPTS

crystallized intelligence (p. 515)

deviation IQ (p. 521)

executive function (p. 511)

fluid intelligence (p. 515)

formal operational stage (p. 508)

hypothetical reasoning (p. 508)

imaginary audience (p. 508)

intelligence quotient (IQ) (p. 521)

judgment bias (p. 513)

menarche (p. 500)

metacognition (p. 511)

personal fable (p. 508)

psychometric model (p. 514)

puberty (p. 500)

skeletal maturity (p. 500)

spermarche (p. 500)

stereotype threat (p. 524)

test bias (p. 524)

triarchic theory (p. 517)

# 15 SOCIAL AND EMOTIONAL DEVELOPMENT

Kelsey burst in the door of her house, dropped her backpack on the floor, and shrieked, "Mom! You'll never guess what happened in school today. I got the lead in the school musical! I am soooo excited! Can you believe it? It's me! Star of the show! Tah dah!" Kelsey was literally skipping around the kitchen, singing a verse from one of the songs she had been so earnestly rehearsing for the past two weeks.

"Honey, that's wonderful," her mother responded, at the same time giving her fourteen-year-old daughter a big bear hug. "I know you worked so hard for this, especially with all of the practicing you've been doing. What great news!"

"Yeah, it is great." But almost in a flash, Kelsey's exuberance waned. Her mother had turned away to finish unpacking groceries, but she wondered about Kelsey's long, silent pause.

"Mom, I forgot to tell you. I actually need to get back to school in half an hour. First rehearsal for everyone who was picked for the cast is actually today. We have to hurry." Kelsey knew that her mother didn't like to have last-minute plans sprung upon her.

development, as well as the development of self and identity, are linked to advances in cognition.

## RISK/RESILIENCE

### What factors promote risk or resilience during adolescence?

Many factors can put adolescents at risk in their social and emotional development. For example, the failure to regulate emotions, genetic propensities for depression and antisocial behaviors, and environments that are unsupportive of positive development are among them. Research has also identified several factors that are protective. Ethnic identity and community service are two examples of positive forces in the lives of adolescents.

# Chapter Review

## EMOTIONAL DEVELOPMENT IN ADOLESCENCE

### What are the distinctive features of emotional development in adolescence?

Adolescents experience more negative emotions and have more negative interactions with their parents than children of other ages.

### What is the relationship between emotion regulation and healthy adaptation in adolescence?

Adolescents who use active emotion regulation strategies, such as problem solving rather than denial or rumination, are less likely to develop adjustment problems, such as *internalizing* or *externalizing*.

### What factors are related to depression in adolescence?

Depression may have a genetic component but is also linked to family conflict, lack of parental warmth, and family violence. Adolescents may be especially prone to depression because of the large number of cognitive, physical, emotional, and social changes that take place at this time.

### How do secure attachments play a role in adolescent development?

Adolescents who have secure attachments display many positive qualities, including high self-esteem, a strong sense of personal identity, fewer depressive symptoms, and social competence. Secure attachments also help adolescents to develop *internal working models of relationships,* which can serve as the basis for the quality of their own relationships with friends, romantic partners, and eventually their own children.

## THE DEVELOPMENT OF SELF IN ADOLESCENCE

### What are the main features of self-definitions in adolescence?

Definitions of self may include conflicting dimensions, probably in response to demands from different social groups (for instance, friends versus parents). A reliance on social comparison diminishes in concepts of self as adolescents develop a firm sense of personal identity.

### In what ways does self as subject change during adolescence?

Adolescents widen the scope of their concepts of agency, individuality, stability, and reflection. They are more likely than younger children to acknowledge the influence of others and to draw on psychological, internal qualities as opposed to physical traits.

### What changes in self-esteem have been reported in adolescence?

Some researchers have reported a drop in self-esteem as children enter adolescence, especially for girls, but others claim that the changes are small and that within-group differences are larger than differences between boys and girls. The most important aspect of self-esteem is that it is associated with a number of positive developmental outcomes, including those that are long term.

### What is an identity crisis? Is there evidence that this is a significant part of adolescent development?

The *identity crisis* refers to the idea that adolescents, in particular, experience a period of uncertainty about who they are and what roles they will fill in society. Although research indicates that this is a time of heightened conflicts with parents as they explore new ways of behaving, most teenagers negotiate this time without undergoing a "crisis."

### How important is ethnic group identity for young people?

*Ethnic identity*, a sense of belonging to one's own cultural group, seems to benefit children and improve their understanding of others. It can also serve as a buffer against perceived discrimination.

## MORAL DEVELOPMENT IN ADOLESCENCE

### What are the main contributors to antisocial behaviors in adolescence?

Researchers have identified genetic, socialization, and contextual factors that contribute to the emergence of antisocial behaviors in youth. A decline in feelings of empathy may play a special role in the development of highly aggressive youth. Contemporary viewpoints emphasize the convergence of multiple risk and protective factors that result in antisocial behaviors.

### How do volunteering and community service promote positive youth development?

A substantial number of young people participate in some form of community service. Volunteering provides opportunities to develop identity, social connectedness, and civic knowledge.

## GENDER ROLES IN ADOLESCENCE

### What is the nature of gender concepts and behaviors during adolescence?

Adolescents show greater flexibility in their gender-role concepts. They show less sex segregation in their interactions with peers and are more tolerant of cross-sex behavior.

### What is the gender intensification hypothesis? Does research provide support for this hypothesis?

Gender intensification refers to a period of heightened adherence to traditional gender-role beliefs during the period of adolescence. Although some studies provide support for this concept, other research indicates that gender differences in beliefs diminish over adolescence.

### What kinds of problems do adolescents experience with sexual harassment?

Sexual harassment is a common occurrence in the lives of adolescents. Victims of harassment evidence a variety of reactions to these episodes, ranging from embarrassment to fear.

## KEY TERMS AND CONCEPTS

**ethnic identity** (p. 541)

**externalizing problem** (p. 533)

**gender intensification** (p. 546)

**identity crisis** (p. 541)

**internalizing problem** (p. 533)

**internal working model of relationships** (p. 535)

# CONTEXTS OF DEVELOPMENT

K evin's mother had come home from work early so that she could get ready for his soccer team's pasta party, scheduled at their house that night. As busy as she was with work, she wanted to participate in this tradition of having a pregame event to build team spirit. She knew that Kevin was incredibly busy, too, with homework, sports, band practice, and a peer tutoring project for which he had just volunteered. As she was thinking about the impossibly rapid pace of their lives, she heard Kevin's car pull into the driveway, and then his steps on the front porch.

"Hi, honey!" she sang out. "How was school today?"

"Fine," Kevin replied. And with that brief statement and a quick smile, he vanished into his room.

"Probably instant-messaging his friends," she thought. She recalled how the very same question about the school day would lead to a full-blown conversation only a few short years ago. She had learned from other parents that this was the way things went in many households with teenagers, both boys and

**SOCIOCULTURAL INFLUENCE** How do sociocultural factors influence the contexts of development in adolescence?

**RISK/RESILIENCE** What factors promote risk or resilience during adolescence?

girls. It was taking her some time to understand the world of adolescence—the need for privacy and independence, spending so much time with friends, and being on that computer! She knew, though, that she and her husband had to make some adjustments in their relationship with their son. He was, after all, about to enter the world as a full-fledged adult in only two years.

Throughout this text, as we have discussed the various contexts that impinge on child development, we have emphasized the primary role of the family in shaping cognitive, social, and emotional development. For adolescents, who are at the life stage at which forging autonomy and independence are pivotal developmental tasks, might it be that the family diminishes in importance as peers, media, and other outside influences assume a more prominent role? Kevin's behaviors, for example, suggest that friends and technology are certainly significant factors in his daily life. And even if the family does not assume a secondary role, how might roles in the family shift in response to adolescents' sometimes dramatic demands that they be treated as mature, responsible individuals, a lesson that Kevin's parents are in the process of learning?

As we discuss the different contexts in which adolescent development occurs, we need to emphasize an important point: the contexts for development are interrelated. This idea was highlighted in a major longitudinal study of the well-being of over 12,000 adolescents in the suburbs of Washington, DC. Children who had warm, supportive parents also tended to have stable friendships with peers who engaged in less deviant behavior. Children who grew up in "good neighborhoods" also had opportunities to attend high-quality schools. Most importantly, while there were statistical effects of families, peers, schools, and neighborhoods on successful academic performance, positive behaviors, and mental health among adolescents, the *combined* effect of these four contexts explained the most variation in positive development (Cook et al., 2002).

## THE FAMILY IN ADOLESCENCE

Perhaps because of the popular idea that adolescence involves rebellion against the adults in their lives, most of the research on family processes during this developmental time has centered on parents, as opposed to siblings or other family members. Do parent-child interactions indeed change during the teen years and, if so, how? Furthermore, what are the most effective parenting strategies for caregivers to use in order to promote healthy social and emotional adjustment and reduce the risky behaviors that some youth begin to manifest?

### RELATIONSHIPS WITH PARENTS

It is precisely adolescents' needs to express autonomy that typically precipitate a change in parent-child relations. As children press for independence, many parents find that they must adjust to form more egalitarian relationships with their children (Adams & Laursen, 2001; Collins, 1995). Perhaps contributing to the shifting nature of power relations within the family are changes in the way adolescents even think about their parents. Rather than seeing their parents as perfect and idealized individuals, they begin to consider them as people with both strengths and weaknesses

sibling backed down, and the submission negatively reinforced the child's aggression. In addition, although parents were observed to nag, scold, or threaten their children, they seldom followed through on their threats. Such sequences between the target child and other family members occurred as often as hundreds of times each day in the aggressive families. Over time, the target boys' aggression escalated in frequency and progressed to physical assaults.

At this point, many parents attempted to control their sons' aggressive behaviors, but in doing so they, too, became highly aggressive. The chains of coercion increased in duration to form long bursts of negative interactions and often resulted in hitting between parent and child. After extended experience in these maladaptive familial exchanges, boys became out of control and acted violently in settings outside the home, such as the school. Aggression in school was related, in turn, to poor peer relations and academic failure, adding to the chain of negative events in the boys' lives.

Can such extreme patterns of aggression be controlled? Patterson and his colleagues have intervened in the maladaptive interactions of aggressive families by training parents in basic child management skills (Patterson et al., 1975; Snyder, Reid, & Patterson, 2003). They focused on teaching parents to use discipline more effectively by dispensing more positive reinforcements for prosocial behaviors, using reasoning, disciplining consistently, and setting clear limits on even minor acts of aggression. Children significantly decreased their rates of deviant behavior after only a few weeks, and the results were maintained for as long as twelve months after the initial training period (Patterson & Fleischman, 1979). As an added benefit, parents' perceptions of their children became more positive (Patterson & Reid, 1973).

**Relationships with Stepparents**    Approximately 75 to 80 percent of divorced individuals remarry, the majority within five years after their divorce (Cherlin, 1992). As a consequence, a significant number of children, often teenagers by virtue of the timing of these events, live with a stepparent. For children who have experienced the separation of their own parents, the introduction of a new "parent" can represent yet another difficult transition, even though parental remarriage holds the promise of greater financial security and emotional support for both parents and children (Zill, Morrison, & Coiro, 1993).

Like divorce, a parent's remarriage often leads to aggression, noncompliance, poor peer relations, and academic difficulties among children (Bray, 1988; Zill, 1988). In fact, children with stepparents often resemble children with single parents on measures of problem behavior, academic success, and psychological adjustment (Hetherington & Henderson, 1997). As Figure 16.2 shows, a survey of more than

◑━ **KEY THEME**
**RISK/RESILIENCE**

◑━ **KEY THEME**
**RISK/RESILIENCE**

◁ **FIGURE 16.2**

**Family Type and Percentage of Children Experiencing Problems in School**

According to a national study involving more than 10,000 children in grades six though twelve, children living in stepfamilies resemble those living in single-parent homes (with their mother) in the patterns of difficulties they show in school. Both groups have more problems than children living in two-parent families, probably due to differences in parenting style among the groups.

*Source:* Adapted from Zill (1994).

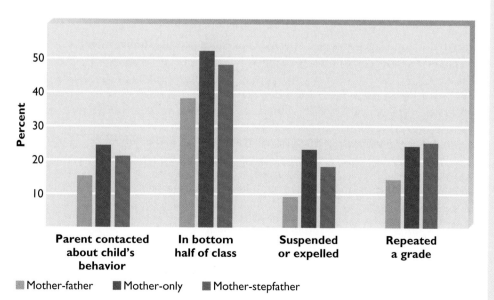

■ Mother-father  ■ Mother-only  ■ Mother-stepfather

10,000 children in grades six through twelve showed that children in stepfamilies look similar to children from single-parent families in the number of school-related problems experienced; both groups have more problems than children from two-parent families (Zill, 1994). The child usually has more difficulty adjusting when stepparents have larger numbers of their own children, when children from two previous marriages are assimilated into one family, and when the custodial parent and stepparent have a new biological child of their own (Hetherington, 1999; Hetherington, Henderson, & Reiss, 1999; Santrock & Sitterle, 1987; Zill, 1988). Adolescents have more problems adjusting to their new family than younger children, perhaps because their growing autonomy leads them to be more confrontational with parents (Brand, Clingempeel, & Bowen-Woodward, 1988; Hetherington & Jodl, 1994). Even if children had shown previous adjustment to the remarriage of their parents, problems can resurface in adolescence (Bray, 1999). In addition, girls in the middle school and adolescent years do not adjust as well as boys to parental remarriage; girls especially withdraw from their stepfather (Brand et al., 1988; Vuchinich et al., 1991).

Drawing from data collected in a national survey of parent-adolescent relations, Frank Furstenberg (1987) found that stepparents had reservations about their ability to discipline and provide affection to stepchildren. At the same time, stepchildren corroborated that stepparents were less involved than their biological parents in care and supervision. Other researchers examining stepparent-stepchild relationships over time confirm that stepparents typically do not fit the profile of authoritative parenting described earlier in this chapter (Hetherington & Jodl, 1994), and thus the benefits of that parenting style for children are not realized. If anything, stepparents often look like the disengaged parents described earlier in this book; they provide less support for and control over the behavior of their stepchildren compared with their biological children (Mekos, Hetherington, & Reiss, 1996). Moreover, when stepparents do exert control, adolescents tend to show greater aggression, noncompliance, and other problem behaviors (Kim, Hetherington, & Reiss, 1999).

Some difficulties in stepfamilies may stem from the uncertain social roles of stepparents. Stepparents believe that they should play an active role in parenting but are also reluctant to become too involved with their stepchildren (Fine, Coleman, & Ganong, 1999). The advice given by one sixteen-year-old stepson reveals just how precise a balance stepparents must strike.

> The stepparent first would be to give room to the children, but still on the same spectrum, keep control basically, keep disciplining but I wouldn't say that you should make them, kinda let them ease into it. You shouldn't jump into something right away which is completely new. (Fine et al., 1999, p. 283)

Parental remarriage presents special challenges to all family members, which researchers are just beginning to explore.

## F O R ◆ Y O U R ◆ R E V I E W

◆ How do relationships with parents change during adolescence?

◆ What are the elements of successful parenting of adolescents?

◆ What social class and ethnic group differences have been observed in parenting?

◆ How do coercive cycles in parenting develop?

◆ What issues arise in children's relationships with stepparents?

**Table 16.1   How Do Adolescents Spend Their Free Time?**

Reed Larson compiled the results of forty-five studies of how adolescents in various cultures spend their work and free-time hours per day. A portion of the results is shown here. You should note that several of the activities in the "free time" category include opportunities to interact with peers. What do the data suggest about cross-cultural differences in how adolescents spend their time?

| Activity | United States | Europe | East Asia |
|---|---|---|---|
| Household labor | 20–40 min | 20–40 min | 10–20 min |
| Paid labor | 40–60 min | 10–20 min | 1–10 min |
| Schoolwork | 3.0–4.5 hr | 4.0–5.5 hr | 5.5–7.5 hr |
| **Total work time** | **4–6 hr** | **4.5–6.5 hr** | **6–8 hr** |
| TV viewing | 1.5–2.5 hr | 1.5–2.5 hr | 1.5–2.5 hr |
| Talking | 2–3 hr | Insufficient data | 45–60 min |
| Sports | 30–60 min | 20–80 min | 1–20 min |
| Structured voluntary activities | 10–20 min | 1.0–20 min | 0–10 min |
| **Total free time** | **6.5–8.0 hr** | **5.5–7.5 hr** | **4.0–5.5 hr** |

*Source:* Larson (2001).

## PEER RELATIONSHIPS IN ADOLESCENCE

By the time they reach adolescence, children spend considerable free time with their peers, at least in the United States. In a review of forty-five studies of how adolescents in different countries spend their daily time (see Table 16.1), Reed Larson found that American youth have more unrestricted time than children in Europe or Asia and that much of this time is spent with friends (Larson, 2001). Although time spent with peers might provide important opportunities to develop social skills and supportive relationships, some research is beginning to indicate that the amount of unstructured time spent with peers without adult supervision is related to depression, conduct problems, and lower grades in school. On the other hand, free time spent with parents and other adults or participating in such structured activities as hobbies, sports, and extracurricular activities at school predicts better school success and fewer conduct problems (Mahoney, 2000; McHale, Crouter, & Tucker, 2001).

Peer relations during adolescence become more intense on one level and involve larger networks on another level. Adolescents form close, intimate friendships with a subset of their peers, often those who resemble themselves in certain traits, such as an orientation to academics (Iervolino et al., 2002). Many children also form **cliques**, groups of five to ten children, usually in the same class at school, who frequently interact together (Brown, 1989). Clique membership is frequently supplemented by identification with a **crowd**, a larger group of peers with a specific reputation, such as "jocks" or "brains" Members of crowds do not necessarily spend time together but share a label based on a stereotype. Interestingly, even though youngsters may see themselves as members of particular cliques, their membership in crowds is often identified or labeled by others (Brown, 1989). In other words, a girl may not see herself as a "brain" but receive that label from peers who observe her academic achievements and studious behaviors. Membership in cliques and crowds in the middle and later school years reflects the child's growing need for group belonging at a time when he is orienting away from parents and other adults. At the same time, the values that parents encourage can influence the crowds with which their adolescent children affiliate themselves. If a parent encourages achievement, for example, the child's academic success may place her in the group of "brains" (Brown et al., 1993). The norms of cliques and crowds can be powerful shapers of behavior; they often provide the adolescent with prescriptions on how

**clique**   Peer group of five to ten children who frequently interact together.

**crowds**   Large group of peers characterized by specific traits or reputation.

Adolescents who spend time with their peers in structured activities such as extracurricular clubs at school (as opposed to unstructured time with peers) are at less risk for academic and behavioral problems.

to dress, act, and even what ambitions to have for the future. However, the degree to which the group has influence depends on how strongly the adolescent identifies with that group (Kiesner et al., 2002).

As adolescents approach young adulthood and feel more secure about their self-identity, they are less interested in cliques and crowds, and become oriented once again toward relationships with individuals. In one study, third- through twelfth-graders were asked to list their closest friends in the entire school, as well as the people they spent time with (Shrum & Cheek, 1987). Analysis of the patterns of relationships among children showed a sharp decline toward later adolescence in the percentage of students who were members of cliques.

One other significant change in adolescence is that some peer relations begin to reflect interest in the opposite sex. The time spent with same-sex peers does not decline in adolescence, but time spent with an opposite-sex peer increases substantially during high school (Richards et al., 1998). As they grow older, and as they begin to spend increasing time with their romantic partners, adolescents spend less time with family members. Nonetheless, they still maintain close emotional ties with the family, rating parents and romantic partners as their most influential relationships (Laursen & Williams, 1997).

## PEER PRESSURE AND CONFORMITY

One of the most widely accepted beliefs about peer groups is that they control the behavior of children, sometimes more than parents and other adults would like. In fact, peer pressure *is* a very real phenomenon. When seventh- through twelfth-graders were asked to rate how much pressure they felt from agemates in several domains, they did report pressure, and the greatest pressure was simply to be involved with peers: spend time with them, go to parties, and otherwise associate with them (Brown, Clasen, & Eicher, 1986; Clasen & Brown, 1985). They also felt pressure to excel and to complete their education. Contrary to popular opinion, however, they reported the least peer pressure to engage in misconduct, such as smoking, drinking, or having sexual relations. Older adolescents, however, felt more pressure to engage in misconduct than younger adolescents did.

How willing are children to conform to these peer pressures? Again, when researchers ask them, children give different answers depending on their age (Berndt, 1979; Brown, Clasen, & Eicher, 1986; Gavin & Furman, 1989). Relative to

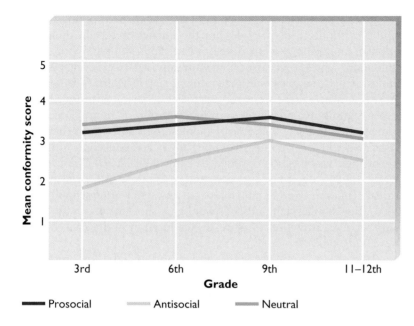

◀ **FIGURE 16.3**

**Developmental Changes in Conformity to Peer Pressure**

Conformity to peer pressure, whether it involves prosocial, antisocial, or neutral behavior, peaks in early adolescence, then declines. The higher numbers in this graph represent greater willingness to conform.

*Source:* Adapted from Berndt (1979).

other ages, vulnerability to peer pressure peaks in early adolescence, usually between the sixth and ninth grades (see Figure 16.3). However, note in Figure 16.3 that, in terms of actual conformity scores, most children would not succumb to peer pressure; their average ratings are in the middle of the rating scale and correspond to a neutral response (Berndt, 1999). By late adolescence the influence of peers on conformity declines even further.

For some children, though, the peer group plays an important part in influencing behaviors and choices. By virtue of their style of parenting, parents may be responsible for adolescents' tendencies to seek out the peer group. When parents of adolescents are unresponsive to their children and maintain their power and restrictiveness, their children tend to be more noticeably oriented to their peer group (Bogenschneider et al., 1998; Fuligni & Eccles, 1993). Adolescents who develop an extreme orientation to their peer group, to the extent that they will ignore parents and schoolwork in order to remain popular, are more likely to become involved with alcohol and drug use, to skip classes, and to demonstrate other problem behaviors (Fuligni et al., 2001).

Researchers now believe that studying "peer pressure" as a general phenomenon is not as revealing as examining the roles that *specific* peers play in the child's development. For example, some friends may be more influential than others, and their influence may be greater in some domains than in others, such as aggression as opposed to school achievement. In addition, a child's vulnerability to peer influences probably depends to some degree on his level of emotional and cognitive development (Berndt, 1999; Hartup, 1999). Thus a full understanding of peer influences will have to take these complexities into account.

## PEER POPULARITY

Peer popularity has both positive and negative consequences associated with it. In one study, popular teens tended to show good self-control, sensitivity to the views of others, and healthy emotional relationships with parents and friends. At the same time, those who were popular at age thirteen were more likely to show increases in alcohol and marijuana use and minor delinquent behavior a year later. According to the *popularity-socialization hypothesis*, popular teens experience more opportunities to be socialized by their agemates than those who are less popular, subjecting them to both the positive and the negative influences of peers (Allen et al., 2005).

What personal qualities are associated with peer popularity? Social skills, no doubt, continue to play a role, but the impact of certain dimensions of personal behavior may change with development. For example, we noted that, in middle childhood, aggression is associated with unpopularity among peers. To some degree, things change in adolescence. According to Terrie Moffit (1993), the adolescent years are a time when some teens see antisocial behavior as more desirable because it is a clear sign of breaking away from the control of parents. Consistent with this idea, some studies indicate that, in early adolescence, antisocial behavior may actually be associated with peer popularity, especially if it is conceived of as *perceived popularity*, or high visibility (as opposed to being well liked). Thus, for example, eighth-grade children described by peers and teachers as antisocial were named as individuals children would want to spend time with after school (Kiesner & Pastore, 2005). In a similar vein, middle school girls show attraction to aggressive boys, and boys show an attraction to aggressive children of both sexes (Bukowski, Sippola, & Newcomb, 2000).

Two recent studies provide some additional clues about the social dynamics of aggression and popularity. Thomas Farmer and his colleagues (Farmer et al., 2003) surveyed seventh- and eighth-graders, as well as their peers and teachers, and found two types of aggressive children: "tough" boys who were aggressive but also popular and socially skilled, and "troubled boys" who were aggressive, unpopular, and unskilled socially. The first group, more than the second, tended to be leaders who were involved in extracurricular activities and were very influential in peer groups. Other researchers have also shown that overt, but especially *relational*, aggression is associated with perceived popularity (Cillessen & Mayeux, 2004; Rose et al., 2004). Recall that relational aggression refers to tactics such as ignoring others or leaving them out of social activities. Together, these research findings seem to tell a more complicated story: that, in the transition from elementary school to middle school, when many peer groups become shifted or realigned, some children find forceful ways to exert social power. They manipulate others, assert themselves, and generally "call the shots" with their peers. In many cases, their efforts at using aggression to attain social status are successful, at least in the short run. However, the long-term outcomes of behaving in this way are still not known (Cillessen & Rose, 2005).

## FRIENDSHIPS

By adolescence, the importance of close friendship is firmly solidified. Adolescents from such diverse cultures as China and Iceland claim strong loyalty to their close friends (Keller et al., 1998). Why are friends important? In our culture, adolescents say they value the ability to share thoughts and feelings with friends and expect mutual understanding and self-disclosure in friendships (Bigelow & LaGaipa, 1975; Furman & Bierman, 1984). They share problems, solutions to those problems, and private feelings with friends. These qualities fit the needs of individuals who are struggling to define who they are and who they will become. A sample exchange between two adolescent friends drawn from Parker and Gottman's (1989) research illustrates these themes:

A: *I don't know. Gosh, I have no idea what I want to do. And it really doesn't bother me that much that I don't have my future planned.* [laughs]

B: [laughs]

A: [laughs] *Like it bothers my Dad a lot, but it doesn't bother me.*

B: *Just tell your dad what I always tell my Dad: "Dad, I am."*

A: [laughs] *Exactly!*

B: *And whatever happens tomorrow, I still will be!*

Adolescents continue to prefer same-sex friends, although the frequency of boy-girl interactions increases. At this age, similarities in attitudes about academics, dating, drinking, smoking, and drug use influence whether children become friends (Dishion, Andrews, & Crosby, 1995; Epstein, 1983; Tolson & Urberg, 1993). Adolescent friendships become more selective with age; teenagers have fewer mutual friends than younger children do, but mutual friends comprise a greater proportion of their total network of friends. The tendency for girls to have smaller friendship networks than boys, observed earlier in childhood, disappears to some degree, but girls' friendships remain marked by emotional intensity and, perhaps because of this, even fragility (Benenson & Christakos, 2003; Urberg et al., 1995). Adolescents also say that the time they spend with their friends is the most enjoyable part of their day (Csikszentmihalyi & Larson, 1984). Friendship is thus a key element in the social and emotional life of the older child.

The relationship styles cultivated in friendships may extend to relations with others later in life. Harry Stack Sullivan (1953) believed that the capacity for intimacy nurtured by same-sex friendships in childhood provides the foundation for intimacy in more mature adult relationships. The failure to acquire this capacity in the formative years of childhood may impair a person's later functioning as a romantic partner, spouse, or parent. More recent studies confirm that there is a correlation between relational styles used with friends and romantic partners (Furman, 1999). For example, adolescents who perceive their friendships as supportive also tend to see their romantic relationships as supportive (Connolly, Furman, & Konarski, 2000).

Friends can encourage many positive qualities, such as the tendency to engage in prosocial behavior. When their friends are prosocial, adolescents express altruistic goals (for instance, they say that they try to share or cheer someone up if something has gone wrong), and are described by peers as behaving prosocially a year later (Barry & Wentzel, 2006). But research has also revealed that friendships may not always be positive and emotionally supportive. Among rejected children, for example, interactions with their friends tend to be more negative than among other children (Rubin, Bukowski, & Parker, 1998). Friends can also be a factor in deviant behavior, especially among children who are predisposed to have conduct problems themselves. Thomas Dishion and his colleagues (Dishion, Patterson, & Griesler, 1994) observed that ten-year-old aggressive boys who had been rejected by most of their peers often became friends with other aggressive boys. Over time, they conversed more about deviant behavior, such as substance abuse and delinquency, a form of talk for which deviant peers typically reward one another (Dishion et al., 1996). By age fourteen, association with antisocial friends was found to contribute statistically to the tendency to engage in deviant behaviors. These findings suggest that breaking the cycle of antisocial behavior may require more than intervening in an individual child's pattern of behaviors; monitoring his or her friendship networks may be just as important. Adolescence is an especially vulnerable time for the negative influences of antisocial friends (Berndt, Hawkins, & Jiao, 1999). In addition, association with deviant friends is especially likely when parents fail to be nurturant and involved and to monitor their adolescents' behaviors (Ary et al., 1999; Scaramella et al., 2002).

**KEY THEME**
RISK/RESILIENCE

## ROMANTIC RELATIONSHIPS

Romantic relationships seem to grow in a specific sequence for many adolescents. They usually begin with mixed-sex interactions that involve casual and informal boy-girl groups in early adolescence. This type of interaction is often followed by group dating, and finally romantic relationships with a single partner (Connolly et al., 2004). Most teens report that they have "fallen in love" and that they have been involved in a serious romantic relationship in high school, according to the results of one study (Regan et al., 2004). However, although teenagers are deeply interested in romantic relationships, their relationships are generally not long-enduring, especially early in adolescence (Davies & Windle, 2000). Only about 33 percent report having a current girlfriend or boyfriend by age 15 or 16 (Connolly & Johnson, 1996).

Unlike more mature romantic relationships, which offer mutual support and caregiving, romantic relationships at this time take on significance merely because adolescents feel it is important to be involved with someone romantically (Furman, 2002). Early romantic relationships function as opportunities to explore sexuality and are a source of companionship. Later in adolescence, however, romantic relationships take on a greater caregiving and mutual support function, qualities associated with mature relationships in adulthood (Furman & Wehner, 1994).

F O R • Y O U R • R E V I E W

* What are the characteristics of peer relationships during adolescence?

* When does peer pressure reach its peak? What factors are related to vulnerability to peer pressure?

* What factors are related to peer popularity in adolescence?

* What are the qualities of children's friendships during adolescence?

* What are the qualities of romantic relationships in adolescence?

## SCHOOL

Clearly, a significant part of most adolescents' daily life continues to be the school experience. Academic demands increase, as do opportunities to explore personal interests, such as sports, drama, music, and other domains, through formal study or extracurricular activities. There is much more that can be said about teenagers' experiences in the educational system than can be discussed in this book. In this section, we take the opportunity to describe two school-related topics that seem to be especially relevant to development in adolescence.

### SCHOOL TRANSITIONS

Aside from the transition to kindergarten, a second important shift occurs when children move from elementary school to a middle or junior high school. In the United States, this transition is usually the visible signal of childhood's end and the beginning of adolescence. Children must adapt to a new physical environment, new teachers, and, often, new peers; and now, rather than staying with the same classmates in the same room for most of the school day, they move from class to class, each usually with its own set of students. Frequently the difference in student body size is dramatic. In one study, the mean school size from grade six to grade seven increased from 466 to 1,307, and the mean number of children in each grade went from 59 to 403 (Simmons et al., 1987). It is no wonder that many researchers report a decline in school satisfaction and academic motivation in pre- and early adolescence, as well as a drop in grades and participation in extracurricular activities (Eccles, Midgley, et al., 1993; Hirsch & Rapkin, 1987; Schulenberg, Asp, & Petersen, 1984; Simmons & Blyth, 1987).

We have already noted that some researchers have observed a decline in self-esteem at this time, particularly among preadolescent girls (Hirsch & Rapkin, 1987; Simmons et al., 1979). Early-maturing sixth-grade girls display better images of themselves when they attend schools with kindergarten through eighth-grade classes, presumably because they feel less pressured to adopt dating and other activities that become prevalent among seventh- and eighth-graders. On the other hand, those girls entering puberty at more typical ages and at about the same time that they

## NEIGHBORHOODS

### What aspects of development are known to be influenced by neighborhoods?

The neighborhoods in which children grow up have an effect on academic success, mental health, and sexual behavior. Neighborhoods influence development through the institutional resources they provide, the parenting styles practiced in response to safety, the support network perceived to exist in the neighborhood, and the individual and collective efforts of community residents to supervise and monitor the development of youth.

### What is the impact on adolescents of exposure to violence? What factors promote successful adaptation to this exposure?

Exposure to violence is linked to PTSD, depression, anxiety, substance use, and the tendency to commit aggressive acts. Modeling and coaching youth in active, problem-focused coping strategies can help to mitigate these effects, as does the practice of religious and spiritual behaviors.

### What adverse developmental outcomes do some children from affluent families manifest?

For some children from affluent families, high pressures to achieve, combined with lack of emotional connection to parents, are associated with depression, anxiety, and substance use.

### What are the most serious consequences for children experiencing war, and what procedures may be most effective in dealing with those consequences?

Children who witness war evidence the symptoms of PTSD, especially within the first year of their exposure. Successful interventions have involved placing children in a secure environment, as well as providing support to caregivers, who have the potential to, in turn, be helpful to their children.

## KEY TERMS AND CONCEPTS

**clique** (p. 559)

**coercive cycle** (p. 556)

**crowds** (p. 559)

# Pathways: Connecting the Story of Development

| | Infancy (0–2 years) | Early Childhood (2–6 years) |
|---|---|---|
| **Physical Development** | • Evidences rapid gains in height and weight, with faster rates of growth in the head region and regions nearer the center of the body<br>• Shows period of rapid brain development, including formation and pruning of synapses<br>• Shows basic learning capabilities in the form of habituation, operant and classical conditioning, and imitation<br>• Shows improvements in visual accommodation, saccadic movements, acuity, and vergence<br>• Attracted first to external features of objects and to movement, and later to internal features of objects<br>• Localizes sounds<br>• Recognizes melodic rhythms and other features of music<br>• Shows sensitivity to smells, tastes, and tactile stimuli | • Shows advances in gross motor skills such as running, jumping, and skipping<br>• Evidences slower but regular increases in size<br>• Shows evidence of implicit learning |
| **Cognitive/ Language Development** | • Attends to increasingly complex patterns including those with facelike organization<br>• Responsive to biological motion<br>• Shows signs of depth perception<br>• Shows intermodal perception<br>• Develops *means-ends behavior*<br>• Attains the *object concept*<br>• Shows sensitivity to changes in number<br>• Relies on egocentric and landmark cues to locate objects<br>• Classifies objects according to physical similarities, as well as thematic and simple taxonomic relations<br>• Distinguishes between animate and inanimate objects<br>• Shows recognition memory for simple stimuli<br>• Shows long-term recall in elicited imitation tasks<br>• Shows simple problem-solving behaviors, including transfer<br>• Discriminates among phonemes<br>• Discriminates own language from others<br>• Detects words in speech stream<br>• Produces gestures to communicate<br>• Comprehends many words<br>• Speaks in single-word utterances | • Shows gains in ability to make perceptual discriminations<br>• Can classify according to basic-level concepts<br>• Understands the meaning of simple number terms, and eventually the basic principles of counting<br>• Displays good intuitions about mathematical operations such as addition and forming fractions<br>• Uses landmark cues to negotiate spatial environments<br>• Uses geometric cues to aid spatial location<br>• Begins to be able to read maps<br>• Realizes that others can have different visual perspectives<br>• Develops a *theory of mind*<br>• Shows elementary planning activities<br>• Displays knowledge of scripts<br>• Displays autobiographical memory<br>• By age three, attains *representational insight*<br>• Uses two- and then multiword utterances<br>• Uses morphemes, negatives, questions, and passive voice<br>• Shows rapid growth in vocabulary and use of syntax<br>• Displays overregularizations<br>• Shows growth in referential communication and other aspects of pragmatics |
| **Social/ Emotional Development** | • Displays basic emotions<br>• Imitates emotional expressions of others<br>• Recognizes others' emotions<br>• Begins to regulate own emotions through withdrawal or distraction<br>• Forms attachments<br>• Recognizes self<br>• Begins to be able to delay gratification<br>• Shows early signs of agency<br>• Shows intersubjectivity<br>• Shows early signs of empathy | • Displays self-conscious emotions<br>• Uses language to express emotions<br>• Understands causes and consequences of emotions<br>• Shows more effective emotion regulation strategies and, eventually, a decline in tantrums<br>• Displays more complex aspects of attachment by considering motives, feelings of caregiver<br>• Shows decline in separation distress and other attachment behaviors typical of infants<br>• Has notion of categorical self<br>• Displays overt behaviors signaling independence<br>• Shows first signs of self-control<br>• Shows early signs of conscience and altruism<br>• Thinks in terms of preconventional ideas<br>• Shows awareness of own gender and gender stereotypes |

| MIDDLE CHILDHOOD (6–11 YEARS) | ADOLESCENCE (11–18 YEARS) | |
|---|---|---|
| • Shows more efficient and better-controlled motor skills<br>• Becomes more adept at fine-motor coordination<br>• Shows steady growth in physical size | • Shows a physical growth spurt that does not conform to the principles of cephalocaudal and proximodistal development<br>• Shows signs of sexual maturity and gains the ability to reproduce<br>• Evidences maturation of frontal regions of the brain | **Physical Development** |
| • Shows systematic and efficient attention strategies<br>• Shows logical thought on conservation tasks but only in the presence of real objects or images<br>• Develops increasing memory span<br>• Produces various kinds of memory strategies to enhance recall<br>• Shows greater control of cognitive processing<br>• Shows gains in ability to plan the steps in problem solving<br>• Becomes more flexible in strategy use<br>• Shows growth in metacognition<br>• Shows metalinguistic awareness including appreciation of humor and metaphor | • Can think abstractly and *hypothetically*, generating multiple solutions to a problem<br>• May display beliefs in the *imaginary audience* and the *personal fable*<br>• Shows growth in scientific reasoning skills<br>• Shows growth in *executive function*<br>• Shows evidence of *judgment biases* | **Cognitive/ Language Development** |
| • Shows understanding of display rules<br>• Engages in social-comparison<br>• Displays global self-esteem<br>• Shows mastery orientation<br>• Exercises self-regulation through internalized language<br>• Thinks in terms of moral realism or conventional ideas<br>• Shows greater knowledge of and greater flexibility toward gender stereotypes | • Shows more negative emotions than before<br>• Uses early attachments as basis for more mature relationships<br>• Defines self in terms of social roles<br>• Views self from multiple and conflicting perspectives<br>• Period of identity formation<br>• Thinks in terms of moral relativism or postconventional ideas<br>• Shows signs of gender intensification | **Social/ Emotional Development** |

# GLOSSARY

**Accommodation**   In Piagetian theory, a component of adaptation; process of modification in thinking (schemes) that takes place when old ways of understanding something no longer fit.

**Adaptation**   In Piagetian theory, the inborn tendency to adjust or become more attuned to conditions imposed by the environment; takes place through assimilation and accommodation.

**Age-history confound**   In longitudinal studies, the co-occurrence of historical factors with changes in age; affects the ability to interpret results.

**Allele**   Alternate form of a specific gene; provides a genetic basis for many individual differences.

**Altruism**   Behavior carried out to help another without expectation of reward.

**Ambivalent (resistant) attachment**   Insecure attachment in which the infant shows separation protest but also distress upon the caregiver's return.

**Amniocentesis**   Method of sampling the fluid surrounding the developing fetus through insertion of a needle; used to diagnose fetal genetic and developmental disorders.

**Amniotic sac**   Fluid-filled, transparent protective membrane surrounding the fetus.

**Analogical transfer**   Ability to employ the solution to one problem in other, similar problems.

**Androgen**   Class of male or masculinizing hormones.

**Animism**   Attribution of lifelike qualities to inanimate objects.

**A-not-B error**   Error that an infant makes when an object is hidden in location A, found by the infant, and then, in full view of the infant, moved to location B. Piaget observed that the child will mistakenly but persistently search for the object in location A.

**Artificialism**   Belief that naturally occurring events are caused by people.

**Assimilation**   In Piagetian theory, a component of adaptation; process of interpreting an experience in terms of current ways (schemes) of understanding things.

**Attachment**   Strong emotional bond that emerges between infant and caregiver.

**Attention**   State of alertness or arousal that allows the individual to focus on a selected aspect of the environment.

**Authoritarian parent**   Parent who relies on coercive techniques to discipline the child and displays a low level of nurturance.

**Authoritative parent**   Parent who sets limits on a child's behavior using reasoning and explanation and displays a high degree of nurturance.

**Autobiographical memory**   Memory for specific events in one's own life.

**Autosome**   One of twenty-two pairs of homologous chromosomes. The two members of each pair are similar in size, shape, and genetic function. The two sex chromosomes are excluded from this class.

**Babbling**   Consonant-vowel utterances that characterize the infant's first attempts to vocalize.

**Basic (primary) emotion**   Emotion, such as joy, sadness, or surprise, that appears early in infancy and seems to have a biological foundation.

**Behavior analysis**   Learning theory perspective that explains the development of behavior according to the principles of classical and operant conditioning.

**Behavior genetics**   Study of how characteristics and behaviors of individuals, such as intelligence and personality, are influenced by the interaction between genotype and experience.

**Broca's area**   Portion of the cerebral cortex that controls expressive language.

**Canalization**   Concept that the development of some attributes is governed primarily by the genotype and that only extreme environmental conditions will alter the phenotypic pattern for these attributes.

**Canonical babbling**   Repetition of simple consonant-vowel combinations in well-formed syllables.

**Cardinality**   Principle that the last number in a set of counted numbers refers to the number in that set.

**Case study**   In-depth description of psychological characteristics and behaviors of an individual, often in the form of a narrative.

**Catch-up growth**   Increase in growth rate after some factor, such as illness or poor nutrition, has disrupted the expected, normal growth rate.

**Categorical perception**   Inability to distinguish among sounds that vary on some basic physical dimension except when those sounds lie at opposite sides of a critical juncture point on that dimension.

**Categorical self**   Self-classification in terms of membership in certain groups based on sex, age, skills, what one owns, where one lives, and who one's friends are.

**Centration**   In Piagetian theory, tendency of the child to focus on only one aspect of a problem.

**Cephalocaudal development**   Pattern in which organs, systems, and motor movements near the head tend to develop earlier than those near the feet.

**Chorionic villus sampling**   Method of sampling fetal chorionic cells; used to diagnose embryonic genetic and developmental disorders.

**Chromosome**   Threadlike structure of DNA, located in the nucleus of cells, which forms a collection of genes. A human body cell normally contains forty-six chromosomes.

**Chronosystem**   In Bronfenbrenner's ecological systems theory, the constantly changing temporal component of the environment that can influence development.

**Clinical method**   Flexible, open-ended interview method in which questions are modified in reaction to the child's responses.

**Clique**   Peer group of five to ten children who frequently interact together.

**Codominance**   Condition in which individual, unblended characteristics of two alleles are reflected in the phenotype.

**Coercive cycle**   Pattern of escalating negative reciprocal interactions.

**Cognition**   Processes involved in thinking and mental activity, such as attention, memory, and problem solving.

**Cognitive-developmental theory**   Theoretical orientation, most frequently associated with Piaget, emphasizing the active construction of psychological structures to interpret experience.

**Cohort effect**   All the characteristics shared by individuals growing up in a specific social and historical context.

**Collaborative learning**   Peer-centered learning in which students work together on academic problems with the goal of arriving at solutions that are more effective than solutions that could have been derived from individual effort alone.

**Concepts**   Definition of a set of information on the basis of some general or abstract principle.

**Concordance rate**   Percentage of pairs of twins in which both members have a specific trait identified in one twin.

**Concrete operational stage**   In Piagetian theory, the third stage of development, from approximately seven to eleven years of age, in which thought is logical when stimuli are physically present.

**Conditioned response (CR)**   Learned response that is exhibited to a previously neutral stimulus (CS) as a result of pairing the CS with an unconditioned stimulus (UCS).

**Conditioned stimulus (CS)**   Neutral stimulus that begins to elicit a response similar to the unconditioned stimulus (UCS) with which it has been paired.

**Conservation task**   Problem that requires the child to make judgments about the equivalence of two displays; used to assess stage of cognitive development.

**Contextual models**   theories of development that are concerned with the effects of a broad range of biological, physical, and socio-cultural settings on the process of development.

**Control theory**   Hypothesis about parent-child interactions suggesting that the intensity of one partner's behavior affects the intensity of the other's response.

**Conventional level**   In Kohlberg's theory, the second level of moral reasoning, in which the child conforms to the norms of the majority and wishes to preserve the social order.

**Cooing**   Vowel-like utterances that characterize the infant's first attempts to vocalize.

**Cooperative learning**   Peer-centered learning experience in which students work together in small groups to solve academic problems.

**Cooperative play**   Interactive play in which children's actions are reciprocal.

**Core knowledge hypothesis**   The idea that infants possess innate knowledge of certain properties of objects.

**Correlation coefficient ($r$)**   Statistical measure, ranging from +1.00 to −1.00, that summarizes the strength and direction of the relationship between two variables; does not provide information about causation.

**Correlational study**   Study that assesses whether changes in one variable are accompanied by systematic changes in another variable.

**Cross-cultural study**   Study that compares individuals in different cultural contexts.

**Crossing over**   Process during the first stage of meiosis when genetic material is exchanged between autosomes.

**Cross-sectional study**   Study in which individuals of different ages are examined at the same point in time.

**Crowds**   Large group of peers characterized by specific traits or reputation.

**Crystallized intelligence**   Mental skills derived from cultural experience.

**Cultural compatibility hypothesis**   Theory that school instruction is most effective if it is consistent with the practices of the child's background culture.

**Debriefing**   Providing research participants with a statement of the true goals of a study after initially deceiving them or omitting information about its purposes.

**Deferred imitation**   Ability to imitate a model's behavior hours, days, and even weeks after observation.

**Delay of gratification**   Capacity to wait before performing a tempting activity or attaining some highly desired outcome; a measure of ability to regulate one's own behavior.

**Deoxyribonucleic acid (DNA)**   Long, spiral staircaselike sequence of molecules created by nucleotides identified with the blueprint for genetic inheritance.

**Dependent variable**   Behavior that is measured; suspected effect of an experimental manipulation.

**Development**   Physical and psychological changes in the individual over a lifetime.

**Developmental delay**   The condition children are said to have when they deviate noticeably from motor, cognitive, or language milestones in one or more areas.

**Developmental psychology**   Systematic and scientific study of changes in human behaviors and mental activities over time.

**Deviation IQ**   IQ score computed by comparing the child's performance with that of a standardization sample

**Disorganized/disoriented attachment**   Infant-caregiver relations categorized by the infant's fear of the caregiver, confused facial expressions, and a combination of avoidant and ambivalent attachment behaviors.

**Display rule**   Cultural guideline concerning when, how, and to what degree to display emotions.

**Dominant allele**   Allele whose characteristics are reflected in the phenotype even when part of a heterozygous genotype. Its genetic characteristics tend to mask the characteristics of other alleles.

**Down syndrome**   Disorder resulting from an extra chromosomal material on pair number twenty-one; associated with mental retardation and distinct physical features.

**Dynamic systems theory**   Theoretical orientation that explains development as the emerging organization arising from the interaction of many different processes.

**Ecological systems theory**   Bronfenbrenner's theory that development is influenced by experiences arising from broader social and cultural systems as well as a child's immediate surroundings.

**Effectance motivation**   Inborn desire theorized by Robert White to be the basis for the infant's and child's efforts to master and gain control of the environment.

**Effortful control**   Ability to suppress undesirable responses for less dominant ones that are considered socially or morally more acceptable.

**Egocentric**   Term applied to the preoperational child's inability to separate his or her own perspective from those of others.

**Elaboration**   Memory strategy in which individuals link items to be remembered in the form of an image or a sentence.

**Elicited imitation**   Method in which older infants and preschoolers must repeat a sequence of actions demonstrated by the experimenter.

**Embryonic period**   Period of prenatal development during which major biological organs and systems form; begins about the tenth to fourteenth day after conception and ends about the eighth week after conception.

**Emotion**  Complex behavior involving physiological, expressive, and experiential components produced in response to some internal or external event.

**Empathy**  Understanding and sharing of the feelings of others.

**Empiricism**  Theory that environmental experiences shape the individual; more specifically, that all knowledge is derived from sensory experiences.

**Episodic memory**  Memory for events that took place at a specific time and place.

**Equilibration**  In Piagetian theory, an innate self-regulatory process that, through accommodation and assimilation, results in more organized and powerful schemes for adapting to the environment.

**Ethnic identity**  The sense of belonging to a particular cultural group.

**Ethnography**  Set of methods, including observations and interviews, used by researchers to describe the behaviors and underlying meaning systems within a given culture.

**Ethology**  Theoretical orientation and discipline concerned with the evolutionary origins of behavior and its adaptive and survival value in animals, including humans.

**Executive function**  Portion of the information-processing system that coordinates various component processes in order to achieve some goal.

**Exosystem**  In Bronfenbrenner's ecological systems theory, environmental settings that indirectly affect the child by influencing the various microsystems forming the child's immediate environment.

**Expansion**  Repetition of a child's utterance along with more complex forms.

**Experimental design**  Research method in which one or more independent variables are manipulated to determine the effect on other, dependent variables.

**Explicit memory**  Conscious recollection of a past event or experience.

**Expressive aphasia**  Loss of the ability to speak fluently.

**Expressive characteristics**  Characteristics associated with emotions or relationships with people; usually considered feminine.

**Expressive style**  Type of early language production in which the child uses many social words.

**Externality effect**  Tendency for infants younger than two months to focus on the external features of a complex stimulus and explore the internal features less systematically.

**Externalizing problem**  Outward-directed behavioral manifestation, usually aggression or a temper tantrum, which is typically driven by anger.

**Failure to thrive**  Label applied to any child whose growth in height or weight is below the third percentile for children of the same age.

**Fast-mapping**  Process through which the context in which the child hears words spoken provides the key to their meanings.

**Fetal alcohol syndrome (FAS)**  Cluster of fetal abnormalities stemming from mother's consumption of alcohol; includes growth retardation, defects in facial features, and intellectual retardation.

**Fetal blood sampling**  Method of withdrawing blood from the umbilical cord of the fetus; used to diagnose genetic disorders, especially those that affect the blood.

**Fetal monitoring device**  Medical device used to monitor fetal heartbeat during delivery.

**Fetal period**  Period of prenatal development, from about the eighth week after conception to birth, marked by rapid growth and preparation of body systems for functioning in the postnatal environment.

**Field experiment**  Study in which the experimental manipulations are carried out in a natural setting.

**Fluid intelligence**  Biologically based mental abilities that are relatively uninfluenced by cultural experiences.

**Focus on states**  Preoperational child's tendency to treat two or more connected events as unrelated.

**Formal operational stage**  In Piagetian theory, the last stage of development, from approximately eleven to fifteen years of age, in which thought is abstract and hypothetical.

**Fragile X syndrome**  Disorder associated with a pinched region of the X chromosome; a leading genetic cause of mental retardation in males.

**Fraternal twins**  Siblings who share the same womb at the same time but originate from two different eggs fertilized by two different sperm cells. Also called *dizygotic twins*.

**Gamete**  Sperm cell in males, egg cell in females, normally containing only twenty-three chromosomes.

**Gender constancy**  Knowledge, usually gained around age six or seven years, that one's gender does not change as a result of alterations in appearance, behaviors, or desires.

**Gender identity**  Knowledge, usually gained by age three years, that one is male or female.

**Gender intensification**  Return to traditional beliefs about gender during adolescence.

**Gender-role development**  Process by which individuals acquire the characteristics and behaviors prescribed by their culture for their sex. Also called *sex typing*.

**Gender schema**  Cognitive organizing structure for information relevant to sex typing.

**Gender schema theory**  Cognitive-developmental theory that stresses the importance of the acquisition of gender identity and children's intrinsic motivations to behave in a gender-typical manner.

**Gender stability**  Knowledge, usually gained by age four years, that one's gender does not change over time.

**Gender stereotype**  Expectation or belief that individuals within a given culture hold about the behaviors characteristic of males and females.

**Gene**  Large segment of nucleotides within a chromosome that codes for the production of proteins and enzymes. These proteins and enzymes underlie traits and characteristics inherited from one generation to the next.

**Genetic counseling**  Medical and counseling specialty concerned with determining and communicating the likelihood that prospective parents will give birth to a baby with a genetic disorder.

**Genetic screening**  Systematic search using a variety of tests to detect developmental risk due to genetic anomalies.

**Genomic imprinting**  Instances of genetic transmission in which the expression of a gene is determined by whether the particular allelic form has been inherited from the mother or the father.

**Genotype**  Total genetic endowment inherited by an individual.

**Germinal period**  Period lasting about ten to fourteen days following conception before the fertilized egg becomes implanted in the uterine wall. Also called *period of the zygote*.

**Gestational age** Age of fetus derived from onset of mother's last menstrual period.

**Glial cell** Brain cell that provides the material from which myelin is created, nourishes neurons, and provides a scaffolding for neuron migration.

**Grammar** Rules pertaining to the structure of language.

**Habituation** Gradual decline in the intensity, frequency, or duration of a response over repeated or lengthy occurrences of the same stimulus.

**Heritability** Proportion of variability in the phenotype that is estimated to be accounted for by genetic influences within a known environmental range.

**Heterozygous** Genotype in which two alleles of a gene are different. The effects on a trait will depend on how the two alleles interact.

**Homozygous** Genotype in which two alleles of a gene are identical, thus having the same effects on a trait.

**Hormones** Chemicals produced by various glands which are secreted directly into the bloodstream and can therefore circulate to influence cells in other locations of the body.

**Human genome** Entire inventory of nucleotide base pairs that compose the genes and chromosomes of humans.

**Hypothetical reasoning** Ability to systematically generate and evaluate potential solutions to a problem.

**Identical twins** Two individuals who originate from a single zygote (one egg fertilized by one sperm), which early in cell division separates to form two separate cell masses. Also called *monozygotic twins*.

**Identity** In Eriksonian psychosocial theory, the acceptance of both self and society, a concept that must be achieved at every stage but is especially important during adolescence.

**Identity crisis** Period, usually during adolescence, characterized by considerable uncertainty about the self and the role the individual is to fulfill in society.

**Imaginary audience** Individual's belief that others are examining and evaluating him or her.

**Immanent justice** Young child's belief that punishment will inevitably follow a transgression.

**Implicit learning** Abstract knowledge not available to conscious reflection; acquired accidentally from processing structured information.

**Implicit memory** Nonconscious recollections of how to do something behaviorally.

**Imprinting** Form of learning, difficult to reverse, during a sensitive period in development in which an organism tends to stay near a particular stimulus.

**Independent variable** Variable manipulated by the experimenter; the suspected cause.

**Individual differences** Unique characteristics that distinguish a person from other members of a larger group.

**Induction** Parental control technique that relies on the extensive use of reasoning and explanation as well as the arousal of empathic feelings.

**Infantile amnesia** Failure to remember events from the first two to three years of one's life.

**Information processing** Theoretical approach that views humans as having a limited ability to process information, much like computers.

**Informed consent** Participant's formal acknowledgment that he or she understands the purposes, procedures, and risks of a study, and agrees to participate in it.

**Inner speech** Interiorized form of private speech.

**Instrumental characteristics** Characteristics associated with acting on the world; usually considered masculine.

**Instrumental competence** Child's display of independence, self-control, achievement orientation, and cooperation.

**Intelligence quotient (IQ)** Numerical score received on an intelligence test.

**Interactive synchrony** Reciprocal, mutually engaging cycles of caregiver-child behaviors.

**Interagent consistency** Consistency in application of disciplinary strategies among different caregivers.

**Intermodal perception** Coordination of sensory information to perceive or make inferences about the characteristics of an object.

**Internal working model of relationships** Mental framework of the quality of relationships with others, developed as a result of early ongoing interactions with caregivers.

**Internalizing problem** Disturbance of mood, such as guilt and sadness, and, in more severe cases, anxiety and depression.

**Intersubjectivity** Mutual attention and shared communication that take place between two individuals.

**Intra-agent consistency** Consistency in a single caregiver's application of discipline from one situation to the next.

**Joint attention** Episodes in which the child and another individual share the same "psychological space" as they encounter experiences in the world.

**Judgment bias** Tendency to be influenced by inappropriate information at the expense of important and perhaps more relevant facts.

**Karyotype** Pictorial representation of an individual's chromosomes.

**Lagging-down growth** Decrease in growth rate after some factor, such as a congenital or hormonal disorder, has accelerated the expected normal growth rate.

**Lateralization** Process by which one hemisphere of the brain comes to dominate the other; for example, processing of language in the left hemisphere or of spatial information in the right hemisphere.

**Learned helplessness** Belief that one has little control over situations, perhaps because of lack of ability or inconsistent outcomes.

**Learning** Relatively permanent change in behavior as a result of such experiences as exploration, observation, and practice.

**Limited-resource model** Information-processing model that emphasizes the allocation of finite energy within the cognitive system.

**Longitudinal study** Research in which the same participants are repeatedly tested over a period of time, usually years.

**Long-term memory** Memory that holds information for extended periods of time.

**Macrosystem** In Bronfenbrenner's ecological systems theory, major historical events and the broad values, practices, and customs shared by a culture.

**Mastery orientation** Belief that achievements are based on one's own efforts rather than on luck or other factors beyond one's control.

**Maternal blood screening**  Tests performed on a woman's blood to determine whether the fetus she is carrying has an increased risk for some types of chromosomal and metabolic disorders.

**Means-ends behavior**  Deliberate behavior employed to attain a goal.

**Meiosis**  Process of cell division that forms the gametes; normally results in twenty-three chromosomes in each human egg and sperm cell rather than the full complement of forty-six.

**Memory span**  Number of stimulus items that can be recalled after a brief interval of time.

**Memory strategy**  Mental activity, such as rehearsal, that enhances memory performance.

**Menarche**  First occurrence of menstruation.

**Mesosystem**  In Bronfenbrenner's ecological systems theory, the environment provided by the interrelationships among the various settings of the microsystem.

**Meta-analysis**  Statistical examination of a body of research studies to assess the effect of the common central variable.

**Metacognition**  Awareness and knowledge of cognitive processes.

**Metalinguistic awareness**  Ability to reflect on language as a communication tool and on the self as a user of language.

**Metamemory**  The child's understanding of his or her own memory.

**Metaphor**  Figurative language in which a term is transferred from the object it customarily designates to describe a comparable object or event.

**Microgenetic study**  A research approach in which close observations are made of the individual child's behavior from one trial to the next.

**Microsystem**  In Bronfenbrenner's ecological systems theory, the immediate environment provided in such settings as the home, school, workplace, and neighborhood.

**Mitosis**  Process of cell division that takes place in most cells of the human body and results in a full complement of identical material in the forty-six chromosomes in each cell.

**Moral realism**  In Piaget's theory of moral development, the first stage of moral reasoning, in which moral judgments are made on the basis of the consequences of an act. Also called *heteronomy*.

**Moral relativism**  In Piaget's theory of moral development, the second stage of moral reasoning, in which moral judgments are made on the basis of the actor's intentions. Also called *autonomy*.

**Morality of care and responsibility**  Tendency to make moral judgments on the basis of concern for others.

**Morality of justice**  Tendency to make moral judgments on the basis of reason and abstract principles of equity.

**Morphology**  Rules of how to combine the smallest meaningful units of language to form words.

**Motherese (parentese)**  Simple, repetitive, high-pitched speech of caregivers to young children; includes many questions.

**Multistore model**  Name for many traditional information-processing models which posit several mental structures through which information flows.

**Mutation**  Sudden change in molecular structure of a gene; may occur spontaneously or be caused by an environmental event such as radiation.

**Mutual exclusivity bias**  Tendency for children to assume that unfamiliar words label new objects.

**Myelin**  Sheath of fatty cells that insulates and speeds neural impulses by about tenfold.

**Natural domain**  Concept or category that children acquire especially rapidly and effortlessly.

**Naturalistic observation**  Study in which observations of naturally occurring behavior are made in real-life settings.

**Nature-nurture debate**  Ongoing theoretical controversy over whether development is the result of the child's genetic endowment or environmental influences.

**Negative correlation**  Relationship in which changes in one variable are accompanied by systematic changes in another variable in the opposite direction.

**Negative punishment**  Removal or loss of a desired stimulus or reward, which weakens or decreases the frequency of a preceding response.

**Negative reinforcement**  Removal of an aversive stimulus, which strengthens a preceding response.

**Neuron**  Nerve cell within the central nervous system that is electrochemically designed to transmit messages between cells.

**Niche picking**  Tendency to actively select an environment compatible with a genotype.

**Nominal**  Word that labels objects, people, or events; the first type of word most children produce.

**Norm**  Quantitative measure that provides typical values and variations in such characteristics as height and weight for children.

**Nucleotide**  Repeating basic building block of DNA consisting of nitrogen-based molecules of adenine, thymine, cytosine, and guanine.

**Object concept**  Realization that objects exist even when they are not within view. Also called *object permanence*.

**Observational learning**  Learning that takes place by simply observing another person's behavior.

**Observer bias**  Tendency of researchers to interpret ongoing events as being consistent with their research hypotheses.

**One-to-one correspondence**  Understanding that two sets are equivalent in number if each element in one set can be mapped onto a unique element in the second set with none left over.

**Operation**  In Piagetian theory, a mental action that allows a child to reason about events that have transpired.

**Operational definition**  Specification of variables in terms of measurable properties.

**Ordinality**  Principle that a number refers to an item's order within a set.

**Organization**  In Piagetian theory, the inborn tendency for structures and processes to become more systematic and coherent; tendency to reorder items to fit some category or higher-order scheme.

**Overextension**  Tendency to apply a label to a broader category than the term actually signifies.

**Overregularization**  Inappropriate application of grammatical rules to words that require exceptions to those rules.

**Parallel play**  Side-by-side, independent play that is not interactive.

**Participant reactivity**  Tendency of individuals who know they are under observation to alter natural behavior.

**Perception**  Process of organizing and interpreting sensory information.

**Perceptual differentiation**  Process postulated by Eleanor and James Gibson in which experience contributes to the ability to make increasingly finer perceptual discriminations and to distinguish stimulation arising from each sensory modality.

**Perinatal period** Period beginning about the seventh month of pregnancy and continuing until about four weeks after birth.

**Permissive parent** Parent who sets few limits on the child's behavior.

**Personal fable** Belief that one is unique and perhaps even invulnerable.

**Perspective taking** Ability to take the role of another person and understand what that person is thinking, is feeling, or knows.

**Phenotype** Observable and measurable characteristics and traits of an individual; a product of the interaction of the genotype with the environment.

**Phenylketonuria (PKU)** Recessive genetic disorder in which phenylalanine, an amino acid, fails to be metabolized. Unless dietary changes are made to reduce intake of phenylalanine, severe mental retardation occurs.

**Phoneme** Smallest unit of sound that changes the meanings of words.

**Phonology** Fundamental sound units and combinations of units in a given language.

**Placenta** Support organ formed by cells from both blastocyst and uterine lining; serves as exchange site for oxygen, nutrients, and waste products.

**Plasticity** Capacity of immature systems, including regions of the brain and the individual neurons within those regions, to take on different functions as a result of experience.

**Polygenic** Phenotypic characteristic influenced by two or more genes.

**Positive correlation** Relationship in which changes in one variable are accompanied by systematic changes in another variable in the same direction.

**Positive punishment** Occurrence of an aversive stimulus that serves to weaken or decrease the frequency of a preceding response.

**Positive reinforcement** Occurrence of a stimulus that strengthens a preceding response. Also known as a *reward*.

**Postconventional level** In Kohlberg's theory, the third level of moral reasoning, in which laws are seen as the result of a social contract and individual principles of conscience may emerge.

**Postnatal period** Period in development following birth.

**Power assertion** Parental control technique that relies on the use of forceful commands, physical punishment, and removal of material objects or privileges.

**Pragmatics** Rules for using language effectively within a social context.

**Preconventional level** In Kohlberg's theory, the first level of moral reasoning, in which morality is motivated by the avoidance of punishments and attainment of rewards.

**Prenatal development** Period in development from conception to the onset of labor.

**Preoperational stage** In Piagetian theory, the second stage of development, from approximately two to seven years of age, in which thought becomes symbolic in form.

**Prepared (natural) childbirth** Type of childbirth that involves practicing procedures during pregnancy and childbirth that are designed to minimize pain and reduce the need for medication during delivery.

**Primacy effect** Tendency for individuals to display good recall for early items in a list.

**Primary reinforcer** Reward that gratifies biological need or drives.

**Private speech** Children's vocalized speech to themselves that directs behavior.

**Processing speed** Rapidity with which cognitive activities are carried out.

**Productive language** Meaningful language spoken or otherwise produced by an individual.

**Prosocial behavior** Positive social action performed to benefit others.

**Prosody** Patterns of intonation, stress, and rhythm that communicate meaning in speech.

**Protodeclarative communication** Use of a gesture to call attention to an object or event.

**Protoimperative communication** Use of a gesture to issue a command or request.

**Proximodistal development** Pattern in which organs and systems of the body near the middle tend to develop earlier than those near the periphery.

**Psychometric model** Model of intelligence based on the testing of large groups of individuals to quantify differences in abilities.

**Psychosocial theory of development** Erikson's theory that personality develops through eight stages of adaptive functioning to meet the demands framed by society.

**Puberty** Developmental period during which a sequence of physical changes takes place that transforms the person from an immature individual to one capable of reproduction.

**Quasi-experiment** Study in which researchers investigate the effects of independent variables that they do not manipulate themselves but that occur as a result of participants' natural experiences.

**Questionnaire** Set of standardized questions administered to participants in written form.

**Random assignment** Use of principles of chance to assign participants to treatment and control groups; avoids systematic bias.

**Range of reaction** Range of phenotypic differences possible as a result of different environments' interacting with a specific genotype.

**Realism** Inability to distinguish between mental and physical abilities.

**Recall memory** Ability to reproduce stimuli that one has previously encountered.

**Recast** Repetition of a child's utterance along with grammatical corrections.

**Recency effect** Tendency for individuals to show good recall for the last few items in a list.

**Receptive aphasia** Loss of the ability to comprehend speech.

**Receptive language** Ability to comprehend spoken speech.

**Recessive allele** Allele whose characteristics do not tend to be expressed when part of a heterozygous genotype. Its genetic characteristics tend to be masked by other alleles.

**Recognition memory** Ability to identify whether a stimulus has previously been encountered.

**Recovery from habituation (dishabituation)** Renewed response to a change in a stimulus, which indicates that the infant has detected that change.

**Referential communication** Communication in situations that require the child to describe an object to a listener or to evaluate the effectiveness of a message.

**Referential style**   Type of early language production in which the child uses mostly nominals.

**Reflex**   Involuntary reaction to touch, light, sound, and other kinds of stimulation.

**Rehearsal**   Memory strategy that involves repetition of items to be remembered.

**Reliability**   Degree to which a measure will yield the same results if administered repeatedly.

**Representational insight**   The child's ability to understand that a symbol or model can stand for a real-life event.

**Reunion behavior**   The child's style of greeting a caregiver after a separation.

**Reversibility**   In Piagetian theory, the ability to mentally reverse or negate an action or a transformation.

**Rhythmical stereotypy**   Repeated sequence of movements, such as leg kicking, hand waving, or head banging, that has no apparent goal.

**Saccades**   Rapid eye movement to inspect an object or view a stimulus in the periphery of the visual field.

**Scaffolding**   Temporary aid provided by one person to encourage, support, and assist a lesser-skilled person in carrying out a task or completing a problem. The model provides knowledge and skills that are learned and gradually transferred to the learner.

**Scheme**   In Piagetian theory, the mental structure underlying a coordinated and systematic pattern of behaviors or thinking applied across similar objects or situations.

**Scientific method**   Use of objective, measurable, and repeatable techniques to gather information.

**Script**   Organized scheme or framework for commonly experienced events.

**Secondary reinforcer**   Object or person that attains rewarding value because of its association with a primary reinforcer.

**Secular trend**   Consistent pattern of change over generations.

**Secure attachment**   Attachment category defined by the infant's distress at separation from the caregiver and enthusiastic greeting upon his or her return. The infant also displays stranger anxiety and uses the caregiver as a secure base for exploration.

**Secure base**   An attachment behavior in which the infant explores the environment but periodically checks back with the caregiver.

**Self-conscious emotion**   Emotion, such as guilt and envy, that appears later in childhood and requires more knowledge about the self as related to others.

**Self-control**   Ability to comply with sociocultural prescriptions concerning ethical or moral behavior.

**Self-esteem**   One's feelings of worth; extent to which one senses that one's attributes and actions are good, desired, and valued.

**Self-regulation**   Process by which children come to control their own behaviors in accordance with the standards of their caregivers and community, especially in the absence of other adults.

**Semantic bootstrapping hypothesis**   Idea that children derive information about syntax from the meaning of words.

**Semantic memory**   Memory for general concepts or facts.

**Semantics**   Meanings of words or combinations of words.

**Sensation**   Basic information in the external world that is processed by the sensory receptors.

**Sensitive period**   Brief period during which specific kinds of experiences have significant positive or negative consequences for development and behavior; also called *critical period*.

**Sensorimotor stage**   In Piagetian theory, the first stage of cognitive development, from birth to approximately two years of age, in which thought is based primarily on action.

**Sensory register**   Memory store that holds information for very brief periods of time in a form that closely resembles the initial input.

**Separation anxiety**   Distress that the infant shows when the primary caregiver leaves the immediate environment.

**Sequential study**   Study that examines groups of individuals of different ages over a period of time; usually shorter than a longitudinal study.

**Sex segregation**   Clustering of individuals into same-sex groups.

**Sex typicality**   Extent to which a behavior is usually associated with one sex as opposed to the other.

**Shape bias**   The child's assumption that a new word labels an entire object, specifically its form.

**Sickle cell disease**   Genetic blood disorder common in regions of Africa and other areas where malaria is found and among descendants of the people of these regions. Abnormal blood cells carry insufficient oxygen.

**Sickle cell trait**   Symptoms shown by those possessing a heterozygous genotype for sickle cell anemia.

**Single-case design**   Study that follows only one or a few participants over a period of time, with an emphasis on systematic collection of data.

**Skeletal maturity**   Extent to which cartilage has ossified to form bone; provides the most accurate estimate of how much additional growth will take place in the individual.

**Smooth visual pursuit**   Consistent, unbroken tracking by the eyes that serves to maintain focus on a moving visual target.

**Social comparison**   Process in which individuals define themselves in relation to the skills, attributes, and qualities of others; an important contributor to self-concept during middle childhood.

**Social convention**   Behavioral rules that regulate social interactions, such as dress codes and degrees of formality in speech.

**Social learning theory**   Theoretical approach emphasizing the importance of learning through observation and imitation of behaviors modeled by others.

**Social policy**   Programs and plans established by local, regional, or national public and private organizations and agencies designed to achieve a particular social purpose or goal.

**Social pretend play**   Play that makes use of imaginary and symbolic objects and social roles, often enacted among several children. Also called *sociodramatic play*.

**Social referencing**   Looking to another individual for emotional cues in interpreting a strange or ambiguous event.

**Socialization**   Process by which children acquire the social knowledge, skills, and attitudes valued by the larger society.

**Sociohistorical theory**   Vygotsky's developmental theory emphasizing the importance of cultural tools, symbols, and ways of thinking that the child acquires from more knowledgeable members of the community.

**Sociometric nomination**   Peer assessment measure in which children are asked to name a specified number of peers who fit a certain criterion, such as "peers you would like to walk home with."

**Sociometric rating scale**   Peer assessment measure in which children rate peers on a number of social dimensions.

**Solitary play**   Individual play, performed without regard for what others are doing.

**Sound localization**   Ability to determine a sound's point of origin.

**Spermarche**   The first ejaculation of sperm by males entering puberty.

**Stage**   Developmental period during which the organization of thought and behavior is qualitatively different from that of an earlier or later period.

**Stereopsis**   The ability to fuse the two distinct images from the eyes to perceive a single object.

**Stereotype threat**   The psychological impact of negative social stereotypes in an individual.

**Strange Situation**   Standardized test that assesses the quality of infant-caregiver attachment.

**Stranger anxiety**   Fear or distress that an infant shows at the approach of an unfamiliar person.

**Structured interview**   Standardized set of questions administered orally to participants.

**Structured observation**   Study in which behaviors are recorded as they occur within a situation constructed by the experimenter, usually in the laboratory.

**Sudden infant death syndrome (SIDS)**   Sudden, unexplained death of an infant or a toddler as a result of cessation of breathing during sleep.

**Syntax**   Grammatical rules that dictate how words can be combined.

**Systems theory**   Model for understanding the family that emphasizes the reciprocal interactions among various members.

**Telegraphic speech**   Early two-word speech that contains few modifiers, prepositions, or other connective words.

**Temperament**   Stable, early-appearing constellation of individual personality attributes believed to have a hereditary basis; includes sociability, emotionality, and activity level.

**Teratogen**   Any environmental agent that can cause deviations in prenatal development. Consequences may range from behavioral problems to death.

**Test bias**   Idea that the content of traditional standardized tests does not adequately measure the competencies of children from diverse cultural backgrounds.

**Theory**   Set of ideas or propositions that helps to organize or explain observable phenomena.

**Theory of mind**   Awareness of the concept of mental states, both one's own and those of others.

**Time-out**   Disciplinary technique that involves immediately removing a child from all possible sources of reward and leaving the child alone in a quiet, neutral place for a short time.

**Triarchic theory**   Theory developed by Robert Sternberg that intelligence consists of three major components: (1) the ability to adapt to the environment, (2) the ability to employ fundamental information-processing skills, and (3) the ability to deal with novelty and automatize processing.

**Trisomy**   Inheritance of an extra chromosome.

**Turn taking**   Alternating vocalization by parent and child.

**Turnabout**   Element of conversation that requests a response from the child.

**Ultrasonography**   Method of using sound wave reflections to obtain a representation of the developing fetus; used to estimate gestational age and detect fetal physical abnormalities.

**Umbilical cord**   Conduit of blood vessels through which oxygen, nutrients, and waste products are transported between placenta and embryo.

**Unconditioned response (UCR)**   Response that is automatically elicited by the conditioned stimulus (CS).

**Unconditioned stimulus (UCS)**   Stimulus that, without prior training, elicits a reflexlike response (unconditioned response).

**Underextension**   Application of a label to a narrower class of objects than the term signifies.

**Uninvolved parent**   Parent who is emotionally detached from the child and focuses on his or her own needs as opposed to the child's.

**Validity**   Degree to which an assessment procedure actually measures the variable under consideration.

**Variable**   Factor having no fixed or constant value in a given situation.

**Vergence**   Ability of the eyes to rotate in opposite directions to fixate on objects at different distances; improves rapidly during first few months after birth.

**Viability**   Ability of the baby to survive outside the mother's womb.

**Visual accommodation**   Visuomotor process by which small involuntary muscles change the shape of the lens of the eye so that images of objects seen at different distances are brought into focus on the retina.

**Visual acuity**   Ability to make fine discriminations among elements in a visual array by detecting contours, transitions in light patterns that signal borders and edges.

**Visual cliff**   Experimental apparatus used to test depth perception, in which the surface on one side of a glass-covered table is made to appear far below the surface on the other side.

**Vocabulary spurt**   Period of rapid word acquisition that typically occurs early in language development.

**Wernicke's area**   Portion of the cerebral cortex that controls language comprehension.

**Williams syndrome**   Dominant genetic disorder involving the deletion of a set of genes, which results in affected individuals' typically having a strong social orientation, good musical ability, and some unusual linguistic capabilities; accompanied by mental retardation and severe deficits in numerical and spatial ability.

**Working memory**   Short-term memory store in which mental operations such as rehearsal and categorization take place.

**X chromosome**   Larger of the two sex chromosomes associated with genetic determination of sex. Normally females have two X chromosomes and males, only one.

**Y chromosome**   Smaller of the two sex chromosomes associated with genetic determination of sex. Normally males have one Y chromosome and females, none.

**Zone of proximal development**   Range of various kinds of support and assistance provided by an expert (usually an adult) who helps children to carry out activities they currently cannot complete but will later be able to accomplish independently.

**Zygote**   Fertilized egg cell.

# REFERENCES

Abbassi, V. (1998). Growth and normal puberty. *Pediatrics, 102, 507–511.*

Abel, E. L. (1989). *Behavioral teratogenesis and behavioral mutagenesis: A primer in abnormal development.* New York: Plenum Press.

Aboud, F. E., & Skerry, S. (1983). Self and ethnic concepts in relation to ethnic constancy. *Canadian Journal of Behavioral Science, 15, 14–26.*

Achenbach, T. M., Howell, C. T., Aoki, M. F., & Rauh, V. A. (1993). Nine-year outcome of the Vermont Intervention Program for Low Birth Weight Infants. *Pediatrics, 91, 45–55.*

Ackerman, B. P., Abe, J. A., & Izard, C. E. (1998). Differential emotions theory and emotional development. In M. F. Mascolo & S. Griffin (Eds.), *What develops in emotional development?* (pp. 85–106). New York: Plenum.

Acredolo, L. P., & Goodwyn, S. W. (1988). Symbolic gesturing in normal infants. *Child Development, 59, 450–466.*

Acredolo, L. P., & Goodwyn, S. W. (1990a). Sign language among hearing infants: The spontaneous development of symbolic gestures. In V. Volterra & C. J. Erting (Eds.), *From gesture to language in hearing and deaf children.* New York: Springer-Verlag.

Acredolo, L. P., & Goodwyn, S. W. (1990b). Sign language in babies: The significance of symbolic gesturing for understanding language development. In R. Vasta (Ed.), *Annals of child development* (Vol. 7, pp. 1–42). Greenwich, CT: JAI Press.

Acredolo, L. P., Pick, H. L., Jr., & Olsen, M. G. (1975). Environmental differentiation and familiarity as determinants of children's memory for spatial location. *Developmental Psychology, 11, 495–501.*

Adams, R. J., & Courage, M. L. (1998). Human newborn color vision: Measurement with chromatic stimuli varying in excitation purity. *Journal of Experimental Child Psychology, 68, 22–34.*

Adams, R., & Laursen, B. (2001). The organization and dynamics of adolescent conflict with parents and friends. *Journal of Marriage and the Family, 63, 97–110.*

Adams, S., Kuebli, J., Boyle, P. A., & Fivush, R. (1995). Gender differences in parent-child conversations about past emotions: A longitudinal investigation. *Sex Roles, 33, 309–323.*

Adi-Japha, E., & Freeman, N. H. (2001). Development of differentiation between writing and drawing systems. *Developmental Psychology, 37, 101–114.*

Adler, S. P. (1992). Cytomegalovirus and pregnancy. *Current Opinions in Obstetrics and Gynecology, 4, 670–675.*

Adoh, T. O., & Woodhouse, J. M. (1994). The Cardiff Acuity Test used for measuring visual acuity development in toddlers. *Vision Research, 34, 555–560.*

Adolph, K. E. (1997). Learning in the development of infant locomotion. *Monographs of the Society for Research in Child Development, 62(3, Serial No. 251).*

Adolph, K. E. (2000). Specificity of learning: Why infants fall over a veritable cliff. *Psychological Science, 11, 290–295.*

Adolph, K. E., Vereijken, B., & Denny, M. A. (1998). Learning to crawl. *Child Development, 69, 1299–1312.*

Adolph, K. E., Vereijken, B., & Shrout, P. E. (2003). What changes in infant walking and why. *Child Development, 74, 475–497.*

Agustines, L. A., Lin, Y. G., Rumney, P. J., Lu, M. C., Bonebrake, R., Asrat, T., & Nageotte, M. (2000). Outcomes of extremely low-birth-weight infants between 500 and 750 g. *American Journal of Obstetrics and Gynecology, 182, 1114–1116.*

Ahmed, A., & Ruffman, T. (1998). Why do infants make A not B errors in a search task, yet show memory for location of hidden objects in a nonsearch task? *Developmental Psychology, 34, 441–453.*

Ahnert, L., Rickert, H., & Lamb, M. E. (2000). Shared caregiving: Comparisons between home and child-care settings. *Developmental Psychology, 36, 339–351.*

Ainsworth, M. D. S., Bell, S. M., & Stayton, D. J. (1971). Individual differences in Strange Situation behavior of one-year-olds. In H. R. Schaffer (Ed.), *The Origins of human social relations.* London: Academic Press.

Ainsworth, M. D. S., Bell, S. M., & Stayton, D. J. (1972). Individual differences in the development of some attachment behaviors. *Merrill-Palmer Quarterly, 18, 123–143.*

Ainsworth, M. D. S., Bell, S. M., & Stayton, D. J. (1974). Infant-mother attachment and social development: "Socialization" as a product of reciprocal responsiveness to signals. In M. R. Richards (Ed.), *The integration of the child into a social world.* London: Cambridge University Press.

Ainsworth, M. D. S., Blehar, M. C., Waters, E., & Wall, S. (1978). *Patterns of attachment: A psychological study of the strange situation.* Hillsdale, NJ: Erlbaum.

Akhtar, N., Carpenter, M., & Tomasello, M. (1996). The role of discourse novelty in early word learning. *Child Development, 67, 635–645.*

Akhtar, N., Jipson, J., & Callanan, M. A. (2001). Learning words through overhearing. *Child Development, 72, 416–430.*

Aksan, N., & Kochanska, G. (2005). Conscience in childhood: Old questions, new answers. *Developmental Psychology, 41, 506–516.*

Alaimo, K., Olson, C. M., & Frongillo, E. A., Jr. (2001). Food insufficiency and American school-aged children's cognitive, academic, and psychosocial development. *Pediatrics, 108, 44–53.*

Alan Guttmacher Institute. (1993). *Facts in Brief, March* (pp. 1–2). Chicago: Alan Guttmacher Innstitute.

Alessandri, S. M., & Lewis, M. (1993). Parental evaluation and its relation to shame and pride in young children. *Sex Roles, 29, 335–343.*

Alexander, J. M., Carr, M., & Schwanenflugel, P. J. (1995). Development of metacognition in gifted children: Directions for future research. *Developmental Review, 15, 1–37.*

Alexander, K. L., & Entwisle, D. R. (1988). Achievement in the first 2 years of school: Patterns and processes. *Monographs of the Society for Research in Child Development, 53(2, Serial No. 218).*

Alexander, K. L., Entwisle, D. R., & Bedinger, S. D. (1994). When expectations work: Race and socioeconomic differences in school performance. *Social Psychology Quarterly, 57, 283–299.*

Alfieri, T., Ruble, D. N., & Higgins, E. T. (1996). Gender stereotypes during adolescence: Developmental changes and the transition to junior high school. *Developmental Psychology, 32, 1129–1137.*

Allaire, A. D. (2001). Complementary and alternative medicine in the labor and delivery suite. *Clinical Obstetrics and Gynecology, 44, 681–691.*

Allanson, J., & Graham, G. (2002). Sex chromosome abnormalities. In D. L. Rimoin, J. M. Connor, R. E. Pyeritz, & B. R. Korf (Eds.), *Emery and Rimoin's principles and practice of medical genetics* (4th ed., Vol. 1, pp. 1184–1201). London: Churchill Livingston.

Allen, J. P., & Land, D. (1999). Attachment in adolescence. In J. Cassidy & P. R. Shaver (Eds.), *Handbook of attachment: Theory, research, and clinical applications* (pp. 319–335). New York: Guilford.

Allen, J. P., McElhaney, K. B., Land, D. J., Kuperminc, G. P., Moore, C. W., O'Beirne-Kelly, H., & Kilmer, S. L. (2003). A secure base in adolescence: Markers of attachment security in the mother-adolescent relationship. *Child Development, 74, 292–307.*

Allen, J. P., Philliber, S., Herrling, S., & Kuperminc, G. P. (1997). Preventing teen pregnancy and academic failure: Experimental evaluation of a developmentally based approach. *Child Development, 64, 729–742.*

Allen, J. P., Porter, M. R., McFarland, F. C., Marsh, P., & McElhaney, K. B. (2005). The two faces of adolescents' success with peers: Adolescent popularity, social adaptation, and deviant behavior. *Child Development, 76, 747–760.*

Allwood, M. A., Bell-Dolan, D., & Husain, S. A. (2002). Children's trauma and adjustment reactions to violent and nonviolent war experiences.

*Journal of the American Academy of Child and Adolescent Psychiatry, 41*, 450–457.

Als, H., Lawhon, G., Duffy, F. H., McAnulty, G. B., Gibes-Grossman, R., Blickman, J. G. (1994). Individualized developmental care for the very low-birth-weight preterm infants: Medical and neurofunctional effects. *Journal of the American Medical Association, 272*, 853–858.

Alsaker, F. D. (1992). Pubertal timing, overweight, and psychological adjustment. *Journal of Early Adolescence, 12*, 396–419.

Altermatt, E. R., Pomerantz, E. M., Ruble, D. N., Frey, K., & Greulich, F. K. (2002). Predicting changes in children's self-perceptions of academic competence: A naturalistic examination of evaluative discourse among class mates. *Developmental Psychology, 38*, 903–917.

Alwitt, L. F., Anderson, D. R., Lorch, E. P., & Levin, S. R. (1980). Preschool children's visual attention to attributes of television. *Human Communication Research, 7*, 52–67.

Amato, P. R. (1999). Children of divorced parents as young adults. In E. M. Hetherington (Ed.), *Coping with divorce, single parenting, and remarriage* (pp. 147–163). Mahwah, NJ: Erlbaum.

Amato, P. R. (2001). Children of divorce in the 1990s: An update of the Amato and Keith (1990) meta-analysis. *Journal of Family Psychology, 15*, 355–370.

Amato, P. R., & Rezac, S. J. (1994). Contact with nonresident parents, in-terparental conflict, and children's behavior. *Journal of Family Issues, 15*, 191–207.

Ambady, N., Shih, M., Kim, A., & Pittinsky, T. L. (2001). Stereotype susceptibility in children: Effects of identity activation on quantitative performance. *Psychological Science, 12*, 385–390.

American Academy of Pediatrics Committee on Drugs. (2001). The transfer of drugs and other chemicals into human milk. *Pediatrics, 108*, 776–789.

American Academy of Pediatrics Committee on Environmental Health. (1997). Environmental tobacco smoke: A hazard to children. *Pediatrics, 99*, 639–642.

American Academy of Pediatrics Task Force on Infant Sleep Position and Sudden Infant Death Syndrome. (2000). Changing concept of sudden infant death syndrome: Implications for infant sleeping environment and sleep position. *Pediatrics, 105*, 650–656.

American Academy of Pediatrics, Committee on Substance Abuse and Committee on Children with Disabilities. (2000). Fetal alcohol syndrome and alcohol-related neurodevelopmental disorders. *Pediatrics, 106*, 358–361.

American Academy of Pediatrics. (2001). Developmental surveillance and screening of infants and young children. *Pediatrics, 108*, 192–196.

American Academy of Pediatrics. (2005). *AAP revises recommendations on reducing the risk of SIDS*. Retrieved May 12, 2006, from www.aap.org/ncepr/sids.htm.

American Association of University Women. (1992). *How schools shortchange girls*. Washington, DC: AAUW Educational Foundation.

American College of Obstetricians and Gynecologists Committee on Ethics. (2002). Sex selection. *Ethics in Obstetrics and Gynecology* (pp. 85–88). Washington, DC: The American College of Obstetricians and Gynecologists.

American College of Obstetricians and Gynecologists. (1994). Substance abuse in pregnancy. *ACOG Technical Bulletin No. 195*.

American Psychiatric Association. (1994). *Diagnostic and statistical manual of mental disorders* (4th ed.). Washington, DC.

American Psychiatric Association. (2000). *Diagnostic and statistical manual of mental disorders–TR* (4th ed.). Arlington, VA: Author.

American Psychiatric Association. (2002). *Fact sheet: Attention deficit/hyperactivity disorder*. Retrieved December 9, 2002, from www.psych.org/publicinfo/adhdfactsheet42401.pdf

Anand, K. J. S., and the International Evidence-Based Group for Neonatal Pain. (2001). Consensus statement for the prevention and management of pain in the newborn. *Archives of Pediatric and Adolescent Medicine, 155*, 173–180.

Andersen, R. E., Crespo, C. J., Bartlett, S. J., Cheskin, L. J., & Pratt, M. (1998). Relationship of physical activity and television watching with body weight and level of fatness among children: Results from the Third National Health and Nutrition Examination Survey. *Journal of the American Medical Association, 279*, 938–942.

Anderson, C. A., Berkowitz, L., Donnerstein, E., Huesmann, L. R., Johnson, J. D., Linz, D., et al. (2003). The influence of media violence on youth. *Psychological Science in the Public Interest, 4*, 81–110.

Anderson, D. R., & Burns, J. (1991). Paying attention to television. In J. Bryant & D. Zillmann (Eds.), *Responding to the screen: Reception and reaction processes* (pp. 3–25). Hillsdale, NJ: Erlbaum.

Anderson, D. R., Huston, A. C., Schmitt, K. L., Lineberger, D. L., & Wright, J. C. (2001). Early childhood television viewing and adolescent behavior: The recontact study. *Monographs of the Society for Research in Child Development, 66*(Serial No. 264).

Anderson, D. R., Lorch, E. P., Field, D. E., & Sanders, J. (1981). The effects of TV program comprehensibility on preschool children's television viewing behavior. *Child Development, 52*, 151–157.

Anderson, M., Kaufman, J., Simon, T. R., Barrios, L., Paulozzi, L., Ryan, G., et al. (2001). School-associated violent deaths in the United States, 1994–1999. *Journal of the American Medical Association, 286*, 2695–2702.

Andersson, B. (1992). Effects of day-care on cognitive and socioemotional competence of thirteen-year-old Swedish schoolchildren. *Child Development, 63*, 20–36.

Anglin, J. M. (1993). Vocabulary development: A morphological analysis. *Monographs of the Society for Research in Child Development, 59* (5, Serial No. 242).

Angoff, W. H. (1988). The nature-nurture debate: Aptitudes and group differences. *American Psychologist, 43*, 713–720.

Anisfeld, M. (1996). Only tongue protrusion modeling is matched by neonates. *Developmental Review, 16*, 149–161.

Annett, M. (1973). Laterality of childhood hemiplegia and the growth of speech and intelligence. *Cortex, 9*, 4–33.

Antell, S. E., & Keating, D. P. (1983). Perception of numerical invariance in neonates. *Child Development, 54*, 695–701.

Antill, J. K., Goodnow, J. J., Russell, G., & Cotton, S. (1996). The influence of parents and family context on children's involvement in household tasks. *Sex Roles, 34*, 215–236.

Antonov, A. N. (1947). Children born during the siege of Leningrad in 1942. *Journal of Pediatrics, 30*, 250–259.

Apgar, V. (1953). A proposal for a new method of evaluation of the newborn infant. *Anesthesia and Analgesia: Current Researches, 32*, 260–267.

Arend, R., Gove, F. L., & Sroufe, L. A. (1979). Continuity of individual adaptation from infancy to kindergarten: A predictive study of ego-resiliency and curiosity in preschoolers. *Child Development, 50*, 950–959.

Ariès, P. (1962). *Centuries of childhood: A social history of family life* (R. Baldick, Trans.). New York: Vintage.

Arnett, J. J. (1999). Adolescent storm and stress, reconsidered. *American Psychologist, 54*, 317–326.

Arnold, D. S., & Whitehurst, G. J. (1994). Accelerating language development through picture book reading: A summary of dialogic reading and its effects. In D. K. Dickinson (Ed.), *Bridges to literacy: Children, families, and schools* (pp. 103–128). Cambridge, MA: Blackwell.

Aronfreed, J. (1976). Moral development from the standpoint of a general psychological theory. In T. Lickona (Ed.), *Moral development and moral behavior*. New York: Holt, Rinehart & Winston.

Arsenio, W. F., Cooperman, S., & Lover, A. (2000). Affective predictors of preschoolers' aggression and peer acceptance: Direct and indirect effects. *Developmental Psychology, 36*, 438–448.

Arsenio, W. F., & Ford, M. E. (1985). The role of affective information in social-cognitive development: Children's differentiation of moral and conventional events. *Merrill-Palmer Quarterly, 31*, 1–17.

Arsenio, W. F., & Lemerise, E. A. (2004). Aggression and moral development: Integrating social information processing and moral domain models. *Child Development, 75*, 987–1002.

Artigal, J. M. (1991). *The Catalan immersion program: A European point of view*. Norwood, NJ: Ablex.

Ary, D. V., Duncan, T. E., Biglan, A., Metzler, C. W., Noell, J. W., & Smolkowski, K. (1999). Development of adolescent problem behavior. *Journal of Abnormal Child Psychology, 27*, 141–150.

Asendorpf, J. B., & Baudonnière, P-M. (1993). Self-awareness and other-awareness: Mirror self-recognition and synchronic imitation among unfamiliar peers. *Developmental Psychology, 29*, 88–95.

Asher, S. R. (1983). Social competence and peer status: Recent advances and future directions. *Child Development, 54,* 1427–1434.

Asher, S. R., & Dodge, K. A. (1986). The identification of socially rejected children. *Developmental Psychology, 22,* 444–449.

Ashima-Takane, Y., Goodz, E., & Derevensky, J. L. (1996). Birth order effects on early language development: Do secondborn children learn from overheard speech? *Child Development, 67,* 621–634.

Ashley-Koch, A., Yang, Q., & Olney, R. S. (2000). Sickle hemoglobin (HbS) allele and sickle cell disease: A HuGE review. *American Journal of Epidemiology, 151,* 839–845.

Ashmead, D. H., Clifton, R. K., & Perris, E. E. (1987). Precision of auditory localization in human infants. *Developmental Psychology, 23,* 641–647.

Ashmead, D. H., Hill, E. W., & Talor, C. R. (1989). Obstacle perception by congenitally blind children. *Perception & Psychophysics, 46,* 425–433.

Aslin, R. N. (1987a). Motor aspects of visual development in infancy. In P. Salapatek & L. Cohen (Eds.), *Handbook of infant perception: From sensation to perception* (Vol. 1). Orlando, FL: Academic Press.

Aslin, R. N. (1987b). Visual and auditory development in infancy. In J. D. Osofsky (Ed.), *Handbook of infant development* (2nd ed., pp. 5–97). New York: Wiley.

Aslin, R. N. (1993). Perception of visual direction in human infants. In C. Granrud (Ed.), *Visual perception and cognition in infancy* (pp. 91–119). Hillsdale, NJ: Erlbaum.

Aslin, R. N. (2000). Why take the cog out of infant cognition? *Infancy, 1,* 463–470.

Aslin, R. N., & Smith, L. B. (1988). Perceptual development. *Annual Review of Psychology, 39,* 435–473.

Astington, J. W., Harris, P. L., & Olson, D. R. (1988). *Developing theories of mind.* New York: Cambridge University Press.

Atkinson, R. C., & Shiffrin, R. M. (1968). Human memory: A proposed system and its control processes. In K. W. Spence & J. T. Spence (Eds.), *The psychology of learning and motivation: Advances in research and theory* (Vol. 2, pp. 90–95). New York: Academic Press.

Au, T. K.-F., Knightly, L. M., Jun, S.-A., & Oh, J. S. (2002). Overhearing a language during childhood. *Psychological Science, 13,* 238–243.

Avenevoli, S., Sess, F. M., & Steinberg, L. (1999). Family structure, parenting practices, and adolescent adjustment: An ecological examination. In E. M. Hetherington (Ed.), *Coping with divorce, single parenting, and remarriage* (pp. 65–90). Mahwah, NJ: Erlbaum.

Aviezer, O., Sagi, A., Joels, T., & Ziv, Y. (1999). Emotional availability and attachment representations in kibbutz infants and their mothers. *Developmental Psychology, 35,* 811–821.

Avis, J., & Harris, P. L. (1991). Belief-desire reasoning among Baka children: Evidence for a universal conception of mind. *Child Development, 62,* 460–467.

Aylward, G. P., Pfeiffer, S. I., Wright, A., & Verhulst, S. J. (1989). Outcome studies of low birth weight infants published in the last decade: A metaanalysis. *Journal of Pediatrics, 115,* 515–520.

Bachevalier, J., Brickson, M., & Hagger, C. (1993). Limbic-dependent recognition memory in monkeys develops early in infancy. *Neuro Report, 4,* 77–80.

Bachevalier, J., Hagger, C., & Mishkin, M. (1991). Functional maturation of the occipitotemporal pathway in infant rhesus monkeys. In N. A. Lassen, D. H. Ingvar, M. E. Raichle, & L. Friberg (Eds.), *Brain work and mental activity* (pp. 231–240). Copenhagen: Munksgaard.

Backscheider, A. G., Shatz, M., & Gelman, S. A. (1993). Preschoolers' ability to distinguish living kinds as a function of regrowth. *Child Development, 64,* 1242–1257.

Bader, A. P., & Phillips, R. D. (1999). Father's proficiency at recognizing their newborns by tactile cues. *Infant Behavior and Development, 22,* 405–409.

Bagwell, C. L., Newcomb, A. F., & Bukowski, W. M. (1998). Preadolescent friendship and peer rejection as predictors of adult adjustment. *Child Development, 69,* 140–153.

Bahrick, L. E. (2002). Generalization of learning in three-and-a-half-month-old infants on the basis of amodal relations. *Child Development, 73,* 667–681.

Bahrick, L. E., & Lickliter, R. (2000). Intersensory redundancy guides attentional selectivity and perceptual learning in infancy. *Developmental Psychology, 36,* 190–201.

Bahrick, L. E., Netto, D., & Hernandez-Reif, M. (1998). Intermodal perception of adult and child faces and voices by infants. *Child Development, 69,* 1263–1275.

Baillargeon, R. (1987a). Object permanence in 31/2- and 41/2-month-old infants. *Developmental Psychology, 23,* 655–664.

Baillargeon, R. (1987b). Young children's reasoning about the physical and spatial characteristics of a hidden object. *Cognitive Development, 2,* 179–200.

Baillargeon, R. (1995). Physical reasoning in infancy. In M. S. Gazzaniga (Ed.), *The cognitive neurosciences* (pp. 181–204). Cambridge, MA: MIT Press.

Baillargeon, R. (2001). Infants' physical knowledge: Of acquired expectations and core principles. In E. Dupoux (Ed.), *Language, brain, and cognitive development: Essays in honor of Jacques Mehler* (pp. 341–361). Cambridge, MA: MIT Press.

Baillargeon, R., & DeVos, J. (1991). Object permanence in young infants: Further evidence. *Child Development, 62,* 1227–1246.

Baille, M.-F., Arnaud, C., Cans, C., Grandjean, H., du Mazaubrun, C., & Rumeau-Rouquette, C. (1996). Prevalence, aetiology, and care of severe and profound hearing loss. *Archives of Disease in Childhood, 75,* 129–132.

Baker-Sennett, J., Matusov, E., & Rogoff, B. (1993). Planning as a developmental process. In H. W. Reese (Ed.), *Advances in child development and behavior* (Vol. 24). San Diego, CA: Academic Press.

Balaban, M. T., Anderson, L. M., & Wisniewski, A. B. (1998). Lateral asymmetries in infant melody perception. *Developmental Psychology, 34,* 39–48.

Baldwin, J. M. (1930). [Autobiography]. In C. Murchison (Ed.), *A history of psychology in autobiography* (Vol. 1). Worcester, MA: Clark University Press.

Bales, D. W., & Sera, M. D. (1995). Preschoolers' understanding of stable and changeable characteristics. *Cognitive Development, 10,* 69–107.

Balint, J. P. (1998). Physical findings in nutritional deficiencies. *Pediatric Clinics of North America, 45,* 245–260.

Ballard, B. D., Gipson, M. T., Guttenberg, W., & Ramsey, K. (1980). Palatability of food as a factor influencing obese and normal-weight children's eating habits. *Behavior Research and Therapy, 18,* 598–600.

Bandura, A. (1965). Vicarious processes: A case of no-trial learning. In L. Berkowitz (Ed.), *Advances in experimental social psychology* (Vol. 2, pp. 1–55). New York: Academic Press.

Bandura, A. (1969). *Principles of behavior modification.* New York: Holt, Rinehart & Winston.

Bandura, A. (1977a). Self-efficacy: Toward a unifying theory of behavioral change. *Psychological Review, 84,* 191–215.

Bandura, A. (1977b). *Social learning theory.* Englewood Cliffs, NJ: Prentice-Hall.

Bandura, A. (1986). *Social foundations of thought and action: A social cognitive theory.* Englewood Cliffs, NJ: Prentice-Hall.

Bandura, A. (1989). Social cognitive theory. In R. Vasta (Ed.), *Annals of child development: Vol. 6. Six theories of child development: Revised formulations and current issues* (pp. 1–60). Greenwich, CT: JAI Press.

Bandura, A., Barbaranelli, C., Caprara, G. V., & Pastorelli, C. (1996). Multifaceted impact of self-efficacy beliefs on academic functioning. *Child Development, 67,* 1206–1222.

Bandura, A., Barbaranelli, C., Caprara, G. V., & Pastorelli, C. (2001). Self-efficacy beliefs as shapers of children's aspirations and career trajectories. *Child Development, 72,* 187–206.

Bandura, A., Ross, D., & Ross, S. A. (1963a). Imitation of film-mediated aggressive models. *Journal of Abnormal and Social Psychology, 66,* 3–11.

Bandura, A., Ross, D., & Ross, S. A. (1963b). Vicarious reinforcement and imitative learning. *Journal of Abnormal and Social Psychology, 67,* 601–607.

Bandura, A., & Walters, R. H. (1959). *Adolescent aggression.* New York: Ronald Press.

Bandura, A., & Walters, R. H. (1963). *Social learning and personality development.* New York: Holt, Rinehart & Winston.

Banks, M. S., Aslin, R. N., & Letson, R. D. (1975). Sensitive period for the development of human binocular vision. *Science, 190,* 675–677.

Barber, B. K., & Harmon, E. L. (2002). Violating the self: Parental psychological control of children and adolescents. In B. K. Barber (Ed.), *Parental psychological control of children and adolescents* (pp. 15–52). Washington, DC: American Psychological Association.

Barber, B. L., & Eccles, J. S. (1992). Long-term influence of divorce and single-parenting on adolescent family- and work-related values, behaviors, and aspirations. *Psychological Bulletin, 111,* 108–126.

Barden, R. C., Zelko, F., Duncan, S. W., & Masters, J. C. (1980). Children's consensual knowledge about the experiential components of emotion. *Journal of Personality and Social Psychology, 39,* 968–976.

Barela, J. A., Jeka, J. J., & Clark, J. E. (1999). The use of somatosensory information during the acquisition of independent upright stance. *Infant Behavior and Development, 22,* 87–102.

Barkeling, B., Ekman, S., & Rössner, S. (1992). Eating behaviour in obese and normal weight 11-year-old children. *International Journal of Obesity, 16,* 355–360.

Barkley, R. A. (1997). *ADHD and the nature of self-control.* New York: Guilford Press.

Barnes, K. (1971). Preschool play norms: A replication. *Developmental Psychology, 5,* 99–103.

Barnhart, H. X., Caldwell, M. B., Thomas, P., Mascola, L., Ortiz, I., Hus, H. W., et al. (1996). Natural history of human immunodeficiency virus disease in perinatally infected children: An analysis from the Pediatric Spectrum of Disease Project. *Pediatrics, 97,* 710–716.

Baron-Cohen, S. (1995). *Mindblindness: An essay on autism and theory of mind.* Cambridge, MA: MIT Press.

Baron-Cohen, S., Tager-Flusberg, H., & Cohen, D. J. (1993). *Understanding other minds: Perspectives from autism.* New York: Oxford University Press.

Barr, R., Dowden, A., & Hayne, H. (1996). Developmental change in deferred imitation by 6- to 24-month-old infants. *Infant Behavior and Development, 19,* 159–170.

Barrett, K. C. (1998). A functionalist perspective to the development of emotions. In M. F. Mascolo & S. Griffin (Eds.), *What develops in emotional development?* (pp. 109–133). New York: Plenum.

Barrett, M. D. (1985). Issues in the study of children's single-word speech. In M. D. Barrett (Ed.), *Children's single-word speech.* Chichester, UK: Wiley.

Barrett, M. D. (1986). Early semantic representations and early word usage. In S. A. Kuczaj & M. D. Barrett (Eds.), *The development of word meaning.* New York: Springer-Verlag.

Barrett, M. D. (1989). Early language development. In A. Slater & G. Bremner (Eds.), *Infant development.* London: Erlbaum.

Barry, C. M., & Wentzel, K. R. (2006). Friend influence on prosocial behavior: The role of motivational factors and friendship characteristics. *Developmental Psychology, 42,* 153–163.

Barth, J. M. (1989, April). *Parent-child relationships and children's transition to school.* Paper presented at the biennial meeting of the Society for Research in Child Development, Kansas City, MO.

Bartlett, N. H., Vasey, P. L., & Bukowski, W. M. (2000). Is gender identity disorder in children a mental disorder? *Sex Roles, 43,* 753–785.

Baruch, C., & Drake, C. (1997). Tempo discrimination in infants. *Infant Behavior and Development, 20,* 573–577.

Basser, L. S. (1962). Hemiplegia of early onset and the faculty of speech with special reference to the effects of hemispherectomy. *Brain, 85,* 427–460.

Bates, E. (1979). *The emergence of symbols: Cognition and communication in infancy.* New York: Academic Press.

Bates, E., Bretherton, I., & Snyder, L. (1988). *From first words to grammar.* Cambridge, UK: Cambridge University Press.

Bates, E., Camaioni, L., & Volterra, V. (1975). The acquisition of performatives prior to speech. *Merrill-Palmer Quarterly, 21,* 205–224.

Bates, J., Marvinney, D., Kelly, T., Dodge, K., Bennett, T., & Pettit, G. (1994). Child-care history and kindergarten adjustment. *Developmental Psychology, 30,* 690–700.

Bates, J. E., Maslin, C. A., & Frankel, K. A. (1985). Attachment security, mother-child interaction, and temperament as predictors of behavior-problem ratings at age three years. In I. Bretherton & E. Waters (Eds.), *Growing points of attachment theory and research. Monographs of the Society for Research in Child Development, 50*(1–2, Serial No. 209).

Bauer, P. J. (1993). Memory for gender-consistent and gender-inconsistent event sequences by twenty-five-month-old children. *Child Development, 64,* 285–297.

Bauer, P. J. (2002). Long-term recall memory: Behavioral and neurodevelopmental changes in the first 2 years of life. *Current Directions in Psychological Science, 11,* 137–141.

Bauer, P. J. (2004). Getting explicit memory off the ground: Steps toward construction of a neuro-developmental account of changes in the first two years of life. *Developmental Review, 24,* 347–373.

Bauer, P. J., Liebl, M., & Stennes, L. (1998). PRETTY is to DRESS as BRAVE is to SUITCOAT: Gender-based property-to-property inferences by 4-1/2-year-old children. *Merrill-Palmer Quarterly, 44,* 355–377.

Bauer, P. J., Wenner, J. A., Dropik, P. L., & Wewerka, S. S. (2000). Parameters of remembering and forgetting in the transition from infancy to early childhood. *Monographs of the Society for Research in Child Development, 65*(4, Serial No. 263).

Baumrind, D. (1971). Current patterns of parental authority. *Developmental Psychology Monographs, 4*(1, Pt. 2).

Baumrind, D. (1972). From each according to her ability. *School Review, 80,* 161–197.

Baumrind, D. (1991). The influence of parenting style on adolescent competence and substance abuse. *Journal of Early Adolescence, 11,* 56–94.

Baumrind, D. (1993). The average expectable environment is not good enough: A response to Scarr. *Child Development, 64,* 1299–1317.

Baumrind, D. (1996). Parenting: The discipline controversy revisited. *Family Relations, 45,* 405–414.

Baumrind, D., Larzelere, R. E., & Cowan, P. A. (2002). Ordinary physical punishment: Is it harmful? Comment on Gershoff (2002). *Psychological Bulletin, 128,* 580–589.

Bauserman, R. (2002). Child adjustment in joint-custody versus sole-custody arrangements: A meta-analytic review. *Journal of Family Psychology, 16,* 91–102.

Baydar, N., & Brooks-Gunn, J. (1991). Effects of maternal employment and child care arrangements on preschoolers' cognitive and behavioral outcomes: Evidence from the children of the National Longitudinal Survey of Youth. *Developmental Psychology, 27,* 932–945.

Bayley, N. (1993). *Bayley Scales of Infant Development* (2nd ed.). San Antonio: The Psychological Corporation.

Beauchamp, G. K., & Cowart, B. J. (1990). Preference for high salt concentrations among children. *Developmental Psychology, 26,* 539–545.

Beauchamp, G. K., & Moran, M. (1982). Dietary experience and sweet taste preferences in human infants. *Appetite, 3,* 139–152.

Beauchamp, T. L., Faden, R. R., Wallace, R. J., Jr., & Walters, L. (1982). *Ethical issues in social science research.* Baltimore, MD: Johns Hopkins University Press.

Beaudet, A. L., Scriver, C. R., Sly, W. S., & Valle, D. (2001). Genetics, biochemistry, and molecular bases of variant human phenoypes. In C. R. Scriver, A. L. Beaudet, W. S. Sly, & D. Valle (Eds.), *The metabolic and molecular bases of inherited disease* (8th ed., Vol. 1, pp. 3–45). New York: McGraw-Hill.

Beck, R. W., & Beck, S. H. (1989). The incidence of extended households among middle-aged black and white women. *Journal of Family Issues, 10,* 147–168.

Becker, A. B., Manfreda, J., Ferguson, A. C., Dimich-Ward, H., Watson, W. T. A., Chan-Yeung, M. (1999). Breast-feeding and environmental tobacco smoke exposure. *Archives of Pediatric and Adolescent Medicine, 153,* 689–691.

Becker, J. (1989). Preschoolers' use of number words to denote one-to-one correspondence. *Child Development, 60,* 1147–1157.

Beckett, K. (1995). Fetal rights and "crack moms": Pregnant women in the war on drugs. *Contemporary Drug Problems, 22,* 587–612.

Coie, J. D., Dodge, K. A., & Coppotelli, H. (1982). Dimensions and types of social status: A cross-age perspective. *Developmental Psychology, 18,* 557–570.

Colby, A., & Damon, W. (1992). *Some do care: Contemporary lives of moral commitment.* New York: Free Press.

Colby, A., Kohlberg, L., Gibbs, J., & Lieberman, M. (1983). A longitudinal study of moral judgment. *Monographs of the Society for Research in Child Development, 48*(1–2, Serial No. 200).

Cole, D. A., Martin, J. M., Peeke, L. A., Seroczynski, A. D., & Fier, J. (1999). Children's over- and underestimation of academic competence: A longitudinal study of gender differences, depression, and anxiety. *Child Development, 70,* 459–473.

Cole, D. A., Maxwell, S. E., Martin, J. M., Peeke, L. G., Seroczynski, A. D., Tram, J. M., et al. (2001). The development of multiple domains of child and adolescent self-concept: A cohort sequential longitudinal design. *Child Development, 72,* 1723–1746.

Cole, P. M., Bruschi, C. J., & Tamang, B. L. (2002). Cultural differences in children's emotional reactions to difficult situations. *Child Development, 73,* 983–996.

Cole, P. M., Zahn-Waxler, C., & Smith, K. D. (1994). Expressive control during a disappointment: Variations related to preschoolers' behavior problems. *Developmental Psychology, 30,* 835–846.

Coleman, P. K., & Karraker, K. H. (1998). Self-efficacy and parenting quality: Findings and future applications. *Developmental Review, 18,* 47–85.

Coley, R. L. (1998). Children's socialization experiences and functioning in single-mother households: The importance of fathers and other men. *Child Development, 69,* 219–230.

Coley, R. L., & Chase-Lansdale, P. L. (1998). Adolescent pregnancy and parenthood: Recent evidence and future directions. *American Psychologist, 53,* 152–166.

Collaer, M. L., & Hines, M. (1995). Human behavioral sex differences: A role for gonadal hormones during early development? *Psychological Bulletin, 118,* 55–107.

Collins, J. A. (1995). A couple with infertility. *Journal of the American Medical Association, 274,* 1159–1164.

Collins, W. A., (1995). Relationships and development: Family adaptation to individual change. In S. Shulman (Ed.), *Close relationships and socioemotional development* (pp. 128–154). New York: Ablex.

Collins, W. A., & Laursen, B. (2004a). Parent-adolescent relationships and influences. In R. M. Lerner & L. Steinberg (Eds.), *Handbook of adolescent psychology* (2nd ed., pp. 331–361). Hoboken, NJ: Wiley.

Collins, W. A., & Laursen, B. (2004b). Changing relationships, changing youth: Interpersonal contexts of adolescent development. *Journal of Early Adolescence, 24,* 55–62.

Collins, W. A., Maccoby, E. E., Steinberg, L., Hetherington, E. M., & Bornstein, M. H. (2000). Contemporary research on parenting: The case for nature and nurture. *American Psychologist, 55,* 218–232.

Collins, W. A., & Steinberg, L. (2006). Adolescent development in interpersonal context. In W. Damon & R. M. Lerner (Editors-in-Chief) & N. Eisenberg (Vol. Ed.), *Handbook of child psychology: Vol. 3. Social, emotional, and personality development* (6th ed., pp. 1003–1067). Hoboken, NJ: Wiley.

Collis, B., & Ollila, L. (1990). The effects of computer use on grade 1 children's gender stereotypes about reading, writing, and computer use. *Journal of Research and Development in Education, 24,* 14–20.

Coltrane, S. (2000). Research on household labor: Modeling and measuring the social embeddedness of routine family work. *Journal of Marriage and the Family, 62,* 1208–1233.

Comeau, L., Cormier, P., Grandmaison, È., & Lacroix, D. (1999). A longitudinal study of phonological processing skills in children learning to read in a second language. *Journal of Educational Psychology, 91,* 29–43.

Committee on Genetics. (1996). Newborn screening fact sheet. *Pediatrics, 98,* 473–501.

Compas, B. E. (2004). Processes of risk and resilience during adolescence: Linking contexts and individuals. In R. M. Lerner & L. Steinberg (Eds.), *Handbook of adolescent psychology* (2nd ed., pp. 263–296). Hoboken, NJ: Wiley.

Compas, B. E., Langrock, A. M., Keller, G., Merchant, M. J., & Copeland, M. E. (2002). Coping with parental depression: Processes of adaptation to chronic stress. In S. H. Goodman & I. H. Gotlib (Eds.), *Children of depressed parents: Mechanisms of risk and implications for treatment* (pp. 227–252). Washington, DC: American Psychological Association.

Comstock, G. (1991). *Television and the American child.* Orlando, FL: Academic Press.

Comstock, G., & Scharrer, E. A. (2006). Media and popular culture. In W. Damon & R. M. Lerner (Editors-in-Chief) & K. A. Renninger & I. E. Sigel (Vol. Eds.), *Handbook of child psychology: Vol. 4. Child psychology in practice* (6th ed., pp. 817–863). Hoboken, NJ: Wiley.

Conger, R. D., Conger, K. J., Elder, G. H., Jr., Lorenz, F. O., Simons, R. L., & Whitbeck, L. B. (1992). A family process model of economic hardship and adjustment of early adolescent boys. *Child Development, 63,* 526–541.

Conger, R. D., Wallace, L. E., Sun, Y., Simons, R. L., McLoyd, V. C., & Brody, G. H. (2002). Economic pressure in African American families: A replication and extension of the family stress model. *Developmental Psychology, 38,* 179–193.

Connolly, J. A., Craig, W., Goldberg, A., & Pepler, D. (2004). Mixed gender groups, dating, and romantic relationships in early adolescence. *Journal of Research on Adolescence, 14,* 185–207.

Connolly, J., Furman, W., & Konarski, R. (2000). The role of peers in the emergence of heterosexual romantic relationships in adolescence. *Child Development, 71,* 1395–1408.

Connolly, J. A., & Johnson, A. (1996). Adolescents' romantic relationships and the structure and quality of their close interpersonal ties. *Personal Relationships, 3,* 185–195.

Connors, F., & Olson, R. K. (1990). Reading comprehension in dyslexic and normal readers: A component-skills analysis. In D. A. Balota, G. B. Flores d'Arcais, & K. Rayner (Eds.), *Comprehension processes in reading.* Hillsdale, NJ: Erlbaum.

Conway, A. R. A., Cowan, N., Bunting, M. F., Therriault, D. J., & Minkoff, S. R. B. (2002). A latent variable analysis of working memory capacity, short-term memory capacity, processing speed, and general fluid intelligence. *Intelligence, 30,* 163–184.

Cook, E. T., Greenberg, M. T., & Kusche, C. (1994). The relations between emotional understanding, intellectual functioning, and disruptive behavior problems in elementary-school-aged children. *Journal of Abnormal Child Psychology, 22,* 205–219.

Cook, T. D., Herman, M. R., Phillips, M., & Settersten, Jr., R. A. (2002). Some ways in which neighborhoods, nuclear families, friendship groups, and schools jointly affect changes in early adolescent development. *Child Development, 73,* 1283–1309.

Cooley, C. H. (1902). *Human nature and the social order.* New York: Scribner's.

Cooper, M. L., Shaver, P. R., & Collins, N. L. (1998). Attachment styles, emotion regulation, and adjustment in adolescence. *Journal of Personality and Social Psychology, 74,* 1380–1397.

Copper, R. L., Goldenberg, R. L., Cliver, S. P., DuBard, M. B., Hoffman, H. J., & Davis, R. O. (1993). Anthropometric assessment of body size differences of full-term male and female infants. *Obstetrics and Gynecology, 81,* 161–164.

Corina, D. P., McBurney, S. L., Dodrill, C., Hinshaw, K., Brinkley, J., & Ojemann, G. (1999). Functional roles of Broca's area and supramarginal gyrus: Evidence from cortical stimulation mapping of a deaf signer. *NeuroImage, 10,* 570–581.

Correa-Chávez, M., Rogoff, B., & Mejía Arauz, R. (2005). Cultural patterns in attending to two events at once. *Child Development, 76,* 664–678.

Costanzo, P. R., & Woody, E. Z. (1979). Externality as a function of obesity in children: Pervasive style or eating-specific attribute? *Journal of Personality and Social Psychology, 37,* 2286–2296.

Courage, M. L., & Howe, M. L. (2004). Advances in early memory development research: Insights about the dark side of the moon. *Developmental Review, 24,* 6–32.

Cournoyer, M., & Trudel, M. (1991). Behavioral correlates of self-control at 33 months. *Infant Behavior and Development, 14,* 497–503.

Coustan, D. R., & Felig, P. (1988). Diabetes mellitus. In G. N. Burrow & T. F. Ferris (Eds.), *Medical complications during pregnancy* (3rd ed.). Philadelphia: W.B. Saunders.

Cowan, N. (1999). The differential maturation of two processing rates related to digit span. *Journal of Experimental Child Psychology, 72,* 193–209.

Cowan, N., Wood, N. L., Wood, P. K., Keller, T. A., Nugent, L. D., & Keller, C. V. (1998). Two separate verbal processing rates contribute to short-term memory span. *Journal of Experimental Psychology: General, 127,* 141–160.

Cowan, W. M. (1979, September). The development of the brain. *Scientific American, 241,* 113–133.

Cox, M., & Harter, K. S. M. (2003). Parent-child relationships. In M. H. Bornstein & L. Davidson, C. Keyes, & K. Moore (Eds.), *Well-being: Positive development across the lifespan.* Mahwah, NJ: Erlbaum.

Cox, M. J., Owen, T. J., Henderson, V. K., & Margand, N. A. (1992). Prediction of infant-father and infant-mother interaction. *Developmental Psychology, 28,* 474–483.

Cox, M. J., & Paley, B. (2003). Understanding families as systems. *Current Directions in Psychological Science, 5,* 193–196.

Coyle, T. R., & Bjorklund, D. F. (1997). Age differences in, and consequences of, multiple- and variable-strategy use on a multitrial sort-recall task. *Developmental Psychology, 33,* 372–380.

Crain-Thoreson, C., & Dale, P. S. (1992). Do early talkers become early readers? Linguistic precocity, preschool language, and emergent literacy. *Developmental Psychology, 28,* 421–429.

Crandall, V. C. (1969). Sex differences in expectancy of intellectual and academic reinforcement. In C. P. Smith (Ed.), *Achievement-related motives in children.* New York: Russell Sage.

Crawford, P. B., Story, M., Wang, M. C., Ritchie, L. D., & Sabry, Z. I. (2001). Ethnic issues in the epidemiology of childhood obesity. *Pediatric Clinics of North America, 48,* 855–875.

Crick, N. R., Casas, J. F., & Mosher, M. (1997). Relational and overt aggression in preschool. *Developmental Psychology, 33,* 579–588.

Crick, N. R., & Dodge, K. A. (1994). A review and reformulation of social information-processing mechanisms in children's social adjustment. *Psychological Bulletin, 115,* 74–101.

Crick, N. R., & Dodge, K. A. (1996). Social information-processing mechanisms in reactive and proactive aggression. *Child Development, 67,* 993–1002.

Crick, N. R., & Grotpeter, J. K. (1995). Relational aggression, gender, and social-psychological adjustment. *Child Development, 66,* 710–722.

Crick, N. R., & Ladd, G. W. (1993). Children's perceptions of their peer experiences: Attributions, loneliness, social anxiety, and social avoidance. *Developmental Psychology, 29,* 244–254.

Criss, M. M., Pettit, G. S., Bates, J. E., Dodge, K. A., & Lapp, A. L. (2002). Family adversity, positive peer relationships, and children's externalizing behavior: A longitudinal perspective on risk and resilience. *Child Development, 73,* 1220–1237.

Crook, C. (1992). Cultural artifacts in social development: The case of computers. In H. McGurk (Ed.), *Childhood social development: Contemporary perspectives* (pp. 207–231). Hove, UK: Erlbaum.

Crouter, A. C., & Bumpus, M. F. (2001). Linking parents' work stress to children's and adolescents' psychological adjustment. *Current Directions in Psychological Science, 10,* 156–159.

Crouter, A. C., Bumpus, M. F., Davis, K. D., & McHale, S. M. (2005). How do parents learn about adolescents' experiences? Implications for parental knowledge and adolescent risky behavior. *Child Development, 76,* 869–882.

Crouter, A. C., Manke, B. A., & McHale, S. M. (1995). The family context of gender intensification in early adolescence. *Child Development, 66,* 317–329.

Crouter, A. C., McHale, S. M., & Tucker, C. J. (1999). Does stress exacerbate parental differential treatment of siblings? A pattern-analytic approach. *Journal of Family Psychology, 13,* 286–299.

Crowley, K., & Siegler, R. S. (1998). Explanation and generalization in young children's strategy learning. *Child Development, 70,* 304–316.

Csikszentmihalyi, M., & Larson, R. (1984). *Being adolescent.* New York: Basic Books.

Culley, L. (1993). Gender equity and computing in secondary schools. In J. Benyon & H. McKay (Eds.), *Computers into classrooms* (pp. 73–95). London: Falmer Press.

Cummings, E. M. (1995). Security, emotionality, and parental depression: A commentary. *Developmental Psychology, 31,* 425–427.

Cummings, E. M., Zahn-Waxler, C., & Radke-Yarrow, C. (1981). Young children's responses to expressions of anger and affection by others in the family. *Child Development, 52,* 1274–1282.

Cuniff, C., & Committee on Genetics. (2004). Prenatal screening and diagnosis for pediatricians. *Pediatrics, 114,* 889–894.

Cunningham, J. D. (1993). Experiences of Australian mothers who gave birth either at home, at a birth centre, or in hospital labour wards. *Social Science and Medicine, 36,* 475–483.

Curtiss, S. (1977). *Genie: A psycholinguistic study of a modern-day "wild child."* New York: Academic Press.

Cuttler, L., Silvers, J. B., Singh, J., Marrero, U., Finkelstein, B., Tannin, G., & Neuhauser, D. (1996, August 21). Short stature and growth hormone therapy: A national study of physician recommendation patterns. *Journal of the American Medical Association, 276,* 531–537.

Dahl, R. E., & Lewin, D. S. (2002). Pathways to adolescent health: Sleep regulation and behavior. *Journal of Adolescent Health, 31,* 175–184.

Dahl, R. E., Scher, M. S., Williamson, D. E., Robles, N., & Day, N. (1995). A longitudinal study of prenatal marijuana use: Effects on sleep and arousal at age 3 years. *Archives of Pediatric and Adolescent Medicine, 149,* 145–150.

Daley, T. C., Whaley, S. E., Sigman, M. D., Espinosa, M. P., & Neumann, C. (2003). IQ on the rise: The Flynn effect in rural Kenyan children. *Psychological Science, 14,* 215–219.

Dalterio, S., & Bartke, A. (1979). Perinatal exposure to cannabinoids alters male reproductive function in mice. *Science, 205,* 1420–1422.

Damon, W. (1983). *Social and personality development: Infancy through adolescence.* New York: W. W. Norton.

Damon, W., & Hart, D. (1988). *Self-understanding in childhood and adolescence.* New York: Cambridge University Press.

Daniels, K. (1989). Waterbirth: The newest form of safe, gentle and joyous birth. *Journal of Nurse-Midwifery, 34,* 198–205.

Daniels, K., & Taylor, K. (1993). Formulating selection policies for assisted reproduction. *Social Science & Medicine, 37,* 1473–1480.

Dapretto, M., & Bjork, E. L. (2000). The development of word retrieval abilities in the second year and its relation to early vocabulary growth. *Child Development, 71,* 635–648.

Dark, V. J., & Benbow, C. P. (1993). Cognitive differences among the gifted: A review and new data. In D. K. Detterman (Ed.), *Current topics in human intelligence. Vol. 3. Individual differences and cognition* (pp. 85–120). Norwood, NJ: Ablex.

Darnovsky, M. (2004). Revisiting sex selection: The growing popularity of new sex selection methods revives an old debate. *Gene Watch, 17,* 3–6.

Darwin, C. (1877). A biographical sketch of an infant. *Mind, 2,* 285–294.

Dasen, P. R. (1972). Cross-cultural Piagetian research: A summary. *Journal of Cross-Cultural Psychology, 3,* 23–39.

Davidoff, M. J., Dias, T., Damus, K., Russell, R., Bettegowda, V. R., et al. (2006). Changes in gestational age distribution among U. S. singleton births: Impact on rates of late preterm birth, 1992–2002. *Seminars in Perinatology, 30,* 8–15.

Davies, P. T., & Scummings, E. M. (1998). Exploring children's emotional security as a mediator of the link between marital relations and child adjustment. *Child Development, 69,* 124–139.

Davies, P. T., & Windle, M. (2000). Middle adolescents' dating pathways and psychosocial adjustment. *Merrill-Palmer Quarterly, 44,* 231–337.

Davis, B. L., MacNeilage, P. F., Matyear, C. L., & Powell, J. K. (2000). Prosodic correlates of stress in babbling: An acoustic study. *Child Development, 71,* 1258–1270.

Davis, S. C., & Roberts, I. A. G. (1996). Bone marrow transplant for sickle cell disease: An update. *Archives of Disease in Childhood, 75,* 448–450.

Davis-Kean, P. E., & Sandler, H. M. (2001). A meta-analysis of measures of self-esteem for young children: A framework for future measures. *Child Development, 72,* 887–906.

Davison, K. K., & Birch, L. L. (1999). Weight status, parent reaction, and self-concept in five-year-old girls. *Pediatrics, 107,* 46–53.

Davison, K. K., & Birch, L. L. (2002). Processes linking weight status and self-concept among girls from ages 5 to 7 years. *Developmental Psychology, 38,* 735–748.

Dawson, G. (1994). Development of emotion expression and emotion regulation in infancy. In G. Dawson & K. W. Fischer (Eds.), *Human behavior and the developing brain* (pp. 346–379). New York: Guilford.

Dawson, G., Munson, J., Estes, A., Osterling, J., McPartland, J., Toth, K., et al. (2002). Neurocognitive function and joint attention ability in young children with autism spectrum disorder versus developmental delay. *Child Development, 73,* 345–358.

Day, N. L., & Richardson, G. A. (1994). Comparative teratogenicity of alcohol and other drugs. *Alcohol Health and Research World, 18,* 42–48.

de Fockert, J. W., Rees, G., Frith, C. D., & Lavie, N. (2001). The role of working memory in visual selective attention. *Science, 291,* 1803–1806.

de Haan, M., & Nelson, C. A. (1997). Brain activity differentiates face and object processing in 6-month-olds. *Developmental Psychology, 35,* 1113–1121.

de Villiers, P. A., & de Villiers, J. G. (1979). Form and function in the development of sentence negation. *Papers and Reports in Child Language, 17,* 57–64.

De Wolff, M. S., & van IJzendoorn, M. H. (1997). Sensitivity and attachment: A meta-analysis on parental antecedents of attachment. *Child Development, 68,* 571–591.

Deák, G. O., & Bauer, P. J. (1996). The dynamics of preschoolers' categorization choices. *Child Development, 67,* 740–767.

Deater-Deckard, K., & Dunn, J. (1999). Multiple risks and adjustment in young children growing up in different family settings: A British community study of stepparent, single mother, and nondivorced families. In E. M. Hetherington (Ed.), *Coping with divorce, single parenting, and remarriage* (pp. 65–90). Mahwah, NJ: Erlbaum.

Deater-Deckard, K., Pike, A., Petrill, S. A., Cutting, A. L., Hughes, C., & O'Connor, T. G. (2001). Nonshared environmental processes in social-emotional development: An observational study of identical twin differences in the preschool period. *Developmental Science, 4,* F1–F6.

DeBaryshe, B. D. (1993). Joint picture-book reading correlates of early oral language skill. *Journal of Child Language, 20,* 455–461.

DeBaryshe, B. D., Patterson, G. R., & Capaldi, D. M. (1993). A performance model for academic achievement in early adolescent boys. *Developmental Psychology, 29,* 795–804.

DeBell, M., & Chapman, C. (2003). U.S. Department of Education, National Center for Education Statistics. *Computer and Internet use by children and adolescents in 2001* (NCES 2001–014). Washington, DC: U.S. Government Printing Office.

DeCasper, A. J., & Fifer, W. P. (1980). Of human bonding: Newborns prefer their mothers' voices. *Science, 208,* 1174–1176.

DeCasper, A. J., Lecanuet, J.-P., Busnel, M.-C., Granier-Deferre, C., & Maugeais, R. (1994). Fetal reactions to recurrent maternal speech. *Infant Behavior and Development, 17,* 159–164.

DeCasper, A. J., & Spence, M. J. (1986). Prenatal maternal speech influences newborns' perception of speech sounds. *Infant Behavior and Development, 9,* 133–150.

Declercq, E. R. (1993). Where babies are born and who attends their births: Findings from the revised 1989 United States Standard Certificate of Live Birth. *Obstetrics and Gynecology, 81,* 997–1004.

DeFries, J. C., Gervais, M. C., & Thomas, E. A. (1978). Response to 30 generations of selection for open-field activity in laboratory mice. *Behavior Genetics, 8,* 3–13.

Dekovic, M., & Janssens, J. (1992). Parents' child-rearing style and child's sociometric status. *Developmental Psychology, 28,* 925–932.

DeLisi, R., & Gallagher, A. M. (1991). Understanding of gender stability and constancy in Argentinian children. *Merrill-Palmer Quarterly, 37,* 483–502.

DeLoache, J. (1987). Rapid change in the symbolic functioning of young children. *Science, 238,* 1556–1557.

DeLoache, J. S. (2000). Dual representation and young children's use of scale models. *Child Development, 71,* 329–338.

DeLoache, J. S. (2004). Becoming symbol-minded. *Trends in Cognitive Sciences, 8,* 66–70.

DeLoache, J. S., & Smith, C. M. (1999). Early symbolic representation. In I. E. Sigel (Ed.), *Development of mental representation: Theories and applications* (pp. 61–86). Mahwah, NJ: Erlbaum.

Demany, L., McKenzie, B., & Vurpillot, E. (1977). Rhythm perception in early infancy. *Nature, 266,* 718–719.

Demetriou, H., & Hay, D. F. (2004). Toddlers' reactions to the distress of familiar peers: The importance of context. *Infancy, 6,* 299–318.

Demo, D. H., & Acock, A. C. (1996). Family structure, family process, and adolescent well-being. *Journal of Research on Adolescence, 6,* 457–488.

Dempster, F. N. (1981). Memory span: Sources of individual and developmental differences. *Psychological Bulletin, 89,* 63–100.

DeMulder, E. K., Denham, S., Schmidt, M., & Mitchell, J. (2000). Q-sort assessment of attachment security during the preschool years: Links from home to school. *Developmental Psychology, 36,* 274–282.

DeNavas-Walt, C., Proctor, B. D., & Lee, C. H. (2005). Income, poverty, and health insurance coverage in the United States: 2004. *Current Population Reports* (P60-229). Washington, DC: U.S. Government Printing Office.

Denham, S. A. (1998). *Emotional development in young children.* New York: Guilford.

Denham, S. A., McKinley, M., Couchoud, E. A., & Holt, R. (1990). Emotional and behavioral predictors of preschool ratings. *Child Development, 61,* 1145–1152.

Denham, S. A., Mitchell-Copeland, J., Strandberg, K., Auerbach, S., & Blair, K. (1997). Parental contributions to preschoolers' emotional competence: Direct and indirect effects. *Motivation and Emotion, 21,* 65–86.

Dennis, W. (1960). Causes of retardation among institutional children: Iran. *Journal of Genetic Psychology, 96,* 47–59.

Dennis, W., & Dennis, M. G. (1940). The effect of cradling practices upon the onset of walking in Hopi children. *Journal of Genetic Psychology, 56,* 77–86.

Desrochers, S., Ricard, M., Decarie, T. G., & Allard, L. (1994). Developmental synchrony between social referencing and Piagetian sensorimotor causality. *Infant Behavior and Development, 17,* 303–309.

Deur, J. L., & Parke, R. D. (1970). Effects of inconsistent punishment on aggression in children. *Developmental Psychology, 2,* 403–411.

Deutsch, M., Katz, I., & Jensen, A. R. (1968). *Social class, race, and psychological development.* New York: Holt, Rinehart & Winston.

Devoe, L. D., Murray, C., Youssif, A., & Arnaud, M. (1993). Maternal caffeine consumption and fetal behavior in normal third-trimester pregnancy. *American Journal of Obstetrics and Gynecology, 168,* 1105–1112.

Dhont, M., De Sutter, P., Ruyssinck, G., Martens, G., & Bekaert, A. (1999). Perinatal outcome of pregnancies after assisted reproduction: A case-control study. *American Journal of Obstetrics and Gynecology, 181,* 688–695.

Diamond, A. (1985). The development of the ability to use recall to guide action as indicated by infants' performance on A–B. *Child Development, 56,* 868–883.

Diamond, A. (1991). Neuropsychological insights into the meaning of object concept development. In S. Carey & R. Gelman (Eds.), *The epigenesis of mind: Essays on biology and cognition* (pp. 67–110). Hillsdale, NJ: Erlbaum.

Diamond, A., & Goldman-Rakic, P. S. (1989). Comparison of human infants and rhesus monkeys on Piaget's A–B task: Evidence for dependence on dorsolateral prefrontal cortex. *Experimental Brain Research, 74,* 24–40.

Diamond, A., Prevor, M. B., Callender, G., & Druin, D. P. (1997). Prefrontal cortex cognitive deficits in children treated early and continuously for PKU. *Monographs of the Society for Research in Child Development, 62*(4, Serial No. 252).

Diaz, R. M., & Klingler, C. (1991). Towards an explanatory model of the interaction between bilingualism and cognitive development. In E. Bialystok (Ed.), *Language processing in bilingual children.* Cambridge, UK: Cambridge University Press.

Diaz, R. M., Neal, C. J., & Vachio, A. (1991). Maternal teaching in the zone of the proximal development: A comparison of low- and high-risk dyads. *Merrill-Palmer Quarterly, 37,* 83–108.

Dick, D. M., Rose, R. J., Viken, R. J., & Kaprio, J. (2000). Pubertal timing and substance use: Associations between and within families across late adolescence. *Developmental Psychology, 36,* 180–189.

Dickens, W. T., & Flynn, J. R. (2001). Heritability estimates versus large environmental effects: The IQ paradox resolved. *Psychological Review, 108,* 346–369.

Dick-Read, G. (1959). *Childbirth without fear.* New York: Harper & Row.

Dien, D. S. (1982). A Chinese perspective on Kohlberg's theory of moral development. *Developmental Review, 2,* 331–341.

Dien, D. S.-F. (2000). The evolving nature of self-identity across four levels of history. *Human Development, 43,* 1–18.

Dietz, T. L. (1998). An examination of violence and gender role portrayals in video games: Implications for gender socialization and aggressive behavior. *Sex Roles, 38,* 425–442.

DiMatteo, M. R., Lepper, H. S., Damush, T. M., Morton, S. C., Carney, M. F., Pearson, M., & Kahn, K. L. (1996). Cesarean childbirth and psychosocial outcomes: A meta-analysis. *Health Psychology, 15,* 303–314.

Dion, K. K., & Berscheid, E. (1974). Physical attractiveness and peer perception among children. *Sociometry, 37,* 1–12.

Dishion, T. J., Andrews, D. W., & Crosby, L. (1995). Anti-social boys and their friends in early adolescence: Relationship characteristics, quality, and interactional process. *Child Development, 66,* 139–151.

Dishion, T. J., Patterson, G. R., & Griesler, P. C. (1994). Peer adaptations in the development of antisocial behavior: A confluence model. In L. R. Huesmann (Ed.), *Aggressive behavior: Current perspectives* (pp. 61–95). New York: Plenum.

Dishion, T.J., Spracklen, K. M., Andrews, D. W., & Patterson, G. R. (1996). Deviancy training in male adolescent friendships. *Behavior Therapy, 27,* 373–390.

DiVitto, B., & Goldberg, S. (1979). The effect of newborn medical status on early parent-infant interactions. In T. M. Field, A. M. Sostek, S. Goldberg, & H. H. Shuman (Eds.), *Infants born at risk.* New York: S. P. Medical & Scientific Books.

Dix, T. (1993). Attributing dispositions to children: An interactional analysis of attribution in socialization. *Personality and Social Psychology Bulletin, 19,* 633–643.

Dix, T. H., & Grusec, J. E. (1985). Parent attribution processes in the socialization of children. In I. E. Sigel (Ed.), *Parental belief systems: The psychological consequences for children.* Hillsdale, NJ: Erlbaum.

Dix, T. H., Ruble, D. N., Grusec, J. E., & Nixon, S. (1986). Social cognition in parents: Inferential and affective reactions to children of three age levels. *Child Development, 57,* 879–894.

Dix, T. H., Ruble, D. N., & Zambarano, R. J. (1989). Mothers' implicit theories of discipline: Child effects, parent effects, and the attribution process. *Child Development, 60,* 1373–1391.

Dixon, S., Tronick, E., Keeler, C., & Brazelton, T. B. (1981). Mother-infant interaction among the Gusii of Kenya. In T. M. Field, A. M. Sosteck, P. Vietze, & P. H. Leiderman (Eds.), *Culture and early interactions.* Hillsdale, NJ: Erlbaum.

Dixon, W. E., Jr., & Shore, C. (1997). Temperamental predictors of linguistic style during multiword acquisition. *Infant Behavior and Development, 20,* 99–103.

Dixon, W. E., Jr., & Smith, P. H. (2000). Links between early temperament and language acquisition. *Merrill-Palmer Quarterly, 46,* 417–440.

Dodge, K. A., Coie, J. D., & Lynam, D. (2006). Aggression and antisocial behavior in youth. In W. Damon & R. M. Lerner (Editors-in-Chief) & N. Eisenberg (Vol. Ed.), *Handbook of child psychology: Vol. 3. Social, emotional, and personality development* (6th ed., pp. 719–788). Hoboken, NJ: Wiley.

Dodge, K. A., Lansford, J. E., Burks, V. S., Bates, J. E., Pettit, G. S., et al. (2003). Peer rejection and social information-processing factors in development of aggressive behavior problems in children. *Child Development, 74,* 374–393.

Dodge, K. A., Murphy, R. R., & Buchsbaum, K. (1984). The assessment of intention-cue detection skills in children: Implications for developmental psychopathology. *Child Development, 55,* 163–173.

Dodge, K. A., & Pettit, G. S. (2003). A biopsychosocial model of the development of chronic conduct problems in adolescence. *Developmental Psychology, 39,* 349–371.

Dodge, K. A., Pettit, G. S., & Bates, J. E. (1994). Socialization mediators of the relation between socioeconomic status and child conduct problems. *Child Development, 65,* 649–665.

Doherty, W. J., & Needle, R. H. (1991). Psychological adjustment and substance use among adolescents before and after parental divorce. *Child Development, 62,* 328–337.

Donnelly, M., & Wilson, R. (1994). The dimensions of depression in early adolescence. *Personality and Individual Differences, 17,* 425–430.

Dooley, S. L. (1999). Routine ultrasound in pregnancy. *Clinical Obstetrics and Gynecology,* 737–748.

Dornbusch, S. M., Ritter, P. L., Leiderman, P. H., Roberts, D. F., & Fraleigh, M. J. (1987). The relation of parenting style to adolescent school performance. *Child Development, 58,* 1244–1257.

Dowling, J. E. (1998). *Creating mind: How the brain works.* New York: Norton.

Downey, G., Feldman, S., Khuri, J., & Friedman, S. (1994). Maltreatment and childhood depression. In W. M. Reynolds & H. F. Johnston (Eds.), *Handbook of depression in children and adolescents: Issues in clinical child psychology* (pp. 481–508). New York: Plenum.

Dozier, M., Stovall, K. C., Albus, K. E., & Bates, B. (2001). Attachment for infants in foster care: The role of caregiver state of mind. *Child Development, 72,* 1467–1477.

Dreher, M. C., Nugent, K., & Hudgins, R. (1994). Prenatal marijuana exposure and neonatal outcomes in Jamaica: An ethnographic study. *Pediatrics, 93,* 254–260.

Drewett, R., Wolke, D., Asefa, M., Kaba, M., & Tessema, F. (2001). Malnutrition and mental development: Is there a sensitive period? A nested case-control study. *Journal of Child Psychology and Psychiatry, 42,* 181–187.

Dromi, E. (1999). Early lexical development. In M. Barrett (Ed.), *The development of language* (pp. 99–131). East Sussex, UK: Psychology Press.

Drotar, D., & Robinson, J. (2000). Developmental psychopathology of failure to thrive. In A. J. Sameroff & M. L. Lewis (Eds.), *Handbook of developmental psychopathology* (2nd ed., pp. 351–364). Dordrecht, Netherlands: Kluwer.

Drug and Therapeutics Committee of the Lawson Wilkins Pediatric Endocrine Society. (1995). Guidelines for the use of growth hormone in children with short stature. *Journal of Pediatrics, 127,* 857–867.

Dubner, A. E., & Motta, R. W. (1999). Sexually and physically abused foster care children and posttraumatic stress disorder. *Journal of Consulting and Clinical Psychology, 67,* 367–373.

DuBois, D. L., Burk-Braxton, C., Swenson, L. P., Tevendale, H. D., Lockerd, E. M., & Moran, B. L. (2002). Getting by with a little help from self and others: Self-esteem and social support as resources in early adolescence. *Developmental Psychology, 38,* 822–839.

DuBois, D. L., Tevendale, H. D., Burk-Braxton, C., Swenson, L. P., & Hardesty, J. L. (2000). Self-system influences during early adolescence: Investigation of an integrative model. *Journal of Early Adolescence, 20,* 12–43.

Dubow, E. F., Tisak, J., Causey, D., Hryshko, A., & Reid, G. (1991). A two-year longitudinal study of stressful life events, social support, and social problem-solving skills: Contributions to children's behavioral and academic adjustment. *Child Development, 62,* 583–599.

Dunham, P., & Dunham, F. (1995). Developmental antecedents of taxonomic and thematic strategies at 3 years of age. *Developmental Psychology, 31,* 483–493.

Dunn, J. (1988). Connections between relationships: Implications of research on mothers and siblings. In R. A. Hinde & J. Stevenson-Hinde (Eds.), *Relationships within families: Mutual influences.* Oxford: Clarendon Press.

Dunn, J. (1996). Brothers and sisters in middle childhood and early adolescence: Continuity and change in individual differences. In G. H. Brody (Ed.), *Sibling relationships: Their causes and consequences.* Norwood, NJ: Ablex.

Dunn, J., Bretherton, I., & Munn, P. (1987). Conversations about feeling states between mothers and their young children. *Developmental Psychology, 23,* 132–139.

Dunn, J., & Brown, J. R. (1994). Affect expression in the family, children's understanding of emotions, and their interactions with others. *Merrill Palmer Quarterly, 40,* 120–137.

Dunn, J., Brown, J. R., & Maguire, M. (1995). The development of children's moral sensibility: Individual differences and emotion understanding. *Developmental Psychology, 31,* 649–659.

Dunn, J., & Cutting, A. L. (1999). Understanding others, and individual differences in friendship interactions in young children. *Social Development, 8,* 201–219.

Dunn, J., & Hughes, C. (2001). "I got some swords and you're dead!": Violent fantasy, antisocial behavior, and moral sensibility in young children. *Child Development, 72,* 491–505.

Dunn, J., & Kendrick, C. (1982). *Siblings: Love, envy, and understanding.* Cambridge, MA: Harvard University Press.

Dunn, J., & McGuire, S. (1994). Young children's nonshared experiences: A summary of studies in Cambridge and Colorado. In E. M. Hetherington, D. Reiss, & R. Plomin (Eds.), *Separate social worlds of siblings: The impact of nonshared environment on development* (pp. 111–128). Hillsdale, NJ: Erlbaum.

Dunn, J., Slombowski, C., & Beardsall, L. (1994). Sibling relationships from the preschool period through middle childhood and early adolescence. *Developmental Psychology, 30,* 315–324.

Durik, A. M., Hyde, J. S., & Clark, R. (2000). Sequelae of Cesarean and vaginal deliveries: Psychosocial outcomes for mothers and infants. *Developmental Psychology, 36,* 251–260.

Durston, S., Davidson, M. C., Tottenham, N., Galvan, A., Spicer, J., et al. (2006). A shift from diffuse to focal cortical activity with development. *Developmental Science, 9,* 1–8.

Durston, S., Hulshoff, H. E., Casey, B. J., Giedd, J. N., Buitelaar, J. K., & van Engeland, H. (2001). Anatomical MRI of the developing human brain: What have we learned? *Journal of the American Academy of Adolescent Psychiatry, 40* 1012–1020.

Durston, S., Thomas, K. M., Yang, Y., Ulug, A. M., Zimmerman, R. D., & Casey, B. J. (2002). A neural basis for the development of inhibitory control. *Developmental Science, 5,* F9–F16.

Dusek, J. B. (2000). Commentary on the special issue: The maturing of self-esteem research with early adolescents. *Journal of Early Adolescence, 20,* 231–240.

Dweck, C. S. (1986). Motivational processes affecting learning. *American Psychologist, 41,* 1040–1048.

Dweck, C. S. (1991). Self-theories and goals: Their role in motivation, personality, and development. In R. Diestbier (Ed.), *Nebraska Symposium on Motivation, 1990* (Vol. 36, pp. 199–235). Lincoln: University of Nebraska Press.

Dweck, C. S. (1999). *Self-theories: Their role in motivation, personality, and development.* Philadelphia, PA: Psychology Press.

Dweck, C. S., & Elliott, E. S. (1983). Achievement motivation. In E. M. Hetherington (Ed.), *Handbook of child psychology: Vol. IV. Socialization, personality, and social development* (4th ed., pp. 643–691). New York: Wiley.

Dweck, C. S., Goetz, T. E., & Strauss, N. L. (1980). Sex differences in learned helplessness: IV. An experimental and naturalistic study of failure generalization and its mediators. *Journal of Personality and Social Psychology, 38,* 441–452.

Dybdahl, R. (2001). Children and mothers in war: An outcome study of a psychosocial intervention program. *Child Development, 72,* 1214–1230.

Dye, N. S. (1986). The medicalization of birth. In P. S. Eakins (Ed.), *The American way of birth.* Philadelphia: Temple University Press.

Eagly, A. H., & Steffen, V. J. (1986). Gender and aggressive behavior: A meta-analytic review of the social psychological literature. *Psychological Bulletin, 100,* 309–330.

East, P. L., & Jacobson, L. J. (2001). The younger siblings of teenage mothers: A follow-up of their pregnancy risk. *Developmental Psychology, 37,* 254–264.

Ebrahim, S. H., Luman, E. T., Floyd, R. L., Murphy, C. C., Bennett, D. M., & Boyle, C. A. (1998). Alcohol consumption by pregnant women in the United States during 1988–1995. *Obstetrics and Gynecology, 92,* 187–192.

Eccles, J. (1983). Expectancies, values, and academic behaviors. In J. T. Spence (Ed.), *Achievement and achievement motives: Psychological and sociological approaches.* San Francisco: W.H. Freeman.

Eccles, J. S. (1987). Adolescence: Gateway to androgyny? In D. B. Carter (Ed.), *Current conceptions of sex roles and sex typing: Theory and research* (pp. 225–241). New York: Praeger.

Eccles, J. S., & Barber, B. L. (1999). Student council, volunteering, basketball, or marching band: What kind of extracurricular involvement matters? *Journal of Adolescent Research, 14,* 10–43.

Eccles, J., Barber, B., Jozefowicz, D., Malenchuk, O., & Vida, M. (1999). Self-evaluations of competence, task values, and self-esteem. In N. G. Johnson, M. C. Roberts, & J. Worell (Eds.), *Beyond appearance: A new look at adolescent girls* (pp. 53–83). Washington, DC: American Psychological Association.

Eccles, J. S., Lord, S. E., Roeser, R. W., Barber, B. L., & Jozefowicz, D. M. H. (1997). The association of school transitions in early adolescence with developmental trajectories through high school. In J. Schulenberg, J. Maggs, & K. Hurrelmann (Eds.), *Health risks and developmental transitions during adolescence* (pp. 283–320). New York: Cambridge University Press.

Eccles, J. S., & Midgley, C. (1989). Stage/environment fit: Developmentally appropriate classrooms for early adolescents. In R. E. Ames & C. Ames (Eds.), *Research on motivation in education* (Vol. 3, pp. 139–186). San Diego, CA: Academic Press.

Eccles, J. S., Midgley, C., Wigfield, A., Buchanan, C. M., Reuman, D., Flanagan, C., & Mac Iver, D. (1993). Development during adolescence: The impact of stage-environment fit on young adolescents' experiences in schools and families. *American Psychologist, 48,* 90–101.

Eccles, J. S., & Roeser, R. W. (1999). School and community influences on human development. In M. H. Bornstein & M. E. Lamb (Eds.), *Developmental psychology: An advanced textbook* (4th ed., pp. 503–554). Mahwah, NJ: Erlbaum.

Eccles, J., Wigfield, A., Harold, R. D., & Blumenfeld, P. (1993). Age and gender differences in children's self- and task perceptions during elementary school. *Child Development, 64,* 830–847.

Eckenrode, J., Laird, M., & Doris, J. (1993). School performance and disciplinary problems among abused and neglected children. *Developmental Psychology, 29,* 53–62.

Eckerman, C. O., Whatley, J. L., & Kutz, S. L. (1975). Growth of social play with peers during the second year of life. *Developmental Psychology, 11,* 42–49.

Eder, D., & Hallinan, M. T. (1978). Sex differences in children's friendships. *American Sociological Review, 43,* 237–250.

Egan, S. K., & Perry, D. G. (1998). Does low self-regard invite victimization? *Developmental Psychology, 34,* 299–309.

Egan, S. K., & Perry, D. G. (2001). Gender identity: A multidimensional analysis with implications for psychosocial adjustment. *Developmental Psychology, 37,* 451–463.

Egeland, B., & Sroufe, L. A. (1981). Attachment and early maltreatment. *Child Development, 52,* 44–52.

Egeland, B., Jacobvitz, D., & Papatola, K. (1987). Intergenerational continuity of abuse. In R. J. Gelles & J. B. Lancaster (Eds.), *Child abuse and neglect: Biosocial dimensions.* Hawthorne, NY: Aldine de Gruyter.

Ehrenberg, R. G., Brewer, D. J., Gamoran, A., & Willms, J. D. (2001a). Class size and student achievement. *Psychological Science in the Public Interest, 2,* 1–30.

Ehrenberg, R. G., Brewer, D. J., Gamoran, A., & Willms, J. D. (2001b, November). Does class size matter? *Scientific American, 285,* 79–85.

Ehri, L. C. (1998). Grapheme-phoneme knowledge is essential for learning to read words in English. In J. L. Metsala & L. C. Ehri (Eds.), *Word recognition in beginning literacy* (pp. 3–40). Mahwah, NJ: Erlbaum.

Eigsti, I., & Cicchetti, D. (2004). The impact of child maltreatment on expressive syntax at 60 months. *Developmental Science, 7,* 88–102.

Eilers, R. E., & Berlin, C. (1995). Advances in early detection of hearing loss in infants. *Current Problems in Pediatrics, 25,* 60–66.

Eimas, P. D., Siqueland, E. R., Jusczyk, P., & Vigorito, J. (1971). Speech perception in infants. *Science, 171,* 303–306.

Eisenberg, N. (1986). *Altruistic emotion, cognition, and behavior.* Hillsdale, NJ: Erlbaum.

Eisenberg, N., Boehnke, K., Schuhler, P., & Silbereisen, R. K. (1985). The development of prosocial behavior and cognition in German children. *Journal of Cross-Cultural Psychology, 16,* 69–82.

Eisenberg, N., Carol, G., Murphy, B., & Van Court, P. (1995). Prosocial development in late adolescence: A longitudinal study. *Child Development, 66,* 1179–1197.

Eisenberg, N., & Fabes, R. A. (1998). Prosocial development. In W. Damon (Series Ed.) & N. Eisenberg (Vol. Ed.), *Handbook of child psychology: Vol. 3. Social, emotional, and personality development* (5th ed., pp. 701–778). New York: Wiley.

Eisenberg, N., Fabes, R. A., Shepard, S. A., Guthrie, I. K., Murphy, B. C., & Reiser, M. (1999). Parental reactions to children's negative emotions: Longitudinal reactions to the quality of children's social functioning. *Child Development, 70,* 513–534.

Eisenberg, N., Fabes, R. A., Shepard, S. A., Murphy, B. C., Guthrie, I. K., Jones, S., et al. (1997). Contemporaneous and longitudinal prediction of children's social functioning from regulation and emotionality. *Child Development, 68,* 642–664.

Eisenberg, N., Fabes, R. A., & Spinrad, T. L. (2006). Prosocial development. In W. Damon & R. M. Lerner (Editors-in-Chief) & N. Eisenberg (Vol. Ed.), *Handbook of child psychology: Vol. 3. Social, emotional, and personality development* (6th ed., pp. 646–718). Hoboken, NJ: Wiley.

Eisenberg, N., Gershoff, E. T., Fabes, R. A., Shepard, S. A., Cumberland, A. J., Losoya, S. H., et al. (2001). Mother's emotional expressivity and children's behavior problems and social competence: Mediation through children's regulation. *Developmental Psychology, 37,* 475–490.

Eisenberg, N., Hertz-Lazarowitz, R., & Fuchs, I. (1990). Prosocial moral judgment in Israeli kibbutz and city children: A longitudinal study. *Merrill-Palmer Quarterly, 36,* 273–285.

Eisenberg, N., & Lennon, R. (1983). Sex differences in empathy and related capacities. *Psychological Bulletin, 94,* 100–131.

Eisenberg, N., & Miller, P. A. (1987). The relation of empathy to prosocial and related behaviors. *Psychological Bulletin, 101,* 91–119.

Eisenberg, N., & Mussen, P. H. (1989). *The roots of prosocial behavior in children.* Cambridge, UK: Cambridge University Press.

Eisenberg, N., Pidada, S., & Liew, J. (2001). The relations of regulation and negative emotionality to Indonesian children's social functioning. *Child Development, 72,* 1747–1763.

Eisenberg, N., & Shell, R. (1986). Prosocial moral judgment and behavior in children: The mediating role of cost. *Personality and Social Psychology Bulletin, 12,* 426–433.

Eisenberg, N., Valiente, C., Morris, A. S., Fabes, R. A., Cumberland, A., et al. (2003). Longitudinal relations among parental emotional expressivity, children's regulation, and quality of socioemotional functioning. *Developmental Psychology, 39,* 3–19.

Eisenberg, N., Zhou, Q., Losoya, S. H., Fabes, R. A., Shepard, S. A., et al. (2003). The relations of parenting, effortful control, and ego control to children's emotional expressivity. *Child Development, 74,* 875–895.

Eisenberg, N., Zhou, Q., Spinrad, T., Valiente, C., Fabes, R. A., & Liew, J. (2005). Relations among positive parenting, children's effortful control, and externalizing problems: A three-wave longitudinal study. *Child Development, 76,* 1055–1071.

Eizenman, D. R., & Bertenthal, B. I. (1998). Infants' perception of object unity in translating and rotating displays. *Developmental Psychology, 34,* 426–434.

Ekman, P. (1972). Universals and cultural differences in facial expressions of emotion. In J. K. Cole (Ed.), *Nebraska symposium on motivation, 1971.* Lincoln: University of Nebraska Press.

Ekman, P. (1973). Cross-cultural studies of facial expression. In P. Ekman (Ed.), *Darwin and facial expression.* New York: Academic Press.

Elardo, R., & Bradley, R. H. (1981). The Home Observation for Measurement of the Environment (HOME) scale: A review of research. *Developmental Review, 1,* 113–145.

Elardo, R., Bradley, R. H., & Caldwell, B. M. (1975). The relation of infants' home environments to mental test performance from six to thirty-six months: A longitudinal analysis. *Child Development, 46,* 71–76.

Elardo, R., Bradley, R., & Caldwell, B. M. (1977). A longitudinal study of the relation of infants' home environments to language development at age three. *Child Development, 48,* 595–603.

Eley, T. C. (1997). General genes: A new theme in developmental psychopathology. *Current Directions in Psychological Science, 6,* 90–95.

Elfenbein, H. A., & Ambady, N. (2002). On the universality and cultural specificity of emotion recognition: A meta-analysis. *Psychological Bulletin, 128,* 203–235.

Elias, S., Simpson, J. L., & Shulman, L. P. (2002). Techniques for prenatal diagnosis. In D. L. Rimoin, J. M. Connor, R. E. Pyeritz, & B. R. Korf (Eds.), *Emery and Rimoin's principles and practice of medical genetics* (4th ed., Vol. 1, pp. 802–825). London: Churchill Livingston.

Eliez, S., & Reiss, A. L. (2000). Genetics of childhood disorders: 77 Fragile X syndrome. *Journal of the American Academy of Child and Adolescent Psychiatry, 39,* 264–266.

Elkind, D. (1976). *Child development and education.* New York: Oxford.

Elkind, D. (1981). *Children and adolescents: Interpretive essays on Jean Piaget* (3rd ed.). New York: Oxford University Press.

Ellemberg, D., Lewis, T. L., Liu, C. H., & Maurer, D. (1999). Development of spatial and temporal vision during childhood. *Vision Research, 39,* 2325–2333.

Elliott, D. S., Wilson, W. J., Huizinga, D., Sampson, R. J., Elliott, A., & Rankin, B. (1996). The effects of neighborhood disadvantage on adolescent development. *Journal of Crime and Delinquency, 33,* 389–426.

Ellis, B. J., & Garber, J. (2000). Psychosocial antecedents of variation in girls' pubertal timing: Maternal depression, stepfather presence, and marital and family stress. *Child Development, 71,* 273–287.

Emde, R. N., & Koenig, K. L. (1969). Neonatal smiling, frowning and rapid eye movement states. *Journal of the American Academy of Child Psychiatry, 8,* 57–67.

Emde, R. N., Plomin, R., Robinson, J., Corley, R., DeFries, J., Walker, D. W., et al. (1992). Temperament, emotion, and cognition at fourteen months: The MacArthur longitudinal twin study. *Child Development, 63,* 1427–1455.

Emery, R. E. (1999a). Changing the rules for determining child custody in divorce cases. *Clinical Psychology: Science and Practice, 6,* 323–327.

Emery, R. E. (1999b). *Marriage, divorce, and children's adjustment* (2nd ed.). Thousand Oaks, CA: Sage.

Emery, R. E., Otto, R. K., & O'Donohue (2005). A critical assessment of child custody evaluations. *Psychological Science in the Public Interest, 6,* 1–29.

Emmons, L. (1996). The relationship of dieting to weight in adolescents. *Adolescence, 31,* 167–178.

Emory, E. K., Schlackman, L. J., & Fiano, K. (1996). Drug-hormone interactions on neurobehavioral responses in human neonates. *Infant Behavior and Development, 19,* 213–220.

Eng, T. R., & Butler, W. T. (Eds.). (1997). *The hidden epidemic: Confronting sexually transmitted disease.* Washington, DC: Institute of Medicine, National Academy Press.

Engle, R. W. (2002). Working memory capacity as executive attention. *Current Directions in Psychological Science, 11,* 19–23.

Engle, R. W., Kane, M. J., & Tuholski, S. W. (1999). Individual differences in working memory capacity and what they tell us about controlled attention, general fluid intelligence, and functions of the prefrontal cortex. In A. Miyake & P. Shah (Eds.), *Models of working memory: Mechanisms of active maintenance and executive control* (pp. 102–134). New York: Cambridge University Press.

Enright, M. K., Rovee-Collier, C. K., Fagen, J. W., & Caniglia, K. (1983). The effects of distributed training on retention of operant conditioning in human infants. *Journal of Experimental Child Psychology, 36,* 512–524.

Ensembl Human. (2006). *Explore the* Homo sapiens *genome.* Retrieved May 5, 2006, from www.ensembl.org/Homo_sapiens/index.html.

Entwisle, D. (1995). The role of schools in sustaining early childhood program benefits. *The Future of Children: Long-term Outcomes of Early Childhood Programs, 5,* 133–143.

Epstein, C. J. (2001). Down syndrome (Trisomy 21). In C. R. Scriver, A. L. Beaudet, W. S. Sly, & D. Valle (Eds.), *The metabolic and molecular bases of inherited disease* (8th ed., Vol. 1, pp.1223–1256). New York: McGraw-Hill.

Epstein, J. L. (1983). Examining theories of adolescent friendship. In J. L. Epstein & N. L. Karweit (Eds.), Friends in school. San Diego: Academic Press.

Erbe, R. W., & Levy, H. L. (2002). Neonatal screening. In D. L. Rimoin, J. M. Connor, R. E. Pyeritz, & B. R. Korf (Eds.), *Emery and Rimoin's principles and practice of medical genetics* (4th ed., Vol. 1, pp. 826–841). London: Churchill Livingston.

Erdley, C. A., Cain, K. M., Loomis, C. C., Dumas-Hines, F., & Dweck, C. S. (1997). Relations among children's social goals, implicit personality theories, and responses to social failure. *Developmental Psychology, 33,* 263–272.

Erhardt, D., & Hinshaw, S. P. (1994). Initial sociometric impressions of attention-deficit hyperactivity disorder and comparison boys: Predictions from social behaviors and from nonbehavioral variables. *Journal of Consulting and Clinical Psychology, 62,* 833–842.

Erickson, M. F., Sroufe, L. A., & Egeland, B. (1985). The relationship between quality of attachment and behavior problems in preschool in a high-risk sample. In I. Bretherton & E. Waters (Eds.), *Growing points of attachment theory and research. Monographs of the Society for Research in Child Development, 50*(1–2, Serial No. 209).

Erikson, E. H. (1950). *Childhood and society.* New York: W. W. Norton.

Ernst, M., Moolchan, E. T., & Robinson, M. L. (2001). Behavioral and neural consequences of prenatal exposure to nicotine. *Journal of the Academy of Adolescent Psychiatry, 40,* 630–641.

Eron, L. D., Huesmann, L. R., & Zelli, A. (1991). The role of parental variables in the learning of aggression. In D. J. Pepler & K. H. Rubin (Eds.), *The development and treatment of childhood aggression* (pp. 169–188). Hillsdale, NJ: Erlbaum.

Erwin, P. (1985). Similarity of attitudes and constructs in children's friendships. *Journal of Experimental Child Psychology, 40,* 470–485.

Eskenazi, B., Stapleton, A. L., Kharrazi, M., & Chee, W. Y. (1999). Associations between maternal decaffeinated and caffeinated coffee consumption and fetal growth and gestational duration. *Epidemiology, 10,* 242–249.

Eskritt, M., & Lee, K. (2002). "Remember where you last saw that card": Children's production of external symbols as a memory aid. *Developmental Psychology, 38,* 254–266.

Espy, K. A., & Kaufmann, P. M. (2002). Individual differences in the development of executive function in children: Lessons from the delayed response and A-not-B tasks. In D. L. Molfese & V. J. Molfese (Eds.), *Developmental variations in learning: Applications to social, executive function, language, and reading skills* (pp. 113–137). Mahwah, NJ: Erlbaum.

European Collaborative Study. (2001). Fluctuations in symptoms in human immunodeficiency virus-infected children: The first 10 years of life. *Pediatrics, 108,* 116–122.

Eveleth, P. B., & Tanner, J. M. (1990). *Worldwide variation in human growth* (2nd ed.). Cambridge, UK: Cambridge University Press.

Everman, D. B., & Cassidy, S. B. (2000). Genetics of childhood disorders: 12 Genomic imprinting: Breaking the rules. *Journal of the American Academy of Child and Adolescent Psychiatry, 39,* 386–389.

Eyler, F. D., Behnke, M., Conlon, M., Woods, N. W., & Wobie, K. (1998). Birth outcomes from a prospective matched study of prenatal crack cocaine use: II. Interactive and dose effects on neurobehavioral assessment. *Pediatrics, 101,* 237–241.

Ezzell, C. (2000, July). Beyond the human genome. *Scientific American, 283,* 64–69.

Fabes, R. A., Eisenberg, N., Hanish, L. D., & Spinrad, T. L. (2001). Preschoolers' spontaneous emotion vocabulary: Relations to likability. *Early Education and Development, 12,* 11–27.

Fabes, R. A., Eisenberg, N., Jones, S., Smith, M., Guthries, I, Poulin, R., et al. (1999). Regulation, emotionality, and preschoolers' socially competent peer interactions. *Child Development, 70,* 432–442.

Fabes, R. A., Eisenberg, N., Karbon, M., Troyer, D., & Switzer, G. (1994). The relations of children's emotion regulation to their vicarious emotional responses and comforting behaviors. *Child Development, 65,* 1678–1693.

Fabes, R. A., Eisenberg, N., McCormick, S. E., & Wilson, M. S. (1988). Preschoolers' attributions of the situational determinants of others' naturally occurring emotions. *Developmental Psychology, 24,* 376–385.

Fabes, R. A., Hanish, L. D., Martin, C. L., & Eisenberg, N. (2002). Young children's negative emotionality and social isolation: A latent growth curve analysis. *Merrill Palmer Quarterly, 48,* 284–307.

Fabes, R. A., Leonard, S. A., Kupanoff, K., & Martin, C. L. (2001). Parental coping with children's negative emotions: Relations with children's emotional and social responding. *Child Development, 72,* 907–920.

Fackelmann, K. (1998). It's a girl! Is sex selection the first step to designer children? *Science News, 154,* 350–351.

Fagan, J. F., III. (1974). Infant recognition memory: The effects of length of familiarization and type of discrimination task. *Child Development, 45,* 351–356.

Fagan, J. F., & Holland, C. R. (2002). Equal opportunity and racial differences in IQ. *Intelligence, 30,* 361–387.

Fagot, B. I. (1977). Consequences of moderate cross-gender behavior in preschool children. *Child Development, 48,* 902–907.

Fagot, B. I. (1978). The influence of sex of child on parental reactions to toddler children. *Child Development, 49,* 459–465.

Fagot, B. I. (1985). Changes in thinking about early sex role development. *Developmental Review, 5,* 83–98.

Fagot, B. I., & Leinbach, M. D. (1987). Socialization of sex roles within the family. In D. B. Carter (Ed.), *Current conceptions of sex roles and sex typing: Theory and research.* New York: Praeger.

Fagot, B. I., & Leinbach, M. D. (1989). The young child's gender schema: Environmental input, internal organization. *Child Development, 60,* 663–672.

Fagot, B. I., & Leinbach, M. D. (1995). Gender knowledge in egalitarian and traditional families. *Sex Roles, 32,* 513–526.

Fagot, B. I., Leinbach, M. D., & O'Boyle, C. (1992). Gender labeling, gender stereotyping, and parenting behaviors. *Developmental Psychology, 28,* 225–230.

Falbo, T., & Cooper, C. R. (1980). Young children's time and intellectual ability. *Journal of Genetic Psychology, 173,* 299–300.

Falbo, T., & Polit, D. F. (1986). Quantitative review of the only child literature: Research evidence and theory development. *Psychological Bulletin, 100,* 176–189.

Famularo, R., Fenton, T., Kinscherff, R., Ayoub, C., & Barnum, R. (1994). Maternal and child posttraumatic disorder in cases of child maltreatment. *Child Abuse and Neglect, 18,* 27–36.

Fancher, R. E. (1998). Alfred Binet, general psychologist. In G. A. Kimble & M. Wertheimer (Eds.), *Portraits of pioneers in psychology* (Vol. 3, pp. 67–83). Washington, DC: American Psychological Association.

Fangman, J. J., Mark, P. M., Pratt, L., Conway, K. K., Healey, M. L., Oswald, J. W., & Uden, D. L. (1994). Prematurity prevention programs: An analysis of successes and failures. *American Journal of Obstetrics and Gynecology, 170,* 744–750.

Fantz, R. L. (1961, May). The origin of form perception. *Scientific American, 204,* pp. 66–72.

Farmer, T. W., Estell, D. B., Bishop, J. L., O'Neal, K. K., & Cairns, B. D. (2003). Rejected bullies or popular leaders? The social relations of aggressive subtypes of rural African American early adolescents. *Developmental Psychology, 39,* 992–1004.

Farooqi, I. S., & O'Rahilly, S. (2000). Recent advances in the genetics of severe childhood obesity. *Archives of Disease in Childhood, 83,* 31–34.

Farr, K. A. (1995). Fetal abuse and the criminalization of behavior during pregnancy. *Crime and Delinquency, 41,* 235–245.

Farrar, M. J. (1992). Negative evidence and grammatical morpheme acquisition. *Developmental Psychology, 28,* 90–98.

Farrell, A. D., & Bruce, S. E. (1997). Impact of exposure to community violence on violent behavior and emotional distress among urban adolescents. *Journal of Clinical Child Psychology, 26,* 2–17.

Farrell, S. P., Hains, A. A., & Davies, W. H. (1998). Cognitive behavioral interventions for sexually abused children exhibiting PTSD symptomology. *Behavior Therapy, 29,* 241–255.

Farrington, D. P. (1991). Childhood aggression and adult violence: Early precursors and later-life outcomes. In D. J. Pepler & K. H. Rubin (Eds.), *The development and treatment of childhood aggression* (pp. 5–29). Hillsdale, NJ: Erlbaum.

Farver, J. M., Kim, Y. K., & Lee, Y. (1995). Cultural differences in Korean- and Anglo-American preschoolers' social interaction and play behaviors. *Child Development, 66,* 1088–1099.

Farver, J. M., & Shin, Y. L. (1997). Social pretend play in Korean- and Anglo-American preschoolers. *Child Development, 68,* 544–556.

Farver, J. M., & Wimbarti, S. (1995). Paternal participation in toddlers' pretend play. *Social Development, 4,* 17–31.

Fausto-Sterling, A. (1992). *Myths of gender: Biological theories about women and men* (2nd ed.). New York: Basic Books.

Federman, J. (1998). *National Television Violence Study III.* Thousand Oaks, CA: Sage.

Federal Interagency Forum on Child and Family Statistics. (2005). *Backgrounder: Healthy eating index shows most children and adolescents have a diet that is poor or needs improvement.* Retrieved January 13, 2003, from childstats.gov/ac1999/heirel.asp

Federal Interagency Forum on Child and Family Statistics. (2005). *America's children: Key national indicators of well-being 2005.* Washington, DC: U.S. Government Printing Office.

Feinberg, M. E., & Hetherington, E. M. (2000). Sibling differentiation in adolescence: Implications for behavioral genetic theory. *Child Development, 71,* 1512–1524.

Feingold, A. (1988). Cognitive gender differences are disappearing. *American Psychologist, 43,* 95–103.

Feingold, A. (1992). Sex differences in variability in intellectual abilities: A new look at an old controversy. *Review of Educational Research, 62,* 61–84.

Feingold, A. (1993). Cognitive gender differences: A developmental perspective. *Sex Roles, 29,* 91–112.

Feingold, A. (1994). Gender differences in personality: A meta-analysis. *Psychological Bulletin, 116,* 429–456.

Feldman, D. (1979). The mysterious case of extreme giftedness. In H. Passow (Ed.), *The gifted and talented.* Chicago: University of Chicago Press.

Feldman, H., Goldin-Meadow, S., & Gleitman, L. (1978). Beyond Herodotus: The creation of language by linguistically deprived children. In A. Locke (Ed.), *Action, gesture, and symbol: The emergence of language.* New York: Academic Press.

Feldman, P. J., Dunkel-Schetter, C., Sandman, C. A., & Wadhwa, P. D. (2000). Maternal social support predicts birth weight and fetal growth in human pregnancy. *Psychosomatic Medicine, 62,* 715–725.

Feldman, R., Weller, A., Sirota, L., & Eidelman, A. I. (2002). Skin-to-skin contact (kangaroo care) promotes self-regulation in premature infants: Sleep-wake cyclicity, arousal modulation, and sustained exploration. *Developmental Psychology, 38,* 194–207.

Feldman, W., Feldman, E., & Goodman, J. T. (1988). Culture versus biology: Children's attitudes toward fatness and thinness. *Pediatrics, 81,* 190–194.

Felner, R. D., & Adan, A. M. (1988). The School Transitional Environment Project: An ecological intervention and evaluation. In R. H. Price, E. L. Cowan, R. P. Lorion, I. Serrano-Garcia, & J. Ramos-McKay (Eds.), *14 ounces of prevention: A casebook for practitioners.* Washington, DC: American Psychological Association.

Felner, R. D., Ginter, M., & Primavera, J. (1982). Primary prevention during school transitions: Social support and environmental structure. *American Journal of Community Psychology, 10,* 277–290.

Felson, R. B. (1993). The (somewhat) social self: How others affect self-appraisals. In J. Suls (Ed.), *Psychological perspectives on the self* (Vol. 4, pp. 1–26). Hillsdale, NJ: Erlbaum.

Fenson, L., Dale, P. S., Reznick, J. S., Bates, E., Thal, D. J., & Pethick, S. J. (1994). Variability in early communicative development. *Monographs of the Society for Research in Child Development, 59* (5, Serial No. 242).

Fergusson, D. M., Lynskey, M., & Horwood, L. J. (1995). The adolescent outcomes of adoption: A 16-year longitudinal study. *Journal of Child Psychology and Psychiatry and Allied Disciplines, 36,* 597–615.

Fergusson, D. M., Woodward, L. J., & Horwood, L. J. (1998). Maternal smoking during pregnancy and psychiatric adjustment in late adolescence. *Archives of General Psychiatry, 55,* 721–727.

Fernald, A. (1985). Four-month-olds prefer to listen to motherese. *Infant Behavior and Development, 8,* 181–195.

Fernald, A. (1991). Prosody in speech to children: Prelinguistic and linguistic features. In R. Vasta (Ed.), *Annals of child development: Vol. 8.* London: Jessica Kingsley.

Fernald, A., & Mazzie, C. (1991). Prosody and focus in speech to infants and adults. *Developmental Psychology, 27,* 209–221.

Fernald, A., & Morikawa, H. (1993). Common themes and cultural variations in Japanese and American mothers' speech to infants. *Child Development, 64,* 637–656.

Fernald, A., Perfors, A., & Marchman, V. A. (2006). Picking up speed in understanding: Speech processing efficiency and vocabulary growth across the 2nd year. *Developmental Psychology, 42,* 98–116.

Fernald, A., Swingley, D., & Pinto, J. P. (2001). When half a word is enough: Infants can recognize spoken words using partial phonetic information. *Child Development, 72,* 1003–1015.

Ferrier, S., Dunham, P., & Dunham, F. (2000). The confused robot: Two-year-olds' responses to breakdowns in conversation. *Social Development, 9,* 337–347.

Feuerstein, R., Rand, Y., & Rynders, J. (1988). *Don't accept me as I am: Helping "retarded" people to excel.* New York: Plenum.

Field, J., Muir, D., Pilon, R., Sinclair, M., & Dodwell, P. (1980). Infants' orientation to lateral sounds from birth to three months. *Child Development, 51,* 295–298.

Field, T. (1979). Differential behavior and cardiac responses of 3-month-olds to a mirror and a peer. *Infant Behavior and Development, 2,* 179–184.

Field, T. (1995). Infants of depressed mothers. *Infant Behavior and Development, 18,* 1–13.

Field, T. (2001). Massage therapy facilitates weight gain in preterm infants. *Current Directions in Psychological Science, 10,* 51–54.

Field, T. M. (1977). Effects of early separation, interactive deficits, and experimental manipulations on infant-mother face-to-face interactions. *Child Development, 48,* 763–771.

Field, T. M. (1982). Affective displays of high-risk infants during early interactions. In T. Field & A. Fogel (Eds.), *Emotion and early interaction.* Hillsdale, NJ: Erlbaum.

Field, T. M., Cohen, D., Garcia, R., & Greenberg, R. (1984). Mother-stranger face discrimination by the newborn. *Infant Behavior and Development, 7,* 19–25.

Field, T., Fox, N. A., Pickens, J., & Nawrocki, T. (1995). Relative right frontal EEG activation in 3- to 6-month-old infants of "depressed" mothers. *Developmental Psychology, 31,* 358–363.

Field, T., Healy, B., Goldstein, S., Perry, S., Bendell, D., Schanberg, S., et al. (1988). Infants of depressed mothers show "depressed" behavior even with nondepressed adults. *Child Development, 59,* 1569–1579.

Field, T., Scafidi, F., Pickens, J., Prodromidis, M., Pelaez-Nogueras, M., Torquati, J., et al. (1998). Polydrug-using adolescent mothers and their infants receiving early intervention. *Adolescence, 33,* 117–143.

Field, T. M., Woodson, R., Cohen, D., Greenberg, R., Garcia, R., & Collins, K. (1983). Discrimination and imitation of facial expressions by term and preterm neonates. *Infant Behavior and Development, 6,* 485–489.

Field, T. M., Woodson, R., Greenberg, R., & Cohen, D. (1982). Discrimination and imitation of facial expressions by neonates. *Science, 218,* 179–181.

Fillmore, L. W., & Meyer, L. (1992). The curriculum and linguistic minorities. In P. Jackson (Ed.), *Handbook of research on curriculum.* New York: Macmillan.

Finch, E. (1978). *Clinical assessment of short stature.* Unpublished medical school thesis, Yale University.

Fine, M. A., Coleman, M., & Ganong, L. H. (1999). A social constructionist multi-method approach to understanding the stepparent role. In E. M. Hetherington (Ed.), *Coping with divorce, single parenting, and remarriage* (pp. 273–294). Mahwah, NJ: Erlbaum.

Finn, J. D., & Achilles, C. M. (1990). Answers and questions about class size: A statewide experiment. *American Educational Research Journal, 27,* 557–577.

Finnie, V., & Russell, A. (1988). Preschool children's social status and their mothers' behavior and knowledge in the supervisory role. *Developmental Psychology, 24,* 789–801.

Fioravanti, F., Inchingolo, P., Pensiero, S., & Spanio, M. (1995). Saccadic eye movement conjugation in children. *Vision Research, 35,* 3217–3228.

Fischbein, S. (1981). Heredity-environment influences on growth and development during adolescence. In L. Gedda, P. Parisi, & W. E. Nance (Eds.), *Twin research 3: Pt. B. Program in clinical and biological research.* New York: Liss.

Fischer, K. W., & Bidell, T. R. (2006). Dynamic development of action and thought. In W. Damon & R. M. Lerner (Editors-in-Chief) & R. M. Lerner (Vol. Ed.), *Handbook of child psychology: Vol. 1. Theoretical models of human development* (6th ed., pp. 313–399). Hoboken, NJ: Wiley.

Fisher, C. (2002). Structural limits on verb mapping: The role of abstract structure in 2.5-year-olds' interpretations of novel verbs. *Developmental Science, 5,* 55–64.

Fisher, C. B. (1994). Reporting and referring research participants: Ethical challenges for investigators studying children and youth. *Ethics & Behavior, 4,* 87–95.

Fisher, C. B., Higgins D'Alessandro, A., Rau, J. M. B., Kuther, T. L., & Belanger, S. (1996). Referring and reporting research participants at risk: Views from urban adolescents. *Child Development, 67,* 2086–2100.

Fishkin, J., Keniston, K., & MacKinnon, C. (1973). Moral reasoning and political ideology. *Journal of Personality and Social Psychology, 27,* 109–119.

Fivush, R. (1984). Learning about school: The development of kindergartners' school scripts. *Child Development, 55,* 1697–1709.

Fivush, R. (1997). Event memory in early childhood. In N. Cowan (Ed.), *The development of memory in childhood* (pp. 139–161). East Sussex, UK: Psychology Press.

Fivush, R., & Schwarzmueller, A. (1998). Children remember childhood: Implications for childhood amnesia. *Applied Cognitive Psychology, 12,* 455–473.

Fivush, R., Haden, C., & Adam, S. (1995). Structure and coherence of preschoolers' personal narratives over time: Implications for childhood amnesia. *Journal of Experimental Child Psychology, 60,* 32–56.

Fivush, R., Kuebli, J., & Clubb, P. A. (1992). The structure of events and event representations: A developmental analysis. *Child Development, 63,* 188–201.

Flanagan, C. A. (1990). Change in family work status: Effects on parent-adolescent decision making. *Child Development, 61,* 163–177.

Flannagan, D., & Hardee, S. D. (1994). Talk about preschoolers' interpersonal relationships: Patterns related to culture, SES, and gender of child. *Merrill-Palmer Quarterly, 40,* 523–537.

Flavell, J. H. (1963). *The developmental psychology of Jean Piaget.* New York: Van Nostrand Reinhold.

Flavell, J. H. (1970). Developmental studies of mediated memory. In H. W. Reese & L. P. Lipsitt (Eds.), *Advances in child development and behavior* (Vol. 5). New York: Academic Press.

Flavell, J. H. (1978). The development of knowledge about visual perception. In C. B. Keasey (Ed.), *Nebraska symposium on motivation* (Vol. 25). Lincoln: University of Nebraska Press.

Flavell, J. H. (1993). Young children's understanding of thinking and consciousness. *Current Directions in Psychological Science, 2,* 40–43.

Flavell, J. H. (1996). Piaget's legacy. *Psychological Science, 7,* 200–203.

Flavell, J. H., Beach, D. H., & Chinsky, J. M. (1966). Spontaneous verbal rehearsal in a memory task as a function of age. *Child Development, 37,* 283–299.

Flavell, J. H., Flavell, E. R., Green, F. L., & Korfmacher, J. E. (1990). Do young children think of television images as pictures or real objects? *Journal of Broadcasting & Electronic Media, 34,* 399–419.

Flavell, J. H., & Wellman, H. M. (1977). Metamemory. In R. V. Kail & J. W. Hagen (Eds.), *Perspectives on the development of memory and cognition* (pp. 3–33). Hillsdale, NJ: Erlbaum.

Flavell, J. H., Green, F. L., & Flavell, E. R. (1995). The development of children's knowledge about attentional focus. *Developmental Psychology, 31,* 706–712.

Flavell, J. H., Zhang, X-D, Zou, H., Dong, Q., & Qi, S. (1983). A comparison of the appearance-reality distinction in the People's Republic of China and the United States. *Cognitive Psychology, 15,* 459–466.

Fletcher, A. C., Steinberg, L., & Williams-Wheeler, M. (2004). Parental influences on adolescent problem behavior: Revisiting Stattin and Kerr. *Child Development, 75,* 781–796.

Fletcher-Flinn, C. M., & Thompson, G. B. (2000). Learning to read with underdeveloped phonemic awareness but lexicalized phonological recoding: A case study of a 3-year-old. *Cognition, 74,* 177–208.

Flick, L., Vemulapalli, C., Stulac, B. B., & Kemp, J. S. (2001). The influence of grandmothers and other senior caregivers on sleep position used by African American infants. *Archives of Pediatrics and Adolescent Medicine, 155,* 1231–1237.

Flieller, A. (1999). Comparison of the development of formal thought in adolescent cohorts aged 10 to 15 years (1967–1996 and 1972–1993). *Developmental Psychology, 35,* 1048–1058.

Florsheim, P., Tolan, P., & Gorman-Smith, D. (1998). Family relationship, parenting practices, the availability of male family members, and the behavior of inner-city boys in single-mother and two-parent families. *Child Development, 69,* 1437–1447.

Flynn, J. R. (1998). IQ gains over time: Toward finding the causes. In U. Neisser (Ed.), *The rising curve: Long-term gains in IQ and related measures* (pp. 25–66). Washington, DC: American Psychological Association.

Flynn, J. R. (1999). Searching for justice: The discovery of IQ gains over time. *American Psychologist, 54,* 5–20.

Foa, E. B., & Meadows, E. A. (1997). Psychosocial treatments for post-traumatic stress disorder: A critical review. *Annual Review of Psychology, 48,* 449–480.

Fodor, J. A . (1992). A theory of the child's theory of mind. *Cognition, 44,* 283–296.

Fodor, J. A. (1983). *The modularity of mind.* Cambridge, MA: MIT Press.

Fogel, A. (1979). Peer- vs. mother-directed behavior in 1- to 3-month-old infants. *Infant Behavior and Development, 2,* 215–226.

Fogel, A. (1982). Early adult-infant face-to-face interaction: Expectable sequences of behavior. *Journal of Pediatric Psychology, 7,* 1–22.

Fomon, S. J. (1993). *Nutrition of normal infants.* St. Louis, MO: Mosby-Yearbook.

Food and Drug Aministration. (2005). *Public Health Advisory: Strengthened risk management program for isotretinoin.* Retrieved May 3, 2006, from www.fda.gov/cder/drug/advisory/isotretinoin2005.htm.

Forbes, E. E., Cohn, J. F., Allen, N. B., & Lewinsohn, P. M. (2004). Infant affect during parent-infant interaction at 3 and 6 months: Differences between mothers and fathers and influence of parent history of depression. *Infancy, 5,* 61–84.

Forman, D. R., & Kochanska, G. (2001). Viewing imitation as child responsiveness: A link between teaching and discipline domains of socialization. *Developmental Psychology, 37,* 198–206.

Forman, D. R., Aksan, N., & Kochanska, G. (2004). Toddlers' responsive imitation predicts preschool-age conscience. *Psychological Science, 15,* 699–704.

Foulon, W., Villena, I., Stray-Pedersen, B., Decoster, A., Lappalainen, M., Pinon, J.-M., et al. (1999). Treatment of toxoplasmosis during pregnancy: A multicenter study of impact on fetal transmission and children's sequelae at age 1 year. *American Journal of Obstetrics and Gynecology, 180,* 410–415.

Fox, N. A. (1991). If it's not left, it's right: Electroencephalograph asymmetry and the development of emotion. *American Psychologist, 46,* 863–872.

Fox, N. A. (1994). Dynamic cerebral processes underlying emotion regulation. In N. A. Fox (Ed.), *The development of emotion regulation: Biological and behavioral considerations. Monographs of the Society for Research in Child Development, 59* (Nos. 2–3, Serial No. 240).

Fox, N. A., & Davidson, R. J. (1986). Psychophysiological measures of emotion: New directions in developmental research. In C. E. Izard & P. B. Read (Eds.), *Measuring emotions in infants and children* (Vol. 2). Cambridge, UK: Cambridge University Press.

Fox, R., Aslin, R. N., Shea, S. L., & Dumais, S. T. (1980). Stereopsis in human infants. *Science, 207,* 323–324.

Fraiberg, S. (1977). *Insights from the blind.* New York: Basic Books.

Franco, P., Groswasser, J., Hassid, S., Lanquart, J. P., Scaillet, S., & Kahn, A. (1999). Prenatal exposure to cigarette smoking is associated with a decrease in arousal in infants. *Journal of Pediatrics, 135,* 34–38.

Frank, D. A., Augustyn, M., Knight, W. G., Pell, T., & Zuckerman, B. (2001). Growth, development, and behavior in early childhood following prenatal cocaine exposure: A systematic review. *Journal of the American Medical Association, 285,* 1613–1625.

Franklin, C., Grant, D., Corcoran, J., O'Dell-Miller, P., & Bultman, L. (1997). Effectiveness of prevention programs for adolescent pregnancy: A meta-analysis. *Journal of Marriage and the Family, 59,* 551–567.

Fraser, S. (1995). *The bell curve wars: Race, intelligence, and the future of America.* New York: Basic Books.

Frauenglass, M. H., & Diaz, R. M. (1985). Self-regulatory functions of children's private speech: A critical analysis of recent challenges to Vygotsky's theory. *Developmental Psychology, 21,* 357–364.

Frazier, J. A., & Morrison, F. J. (1998). The influence of extended-year schooling on growth of achievement and perceived competence in early elementary school. *Child Development, 69,* 495–517.

Fredricks, J. A., & Eccles, J. S. (2002). Children's competence and value beliefs from childhood through adolescence: Growth trajectories in two male-sex-typed domains. *Developmental Psychology, 38,* 519–533.

Fredriks, A. M., Van Buren, S., Burgmeijer, R. J. F., Meulmeester, J. F., Beuker, R. J., Brugman, E., et al. (2000). Continuing positive secular growth change in the Netherlands 1955–1997. *Pediatric Research, 47,* 316–323.

Fredriksen, K., Rhodes, J., Reddy, R., & Way, N. (2004). Sleepless in Chicago: Tracking the effects of adolescent sleep loss during the middle school years. *Child Development, 75,* 84–95.

Freedland, R. L., & Bertenthal, B. I. (1994). Developmental changes in interlimb coordination: Transition to hands-and-knees crawling. *Psychological Science, 5,* 26–32.

French, S. E., Seidman, E., Allen, L., & Aber, J. L. (2000). Racial/ethnic identity, congruence with the social context, and the transition to high school. *Journal of Adolescent Research, 15,* 587–602.

French, S. E., Seidman, E., Allen, L., & Aber, J. L. (2006). The development of ethnic identity during adolescence. *Developmental Psychology, 42,* 1–10.

Frey, K. S., Hirschstein, M. K., Snell, J. L., Edstrom, L. V. S., MacKenzie, E. P., & Broderick, C. J. (2005). Reducing playground bullying and supporting beliefs: An experimental trial of the *Steps to Respect* program. *Developmental Psychology, 41,* 479–491.

Frey, K. S., & Ruble, D. N. (1987). What children say about classroom performance: Sex and grade differences in perceived competence. *Child Development, 58,* 1066–1078.

Fried, P. A., Watkinson, B., & Gray, R. (1998). Differential effects on cognitive functioning in 9- to 12-year-olds prenatally exposed to cigarettes and marijuana. *Neurotoxicology and Teratology, 20,* 293–306.

Friedman, J. M., & Hanson, J. W. (2002). Clinical teratology. In D. L. Rimoin, J. M. Connor, R. E. Pyeritz, & B. R. Korf (Eds.), *Emery and Rimoin's principles and practice of medical genetics* (4th ed., Vol. 1, pp. 1011–1045). London: Churchill Livingston.

Friedman, J. M., & Polifka, J. E. (1996). *The effects of drugs on the fetus and nursing infant: A handbook for health care professionals.* Baltimore: Johns Hopkins University Press.

Frith, U., & Happé, F. (1999). Theory of mind and self-consciousness: What is it like to be autistic? *Mind & Language, 14,* 1–22.

Frodi, A. M., & Lamb, M. E. (1980). Child abusers' responses to infant smiles and cries. *Child Development, 51,* 238–241.

Frodi, A. M., Lamb, M. E., Leavitt, L. A., & Donovan, W. L. (1978). Fathers' and mothers' responses to infant smiles and cries. *Infant Behavior and Development, 1,* 187–198.

Frodi, A. M., & Thompson, R. (1985). Infants' affective responses in the strange situation: Effects of prematurity and of quality of attachment. *Child Development, 56,* 1280–1290.

Fuligni, A. J. (1997). The academic achievement of adolescents from immigrant families: The roles of family background, attitudes, and behavior. *Child Development, 68,* 351–363.

Fuligni, A. J., & Eccles, J. S. (1993). Perceived parent-child relationships and early adolescents' orientation toward peers. *Developmental Psychology, 29,* 622–632.

Fuligni, A. J., & Stevenson, H. W. (1995). Time use and mathematics achievement among American, Chinese, and Japanese high school students. *Child Development, 66,* 830–842.

Fuligni, A. J., Eccles, J. S., Barber, B. L., & Clements, P. (2001). Early adolescent peer orientation and adjustment during high school. *Developmental Psychology, 37,* 28–36.

Fuligni, A. J., Witkow, M., & Garcia, C. (2005). Ethnic identity and the academic adjustment of adolescents from Mexican, Chinese, and European backgrounds. *Developmental Psychology, 41,* 799–811.

Fulker, O. W., & Eysenck, H. J. (1979). Nature, nurture and socioeconomic status. In H. J. Eysenck (Ed.), *The structure and measurement of intelligence.* Berlin: Springer-Verlag.

Furman, W. (1999). Friends and lovers: The role of peer relationships in adolescent romantic relationships. In W. A. Collins & B. Laursen (Eds.), *Minnesota symposia on child psychology: Vol. 30. Relationships as developmental contexts* (pp. 133–154). Mahwah, NJ: Erlbaum.

Furman, W. (2002). The emerging field of adolescent romantic relationships. *Current Directions in Psychological Science, 11,* 177–180.

Furman, W., & Bierman, K. L. (1984). Children's conceptions of friendship: A multimethod study of developmental changes. *Developmental Psychology, 20,* 925–931.

Furman, W., & Buhrmester, D. (1992). Age and sex differences in perceptions of networks of personal relationships. *Child Development, 63,* 103–115.

Furman, W., Somin, V. A., Shaffer, L., & Bouchey, H. A. (2002). Adolescents' working models and styles for relationships with parents, friends, and romantic partners. *Child Development, 73,* 241–255.

Furman, W., & Wehner, E. A. (1994). Romantic views: Toward a theory of adolescent romantic relationships. In R. Montemayor, G. R. Adams, & G. P. Gullota (Eds.), *Advances in adolescent development: Vol. 6. Relationships during adolescence* (pp. 168–175). Thousand Oaks, CA: Sage.

Furnham, A., & Mak, T. (1999). Sex-role stereotyping in television commercials: A review and comparison of fourteen studies done on five continents over 25 years. *Sex Roles, 41,* 413–437.

Furstenberg, F. F. (1994). History and current status of divorce in the United States. *The Future of Children, 4,* 29–43.

Furstenberg, F. F., Jr. (1987). The new extended family: The experience of parents and children after remarriage. In K. Paley & M. Ihinger-Tallman (Eds.), *Remarriage and stepparenting.* New York: Guilford Press.

Furstenberg, F. F., Jr., Brooks-Gunn, J., & Chase-Lansdale, L. (1989). Teenaged pregnancy and childbearing. *American Psychologist, 44,* 313–320.

Fuson, K. C., & Kwon, Y. (1992). Korean children's understanding of multidigit addition and subtraction. *Child Development, 63,* 491–506.

Gabbe, S. G., & Turner, L. P. (1997). Reproductive hazards of the American lifestyle: Work during pregnancy. *American Journal of Obstetrics and Gynecology, 176,* 826–832.

Gabel, S. (1997). Conduct disorder in grade-school children. In J. D. Noshpitz (Series Ed.) & P. F. Kernberg & J. R. Bemporad (Vol. Eds.), *Handbook of child and adolescent psychiatry* (Vol. 2, pp. 309–401). New York: Wiley.

Gaddis, A., & Brooks-Gunn, J. (1985). The male experience of pubertal change. *Journal of Youth and Adolescence, 14,* 61–69.

Gagnon, M., & Ladouceur, R. (1992). Behavioral treatment of child stutterers: Replication and extension. *Behavior Therapy, 23,* 113–129.

Galambos, N. L. (2004). Gender and gender role development in adolescence. In R. M. Lerner & L. Steinberg (Eds.), *Handbook of adolescent psychology* (2nd ed., pp. 233–262). Hoboken, NJ: Wiley.

Gallahue, D. L. (1989). *Understanding motor development: Infants, children, adolescents.* Indianapolis, IN: Benchmark Press.

Galler, J. R., Ramsey, F. C., Morley, D. S., Archer, E., & Salt, P. (1990). The long-term effects of early kwashiorkor compared with marasmus. IV. Performance on the National High School Entrance Exam. *Pediatric Research, 28,* 235–239.

Gallistel, C. R., Brown, A. L., Carey, S., Gelman, R., & Keil, F. C. (1991). Lessons from animal learning for the study of cognitive development. In S. Carey & R. Gelman (Eds.), *The epigenesis of mind: Essays on biology and cognition* (pp. 3–36). Hillsdale, NJ: Erlbaum.

Galton, F. (1883). *Inquiries into human faculty and its development.* London: Macmillan.

Gannon, P. J., Holloway, R. L., Broadfield, D. C., & Braun, A. R. (1998). Asymmetry of chimpanzee planum temporale: Humanlike pattern of Wernicke's brain language area homolog. *Science, 279,* 220–222.

Garabino, J. (1982). Sociocultural risk: Dangers to competence. In C. Kopp & J. Krakow (Eds.), *Child development in a social context.* Reading, MA: Addison-Wesley.

Garcia, M. M., Shaw, D. S., Winslow, E. B., & Yaggi, K. E. (2000). Destructive sibling conflict and the development of conduct problems in young boys. *Developmental Psychology, 36,* 44–53.

Gardner, B. T., & Gardner, R. A. (1971). Two-way communication with an infant chimpanzee. In A. M. Schrier & F. Stollnitz (Eds.), *Behavior of nonhuman primates.* New York: Academic Press.

Gardner, D., Harris, P. L., Ohmoto, M., & Hamasaki, T. (1988). Japanese children's understanding of the distinction between real and apparent emotion. *International Journal of Behavioral Development, 11,* 203–218.

Gardner, H. (1983). *Frames of mind: The theory of multiple intelligences.* New York: Basic Books.

Gardner, H. (1986). The waning of intelligence tests. In R. J. Sternberg & D. K. Detterman (Eds.), *What is intelligence?* (pp. 73–76). Norwood, NJ: Ablex.

Gardner, H. (1998). Are there additional intelligences? The case for naturalistic, spiritual, and existential intelligences. In J. Kane (Ed.), *Education, information, and transformation: Essays on learning and thinking* (pp. 111–131). Upper Saddle River, NJ: Prentice Hall.

Gardner, M., & Steinberg, L. (2005). Peer influence on risk taking, risk preference, and risky decision making in adolescence and adulthood: An experimental study. *Developmental Psychology, 41,* 625–635.

Gardner, W., & Rogoff, B. (1990). Children's deliberateness of planning according to task circumstances. *Developmental Psychology, 26,* 480–487.

Garland, A. F., & Zigler, E. (1993). Adolescent suicide prevention: Current research and social policy implications. *American Psychologist, 48,* 169–182.

Gash, H., & Morgan, M. (1993). School-based modifications of children's gender-related beliefs. *Journal of Applied Developmental Psychology, 14,* 277–287.

Gavin, L. A., & Furman, W. (1989). Age differences in adolescent's perceptions of their peer groups. *Developmental Psychology, 25,* 827–834.

Gazelle, H., & Ladd, G. W. (2003). Anxious solitude and peer exclusion: A diathesis-stress model of internalizing trajectories in childhood. *Child Development, 74,* 257–278.

Gazelle, H., & Rudolph, K. D. (2004). Moving toward and away from the world: Approach and avoidance trajectories in anxious solitary youth. *Child Development, 75,* 829–849.

Ge, X., Best, K. M., Conger, R. D., & Simons, R. L. (1996). Parenting behaviors and the occurrence and co-occurrence of adolescent depressive symptoms and conduct problems. *Developmental Psychology, 32,* 717–731.

Ge, X., Conger, R. D., & Elder, G. H., Jr. (1996). Coming of age too early: Pubertal influences on girls' vulnerability to psychological distress. *Child Development, 67,* 3386–3400.

Ge, X., Kim, I. J., Brody, G. H., Conger, R. D., Simons, R. L., et al. (2003). It's about timing and change: Pubertal transition effects on symptoms of major depression among African American youths. *Developmental Psychology, 39,* 430–439.

Ge, X., Lorenz, F. O., Conger, R. D., Elder, G. H., Jr., & Simons, R. L. (1994). Trajectories of stressful life events and depressive symptoms during adolescence. *Developmental Psychology, 30,* 467–483.

Geary, D. C., Bow-Thomas, C. C., Fan, L., & Siegler, R. S. (1993). Even before formal instruction, Chinese children outperform American children in mental addition. *Cognitive Development, 8,* 517–529.

Geldart, S., Maurer, D., & Carney, K. (1999). Effects of the height of the internal features of faces on adult's aesthetic ratings and 5-month-old's looking times. *Perception, 28,* 839–850.

Gelman, R. (1969). Conservation acquisition: A problem of learning to attend to relevant attributes. *Journal of Experimental Child Psychology, 7,* 167–187.

Gelman, R., & Gallistel, C. R. (1978). *The child's understanding of number.* Cambridge, MA: Harvard University Press.

Gelman, R., & Meck, E. (1983). Preschoolers' counting: Principles before skill. *Cognition, 13,* 343–359.

Gelman, R., Spelke, E. S., & Meck, E. (1983). What preschoolers know about animate and inanimate objects. In D. Rogers & J. A. Sloboda (Eds.), *The acquisition of symbolic skills.* New York: Plenum.

Gelman, R., & Williams, E. M. (1998). Enabling constraints for cognitive development: Domain specificity and epigenesis. In W. Damon (Series Ed.) & D. Kuhn & R. S. Siegler (Vol. Eds.), *Handbook of child psychology: Vol. 2. Cognition, perception, and language* (5th ed., pp. 575–630). New York: Wiley.

Gelman, S. A., Coley, J. D., Rosengren, K. S., Hartman, E., & Pappas, A. (1998). Beyond labeling: The role of maternal input in the acquisition of richly structured categories. *Monographs of the Society for Research in Child Development, 63*(1, Serial No. 253).

Gelman, S. A., & Kalish, C. W. (2006). Conceptual development. In W. Damon & R. M. Lerner (Editors-in-Chief) & D. M. Kuhn & R. S. Siegler (Vol. Eds.), *Handbook of child psychology: Vol. 2. Cognition, perception, and language* (6th ed., pp. 687–733). Hoboken, NJ: Wiley.

Gelman, S. A., & Kremer, K. E. (1991). Understanding natural cause: Children's explanations of how objects and their properties originate. *Child Development, 62,* 396–414.

Gelman, S. A., Taylor, M. G., & Nguyen, S. P. (2004). Mother-child conversations about gender. *Monographs of the Society for Research in Child Development, 69*(1, Serial No. 275).

Gershkoff-Stowe, L. (2001). The course of children's naming errors in early word learning. *Journal of Cognition and Development, 2,* 131–155.

Gershkoff-Stowe, L., & Smith, L. B. (1997). A curvilinear trend in naming errors as a function of early vocabulary growth. *Cognitive Psychology, 34,* 37–71.

Gershoff, E. T. (2002). Corporal punishment by parents and associated child behaviors and experiences: A meta-analytic and theoretical review. *Psychological Bulletin, 128,* 539–579.

Geschwind, M., & Galaburda, A. M. (1987). *Cerebral lateralization.* Cambridge, MA: MIT Press.

Gesell, A., & Thompson, H. (1934). *Infant behavior: Its genesis and growth.* New York: McGraw-Hill.

Gesell, A., & Thompson, H. (1938). *The psychology of early growth.* New York: Macmillan.

Gewirtz, J. L., & Peláez-Nogueras, M. (1992). B. F. Skinner's legacy to human infant behavior and development. *American Psychologist, 47,* 1411–1422.

Ghim, H-R. (1990). Evidence for perceptual organization in infants: Perception of subjective contours by young infants. *Infant Behavior and Development, 13,* 221–248.

Gibson, E. J. (1969). *Principles of perceptual learning and development.* New York: Appleton.

Gibson, E. J. (1982). The concept of affordances in development: The renascence of functionalism. In W. A. Collins (Ed.), *The Minnesota symposia on child psychology: Vol. 15. The concept of development.* Hillsdale, NJ: Erlbaum.

Gibson, E. J. (1988). Exploratory behavior in the development of perceiving, acting, and the acquiring of knowledge. *Annual Review of Psychology, 39,* 1–41.

Gibson, E. J., Gibson, J. J., Pick, A. D., & Osser, H. (1962). A developmental study of the discrimination of letter-like forms. *Journal of Comparative and Physiological Psychology, 55,* 897–906.

Gibson, E. J., & Walker, A. (1984). Development of knowledge of visual-tactual affordances of substance. *Child Development, 55,* 453–460.

Gibson, J. J. (1966). *The senses considered as perceptual systems.* Boston: Houghton Mifflin.

Gibson, J. J. (1979). *The ecological approach to visual perception.* Boston: Houghton Mifflin.

Gibson, M., & Ogbu, J. (Eds.). (1991). *Minority status and schooling: A comparative study of immigrant and involuntary minorities.* New York: Garland.

Giedd, J. N., Blumenthal, J., Molloy, E., & Castellanos, F. X. (2001). Brain imaging of attention deficit/hyperactivity disorder. *Annals of the New York Academy of Sciences, 931,* 33–49.

Gilbert, S. F. (2003). *Developmental biology* (7th ed.). Sunderland, MA: Sinauer Associates.

Gilbert, W. M., Nesbitt, T. S., & Danielsen, B. (1999). Childbearing beyond age 40: Pregnancy outcome in 24,032 cases. *Obstetrics and Gynecology, 93,* 9–14.

Giles, J. W., Gopnik, A., & Heyman, G. D. (2002). Source monitoring reduces the suggestibility of preschool children. *Psychological Science, 13,* 288–291.

Gilligan, C. (1982). *In a different voice: Psychological theory and women's development.* Cambridge, MA: Harvard University Press.

Gilligan, C. (1988). Remapping the moral domain: New images of self in relationship. In C. Gilligan, J. V. Ward, J. M. Taylor, & B. Bardige (Eds.), *Mapping the moral domain.* Cambridge, MA: Harvard University Press.

Gilligan, C., & Attanucci, J. (1988). Two moral orientations: Gender differences and similarities. *Merrill-Palmer Quarterly, 34,* 223–237.

Gilliom, M., Shaw, D. S., Beck, J. E., Schonberg, M. A., & Lukon, J. L. (2002). Anger regulation in disadvantaged preschool boys: Strategies, antecedents, and the development of self-control. *Developmental Psychology, 38,* 222–235.

Ginsberg, H. P. (1972). *The myth of the deprived child: Poor children's intellect and education.* Englewood Cliffs, NJ: Prentice-Hall.

Ginsburg, H. P. & Opper, S. (1988). *Piaget's theory of intellectual development* (3rd ed.). Englewood Cliffs, NJ: Prentice-Hall.

Ginsburg, H. P., Pappas, S., & Seo, K. H. (2001). Everyday mathematical knowledge: Asking young children what is developmentally appropriate. In S. L. Golbeck (Ed.), *The Rutgers invitational symposium on education series: Psychological perspectives on early childhood education: Reframing dilemmas in research and practice* (pp. 181–219). Mahwah, NJ: Erlbaum.

Glasgow, K. L., Dornbusch, S. N., Troyer, L., Steinberg, L., & Ritter, P. (1997). Parenting styles, adolescents' attributions, and educational outcomes in nine heterogeneous high schools. *Child Development, 68,* 507–529.

Glass, D. C., Neulinger, J., & Brim, O. G. (1974). Birth order, verbal intelligence, and educational aspiration. *Child Development, 45,* 807–811.

Glassman, M., & Zan, B. (1995). Moral activity and domain theory: An alternative interpretation of research on young children. *Developmental Review, 15,* 434–457.

Gleason, J. B., & Perlmann, R. Y. (1985). Acquiring social variation in speech. In H. Giles & R. N. St. Clair (Eds.), *Recent advances in language, communication, and social psychology.* London: Erlbaum.

Gleason, J. B., & Weintraub, S. (1978). Input language and the acquisition of communicative competence. In K. Nelson (Ed.), *Children's language* (Vol. 1). New York: Gardner Press.

Gleitman, L. R., Gleitman, H., & Shipley, E. F. (1972). The emergence of the child as grammarian. *Cognition, 1,* 137–164.

Gleitman, L. R., Newport, E. L., & Gleitman, H. (1984). The current status of the motherese hypothesis. *Journal of Child Language, 11,* 43–79.

Glynn, L. M., Wadhwa, P. O., Dunkel-Schetter, C., Chicz-DeMet, A., & Sandman, C. A. (2001). When stress happens matters: Effects of earthquake timing on stress responsivity in pregnancy. *American Journal of Obstetrics & Gynecology, 184,* 637–642.

Gogate, L. J., Bahrick, L. E., & Watson, J. D. (2000). A study of multi-modal motherese: The role of temporal synchrony between verbal labels and gestures. *Child Development, 71,* 878–894.

Goldberg, M. C., Maurer, D., & Lewis, T. L. (2001). Developmental changes in attention: The effects of endogenous cueing and of distractors. *Developmental Science, 4,* 209–219.

Goldberg, S. (1979). Premature birth: Consequences for the parent-infant relationship. *American Scientist, 67,* 582–590.

Goldberg, W. A., Greenberger, E., & Nagel, S. K. (1996). Employment and achievement: Mothers' work involvement in relation to children's achievement behaviors and mothers' parenting behaviors. *Child Development, 67,* 1512–1527.

Golden, F. (1998, September 21). Boy? Girl? Up to you. *Time,* pp. 82–83.

Goldenberg, R. L., Clivar, S. P., Cutter, G. R., Hoffman, H. J., Cassady, G., Davis, R. O., & Nelson, K. G. (1991). Black-white differences in newborn anthropometric measurements. *Obstetrics and Gynecology, 78,* 782–788.

Goldfield, B. A., & Reznick, J. S. (1990). Early lexical acquisition: Rate, content, and the vocabulary spurt. *Journal of Child Language, 17,* 171–183.

Goldin-Meadow, S. (2006). Nonverbal communication: The hand's role in talking and thinking. In W. Damon & R. M. Lerner (Editors-in-Chief) & D. M. Kuhn & R. S. Siegler (Vol. Eds.), *Handbook of child psychology: Vol. 2. Cognition, perception, and language* (6th ed., pp. 336–369). Hoboken, NJ: Wiley.

Goldsmith, H. H., & Alansky, J. A. (1987). Maternal and infant temperamental predictors of attachment: A meta-analytic review. *Journal of Consulting and Clinical Psychology, 55,* 805–816.

Goldsmith, H. H., Buss, K. A., & Lemery, K. S. (1997). Toddler and childhood temperament: Expanded content, stronger genetic evidence, new evidence for the importance of environment. *Developmental Psychology, 33,* 891–905.

Goldstein, S. E., Davis-Kean, P. E., & Eccles, J. S. (2005). Parents, peers, and problem behavior: A longitudinal investigation of the impact of relationship perceptions and characteristics on the development of adolescent problem behavior. *Developmental Psychology, 41,* 401–413.

Golier, J., & Yehuda, R. (1998). Neuroendocrine activity and memory-related impairments in posttraumatic stress disorder. *Development and Psychopathology, 10,* 857–869.

Golinkoff, R. M., Harding, C. G., Carlson, V., & Sexton, M. E. (1984). The infant's perception of causal events: The distinction between animate and inanimate objects. In L. L. Lipsitt & C. Rovee-Collier (Eds.), *Advances in infancy research. Vol. 3.* Norwood, NJ: Ablex.

Golinkoff, R. M., Mervis, C. B., & Hirsh-Pasek, K. (1994). Early object labels: The case for a developmental lexical principles framework. *Journal of Child Language, 21,* 125–155.

Golombok, S., Cook, R., Bish, A., & Murray, C. (1995). Families created by the new reproductive technologies: Quality of parenting and social and emotional development of the children. *Child Development, 66,* 285–298.

Golombok, S., MacCallum, F., & Goodman, E. (2001). The "test-tube" generation: Parent-child relationships and the psychological well-being of in vitro fertilization in children at adolescence. *Child Development, 72*, 599–608.

Golombok, S., MacCallum, F., Goodman, E., & Rutter, M. (2002). Families with children conceived by donor insemination: A follow-up at stage twelve. *Child Development, 73*, 952–968.

Golombok, S., Perry, B., Burston, A., Murray, C., Mooney-Somers, J., Stevens, M., & Golding, J. (2003). Children with lesbian parents: A community study. *Developmental Psychology, 39*, 20–33.

Goncu, A., Patt, M. B., & Kouba, E. (2002). Understanding young children's pretend play in context. In P. K. Smith & C. H. Hart (Eds.), *Blackwell handbook of childhood social development* (pp. 418–437). Malden, MA: Blackwell.

Gonzalez, P., Guzman, J. C., Partelow, L., Pahlke, E., Jocelyn, L., Kastberg, D., & Williams, T. (2004). *Highlights from the Trends in International Mathematics and Science Study (TIMMS) 2003* (NCES 2005–05). U.S. Department of Education, National Center for Education Statistics. Washington, DC: U.S. Government Printing Office.

Goodnow, J. (1988). Children's household work: Its nature and functions. *Psychological Bulletin, 103*, 5–26.

Goodwin, S. W., & Acredolo, L. P. (1993). Symbolic gesture versus word: Is there a modality advantage for onset of symbol use? *Child Development, 64*, 688–701.

Gopnik, A. (1996). The post-Piaget era. *Psychological Science, 7*, 221–225.

Gopnik, A., & Meltzoff, A. N. (1986). Relations between semantic and cognitive development in the one-word stage: The specificity hypothesis. *Child Development, 57*, 1040–1053.

Gopnik, A., & Meltzoff, A. N. (1987). The development of categorization in the second year and its relation to other cognitive and linguistic attainments. *Child Development, 58*, 1523–1531.

Gopnik, A., & Rosati, A. (2001). Duck or rabbit? Reversing ambiguous figures and understanding ambiguous representations. *Developmental Science, 4*, 175–183.

Gordin, D., & Pea, R. D. (1995). Prospects for scientific visualization as an educational technology. *The Journal of Learning Science, 4*, 249–279.

Gordon, I., & Slater, A. (1998). Nativism and empiricism: The history of two ideas. In A. Slater (Ed.), *Perceptual development: Visual, auditory, and speech perception in infancy* (pp. 73–103). East Sussex, UK: Psychology Press.

Gorman-Smith, D., & Tolan, P. (1998). The prevalence and consequences of exposure to violence among African-American youth. *Development and Psychopathology, 10*, 101–116.

Gorski, P. A. (1991). Developmental intervention during neonatal hospitalization: Critiquing the state of the science. *Pediatric Clinics of North America, 38*, 1469–1479.

Gorski, R. A. (1980). Sexual differentiation of the brain. In D. T. Krieger & J. C. Hughes (Eds.), *Neuroendocrinology.* New York: Rockefeller University Press.

Gortmaker, S. L., Must, A., Sobol, A. M., Peterson, K., Colditz, G. A., & Dietz, W. H. (1996). Television viewing as a cause of increasing obesity among children in the United States, 1886–1990. *Archives of Pediatrics and Adolescent Medicine, 150*, 356–362.

Gottesman, I. I., & Shields, J. (1982). *Schizophrenia: The epigenetic puzzle.* Cambridge, UK: Cambridge University Press.

Gottfried, A. E., Bathurst, K., & Gottfried, A. W. (1994). Role of maternal and dual-earner employment status in children's development. In A. E. Gottfried, & A. W. Gottfried (Eds.), *Redefining families: Implications for children's development.* New York: Plenum.

Gottfried, G. M. (1997). Using metaphors as modifiers: Children's production of metaphoric compounds. *Journal of Child Language, 24*, 567–601.

Gottlieb, G. (1991). Experimental canalization of behavioral development: Theory. *Developmental Psychology, 27*, 4–13.

Gottlieb, G. (2000). Environmental and behavioral influences on gene activity. *Current Directions in Psychological Science, 9*, 93–97.

Gottlieb, G., Wahlsten, D., & Lickliter, R. (2006). The significance of biology for human development: A developmental psychobiological sys-

tems view. In W. Damon & R. M. Lerner (Editors-in-Chief) & R. M. Lerner (Vol. Ed.), *Handbook of child psychology: Vol. 1. Theoretical models of human development* (6th ed., pp. 210–257). Hoboken, NJ: Wiley.

Gottman, J. M. (1983). How children become friends. Monographs of the Society for Research in Child Development, 48(2, Serial No. 201).

Gottman, J. M., Gonso, J., & Rasmussen, B. (1975). Social interaction, social competence, and friendship in children. *Child Development, 46*, 709–718.

Gottman, J. M., Katz, L. F., & Hooven, C. (1997). *Metaemotion: How families communicate emotionally.* Mahwah, NJ: Erlbaum.

Gottman, J. M., & Parkhurst, J. T. (1980). A developmental theory of friendship and acquaintanceship processes. In W. A. Collins (Ed.), *The Minnesota symposia on child development: Vol. 13. Development of cognition, affect, and social relations.* Hillsdale, NJ: Erlbaum.

Goubet, N., & Clifton, R. K. (1998). Object and event representation in 6 1/2-month-old infants. *Developmental Psychology, 34*, 63–76.

Goy, R. (1970). Early hormonal influences on the development of sexual and sex-related behavior. In F. Schmitt, G. Quarton, T. Melnechuck, & G. Adelman (Eds.), *The neurosciences: Second study program.* New York: Rockefeller University Press.

Graham, S. A., & Poulin-Dubois, D. (1999). Infants' reliance on shape to generalize novel labels to animate and inanimate objects. *Journal of Child Language, 26*, 295–320.

Gralinski, J. H., & Kopp, C. B. (1993). Everyday rules for behavior: Mothers' requests to young children. *Developmental Psychology, 29*, 573–584.

Grandjean, H., Larroque, D., Levi, S., and the Eurofetus Study Group. (1999). The performance of routine ultrasonographic screening of pregnancies in the Eurofetus Study. *American Journal of Obstetrics and Gynecology, 181*, 446–454.

Grantham-McGregor, S., Powell, C., Walker, S., Change, S., & Fletcher, P. (1994). The long-term follow-up of severely malnourished children who participated in an intervention program. *Child Development, 65*, 428–439.

Graves, S. B. (1993). Television, the portrayal of African Americans, and the development of children's attitudes. In G. L. Berry & J. K. Asamen (Eds.), *Children and television: Images in a changing sociocultural world* (pp. 179–190). Newbury Park, CA: Sage.

Graves, N. B., & Graves, T. D. (1983). The cultural context of prosocial development: An ecological model. In D. L. Bridgeman (Ed.), *The nature of prosocial development: Interdisciplinary theories and strategies.* New York: Academic Press.

Gray, M., & Steinberg, L. (1999). Unpacking authoritative parenting: Reassessing a multidimensional construct. *Journal of Marriage and the Family, 61*, 574–587.

Gray-Little, B., & Hafdahl, A. R. (2000). Factors influencing racial comparisons of self-esteem: A quantitative review. *Psychological Bulletin, 126*, 26–54.

Greenberg, B. S. (1986). Minorities and the mass media. In J. Bryant & D. Zillman (Eds.), *Perspectives on mass media effects.* Hillsdale, NJ: Erlbaum.

Greenberg, B. S., & Brand, J. E. (1994). Minorities and the mass media: 1970s to 1990s. In J. Bryant & D. Zillmann (Eds.), *Media effects: Advances in theory and research* (pp. 273–314). Hillsdale, NJ: Erlbaum.

Greenberger, E., & Chen, C. (1996). Perceived family relationships and depressed mood in early and late adolescence: A comparison of European and Asian Americans. *Developmental Psychology, 32*, 707–716.

Greene, M. L., Way, N., & Pahl, K. (2006). Trajectories of perceived adult and peer discrimination among Black, Latino, and Asian American adolescents: Patterns and psychological correlates. *Developmental Psychology, 42*, 218–236.

Greenfield, P. M. (1984). A theory of the teacher in the learning activities of everyday life. In B. Rogoff & J. Lave (Eds.), *Everyday cognition: Its development in social context.* Cambridge, MA: Harvard University Press.

Greenfield, P. M. (1997). You can't take it with you: Why ability assessments don't cross cultures. *American Psychologist, 52,* 1115–1124.

Greenfield, P. M. (1998). The cultural evolution of IQ. In U. Neisser (Ed.), *The rising curve: Long-term gains in IQ and related measures* (pp. 85–94). Washington, DC: American Psychological Association.

Greenfield, P. M., & Cocking, R. R. (Eds.). (1996). *Interacting with video.* Norwood, NJ: Ablex.

Greenhoot, A. F., Ornstein, P. A., Gordon, B. N., & Baker-Ward, L. (1999). Acting out the details of a pediatric check-up: The impact of interview condition and behavioral style on children's memory reports. *Child Development, 70,* 363–380.

Greenhouse, L. (2000, October 5). Justices consider limits of the legal response to risky behavior by pregnant women. *New York Times,* p. A6.

Greenough, W. T., Black, J. E., & Wallace, C. S. (1987). Experience and brain development. *Child Development, 58,* 539–559.

Gregg, V., Gibbs, J. C., & Basinger, K. S. (1994). Patterns of developmental delay in moral judgment by male and female delinquents. *Merrill-Palmer Quarterly, 40,* 538–553.

Greif, E. B., & Gleason, J. B. (1980). Hi, thanks, and goodbye: More routine information. *Language in Society, 9,* 159–166.

Greif, E. B., & Ulman, K. J. (1982). The psychological impact of menarche on early adolescent females: A review of the literature. *Child Development, 53,* 1413–1430.

Gressens, P. (2000). Mechanisms and disturbances of neuronal migration. *Pediatric Research, 48,* 725–730.

Grimshaw, G. M., Adelstein, A., Bryden, M. P., & MacKinnon, G. E. (1998). First-language acquisition in adolescence: Evidence for a critical period for language development. *Brain and Language, 63,* 237–255.

Grolnick, W. S., Bridges, L. J., & Connell, J. P. (1996). Emotion regulation in two-year-olds: Strategies and emotional expression in four contexts. *Child Development, 67,* 928–941.

Grolnick, W. S., Ryan, R. M., & Deci, E. L. (1991). Inner resources for school achievement: Motivational mediators of children's perceptions of their parents. *Journal of Educational Psychology, 83,* 508–517.

Grolnick, W. S., & Slowiaczek, M. L. (1994). Parents' involvement in children's schooling: A multidimensional conceptualization and motivation model. *Child Development, 65,* 237–252.

Groome, L. J., Swiber, M. J., Atterbury, J. L., Bentz, L. S., & Holland, S. B. (1997). Similarities and differences in behavioral state organization during sleep periods in the perinatal infant before and after birth. *Child Development, 68,* 1–11.

Grossmann, K., Grossmann, K. E., Fremmer-Bombik, E., Kindler, H., Scheuer-Englisch, H., & Zimmermann, P. (2002). The uniqueness of the child-father attachment relationship: Fathers' sensitive and challenging play as a pivotal variable in a 16-year longitudinal study. *Social Development, 11,* 307–331.

Grossmann, K., Grossmann, K. E., Spangler, G., Suess, G., & Unzner, L. (1985). Maternal sensitivity and newborns' orientation responses as related to quality of attachment in northern Germany. In I. Bretherton & E. Waters (Eds.), *Growing points of attachment theory and research. Monographs of the Society for Research in Child Development, 50* (1–2, Serial No. 209).

Grotevant, H. D., & Cooper, C. R. (1986). Individuation in family relationships. *Human Development, 29,* 82–100.

Gruen, G., Ottinger, D., & Zigler, E. (1970). Level of aspiration and the probability learning of middle- and lower-class children. *Developmental Psychology, 3,* 133–142.

Grunseit, A., Kippax, S., Aggleton, P., & Baldo, M.,& Slutkin, G. (1997). Sexuality education and young people's sexual behavior: A review of studies. *Journal of Adolescent Research, 12,* 421–453.

Grusec, J. E. (1982). The socialization of altruism. In N. Eisenberg (Ed.), *The development of prosocial behavior.* New York: Academic Press.

Grusec, J. E. (1991). Socializing concern for others in the home. *Developmental Psychology, 27,* 338–342.

Grusec, J. E. (1992). Social learning theory and developmental psychology: The legacies of Robert Sears and Albert Bandura. *Developmental Psychology, 28,* 776–786.

Grusec, J. E., & Goodnow, J. J. (1994). Impact of parental discipline methods on the child's internalization of values: A reconceptualization of current points of view. *Developmental Psychology, 30,* 4–19.

Grusec, J. E., Goodnow, J. J., & Cohen, L. (1996). Household work and the development of concern for others. *Developmental Psychology, 32,* 999–1007.

Grusec, J. E., Hastings, P., & Mammone, N. (1994). Parenting cognitions and relationship schemas. In J. G. Smetana (Ed.), *Beliefs about parenting: Origins and developmental implications* (pp. 5–19). San Francisco: Jossey-Bass.

Grusec, J. E., & Skubiski, L. (1970). Model nurturance, demand characteristics of the modeling experiment, and altruism. *Journal of Personality and Social Psychology, 14,* 352–359.

Grych, J. H., Harold, G. T., & Miles, C. J. (2003). A prospective investigation of appraisals as mediators of the link between interparental conflict and child adjustment. *Child Development, 74,* 1176–1193.

Guerra, B., Lazzarotto, T., Quarta, S., Lanari, M., Bovicelli, L., Nicolosi, A., & Landini, M. P. (2000). Prenatal diagnosis of symptomatic congenital cytomegalovirus infection. *American Journal of Obstetrics and Gynecology, 183,* 476–482.

Guinan, M. E. (1995). Artificial insemination by donor: Safety and secrecy. *Journal of the American Medical Association, 273,* 890–891.

Gunnar, M. R. (1998). Quality of early care and buffering of neuroendocrine stress reactions: Potential effects on the developing brain. *Preventive Medicine, 27,* 208–211.

Gunnar, M. R., Porter, F., Wolf, C., Rigatuso, J., & Larson, M. (1995). Neonatal stress reactivity: Predictions to later emotional development. *Child Development, 66,* 1–13.

Gunnar, M. R., & White, B. P. (2001). Salivary cortisol measures in infant and child assessment. In L. T. Singer & P. S. Zeskind (Eds.), *Biobehavioral assessment of the infant* (pp. 167–189). New York: Guilford Press.

Gunston, G. D., Burkimsher, D., Malan, H, & Sive, A. A. (1992). Reversible cerebral shrinkage in kwashiorkor: An MRI study. *Archives of Disease in Childhood, 67,* 1030–1032.

Guntheroth, W. G., & Spiers, P. S. (2001). Thermal stress in sudden infant death: Is there an ambiguity with the rebreathing hypothesis? *Pediatrics, 107,* 693–698.

Gutman, L. M. , & Eccles, J. S. (1999). Financial strain, parenting behaviors, and adolescents' achievement: Testing model equivalence between African American and European American single- and two-parent families. *Child Development, 70,* 1464–1476.

Guttentag, R. E. (1987). Memory and aging: Implications for theories of memory development during childhood. *Developmental Review, 5,* 56–82.

Hafner-Eaton, C., & Pearce, L. K. (1994). Birth choices, the law, and medicine: Balancing individual freedoms and protection of the public's health. *Journal of Health Politics, Policy and Law, 19,* 813–835.

Hagay, Z. J., Biran, G., Ornoy, A., & Reece, E. A. (1996). Congenital cytomegalovirus infection: A long-standing problem still seeking a solution. *American Journal of Obstetrics and Gynecology, 174,* 241–245.

Hahn, C.-S., & DiPietro, J. A. (2001). In vitro fertilization and the family: Quality of parenting, family functioning, and child psychosocial adjustment. *Developmental Psychology, 37,* 37–48.

Haight, W. L., Wang, X., Fung, H., Williams, K., & Mintz, J. (1999). Universal, developmental, and variable aspects of young children's play: A cross-cultural comparison of pretending at home. *Child Development, 70,* 1477–1488.

Hainline, L. (1998). The development of basic visual abilities. In A. Slater (Ed.), *Perceptual development: Visual, auditory, and speech perception in infancy* (pp. 5–50). East Sussex, UK: Psychology Press.

Hainline, L., & Riddell, P. M. (1995). Binocular alignment and vergence in early infancy. *Vision Research, 35,* 3229–3236.

Haith, M. M. (1997). The development of future thinking as essential for the emergence of skill in planning. In S. L. Friedman & E. K. Scholnick (Eds.), *The developmental psychology of planning: Why, how, and when do we plan?* (pp. 25–42). Mahwah, NJ: Erlbaum.

Haith, M. M. (1998). Who put the cog in cognition? Is rich interpretation too costly? *Infant Behavior and Development, 21,* 167–179.

Hakuta, K. (1999). The debate on bilingual education. *Journal of Developmental & Behavioral Pediatrics, 20,* 36–37.

Hakuta, K., & Diaz, R. M. (1985). The relationship between degree of bilingualism and cognitive ability: A critical discussion and some new longitudinal data. In K. E. Nelson (Ed.), *Children's language* (Vol. 5). Hillsdale, NJ: Erlbaum.

Hakuta, K., & Mostafapour, E. F. (1996). Perspectives from the history and politics of bilingualism amd bilingual education in the United States. In I. Parasnis (Ed.), *Cultural and language diversity and the deaf experience* (pp. 38–50). Cambridge, UK: Cambridge University Press.

Haley, D. W., & Stansbury, K. (2003). Infant stress and parent responsiveness: Regulation of physiology and behavior during still-face and reunion. *Child Development, 74,* 1534–1546.

Hall, G. S. (1891). The contents of children's minds on entering school. *Pedagogical Seminary, 1,* 139–173.

Hall, J. A. (1984). *Nonverbal sex differences: Communication accuracy and expressive style.* Baltimore: Johns Hopkins University Press.

Hall, J. A., & Halberstadt, A. G. (1986). Smiling and gazing. In J. S. Hyde & M. C. Linn (Eds.), *The psychology of gender: Advances through meta-analysis.* Baltimore: Johns Hopkins University Press.

Halpern, C. T., Udry, J. R., Campbell, B., & Suchindran, C. (1999). Effects of body fat on weight concerns, dating, and sexual activity: A longitudinal analysis of black and white adolescent girls. *Developmental Psychology, 35,* 721–736.

Halpern, D. F. (1986). *Sex differences in cognitive abilities.* Hillsdale, NJ: Erlbaum.

Halpern, L. F., MacLean, W. E., Jr., & Baumeister, A. A. (1995). Infant sleep-wake characteristics: Relation to neurological status and the prediction of developmental outcome. *Developmental Review, 15,* 255–291.

Hamilton, B. E., Martin, J. A., Ventura, S. J., Sutton, P. D., & Menacker, F. (2005). *Births: Preliminary data for 2004* (National Vital Statistics Reports, Vol. 54, No. 8). Hyattsville, MD: National Center for Health Statistics.

Hampson, E., Rovet, J. F., & Altmann, D. (1998). Spatial reasoning in children with congential adrenal hyperplasia due to 21-hydroxylase deficiency. *Developmental Neuropsychology, 14,* 299–320.

Hamre, B. K., & Pianta, R. C. (2001). Early teacher-child relationships and the trajectory of children's outcomes through eighth grade. *Child Development, 72,* 625–638.

Han, J. J., Leichtman, M. D., & Wang, Q. (1998). Autobiographical memory in Korean, Chinese, and American children. *Developmental Psychology, 34,* 701–713.

Han, W. J. (2004). Nonstandard work schedules and child care decisions: Evidence from the NICHD Study of Early Child Care. *Early Childhood Research Quarterly, 19,* 231–256.

Hand, J. Z., & Sanchez, L. (2000). Badgering or bantering? Gender differences in experience of, and reaction to, sexual harassment among U.S. high school students. *Gender & Society, 14,* 718–746.

Hansen, J. D. L. (1990). Malnutrition review. *Pediatric Reviews and Communication, 4,* 201–212.

Hansen, M., Bower, C., Milne, E., de Klerk, N., & Kurinczuk, J. J. (2005). Assisted reproductive technologies and the risk of birth defects—a systematic review. *Human Reproduction, 20,* 328–338.

Hanson, J. W. (1986). Teratogen update: Fetal hydantoin effects. *Teratology, 33,* 349–353.

Hanson, J. W. (1997). Human teratology. In D. L. Rimoin, J. M. Connor, & R. E. Pyeritz (Eds.), *Emory and Rimoin's principles and practices of medical genetics* (3rd Ed., Vol. 1, pp. 697–724). New York: Churchill Livingstone.

Harbison, R. D., & Mantilla-Plata, B. (1972). Prenatal toxicity, maternal distribution and placental transfer of tetrahydrocannabinol. *Journal of Pharmacology and Experimental Therapeutics, 180,* 446–453.

Hareven, T. (1985). Historical changes in the family and the life course: Implications for child development. In A. B. Smuts & J. W. Hagen (Eds.), *History and research in child development. Monographs of the Society for Research in Child Development, 50*(4–5, Serial No. 211).

Harley, K., & Reese, E. (1999). Origins of autobiographical memory. *Developmental Psychology, 35,* 1338–1348.

Harlow, H. F., & Zimmerman, R. R. (1959). Affectional responses in the infant monkey. *Science, 130,* 421–432.

Harman, C., Rothbart, M. K., & Posner, M. I. (1997). Distress and attention interactions in early infancy. *Motivation and Emotion, 21,* 27–43.

Harnishfeger, K. K., & Pope, S. (1996). Intending to forget: The development of cognitive inhibition in directed forgetting. *Journal of Experimental Child Psychology, 62,* 292–315.

Harold, G. T., Fincham, F. D., Osborne, L. N., & Conger, R. D. (1997). Mom and Dad are at it again: Adolescent perceptions of marital conflict and adolescent psychological distress. *Developmental Psychology, 33,* 333–350.

Harpin, V., Chellappah, G., & Rutter, N. (1983). Responses of the newborn infant to overheating. *Biology of the Neonate, 44,* 65–75.

Harriman, A. E., & Lukosius, P. A. (1982). On why Wayne Dennis found Hopi children retarded in age at onset of walking. *Perceptual and Motor Skills, 55,* 79–86.

Harris, J. R. (1995). Where is the child's environment? A group socialization theory of development. *Psychological Review, 102,* 458–489.

Harris, J. R. (1998). *The nurture assumption: Why children turn out the way they do.* New York: Free Press.

Harris, J. R. (2000). Socialization, personality development, and the child's environments: Comment on Vandell (2000). *Developmental Psychology, 36,* 711–723.

Harris, P. L., Donnelly, K., Guz, G. R., & Pitt-Watson, R. (1986). Children's understanding of the distinction between real and apparent emotion. *Child Development, 57,* 895–909.

Harris, P. L., Olthof, T., & Meerum Terwogt, M. (1981). Children's knowledge of emotion. *Journal of Child Psychology and Psychiatry, 22,* 247–261.

Harris, R. T. (1991, March). Anorexia nervosa and bulimia nervosa in female adolescents. *Nutrition Today* pp. 30–34.

Harrison, L. J., & Ungerer, J. A. (2002). Maternal employment and infant-mother attachment security at 12 months postpartum. *Developmental Psychology, 38,* 758–773.

Harrison, M. R. (1996). Fetal surgery. *American Journal of Obstetrics and Gynecology, 174,* 1255–1264.

Hart, C. H., De Wolf, D. M., Wozniak, P., & Burts, D. C. (1992). Maternal and paternal disciplinary styles: Relations with preschoolers' playground behavioral orientations and peer status. *Child Development, 63,* 879–892.

Hart, D., & Fegley, S. (1995). Prosocial behavior and caring in adolescence: Relations to self-understanding and social judgment. *Child Development, 66,* 1346–1359.

Hart, D., Fegley, S., & Brengelman, D. (1993). Perceptions of past, present and future selves among children and adolescents. *British Journal of Developmental Psychology, 11,* 265–282.

Hart, E. L., Lahey, B. B., Loeber, R., Applegate, B., & Frick, P. J. (1995). Developmental change in attention-deficit hyperactivity disorder in boys: A four-year longitudinal study. *Journal of Abnormal Child Psychology, 23,* 729–749.

Hart, S. N., & Brassard, M. R. (1987). A major threat to children's mental health. *American Psychologist, 42,* 160–165.

Harter, S. (1986a). Cognitive-developmental processes in the integration of concepts about emotions and the self. *Social Cognition, 4,* 119–151.

Harter, S. (1986b). Processes underlying the construct, maintenance and enhancement of the self-concept in children. In J. Suls & A. Greenwald (Eds.), *Psychological perspectives on the self* (Vol. 3, pp. 136–182). Hillsdale, NJ: Erlbaum.

Harter, S. (1987). The determinants and mediational role of global self-worth in children. In N. Eisenberg (Ed.), *Contemporary topics in developmental psychology.* New York: Wiley.

Harter, S. (1998). The development of self-representations. In W. Damon (Series Ed.) & N. Eisenberg (Vol. Ed.), *Handbook of child psychology: Vol. 3. Social, emotional, and personality development* (5th ed., pp. 553–617). New York: Wiley.

Harter, S. (1999). *The construction of the self: A developmental perspective.* New York: Guilford Press.

Harter, S. (2006). The self. In W. Damon & R. M. Lerner (Editors-in-Chief) & N. Eisenberg (Vol. Ed.), *Handbook of child psychology: Vol. 3. Social, emotional, and personality development* (6th ed., pp. 505–570). Hoboken, NJ: Wiley.

Harter, S., Marold, D. B., Whitesell, N. R., & Cobbs, G. (1996). A model of the effects of perceived parent and peer support on adolescent false self behavior. *Child Development, 67,* 360–374.

Harter, S., & Monsour, A. (1992). Developmental analysis of conflict caused by opposing attributes in the adolescent self-portrait. *Developmental Psychology, 28,* 251–260.

Harter, S., Waters, P., & Whitesell, N. R. (1998). Relational self-worth: Differences in perceived worth as a person across interpersonal contexts among adolescents. *Child Development, 69,* 756–766.

Harter, S., & Whitesell, N. R. (1989). Developmental changes in children's understanding of single, multiple, and blended emotion concepts. In C. Saarni & P. Harris (Eds.), *Children's understanding of emotion* (pp. 81–116). Cambridge, UK: Cambridge University Press.

Hartshorn, K., Rovee-Collier, C., Gerhardstein, P., Bhatt, R. S., Klein, P. J., Aaron, F., et al. (1998). Developmental changes in the specificity of memory over the first year of life. *Developmental Psychobiology, 33,* 61–78.

Hartup, W. W. (1983). Peer relations. In E. M. Hetherington (Ed.), *Handbook of child psychology: Vol. IV. Socialization, personality, and social development* (4th ed., pp. 103–196). New York: Wiley.

Hartup, W. W. (1996). The company they keep: Friendships and their developmental significance. *Child Development, 67,* 1–13.

Hartup, W. W. (1999). Constraints on peer socialization: Let me count the ways. *Merrill-Palmer Quarterly, 45,* 172–183.

Hartup, W. W., French, D. C., Laursen, B., Johnston, M. K., & Ogawa, J. R. (1993). Conflict and friendship relations in middle childhood: Behavior in a closed field situation. *Child Development, 64,* 445–454.

Hartup, W. W., & Sancilio, M. F. (1986). Children's friendships. In E. Shopler & G. B. Mesibov (Eds.), *Social behavior in autism.* New York: Plenum Press.

Hartup, W. W., & Stevens, N. (1999). Friendships and adaptation across the life span. *Current Directions in Psychological Science, 3,* 76–79.

Harvey, E. (1999). Short-term and long-term effects of early parental employment on children of the National Longitudinal Survey of Youth. *Developmental Psychology, 35,* 445–459.

Hasebe, Y., Nucci, L., & Nucci, M. S. (2004). Parental control of the personal domain and adolescent symptoms of psychopathology: A cross-national study in the United States and Japan. *Child Development, 75,* 815–828.

Haselager, G. J. T., Hartup, W. W., van Lieshout, C. F. M., & Riksen-Walraven, J. M. A. (1998). Similarities between friends and nonfriends in middle childhood. *Child Development, 69,* 1198–1208.

Hastings, P. D., & Grusec, J. E. (1998). Parenting goals as organizers of responses to parent-child disagreement. *Developmental Psychology, 34,* 465–479.

Hastings, P. D., Zahn-Waxler, C., Robinson, J., Usher, B., & Bridges, D. (2000). The development of concern for others in children with behavior problems. *Developmental Psychology, 36,* 531–546.

Hatfield, J. S., Ferguson, L. R., & Alpert, R. (1967). Mother-child interaction and the socialization process. *Child Development, 38,* 365–414.

Haubenstricker, J., & Seefeldt, V. (1986). Acquisition of motor skills during childhood. In V. Seefeldt (Ed.), *Physical activity and well-being.* Reston, VA: American Alliance for Health, Education, Recreation, and Dance.

Hauck, F. R., & Hunt, C. E. (2000). Sudden infant death syndrome in 2000. *Current Problems in Pediatrics, 30,* 241–261.

Hauk, F. R. (2001). Changing epidemiology. In R. W. Byard & H. F. Kraus (Eds.), *Sudden infant death syndrome: Problems, progress, & possibilities* (pp. 31–57). London: Arnold.

Hauk, F. R., Omojokun, O. O., & Siadaty, M. S. (2005). Do pacifiers reduce the risk of Sudden Infant Death Syndrome? A meta-analysis. *Pediatrics, 116,* 716–723.

Hauser, S. T., Powers, S. I., Noam, G. G., & Bowlds, M. K. (1987). Family interiors of adolescent ego development trajectories. *Family Perspectives, 21,* 263–282.

Hawkins, J., Sheingold, K., Gearhart, M., & Berger, C. (1982). Microcomputers in classrooms: Impact on the social life of elementary classrooms. *Journal of Applied Developmental Psychology, 3,* 361–373.

Hawn, P. R., & Harris, L. J. (1983). Hand differences in grasp duration and reaching in two- and five-month old infants. In G. Young, S. Segalowitz, C. M. Carter, & S. E. Trehub (Eds.), *Manual specialization and the developing brain.* New York: Academic Press.

Hay, D. F. (1985). Learning to form relationships in infancy: Parallel attainments with parents and peers. *Developmental Review, 5,* 122–161.

Hay, D. F., Castle, J., Davies, L., Demetriou, H., & Stimson, C. A. (1999). Prosocial action in very early childhood. *Journal of Child Psychology and Psychiatry, 40,* 905–916.

Hay, D. F., Nash, A., & Pedersen, J. (1983). Interaction between 6-month-old peers. *Child Development, 54,* 557–562.

Hayne, H. (2004). Infant memory development: Implications for childhood amnesia. *Developmental Review, 24,* 33–73.

Hayne, H., & Rovee-Collier, C. (1995). The organization of reactivated memory. *Child Development, 66,* 893–906.

Heath, S. B. (1989). Oral and literate traditions among black Americans living in poverty. *American Psychologist, 44,* 367–373.

Hebb, D. O. (1980). *Essay on mind.* Hillsdale, NJ: Erlbaum.

Held, R., Birch, E., & Gwiazda, J. (1980). Stereoacuity in human infants. *Proceedings of the National Academy of Sciences of the U.S.A., 77,* 5572–5574.

Helwig, C. C., Zelazo, P. D., & Wilson, M. (2001). Children's judgments of psychological harm in normal and noncanonical situations. *Child Development, 72,* 66–81.

Henderlong, J., & Lepper, M. R. (2002). The effects of praise on children's intrinsic motivation: A review and synthesis. *Psychological Bulletin, 128,* 774–795.

Henifin, M. S. (1993). New reproductive technologies: Equity and access to reproductive health care. *Journal of Social Issues, 49,* 61–74.

Hepper, P. G., & Shahidullah, B. S. (1994). Development of fetal hearing. *Archives of Disease in Childhood, 71,* F81–F87.

Hepper, P. G., Wells, D. L., & Lynch, C. (2005). Prenatal thumbsucking is related to postnatal handedness. *Neuropsychologia, 43,* 313–315.

Herman, M. R., Dornbusch, S. M., Herron, M. C., & Herting, J. R. (1997). The influence of family regulation, connection, and psychological autonomy on six measures of adolescent functioning. *Journal of Adolescent Research, 12,* 34–67.

Hernandez-Reif, M., Field, T., Diego, M., & Largie, S. (2003). Haptic habituation to temperature is slower in newborns of depressed mothers. *Infancy, 4,* 47–63.

Herpetz-Dahlmann, B., Müller, B., Herpetz, S., Heussen, N., Hebebrand, J., & Remschmidt, H. (2001). Prospective 10-year follow-up in adolescent anorexia nervosa: Course, outcome, psychiatric comorbidity, and psychosocial adaptation. *Journal of Child Psychology and Psychiatry, 42,* 603–612.

Herrnstein, R. J., & Murray, C. (1994). *The bell curve: Intelligence and class structure in American life.* New York: Free Press.

Hertsgaard, L., Gunnar, M., Erickson, M. F., & Nachmias, M. (1996). Adrenocortical responses to the Strange Situation in infants with disorganized/disoriented attachment relationships. *Child Development, 66,* 1100–1106.

Hetherington, E. M. (1989). Coping with family transitions: Winners, losers, and survivors. *Child Development, 60,* 1–14.

Hetherington, E. M., Cox, M., & Cox, R. (1982). Effects of divorce on parents and children. In M. Lamb (Ed.), *Nontraditional families.* Hillsdale, NJ: Erlbaum.

Hetherington, E. M., & Henderson, S. H. (1997). The effects of divorce on fathers and their children. In M. E. Lamb (Ed.), *The role of the father in child development* (pp. 191–211). New York: Wiley.

Hetherington, E. M., Henderson, S. H., & Reiss, D. (1999). Adolescent siblings in stepfamilies: Family functioning and adolescent adjustment. *Monographs of the Society for Research in Child Development, 64*(4, Serial No. 259).

Hetherington, E. M., & Jodl, K. M. (1994). Stepfamilies as settings for child development. In A. Booth & J. Dunn (Eds.), *Stepfamilies: Who benefits? Who does not?* (pp. 55–79). Hillsdale, NJ: Erlbaum.

Hetherington, E. M., & Kelly, J. (2002). *For better or for worse: Divorce reconsidered.* New York: Norton.

Heyman, G. D., & Dweck, C. S. (1998). Children's thinking about traits? Implications for judgments of the self and others. *Child Development, 69,* 391–403.

Heynen, A. J., Yoon, B-J., Liu, C-H., Chung, H. J., Huganir, R. L., & Bear, M. F. (2003). Molecular mechanism for loss of visual cortical responsiveness following brief monocular deprivation. *Nature Neuroscience, 8,* 854–862.

Hilgard, J. R. (1932). Learning and maturation in preschool children. *Journal of Genetic Psychology, 41,* 36–56.

Hill, C. R., & Stafford, F. P. (1980). Parental care of children: Time diary estimates of quantity, predictability, and variety. *Journal of Human Resources, 15,* 219–289.

Hill, J. P. (1987). Research on adolescents and their families: Past and prospect. In C. E. Irwin (Ed.), *Adolescent social behavior and health.* San Francisco: Jossey-Bass.

Hill, J. P., & Lynch, M. E. (1983). The intensification of gender-related role expectations during early adolescence. In J. Brooks-Gunn & A. C. Petersen (Eds.), *Girls at puberty: Biological and psychosocial perspectives* (pp. 201–228). New York: Academic Press.

Hill, N. E., & Taylor, L. C. (2004). Parental school involvement and children's academic achievement: Pragmatics and issues. *Current Directions in Psychological Science, 13,* 161–164.

Hinde, R. A. (1989). Ethological and relationships approaches. In R. Vasta (Ed.), *Annals of child development: Six theories of child development: Revised formulations and current issues* (Vol. 6, pp. 251–285). Greenwich, CT: JAI Press.

Hinde, R. A., Titmus, G., Easton, D., & Tamplin, A. (1985). Incidence of "friendship" and behavior to strong associates versus non-associates in preschoolers. *Child Development, 56,* 234–245.

Hines, M., Golombok, S., Rust, J., Johnston, K. J., Golding, J., & ALSPAC Study Team. (2002). Testosterone during pregnancy and gender role behavior of preschool children: A longitudinal population study. *Developmental Psychology, 73,* 1678–1687.

Hirsch, B. J., & Rapkin, B. D. (1987). The transition to junior high school: A longitudinal study of self-esteem, psychological symptomatology, school life, and social support. *Child Development, 58,* 1235–1243.

Hirschfeld, L. A., & Gelman, S. A. (1994). Toward a topography of mind: An introduction to domain specificity. In L. A. Hirschfeld & S. A. Gelman (Eds.), *Mapping the mind: Domain specificity in cognition and culture* (pp. 3–35). Oxford, UK: Oxford University Press.

Hirsch-Pasek, K., Gleitman, L. R., & Gleitman, H. (1978). What does the brain say to the mind? A study of the detection and report of ambiguity by young children. In A. Sinclair, R. J. Jarvella, & W. J. M. Levelt (Eds.), *The child's conception of language.* Berlin: Springer-Verlag.

Ho, C. S., & Bryant, P. (1997). Phonological skills are important in learning to read Chinese. *Developmental Psychology, 33,* 946–951.

Hock, E., & DeMeis, D. K. (1990). Depression in mothers of infants: The role of maternal employment. *Developmental Psychology, 26,* 285–291.

Hoff, E., & Naigles, L. (2002). How children use input to acquire a lexicon. *Child Development, 73,* 418–433.

Hoff, T. L. (1992). Psychology in Canada one hundred years ago: James Mark Baldwin at the University of Toronto. *Canadian Psychology, 33,* 683–694.

Hofferth, S. (1996). Child care in the United States today. *The Future of Children, 6*(2), 41–61.

Hoff-Ginsberg, E. (1986). Function and structure in maternal speech: Their relation to the child's development of syntax. *Developmental Psychology, 22,* 155–163.

Hoff-Ginsberg, E. (1991). Mother-child conversation in different social classes and communicative settings. *Child Development, 62,* 782–796.

Hoffman, L. W. (1979). Maternal employment: 1979. *American Psychologist, 34,* 859–865.

Hoffman, L. W. (1984). Maternal employment and the young child. In M. Perlmutter (Ed.), *The Minnesota symposia on child psychology: Vol. 17. Parent-child interaction and parent-child relations in child development.* Hillsdale, NJ: Erlbaum.

Hoffman, L. W. (1989). Effects of maternal employment in the two-parent family. *American Psychologist, 44,* 283–292.

Hoffman, L. W., & Kloska, D. D. (1995). Parents' gender-based attitudes toward marital roles and child rearing: Development and validation of new measures. *Sex Roles, 32,* 273–295.

Hoffman, M. L. (1970). Moral development. In P. H. Mussen (Ed.), *Carmichael's manual of child psychology* (Vol. 2, pp. 261–359). New York: Wiley.

Hoffman, M. L. (1975). Altruistic behavior and the parent-child relationship. *Journal of Personality and Social Psychology, 31,* 937–943.

Hoffman, M. L. (1976). Empathy, role-taking, guilt, and the development of altruistic motives. In T. Lickona (Ed.), *Moral development and moral behavior: Theory, research, and social issues.* New York: Holt, Rinehart & Winston.

Hoffman, M. L. (1982). Development of prosocial motivation: Empathy and guilt. In N. Eisenberg (Ed.), *The development of prosocial behavior.* New York: Academic Press.

Hoffman-Plotkin, D., & Twentyman, C. (1984). A multimodal assessment of behavioral and cognitive deficits in abused and neglected preschoolers. *Child Development, 52,* 13–30.

Høien, T., Lundberg, I., Stanovich, K. E., & Bjaalid, I. K. (1995). Components of phonological awareness. *Reading and Writing: An Interdisciplinary Journal, 7,* 171–188.

Holden, G. W. (1983). Avoiding conflict: Mothers as tacticians in the supermarket. *Child Development, 54,* 233–240.

Holden, G. W., & West, M. J. (1989). Proximate regulation by mothers: A demonstration of how differing styles affect young children's behavior. *Child Development, 60,* 64–69.

Hollenbeck, A. R., & Slaby, R. G. (1979). Infant visual and vocal responses to television. *Child Development, 50,* 41–45.

Holowka, S., & Petitto, L. A. (2002). Left hemisphere cerebral specialization for babies while babbling. *Science, 297,* 1515.

Hood, K. E., Draper, P., Crockett, L. J., & Petersen, A. C. (1987). The ontogeny and phylogeny of sex differences in development: A biopsychosocial synthesis. In D. B. Carter (Ed.), *Current conceptions of sex roles and sex typing: Theory and research.* New York: Praeger.

Hooper, C. J., Luciana, M., Conklin, H. M., & Yarger, R. S. (2004). Adolescents' performance on the Iowa Gambling Task: Implications for the development of decision making and ventromedial prefrontal cortex. *Developmental Psychology, 40,* 1148–1158.

Hopkins, B., & Westra, T. (1990). Motor development, maternal expectations, and the role of handling. *Infant Behavior and Development, 13,* 117–122.

Hops, H., & Finch, M. (1985). Social competence and skill: A reassessment. In B. H. Schneider, K. H. Rubin, & J. E. Ledingham (Eds.), *Children's peer relations: Issues in assessment and intervention.* New York: Springer-Verlag.

Horn, J. L. (1968). Organization of abilities and the development of intelligence. *Psychological Review, 75,* 242–259.

Horn, J. L., & Cattell, R. B. (1967). Refinement and test of the theory of fluid and crystallized ability intelligences. *Journal of Educational Psychology, 57,* 253–270.

Horn, J. M., & Packard, T. (1985). Early identification of learning problems: A meta-analysis. *Journal of Educational Psychology, 77,* 349–360.

Horne, A. M., Glaser, B. A., & Calhoun, G. B. (1999). Conduct disorders. In R. T. Ammerman, M. Hersen, & C. G. Last (Eds.), *Handbook of prescriptive treatments for children and adolescents* (2nd ed., pp. 84–101). Boston: Allyn & Bacon.

Horowitz, F. D. (2000). Child development and the PITS: Simple questions, complex answers, and developmental theory. *Child Development, 71,* 1–10.

Hosmer, L. (2001). Home birth. *Clinical Obstetrics and Gynecology, 44,* 671–680.

Hossain, Z., & Roopnarine, J. L. (1994). African-American fathers' involvement with infants: Relationship to their functioning style, support, education, and income. *Infant Behavior and Development, 17,* 175–184.

Hossain, Z., Field, T., Gonzalez, J., Malphurs, J., Del Valle, C., & Pickens, J. (1994). Infants of "depressed" mothers interact better with their non-depressed fathers. *Infant Mental Health Journal, 15,* 348–357.

Hotz, V. J., McElroy, S. W., & Sanders, S. G. (1997). The costs and consequences of teenage childbearing for mothers. In R. A. Maynard (Ed.), *Kids having kids* (pp. 55–94). Washington, DC: Urban Institute.

Howe, M. L. & Courage, M. L. (1993). On resolving the enigma of infantile amnesia. *Psychological Bulletin, 113,* 305–326.

Howe, M. L., & Courage, M. L. (1997). The emergence and early development of autobiographical memory. *Psychological Review, 104,* 499–523.

Howes, C. (1987a). Peer interaction of young children. *Monographs of the Society for Research in Child Development, 53* (1, Serial No. 217).

Howes, C. (1987b). Social competence with peers in young children. *Developmental Review, 7,* 252–272.

Howes, C. (1990). Can age of entry and the quality of childcare predict adjustment in kindergarten? *Developmental Psychology, 26,* 292–303.

Howes, C., Phillips, D. A., & Whitebook, M. (1992). Thresholds of quality: Implications for the social development of children in center-based child care. *Child Development, 63,* 449–460.

Howes, C., Unger, O., & Seidner, L. B. (1989). Social pretend play in toddlers: Parallels with social play and with solitary pretend. *Child Development, 60,* 77–84.

Hoyert, D. L., Freedman, M. A., Strobino, D. M., & Guyer, B. (2001). Annual summary of vital statistics: 2000. *Pediatrics, 108,* 1241–1255.

Hoyert, D. L., Kung, H., & Smith, B. L. (2005). Deaths: Preliminary data for 2003. *National Vital Statistics Reports, Vol. 53, No. 15.* Bethesda, MD: National Center for Health Statistics.

Hsieh, F.-J., Shyu, M.-K., Sheu, B.-C., Lin, S.-P., Chen, C.-P., & Huang, F.-Y. (1995). Limb defects after chorionic villus sampling. *Obstetrics and Gynecology, 85,* 84–88.

Hsu, H.-C., & Fogel, A. (2001). Infant vocal development in a dynamic mother-infant communication system. *Infancy, 2,* 87–109.

Hsu, H-C., & Fogel, A. (2003). Stability and transitions in mother-infant face-to-face communication during the first 6 months: A microhistorical approach. *Developmental Psychology, 39,* 1061–1082.

Hubbard, J. A. (2001). Emotion expression processes in children's peer interaction: The role of peer rejection, aggression, and gender. *Child Development, 72,* 1426–1438.

Hubbs-Tait, L., Nation, J. R., Krebs, N. F., & Bellinger, D. C. (2005). Neurotoxicants, micronutrients, and social environments: Individual effects on children's development. *Psychological Science in the Public Interest, 6,* 57–121.

Hubel, D. H., & Wiesel, T. N. (1979, September). Brain mechanisms of vision. *Scientific American, 241,* pp. 150–162.

Hudson, J. A., Shapiro, L. R., & Sosa, B. B. (1995). Planning in the real world: Preschool children's scripts and plans for familiar events. *Child Development, 66,* 984–998.

Huebner, A., & Garrod, A. (1991). Moral reasoning in a karmic world. *Human Development, 34,* 341–352.

Huesmann, L. R., Lagerspetz, K., & Eron, L. D. (1984). Intervening variables and the TV violence-aggression relation: Evidence from two countries. *Developmental Psychology, 20,* 746–775.

Huffman, L. C., Bryan, Y. E., del Carmen, R., Pedersen, F. A., Doussrad-Roosevelt, J. A., & Porges, S. W. (1998). Infant temperament and cardiac vagal tone: Assessments at twelve weeks of age. *Child Development, 69,* 624–635.

Hughes, C., & Russell, J. (1993). Autistic children's difficulty with mental disengagement from an object: Its implications for theories of autism. *Developmental Psychology, 29,* 498–510.

Human Genome Project Information. (2006). *Gene therapy.* Retrieved May 5. 2006, from www.ornl.gov/sci/techresources/Human_Genome/medicine/genetherapy.shtml.

Hur, Y.-M., & Bouchard, T. J., Jr. (1995). Genetic influences on perceptions of childhood family environment: A reared apart twin study. *Child Development, 1995,* 330–345.

Hurley, J. C., & Underwood, M. K. (2002). Children's understanding of their research rights before and after debriefing: Informed assent, confidentiality, and stopping participation. *Child Development, 73,* 132–143.

Husain, M., & Kennard, C. (1997). Distractor-dependent frontal neglect. *Neuropsychologia, 35,* 829–841.

Huston, A. C. (1983). Sex typing. In E. M. Hetherington (Ed.), *Handbook of child psychology: Vol. IV. Socialization, personality, and social development* (4th ed., pp. 387–467). New York: Wiley.

Huston, A. C. (1985). The development of sex typing: Themes from recent research. *Developmental Review, 5,* 1–17.

Huston, A. C., & Alvarez, M. M. (1990). The socialization context of gender role development in early adolescence. In R. Montemayor, G. R. Adams, & T. P. Gullota (Eds.), *From childhood to adolescence: A transitional period?* (pp. 156–179). Newbury Park, CA: Sage.

Huston, A. C., & Wright, J. C. (1998). Mass media and children's development. In W. Damon (Series Ed.) & R. Lerner (Vol. Ed.), *Handbook of child psychology: Vol. 4. Child psychology in practice* (5th ed., pp. 999–1058). New York: Wiley.

Huston, A. C., Wright, J. C., Marquis, J., & Green, S. B. (1999). How young children spend their time: Television and other activities. *Developmental Psychology, 35,* 912–925.

Huston, A. C., Wright, J. C., Rice, M. L., Kerkman, D., & St. Peters, M. (1990). Development of television viewing patterns in early childhood: A longitudinal investigation. *Developmental Psychology, 26,* 409–420.

Huttenlocher, J., Haight, W., Bryk, A., Seltzer, M., & Lyons, T. (1991). Early vocabulary growth: Relation to language input and gender. *Developmental Psychology, 27,* 236–248.

Huttenlocher, P. R. (1979). Synaptic density in human frontal cortex—developmental changes and effects of aging. *Brain Research, 163,* 195–205.

Huttenlocher, P. R. (1994). Synaptogenesis in human cerebral cortex. In G. Dawson & K. W. Fischer (Eds.), *Human behavior and the developing brain* (pp. 137–152). New York: Guilford.

Hyde, J. S. (1984). How large are gender differences in aggression? A developmental meta-analysis. *Developmental Psychology, 20,* 722–736.

Hyde, J. S. (1986). Gender differences in aggression. In J. S. Hyde & M. C. Linn (Eds.), *The psychology of gender: Advances through meta-analysis.* Baltimore: Johns Hopkins University Press.

Hyde, J. S., Fennema, E., & Lamon, S. J. (1990). Gender differences in mathematics performance: A meta-analysis. *Psychological Bulletin, 107,* 139–155.

Hyde, J. S., & Linn, M. C. (1988). Gender differences in verbal ability: A meta-analysis. *Psychological Bulletin, 104,* 53–69.

Hymel, S., LeMare, L., Ditner, E., & Woody, E. Z. (1999). Assessing self-concept in children: Variations across self-concept domains. *Merrill-Palmer Quarterly, 45,* 602–623.

Iervolino, A. C., Pike, A., Manke, B., Reiss, D., Hetherington, E. M., & Plomin, R. (2002). Genetic and environmental influences in adolescent peer socialization: Evidence from two genetically sensitive designs. *Child Development, 73,* 162–174.

Ingram, D. (1999). Phonological acquisition. In M. Barrett (Ed.), *The development of language.* Hove, UK: Psychology Press.

Inhelder, B., & Piaget, J. (1958). *The growth of logical thinking from childhood to adolescence.* New York: Basic Books.

International Human Genome Sequencing Consortium. (2004). Finishing the euchromatic sequence of the human genome. *Nature, 431,* 931–945.

Isabella, R. A. (1993). Origins of attachment: Maternal interactive behavior across the first year. *Child Development, 64,* 605–621.

Isabella, R. A., Belsky, J., & von Eye, A. (1989). Origins of infant-mother attachment: An examination of interactional synchrony during the infant's first year. *Developmental Psychology, 25,* 12–21.

Isensee, W. (1986, September 3). *The Chronicle of Higher Education, 33.*

Ishii-Kuntz, M. (1994). Paternal involvement and perception toward fathers' roles: A comparison between Japan and the United States. *Journal of Family Issues, 15,* 30–48.

Isley, S. L., O'Neil, R., Clatfelter, D., & Parke, R. D. (1999). Parent and child expressed affect and children's social competence: Modeling direct and indirect pathways *Developmental Psychology, 35,* 547–560.

Iverson, J. M., & Goldin-Meadow, S. (2001). The resilience of gesture in talk: Gesture in blind speakers and listeners. *Developmental Science, 4,* 416–422.

Iverson, J. M., & Goldin-Meadow, S. (2005). Gesture paves the way for language development. *Psychological Science, 16,* 367–371.

Izard, C. E. (1978). On the ontogenesis of emotions and emotion-cognition relationships in infancy. In M. Lewis & L. A. Rosenblum (Eds.), *The development of affect.* New York: Plenum Press.

Izard, C., & Ackerman, B. P. (2000). Motivational, organizational, and regulatory functions of discrete emotions. In M. Lewis & J. M. Haviland-Jones (Eds.), *Handbook of emotions* (2nd ed., pp. 253–280). New York: Guilford Press.

Izard, C. E., & Dougherty, L. M. (1982). Two complementary systems for measuring facial expressions in infants and children. In C. E. Izard (Ed.), *Measuring emotions in infants and children* (Vol. 1). Cambridge, UK: Cambridge University Press.

Izard, C. E., Fantauzzo, C. A., Castle, J. M., Haynes, O. M., Rayias, M. F., & Putnam, P. H. (1995). The ontogeny and significance of infants' facial expressions in the first 9 months of life. *Developmental Psychology, 31,* 997–1013.

Izard, C., Fine, S., Schultz, D., Mostow, A., Ackerman, B., & Youngstrom, E. (2001). Emotion knowledge as a predictor of social behavior and academic competence in children at risk. *Psychological Science, 12,* 18–23.

Izard, C. E., Haynes, O. M., Chisolm, G., & Baak, K. (1991). Emotional determinants of infant-mother attachment. *Child Development, 62,* 906–917.

Izard, C. E., Huebner, R. R., Risser, D., McGinnes, G., & Dougherty, L. (1980). The young infant's ability to produce discrete emotion expressions. *Developmental Psychology, 16,* 132–140.

Izard, C. E., Kagan, J., & Zajonc, R. B. (1984). Introduction. In C. E. Izard, J. Kagan, & R. B. Zajonc (Eds.), *Emotions, cognition, and behavior.* Cambridge, UK: Cambridge University Press.

Izard, C. E., & Malatesta, C. Z. (1987). Perspectives on emotional development: I. Differential emotions theory of early emotional development. In J. D. Osofsky (Ed.), *Handbook of infant development* (2nd ed., pp. 494–554). New York: Wiley.


Jaccard, J., Dittus, P. J., & Gordon, V. V. (1998). Parent-adolescent congruency in reports of adolescent sexual behavior and in communications about sexual behavior. *Child Development, 69,* 247–261.

Jacklin, C. N. (1989). Female and male: Issues of gender. *American Psychologist, 44,* 127–133.

Jacklin, C. N., DiPietro, J. A., & Maccoby, E. E. (1984). Sex-typing behavior and sex-typing pressure in child/parent interaction. *Archives of Sexual Behavior, 13,* 413–425.

Jacklin, C. N., & Maccoby, E. E. (1978). Social behavior at thirty-three months in same-sex and mixed-sex dyads. *Child Development, 49,* 557–569.

Jackson, A. P., Brooks Gunn, J., Huang, C. C., & Glassman, M. (2000). Single mothers in low-wage jobs: Financial strain, parenting, and preschoolers' outcomes. *Child Development, 71,* 1409–1423.

Jackson, A. W., & Hornbeck, D. W. (1989). Educating young adolescents: Why we must restructure middle grade schools. *American Psychologist, 44,* 831–836.

Jackson, J. F. (1993). Human behavioral genetics, Scarr's theory, and her views on interventions: A critical review and commentary on their implications for African American children. *Child Development, 64,* 1318–1332.

Jacobs, J. E., & Klaczynski, P. A. (2002). The development of judgment and decision making during childhood and adolescence. *Current Directions in Psychological Science, 11,* 145–149.

Jacobs, J. E., & Potenza, M. (1991). The use of judgment heuristics to make social and object decisions: A developmental perspective. *Child Development, 62,* 166–178.

Jacobs, J. E., Lanza, S., Osgood, D. W., Eccles, J. S., & Wigfield, A. (2002). Changes in children's self-competence and values: Gender and domain differences across grades one through twelve. *Child Development, 73,* 509–527.

Jacobs, P. A., & Hassold, T. J. (1995). The origin of numerical chromosome abnormalities. *Advances in Genetics, 33,* 101–133.

Jacobsen, T., Edelstein, W., & Hofman, V. (1994). A longitudinal study of the relation between representations of attachment in childhood and cognitive functioning in childhood and adolescence. *Developmental Psychology, 30,* 112–124.

Jacobson, J. L., & Jacobson, S. W. (1996). Methodological considerations in behavioral toxicology in infants and children. *Developmental Psychology, 32,* 390–403.

Jaffee, S. R., Moffitt, T. E., Caspi, A., & Taylor, A. Life with (or without) father: The benefits of living with two biological parents depend on the father's antisocial behavior. *Child Development, 74,* 109–126.

Jaglom, L. M., & Gardner, H. (1981). The preschool television viewer as anthropologist. In H. Kelly & H. Gardner (Eds.), *New directions in child development: Viewing children through television* (pp. 9–30). San Francisco: Jossey-Bass.

Jahns, L., Siega-Riz, A. M., & Popkin, B. M. (2001). The increasing prevalence of snacking among U.S. children from 1977 to 1996. *Journal of Pediatrics, 138,* 493–498.

Jahromi, L. B., Putnam, S. P., & Stifter, C. A. (2004). Maternal regulation of infant reactivity from 2 to 6 months. *Developmental Psychology, 40,* 477–487.

James, S. (1978). Effect of listener age and situation on the politeness of children's directives. *Journal of Psycholinguistic Research, 7,* 307–317.

James, W. (1890). *The principles of psychology.* New York: Henry Holt.

James, W. (1892). *Psychology: The briefer course.* New York: Henry Holt.

Janicki, M. P., & Dalton, A. J. (2000). Prevalence of dementia and impact on intellectual disability services. *Mental Retardation, 38,* 276–288.

Jarrett, R. L. (1997). Bringing families back in: Neighborhoods' effects on child development. In J. Brooks-Gunn, G. J. Duncan, & J. L. Aber (Eds.), *Neighborhood poverty: Vol. 2. Policy implications in studying neighborhoods* (pp. 48–64). New York: Russell Sage Foundation.

Jegalian, K., & Lahn, B. T. (2001, February). Why the Y is so weird. *Scientific American, 284,* pp. 56–61.

Jencks, C. (1972). *Inequality: A reassessment of the effect of family and schooling in America.* New York: Basic Books.

Jencks, C., & Mayer, S. (1990). The social consequences of growing up in a poor neighborhood. In L. E. Lynn & M. F. H. McGeary (Eds.), *Inner-city poverty in the United States* (pp. 111–186). Washington, DC: National Academy Press.

Jenkins, J. (1992). Sibling relationships in disharmonious homes: Potential difficulties and protective effects. In R. A. Hinde & J. Stevenson-Hinde (Eds.), *Children's sibling relationships: Developmental and clinical issues* (pp. 125–138). Hillsdale, NJ: Erlbaum.

Jensen, A. R. (1969). How much can we boost IQ and scholastic achievement? *Harvard Educational Review, 39,* 1–123.

Jensen, A. R. (1980). *Bias in mental testing.* New York: Free Press.

Jensen, A. R. (1982). The chronometry of intelligence. In R. J. Sternberg (Ed.), *Advances in the psychology of human intelligence* (Vol. 1). Hillsdale, NJ: Erlbaum.

Jensen, A. R., & Munroe, E. (1979). Reaction time, movement time, and intelligence. *Intelligence, 3,* 121–126.

Johnson, J., & Newport, E. (1989). Critical period effects in second language learning: The influence of maturational state on the acquisition of English as a second language. *Cognitive Psychology, 21,* 60–99.

Johnson, K. E., & Mervis, C. M. (1997). First steps in the emergence of verbal humor: A case study. *Infant Behavior & Development, 20,* 187–196.

Johnson, M. H. (1992). Imprinting and the development of face recognition: From chick to man. *Current Directions in Psychological Science, 1,* 52–55.

Johnson, M. H. (2000). Functional brain development in infants: Elements of an interactive specialization framework. *Child Development, 71*, 75–81.

Johnson, M. H., Dziurawiec, S., Ellis, H. D., & Morton, J. (1991). Newborns' preferential tracking of face-like stimuli and its subsequent decline. *Cognition, 40*, 1–21.

Johnson, M. H., Farroni, T., Brockbank, M., & Simion, F. (2000). Preferential orienting to faces in 4-month-olds: Analysis of temporal-nasal visual field differences. *Developmental Science, 3*, 41–45.

Johnson, S. P. (2004). Development of perceptual completion in infancy. *Psychological Science, 15*, 769–775.

Johnson, S. P., Bremner, J. G., Slater, A. M., & Mason, U. C. (2000). The role of good form in young infant's perception of partly occluded objects. *Journal of Experimental Child Psychology, 76*, 1–25.

Johnson, S. P., & Mason, U. (2002). Perception of kinetic illusory contours by two-month-old infants. *Child Development, 73*, 22–34.

Johnston, J., Brzezinski, E. J., & Anderman, E. M. (1994). *Taking the measure of Channel One: A three year perspective*. Ann Arbor, MI: University of Michigan, Institute for Social Research.

Joint Committee on Infant Hearing. (2000). Year 2000 Position Statement: Principles and Guidelines for Early Hearing Detection and Intervention Program. *Pediatrics, 106*, 798–817.

Jones, D. C. (2004). Image among adolescent girls and boys: A longitudinal study. *Developmental Psychology, 40*, 823–835.

Jones, G. P., & Dembo, M. H. (1989). Age and sex role differences in intimate friendships during childhood and adolescence. *Merrill-Palmer Quarterly, 35*, 445–462.

Jones, K. L., & Smith, D. W. (1973). Recognition of the fetal alcohol syndrome in early infancy. *Lancet, 2*, 999–1001.

Jones, M. C. (1965). Psychological correlates of somatic development. *Child Development, 36*, 899–911.

Jones, S. S. (1996). Imitation or exploration? Young infants' matching of adults' oral gestures. *Child Development, 67*, 1952–1969.

Joseph, R. (2000). Fetal brain behavior and cognitive development. *Developmental Review, 20*, 81–98.

Joyce, B. A., Keck, J. F., & Gerkensmeyer, J. (2001). Evaluation of pain management interventions for neonatal circumcision pain. *Journal of Pediatric Health Care, 15*, 105–114.

Juffer, F., & van IJzendoorn, M. A. (2005). Behavior problems and mental health referrals of international adoptees. *Journal of the American Medical Association, 293*, 2501–2515.

Jusczyk, P. W., Cutler, A., & Redanz, L. (1993). Infants' sensitivity to predominant stress patterns in English. *Child Development, 64*, 675–687.

Jusczyk, P. W., Friederici, A. D., Wessels, J. M. I., Svenkerud, V. Y., & Jusczyk, A. M. (1993). Infants' sensitivity to the sound patterns of native language words. *Journal of Memory and Language, 32*, 402–420.

Jusczyk, P. W., Hirsh-Pasek, K., Kemler Nelson, D. G., Kennedy, L. J., Woodward, A. & Piwoz, J. (1992). Perception of acoustic correlates of major phrasal units by young infants. *Cognitive Psychology, 24*, 252–293.

Kagan, J. (1981). *The second year: The emergence of self-awareness*. Cambridge, MA: Harvard University Press.

Kagan, J. (1994). *Galen's prophecy: Temperament in human nature*. New York: Basic Books.

Kagan, J., Arcus, D., Snidman, N., Feng, W. Y., Hendler, J., & Greene, S. (1994). Reactivity in infants: A cross-national comparison. *Developmental Psychology, 30*, 342–345.

Kagan, J., & Fox, N. A. (2006). Biology, culture, and temperamental biases. In W. Damon & R. M. Lerner (Editors-in-Chief) & N. Eisenberg (Vol. Ed.), *Handbook of child psychology: Vol. 3. Social, emotional, and personality development* (6th ed., pp. 167–225). Hoboken, NJ: Wiley.

Kagan, J., Reznick, J. S., & Snidman, N. (1988). Biological basis of childhood shyness. *Science, 240*, 167–171.

Kagan, J., Snidman, N., & Arcus, D. M. (1992). Initial reactions to unfamiliarity. *Current Directions in Psychological Science, 1*, 171–174.

Kagan, J., Snidman, N., & Arcus, D. (1993). On the temperamental categories of inhibited and uninhibited children. In K. H. Rubin & J. B. Asendorpf (Eds.), *Social withdrawal, inhibition, and shyness in children* (pp. 19–28). Hillsdale, NJ: Erlbaum.

Kahn, P. H., Jr. (1992). Children's obligatory and discretionary moral judgments. *Child Development, 63*, 416–430.

Kail, R. (1986). Sources of age differences in speed of processing. *Child Development, 57*, 969–987.

Kail, R. (1990). *The development of memory in children* (3rd ed.). New York: W.H. Freeman.

Kail, R. (1991a). Development of processing speed in childhood and adolescence. In H. W. Reese (Ed.), *Advances in child development and behavior* (Vol. 23). San Diego, CA: Academic Press.

Kail, R. (1991b). Processing time declines exponentially during childhood and adolescence. *Developmental Psychology, 27*, 259–266.

Kail, R. V., & Miller, C. A. (2006). Developmental change in processing speed: Domain specificity and stability during childhood and adolescence. *Journal of Cognition and Development, 7*, 119–137.

Kaiser, J. (2005). An early look at baby's genes. *Science, 309*, 1476–1478.

Kaiser Family Foundation. (2004). *Sex education in America: General public/Parents survey*. Washington, DC: Kaiser Family Foundation.

Kaiser Family Foundation. (2005). *U. S. teen sexual activity*. Washington, DC: Henry J. Kaiser Family Foundation.

Kaitz, M., Lapidot, P., Bronner, R., & Eidelman, A. I. (1992). Parturient women can recognize their infants by touch. *Developmental Psychology, 28*, 35–39.

Kaitz, M., Shiri, S., Danziger, S., Hershko, Z., & Eidelman, A. I. (1994). Fathers can also recognize their newborns by touch. *Infant Behavior and Development, 17*, 205–207.

Kajii, T., Kida, M., & Takahashi, K. (1973). The effect of thalidomide intake during 113 human pregnancies. *Teratology, 8*, 163–166.

Kamins, M. L., & Dweck, C. S. (1999). Person versus process praise and criticism: Implications for contingent self-worth and coping. *Developmental Psychology, 35*, 835–847.

Kanner, L. (1943). Autistic disturbances of affective contact. *Nervous Children, 2*, 217–250.

Kaplan, H., & Dove, H. (1987). Infant development among the Ache of Eastern Paraguay. *Developmental Psychology, 23*, 190–196.

Kaplowitz, P. B., Slora, E. J., Wasserman, R. C., Pedlow, S. E., & Herman-Giddens, M. E. (2001). Earlier onset of puberty in girls: Relation to increased body mass index and race. *Pediatrics, 108*, 347–353.

Karmiloff-Smith, A. (1995). Annotation: The extraordinary cognitive journey from foetus through infancy. *Journal of Child Psychology and Psychiatry, 36*, 1293–1313.

Karraker, K. H., Vogel, D. A., & Lake, M. A. (1995). Parents' gender-stereotyped perceptions of newborns: The eye of the beholder revisited. *Sex Roles, 33*, 687–701.

Karrass, J., & Braungart-Rieker, J. M. (2005). Effects of shared parent-infant book reading on early language acquisition. *Applied Developmental Psychology, 26*, 133–148.

Katz, P. A. (1987). Variations in family constellation: Effects on gender schemata. In L. S. Liben & M. L. Signorella (Eds.), *New directions for child development: No. 38. Children's gender schemata*. San Francisco: Jossey-Bass.

Katz, P. A., & Ksansnak, K. R. (1994). Developmental aspects of gender role flexibility and traditionality in middle childhood and adolescence. *Developmental Psychology, 30*, 272–282.

Katz, P., Natchtigall, R., & Showstack, J. (2002). The economic impact of the assisted reproductive technologies. *Nature Cell Biology, 4*, s29–32.

Katzman, D. K., Golden, N. H., Neumark-Sztainer, D., Yager, J., & Strober, M. (2000). From prevention to prognosis: Clinical research update on adolescent eating disorders. *Pediatric Research, 47*, 709–712.

Kaufman, A. S. (2001). WAIS-III IQs, Horn's theory, and generational changes from young adulthood to old age. *Intelligence, 29*, 131–167.

Kaufman, A. S., Kamphaus, R. W., & Kaufman, N. L. (1985). New directions in intelligence testing: The Kaufman Assessment Battery for Children (K-ABC). In B. B. Wolman (Ed.), *Handbook of intelligence* (pp. 663–698). New York: Wiley.

Kaye, K., & Marcus, J. (1981). Infant imitation: The sensorimotor agenda. *Developmental Psychology, 17,* 258–265.

Kayne, M. A., Greulich, M. B., & Albers, L. L. (2001). Doulas: An alternative yet complementary addition to care during childbirth. *Clinical Obstetrics and Gynecology, 44,* 692–703.

Kazdin, A., & Benjet, C. (2003). Spanking children: Evidence and issues. *Current Directions in Psychological Science, 12,* 99–103.

Keel, P. K., Fulkerson, J. A., & Leon, G. R. (1997). Disordered eating precursors in pre- and early adolescent girls and boys. *Journal of Youth and Adolescence, 26,* 203–216.

Keen, R. E., & Berthier, N. E. (2004). Continuities and discontinuities in infants' representation of objects and events. In R. V. Kail (Ed.), *Advances in child development and behavior* (Vol. 32, pp. 243–279). San Diego: Elsevier.

Keil, F. C. (1989). *Concepts, kinds, and cognitive development.* Cambridge, MA: MIT Press.

Keller, M., Edelstein, W., Schmid, C., Fang, F., & Fang, G. (1998). Reasoning about responsibilities and obligations in close relationships: A comparison across two cultures. *Developmental Psychology, 34,* 731–741.

Kelley, M. L., Power, T. G., & Wimbush, D. D. (1992). Determinants of disciplinary practices in low-income black mothers. *Child Development, 63,* 573–582.

Kelley, S. A., Brownell, C. A., & Campbell, S. B. (2000). Mastery motivation and self-evaluative affect in toddlers: Longitudinal relations with maternal behavior. *Child Development, 71,* 1061–1071.

Kellman, P. J. (1996). The origins of object perception. In R. Gelman & T. Au (Eds.), *Perceptual and cognitive development* (pp. 3–48). New York: Academic Press.

Kellman, P. J., & Arterberry, M. E. (1998). *The cradle of knowledge: Development of perception in infancy.* Cambridge, MA: MIT Press.

Kellman, P. J., & Arterberry, M. E. (2006). Infant visual perception. In W. Damon & R. M. Lerner (Editors-in-Chief) & D. M. Kuhn & R. S. Siegler (Vol. Eds.), *Handbook of child psychology: Vol. 2. Cognition, perception, and language* (6th ed., pp. 109–160). Hoboken, NJ: Wiley.

Kellman, P. J., & Banks, M. S. (1998). Infant visual perception. In W. Damon (Series Ed.) & R. Siegler & D. Kuhn (Vol. Eds.), *Handbook of child psychology: Vol. 2. Cognition, perception, and language* (5th ed., pp. 103–146). New York: Wiley.

Kellman, P. J., & Spelke, E. S. (1983). Perception of partly occluded objects in infancy. *Cognitive Psychology, 15,* 483–524.

Kelly, M. H. (1992). Using sound to solve syntactic problems: The role of phonology in grammatical category assignments. *Psychological Review, 99,* 349–364.

Kemler Nelson, D. G., Hirsh-Pasek, K., Jusczyk, P. W., & Cassidy, K. W. (1989). How the prosodic cues in motherese might assist language learning. *Journal of Child Language, 16,* 55–68.

Kemp, J. S., Livne, M., White, D. K., & Arfken, C. L. (1998). Softness and potential to cause rebreathing: Differences in bedding used by infants at high and low risk for sudden infant death syndrome. *Journal of Pediatrics, 132,* 234–239.

Kendler, K. S., Prescott, C. A., Neale, M. C., & Pedersen, N. L. (1997). Temperance Board registration for alcohol abuse in a national sample of Swedish male twins, born 1902–1949. *Archives of General Psychiatry, 54,* 178–184.

Kennedy, C. R. (2000). Neonatal screening for hearing impairment. *Archives of Disease in Childhood, 83,* 377–383.

Keogh, J., & Sugden, D. (1985). *Movement skill development.* New York: Macmillan.

Kerig, P. K., Cowan, P. A., & Cowan, C. P. (1993). Marital quality and gender differences in parent-child interaction. *Developmental Psychology, 29,* 931–939.

Kersten, A. W., & Smith, L. B. (2002). Attention to novel objects during verb learning. *Child Development, 73,* 93–109.

Kieras, J. E., Tobin, R. T., Graziano, W. G., & Rothbart, M. K. (2005). You can't always get what you want: Effortful control and children's responses to undesirable gifts. *Psychological Science, 16,* 391–396.

Kiesner, J., Cadinu, M., Poulin, F., & Bucci, M. (2002). Group identification in early adolescence: Its relation with peer adjustment and its moderator effect on peer influence. *Child Development, 73,* 196–208.

Kiesner, J., & Pastore, M. (2005). Differences in the relations between antisocial behavior and peer acceptance across contexts and across adolescence. *Child Development, 76,* 1278–1293.

Kilbride, H., Castor, C., Hoffman, E., & Fuger, K. L. (2000). Thirty-six-month outcome of prenatal cocaine exposure for term or near-term infants: Impact of early case management. *Journal of Developmental and Behavioral Pediatrics, 21,* 19–26.

Killen, M., Pisacane, K., Lee Kim, J., & Ardila Rey, A. (2001). Fairness or stereotypes? Young children's priorities when evaluating group exclusion and inclusion. *Developmental Psychology, 37,* 587–596.

Kim, J. E., Hetherington, E. M., & Reiss, D. (1999). Associations among family relationships., antisocial peers, and adolescents' externalizing behaviors: Gender and family type differences. *Child Development, 70,* 1209–1230.

Kim, K. H. S., Relkin, N. R., Lee, K., & Hirsch, J. (1997). Distinct cortical areas associated with native and second languages. *Nature, 388,* 171–174.

Kim, K. J., Conger, R. D., Lorenz, F. O., & Elder, G. H., Jr. (2001). Parent-adolescent reciprocity in negative affect and its relation to early adult social development. *Developmental Psychology, 37,* 775–790.

Kinsman, S. B., Romer, D., Furstenberg, F. F., & Schwartz, D. F. (1998). Early sexual initiation: The role of peer norms. *Pediatrics, 102,* 1185–1192.

Kirby, D. (1997). *No easy answers: Research findings on programs to reduce teen pregnancy.* Washington, DC: National Campaign to Prevent Teen Pregnancy.

Kirkpatrick, S. W., & Sanders, D. M. (1978). Body image stereotypes: A developmental comparison. *Journal of Genetic Psychology, 132,* 87–95.

Kisilevsky, B. S., Hains, S. M. J., & Low, J. A. (1999). Differential maturation of fetal responses to vibroacoustic stimulation in a high risk population. *Developmental Science, 2,* 234–245.

Kisilevsky, B. S., & Low, J. A. (1998). Human fetal behavior: 100 years of study. *Developmental Review, 18,* 1–29.

Kisilevsky, B. S., & Muir, D. W. (1991). Human fetal and subsequent newborn responses to sound and vibration. *Infant Behavior and Development, 14,* 1–26.

Klaczynski, P. A. (2000). Motivated scientific reasoning biases, epistemological beliefs, and theory polarization: A two-process approach to adolescent cognition. *Child Development, 71,* 1347–1366.

Klaczynski, P. A. (2001). Analytic and heuristic processing influences on adolescent reasoning and decision-making. *Child Development, 72,* 844–861.

Klaczynski, P. A. (2004). A dual-process model of adolescent development: Implications for decision making, reasoning, and identity. In R. V. Kail (Ed.), *Advances in child development and behavior* (Vol. 32, pp. 73–123). San Diego, CA: Elsevier.

Klahr, D. (1978). Goal formation, planning, and learning by preschool problem solvers or: "My socks are in the dryer." In R. S. Siegler (Ed.), *Children's thinking: What develops?* (pp. 181–212). Hillsdale, NJ: Erlbaum.

Klahr, D. (1989). Information-processing approaches. In R. Vasta (Ed.), *Annals of child development: Vol 6. Six theories of child development: Revised formulations and current issues.* Greenwich, CT: JAI Press.

Klahr, D., Chen, Z., & Toth, E. E. (2001). Cognitive development and science education: Ships that pass in the night or beacons of mutual illumination? In S. M. Carver & D. Klahr (Eds.), *Cognition and instruction: Twenty-five years of progress* (pp. 75–119). Mahwah, NJ: Erlbaum.

Klahr, D., & Dunbar, K. (1988). Dual space search during scientific reasoning. *Cognitive Science, 12,* 1–55.

Klahr, D., Fay, A. L., & Dunbar, K. (1993). Heuristics for scientific experimentation: A developmental study. *Cognitive Psychology, 25,* 111–146.

Klahr, D., & MacWhinney, B. (1998). Information processing. In W. Damon (Series Ed.) & D. Kuhn & R. S. Siegler (Vol. Eds.), *Handbook of child psychology: Vol. 2. Cognition, perception, and language* (5th ed., pp. 631–678). New York: Wiley.

Klahr, D., & Robinson, M. (1981). Formal assessment of problem solving and planning processes in preschool children. *Cognitive Psychology, 13,* 113–148.

Klaus, M., & Kennell, J. (1982). *Parent-infant bonding.* St. Louis: C. V. Mosby.

Klebanov, P. K., Brooks-Gunn, J., & McCormick, M. C. (1994). Classroom behavior of very low birth weight elementary school children. *Pediatrics, 94,* 700–708.

Klein, P. D. (1997). Multiplying the problems of intelligence by eight: A critique of Gardner's theory. *Canadian Journal of Education, 22,* 377–394.

Klesges, R. C., Haddock, C. K., Stein, R. J., Klesges, L. M., Eck, L. H., & Hanson, C. L. (1992). Relationship between psychosocial functioning and body fat in preschool children: A longitudinal investigation. *Journal of Consulting and Clinical Psychology, 60,* 793–796.

Kliewer, W., Adams Parrish, K., Taylor, K. W., Jackson, K., Walker, J. M., & Shivy, V. A. (2006). Socialization of coping with community violence: Influences of caregiver coaching, modeling, and family context. *Child Development, 77,* 605–623.

Klima, E. S., & Bellugi, U. (1966). Syntactic regularities in the speech of children. In J. Lyons & R. J. Wales (Eds.), *Psycholinguistic papers: The proceedings of the 1966 Edinburgh conference.* Edinburgh: Edinburgh University Press.

Kling, K. C., Hyde, J. S., Showers, C. J., & Buswell, B. N. (1999). Gender differences in self-esteem: A meta-analysis. *Psychological Bulletin, 125,* 470–500.

Knowles, R. V. (1985). *Genetics, society and decisions.* Columbus, OH: Merrill.

Kobak, R. R., Cole, H. E., Ferenz-Gillies, R., & Fleming, W. S. (1993). Attachment and emotion regulation during mother-teen problem-solving: A control theory analysis. *Child Development, 64,* 231–245.

Kobayashi-Winata, H., & Power, T. G. (1989). Child rearing and compliance: Japanese and American families in Houston. *Journal of Cross-Cultural Psychology, 20,* 333–356.

Kochanek, K. D., Murphy, S. L., Anderson, R. N., & Scott, C. (2004). *Deaths: Final data for 2002. National Vital Statistics Report, 53*(5), 1–116.

Kochanska, G. (1994). Beyond cognition: Expanding the search for the early roots of internalization and conscience. *Developmental Psychology, 30,* 20–22.

Kochanska, G. (1997). Mutually responsive orientation between mothers and their young children: Implications for early socialization. *Child Development, 68,* 94–112.

Kochanska, G. (2001). Emotional development in children with different attachment histories: The first three years. *Child Development, 72,* 474–490.

Kochanska, G. (2002). Committed compliance, moral self, and internalization: A mediational model. *Developmental Psychology, 38,* 339–351.

Kochanska, G., Aksan, N., Knaack, A., & Rhines, H. M. (2004). Maternal parenting and children's conscience: Early security as a moderator. *Child Development, 75,* 1229–1242.

Kochanska, G., Aksan, N., & Koenig, A. L. (1995). A longitudinal study of the roots of preschoolers' conscience: Committed compliance and emerging internalizations. *Child Development, 66,* 1752–1769.

Kochanska, G., Casey, R. J., & Fukumoto, A. (1995). Toddlers' sensitivity to standard violation. *Child Development, 66,* 643–656.

Kochanska, G., Coy, K. C., & Murray, K. T. (2001). The development of self-regulation in the first four years of life. *Child Development, 72,* 1091–1111.

Kochanska, G., Gross, J. N., Lin, M.-H., & Nichols, K. E. (2002). Guilt in young children: Development, determinants, and relations with a broader system of standards. *Child Development, 73,* 461–482.

Kochanska, G., & Murray, K. T. (2000). Mother-child responsive orientation and conscience development: From toddler to early school age. *Child Development, 71,* 417–431.

Kochanska, G., Murray, K., & Coy, K. C. (1997). Inhibitory control as a contributor to conscience in childhood: From toddler to early school age. *Child Development, 68,* 263–277.

Kochanska, G., Murray, K. T., & Harlan, E. T. (2000). Effortful control in early childhood: Continuity and change, antecedents, and implications for social development. *Developmental Psychology, 36,* 220–232.

Kochanska, G., Tjebkes, T. L., & Forman, D. R. (1998). Children's emerging regulation of conduct: Restraint, compliance, and internalization from infancy to the second year. *Child Development, 69,* 1378–1389.

Kochenderfer, B. J., & Ladd, G. W. (1996). Peer victimization: Cause or consequence of school maladjustment? *Child Development, 67,* 1305–1317.

Koff, E., & Rierdan, J. (1995). Preparing girls for menstruation: Recommendations from adolescent girls. *Adolescence, 30,* 795–811.

Kohlberg, L. (1966). A cognitive-developmental analysis of children's sex-role concepts and attitudes. In E. E. Maccoby (Ed.), *The development of sex differences* (pp. 82–173). Stanford, CA: Stanford University Press.

Kohlberg, L. (1969). Stage and sequence: The cognitive-developmental approach to socialization. In D. A. Goslin (Ed.), *The handbook of socialization theory and research* (pp. 347–380). Chicago: Rand McNally.

Kohlberg, L. (1976). Moral stages and moralization: The cognitive developmental approach. In T. Lickona (Ed.), *Moral development and moral behavior: Theory, research, and social issu*es (pp. 31–53). New York: Holt, Rinehart & Winston.

Kohlberg, L. (1984). *Essays on moral development: Vol. 2. The psychology of moral development.* San Francisco: Harper & Row.

Kohlberg, L., & Kramer, R. (1969). Continuities and discontinuities in childhood moral development. *Human Development, 12,* 93–120.

Kolata, G. (2001, September 28). Fertility ethics authority approves sex selection. *New York Times,* p. A16.

Kopp, C. (1989). Regulation of distress and negative emotions: A developmental view. *Developmental Psychology, 25,* 343–354.

Kopp, C. B. (1987). The growth of self-regulation: Caregivers and children. In N. Eisenberg (Ed.), *Contemporary topics in developmental psychology* (pp. 34–55). New York: Wiley.

Kopp, C. B. (1992). Emotional distress and control in young children. In N. Eisenberg & R. A. Fabes (Eds.), *Emotion and its regulation in early development (New Directions in Child Development,* No. 55). San Francisco: Jossey-Bass.

Korner, A. F. (1972). State as a variable, as obstacle, and mediator of stimulation in infant research. *Merrill-Palmer Quarterly, 18,* 77–94.

Korner, A. F. (1987). Preventive intervention with high-risk newborns: Theoretical, conceptual, and methodological perspectives. In J. D. Osofsky (Ed.), *Handbook of infant development* (2nd ed.). New York: Wiley.

Kotelchuk, M. (1976). The infant's relationship to the father: Experimental evidence. In M. E. Lamb (Ed.), *The role of the father in child development.* New York: Wiley.

Kovacs, D. M., Parker, J. G., & Hoffman, L. W. (1996). Behavioral, affective, and social correlates of involvement in cross-sex friendship in elementary school. *Child Development, 67,* 2269–2286.

Kowal, A., & Kramer, L. (1997). Children's understanding of potential differential treatment. *Child Development, 68,* 113–126.

Kraemer, H. C., Korner, A., Anders, T., Jacklin, C. N., & Dimiceli, S. (1985). Obstetric drugs and infant behavior: A re-evaluation. *Journal of Pediatric Psychology, 10,* 345–353.

Krafchuk, E. E., Tronick, E. Z., & Clifton, R. K. (1983). Behavioral and cardiac responses to sound in preterm infants varying in risk status: A hypothesis of their paradoxical reactivity. In T. Field & A. Sostek (Eds.), *Infants born at risk: Physiological, perceptual, and cognitive processes.* New York: Grune & Stratton.

Kramer, A. F., Gonzalez de Sather, J. C. M., & Cassavaugh, N. D. (2005). Development of attentional and oculomotor control. *Developmental Psychology, 41,* 760–772.

Kramer, L., Perozynski, L. A., & Chung, T. (1999). Parental responses to sibling conflict: The effects of development and parent gender. *Child Development, 70,* 1401–1414.

Kranzler, J. H., Rosenbloom, A. L., Proctor, B., Diamond, F. B., Jr., & Watson, M. (2000). Is short stature a handicap? A comparison of the psychosocial functioning of referred and nonreferred children with normal short stature and children with normal stature. *Journal of Pediatrics, 136,* 96–102.

Krascum, R. M., & Andrews, S. (1998). The effects of theories on children's acquisition of family-resemblance structures. *Child Development, 69,* 333–346.

Krauss, R. H., & Glucksberg, S. (1969). The development of communication. *Child Development, 40,* 255–266.

Krebs, D. L., & Van Hesteren, F. (1994). The development of altruism: Toward an integrative model. *Developmental Review, 14,* 103–158.

Krendl, K. A., & Broihier, M. (1992). Student responses to computers: A longitudinal study. *Journal of Educational Computing Research, 8,* 215–227.

Kreutzer, M. A., Leonard, S. C., & Flavell, J. H. (1975). An interview study of children's knowledge about memory. *Monographs of the Society for Research in Child Development, 40*(1, Serial No. 159).

Krevans, J., & Gibbs, J. C. (1996). Parents' use of inductive discipline: Relations to children's empathy and prosocial behavior. *Child Development, 67,* 3263–3277.

Kroll, J. (1977). The concept of childhood in the Middle Ages. *Journal of the History of the Behavioral Sciences, 13,* 384–393.

Krowchuck, D. P., Kreiter, S. R., Woods, C. R., Sinal, S. H., & DuRant, R. H. (1998). Problem dieting behavior among young adolescents. *Archives of Pediatric and Adolescent Medicine, 152,* 884–888.

Krumhansl, C. L., & Jusczyk, P. W. (1990). Infants' perception of phrase structure in music. *Psychological Science, 1,* 70–73.

Kuczaj, S. A., Borys, R. H., & Jones, M. (1989). On the interaction of language and thought: Some thoughts and developmental data. In A. Gellatly, D. Rogers, & J. A. Sloboda (Eds.), *Cognition and social worlds.* Oxford: Clarendon Press.

Kuczynski, L., & Kochanska, G. (1995). Function and content of maternal demands: Developmental significance of early demands for competent action. *Child Development, 66,* 616–628.

Kuebli, J., Butler, S., & Fivush, R. (1995). Mother-child talk about past emotions: Relations of maternal language and child gender over time. *Cognition and Emotion, 9,* 265–283.

Kuhl, P. K. (1987). Perception of speech and sound in early infancy. In P. Salapatek & L. Cohen (Eds.), *Handbook of infant perception: From perception to cognition* (Vol. 2). Orlando, FL: Academic Press.

Kuhl, P. K., & Miller, J. D. (1978). Speech perception by the chinchilla: Identification functions for synthetic VOT stimuli. *Journal of the Acoustical Society of America, 63,* 905–917.

Kuhl, P. K., & Padden, D. M. (1983). Enhanced discriminability at the phonetic boundary for the place feature in macaques. *Journal of the Acoustical Society of America, 73,* 1003–1010.

Kuhl, P. K., Stevens, E., Hayashi, A., Deguchi, T., Kiritani, S., & Iverson, P. (2006). Infants show a facilitation effect for native language phonetic perception between 6 and 12 months. *Developmental Science, 9,* F13–F22.

Kuhl, P. K., Williams, K. A., Lacerda, F., Stevens, K. N., & Lindblom, B. (1992). Linguistic experience alters phonetic perception in infants by 6 months of age. *Science, 255,* 606–608.

Kuhn, D. (2000a). Metacognitive development. *Current Directions in Psychological Science, 9,* 178–181.

Kuhn, D. (2000b). Theory of mind, metacognition, and reasoning: A lifespan perspective. In P. Mitchell & K. J. Riggs (Eds.), *Children's reasoning and the mind* (pp. 301–326). Hove, UK: Psychology Press.

Kuhn, D. (2006). Do cognitive changes accompany developments in the adolescent brain? *Perspectives on Psychological Science, 1,* 59–67.

Kuhn, D., & Dean, D., Jr. (2005). Is developing scientific thinking all about learning to control variables? *Psychological Science, 16,* 866–870.

Kuhn, D., Garcia-Mila, M., Zohar, A., & Andersen, C. (1995). Strategies of knowledge acquisition. *Monographs of the Society for Research in Child Development, 60* (No. 4, Serial No. 245).

Kuhn, D., & Pearsall, S. (2000). Developmental origins of scientific thinking. *Journal of Cognition and Development, 1,* 113–129.

Kuhn, D., Schauble, L., & Garcia-Mila, M. (1992). Cross-domain development of scientific reasoning. *Cognition and Instruction, 9,* 285–327.

Kuklinski, M. R., & Weinstein, R. S. (2001). Classroom and developmental differences in a path model of teacher expectancy effects. *Child Development, 72,* 1554–1578.

Kunkel, D. (2001). Children and television advertising. In D. Singer & J. Singer (Eds.), *Handbook of children and the media* (pp. 375–393). Thousand Oaks, CA: Sage.

Kunkel, D., & Roberts, D. (1991). Young minds and marketplace values: Issues in children's television advertising. *Journal of Social Issues, 47,* 57–72.

Kunzig, R. (1998, August). Climbing through the brain. *Discover, 19,* 61–69.

Kuppermann, M., Gates, E., & Washington, A. E. (1996). Racial ethnic differences in prenatal diagnostic test use and outcomes: Preferences, socioeconomics, or patient knowledge? *Obstetrics and Gynecology, 87,* 675–682.

Kurdek, L. A. (1989). Siblings' reactions to parental divorce. *Journal of Divorce, 12,* 203–219.

Kurdek, L. A., Fine, M. A., & Sinclair, R. J. (1995). School adjustment in sixth graders: Parenting transitions, family climate, and peer norm effects. *Child Development, 66,* 430–445.

LaBarbera, J. D., Izard, C. E., Vietze, P., & Parisi, S. A. (1976). Four- and six-month-old infants' visual responses to joy, anger, and neutral expressions. *Child Development, 47,* 535–538.

Lackey, P. N. (1989). Adults' attitudes about assignments of household chores to male and female children. *Sex Roles, 20,* 271–281.

Ladd, G. W. (1983). Social networks of popular, average, and rejected children in school settings. *Merrill-Palmer Quarterly, 29,* 283–307.

Ladd, G. W., Birch, S. H., & Buhs, E. S. (1999). Children's social and scholastic lives in kindergarten: Related spheres of influence? *Child Development, 70,* 1373–1400.

Ladd, G. W., & Burgess, K. B. (1999). Charting the relationship trajectories of aggressive, withdrawn, and aggressive/withdrawn children during early grade school. *Child Development, 70,* 910–929.

Ladd, G. W., & Golter, B. S. (1988). Parents' management of preschooler's peer relations: Is it related to children's social competencies? *Developmental Psychology, 24,* 109–117.

Ladd, G. W., & Hart, C. H. (1992). Creating informal play opportunities: Are parents' and preschoolers' initiations related to children's competence with peers? *Developmental Psychology, 28,* 1179–1187.

Ladd, G. W., Kochenderfer, B. J., & Coleman, C. C. (1996). Friendship quality as a predictor of young children's early school adjustment. *Child Development, 67,* 1103–1118.

Ladd, G. W., & Price, J. M. (1987). Predicting children's social and school adjustment following the transition from preschool to kindergarten. *Child Development, 58,* 1168–1189.

Lahey, B. B., Hammer, D., Crumrine, P. L., & Forehand, R. L. (1980). Birth order sex interactions in child behavior problems. *Developmental Psychology, 16,* 608–615.

Laible, D. J., & Thompson, R. A. (2000). Mother-child discourse, attachment security, shared positive affect, and early conscience development. *Child Development, 71,* 1424–1440.

Laible, D. J., & Thompson, R. A. (2002). Mother-child conflict in the toddler years: Lessons in emotion, morality, and relationships. *Child Development, 73,* 1187–1203.

Lamaze, F. (1970). *Painless childbirth: Psychoprophylactic method.* Chicago: Henry Regnery.

Lamb, M. E. (1981). *The role of the father in child development* (rev. ed.). New York: Wiley.

Lamb, M. E. (1987). Introduction: The emergent American father. In M. E. Lamb (Ed.), *The father's role: Cross-cultural perspectives.* Hillsdale, NJ: Erlbaum.

Lamb, M. E. (1997). The development of father–infant relationships. In M. E. Lamb (Ed.), *The role of the father in child development* (3rd ed., pp. 104–120). New York: Wiley.

Lamb, M. E. (1998). Nonparental child care: Context, quality, correlates, and consequences. In W. Damon (Series Ed.) & I. E. Sigel & K. A. Renninger (Vol. Eds.), *Handbook of child psychology: Vol. 4. Child psychology in practice* (5th ed., pp. 73–133). New York: Wiley.

Lamb, M. E., & Ahnert, L. (2006). Nonparental child care: Context, concepts, correlates, and consequences. In W. Damon & R. M. Lerner (Editors-in-Chief) & K. A. Renninger & I. E. Sigel (Vol. Eds.), *Handbook of child psychology: Vol. 4. Child psychology in practice* (6th ed., pp. 950–1016). Hoboken, NJ: Wiley.

Lamb, M. E., Easterbrooks, M. A., & Holden, G. (1980). Reinforcement and punishment among preschoolers: Characteristics and correlates. *Child Development, 51,* 1230–1236.

Lamb, M. E., Pleck, J. H., Charnov, E. L., & Levine, J. A. (1987). A biosocial perspective on paternal behavior and involvement. In J. B. Lancaster, J. Altmann, A. S. Rossi, & L. R. Sherrod (Eds.), *Parenting across the life span: Biosocial dimensions.* New York: Aldine de Gruyter.

Lamb, M. E., & Roopnarine, J. L. (1979). Peer influences on sex-role development in preschoolers. *Child Development, 50,* 1219–1222.

Lamborn, S. D., Mounts, N. S., Steinberg, L., & Dornbusch, S. M. (1991). Patterns of competence and adjustment among adolescents from authoritative, authoritarian, indulgent, and neglectful families. *Child Development, 62,* 1049–1065.

Lammer, E. J., Chen, D. T., Hoar, R. M., Agnish, N. D., et al. (1985). Retinoic acid embryopathy. *New England Journal of Medicine, 313,* 837–841.

Lampl, M., Veldhuis, J. D., & Johnson, M. L. (1992). Saltation and stasis: A model of human growth. *Science, 258,* 801–803.

Landau, S., Lorch, E. P., & Milich, R. (1992). Visual attention to and comprehension of television in attention-deficit hyperactivity disordered and normal boys. *Child Development, 63,* 928–937.

Landry, M. L. (2004). Viral infections. In G. N. Burrow, T. P. Duffy, & J. Copel (Eds.), *Medical complications during pregnancy* (6th ed., pp. 347–374). Philadelphia: Saunders.

Langlois, J. H., & Stephan, C. (1981). Beauty and the beast: The role of physical attractiveness in the development of peer relations and social behavior. In S. S. Brehm, S. H. Kassin, & F. X. Gibbons (Eds.), *Developmental social psychology* (pp. 152–168). New York: Oxford University Press.

Larkin, R. W. (1979). *Suburban youth in cultural crisis.* New York: Oxford University Press.

Larsen, J. T., To, Y. M., & Fireman, G. (2006). Children's understanding and experience of mixed emotions. *Psychological Science.*

Larson, R. W. (2001). How U.S. children and adolescents spend time: What it does (and doesn't) tell us about development. *Current Directions in Psychological Science, 10,* 160–164.

Larson, R. W., & Ham, M. (1993). Stress and "storm and stress" in early adolescence: The relationship of negative events with dysphoric affect. *Developmental Psychology, 29,* 130–140.

Larson, R. W., & Lampman-Petraitis, C. (1989). Daily emotional stress as reported by children and adolescents. *Child Development, 60,* 1250–1260.

Larson, R. W., Moneta, G., Richards, M. H., & Wilson, S. (2002). Continuity, stability, and change in daily emotional experience across adolescence. *Developmental Psychology, 73,* 1151–1165.

Laskari, A., Smith, A. K., & Graham, J. M., Jr. (1999). Williams-Beuren syndrome: An update and review for the primary physician. *Clinical Pediatrics, 38,* 189–208.

Latz, S., Wolf, A. W., & Lozoff, B. (1999). Cosleeping in context: Sleep practices and problems in young children in Japan and the United States. *Archives of Pediatrics and Adolescent Medicine, 153,* 339–346.

Laursen, B., Coy, K. C., & Collins, W. A. (1998). Reconsidering changes in parent-child conflict across adolescence: A meta-analysis. *Child Development, 69,* 817–832.

Laursen, B., & Williams, V. A. (1997). Perceptions of interdependence and closeness in family and peer relationships among adolescents with and without romantic partners. In S. Shulman & W. Andrew Collins (Eds.), *New Directions for Child Development: No. 78. Romantic relationships in adolescence: Developmental perspectives* (pp. 3–20). San Francisco: Jossey-Bass.

Lawson, M. (1980). Development of body build stereotypes, peer ratings, and self-esteem in Australian children. *Journal of Psychology, 104,* 111–118.

Lazar, I., & Darlington, R. (1982). Lasting effects of early education: A report from the Consortium for Longitudinal Studies. *Monographs of the Society for Research in Child Development, 47* (2–3, Serial No. 195).

Leaper, C. (2000). Gender, affiliation, assertion, and the interactive context of parent-child play. *Developmental Psychology, 36,* 381–393.

Learmonth, A. E., Nadel, L., & Newcombe, N. S. (2002). Children's use of landmarks: Implications for modularity theory. *Psychological Science, 13,* 337–341.

LeBoyer, F. (1975). *Birth without violence.* New York: Knopf.

Lecanuet, J.-P. (1998). Foetal responses to auditory and speech stimuli. In A. Slater (Ed.), *Perceptual development: Visual, auditory, and speech perception in infancy* (pp. 317–355). East Sussex, UK: Psychology Press.

Lederberg, A. R., Prezbindowski, A. K., & Spencer, P. E. (2000). Word-learning skills of deaf preschoolers: The development of novel mapping and rapid word-learning strategies. *Child Development, 71,* 1571–1585.

Lee, B. C. P., Kuppusamy, K. G. R., El-Ghazzawy, O., Gordon, R. E., Lin, W., & Haacke, M. (1999). Hemispheric language dominance in children demonstrated by functional magnetic resonance imaging. *Journal of Child Neurology, 14,* 78–82.

Lee, K., Cameron, C. A., Xu, F., Fu, G., & Board, J. (1997). Chinese and Canadian children's evaluations of lying and truth telling: Similarities and differences in the context of pro- and antisocial behavior. *Child Development, 68,* 924–934.

Lee, L. C. (1971). The concommitant development of cognitive and moral modes of thought: A test of selected deductions from Piaget's theory. *Genetic Psychology Monographs, 83,* 93–146.

Lee, R. V. (1988). Sexually transmitted infections. In G. N. Burrow & T. F. Ferris (Eds.), *Medical complications during pregnancy.* Philadelphia: W.B. Saunders.

Leekam, S. R., Lopez, B., & Moore, C. (2000). Attention and joint attention in preschool children with autism. *Developmental Psychology, 36,* 261–273.

Legerstee, M., Anderson, D., & Schaffer, A. (1998). Five- and eight-month-old infants recognize their faces and voices as familiar and social stimuli. *Child Development, 69,* 37–50.

Leinbach, M. D., Hort, B. E., & Fagot, B. I. (1997). Bears are for boys: Metaphorical associations in young children's gender stereotypes. *Cognitive Development, 12,* 107–130.

Lemish, D., & Rice, M. (1986). Television as a talking picture book: A prop for language acquisition. *Journal of Child Language, 13,* 251–274.

Lenneberg, E. (1967). *Biological foundations of language.* New York: Wiley.

Leonard, L. B. (1998). *Children with specific language impairment.* Cambridge, MA: MIT Press.

Leonard, L. B., Newhoff, M., & Meselam, L. (1980). Individual differences in early child phonology. *Applied Psycholinguistics, 1,* 7–30.

Lerner, R. M., & Lerner, J. V. (1977). Effects of age, sex, and physical attractiveness on child-peer relations, academic performance, and elementary school adjustment. *Developmental Psychology, 13,* 585–590.

Lesser, G. S., Fifer, F., & Clark, D. H. (1965). Mental abilities of children of different social-class and cultural groups. *Monographs of the Society for Research in Child Development, 30*(4, Serial No. 102).

Lester, B. M., & Brazelton, T. B. (1982). Cross-cultural assessment of neonatal behavior. In D. Wagner & H. W. Stevenson (Eds.), *Cultural perspectives on child development.* San Francisco: W.H. Freeman.

Lester, B. M., & Dreher, M. (1989). Effects of marijuana use during pregnancy on newborn cry. *Child Development, 60,* 765–771.

LeVay, S., & Hamer, D. H. (1994, May). Evidence for a biological influence in male homosexuality. *Scientific American, 270,* 43–57.

Leventhal, T., & Brooks-Gunn, J. (2000). The neighborhoods they live in: The effects of neighborhood residence on child and adolescent outcomes. *Psychological Bulletin, 126,* 309–337.

Levine, R., & White, M. (1986). *Human conditions: The cultural basis for educational development.* New York: Routledge & Kegan Paul.

Levine, R., Dixon, S., LeVine, S., Richman, A., Leiderman, P. M., Keefer, C. H., & Brazelton, T. B. (1994). *Child care and culture: Lessons from Africa.* New York: Cambridge University Press.

Levine, S. C., Huttenlocher, J., Taylor, A., & Langrock, A. (1999). Early sex differences in spatial skill. *Developmental Psychology, 35,* 940–949.

Levine, S. C., Jordan, N. C., & Huttenlocher, J. (1992). Development of calculation abilities in young children. *Journal of Experimental Child Psychology, 53,* 72–103.

Levitin, D. J., & Bellugi, U. (1998). Musical abilities in individuals with Williams' syndrome. *Music Perception, 15(4),* 357–389.

Levitt, M. J., Guacci-Franco, N., & Levitt, J. L. (1993). Convoys of social support in childhood and early adolescence: Structure and function. *Developmental Psychology, 29,* 811–818.

Levy, G. D., Taylor, M. G., & Gelman, S. A. (1995). Traditional and evaluative aspects of flexibility in gender roles, social conventions, moral rules, and physical laws. *Child Development, 66,* 515–531.

Levy, Y. (1999). Early metalinguistic competence: Speech monitoring and repair behavior. *Developmental Psychology, 35,* 822–834.

Lew, A. R., Bremner, J. G., & Lefkovitch, L. P. (2000). The development of relational landmark use in six- to twelve-month old infants in a spatial orientation task. *Child Development, 71,* 1179–1190.

Lew, A. R., & Butterworth, G. (1997). The development of hand-mouth coordination in 2- to 5-month-old infants: Similarities with reaching and grasping. *Infant Behavior and Development, 20,* 59–69.

Lewis, M. (1983). On the nature of intelligence. In M. Lewis (Ed.), *Origins of intelligence.* New York: Plenum Press.

Lewis, M. (1989, April). *Self and self-conscious emotions.* Paper presented at the biennial meeting of the Society for Research in Child Development, Kansas City, MO.

Lewis, M. (1993). Early socioemotional predictors of cognitive competency at 4 years. *Developmental Psychology, 29,* 1036–1045.

Lewis, M., Alessandri, S., & Sullivan, M. (1992). Differences in shame and pride as a function of children's gender and task difficulty. *Child Development, 63,* 630–638.

Lewis, M., & Feiring, C. (1982). Some American families at dinner. In L. M. Laosa & I. E. Sigel (Eds.), *Families as learning environments for children.* New York: Plenum Press.

Lewis, M., Hitchcock, D. F. A., & Sullivan, M. W. (2004). Physiological and emotional reactivity to learning and frustration. *Infancy, 6,* 121–143.

Lewis, M. D., Lamm, C., Segalowitz, S. A., Stieben, J., & Zelazo, P. D. (2006). Neurophysiological correlates of emotion regulation in children and adolescents. *Journal of Cognitive Neuroscience, 18,* 1–17.

Lewis, M., & Michalson, L. (1983). *Children's emotions and moods: Developmental theory and measurement.* New York: Plenum Press.

Lewis, M., & Ramsay, D. (2002). Cortisol response to embarrassment and shame. *Child Development, 73,* 1034–1045.

Lewis, M., Sullivan, M. W., Stanger, C., & Weiss, M. (1989). Self development and self-conscious emotions. *Child Development, 60,* 146–156.

Lewis, T. L., Maurer, D., & Kay, D. (1978). Newborns' central vision: Whole or hole? *Journal of Experimental Child Psychology, 26,* 193–203.

Lewkowicz, D. J. (2000). The development of intersensory temporal perception: An epigenetic systems/limitations view. *Psychological Bulletin, 126,* 281–308.

Li, J. (2006). Self in learning: Chinese adolescents' goals and sense of agency. *Child Development, 77,* 482–501.

Li, X., Stanton, B., & Feigelman, S. (2000). Impact of perceived parental monitoring on adolescent risk behavior. *Journal of Adolescent Health, 27,* 49–56.

Liben, L. S., & Bigler, R. S. (2002). The developmental course of gender differentiation: Conceptualizing, measuring, and evaluating constructs and pathways. *Monographs of the Society for Research in Child Development, 67*(2, Serial no. 269).

Liben, L. S., & Downs, R. M. (1993). Understanding person-space-map relations: Cartographic and developmental perspectives. *Developmental Psychology, 29,* 739–752.

Liben, L. S., Susman, E. J., Finkelstein, J. W., Chinchilli, V. M., Kunselman, S., Schwab, J., et al. (2002). The effects of sex steroids on spatial performance: A review and an experimental clinical investigation. *Developmental Psychology, 38,* 236–253.

Lickliter, R., & Bahrick, L. E. (2000). The development of infant intersensory perception: Advantages of a comparative convergent-operations approach. *Psychological Bulletin, 126,* 260–280.

Lickona, T. (1976). Research on Piaget's theory of moral development. In T. Lickona (Ed.), *Moral development and behavior: Theory, research, and social issues* (pp. 219–240). New York: Holt, Rinehart & Winston.

Lieberman, D. (1985). Research on children and microcomputers: A review of utilization and effect studies. In M. Chen & W. Paisley (Eds.), *Children and microcomputers: Research on the newest medium.* Beverly Hills: Sage.

Lien, W., Klezovitch, O., Fernandez, T. E., Delrow, J., & Vasioukhin, V. (2006). E–catenin controls cerebral cortical size by regulating the hedgehog signaling pathway. *Science, 311,* 1609–1612.

Lightfoot, D. (1982). *The language lottery: Toward a biology of grammars.* Cambridge, MA: MIT Press.

Lillard, A. S. (1997). Other folks' theories of mind and behavior. *Psychological Science, 8,* 268–274.

Lillard, A. S. (1998). Ethnopsychologies: Cultural variation in theories of mind. *Psychological Bulletin, 123,* 3–32.

Limb, C. J., & Holmes, L. B. (1994). Anencephaly: Changes in prenatal detection and birth status, 1972 through 1990. *American Journal of Obstetrics and Gynecology, 170,* 1333–1338.

Lin, C. C., & Fu, V. R. (1990). A comparison of child-rearing practices among Chinese, immigrant Chinese, and Caucasian-American parents. *Child Development, 61,* 429–433.

Lindegren, M. L., Steinberg, S., & Byers, R. H. (2000). Epidemiology of HIV/AIDS in children. *Pediatric Clinics of North America, 47,* 1–20.

Lindsay, E. W., Mize, J., & Pettit, G. S. (1997). Differential play patterns of mothers and fathers of sons and daughters: Implications for children's gender role development. *Sex Roles, 37,* 643–661.

Linn, M. C., & Petersen, A. C. (1985). Emergence and characterization of sex differences in spatial ability: A meta-analysis. *Child Development, 56,* 1479–1498.

Linn, M. C., & Petersen, A. C. (1986). A meta-analysis of differences in spatial ability: Implications for mathematics and science achievement. In J. S. Hyde & M. C. Linn (Eds.), *The psychology of gender: Advances through meta-analysis.* Baltimore: Johns Hopkins University Press.

Linney, J. A., & Seidman, E. N. (1989). The future of schooling. *American Psychologist, 44,* 336–340.

Lips, H. M. (2004). The gender gap in possible selves: Divergence of academic self-views among high school and university students. *Sex Roles, 50,* 357–371.

Little, T. D., & Lopez, D. F. (1997). Regularities in the development of children's causality beliefs about school performance across six sociocultural contexts. *Developmental Psychology, 33,* 165–175.

Littleton, K., & Häkkinen, P. (1999). Learning together: Understanding the processes of computer-based collaborative learning. In P. Dillenbourg (Ed.), *Collaborative learning: Cognitive and computational approaches* (pp. 20–30). New York: Pergamon.

Littschwager, J. C., & Markman, E. M. (1994). Sixteen- and 24-month-olds' use of mutual exclusivity as a default assumption in second-label learning. *Developmental Psychology, 30,* 955–958.

Liu, H., Kuhl, P. K., & Tsao, F. (2003). An association between mothers' speech clarity and infants' discrimination skills. *Developmental Science, 6,* F1–F10.

Lobel, T. E., Gruber, R., Govrin, N., & Mashraki Pedhatzur, S. (2001). Children's gender-related inferences and judgments: A cross-cultural study. *Developmental Psychology, 37,* 839–846.

Locke, J. (1961). *An essay concerning human understanding.* London: J. M. Deut and Sons. (Original work published in 1690)

Locke, J. (1964). Some thoughts concerning education. In P. Gay (Ed.), *John Locke on education.* New York: Teacher's College. (Original work published in 1693).

Lockman, J. J., & Thelen, E. (1993). Developmental biodynamics: Brain, body, behavior connections. *Child Development, 64,* 953–959.

Loeb, R. C., Horst, L., & Horton, P. J. (1980). Family interaction patterns associated with self-esteem in preadolescent girls and boys. *Merrill-Palmer Quarterly, 26,* 203–217.

Loeber, R., & Hay, D. F. (1997). Key issues in the development of aggression and violence from childhood to early adulthood. *Annual Review of Psychology, 48,* 371–410.

Loehlin, J. C., Lindzey, G., & Spuhler, J. N. (1975). *Racial differences in intelligence.* San Francisco: W.H. Freeman.

Loewenstein, J., & Gentner, D. (2001). Spatial mapping in preschoolers: Close comparisons facilitate far mappings. *Journal of Cognition and Development, 2,* 189–219.

Lombroso, P. J. (2000). Genetics of childhood disorders: 16. Angleman syndrome: A failure to process. *Journal of the American Academy of Child and Adolescent Psychiatry, 39,* 931–933.

López-Camelo, J. S., Orioli, I. M., da Graça Dutra, M., Nazer-Herrera, J., Rivera, N., Ojeda, M. E., et al. (2005). Reduction of birth prevalence rates of neural tube defects after folic acid fortification in Chile. *American Journal of Medical Genetics: Part A, 135,* 120–125.

Lorch, E. P., Bellack, D. R., & Augsbach, L. H. (1987). Young children's memory for televised stories: Effects of importance. *Child Development, 58,* 453–463.

Lord, S. E., Eccles, J. S., & McCarthy, K. A. (1994). Surviving the junior high school transition: Family processes and self-perceptions as protective and risk factors. *Journal of Early Adolescence, 14,* 162–199.

Lorenz, J. M., Wooliever, D. E., Jetton, J. R., & Paneth, N. (1997). A quantitative review of mortality and developmental disability in extremely premature newborns. *Archives of Pediatric and Adolescent Medicine, 152,* 425–435.

Lorenz, K. Z. (1966). *On aggression* (M. K. Wilson, Trans.). New York: Harcourt, Brace, & World. (Original work published 1963)

Love, J. M., Harrison, L., Sagi-Schwartz, A., van IJzendoorn, M. H., Ross, C., et al. (2003). Child care quality matters: How conclusions may vary with context. *Child Development, 74,* 1021–1033.

Love, J. M., Kisker, E. E., Ross, C., Raikes, H., Constantine, J., et al. (2005). The effectiveness of Early Head Start for 3-year-old children and their parents: Lessons for policy and programs. *Developmental Psychology, 41,* 885–901.

Lovdal, L. T. (1989). Sex role messages in television commercials: An update. *Sex Roles, 21,* 715–724.

Lu, G. C., Rouse, D. J., DuBard, M., Cliver, S., Kimberlin, D., & Hauth, J. C. (2001). The effect of the increasing prevalence of maternal obesity on prenatal morbidity. *American Journal of Obstetrics and Gynecology, 185,* 845–849.

Lubinski, D., Webb, R. M., Morelock, M. J., & Benbow, C. P. (2001). Top 1 in 10,000: A 10-year follow-up of the profoundly gifted. *Journal of Applied Psychology, 86,* 718–729.

Luciana, M., Conklin, H. M., Hooper, C. J., & Yarger, R. S. (2005). The development of nonverbal working memory and executive control processes in adolescents. *Child Development, 76,* 697–712.

Ludington-Hoe, S. M., & Swinth, J. Y. (1996). Developmental aspects of kangaroo care. *Journal of Obstetric and Gynecological Neonatal Nursing, 25,* 691–703.

Luecke-Aleksa, D. R., Anderson, D. R., Collins, P. A., & Schmitt, K. L. (1995). Gender constancy and television viewing. *Developmental Psychology, 31,* 773–780.

Luke, B., Avni, M., Min, L., & Misiumas, R. (1999). Work and pregnancy: The role of fatigue and the "second shift" on antenatal morbidity. *American Journal of Obstetrics and Gynecology, 181,* 1172–1179.

Lummis, M., & Stevenson, H. W. (1990). Gender differences in beliefs and achievement: A cross-cultural study. *Developmental Psychology, 26,* 254–263.

Luna, B., Garver, K. E., Urban, T. A., Lazar, N. A., & Sweeney, J. A. (2004). Maturation of cognitive processes from late childhood to adulthood. *Child Development, 75,* 1357–1372.

Luna, B., Thulborn, K. R., Munoz, D. P., Merriam, E. P., Garver, K. E., et al. (2001). Maturation of widely distributed brain function subserves cognitive development. *Neuroimage, 13,* 786–793.

Luria, A. R. (1961). *The role of speech in the regulation of normal and abnormal behavior.* New York: Liveright.

Luria, A. R. (1969). Speech and formation of mental processes. In M. Cole & I. Maltzman (Eds.), *A handbook of contemporary Soviet psychology.* New York: Basic Books.

Lussier, G., Deater-Deckard, K., Dunn, J., & Davies, L. (2002). Support across two generations: Children's closeness to grandparents following parental divorce and remarriage. *Journal of Family Psychology, 16,* 363–376.

Luster, T., & McAdoo, H. P. (1994). Factors related to the achievement and adjustment of young African American children. *Child Development, 65,* 1080–1994.

Luster, T., & McAdoo, H. P. (1996). Family and child influences on educational attainment: A secondary analysis of the High/Scope Perry Preschool data. *Developmental Psychology, 32,* 26–39.

Luthar, S. S., & Becker, B. E. (2002). Privileged but pressured? A study of affluent youth. *Child Development, 73,* 1593–1610.

Luthar, S. S., Cicchetti, D., & Becker, B. (2000). The construct of resilience: A critical evaluation and guidelines for future work. *Child Development, 71,* 543–562.

Luthar, S. S., & D'Avanzo, K. (1999). Contextual factors in substance use: A study of suburban and inner-city adolescents. *Development and Psychopathology, 11,* 845–867.

Luthar, S. S., & Latendresse, S. J. (2005). Children of the affluent: Challenges to well-being. *Current Directions in Psychological Science, 14,* 49–53.

Lutkenhaus, P., Bullock, M., & Geppert, U. (1987). Toddlers' actions: Knowledge, control, and the self. In F. Halisch & J. Kuhl (Eds.), *Motivation, intention, and volition.* Berlin: Springer.

Lykken, D. T., McGue, M. Tellegen, A., & Bouchard, T. J., Jr. (1992). Emer-genesis: Genetic traits that may not run in families. *American Psychologist, 47,* 1565–1577.

Lyon, T. D., & Flavell, J. H. (1993). Young children's understanding of forgetting over time. *Child Development, 64,* 789–800.

Lyons-Ruth, K., Alpern, L., & Repacholi, B. (1993). Disorganized infant attachment classification and maternal psychosocial problems as predictors of hostile-aggressive behavior in preschool children. *Child Development, 64,* 572–585.

Lyons-Ruth, K., & Jacobvitz, D. (1999). Attachment disorganization: Unresolved loss, relational violence, and lapses in behavioral and attentional strategies. In J. Cassidy & P. R. Shaver (Eds.), *Handbook of attachment: Theory, research, and clinical applications* (pp. 520–554). New York: Guilford Press.

Lytton, H., & Romney, D. M. (1991). Parents' differential socialization of boys and girls: A meta-analysis. *Psychological Bulletin, 109,* 267–296.

Ma, H. K., & Cheung, C.-K. (1996). A cross-cultural study of moral stage structure in Hong Kong Chinese, English, and Americans. *Journal of Cross-Cultural Psychology, 27,* 700–713.

Maccoby, E. E. (1984). Socialization and developmental change. *Child Development, 55,* 317–328.

Maccoby, E. E. (1988). Gender as a social category. *Developmental Psychology, 24,* 755–765.

Maccoby, E. E. (1990). Gender and relationships: A developmental account. *American Psychologist, 45,* 513–520.

Maccoby, E. E. (2002). Gender and group process: A developmental perspective. *Current Directions in Psychological Science, 11,* 54–58.

Maccoby, E. E., & Jacklin, C. N. (1974). *The psychology of sex differences.* Stanford, CA: Stanford University Press.

Maccoby, E. E., & Jacklin, C. N. (1987). Gender segregation in childhood. In H. W. Reese (Ed.), *Advances in child development and behavior* (Vol. 20). Orlando, FL: Academic Press.

Maccoby, E. E., & Martin, J. A. (1983). Socialization in the context of the family: Parent-child interaction. In E. M. Hetherington (Ed.), *Handbook of child psychology: Vol. IV. Socialization, personality, and social development* (4th ed., pp. 1–101). New York: Wiley.

MacFarlane, J. A. (1975). Olfaction in the development of social preferences in the human neonate. In M. A. Hofer (Ed.), *Parent-infant interaction.* Amsterdam: Elsevier.

MacKinnon, C. E. (1988). Influences on sibling relations in families with married and divorced parents. *Journal of Social Issues, 9,* 469–477.

MacKinnon, C. E. (1989). Sibling interactions in married and divorced families: Influence of ordinal position, socioeconomic status, and play context. *Journal of Divorce, 12,* 221–251.

MacKinnon-Lewis, C., Rabiner, D., & Starnes, R. (1999). Predicting boys' social acceptance and aggression: The role of mother-child interactions and boys' beliefs about peers. *Developmental Psychology, 35,* 632–639.

MacKinnon-Lewis, C., Volling, B. L., Lamb, M. E., Dechman, K., Rabiner, D., & Curtner, M. E. (1994). A cross-contextual analysis of boys' social competence: From family to school. *Developmental Psychology, 30,* 325–333.

MacLusky, N. J., & Naftolin, F. (1981). Sexual differentiation of the nervous system. *Science, 211,* 1294–1303.

MacMillan, H. L., MacMillan, J. H., Offord, D. R., Griffith, L., & MacMillan, A. (1994). Primary prevention of child abuse and neglect: A critical review. Part I. *Journal of Child Psychology, Psychiatry, and Allied Disciplines, 35,* 835–856.

Madi, B. C., Sandall, J., Bennett, R., & MacLeod, C. (1999). Effects of female relative support in labor: A randomized controlled trial. *Birth, 26,* 4–8.

Madigan, S., Moran, G., & Pederson, D. R. (2006). Unresolved states of mind, disorganized attachment relationships, and disrupted interactions of adolescent mothers and their infants. *Developmental Psychology, 42,* 293–304.

Maffeis, C., Schutz, Y., Zaffanello, M., Piccoli, R., & Pinelli, L. (1994). Elevated energy expenditure and reduced energy intake in obese prepubertal children: Paradox of poor dietary reliability in obesity? *Journal of Pediatrics, 124,* 348–354.

Magnusson, D., Stattin, H., & Allen, V. (1986). Differential maturation among girls and its relations to social adjustment: A longitudinal perspective. In P. B. Baltes, D. L. Featherman, & R. M. Lerner (Eds.), *Lifespan development and behavior* (Vol. 7). Hillsdale, NJ: Erlbaum.

Mahoney, J. L. (2000). School extracurricular activity participation as a moderator in the development of antisocial behavior patterns. *Child Development, 71,* 502–516.

Main, M., Kaplan, N., & Cassidy, J. (1985). Security in infancy, childhood, and adulthood: A move to the level of representation. In I. Bretherton & E. Waters (Eds.), *Growing points of attachment theory and research. Monographs of the Society for Research in Child Development, 50*(1–2, Serial No. 209).

Main, M., & Solomon, J. (1986). Discovery of a disorganized/disoriented attachment pattern. In T. B. Brazelton & M. W. Yogman (Eds.), *Affective development in infancy.* Norwood, NJ: Ablex.

Malatesta, C. Z., Culver, C., Tesman, J. R., & Shepard, B. (1989). The development of emotion expression during the first two years of life. *Monographs of the Society for Research in Child Development, 54*(1–2, Serial No. 219).

Malina, R. M. (1980). Biosocial correlates of motor development during infancy and early childhood. In L. S. Greene & F. E. Johnstone (Eds.), *Social and biological predictors of nutritional status, physical growth, and neurological development.* New York: Academic Press.

Malone, F. D., Canick, J. A., Ball, R. H. Nyberg, D. A., Comstock, C. H., Bukowski, R., et al. (2005). First-trimester or second-trimester screening, or both, for Down's syndrome. *New England Journal of Medicine, 353,* 2001–2011.

Mandler, J. M. (1988). How to build a baby: On the development of an accessible representational system. *Cognitive Development, 3,* 113–136.

Mandler, J. M. (1998). Representation. In W. Damon (Series Ed.) & D. Kuhn & R. S. Siegler (Vol. Eds.), *Handbook of child psychology: Vol. 2. Cognition, perception, and language* (5th ed., pp. 255–308). New York: Wiley.

Mandler, J. M. (2004). *The foundations of mind: The origins of the conceptual system.* New York: Oxford University Press.

Mandler, J. M., Fivush, R., & Reznick, J. S. (1987). The development of contextual categories. *Cognitive Development, 2,* 339–354.

Mandler, J. M., & McDonough, L. (1993). Concept formation in infancy. *Cognitive Development, 8,* 291–318.

Mandler, J. M., & McDonough, L. (1998). Studies in inductive inference in infancy. *Cognitive Psychology, 37,* 60–96.

Mandler, J. M., & McDonough, L. (2000). Advancing downward to the basic level. *Journal of Cognition and Development, 1,* 379–403.

Mangelsdorf, S. C., Plunkett, J. W., Dedrick, C. F., Berlin, M., Meisels, S. J., McHale, J. L., & Dichtellmiller, M. (1996). Attachment security in very low birth weight infants. *Developmental Psychology, 32,* 914–920.

Mannarino, A. P. (1978). Friendship patterns and self-concept development in preadolescent males. *Journal of Genetic Psychology, 133,* 105–110.

Maratsos, M. P. (1983). Some current issues in the study of the acquisition of grammar. In J. H. Flavell & E. M. Markman (Eds.), *Handbook of child psychology: Vol. III. Cognitive development* (4th ed., pp. 707–786). New York: Wiley.

Maratsos, M. P. (1989). Innateness and plasticity in language acquisition. In M. L. Rice & R. L. Schiefelbusch (Eds.), *The teachability of language.* Baltimore: Paul H. Brookes.

Marcus, G. F. (1996). Why do children say "breaked"? *Current Directions in Psychological Science, 5,* 81–85.

Marcus, G. F., Pinker, S., Ullman, M., Hollander, M., Rosen, T. J., & Xu, F. (1992). Overregularization in language acquisition. *Monographs of the Society for Research in Child Development, 57*(4 Serial No. 228).

Marcus, G. F., Vijayan, S., Bandi Rao, S., & Vishton, P. M. (1998). Rule learning by seven-month-old infants. *Science, 283,* 77–80.

Marean, G. C., Werner, L. A., & Kuhl, P. K. (1992). Vowel categorization by very young infants. *Developmental Psychology, 28,* 395–405.

Mareschal, D., & Johnson, S. P. (2002). Learning to perceive object unity: A connectionist account. *Developmental Science, 5,* 151–172.

Markman, E. M. (1987). How children constrain the possible meanings of words. In U. Neisser (Ed.), *Concepts and conceptual development: Ecological and intellectual factors in categorization.* Cambridge, UK: Cambridge University Press.

Markman, E. M. (1990). Constraints children place on word meanings. *Cognitive Science, 14,* 57–77.

Markman, E. M., & Hutchinson, J. E. (1984). Children's sensitivity to constraints on word meaning: Taxonomic versus thematic relations. *Cognitive Psychology, 16,* 1–27.

Markman, E. M., & Wachtel G. F. (1988). Children's use of mutual exclusivity to constrain the meanings of words. *Cognitive Psychology, 20,* 121–157.

Marlier, L., & Schaal, B. (2005). Human newborns prefer human milk: Conspecific milk odor is attractive without postnatal exposure. *Child Development, 76,* 155–168.

Marlier, L., Schaal, B., & Soussignan, R. (1998). Neonatal responsiveness to the odor of amniotic and lacteal fluids: A test of perinatal chemosensory continuity. *Child Development, 69,* 611–623.

Marr, D. B., & Sternberg, R. J. (1987). The role of mental speed in intelligence: A triarchic perspective. In P. A. Vernon (Ed.), *Speed of information-processing and intelligence.* Norwood, NJ: Ablex.

Marsh, H. W., Craven, R., & Debus, R. (1998). Structure, stability, and development of young children's self-concepts: A multicohort-multioccasion study. *Child Development, 69,* 1030–1053.

Marshall, N. (2004). The quality of early child care and children's development. *Current Directions in Psychological Science, 13,* 165–168.

Marshall, S. (1995). Ethnic socialization of African American children: Implications for parenting, identity development, and academic achievement. *Journal of Youth and Adolescence, 24,* 377–396.

Martin, C. L. (1995). Stereotypes about children with traditional and nontraditional gender roles. *Sex Roles, 33,* 727–751.

Martin, C. L., Eisenbud, L., & Rose, H. (1995). Children's gender-based reasoning about toys. *Child Development, 66,* 1453–1471.

Martin, C. L., & Fabes, R. A. (2001). The stability and consequences of young children's same-sex peer interactions. *Developmental Psychology, 37,* 431–446.

Martin, C. L., & Halverson, C. F. (1981). A schematic processing model of sex typing and stereotyping in children. *Child Development, 52,* 1119–1134.

Martin, C. L., & Halverson, C. F. (1987). The roles of cognition in sex role acquisition. In D. B. Carter (Ed.), *Current conceptions of sex roles and sex typing: Theory and research* (pp. 123–137). New York: Praeger.

Martin, C. L. , & Ruble, D. N. (1997). A developmental perspective of self-construals and sex differences: Comment on Cross and Madson (1997). *Psychological Bulletin, 122,* 45–50.

Martin, J., Martin, D. C., Lund, C. A., & Streissguth, A. P. (1977). Maternal alcohol ingestion and cigarette smoking and their effects on newborn conditioning. *Alcoholism: Clinical and Experimental Research, 1,* 243–247.

Martinez de Villarreal, L., Perez, J. Z., Vazquez, P. A., Herrera, P. H., Campos Mdel, R., Lopez, R. A., et al. (2002). Decline of neural tube defects after a folic acid campaign in Nuevo Leon, Mexico. *Teratology, 66,* 249–256.

Marvin, R. S. (1977). An ethological-cognitive model for the attenuation of mother-child attachment behavior. In T. M. Alloway, L. Krames, & P. Pliner (Eds.), *Advances in the study of communication and affect: Vol. 3. The development of social attachments.* New York: Plenum Press.

Masataka, N. (1996). Perception of motherese in a signed language by 6-month-old infants. *Developmental Psychology, 32,* 874–879.

Mason, C. A., Cauce, A. M., Gonzales, N., & Hiraga, Y. (1996). Neither too sweet nor too sour: Problem peers, maternal control, and problem behavior in African American adolescents. *Child Development, 67,* 2115–2130.

Massaro, D. W., & Cowan, N. (1993). Information processing models: Microscopes of mind. In L. W. Porter & M. R. Rosenzweig (Eds.), *Annual Review of Psychology, 34,* 383–425.

Masten, A. S., & Coatsworth, J. D. (1998). The development of competence in favorable and unfavorable environments: Lessons from research on successful children. *American Psychologist, 53,* 205–220.

Masur, E. F. (1982). Mothers' responses to infants' object-related gestures: Influences on lexical development. *Journal of Child Language, 9,* 23–30.

Matas, L., Arend, R. A., & Sroufe, L. A. (1978). Continuity of adaptation in the second year: The relationship between quality of attachment and later competence. *Child Development, 49,* 547–556.

Mathews, T. J., Honein, M. A., & Erickson, J. D. (2002). Spina bifida and anencephaly prevalence—United States. *MMWR Recommendations and Reports,* Rep 51(RR-13), pp. 9–11.

Matias, R., & Cohn, J. F. (1993). Are max-specified infant facial expressions during face-to-face interaction consistent with differential emotions theory? *Developmental Psychology, 29,* 524–531.

Mattson, S. N., Riley, E. P., Gramling, L., Delis, D. C., & Jones, K. L. (1997). Heavy prenatal alcohol exposure with or without physical features of fetal alcohol syndrome leads to IQ deficits. *Journal of Pediatrics, 131,* 718–721.

Mattys, S. L., & Jusczyk, P. W. (2001). Do infants segment words or recurring contiguous patterns? *Journal of Experimental Psychology: Human Perception and Performance, 27,* 644–655.

Matusov, E., Bell, N., & Rogoff, B. (2002). Schooling as cultural process: Working together and guidance by children from schools differing in collaborative practices. In R. V. Kail & H. W. Reese (Eds.), *Advances in child development* (Vol. 29, pp. 129–160). San Diego: Academic Press.

Maurer, D. (1983). The scanning of compound figures by young infants. *Journal of Experimental Child Psychology, 35,* 437–448.

Maurer, D., Lewis, T. L., Brent, H. P., & Levin, A. V. (1999). Rapid improvement in the acuity of infants after visual input. *Science, 286,* 108–110.

May, D. C., Kundert, D. K., & Brent, D. (1995). Does delayed school entry reduce later grade retentions and use of special education services? *Remedial and Special Education, 16,* 288–294.

Mayberry, R. I., & Nicoladis, E. (2000). Gesture reflects language development: Evidence from bilingual children. *Current Directions in Psychological Science, 9,* 192–196.

McAnarney, E. R. (1987). Young maternal age and adverse neonatal outcome. *American Journal of Diseases of Children, 141,* 1053–1059.

McAnarney, E. R., & Stevens-Simon, C. (1990). Maternal psychological stress/depression and low birth weight. *American Journal of Diseases of Children, 144,* 789–792.

McArdle, J. J., Ferrer Caja, E., Hamagami, F., & Woodcock, R. W. (2002). Comparative longitudinal structural analyses of the growth and decline of multiple intellectual abilities over the life span. *Developmental Psychology, 38,* 115–142.

McBride, W. G. (1961). Thalidomide and congenital abnormalities. *Lancet, 2,* 1358.

McCall, R. B. (1979). *Infants.* Cambridge, MA: Harvard University Press.

McCall, R. B., Parke, R. D., & Kavanaugh, R. D. (1977). Imitation of live and televised models in children one to three years of age. *Monographs of the Society for Research in Child Development, 42*(3, Serial No. 171).

McCartney, K., Harris, M. J., & Bernieri, F. (1990). Growing up and growing apart: A developmental meta-analysis of twin studies. *Psychological Bulletin, 107,* 226–237.

McCartney, K., & Nelson, K. (1981). Children's use of scripts in story recall. *Discourse Processes, 4,* 59–70.

McCartney, K., Scarr, S., Phillips, D., & Grajek, S. (1985). Day care as intervention: Comparisons of varying quality programs. *Journal of Applied Developmental Psychology, 6,* 247–260.

McCarty, M. E., Clifton, R. K., Ashmead, D. H., Lee, P., & Goubet, N. (2001) How infants use vision for grasping objects. *Child Development, 72,* 973–987.

McClelland, D. C. (1973). Testing for competence rather than for "intelligence." *American Psychologist, 28,* 1–14.

McClintock, M. K., & Herdt, G. (1996). Rethinking puberty: The development of sexual attraction. *Current Directions in Psychological Science, 5,* 178–183.

McCord, J. (1977). A comparative study of two generations of native Americans. In R. F. Meier (Ed.), *Theory in criminology* (pp. 83–92). Beverly Hills, CA: Sage.

McCormick, M. C. (1997). The outcomes of very low birth weight infants: Are we asking the right questions? *Pediatrics, 99,* 869–875.

McCormick, M. C., McCarton, C., Tonascia, J., & Brooks-Gunn, J. (1993). Early educational intervention for very low birth weight infants: Results from the Infant Health and Development Program. *Journal of Pediatrics, 123,* 527–533.

McDermott, S., & Greenberg, B. (1984). Parents, peers and television as determinants of Black children's esteem. In R. Bostrom (Ed.), *Communication yearbook* (Vol. 8, pp. 164–177). Beverly Hills, CA: Sage.

McDonald, M. A., Sigman, M., Espinosa, M. P., & Neumann, C. G. (1994). Impact of temporary food shortage on children and their mothers. *Child Development, 65,* 404–415.

McGhee, P. E. (1979). *Humor: Its origin and development.* San Francisco: W.H. Freeman.

McGinniss, M. J., & Kaback, M. M. (2002). Heterozygote testing and carrier screening. In D. L. Rimoin, J. M. Connor, R. E. Pyeritz, & B. R. Korf (Eds.), *Emery and Rimoin's principles and practice of medical genetics* (4th ed., Vol. 1, pp. 752–762). London: Churchill Livingston.

McGraw, M. B. (1935). *Growth: A study of Johnny and Jimmy.* New York: Appleton-Century-Crofts.

McGraw, M. B. (1939). Swimming behavior of the human infant. *Journal of Pediatrics, 15,* 485–490.

McGregor, J. A., & French, J. I. (1991). *Chlamydia trachomatis* infection during pregnancy. *American Journal of Obstetrics and Gynecology, 165,* 1782–1789.

McGue, M. (1999). The behavioral genetics of alcoholism. *Current Directions in Psychological Science, 8,* 109–115.

McGue, M., Elkins, I., Walden, B., & Iacono, W. G. (2005). Perceptions of parent-adolescent relationship: A longitudinal investigation. *Developmental Psychology, 41,* 971–984.

McGuire, J. (1988). Gender stereotypes of parents with two-year-olds and beliefs about gender differences in behavior. *Sex Roles, 19,* 233–240.

McGuire, K. D., & Weisz, J. R. (1982). Social cognition and behavior correlates of preadolescent chumship. *Child Development, 53,* 1478–1484.

McGuire, P. K., Robertson, D. A. T., David, A. S., Kitson, N., Frackowiak, R. S. J., & Frith, C. D. (1997). Neural correlates of thinking in sign language. *NeuroReport, 8,* 695–697.

McGurk, H., & MacDonald, J. (1976). Hearing lips and seeing voices. *Nature* (London), *264,* 746–748.

McHale, S. M., Crouter, A. C., McGuire, S. A., & Updegraff, K. A. (1995). Congruence between mothers' and fathers' differential treatment of siblings: Links with family relations and children's well-being. *Child Development, 66*, 116–128.

McHale, S. M., Crouter, A. C., & Tucker, C. J. (1999). Family context and gender role socialization in middle childhood: Comparing boys to girls and sisters to brothers. *Child Development, 70*, 990–1004.

McHale, S. M., Crouter, A. C., & Tucker, C. J. (2001). Free-time activities in middle childhood: Links with adjustment in early adolescence. *Child Development, 72*, 1764–1778.

McHale, S. M., Kim, J., Whiteman, S., & Crouter, A. C. (2004). Links between sex-typed time use in middle childhood and gender development in early adolescence. *Developmental Psychology, 40*, 868–881.

McHale, S. M., Shanahan, L., Updegraff, K. A., Crouter, A. C., & Booth, A. (2004). Developmental and individual differences in girls' sex-typed activities in middle childhood and adolescence. *Child Development, 75*, 1575–1593.

McHale, S. M., Updegraff, K. A., Jackson-Newsom, J., Tucker, C. J., & Crouter, A. C. (2000). When does parents' differential treatment have negative implications for siblings? *Social Development, 9*, 149–172.

McIlhaney, J. S., Jr. (2000). Sexually transmitted infection and teenage sexuality. *American Journal of Obstetrics and Gynecology, 183*, 334–339.

McKenna, J., & McDade, T. (2005). Why babies should never sleep alone: A review of the co-sleeping controversy in relation to SIDS, bedsharing and breast feeding. *Paediatric Respiratory Reviews, 6*, 134–152.

McKey, R. H., Condelli, L., Granson, H., Barrett, B., McConkey, C., & Plantz, M. (1985). *The impact of Head Start on children, families and communities* (Final report of the Head Start Evaluation, Synthesis and Utilization Project). Washington, DC: U.S. Government Printing Office.

McKusick, V. A., & Amberger, J. S. (2002). Morbid anatomy of the human genome. In D. L. Rimoin, J. M. Connor, R. E. Pyeritz, & B. R. Korf (Eds.), *Emery and Rimoin's principles and practice of medical genetics* (4th ed., Vol. 1, pp. 174–298). London: Churchill Livingston.

McLoyd, V. C. (1990). The impact of economic hardship on black families and children: Psychological distress, parenting, and socioemotional development. *Child Development, 61*, 311–346.

McLoyd, V. C. (1998). Changing demographics in the American population: Implications for research on minority children and adolescents. In V. C. McLoyd & L. Steinberg (Eds.), *Studying minority adolescents* (pp. 3–28). Mahwah, NJ: Erlbaum.

McLoyd, V. C., Epstein Jayaratne, T., Ceballo, R., & Borquez, J. (1994). Unemployment and work interruption among African American single mothers: Effects on parenting and adolescent socioemotional functioning. *Child Development, 65*, 562–589.

McManus, I. C., & Bryden, M. P. (1991). Geschwind's theory of cerebral lateralization: Developing a formal, causal model. *Psychological Bulletin, 110*, 237–253.

Mead, G. H. (1934). *Mind, self, and society.* Chicago: University of Chicago Press.

Medin, D. L. (1989). Concepts and conceptual structure. *American Psychologist, 44*, 1469–1481.

Meichenbaum, D. (1977). *Cognitive-behavior modification: An integrative approach.* New York: Plenum Press.

Meins, E. (1998). The effects of security of attachment and maternal attribution of meaning on children's linguistic acquisitional style. *Infant Behavior and Development, 21*, 237–252.

Mekos, D., Hetherington, E. M., & Reiss, D. (1996). Sibling differences in problem behavior and parental treatment in nondivorced and remarried families. *Child Development, 67*, 2148–2165.

Meltzoff, A. N. (1995). What infant memory tells us about infantile amnesia: Long-term recall and deferred imitation. *Journal of Experimental Child Psychology, 59*, 497–515.

Meltzoff, A. N., & Moore, M. K. (1999). Persons and representation: Why infant imitation is important for theories of human development. In J. Nadel & G. Butterworth (Eds.), *Imitation in infancy* (pp. 9–35). Cambridge, UK: Cambridge University Press.

Mennella, J. A., & Beauchamp, G. K. (1996). The human infant's response to vanilla flavors in mother's milk and formula. *Infant Behavior and Development, 19*, 13–19.

Mennella, J. A., Griffin, C. E., & Beauchamp, G. K. (2004). Flavor programming during infancy. *Pediatrics, 113*, 840–845.

Mennella, J. A., Pepino, M. Y., & Reed, D. R. (2005). Genetic and environmental determinants of bitter perception and sweet preferences. *Pediatrics, 115*, 216–222.

Merimee, T. J., Zapf, J., & Froesch, E. R. (1981). Dwarfism in the Pygmy: An isolated deficiency of insulin-like Growth Factor I. *New England Journal of Medicine, 305*, 965–968.

Mervis, C. B. (2003). Williams syndrome: 15 years of psychological research. *Developmental Neuroscience, 23*, 1–12.

Messer, D. J. (1981). The identification of names in maternal speech to infants. *Journal of Psycholinguistic Research, 10*, 69–77.

Messer, S. C., & Gross, A. M. (1995) Childhood depression and family interaction: A naturalistic observation study. *Journal of Clinical Child Psychology, 24*, 77–88.

Messinger, D. S., & Fogel, A. (1998). Give and take: The development of conventional infant gestures. *Merrill-Palmer Quarterly, 44*, 566–590.

Messinger, D. S., Fogel, A., & Dickson, K. L. (1999). What's in a smile? *Developmental Psychology, 35*, 701–708.

Messinger, D. S., Fogel, A., & Dickson, K. L. (2001). All smiles are positive, but some smiles are more positive than others. *Developmental Psychology, 37*, 642–653.

Meyer, M., & Fienberg, S. (1992). *Assessing evaluation studies: The case of bilingual education strategies.* Washington, DC: National Academy Press.

Meyer, M. B., & Tonascia, J. A. (1977). Maternal smoking, pregnancy complications, and perinatal mortality. *American Journal of Obstetrics and Gynecology, 128*, 494–502.

Michel, G. F. (1988). A neuropsychological perspective on infant sensorimotor development. In C. Rovee-Collier & L. P. Lipsitt (Eds.), *Advances in infancy research* (Vol. 5). Norwood, NJ: Ablex.

Michelsson, K., Sirvio, P., & Wasz-Hockert, D. (1977). Pain cry in fullterm asphyxiated newborn infants correlated with late findings. *Acta Paediatrica Scandinavica, 66*, 611–616.

Miech, R. A., Kumanyika, S. K., Stettler, N., Link, B. G., Phelan, J. C., & Chang, V. W. (2006). Trends in the association of poverty with overweight among US adolescents, 1971–2004. *Journal of the American Medical Association, 295*, 2385–2393.

Milgram, N. A. (1998). Children under stress. In T. H. Ollendick & M. Hersen (Eds.), *Handbook of child psychopathology* (3rd ed., pp. 505–533). New York: Plenum.

Miller, A. L., Volling, B. L., & McElwain, N. L. (2000). Sibling jealousy in a triadic context with mothers and fathers. *Social Development, 9*, 433–457.

Miller, B. C., Benson, B., & Galbraith, K. A. (2001). Family relationships and adolescent pregnancy risk: A research synthesis. *Developmental Review, 21*, 1–38.

Miller, B. C., Fan, X., Christensen, M., Grotevant, H. D., & van Dulmen, M. (2000). Comparison of adopted and nonadopted adolescents in a large, nationally representative sample. *Developmental Psychology, 71*, 1458–1473.

Miller, J. G. (1999). Cultural Psychology: Implications for basic psychological theory. *Psychological Science, 10*, 85–91.

Miller, J. M., Jr., & Boudreaux, M. C. (1999). A study of antenatal cocaine use—chaos in action. *American Journal of Obstetrics and Gynecology, 180*, 1427–1431.

Miller, L. T., & Vernon, P. A. (1996). Intelligence, reaction time, and working memory in 4- to 6-year-old children. *Intelligence, 22*, 155–190.

Miller, N. B., Cowan, P. A., Cowan, C. P., Hetherington, E. M., & Clingempeel, W. G. (1993). Externalizing in preschoolers and early adolescents: A cross-study replication of a family model. *Developmental Psychology, 29*, 3–18.

Miller, N., & Maruyama, G. (1976). Ordinal position and peer popularity. *Journal of Personality and Social Psychology, 33*, 123–131.

Miller, P. A., Eisenberg, N., Fabes, R. A., & Shell, R. (1996). Relations of moral reasoning and vicarious emotion to young children's prosocial behavior toward peers and adults. *Developmental Psychology, 32*, 210–219.

Miller, W. L., & Levine, L. S. (1987). Molecular and clinical advances in congenital adrenal hyperplasia. *Journal of Pediatrics, 111,* 1–17.

Miller-Jones, D. (1989). Culture and testing. *American Psychologist, 44,* 360–366.

Mills, D. L., Coffey-Corina, S. A., & Neville, H. J. (1993). Language acquisition and cerebral specialization in 20-month-old infants. *Journal of Cognitive Neuroscience, 5,* 317–334.

Mills, D. L., Coffey-Corina, S. A., & Neville, H. J. (1994). Variability in cerebral organization during primary language acquisition. In G. Dawson & K. W. Fischer (Eds.), *Human behavior and the developing brain* (pp. 427–455). New York: Guilford.

Mills, D. L., Coffey-Corina, S., & Neville, H. J. (1997). Language comprehension and cerebral specialization from 13 to 20 months. *Developmental Neuropsychology, 13,* 397–445.

Mills, R. S. L., & Grusec, J. E. (1989). Cognitive, affective, and behavioral consequences of praising altruism. *Merrill-Palmer Quarterly, 35,* 299–326.

Mills, R. S. L., & Rubin, K. H. (1993). Socialization factors in the development of social withdrawal. In K. H. Rubin & J. B. Asendorpf (Eds.), *Social withdrawal, inhibition, and shyness in childhood* (pp. 117–148). Hillsdale, NJ: Erlbaum.

Minuchin, P. P. (1988). Relationships within the family: A systems perspective on development. In R. A. Hinde & J. Stevenson-Hinde (Eds.), *Relationships within families: Mutual influences.* Oxford: Clarendon Press.

Minuchin, P. P., & Shapiro, E. K. (1983). The school as a context for social development. In E. M. Hetherington (Ed.), *Handbook of child psychology: Vol. IV. Socialization, personality, and social development* (pp. 197–274). New York: Wiley.

Mischel, H. N., & Mischel, W. (1983). The development of children's knowledge of self-control strategies. *Child Development, 54,* 603–619.

Mischel, W. (1966). A social learning view of sex differences in behavior. In E. E. Maccoby (Ed.), *The development of sex differences.* Stanford, CA: Stanford University Press.

Mischel, W., Ebbesen, E. B., & Zeiss, A. R. (1972). Cognitive and attentional mechanisms in delay of gratification. *Journal of Personality and Social Psychology, 21,* 204–218.

Mischel, W., Shoda, Y., & Rodriguez, M. L. (1989). Delay of gratification in children. *Science, 244,* 933–938.

Mitchell, E. A., & Milerad, J. (1999). *Smoking and sudden infant death syndrome.* Paper series prepared for International Consultation on Environmental Tobacco Smoke and Child Health. Geneva, Switzerland. Retrieved October 21, 2002, from www5.who.int/tobacco/repository/tld67/mitchell.pdf

Mitchell, E. A., Thach, B. T., Thompson, J. M. D., Williams, S. (1999). Changing infants' sleep position increases risk of sudden infant death syndrome. *Archives of Pediatrics and Adolescent Medicine, 153,* 1136–1141.

Mitchell, E. A., Tuohy, P. G., Brunt, J. M., Thompson, J. M. D., Clements, M. S., Stewart, A. W., et al. (1997). Risk factors for sudden infant death syndrome following the prevention campaign in New Zealand: A prospective study. *Pediatrics, 100,* 835–840.

Mittendorf, R., Williams, M. A., Berkey, C. S., & Cotter, P. F. (1990). The length of uncomplicated human gestation. *Obstetrics and Gynecology, 75,* 929–932.

Mittendorf, R., Williams, M. A., Berkley, C. S., Lieberman, E., & Monson, R. R. (1993). Predictors of human gestational length. *American Journal of Obstetrics and Gynecology, 168,* 480–484.

Mix, K. S., Huttenlocher, J., & Levine, S. C. (2002). *Quantitative development in infancy and early childhood*: London, Oxford University Press.

Mix, K. S., Levine, S. C., & Huttenlocher, J. (1999). Early fraction calculation ability. *Developmental Psychology, 35,* 164–174.

Miyake, A., Friedman, N. P., Rettinger, D. A., Shah, P., & Hegarty, M. (2001). How are visuospatial working memory, executive functioning, and spatial abilities related? A latent variable analysis. *Journal of Experimental Psychology: General, 130,* 621–640.

Miyake, K., Chen, S., & Campos, J. J. (1985). Infant temperament, mother's mode of interaction, and attachment in Japan: An interim report. In I. Bretherton & E. Waters (Eds.), *Growing points of attachment theory and research. Monographs of the Society for Research in Child Development, 50*(1–2, Serial No. 209).

Moely, B. E., Olson, F. A., Halwes, T. G., & Flavell, J. H. (1969). Production deficiency in young children's clustered recall. *Developmental Psychology, 1,* 26–34.

Moffat, R., & Hackel, A. (1985). Thermal aspects of neonatal care. In A. Gottfried & J. Gaiter (Eds.), *Infant stress under intensive care.* Baltimore: University Park Press.

Moffitt, T. E. (1993). Life-course-persistent and adolescence-limited antisocial behavior: A developmental taxonomy. *Psychological Review, 100,* 674–701.

Moldavsky, M., Lev, D., & Lerman-Sagie, T. (2001). Behavioral phenotypes of genetic syndromes: A reference guide to physicians. *Journal of the American Academy of Adolescent Psychiatry, 40,* 749–761.

Mondloch, C. J., Lewis, T. L., Budreau, D. R., Maurer, D., Dannemiller, J. L., Stephens, B. R., & Kleiner-Gathercoal, K. A. (1999). Face perception during early infancy. *Psychological Science, 10,* 419–422.

Monfries, M. M., & Kafer, N. F. (1987). Neglected and rejected children: A social-skills model. *Journal of Psychology, 121,* 401–407.

Montague, D. P. F., & Walker-Andrews, A. S. (2001). Peekaboo: A new look at infants' perception of emotion expressions. *Developmental Psychology, 37,* 826–838.

Moon, C., Cooper, R. P., & Fifer, W. P. (1993). Two-day-olds prefer their native language. *Infant Behavior and Development, 16,* 494–500.

Moon, R. Y., & Biliter, W. M. (2001). Infant sleep position policies in licensed child care centers after Back to Sleep campaign. *Pediatrics, 106,* 576–580.

Moon, R. Y., Patel, K. M., & McDermott Shaefer, S. J. (2000). Sudden infant death syndrome in child care settings. *Pediatrics, 106,* 295–300.

Moore, K. L., & Persaud, T. V. N. (1998). *Before we are born: Essentials of embryology and birth defects* (5th ed.). Philadelphia: W.B. Saunders.

Moore, K. L., & Persaud, T. V. N. (2003). *The developing human: Clinically oriented embryology.* Philadelphia: Saunders.

Morison, P., & Masten, A. S. (1991). Peer reputation in middle childhood as a predictor of adaptation in adolescence: A seven-year follow-up. *Child Development, 62,* 991–1007.

Morrelli, G., Rogoff, B., Oppenheim, D., & Goldsmith, D. (1992). Cultural variation in infants' sleeping arrangements: Questions of independence. *Developmental Psychology, 28,* 604–613.

Morris, R., & Kratchowill, T. (1983). *Treating children's fears and phobias.* New York: Pergamon Press.

Morrison, F. J., Griffith, E. M., & Alberts, D. M. (1997). Nature-nurture in the classroom: Entrance age, school readiness, and learning in children. *Developmental Psychology, 33,* 254–262.

Morrison, F. J., Smith, L., & Dow-Ehrensberger, M. (1995). Education and cognitive development: A natural experiment. *Developmental Psychology, 31,* 789–799.

Morrongiello, B. A. (1984). Auditory temporal pattern perception in 6- and 12-month-old infants. *Developmental Psychology, 20,* 441–448.

Morrongiello, B. A., Fenwick, K. D., & Chance, G. (1990). Sound localization acuity in very young infants: An observer-based testing procedure. *Developmental Psychology, 26,* 75–84.

Morrongiello, B. A., Fenwick, K. D., & Chance, G. (1998). Crossmodal learning in newborn infants: Inferences about properties of auditory-visual events. *Infant Behavior and Development, 21,* 543–554.

Moses, L. J., Baldwin, D. A., Rosicky, J. G., & Tidball, G. (2001). Evidence for referential understanding in the emotions domain at twelve and eighteen months. *Child Development, 72,* 718–735.

Mosko, S., Richard, C., & McKenna, J. (1997). Infant arousals during mother-infant bed sharing: Implications for infant sleep and sudden infant death syndrome research. *Pediatrics, 100,* 841–849.

Moss, E., Rousseau, D., Parent, S., St.-Laurent, D., & Saintonge, J. (1998). Correlates of attachment at school age: Maternal reported stress, mother-child interaction, and behavior problems. *Child Development, 69,* 1390–1405.

Mosteller, F. (1995, Summer/Fall). The Tennessee study of class size in the early school grades. *The Future of Children, 5*(2), pp. 113–127.

Petitto, L. A., & Marentette, P. F. (1991). Babbling in the manual code: Evidence for the ontogeny of language. *Science, 251,* 1493–1496.

Pettit, G. S. (2004). Violent children in developmental perspective: Risk and protective factors and the mechanisms through which they (may) operate. *Current Directions in Psychological Science, 13,* 194–197.

Pettit, G. S., Bates, J. E., Dodge, K. A., & Meece, D. W. (1999). The impact of after-school peer contact on early adolescent externalizing problems is moderated by parental monitoring, neighborhood safety, and prior adjustment. *Child Development, 70,* 768–778.

Pettit, G. S., Clawson, M. A., Dodge, K. A. & Bates, J. E. (1996). Stability and change in peer-rejected status: The role of child behavior, parenting, and family ecology. *Merrill-Palmer Quarterly, 42,* 267–294.

Pettit, G. S., Laird, R. D., Dodge, K. A., Bates, J. E., & Criss, M. M. (2001). Antecedents and behavior-problem outcomes of parental monitoring and psychological control in early adolescence. *Child Development, 72,* 583–598.

Pew Internet & American Life Project (2005). Generations on line. Retrieved June 7, 2006 from www.pewinternet.org/pdfs/PIP_Generations_Memo.pdf.

Phelps, E., & Damon, W. (1989). Problem solving with equals: Peer collaboration as a context for learning mathematics and spatial concepts. *Journal of Educational Psychology, 81,* 639–646.

Phenylketonuria. (2000, October 16–18). Phenylketonuria (PKU): Screening and management. *NIH Consensus Statement, 17,* 1–33.

Phillips, D. (1984). The illusion of incompetence among academically competent children. *Child Development, 55,* 2000–2016.

Phinney, J. S. (1990). Ethnic identity in adolescents and adults: Review of research. *Psychological Bulletin, 108,* 499–514.

Phinney, J. S., Ferguson, D. L., & Tate, J. D. (1997). Intergroup attitudes among ethnic minority adolescents: A causal model. *Child Development, 68,* 955–969.

Phinney, J. S., & Rosenthal, D. A. (1992). Ethnic identity in adolescence: Process, context and outcome. In G. R. Adams, T. P. Gullotta, & R. Montemayor (Eds.), *Adolescent identity formation.* Newbury Park, CA: Sage.

Piaget, J. (1929). *The child's conception of the world.* London: Routledge & Kegan Paul.

Piaget, J. (1952a). *The child's conception of number.* New York: W. W. Norton.

Piaget, J. (1952b). *The origins of intelligence in children.* New York: W. W. Norton.

Piaget, J. (1954). *The construction of reality in the child.* New York: Basic Books.

Piaget, J. (1962). *Play, dreams, and imitation in childhood.* New York: W. W. Norton.

Piaget, J. (1965). *The moral judgment of the child.* New York: Free Press. (Original work published 1932)

Piaget, J. (1971). *Biology and knowledge: An essay on the relationship between organic regulations and cognitive processes.* Chicago: University of Chicago Press.

Piaget, J., & Inhelder, B. (1956). *The child's conception of space.* London: Routledge & Kegan Paul.

Pick, A. D. (1965). Improvement of visual and tactual discrimination. *Journal of Experimental Psychology, 69,* 331–339.

Pick, H. L., Jr. (1987). Information and the effects of early perceptual experience. In N. Eisenberg (Ed.), *Contemporary topics in developmental psychology.* New York: Wiley.

Pick, H. L., Jr. (1992). Eleanor J. Gibson: Learning to perceive and perceiving to learn. *Developmental Psychology, 28,* 787–794.

Pickens, J. (1994). Perception of auditory-visual distance relations by 5-month-old infants. *Developmental Psychology, 30,* 537–544.

Pickens, J., & Field, T. (1993). Facial expressivity in infants of depressed mothers. *Developmental Psychology, 29,* 986–988.

Piecuch, R. E., Leonard, C. H., & Cooper, B. A. (1998). Infants with birth weight 1,000–1,499 grams born in three time periods: Has outcome changed over time? *Clinical Pediatrics, 37,* 537–546.

Pierce, J. W., & Wardle, J. (1997). Cause and effect beliefs and self-esteem of overweight children. *Journal of Child Psychology and Psychiatry, 38,* 645–650.

Pike, A., McGuire, S., Hetherington, E. M., Reiss, D., & Plomin, R. (1996). Family environment and adolescent depressive symptoms and antisocial behavior: A multivariate genetic analysis. *Developmental Psychology, 32,* 590–603.

Pillemer, D. B. (1998). *Momentous events, vivid memories.* Cambridge, MA; Harvard University Press.

Pillemer, D. B., & White, S. H. (1989). Childhood events recalled by children and adults. In H. W. Reese (Ed.), *Advances in child development and behavior* (Vol. 21, pp. 297–340). San Diego: Academic Press.

Pineau, A., & Streri, A. (1990). Intermodal transfer of spatial arrangement of the component parts of an object in infants aged 4–5 months. *Perception, 19,* 795–804.

Pinker, S. (1984). *Language learnability and language development.* Cambridge, MA: Harvard University Press.

Pinker, S. (1987). The bootstrapping problem in language acquisition. In B. MacWhinney (Ed.), *Mechanisms of language acquisition.* Hillsdale, NJ: Erlbaum.

Pinyerd, B. J. (1992). Assessment of infant growth. *Journal of Pediatric Health Care, 6,* 302–308.

Pipe, M., Gee, S., Wilson, J. C., & Egerton, J. M. (1999). Children's recall 1 or 2 years after an event. *Developmental Psychology, 35,* 781–789.

Platt, L. D., Koch, R., Hanley, W. B., Levy, H. L., Matalon, R., Rouse, B., et al. (2000). The International Study of Pregnancy Outcome in Women with Maternal Phenylketonuria: Report of a 12-year study. *American Journal of Obstetrics and Gynecology, 182,* 326–333.

Pleck, E. H., & Pleck, J. H. (1997). Fatherhood ideals in the United States: Historical dimensions. In M. E. Lamb (Ed.), *The role of the father in child development* (3rd ed., pp. 33–48). New York: Wiley.

Plomin, R., DeFries, J. C., & Fulker, D. (1988). The Colorado Adoption Project. In R. Plomin, J. C. DeFries, & D. Fulker (Eds.), *Nature and nurture during infancy and early childhood* (pp. 37–76). Cambridge, UK: Cambridge University Press.

Plomin, R., DeFries, J. C., McClearn, G. E., & McGuffin, P. (2001). *Behavioral genetics* (4th ed.). New York: Worth.

Plomin, R., Owen, M. J., & McGuffin, P. (1994). The genetic basis of complex human behaviors. Science, 264, 1733–1739.

Plomin, R., Reiss, D., Hetherington, E. M., & Howe, G. W. (1994). Nature and nurture: Genetic contributions to measures of the family environment. *Developmental Psychology, 30,* 32–43.

Plomin, R., & Rutter, M. (1998). Child development, molecular genetics, and what to do with genes once they are found. *Child Development, 69,* 1223–1242.

Polka, L. M., & Werker, J. F. (1994). Developmental changes in perception of nonnative vowel contrasts. *Journal of Experimental Psychology: Human Perception and Performance, 20,* 421–435.

Pollak, S. D., Cicchetti, D., Hornung, K., & Reed, A. (2000). Recognizing emotion in faces: Developmental effects of child abuse and neglect. *Developmental Psychology, 36,* 679–688.

Pollard, I. (2000). Substance abuse and parenthood: Biological mechanisms–bioethical challenges. *Women & Health, 30,* 1–24.

Pollitt, E. (1994). Poverty and child development: Relevance of research in developing countries to the United States. *Child Development, 65,* 283–295.

Pollitt, E. (1996). Timing and vulnerability in research on malnutrition and cognition. *Nutrition Reviews, 54,* S49-S55.

Pollock, L. A. (1983). *Forgotten children: Parent-child relations from 1500–1900.* Cambridge, UK: Cambridge University Press.

Pomerantz, E. M., Ruble, D. N., Frey, K. S., & Greulich, F. (1995). Meeting goals and confronting conflict: Children's changing perceptions of social comparison. *Child Development, 66,* 723–738.

Pomerleau, A., Bolduc, D., Malcuit, G., & Cossette, L. (1990). Pink or blue: Environmental gender stereotypes in the first two years of life. *Sex Roles, 22,* 359–367.

Poole, D. A., & Lindsay, D. S. (2002). Reducing child witnesses' false reports of misinformation from parents. *Journal of Experimental Child Psychology, 81,* 117–140.

Poole, D. A., & White, L. T. (1991). Effects of question repetition on the eyewitness testimony of children and adults. *Developmental Psychology, 27,* 975–986.

Poole, D. A., & White, L. T. (1993). Two years later: Effects of question repetition and retention interval on the eyewitness testimony of children and adults. *Developmental Psychology, 29,* 844–853.

Pope, A. W., & Bierman, K. L. (1999). Predicting adolescent peer problems and antisocial activities: The relative roles of aggression and dysregulation. *Developmental Psychology, 35,* 335–346.

Pope, S., & Kipp, K. K. (1998). The development of efficient forgetting: Evidence from directed-forgetting tasks. *Developmental Review, 18,* 86–123.

Porges, S. W., Doussard-Roosevelt, J. A., & Maiti, A. K. (1994). Vagal tone and the physiological regulation of emotion. In N. A. Fox (Ed.), The development of emotion regulation: Biological and behavioral considerations. *Monographs of the Society for Research in Child Development, 59*(2–3, Serial No. 240).

Porter, F. L., Grunau, R. E., & Anand, K. J. S. (1999). Long-term effects of pain in infants. *Journal of Developmental and Behavioral Pediatrics, 20,* 253–261.

Porter, R. H., Balogh, R. D., & Makin, J. W. (1988). Olfactory influences on mother-infant interaction. In C. Rovee-Collier & L. P. Lipsitt (Eds.), *Advances in infancy research* (Vol. 5). Norwood, NJ: Ablex.

Posada, G., Gao, Y., Wu, F., Posada, R., Tascon, M., Schoelmerich, A., et al. (1995). The secure-base phenomenon across cultures: Children's behaviors, mothers' preferences, and experts' concepts. In E. Waters, B. E. Vaughn, G. Posada, & K. Kondo-Ikemura (Eds.), *Caregiving, cultural, and cognitive perspectives on secure-base behavior and working models: New growing points of attachment theory and research. Monographs of the Society for Research in Child Development, 60* (Nos. 2–3, Serial No. 244).

Post, R. M., & Weiss, S. R. B. (1997). Emergent properties of neural systems: How focal molecular neurobiological alterations can affect behavior. *Development and Psychopathology, 9,* 907–929.

Poulin-Dubois, D., Lepage, A., & Ferland, D. (1996). Infants' concept of animacy. *Cognitive Development, 11,* 19–36.

Poulin-Dubois, D., Serbin, L. A., & Derbyshire, A. (1998). Toddlers' intermodal and verbal knowledge about gender. *Merrill-Palmer Quarterly, 44,* 338–354.

Poulin-Dubois, D., Serbin, L. A., Eichstedt, J. A., Sen, M. G., & Beissel, C. F. (2002). Men don't put on make-up: Toddlers' knowledge of the gender stereotyping of household activities. *Social Development, 11,* 166–181.

Povinelli, D. (2001). The self: Elevated in consciousness and extended in time. In C. Moore & K. Lemmon (Eds.), *The self in time* (pp. 75–95). Mahwah, NJ: Erlbaum.

Power, T. G., & Chapieski, M. L. (1986). Childrearing and impulse control in toddlers: A naturalistic investigation. *Developmental Psychology, 22,* 271–275.

Powers, S. I., Hauser, S. T., & Kilner, L. A. (1989). Adolescent mental health. *American Psychologist, 44,* 200–208.

Prader, A. (1978). Catch-up growth. *Postgraduate Medical Journal, 54,* 133–146.

Pratt, M. W., Green, D., MacVicar, J., & Bountrogianni, M. (1992). The mathematical parent: Parental scaffolding, parenting style, and learning outcomes in long-division mathematics homework. *Journal of Applied Developmental Psychology, 13,* 17–34.

Premack, D. (1971). Language in chimpanzee? *Science, 172,* 808–822.

Pressley, M., & Levin, J. R. (1977). Task parameters affecting the efficacy of a visual imagery learning strategy in younger and older children. *Journal of Experimental Child Psychology, 24,* 53–59.

Preyer, W. (1888–1889). *The mind of the child* (H. W. Brown, Trans.). New York: Appleton. (Original work published in 1882)

Pride, P. G., Drugan, A., Johnson, M. P., Isada, N. B., & Evans, M. I. (1993). Prenatal diagnosis: Choices women make about pursuing testing and acting on abnormal results. *Clinical Obstetrics and Gynecology, 36,* 496–509.

Proffitt, D. R., & Bertenthal, B. I. (1990). Converging operations revisited: Assessing what infants perceive using discrimination measures. *Perception & Psychophysics, 47,* 1–11.

Pulkkinen, L. (1982). Self-control and continuity from childhood to adolescence. In P. B. Baltes & O. G. Brim (Eds.), *Life-span development and behavior* (Vol. 4, pp. 63–105). New York: Academic Press.

Purcell, P., & Stewart, L. (1990). Dick and Jane in 1989. *Sex Roles, 22,* 177–185.

Putallaz, M. (1987). Maternal behavior and children's sociometric status. *Child Development, 58,* 324–340.

Quinn, P. C., Eimas, P. D., & Rosenkranz, S. L. (1993). Evidence for representations of perceptually similar natural categories by 3-month-old and 4-month-old infants. *Perception, 22,* 463–475.

Radin, N. (1981). The role of the father in cognitive, academic, and intellectual development. In M. E. Lamb (Ed.), *The role of the father in child development.* New York: Wiley.

Radin, N. (1994). Primary-caregiving fathers in intact families. In A. E. Gottfried & A. W. Gottfried (Eds.), *Redefining families: Implications for children's development* (pp. 11–49). NY: Plenum Press.

Radke-Yarrow, M., & Zahn-Waxler, C. (1984). Roots, motives, and patterns of children's prosocial behavior. In E. Staub, D. Bar-Tel, J. Karylowski, & J. Reykowski (Eds.), *Development and maintenance of prosocial behavior.* New York: Plenum Press.

Radke-Yarrow, M., Zahn-Waxler, C., & Chapman, M. (1983). Children's prosocial dispositions and behavior. In E. M. Hetherington (Ed.), *Handbook of child psychology: Vol. IV. Socialization, personality, and social development* (4th ed., pp. 469–545). New York: Wiley.

Radziszewska, B., Richardson, J. L., Dent, C. W., & Flay, B. R. (1996). Parenting style and adolescent depressive symptoms, smoking, and academic achievement: Ethnic, gender, and SES differences. *Journal of Behavioral Medicine, 19,* 289–305.

Radziszewska, B., & Rogoff, B. (1988). Influence of adult and peer collaborators on children's planning skills. *Developmental Psychology, 24,* 840–848.

Radziszewska, B., & Rogoff, R. (1991). Children's guided participation in planning imaginary errands with skilled adult or peer partners. *Developmental Psychology, 27,* 381–389.

Rallison, M. L. (1986). *Growth disorders in infants, children, and adolescents.* New York: Wiley.

Ram, A., & Ross, H. S. (2001). Problem-solving, contention, and struggle: How siblings resolve a conflict of interests. *Child Development, 72,* 1710–1722.

Ramey, C. T., Bryant, D. M., & Suarez, T. M. (1987). Early intervention: Why, for whom, how, at what cost? In N. Gunzenhauser (Ed.), *Infant stimulation: For whom, what kind, when, and how much?* (Johnson & Johnson Baby Products Company Pediatric Round Table Series No. 13). Skilman, NJ: Johnson & Johnson.

Ramey, C. T., Bryant, D. M., Wasik, B. H., Sparling, J. J., Fendt, K. H., & LaVange, L. M. (1992). Infant Health and Development Program for low birth weight, premature infants: Program elements, family participation, and child intelligence. *Pediatrics, 89,* 454–465.

Ramey, C. T., & Campbell, F. A. (1981). Educational intervention for children at risk for mild retardation: A longitudinal analysis. In P. Mittler (Ed.), *Frontiers of knowledge in mental retardation: Vol. 1. Social, educational, and behavioral aspects.* Baltimore: University Park Press.

Ramey, C. T., Lee, M. W., & Burchinal, M. R. (1989). Developmental plasticity and predictability: Consequences of ecological change. In M. H. Bornstein & N. A. Krasnegor (Eds.), *Stability and continuity in mental development: Behavioral and biological perspectives.* Hillsdale, NJ: Erlbaum.

Ramey, C. T., & Ramey, S. L. (1998). Early intervention and early experience. *American Psychologist, 53,* 109–120.

Rao, N., & Stewart, S. M. (1999). Cultural influences on sharer and recipient behavior: Sharing in Chinese and Indian preschool children. *Journal of Cross-Cultural Psychology, 30,* 219–241.

Rapport, M. D. (1995). Attention-deficit hyperactivity disorder. In M. Hersen & R. T. Ammerman (Eds.), *Advanced abnormal psychology* (pp. 353–373). Hillsdale, NJ: Erlbaum.

Raven, J. C. (1962). *Coloured progressive matrices.* London: H. K. Lewis and Co.

Reece, E. A., Hobbins, J. C., Mahoney, M. J., & Petrie, R. H. (1995). *Handbook of medicine of the fetus & mother*. Philadelphia: J. B. Lippincott.

Reese, E., & Fivush, R. (1993). Parental styles for talking about the past. *Developmental Psychology, 29*, 596–606.

Reese, E., Haden, C. A., & Fivush, R. (1993). Mother-child conversations about the past: Relationships of style and memory over time. *Cognitive Development, 8*, 403–430.

Regan, P. C., Durvasula, R., Howell, L., Ureno, O., & Rea, M. (2004). Romance seems to be alive and well during the high school years. *Social Behavior and Personality, 32*, 667–676.

Reilly, J. J., & Dorosty, A. R. (1999). Epidemic of obesity in UK children. *Lancet, 354*, 1874–1875.

Reisman, J. E. (1987). Touch, motion, and proprioception. In P. Salapatek & L. Cohen (Eds.), *Handbook of infant perception: From sensation to perception* (Vol. 1). Orlando, FL: Academic Press.

Reiss, D., Neiderhiser, J. M., Hetherington, E. M., & Plomin, R. (2000). *The relationship code: Deciphering genetic and social patterns in adolescent development*. Cambridge, MA: Harvard University Press.

Reissland, N. (1988). Neonatal imitation in the first hour of life: Observations in rural Nepal. *Developmental Psychology, 24*, 464–469.

Remafedi, G., French, S., Story, M., Resnick, M. D., & Blum, R. (1998). The relationship between suicide risk and sexual orientation: Results of a population-based study. *American Journal of Public Health, 88*, 57–60.

Renshaw, P. D. & Brown, P. J. (1993). Loneliness in middle childhood: Concurrent and longitudinal predictors. *Child Development, 64*, 1271–1284.

Resnick, L. B. (1986). The development of mathematical intuition. In M. Perlmutter (Ed.), *Perspectives on intellectual development: The Minnesota symposia on child psychology* (Vol. 19). Hillsdale, NJ: Erlbaum.

Resnick, L. B. (1995). Inventing arithmetic: Making children's intuitions work at school. In C. A. Nelson (Ed.), *Basic and applied perspectives on learning, cognition, and development. Minnesota Symposia on Child Psychology* (Vol. 28, pp. 75–101). Mahwah, NJ: Erlbaum.

Resnick, L. B., & Singer, J. A. (1993). Protoquantitative origins of ratio reasoning. In T. P. Carpenter, E. Fennema, & T. A. Romberg (Eds.), *Rational numbers: An integration of research* (pp. 107–130). Hillsdale, NJ: Erlbaum.

Reyna, V. F., & Brainerd, C. J. (1995). Fuzzy-trace theory: An interim synthesis. *Learning and Individual Differences, 7*, 1–75.

Reynolds, A. J., Ou, S., & Topitzes, J. W. (2004). Paths of effects of early childhood intervention on educational attainment and delinquency: A confirmatory analysis of the Chicago Child-Parent Centers. *Child Development, 75*, 1299–1328.

Reynolds, A. J., Temple, J. A., Robertson, D. L., & Mann, E. A. (2001). Long-term effects of an early childhood intervention on educational achievement and juvenile arrest: A 15-year follow-up of low income children in public schools. *Journal of the American Medical Association, 285*, 2339–2346.

Reznick, J. S., & Goldfield, B. A. (1992). Rapid change in lexical development in comprehension and production. *Developmental Psychology, 28*, 406–413.

Rheingold, H. L., & Cook, K. V. (1975). The contents of boys' and girls' rooms as an index of parents' behavior. *Child Development, 46*, 459–463.

Rice, K. G. (1990). Attachment in adolescence: A narrative and meta-analytic review. *Journal of Youth and Adolescence, 19*, 511–538.

Rice, M. L. (1983). The role of television in language acquisition. *Developmental Review, 3*, 211–224.

Rice, M. L., Huston, A. C., Truglio, R., & Wright, J. (1990). Words from "Sesame Street": Learning vocabulary while viewing. *Developmental Psychology, 26*, 421–428.

Rice, M. L., & Woodsmall, L. (1988). Lessons from television: Children's word learning when viewing. *Child Development, 59*, 420–429.

Richards, H. G., Frentzen, B., Gerhardt, K. J., McCann, M. E., & Abrams, R. M. (1992). Sound levels in the human uterus. *Obstetrics and Gynecology, 80*, 186–190.

Richards, J. E., & Holley, F. B. (1999). Infant attention and the development of smooth pursuit tracking. *Developmental Psychology, 35*, 856–867.

Richards, M. H., Crowe, P. A., Larson, R., & Swarr, A. (1998). Developmental patterns and gender differences in the experience of peer companionship during adolescence. *Child Development, 69*, 154–163.

Richards, M. H., & Duckett, E. (1994). The relationship of maternal employment to early adolescent daily experience with and without parents. *Child Development, 65*, 225–236.

Rimoin, D. L., Connor, J. M., Pyeritz, R. E., & Korf, B. R. (2002). Nature and frequency of genetic disease. In D. L. Rimoin, J. M. Connor, R. E. Pyeritz, & B. R. Korf (Eds.), *Emery and Rimoin's principles and practice of medical genetics* (4th ed., Vol. 1, pp. 55–59). London: Churchill Livingston.

Ris, M. D., Williams, S. E., Hunt, M. M., Berry, H. K., & Leslie, N. (1994). Early-treated phenylketonuria: Adult neuropsychologic outcome. *Journal of Pediatrics, 124*, 388–392.

Robbins, W. J., Brody, S., Hogan, A. G., Jackson, C. M., & Green, C. W. (Eds.). (1928). *Growth*. New Haven: Yale University Press.

Roberts, D. F., & Foehr, U. G. (2004). *Kids and media in America*. New York: Cambridge University Press.

Roberts, D. F., Foehr, U. G., & Rideout, V. (2005). *Generation M: Media in the lives of 8- to 18-year-olds*. Menlo Park, CA: Kaiser Family Foundation.

Roberts, D. F., Foehr, U. G., Rideout, V. J., & Brodie, M. (1999). *Kids and media at the new millennium: A comprehensive national analysis of children's media use*. Menlo Park, CA: The Henry J. Kaiser Family Foundation.

Roberts, L. (1991). Does the egg beckon sperm when the time is right? *Science, 252*, 214.

Roberts, W., & Strayer, J. (1996). Empathy, emotional expressiveness, and prosocial behavior. *Child Development, 67*, 449–470.

Robin, D. J., Berthier, N. E., & Clifton, R. K. (1996). Infants' predictive reaching for moving objects in the dark. *Developmental Psychology, 32*, 824–835.

Robinson, A., & Clinkenbeard, P. R. (1998). Giftedness: An exceptionality examined. *Annual Review of Psychology, 49*, 117–139.

Robinson, J. L., Kagan, J., Reznick, J. S., & Corley, R. (1992). The heritability of inhibited and uninhibited behavior: A twin study. *Developmental Psychology, 28*, 1030–1037.

Robinson, J. L., Zahn-Waxler, C., & Emde, R. N. (1994). Patterns of development in early empathic behavior: Environmental and child constitutional influences. *Social Development, 3*, 125–145.

Robinson, T. N. (2001). Television viewing and childhood obesity. *Pediatric Clinics of North America, 48*, 1017–1026.

Robinson, T. N., Chang, J. Y., Haydel, K. F., & Killen, J. D. (2001). Overweight concerns and body dissatisfaction among third-grade children: The impacts of ethnicity and socioeconomic status. *Journal of Pediatrics, 138*, 181–187.

Rochat, P. (1993). Hand-mouth coordination in the newborn: Morphology, determinants, and early development of a basic act. In G. J. P. Savelsbergh (Ed.), *The development of coordination in infancy* (pp. 265–288). Amsterdam, The Netherlands: Elsevier.

Rochat, P. (2001). *The infant's social world*. Cambridge, MA: Harvard University Press.

Rochat, P., & Goubet, N. (1995). Development of sitting and reaching in 5- to 6-month-old infants. *Infant Behavior and Development, 18*, 53–68.

Rochat, P., & Morgan, R. (1995). Spatial determinants in perception of self-produced leg movements by 3- to 5-month-old infants. *Developmental Psychology, 31*, 626–636.

Rochat, P., & Morgan, R. (1998). Two functional orientations of self-exploration in infancy. *British Journal of Developmental Psychology, 16*, 139–154.

Rochat, P., & Striano, T. (1999). Social-cognitive development in the first year. In P. Rochat (Ed.), *Early social cognition: Understanding in the first months of life* (pp. 3–34). Mahwah, NJ: Erlbaum.

Rochat, P., & Striano, T. (2002). Who's in the mirror? Self-other discrimination in specular images by four- and nine-month-old infants. *Child Development, 73*, 35–46.

Roffwarg, H. P., Muzio, J. N., & Dement, W. C. (1966). Ontogenetic development of the human sleep-dream cycle. *Science, 152*, 604–619.

Rogeness, G. A., & McClure, E. B. (1996). Development and neurotransmitter-environmental interactions. *Development and Psychopathology, 8,* 183–199.

Rogoff, B. (1981). Schooling and the development of cognitive skills. In H. C. Triandis & A. Heron (Eds.), *Handbook of cross-cultural psychology: Developmental psychology* (Vol. 4). Boston: Allyn & Bacon.

Rogoff, B. (1998). Cognition as a collaborative process. In W. Damon (Series Ed.) & D. Kuhn & R. S. Siegler (Vol. Eds.), *Handbook of child psychology: Vol. 2. Cognition, perception, and language* (5th ed., pp. 679–744). New York: Wiley.

Rogoff, B., Mistry, J., Göncü, A., & Mosier, C. (1993). Guided participation in cultural activity by toddlers and caregivers. *Monographs of the Society for Research in Child Development, 58*(8, Serial No. 236).

Roid, G. (2003). *Stanford-Binet Intelligence Scales.* Boston: Houghton Mifflin.

Rönnqvist, L., & von Hofsten, C. (1994). Neonatal finger and arm movements as determined by a social and an object context. *Early Development & Parenting, 3,* 81–94.

Rosch, E., Mervis, C. B., Gray, W. D., Johnson, D. M., & Boyes-Braem, P. (1976). Basic objects in natural categories. *Cognitive Psychology, 8,* 382–439.

Roschelle, J. M., Pea, R. D., Hoadley, C. M., Gordin, D. N., & Means, B. M. (2000, Fall/Winter). Changing how and what children learn in school with computer-based technologies. *Future of Children, 10*(2), 76–101.

Rose, A. J., & Asher, S. R. (1999). Children's goals and strategies in response to conflicts within a friendship. *Developmental Psychology, 35,* 69–79.

Rose, A. J., & Asher, S. R. (2004). Children's strategies and goals in response to help-giving and help-seeking tasks within a friendship. *Child Development, 75,* 749–763.

Rose, A. J., Swenson, L. P., & Waller, E. M. (2004). Overt and relational aggression and perceived popularity: Developmental differences in concurrent and prospective relations. *Developmental Psychology, 40,* 378–387.

Rose, S. A., Feldman, J. F., & Jankowski, J. J. (2001). Visual short-term memory in the first year of life: Capacity and recency effects. *Developmental Psychology, 37,* 539–549.

Rose, S. A., Gottfried, A. W., & Bridger, W. H. (1981). Cross-modal transfer in 6-month-old infants. *Developmental Psychology, 17,* 661–669.

Rosen, K. S., & Burke, P. B. (1999). Multiple attachment relationships within families: Mothers and fathers with two young children. *Developmental Psychology, 35,* 436–444.

Rosenberg, K. R., & Trevathen, W. R. (2001, November). The evolution of human birth. *Scientific American, 285,* 72–77.

Rosengren, K. S., Gelman, S. A., Kalish, C. W., & McCormick, M. (1991). As time goes by: Children's early understanding of growth in animals. *Child Development, 62,* 1302–1320.

Rosenkoetter, L. I. (1973). Resistance to temptation: Inhibitory and disinhibitory effects of models. *Developmental Psychology, 8,* 80–84.

Rosenthal, R., & Jacobson, L. (1968). *Pygmalion in the classroom: Teacher expectation and pupils' intellectual development.* New York: Holt, Rinehart & Winston.

Ross, G. S. (1980). Categorization in infancy. *Developmental Psychology, 16,* 391–396.

Roth, J., & Brooks-Gunn, J. (2000). What do adolescents need for healthy development? Implications for youth policy. *Social Policy Report, 14,* 3–19.

Rothbart, M. K. (1986). Longitudinal home observations of infant temperament. *Developmental Psychology, 22,* 356–365.

Rothbart, M. K., Ahadi, S. A., & Evans, D. E. (2000). Temperament and personality: Origins and outcomes. *Journal of Personality and Social Psychology, 78,* 122–135.

Rothbart, M. K., Ahadi, S. A., & Hershey, K. L. (1994). Temperament and social behavior in childhood. *Merrill-Palmer Quarterly, 40,* 21–39.

Rothbart, M. K., & Bates, J. E. (2006). Temperament. In W. Damon & R. M. Lerner (Editors-in-Chief) & N. Eisenberg (Vol. Ed.), *Handbook of child psychology: Vol. 3. Social, emotional, and personality development* (6th ed., pp. 99–166). Hoboken, NJ: Wiley.

Rothbart, M. K., Derryberry, D., & Posner, M. I. (1994). A psychobiological approach to the development of temperament. In J. E. Bates & T. D. Wachs (Eds.), *Temperament: Individual differences at the interface of biology and behavior* (pp. 83–116). Washington, DC: American Psychological Association.

Rothbaum, F., Weisz, J., Pott, M., Miyake, K., & Morelli, G. (2000). Attachment and culture: Security in the United States and Japan. *American Psychologist, 55,* 1093–1104.

Rothberg, A. D., & Lits, B. (1991). Psychosocial support for maternal stress during pregnancy: Effect on birth weight. *American Journal of Obstetrics and Gynecology, 165,* 403–407.

Rouse, B., Matalon, R., Koch, R., Azen, C., Levy, H., Hanley, W., et al. (2000). Maternal phenylketonuria syndrome: Congenital heart defects, microcephaly, and developmental outcomes. *Journal of Pediatrics, 136,* 57–61.

Rousseau, J. J. (1895). *Émile or treatise on education* (W. H. Payne, Trans.). New York: Appleton. (Original work published 1762)

Rovee-Collier, C. (1999). The development of infant memory. *Current Directions in Psychological Science, 8,* 80–85.

Rovee-Collier, C. K. (1987). Learning and memory in infancy. In J. D. Osofsky (Ed.), *Handbook of infant development* (2nd ed., pp. 98–148). New York: Wiley.

Rovee-Collier, C. K., & Hayne, H. (1987). Reactivation of infant memory: Implications for cognitive development. In H. W. Reese (Ed.), *Advances in child development and behavior* (Vol. 20, pp. 185–238). San Diego, CA: Academic Press.

Rovee-Collier, C., Schechter, A., Shyi, G. C. W., & Shields, P. (1992). Perceptual identification of contextual attributes and infant memory retrieval. *Developmental Psychology, 28,* 307–318.

Rovee-Collier, C. K., & Shyi, G. (1992). A functional and cognitive analysis of infant long-term retention. In M. L. Howe, C. J. Brainerd, & V. F. Reyna (Eds.), *Development of long-term retention* (pp. 3–55). New York: Springer-Verlag.

Rowe, D. C., Jacobson, K. C., & Van den Oord, E. J. C. G. (1999). Genetic and environmental influences on vocabulary IQ: Parental education level as moderator. *Child Development, 70,* 1151–1162.

Rozin, P. (1990). Development in the food domain. *Developmental Psychology, 26,* 555–562.

Rubin, K. H. (1993). The Waterloo Longitudinal Project: Correlates and consequences of social withdrawal from childhood to adolescence. In K. H. Rubin & J. B. Asendorpf (Eds.), *Social withdrawal, inhibition, and shyness in childhood* (pp. 291–314). Hillsdale, NJ: Erlbaum.

Rubin, K. H., & Asendorpf, J. B. (1993). Social withdrawal, inhibition, and shyness in childhood: Conceptual and definitional issues. In K. H. Rubin & J. B. Asendorpf (Eds.), *Social withdrawal, inhibition, and shyness in childhood* (pp. 3–17). Hillsdale, NJ: Erlbaum.

Rubin, K. H., Bukowski, W., & Parker, J. G. (1998). Peer interactions, relationships, and groups. In W. Damon (Series Ed.) & N. Eisenberg (Vol. Ed.), *Handbook of child psychology. Vol. 3. Social, emotional, and personality development* (5th ed., pp. 619–700). New York: Wiley.

Rubin, K. H., Burgess, K. B., Dwyer, K. M., & Hastings, P. D. (2003). Predicting preschoolers' externalizing behaviors from toddler temperament, conflict, and maternal negativity. *Developmental Psychology, 39,* 164–176.

Rubin, K. H., Fein, G. G., & Vandenberg, B. (1983). Play. In E. M. Hetherington (Ed.), *Handbook of child psychology: Vol. IV. Socialization, personality, and social development* (4th ed., pp. 693–744). New York: Wiley.

Rubin, K. H., Hymel, S., & Mills, R. S. L. (1989). Sociability and social withdrawal in childhood: Stability and outcomes. *Journal of Personality, 57,* 238–255.

Rubin, K. H., & Krasnor, L. R. (1986). Social-cognitive and social behavioral perspectives on problem-solving. In M. Perlmutter (Ed.), *The Minnesota symposia on child psychology: Vol. 18. Cognitive perspectives on children's social and behavioral development.* Hillsdale, NJ: Erlbaum.

Rubin, K. H., Lynch, D., Coplan, R., Rose-Krasnor, L., & Booth, C. L. (1994). "Birds of a feather…": Behavioral concordances and preferential personal attraction in children. *Child Development, 65,* 1778–1785.

Rubin, K. H., Maioni, T. L., & Hornung, M. (1976). Free play behaviors in middle- and lower-class preschoolers: Parten and Piaget revisited. *Child Development, 47,* 414–419.

Ruble, D. N. (1983). The development of social-comparison processes and their role in achievement-related self-socialization. In E. T. Higgins, D. Ruble, & W. W. Hartup (Eds.), *Social cognition and social development: A sociocultural perspective.* Cambridge, UK: Cambridge University Press.

Ruble, D. N. (1987). The acquisition of self-knowledge: A self-socialization perspective. In N. Eisenberg (Ed.), *Contemporary topics in developmental psychology.* New York: Wiley.

Ruble, D. N., Boggiano, A. K., Feldman, N. S., & Loebl, J. H. (1980). Developmental analysis of the role of social comparison in self-evaluation. *Developmental Psychology, 16,* 105–115.

Ruble, D. N., & Brooks-Gunn, J. (1982). The experience of menarche. *Child Development, 53,* 1557–1566.

Ruble, D. N., Eisenberg, R., & Higgins, E. T. (1994). Developmental changes in achievement evaluation: Motivational implications of self-other differences. *Child Development, 65,* 1095–1110.

Ruble, D. N., & Flett, G. L. (1988). Conflicting goals in self-evaluative information seeking: Developmental and ability level analyses. *Child Development, 59,* 97–106.

Ruble, D. N., Martin, C. L., & Berenbaum, S. A. (2006). Gender development. In W. Damon & R. M. Lerner (Editors-in-Chief) & N. Eisenberg (Vol. Ed.), *Handbook of child psychology: Vol. 3. Social, emotional, and personality development* (6th ed., pp. 858–932). Hoboken, NJ: Wiley.

Rudolph, K. D., Caldwell, M., & Conley, C. S. (2005). Need for approval and children's well-being. *Child Development, 76,* 309–323.

Rudolph, K. D., & Hammen, C. (1999). Age and gender as determinants of stress exposure, generation, and reactions in youngsters: A transactional perspective. *Child Development, 70,* 660–677.

Rudolph, K. D., Hammen, C., & Burge, D. (1995). Cognitive representations of self, family, and peers in school-age children: Links with social competence and sociometric status. *Child Development, 66,* 1385–1402.

Rudolph, K. D., Lambert, S. F., Clark, A. G., & Kurlakowsky, K. D. (2001). Negotiating the transition to middle school: The role of self-regulatory processes. *Child Development, 72,* 929–946.

Ruff, H. A., & Kohler, C. J. (1978). Tactual visual transfer in 6-month-old infants. *Infant Behavior and Development, 1,* 259–264.

Ruff, H. A., & Rothbart, M. K. (1996). *Attention and early development: Themes and variations.* New York: Oxford University Press.

Ruffman, T., Slade, L., & Crowe, E. (2002). The relation between children's and mothers' mental state language and thoery-of-mind understanding. *Child Development, 73,* 734–751.

Rumbaugh, D. M., Gill, T. V., & von Glasersfeld, E. C. (1973). Reading and sentence completion by a chimpanzee (*Pan*). *Science, 182,* 731–733.

Runyan, D. K., Hunter, W. M., Socolar, R. R. S., Amaya-Jackson, L., English, D., Landsverk, J., et al. (1998). Children who prosper in unfavorable environments: The relationship to social capital. *Pediatrics, 101,* 12–18.

Rutter, M. (1983). School effects on pupil progress: Research findings and policy implications. *Child Development, 54,* 1–29.

Rutter, M. (1986). Meyerian psychobiology, personality development, and the role of life experiences. *American Journal of Psychiatry, 143,* 1077–1087.

Rutter, M. (1990). Psychosocial resilience and protective mechanisms. In J. Rolf, A. S. Masten, D. Cicchetti, K. H. Neuchterlein, & S. Weintraub (Eds.), *Risk and protective factors in the development of psychopathology* (pp. 79–101). New York: Cambridge University Press.

Rutter, M. (1991). Age changes in depressive disorders: Some developmental considerations. In J. Garber & K. A. Dodge (Eds.), *The development of emotion regulation and dysregulation* (pp. 273–300). Cambridge, UK: Cambridge University Press.

Rutter, M. (2002). Nature, nurture, and development: From evangelism through science toward policy and practice. *Child Development, 73,* 1–21.

Rutter, M. (2003). Commentary: Causal processes leading to antisocial behavior. *Developmental Psychology, 39,* 372–378.

Rutter, M., & Garmezy, N. (1983). Developmental psychopathology. In E. M. Hetherington (Ed.), *Handbook of child psychology: Vol. IV. Socialization, personality, and social development* (4th ed., pp. 775–911). New York: Wiley.

Rutter, M., & Madge, N. (1976). *Cycles of disadvantage.* London: Heinemann.

Rutter, M., & Silberg, J. (2002). Gene-environment interplay in relation to emotional and behavioral disturbance. *Annual Review of Psychology, 53,* 463–490.

Rutter, M., Silberg, J., O'Connor, T., & Simonoff, E. (1999a). Genetics and child psychiatry: I. Advances in quantitative and molecular genetics. *Journal of Child Psychology and Psychiatry, 40,* 3–18.

Rutter, M., Silberg, J., O'Connor, T., & Simonoff, E. (1999b). Genetics and child psychiatry: II. Empirical research findings. *Journal of Child Psychology and Psychiatry, 40,* 19–55.

Ryan, R. M., & Grolnick, W. S. (1986). Origins and pawns in the classroom: Self-report and projective assessments of individual differences in children's perceptions. *Journal of Personality and Social Psychology, 50,* 550–558.

Saarni, C. (1998). Issues of cultural meaningfulness in emotional development. *Developmental Psychology, 34,* 647–652.

Saarni, C. (1999). *The development of emotional competence.* New York: Guilford.

Saarni, C., Campos, J. J., Camras, L. A., & Witherington, D. (2006). Emotional development: Action, communication, and understanding. In W. Damon & R. M. Lerner (Editors-in-Chief) & N. Eisenberg (Vol. Ed.), *Handbook of child psychology: Vol. 3. Social, emotional, and personality development* (6th ed., pp. 226–299). Hoboken, NJ: Wiley.

Saarni, C., Mumme, D. L., & Campos, J. L. (1998). Emotional development: Action, communication, and understanding. In W. Damon (Series Ed.) & N. Eisenberg (Vol. Ed.), *Handbook of child psychology: Vol. 3. Social, emotional, and personality development* (5th ed., pp. 237–309). New York: Wiley.

Sachs, S. (2001, August 15). Clinic's pitch to Indian emigres: It's a boy. *New York Times,* pp. A1, B6.

Sadker, M. & Sadker, D. (1994). *Failing at fairness: How America's schools cheat girls.* New York: Charles Scribner's Sons.

Sadler, T. M. (2004). *Langman's medical embryology* (9th ed.). Philadelphia: Lippincott Williams & Wilkins.

Saffran, J. R. (2001). Words in a sea of sounds: The output of infant statistical learning. *Cognition, 81,* 149–169.

Saffran, J. R., Aslin, R. N., & Newport, E. (1996). Statistical learning by 8-month-olds. *Science, 274,* 1926–1928.

Saffran, J. R., & Griepentrog, G. J. (2001). Absolute pitch in infant auditory learning: Evidence for developmental reorganization. *Developmental Psychology, 37,* 74–85.

Saffran, J. R., Loman, M. M., & Robertson, R. R. W. (2000). Infant memory for musical experiences. *Cognition, 77,* B15–B23.

Saffran, J. R., Werker, J. F., & Werner, L. A. (2006). The infant's auditory world: Hearing, speech, and the beginnings of language. In W. Damon & R. M. Lerner (Editors-in-Chief) & D. M. Kuhn & R. S. Siegler (Vol. Eds.), *Handbook of child psychology: Vol. 2. Cognition, perception, and language* (6th ed., pp. 58–108). Hoboken, NJ: Wiley.

Sagi, A., Lamb, M. E., Lewkowicz, K. S., Shoham, R., Dvir, R., & Estes, D. (1985). Security of infant-mother, -father, and -metapelet attachments among kibbutz-reared Israeli children. In I. Bretherton & E. Waters (Eds.), *Growing points of attachment theory and research. Monographs of the Society for Research in Child Development, 50*(1–2, Serial No. 209).

Sagi, A., Van IJzendoorn, M. H., Aviezer, O., Donnell, F., & Mayseless, O. (1994). Sleeping out of home in a kibbutz communal arrangement: It makes a difference for mother-child attachment. *Child Development, 65,* 991–1004.

Saigal, S., Hoult, L. A., Streiner, D. L., Stoskopf, B. L., & Rosenbaum, P. L. (2000). School difficulties at adolescence in a regional cohort of children who were extremely low birth weight. *Pediatrics, 105,* 325–331.

Sakala, C. (1993). Midwifery care and out-of-hospital birth settings: How do they reduce unnecessary cesarean section births? *Social Science and Medicine, 37,* 1233–1250.

Salapatek, P. (1975). Pattern perception in early infancy. In L. B. Cohen & P. Salapatek (Eds.), *Infant perception: From sensation to cognition* (Vol. 1). New York: Academic Press.

Salzinger, S., Feldman, R. S., Hammer, M., & Rosario, M. (1993). The effects of physical abuse on children's social relationships. *Child Development, 64,* 169–187.

Samarapungavan, A. (1992). Children's judgments in theory choice tasks: Scientific rationality in childhood. *Cognition, 45,* 1–32.

Sameroff, A. J. (1972). Learning and adaptation in infancy: A comparison of models. In H. W. Reese (Ed.), *Advances in child development and behavior* (Vol. 7). New York: Academic Press.

Sameroff, A. J. (1994). Developmental systems and family functioning. In R. D. Parke & S. G. Kellam (Eds.), *Exploring family relationships with other social contexts* (pp. 199–214). Hillsdale, NJ: Erlbaum.

Sameroff, A. J. (2005). The science of infancy: Academic, social, and political agendas. *Infancy, 7,* 219–242.

Sameroff, A. J., & Chandler, P. J. (1975). Reproductive risk and the continuum of caretaking casualty. In F. D. Horowitz (Ed.), *Review of child development research* (Vol. 4, pp. 187–244). Chicago: University of Chicago Press.

Sampson, P. D., Streissguth, A. P., Bookstein, F. L., Little, R. E., Clarren, S. K., Dehaene, P., et al. (1997). The incidence of fetal alcohol syndrome and the prevalence of alcohol-related neurodevelopmental disorder. *Teratology, 56,* 317–326.

Sampson, R. J., Raudenbush, S. W., & Earls, F. (1997). Neighborhoods and violent crime: A multilevel study of collective efficacy. *Science, 277,* 918–924.

Samuels, M., & Samuels, N. (1996). *The new well pregnancy book.* New York: Simon & Schuster.

Samuelson, L. K., & Smith, L. B. (1998). Memory and attention make smart word learning: An alternative account of Akhtar, Carpenter, and Tomasello. *Child Development, 69,* 94–104.

Samuelson, L. K., & Smith, L. B. (2000). Children's attention to rigid and deformable shape in naming and non-naming tasks. *Child Development, 71,* 1555–1570.

Sandberg, D. E., Brook, A. E., & Campos, S. P. (1994). Short stature: A psychosocial burden requiring growth hormone therapy? *Pediatrics, 94,* 832–840.

Sandberg, D. E., Meyer-Bahlburg, H. F., Ehrhardt, A. A., & Yager, T. J. (1993). The prevalence of gender-atypical behavior in elementary school. *Journal of the American Academy of Child and Adolescent Psychiatry, 32,* 306–314.

Sandberg, E. H., & Huttenlocher, J. (2001). Advanced spatial skills and advance planning: Components of 6-year-olds' navigational map use. *Journal of Cognition and Development, 2,* 51–70.

Sanders, C. E., Field, T. M., Diego, M., & Kaplan, M. (2000). The relationship of Internet use to depression and social isolation among adolescents. *Adolescence, 35,* 237–242.

Santrock, J. W., & Sitterle, K. A. (1987). Parent-child relationships in step-mother families. In K. Pasley & M. Ihinger-Tallman (Eds.), *Remarriage and stepparenting: Current research and theory.* New York: Guilford Press.

Saudino, K. J. (1997). Moving beyond the heritability question: New directions in behavioral genetic studies of personality. *Current Directions in Psychological Science, 6,* 86–90.

Savage, D. D., Becher, M., de la Torre, A. J., & Sutherland, R. J. (2002). Dose-dependent effects of prenatal ethanol exposure on synaptic plasticity and learning in mature offspring. *Alcoholism: Clinical and Experimental Research, 26,* 1752–1758.

Savage-Rumbaugh, E. S., Murphy, J., Sevcik, R. A., Brakke, K. E., Williams, S. L., & Rumbaugh, D. M. (1993). Language comprehension in ape and child. *Monographs of the Society for Research in Child Development, 58*(3–4, Serial No. 233).

Sawin, D. B., & Parke, R. D. (1979). The effects of interagent inconsistent discipline on children's aggressive behavior. *Journal of Experimental Child Psychology, 28,* 525–538.

Saxe, G. B., Guberman, S. R., & Gearhart, M. (1987). Social processes in early number development. *Monographs of the Society for Research in Child Development, 52* (2, Serial No. 216).

Saxton, M. (1997). The contrast theory of negative input. *Journal of Child Language, 24,* 139–161.

Scaramella, L. V., Conger, R. D., & Simons, R. L. (1999). Parental protective influences and gender-specific increases in adolescent internalizing and externalizing problems. *Journal of Research on Adolescence, 9,* 111–141.

Scaramella, L. V., Conger, R. D., Spoth, R., & Simons, R. L. (2002). Evaluation of a social contextual model of delinquency: A cross-study replication. *Child Development, 73,* 175–195.

Scarborough, H. S., & Dobrich, W. (1993). On the efficacy of reading to preschoolers. *Developmental Review, 14,* 245–302.

Scarr, S. (1992). Developmental theories for the 1990s: Development and individual differences. *Child Development, 63,* 1–19.

Scarr, S. (1993). Biological and cultural diversity: The legacy of Darwin for development. *Child Development, 64,* 1333–1353.

Scarr, S., & McCartney, K. (1983). How people make their own environments: A theory of genotype environment effects. *Child Development, 54,* 424–435.

Scarr, S., & Weinberg, R. A. (1976). IQ test performance of black children adopted by white families. *American Psychologist, 31,* 726–739.

Scarr, S., & Weinberg, R. A. (1977). Intellectual similarities within families of both adopted and biological children. *Intelligence, 1,* 170–191.

Scarr, S., & Weinberg, R. A. (1978). The influence of "family background" on intellectual attainment. *American Sociological Review, 43,* 674–692.

Scarr, S., & Weinberg, R. A. (1983). The Minnesota adoption studies: Genetic differences and malleability. *Child Development, 54,* 260–267.

Schachar, R., Mota, V., Logan, G. D., Tannock, R., & Klim, P. (2000). Confirmation of an inhibitory control deficit in attention-deficit/hyperactivity disorder. *Journal of Abnormal Child Psychology, 28,* 227–235.

Schachter, F. F. (1982). Sibling deidentification and split-parent identification: A family tetrad. In M. E. Lamb & B. Sutton-Smith (Eds.), *Sibling relationships: Their nature and significance across the life-span.* Hillsdale, NJ: Erlbaum.

Schaffer, H. R., & Emerson, P. E. (1964). The development of social attachments in infancy. *Monographs of the Society for Research in Child Development, 29*(3, Serial No. 94).

Schauble, L. (1996). The development of scientific reasoning in knowledge-rich contexts. *Developmental Psychology, 32,* 102–119.

Scheper-Hughes, N. (1992). *Death without weeping: The violence of everyday life in Brazil.* Berkeley: University of California Press.

Schieffelin, B. B., & Ochs, E. (1983). A cultural perspective on the transition from prelinguistic to linguistic communication. In R. M. Golinkoff (Ed.), *The transition from prelinguistic to linguistic communication.* Hillsdale, NJ: Erlbaum.

Schlegel, A., & Barry, H. III. (1991). *Adolescence: An anthropological inquiry.* New York: Free Press.

Schlinger, H.D., Jr. (1992). Theory in behavior analysis: An application to child development. *American Psychologist, 47,* 1396–1410.

Schmitt, K. L., Anderson, D. R., & Collins, P. A. (1999). Form and content: Looking at visual features of television. *Developmental Psychology, 35,* 1156–1167.

Schmuckler, M. A., & Fairhall, J. L. (2001). Visual-proprioceptive intermodal perception using point light displays. *Child Development, 72,* 949–962.

Schneider, B. H., Atkinson, L., & Tardif, C. (2001). Child-parent attachment and children's peer relations: A quantitative review. *Developmental Psychology, 37,* 86–100.

Schneider, W. (2000). Research on memory development: Historical trends and current themes. *International Journal of Behavioral Development, 24,* 407–420.

Schneider, W., & Lockl, K. (2002). The development of metacognitive knowledge in children and adolescents. In B. L. Schwartz & T. J. Perfect (Eds.), *Applied metacognition* (pp. 224–260). Cambridge, UK: Cambridge University Press.

Schneider-Rosen, K., Braunwald, K., Carlson, V., & Cicchetti, D. (1985). Current perspectives on attachment theory: Illustrations from the study of maltreated infants. In I. Bretherton & E. Waters (Eds.), *Growing points of attachment theory and research. Monographs of the Society for Research in Child Development, 50*(1–2, Serial No. 209).

Scholmerich, A., Fracasso, M. P., Lamb, M. E., & Broberg, A. (1995). Interactional harmony at 7- and 10-months-of-age predicts security of attachment as measured by Q-sort ratings. *Social Development, 4,* 62–74.

Schore, A. N. (1994). *Affect regulation and the origin of the self: The neurobiology of emotional development.* Hillsdale, NJ: Erlbaum.

Schore, A. N. (1996). The experience-dependent maturation of a regulatory system in the orbital prefrontal cortex and the origin of developmental psychopathology. *Development and Psychopathology, 8,* 59–87.

Schreck, R., & Silverman, N. (2002). Fetal loss. In D. L. Rimoin, J. M. Connor, R. E. Pyeritz, & B. R. Korf (Eds.), *Emery and Rimoin's principles and practice of medical genetics* (4th ed., Vol. 1, pp. 982–997). London: Churchill Livingston.

Schulenberg, J., Asp, C. E., & Petersen, A. (1984). School from the young adolescent's perspective: A descriptive report. *Journal of Early Adolescence, 4,* 107–130.

Schulting, A. B., Malone, P. S., & Dodge, K. A. (2005). The effect of school-based kindergarten transition policies and practices on child academic outcomes. *Developmental Psychology, 41,* 860–871.

Schwartz, D., Chang, L., & Farver, J. M. (2001). Correlates of victimization in Chinese children's peer groups. *Developmental Psychology, 37,* 520–532.

Schwartz, D., Dodge, K. A., & Coie, J. D. (1993). The emergence of chronic peer victimization in boys' play groups. *Child Development, 64,* 1755–1772.

Schwartz, D., Dodge, K. A., Pettit, G. S., Bates, J. E., & Conduct Problems Prevention Research Group. (2000). Friendship as a moderating factor in the pathway between early harsh home environment and later victimization in the peer group. *Developmental Psychology, 36,* 646–662.

Scott, K. D., Berkowitz, G., & Klaus, M. (1999). A comparison of intermittent and continuous support during labor: A meta-analysis. *American Journal of Obstetrics and Gynecology, 180,* 1054–1059.

Scoville, R. (1983). Development of the intention to communicate: The eye of the beholder. In L. Feagans, C. Garvey, & R. Golinkoff (Eds.), *The origins and growth of communication.* Norwood, NJ: Ablex.

Scriver, C. R., Beaudet, A. L., Sly, W. S., & Valle, D. (2001). *The metabolic and molecular bases of inherited disease* (8th ed., Vol. 1). New York: McGraw-Hill.

Sebanc, A. M. (2003). The friendship features of preschool children: Links with prosocial behavior and aggression. *Social Development, 12,* 249–268.

Secker-Walker, R. H., Vacek, P. M., Flynn, B. S., & Mead, P. B. (1997). Smoking in pregnancy, exhaled carbon monoxide, and birth weight. *Obstetrics and Gynecology, 89,* 648–653.

Segall, M. H., Campbell, D. T., & Herskovits, M. J. (1966). *The influence of culture on perception.* New York: Bobbs-Merrill.

Seidman, E., Allen, L., Aber, J. L., Mitchell, C., & Feinman, J. (1994). The impact of school transitions in early adolescence on the self-system and perceived social context of poor urban youth. *Child Development, 65,* 507–522.

Seitz, V., & Apfel, N. H. (1994). Effects of a school for pregnant students on the incidence of low-birthweight deliveries. *Child Development, 65,* 666–676.

Selman, R. L. (1980). *The growth of interpersonal understanding: Developmental and clinical analysis.* New York: Academic Press.

Selzer, J. A. (1991). Relationships between fathers and children who live apart: The father's role after separation. *Journal of Marriage and the Family, 53,* 79–101.

Senghas, A., & Coppola, M. (2001). Children creating language: How Nicaraguan Sign Language acquired a spatial grammar. *Psychological Science, 12,* 323–328.

Serbin, L. A., Connor, J. M., & Iler, I. (1979). Sex-stereotyped and nonstereotyped introductions of new toys in the preschool classroom: An observational study of teacher behavior and its effects. *Psychology of Women Quarterly, 4,* 261–265.

Serbin, L. A., O'Leary, K. D., Kent, R. N., & Tonick, I. J. (1973). A comparison of teacher response to the preacademic and problem behavior of boys and girls. *Child Development, 44,* 796–804.

Serbin, L. A., Poulin-Dubois, D., Colburne, K. A., Sen, M. G., & Eichstedt, J. A. (2001). Gender stereotyping in infancy: Visual preferences for and knowledge of gender-stereotyped toys in the second year. *International Journal of Behavioral Development, 25,* 7–15.

Serbin, L. A., Powlishta, K. K., & Gulko, J. (1993). The development of sex typing in middle childhood. *Monographs of the Society for Research in Child Development, 58* (No. 2, Serial No. 232).

Serbin, L. A., Tonick, I. J., & Sternglanz, S. H. (1977). Shaping cooperative cross-sex play. *Child Development, 48,* 924–929.

Shachar, H., & Sharan, S. (1994). Talking, relating, and achieving: Effects of cooperative learning and whole-class instruction. *Cognition and Instruction, 12,* 313–353.

Shah, N. R., & Bracken, M. B. (2000). A systematic review and meta-analysis of prospective studies on the association between maternal cigarette smoking and preterm delivery. *American Journal of Obstetrics and Gynecology, 182,* 465–472.

Shahar, S. (1990). *Childhood in the Middle Ages.* London: Routledge.

Shannon, J. D., Tamis-LeMonda, C. S., & Margolin, A. (2005). Father involvement in infancy: Influences of past and current relationships. *Infancy, 8,* 21–41.

Shantz, C. (1983). Social cognition. In J. H. Flavell & E. M. Markman (Eds.), *Handbook of child psychology: Vol. III. Cognitive development* (4th ed., pp. 495–555). New York: Wiley.

Sharma, A. R., McGue, M. K., & Benson, P. L. (1998). The psychological adjustment of United States adopted adolescents and their nonadopted siblings. *Child Development, 69,* 791–802.

Sharon, T. (2005). Made to symbolize: Intentionality and children's early understanding of symbols. *Journal of Cognition and Development, 6,* 163–178.

Sharp, D., Cole, M., & Lave, C. (1979). Education and cognitive development: The evidence from experimental research. *Monographs of the Society for Research in Child Development, 44*(1–2, Serial No. 178).

Shatz, M., & Gelman, R. (1973). The development of communication skills: Modification in the speech of young children as a function of listener. *Monographs of the Society for Research in Child Development, 38*(5, Serial No. 152).

Shaw, E., & Darling, J. (1985). *Strategies of being female.* Brighton, UK: Harvester Press.

Shepard, L. A., & Smith, M. L. (1986). Synthesis of research on school readiness and kindergarten retention. *Educational Leadership, 44,* 78–86.

Sherif, M., Harvey, O. J., White, B. J., Hood, W. R., & Sherif, C. W. (1961). *Inter-group conflict and cooperation: The Robber's Cave experiment.* Norman: University of Oklahoma Press.

Shinskey, J. L., & Munakata, Y. (2001). Detecting transparent barriers: Clear evidence against the means-end deficit account of search failures. *Infancy, 2,* 395–404.

Shoda, Y., Mischel, W., & Peake, P. K. (1990). Predicting adolescent cognitive and self-regulatory competencies from preschool delay of gratification: Identifying diagnostic conditions. *Developmental Psychology, 26,* 978–986.

Shonk, S. M., & Cicchetti, D. (2001). Maltreatment, competency deficits, and risk for academic and behavioral maladjustment. *Developmental Psychology, 37,* 3–17.

Shore, R. (1997). *Rethinking the brain: New insights into early development.* New York: Families and Work Institute.

Shostak, M. (1981). *Nisa: The life and words of a !Kung woman.* Cambridge, MA: Harvard University Press.

Shrum, W., & Cheek, N. H. (1987). Social structure during the school years: Onset of the degrouping process. *American Sociological Review, 52,* 218–223.

Shwalb, B. J., Shwalb, D. W., & Shoji, J. (1994). Structure and dimensions of maternal perceptions of Japanese infant temperament. *Developmental Psychology, 30,* 131–141.

Shwe, H. I., & Markman, E. M. (1997). Young children's appreciation of the mental impact of their communicative signals. *Developmental Psychology, 33*, 630–636.

Shweder, R., Goodnow, J., Hatano, G., LeVine, R., Markus, H., & Miller, P. (2006). The cultural psychology of development: One mind, many mentalities. In W. Damon & R. M. Lerner (Editors-in-Chief) & R. M. Lerner (Vol. Ed.), Handbook of child psychology: Vol. 1. Theoretical models of human development (6th ed., pp. 716–792). Hoboken, NJ: Wiley.

Shweder, R. A., Mahapatra, M., & Miller, J. G. (1987). Culture and moral development. In J. Kagan & S. Lamb (Eds.), *The emergence of morality in young children.* Chicago: University of Chicago Press.

Siegal, M. (1988). Children's knowledge of contagion and contamination as causes of illness. *Child Development, 59*, 1353–1359.

Siegel, L. S. (1993). Phonological processing deficits as the basis of a reading disability. *Developmental Review, 13*, 246–257.

Siegel, L. S. (1998). Phonological processing deficits and reading disabilities. In J. L. Metsala & L. C. Ehri (Eds.), *Word recognition in beginning literacy* (pp. 191–160). Mahwah, NJ: Erlbaum.

Siegler, R. S. (1989). Mechanisms of cognitive development. In M. R. Rosenzweig & L. W. Porter (Eds.), *Annual Review of Psychology, 40*, 353–379.

Siegler, R. S. (1994). Cognitive variability: A key to understanding cognitive development. *Current Directions in Psychological Science, 3*, 1–5.

Siegler, R. S. (1996). *Emerging minds: The process of change in children's thinking.* New York: Oxford University Press.

Siegler, R. S. (1997). Concepts and methods for studying cognitive change. In E. Amsel & K. A. Renninger (Eds.), *Change and development: Issues of theory, method, and application* (pp. 77–97). Mahwah, NJ: Erlbaum.

Siegler, R. S. (1998). *Children's thinking* (3rd ed.). Upper Saddle River, NJ: Prentice-Hall.

Siegler, R. S., & Crowley, K. (1991). The microgenetic method: A direct means for studying cognitive development. *American Psychologist, 46*, 606–620.

Siegler, R. S., & Ellis, S. (1996). Piaget on childhood. *Psychological Science, 7*, 211–215.

Siegler, R. S., & Jenkins, E. (1989). *How children discover new strategies.* Hillsdale, NJ: Erlbaum.

Siegler, R. S., & Richards, D. D. (1982). The development of intelligence. In R. J. Sternberg (Ed.), *Handbook of human intelligence.* Cambridge, UK: Cambridge University Press.

Siegler, R. S., & Robinson, M. (1982). The development of numerical understandings. In H. W. Reese & L. P. Lipsitt (Eds.), *Advances in child development and behavior* (Vol. 16). New York: Academic Press.

Siegler, R. S., & Shrager, J. (1984). Strategy choices in addition and subtraction: How do children know what to do? In C. Sophian (Ed.), *Origins of cognitive skills.* Hillsdale, NJ: Erlbaum.

Siegler, R. S., & Stern, E. (1998). Conscious and unconscious strategy discoveries: A microgenetic analysis. *Journal of Experimental Psychology: General, 127*, 377–397.

Signorella, M. L. (1987). Gender schemata: Individual differences and context effects. In L. S. Liben & M. L. Signorella (Eds.), *New directions for child development: No. 38. Children's gender schemata.* San Francisco: Jossey-Bass.

Signorielli, N., & Bacue, A. (1999). Recognition and respect: A content analysis of prime-time television characters across three decades. *Sex Roles, 40*, 527–544.

Silberstein, L., Gardner, H., Phelps, E., & Winner, E. (1982). Autumn leaves and old photographs: The development of metaphor preferences. *Journal of Experimental Child Psychology, 34*, 135–150.

Silk, J. S., Steinberg, L., & Morris, A. S. (2003). Adolescents' emotion regulation in daily life: Links to depressive symptoms and problem behavior. *Child Development, 74*, 1869–1880.

Silver, L. M. (1998, September 21). A quandary that isn't: Picking a baby's sex won't lead to disaster. *Time*, p. 83.

Simcock, G., & Hayne, H. (2002). Breaking the barrier? Children fail to translate their preverbal memories into language. *Psychological Science, 13*, 225–231.

Simmons, R. G., & Blyth, D. A. (1987). *Moving into adolescence: The impact of pubertal change and school context.* Hawthorne, NY: Aldine de Gruyter.

Simmons, R. G., Blyth, D. A., & McKinney, K. L. (1983). The social and psychological effects of puberty on white females. In J. Brooks-Gunn & A. C. Petersen (Eds.), *Girls at puberty.* New York: Plenum Press.

Simmons, R. G., Blyth, D. A., Van Cleave, E. F., & Bush, D. M. (1979). Entry into early adolescence: The impact of school structure, puberty, and early dating on self-esteem. *American Sociological Review, 44*, 948–967.

Simmons, R. G., Burgeson, R., Carlton-Ford, S., & Blyth, D. A. (1987). The impact of cumulative change in early adolescence. *Child Development, 58*, 1220–1234.

Simner, M. L. (1971). Newborn's response to the cry of another infant. *Developmental Psychology, 5*, 136–150.

Simon, T. J., Hespos, S. J., & Rochat, P. (1995). Do infants understand simple arithmetic? A replication of Wynn (1992). *Cognitive Development, 10*, 253–269.

Simons, R., Chao, W., Conger, R., & Elder, G. H. (2001). Quality of parenting as a mediator of the effect of childhood defiance on adolescent friendship choices and delinquency. *Journal of Marriage and Family, 63*, 63–79.

Sinclair, D. (1985). *Human growth after birth* (4th ed.). New York: Oxford University Press.

Singer, J. D., Fuller, B., Keiley, M. K., & Wolf, A. (1998). Early child-care selection: Variation by geographic location, maternal characteristics, and family structure. *Developmental Psychology, 34*, 1129–1144.

Singer, L. M., Brodzinsky, D. M., Ramsay, D., Steir, M., & Waters, E. (1985). Mother-infant attachment in adoptive families. *Child Development, 56*, 1543–1551.

Singer, L. T., Arendt, R., Minnes, S., Salvator, A., Siegel, A. C., & Lewis, B. A. (2001). Developing language skills of cocaine-exposed infants. *Pediatrics, 107*, 1057–1064.

Singer, L. T., Salvator, A., Guo, S., Collin, M., Lilien, L., & Baley, J. (1999). Maternal psychological distress and parenting after the birth of a very low-birth-weight infant. *Journal of the American Medical Association, 281*, 799–805.

Singh, L. Morgan, J. L., & Best, C. T. (2002). Infants listening preferences. Baby talk or happy talk? *Infancy, 3*, 365–394.

Sininger, Y. S., Doyle, K. J., & Moore, J. K. (1999). The case for early identification of hearing loss in children: Auditory system development, experimental auditory deprivation, and development of speech and hearing. *Pediatric Clinics of North America, 46*, 1–14.

Siqueland, E. R., & Lipsitt, L. P. (1966). Conditioned head turning in human newborns. *Journal of Experimental Child Psychology, 4*, 356–376.

Sireteanu, R. (1999). Switching on the infant brain. *Science, 286*, 59–61.

Skinner, B. F. (1953). *Science and human behavior.* New York: Macmillan.

Skinner, B. F. (1971). *Beyond freedom and dignity.* New York: Knopf.

Skinner, B. F. (1974). *About behaviorism.* New York: Knopf.

Skinner, E. A., & Belmont, M. J. (1993). Motivation in the classroom: Reciprocal effects of teacher behavior and student engagement across the school year. *Journal of Educational Psychology, 85*, 571–581.

Skinner, E. A., Zimmer-Gembeck, M. J., & Connell, J. P. (1998). Individual differences and the development of perceived control. *Monographs of the Society for Research in Child Development, 63*(2–3, Serial No. 254).

Skodak, M., & Skeels, H. M. (1949). A final follow-up study of one hundred adopted children. *Pedagogical Seminary and Journal of Genetic Psychology, 75*, 85–125.

Slaby, R. G., & Frey, K. S. (1975). Development of gender constancy and selective attention to same-sex models. *Child Development, 46*, 849–856.

Slade, A., Belsky, J., Aber, J. L., & Phelps, J. L. (1999). Mothers' representations of their relationships with their toddlers: Links to adult attachment and observed mothering. *Developmental Psychology, 35*, 611–619.

Slater, A., Quinn, P. C., Brown, E., & Hayes, R. (1999). Intermodal perception at birth: Intersensory redundancy guides newborn infant's learning of arbitrary auditory-visual pairings. *Developmental Science, 2,* 333–338.

Slater, A., Rose, D., & Morison, V. (1984). New-born infants' perception of similarities and differences between two- and three-dimensional stimuli. *British Journal of Developmental Psychology, 3,* 211–220.

Slater, A., Von der Schulenburg, C., Brown, E., Badenoch, M., Butterworth, G., Parsons, S., & Samuels, C. (1998). Newborn infants prefer attractive faces. *Infant Behavior and Development, 21,* 345–354.

Slaughter-Defoe, D. T., Nakagawa, K., Takanishi, R., & Johnson, D. J. (1990). Toward cultural/ecological perspectives on schooling and achievement in African- and Asian-American children. *Child Development, 61,* 363–383.

Slavin, R. E. (1990). *Cooperative learning: Theory, research, and practice.* Englewood Cliffs, NJ: Prentice Hall.

Slomkowski, C., & Dunn, J. (1996). Young children's understanding of other people's beliefs and feelings and their connected communication with friends. *Developmental Psychology, 32,* 442–447.

Smetana, J. G. (1988). Concepts of self and social conventions: Adolescents' and parents' reasoning about hypothetical and actual family conflicts. In M. R. Gunnar & W. A. Collins (Eds.), *The Minnesota symposia on child psychology: Vol. 21. Development during the transition to adolescence.* Hillsdale, NJ: Erlbaum.

Smetana, J. G., & Braeges, J. L. (1990). The development of toddlers' moral and conventional judgments. *Merrill-Palmer Quarterly, 36,* 329–346.

Smetana, J. G., Campione-Barr, N., & Daddis, C. (2004). Longitudinal development of family decision making: Defining healthy behavioral autonomy for middle-class African American adolescents. *Child Development, 75,* 1418–1434.

Smetana, J. G., Metzger, A., Gettman, D. C., & Campione-Barr, N. (2006). Disclosure and secrecy in adolescent-parent relationships. *Child Development, 77,* 201–217.

Smetana, J. G., Schlagman, N., & Adams, P. W. (1993). Preschool judgments about hypothetical and actual transgressions. *Child Development, 64,* 202–214.

Smilkstein, G., Helsper-Lucas, A., Ashworth, C., Montano, D., & Pagel, M. (1984). Prediction of pregnancy complications: An application of the biopsychosocial model. *Social Sciences & Medicine, 18,* 315–321.

Smith, D. (2001). Harassment in the hallways. *Monitor in Psychology.* Retrieved July 24, 2006 from apa.org/monitor/sep01/harassment.html.

Smith, L. B. (1989). From global similarities to kinds of similarities: The construction of dimensions in development. In S. Vosniadou & A. Ortony (Eds.), *Similarity and analogical reasoning.* New York: Cambridge University Press.

Smith, L. B. (1995). Self-organizing processes in learning to learn words: Development is not induction. In C. A. Nelson (Ed.), *Basic and applied perspectives on learning, cognition, and development. The Minnesota symposia in child psychology* (Vol. 28). Mahwah, NJ: Erlbaum.

Smith, L. B. (1999a). Children's noun learning: How general learning processes make specialized learning mechanisms. In B. MacWhinney (Ed.), *The emergence of language* (pp. 277–303). Mahwah, NJ: Erlbaum.

Smith, L. B. (1999b). Do infants possess innate knowledge structures? The con side. *Developmental Science, 2,* 133–144.

Smith, L. B., Thelen, E., Titzer, R., & McLin, D. (1999). Knowing in the context of acting: The task dynamics of the A-not-B error. *Psychological Review, 106,* 235–260.

Smith, P., Perrin, S., Yule, W., & Rabe-Hesketh, S. (2001). War exposure and maternal reactions in the psychological adjustment of children from Bosnia-Hercegovina. *Journal of Child Psychology and Psychiatry, 42,* 395–404.

Smith, R. (1999, March). The timing of birth. *Scientific American, 280,* 68–75.

Smith, T. E. (1988). Parental control techniques: Relative frequencies and relationships with situational factors. *Journal of Family Issues, 9,* 155–176.

Snarey, J. R. (1985). Cross-cultural universality of social-moral development: A critical review of Kohlbergian research. *Psychological Bulletin, 97,* 202–232.

Snow, C. E. (1977). The development of conversation between babies and mothers. *Journal of Child Language, 4,* 1–22.

Snow, C. E. (1984). Parent-child interaction and the development of communicative ability. In R. L. Schiefelbusch & J. Pickar (Eds.), *The acquisition of communicative competence.* Baltimore: University Park Press.

Snow, C. E. (1987). Relevance of the notion of a critical period to language acquisition. In M. H. Bornstein (Ed.), *Sensitive periods in development.* Hillsdale, NJ: Erlbaum.

Snow, C. E. (1993). Families as social contexts for literacy development. In C. Daiute (Ed.), *The development of literacy through social interaction. New Directions for Child Development. No. 61* (pp. 11–24). San Francisco: Jossey-Bass.

Snow, C. E., & Kang, J. Y. (2006). Becoming bilingual, biliterate, and bicultural. In W. Damon & R. M. Lerner (Editors-in-Chief) & K. A. Renninger & I. E. Sigel (Vol. Eds.), *Handbook of child psychology: Vol. 4. Child psychology in practice* (6th ed., pp. 75–102). Hoboken, NJ: Wiley.

Snow, D. (2006). Regression and reorganization of intonation between 6 and 23 months. *Child Development, 77,* 281–296.

Snyder, J., Reid, J., & Patterson, G. (2003). A social learning model of child and adolescent antisocial behavior. In B. B. Lahey, T. E. Moffitt, & A. Caspi (Eds.), *Causes of conduct disorder and juvenile delinquency* (pp. 27–48). New York: Guilford.

Sobal, J., & Stunkard, A. J. (1989). Socioeconomic status and obesity: A review of the literature. *Psychological Bulletin, 105,* 260–275.

Society for Research in Child Development. (1996). Ethical standards for research with children. In *Directory of members.* Ann Arbor, MI: Author.

Society for Research in Child Development. (2002). *About the society.* Retrieved September 23, 2002, from www.srcd.org/index.html

Sodian, B., Zaitchik, D., & Carey, S. (1991). Young children's differentiation of hypothetical beliefs from evidence. *Child Development, 62,* 753–766.

Soenens, B., Vansteenkiste, M., Luyckx, K., & Goossens, L. (2006). Parenting and adolescent problem behavior: An integrated model with adolescent self-disclosure and perceived parental knowledge as intervening variables. *Developmental Psychology, 42,* 305–318.

Sophian, C., Garyantes, D., & Chang, C. (1997). When three is less than two: Early developments in children's understanding of fractional quantities. *Developmental Psychology, 33,* 731–744.

Sorce, J. F., Emde, R. N., Campos, J., & Klinnert, M. D. (1985). Maternal emotional signaling: Its effect on the visual cliff behavior of 1-year-olds. *Developmental Psychology, 21,* 195–200.

Southwick, S. M., Yehuda, R., & Charney, D. S. (1997). Neurobiological alterations in PTSD: Review of the clinical literature. In C. S. Fullerton & R. J. Ursano (Eds.), *Posttraumatic stress disorder: Acute and long-term responses to trauma and disaster* (pp. 241–266). Washington, DC: American Psychiatric Press.

Spear, L. P. (2000). Neurobehavioral changes in adolescence. *Current Directions in Psychological Science, 9,* 111–114.

Spear, L. P. (2003). Neurodevelopment during adolescence. In D. Cicchetti & E. F. Walker (Eds.), *Neurodevelopmental mechanisms in psychopathology* (pp. 62–83). Cambridge, UK: Cambridge University Press.

Spear, L. S. (2000). The adolescent brain and age-related behavioral manifestations. *Neuroscience and Biobehavioral Reviews, 24,* 417–463.

Spears, W., & Hohle, R. (1967). Sensory and perceptual processes in infants. In Y. Brackbill (Ed.), *Infancy and early childhood.* New York: Free Press.

Spehr, M., Gisselmann, G., Poplawski, A., Riffell, J. A., Wetzel, C. H., Zimmer, R. K., & Hatt, H. (2003) Identification of a testicular odorant receptor mediating human sperm chemotaxis. *Science, 299,* 2054–2058.

Spelke, E. S. (1976). Infants' intermodal perception of events. *Cognitive Psychology, 8,* 553–560.

Spelke, E., Breinlinger, K., Macomber, J., & Jacobson, K. (1992). Origins of knowledge. *Psychological Review, 99,* 605–632.

Spelke, E., & Hespos, S. (2001). Continuity, competence, and the object concept. In E. Dupoux (Ed.), *Language, brain, and cognitive development: Essays in honor of Jacques Mehler* (pp. 325–340). Cambridge, MA: MIT Press.

Spelke, E. S., & Newport, E. L. (1998). Nativism, empiricism, and the development of knowledge. In W. Damon (Series Ed.) & R. Lerner (Vol. Ed.), *Handbook of child psychology: Vol. 1. Theoretical models of human development* (5th ed., pp. 275–340). New York: Wiley.

Spelke, E. S., & Owsley, C. J. (1979). Intermodal exploration and knowledge in infancy. *Infant Behavior and Development, 2*, 13–27.

Spence, M. J., & Freeman, M. S. (1996). Newborn infants prefer the maternal low-pass filtered voice, but not the maternal whispered voice. *Infant Behavior and Development, 19*, 199–212.

Spencer, J. P., Smith, L. B., & Thelen, E. (2001). Tests of a dynamic systems account of the A-not-B error: The influence of prior experience on the spatial memory abilities of two-year-olds. *Child Development, 72*, 1327–1346.

Spencer, J. P., Vereijken, B., Diedrich, F. J., & Thelen, E. (2000). Posture and the emergence of manual skills. *Developmental Science, 3*, 216–233.

Spinrad, T. L., Eisenberg, N., Harris, H., Hanish, L., Fabes, R. A., et al. (2004). The relation of children's everyday nonsocial peer play behavior to their emotionality, regulation, and social functioning. *Developmental Psychology, 40*, 67–80.

Spinrad, T. L., Stifter, C. A., Donelan-McCall, N., & Turner, L. (2004). Mothers' regulation strategies in response to toddlers' affect: Links to later emotion self-regulation. *Social Development, 13*, 40–55.

Spitz, H. H. (1986). *The raising of intelligence.* Hillsdale, NJ: Erlbaum.

Spitz, R. (1946a). Anaclitic depression. *Psychoanalytic Study of the Child, 2*, 313–342.

Sprauve, M. E. (1996) Substance abuse and HIV in pregnancy. *Clinical Obstetrics and Gynecology, 39*, 316–332.

Spreen, O., Risser, A. H., & Edgell, D. (1995). *Developmental neuropsychology.* New York: Oxford University Press.

Spreen, O., Tupper, D., Risser, A., Tuokko, H., & Edgell, D. (1984). *Human developmental neuropsychology.* New York: Oxford University Press.

Sroufe, L. A. (1983). Infant-caregiver attachment and patterns of adaptation in preschool: The roots of maladaptation and competence. In M. Perlmutter (Ed.), *The Minnesota symposia on child psychology: Vol. 16. Development and policy concerning children with special needs.* Hillsdale, NJ: Erlbaum.

Sroufe, L. A. (1996). *Emotional development: The organization of life in the early years.* New York: Cambridge University Press.

Sroufe, L. A., Egeland, B., & Carlson, E. A. (1999). One social world: The integrated development of parent-child and peer relationships. In W. A. Collins & B. Laursen (Eds.), *Minnesota symposia on child psychology: Vol. 30. Relationships as developmental contexts* (pp. 241–261). Mahwah, NJ: Erlbaum.

Staffieri, J. R. (1967). A study of social stereotypes of body image in children. *Journal of Personality and Social Psychology, 7*, 101–104.

Stagno, S., & Cloud, G. A. (1994). Working parents: The impact of day care and breast-feeding on cytomegalovirus infections in offspring. *Proceedings of the National Academy of Science, USA, 91*, 2384–2389.

Stams, G. J. M., Juffer, F., & van IJzendoorn, M. H. (2002). Maternal sensitivity, infant attachment, and temperament in early childhood predict adjustment in middle childhood: The case of adopted children and their biologically unrelated parents. *Developmental Psychology, 38*, 806–821.

Stanovich, K. E. (1993). A model for studies of reading disability. *Developmental Review, 13*, 225–245.

Stansbury, K., & Gunnar, M. R. (1994). Adrenocortical activity and emotion regulation. In N. A. Fox (Ed.), The development of emotion regulation: Biological and behavioral considerations. *Monographs of the Society for Research in Child Development, 59*(2–3, Serial No. 240).

Stanwood, G. D., & Levitt, P. (2001). The effects of cocaine on the developing nervous system. In C. A. Nelson & M. Luciana (Eds.), *Handbook of developmental cognitive neuroscience* (pp. 519–536). Cambridge, MA: MIT Press.

Stark, R. E. (1986). Prespeech segmental feature detection. In P. Fletcher & M. Garman (Eds.), *Language acquisition: Studies in first language development.* Cambridge, UK: Cambridge University Press.

Statistics Canada. (1999). Retreived January 13, 2003, from http:\\www.statcan.ca

Statistics Canada. (2005). *Visible minority population, by age group (2001 Census).* Retrieved October 27, 2005 from www40.statcan.ca/l01/cst01/demo50a.htm.

Stätten, H., & Kerr, M. (2000). Parental monitoring: A reinterpretation. *Child Development, 71*, 1072–1085.

Steele, C. M., & Aronson, J. (1995). Stereotype threat and the intellectual test performance of African Americans. *Journal of Personality and Social Psychology, 69*, 797–811.

Steele, H., Steele, M., & Fonagy, P. (1996). Associations among attachment classifications of mothers, fathers, and their infants. *Child Development, 67*, 541–555.

Stein, J. H., & Reiser, L. W. (1994). A study of white middle-class adolescent boys' responses to "semenarche" (the first ejaculation). *Journal of Youth and Adolescence, 23*, 373–384.

Stein, L. K. (1999). Factors influencing the efficacy of universal newborn hearing screening. *Pediatric Clinics of North America, 46*, 95–105.

Stein, N. (1995). Sexual harassment in the school: The public performance of gendered violence. *Harvard Educational Review, 65*, 145–162.

Stein, N., & Cappello, D. (1999). *Gender violence/Gender justice: An interdisciplinary teaching guide for teachers of English, literature, social studies, psychology, health, peer counseling, and family and consumer sciences (grades 7–12).* Wellesley, MA: Wellesley College Center for Research on Women.

Steinberg, L. (1996). *Beyond the classroom: Why school reform has failed and what parents need to do.* New York: Simon & Schuster.

Steinberg, L. (2001). We know some things: Adolescent-parent relationships in retrospect and prospect. *Journal of Research on Adolescence, 11*, 1–19.

Steinberg, L., Elmen, J. D., & Mounts, N. S. (1989). Authoritative parenting, psychosocial maturity, and academic success among adolescents. *Child Development, 60*, 1424–1436.

Steinberg, L., Greenberger, E., Garduque, L., & McAuliffe, S. (1982). High school students in the labor force: Some costs and benefits to schooling and learning. *Educational Evaluation and Policy Analysis, 4*, 363–372.

Steinberg, L., Lamborn, S. D., Darling, N., Mounts, N. S., & Dornbusch, S. (1994). Over-time changes in adjustment and competence among adolescents from authoritative, authoritarian, indulgent, and neglectful families. *Child Development, 65*, 754–770.

Steiner, J. E. (1979). Human facial expressions in response to taste and smell stimulation. In H. W. Reese & L. P. Lipsitt (Eds.), *Advances in child development and behavior* (Vol. 13). New York: Academic Press.

Stern, D. N. (1974). The goal and structure of mother-infant play. *Journal of the American Academy of Child Psychiatry, 13*, 402–421.

Sternberg, K. J., Lamb, M. E., Greenbaum, C., Cichetti, D., Dawud, S., Cortes, R. M., et al. (1993). Effects of domestic violence on children's behavior problems and depression. *Developmental Psychology, 29*, 44–52.

Sternberg, R. J. (1981). A componential theory of intellectual giftedness. *Gifted Child Quarterly, 25*, 86–93.

Sternberg, R. J. (1982). *Intelligence applied.* New York: Harcourt.

Sternberg, R. J. (1985). *Beyond IQ: A triarchic theory of human intelligence.* Cambridge, UK: Cambridge University Press.

Sternberg, R. J. (1986). Triarchic theory of intellectual giftedness. In R. J. Sternberg & J. E. Davidson (Eds.), *Conceptions of giftedness* (pp. 223–243). Cambridge, UK: Cambridge University Press.

Sternberg, R. J. (1995). Testing common sense. *American Psychologist, 50*, 912–927.

Sternberg, R. J. (1998). Applying the triarchic theory of human intelligence in the classroom. In R. J. Sternberg & W. M. Williams (Eds.), *Intelligence, instruction, and assessment: Theory into practice* (pp. 1–15). Mahwah, NJ: Erlbaum.

Sternberg, R. J. (2001). Successful intelligence: Understanding what Spearman had rather than what he studied. In J. M. Collis & S. Messick (Eds.), *Intelligence and personality: Bridging the gap in theory and measurement* (pp. 347–373). Mahwah, NJ: Erlbaum.

Sternberg, R. J., Conway, B. E., Ketron, J. L., & Bernstein, M. (1981). People's conceptions of intelligence. *Journal of Personality and Social Psychology, 41*, 37–55.

Sternberg, R. J., & Frensch, P. A. (1993). Mechanisms of transfer. In D. K. Detterman & R. J. Sternberg (Eds.), *Transfer on trial: Intelligence, cognition, and instruction* (pp. 25–38). Norwood, NJ: Ablex.

Sternberg, R. J., & Kaufman, J. C. (1998). Human abilities. *Annual Review of Psychology, 49,* 479–502.

Sternberger, J. (1992). A performance constraint on compensatory lengthening in child phonology. *Language and Speech, 35,* 207–218.

Stetsenko, A., Little, T. D., Gordeeva, T., Grasshof, M., & Oettingen, G. (2000). Gender effects in children's beliefs about school performance: A cross-cultural study. *Child Development, 71,* 517–527.

Stetsenko, A., Little, T. D., Oettingen, G., & Baltes, P. B. (1995). Agency, control, and means-ends beliefs about school performance in Moscow children: How similar are they to beliefs of western children? *Developmental Psychology, 31,* 285–299.

Stevenson, D. K., et al. (1998). Very low birth weight outcomes of the National Institute of Child Health and Human Development Neonatal Research Network, January 1993 through December 1994. *American Journal of Obstetrics and Gynecology, 179,* 1632–1639.

Stevenson, H. W., Chen, C., & Lee, S. (1993). Mathematics achievement of Chinese, Japanese, and American children: Ten years later. *Science, 259,* 53–58.

Stevenson, H. W., Lee, S., & Stigler, J. W. (1986). Mathematics achievement of Chinese, Japanese, and American children. *Science, 231,* 693–699.

Stevenson, H. W., Stigler, J. W., Lee, S., Lucker, G. W., Kitamura, S., & Hsu, C. (1985). Cognitive performance and academic achievement of Japanese, Chinese, and American children. *Child Development, 56,* 718–734.

Stevenson, J., Asherson, P., Hay, D., Levy, F., Swanson, J., Thapar, A., & Willcutt, E. (2005). Characterizing the ADHD phenotype for genetic studies. *Developmental Science, 8,* 115–121.

Stevenson-Hinde, J., & Shouldice, A. (1995). Maternal interactions and self-reports related to attachment classifications at 4.5 years. *Child Development, 66,* 583–596.

Stice, E., Presnell, K., & Bearman, S. K. (2001). Relation of early menarche to depression, eating disorders, substance abuse, and comorbid psychopathology among adolescent girls. *Developmental Psychology, 37,* 608–619.

Stice, E., & Whitenton, K. (2002). Risk factors for body dissatisfaction in adolescent girls: A longitudinal investigation. *Developmental Psychology, 38,* 669–678.

Stifter, C. A., Fox, N. A., & Porges, S. W. (1989). Facial expressivity and vagal tone in five- and ten-month-old infants. *Infant Behavior and Development, 12,* 127–137.

Stigler, J. W., Lee, S., & Stevenson, H. W. (1987). Mathematics classrooms in Japan, Taiwan, and the United States. *Child Development, 58,* 1272–1285.

Stigler, J. W., Smith, S., & Mao, L.-W. (1985). The self-perception of competence by Chinese children. *Child Development, 56,* 1259–1270.

Stipek, D., & Hoffman, J. M. (1980). Children's achievement related expectancies as a function of academic performance histories and sex. *Journal of Educational Psychology, 72,* 861–865.

Stipek, D., Recchia, S., & McClintic, S. (1992). Self-evaluation in young children. *Monographs of the Society for Research in Child Development, 57*(1, Serial No. 226).

Stoel-Gammon, C., & Otomo, K. (1986). Babbling development of hearing-impaired and normally hearing subjects. *Journal of Speech and Hearing Disorders, 51,* 33–41.

Stolberg, A. L., & Anker, J. M. (1984). Cognitive and behavioral changes in children resulting from parental divorce and consequent environmental changes. *Journal of Divorce, 8,* 184–197.

Stoolmiller, M. (2001). Synergistic interaction of child manageability problems and parent-discipline tactics in predicting future growth in externalizing behavior for boys. *Developmental Psychology, 37,* 814–825.

Stormshak, E. A., Bellanti, C. J., Bierman, K. L., & the Conduct Problems Prevention Group. (1996). The quality of sibling relationships and the development of social competence and behavioral control in aggressive children. *Developmental Psychology, 32,* 79–89.

Strasburger, V. C. (1993). Children, adolescents, and the media: Five crucial issues. Adolescent Medicine: State of the Art Review, 4, 479–493.Stratton, K. R., Howe, C. J., & Battaglia, F. C. (Eds.). (1996). *Fetal alcohol syndrome: Diagnosis, epidemiology, prevention and treatment.* Washington, DC: National Academy Press.

Straus, M. A., & Donnelly, D. A. (1993). Corporal punishment of adolescents by American parents. *Youth and Society, 24,* 419–442.

Straus, M. A., & Stewart, J. H. (1999). Corporal punishment by American parents: National data on prevalence, chronicity, severity, and duration, in relation to child and family characteristics. *Clinical Child and Family Psychology Review, 2,* 55–70.

Strauss, R. (1999). Childhood obesity. *Current Problems in Pediatrics, 29,* 5–29.

Streiner, D. L., Saigal, S., Burrows, E., Stoskopf, B., & Rosenbaum, P. (2001). Attitudes of parents and health care professionals toward active treatment of extremely premature infants. *Pediatrics, 108,* 152–157.

Streissguth, A. P., Barr, H. M., Bookstein, F. L., Sampson, P. D., & Olson, H. C. (1999). The long-term neurocognitive consequences of prenatal alcohol exposure: A 14-year study. *Psychological Science, 10,* 186–190.

Streissguth, A. P., Bookstein, F. L., Sampson, P. D., & Barr, H. M. (1995). Attention: Prenatal alcohol and continuities of vigilence and attentional problems from 4 through 14 years. *Development and Psychopathology, 7,* 419–446.

Streissguth, A. P., Sampson, P. D., Barr, H. M., Bookstein, F. L., & Olson, H. C. (1994). The effects of prenatal exposure to alcohol and tobacco: Contributions from the Seattle Longitudinal Prospective Study and implications for public policy. In H. L. Needleman & D. Bellinger (Eds.), *Prenatal exposure to toxicants: Developmental consequences* (pp. 148–183). Baltimore: Johns Hopkins University Press.

Streissguth, A. P., Treder, R., Barr, H. M., Shepard, T., Bleyer, A., & Martin, D. (1984). Prenatal aspirin and offspring IQ in a large group. *Teratology, 29,* 59A–60A.

Stricker, J. M., Miltenberger, R. G., Garlinghouse, M. A., Deaver, C. M., & Anderson, C. A. (2001). Evaluation of an awareness enhancement device for the treatment of thumb sucking in children. *Journal of Applied Behavior Analysis, 34,* 77–80.

Strough, J., & Berg, C. A. (2000). Goals as a mediator of gender differences in high-affiliation dyadic conversations. *Developmental Psychology, 36,* 117–125.

Strutt, G. F., Anderson, D. R., & Well, A. D. (1975). A developmental study of the effects of irrelevant information on speeded classification. *Journal of Experimental Child Psychology, 20,* 127–135.

Styne, D. M. (2001). Childhood and adolescent obesity. *Pediatric Clinics of North America, 48,* 832–862.

Suarez-Orozco, C., & Suarez-Orozco, M. (1996). *Transformations: Migration, family life and achievement motivation among Latino adolescents.* Palo Alto, CA: Stanford University Press.

Subrahmanyam, K., & Greenfield, P. M. (1998). Computer games for girls: What makes them play? In J. Cassell & H. Jenkins (Eds.), *From Barbie to Mortal Kombat: Gender and computer games* (pp. 46–71). Cambridge, MA: MIT Press.

Subrahmanyam, K., Greenfield, P., Kraut, R., & Gross, E. (2001). The impact of computer use on children's and adolescents' development. *Journal of Applied Developmental Psychology, 22,* 7–30.

Subrahmanyam, K., Kraut, R. E., Greenfield, P. M., & Gross, E. F. (2000, Fall/Winter). The impact of computer use on children's activities and development. *Future of Children, 10*(2), 123–144.

Subrahmanyam, K., Smahel, D., & Greenfield, P. (2006). Connecting developmental constructions to the Internet: Identity presentation and sexual exploration in online teen chat rooms. *Developmental Psychology, 42,* 395-406.

Sugarman, S. (1982). Developmental change in early representational intelligence: Evidence from spatial classification strategies and related verbal expressions. *Cognitive Psychology, 14,* 410–449.

Sugarman, S. (1983). *Children's early thought: Developments in classification.* New York: Cambridge University Press.

Sullivan, H. S. (1953). *The interpersonal theory of psychiatry.* New York: W. W. Norton.

Sullivan, T. N., Kung, E. M., & Farrell, A. D. (2004). Relation between witnessing violence and drug use initiation among rural adolescents: Parental monitoring and family support as protective factors. *Journal of Clinical and Adolescent Psychology, 33,* 488–498.

Sun, L. C., & Roopnarine, J. L. (1996). Mother-infant, father-infant interaction and involvement in childcare and household labor among Taiwanese families. *Infant Behavior and Development, 19,* 121–129.

Super, C. M. (1976). Environmental effects on motor development: The case of "African infant precocity." *Developmental Medicine and Child Neurology, 18,* 561–567.

Super, C. M., & Harkness, S. (1982). The infant's niche in rural Kenya and metropolitan America. In L. Adler (Ed.), *Cross-cultural research at issue* (pp. 247–255). New York: Academic Press.

Super, C. M., & Harkness, S. (1997). The cultural structuring of child development. In J. W. Berry (Ed.), *Handbook of cross-cultural psychology: Vol. 2. Basic processes and human development* (2nd ed., pp. 1–39). Boston: Allyn & Bacon.

Sutton-Smith, B., & Rosenberg, B. G. (1970). *The sibling.* New York: Holt, Rinehart & Winston.

Swain, I. U., Zelazo, P. R., & Clifton, R. K. (1993). Newborn infants' memory for speech sounds retained over 24 hours. *Developmental Psychology, 29,* 312–323.

Swanson, H. L., Mink, J., & Bocian, K. M. (1999). Cognitive processing deficits in poor readers with symptoms of reading disabilities and ADHD: More alike than different? *Journal of Educational Psychology, 91,* 321–333.

Szkrybalo, J., & Ruble, D. N. (1999). "God made me a girl": Sex-category constancy judgments and explanation revisited. *Developmental Psychology, 35,* 392–402.

Taddio, A., Goldbach, M., Ipp, M., Stevens, B., & Koren, G. (1995). Effect of neonatal circumcision on pain responses during vaccination in boys. *Lancet, 345,* 291–292.

Tager-Flusberg, H. (1985). Putting words together: Morphology and syntax in the preschool years. In J. B. Gleason (Ed.), *The development of language.* Columbus, OH: Charles E. Merrill.

Takahashi, K. (1990). Are the key assumptions of the Strange Situation procedure universal? A view from Japanese research. *Human Development, 33,* 23–30.

Takei, W. (2001). How do deaf infants attain first signs? *Developmental Science, 4,* 71–78.

Tallal, P., Miller, S. L., Bedi, G., Byma, G., Wang, X., Nagarajan, S. S., et al. (1996). Language comprehension in language-learning impaired children improved with acoustically modified speech. *Science, 271,* 81–84.

Tallal, P., Miller, S. L., Jenkins, W. M., & Merzenich, M. M. (1997). The role of temporal processing in developmental language-based learning disorders: Research and clinical implications. In B. Blachman (Ed.), *Foundations of reading acquisition and dyslexia: Implications for early intervention* (pp. 49–66). Mahwah, NJ: Erlbaum.

Tam, C. W. Y., & Stokes, S. F. (2001). Form and function of negation in early developmental Cantonese. *Journal of Child Language, 28,* 373–391.

Tamis-LeMonda, C. S., Bornstein, M. H., & Baumwell, L. (2001). Maternal responsiveness and children's achievement of language milestones. *Child Development, 72,* 748–767.

Tanapat, P., Hastings, N. B., & Gould, E. (2001). Adult neurogenesis in the hippocampal formation. In C. A. Nelson & M. Luciana (Eds.), *Handbook of developmental cognitive neuroscience* (pp. 93–105). Cambridge, MA: MIT Press.

Tanner, J. M. (1978). *Fetus into man: Physical growth from conception to maturity.* Cambridge, MA: Harvard University Press.

Tanner, J. M. (1990). *Foetus into man: Physical growth from conception to maturity* (rev. ed.). Cambridge, MA: Harvard University Press.

Tannock, R., & Martinussen, R. (2001). Reconceptualizing ADHD. *Educational Leadership, 59,* 20–25.

Tappin, D., Ecob, R., & Brooke, H. (2005). Bedsharing, roomsharing and sudden infant death syndrome in Scotland. *Journal of Pediatrics, 147,* 32–37.

Taras, H. L., Sallis, J. F., Patterson, T. L., Nader, P. R., & Nelson, J. A. (1989). Television's influence on children's diet and physical activity. *Journal of Developmental and Behavioral Pediatrics, 10,* 176–180.

Tardieu, M., Mayaux, M.-J., Seibel, N., Funck-Brentano, I., Straub, E., Teglas, J. P., & Blanche, S. (1995). Cognitive assessment of school-age children infected with maternally transmitted human immunodeficiency virus type 1. *Journal of Pediatrics, 126,* 375–379.

Tardif, T. (1996). Nouns are not always learned before verbs: Evidence from Mandarin speakers' early vocabularies. *Developmental Psychology, 32,* 492–504.

Tardif, T., Gelman, S. A., & Xu, F. (1999). Putting the "noun bias" in context: A comparison of English and Mandarin. *Child Development, 70,* 620–635.

Tardif, T., & Wellman, H. M. (2000). Acquisition of mental state language in Mandarin-speaking and Cantonese-speaking children. *Developmental Psychology, 36,* 25–43.

Taubes, G. (1998). As obesity rates rise, experts struggle to explain why. *Science, 1998,* 1367–1368.

Taylor, H. G., Klein, N., & Hack, M. (2000). School-age consequences of birth-weight less than 750g: A review and update. *Developmental Neuropsychology, 17,* 289–321.

Taylor, H. G., Klein, N., Minich, N. M., & Hack, M. (2001). Long-term family outcomes for children with very low birth weights. *Archives of Pediatrics & Adolescent Medicine, 155,* 155–161.

Taylor, R. D. (1996). Adolescents' perceptions of kinship support and family management practices: Association with adolescent adjustment in African American families. *Developmental Psychology, 32,* 687–695.

Teller, D. Y. (1998). Spatial and temporal aspects of infant color vision. *Vision Research, 38,* 3275–3282.

Tenenbaum, H. R., & Leaper, C. (2002). Are parents' gender schemas related to their children's gender-related cognitions? A meta-analysis. *Developmental Psychology, 38,* 615–630.

Teratology Society. (2005). *Teratology primer.* Reston, VA: Author.

Terman, L. M. (1916). *The measurement of intelligence.* Boston: Houghton Mifflin.

Terman, L. M. (1925). *Genetic studies of genius: Vol. 1. Mental and physical traits of a thousand gifted children.* Stanford, CA: Stanford University Press.

Terman, L. M. (1954). The discovery and encouragement of exceptional talent. *American Psychologist, 9,* 221–238.

Terman, L. M., & Oden, M. H. (1959). *Genetic studies of genius: Vol. 4. The gifted group at midlife.* Stanford, CA: Stanford University Press.

Terrace, H. S., Pettito, L. A., Sanders, R. J., & Bever, T. G. (1979). Can an ape create a sentence? *Science, 206,* 891–900.

Terrance, C., Logan, A. & Peters, D. (2004). Perceptions of peer sexual harassment among high school students. *Sex Roles, 51,* 479–490.

Teti, D. M., & Gelfand, D. M. (1991). Behavioral competence among mothers of infants in the first year: The mediational role of maternal self-efficacy. *Child Development, 62,* 918–929.

Teti, D. M., Gelfand, D. M., Messinger, D. S., & Isabella, R. (1995). Maternal depression and the quality of early attachment: An examination of infants, preschoolers, and their mothers. *Developmental Psychology, 31,* 364–376.

Teti, D. M., Sakin, J. W., Kucera, E., & Corns, K. M. (1996). And baby makes four: Predictors of attachment security among preschool age firstborns during the transition to siblinghood. *Child Development, 67,* 579–596.

Thabet, A. A., & Vostanis, P. (2000). Posttraumatic stress disorder reactions in children of war: A longitudinal study. *Child Abuse & Neglect, 24,* 291–298.

Tharp, R. G. (1989). Psychocultural variables and constants: Effects on teaching and learning in schools. *American Psychologist, 44,* 349–359.

Thelen, E. (1996). The improvising infant: Learning about learning to move. In M. R. Merrens & G. G. Brannigan (Eds.), *The developmental psychologists: Research adventures across the life span* (pp. 21–36). New York: McGraw-Hill.

Thelen, E., Skala, K. D., & Kelso, J. A. S. (1987). The dynamic nature of early coordination: Evidence from bilateral leg movements in young infants. *Developmental Psychology, 23,* 179–186.

Thelen, E., & Smith, L. B. (1994). *A dynamic systems approach to the development of cognition and action.* Cambridge, MA: MIT Press.

Thelen, E., & Smith, L. B. (2006). Dynamic systems theories. In W. Damon & R. M. Lerner (Editors-in-Chief) & R. M. Lerner (Vol. Ed.), *Handbook of child psychology: Vol. 1. Theoretical models of human development* (6th ed., pp. 258–312). Hoboken, NJ: Wiley.

Thelen, E., & Ulrich, B. D. (1991). Hidden skills: A dynamic systems analysis of treadmill stepping during the first year. *Monographs of the Society for Research in Child Development, 56*(1, Serial No. 223).

Thierry, K. L., & Spence, M. J. (2002). Source-monitoring training facilitates preschoolers' eyewitness memory performance. *Developmental Psychology, 38,* 428–437.

Thiessen, E. D., Hill, E. A., & Saffran, J. R. (2005). Infant-directed speech facilitates word segmentation. *Infancy, 7,* 53–71.

Thoman, A. (1993). Obligation and option in the premature nursery. *Developmental Review, 13,* 1–30.

Thomas, D. G., & Lykins, M. S. (1995). Event-related potential measures of 24-hour retention in 5-month-old infants. *Developmental Psychology, 31,* 946–957.

Thompson, C. (1982). Cortical activity in behavioural development. In J. W. T. Dickerson & H. McGurk (Eds.), *Brain and behavioural development.* London: Surrey University Press.

Thompson, R. A. (1990). Vulnerability in research: A developmental perspective on risk research. *Child Development, 61,* 1–16.

Thompson, R. A. (1994). Emotion regulation: A theme in search of definition. In N. A. Fox (Ed.), *The development of emotion regulation. Monographs of the Society for Research in Child Development, 59* (Nos. 2–3, Serial No. 240).

Thompson, R. A. (1996). Attachment and emotional development: From clinic to research to policy. In M. R. Merrens & G. G. Brannigan (Eds.), *The developmental psychologists: Research adventures across the life span* (pp. 69–87). New York: McGraw-Hill.

Thompson, R. A. (2006). The development of the person: Social understanding, relationships, conscience, self. In W. Damon & R. M. Lerner (Editors-in-Chief) & N. Eisenberg (Vol. Ed.), *Handbook of child psychology: Vol. 3. Social, emotional, and personality development* (6th ed., pp. 24–98). Hoboken, NJ: Wiley.

Thompson, R. A., & Nelson, C. A. (2001). Developmental science and the media: Early brain development. *American Psychologist, 56,* 5–15.

Thompson, V. D. (1974). Family size: Implicit policies and assumed psychological outcomes. *Journal of Social Issues, 30,* 93–124.

Thorn, F., Gwiazda, J., Cruz, A. V., Bauer, J. A., & Held, R. (1994). The development of eye alignment, convergence and sensory binocularity in young infants. *Investigative Ophthalmology and Visual Science, 35,* 544–553.

Thornton, S. (1999). Creating the conditions for cognitive change: The interaction between task structures and specific strategies. *Child Development, 70,* 588–603.

Thurstone, L. L. (1938). *Primary mental abilities.* Chicago: University of Chicago Press.

Tieger, T. (1980). On the biological basis of sex differences in aggression. *Child Development, 51,* 943–963.

Tietjen, A. M. (1986). Prosocial moral reasoning among children and adults in a Papua New Guinea society. *Developmental Psychology, 22,* 861–868.

Tincoff, R., & Jusczyk, P. W. (1999). Some beginnings of word comprehension in 6-month-olds. *Psychological Science, 10,* 172–175.

Toda, S., & Fogel, A. (1993). Infant response to the still-face situation at 3 and 6 months. *Developmental Psychology, 29,* 532–538.

Toda, S., Fogel, A., & Kawai, M. (1990). Maternal speech to three-month-old infants in the United States and Japan. *Journal of Child Language, 17,* 279–294.

Tolmie, J. L. (2002). Down syndrome and other autosomal trisomies. In D. L. Rimoin, J. M. Connor, R. E. Pyeritz, & B. R. Korf (Eds.), *Emery and Rimoin's principles and practice of medical genetics* (4th ed., Vol. 1, pp. 1129–1183). London: Churchill Livingston.

Tolson, J. M., & Urberg, K. A. (1993). Similarity between adolescent best friends. *Journal of Adolescent Research, 8,* 274–288.

Tomasello, M. (1995). Understanding the self as social agent. In P. Rochat (Ed.), *The self in infancy: Theory and research* (pp. 449–460). Amsterdam: North Holland-Elsevier.

Tomasello, M. (1998). Uniquely primate, uniquely human. *Developmental Science, 1,* 1–16.

Tomasello, M. (2000). Do young children have adult syntactic competence? *Cognition, 74,* 209–253.

Tomasello, M., Akhtar, N., Dodson, K., & Rekau, L. (1997). Differential productivity in young children's use of nouns and verbs. *Journal of Child Language, 24,* 373–387.

Tomasello, M., & Brooks, P. (1998). Young children's earliest transitive and intransitive contructions. *Cognitive Linguistics, 8,* 375–395.

Tomasello, M., & Brooks, P. J. (1999). Early syntactic development: A construction grammar approach. In M. Barrett (Ed.), *The development of language* (pp. 161–190). Hove, UK: Psychology Press.

Tomasello, M., Conti-Ramsden, G., & Ewert, B. (1990). Young children's conversations with their mothers and fathers: Differences in breakdown and repair. *Journal of Child Language, 17,* 115–130.

Tomasello, M., & Farrar, M. J. (1986). Joint attention and early language. *Child Development, 57,* 1454–1463.

Tomasello, M., Strosberg, R., & Akhtar, N. (1996). Eighteen-month-old children learn words in non-ostensive contexts. *Journal of Child Language, 23,* 157–176.

Tongsong, T., Wanapirak, C., Sirivatanapa, P., Piyamongkol, W., Sirichotiyakul, S. & Yampochai, A. (1998). Amniocentesis-related fetal loss: A cohort study. *Obstetrics and Gynecology, 92,* 64–67.

Tough, S. C., Greene, C. A., Svenson, L. W., & Belik, J. (2000). Effects of in vitro fertilization on low birth weight, preterm delivery, and multiple birth. *Journal of Pediatrics, 136,* 618–622.

Touwen, B. C. L. (1974). The neurological development of the infant. In J. A. Davis & J. Dobbing (Eds.), *Scientific foundations of paediatrics.* Philadelphia: W.B. Saunders.

Trainor, L. J. (1996). Infant preferences for infant-directed versus non-infant-directed play songs and lullabies. *Infant Behavior and Development, 19,* 83–92.

Trainor, L. J., & Heinmiller, B. M. (1998). The development of evaluative responses to music: Infants prefer to listen to consonance over dissonance. *Infant Behavior and Development, 21,* 77–88.

Trehub, S. E., Bull, D., & Thorpe, L. A. (1984). Infants' perception of melodies: The role of melodic contour. *Child Development, 55,* 821–830.

Trehub, S. E., Thorpe, L. A., & Morrongiello, B. A. (1985). Infants' perception of melodies: Changes in a single tone. *Infant Behavior and Development, 8,* 213–223.

Trehub, S. E., Unyk, A. M., & Trainor, L. J. (1993). Maternal singing in cross-cultural perspective. *Infant Behavior and Development, 16,* 285–295.

Treiber, F., & Wilcox, S. (1980). Perception of a "subjective" contour by infants. *Child Development, 51,* 915–917.

Trevarthen, C., & Aitken, K. J. (2001). Infant intersubjectivity: Research, theory, and clinical applications. *Journal of Child Psychology & Psychiatry & Allied Disciplines, 42,* 3–48.

Trevathen, W. R. (1987). *Human birth: An evolutionary perspective.* New York: Aldine de Gruyter.

Tronick, E. Z. (1987). The Neonatal Behavioral Assessment Scale as a biomarker of the effects of environmental agents on the newborn. *Environmental Health Perspectives, 74,* 185–189.

Tronick, E. Z., Als, H., Adamson, L., Wise, S., & Brazelton, T. E. (1978). The infant's response to entrapment between contradictory messages in face-to-face interaction. *Journal of the American Academy of Child Psychiatry, 17,* 1–13.

Tronick, E. Z., & Cohn, J. F. (1989). Infant-mother face-to-face interaction: Age and gender differences in coordination and the occurrence of miscoordination. *Child Development, 60,* 85–92.

Tronick, E. Z., Ricks, M., & Cohn, J. F. (1982). Maternal and infant affective exchange: Patterns of adaptation. In T. Field & A. Fogel (Eds.), *Emotion and early interaction.* Hillsdale, NJ: Erlbaum.

Troseth, G. L. (2003). TV guide: Two-year-old children learn to use video as a source of information. *Developmental Psychology, 39,* 140–150.

Tröster, H., & Brambring, M. (1993). Early motor development in blind infants. *Journal of Applied Developmental Psychology, 14,* 83–106.

True, M. M., Pisani, L., & Oumar, F. (2001). Infant-mother attachment among the Dogon of Mali. *Child Development, 72,* 1451–1466.

Trzesniewski, K. H., Brent Donnellan, M. B., Moffitt, T. E., Robins, R. W., Poulton, R., & Caspi, A. (2006). Low self-esteem during adolescence predicts poor health, criminal behavior, and limited economic prospects during adulthood. *Developmental Psychology, 42,* 382–290.

Tschopp, C., Viviani, P., Reicherts, M., Bullinger, A., Rudaz, N., Mermoud, C., & Safran, A. B. (1999). Does visual sensitivity improve between 5 and 8 years? A study of automated visual field examination. *Vision Research, 39,* 1107–1119.

Tucker, D. M. (1981). Lateral brain function, emotion, and conceptualization. *Psychological Bulletin, 89,* 19–46.

Tucker, G. R., & d'Anglejan, A. (1972). An approach to bilingual education: The St. Lambert experiment. In M. Swain (Ed.), *Bilingual schooling: Some experiences in Canada and the United States.* Ontario: Ontario Institute for Studies in Education.

Turiel, E. (1998). The development of morality. In W. Damon (Series Ed.) & N. Eisenberg (Vol. Ed.), *Handbook of child psychology: Vol. 3. Social, emotional, and personality development* (5th ed., pp. 863–932). New York: Wiley.

Turiel, E. (2006). The development of morality. In W. Damon & R. M. Lerner (Editors-in-Chief) & N. Eisenberg (Vol. Ed.), *Handbook of child psychology: Vol. 3. Social, emotional, and personality development* (6th ed., pp. 789–857). Hoboken, NJ: Wiley.

Turiel, E., & Wainryb, C. (1994). Social reasoning and the varieties of social experiences in cultural contexts. In H. Reese (Ed.), *Advances in child development and behavior* (Vol. 25, pp. 289–326).

Turkheimer, E., Goldsmith, H. H., & Gottesman, I. I. (1995). Commentary. *Human Development, 38,* 142–153.

Turner, R. A., Irwin, C. E., & Millstein, S. G. (1991). Family structure, family processes, and experimenting with substances during adolescence. *Journal of Research on Adolescence, 1,* 93–106.

Turner, S. M., & Mo, L. (1984). Chinese adolescents' self-concept as measured by the Offer Self-Image Questionnaire. *Journal of Youth and Adolescence, 13,* 131–142.

Turner-Bowker, D. M. (1996). Gender stereotyped descriptors in children's picture books: Does "Curious Jane" exist in the literature? *Sex Roles, 35,* 461–488.

Twenge, J. M., & Crocker, J. (2002). Race and self-esteem: Meta-analyses comparing Whites, Blacks, Hispanics, Asians, and American Indians and comment on Gray-Little and Hafdahl (2000). *Psychological Bulletin, 128,* 371–408.

Ullian, E. M., Sapperstein, S. K., Christopherson, K. S., & Barres, B. A. (2001). Control of synapse number by glia. *Science, 291,* 657–661.

Underwood, L. E. (1991, March/April). Normal adolescent growth and development. *Nutrition Today,* pp. 11–16.

Underwood, M. K., Schockner, A. E., & Hurley, J. C. (2001). Children's responses to same- and other-gender peers: An experimental investigation with 8-, 10-, and 12-year-olds. *Developmental Psychology, 37,* 362–372.

UNICEF. (2002). *The State of the World's Children 2002.* Retrieved November 27, 2002, from www.unicef.org/sowc02/

United Nations. (2001, October). *Population and vital statistics report* (Series A, Vol. 53, No. 4). New York: Author.

United Nations. (2005). *Population and vital statistics report.* Retrieved October 2, 2005, from unstats.un.org/unsd/demographic/products/vitstats/seriesa2.htm.

U.S. Bureau of the Census. (2001). *Statistical abstract of the United States* (121st ed.). Washington, DC: U.S. Government Printing Office.

U.S. Bureau of the Census. (2005a). *National population estimates—characteristics.* Retrieved October 27, 2005 from www.census.gov/popest/national/asrh/NC-EST2004-asrh.html.

U.S. Bureau of the Census. (2005b). *Statistical abstract of the United States, 2006: The national data book* (125th ed.). Washington, DC: U.S. Government Printing Office. Retrieved October 30, 2005, from www.census.gov/prod/2004pubs/04statab/labor.pdf.

U.S. Department of Education. (1993). *National excellence: A case for developing America's talent.* Washington, DC: Office of Educational Research and Improvement.

U.S. Department of Education. (1996). *1996 trends in academic programs.* Washington, DC: U.S. Government Printing Office.

U.S. Department of Health and Human Services. (2004). *What you need to know about mercury in fish and shellfish.* Retrieved May 10, 2006, from www.cfsan.fda.gov/~dms/admehg3.html.

U.S. Department of Health and Human Services. (2005). *Child maltreatment 2003.* Washington, DC: U.S. Government Printing Office.

U.S. Department of Justice. (2005). *Juvenile victimization and offending, 1993–2003.* Bureau of Justice Special Report, NCJ 209468.

Urberg, K. A., Degirmencioglu, S. M., Tolson, J. M., & Halliday-Scher, K. (1995). The structure of adolescent peer networks. *Developmental Psychology, 31,* 540–547.

Uttal, D. H., & Wellman, H. M. (1989). Young children's representation of spatial information acquired from maps. *Developmental Psychology, 25,* 128–138.

Uttal, D. H., Gregg, V. H., Tan, L. S., Chamberlin, M. H., & Sines, A. (2001). Connecting the dots: Children's use of a systematic figure to facilitate mapping and search. *Developmental Psychology, 37,* 338–350.

Valdez-Menchaca, M. C., & Whitehurst, G. J. (1992). Accelerating language development through picture book reading: A systematic extension to Mexican day care. *Developmental Psychology, 28,* 1106–1114.

Valeski, T. N., & Stipek, D. J. (2001). Young children's feelings about school. *Child Development, 72,* 1198–1213.

Valian, V. (1986). Syntactic categories in the speech of young children. *Developmental Psychology, 22,* 562–579.

Valk, A. (2000). Ethnic identity, ethnic attitudes, self-esteem, and esteem toward others among Estonian and Russian adolescents. *Journal of Adolescent Research, 15,* 637–651.

Valsiner, J. (2006). Developmental epistemology and implications for methodology. In W. Damon & R. M. Lerner (Editors-in-Chief) & R. M. Lerner (Vol. Ed.), *Handbook of child psychology: Vol. 1. Theoretical models of human development* (6th ed., pp. 166–209). Hoboken, NJ: Wiley.

Van Balen, F. (1998). Development of IVF children. *Developmental Review, 18,* 30–46.

van den Boom, D. C. (1994). The influence of temperament and mothering on attachment and exploration: An experimental manipulation of sensitive responsiveness among lower-class mothers with irritable infants. *Child Development, 65,* 1457–1477.

van den Boom, D. C. (1995). Do first-year intervention effects endure? Follow-up during toddlerhood of a sample of Dutch irritable infants. *Child Development, 66,* 1798–1816.

van den Boom, D. C., & Hoeksma, J. B. (1994). The effects of infant irritability on mother-infant interaction: A growth-curve analysis. *Developmental Psychology, 30,* 581–590.

Van IJzendoorn, M. H. (1995). Adult attachment representations, parental responsiveness and infant attachment: A meta-analysis on the predictive validity of the Adult Attachment Interview. *Psychological Bulletin, 117,* 387–403.

van IJzendoorn, M. H., Moran, G., Belsky, J., Pederson, D., Bakermans Kranenburg, M. J., & Kneppers, K. (2000). The similarity of siblings' attachments to their mother. *Child Development, 71,* 1086–1098.

van IJzendoorn, M. H., & Sagi, A. (1999). Cross-cultural patterns of attachment. In J. Cassidy & P. R. Shaver (Eds.), *Handbook of attachment: Theory, research, and clinical applications* (pp. 713–734). New York: Guilford Press.

Van Rooy, C., Stough, C., Pipingas, A., Hocking, C., & Silberstein, R. B. (2001). Spatial working memory and intelligence: Biological correlates. *Intelligence, 29,* 275–292.

Vandell, D. L. (2000). Parents, peers, and other socializing influences. *Developmental Psychology, 36,* 699–710.

Vandell, D. L., & Mueller, E. C. (1980). Peer play and friendships during the first two years. In H. C. Foot, A. J. Chapman, & J. R. Smith (Eds.), *Friendship and social relations in children.* New York: Wiley.

Vandell, D. L., & Ramanan, J. (1992). Effects of early and recent maternal employment on children from low-income families. *Child Development, 63,* 938–949.

Vandell, D. L., & Wilson, K. S. (1982). Social interaction in the first year of life: Infants' social skills with peers versus mother. In K. H. Rubin & H. S. Ross (Eds.), *Peer relationships and social skills in childhood.* New York: Springer-Verlag.

Vandell, D. L., Wilson, K. S., & Buchanan, N. R. (1980). Peer interaction in the first year of life: An examination of its structure, content, and sensitivity to toys. *Child Development, 51,* 481–488.

Vandenberg, S. G., & Vogler, G. P. (1985). Genetic determinants of intelligence. In B. B. Wolman (Ed.), *Handbook of intelligence.* New York: Wiley.

Varni, J. W. (1983). *Clinical behavioral pediatrics: An interdisciplinary biobehavioral approach.* New York: Pergamon Press.

Vaughn, B. E., Kopp, C. B., & Krakow, J. B. (1984). The emergence and consolidation of self-control from eighteen to thirty months of age: Normative trends and individual differences. *Child Development, 55,* 990–1004.

Vaughn, B. E., Taraldson, B., Crichton, L., & Egeland, B. (1980). Relationships between neonatal behavioral organization and infant behavior during the first year of life. *Infant Behavior and Development, 3,* 78–89.

Vernon, P. A. (1983). Speed of information processing and general intelligence. *Intelligence, 7,* 53–70.

Verschueren, K., & Marcoen, A. (1999). Representation of self and socioemotional competence in kindergartners: Differential and combined effects of attachment to mothers and fathers. *Child Development, 70,* 183–201.

Vihman, M. M. (1998). Early phonological disorders. In J. E. Bernthal & N. W. Bankson (Eds.), *Articulation and phonological development* (4th ed., pp. 63–110). Boston: Allyn & Bacon.

Vinter, A., & Perruchet, P. (2000). Implicit learning in children is not related to age: Evidence from drawing behavior. *Child Development, 71,* 1223–1240.

Vohr, B. R., Wright, L. L., Dusick, A. M., Mele, L., Verter, J., Steichen, J. J., et al. (2000). Neurodevelopmental and functional outcomes of extremely low birth weight infants in the National Institute of Child Health and Human Development Neonatal Research Network, 1993–1994. *Pediatrics, 105,* 1216–1226.

Volling, B. L., MacKinnon-Lewis, C., Rabiner, D., & Baradaran, L. P. (1993). Children's social competence and sociometric status: Further exploration of aggression, social withdrawal, and peer rejection. *Development and Psychopathology, 5,* 459–483.

von Hofsten, C., & Rönnqvist, L. (1993). The structuring of neonatal arm movement. *Child Development, 64,* 1046–1057.

von Hofsten, C., & Rosander, K. (1997). Development of smooth pursuit tracking in young infants. *Vision Research, 37,* 1799–1810.

Vorhees, C. V. (1986). Principles of behavioral teratology. In E. P. Riley & C. V. Vorhees (Eds.), *Handbook of behavioral teratology.* New York: Plenum Press.

Vouloumanos, A., & Werker, J. F. (2004). Tuned to the signal: The privileged status of speech for young infants. *Developmental Science, 3,* 270–276.

Voyer, D., Voyer, S., & Bryden, M. P. (1995). Magnitude of sex differences in spatial abilities: A meta-analysis and consideration of critical variables. *Psychological Bulletin, 117,* 250–270.

Vuchinich, S., Hetherington, E. M., Vuchinich, R. A., & Clingempeel, W. G. (1991). Parent-child interaction and gender differences in early adolescents' adaptation to stepfamilies. *Developmental Psychology, 27,* 618–626.

Vuyk, R. (1981). *Overview and critique of Piaget's genetic epistemology 1965–1980* (Vols. 1 & 2). New York: Academic Press.

Vygotsky, L. S. (1962). *Thought and language* (E. Hanfmann & G. Vakar, Trans.). Cambridge, MA: MIT Press.

Vygotsky, L. S. (1978). *Mind in society: The development of higher psychological processes.* Cambridge, MA: Harvard University Press.

Wachs, T. D., & Combs, T. T. (1995). The domains of infant mastery motivation. In R. H. McTurk & G. A. Morgan (Eds.), *Mastery motivation: Origins, conceptualizations, and applications* (pp. 147–164). Norwood, NJ: Ablex.

Waddington, C. H. (1971). Concepts of development. In E. Tobach, L. R. Aronson, & E. Shaw (Eds.), *The biopsychology of development.* San Diego, CA: Academic Press.

Wadhwa, P. D., Sandman, C. A., Porto, M., Dunkel-Schetter, C., & Garite, T. J. (1993). The association between prenatal stress and infant birth weight and gestational age at birth: A prospective investigation. *American Journal of Obstetrics and Gynecology, 169,* 858–865.

Wagner, B. M., & Phillips, D. A. (1992). Beyond beliefs: Parent and child behaviors and children's perceived academic competence. *Child Development, 63,* 1380–1391.

Wagner, L. (2001). Aspectual influences on early tense comprehension. *Journal of Child Language, 28,* 661–681.

Wagner, M. E., Schubert, H. J. P., & Schubert, D. S. P. (1985). Family size effects: A review. *Journal of Genetic Psychology, 146,* 65–78.

Wahlstrom, K. (2002). Changing times: Findings from the first longitudinal study of later high school start times. *NASSP Bulletin, 86,* 3–21.

Wainright, J. L., Russell, S. T., & Patterson, C. J. (2004). Psychosocial adjustment, school outcomes, and romantic relationships of adolescents with same-sex parents. *Child Development, 75,* 1886–1898.

Wainryb, C., Shaw, L. A., Laupa, M., & Smith, K. R. (2001). Children's, adolescents', and young adults' thinking about different types of disagreements. *Developmental Psychology, 37,* 373–386.

Walden, T. A., & Smith, M. C. (1997). Emotion regulation. *Motivation and Emotion, 21,* 7–25.

Waldenström, U. (1999). Experience of labor and birth in 1111 women. *Journal of Psychosomatic Research, 47,* 471–482.

Waldrop, M. F., & Halverson, C. F. (1975). Intensive and extensive peer behavior: Longitudinal and cross-sectional analyses. *Child Development, 46,* 19–26.

Walk, R. D. (1968). Monocular compared to binocular depth perception in human infants. *Science, 162,* 473–475.

Walker, E. F. (2002). Adolescent neurodevelopment and psychopathology. *Current Directions in Psychological Science, 11,* 24–28.

Walker, L. J. (1984). Sex differences in the development of moral reasoning: A critical review. *Child Development, 55,* 677–691.

Walker, L. J. (1989). A longitudinal study of moral reasoning. *Child Development, 60,* 157–166.

Walker, L. J. (1991). Sex differences in moral reasoning. In W. M. Kurtines & J. L. Gewirtz (Eds.), *Handbook of moral behavior and development: Vol. 2. Research* (pp. 333–364). Hillsdale, NJ: Erlbaum.

Walker, L. J. (1996). Is one sex morally superior? In M. R. Merrens & G. G. Brannigan (Eds.), *The developmental psychologists: Research adventures across the life span.* New York: McGraw-Hill.

Walker, L., Hennig, K. H., & Krettenauer, T. (2000). Parent and peer contexts for children's moral reasoning development. *Child Development, 71,* 1033–1048.

Walker, L. J., & Pitts, R. C. (1998). Naturalistic conceptions of moral maturity. *Developmental Psychology, 34,* 403–419.

Walker-Andrews, A. S., Bahrick, L. E., Raglioni, S. S., & Diaz, I. (1991). Infant's bimodal perception of gender. *Ecological Psychology, 3,* 55–75.

Walker-Andrews, A. S., & Lennon, E. M. (1985). Auditory-visual perception of changing distance by human infants. *Child Development, 56,* 544–548.

Wallerstein, J. S., Corbin, S. B., & Lewis, J. M. (1988). Children of divorce: A ten-year study. In E. M. Hetherington & J. Arasteh (Eds.), *Impact of divorce, single-parenting, and stepparenting on children* (pp. 198–214). Hillsdale, NJ: Erlbaum.

Wallerstein, J. S., & Kelly, J. B. (1980). *Surviving the breakup: How children and parents cope with divorce.* New York: Basic Books.

Walsh, B. T., & Devlin, M. J. (1998). Eating disorders: Progress and problems. *Science, 280,* 1387–1390.

Wang, Q. (2004). The emergence of cultural self-constructs: Autobiographical memory and self-description in European American and Chinese children. *Developmental Psychology, 40,* 3–15.

Ward, L. M. (2004). Wading through stereotypes: Positive and negative associations between media use and Black adolescents' conceptions of self. *Developmental Psychology, 40,* 284–294.

Ward, S., Reale, G., & Levinson, D. (1972). Children's perceptions, explanations, and judgments of television advertising. In E. A. Rubenstein, G. A. Comstock, & J. P. Murray (Eds.), *Television and social behavior: Vol. 4. Television in day-to-day life: Patterns of use.* Washington, DC: U.S. Government Printing Office.

Wark, G. R., & Krebs, D. L. (1996). Gender and dilemma differences in real-life moral judgment. *Developmental Psychology, 32,* 220–230.

Warkany, J., & Schraffenberger, E. (1947). Congenital malformations induced in rats by roentgen rays. *American Journal of Roentgenology and Radium Therapy, 57,* 455–463.

Warren, S. L., Huston, L., Egeland, B., & Sroufe, L. A. (1997). Child and adolescent anxiety disorders and early attachment. *Journal of the American Academy of Child and Adolescent Psychiatry, 36,* 637–644.

Wass, T. S., Persutte, W. H., & Hobbins, J. C. (2001). The impact of prenatal alcohol exposure on frontal cortex development in utero. *American Journal of Obstetrics and Gynecology, 185,* 737–742.

Waterhouse, L., Fein, D., & Modahl, C. (1996). Neurofunctional mechanisms in autism. *Psychological Review, 103,* 457–489.

Waters, E., & Deane, K. E. (1985). Defining and assessing individual differences in attachment relationships: Q-methodology and the organization of behavior in infancy and early childhood. In I. Bretherton & E. Waters (Eds.), *Growing points of attachment theory and research. Monographs of the Society for Research in Child Development, 50* (1–2, Serial No. 209).

Waters, E., Wippman, J., & Sroufe, L. A. (1979). Attachment, positive affect, and competence in the peer group: Two studies in construct validation. *Child Development, 50,* 821–829.

Watson, A. C., Nixon, C. L., Wilson, A., & Capage, L. (1999). Social interaction skills and theory of mind in young children. *Developmental Psychology, 35,* 386–391.

Watson, J. B. (1930). *Behaviorism.* New York: W. W. Norton.

Watson, J. S. (1971). Cognitive-perceptual development in infancy: Settings for the seventies. *Merrill-Palmer Quarterly, 17,* 139–152.

Watson, J. S., & Ramey, C. T. (1972). Reactions to response-contingent stimulation in early infancy. *Merrill-Palmer Quarterly, 18,* 219–227.

Waxman, S. R., & Booth, A. E. (2000). Principles that are invoked in the acquisition of words, but not facts. *Cognition, 77,* B33–B43.

Weber-Fox, C. M., & Neville, H. J. (1996). Maturational contraints on functional specializations for language processing: ERP and behavioral evidence in bilingual speakers. *Journal of Cognitive Neuroscience, 8,* 231–256.

Wechsler, D. (1991). *Wechsler intelligence scale for children—Third edition: Manual.* New York: The Psychological Corporation.

Weinberg, M. K., & Tronick, E. Z. (1994). Beyond the face: An empirical study of infant affective configurations of facial, vocal, gestural, and regulatory behaviors. *Child Development, 65,* 1503–1515.

Weinberg, W. K., Tronick, E. Z., Cohn, J. F., & Olson, K. L. (1999). Gender differences in emotional expressivity and self-regulation during early infancy. *Developmental Psychology, 35,* 175–188.

Weinberger, S. E., & Weiss, S. T. (1988). Pulmonary diseases. In G. N. Burrow & T. F. Ferris (Eds.), *Medical complications of pregnancy* (3rd ed., pp. 448–484). Philadelphia: W.B. Saunders.

Weiner, B., & Handel, S. J. (1985). A cognition-emotion-action sequence: Anticipated emotional consequences of causal attributions and reported communication strategy. *Developmental Psychology, 21,* 102–107.

Weinfield, N. S., Ogawa, J. R., & Sroufe, L. A. (1997). Early attachment as a pathway to adolescent peer competence. *Journal of Research on Adolescence, 7,* 241–265.

Weisner, T. S. (1996). Why ethnography should be the most important method in the study of human development. In A. C. R. Jessor & R. A. Shweder (Eds.), *Ethnography and human development* (pp. 305–324). Chicago: University of Chicago Press.

Weiss, L. H., & Schwarz, J. C. (1996). The relationship between parenting types and older adolescents' personality, academic achievement, adjustment, and substance abuse. *Child Development, 67,* 2101–2114.

Weitzman, L. J. (1985). *The divorce revolution: The unexpected social and economic consequences for women and children in America.* New York: Free Press.

Weitzman, M., Gortmaker, S., & Sobol, A. (1992). Maternal smoking and behavior problems of children. *Pediatrics, 90,* 342–349.

Welch-Ross, M. K. (1995). An integrative model of the development of autobiographical memory. *Developmental Review, 15,* 338–365.

Welch-Ross, M. K., & Schmidt, C. R. (1996). Gender-schema development and children's constructive story memory: Evidence for a developmental model. *Child Development, 67,* 820–835.

Wellman, H. M. (1977). The early development of intentional memory. *Human Development, 20,* 86–101.

Wellman, H. M. (1990). *The child's theory of mind.* Cambridge, MA: MIT Press.

Wellman, H. M., Cross, D., & Watson, J. (2001). Meta-analysis of theory-of-mind development: The truth about false belief. *Child Development, 72,* 655–684.

Wellman, H. M., & Estes, D. (1986). Early understanding of mental entities: A reexamination of childhood realism. *Child Development, 57,* 910–923.

Wellman, H. M., & Lempers, J. D. (1977). The naturalistic communicative abilities of two-year-olds. *Child Development, 48,* 1052–1057.

Wellman, H. M., & Liu, D. (2004). Scaling of theory-of-mind tasks. *Child Development, 75,* 523–541.

Welsh, M. C. (2002). Developmental and clinical variations in executive functions. In D. L. Molfese & V. J. Molfese (Eds.), *Developmental variations in learning: Applications to social, executive function, language, and reading skills* (pp. 139–185). Mahwah, NJ: Erlbaum.

Wenglinsky, H. (1998). *Does it compute? The relationship between educational technology and student achievement in mathematics.* Princeton, NJ: Educational Testing Service.

Wentzel, K. R. (2002). Are effective teachers like good parents? Teaching styles and student adjustment in early adolescence. *Child Development, 73,* 287–301.

Wentzel, K. R., & Erdley, C. A. (1993). Strategies for making friends: Relations to social behavior and peer acceptance in early adolescence. *Developmental Psychology, 29,* 819–826.

Werker, J. F., & Desjardins, R. N. (1995). Listening to speech in the 1st year of life: Experiential influences on phoneme perception. *Current Directions in Psychological Science, 4,* 76–81.

Werker, J. F., & Lalonde, C. E. (1988). Cross-language speech perception: Initial capabilities and developmental change. *Developmental Psychology, 24,* 672–683.

Werker, J. F., & Tees, R. C. (1984). Cross-language speech perception: Evidence for perceptual reorganization during the first year of life. *Infant Behavior and Development, 7,* 49–63.

Werner, E. E. (1972). Infants around the world: Cross-cultural studies of psychomotor development from birth to two years. *Journal of Cross-Cultural Psychology, 3,* 111–134.

Werner, E. E. (1995). Resilience in development. *Current Directions in Psychological Science, 4,* 81–85.

Wertsch, J. V. (1985). *Vygotsky and the social formation of mind.* Cambridge, MA: Harvard University Press.

Wertsch, J. V., & Tulviste, P. (1992). L. S. Vygotsky and contemporary developmental psychology. *Developmental Psychology, 28,* 548–557.

Wertz, D. C., & Fletcher, J. C. (1993). Feminist criticism of prenatal diagnosis: A response. *Clinical Obstetrics and Gynecology, 36,* 541–567.

Wertz, D. C., & Fletcher, J. C. (1998). Ethical and social issues in prenatal sex selection: A survey of geneticists in 37 nations. *Social Science & Medicine, 46,* 255–273.

West, T. A., & Bauer, P. J. (1999). Assumptions of infantile amnesia: Are there differences between early and later memories? *Memory, 7,* 257–278.

Westinghouse Learning Corporation. (1969). *Impact of Head Start: Evaluation of the effects of Head Start on children's cognitive and affective development.* Washington, DC: Clearinghouse for Federal, Scientific, and Technical Information.

Wexler, K. (1982). A principle theory for language acquisition. In E. Wanner & L. Gleitman (Eds.), *Language acquisition: The state of the art* (pp. 288–315). Cambridge: Cambridge University Press.

Whalen, C. K., Jamner, L. D., Henker, B., Delfino, R. J., & Lozano, J. M. (2002). The ADHD Spectrum and everyday life: Experience sampling of adolescent moods, activities, smoking, and drinking. *Child Development, 73,* 209–227.

Whalen, R. E. (1984). Multiple actions of steroids and their antagonists. *Archives of Sexual Behavior, 13,* 497–502.

Whitaker, R. C., Wright, J. A., Pepe, M. S., Seidel, K. D., & Dietz, W. H. (1997). Predicting obesity in young adulthood from childhood and parental obesity. *New England Journal of Medicine, 337,* 869–873.

White, B. Y., & Fredriksen, J. R. (1998). Inquiry, modeling, and metacognition: Making science accessible to all students. *Cognition and Instruction, 16*(63), 90–91.

White, R. W. (1959). Motivation reconsidered: The concept of competence. *Psychological Review, 66,* 297–333.

Whitehurst, G. J., Arnold, D. S., Epstein, J. N., Angell, A. L., Smith, M., & Fischel, J. E. (1994). A picture book reading intervention in day care and home for children from low-income families. *Developmental Psychology, 30,* 679–689.

Whitehurst, G. J., & Fischel, J. E. (2000). Reading and language impairments in conditions of poverty. In D. V. M. Bishop & L. B. Leonard (Eds.), *Speech and language impairments in children: Causes, characteristics, intervention and outcome* (pp. 53–71). Hove, UK: Psychology Press.

Whiteman, S. D., & Buchanan, C. M. (2002). Mothers' and children's expectations for adolescence: The impact of perceptions of an older sibling's experience. *Journal of Family Psychology, 16,* 157–171.

Whiting, B. B., & Edwards, C. P. (1988). *Children of different worlds.* Cambridge, MA: Harvard University Press.

Whiting, B. B., & Whiting, J. W. M. (1975). *Children of six cultures: A psychocultural analysis.* Cambridge, MA: Harvard University Press.

Whitlock, J. L., Powers, J. L., & Eckenrode, J. (2006). The virtual cutting edge: The Internet and adolescent self-injury. *Developmental Psychology, 42,* 407–417.

Wichstrøm, L. (1999). The emergence of gender difference in depressed mood during adolescence: The role of intensified gender socialization. *Developmental Psychology, 35,* 232–245.

Widom, C. S. (1989). The cycle of violence. *Science, 244,* 160–166.

Wigfield, A., & Eccles, J. S. (1994). Children's competence beliefs, achievement values, and general self-esteem: Changes across elementary and middle school. *Journal of Early Adolescence, 14,* 107–138.

Willats, P. (1990). Development of problem-solving strategies in infancy. In D. F. Bjorklund (Ed.), *Children's strategies: Contemporary views of cognitive development* (pp. 23–66). Hillsdale, NJ: Erlbaum.

Williams, J. E., & Best, D. L. (1982). *Measuring sex stereotypes: A thirty nation study.* Beverly Hills, CA: Sage.

Williams, J. M., & Currie, C. (2000). Self-esteem and physical development in early adolescence: Pubertal timing and body image. *Journal of Early Adolescence, 20,* 120–149.

Williams, L. J., Rasmussen, S. A., Flores, A., Kirby, R. S., & Edmonds, L. D. (2005). Decline in the prevalence of spina bifida and anencephaly by race/ethnicity: 1995–2002. *Pediatrics, 116,* 580–586.

Willig, A. C., & Ramirez, J. D. (1993). The evaluation of bilingual education. In M. B. Arias & U. Casanova (Eds.), *Bilingual education: Politics, practice, research.* Chicago: National Society for the Study of Education.

Willinger, M., Ko, C.-W., Hoffman, H. J., Kessler, R. C., & Corwin, M. J. (2000). Factors associated with caregivers' choice of infant sleep position, 1994–1998: The National Infant Sleep Position Study. *Journal of the American Medical Association, 283,* 2135–2142.

Willinger, M., Ko, C-W., Hoffman, H. J., Kessler, R. C., & Corwin, M. J. (2003). Trends in infant bed sharing in the United States, 1993–2000: The National Infant Sleep Position Study. *Archives of Pediatrics & Adolescent Medicine, 157,* 43–49.

Wilson, B. J., & Weiss, A. J. (1992). Developmental differences in children's reactions to a toy advertisement linked to a toy-based cartoon. *Journal of Broadcasting and Electronic Media, 36,* 371–394.

Wilson, J. G. (1977). Current status of teratology: General principles and mechanisms derived from animal studies. In J. G. Wilson & F. C. Fraser (Eds.), *Handbook of teratology: Vol. 1. General principles and etiology.* New York: Plenum Press.

Wilson, M. N. (1986). The black extended family: An analytical consideration. *Developmental Psychology, 22,* 246–258.

Wimmer, H., & Perner, J. (1983). Beliefs about beliefs: Representation and constraining function of wrong beliefs in young children's understanding of deception. *Cognition, 13,* 103–128.

Winner, E. (1979). New names for old things: The emergence of metaphoric language. *Journal of Child Language, 6,* 469–491.

Winner, E. (1996). *Gifted children: Myths and realities.* New York: Basic Books.

Winner, E. (1997). Exceptionally high intelligence and schooling. *American Psychologist, 52,* 1070–1081.

Winner, E. (2000). The origins and ends of giftedness. *American Psychologist, 55,* 159–169.

Winsler, A., Carlton, M. P., & Barry, M. J. (2000). Age-related changes in preschool children's systematic use of private speech in a natural setting. *Journal of Child Language, 27,* 665–687.

Winsler, A., Diaz, R. M., Atencio, D. J., McCarthy, E. M., & Chabay, L. A. (2000). Verbal self-regulation over time in preschool children at risk for attention and behavior problems. *Journal of Child Psychology and Psychiatry, 41,* 875–886.

Winsler, A., & Naglieri, J. (2003). Overt and covert verbal problem–solving strategies: Developmental trends in use, awareness, and relations with task performance in children aged 5 to 17. *Child Development, 74,* 659–678.

Winstead, B. A. (1986). Sex differences in same-sex friendships. In V. J. Derlaga & B. A. Winstead (Eds.), *Friendship and social interaction.* New York: Springer-Verlag.

Wolchik, S. A., West, S. G., Westover, S., Sandler, I. N., Martin, A., Lustig, J., et al. (2002). The children of divorce parenting intervention: Outcome evaluation of an empirically based program. In T. A. Revenson & A. R. D'Augelli (Eds.), *A quarter century of community psychology: Readings from the American Journal of Community Psychology* (pp. 409–444). New York: Kluwer Academic/Plenum Publishers.

Wolfe, D. A. (1985). Child-abusive parents: An empirical review and analysis. *Psychological Bulletin, 97,* 462–482.

Wolfe, D. A., Fairbank, J., Kelly, J. A., & Bradlyn, A. S. (1983). Child abusive parents' physiological responses to stressful and non-stressful behavior in children. *Behavioral Assessment, 5,* 363–371.

Wolfe, D. A., Sas, L., & Wekerle, C. (1994). Factors associated with the development of post-traumatic stress disorder among child victims of sexual abuse. *Child Abuse and Neglect, 18,* 37–50.

Wolff, P. H. (1969). The natural history of crying and other vocalizations in early infancy. In B. Foss (Ed.), *Determinants of infant behavior* (Vol. 4). London: Methuen.

Wolff, P. H. (1987). *The development of behavioral states and the expression of emotions in early infancy.* Chicago: University of Chicago Press.

Wolfner, G. D., & Gelles, R. J. (1993). A profile of violence toward children: A national study. *Child Abuse and Neglect, 17,* 197–212.

Wolfson, A. R., & Carskadon, M. A. (1998). Sleep schedules and daytime functioning in adolescents. *Child Development, 69,* 875–887.

Wood, D. J., Bruner, J. S., & Ross, G. (1976). The role of tutoring in problem solving. *Journal of Child Psychology and Psychiatry, 17,* 89–100.

Woolfe, T., Want, S. C., & Siegal, M. (2002). Signposts to development: Theory of mind in deaf children. *Child Development, 73,* 768–778.

Worobey, J. (1985). A review of Brazelton-based interventions to enhance parent-infant interaction. *Journal of Reproductive and Infant Psychology, 3,* 64–73.

Wright, J. C., Huston, A. C., Murphy, K. C., St. Peters, M., Piñon, M., Scantlin, R., & Kotler, J. (2001). The relations of early television viewing to school readiness and vocabulary of children from low-income families: The Early Window Project. *Child Development, 72,* 1347–1366.

Wright, J. C., Huston, A. C., Reitz, A. L., & Piemyat, S. (1994). Young children's perceptions of television reality: Determinants and developmental differences. *Developmental Psychology, 30,* 229–239.

Wright, K. (1998, May). Human in the age of mechanical reproduction. *Discover, 19,* pp. 79–84.

Wright, M. O., & Masten, A. S. (2005). Resilience processes in development. In S. Goldstein & R. B. Brooks (Eds.), *Handbook of resilience in children* (pp. 17–37). New York: Klewar/Plenum.

Wynn, K. (1992a). Addition and subtraction by human infants. *Nature, 358,* 749–750.

Wynn, K. (1992b). Children's acquisition of the number words and the counting system. *Cognitive Psychology, 24,* 220–251.

Wynn, K. (1998). Psychological foundations of number: Numerical competence in human infants. *Trends in Cognitive Science, 2,* 296–303.

Xu, F., & Spelke, E. S. (2000). Large number discrimination in 6-month-olds. *Cognition, 74,* B1–B11.

Yakovlev, P. I., & Lecours, A. R. (1967). The myelogenetic cycles of regional maturation of the brain. In A. Minkowski (Ed.), *Regional development of the brain in early life.* Oxford: Blackwell.

Yale, M. E., Messinger, D. S., Cobo-Lewis, A. B., Oller, D. K., & Eilers, R. E. (1999). An event-based analysis of the coordination of early child vocalizations and facial actions. *Developmental Psychology, 35,* 505–513.

Yarrow, L. J., Goodwin, M. S., Manheimer, H., & Milowe, I. D. (1973). Infancy experiences and cognitive and personality development at 10 years. In L. J. Stone, H. T. Smith, & L. B. Murphy (Eds.), *The competent infant: Research and commentary.* New York: Basic Books.

Yates, M., & Youniss, J. (1996a). Community service and political-moral identity in adolescents. *Journal of Research on Adolescence, 6,* 271–284.

Yates, M., & Youniss, J. (1996b). A developmental perspective on community service in adolescence. *Social Development, 5,* 85–111.

Yogman, M. W. (1982). Observations on the father-infant relationship. In S. H. Cath, A. R. Gurwitt, & J. M. Ross (Eds.), *Father and child: Developmental and clinical perspectives.* Boston: Little, Brown.

Yogman, M. W., Dixon, S., Tronick, E., Als, H., Adamson, L., Lester, B. M., & Brazelton, T. B. (1977, April). *The goals and structure of face-to-face interaction between infants and their fathers.* Paper presented at the biennial meeting of the Society for Research in Child Development, New Orleans.

Yonas, A., & Owsley, C. (1987). Development of visual space perception. In P. Salapatek & L. Cohen (Eds.), *Handbook of infant perception: From perception to cognition* (Vol. 2). Orlando, FL: Academic Press.

Yoon, P. W., Olney, R. S., Khoury, M. J., Sappenfield, W. M., Chavez, G. F., & Taylor, D. (1997). Contribution of birth defects and genetic diseases to pediatric hospitalizations. *Archives of Pediatrics & Adolescent Medicine, 151,* 1096–1103.

Young, S. K., Fox, N. A., & Zahn-Waxler, C. (1999). The relations between temperament and empathy in 2-year-olds. *Developmental Psychology, 35,* 1189–1197.

Youngblade, L. M., & Belsky, J. (1992). Parent-child antecedents of 5-year-olds' close friendships: A longitudinal analysis. *Developmental Psychology, 28,* 700–713.

Young-Browne, G., Rosenfeld, H. M., & Horowitz, F. D. (1977). Infant discrimination of facial expression. *Child Development, 48,* 555–562.

Younger, A., Gentile, C., & Burgess, K. (1993). Children's perceptions of social withdrawal: Changes across age. In K. H. Rubin & J. B. Asend-orpf (Eds.), *Social withdrawal, inhibition, and shyness in childhood* (pp. 215–235). Hillsdale, NJ: Erlbaum.

Younger, B. A. (2003). Parsing objects into categories: Infants' perception and use of correlated attributes. In D. H. Rakison & L. M. Oakes (Eds.), *Early category and concept development* (pp. 77–102). New York: Oxford University Press.

Youniss, J., McLellan, J., & Mazur, B. (2004). Voluntary service, peer group orientation, and civic engagement. *Journal of Adolescent Research, 16,* 456-468.

Youniss, J., McLellan, J., Su, Y., & Yates, M. (1999). The role of community service in identity development: Normative, unconventional, and deviant orientations. *Journal of Adolescent Research, 14,* 248–261.

Youniss, J., McLellan, J., & Yates, M. (1999). Religion, community service, and identity in American youth. *Journal of Adolescence, 22,* 243–253.

Yule, W. (1998). Posttraumatic stress disorder in children and its treatment. In T. W. Miller (Ed.), *Children of trauma: Stressful life events and their effects on children and adolescents* (pp. 219–243). Madison, CT: International Universities Press.

Yule, W. (2000). Emmanuel Miller lectures from pogroms to "ethnic cleansing": Meeting the needs of war affected children. *Journal of Child Psychology and Psychiatry, 41,* 695–702.

Yunger, J. L., Carver, P. R., & Perry, D. G. (2004). Does gender identity influence children's psychological well-being? *Developmental Psychology, 40,* 572–582.

Zagon, I. S., & McLaughlin, P. J. (1984). An overview of the neurobehavioral sequelae of perinatal opiod exposure. In J. Yanai (Ed.), *Neurobehavioral teratology.* New York: Elsevier.

Zahn-Waxler, C., Friedman, S. L., & Cummings, E. M. (1983). Children's emotions and behaviors in response to infants' cries. *Child Development, 54,* 1522–1528.

Zahn-Waxler, C., Radke-Yarrow, M., Wagner, E., & Chapman, M. (1992). Development of concern for others. *Developmental Psychology, 28,* 126–136.

Zajonc, R. B., Markus, H., & Markus, G. B. (1979). The birth order puzzle. *Journal of Personality and Social Psychology, 37,* 1325–1341.

Zaslow, M. J., Dion, M. R., Morrison, D. R., Weinfield, N., Ogawa, J., & Tabors, P. (1999). Protective factors in the development of preschool-age children of young mothers receiving welfare. In E. M. Hetherington (Ed.), *Coping with divorce, single parenting, and remarriage* (pp. 193–223). Mahwah, NJ: Erlbaum.

Zeanah, C. H., Smyke, A. T., Koga, S. F., Carlson, E., & The Bucharest Early Intervention Project. (2005). Attachment in institutionalized and community children in Romania. *Child Development, 76,* 1015–1028.

Zebrowitz, L. A., Kendall-Tackett, K., & Fafel, J. (1991). The influence of children's facial maturity on parental expectations and punishments. *Journal of Experimental Child Psychology, 52,* 221–238.

Zelazo, N. A., Zelazo, P. R., Cohen, K. M., & Zelazo, P. D. (1993). Specificity of practice effects on elementary neuromotor patterns. *Developmental Psychology, 29,* 686–691.

Zelazo, P. D., Helwig, C. C. & Lau, A. (1996). Intention, act, and outcome in behavioral prediction and moral judgment. *Child Development, 67,* 2478–2492.

Zelazo, P. R. (1983). The development of walking: New findings and old assumptions. *Journal of Motor Behavior, 15,* 99–137.

Zelazo, P. R. (1998). McGraw and the development of unaided walking. *Developmental Review, 18,* 449–471.

Zeskind, P. S. (1981). Behavioral dimensions and cry sounds of infants of differential fetal growth. *Infant Behavior and Development, 4,* 297–306.

Zhou, Q., Eisenberg, N., Losoya, S. H., Fabes, R. A., Reiser, M., Guthrie, I. K., et al. (2002). The relations of parental warmth and positive expressiveness to children's empathy-related responding and social functioning: A longitudinal study. *Developmental Psychology, 73,* 893–915.

Zhou, Q., Eisenberg, N., Wang, Y., & Reiser, M. (2004). Chinese children's effortful control and dispositional anger/frustration: Relations to parenting styles and children's social functioning. *Developmental Psychology, 40,* 352–366.

Zhu, J. L., Madsen, K. M., Vestergaard, M., Olesen, A. V., Basso, O., & Olsen, J. (2005). Paternal age and congenital malformations. *Human Reproduction, 20,* 3173–3177.

Ziegert, D. I., Kistner, J. A., Castro, R., & Robertson, B. (2001). Longitudinal study of young children's responses to challenging achievement situations. *Child Development, 72,* 609–624.

Zigler, E. (1967). Familial mental retardation: A continuing dilemma. *Science, 155,* 292–298.

Zigler, E., & Butterfield, E. C. (1968). Motivational aspects of changes in IQ test performance of culturally deprived nursery school children. *Child Development, 39,* 1–14.

Zill, N. (1988). Behavior, achievement, and health problems among children in stepfamilies: Findings from a national survey of child health. In E. M. Hetherington & J. D. Arasteh (Eds.), *Impact of divorce, single-parenting, and stepparenting on children.* Hillsdale, NJ: Erlbaum.

Zill, N. (1994). Understanding why children in stepfamilies have more learning and behavior problems than children in nuclear families. In A. Booth & J. Dunn (Eds.), *Stepfamilies: Who benefits? Who does not?* (pp. 97–106) Hillsdale, NJ: Erlbaum.

Zill, N., Morrison, D. R., & Coiro, M. J. (1993). Long-term effects of parental divorce on parent-child relationships, adjustment, and achievement in young adulthood. *Journal of Family Psychology, 7,* 1–13.

Zimet, G. D., Owens, R., Dahms, W., Cutler, M., Litvene, M., & Cuttler, L. (1997). Psychosocial outcome of children evaluated for short stature. *Archives of Pediatric and Adolescent Medicine, 151,* 1017–1023.

Zimmerman, M. A., Copeland, L. A., Shope, J. T., & Dielman, T. E. (1997). A longitudinal study of self-esteem: Implications for adolescent development. *Journal of Youth and Adolescence, 26,* 117–142.

Zucker, K. J., & Bradley, S. J. (2000). Gender identity disorder. In C. H. Zeanah, Jr. (Ed.), *Handbook of infant mental health* (2nd ed., pp. 412–424). New York: Guilford Press.

Zuckerman, B., & Bresnahan, K. (1991). Developmental and behavioral consequences of prenatal drug and alcohol exposure. *Pediatric Clinics of North America, 38,* 1387–1406.

# CREDITS

## Text Credits

**Chapter 1:** p. 8 *Figure 1.1* From Robert S. Siegler, *Emerging Minds: The Process of Change in Children's Thinking.* Copyright © 1996. Reprinted by Oxford University Press, England. p. 29 *Figure 1.4* From Garabino, J., "Sociocultural Risk: Dangers to Competence," in C. Kopp and J. Krakow (Eds.), *Child Development in a Social Context.* Copyright © 1982. Reprinted by permission of Pearson Education, Inc.

**Chapter 2:** p. 44 *Figure 2.1* Adapted from Ram, A., & Ross, H. S. "Problem-solving, contention, and struggle: How siblings resolve a conflict of interests," *Child Development, 72,* 2001, p.1715 (Table 3). Reprinted with permission from the Society for Research in Child Development. p. 50 *Figure 2.2* From Sheldrick, R.C. (2004). Social networks and degree of psychopathy among adolescent offenders (Doctoral dissertation, Temple University, 1990). Dissertation Abstracts International, 65, 1964. Reprinted by permission of the author. p. 51 *Figure 2.3* From M. Gardner & L. Steinberg, "Peer influence on risk taking, risk preference, and risky decision making in adolescence and adulthood: An experimental study," *Developmental Psychology, 41,* pp. 625–635. Reprinted with permission of the publisher, American Psychological Association. p. 54 From Gagnon, M. & Ladouceur, R., "Behavioral treatment of child stutterers: Replication and extension," *Behavior Therapy, 23,* 1992, pp. 113–129. Copyright 1992 by the Association for Advancement of Behavior Therapy. Reprinted by permission of the publisher. p. 58 *Figure 2.7* From Cole, D. A., Maxwell, S. E., Martin, J. M., Peeke, L. G., Seroczynski, A. D., Tram, J. M., Hoffman, K. B., Ruiz, M. D., Jacquez, F., & Maschman, T., "The development of multiple domains of child and adolescent self-concept: A cohort sequential longitudinal design," *Child Development, 72,* 2001, p. 1735 (Figure 3). Reprinted with permission from the Society for Research in Child Development. p. 60 *Figure 2.8* Data from R. S. Siegler & E. Stern, "Conscious and unconscious strategy discoveries: A microgenetic analysis," *Journal of Experimental Psychology, General, 127,* 1998, pp. 377–397. Reprinted with permission of the publisher, American Psychological Association.

**Chapter 3:** p. 72 *Figure 3.1* Adapted from Warren Isensee, *The Chronicle of Higher Education,* September 3, 1986. Reprinted by permission of Warren Isensee. p. 100 *Table 3.5* Intelligence, Genes, and Success: Scientists Respond to The Bell Curve, 1997, pp. 45–70, "IQ and Degrees of Relatedness: Similarities of Genetically Related and Unrelated Individuals Who Live Together and Apart," B. Devlin, S. E. Feinberg, D. P. Resnick, & K. Roder (Eds.). With kind permission of Springer Science and Business Media, and the author.

**Chapter 4:** p. 120 *Figure 4.3* Reprinted from *The Developing Human* by Keith L. Moore, Ph.D. Copyright 1998, with permission from Elsevier. p. 131 *Figure 4.4* Reprinted from Pediatric Clinics of North America, 47, Lindegren, Steinberg, & Byers, "Epidemiology of HIV/AIDS in children," pp. 1–20, Copyright 2000, with permission from Elsevier. p. 133 *Table 4.4* From Reece, E. A., Hobbins, J. C., Mahoney, M. J., and Petrie, R. H., *Handbook of Medicine of the Fetus and the Mother.* Copyright © 1995. Reprinted by permission of Dr. Albert Reece. p. 143 *Figure 4.7* From Brooks-Gunn, Kiebanov, Liaw, & Spiker, "Enha-ncing the Development of Low-Birthweight, Premature Infants: Changes in Cognition and Behavior Over the First Three Years," *Child Development, 64,* 736–754. Reprinted with permission from the Society for Research in Child Development.

p. 144 *Table 4.5* From V. Apgar, "A Proposal for a New Method of Evaluation of the Newborn Infant," *Anesthesia and Analgesia: Current Researches, 32,* 1953, 260–267. Reprinted by permission of Lippincott Williams & Wilkins.

**Chapter 5:** p. 156 *Figure 5.4* Illustration copyright 1998 John W. Karapelou. Reprinted by permission of John W. Karapelou. p. 157 *Figure 5.5* Reprinted from *Neuropsychologia, 28,* Huttenlocher, P. R., "Morphometric Study of Human Cerebral Cortex Development," pp. 517–527, Copyright 1990, with permission from Elsevier. p. 175 *Figure 5.8* Reprinted from *Infant Perception: From Sensation to Cognition,* Vol. 1 by L. B. Cohen and P. Salapatek (Eds.), "Pattern Perception in Early Infancy" by P. Salapatek, Copyright 1975, with permission from Elsevier.

**Chapter 6:** p. 191 *Figure 6.1* From Treiber et al., "Perception of a 'Subjective' Contour by Infants," *Child Development, 51,* 915–917. Reprinted by permission of Blackwell Publishing. p. 192 *Figure 6.2* From V. M. Cassia, C. Turati, & F. Simon, "A nonspecific bias explains newborns' face preferences," *Psychological Science, 15,* 2004, pp. 379–383. Reprinted by permission of Blackwell Publishing. p. 193 *Figure 6.3* Adapted from Spelke, E. S., "Perception of Unity, Persistence and Identity: Thoughts on Infants' Conceptions of Objects," in J. Mehler and R. Fox (Eds.), *Neonate Cognition: Beyond the Blooming, Buzzing Confusion,* 1985. Reprinted by permission. p. 195 *Figure 6.4* From Adolph, K. E., "Specificity of learning: Why infants fall over a veritable cliff," *Psychological Science, 11,* 2000, p. 292. Reprinted by permission of Blackwell Publishing. p. 203 *Figure 6.6* Adapted from Baillargeon, R. (1987). "Object Permanence in 3 1/2 – 4 1/2 month-old infants," *Developmental Psychology, 23,* pp. 655–664, 1987. Adapted with permission. p. 204 *Figure 6.7* From Spelke, E., Breinlinger, K., Macomber, J., & Jacobson, K., "Origins of knowledge," *Psychological Review, 99,* pp. 605–632, 1992. Reprinted with permission. p. 209 *Figure 6.9* Nature by K. Wynn. Copyright 1992 by Nature Pubg Group. Reproduced with permission of Nature Pubg Group in the format Textbook via Copyright Clearance Center. p. 210 *Figure 6.10* From J. F. Fagan, "Infant Recognition Memory: The Effects of Length ...," *Child Development, 45,* 1974, pp. 351–356. Reprinted by permission of Blackwell Publishing. p. 213 *Figure 6.13* Adapted from Z. Chen, R. P. Sanchez, and T. Campbell, "From beyond to within their grasp: The rudiments of analogical problem solving in 10- and 13-month-olds," *Developmental Psychology, 33,* pp. 790–801, 1997. Adapted with permission. p. 218 *Figure 6.14* Reprinted from *Infant Behavior & Development, 8,* Fernald, A., "Four-month-olds Prefer to Listen to Motherese," pp. 181–195, Copyright 1985, with permission from Elsevier. p. 222 *Figure 6.15* From Bates, Thal, Fenson, Dale, Reznick, Reilley, & Hartung, "Developmental and Stylistic Variation in the Composition of Early Vocabulary," *Journal of Child Language, 21,* 1994, pp. 85–123. Reprinted with the permission of Cambridge University Press. p. 223 *Figure 6.16* Adapted from Goldfield, B. A. & Reznick, J. S., "Early Lexical Acquisition: Rate, Content, & the Vocabulary Spurt," *Journal of Child Language, 17,* 1990, pp. 171–183. Reprinted with the permission of Cambridge University Press. p. 226 *Table 6.2* Bayley Scales of Infant Development. Copyright © 1993, 1984, 1969 by Harcourt Assessment, Inc. Reproduced with permission. All rights reserved.

**Chapter 7:** p. 258 *Figure 7.3* Adapted from T. M. Field, "Affective Displays of High-Risk Infants During Early Interactions," in T. Field and A. Fogel (Eds.), *Emotion and Early Interaction,* 1982, p. 109. Reprinted by permission of Erlbaum, and the author.

Science and Business Media.    p. 502 *Figure 14.4* From X. Ge, R. D. Conger, & G. H. Elder, Jr., "Coming of age too early: Pubertal influences on girls' vulnerability to psychological distress," *Child Development, 67,* 1996, p. 3394. Reprinted by permission of Blackwell Publishing.    p. 522 *Figure 14.7* Wechsler Intelligence Scale for Children - Third Edition. Copyright © 1990 by Harcourt Assessment, Inc. Reproduced with permission. All rights reserved. p. 525 *Figure 14.8* From N. Ambady, M. Shih, A. Kim, and T. L. Pittinsky, "Stereotype susceptibility in children: Effects of identity activation on quantitative performance," *Psychological Science, 12,* pp. 385–390. Copyright © 2001. Reprinted by permission of Blackwell Publishing Ltd.

**Chapter 15:**    p. 532 *Figure 15.1* From R. Larson & M. Ham, "Stress and 'Storm and Stress' in Early Adolescence: The Relationship of Negative Effects with Dysphoric Affect," *Developmental Psychology, 29,* p. 136, 1993, published by American Psychological Association. Reprinted with permission.    p. 537 *Figure 15.2* From Harter, S., & Monsour, A., "Developmental Analysis of Conflict Caused by Opposing Attributes in the Adolescent Self-Portrait," *Developmental Psychology, 28,* pp. 251–260, 1992, published by American Psychological Association. Reprinted with permission. p. 542 *Figure 15.3* From S. E. French, E. Seidman, L. Allen, & J. L. Aber, "The development of ethnic identity during adolescence," *Developmental Psychology, 42,* pp. 1–10, 2006, published by American Psychological Association. Reprinted with permission.

**Chapter 16:**    p. 555 *Figure 16.1* From Mason, C. A., Cauce, A. M., Gonzales, N., & Hiraga, Y. "Neither Too Sweet Nor Too Sour: Problem Peers, Maternal Control, and Problem Behavior in African American Adolescents," *Child Development, 67,* pp. 2115–2130. Copyright © 1996. Reprinted by permission.    p. 557 *Figure 16.2* From Nicholas Zill, Ph.D., "Understanding Why Children in Stepfamilies Have More Learning and Behavior Problems Than Children in Nuclear Families," in A. Booth & J. Dunn (Eds.), *Stepfamilies: Who Benefits? Who Does Not?* Copyright © 1994. Reprinted by permission.    p. 561 *Figure 16.3* Adapted from Berndt, "Developmental Changes in Conformity to Peers and Parents," *Developmental Psychology, 15,* 1979, pp. 608–616. Reprinted by permission of the American Psychological Association.

## Photo Credits

**Research Applied to Parenting/Education features:** © Royalty-Free Getty Images.

**Chapter 1:**    p. 1 © Gavriel Jecan/Corbis. p. 2 © Richard Koek/Taxi/ Getty Images.    p. 7 © Don Smetzer/Stone/Getty Images.    p. 9 © Mark Richards/PhotoEdit.    p. 11 © Sean Sprague/The Image Works.    p. 12 Erich Lessing/Art Resource.    p. 14 Archives of the History of American Psychology - The University of Akron. p. 16 Photo courtesy of Mitzi M. Wertheim.    p. 18 © Laura Dwight.    p. 21 © Bill Anderson/Photo Researchers. p. 25 © Erik Homburger/Stock Montage. p. 28 © Earl & Nazima Kowall/ Corbis. p. 30 © Elizabeth Harris/Stone/Getty Images.    p. 33 Thomas McAvoy/Time & Life Pictures/Getty Images.

**Chapter 2:**    p. 39 © Ariel Skelley/Corbis.    p. 41 © Spencer Grant/ PhotoEdit.    p. 42 © Laura Dwight.    p. 45 © Royalty-Free/Corbis. p. 56 (left and right) © Elizabeth Crews.    p. 61 © Lindsay Hebberd/Corbis.

**Chapter 3:**    p. 69 © Royalty-Free/Corbis.    p. 73 *Figure 3.2* © CNRI/ Science Photo Library/Photo Researchers.    p. 82 Photo property of Williams Syndrome Association, Inc.    p. 83 © Rosenan/ Custom Medical Stock Photo.    p. 8.5 *Figure 3.7* Billie Carstens/ Denver Children's Hospital.    p. 87 © Laura Dwight.

p. 91 © B. E. Barnes/PhotoEdit.    p. 95 © Rachel Epstein/The Image Works.    p. 99 © Larry Williams/Corbis.    p. 103 © Robert Brenner/PhotoEdit.

**Chapter 4:**    p. 109 © Dave LaBelle/The Image Works.    p. 111 © David Philips/SS/Photo Researchers.    p. 121 © George Steinmetz.    p. 132 © David Young-Wolff/PhotoEdit.    p. 135 © Jessie Casson/Corbis.    p. 136 © Jules Perrier/Corbis.    p. 137 © Jules Perrier/Corbis.    p. 142 © Lisa Spindler Photography Inc./ Photonica/Getty Images.    p. 145 © Elizabeth Crews.

**Chapter 5:**    p. 149 © Laurence Monneret/Stone/Getty Images. p. 150 © Myrleen Ferguson Cate/PhotoEdit.    p. 153 Courtesy of Dr. Joy Hirsch, Head, The Functional MRI Laboratory, Memorial Sloan-Kettering Cancer Center, New York.    p. 155 © Oliver Meckes/Ottawa/Photo Researchers.    p. 159 © Morgan McCauley/ Corbis.    p. 163 © Laura Dwight.    p. 164 © Lionel Delevingne/ Stock Boston.    p. 168 © Myrleen Ferguson Cate/PhotoEdit. p. 172 *Figure 5.7* Nadja Reissland.    p. 178 *Figure 5.9* © Photo-Disc/Getty Images.    p. 181 *Figure 5.10* Steiner, J.E. (1979). Human facial expressions in response to taste and smell stimulation. In H. W. Reese & L. P. Lipsitt (eds.), Advances in child development and behavior (Vol. 13, pp. 257–295). New York: Academic Press.

**Chapter 6:**    p. 188 © Elizabeth Crews.    p. 192 *Figure 6.2* Cassia et al. A nonspecific bias explains newborns' face preferences. *Psychological Science 15* 379–383.    p. 202 © Laura Dwight/PhotoEdit. p. 206 *Figure 6.8* Adele Diamond.    p. 211 *Figure 6.11* Courtesy of Carolyn Rovee-Collier.    p. 221 © Laura Dwight.    p. 225 © Bruce Dale/National Geographic Society Image Collection.

**Chapter 7:**    p. 236 © Caroline Penn/Panos Pictures.    p. 243 *Figure 7.1* Reprinted with permission from Field, T. M., Woodson, R., Greenberg, R., & Cohen, D. (1982). Discrimination and imitation of facial expressions by neonates. *Science, 218,* 179–181. Copyright 1982 American Association for the Advancement of Science. p. 249 Harlow Primate Laboratory, University of Wisconsin. p. 253 © Laura Dwight/PhotoEdit.    p. 262 © Laura Dwight/ PhotoEdit.    p. 263 © Ron Dahlquist/SuperStock.

**Chapter 8:**    p. 269 © Laura Dwight.    p. 280 © Laura Dwight. p. 282 *Figure 8.6* Mandler, J. M. (1997). Development of categorization: Perceptual and conceptual categories. In G. Bremner, A. Slater, & G. Butterworth (Eds.), *Infant development: Recent advances.* East Sussex, UK: Psychology Press. Reprinted by permission of Psychology Press Limited, Hove, UK.    p. 284 © Myrleen Ferguson Cate/PhotoEdit.    p. 294 © Michael Newman/PhotoEdit.

**Chapter 9:**    p. 308 © Laura Dwight.    p. 310 © David Young-Wolff/ PhotoEdit.    p. 311 © Tony Freeman/PhotoEdit.    p. 312 © Laura Dwight.    p. 319 © Laura Dwight/Corbis.    p. 321 © Elizabeth Crews. p. 324 © Syracuse Newspapers /Gary Walts/The Image Works.

**Chapter 10:**    p. 340 © Digital Vision/Getty Images.    p. 342 © Bob Daemmrich/The Image Works.    p. 346 © A. Inden/zefa/Corbis. p. 347 © Goodman/Photo Researchers.    p. 356 © Philip & Karen Smith/Stone/Getty Images.    p. 361 © Cindy Charles/PhotoEdit. p. 362 © Paul Conklin.

**Chapter 11:**    p. 377 Kevin Taylor/Alamy.    p. 380 © David Young-Wolff/PhotoEdit.    p. 381 © Ariel Skelley/Corbis.    p. 396 © Syracuse Newspapers/Michelle Gabel/The Image Works.    p. 400 © Rachel Epstein/The Image Works.    p. 402 © Royalty-Free/ Corbis.    p. 406 *Figure 11.10 Nature* by K. H. S. Kim, N. R. Relkin, K. Lee, J. Hirsch. Copyright 1997 by Nature Publishing Group (Permission). Reproduced with permission of Nature Publishing Group (Permission) in the format Textbook via Copyright Clearance Center.

**Chapter 12:** p. 414 BananaStock/Alamy. p. 416 © Royalty-Free/ Corbis. p. 421 © Rachel Epstein/The Image Works. p. 433 © R. Lord/The Image Works. p. 438 © Sean Sprague/The Image Works. p. 441 © Hazel Hankin/Stock Boston. p. 442 © Bob Daemmrich.

**Chapter 13:** p. 448 © Elizabeth Crews. p. 450 © Victor Englebert. p. 451 © Geri Engberg/The ImageWorks. p. 458 © Bob Daemmrich/Stock Boston. p. 466 © Tony Freeman/PhotoEdit. p. 467 (**left**) © Laura Dwight. (**right**) © Myrleen Ferguson Cate/ PhotoEdit. p. 476 © Elizabeth Crews/The Image Works.

**Chapter 14:** p. 495 © Larry Dale Gordon/The Image Bank/Getty Images. p. 496 © Suzanne Arms/The Image Works. p. 504 © Laura Dwight. p. 509 © Michael Newman/PhotoEdit. p. 510 © Elizabeth Crews. p. 512 © Ted Horowitz/Corbis.

**Chapter 15:** p. 530 © Richard Hutchings/Corbis. p. 540 © M. Fredericks/The Image Works. p. 544 © Jeff Greenberg/The Image Works. p. 546 © Jonathan Nourok/PhotoEdit. p. 547 Steve Skjold/Alamy.

**Chapter 16:** p. 551 Dynamic Graphics Group/Creatas/Alamy. p. 553 © SW Productions/PhotoDisc/Getty Images. p. 560 © Robin Nelson/PhotoEdit. p. 569 © Charles Gupton/Corbis. p. 570 © Jeff Greenberg/PhotoEdit.

# Name Index

# SUBJECT INDEX

# THE AMERICAN
## BATTLESHIP

SAMUEL LORING MORISON
WITH NORMAN POLMAR

MBI

First published in 2003 by MBI Publishing Company,Galtier Plaza, Suite 200, 380 Jackson Street, St. Paul, MN 55101-3885 USA

The information in this book is true and complete to the best of our knowledge. All recommendations are made without any guarantee on the part of the author or Publisher, who also disclaim any liability incurred in connection with the use of this data or specific details.

We recognize that some words, model names, and designations, for example, mentioned herein are the property of the trademark holder. We use them for identification purposes only. This is not an official publication.

MBI Publishing Company titles are also available at discounts in bulk quantity for industrial or sales-promotional use. For details write to Special Sales Manager at Motorbooks International Wholesalers & Distributors, Galtier Plaza, Suite 200, 380 Jackson Street, St. Paul, MN 55101-3885 USA

ISBN 0-7603-0989-2

**On the frontispiece:** The end of a long line: The battleships *New Jersey* and *Missouri* lead a line of ships in October 1989 during a Pacific Fleet exercise; steaming behind the dreadnoughts are the command ship *Blue Ridge*, nuclear-propelled missile cruiser *Long Beach*, and several destroyers and cruisers. The photo was taken from the nuclear-propelled carrier *Enterprise* (CVN 65). *U.S. Navy*

**On the title page:** The *Missouri* steams out of Pearl Harbor with her crew manning the rail. She was steaming from the Persian Gulf to her home port of Long Beach after seeing action in Operation Desert Storm. She has a communications dome mounted on her second funnel. The *Missouri* and *Wisconsin* both operated Pioneer Unmanned Aerial Vehicles (UAVs) during Desert Storm. *John Bouvia/U.S. Navy*

**On the back cover:** *Lower Left:* "Doughboys" (the World War I term for American soldiers) and sailors crowd the deck of the *Louisiana* as she steams into New York Harbor in 1919. Battleships supplemented the limited number of transports available to bring home the American Expeditionary Force that fought in France. The life rafts in this photo (which was printed from a stereograph card) exemplifies the rafts that inundated ships during wartime. *Keystone View Co./U.S. Navy*

*Top Right:*
The long, lean lines of the *Iowa* imply the power of her big guns as she slides through Pacific waters with Task Force 38 in December 1944. Except for the two Japanese *Yamato*-class dreadnoughts, the four ships of the *Iowa* class were the largest battleships ever built. *Charles F. Jacobs/U.S. Navy*

*Bottom Right:*
This dramatic Chromolithoraph was based on an 1893 painting by Fred S. Cozzens. Shown (from left) are the brig *Enterprise*, firing a salute; the ships-of-the-line *Pennsylvania* and *North Carolina*; and the brig *Hornet*. The brig names were later carried by two famous aircraft carriers of World War II, while the ships-of-the-line gave their names to two steel battleships. *Armstrong & Co./U.S. Navy*

Edited by Steve Gansen
Designed by LeAnn Kuhlmann

Printed in China

# CONTENTS

# INTRODUCTION

F or more than four centuries, the term *battleship* has brought to mind the majestic sight of large warships—under sail or steam—in line, guns poised to destroy an enemy. For much of that period the battleship was the principal measure of sea power; indeed, for many countries it was *the* measure of military power.

These majestic, ruggedly built ships captured the public's fancy with their enormous guns, heavy armor, and beautiful lines. To many, both civilian and sailor, they were more than just a collection of wood, sail, steel, or machinery. They were floating cities, the homes and workplaces for several generations of navy men and marines. Battleships brought a great deal of pride to those men who served on them. These ships were more than inanimate objects; they were living entities with souls.

This book tells the two-century history of the American battleship, from the ships-of-the-line to the present. The *Texas* and the *Maine* were the first in a long line of 59 steel U.S. battleships that from 1900 to 1943 formed the backbone of the U.S. Navy. With the Spanish-American War, the new navy received its first baptism of fire. The 57 battleships that succeeded the *Texas* and the *Maine* went on to bigger and better things and played an important part in the rise of the United States as a naval power. The following is the story of these magnificent ships.

# CHAPTER ONE

# SHIPS-OF-THE-LINE

## THE SAILING NAVY

The term *battleship* was derived from a warship intended to sail in a line of battle. Ships-of-the-line were expensive to build and operate. A Napoleonic-period 74-gun ship, for example, would require a crew of at least 450 men to sail and man her guns. In addition, she would carry on board perhaps 50 or more marines to form the core of landing parties, to be carried ashore by the ship's longboats, or to provide musket fire when alongside an enemy warship in mortal combat.

The actual birth of the battleship in the U.S. Navy began with the wooden sailing ship during the Revolutionary War. The 13 colonies were in an escalating rebellion against Great Britain, whose Royal Navy was the world's largest. As part of its military buildup, the Continental Congress authorized the first ship-of-the-line to be built in America on 20 November 1776. Congress approved three ships-of-the-line, each to mount approximately 74 guns.

The *America* was laid down in May 1777 at Portsmouth, New Hampshire. Plans to build a second ship in Philadelphia were aborted when that city fell to the British, and the third ship appears not to have been started. The *America*'s construction was continually delayed by shortages of funds and materials. While she was still under construction,

**Left:** The ship-of-the-line was the most formidable weapon built by man prior to the twentieth century. Here the ship-of-the-line *North Carolina*, the frigates *Constitution* and *Brandywine*, and sloops *Erie* and *Ontario* depart Port Mahon, Minorca, in 1825. They comprise the U.S. Mediterranean Squadron, a precursor of the current forward-deployment of U.S. warships. *A. Carlotta/U.S. Navy*

John Paul Jones was named her captain and went about designing the figurehead on her bow. It was to be a "Goddess of Liberty," crowned with laurels, her right arm raised and forefinger pointing to heaven, an appeal to a higher tribunal on behalf of the American cause. Her left arm was to carry a blue shield studded with 13 stars.

In the spring of 1781 Jones learned that the British planned to destroy the *America* while she was still under construction. He provided extra pay to workmen to stand guard and took his own turn every third night. However, the *America* was not to sail under the Stars and Stripes. The Continental Congress gave her to France on 3 September 1782 as a mark of gratitude for that country's assistance during the Revolutionary War. The *America* was launched on 5 November 1782, and she departed from Boston for France on 24 June 1783.

The U.S. Navy did not get funds to construct its first ships-of-the-line until the War of 1812. This was due to America's isolation from European wars and politics. Congress authorized six frigates—the largest U.S. warships at the time—in 1794, including the famed *Constitution* and its 44 guns. On 2 January 1813 "four ships to rate not less than 74 guns" were authorized—the *Columbus*, the *Franklin*, the *Independence*, and the *Washington*. The latter three of these battleships were completed by 1815, but the *Columbus* was delayed when the British burned Washington, D.C., and the Washington Navy Yard—where she was under

**Above:** The *Constitution* (74 guns) was one of the six original American frigates. After an exemplary career, she was removed from active service in 1882. She has been preserved afloat as an artifact since 1905. Except for a tour of American cities in 1931, she has been in Boston Harbor. The *Constitution* is shown firing a salute during her semiannual turning-around exercise. *U.S. Navy*

**Right:** The *United States* (66 guns) was the first of six frigates authorized in 1794—the first warships to be built by the U.S. government. These were outstanding ships, superior to their British counterparts (and carried more guns than their 44-gun rate). Here the *United States* is portrayed in her capture of HMS *Macedonian* on 25 October 1812. *E. Tufnell/U.S. Navy*

**U. S. SHIP OF THE LINE PENNSYLVANIA.** *140 Guns.*

construction—in 1814. She was finally laid down in May 1816, launched by the yard on 1 March 1819, and commissioned on 7 September 1819. Larger than the other ships, she was rated at 92 guns. These ships supported U.S. political and economic interests around the world during the first half of the nineteenth century.

Congress authorized two more ships-of-the-line on 3 March 1813. These were the *Chippewa* and the *New Orleans*, both of which were laid down in January 1815 at a Sacketts Harbor shipyard on the New York shore of Lake Ontario. Their contract called for the ships to carry 102 and 106 guns, respectively. Never completed, the *Chippewa* was sold for scrap on 1 November 1833. The *New Orleans* remained unfinished for another 50 years until sold for scrap on 24 September 1883.

Soon after the conflict with Great Britain, on 29 April 1816 the Congress authorized "nine ships to rate not less than 74 guns each." This included the building of one—the *Columbus*—previously authorized on 2 January 1813.

Establishing the policy of naming battleships for states, the eight new ships were named the *Delaware* (commissioned 27 July 1827), the *New Hampshire* (commissioned 13 May 1864), the *North Carolina* (commissioned 24 June 1824), the *Ohio* (launched 30 May 1820), the *Pennsylvania* (launched 18 July 1837), the *Vermont* (commissioned 30 January 1862), and the two ships *New York* and *Virginia*. Some of the aforementioned ships, such as the *Pennsylvania*, ended up commissioned for duty other than their intended purpose. The *Pennsylvania*'s one sailing trip was from her builder to Gosport (Norfolk) Navy Yard. At the end of that voyage her officers reported her to be " not an unqualified success after her launch; some officers thought her 'cumbersome, leewardly and crank. . . . However, she occasionally showed surprising speed in proper trim.'" She was commissioned incomplete as a receiving ship at Gosport (Norfolk) Navy Yard. Others were commissioned incomplete as receiving or storeships.

As evident from their completion dates, there was no hurry. These ships, as frigates and lesser warships,

This dramatic chromolithograph was based on an 1893 painting by Fred S. Cozzens. Shown (from left) are the brig *Enterprise*, firing a salute; the ships-of-the-line *Pennsylvania* and *North Carolina*; and the brig *Hornet*. The brig names were later carried by two famous aircraft carriers of World War II, while the ships-of-the-line gave their names to two steel battleships. *Armstrong & Co./U.S. Navy*

were able to carry out U.S. interests in foreign waters. The navy employed several ships-of-the-line against the Confederacy during the Civil War, but not as warships. The *Virginia*, laid down in May 1822, was almost completed in 1825 when the decision was made to suspend construction for the moment, to be launched at a later date should national interests require her. She remained on the building ways at Boston Navy Yard until finally broken up in 1884.

The *Pennsylvania*, with 120 guns, would have been the largest and most powerful sailing warship ever constructed for the U.S. Navy. However, she only received 34 of her guns and made one short sail from her builders to Gosport Navy Yard before being

commissioned incomplete as a receiving ship. She was burned on 20 April 1861 to prevent her capture by Confederate forces.

The Civil War marked the end for ships powered solely by sail. By the mid-1800s, steam propulsion had become practical for warships. Steam propulsion meant that warships could maneuver so as best to bring their guns to bear on an enemy (or to escape) regardless of the wind.

Initially, steam warships were propelled by huge paddle wheels on each side (beam). Those paddle-wheel structures were both vulnerable to enemy fire and took up space that could be used for broadside guns. The underwater screw propeller proved to be less vulnerable to enemy fire and was more efficient in moving warships.

The March 1862 Battle of Hampton Roads, Virginia, fought between the Confederate ironclad *Virginia* (formerly the USS *Merrimack*) and the Union ship *Monitor*, demonstrated both the effectiveness and the relative invulnerability of "modern" warships. Armor—mounted over wood in the *Virginia*—could resist most existing cannonballs. The revolving two-gun turret of the *Monitor* permitted the ship to fire in any direction without maneuvering, an important factor even with steam-powered warships. The two "ironclads" fought a long and frustrating battle on 9 March. Both suffered some damage, but the Confederates, realizing that the *Monitor* could defend the wooden sailing ships that the *Virginia* sought to destroy, was held back from engaging the Union ship. Finally, the stalemate ended when, forced to abandon Norfolk, the Confederates set the *Virginia* afire and destroyed her on 11 May 1862. The Union *Monitor* was victorious in the first battle between ironclad warships.

The U.S. Navy began the transition from sail to steam in the mid-1800s. This painting by DeSimone shows the armed side-wheel steamer *Susquehanna* (left) and the frigate *Congress* at Naples in 1957. Although her propulsion was reliable, the *Susquehanna*'s engines were removed after the Civil War. She had a bark rig and carried a variety of armament during her brief career, from 1851 to 1868. *U.S. Navy*

Swedish-born engineer John Ericsson (1803–89) had long proposed steel ships. Ericsson built his "monitor" in record time—she was four months from her keel laying to completion in late February 1862. Hurried to completion, the *Monitor* was towed from Greenpoint, New York, for Hampton Roads with workmen still on board. *Thomas P. Rossiter/U.S. Navy*

The Confederate ironclad *Virginia*, built on the hulk of the U.S. steam frigate *Merrimack*, was the world's first armored ship to see combat. She ravaged Union ships off Hampton Roads— here she sinks the Union sloop *Cumberland*, which goes down with her battle flags flying on 8 March 1862. The *Cumberland*'s shot bounced off the sides of the CSS *Virginia*. *Currier & Ives/U.S. Navy*

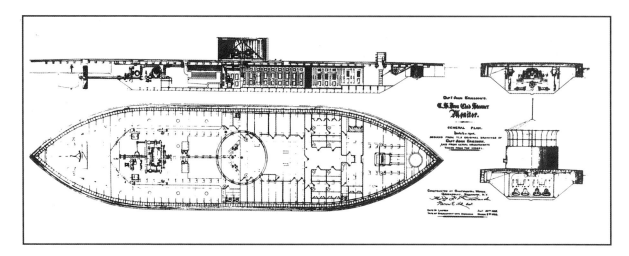

A drawing of the *Monitor* showing the simplicity of her design. She was an iron "box" with a flat bottom and pointed ends. In this perspective the propulsion machinery is at left and the crew's accommodations are at right. Unlike the *Virginia*, the *Monitor* had a relatively shallow draft—10 feet compared to the Confederate ship's 22 feet. *U.S. Navy*

*Below:* The USS *Monitor* was a low-lying, steel warship, her deck penetrated only by a small conning tower (left), a two-gun revolving turret (center), and (after March 1862) two square funnels. Thus, she presented a small target for Confederate gunners. Further, she was highly maneuverable. Such warships were not intended for ocean voyages, and she foundered at sea on 31 December 1862. *U.S. Navy*

European navies, which had already begun to build seagoing ironclads, were quick to learn lessons from the American experience and adopted some of the American design features in their warships, including ships-of-the-line. However, shortly after the war the United States lost interest in the need for a modern navy.

It was not until 1883 tha Congress would fund "modern" warships. At that time the navy had only wooden ships, except for a few coastal monitors and gunboats with iron hulls. The incentive for these new warships came from the expanding U.S. foreign trade, especially in the Far East; increasing difficulties with Spain over Spanish-controlled Cuba, 90 miles south of

Florida; and the intellectual awakening of Americans to the importance of sea power. Occasioning that awakening were the writings of Captain Alfred Thayer Mahan and other "navalists," many of whom were stimulated by the discussions and debates at the U.S. Naval Institute, a professional forum established in 1871, and the Naval War College, founded in 1884.

The *Monitor* was the first warship to mount guns in a revolving turret. Two 11-inch smoothbore guns were fitted; they withdrew into the armored turret to reload. This halftone reproduction of an engraving depicts the turret after the Battle of Hampton Roads, showing the minimal damage caused by the *Virginia*'s gunfire. The men indicate the size of the turret. *U.S. Navy*

The writings of Captain Alfred Thayer Mahan, especially his *Influence of Sea Power upon History, 1660–1783*, led many national leaders as well as senior officers to gain a new understanding of the role of naval forces. He coined the term *sea power* to include a nation's dockyards, merchant marine, naval fleet, seagoing personnel, and supporting industries. *U.S. Navy*

## THE NEW STEEL NAVY

William Henry Hunt was secretary of the navy for only a short time during the administration of President James Garfield, but it is he who deserves the title "Father of the Steel Navy." It was Hunt who moved Congress to authorize the first steel ships on 3 March 1883. These were known as the "A-B-C-D ships": the protected cruisers *Atlanta*, *Baltimore*, and *Chicago*, and the smaller gunboat *Dolphin*. These warships were completed between 1885 and 1889. The largest, the *Chicago*, displaced 4,500 tons and carried four 8-inch guns. The *Atlanta* and the *Boston* both displaced about 3,200 tons and mounted two 8-inch guns. The cruisers were built to serve as commerce raiders. The smaller *Dolphin* was a "dispatch boat" displacing 1,486 tons and armed with two 4-inch guns. All four ships were

*Top:* The USS *Texas* was a second-class battleship, and the first U.S. steel warship to have that designation, although by international standards she was more accurately classed as an armored cruiser. Her main battery was two 12-inch and six 6-inch guns plus lighter weapons. At the time she was designed, her bow ram was considered by many naval officers to be her principal armament. *U.S. Navy*

*Above:* The USS *Maine* at Bar Harbor in her namesake state. Her primary armament consisted of four 10-inch guns and six 6-inch weapons; again, she was more akin to foreign armored cruisers than battleships. The ship's boats are rigged out; note the small gun on her fantail (beneath the boat). Another light gun is visible in the crow's nest on the main (after) mast. *U.S. Navy*

officially considered a disappointment in comparison with foreign contemporaries.

On 24 July 1886 the House Naval Affairs Committee recommended construction of a modest number of new ships, including two "sea-going armored vessels." Subsequently, the committee recommended a smaller type of "armored cruising and battle ship," with a considerably lighter displacement and a corresponding reduction in weight allocated to ordnance and armor. High speed, endurance, and sea-keeping ability were also cited as characteristics of this "super cruiser." The committee emphasized the offensive capabilities of this new armored cruiser type. The original intent of Congress was to provide the United States with a "respectable" offensive-oriented navy, not to forge a first-class battle fleet. The authorization act was passed with little debate on the floors of the House of Representatives and the Senate and signed

Church services were prescribed for all U.S. Navy ships on Sunday. Here services are conducted aboard the USS *Texas* as the fleet lies at anchor at Key West, Florida, in 1898. This is a colored print based on a painting by Howard Chandler Christy. *U.S. Navy*

U.S. Navy divers examine the hulk of the battleship *Maine* after she blew up in Havana harbor. This is the view from aft, looking forward. The funnel in the background is from a ship alongside her hulk. *U.S. Navy*

into law on 6 August 1883, authorizing the navy to build two "armored cruisers," the *Texas* and the *Maine*.

The armored cruiser of the 1880s was designed to be a fast, far-ranging destroyer of enemy commerce and to locate and harass an approaching hostile battle line. It had insufficient strength to stand in the line of battle against enemy battleships. The armored cruiser depended for safety on superior speed and maneuverability. The *Texas* and the *Maine* were more accurately considered armored cruisers rather than battleships, although they carried much larger guns than foreign cruisers. Within the U.S. Navy they were labeled as second-class battleships.

The tactical concepts of the day called for reliance on the use of the ram, thus stressing the importance of heavy forward fire, with broadside fire considered less important. With centerline turrets, only one-half of a ship's main battery could fire ahead and would, in the kind of decisive fleet action envisioned, provide limited offensive support. This shortcoming could have been overcome by using superfiring forward turrets (i.e., one firing over the other), but this design would not be accepted as practicable for years to come because of the uncertainty about what muzzle blast would do to the turret below.

The solution was to place both forward and after turrets as far as possible to either side, and to group the superstructure closely along the centerline. Theoretically at least, both turrets could then be fired either dead ahead or astern. By leaving a "break" in the ship's superstructure abeam each turret, each ship could also in theory fire across (from port to starboard or vice versa) to the opposite beam. In practice, this "crossover" fire was rarely used because of the damaging effect of muzzle blast on the firing ship's own superstructure. Firing of the inboard gun in each turret was also limited at extreme fore or aft train for the same reason. The *Maine* and the *Texas* were the first and last U.S. warships to be built to this pattern. Their successors, the *Indiana* class, would have the centerline main-battery turret configuration, which was to remain the standard practice in American battleships.

Lack of U.S. experience in creating a new navy prompted the Department of the Navy to announce a $15,000 international competition for the best design for a battleship "on a par with the best of other countries." In the end, the design of William John, a distinguished architect employed by the Naval Armaments

and Construction Company, Barrow-in-Furness, Great Britain, was selected for the *Texas*. For the *Maine*, the navy's Bureau of Construction and Repair's design was chosen.

Construction of the *Texas* was assigned to the Norfolk Navy Yard. Using a British design caused delays in obtaining materials. The time required to prepare the shipbuilding facilities at Norfolk, as well as a heated controversy over the merits of the ship's unusual design, resulted in additional delays, and her keel was not laid until 1889. Belated delivery of the engines and armor plate by American civilian contractors further slowed construction and, by the time the *Texas* was commissioned on 15 August 1895, she had become something of an anachronism.

A series of minor mishaps dogged the *Texas* during her early operations, and she acquired a reputation for bad luck. Nevertheless, she was a very steady gun platform and her top speed of nearly 18 knots substantially exceeded that of any other U.S. battleship until after 1900.

The second of the armored ships, the 6,682-ton *Maine*, was even more of a hybrid. She bore a superficial resemblance to the *Texas* in that her two turrets were mounted in echelon, in this instance the forward turret being to starboard and the after one to port. Each turret's two 10-inch guns could be fired through an arc extending from directly ahead to directly astern, as well as across the centerline. The *Maine* and the *Texas* also shared the weakness of carrying inadequate topside armor protection, having been designed before the navy knew the full destructive effects of rapid-fire guns and high-explosive shells. Also, when the main guns were fired inboard across the centerline, the muzzle blasts tended to spring the deck plating badly out of shape and damage the adjacent superstructure and fittings. The off-center arrangement of the turrets was therefore not repeated in subsequent U.S. warships, as the design's practical advantages could not justify these drawbacks.

Both the *Texas* and the *Maine* were originally designed to carry two 61-foot, 8-inch, 14.8-ton steam-powered torpedo boats. These were intended to enter restricted waters and attack enemy targets when they were out of range of the battleships' guns. These boats were to have a single one-pounder gun, and a single 18-inch, trainable torpedo tube firing a Whitehead torpedo. Although the builders completed the *Maine*'s two torpedo boats, the boats proved much too slow for their intended purpose, so the navy employed them as practice boats at its torpedo station in Newport, Rhode Island.

While laid down at the New York Navy Yard, the *Maine* was subject to delays in the delivery of armor plate. By the time of her commissioning on 17 September 1895 she was far outdated. Still, she was considered a smart ship. Her uneventful service career in the North Atlantic Squadron took a dramatic turn in January 1898. A garbled press dispatch on riots in strife-torn Havana, Cuba, led U.S. officials to believe that the American consulate was in danger. To protect American lives and property, the Navy Department ordered Rear Admiral Montgomery Sicard, commanding the fleet off Key West, to immediately send a warship to Spain's rebellious colony. The *Maine* got under way immediately and reached Havana on 25 January. Although U.S.–Spanish relations were tense, this was ostensibly a friendly visit, and the Spanish government reciprocated by ordering one of its armored cruisers to New York.

At 9:40 P.M. on Tuesday, 15 February 1898, the battleship *Maine* blew up in Havana harbor. More than five tons of brown prismatic powder charges for the ship's 6-inch and 10-inch guns ignited in the ship's forward magazine. The explosion burst and twisted bulkheads in the forward third of the ship, effectively sinking it. Out of the 350 officers and men on board, 252 men died that night and another eight died of their wounds in Havana hospitals over the next few days. Four days later, the Spanish cruiser *Vizcaya* entered New York harbor for her "friendly" visit, but found instead a city buzzing with rumors and preparations for war.

A board of inquiry, headed by Captain William T. Sampson, was appointed to investigate the cause of the *Maine*'s explosion. The board began its investigation in Havana on 21 February 1898. After an exhaustive examination of the wreck and after taking testimony from eyewitnesses and experts, the board reported on 21 March that the *Maine* had been destroyed by a double magazine detonation set off from the exterior of the ship, which "could have been produced only by [a] . . . mine situated under the ship." The board of inquiry was unable to fix responsibility for the disaster, but a furious American populace, fueled by an active press—most notably, the newspapers of William Randolph Hearst—concluded that the Spanish were the culprits and demanded revenge (recent research indi-

cates that the explosion was caused by a fire in a coal bunker that ignited an adjacent magazine).

## THE SPANISH-AMERICAN WAR

Fearing war was close at hand, a U.S. "Flying Squadron" was formed for the defense of the eastern seaboard under the command of Acting Commodore Winfield Scott Schley. The squadron consisted of the armored cruiser *Brooklyn* (flagship), the battleships *Massachusetts* and *Texas*, and the cruisers *Columbia* and *Minneapolis*.

The Navy Department realized that Spain was sure to sail a large naval squadron to Cuba for protection, so the top brass decided to amass as much power as possible in the Atlantic. Not wanting to leave a heavily gunned and armored ship in the Pacific away from the forthcoming war, the Navy Department ordered the battleship *Oregon* to sail for the Atlantic to reinforce Acting Rear Admiral William T. Sampson's North Atlantic Squadron, which was based at Key West, Florida. Having no powder and ammunition on board and very little coal, the *Oregon* steamed from the Puget Sound Navy Yard in Bremerton, Washington, on 6 March 1898 and proceeded to San Francisco to take on a full load of coal, powder, and projectiles. The *Oregon* steamed out of San Francisco, California, on 19 March on a remarkable voyage around Cape Horn, through the treacherous Straits of Magellan. Except for stops for coaling and one night's delay because of a violent gale in the Straits of Magellan, there were no delays due to machinery breakdowns. This was a remarkable achievement for the time. En route, the crew prepared for war by painting the ship a dark gray and ripping out the mahogany pilothouse and anything else that might prove to be a fire hazard. The *Oregon* arrived at Key West Naval Station on 26 May after steaming 14,500 nautical miles.

On 21 April, after fruitless diplomatic exchanges, the United States declared war on Spain, and a day later, a blockade of Cuba. On 25 April Secretary of the Navy John D. Long cabled Commodore George Dewey, commander of the Asiatic Squadron, which was anchored in Mirs Bay, near Hong Kong, "Proceed at once to Philippine Islands. Commence operations . . . against Spanish Fleet. You must capture vessels or destroy." On 27 April Dewey's flagship, the cruiser *Olympia*, followed by three other cruisers, two gunboats, and a revenue cutter, departed for Manila. Arriving off of the Philippine island of Luzon, the Asiatic Squadron searched Subic Bay and found nothing.

The squadron then headed for Manila harbor. Dewey led his squadron past the shore batteries into Manila Bay under cover of darkness, accepting the risk that the channel might be mined. Most of the ships had passed the batteries before the Spanish opened fire, so no damage was done to any U.S. ship. At dawn the fleet of Rear Admiral Patricio Montojo y Parason was found lying at anchor off the Cavite Navy Yard.

The odds were distinctly in Dewey's favor. The combined broadsides of his squadron's ships weighed 3,700 pounds. The Spanish Fleet consisted of one modern but unseaworthy steel cruiser, the *Reina Maria Cristina* (flag); an old wooden cruiser, the *Castillo*; and five small cruisers and gunboats. The Spanish Fleet's combined broadside was only 1,273 pounds. Because of this disparity, Admiral Montojo elected to fight at anchor, where his ships could be supported by the Spanish shore fortifications. His tactic was reasonable but unavailing. Spanish losses, afloat and ashore, were 91 men killed and 280 wounded. American casualties were two officers and six men slightly wounded.

Informing the Navy Department of his victory, Dewey explained that he could take Manila at any time, but lacked enough men to hold it. Plans were then set in motion to dispatch an army expeditionary force from the West Coast.

Meanwhile, in the Atlantic, the main action was about to take place. Having established a blockade of the coast of Cuba from Havana to Cienfuegos, on 1 May U.S. forces learned that a Spanish squadron of four cruisers and three destroyers, commanded by Rear Admiral Pascal Cervera y Topete, had sailed from the Cape Verde Islands for Cuba on 29 April.

Assuming that Admiral Cervera was heading for Puerto Rico, Admiral Sampson took the North Atlantic Squadron there. Some U.S. officials believed that Cervera would head farther north and attack New York City. At the time, the U.S. squadron consisted of the armored cruiser *New York* (flagship), the battleships *Indiana* and *Iowa*, the monitors *Amphitrite*, and

The U.S. cruiser *Olympia* (Cruiser No. 6) leads the squadron commanded by Commodore George Dewey at Manila Bay in the first action of the Spanish-American War. In the engagement with the Spanish squadron the U.S. Navy suffered only a few men injured—a small cost to gain a Pacific empire. Dewey went on to become the first—and only—U.S. Admiral of the fleet. *Fred S. Cozzens/U.S. Navy*

The USS *Indiana* in light ice—far from the warm waters off Cuba where she helped to defeat the Spanish Fleet in the Battle of Santiago on 3 July 1898. The *Indiana* mounted four 13-inch guns. U.S. battleship gun caliber did not exceed that size until the *Oklahoma* was commissioned in 1916. Note the *Indiana*'s main gun turret and amidships twin 8-inch turret. *U.S. Navy*

*Right:* The USS *Massachusetts* was the third ship of the *Indiana* class—the first "modern" steel battleships built by the U.S. Navy. In this view the cover of the ship's bow torpedo tube is visible above the (submerged) ram and below the ship's elaborate crest. Only one anchor is fitted. The sailor on the alongside raft is doing what sailors always do aboard steel ships— chipping and painting. *U.S. Navy*

*Below:* The crew of the battleship *Oregon* cheers as the Spanish auxiliary armored cruiser *Cristóbal Colón* strikes her colors during the Battle of Santiago on 3 July 1898. The *Oregon* was the only U.S. battleship on the scene to have all boilers lit and ready to make full steam when the Spanish force broke for the sea. The *Oregon* and the cruiser *Brooklyn* chased the *Cristóbal Colón* and drove her aground. *U.S. Navy*

Admiral Sampson hastened to Key West to telegraph the Navy Department the news. He then set off for Santiago with the *New York* to join Commodore Schley in the blockade of the Spanish fleet, collecting en route the battleship *Oregon*, the torpedo boat *Porter*, and the auxiliary destroyer *Mayflower*. The *Iowa* reached Santiago on 1 June.

Then, the strategic situation stalemated. Sampson could not enter the harbor, located at the end of a narrow, twisting channel and commanded by powerful shore fortifications. Cervera could not leave without encountering the greatly superior American fleet. For the rest of the month, the blockading American fleet started bombarding the fortifications covering the channel into Santiago harbor.

Admiral Sampson left the blockade with his flagship on 3 July to meet with Major General William T. Shafter, commander of the 17,000-man U.S. Army Expeditionary Force, at Siboney. Almost immediately, the Spanish squadron solved Sampson's strategic problem by staging a desperate attempt to escape.

Against Admiral Cervera's objections, the governor-general of Cuba issued orders for a sortie. At 9:31 A.M., the cruiser *Infanta María Teresa*, Cervera's flagship, was sighted leading the squadron

*Terror*, the cruisers *Detroit* and *Montgomery*, and two auxiliary ships. They arrived off of San Juan, Puerto Rico, just before dawn on 23 June. Sampson found nothing, but to make sure the trip wasn't a total loss he bombarded the Spanish fortifications. He then departed for Key West.

A dispatch boat informed him that Commodore Schley, commander of the Flying Squadron, had located the Spanish fleet in the harbor of Santiago, Cuba.

out of the channel. The *Iowa* was the first to sight her and the first to open fire. On her approach, Commodore Schley's flagship, the *Brooklyn*, turned to port, away from the Spanish ship. Schley later received considerable criticism for this maneuver. Upon reaching deep water, the *María Teresa* turned west, on a course paralleling the Cuban coast. Cervera's three other cruisers followed.

Smothered by fire from the battleships *Indiana*, *Iowa*, *Oregon*, *Texas*, and *Brooklyn*, the Spanish flagship beached herself 6 miles down the coast at 10:15 A.M. The *Almirante Oquendo*, the last cruiser in the Spanish line, was driven ashore at 10:35. The *Vizcaya* and the *Cristóbal Colón* continued their flight to the west, pursued by the *Oregon*, the only battleship to have all her boilers lit when the Spanish fleet tried to make its escape. Around 11:00, the *Vizcaya* turned toward the coast with the evident intention of beaching. Admiral Sampson, whose flagship had gradually overtaken the action, signaled the *Iowa* to follow and finish her.

The action settled into a stern chase in which the *Colón* drew away from all her pursuers except the *Oregon*, "the bulldog of the fleet," and the *Brooklyn*. At 1:10 P.M., a 13-inch shell fired at maximum elevation from the *Oregon*'s forward turret struck beside the *Colón*, whose speed had begun to slacken, and the cruiser ran aground off the mouth of the Río Tarquino river. The two destroyers that followed the cruisers out of Santiago had already been destroyed: the *Plutón* by a direct hit from a battleship, probably the *Indiana*;, and the *Furor* in a close action with Lieutenant Commander Richard Wainwright's auxiliary gunboat the *Gloucester*. Spanish losses were 323 dead and 151 wounded; the latter and most of the other 1,800 survivors, including Admiral Cervera, were rescued by Sampson's ships. American casualties were one man killed and one seriously wounded. In filing his after-action report, Sampson opened his report of the action with the words, "The fleet under my command offers the nation as a Fourth-of-July present the whole of Cervera's fleet."

After nightfall, the Spanish attempted to block the channel to Santiago by scuttling the cruiser *Reina Mercedes* across it. The movement was detected, and the Spanish ship was quickly sunk by fire from the *Massachusetts* and the *Texas*.

On 10 July the battleships *Indiana* and *Texas* and the armored cruisers *Brooklyn* and *New York* bombarded Santiago. Santiago fell to the forces of General Shafter on 17 July.

On 12 August in Washington, D.C., representatives of the United States and Spain signed an armistice ending the Spanish-American War. Spain agreed to free Cuba and to cede Puerto Rico and Guam to the United States. Peace treaty negotiations with Spain began in Paris in October, with the treaty eventually signed on 10 December. During the negotiations, American public opinion strongly influenced the decision to annex the Philippines, although President William McKinley did not intend to keep the archipelago. He knew such distant territories could only be defended by a battle fleet dedicated to Mahan's concept of command of the sea. By annexing the Philippines, America committed itself to becoming a sea power.

Hail to the conquering heroes: A fleet review in New York Harbor on 21 August 1898 honored the North Atlantic Squadron and Flying Squadron. The warship in the foreground is the armored cruiser *New York* followed by the battleship *Iowa*. The *New York* flies the two-star flag of Rear Admiral William T. Sampson at her main (after) mast. *U.S. Navy*

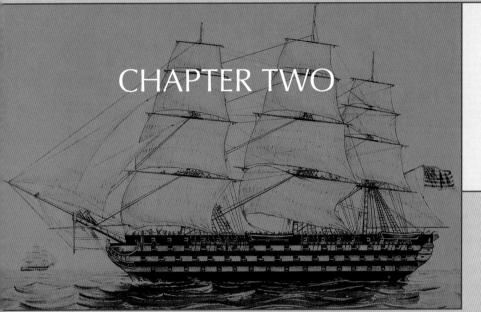

# CHAPTER TWO

# PRE-DREAD-NOUGHT BATTLESHIPS

Secretaries of the Navy William H. Hunt, William E. Chandler, and William C. Whitney had laid the foundations of the Steel Navy, but it would take yet another secretary to create the modern battleships that would bring the fleet into being. Before he took office, few navy men could have imagined Benjamin F. Tracy as a strong secretary. Certainly President Benjamin Harrison, on taking office in 1889, selected Tracy more for reasons of practical politics than for his strategic vision.

Tracy surprised everyone. The former lawyer, Civil War general, and Republican party stalwart turned out to be an outstanding administrator with an open mind. He was the first Secretary of the Navy to adopt Mahan's doctrine that control of the sea is the key to national power, and the first to acknowledge the capital ship as the key to control of the sea. He put these doctrines into effect in the navy with great efficiency and ruthlessness. "We must have armored battleships," he strongly emphasized in his first Navy Department annual report to Congress, and navy men vigorously supported him. The argument for the battleship as "the real bone and sinew of any naval force" was perhaps best stated by Rear Admiral Philip Hichborn of the Bureau of Construction

This photo of the *Indiana*, taken in October 1900, shows the low freeboard of these early steel battleships. Although intended for coastal defense, as the *Oregon* demonstrated in her transit around South America, these ships could steam in the open seas. White hulls were a hallmark of U.S. battleships of the early 1900s, hence the term Great White Fleet during their circumnavigation. *U.S. Navy*

The forward, starboard-side 8-inch gun turret of the *Indiana*. Pre-dreadnought battleships had "mixed" main batteries—this class had four 13-inch and eight 8-inch guns. This arrangement complicated battle tactics and made spotting of the fall of shot difficult. The railing above the turret would be removed before entering battle. *U.S. Navy*

and Repair when he pointed out that "it is only through battleships that an enemy can be met and vanquished before he has even sighted our coast."

In 1889 Tracy convened a special policy board to study the U.S. naval situation. The board's report was described as a "general exposition of . . . views touching the problem of naval defense . . . not made with any expectation or desire that the United States should at this time adopt or commit itself to an exactly defined policy reaching so far out into the future. . . ." The board recommended a 15-year naval construction program to include 10 "first-class battleships of great endurance," comparable in design to their foreign contemporaries, with a range of 5,400 nautical miles at 10 knots. Another 25 battleships called for by the board were to be "limited endurance" ships, designed for operations in an area of the western Atlantic between the Gulf of Saint Lawrence and the Isthmus of Panama. These ships were to be defensive oriented and would back up the 10 first-class battleships.

In his 1889 annual report to Congress, Tracy urged the immediate construction of two groups of battleships—eight ships to be assigned to the Pacific and 12 to the Atlantic and Gulf coasts. However, so ambitious a program was obviously more than Congress could accept. The navy's legislative supporters dared ask for no more than three capital ships, and bowed to coast-defense strategists by labeling the ships "sea-going coast-line battleships" and limiting their size and endurance.

The board's proposal stirred considerable resistance in Congress, where the mere mention of battleships engendered dark thoughts of imperialism and aggression. Congress shelved the board's report for that session, but on 3 June 1890 authorized three "sea-going, coast-line battleships." These ships were to "carry the heaviest ordnance upon a displacement of about 8,500 tons." The design selected resembled in general that drawn up by the policy board for a "1st class Battle Ship of Limited Coal Endurance."

The Navy Department prepared designs for the three authorized battleships under the supervision of Lieutenant Lewis Nixon, a brilliant young naval constructor who in later life as a civilian would head his own shipyard. The Philadelphia company William Cramp and Sons was low bidder on two of the ships, and the Union Iron Works of San Francisco was awarded the remaining contract in accordance with an authorizing act provision that directed that one of the ships be built on the West Coast.

These ships became the *Indiana* class. They were the first U.S. battleships assigned hull numbers with the designation "BB" later indicating Battleship. Designated as Battleships Number 1 through 3, the ships in this class were low-freeboard coast-defense battleships, but they were the first ships of the U.S. Navy that approached their contemporaries in fighting power.

The Cramp bid proposed a battleship 12 feet longer than that envisioned by the department. This 348-foot-long hull was subsequently adopted for all three ships. These 10,288-ton battleships, the *Indiana*, the *Massachusetts*, and the *Oregon*, proved to be outstanding ships on paper, especially when it came to their armament. Although displacing considerably less than many contemporary foreign battleships, each mounted a heavy main battery of four 13-inch guns in a pair of turrets, an intermediate battery of eight 8-inch guns in four wing turrets, a secondary battery of four 6-inch guns on the main deck, and six torpedo tubes. The added weight of fire provided by the intermediate battery—a feature not adopted by the British Navy for another decade—made these the most powerful battleships in the world. To provide more accurate gunfire control for the main battery, a newly developed range finder, designed by Lieutenant Bradley Fiske, was installed in the completed *Indiana*, the first ship in the U.S. Navy to be so fitted. This system afforded some improvement over the "seaman's eye" estimation of ranges previously used.

After the initial sea trials of the *Indiana* in 1895, one report predicted that she "will prove an excellent gun platform." The ships later had problems with their gunnery that were to disprove this assertion. None of the ships' intermediate gun battery could be fired at the extreme fore-and-aft train without their muzzle blasts injuring the adjacent gun positions and crews.

Because of their low freeboard, the *Indianas* were usually awash in heavy seas. This characteristic greatly hampered the use of the 13-inch turrets and the four 6-inch casemate guns during rough weather. In addition, the main turrets of the class were "unbalanced"—similar to the main battery turrets in the *Maine* and the *Texas,* the center of gravity of each turret was some distance from the turret's axis of rotation. As a result of being unbalanced, the turrets were found to be particularly unsatisfactory. When trained abeam, they pulled the ship so far over that the main armor belt on that

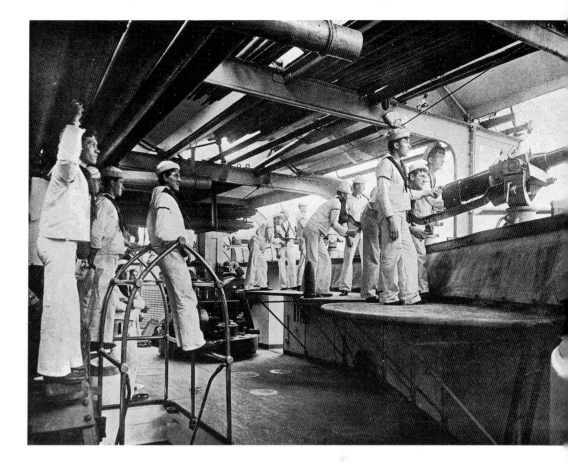

side was brought under water. Concurrently, the belt on the unengaged side was brought far enough out of the water to expose the ship's unarmored bottom. Training the 13-inch guns abeam also reduced their arc of elevation by about five degrees, shortening their range. During the Spanish-American War, these problems were considered to be so serious that these ships were ordered to keep their turrets trained away from the enemy when not actually shooting. This usually meant training them fore or aft.

The navy considered various schemes for solving the problems in the gunnery of the *Indiana* class. In 1901 plans were drawn up for balanced replacement 13-inch turrets of the same general design as those being built into later battleships. These new turrets were rejected, however, as being too costly for the already obsolescent ships. Instead, as a partial solution, 28 tons of lead ballast were loaded into the backs of the old turrets.

Complementing each ship's armament was a defensive shield totaling more than 2,700 tons of steel

Sailors man a light gun aboard the *Massachusetts*. Battleships had 6-inch and lighter guns to fight off torpedo boats, which became a serious threat at the beginning of the century, and other small craft. One of the ship's boats is stowed above this gun. Gunnery proficiency was the major competition between battleships. *U.S. Navy*

armor. Waterline armor belts, 7 feet high and 8 to 18 inches in thickness, protected the battleship's vitals between her main turrets. The powder and ammunition handling rooms below the turrets were encased in armor 17 inches thick, and the turrets themselves were of 15-inch armor. Five inches of steel plating also shielded much of the hull and superstructure above the main belts, including the 6-inch batteries, and the wing turrets had 6 inches of armor protection. The Harvey steel face-hardening process was perfected during construction of this class, and for much of the armor in the *Indiana* and the *Oregon* the navy was able to substitute the superior Harvey processed steel in place of the conventional nickel-steel originally specified.

For additional protection, the hull along the waterline forward and aft of the main armor belts was fitted with cofferdams packed with cocoa fiber cellulose, which was supposed to swell and plug any leak caused by a shell penetrating the ship's skin. It would take the department a number of years to learn that this scheme was in fact ineffective as well as terribly messy whenever the cellulose got wet and rotted, or had to be removed during repairs.

Preliminary plans had specified conical-shaped turrets with thick, sloping sides, based on an old design by famed Civil War engineer James Eads. The Bureau of Ordnance soon realized that such turrets would not provide enough space for working the guns and that they would be difficult to manufacture, so large cylindrical turrets with vertical faces were substituted. Even this created some unforeseen problems. To obtain

**Above:** The *Oregon* in dry dock at the Mare Island (San Francisco) Navy Yard shows the large, twin propellers of this class. She has been refitted with a cage (lattice) main mast. There are two 3-inch anti-boat guns mounted atop the after 13-inch gun turret. Note the movable blocks on the bottom of the dry dock; the *Oregon* rests on these blocks. *U.S. Navy*

**Right:** The *Oregon* at a later stage, painted gray, with a cage main mast, and 3-inch anti-boat guns replacing her earlier battery of light guns. There are large searchlights visible between the funnels and on the lower levels of the cage masts. Searchlights were intended primarily to enable warships to fight off small torpedo craft at night. *U.S. Navy*

adequate elevation of the 13-inch guns without making the port openings too large, the gun mountings had to be placed near the front of the turrets, thus moving each turret's center of balance nearly 4 feet forward of its axis of rotation. Whenever the big guns were trained to either beam, the resulting shift in mass caused the ship to list several degrees toward the engaged side, making gun-pointing difficult, straining the turret-turning machinery, and submerging the armor belt on that side. During a storm at sea in 1896, the unbalanced main turrets aboard the *Indiana* broke free from their stops and, swinging wildly to and fro, required the combined efforts of more than a hundred of the crew to lash them down.

The 8-inch guns were mounted a full 26 feet above the waterline, giving them a commanding field of fire and permitting each pair to be trained across the top of the adjacent 13-inch turret, as far as 14 degrees beyond the ship's centerline. In practice, however, it was discovered that when fired any more than 10 degrees from the centerline, their muzzle blasts rendered the sighting hoods of the larger turrets untenable. A similar interference was discovered to exist between the 13- and 6-inch guns when the big turrets were trained abeam.

So many heavy guns and so much armor on a limited displacement naturally exacted compromises in other areas, and in the *Indiana* class the top speed was only about 16 knots, less than that of either the *Texas* or the *Maine*, and the accommodations and the capacity of the coal bunkers were limited. The ships had a freeboard of only 12 feet, making them wet in a seaway, and in some conditions they were heavy rollers. The limited capacity of existing U.S. dry docks caused a delay of several years in installing the bilge keels specified in the ships' designs, which could rectify the rolling problem.

On 19 July 1892 a fourth battleship, the *Iowa*, was authorized and awarded to the Cramp yard. This design's increase of 12 feet in length and of about 1,000 tons in displacement over the *Indiana* class permitted incorporation of a higher freeboard forward, greater coal and berth-deck capacity, and generally better seakeeping qualities. The new battleship also had a top speed of more than 17 knots.

In the *Iowa* the caliber of the main-battery guns was reduced from 13 to 12 inches, but a more rapid rate of fire helped to compensate for the reduced weight of projectile. The lighter guns could also be ele-

vated or depressed by hand power in the event of machinery failure, a desirable precautionary feature. The oval-shaped balanced turret of new design could also be trained by hand in an emergency. The *Iowa*'s 8-inch and main-battery guns were placed farther apart than in her predecessors, reducing blast interference, and six 4-inch rapid-fire guns replaced the heavier 6-inch rifles of the *Indiana* class. Use of the Harvey processed steel permitted the main armor belts to be reduced to 14 inches in thickness, and they were consequently extended to protect more than three-fourths of the battleship's waterline. The Sino-

A recruiting poster of about 1909 showing a petty officer first class and—almost a requirement—a battleship in the background. The ship represents the then-new *South Carolina* class. Battleships had large crews, but many sailors manned the cruisers and destroyers of the fleet, while significant numbers were also stationed ashore. *U.S. Navy*

Painted a business-like gray, the *Iowa* shows off her appearance during World War I. She was a one-of-a-kind design, slightly larger than the *Indiana* class with a higher freeboard forward, greater coal and berth-deck capacity, and generally better sea-keeping qualities. The last was becoming important for the far-reaching U.S. fleet. *U.S. Navy*

Japanese Battle of the Yalu in 1894 demonstrated the havoc wrought by wood splinters from rapid-fire gun hits, and in the *Iowa* and succeeding battleships much of the traditional ornamental woodwork was replaced by joiner steel, while the wood that remained was fireproofed.

Probably the most striking features of the *Iowa* were her two towering, 100-foot stacks. As in the armored cruiser *Brooklyn*, these served to give the boilers a superior natural draft, reducing the need for operations with pressurized firerooms.

The four battleships of the *Indiana* class provided the backbone for the navy's blockading force during the Spanish-American War. Of the four, the *Oregon* achieved perhaps the greatest fame, particularly for her dramatic 14,500-nautical-mile dash around South America from the West Coast to join the fleet off Cuba. She also outraced the other battleships, including

The *Oregon* caught on the rocks off Hankow Light in the summer of 1900 when she was employed to support Allied operations during he Boxer Rebellion in China. "Boxer" was the Western name for the members of the secret Chinese organization *Yi He Tuan* (the Society of Harmonious Fists). They vowed to overthrow the Manchu dynasty and drive out the Westerners who were taking over China. *Allan J. Drugan/U.S. Navy*

the speedier *Iowa*, during the chase after Cervera's fleeing warships at the Battle of Santiago. This feat was due mainly to her engineering officer's foresight in keeping fires spread thin under all boilers during blockade duty, in contrast to the other warships' policy of "cold iron" under half of the boilers in accordance with normal practice, and in storing the best coal near the firerooms, under lock, for use at a time of supreme need.

After the turn of the century, all four ships became completely outclassed by newer and faster battleships, but the weight of an *Indiana*-class broadside would not be exceeded until the introduction of the dreadnought *Michigan* in 1910. The United States had been slow in entering the battleship race, but its first entries took second place to none.

Following the authorization of the *Iowa* in 1892, a hiatus of several years ensued during which no battleships were added to the navy. The tide of expansionism that had begun during the administration of

**Above:** The *Kentucky*, here at anchor, and her sister ship the *Kearsarge*, were both launched on 24 March 1898 by the Newport News Shipbuilding and Dry dock Company—a unique occurrence in U.S. battleship history. In these ships the 8-inch turrets were mounted directly above the 13-inch turrets, an arrangement that complicated tactics. Each ship also had a battery of seven 5-inch guns along each side. *U.S. Navy*

**Left:** British "tars" raise their caps in salute to the battleship *Kearsarge* at Spithead. The U.S. Navy owes many of its customs and traditions to the Royal Navy. However, the two navies diverged greatly in warship design during the twentieth century, with the significant exception of the three battleships of the *Illinois* class. *U.S. Navy*

The *Alabama* in 1902. She has extended, two-level bridge wings and side-by-side funnels. Most of her starboard 6-inch guns are hidden by the gangplanks. Smaller guns are seen on the forward mast. Battleships carried a large number of boats in part to provide for landing parties. *U.S. Navy*

President Benjamin Harrison slackened during that of Grover Cleveland, who returned to the presidency for a second term in 1893. His new Secretary of the Navy, Hilary A. Herbert, came into office as an opponent to the battleship theory of sea power, but he was soon converted to the doctrines of Captain Mahan. Unfortunately, an economic depression precluded any opportunity for large shipbuilding appropriations, and it was not until 1895 that Congress authorized two additional battleships. On 2 February 1894 the steam sloop *Kearsarge* had run aground on Roncador Reef off Central America and, despite salvage efforts, was lost. Sentimental attachment to the famous veteran of the Civil War was so strong that Congress legislated that one of the new battleships be named *Kearsarge*. The other ship was named for a state, Kentucky, in accordance with traditional practice. Both ships were awarded to a new builder, the Newport News Shipbuilding and Dry Dock Company of Virginia.

Both the *Kearsarge* and the *Kentucky* were launched on the same day, 24 March 1898, barely a month after the sinking of the *Maine*. This was the only twin launching of battleships in U.S. history. Both also had their keels laid the same date, 30 June 1896.

In size, displacement, and speed, the *Kearsarge* and the *Kentucky* were quite conventional, and they suffered from almost as low a freeboard as the *Indiana*-class battleships. Aspects of their armament and machinery were highly innovative. For the main-battery guns, designers returned to four 13-inch guns. Previous tests at the Navy Proving Ground revealed that the 12-inch guns of the type mounted in the *Iowa* were incapable of penetrating the armor carried in most new battleships. An intermediate battery of 8-inch guns was also specified, but the blast interference problems discovered in the *Indiana*-class guns ruled out a duplication of their arrangement. Naval constructors recommended placing a smaller turret above and behind each of the main-battery ones, but they were overruled by ordnance experts who devised the radical scheme of mounting an 8-inch turret directly on top of each 13-inch turret.

This daring departure stirred up a controversy that would continue for years. Those in favor of the superposed turret arrangement argued that the problem of blast interference was overcome, that the efficiency of the intermediate batteries was greatly improved, and that several sets of heavy turret-turning machinery were eliminated. Those objecting to the system pointed out that a single hit could disable four guns, that both the 8- and 13-inch guns would have to be pointed at the same target even though tactical requirements might dictate otherwise, and that their combined firing rate would be reduced because of one set of guns having to wait for the other to fire.

Still, the *Kearsarge* and the *Kentucky* were formidably armed ships for their size and proved to be well-protected, stable gun platforms. As in the *Indiana* class, their low freeboard caused them to become awash in heavy seas. Turret No. 1 could be worked, at best, only with difficulty in a head sea. Coal bunker capacity was some 200 tons less than that of the *Iowa*, and trial speed was a fraction of a knot slower. Another problem with the two new ships was that they had a combined 8-inch and 13-inch shell hoist that was unduly complex. These drawbacks were the result of an attempt to provide first-rate armor and guns on a relatively small ship of limited range with a politically inspired coast-defense mission.

Each of the battleships also carried a huge broadside secondary battery of fourteen 5-inch rapid-fire guns, a substantial advance over both the light 4-inch guns of the *Iowa* and the slow-firing 6-inch rifles of the

Indiana class. In foul weather, the 5-inch broadside guns were unusable.

The ships' main propulsion plants were conventional in design, but in the widespread employment of electricity for the operation of auxiliary machinery, the *Kearsarge* and the *Kentucky* were a great step forward. Gun-elevation and turret-turning machinery, ammunition hoists, deck winches, boat cranes, and ventilation systems were all electrically powered.

During the Spanish-American War, construction work on the new battleships surged ahead, but with the arrival of the peace, work slowed again, and the *Kearsarge* and the *Kentucky* were not commissioned until 20 February 1900 and 15 May 1900, respectively. Both served for several years as flagships and participated in the around-the-world cruise of the "Great White Fleet" from 1907 to 1909. By that time they were outdated, and thereafter served mainly as training ships. The *Kentucky* was scrapped in 1924, but the *Kearsarge* survived until 1956, serving her last 35 years in the unique capacity of the navy's only crane ship.

During President Theodore Roosevelt's first term in office (1901–05), 11 new battleships joined the fleet under naval acts passed by Congress between 1895 and 1899. They were the backbone of his policy of "speak softly and carry a big stick." During his tenure as president, a series of congressional acts provided for important buildup of the navy, including 16 additional battleships, more than half of which were commissioned before the sea-power-minded chief executive left office in 1909.

The momentum gained with authorization of the two *Kearsarge*-class battleships on 2 March 1895 continued the following year when Congress approved funds for three more, to be known as the *Illinois* class, on 10 June 1896. Building contracts for these new 11,565-ton battleships—the *Illinois*, the *Alabama*, and the *Wisconsin*—were awarded to the Newport News Shipbuilding and Dry Dock Company; William Cramp, and Sons; and the Union Iron Works, San Francisco, respectively.

The design for the *Illinois* class was strongly influenced by British designer Sir William White's *Majestic* class, as can be seen from their silhouettes. The U.S. authorization act termed the ships "seagoing coastline battle ships" and called for a combination of the heaviest armor and most powerful armament on a displacement of about 11,000 tons, an increase of 1,000 tons over the *Kearsarge*s. The designers of the *Illinois* class were able to produce a seaworthy ship by the simple expedient of eliminating the 8-inch intermediate

The *Illinois* at high speed with black smoke bellowing forth from her side-by-side funnels. Her compact appearance reveals the strong influence of British designer Sir William White's *Majestic*-class battleships. Of particular interest is the shape of the 13-inch main-battery turrets, which have flat sides and angled fronts. The 8-inch guns were dispensed with, replaced by a large 6-inch battery.
*U.S. Navy*

armament. All three ships were good steamers and exceeded 17 knots on their trials.

These ships bore somewhat the same design relationship to the *Kearsarge*-class battleships that the *Iowa* class had shared with the *Indiana* class. The general hull form and dimensions were the same as in the *Kearsarge*, but freeboard was increased by the addition of a long forecastle and spar deck extending aft for nearly three-quarters of the length of each ship. As in the *Iowa*, this refinement gave the forward turret a more commanding prospect, improved the ship's sea-keeping qualities, and provided more spacious berthing facilities for the crew. There was almost no increase in displacement, and the draft, as in previous U.S. battleships, was necessarily limited to less than 24 feet by the shallow depth of most principal U.S. harbors. In armament and boiler arrangement the ships were strikingly similar to contemporary British battleships, but they were smaller, slower, and had shorter cruising ranges, reflecting the differing strategic and operational requirements of the two navies.

As in the *Kearsarge* class, the main-battery guns were of 13-inch caliber, but in these ships the turrets were elliptical in shape, with an inclined front and an

***Above:*** The new *Maine*—a congressional requirement was that she be named for her predecessor destroyed in Havana Harbor. Larger than the previous *Illinois* class, the three *Maine*-class ships had 12-inch guns using a smokeless powder and firing with a higher muzzle velocity than the earlier 13-inch guns. Note the three-funnel configuration. *U.S. Navy*

***Right:*** The *Ohio* with her crew's bedding airing out. Several of her boats are gone and ladders are rigged, probably indicating that some of her crew are ashore on leave. Radio antennas are rigged on both of her masts. *U.S. Navy*

The *Missouri*, left, and the *Ohio* in the Miraflores Locks of the Panama Canal—"locking north"—on 31 August 1915. The *Wisconsin* is in the distance. All have been refitted with the large cage masts that marked most U.S. battleships and cruisers until the late 1930s. Theodore Roosevelt built the Panama Canal to move the fleet rapidly between the Atlantic and Pacific Oceans. *U.S. Navy*

overhang at the rear. This design provided a turret that was fully balanced for ease of train under all conditions of roll or list—a design that had substantially smaller gun-port openings and much greater resistance to penetration. This turret was lighter and more efficient than the traditional cylindrical turret, which had working room to spare at the sides of the guns but too little at the breeches, and which presented an unnecessarily large target to the enemy.

Although the propulsion machinery in the *Illinois* and her sisters was essentially the same as in the previous class, the steam-plant arrangement was completely revised, with all boilers being mounted fore and aft, with the firerooms outboard of them to either side. This disposition, which was intended to provide easier access to the coal bunkers and better communications between firerooms, necessitated placing the two stacks side by side, which was a common British practice but unique in the U.S. Navy.

Congress provided for no new battleships in 1897, but authorized funds for the construction of three more on 4 May 1898 as part of the major fleet expan-

sion program stemming from the war crisis. These new *Maine*-class ships were at first intended to be near repeats of the *Illinois* class, but subsequently, in hopes of bringing U.S. battleship speed and endurance more in line with contemporary foreign practice, the department invited bidders to submit their own proposals for designs. The resulting accepted plans were for a battleship 20 feet longer than her predecessors, over 700 tons greater in displacement, and having increased bunker capacity and a top speed in excess of 18 knots. The navy dropped the unusual athwartships fireroom arrangement of the *Illinois*-class battleships, adopted modern water-tube boilers, and increased the number of boilers from eight to 24. A third stack was added to accommodate them.

The lead ship of the new class was named *Maine* by order of congress, and her keel was laid on 15 February 1899, exactly one year after the loss of her namesake at Havana. The authorization required that one of the three battleships be named *Maine*. The other ships were named *Missouri* and *Ohio*. As before, one ship was awarded to each major private shipyard.

Sailors aboard the *Missouri* take a break while preparing 12-inch ammunition for target practice, about 1918. The "bullets" have different colors and bands to distinguish different types of ammunition. Several marines in khaki uniforms are visible just forward of the port-side ventilator. Marines aboard battleships formed the core of landing parties and manned secondary guns. *U.S. Navy*

A new 12-inch gun, designed expressly for use with newly developed smokeless powder, was employed for the first time in these ships. In spite of the new projectile being considerably lighter than that for 13-inch guns (850 pounds versus 1,100 pounds), a substantial increase in muzzle velocity resulted in greater overall destructive power. The increased length of the *Maine*-class battleships permitted designers to add two 6-inch rapid-fire guns to the secondary battery, increasing the number of these guns to 16.

The United States used armor hardened by the Krupp process for the first time on the *Maine*-class battleships, and its great toughness allowed the thickness of the armor belt to be reduced from the more than 16 inches of the Harvey-type steel in the *Illinois* class to 11 inches in the *Maine* class without a sacrifice in protection. Another new development was the use of submerged torpedo tubes in place of above-surface mounts, which had been found vulnerable to shellfire. Because of the relative complexity of underwater launch tubes, the U.S. Navy had been late in adopting them, but henceforth this type would be a standard battleship feature in the Steel Navy.

When completed, all three of the *Maines* were overweight and were rather mediocre sea keepers, shipping a great deal of water in bad weather. The

*Maine*'s Niclausse boilers were unsatisfactory in service, and she proved to be what *Jane's Fighting Ships* called a "coal eater." Rear Admiral Robley Evans, who commanded the Great White Fleet during the first leg of the around-the-world voyage from 1907 to 1909, told the Secretary of the Navy that the *Maine* had no "economical speed," and even in port burned coal at the excessive rate of more than 30 tons a day. On the journey from Hampton Roads, Virginia, to California, the *Maine* had to carry bagged coal on deck to supplement her fully loaded bunkers in order to keep pace with the other battleships. This consumption rate caused her to be left behind when the fleet set out across the Pacific.

Both the *Illinois* and the *Maine* classes were designed for the recently fought Spanish-American War, but were soon outdated by the rapid pace of naval progress. The great cruise around the world came just in time for the two classes to display their apparent power to nations that had yet to realize that new developments had already doomed such ships to second-line utilitarian service for the remainder of their days.

Battleship construction continued apace during the expansionist years under President Roosevelt following the Spanish-American War, as the United States moved to acquire the trappings of empire in the Pacific and the Caribbean. On 3 March 1899 Congress appropriated funds for three new battleships, the *Virginia* class, and the following year, before work had even begun on these, the construction of two more of the same class was approved on 7 June 1900. The designs for these warships abandoned all pretense of a limited coast-defense mission—they were to be first-class battleships in every respect, with a length of 435 feet, displacement of nearly 15,000 tons, and a speed of 19 knots.

While new and improved battleships were emerging from American shipyards during President Roosevelt's tenure, the older ones were used in a variety of roles. For example, after the *Oregon*'s triumph of 1898, she spent several years in the Far East. Her travels took her to China, Japan, the Philippines, and Hong Kong. Readily apparent was the *Oregon*'s run-down condition following years without sufficient maintenance. At her best, she had been able to steam at 17 knots. Now, following the steady degradation of her boilers and other equipment, she could manage no more than 10. Her small size, only 351 feet long, posed another type of problem when her big guns, which were 13 inches in diameter and nearly 40 feet long, were trained off the beam, perpendicular to her keel. The entire ship could list as much as 5 degrees in the direction the guns were pointed. Sometimes when the *Oregon* was taking on coal and bunkers filled up more quickly on one side, the guns were trained toward the other side to keep the ship on an even keel. This problem would be eliminated in later battleships with the introduction of counterbalanced turrets.

In 1900 a special Board of Construction, composed of senior officers from the various concerned bureaus, convened to determine the final specifications for the new battleships. The members were in agreement on the selection of 12- and 6-inch guns for the main and secondary batteries, and also on the reintroduction of an intermediate battery of 8-inch guns, which had been omitted from the last two classes. There were strong differences of opinion, however, particularly between the heads of the Bureau of Ordnance and the Bureau of Construction and Repair, regarding the most suitable disposition of the four two-gun turrets of the intermediate battery. In a compromise solution, the board finally recommended that two of the ships should have 8-inch turrets in a quadrilateral arrangement as in the *Indiana* class, while in the other three ships an 8-inch turret should be superposed on each of the two main-battery turrets, as in the *Kearsarge* class, with the remaining pair of 8-inch turrets flanking the superstructure amidships.

Arguments pro and con flared anew a few months later, however, and the Secretary of the Navy appointed a new board with firm instructions to settle on one design for all five battleships. As a result, the board adopted the superposed arrangement plus wing turrets for the entire class. The rationale was that this dual approach afforded more gunpower to be fired in a given direction. Reinforcing the potential of this approach was the success of the 8-inch guns in the Battle of Santiago. There were major drawbacks, however. If one of the dual turrets was knocked out in battle, the ship would lose half of her big-gun capability all at once. And the arrangement lacked flexibility; since the turrets had to turn together, the guns couldn't be aimed at different targets. The first commanding officer of the *Virginia* discovered another problem. The turrets of two different sizes interfered with each other, ironically, because of an increase in the rapidity of fire. In the past, there might have been one shot per gun every three minutes; now it was possible to fire more than

one round per gun in less than a minute. It took time for the smoke and gases to clear, so that a round might be loaded and ready in a 12-inch gun, but in order to see well enough to aim, the crew had to wait to fire until the residue powder from the 8-inch gun had dissipated. Each ship tried different combinations, but essentially the more rapid the fire of the 12-inch gun, the more the superimposed turret became an ineffective weapon.

During President Roosevelt's eight-year administration, four battleships were commissioned and the keels for 16 more were laid down. On 2 September 1906, in a vivid display of the might of the U.S. Navy, all available ships gathered near President Roosevelt's summer home on Oyster Bay in Long Island Sound. The ships anchored in two parallel rows; there were 11 battleships, four armored cruisers, four protected cruisers, a double-turreted monitor, and several destroyers. The weather was awful. At 11:00 A.M. on 6 September, the appointed hour, the presidential yacht, the *Mayflower*, emerged from Oyster Bay. At the same moment, the sky cleared, the sun emerged, and the wind shifted so the ships were lined up in two neat columns. The *Mayflower* proceeded to steam majestically between the two rows as ships in both rows rendered honors. It was as if a higher power was on the side of American naval power.

The large crowd cheers as the battleship *Virginia* slides down the ways at Newport News Shipbuilding on 5 April 1904. Although the bow ram is gone from battleship design, the underwater hull retains the vestiges of that feature. Launchings were great public events—often used by politicians to demonstrate their support of military preparedness. *Newport News Shipbuilding*

The *Virginia*-class battleships authorized in 1898 were fine ships for their day, with good armor protection, but their rolling and their cumbersome double turrets gave them a great disadvantage against the ships they were intended to match. Construction of the lead ship, the *Virginia*, was entrusted to the experienced Newport News Shipbuilding and Dry Dock Company, but other major civilian yards were already busy with existing contracts, and new builders had to be found. The *Nebraska* was thus awarded to the Moran Brothers of Seattle, Washington; the *Georgia* to Bath Iron Works of Bath, Maine; and the *New Jersey* and the *Rhode Island* to the Fore River Shipbuilding Company of Quincy, Massachusetts.

The superposed turrets also turned out to be much less effective than had been hoped. Improvements in loading arrangements and fire control, along with emphasis on target practice, soon increased the firing rate of the 12-inch batteries so much that the 8-inch rifles above could not be employed at their best rate without disrupting the aim or delaying the firing of the larger guns. As a result of this and other problems, the double-decked turret was never repeated.

Torpedo armament was improved over that in previous classes, each ship having four launch tubes designed for new turbine-driven models having long

**Above:** Installing 12-inch guns in the forward turret of the *Connecticut* at the New York Navy Yard in January 1906. The shipyard, located in Brooklyn, was a major builder of battleships for the U.S. Navy through the USS *Missouri*, completed in 1944; she was the penultimate battleship to be constructed for the United States. *U.S. Navy*

**Right:** The *Connecticut* during a high-speed run in 1907. Her hull is white in the style of the period (with gray superstructure); most battleships of the period had an ornate bow insignia with a state motif. The *Connecticut* was rated at 18.78 knots, an achievement that consumed vast amounts of coal and produced tremendous billows of black smoke. *Enrique Muller/U.S. Navy*

range and great destructive power. Armor protection was also more extensive, with the main waterline belts extending the full length of the hull. It was at first planned that three of the battleships would have wood-sheathed and coppered bottoms for resistance to fouling, but this idea was dropped.

The *Virginia* was originally built with inward-turning propellers on the theory that this would improve her steering qualities, but in fact she was found to be most difficult to manage at low speeds or when docking. Her screws sucked a passing steamer into a sideswiping collision at Hampton Roads in 1906, and the scheme was so unsatisfactory that conventional outward-turning screws were installed after the *Virginia* returned from the around-the-world cruise of the Great White Fleet.

During World War I, all *Virginia*-class battleships were relegated to training, transport, or convoy escort roles, and most were sold for scrap a few years later. The *Virginia* and the *New Jersey* were sunk as targets on 5 September 1923 during Army Brigadier General William L. "Billy" Mitchell's spectacular demonstration of airpower.

The *Connecticut* class marked the zenith of American pre-dreadnought battleship designs. It was the largest and most highly developed of the pre-dreadnought battleships. This class was an improved version of the *Virginia* class. After years of "seagoing coastline battleships," the United States finally produced a true ocean-going battleship that compared favorably with its foreign contemporaries. Ironically, by the time the *Connecticuts* were commissioned, they, like the *Virginias* before them, had been rendered obsolete by the rapid pace of technical development.

Two *Connecticut*-class ships were authorized on 1 July 1902. Under the supervision of model-testing pioneer David W. Taylor, the hull form for these ships was worked out in a new model basin at the Washington Navy Yard, the first time such a method had been employed in the calculations for a major class of U.S. warships. Results of the experiments showed that at high speeds a long hull form was more efficient than a short one; consequently, the new battleships were designed with a load-waterline length of 450 feet, 15 feet longer than that of the preceding class. Displacement was also significantly increased over that of earlier U.S. battleships, to 16,000 tons, and the previous limitation on draft was eased to 24 feet. Although the design speed of 18 knots was the same as in the *Virginia* class, this was actually to be achieved with less expenditure of power; the cruising range was to be greater.

In choosing the armament for the proposed *Connecticut*-class battleships during the summer of 1901, the Navy Board of Construction experienced the same strong differences of opinion that had hampered the selection of guns for the earlier *Virginia* and her sisters.

The *Kansas* running speed trials in 1906, prior to her being completed and placed in commission. The main-battery 12-inch guns and intermediate-battery 8-inch guns are installed (all in twin turrets); however, her 3-inch casement guns along the hull have not yet been installed. These ships were unusual in U.S. battleship development by having three funnels. *U.S. Navy*

The *Mississippi*, above, and the *Idaho* represented an effort to arrest the continuing growth of battleship size. Although fitted with the same main and intermediate gun batteries as the previous *Connecticut* class, these ships were 3,000 tons smaller—and were unsuccessful. The ships had a low freeboard. They were in commission from 1908 to 1914. *U.S. Navy*

Although the majority of the board recommended a main battery of four 12-inch guns and a secondary battery of twenty 7-inch rapid-fire guns, a single member held out for a near repeat of the superposed-turret, mixed-battery arrangement of the *Virginia* class. Thus, the board failed to reach agreement. During new deliberations a few months later, the board unanimously agreed upon a third design consisting of four 12-inch guns in a pair of turrets, eight 8-inch guns in four wing turrets, and twelve 7-inch rapid-fire guns in casemates. This arrangement was somewhat reminiscent of the much smaller ships of the *Indiana* class.

The 12-inch guns of the main battery were of the same general design as in the preceding *Maine* and *Virginia* classes, but were 5 feet longer to provide a modest increase in muzzle velocity and to reduce the muzzle blasts' effects on the crews of the smaller guns below when fired to either beam. The 7-inch rapid-fire guns of the secondary battery were of an entirely new design and were considered the largest ones for which crews could hand-load powder and projectile.

In 1902 the Navy Department decided to omit torpedo tubes from all future battleships and armored cruisers, but in light of recent increases in torpedo ranges and accuracy, the department soon reversed this decision. The new battleships each had four underwater launch tubes. Armor protection included full-length waterline belts with a maximum thickness of 11 inches, tapering to 4 inches at the ends. Besides providing builders more detailed plans and specifications to speed construction, innovations in the *Connecticut*

class included the first use of centrifugal pumps for auxiliary purposes and conforming the plates and shapes used in the ships to standard commercial sizes of steel material.

Construction of the *Connecticut* was assigned to the New York Navy Yard; thus, it was the first battleship since the old *Maine* and *Texas* to be built in a government facility. Her sister ship, the *Louisiana,* was awarded to the Newport News Shipbuilding and Dry Dock Company. The Navy Department observed the progress on these two ships with special interest to determine the relative efficiency and cost of construction in the two types of yards. Although government workers had shorter workdays and costs in the navy yards were generally higher, construction of the *Connecticut* was unexpectedly competitive and the quality of work excellent. Navy yards would be involved in future battleship construction on a regular basis.

Three additional battleships of this class were authorized by Congress on 3 March 1903. The *Vermont* was awarded to Fore River Shipbuilding; the *Kansas* to New York Shipbuilding; and the *Minnesota* to Newport News. These battleships were identical to the *Connecticut* in most respects, but the maximum thickness of the waterline armor belts was reduced to only 9 inches, an amount of protection that was clearly substandard for 12-inch-gun battleships. Finally, on 27 April 1904, a sixth ship, the *New Hampshire,* was authorized and awarded to New York Shipbuilding. Although a sister to the other five, her hull number did not fall in sequence because of the simultaneous introduction of two battleships of a new class.

The *Connecticut*-class ships were generally considered to be good, reasonably economical steamers, with a respectable range and sea-keeping ability. Carrying the weight of their 8-inch turrets at the upper-deck level made them more stable than the *Virginias.* The *Connecticut*'s trial board reported that "the steering qualities, steadiness, and seaworthiness of the vessel are excellent." As in the *Virginia* class, however, the ram bow still tended to scoop water up onto the forecastle in heavy seas. The *Connecticut* and *Mississippi* classes were the last American battleships fitted with a ram bow. Forward 3-inch casemate guns, which were almost continually wet, were as useless as those in earlier battleships, the stern guns being only somewhat less so. Internal shutters designed to keep burning fragments from falling into powder-handling rooms in case of flareback in a turret did not work well, and accidental combustion in 12-inch and 8-inch turrets and hoists was a problem throughout the service of the class. Their conning towers and bridges were criticized greatly. Vision slits in the towers were considered to be too small to provide adequate visibility to conn the ship, while the massive foremast and bridge structure was believed to provide too much target area for enemy shells. Further, it was predicted that a hit to the prominent forward superstructure would bury the conning tower under its wreckage and block the vision of the officers trying to fight the ship from this station. The *Connecticut*'s trial report noted that fire in "the highly oiled and varnished woodwork of the chart-house, emergency cabin, and bridges would quickly render the present conning tower untenable, would paralyze the present interior communication system, and compel the ship to be handled from a station below, with no means of communication from deck, which condition during an engagement would be fatal." In taking into account the evaluations of other battleships of the period, the report called for removal of topside clutter.

By 1903 the rapid growth in the size and cost of warships led to one of those periodic reactions whereby legislative action attempts to limit technological progress. In the same act that authorized the *Vermont*, the *Kansas,* and the *Minnesota*, Congress authorized two additional first-class battleships but decreed that they should not exceed 13,000 tons in displacement or $3.5 million in cost.

These two ships were the *Mississippi* and the *Idaho*; they comprised the *Mississippi* class. Their birth had a rather complex background. Late in 1902, the Secretary of the Navy presented the shipbuilding program for fiscal year 1903 to Congress. The House Committee on Naval Affairs approved the navy's program and reported a bill calling for three 16,000-ton battleships of the same design as the *Connecticut's*, plus one 14,500-ton cruiser. During the committee's hearings, an issue arose that had been debated in England for the past decade and was now becoming an issue in the United States Battleships were steadily increasing in size, both domestically and abroad. A growing number of politicians who objected to the correspondingly greater naval appropriations and naval officers who did not believe that larger ships were tactically superior to smaller ships opposed this increase. Partisans of smaller ships contended that a larger number of small battleships would achieve better results than a smaller

The *Idaho* under construction at the William Cramp & Sons yard in Philadelphia, in 1907. A ship in a yard, whether under construction or in overhaul, invariably appears a mass of clutter. She will soon go under a crane for the fitting of her masts, guns, and turrets. The Cramp yard's last battleship to be completed was the *Wyoming,* completed in 1912. *U.S. Navy*

number of big ships. Concentrating ever-increasing amounts of offensive power in ever-fewer ships, they claimed, was a classic example of putting all one's eggs in one basket. In addition, as battleships increased in size and power, the corresponding increase in their protection impeded them from fulfilling their primary mission as destroyers of the enemy.

Supporters of the bigger ships, on the other hand, contended that larger ships were better sea keepers and gun platforms, and better fulfilled the battleship's *raison d'être*. Bigger ships were less likely to be totally disabled by a single torpedo or shell, and they could carry heavier-caliber guns. Because of the relatively primitive communications of the time, it was difficult to direct the fire of several battleships onto the same target. Therefore, it was argued that a few large ships with heavy guns would be better able to concentrate gunfire on an enemy target than would numerous ships with smaller batteries. The issue was debated hotly by both sides. Despite the many arguments put forth, the House of Representatives authorized the three battleships and one armored cruiser requested by the navy.

The proposed naval program met even greater resistance in the Senate, where the Naval Affairs Committee rejected the House's three 16,000-ton battleships and one 14,500-ton armored cruiser. They substituted four "first-class battleships . . . of the general type of the *Oregon*, upon a trial displacement of not more than 12,000 tons, of a maximum draft and ready for service at sea of not more than 24 feet," and two "first-class armored cruisers, of the general type of the *Brooklyn*, not exceeding 9,500 tons displacement."

The two bills went to a joint conference committee. At the request of the House conferees, members of the Board of Construction testified against the Senate bill. They argued that this measure would represent "a backward step in the evolution and growth of the American Navy." After a "very exhaustive" hearing, the conference committee finally reported a rather unusual compromise. The three 16,000-ton battleships approved by the House were restored to the program, and two 13,000-ton battleships were added, replacing the one large armored cruiser originally requested.

Thus, in the *Mississippi* and the *Idaho*, the department was forced to regress to battleships 75 percent shorter and 3,000 tons lighter than the current standard practice. Nevertheless, the navy's designers managed to repeat essentially the entire armament of the *Connecticut* class less only four secondary guns. This was accomplished at the expense of horsepower, speed, and cruising range at a time when tactical and strategic requirements demanded exactly the opposite.

The two ships of the *Mississippi* class were smaller editions of the *Connecticut* class, some 74 feet shorter, but with the same approximate beam and draft. Horsepower and bunker capacity were both reduced to save weight, and the "broken-deck" design last used in the *Maine* class was adopted to bring Turret No. 2 down one deck level to improve stability. To further reduce topside weight, only one military mast was installed.

These ships carried the same 12-inch and 8-inch batteries as the *Connecticuts*, along with eight 7-inch guns and twelve 3-inch guns. Although 18-inch torpedo tubes were considered, two of the newer, more powerful 21-inch tubes were installed. The bigger ships had four of these tubes. The *Mississippi*'s turrets, gun mounts, and ammunition supply were similar to those of the *Connecticut*.

The experiment in curtailing the size of battleships with this class proved to be a failure. As was to be expected, the *Mississippi* and the *Idaho* were first-class battleships in name only and were thoroughly unpopular in the fleet. In spite of the model tests, the ships were unable to achieve the high speeds that the Bureau of Construction and Repair had optimistically predicted. The relatively disadvantageous length-to-beam ratio of the *Mississippis*, as compared with the *Virginias* and the *Connecticuts*, proved to be too much of a handicap. Although both ships were powered by more than 13,000 horsepower, they were unable to exceed their designed 17-knot speed by more than one-tenth of a knot. Their economical speed was 8 knots, rather than the 10 knots of their contemporaries. With only 75 percent of the coal capacity of the *Connecticut* class, the *Mississippis* also had a shorter range than the other ships, putting them at a further disadvantage in fleet operations.

In addition, the *Mississippi* class proved to be poor sea-keeping ships and gunnery platforms in Atlantic waters. Their motion in a seaway was irregular. Their short length and relatively wide beam made them pitch heavily in comparison with longer ships. Combined with an abnormal fore-and-aft motion, this tendency to roll and pitch produced a yawing movement, which made it extremely difficult to keep the guns on target. Their hulls being cut away to a considerable extent aft, it was difficult to keep them on course even in smooth waters.

The *Mississippis* had a relatively short service with the U.S. Fleet, although the *Mississippi* was distinguished as the first U.S. warship to transport aircraft for combat operations. In late 1913 the navy established its first air station at Pensacola, Florida. The

The Greek battleship *Lemnos*—full dressed, that is, with all flags flying—at Smyrna, Turkey, in 1919. She flies the Greek flag at the foremast and the Italian flag at the mainmast. The *Lemnos* was the former USS *Idaho*, transferred to Greece in 1914 along with her sister ship the *Mississippi*. The two ships had many shortcomings and were not popular with the U.S. Navy. *U.S. Navy*

*Mississippi* was ordered there to act as a tender or "station ship" at the new facility, arriving in January 1914 with an aviation unit of seven planes, 32 officers and enlisted men, and their equipment. The battleship's commanding officer also commanded the new air station. Three months later, U.S. naval forces landed at Veracruz, Mexico, and aviation detachments were ordered to support them. One detachment sailed for Tampico in the cruiser *Birmingham* on 20 April 1914. The *Mississippi* departed for Veracruz the next day with a detachment of four pilots and two early seaplanes. On 25 April Lieutenant Junior Grade P. N. L. Bellinger piloted a Curtis C-3 flying boat on a 50-minute flight reconnoitering the Veracruz area and searching for mines in the harbor. This was the first operational flight by a U.S. Navy airplane. Air operations continued, and on 6 May 1914, the *Mississippi*'s second plane, a Curtis A-3 floatplane, or "hydroaeroplane," became the first navy plane to suffer combat damage when it was hit by rifle fire while on a scouting flight near Veracruz. Subsequently, the combined air detachments resumed the program of flight training that the Mexican operation had interrupted, and the *Mississippi* and her planes returned to Pensacola.

Both the *Mississippi* and the *Idaho* were sold to Greece shortly thereafter. They served in the Greek navy as coast defense battleships long after their contemporaries had disappeared, finally to be sunk by German bombers in 1941. With the funds realized from the sale of the two ships, Congress authorized the construction of a third *New Mexico*–class battleship.

To the *Connecticut* fell the honor of leading the Great White Fleet on its cruise around the world. She and her class formed the backbone of the U.S. Fleet for a few short years, but their status was little more than that of caretakers. Even while they had been under construction, the United States was initiating a naval revolution with the design of the *South Carolina* and the *Michigan*, introducing the concept of "big-gun" battleship armament. The British were independently reaching similar conclusions with their *Dreadnought*, laid down in secrecy and rushed to completion with unprecedented haste to become the symbol of a new battleship era.

## THE GREAT WHITE FLEET

The high point of the pre-dreadnought battleships' careers was the voyage of the Great White Fleet. It had not been called this from the outset. Years later, somebody coined the name and it stuck.

President Roosevelt had very specific goals in mind for this historic trip, and not all of them were made public. Politically, he wanted to influence the 1908 U.S. elections on behalf of his party and to generate increased moral and financial support in Congress for funding for the navy, so "it might vote a dozen or so new battleships." He also wanted to win political and public support for the still-unfinished Panama Canal.

Financially, Roosevelt wanted to calm the panic that had ensued in 1907 when a stock market sell-off had plunged values by $2 billion and triggered tremendous strains on the economy. Wall Street blamed Roosevelt for his "erratic anti-business policies." An international banking panic was also occurring in London, Paris, and Berlin. In the United States, the Justice Department was initiating extensive anti-trust actions against monopolies. A foreign adventure such as the fleet's trip might provide the public with welcome diversion from the economic depression.

Economically, a focus on the fleet would be a boon for the U.S. shipbuilding industry and to Wall Street magnates such as Andrew Carnegie and others who made their fortunes in steel and similar industries. Diplomatically, the fleet's courtesy calls to Japan and China would help temper some of the simmering racial conflicts in the United States Regarding national security, it would impress other countries with the might and power of the U.S. Fleet and stave off swirling war sentiments while generating goodwill among allies such as Australia and New Zealand. It would also emphasize America's interests in the Atlantic and Pacific and its expectation that it was to be considered a major player. The country's leaders also expected this display to generate a groundswell of patriotism and domestic support for the government and military, and to upstage the socialists and anarchists who frequently dominated the news in those times. But the strongest reason for Roosevelt was to garner prestige and significantly influence public opinion.

In the battle for symbolism in 1907, a battleship was the ultimate weapon. Robert A. Hart, the author of *The Great White Fleet: Its Voyage around the World, 1907–1909* (New York: Little, Brown, 1965), described it as "a paradox of power and beauty (that) demanded attention—pride and affection of people whose flag it flew and the envy and fear of adversaries. Why hide

This glass-tinted lantern slide shows American sailors from the Great White Fleet posing with Japanese while on liberty in Japan in October 1908. The Japanese turned out in the thousands to welcome and meet the Americans in a most cordial atmosphere. There were very few incidents during the circumnavigation. *U.S. Naval Institute Collection*

it in a stockpile? Why not place it on display as one usually does with costly and beautiful possessions? The meaning of prestige was quite clear to anyone who watched a parade of ships." It was a proclamation to the world of such intangible virtues as honor, dignity, strength, and respect.

If the Spanish-American War marked the emergence of the United States as a world power, then the world cruise of the Great White Fleet from 1907 to 1909 was visible proof on an international scale of the powerful, mobile might of the U.S. Navy. Without the forceful, energetic 1907 decision of Roosevelt, generally regarded as the most outstanding civilian advocate of the navy and American sea power of his time, there would have been no ambitious world cruise.

Roosevelt summed the mission up clearly and succinctly: He wanted the navy prepared and "all failures, blunders, and shortcomings to be made apparent in time of peace and not in time of war." Further, in his view, the voyage would provide "an answer to the very ugly war talk that had begun to spring up in Japan; and it was the best example of 'speaking softly and carrying a big stick.'"

Fifteen Atlantic Fleet battleships completed training and maneuvers in the fall of 1907, including target practice in Cape Cod Bay, and readied themselves for an extensive cruise. These capital ships, joined by the new *Vermont*, gathered at Hampton Roads, Virginia, in early December 1907. The assembled coal-burning battleships, completed between 1900 and 1907, varied in normal load displacement from 11,550 tons to 16,000 tons, and mounted ordnance of various calibers, with either 12-inch or 13-inch main batteries. Roosevelt called the ships, painted white up to the main decks, "white messengers of peace."

While outwardly this around-the-world-cruise seemed simple enough, it turned out to be a logistic nightmare. Because of the shortage of U.S. Navy colliers, the navy was forced to charter 49 foreign colliers to deliver 430,000 tons of coal to various ports for the battleships to recoal. When coal deliveries occasionally failed to arrive on schedule, the navy realized that continued dependence on foreign shipping for fuel could prove to be an Achilles' heel in future wars.

On 16 December 1907 the band played "The Girl I Left behind Me" as the flagship *Connecticut* with Rear Admiral Robley D. Evans on board led the fleet out of Norfolk and steamed south on the first leg of its journey that would take them more than 14,000 miles. After leaving Port of Spain, Trinidad, the first port of call, the fleet crossed the equator for the first of six times during the cruise, and continued south, stopping at various ports en route. After passing through the Straits of Magellan, the ships headed north along the Pacific coast of South and Central America. At Magdalena Bay, Mexico, the fleet held its annual spring target practice. Here, for three weeks in March, the fleet's guns blazed at various short-range targets and achieved 100 percent gains over results from the first competition in 1903 in both accuracy and rapidity of fire. While at Magdalena, the fleet, the United States, and the world were electrified by Secretary of the Navy Victor Metcalf's announcement that the cruise would continue around the world. The fleet was joined there by the hospital ship *Relief*, which embarked patients for return to San Francisco. The *Relief* rejoined the fleet at San Diego and remained with it until detached in November 1908 at Olongapo, Philippines. During her time with the fleet, the *Relief* provided medical care, treatment, and consultations for over 14,000 officers and men of the Great White Fleet.

In early April the fleet got under way for the West Coast of the United States, where they visited several ports from San Diego to Puget Sound. On 9 May, plagued by rheumatism and confined to a wheelchair, Admiral Evans was forced to relinquish command of the fleet. Rear Admiral C. M. Thomas temporarily succeeded him. By mid-May, Admiral Thomas had reached mandatory retirement age and was succeeded by Rear Admiral Charles S. Sperry, who led the fleet for the remainder of the cruise.

On the West Coast the battleships received shipyard overhauls, and the new *Nebraska* and the older *Wisconsin* replaced the *Alabama* and the *Maine*. The latter two battleships had great limitations because of their huge appetites for coal. However, they did complete a world circumnavigation together as a special service squadron, with the *Maine* arriving in New York on 20 October 1908.

On 7 July the Great White Fleet steamed out of San Francisco. By mid-July the ships had reached Honolulu. During August and September the ships touched at Auckland, New Zealand, and the Australian ports of Sydney, Melbourne, and Albany. Large and enthusiastic receptions greeted them at each port.

The fleet next proceeded to Manila, but crews were prevented from going ashore by a cholera epidemic. The American warships then steamed to Yokohama, Japan, for a crucial visit for achieving one of the voyage's major objectives. During their trip to Japan they ran into a typhoon. The *Kearsarge* and *Virginia* classes fared the worst because their topside heaviness and low freeboards made them highly susceptible to rolling. Some of the ships, such as the *Virginia*, rolled to nearly 90-degree angles, but recovered. The admiral in charge of their division slowed to 8 knots to accommodate the low-freeboard ships, but even that didn't help. The *Kearsarge*, for example, at 8 knots, plunged so heavily into the seas that a shudder ran from the keel all the way to the top of the foremast, which snapped off and took with it the radio antenna. Two men fell overboard during the storm; one was rescued, but the second wasn't. Despite the hardship, the ships arrived at Yokohama in mid-October, welcomed by a crowd of interested Japanese visitors, whose size—numbering in the thousands—and cordiality to the American Fleet fulfilled Roosevelt's highest expectations.

After the visit, the ships returned to the Philippines, where gunnery practice in Manila Bay occupied November. At ranges varying from 6,000 to 9,000 yards, the fleet completed the annual fall target competition. The results were as gratifying as the earlier competition at Magdalena. The 1908 fall gunnery exercise again showed more than a 100 percent improvement over the 1903 competition both in number and rapidity of hits.

The ships transited the Indian Ocean, where at Colombo, Ceylon, Sir Thomas Lipton sent aboard a

While the American warships waited to transit northward through the Suez Canal, some officers and men were able to visit the Great Pyramids and Great Sphinx outside of Cairo, Egypt. They rejoined the fleet in Port Said on the Mediterranean coast. The ships steamed some 43,000 miles in 14 months. *U.S. Naval Institute Collection*

pound of tea for each of the 14,000 officers and men. On New Year's Day 1909 the ships were in the Red Sea. After passing through the Suez Canal in early January, the ships divided into two groups to permit crews to visit almost all of the Mediterranean countries. While passing through the canal, the *Georgia*, commanded by Captain Edward Qualtrough, ran aground. She was able to back off, but the troubles were compounded later when Captain Qualtrough was court-martialed for being drunk at a reception at Tangiers, Morocco. For the remainder of the voyage, he was not allowed on the bridge or the quarterdeck of his own ship and was stripped of all command authority.

To the survivors of an earthquake at Messina, Sicily, the fleet sent storeships and a financial contribution of some $3,000. At the end of January 1909 the separated units gathered at Gibraltar, the last foreign port before departure for home. While at this famous British base, the fleet received formal notification of the 1908 fall gunnery competition results. The *Vermont* had won the battleship gunnery pennant by a substantial margin.

Clearing Gibraltar in early February, the Great White Fleet triumphantly arrived at Hampton Roads on 22 February 1909—coincidentally, George Washington's birthday—with both professional and diplomatic missions accomplished, to the gratification of the nation. Only 10 days before he left the White House to be succeeded in office by William Howard Taft, Roosevelt had the pleasure and satisfaction of reviewing the fleet from the presidential yacht, the *Mayflower,* and of addressing and conversing with the more than 6,000 men who had achieved such notable results. In total, the fleet had covered some 43,000 miles.

The cruise abounded in accomplishments and lessons, both diplomatic and professional. If seeing is believing, many West Coast Americans as well as nationals of Japan and numerous other countries had observed firsthand the impressive peacetime display of

"Welcome home, men" said President Roosevelt, in the last days of his presidency as the Great White Fleet returned to Hampton Roads on 22 February 1909. Each of the 20 battleships fired a 21-gun salute as she steamed past the presidential yacht *Mayflower* to honor George Washington's birthday. Here Roosevelt addresses the crew of the *Connecticut. U.S. Navy*

American naval power as an instrument of national policy. Professionally, the voyage was highly informative. For example, important structural and cosmetic changes to battleships followed an evaluation of the cruise, including adoption of "basket" masts and installation of searchlights in their tops, reduction in the length of the forward bridges, elimination of much "top hamper," and a change in the paint scheme from white and slate to slate alone.

In summary, the 1907 to 1909 world cruise of the Great White Fleet was an invaluable experience that can be seen today as a significant event in the rise of modern American naval power. However, when the ships of the *Connecticut* class and her pre-dreadnought sisters returned to Hampton Roads and paraded in triumphant review in early 1909, they were already on the verge of obsolescence. Stripped of their graceful bow ornaments and painted a businesslike gray, the six battleships gradually slipped into second-line roles during the decade that followed, as the successively larger and more powerful dreadnought-type battleships of the *South Carolina*, *Delaware*, *Florida*, *Wyoming*, *New York*, *Pennsylvania*, and *New Mexico* classes

**Above:** The *Georgia*, also fitted with cage masts, barely under way off Philadelphia in June 1909. Note her twin anchors forward, superfiring turrets forward, large bridge wings, and 3-inch guns mounted in side casements. There are radio aerials running up her cage masts (and, not visible, rigged between them).
*William H. Rau/U.S. Navy*

**Left:** The *Minnesota* was typical of the *Connecticut* class as refitted after the Great White Cruise. The modifications included a rework of the bridge configuration as well as the installation of cage masts. There is a range-finding device visible atop the forward and after 12-inch turrets as she steams out of Hampton Roads. *O. W. Waterman/U.S. Navy*

Coaling ship, or supplying a ship with coal for fueling was a long, hard, and dirty job: The *New Hampshire* takes on coal at the New York Navy Yard about 1909. The coal is bagged on the barge, lifted aboard by the ship's booms, and poured down chutes into the bunkers. A chute opening in the deck is at the lower center of the photo, next to the boom winch at left. The ship's band often played during coaling to encourage the crew. *U.S. Navy*

entered service. At the end of World War I, the once-proud veterans of an era of white-and-gilt naval elegance were even pressed briefly into duty as troop transports, until meeting their fate in 1923 in accordance with the Washington Treaty for the limitation of naval armaments.

## THE APPROACH TO WAR

After the cruise of the Great White Fleet, all battleships were concentrated on the East Coast and followed the same annual routine. In the winter, the fleet headed south to gather at Guantánamo Bay, Cuba. The ships ventured forth from that anchorage for training maneuvers and gunnery practice, and the Caribbean offered off-duty liberty attractions for crews. As spring approached, the ships would return north and spend some time in their home ports. When they did have maneuvers, they often took place off the Virginia Capes, an area then known to the U.S. Navy as the southern drill grounds. During the course of each year,

ships would rotate into navy yards for maintenance and repairs. For the few men who were married, a yard period in the ship's home port was among the few opportunities to be with their wives and families.

As this routine continued, each year brought a steady modernization of the fleet. From January to April 1910, the navy commissioned its first four dreadnought battleships: the *Michigan*, the *South Carolina*, the *Delaware*, and the *North Dakota*. Plans for the first two dated from 1904, but their leisurely construction schedule put them behind their British counterpart, HMS *Dreadnought*. That revolutionary warship was completed and fully manned in December 1906, the same month the United States laid the keels for the *Michigan* and the *South Carolina*. These were the first dreadnought-type battleships in any navy armed with super-firing main-battery gun turrets, meaning the guns of the high turret were fired over the top of an adjacent low turret. This arrangement permitted a higher volume of gunfire forward or aft than the *Dreadnought*'s turrets, which were mounted at the same level.

The year 1912 set the precedent for the U.S. Navy and Marine Corps to act as seagoing policemen. When a group of Cubans took over an American-built and -operated sugar mill near Guantánamo, President William Howard Taft dispatched the warships to deal with the problem. The sailors dyed their white uniforms with coffee to match the color of the official marine uniform. The group of sailors and their officers drilled at Guantánamo and advanced on the disputed sugar mill as a band played. The Americans recaptured the mill, with the only fatality being one Cuban, killed by another Cuban.

In October 1913 the United States stationed naval forces off the gulf coast of Mexico to protect American interests during a revolution in that country. For the most part, U.S. battleships just watched and waited; at times they provided temporary hotel services for American citizens who wanted a safe haven until they could be evacuated from the area. The situation took a turn for the worse in April 1914, when a navy enlisted man was detained ashore. Rear Admiral Henry T. Mayo, commander of the navy force off Mexican shores, demanded an apology and a gun salute to make amends. President Woodrow Wilson strongly backed Admiral Mayo because he was trying to force out Mexican President Victoriano Huerta, a military dictator. The situation was exacerbated when a German ship approached Veracruz with a supply of guns and ammunition for the Mexican government.

A landing force of U.S. Marines and sailors went ashore on 21 April and fought a series of battles with the Mexicans. It was a type of urban warfare for which navy men were not trained, although many had practiced marksmanship. Especially proficient was Ensign Willis A. Lee of the *New Hampshire*'s landing party. He had been a member of the navy's rifle team and seemed to relish the opportunity to fire at live targets. When the landing party halted in its advance through the city, Lee sat on a curb with a rifle across his knees, baiting snipers into firing at him. He was effective in returning fire when it came in his direction. And it was hard to see the Mexicans, for they kept themselves well hidden. Observers could only see a rifle barrel or a hand holding a pistol out of a window or over the edge of a roof. Later in the month, army troops relieved the sailors ashore. The warships stayed in the area until the American occupation ended later that year. In the meantime, World War I had begun in Europe.

In the early years of the century, a naval arms race between Great Britain and Germany began to heat up. By August 1914, the continent of Europe had plunged into the "Great War." Despite this, the Naval Academy sent its midshipmen abroad that summer for a training cruise in several battleships. One of the ships was the *Idaho*. She and her sister, the *Mississippi*, got caught up in a balance-of-power game. In preparing for possible conflict, Turkey had signed a contract with a British shipyard to build a battleship with seven turrets. Its arch rival Greece sought battleships of its own to counter this development. The United States decided to make its two pre-dreadnoughts, the *Idaho* and the *Mississippi*, available for sale. The U.S. Navy considered them to be "lemons," and was happy to get rid of them. The *Idaho* was decommissioned at Villefranche, France, on 30 July 1914 and transferred. The U.S. Navy sent the *Maine* to pick up the midshipmen and crew of the *Idaho*. In an unusual move, the navy transferred the ships to the New York Shipbuilding Company, rather than make a government-to-government transfer. In turn, New York Shipbuilding passed them on to Greece. Surprisingly, when war erupted and Turkey wound up on Germany's side, Britain decided not to let Turkey have its contracted battleship. She became HMS *Agincourt*, widely noted as the only battleship with a turret for each day of the week, because of her seven twin 12-inch turrets.

In the summer of 1915 the U.S. Naval Academy midshipmen embarked in three battleships, the *Ohio*, the *Missouri*, and the *Wisconsin*, bound for the Panama Canal. On 16 July after dredges worked all night to open a channel through a mudslide in Culebra Cut, Rear Admiral William E. Fullam's three-ship squadron became the first American battleships to pass through the canal, which had opened less than a year earlier. The around-the-Horn cruise of the *Oregon* in 1898 had been a considerable factor in the push for a Central American canal. Bands played in celebration as the ships, decorated with signal flags, passed through the canal. U.S. soldiers lined the banks of the canal and cheered for their countrymen.

A line of battleships is led by the *Rhode Island* about 1912. Her crew stands by to man the rail; some of her boats are rigged outboard, indicating that she is near port. Battleship maneuvers were mainly steaming in line, practicing to "cross the T" of an enemy battleship column, to bring all main guns to bear on the enemy, which would have his after guns "masked." *U.S. Navy*

# CHAPTER THREE

# FEAR GOD AND DREAD NOUGHT

**Left:** A line of American battleships steams into the British port of Scapa Flow on 7 December 1917, being cheered by the crew of the battleship cruiser *Queen Elizabeth*. Leading Battleship Division 9 is the USS *New York*, followed by the *Wyoming*, the *Florida*, and the *Delaware*. The original is an oil painting by Bernard F. Gribble, now in the U.S. Navy Art Collection. *U.S. Navy*

Upon retirement, British Admiral Sir John Fisher paraphrased Psalms 38:9: "Fear God and dread nought." This was his way of paying tribute to his prize battleship, HMS *Dreadnought*. When Fisher first conceived of such a ship back in 1900, little did he know he was starting a revolution in battleship design.

After the Spanish-American War, the United States held a colonial empire consisting of Puerto Rico, Hawaii, the Philippines, and Guam. In addition, the United States held de facto control over Cuba. This situation continued well into the 1930s. Top military brass believed the United States needed a two-ocean navy, and public sentiment was strongly on their side. In 1901, when Theodore Roosevelt became president, the United States also gained a strong advocate for becoming a first-rate naval power. Roosevelt gradually expanded the fleet until it was second only to that of Great Britain. However, the completion of the HMS *Dreadnought* in December 1906 shifted the balance of naval power to an unprecedented degree. Before the appearance of HMS *Dreadnought*, battleships had a main battery of large guns plus intermediate guns of medium caliber ranging from eight to 16 in number. Their mixed batteries made ranging of shot difficult because of the types of guns employed—it was hard to tell which caliber fell where and limited the range to which all major guns could be employed because of the primitive fire control then in use. It also required different calibers of ammunition to be carried by each ship. As the first all-big-gun battleship to be commissioned, the *Dreadnought* mounted ten 12-inch guns in five twin turrets with no intermediate gun batteries. Further, she was the fastest battleship yet built, with a maximum speed of 21 knots compared to the 15 to 19 knots of existing American battleships.

When the ships of the *Connecticut* class and her pre-dreadnought sisters returned to Hampton Roads in 1909 after their around-the-world cruise, they were already on the verge of obsolescence because of HMS *Dreadnought*. Stripped of their graceful bow ornaments and painted a businesslike gray, the battleships of the Great White Fleet gradually slipped into second-line roles during the decade that followed, as successively larger and more powerful *dreadnought*-type battleships entered service. The United States had to build anew to keep up with European navies. American designers had anticipated the *Dreadnought*

by planning the single-caliber battleship of the *South Carolina* class in 1905. However, the British must be given credit for completing the first all-big-gun battleships, with the *Dreadnought* being completed four years before the *South Carolina* class. The United States' response to the *Dreadnought* was the two ships of the *Delaware* class.

The U.S. Navy was to have two generations of dreadnought battleships. The first generation consisted of the *South Carolina* through the *Texas* (10 ships). In this generation the vital hull spaces were armored, but there was also armor at various locations around the topside superstructure. The second generation consisted of the *Nevada* through the *Massachusetts* for a total of 19 ships, only 12 of which were ever completed. In this generation the internal vital spaces were protected by armor, but not the topside superstructure. The subsequent "fast battleships," the *North Carolina* through the *Louisiana*, were in reality third-generation U.S. dreadnoughts.

## THE FIRST GENERATION

The first U.S. dreadnoughts, the *South Carolina*s, were in fact the world's first "all big gun" battleships to be designed. The naval appropriations for the class were delayed, however, and the British *Dreadnought* was built within a year. If this had not occurred, then either the *South Carolina* or the *Michigan* might have lent her name to a new type of battleship as the embodiment of a huge jump in offensive power. With the British *Lord Nelsons*, the Japanese *Aki* and *Satsuma*, and other contemporaries, they were the outcome of the ever-increasing efficiency of long-range gunnery.

The *South Carolina*s were also the last U.S. battleships restricted to the 16,000-ton limit mandated by Congress on 1 July 1902, and at 18 knots, they conformed to the speed standard of earlier American battleships. As a result, they could not operate tactically with the later dreadnoughts, and were often listed with the pre-dreadnoughts. They did not, for example, serve with the later ships in European waters during World War I.

The *South Carolina* design resulted from gunnery advances, largely due to the efforts of then-Captain William S. Sims. As leader of the reform movement, Sims benefited by having his president's confidence. The Bureau of Construction and Repair (C&R) had been asked to design a new type of battleship in 1904. Sims and his colleagues found the bureau much too

The *New Hampshire* does what a battleship should do: fire broadsides. But the target here is another U.S. ship—the *San Marcos*, the former battleship *Texas* of 1895. The outdated warship was used as a target ship in Chesapeake Bay—and sunk—in 1911. The *New Hampshire*'s hull number was not consecutive with her sister ships because of the authorization of the *Mississippi* and the *Idaho*. N.G. Moser/U.S. Navy

slow to act. They accused its members of being far too conservative and "hence unlikely to bring the fleet to anything like the required level of efficiency." The Great White Fleet cruise tended to confirm this. The matter came to a head when President Roosevelt convened the Newport Conference of 1908 at the Naval War College at Newport, Rhode Island, where the General Board of the navy received the task of developing battleship characteristics. Very little documentation of the design background of the *South Carolina* class has survived, possibly in part because C&R itself found the episode so embarrassing.

It appears that the bureau's initial approach was a relatively conventional design with twin 12-inch gun turrets on the centerline fore and aft, and four single 8-inch gun turrets replacing the twin gun mounts of earlier pre-dreadnoughts. These designs encountered severe structural problems, which presumably were not helped by Congress' limitations on the new battleships' displacement. Chief constructor Washington L. Camps of C&R then chose the then-radical superfiring arrangement with the second turret firing over the first, both forward and aft. In March 1907 the arrangement was tested on the monitor *Florida*. One of the two 12-inch guns in the ship's turret was removed and mounted to superfire above and behind that turret. Animals and several men were simultaneously placed in the first turret to test the blast effects of the superfiring. By this time, the construction on the *South Carolina* was past the point of making alterations, so a possible justification for the turret tests was to see whether the ship could fire four guns ahead or astern.

This class was also built with the cage masts that would become characteristic of U.S. dreadnoughts. The cage mast was tested on the monitor *Florida* in May 1908 and formally adopted for the entire fleet that summer. The original design incorporated a pair of pole masts with a fire-control bridge mounted between them. The ships under construction were completed with cages fore and aft on the centerline to support fire-control tops. The pole masts were cut down to serve as kingbolts for boat cranes. Those ships already commissioned received their cage masts as they entered the shipyard for refit and overhaul.

The *South Carolina* class had two weaknesses. First, C&R refused to put steam turbines in the class. As a result, the machinery power-to-weight ratio was much inferior to Great Britain's *Dreadnought*, a ratio

that limited the U.S. ships' maximum speed to just under 19 knots. Second, the ships in this class were considered to be heavy rollers. This tendency probably contributed to the collapse of the *Michigan*'s foremast in a gale on 15 January 1918, killing six men and injuring another 13.

The *Delaware* class was the first class of U.S. battleships to match the standard of the British dreadnoughts. The *Delawares* combined a new single-caliber main battery with a steam turbine plant, to achieve the new standard speed of 21 knots. The steam turbine plant was 25 percent larger than those of the *South Carolina* class, and thus the freeboard was reduced because of the increase in weight. In addition, the secondary armament was carried lower on the hull because mounting them any higher would have weakened the upper decks.

The 29 June 1906 authorization act for these ships specified that the navy issue tenders for private designs, then compare them with the C&R design to determine which was best. None of the private designs were even remotely satisfactory. The Fore River yard in Massachusetts, one of the companies that submitted designs, later developed its design into what became the Argentine *Rivadavia*-class dreadnoughts. This navy bureaucratic procedure delayed the laying of the ships' keels until November and December 1907.

The *Delaware*-class design was completed in 1906, the chief constructor producing both a 10-gun,

The *North Dakota*, with her crew manning the rail and flags flying (the 48-star "jack" at the bow), and the *Delaware* were the first U.S. battleships to exceed the congressional limit of 16,000 tons that had previously ruled battleship design. These ships had two more 12-inch guns than the *South Dakota* class in a fifth twin turret. *U.S. Navy*

The *Utah* in her World War I camouflage scheme. Such markings were intended primarily to distort the view of a U-boat commander viewing a warship through his periscope. The dazzling designs made it difficult to estimate the ship's range, size, and even the direction in which she was steaming. There are triangular baffles on the mast to confuse an enemy rangefinder. *U.S. Navy*

20,500-ton version and a 12-gun, 24,000-ton design. The larger ship was rejected as too expensive for the limited firepower it provided, even with its design ultimately reduced to 22,000 tons. The critical improvement over the *South Carolina* class was the addition of a fifth turret, which gave the class a 10-gun main battery, making it the equal of British contemporaries. The addition of the fifth turret added 65 feet to the ships' length. The citadel amidships structure of the *South Carolinas* was abandoned for a British-type raised forecastle deck of restricted width.

The 20,500-ton design was also severely criticized for its heavy secondary gun battery, carried at gun-deck level.

The crew of a 5-inch 51-caliber gun in action on the *Utah* during an exercise in the early 1920s. Their short sleeves will provide little protection against burns. The gun officer at top, the enlisted gun crew, and the ship's executive officer (bottom left) all wear gas masks. World War I left the fear that poison gas would be used in future conflicts. *U.S. Navy*

The two guns sponsored out in the bows were not only wet, they also broke up the bow wave and thus wasted propulsion power. Guns on pre-dreadnought classes similarly situated would get so wet that they could not be used effectively in a seaway, as the fleet learned during its world cruise of 1907 to 1909. Moreover, the secondary guns were unprotected. Also, steam lines passed around the magazine of Turret No. 3. Although magazine refrigeration was provided, the magazine could not be kept cool enough, and there was a fear that its powder might become unstable, particularly in the tropics.

The *Delaware*-class design made the first attempt to do away with permanent bridges. It was hoped that, even in peacetime, the ships could be operated from within their spacious conning towers. As in the *South Carolinas*, plans originally showed a pair of pole masts, with a fire-control bridge fitted in between and another between the two funnels, but the final design incorporated cage masts.

The two ships of the *Delaware* class were competitive sisters due to differences in their engineering components. The *Delaware* had conventional reciprocating engines, while the *North Dakota* had geared turbines. At this stage of development, the principal

effect of the turbine was a sharp reduction in fuel economy at cruising speed. The *Delaware*, on the other hand, was the first American battleship that could steam for 24 hours at full speed without needing repairs, even though she had to rely on earlier-model reciprocating engines.

Both ships of the *Delaware* class remained in first-line service until the completion of the *Colorado* and the *West Virginia*. The *North Dakota* was then converted to a mobile target on 1924 and was scrapped in 1931, having been replaced by the *Utah* in that role. The *Delaware* was scrapped in 1924.

Next, the two-ship *Florida* class was essentially a "repeat" of the *Delawares*. The major design change in these ships was the enlargement of the machinery spaces to fit geared turbines. This led to a 3-foot increase in their beam. They were also the first U.S. warships with four propeller shafts. Although the original intention was to carry eight 14-inch guns in a *South Carolina*-class layout, the delay in supplying the guns and turrets led to the *Floridas* being given the same type of 12-inch guns as the *Delaware* class. As a result of criticism of the

*Delaware* class at the Newport Conference of 1908, the design of the *Floridas* was modified to incorporate light armor protection for the secondary battery. To compensate for the additional weight, the proposed 6-inch gun battery was cut back to 5-inch 51-caliber guns, as used in the *Delaware* class.

The two ships of the *Florida* class were later modernized, the *Florida* between 1924 and 1926 and the *Utah* between 1926 and 1928. An essential objective of the modernization was better protection, both on deck and underwater. The ships were converted to burn fuel oil by replacing the original 12 coal boilers with four oil-fed boilers taken from the canceled *South Dakota*-class battleships and the *Lexington*-class battle cruisers of the 1916 shipbuilding program. Each of the six ships that composed the *Florida*, *Wyoming*, and *New York* classes had a thin, watertight "splinter deck" at about the waterline, which separated the main armor belt from the upper belt. Upon reconstruction, 3 inches of armor were added to the second deck between the end barbettes to cover the upper belt, as in the later oil-burning battleships. The ships were also reboilered.

The *Texas* after her 1925–26 reconstruction. Her cage masts have been superseded by tripods, her boilers converted to burn oil, protection improved, twin funnels replaced by one, and superstructure extensively modified. The previous *Florida* and *Wyoming* classes underwent similar updates. The BB 33–35 would again be modernized during World War II. *U.S. Navy*

This involved reducing the volume of the boiler rooms, thereby increasing considerably the effective depth of torpedo protection added by the bulges.

Another essential objective of modernization was the provision for a catapult on the midships turret for launching aircraft. Previously, some of the ships of the first generation dreadnoughts were fitted with flying-off platforms fixed atop a turret. Each ship that was initially fitted this way, with the *Texas* being the first in 1918, carried Hanriot HD-1 biplane fighter aircraft.

After catapults were invented as a means to launch aircraft from the deck, the *New York* class and all succeeding classes replaced their flying-off platforms with this new device as the ships were modernized. Each battleship would carry three planes, and embark over time a variety of floatplanes as well as the Loening OL-series amphibians.

The addition of a gunpowder-type catapult, designated Type P, Mark IV, or Mark IV-1, required the elimination of the mainmast from the *Wyoming* class. Although the forces afloat demanded two fire-control positions, this was not possible for the *Floridas*, which had to make do with the foremast position.

Finally, the secondary batteries, which had been quite wet, were relocated. However, the new bulges, which increased the beam length to 106 feet, did not improve sea-keeping performance. The ships still remained wet, with a tendency toward quick, "snappy" rolling when disturbed by external forces such as storms and hurricanes.

The *Wyoming*-class design was developed as one of three different alternatives for gun size and placement, with both the *Wyoming* and the *Arkansas* carrying different-sized main armament. As stated previously, on 2 July 1908 President Theodore Roosevelt convened a conference at the Naval War College in Newport. The president was under pressure from a reform group headed by Captain Sims, who sought radical modernization of the navy's organization. Roosevelt addressed the conference, asking whether the U.S. Navy should go from 12-inch to 14-inch guns in constructing the *Wyoming* class. Alternatives proposed for this class were a 12-gun, 12-inch design; an eight-gun, 14-inch design; and a 10-gun, 14-inch design. Even though the attendees of the conference favored a 14-inch gun, the navy chose the 12-inch alternative on 30 December 1908. This was largely because it entailed the least construction delay, and existing docking facilities on both coasts could not handle the larger, 14-inch-gun ships. Moreover, the ship design with ten 14-inch guns could only be docked at Pearl Harbor or Puget Sound, Washington, and at the New York Navy Yard if the dock there could be lengthened by 5 feet. The decision was also made to build and test the 14-inch gun and to enlarge docking facilities, so that the more satisfactory ship could be built later. That design became the *New York* class, which was built under the 1910 program. The *Wyoming* class, an interim solution, was essentially an enlarged *Florida* design, with extra beam and greater length to allow space for a fifth turret.

All of these designs—the *South Carolina, Delaware, Florida,* and *Wyoming* classes—were flushdeckers. The Great White Fleet cruise had already shown the problems of mounting secondary guns too low. The solution was to slope the main deck from a high bow aft, gaining about 4 feet in secondary-battery height amidships.

The *Wyoming* class was modernized from 1925 to 1927. One funnel was removed, the after cage mast was replaced by a tripod, and "blisters" for improved torpedo protection were added to the sides of the hull. The *Wyomings* also were equipped with geared turbines and converted to burn fuel oil. Each ship was fitted to carry aircraft, with an aircraft catapult being fitted atop the third turret.

The last of these first-generation U.S. dreadnought battleships was the *New York* class. The *New York* and the *Texas* were the 10-gun 14-inch design that had originally been developed from 1908 to 1909 as an alternative to the *Wyoming* class. Recurring problems with American turbine designs since the *South Carolina* class came to a head when manufacturers refused to accept the machinery specifications laid down by the Bureau of Ships in its contract solicitation for the *New York* class. After a lengthy and inconclusive argument with the manufacturers, the General Board refused to be blackmailed into accepting machinery below its military requirements and chose to revert to reciprocating engines, even though it was aware that they had no great potential for further development. No long-term harm resulted from this decision, however, and the U.S. Navy eventually became the world leader in the development of warship machinery.

The prototype 14-inch 45-caliber gun fitted in the *New York* class was test-fired in January 1910. The first antiaircraft guns mounted on a U.S. battleship were 3-inch guns placed atop turrets aboard the *Texas* in 1916. The *Texas* was also the first U.S. battleship with flying-off platforms for aircraft. They were fitted on both ships of the class while those ships were assigned to the British Grand Fleet, possibly as early as March 1918. The *Texas* flew off her first airplane at Guantánamo Bay in March 1919.

In the mid-1920s the *New York* (from 1926 to 1927) and the *Texas* (from 1925 to 1926) underwent modernization at Norfolk Navy Yard. The changes to both ships were similar to those made earlier to the *Florida* and *Wyoming* classes. As in the *Florida*, protection and fire control were modernized. Six oil-fired boilers, taken from the scrapped capital ships of the 1916 program, were installed and gave them a performance of 28,000 horsepower and a top speed of 21 knots. This was the first class to be fitted with new fire-control equipment, together with new tripod foremasts. Like the previous ships to undergo modernization, both ships were wet and quite stiff. Moreover, they performed poorly at sea due to their reciprocating engines. They showed particularly severe hull and engineering vibrations, bad enough to threaten to crack their propeller shafts at the standard fleet cruising speed of about 12 to 14 knots.

Thus, from 1910 to 1916, the United States completed 10 first-generation dreadnoughts. Those ships were roughly the equal of their foreign contemporaries and served as an interim step from the pre-dreadnought battleships to those ships that would comprise the battle Force of the U.S. Fleet at the start of World War II. Although the transition between the two generations of dreadnoughts would be smooth—the *New York* and the *Texas* were laid down in 1911 and the "new" *Nevada* and *Oklahoma* were laid down the following year—there were marked differences in their design and capabilities.

By 1917, it had become increasingly obvious that the United States would be drawn into the European war. On 16 January 1916 British codebreakers intercepted and deciphered a secret telegram from German Foreign Minister Arthur Zimmerman to the German ambassador to Mexico. Germany promised to restore to Mexico territory lost to the United States—namely, Texas, New Mexico, Arizona, and California—in return for a military alliance should the United States and Germany go to war. A copy of the deciphered telegram was sent to President Woodrow Wilson, who promptly expelled the German ambassador and released the telegram to the press on 1 March 1917. That same month, President Wilson received congressional approval to arm U.S. merchant ships and sent navy crews to man the guns. Germany responded by sinking American cargo ships.

On 3 April all the U.S. battleships headed for an anchorage in the York River in Virginia, near Yorktown.

The United States sent a squadron of battleships to Britain in 1917 to join the Grand Fleet. But they saw no action against the German High Seas Fleet, which, after the 1916 Battle of Jutland, declined to give battle to the Royal Navy. Here sailors aboard the *Delaware* participate in the ship's gala revue—one of many self-produced entertainments of American sailors. *U.S. Navy*

The ships steamed in divisions and anchored safely behind antisubmarine nets, the newer dreadnoughts in one line and the pre-dreadnoughts, with their distinctive tall smokestacks, in a line closer to Yorktown. Altogether, the assembly of ships occupied 5 miles of the York River. Three days later, Congress overwhelmingly approved President Wilson's request for a declaration of war on Germany. The immediate contribution from the U.S. Navy was in the form of transports to carry American soldiers "over there," and destroyers to fight German U-boats, with little for the American battleships to do at the outset.

In the autumn of 1917 the United States and Great Britain agreed that the U.S. Navy would send a division of coal-burning battleships to Europe to reinforce the British Grand Fleet, which was committed to maintaining a distant blockade of German ports and, more specifically, the German Fleet. The Grand Fleet did not get the newest and most capable oil-burning American battleships. With Britain's supply of coal far more plentiful, the U.S. Navy dispatched its older coal-burning ships. Meanwhile, its newer battleships remained behind for the boring duty of training gunners.

During some of the training, the battleships fired their guns at the target ship, the *San Marcos,* which was partially sunk in Chesapeake Bay. It was quite a comedown for the nation's first steel battleship. On 25 November 1917 Battleship Division 9 (the *New York,* the *Arkansas,* the *Wyoming,* and the *Delaware,* minus the *Texas,* which had run aground and was under repair at New York Navy Yard) set out across the North Atlantic. They steamed in line abreast in the daytime and in a column at night. The four ships were painted in camouflage schemes that drew from an overall plan but allowed variations in the individual ships. The camouflage was to deceive the enemy as to which direction the ships were traveling. It turned out to be deceptive, all right, but instead of the Germans, the Americans victimized themselves. Captain Henry Wiley of the *Wyoming* observed that when the ships were steaming side by side, the *New York*'s paint scheme made her seem as if she were converging with his own ship. Later, the Americans found that the British were also confused by the camouflage, so they repainted all four ship darks gray.

## TOUR WITH THE GRAND FLEET

Crossing the North Atlantic was difficult due to the weather. During a storm, the *Delaware* got separated from her division mates but managed to rejoin them off Scotland. On 7 December 1917 the ships reached Scapa Flow, in the Orkney Islands, the home of the Grand Fleet. Battleship Division 9 was absorbed into the Grand Fleet and became the Sixth Battle Squadron. In the early ventures to sea with the British, the Americans—in unknown waters and on high alert—reported many false sightings of German submarines. The squadron eventually got used to British procedures and routines. In one instance, the British destroyer *Valorous* dropped a depth charge on a suspected U-boat. Even though the *Wyoming* was some distance away, the ship was so rocked by the underwater explosion that those on board were concerned their ship had been damaged. The squadron also came to realize what a demoralizing effect the depth charges had on U-boat crews.

Captain Wiley of the *Wyoming* ran a taut, disciplined ship, but his squadron commander, Rear Admiral Hugh Rodman, was constantly giving him an earful about mistakes and shortcomings. After one incident, in which the *New York* slowed without signaling, and the *Wyoming* got uncomfortably close to her stern,

Rodman sent criticisms to Wiley by flag signals. Once the ships were in port and moored, Wiley went on board the flagship to confront the angry admiral. Wiley presented his side of the story and said Rodman should relieve him of duty if the signals the admiral had sent were justified. Rodman calmed down and had a man-to-man talk with the skipper. He explained that he was so committed to making the squadron perform well while with the Grand Fleet that his complaints to the individual ships were harsher than he had realized. After both men had aired their viewpoints, they shook hands and parted as friends.

In the spring of 1918 the fleet base shifted for a time from dreary Scapa Flow to Rosyth, on the Firth of Forth on Scotland's east coast. German soldiers in France were making a push to the west and looked as if they might break through. The Royal Navy, concerned that they might have to cover an evacuation from the Continent, moved the heavy ships to a position closer to land. At times, the fleet was put on 1 hour's notice to get under way.

One of the principal objectives of the American and British ships based in the British Isles was to try to bait the Germans into emerging from their protected lairs so the guns of Allied dreadnoughts could get at them. In May 1916 British and German battleships and battle cruisers had tangled in the monumental Battle of Jutland, an event that would be studied and restudied by naval officers during the period between the world wars. While the British fulfilled their strategic goal of driving the Germans back into port, the battle was a tactical defeat for the Grand Fleet because it failed to sink or even seriously damage the German High Seas Fleet. The British Navy wanted another tussle, this time aided by the Americans. The U.S. battleships went to sea a number of times to train and perform target practice. The real agenda, however, was to draw the High Seas Fleet out of port. The Germans refused to take the bait.

As the war continued into the summer of 1918, the U.S. Navy increased its forces in Great Britain beyond the initial division of coal-burning battleships sent to the British Isles the previous year. On 23 August Battleship Division 7, composed of the *Utah* and two modern oil-burners, the *Nevada* and the *Oklahoma*, arrived in Bantry Bay, Ireland. The division's function was to protect convoys in the event any German battle cruisers attempted to break out and attack convoys arriving from America.

**Top:** Another camouflage scheme of World War I is worn by the battleship *Nebraska* in this April 1918 photograph. A U-boat skipper would have a difficult time estimating the size and direction of the ship when viewed through the narrow lens of a submarine periscope. There are range finders atop her forward and after 8-inch gun turrets (which are superimposed on the 12-inch turrets). *U.S. Navy*

**Above:** Still another camouflage scheme is this splotchy motif of the *New Jersey*, also seen in 1918. Camouflage was not meant to make ships invisible, but just to confuse anyone trying to attack them. The *New Jersey* has large radio antennas fitted to both of her cage masts. There are square fighting tops on the masts, and both are ringed with searchlight platforms. *U.S. Navy*

*Right:* Doughboys—the World War I term for American soldiers—and sailors crowd the deck of the *Louisiana* as she steams into New York Harbor in 1919. Battleships supplemented the limited number of transports available to bring home the American Expeditionary Force that fought in France. This photo, printed from a stereograph card, shows some of the life rafts that inundate ships in time of war. *Keystone View Co./U.S. Navy*

Breaks in the tedious routine of Scapa, where the wind always blew and it was always cold, came when combined forces of British and American ships went out for week long sweeps of the North Sea. Although German U-boats attacked the American battleships on several occasions, their torpedoes did not hit their marks. The only contact came when the *New York* collided with a submarine as she steamed into Pentland Firth (although the ship's proud captain disputed this conclusion). On 29 October 1918, while on board ships holed up in the ports of Keil and Wilhelmshaven across the North Sea, German sailors faced with the prospect of a suicidal sortie mutinied. The mutiny was a turning point in the war, the end of which was not long in coming. On 21 November, just 10 days after

the armistice, the Grand Fleet steamed out in two parallel columns, each 10 miles long, to meet the defeated German High Seas Fleet as it approached for its surrender and internment. The next day, the nine U.S. battleships jointly departed for New York. They arrived off Ambrose Light on Christmas Day and entered New York on 26 December, anchoring in the Hudson River.

In Europe, the defeated German High Seas Fleet was transferred to the Scapa Flow navy base with their crews remaining on board. The following spring, under provisions in the Treaty of Versailles, the surrendered German ships were to be parceled out among the victorious Allies. Before that could occur, the German sailors then living on board opened the sea cocks on each ship, thus scuttling the High Seas Fleet.

On 13 December 1918, aboard the transport *George Washington* (which was escorted by the battleship *Pennsylvania*), President Wilson arrived from the United States to take part in the postwar peace negotiations.

## BRINGING HOME THE TROOPS

At the end of World War I the proud veterans of an era of white-and-gilt naval elegance were pressed briefly into service as troop transports. Between December 1918 and June 1919, having spent the war in the Chesapeake Bay as training ships, several of the pre-dreadnought battleships were outfitted as troop transports and made runs to Brest, France, to pick up troops of the American Expeditionary Force (AEF) and bring them home. Each ship could carry some 1,400 to 1,500 troops per trip, with an average of four round-trip voyages. Participating in this operation were the *Connecticut* and the *Minnesota* (three trips each); the *Nebraska*, the *New Jersey*, the *Rhode Island*, the *Louisiana*, the *Vermont*, and the *Kansas* (four trips each); the *Virginia* (five trips); and the *New Hampshire* (six). After this duty, they resumed normal battleship duties. In 1923 all met their fate in accordance with the Washington Treaty.

In the spring of 1919 the U.S. Pacific Fleet was established, with Admiral Hugh Rodman as its first commander in chief, hoisting his four-star flag on the brand-new battleship *New Mexico* at the New York Navy Yard. She was the first American battleship with electric-drive propulsion. Rather than using the steam from her boilers to operate reciprocating engines or turbines, steam was fed to generators that produced electricity, which in turn powered the

*Above:* Laid up in reserve at the Philadelphia Navy Yard in 1919 are (from left) the *Iowa*, the *Massachusetts*, the *Indiana*, the *Kearsarge*, the *Kentucky*, and the *Maine*. More of the pre-dreadnoughts and the early ships of that type would soon be scrapped or used as targets, with the notable exception of the *Kearsarge*; converted to the *Crane Ship No. 1* in 1920, she had a long if inglorious career. *U.S. Navy*

*Opposite:* After World War I the United States again looked to the Pacific, with the Panama Canal simplifying the transfer of ships between the Atlantic and the Pacific. The *Wyoming*, is seen here transiting the canal's Gailliard Cut on 26 July 1919, has a deflection scale marked on her No. 5 turret, and a range clock on her after cage mast. Marked from 0 to 10, clocks indicated to ships ahead and behind the distance to the enemy in thousands of yards. *U.S. Navy*

main engines. The *New Mexico* and six other modern battleships—the *Idaho,* the *Mississippi,* the *New York,* the *Texas,* the *Wyoming,* and the *Arkansas*—made their way through the Panama Canal to their new home port of Long Beach, California. Their immediate mission was to show the flag in West Coast ports; the long-range mission was to be available and ready

*Right:* The battleship *Michigan* being dismantled at the Philadelphia Navy Yard in October 1923. Although not formally stricken until the following year, the ship was far outdated by the faster, more heavily armed, and better protected dreadnoughts of the second generation that were commissioned in the early 1920s. The United States did not commission a new battleship from 1923 (West Virgina, BB-48) to 1941(North Larolina, BB-55). *S. L. Morison/U.S. Navy*

*Below:* The ex-*Kearsarge* in her guise as the *Crane Ship No. 1*. Bearing little resemblance above her hull to a battleship, she has a rotating, 250-ton-capacity crane fitted aft of her single funnel. In this configuration the *Kearsarge* survived in the navy until 1956. The world's only battleships in active service after that date were the four dreadnoughts of the *Iowa* class. *U.S. Navy*

in the event that the United States became involved in hostilities with Japan.

Secretary of the Navy Josephus Daniels was in Long Beach in August 1919 to welcome the arriving fleet, as he had done at New York after the armistice. The battleships were a novelty on the West Coast, and cities up and down California lavished their crews with hospitality, including giving barbecues, providing free transportation, and handing out tickets to all manner of entertainment. At San Francisco, Secretary Daniels and President Wilson reviewed the fleet. The navy provided a sentimental gesture by using the old *Oregon*, veteran of the Spanish-American War, as the reviewing ship.

The battleships gradually settled into a routine of operation, based at San Pedro, as they conducted maneuvers and fired gunnery practice. When needed, each ship went for overhaul and repairs to the Puget Sound Navy Yard in Bremerton, Washington, which would serve as the principal West Coast battleship yard through World War II and beyond. For ships home from the war, it was time for more of the always ongoing modernization programs. For example, in 1920 the *Texas* got new directors for her broadside

guns and antiaircraft guns, new torpedo defense lookout stations on her cage masts, a plotting room to improve the tracking of enemy ships and the aiming of her guns, updated radio equipment, and raised searchlight platforms.

However, the face of Dreadnought was about to change with the arrival of its second generation.

**Above:** The *Michigan* entering Honolulu Harbor, Oahu, during an exercise in March 1920. After the war the navy began annual fleet exercises or "problems," which soon evolved into attacks against the Panama Canal or the fledgling naval base at Pearl Harbor on Oahu. From 1925, aircraft carriers participated in the problems, a harbinger of World War II operations. *U.S. Navy*

**Left:** U.S. Naval Academy midshipmen of every era spent summers at sea, often aboard battleships. The *Delaware* in the storm-swept North Atlantic about 1920 gives "middies" a taste of real navy life. Most of the midshipmen on board aspired to someday command such a ship, the pride of the fleet and a stepping stone to flag rank. *U.S. Navy*

# CHAPTER FOUR

# SECOND-GENERATION DREADNOUGHTS

**Left:** The battleship *Oklahoma* at Guantánamo Bay, Cuba, a U.S. naval base from shortly after the Spanish-American War. She has an aircraft takeoff platform atop the No. 2 twin 14-inch gun turret. With ten 14-inch guns, these ships had twin turrets superfiring over three-gun turrets, an arrangement that was also used in the two heavy cruisers of the *Pensacola* class. *U.S. Navy*

Unlike the first generation, the second-generation U.S. dreadnoughts were to have the greatest acceptable firepower mounted on a platform that was protected, "where it mattered," by armor plate up to 18 inches thick on the turrets and 16 inches on the deep underwater belt. These two qualities were obtained at the cost of speed.

The *Nevada* class was a revolutionary design, introducing "all-or-nothing" protection. Since armor-piercing shells did not explode when penetrating thin armor plating, the designers reasoned that there was nothing to be gained from using thin armor. Better, they believed, to choose either the thickest armor, which could not be penetrated, or no armor at all—hence, its distinctive all-or-nothing name. Thus, battleships from the *Nevada* class through the aborted *South Dakota* class were known as the second-generation U.S. dreadnoughts. In addition, the second-generation ships were considerably superior to the first-generation classes in both offensive and defensive firepower. They carried the same number of heavy guns, 10, but they were distributed among four turrets—two twin-gun turrets and two triple-gun—which greatly facilitated fire control. The *Nevada* class were the first U.S. battleships to carry triple-gun turrets.

The *Nevada*, riding at anchor at "Gitmo" in 1919. She carries a large observation kite balloon, a tethered airship used for observation and hunting for submarines. Guantánamo, at the eastern end of Cuba, was an important base and coaling station for U.S. warships exercising in the calm waters and clear skies of the Caribbean area. *U.S. Navy*

These ships were still fast, despite the sacrifices made for firepower and armor. They were designed to General Board characteristics and reflected the new demands of very long-range battle: heavy deck armor and highly centralized fire control.

In the previous *New York* class, the central fire control station had to be placed above the relatively thin protective deck because all of the hull volume below that deck was occupied by machinery and magazines. Therefore, the station was enclosed in light splinter armor. In theory, shells would strike the "lower casemate" and burst before they could reach the "central citadel," and its thin armor would defeat the splinters. As expected, battle ranges increased, and shells might well pass over this upper belt, to strike the central belt directly. This led to a major step in the *Nevada* design, which was to move the main armored deck to the top of the upper armor belt, with a splinter deck placed below it to protect the machinery and magazines from shrapnel of armor-penetrating shells. It followed that the upper and lower belts might as well be merged into a single armor belt. Similarly, the upper casemate armor, which in earlier designs had protected the offside secondary guns and uptakes, was abandoned in favor of having heavy armor around the funnel bases. Armor could also be used more efficiently because the main battery was concentrated into four rather than five turrets. Likewise, a funnel was eliminated. The main belt was 17 feet, 5 inches wide and extended for 400 feet. The turrets had 16 to 18 inches of armor plating, the conning tower 16 inches. The total weight of armor was 11,162 tons, 3,291 tons of which was deck

The battleship *Nevada* after being modernized in 1927–29, as was her sister ship the *Oklahoma*. Tripods replaced her cage masts, main battery elevation was increased to provide a greater range, protective bulges were fitted underwater, and her machinery was updated. Three SOC floatplanes are carried on catapults atop Turret No. 3 and on the fantail. *U.S. Navy*

armor; the equivalent figures for the preceding *New York* class were 8,121 tons and 1,322 tons, respectively.

Fuel oil was first introduced in the *Nevada* class. Its advantages over coal included a reduction in engine-room manning and a consequent saving in berthing space. However, there was no longer any coal protection to the machinery spaces, leaving the underwater portion of the hull vulnerable.

The two ships of this class were built with competitive power plants—turbines in the *Nevada* and triple-expansion reciprocating engines in the *Oklahoma*. Both of those battleships, like the five subsequent battleships of the *Pennsylvania* and *New Mexico* classes, were deficient in underwater protection and in the maximum elevation of their heavy guns. The *Nevada* was modernized at the Norfolk Navy Yard and the *Oklahoma* at the Philadelphia Navy Yard from 1927 to 1929. During their modernization, gun elevation was increased to 30 degrees, which increased the range from 23,000 to 34,000 yards. Also, six of the *Nevada*'s boilers were relocated to increase the depth of underwater protection provided by the new antitorpedo bulges, and she received the geared turbines that had their trial run on the now-scrapped *North Dakota*. Two inches of armor were added to the second (heavy) deck. The former rather wet secondaries were replaced by a deckhouse arrangement similar to that built into the *New Mexico* class. Eight 5-inch 25-caliber antiaircraft and two 5-inch 51-caliber single-purpose guns in open mounts above the deckhouse and the lattice masts were replaced by heavy tripods. In addition, two powder-type aircraft catapults were fitted, one atop the third turret and the second catapult on the stern. Three Vought O2U-3 Corsair biplane spotter aircraft would be carried on each ship.

The subsequent *Pennsylvania* class was essentially an enlarged *Nevada* design, with four triple-gun turrets rather than the previous two twin-gun and two triple-gun turrets of the *Nevada* class. This gave the class 20

Inspection aboard the *Idaho* about 1920. The ship's cage foremast hosts a number of radio antennas. The three *New Mexico*-class ships carried the same 12 main-battery guns as the *Arizona* and the *Pennsylvania*, but the later ships had the longer-range 14-inch 50-caliber vice 45-caliber guns. All five had a large number of 5-inch 51-caliber guns for use against small ships, plus 3-inch antiaircraft guns. *U.S. Navy*

percent more firepower without an increase in displacement. This was what the General Board had originally wanted for the *Nevada* class, but Congress had been unwilling to appropriate enough money for the larger gun battery. The *Pennsylvania* was completed as a flagship, with a special two-level control tower. She was initially flagship of the U.S. Atlantic Fleet from commissioning until 1918, and from 1921 to the 7 December 1941 attack on Pearl Harbor she was flagship of the U.S. Pacific Fleet.

The *Pennsylvania* design was considered one of the best of its time, but the design had some disadvantages that offset many of its fine qualities. The triple 14-inch guns did not prove superior in practice to British and German twin mounts, the turrets being cramped and cumbersome. This class also incorporated special underwater protection, consisting of a 3-inch anti-torpedo bulkhead 9 feet inboard of the shell plating, with a another bulkhead 2 feet farther inboard. Tests showed that this system could withstand about 300 pounds of high explosives. The fuel oil was stored in the double bottom compartments; as this fuel was considered highly inflammable, the protective system was designed to keep torpedo explosions as far away from it as possible.

The *Arizona* was commissioned on 12 June 1916, and the *Pennsylvania* was commissioned on 17 October 1919. Initially, neither of the ships was sent overseas due to the severe shortage of navy oilers with which to refuel them. Both ships were modernized from 1929 to 1931, with changes to machinery, underwater protection, armament, and rig generally the same as the *Nevada*. The *Pennsylvania* was modernized at the Philadelphia Navy Yard and the *Arizona* at Norfolk Navy Yard. Among other things, six boilers and geared turbines were fitted, with machinery originally ordered for the canceled battleship *Washington* split between the two ships. In addition, 1 inch of armor was added to the second (heavy) deck; antitorpedo bulges were fitted; tripod masts replaced the cage masts; and two catapults were added, one on top of Turret No. 3 and one on the stern. The modernization of the two *Pennsylvanias* made the pair nearly homogeneous with the *New Mexico* class.

In 1913 the General Board began calling for an entirely new battleship design, displacing about 35,500 tons, and armed with ten 16-inch guns in five twin-gun turrets. Secretary of the Navy Josephus Daniels refused to countenance any substantial increase in tonnage, and decided that the 1914-program battleships would essentially duplicate the *Pennsylvanias* with whatever improvements that could be incorporated at minimum cost. These ships became the *New Mexico* class. Two ships were originally planned, but proceeds of the 1914 sale to Greece of the pre-dreadnought *Mississippi* and *Idaho* were used for the construction of a third ship.

Two major improvements to the *New Mexico* class were made. The first dealt with the problem of wetness by installing a clipper bow that replaced the ram bow, and by mounting 12 of the 22 5-inch 51-caliber guns in a deckhouse. As planned, ships of the class would still retain four guns in the forecastle deck forward; four more aft, below the main deck; and another pair in the open, atop the deckhouse. One of the three ships was completed with that configuration of 22 5-inch guns, but by that time American experience in the North Sea was showing that only the deckhouse guns would be usable in a seaway. The bow and after gun positions were soon plated in, reducing the number to 14 5-inch guns. The second major improvement to the *New Mexico* class was in the main-battery gunnery. These ships introduced the new 14-inch 50-caliber gun, which elevated independently within each turret, in

The *Tennessee* fires her 14-inch 50-caliber main battery during gunnery practice in the 1920s. The purpose of the 59 steel battleships completed by the United States was to carry big guns to sea and to pound enemy warships or bombard enemy territory. Despite their limitations in the century of aircraft and submarines, those battleships were effective warships. *U.S. Navy*

contrast with the earlier dreadnought-type U.S. battleships. In addition, the elevation of the main battery guns was increased from 15 to 30 degrees.

The Bureau of Steam Engineering wanted turbo-electric propulsion to replace steam turbines both for economy and because the turbines had been giving trouble in the previous class. The Bureau of Construction and Repair saw the new system as a means to improve subdivision, and planned to employ the turbo-electric propulsion in all of its later dreadnoughts and battle cruisers. Before moving forward with the plan to replace the geared turbines, the turbo-electric drive system was tested on the *New Mexico*. The steam from her boilers drove two turbogenerators that transmitted a current to four motors that drove the propeller shafts. Although successful, the system was soon abandoned because of its excessive demands on weight and internal volume and because electrical power was vulnerable to battle damage. As a result, geared turbines became the standard for U.S. warship propulsion by World War II.

The *New Mexico* class was modernized under the 1931 program, the changes being similar to those done in the *Nevada*. The *New Mexico* was modernized at the Philadelphia Navy Yard from March 1931 to January 1933; the *Mississippi* at the Norfolk Navy Yard, March

1931 to August 1932; and the *Idaho* at the Norfolk Navy Yard, September 1931 to October 1934. Each ship received entirely new geared turbine propulsion, six new boilers, two powder-type catapults installed aft, and armor added to the second (heavy) dock. The tripod masts originally planned as replacements for the cage masts were replaced with tower bridges, justified primarily on the basis of resistance to blast and to shellfire. A fire-control tower, topped by a low pole mast, took the place of the after cage mast.

The next U.S. dreadnoughts, the two ships of the *Tennessee* class, were slightly modified *New Mexicos*, the principal improvements being in underwater protection. In a set of caisson experiments, it was shown that a series of layers of liquid-filled and void compartments could absorb the explosive energy of a substantial torpedo warhead. The protective system in these two ships was designed to resist 400 pounds of high explosives. These ships incorporated a series of five bulkheads on the port and starboard sides, the outermost compartment remaining void. Inboard of the void there were three liquid-filled compartments, then an inboard void, into which the inner liquid layer could burst in the event of a hit. By that time, designers had rightly appreciated that in the absence of oxygen, fuel oil was not a fire hazard and could be used in

The *West Virginia,* shown in 1935, and her two sister ships were the last U.S. battleships built under the Washington Treaty. They introduced 16-inch guns to the U.S. Navy with eight main battery guns in four turrets. Otherwise they were very similar to the previous *Tennessee* class in design and appearance. Note the large fighting tops atop her cage masts. *U.S. Navy*

the antitorpedo system. Inboard of the torpedo protection, each boiler was in a separate compartment, the boilers themselves forming a kind of inner protective layer. Two large turbogenerators were positioned on the ship's centerline. The dispersion of the boilers showed externally in the adoption of two funnels, rather than the previous single-trunked funnel.

The pilothouse and forward superstructure were considerably enlarged, the most prominent feature being a big air intake terminating under the pilothouse. The cage masts were of a new and heavier type, with each carrying a two-level enclosed top, the upper level of which was for main-battery control, the lower for the secondary battery.

The *California* and the namesake of her class, the *Tennessee,* were among the most advanced of the pre–World War II battleships. Along with the three ships of the succeeding *Colorado* class, the *Colorado,* the *Maryland,* and the *West Virginia* (the *Washington* was canceled before completion), they would form the "Big Five," a homogeneous group except for their main batteries. All of this class were scheduled to be modernized in the early 1930s, but these plans were deferred, first because of the Great Depression, and then because the ships were too urgently needed for other duties. In the mid-1930s some minor alterations were made to them. The torpedo tubes were removed and two catapults of the powder type added aft (one on Turret No. 3 and the second on the fantail), the sec-

ondary battery was changed to twelve 5-inch 51-caliber guns, and antiaircraft batteries of eight 5-inch 25-caliber and 1.1-inch guns were added to replace the old 3-inch antiaircraft guns. It was also planned to fit them with bulges in the late 1930s, to restore buoyancy and lift their belts out of the water, given the extra weight the ships had accumulated since completion.

Total reconstruction of the two *Tennessees* was finally authorized in the 1939 program. This did not take place until after the 7 December 1941 attack. The *Tennessee,* hit by two bombs and only slightly damaged at Pearl Harbor, was operated for some time in nearly her original configuration before being chosen as the prototype for a major reconstruction. This reconstruction, plus repair of the damage suffered at Pearl Harbor, made the *Tennessee* and the *California* virtually brand-new ships.

In the reconstruction of the two ships, the two cage masts were removed and replaced by a massive modern superstructure. Antitorpedo blisters and heavy antiaircraft batteries were included in the reconstruction. There was also the provision of new main battery directors on modern tower masts. The principal addition to the armor was 3 inches over the magazines; the turret top armor was also reinforced. Wider bulges were fitted in a radical attempt to restore the armored freeboard, estimated before the reconstructions as being 2 to 3 feet below the optimum for gun engagements. By the time the reconstruction was completed, the two ships of this class, as well as the *West Virginia* of the *Colorado* class, could, at a distance, easily be mistaken for fast battleships.

The subsequent *Colorado* class was a repeat of the *Tennessee* design, with twin 16-inch 45-caliber guns in place of the earlier triple 14-inch 50-caliber. The electric generator installation aboard each ship was increased, with every possible item of equipment being run by electricity. There were no other substantial changes in the design, although for many years there were unofficial claims of a considerable increase in belt armor, from a minimum of the 14 inches erroneously credited to the *Tennessee* to an equally incorrect 16 inches claimed to be on the *Colorados*. The new 16-inch 45-caliber guns fired a 2,100-pound shell at a muzzle velocity of 2,600 feet per second, which would penetrate 18.9 inches of armor at 12,000 yards.

The three completed *Colorados* were not modified substantially between the wars, but they did receive the standard two-catapult installation, and their secondary armament was altered to 10 to twelve 5-inch 51-caliber dual-purpose guns and seven or eight 5-inch 25-caliber antiaircraft guns. This class was the first to receive the new compressed air catapults.

One ship of this class, the *Washington*, was 75.9 percent complete when she was suspended under the terms of the Washington Treaty on 8 February 1922. On 25 November 1924 she was used to test a sandwich-type system to protect against underwater explosions. The series of tests began with three 2,000-pound bombs and two 400-pound torpedo warheads being detonated and exploded around the hull at prescribed distances. Afterward, the ship was exposed to heavy seas for three days. Subsequent inspection showed that the ship had a list of 5 degrees. If the ship had been in service, the crew would have been able to patch the leaks without using pumps and maintain the ship on an even keel so that she could have remained in action. After having survived the explosions and heavy seas, without repairs or pumping, the *Washington* remained afloat another five days until finally being sunk by fourteen 14-inch shells fired from the *Texas*.

The *Colorado* almost saw further active service after the war. In the 1948 program, later postponed to the 1950 program and then ultimately canceled, it was planned to convert the battleship to a radio-controlled target ship for the testing of new anti-ship missiles. Conversion would have included removal of all turrets and the massive reduction of topside superstructure.

FORCE PRACTICE U.S. BATTLE FLEET BATTLE SHIP DIVISION FIVE

The 6-foot blisters on both sides of the hull would have been removed and the crew reduced to 25 officers and 515 enlisted men. Maximum speed would have been 22 knots. Under radio control, endurance would have been for six hours at 15 knots.

The subsequent *South Dakota* design amounted to an enlarged *Maryland* class, with triple rather than twin turrets, and with all of the secondary battery above the forecastle deck. Visually, the most unusual feature would have been the massive trunked funnel, uniting four large uptakes emerging from each of the dispersed boiler rooms. This would be the largest and most powerful class of U.S. battleship until the design of the *Iowa* class. Approved under the 1916 program, this class finally achieved what the General Board had wanted since 1914—a jump in battleship capabilities and size. From the start, the board wanted twelve 16-inch guns and a 23-knot speed, the latter partly out of the fear that Japan would acquire fast battleships similar to the British *Queen Elizabeths*. The board considered a 2-knot increase over the previous classes' 21 knots to be the absolute minimum requirement. Finally, given a great increase in displacement, it was natural to go from the existing main battery of 16-inch 45-caliber guns to the much more powerful 16-inch 50-caliber, and from the 5-inch 51-caliber secondary gun to the new 6-inch 53-caliber. Armor thicknesses did not increase, largely because 13 inches was

Battle practice off San Diego, California, in the mid-1920s with the three *Colorado*-class battleships leading the battle line. The Washington Treaty of 1922 gave the United States and Great Britain parity in capital ships, with Japan having slightly less in a 5:5:3 ratio. That led to Japan's stressing innovative tactics as well as aviation and submarines to counter its inferiority. *U.S. Navy*

The subsequent *South Dakota* was essentially an enlarged *Colorado* with twelve 16-inch guns in triple turrets and a secondary battery of twelve 6-inch guns on a larger hull. Visually, the most unusual feature would have been the massive trunked funnel, uniting four large uptakes emerging from each of the dispersed boiler rooms. The Washington Treaty halted their construction. *U.S. Navy*

considered the maximum that could be manufactured with consistent quality. Main battery elevation was increased to 40 degrees.

The *South Dakota* design was frozen in the summer of 1918. At that time the U.S. naval staff in London was much impressed by the design of the British battle cruiser *Hood*, and it proposed that the United States develop its own fast battleships, and that they be armed with 16-inch guns. Several sketches were prepared, but the General Board felt that to build them would make existing ships obsolete, and would not be in the U.S. Navy's best interests. It therefore persevered with the much more conventional *South Dakota* design.

Delayed by the emergency antisubmarine warfare program of World War I, the *South Dakota*'s ships were not laid down until after the war, and none of the ships were very advanced at the time of the Washington Conference, when all were suspended 8 February 1922. All six ships of the class were finally canceled on 17 August 1923—the date the Washington Treaty was formally ratified and came into force—and were broken up on the stocks. Parts of their engineering plants, as noted previously, were preserved and used in battleship modernizations. Armor intended for the *Montana*

was shipped to the Panama Canal between 1941 and 1942 to reinforce the locks there. Other armor destined for this class was used to repair ships in World War II.

Although not dreadnought battleships, among the most interesting of the second-generation designs were the *Lexington*-class battle cruisers. The General Board considered building battle cruisers in 1912 to counter the four Japanese *Kongo*-class battleships, but then withdrew them from consideration. The original proposal would not have been approved by Congress without reducing the number of battleships as a cost-saving measure. This was unacceptable to the board, who considered increasing the number of battleships a more urgent requirement at the time. The ships that had been contemplated would have been relatively heavily armored, and as such were much closer to fast battleships than to the battle cruisers approved in 1916. The *Lexingtons* were ordered as part of the large 1916 program as a major element of a 35-knot scouting force to support a large battle fleet; other elements of the scouting force were flush-deck destroyers and the light cruisers of the *Omaha* class.

If completed, the *Lexingtons* would have been ships powerful enough to press home reconnaissance in the face of enemy battle cruisers. Their design was scaled up from a series of designs for cruisers displacing about 10,000 to 14,000 tons, and so would have been much more lightly built than contemporary U.S. battleships. The 1916 design, for a ship of 34,800 tons, "normal" displacement, was complicated by the relatively limited steam output of existing boilers—there was not enough space below the armored deck for the 24 boilers needed to make 180,000 shaft horsepower. Hence, the very unusual design that was initially adopted had half the boilers above the protective deck, inside armored boxes on the centerline. The remaining boilers were in individual compartments outboard of the electric generators. The uptakes were trunked into no less than seven funnels, of which only five showed in profile, as four were in widely spaced pairs abeam.

The main battery comprised ten 14-inch 50-caliber guns in two twin- and two triple-gun turrets, the triples superfiring over the twins. The secondary armament was eighteen 5-inch 51-caliber guns. Armor was very light: 5 inches on the belt, bulkheads, barbettes, and conning tower, with 2 to 6 inches on each turret. The armored boxes around the upper boilers were 8 inches. Design requirements included provision for aircraft, which probably explains the break in

the main deck right aft. When these ships were designed, the only U.S. catapult was the fixed straight-track type of the old armored cruisers. Although trainable catapults were designed immediately after World War I, no sketches show them in the final design of the *Lexington* class.

All American capital ship construction was suspended in 1917 in favor of merchant and antisubmarine ships. This delay was used progressively to upgrade and refine the design. In 1917 the main armament of the *Lexington* class was increased to eight 16-inch guns because the 1916 authorizing law required ships with "as powerful armament as any vessels of their class," and it was known that battle cruisers with 15-inch guns were being built in Europe, while Japan was planning to build even larger, 16-inch-gunned ships. A reduction in the number of boilers to 20 enabled all to be located below the protective deck. Correspondingly, the number of funnels was reduced to five, of which only three showed in profile, as two were in widely spaced pairs abeam. The secondary armament was increased to fourteen 6-inch 53-caliber guns. These changes increased the "normal" displacement to 35,300 tons at 31-foot, 4-inch draft.

The beam remained at the same 90 feet as in the 1916 design, while power and speed remained unaltered.

The next design modification, in 1918, was to improve protection by widening the hull to incorporate a torpedo protection system and by increasing the vertical belt armor to 9 inches. In a further step, the hull depth was then increased, probably to increase strength, and the armor belt was reduced in thickness and sloped outwards. With the development of small tube boilers, the number in each ship could be further reduced to 16, and the uptakes could be trunked into two large oval funnels. Increased displacement and reduced speed had to be accepted.

The final version of the *Lexington*'s design owes much to U.S. reactions to HMS *Hood*, even though the *Lexington*'s was still very lightly armored, and thus still reflected the original battle cruiser operational concept. The Bureau of Ordnance argued, moreover, that on the basis of British analysis of the Battle of Jutland, the loss of the three battle cruisers had not been due to their lack of armor, but to their poor antiflash protection. Thus, more armor was not needed, but rather better magazine arrangements. The choice of a sloping belt owed much to British practice, as did, most likely,

A phosphorus bomb dropped by an Army twin-engine Martin bomber explodes on the ex-battleship *Alabama* during the September 1921 bombing tests. While bomb hits on ships' superstructures were dramatic, near misses inflicted more serious damage on the ship's hull. Army aviators sought to use such tests as justification for buying bombers rather than battleships. *U.S. Navy*

the decision to supplement the four underwater torpedo tubes with four above water.

All six battle cruiser were canceled under the Washington Treaty, but the *Lexington* and the *Saratoga* were eventually completed as large aircraft carriers. It appears, though, that they were considered by some to be obsolete even before treaty negotiations started. Since early 1921, the conversion of ships to aircraft carriers had been studied several times, as had plans to build carriers from the keel up. In fact, the plans for the keel-up carrier, with necessary modifications, were used to complete the *Lexington* and the *Saratoga* as carriers. Had the keel-up carrier also been built along with the two battle cruisers as carriers, it would have been hard to tell the difference among the three ships.

Construction on all six ships of the *Lexington* class was suspended on 8 February 1922 and finally canceled on 17 August 1923. A report at the time noted that to date only $4 million had been allotted to the four most advanced units between 1921 and 1922, with even less for the other two units. This meant there would have been a five-to-six-year building period

without more generous funding thereafter. The ships had originally been priced at a total of $25.3 million for hull and machinery; by comparison, the *West Virginia* alone cost $15.6 million for hull and machinery as the last battleship in its program to be completed.

## BATTLE FLEET AND BATTLE FORCE ORGANIZATION

The U.S. Fleet was officially established as the "United States Fleet" on 8 December 1922. General Order No. 94 essentially combined the bulk of the major combatant warships under a single command. This reorganization was done to get around the very unpopular Secretary of the Navy Josephus Daniels' desire to designate separate Atlantic and Pacific Fleets.

**Battle Fleet, U.S. Fleet:** Established 8 December 1922 by General Order No. 94, it consisted at the outset of the major combatant units, centered on those battleships formerly assigned to the Pacific Fleet. It was at first subdivided into "type" commands for battleships, aircraft, and destroyers. A type command for submarines was added on 1 July 1923. It was stationed

The ex-USS *Alabama* after being struck by a phosphorus bomb while a target for army bombers in Chesapeake Bay in September 1921. An Army twin-engine Martin bomber is flying over the ship; in the foreground is a Navy F5L flying boat. Other ex-battleship targets are in the background—the *San Marcos* (ex-*Texas*) and the *Indiana*. *U.S. Navy*

in the Pacific Ocean. The Battle Fleet, as well as its successor, the Battle Force, always contained the bulk of the battleship strength of the U.S. Navy. The Pacific Fleet's battleship strength was increased at the expense of the Atlantic Fleet. In June 1919, counting both pre-dreadnoughts and dreadnoughts, the Atlantic Fleet was assigned 15 battleships, and the Pacific Fleet 14 battleships. By October 1921, when the *Utah* was operating in European waters and the *Florida* had become flagship of the Control Force, the Atlantic Fleet had only five battleships while the Pacific Fleet had 15. This tendency to assign more battleships to the Battle Fleet continued between 1922 and 1931. During the modernization program of the late 1920s and early 1930s, replacement ships were sent to the West Coast when Battle Fleet units were in the Navy Yard, but no such replacements were made when Scouting Fleet units were similarly absent.

The Battle Fleet kept up its advantage over the Scouting Fleet with the assignment of the *Langley*. Although plans were to divide the two new carriers *Lexington* and *Saratoga* between the two fleets, this was not done until after the Scouting Fleet was transferred to the Pacific Fleet.

**Battle Force, U.S. Fleet:** Established 1 April 1931 by General Order No. 211, this command was similar to Battle Fleet. It was subdivided into the same type of commands for battleships, destroyers, and aircraft, although some of the titles were changed. For example, Battleship Divisions, Battle Fleet became Battleships,

Battle Force; Aircraft Squadrons, Battle Fleet took the name of Aircraft, Battle Force.

For the greater part of the next decade the tendency was for the Battle Force to be superior to the Scouting Force in battleships, aircraft, and destroyers, but inferior in cruisers. After the Scouting Force was moved to the Pacific in the spring of 1932, this difference had little strategic significance.

At the end of the decade the trend was reversed. New construction was assigned to the Atlantic Squadron and the Patrol Force. Moreover, units already in the Battle Force were sent to the Atlantic.

**Battle Force, U.S. Pacific Fleet:** The existing organization of the Battle Force, United States Fleet was taken over in its entirety, without changes, when the Pacific Fleet was re-created by General Order No. 143 in 1941.

## NAVAL DISARMAMENT

The Anglo-Japanese Alliance of 1902 included an agreement that each country would remain neutral should the other go to war, except when one was attacked by more than one enemy. Great Britain was thus not involved in Japan's war with Russia from 1904 to 1905. After a smashing victory in that war, the newly confident Japanese participated in World War I, and for minimal involvement with the Allies profited greatly from the postwar allocation of former German territories and other settlements throughout the Pacific.

On the other side of the Pacific, the Americans viewed the sudden expansion and military prowess of the Japanese as a threat to their interests in the Philippines and elsewhere—a threat supported by the alliance with Great Britain. Britain tried to reassure the United States that the Anglo-Japanese Alliance would not be valid if Japan should go to war with the United States However, the U.S. wanted a fleet that was second to none, and thus enmeshed it in a naval arms race with Japan. The British, with their own vast interests in the Far East and Pacific, and likewise committed to a "One-Power Standard," began their own new shipbuilding program.

When the Washington Conference opened in Washington on 12 November 1921, the primary objective—to multilaterally rid the United States, Great Britain, and Japan of enormously expensive programs—might have seemed clear. However, America's real objective—to achieve parity with the Royal Navy—was by now an open secret. A second, hidden agenda was to terminate the Anglo-Japanese Alliance, and a third was to bind the Japanese to controllable limits with its navy.

With little preamble, the senior American delegate to the Washington Conference, Secretary of State Charles Evans Hughes, announced a series of proposals that were amazing in their scope. Capital ships—namely, battleships—would be taken as the measure of naval power, with lesser types prorated. The United States, Great Britain, and Japan would be permitted to maintain total capital ship tonnage in the ratio of 5:5:3. After much diplomatic wrangling, the proposal was agreed to, and the Americans instantly achieved two of their hidden aims.

For good measure, the French and Italians also accepted parity, finally agreeing to relative strengths of United States and Great Britain 5 each, Japan 3, and France and Italy 1.75 each. The treaty would be binding for 15 years.

The Royal Navy's leadership was furious at having to scrap 850,000 tons of uncompleted battleships. In contrast, the U.S. Navy only had to scrap 580,000 tons, most of which consisted of the six battleships of the *South Dakota* class and the four battle cruisers of the *Lexington* class. The scrapping process played out to a most curious end. By the terms of the treaty, the U.S. Navy was obligated to dispose of the last of the incomplete battleships by 17 February 1925. Although the treaty permitted completion of two of her sisters, the *Washington* could not be finished. Work on the ship, which was then more than three-fourths complete, had stopped on 8 February, two days after the signing of the Washington Treaty. She was scheduled to serve as a target for gunfire to test the strength of her armor and protection. Despite a last-ditch lawsuit by a civilian who had worked for the navy to save her, on 25 November, the battleship *Texas* finished the job with 14-inch gunfire. She unleashed a 10-gun salvo, and an hour later another salvo found the mark. The *Washington* listed and took on water through holes punched into her hull. Slowly she settled, then her bow lurched and made a roar as it pointed downward. The slender tail of the *Washington* pointed upward and she descended out of sight.

The Washington Treaty agreements proved to be an effective regulator, but with the unforeseen effects of promoting the development of naval airpower and starting a new naval race in heavy and light cruisers. The reductions in American naval strength, combined with restrictions U.S. naval bases in the western Pacific, were a crushing blow to the navy's expansion programs. It rendered the U.S. Navy inferior to that of Japan for operations in the Western Pacific and Far East, thus leaving the security of American interests in these areas dependent upon treaties.

Another disarmament conference was scheduled for 1936 in London, but in 1934 Japan gave two years' notice, as required by the Washington Treaty, that it was terminating the treaty. By coincidence, this was the termination date of the London Treaty. An attempt was made at London in 1936 to renew the two treaties, but Japan insisted on parity with the United States and Great Britain. The latter two countries would not agree to this. As a result, the conference only settled issues of minor consequence, such as the sizes of various types of ships and the size of the guns they could carry. So ended the experimentation with naval disarmament.

## OPERATIONS BETWEEN THE WARS

During the Revolutionary War, George Washington said, "It follows then as certain as night succeeds day that without a decisive naval force, we can do nothing definitive and with it everything honorable and glorious." Unfortunately, between the two world wars, Washington's sage advice was forgotten.

During, and for a few years after, World War I, the United States laid down the keels for 16 battleships, seven of which were canceled. The last completed, the *Colorado*, the *Maryland*, and the *West Vir-*

*ginia*, mounted 16-inch guns, the first ever in American battleships. They were 624 feet long, displaced 32,600 tons, could cruise at 21 knots, and had an 18-inch armor belt. At high speed on variable courses, they could fire an accurate broadside of over 8 tons more than 20 miles.

Amid wishful thinking, especially in the United States, international agreements limited the warships of the major naval powers. Isolationists and pacifists, joined by cost-conscious congressmen, winced at the price the country was paying for a balanced navy including aircraft carrier and battleship construction. In addition, airpower zealots, such as Brigadier General William "Billy" Mitchell, claimed that not only battleships but navies as a whole were obsolete.

Understanding of the U.S. need for adequate strength afloat suffered sorely during the two decades between the world wars, primarily because some vocal men claimed that the airplane had replaced navies, including aircraft carriers. Part of the success of General Mitchell and other zealots in deluding citizens came from their misrepresentations of the sinking of various stationary ships during gunfire and bombing experiments.

Violating agreed-upon army–navy rules established to allow study of shell and bomb effects between attacks, General Mitchell's planes sank the captured German battleship *Ostfriesland* at anchor on 20 July 1921. He then spread extreme claims as to the vulnerability of navies. In retrospect, Mitchell's methodology was of the stacked-deck variety.

Being at anchor, the ships could not maneuver at high speed to avoid hits.

There were no carrier fighter planes to shoot down some or most of the bombers before they could reach the targets, a tactic often successfully demonstrated in World War II.

The ship was not firing at the attackers. By 1944 the massed concentration of antiaircraft guns from 5-inch to 20mm, in conjunction with outstanding fighter-plane defense, would make U.S. task forces safe from most conventional air attacks—so safe, in fact, that the Japanese undertook their desperate kamikaze campaign.

The *Ostfriesland* lacked the watertight integrity that would have prevailed had her crew been on board. During World War II, damage-control parties would save many a damaged ship to fight again.

The U.S. Navy survived, despite General Mitchell and his supporters, and steadily integrated aviation into the fleet. However, in the Depression of the 1930s there was limited funding for warship construction. Even Japan's aggressive invasion of Manchuria in 1931, the rise of Hitler two years later, and the gradual resurgence of German military and naval power did not awaken the American people or spur Congress to significant action. In the critical years before World War II, appropriations for the U.S. Navy sank to under $300 million in 1934. They did not exceed $600 million for all purposes, including construction, until 1939 when World War II erupted. This put a severe strain on American naval strategists, who now had to consider the possibility of a two-ocean war with a limited fleet.

Fortunately for advocates of the U.S. Navy, Franklin D. Roosevelt took office as president in 1933. Roosevelt, an astute naval enthusiast who had been the Assistant Secretary of the Navy in World War I, knew well the dominant role sea power must play in America's destiny. He managed to provide for some ship construction outside of the formal naval budget. Yet, isolationist sentiment so prevailed that he had to proceed slowly in building up the navy. Meanwhile, the fleet struggled on, making the best out of what it had.

The *Alabama* sinking after being struck by several bombs during the September 1921 bombing trials. Her after cage mast has crumpled and her amidships are devastated, as is her stern. Such attacks were instructive in the damage that a warship could sustain, but led to unresolved debates between "battleship admirals" and army aviators. *U.S. Navy*

# CHAPTER FIVE

# THE FAST BATTLESHIPS

## NEW STANDARDS OF DESIGN

The ships of the *North Carolina* class were designed during the last years of the Washington Treaty to replace the *Arkansas* and one other ship. As a result, they were the first U.S. battleships built after the expiration of that treaty. They were the outgrowth of a long and tortuous process of design evolution, which, beginning as an updated version of the traditional U.S. capital ship rather than with fast battleships, concentrated on firepower and armor protection at the expense of speed. In 1935, however, the General Board of the navy decided that it would be useful to evaluate the designs being built abroad (i.e., fast but well-armed and well-protected ships).

What decided the issue in favor of a fast ship was the need to operate carrier task forces. At one point, a combination of two fast battleships with each of the two large carriers of the time—the *Saratoga* and the *Lexington*—was under consideration to form the core of a task group. An important factor was the threat presented by the three 26-knot Japanese *Kongo*-class battleships.

The General Board first approved a 30-knot, nine 14-inch-gun ship, protected against 14-inch fire, using much the same arguments that would later be made in favor of the *Iowa*-class battleships. These arguments centered on Japan's renouncement of the

**Left:** The 10 U.S. fast battleships completed from 1941 to 1944 were armed with nine 16-inch guns, as shown here on the USS *Alabama* , steaming in rough seas in late 1942. Their secondary battery consisted of 20 of the highly effective 5-inch 38-caliber guns in twin mounts, except for the *South Dakota* , which had sixteen 5-inch guns. *U.S. Navy*

The *Indiana* en route to battle in the Pacific in January 1944. Compare the tight grouping of her amidships 5-inch mounts with those of the *North Carolina*, which was almost 50 feet longer. There is a quad 40mm mount on top of the 16-inch No. 2 turret, with another quad 40mm and single 20mm mounts just forward of the 5-inch guns. OS2U floatplanes are on the two stern catapults. *U.S. Navy*

Washington Treaty in 1934 and the intentions of England, France, and Italy to build faster battleships once the treaty lapsed in 1936. At virtually the last minute, Admiral William H. Standley, chief of naval operations, recommended a more traditional 27-knot ship design, armed with twelve 14-inch guns in three quadruple-gun turrets (later 12-inch, in three quadruple turrets).

If the U.S. Navy did not start a program soon, it was in danger of falling behind, so it finally adopted a design featuring 16-inch guns in three triple-gun turrets. Although 16-inch guns had been considered in the earliest sketch designs, the London Naval Disarmament Treaty of 1936 limited new battleships to 14-inch guns, and it was that caliber that determined both the battery and the protection of new ships. The ships were to be immune against 1,500-pound, 14-inch shells up to 33,000 yards. The design made specific allowance for replacing the new quad 14-inch turret with a triple 16-inch turret in the event that the "escalator" clause in the London Treaty was invoked, by which a signatory to the treaty could adopt 16-inch guns if a nonsignatory (e.g., Japan) refused to observe the 14-inch limitation.

As it turned out, Japan refused to agree to the 14-inch gun standard, and the U.S. government invoked

the escalator clause, so that all new American battleships were armed with 16-inch guns. The invocation did not change the armor distribution, which was too basic to the design.

Both ships of the class, the *North Carolina* and the *Washington*, entered service just before the outbreak of World War II. They were not fully operational until early 1942, due in part to severe propeller vibration problems. In retrospect, the *North Carolina* design was superior from an operational viewpoint to the later, more cramped *South Dakota* class. At the end of World War II, each ship of the class had 15 quadruple 40mm antiaircraft mounts. The *North Carolina* had, in addition, 20 single and eight twin 20mm antiaircraft guns. The *North Carolina* was refitted and employed briefly postwar as a training ship.

The four *South Dakota*s were an attempt to achieve effective protection against 16-inch shellfire on a displacement limited to 35,000 tons by the Washington Treaty—even though it was no longer in force—without any sacrifice of the speed achieved in the *North Carolina* design. They represented only a slight improvement over the previous *North Carolina* class. The ships of the *South Dakota* class were shorter and less graceful looking than their predecessors, but had better armor protection. It was also important to protect them against underwater damage, which was expected at very long range from enemy ships. The eventual design was a combination of very steeply sloped internal side armor and a heavily armored deck. The length of the "vitals" was reduced as much as possible in order to save weight, and considerable cramping of upper works such as blast interference between secondary guns and light antiaircraft guns was accepted.

The *North Carolina*, above in April 1942, and the *Washington* established the basic configuration for the succeeding fast battleship classes, although hull and superstructure would vary. The 16-inch guns are in triple turrets and the secondary battery of twenty 5-inch guns are in enclosed twin mounts, five per side, on two levels. More antiaircraft guns were added during the war. *U.S. Navy*

As soon as World War II ended, the navy faced the problem of adapting to a peacetime status. The Curtiss SC-1s were competent aircraft, but their time had passed. Development of the Edo XOSE-1 catapult aircraft was continued into 1948, but it would never see operational service. By the late 1940s all the catapults had been removed along with the aircraft. Considerable thought and planning were given to replacing these aircraft with helicopters on battleships, but they too were removed by 1949 after operational tests proved them inadequate.

## THE DEVELOPMENT OF RADAR

Probably the most important technological development that affected battleships during World War II was radar. Its probing radio beams could penetrate darkness and clouds, and at some angles see farther than the human eye. The beams were reflected back to the radar when reflected off a hard surface, like an enemy ship or aircraft, allowing the radar operator to determine the object's distance and bearing. In time, radar could also distinguish between friendly and enemy aircraft, with the use of a transponder fitted in the friendly aircraft, and could provide an aircraft's altitude as well as range and direction.

Radar was developed almost simultaneously in Great Britain and the United States. The first U.S. operational radar was developed by the Naval Research Laboratory in Anacostia, Washington, D.C. This was the XAF, which was installed in the destroyer *Leary* in the spring of 1937. During subsequent trials in the Caribbean the XAF detected aircraft at a distance of 100 nautical miles, surface ships at 15 nautical miles, and 14-inch shells in flight at 7 nautical miles. The operational model of this air-search radar was the CXAM, with the first one fitted in the battleship *New York* in December 1938. The *New York*'s CXAM antenna is now on exhibit at the Washington Navy Yard, Washington, D.C. At the same time, the CXZ, developed by the Radio Corporation of American (RCA), was fitted in the battleship *Texas*.

After the navy evaluated the XAF, RCA won the contract to produce the model, which was designated CXAM. Deliveries began in May 1941. The first installations in battleships were in the *California*, the *Pennsylvania*, the *North Carolina*, the *Texas* (after removal of the CXZ), the *Washington*, and the *West Virginia*.

In 1941 the new and more efficient SC-series radar, a development of the CXAM, was first installed

in the *West Virginia*. In 1942 an SRA-type radar that served as a general warning device and navigational aid was installed on all the battleships. Starting in January 1943 an SK air-search radar replaced the installed radar fit, and an SC-2 air-search radar replaced the SC installations. By 1944 an improved SK-2 radar replaced previous SK radar installations. In 1944 a more reliable SP air-search radar replaced existing air-search systems.

## ALASKA-CLASS LARGE CRUISERS

The one remaining class of U.S. warships that could be defined as dreadnoughts were the *Alaska*-class large cruisers (CB). Though classified as cruisers, their

The battleship *New York* was the second U.S. Navy ship to be fitted with radar. Here the antenna for CXAM is fitted above the ship's bridge. The square antenna, with a nearly invisible wire mesh, was installed in 1938. By 7 December 1941 several U.S. battleships, cruisers, and carriers had radar installed; by the end of the war every U.S. surface warship and submarine had radar. *U.S. Navy*

**Left:** The *Alaska*, shown at the Philadelphia Navy Yard in July 1944, and her sister ship the *Guam* were the largest cruisers built by the United States—some 10,000 tons larger than the biggest U.S. heavy cruisers. Many historians and analysts consider the *Alaskas* to be properly classified as battle cruisers in view of their speed (31 knots) and main battery (12-inch guns). *U.S. Navy*

**Below:** The *Alaska* in camouflage in September 1944, which she wore throughout her brief operational career. She has a twin 5-inch 38-caliber mount and quad 40mm mount superfiring over the forward 12-inch turrets; also note the "quad 40s" at her bow. She carried her catapults and floatplanes—with twin aircraft hangars—amidships, in the style of the U.S. treaty-era cruisers. *U.S. Navy*

12-inch gun armament and size put them in the battle cruiser category, and at one time in the early design stage they received the "CC" designation of battle cruisers. However, although the ships of this class were commonly and repeatedly referred to as "battle cruisers," that practice was officially discouraged.

In the late 1930s, before the United States entered World War II, the U.S. Navy sought a counter to the German *Scharnhorst*-class battle cruisers and a battle cruiser the Japanese reportedly had under construction (these reports later proved to be false). To counter these threats, the General Board came up with the *Alaska* class.

The *Alaskas* possessed capabilities that put them far beyond even the excellent 17,000-ton *Des Moines* class. These large cruisers were simple developments of U.S. cruiser doctrine and requirements. In effect, they were heavy cruisers unencumbered by the treaty limits of 8-inch guns and a maximum displacement of 10,000 tons. They are often described as white elephants, since by the time two of the six ships that were originally ordered finally appeared in 1944, the tactical and strategic concepts that inspired them were completely outmoded.

A 12-inch-gun cruiser project surfaced in the Bureau of Construction & Repair as early as 1938, and the president may well have inspired it on the basis of his notions of foreign "battle cruiser" and "super cruiser" developments. Discussions always began with the 12-inch-gun ship as one alternative in a spectrum of possible future cruisers.

Cruiser design is evident in the *Alaska* class with the provision of one rather than two rudders, which ensured a very large tactical diameter, and in the requirement for enclosed stowage for aircraft rather than the open fantails of the fast battleships. This stowage feature was responsible for the unusual aircraft arrangement, as the aft hull was too restricted to permit a hangar in the conventional location. In 1945 and 1946 there were proposals to remove the two midships catapults and replace them with an additional pair of twin 5-inch 38-caliber gun mounts, with a single catapult being fitted on the fantail and no hangar.

The battle cruisers' 12-inch 50-caliber guns were of a new design and, because they were unique among wartime U.S. ships, they were the most expensive U.S. heavy guns of their period. The initial *Alaska* design called for eight guns in two triple turrets and one twin

turret. The design finally adopted was that of three triple-gun turrets (i.e., nine guns, as in the fast battleships). This arrangement was justified in part because it simplified turret production.

The *Alaskas* turned out to be very long, flush-decked ships. They had a towering forward superstructure and a tall single funnel. Their 12-inch guns could be elevated to 45 degrees to fire a 1,140-pound shell a distance of 36,000 yards or 18 nautical miles.

Neither ship received modifications during the war or saw further service. The ships of the *Alaska* class were expensive to maintain, and poor substitutes for battleships. After the war, even a *Baltimore*-class heavy cruiser could overpower any Soviet gun cruiser, such as those of the *Sverdlov* class. Left with no worthwhile adversaries, the *Alaskas* became "excess to naval requirements."

The differing lines of the battleship and large cruiser are shown with the *Alaska* (top) and the *Missouri* at rest in 1944. Their relative size, hull design, and catapult arrangements are evident. There were proposals to complete the third large cruiser, the *Hawaii*, as a large command ship or missile cruiser, but, like the two canceled *Iowas*, the proposals were not to be. *U.S. Navy*

# CHAPTER SIX

# PRE–WORLD WAR II OPERATIONS

The U.S. Neutrality Act was passed on 31 August 1935 as a reaction to growing fears of war in Europe. It prohibited U.S. involvement in other nations' conflicts and outlawed the sale of munitions to belligerents. This act was made more restrictive by an amendment in 1937 under which nations the president declared to be in a state of war could not receive U.S. arms or loans. The act empowered the president to forbid U.S. citizens to travel on belligerents' ships; to forbid U.S. ships to carry U.S. goods; and to force belligerents to pay for goods before shipment—a policy called "cash and carry."

When war broke out in Europe in September 1939, President Roosevelt called Congress into special session for the purpose of revising the Neutrality Act. After a stormy debate, Congress passed legislation repealing the embargo on the sale of munitions. The "cash-and-carry" policy was retained.

On 5 September 1939 President Roosevelt issued his first neutrality proclamation, declaring that the use of U.S. territorial waters for hostile operations was unfriendly, offensive, and a violation of U.S. neutrality. A day earlier, the U.S. Chief of Naval Operations, Admiral Harold R. Stark, ordered the establishment of aircraft and ship patrols to observe and report the movement of foreign warships within

**Left:** The battleship *Texas* on neutrality patrol in the North Atlantic in the summer of 1941 silhouetted against the setting sun. The U.S. Navy was already in a shooting war in the Atlantic at that time, although the rest of the country was still at peace. *Dayton A. Seiler/U.S. Navy*

1939. The patrol had several encounters with German U-boats. After a U-boat fired a torpedo at the destroyer USS *Greer*, President Roosevelt issued a "shoot-on-sight" order, authorizing an attack upon any vessel threatening U.S. shipping. In October, U-boats disabled the destroyer USS *Kearny* and sank the destroyer USS *Reuben James*.

## ATLANTIC OPERATIONS

In 1941 the old battleship *New York* operated in the North Atlantic on Neutrality Patrol. The problem was that the Neutrality Patrol had a pro-British inclination. The ship also was part of a July 1941 expedition to deliver U.S. Marines to Iceland to provide a replacement garrison for the British troops that were needed elsewhere. While the *New York* was there, a German plane flew over. Until then, the ship's crew had had trouble getting battle stations manned in a timely fashion when the call for general quarters was sounded. This time, with a genuine threat visible to all, the response was much faster. The plane flew over without attacking because the United States was still officially neutral, but the ship's crew demonstrated it was ready for the real thing.

The *New York* was later based at Argentia, Newfoundland, as a station ship to protect what had become a major U.S. base for the support of convoy operations. Another of the old battleships, the *Arkansas*, was also operating in the Atlantic. In August 1941 she received a most unusual assignment. She steamed from

The *Idaho* and her sister ships of Battleship Division 3 were transferred from the Pacific to the Atlantic in June 1941 to reinforce the Neutrality Patrol. They provided the Atlantic with six battleships, the others being the *Arkansas*, the *New York*, and the *Texas*, which formed Battleship Division 5. *U.S. Navy*

designated areas in the western Atlantic. The reporting areas were soon expanded to the eastern coast of Canada down to the West Indies.

At the time, the predominant U.S. naval strength was in the Pacific under the commander in chief, U.S. Fleet. In January 1939 an Atlantic Squadron had been formed, and on 1 January 1941, the squadron was reorganized as the U.S. Atlantic Fleet under the command of Admiral Ernest J. King.

To enforce provisions of the U.S. Neutrality Act, navy and Coast Guard ships and aircraft began what was officially known as "Neutrality Patrol" on 5 September

There was a seventh U.S. battleship in the Atlantic in 1941, the training ship *Wyoming*. This is her appearance early in the war, with a cage mast forward and mounting six of her original twelve 12-inch guns (three turrets). She also mounts single and twin 5-inch 38-caliber guns and lighter antiaircraft guns. She trained about 35,000 men during the war. *U.S. Navy*

Newport to Argentia and was present when the cruiser *Augusta* arrived with President Roosevelt on board. He had managed to elude members of the press, who had no idea that he had come to Newfoundland for a secret meeting with Britain's Prime Minister Winston Churchill. They had been in frequent communication for months, as Churchill pleaded with Roosevelt for help in fighting off the Nazis. Roosevelt had done as much as he could, given the isolationist sentiment in the United States. From this meeting came the formulation of the Atlantic Charter, a statement of war aims for the two prospective allies.

## THE FAST BATTLESHIPS BEGIN TO EMERGE

When World War II broke out in Europe, 1939 the *North Carolina* was under construction at the New York Navy Yard. There was now a new sense of urgency about her completion. In the spring of 1941 installation and the testing of new equipment, including radar, went on around the clock, six and seven days a week. One of the new innovations on the *North Carolina* was that she could take on oil rapidly because of a series of tanks that were fed from a central tank. The fuel went down a trunk into each master tank, then the other tanks filled automatically as they were opened. With two or three such master tanks receiving oil at the same time, the process was faster than in the older battleships. When the *North Carolina* went out for her engineering trials, she and her sister, the

*Washington*, developed severe vibration problems as they reached higher speeds. To deal with the difficulty, the Bureau of Ships changed propellers and tried various combinations of propellers with different numbers of blades. The fix was eventually successful.

The *North Carolina* was the first U.S. battleship equipped from the outset with radar. Security precautions were still tight, so officers and crew had to be careful in discussing the miraculous new device. Despite security, somehow, a report of the equipment appeared in a New York newspaper, leading the ship's gunnery officer, Lieutenant Commander Tom Hill, to pose a devilish question to the executive officer: "Is it all right now to say that dirty word?" It was certainly all right to use the equipment that went with the word, and it provided a spectacular advance in antiaircraft gunnery—an area in which the fleet had been woefully lacking. Previously, gunners had to try to take visual ranges on moving airplanes and send them to a director—an electromechanical device high in the ship that used target range and bearing to direct aiming. The director calculated settings for projectile fuses, and then gun crews inserted the projectiles into the guns and fired them. Radar and modern directors automated a good deal of the work and enabled much faster solutions for the 5-inch guns. In addition, when the *North Carolina* went out for gunnery trials off Cape May, New Jersey, her new 5-inch 38-caliber guns could shoot down drone aircraft at 12,000 to 13,000 feet,

The *Texas* in her World War II configuration in April 1944. After Atlantic convoy work and seeing combat in the invasions of France, she and her sister ship, the *New York,* departed for combat in the Pacific in late 1944. Her 12-inch main-battery turrets are surrounded by 40mm and 20mm antiaircraft mounts and eight 3-inch guns. Stacks of life rafts have replaced the prewar ship's boats. *U.S. Navy*

The *Arkansas*—at sea with her crew's bedding getting an airing. A pair of OS2U Kingfisher floatplanes rest on the catapult atop her No. 3 main-battery turret. She, too, has had numerous 20mm and 40mm guns installed plus eight 3-inch antiaircraft guns. The old battleships kept all of their main-battery guns while having 5-inch dual-purpose and lesser guns installed. *U.S. Navy*

about double the range of the 5-inch 25-caliber guns on previous battleships.

The *North Carolina* and the *Washington* were commissioned, respectively, on 9 April 1941 and 15 May 1941. Because the *North Carolina* was commissioned in the media hotbed of New York City, she received a great deal of attention as the year 1941 progressed. Reporters accompanied her as she conducted trials at sea and fired her guns. She was so much in the public eye, that she became known as "The Showboat."

When it came time for shakedown training, the *North Carolina* operated with the *Washington* for the first time.

As the *North Carolina* and the *Washington* strutted their stuff as the new kids on the block, the three old battleships in the Atlantic Fleet were becoming genuine relics. One of the ships, the *New York*, had been converted in the 1920s from coal to oil, but she still had those old sewing-machine engines rather than the steam turbines that became the norm soon after

The *Wyoming* in her ultimate World War II configuration as a gunnery training ship in April 1945. Her forward cage mast is gone, as are all of her 12-inch main-battery guns, the last removed in a January–April 1944 refit. Her main battery is now single and twin 5-inch dual-purpose mounts and numerous 20mm and 40mm guns along with their associated fire-control directors and radars. *U.S. Navy*

Admiral Kimmel brought most of the U.S. Fleet into Pearl Harbor every weekend. Along with setting the date for Y-day, Yamamoto delegated responsibility for the Pearl Harbor Striking Force to Vice Admiral Chuichi Nagumo.

Thousands of drums of fuel oil were stowed in every vacant space of the carriers and even topside in case it proved too rough to fuel at sea. The last provisions were taken on board the ships.

On 25 November Admiral Yamamoto issued his order to the Striking Force to sortie next day. It was to "advance into Hawaiian waters, and upon the very opening of hostilities attack the main force of the United States Fleet in Hawaii" and deal it a mortal blow.

At 6 A.M. on 26 November, the "magnificent air fleet" departed from Tankan Bay through heavy fog and rough seas. The six carriers steamed in two parallel columns with a battleship at the rear of each column, two destroyers on the left flank and the three submarines on the right flank, and a heavy cruiser several miles away on either flank. The rest of the destroyers steamed in line several miles ahead in order to detect shipping. Orders were given to sink any American, British, or Dutch merchant ship encountered on sight, and to place a boarding party on any neutral ship to prevent radio transmission. Only one vessel, a Japanese ship, was met on the outward passage. The force continued on its way. America's first "Day of Infamy" was fast approaching.

Arriving at a point 490 miles north of Hawaii without being sighted, the force turned south shortly after 9:00 P.M. on 6 December and headed toward the aircraft launching point at 26 knots. Meanwhile, the heavy cruisers pushed on ahead of the carriers' launching position and catapulted four float-type "Zeros" at about 6:00 A.M. to reconnoiter Pearl Harbor and report whether the Pacific Fleet was really there. There it all was—except for those prize targets, the navy's three aircraft carriers—the *Lexington,* the *Saratoga,* and the *Enterprise.*

Admiral Nagumo reached his launching point slightly before 6:00 A.M. and, as the planes hit Oahu "right on the nose," it is evident that his fleet navigating officer had done an excellent job of dead reckoning. The carriers commenced launching the first wave immediately: 40 "Kates" armed with deadly aerial torpedoes, 49 more equipped as high-level bombers, 51 "Val" dive-bombers, and 43 "Zero" fighters took off and orbited south of the force, waiting for their group commander's signals to go.

Sunday, 7 December 1941, the "date that will live in infamy," dawned bright and fair over Pearl Harbor. According to the *Nautical Almanac,* the time of sunrise was 6:26 A.M. At that time of year, the sun comes up from over Mount Tantalus and Mount Olympus, which were carrying their usual nightcap of trade-wind clouds. Thus, it was almost 7:00 A.M. when the sun actually appeared.

Sharp-eyed Boatswain's Mate Milligan of the destroyer *Allen* noticed 20 to 25 planes orbiting at an altitude of about 5,000 feet at 7:30 A.M., but in view of the frequent air-attack drills recently held, he thought nothing of it. Apparently these were the Val dive-bombers, which had reached the target first due to their superior speed, and were waiting for the torpedo-carrying Kates.

The USS *Oglala* was tied up outboard of the light cruiser *Helena* at Pier 1010. Rear Admiral William R. Furlong, commander, Mine Force Pacific Fleet, pacing the quarterdeck of the *Oglala,* was in an excellent position to survey what followed. A few seconds short of 7:55 A.M., he noticed a plane flying low over Ford Island from the northeast. Then he heard the explosion of a bomb on the seaplane ramp at the south end of Ford Island and saw dust and debris arise, but thought it was an accidental drop by a U.S. plane. The plane turned up the main channel between his ship and Ford Island, and Furlong saw the "meatball" insignia painted on its side. He called for general quarters and, realizing he was the senior officer present afloat (SOPA) in Pearl Harbor, had the signal hoisted: "All Ships in Harbor Sortie."

Almost simultaneous with the fall of the first bomb, the signal tower at Pearl Harbor telephoned to Admiral Kimmel's headquarters: "Enemy air raid—not drill." At 7:58 Rear Admiral Patrick N. L. Bellinger from his headquarters on Ford Island broadcast a message that shook the United States as nothing had since the firing on Fort Sumter:

"Air raid, Pearl Harbor—this is no drill!"

The Sabbath calm was rudely broken by bomb explosions, by the hoarse klaxon sounding general quarters on every ship, and presently by the sharp bark of 5-inch antiaircraft guns and the nervous chatter of machine guns. Colors were raised defiantly, and the Battle of Pearl Harbor was on. In one split second, the United States passed from a precarious neutrality to full-fledged belligerency; 7 December was the first of 1,364 days of war.

## PEARL HARBOR, BATTLESHIP ROW, AND AFTERMATH

The Japanese knew exactly what they wanted. The eight battleships moored at Pearl were the priority targets. The aviators were well briefed with the latest clandestine information from the Japanese consul at Honolulu. They were supplied with accurate charts and knew that the battleships were tied up singly or in pairs to the great mooring quays along the southeast shore of Ford Island. Four separate torpedo-plane attacks were made before 8:25 A.M.—the major one by 12 Kates, which swung in from the southeast over Merry Point, split up, and launched their specially fitted shoal-water torpedoes at altitudes between 40 and 100 feet above the water. The second torpedo attack, by three planes, was made on the same battleships. The third, by a single plane, was directed at the cruiser *Helena*. The fourth attack, by five planes that came in from the northwest, was made on the ships moored to the berths on the north side of Ford Island, two or three of which were normally occupied by carriers. Within five minutes of the first torpedo attack, the battleships were also combed fore and aft by dive-bombers, which, from their steep angles of attack, were very difficult to get at with the few antiaircraft guns then mounted on battle wagons. After launching torpedoes and dropping bombs, the Kates and Vals flew back over their targets, strafing viciously to kill the men. Half an hour after the battle opened, the *Arizona* was a burning wreck, the *Oklahoma* had capsized to port, the *West Virginia* had sunk, the *California* was going down, and every other battleship (except the *Pennsylvania* in dry dock) had been badly damaged. By 8:25 A.M. the Japanese had accomplished about 90 percent of their objective—to wreck the Battle Force of the Pacific Fleet.

To list the events on each ship, one by one:

The **West Virginia**, the youngest battleship present—18 years old on 1 December—was one of the first and hardest hit, and also one of the last to be returned to active duty. "Wee Vee," as her crew called the *West Virginia*, took six or seven torpedoes on her port side—four of them on the armor belt amidships

A panoramic view of Pearl Harbor during the Japanese attack on 7 December 1941. This appears to be late in the attack because of the large number of antiaircraft bursts. The massive cloud of black smoke in the center is primarily from the stricken *Arizona*. Ford Island is beyond the *Arizona*. One of the columns of smoke at left is from the oil fires engulfing two destroyers in dry dock with the *Pennsylvania*. *U.S. Navy*

The smoke pours from the *West Virginia* (outboard) as she sinks to the bottom of Pearl Harbor; the *Tennessee* (inboard) was protected from aerial torpedoes by the former ship. Small boats are taking off survivors; earlier they picked them up from the water as ships sank under them. Many *West Virginia* survivors crossed over to the *Tennessee* and then ashore to Ford Island. *U.S. Navy*

when she was listing heavily—and, for good measure, two bombs, one of which started a fire. The first torpedoes hit before 7:56 A.M.

Two fortunate circumstances, one due to training and the other to chance, saved the *West Virginia* from the fate of battleships that received fewer hits. A group of her younger officers, Lieutenant Claude V. Ricketts and three lieutenants junior grade, H. B. Stark, F. H. White USNR, and R. Beecham, who had discussed a possible air raid on the fleet and damage-control measures thereby required, acted promptly and decisively. The officer of the deck, Ensign Roman L. Brooks, saw the first bomb hit the hangar on Ford Island and thought it was an internal explosion on board the *California*, which was in his line of vision. He promptly gave the order "Away Fire and Rescue Party!" This immediately started the *West Virginia* personnel topside on the run and saved hundreds of lives. Lieutenant White, one of the first to reach the deck, saw a Kate in the act of launching, and gave the general alarm before the first torpedo hit.

These torpedo hits knocked out all power, light, communications, and the antiaircraft guns on the port side. The ship listed so rapidly that the guns on the starboard side, which opened fire within two minutes, could only be served by organizing a double row of ammunition passers, one to pass and the other to hold up the passer.

At Central Station, Lieutenant Commander J. S. Harper gave the order to counter-flood promptly, but it never reached the repair parties because the telephones had gone silent with the loss of power—installation of new sound-powered telephones had not yet been completed. Lieutenant Ricketts, although on the sick list, started counter-flooding on his own initiative, with the aid of Boatswain's Mate Billingsley, who knew how to operate the gear. This counter-flooding, together with the retarding force of the wire cables between the *West Virginia* and the *Tennessee*, corrected a 28-degree list to 15 degrees, and allowed her to sink bodily until the turn of the port bilge hit bottom, and thus saved the ship from capsizing.

In the meantime, Captain Mervyn S. Bennion had been disemboweled by fragments from a bomb that exploded on the *Tennessee* alongside. His last order was to Ricketts and White to leave him, which they refused to do; Chief Pharmacist's Mate Leak administered a hypodermic, and Captain Bennion was moved to another part of the bridge. He expressed concern only for the ship and crew, asking what was going on right up to the moment of his death.

Within a few minutes of opening fire, the ready ammunition for the antiaircraft guns was expended. Ricketts and Ensign Ford organized an ammunition-passing team that continued to operate when the ship was all aflame topside. The *Arizona*'s forward magazines had exploded, showering burning debris on the *West Virginia*'s decks.

For an hour and a half, all hands stood by to fight fires, and only the wounded were evacuated. During much of this time the ship was being dive-bombed and strafed. Antiaircraft gunners stood to their guns despite the list. At 9:40 A.M. the ship was on fire from the bow to Turret No. 1, flames shooting up to the foretop, curiously sparing that end of the bridge where Captain Bennion's body lay. About a hundred men, blown overboard or injured and fallen overboard, were in imminent danger from burning oil or drowning, but most were saved by boats from other ships, notably by a motor launch from the repair ship *Rigel*.

A tug helps fight fires aboard the *West Virginia* as she burns after settling to the bottom of Pearl Harbor. Some U.S. Navy officers believed that the shallow waters of the harbor would deter Japanese aerial torpedoes; the Japanese modified battleship shells to make them effective torpedoes in the harbor. *U.S. Navy*

The battleship *Arizona's* forward tripod mast collapses as a forward magazine detonates, destroying the ship. The *Arizona* was one of two dreadnoughts that were destroyed at Pearl Harbor, and she suffered the heaviest loss of life, including Rear Admiral Isaac C. Kidd, the division commander and the only flag officer killed in the Japanese attack. *U.S. Navy*

At about 10:05 A.M., when all power was lost and the *West Virginia* rested on the bottom and fire swept her superstructure, the damage-control officer ordered "Abandon ship." Survivors went over the side into boats or swam to Ford Island or to the *Tennessee*. Some crossed to her by walking tightrope on a 5-inch gun and remained there to help her gunners. Senior officers then organized a working party that returned on board and, with the aid of others who reported, brought all fires under control during the afternoon.

"Throughout the entire action," reported Commander Roscoe H. Hillenkoetter concerning the *West Virginia*, "there was never the slightest sign of faltering or of cowardice. The actions of the officers and men were wholly commendable; their spirit was marvelous; there was no panic, no shirking or flinching and words fail in attempting to describe the truly magnificent display of courage, discipline and devotion to duty of all." Highly commended was Chief Boatswain's Mate L. M. Jansen, commander of YG-47, who brought his "honey barge" (garbage lighter) alongside and helped fight the fires until they were extinguished. He then performed the same service for the *Arizona*.

Of the 1,454 men on board 1 December, the *West Virginia* lost two officers, and 103 men were killed or missing. Fifty-two out of 87 officers were wounded. In view of the heavy damage sustained by the ship, these casualties were light thanks to the excellent discipline of the crew and the prompt alert by the officer of the deck.

The *Tennessee* (Captain C. E. Reordan commanding), 21 years old, and one of five turbo-electric-drive battleships, was moored inboard of the *West Virginia* and thus protected by her from aerial torpedoes. She received two bomb hits very early in the action, the first of which detonated on the center gun of Turret No. 2. This is the one that killed Captain Bennion of the *West Virginia*. The second hit Turret No. 3, pierced the 5-inch armor, and exploded inside, fortunately with a low-order detonation. Most of her damage, however, came from fires started by flaming debris or burning oil from the *Arizona*, moored only 75 feet astern. The *Tennessee's* crew was able to handle their own fires and render assistance to the other battleship as well. Fire fighting continued all that day and the next night, with the men taking time out only for coffee and sandwiches. Casualties in this ship were light: five men killed or missing, one officer and 20 men wounded out of 94 officers and 1,372 men reported on board on 1 December.

Although the *Tennessee's* power plant remained intact, the ship was so wedged in by the sunken *West Virginia* that it was very difficult to move her. As early as 20 December she got under way, in company with the *Maryland* and the *Pennsylvania*, and steamed to the West Coast, where she was given a complete overhaul and modernization at the West Coast battleship repair center at Bremerton, Puget Sound.

The *Arizona*, moored astern of the *Tennessee*, took the worst beating of any ship in the fleet, suffered the largest number of casualties, and became a total loss. Although moored inboard, she did not enjoy much protection, for the outboard berth was occupied by the repair ship *Vestal* (AR 4), beyond which the *Arizona's* bow projected about 100 feet. The repair ship remained there during the attack on the *Arizona*, took two bomb hits that caused serious flooding, but got under way around 8:45 A.M. and saved herself by beaching on Area Shoal.

The *Arizona* barely had time to sound general quarters, man battle stations, and set Condition Zed (complete watertight integrity) when she received several lethal torpedo and bomb hits. One torpedo passed

ahead of the *Vestal* and hit under Turret No. 1; but the thing that broke her up was a heavy bomb that hit beside the second turret, penetrated the forecastle, and exploded in one of the forward magazines before it could be flooded—so fast had the action occurred. This explosion completely wrecked the forward part of the ship. Flames shot 500 feet into the air; scores of men, including Rear Admiral Isaac C. Kidd, who was on the signal bridge, and Captain Franklin Van Valkenburgh, on the navigation bridge, were killed. This explosion happened, apparently, before 8:10 A.M. Shortly thereafter, a second bomb went right down the stack, a third hit the boat deck, a fourth the faceplate of Turret No. 4; and four more struck the superstructure between the bridge and the tripod mast. The *Arizona* listed radically but settled so fast that she did not capsize. Over a thousand men burned to death or were trapped below and drowned. Machine gunners continued firing at planes until the heat of the flames drove them from their guns, and all able-bodied survivors remained on board fighting fires and evacuating the wounded until 10:32 A.M., although at one time the *Arizona* looked like one mass of flames. The *Arizona* had lost almost four-fifths of her complement: 47 officers and 1,056 men were killed or missing, and five officers and 39 men were wounded, out of 100 officers and 1,411 men on board as of 1 December.

The **Nevada,** moored next astern of the *Arizona* at the easternmost berth in Battleship Row, was lucky in that she had no ship tied up alongside to restrict her movements, and she was superbly handled by Lieutenant Commander Francis J. Thomas USNR, the senior officer on board at the time. The antiaircraft battery, directed by Ensign Joseph K. Taussig Jr., even after he had been severely wounded, opened fire promptly and accurately. The 5-inch battery on the port side, commanded by Ensign T. H. Taylor, shot down one and possibly two of the torpedo-bombers that made for the ship; .50-caliber machine guns accounted for another that splashed off her port quarter. It was probably due to this good shooting that the *Nevada*, despite her exposed position, suffered only one torpedo hit, and that well forward. The torpedo tore a hole 45 feet long and 30 feet high, flooding many compartments but leaving the power plant intact. Around 8:25 A.M. the ship was subjected to a severe dive-bombing attack, which resulted in two or three hits. Thomas, the acting commanding officer, then decided, in spite of the enormous hole made by the

torpedo hit, to stand out. Chief Boatswain E. J. Hill jumped onto the mooring quay, cast off the lines under strafing fire, and swam back to the ship just as she was getting under way.

Shortly before 9:00 A.M. Rear Admiral Furlong in the *Oglala*, having observed explosions that looked like magnetic mines in the main ship channel, signaled the *Nevada* to go around the north side of Ford Island; but she was already committed to the southerly course and passed right over the scene of the explosions without damage. A flight of Val dive-bombers making for the *Pennsylvania*, seeing a battleship under way, concentrated on her instead, and, when the *Nevada* had reached a point opposite the floating dry dock, she looked like a goner. The spray from the exploding near misses almost concealed her from view, and she received more hits here, too. Admiral Furlong hailed two tugs and ordered them to assist the battleship, fearing she might be sunk in the channel; they went alongside, pushed her clear, helped her extinguish fires (for her fire mains had been ruptured by bombs) and beached her on hard bottom at Waipio Point, opposite the southern end of Ford Island, around 9:40 A.M. There the ship's crew brought fires under control and secured.

The *Nevada* had taken at least five bomb hits in addition to the torpedo. The forward part of the ship was pretty thoroughly wrecked, the superstructure was mostly destroyed, and the navigation bridge and charthouse deck were completely burned through. But the

Battered and burning, the *Nevada* was intentionally grounded at Hospital Point to avoid blocking the narrow entrance to the harbor. Here the Navy Yard tug *Hoga* *(which still exists)* helps fight fires on the ship. The pilothouse (below the forward tripod mast) is discolored from the intensive fire that racked the ship. *U.S. Navy*

engineering department was intact. Three officers and 47 men were killed or missing, five officers and 104 men wounded, out of 94 officers and 1,390 men on board 1 December. The *Nevada* was refloated on 12 February 1942 and proceeded to Puget Sound after temporary repairs. She rejoined the fleet before the end of 1943.

The remaining pair of battleships, moored to the next berth forward, were the *Oklahoma* and the *Maryland*. The **Oklahoma,** in the outboard position, was hit very early in the fight. A few moments after the first bomb was seen to explode on the southwest end of Ford Island, and almost simultaneously with the call to general quarters, the *Oklahoma* was struck by three torpedoes in rapid succession and took a list of 25 to 35 degrees. There was no time to set Condition Zed, to counter-flood, or to take other measures to prevent capsizing; and the rapid listing prevented all but one or two machine guns from firing. Captain H. D. Bode was ashore. Within a few minutes the executive officer, Commander Jesse L. Kenworthy Jr., decided after a quick conference with Lieutenant Commander William H. Hobby, the first lieutenant, to abandon ship. The word was passed, and the men were directed to go over the ship's starboard side as she rolled. She received two more torpedo hits above the armor belt as she started to capsize; the men were strafed as they crawled over, and explosions from high-level bombers hit all around. The *Oklahoma* only stopped rolling when her masts caught in the mud of the harbor bottom. Within 20 minutes of the start of the attack she was capsized 150 degrees with the starboard side of the bottom above water and a portion of the keel clear. According to one report, "The conduct of the crew was excellent throughout," and many climbed on board the *Maryland* to assist fighting her antiaircraft batteries. Twenty officers and 395 men were killed or missing, and two officers and 30 men were wounded, out of 82 officers and 1,272 men on board.

The **Maryland,** protected from torpedoes by the *Oklahoma,* was the luckiest battleship. Just as the attack started, Seaman L. V. Short broke off addressing Christmas cards to operate a machine gun and shot down a torpedo plane before it could launch. Only two officers and two men were killed or missing, and 14 men wounded, out of 108 officers and 1,496 men on board. The only damage to the ship was caused by a fragmentation bomb that detonated on the forecastle awning ridgepole, and by a 16-inch armor-piercing bomb that entered the forecastle below the waterline

***Top:*** The *Maryland* (left) was protected from torpedo attack by the *Oklahoma*, which rolled over from torpedo damage, her masts sticking into the bottom of the harbor. Her capsized hull is visible at right. Some men survived inside her for several days until holes could be cut into her double bottom by acetylene torches. They were located by pounding on the hull with hammers. *U.S. Navy*

***Above:*** One of the capsized *Oklahoma's* propellers dominates this view of her hull. Although the *Oklahoma* was salvaged, she and the *Arizona* were the only two of the eight battleships at Pearl Harbor that were not returned to active service. The waters of Pearl Harbor were covered with oil from those and other sunken battleships for several years. *U.S. Navy*

The *California*, the southernmost ship in Battleship Row and flagship of Vice Admiral William. S. Pye, the Battle Force commander, was heavily damaged and slowly sank. Here she is shrouded with smoke from her burning fuel. Her No. 1 main-battery 14-inch turret is slightly elevated to starboard, the No. 2 turret fully trained to starboard. *U.S. Navy*

and detonated in the hold. The Navy Yard at Pearl Harbor completed temporary repairs on the *Maryland* by 20 December without taking her into dry dock, and she was the first of the battle fleet to return to active service, in February 1942.

The oiler **Neosho** got under way promptly and received no hits. Not so fortunate was the **California,** flagship of Vice Admiral William S. Pye, at the southernmost berth. Although the last of the battleships to be hit, she was less prepared than any for the blows. Her material condition as to watertight integrity was bad, too many of her officers were ashore, and some of those aboard failed to act quickly or intelligently.

On the *California*, there was a delay both in sounding general quarters and in ordering Condition Zed, which called for closure of all watertight hatches and doors. At 8:05 A.M., before Condition Zed could be executed, and just as the machine-gun battery opened fire, two deep-running torpedoes hit the *California* below the armor belt, one just forward of the bridge and the other aft, below Turret No. 3.

Their effect, owing to the "unbuttoned" condition of the ship, proved to be far-reaching and disastrous. She began listing to port. Prompt though unorthodox counter-flooding, directed by Ensign Edgar M. Fain USNR, prevented her from capsizing, but the rupture of oil tanks by the forward torpedo let salt water into the fuel system and, before it could be cleared, light and power were lost. It was now 8:10 A.M.; antiaircraft batteries were blazing away, the ammunition supply was being kept up by hand. At 8:25 A.M. a bomb exploded below, setting off the antiaircraft ammunition magazine, spreading blast and fire in the ammunition passageway, and killing about 50 men; a second bomb ruptured the bow plates.

Owing to Herculean efforts, the damage-control party restored light, power, and water pressure at 8:55 A.M.; the men then concentrated on fighting fires that they successfully brought under control. The *California* was ready to get under way by 9:10 A.M., using four boilers, but before Captain Bunkley, who in the meantime had come aboard, could issue orders to unmoor, burning oil from windward floated down and engulfed the stern. So at 10:02 the captain ordered "Abandon ship." Shortly after, the wind blew this pool of burning oil clear, and at 10:15 the captain ordered all hands to return on board. Not everyone obeyed.

Although the minesweepers *Vireo* and *Bobolink* closed the battleships and applied their pumps, and numerous "handy billies" (portable gasoline-driven

The fleet flagship *Pennsylvania* in the large dry dock at Pearl Harbor after the attack; in the foreground are the wrecked destroyers *Cassin* and *Downes*. The *Pennsylvania* suffered a single bomb hit. The machinery and other gear from the burned-out destroyers were transferred back to the mainland for installation in new hulls—given the same names and hull numbers. *U.S. Navy*

pumps) were obtained from other ships, the *California* slowly settled. Her bulkheads were so leaky that the water entering the great gashes made by enemy torpedo hits could not be isolated. Prompt work by the divers might have kept her afloat, but as it was she slowly settled into the mud, with eventually only the superstructure above water. Six officers and 92 men were killed or missing, and three officers and 58 men were wounded, out of 120 officers and 1,546 men on board. The *California* was refloated on 24 March 1942; she then proceeded under her own power to Bremerton for repairs and rejoined the fleet in time for the Marianas operation.

The old battleship **Utah,** converted to a target ship and mistaken by the Japanese for an aircraft carrier, was completely defenseless. Within five minutes of the beginning of the attack she took two torpedo hits; she listed so rapidly that the senior officer aboard ordered, "All hands on deck and abandon ship over starboard side." As the crew crawled over, some of them coming out through ports in the captain's cabin, the Kates returned and strafed them. By 8:12 A.M. the *Utah* was bottom-up—a total loss.

Finally, there was the *Pennsylvania.* Flagship of the Pacific Fleet, she was in the permanent dry dock next to pier 1010, facing shoreward, with the destroyers *Cassin* and *Downes* occupying the space at the head of the dock. These three had a special fight of their own. During the first phase they were attacked by dive-bombers and Zeros that had just made passes at nearby Hickam Field. On board the battleship all antiaircraft batteries were promptly manned and rapidly brought into action; her 3-inch 50-caliber guns "fired fast, quietly and efficiently," reported the skipper of the *Cassin.* Both destroyers and the *Pennsylvania* were further handicapped when a bomb severed their power cables from the yard.

At 8:40 A.M. the second attack of 50 high-level Kates, 80 dive-bombing Vals, and 40 Zeros, launched from the Japanese carriers about an hour after the first wave, began to come in. The high-level bombers crisscrossed their targets from various directions at 10,000 to 12,000 feet altitude, inflicting serious damage on several ships with their converted 16-inch armor-piercing bombs. Up to this time it had been mostly take and no give for the fleet; but the 15-minute lull before 8:40 gave them time to replenish ammunition supplies, organize defense, and give something back.

At about 9:00 A.M., when the *Nevada* on her sortie was off 1010 dock, she attracted the worst of a dive-bombing attack that was initially directed at the *Pennsylvania.* Several of the Vals, however, refused to be diverted. One of them dropped a bomb that hit the destroyer *Shaw* in the floating dry dock only a few yards westward and caused a spectacular explosion. At 9:06 A.M. the *Pennsylvania* suffered a hit that penetrated her boat deck and detonated in the casemate of a 5-inch gun.

In the meantime Captain C. M. Cooke Jr., commanding officer of the *Pennsylvania,* had ordered the dry dock to be flooded, hoping to quench the flames; but this did not mend matters, because burning oil rose on top of the water. The *Pennsylvania,* owing to the bomb hit that exploded below, lost two officers, with 16 men killed and 30 men wounded, out of 81 officers and 1,395 men on board. But she suffered no great damage, left the dry dock on 12 December, and proceeded to the West Coast for overhaul. Here our tale of Battleship Row ends.

By 10 A.M. the battle was over; the last enemy planes rendezvoused over northern Oahu and returned to their carriers. Never in modern history was a war begun with so smashing a victory by one side, and never in recorded history did the initial victor pay so dearly for his calculated treachery. There is some question, however, whether the Japanese attacked the right targets. They knocked out the Battle Force and decimated the striking airpower present; but they neglected permanent installations at Pearl Harbor, including the repair shops, which were able to do an amazingly quick job returning the less severely damaged ships to service. And the Japanese did not even attempt to hit the power plant or the large fuel-oil tank farm, filled to capacity, whose loss (in the opinion of Admiral Thomas C. Hart) would have set back the U.S. advance across the Pacific much longer than did the damage to the fleet.

The heroic efforts of raising four of the five sunken battleships, repairing three damaged battleships, and restoring all to the fleet proudly reflect the motto of the Pearl Harbor Navy Yard: "We keep them fit to fight." Captain Homer N. Wallin was the officer chiefly responsible for these praiseworthy salvage operations. Since the salvage of the four sunken battleships was long and laborious and in varying degrees involved the same techniques, we shall confine ourselves to discussing the cases of the *Oklahoma* and the *West Virginia*; one was beyond rehabilitation, and the other was the most successful of the rehabilitations.

The *Oklahoma*, the toughest and most spectacular of the attempted salvage jobs, was not only sunk but capsized, with keel in the air and masts crumpled in the mud. Under the direction of Chief Watertender R. H. Snow, a scale model, inverted in exactly the position of the ship, was constructed so that divers could orient themselves to an upside-down interior. Divers sealed the great apertures that the torpedoes had torn in her hull, and opened other vents for the water to flow out, so that by the forcing in of air the 29,000-ton ship was given a positive buoyancy of 18,000 tons. In the *Oklahoma*, as in all the sunken ships, decomposing organic matter from provisions, clothing, and bodies of victims generated a gas so deadly that men had to work with gas masks even when water was freed from the compartments. This preparatory work took over a year to accomplish.

When buoyancy was finally restored to the *Oklahoma*, the next problem was to right her. In order to distribute the strain fore and aft, crews erected on her capsized bottom 21 triangular timber frames 40 feet high, of the type known as "bents." From the steel cap at the apex of each bent, six heavy steel cables led to pad eyes welded into the inverted ship's starboard side along a line where the greatest leverage could be exerted. Also, from each cap, two steel cables led to an enormous 16-sheave burton tackle whose pendant was geared at 8000-to-1 ratio to a 5-horsepower electric winch firmly embedded in a deep concrete foundation on Ford Island.

When everything was set, in March 1943, the 21 small motors pulled the big ship over to a 90-degree position in a little over 100 hours. The bents and cables were then removed, a new grip taken by the cables topside, and the *Oklahoma* was righted completely. On 28 December 1943 she was towed to a Pearl Harbor dry dock, but an examination found her unfit for further service. The *Oklahoma* was sold for scrap after the war.

**Left:** The *California* being rearmed at Pearl Harbor in July 1942 before returning to the United States. A large floating crane is alongside her starboard bow, placing a gun in Turret No. 1. Guns are fitted in Turrets No. 3 (without top installed) and No. 4. Her secondary battery and antiaircraft guns would be completely modified when rebuilt. (U.S. Navy)

**Above:** The *West Virginia* ready to depart Pearl Harbor on 30 April 1943 for complete reconstruction at the Puget Sound Navy Yard (Bremerton, Washington). She was rebuilt—to a radically different configuration—and rejoined the fleet for combat operations. The ship's crewmen are in dress whites as they await departure. There are large life rafts on the after 16-inch turrets. *U.S. Navy*

**Upper left:** The salvage of the stricken *Oklahoma*, which had capsized, was the most difficult of the battleship salvage operations. Here, on 8 March 1943, the hull is being slowly righted by 21 triangular timber frames, each 40 feet high, with steel cables rigged to electric winches embedded in concrete on Ford Island (right). A massive amount of pumping and other work had already been accomplished. *U.S. Navy*

The *West Virginia* was perhaps the most successful example of rehabilitation. The six or seven torpedoes that hit her had blown out a 120-foot-long series of gashes 12 to 15 feet high; one of the bomb hits had pushed the third, second, and main decks down so that they came together 10 feet below the original third-deck level. Inside it looked as if a giant had crumpled the ship and then lighted a torch to the remains. Her bottom was wrinkled and bent where it struck the harbor bottom. But she lay almost on an even keel.

As the great slash in her port side was too large for patching, the engineers built a series of huge cofferdams, 50 feet deep, which were weighted, lowered, and bolted to the hull by divers so that they formed one big outer wall. At the bottom, where a snug fitting of timbers to the jagged edges of steel was impossible, the gash was sealed with tremic cement, the kind that hardens under water. This battleship was pumped out, raised, and cleaned largely by her own crew with the aid of civilian technicians, since the common workmen of the yard blanched at the indescribable filth and grisly human remains in her wrecked and soaked interior. On 17 May 1942 she was refloated and towed into the Navy Yard dry dock for temporary repairs. The General Electric Company, which had built the motors and generators for the ship, sent 50 specialists to assist more than a hundred Pearl Harbor electricians in the complex task of rewinding all main generators and motors.

In due course the *West Virginia* proceeded under her own power to Bremerton for a modernization that made her a practically new ship. As the work was frequently interrupted by other tasks of higher priority, she was not ready to rejoin the fleet until the middle of 1944. Her new construction was all welded instead of riveted, and the weight savings raised her waterline by 2 inches. Her deck and turret armor were doubled in thickness and her watertight integrity was greatly improved. Her main battery had to be regunned. A new ventilation system, new fire mains, and new fuel oil-lines were built, and "blisters" on both sides of the hull were added to afford greater stability and antitorpedo protection. These increased her beam from 98 to 114 feet, which meant she could no longer pass through the Panama Canal.

In the early months of the war, the older battleships such as the *Pennsylvania* were not of much use and so spent a good deal of time in San Francisco. The *Tennessee* and the *Maryland*, lightly damaged at Pearl Harbor, had been repaired and restored to duty. They were joined by four ships that had not been at Pearl Harbor: the *Colorado* was at Puget Sound Navy Yard, Bremerton, Washington, for an overhaul, and the *Mississippi*, the *New Mexico*, and the *Idaho*, which had been recalled from the Atlantic. These old ships were too slow to steam with the aircraft carriers and were poorly armed against aerial attack.

In April 1942 came a flicker of activity. On the 14th the *Pennsylvania*, six other battleships, and a squadron of destroyers got under way as Task Force One. They steamed out under the Golden Gate Bridge and headed southwest with no air cover. The *Pennsylvania*'s overloaded condition made her movements sluggish and uncomfortable, even in moderate seas. The ships performed maneuvers, launched their float-planes to perform reconnaissance flights, and practiced firing all their guns. Scuttlebutt concerning the task force's mission was rampant during the time at sea, but nothing came of it. In late April the ships headed back to the West Coast, engaging in war games as they steamed. Far to the west, off Australia, American and Japanese forces were engaging in the Battle of the Coral Sea, an aircraft carrier engagement and the first naval battle in which the opposing ships did not come within sight of each other. The old ships of Task Force One would have only been an impediment in that environment, requiring antiaircraft protection and unable to use their big guns against an enemy far out of range.

On 31 May Vice Admiral William Pye, commander of Task Force One, dispatched the *Maryland*, the *Colorado*, and a screen of three destroyers northwestward from San Francisco following a report that a small force of Japanese aircraft carriers might be approaching the West Coast. In command of the task group on the flagship *Maryland* was Rear Admiral Walter Stratton Anderson. On 5 June Pye and his other five battleships and escorts also steamed west after hearing reports of the momentous Battle of Midway far to the west. The Japanese Combined Fleet had gone to sea in force, sending its attack probes toward both Midway Island and the Aleutians. American carrier-based dive-bombers scored a great victory at Midway by sinking four aircraft carriers. The small carriers that might have threatened San Francisco went to the Aleutians instead. As it was, the two groups of old battleships rendezvoused at sea, then returned to port. Their crews saw only empty ocean, which was just as well. With scant air cover, they would have been easy targets for carrier planes.

Although no U.S. fast battleships were sunk during the war, several suffered battle damage. Here the *South Dakota* (top) gets help from the repair ship *Prometheus*, the photo probably taken at Nouméa, New Caledonia, in November 1942. Two destroyers are also being tended by the *Prometheus*. The Navy kept numerous tenders and repairs ships in forward areas to keep the warships at war. *U.S. Navy*

In early November the *Maryland* and the *Colorado* headed west from Pearl Harbor to provide possible backup support for the Guadalcanal operation. From here on the pace that the old battleships were accustomed to began to speed up.

From 1943 on, the veterans of Battleship Row had useful and valuable careers. The *Nevada* served as Rear Admiral Morton Deyo's flagship in the Normandy invasion. Her big guns more than repaid her total cost of reconstruction in terms of the brilliant fire support she provided in the invasions of Normandy and southern France. Her gunfire was an important reason for the signal from the Normandy beaches, "Thank God for the United States Navy!"

The *Nevada* then returned to the Pacific in time to help pound Iwo Jima. The *West Virginia*, the *Maryland*, the *California*, the *Tennessee,* and the *Pennsylvania* crossed the enemy's "T" at the Battle of Surigao Strait and subsequently participated in the Okinawa operation, where the *Nevada* was damaged by a kamikaze and other air attacks. The *West Virginia* had the proud privilege of entering Sagami Bay, Japan, with the occupation forces on 27 August 1945.

## THE NIGHT ACTIONS OFF GUADALCANAL AND OTHER BATTLES

Fortunately, the new fast battleships were beginning to become available as war engulfed the United States. In the wake of the commissionings of the *North Carolina* and the *Washington* in the spring of 1941, the *South*

*Dakota*, the *Indiana*, the *Massachusetts*, and the *Alabama* were commissioned between March and August 1942. From February 1943 to April 1944, the *Iowa*, the *New Jersey*, the *Missouri*, and the *Wisconsin* would follow. They represented a new breed, and with a designed speed of 33 knots, they bristled with antiaircraft batteries, and their 16-inch guns could fire with remarkable accuracy at a high-speed target far over the horizon.

To give dual big-gun and antiaircraft protection to the flattops, the new battleship *North Carolina* shifted from the Atlantic Fleet. In July 1942, after months in which the first fast battleships had operated in the Atlantic as a support to the Royal Navy, the *North Carolina* arrived in Pearl Harbor, amid the wrecks of some of the old battleships. Bristling topside with dozens of antiaircraft guns, the *North Carolina* was without question the most modern battleship that had ever reached Hawaii. The *North Carolina*'s crew was taken aback by a roaring ovation from the crews of the older ships that ringed the harbor. To the veterans at Pearl, she was more than just a warship at that moment. She was a new symbol of hope, a commodity that the men of the other warships had hungered for in the last few months. Even beyond that, she was a promise of more to come.

The *North Carolina* became the first of the new ships that went into combat when she provided antiaircraft support for the carrier *Enterprise* during the Battle of the Eastern Solomons in late August 1942. U.S. Marines had invaded the island of Guadalcanal on

Rear Admiral Willis A. (Ching) Lee Jr. took command of the navy's fast battleships in August 1942. He led those ships in the Solomons campaign and in subsequent actions across the Pacific until mid-1945, when he was detached from the fleet to help devise methods of countering kamikaze attacks. Lee never returned to his beloved battleships; a heart attack took his life on 25 August 1945. *U.S. Navy*

7 August, and the Japanese had subsequently interjected numerous naval forces in an effort to recapture the island, particularly its airstrip, Henderson Field. Despite the help, the *Enterprise* caught three bombs on 24 August. On 15 September "The Showboat" once again served as a protector, this time steaming with a convoy that included the aircraft carrier *Wasp*. That afternoon, Radioman Alan Campbell was on watch in the flag radio space on the bridge. He witnessed explosions on the *Wasp*, heard a call to general quarters, and then a radio report from the destroyer *O'Brien*: "Torpedo under our ship headed for you." Captain George Fort ordered the battleship's rudder hard to starboard, and Radioman Campbell got a good grip on a nearby railing. The torpedo smacked home on the port bow and threw up a geyser of water higher than the ship's mast.

Two months after Midway the U.S. Navy, in its first amphibious assault of the war against a hostile shore, struck at Guadalcanal in the Solomons to begin the amphibious drive that would surge across the Pacific. Guadalcanal had been seized by the Japanese to dominate Australian sea-lanes. The invasion force under Rear Admiral Richmond Kelly Turner swept into what came to be known as "Iron Bottom Sound" and landed the marines on 7 August 1942. The rugged campaign, with bitter jungle battles and a series of fierce naval engagements, continued until February 1943.

Among the sea fights were Savo Island, Eastern Solomons, Cape Esperance, Santa Cruz, Guadalcanal, Tassafaronga, and Rennell Island.

In August 1942, about the time marines were invading Guadalcanal, the new *South Dakota* left Philadelphia and headed for the Pacific so she could team up with the *North Carolina* to form the first division of 35,000-ton fast battleships in the South Pacific. Rear Admiral Willis A. Lee Jr. was in command as commander, Battleship Division Six; he had taken the empty billet created when Admiral Wilcox was lost overboard the *Washington* a few months earlier. Soon afterward, the *South Dakota* was damaged when she struck a submerged coral pinnacle at Tongatabu; Lee shifted his flag to the *Washington*. On 26 October, after being repaired and taking aboard additional guns, the *South Dakota* steamed with the carrier *Enterprise* in the Battle of Santa Cruz Islands. There she put on an impressive display of firepower with her 5-inch, 40-millimeter, and 20-millimeter array of antiaircraft guns. With no surface targets, antiaircraft guns were the weapons of necessity in that action. Someone be-

gan making chalk marks to indicate Japanese planes that the ship's guns had shot down, or perhaps to note the number of planes that guns of any ship knocked down. The *South Dakota*'s crew eventually claimed to have shot down 32 planes, although others believed the number to be either slightly lower or substantially lower. In any event, the *Enterprise* was well protected that day, while the carrier *Hornet*, which was not protected by a battleship, was sunk.

The Battle of Savo Island took place on 9 August 1942 and was fought just north of Guadalcanal. It ended in near disaster, when the Japanese in a surprise night attack sank four cruisers and damaged another. With control of the seas often in doubt, Admiral Chester W. Nimitz, commander in chief, Pacific Fleet, sent in all ships available. The aircraft carrier *Saratoga* joined the carriers *Enterprise*, *Wasp*, and *Hornet* that had supported the initial landing. In the Battle of the Eastern Solomons, 24–25 August 1942, the *North Carolina* became the first of the new fast battleships into combat when she provided antiaircraft support for the priceless carrier *Enterprise* during the Battle of the Eastern Solomons in late August. After the U.S. invasion of Guadalcanal, the Japanese had tried numerous times to interject numerous naval forces in an effort to recapture the island, particularly its airstrip, Henderson Field. Despite the help, the *Enterprise* caught three bombs on 24 August. On 15 September "The Showboat," as the *North Carolina* was nicknamed, once again served as a protector, this time steaming with a convoy that included the aircraft carrier *Wasp*.

On 12 October, at the Battle of Cape Esperance, not only did the *North Carolina*'s guns again chalk up a heavy toll against the enemy, but she proved that she could take it as well as dish it out. At the peak of the battle, a torpedo from the Japanese submarine *I-19*, initiallly meant for the *Hornet*, hit the *North Carolina* on the port side and tore a 32-by-18-foot hole in the hull of the rugged battleship. The damage-control party promptly sealed off the area, and the ship continued shooting accurately at the enemy planes as if nothing had happened. She even increased her speed to 25 knots. The modern battleship teamed with the aircraft carrier made an almost invulnerable combination. The carrier's fighter planes shot down many of the attacking aircraft. The battleship not only defended against surface attack, but her numerous and highly effective antiaircraft guns saved the carrier from enemy planes that broke through the fighters.

The *North Carolina* later steamed back to Pearl Harbor for repairs. A shortage of ships for all the pressing tasks in the Pacific hurt the U.S. effort desperately in the first years of the war. The limitations placed on the navy in the 1930s paid off in bitter coin of loss of lives and ships.

Late in October 1942, while the land battle raged for Henderson Field, Guadalcanal's prized airstrip, the naval engagement of Santa Cruz was fought. While the *North Carolina* was being repaired, the new battleship *South Dakota* took her place on the front line to defend the *Enterprise*. When the flattop came under attack, the *South Dakota*'s heavy antiaircraft fire saved the *Enterprise* from Japanese dive-bombers. Not so with the *Hornet*, which lacked the massed antiaircraft protection a battleship provides. Pounded by dive-bombers, she was finally abandoned and later sunk by Japanese destroyers. By 12 November American naval reinforcements, including the battleship *Washington*, arrived to operate with the *South Dakota*. Now the United States could match Japan's big guns.

The Japanese now made the supreme effort to recover Guadalcanal, sending in battleships as well as other naval, air, and land forces. The Japanese and U.S. Navies met the evening of 12–13 November as the Naval Battle of Guadalcanal began. The battle raged until dawn. The Japanese battleship *Hiei*, badly damaged during the night, was finished off by navy and marine bombers the next day. On the night of 14 November a formation of four U.S. destroyers and two U.S. battleships (the *Washington* and the *South Dakota*) steamed into the narrow waters between Guadalcanal and nearby Savo Island to intercept a force of Japanese bombardment ships. Those waters were a less-than-ideal location for a gunnery duel between battleships, which were intended to fight at long range on the high seas. But the circumstances were such that Vice Admiral William F. Halsey Jr., commander, South Pacific Force, had few other options but to use his big ships here and now against the Japanese.

Ships on both sides were soon engaged in a slugging match at ranges far shorter than those for which the big-gun ships were designed. When the *Washington* opened up with her big guns, it was the first use of a battleship main battery in anger in the Pacific war. Ensign Bob Reed, in the destroyer *Preston*, saw the 16-inch rounds trace parabolic arcs, glowing cherry red, as

The battleship *Washington* was part of U.S. Task Force 39, which included the aircraft carrier *Wasp,* that operated with the British Home Fleet in April 1942. Here the *Washington* steams through heavy North Atlantic swells. The arrival of Task Force 39 at Scapa Flow was reminiscent of the arrival of U.S. battleships to join the British Grand Fleet in December 1917. *U.S. Navy*

they left the guns. They disappeared for a time into low clouds, then reappeared as they descended on or near the Japanese ships.

The *Washington*'s gunnery was excellent that night, and effective; her 16-inch shells pounded the *Kirishima*, forcing that battleship's crew to scuttle her. Though the *Washington* was unhurt during the battle, a great deal of Japanese response was drawn to the *South Dakota*, as she was silhouetted by the fires from the burning destroyers. She received considerable topside damage and personnel casualties and later sailed for repairs. The night's action derailed the "Tokyo Express" and essentially broke the back of Japanese efforts to recapture Guadalcanal.

## THE BRITISH HOME FLEET AND OPERATION "TORCH"

Though fighting desperately on a shoestring in the Pacific, the U.S. Navy had to keep its strength divided in a two-ocean war. The full U.S. Navy was needed in the Pacific, but Hitler had to be stopped in Europe and Africa. Even as the navy and marines struggled to survive in the Solomons, the strategy called for a multi-pronged invasion of North Africa. This was to be the first step in cracking Hitler's Fortress Europe and preventing German capture of French naval forces and bases in West Africa.

On 8 November 1942 Operation Torch commenced. The Allies were not yet ready for a full-scale invasion of the European continent, but they did establish a toehold in North Africa with Operation Torch. Invasion assaults swept into Algeria at Oran and Algiers, and into Morocco in three landings north and south of Casablanca. The Algerian invasions, with British naval support, sortied from England. The Western Task Force for the Morocco landings sailed from the United States. To support the invasion force, the U.S. Navy used a variety of warships, including the World War I veteran battleships *Texas* and *New York*, along with the *Massachusetts*, commissioned only six months earlier.

As the navy returned to the shores of North Africa where in its infancy it had forged some of its noblest traditions, the two veteran battlewagons covered the forward flanks of the invasion force of over 100 ships under Rear Admiral H. Kent Hewitt. The *Texas*

King George VI inspects the ship's company of the USS *Washington* at Scapa Flow on 7 June 1942. Some of the ship's marines are in the lower right; an OS2U Kingfisher is on the *Washington*'s port catapult. Anchored in the background is the British battleship *Duke of York*. Later in the war a British battleship-carrier force was assigned to the U.S. Pacific Fleet and included the *Duke of York*. *Imperial War Museum*

The unfinished French battleship *Jean Bart*, moored at Casablanca, was the only "enemy" battleship to be engaged by U.S. battleships in the Atlantic theater. In November 1942, during Operation Torch, the USS *Massachusetts* and a heavy cruiser engaged in a one-sided duel with the French ship. As shown here, only the *Jean Bart*'s No. 1 turret with four 15-inch guns was installed. *U.S. Navy*

ported the northern invasion thrust near Port Lyautey; the *New York*, some 200 miles to the south at Safi, helped ensure the success of that landing. In the center, the *Massachusetts*, of Rear Admiral Robert C. Giffen's Covering Group, protected the landings at Fedhala by bombarding the French coastal artillery at Casablanca a few miles to the southwest. The shore batteries were buttressed by the 15-inch guns of the unfinished French battleship *Jean Bart* lying in port. Both had to be silenced, or they could tear the invasion force to pieces. The *Jean Bart* began flinging salvos seaward, which was the signal for the American ships to retaliate. The *Massachusetts*, along with the heavy cruiser *Tuscaloosa*, found the range on the *Jean Bart* from 12 to 15 miles distance. One shell landed on a barbette, causing the turret to jam and putting it out of action for hours. Maneuvering frequently, in part to avoid torpedoes from French destroyers, the *Massachusetts* continued shooting, sinking two destroyers, damaging shore batteries, and generally making a mess of the port. She was hit twice during the engagement and fired about 60 percent of her main battery rounds that day.

Victory in North Africa and in the naval battle of Guadalcanal did not end the call for battleships in the Atlantic-Mediterranean theater. The new fast battleships would be needed to guard the critical shipping lanes to England and Russia, furnishing big-gun, armored-ship protection against German surface-ship

attack on the convoys, the lifeline and very means of existence of all overseas operations. But there were only a finite number of battleships available. The few old battleships not in the Pacific convoyed and trained the rising tide of new men needed in Europe. At Normandy in June 1944 and in the invasion of southern France that autumn, their guns again came into demand to smash shore defenses as part of the relentless onslaught from the sea. The *Texas* would serve well again. The *Arkansas*, so old that many thought her useless, and the *Nevada*, transferred temporarily from the Pacific, would deliver mighty blows. Reaching far inland with their big guns, they would confound the enemy with their accuracy and effect.

In both theaters of war, ground troops appreciated the effect of the battleships' big guns. In the Pacific, "The greatest single factor in the American success is naval gunfire," according to Colonel Y. Saito, Imperial Japanese Army. In the Atlantic, no lesser a personage then Field Marshal Erwin Rommel, commander of the Atlantic Wall, stated that, "our operations in Normandy are tremendously hampered, and in some places even rendered impossible by . . . the effect of heavy naval guns [whose firepower] is so immense that no operation of any kind is possible in that area."

So ended the year 1942. Over 800 more days of war remained.

# CHAPTER EIGHT

# WORLD WAR II

## THE TIDE TURNS

By early 1943, the U.S. Pacific Fleet had an entirely different set of demands than the Atlantic Fleet. The new fast battleships were stalwarts in the fast carrier task forces. Mounting over 100 medium- and small-caliber antiaircraft guns each, with accurate fire control, they were overwhelmingly effective in battle against attacking aircraft. As the war progressed westward, opportunities increased to use their big guns in shore bombardment. Always they were a great comfort and ever sought after by task-force commanders to protect their aircraft carriers.

### THE "VETERANS" AND THE ALEUTIAN ISLANDS

The old veterans of Pearl Harbor's Battleship Row had a different mission. Lacking speed, they could not operate with fast carrier task forces, so they served as backup support in the closing stages of the Guadalcanal campaign and in the drive up the Solomons.

Then, starting in May 1943, several of the old battleships, as part of a task force under Rear Admiral Thomas C. Kinkaid, ventured north to the Aleutians for the seizure of the islands of Attu and Kiska. The Japanese had limited airpower in this area, so the ships were safer than they would have been in a place such as the Solomons; and they

**Left:** The "old battleships"—many of them veterans of the Pearl Harbor attack—saw action in several roles during World War II. Of particular importance was the fire support the provided for the invasions of North Africa (1942), the Aleutians (1943), Normandy (1944), and a dozen landings in the Pacific (1943–45). Here the rejuvenated *West Virginia* bombards Okinawa with her 14-inch guns on 1 April 1945. *U.S. Navy*

were also cooler in the northern climate. They were accompanied by some small escort carriers (CVE) that provided a minimum of air support. On 11 May army troops landed on Attu Island. Submarines were still a concern, and lookouts and sonar men were kept on full alert. On occasion, some reported enemy submarines turned out to be whales. The cool, foggy weather was enlivened at times by an Aleutian phenomenon known as the "williwaw," a sudden gust of wind that could reach speeds as high as 100 knots. The wind churned the seas, sending up waves and spray onto the decks of the battleships and their escorts.

Because the fog was so thick, the ships had to rely heavily on radar to navigate and to maintain position within formation. One day, the fog lifted and the *Mississippi* launched her OS2U Kingfisher floatplane for antisubmarine patrol. The fog soon closed in and the ship lost radar and radio contact with the plane, which was lost with its crew. The radar and radio situation was complicated by unusual atmospheric effects that sometimes made it possible to pick up signals at a far greater range than usual. This phenomenon led to the most unusual "Battle of the Pips" in the early morning hours of 26 July. The *Mississippi* reported surface con-

tacts at a range of 15 miles, and radar operators on board the *Idaho* and the cruisers *Wichita* and *Portland* spotted them as well. Soon, the ships were banging away merrily at the phantom targets. Eventually, the radar operators concluded that the phosphorescent images on their scopes were actually islands a hundred miles away!

## ATLANTIC CONVOY DUTY

In the Atlantic, the old battleships served in the boring duty of being convoy escorts. They accompanied the convoys that ferried fuel, equipment, weapons, ammunition, and soldiers to the European theater. Though they could provide little protection against submarines and absolutely none against attacking aircraft, their 12-inch and 14-inch guns would be invaluable if a surface raider lurked on the convoy's course ready to pounce when it came into view.

Convoy duty on the North Atlantic run meant that the convoy would often encounter fog. The old battleships' 36-inch searchlights were very useful as they were sometimes shone on cargo ships to give them a point of reference. Ships also blew their steam whistles as a way of warning others against steering too close.

The old battleships were not operating alone in the Atlantic; some of the fast battleships were there too. As long as potent German ships, such as the battleship *Tirpitz* and the battle cruiser *Scharnhorst*, could menace Allied convoys, the Allied navies had to keep a careful watch. The U.S. Navy maintained new fast battleships in the Atlantic to support this watch. In May 1943 the new *Alabama* and *South Dakota*, freshly repaired from battle damage sustained in her fight in the Solomon Islands, joined the Royal Navy in Scapa Flow.

In the months that followed, the *Alabama* and the *South Dakota* served as part of the covering force for convoys that operated north of the Arctic Circle, mostly on their way to the Soviet Union. After their deployment with the British, the *South Dakota* and the *Alabama* were released from Atlantic duty and the "*Tirpitz* watch," having been replaced by the newer *Iowa* and *New Jersey*. The *South Dakota* and the *Alabama* then steamed to Norfolk to spend a brief shipyard period before being dispatched to the Pacific.

The *Iowa* was to have a unique piece of equipment for a battleship. Because she was to transport President Franklin Roosevelt, the Joint Chiefs of Staff, and other staff members to Casablanca on the first leg of the president's journey to the Tehran conference for a meeting

The *Idaho* that saw action in the Aleutians bore little outward resemblance to her prewar appearance. This photo, taken in 1944, shows her secondary battery of four 5-inch dual-purpose guns in single mounts per side, plus numerous 40mm and 20mm guns. The catapult previously fitted atop her No. 3 turret has been removed, and the ship's three OS2U Kingfishers use two fantail "cats." *U.S. Navy*

with the Allied leaders. To cross the Atlantic to North Africa, he chose the *Iowa*, which was commanded by his former naval aide, Captain John McCrea. For this passage, the *Iowa* was fitted with a square bathtub was fitted in the captain's quarters for the president to use. That bathtub was the only one ever fitted on a U.S. naval ship, and it still remains on board today.

Following his Armistice Day speech at Arlington National Cemetery 11 November 1943, Roosevelt boarded his presidential yacht, the *Potomac*, and rendezvoused with the *Iowa* upstream from the mouth of the Potomac River. The ship then proceeded to Hampton Roads for fueling. Captain McCrea informed the president that he wanted to get his ship under way for sea at 11:00 P.M. on 12 November because that was the time of high tide, and thus the greatest clearance for the ship's bottom. Roosevelt, who had loved the sea since his youth, recalled the old sailor's superstition against starting an important voyage on a Friday. So he asked McCrea to begin the voyage on Saturday. The *Iowa*'s anchor broke ground just after midnight on 13 November and she began her momentous journey. Whether because of superstition or not, she was able to sail without mishap the following day.

On the sunny but windy Sunday afternoon of 14 November, the battleship steamed eastward. Her original escort had been replaced by four destroyers, the crews of which were unaware that the president was on board the *Iowa*. Suddenly, all of the *Iowa*'s crew were riveted by an announcement over the ship's loudspeaker system: "General quarters. This ain't no drill!" The escorting destroyers had been conducting exercises, and the *William D. Porter*, while simulating a torpedo attack on the *Iowa*, mistakenly launched a live, fully armed torpedo at *Iowa*. Her crew had sent a radio message, "Torpedo on the starboard beam," to warn the battleship, which then went to full speed and turned to starboard to present a bow on target, (as small a target as possible). The torpedo exploded in the turbulence created by the *Iowa*'s wake, only about 100 yards astern. Admiral Ernest J. King, Chief of Naval Operations and commander in chief, United States Fleet, was aboard the *Iowa* for the voyage. While glaring at the offending destroyer and probably trying to think of a suitably cruel punishment for the offending destroyer's skipper, General Hap Arnold, chief of the army air forces and a fellow member of the Joint Chiefs of Staff, yanked the admiral's chain by asking, "Tell me, Ernest, does this happen often in your Navy?"

Fast battleships served in the Atlantic until 1943, mostly on their post-construction shakedown cruises and convoy duty (with the notable exception of Operation Torch). The *Massachusetts* is seen beneath the muzzles of the after 16-inch guns of the *Alabama* while the dreadnoughts were at Casco Bay, Maine, in January 1943. Both ships later went to the Pacific. *U.S. Navy*

The *Alabama,* like many other U.S. fast battleships and old dreadnoughts, served in both the Atlantic and Pacific theaters during World War II. Although ships of both categories suffered battle damage—the older ships primarily from kamikazes—no U.S. battleship was lost after the debacle at Pearl Harbor. In the foreground are the barrels of 20mm Oerlikon antiaircraft guns. *U.S. Navy*

## THE AMPHIBIOUS SUPPORT MISSION

In late 1943, with carrier protection against air threats available, and with an increased number of oilers available to supply fuel, the old battleships finally found a suitable first-line mission with the beginning of the amphibious campaign in the Central Pacific in November 1943. The first target was the Gilbert Islands. The old battleships had two primary roles: bombardment of the islands prior to the invasion force hitting the beach, and gunfire support of soldiers and marines once they were ashore. The battleships weren't required to do any high-speed steaming. Instead, they would get close to the islands and unleash their big guns in concert with the smaller 8-inch, 6-inch, and 5-inch guns carried by heavy cruisers, light cruisers, and destroyers, respectively.

On 20 November 1943 a powerful bombardment force consisting of several old 14-inch-gun battleships and the 16-inch-gun *Maryland* descended on Tarawa and Makin Atolls. While marines were assaulting the bitterly defended island of Betio (part of Tarawa Atoll)

in the Gilberts, army troops were hitting nearby Makin. Included in the fire-support ships at the latter were the *Pennsylvania*, the *Idaho*, the *New Mexico*, and the *Mississippi*. They joined with airpower to shatter the Japanese defenses at Makin, and Rear Admiral Richmond Kelly Turner directed the island's capture from his flagship, the *Pennsylvania*.

Tarawa was a harder nut to crack. Rear Admiral Harry Hill in the battleship *Maryland* led the assault force. The naval bombardment by the *Maryland*, the *Tennessee*, and other ships blanketed the island, cut communications, and silenced most of the enemy's heavy guns. However, concealed defenses, including heavy blockhouses that might have been knocked out in a longer bombardment, and a dodging tide that caused the assault craft to ground well offshore, set up major obstacles for the gallant marines. Nevertheless, they fought on, ably supported by navy guns and planes. On 23 November, after several days of savage fighting, Tarawa fell into American hands.

The *Maryland* was lightly damaged at Pearl Harbor, hence when rebuilt she retained her forward cage mast and twin funnels. Little else in her superstructure resembled the prewar dreadnought. Her 16-inch guns were used for shore bombardment and, at Surigao Strait in October 1944, she and five other old battleships participated in history's last battleship-versus-battleship combat. *U.S. Navy*

During the initial bombardment of the island, a loud hiss of gas and flames shot out of the range-finder ports on either side of Turret No. 2 on the *Mississippi.* The turret had suffered an internal explosion. The report, "Fire in the lower handling room of turret two," was sent to the bridge. The officer of the deck realized that if the fire reached the powder magazines, the ship would blow up. The commanding officer, Captain Lunsford L. Hunter, contemplated flooding the magazines, but first he sent the chief boatswain to investigate. The boatswain reported that the fire had been extinguished, but nearly everybody in the top levels of the turret had been killed or injured by the explosion. The other three 14-inch turrets kept shooting. The eventual death toll was 43. The explosion was probably caused when powder was inserted into a barrel that still contained a smoldering remnant from the previous firing.

In the predawn hours, as part of the normal procedure for observing the effects of gunfire, the *Maryland* prepared to launch an OS2U floatplane in order to have a spotter aloft during the bombardment. While the aircraft was still on the catapult, the plane's observer saw a flash on Betio and then heard a splash near the ship. The Japanese were firing at the ship; the plane's exhaust flames had given the enemy gunners a target in the darkness.

The Gilberts operation proved to be costly in lives. However, the U.S. forces were eventually victorious, thanks in large part to the fire support of the battleships.

The Central Pacific Force, established on 5 August 1943, was renamed the Fifth Fleet on 26 April 1944. It was a formidable armada under the command of Vice Admiral Raymond A. Spruance, hero of Midway. His first huge task was sweeping the Gilbert-Marshall chain free of Japanese forces. The versatile battleship, having proved her worth as a command ship, antiaircraft station, and gun platform for shore bombardment, became a principal part of the Fifth Fleet. With enormous firepower, higher speed, and battle ruggedness, the new battleships of the *North Carolina, South Dakota,* and later *Iowa* classes were perfect consorts for the aircraft carriers. The older battleships likewise went to the forefront in the role of "fire-support powerhouses" in amphibious operations. Before a landing, their deliberate fire knocked out a large part of the enemy's shore defenses. Afterward, they well supported the troops with precise call-fire missions.

In early 1944, while the *Colorado* was bombarding the Marshall Islands, she opened up with a broadside of 16-inch projectiles. The aerial spotter radioed

The *Pennsylvania* was the Pacific Fleet flagship at the time of the Pearl Harbor attack. By August 1944, when this photo was taken, the *Pennsylvania* was bombarding Guam with her 14-inch guns. Major task-force commanders flew their flags in fast battleships, cruisers, or specialized amphibious command ships. Note the main deck lines forward, the single catapult aft. *U.S. Navy*

in an interesting report: "Up five miles, right three islands." The ship had fired at the wrong island. Such wild fire direction was, in fact, an exception to the rule. The heavy casualties inflicted on the marines in the Gilberts led to heavier preinvasion bombardment in later assaults. The old prewar battleships were able to specialize in firing at shore targets and enemy troop concentrations, and became quite skilled. They were also the beneficiaries of reconnaissance photos and even three-dimensional terrain maps, so that gunfire directors on board ship could visualize in advance what the targets would look like from offshore. In contrast to the bloodbath at the Gilberts, the invasion of the Marshalls was a textbook success. After Makin and Tarawa, the old battleships had little time to cool their gun barrels as they trained for the amphibious assaults to come.

The Fifth Amphibious Force struck Kwajalein only two months after the Gilberts. Having to spread resources throughout the Pacific, the Japanese had naturally given less attention to the islands to the west like Eniwetok. While Admiral Spruance was pushing through the Marshalls on the near route to Japan, the Seventh Fleet spearheaded General MacArthur's advance along New Guinea toward the Philippines. During February 1944, the fast carrier task force, including its screen of battleships, demonstrated the mobility and striking power that were to be its trademark throughout the inexorable island-hopping campaign toward Japan. In mid-February carrier planes attacked the Japanese stronghold of Truk in the Caroline Islands, and the *Iowa* and the *New Jersey* joined other surface warships in going after Japanese ships escaping from Truk Lagoon. A week later, the fast battleships were in the carrier screens as they approached the Mariana Islands for a softening-up strike in preparation for yet another step in the road to Japan.

In the darkness on the night of 21 February, the ships of Task Group 58.2 came under air attack. The 5-inch gun mounts of the *Alabama* were under radar control by Mark 37 directors and went into automatic fire when Japanese aircraft came within range. The ship maneuvered during the attack and swung to the right. The 5-inch mounts continued to track the low-flying planes, so their barrels essentially moved to stay on target as the ship rotated under them, until the guns finally reached the limit of their mobility. They stopped shooting because of firing cutout cams, which are devices that prevented guns from shooting

at other parts of the ship. Tragically, a man in gun mount number five on the starboard side overrode the safety feature and fired the mount's two guns directly into the back of mount number nine. The blast killed five men and injured 11. Despite the man's nine months of experience in the gun mount, the reasons for this accident have never been adequately explained.

## "THANK GOD FOR THE UNITED STATES NAVY"

Though the Pacific Fleet grabbed most of the battleships during World War II, and in early June 1944 was preparing for the conquest of the Marianas, a few of the older ones, namely, the *Nevada*, the *Arkansas*, and the *Texas*, remained in the Atlantic and provided shore bombardment in the amphibious assault on a continent. On D-Day, 6 June 1944, as Turner sailed for Saipan, halfway around the world and long before dawn the Normandy invasion unleashed power from the sea like a giant storm. The *Nevada*, damaged at Pearl Harbor and later active in the Attu landings in the Aleutians, was bombing German shore batteries and installations on the Normandy coast. On another quarter, the *Arkansas*, the oldest U.S. battleship in World War II, and the *Texas* also pounded the beaches along with other ships, opening breaches in the enemy coastal defenses that permitted advances inland. In addition, calls for gunfire support from paratroopers started coming in at an ever-increasing pace.

Around 5:30 A.M. there was just enough daylight for the Germans to make out the *Arkansas* a few miles off Omaha Beach, and they opened up on the ship with 88mm guns. The shells didn't hit, but were close enough to throw up shrapnel on deck. The "Arky" responded with gunfire and silenced the German 88s.

Later in the day, as the Allied troops moved ashore, the Germans shifted their gunfire from the ships to the men who were landing. The Germans commanded the heights above Omaha Beach and were able to pour down withering machine-gun fire on the men as they stepped out of their landing craft. The battleships elevated their guns to destroy these fortifications, as well as enemy rail lines, truck convoys, artillery batteries, and troop concentrations well inland. This won the warm gratitude of the assault troops. That evening Major General Leonard T. Gerow drafted and sent this simple message: "Thank God for the United States Navy."

The 12-inch guns of the *Arkansas* complemented the 14-inch guns on the *Texas* in pouring rounds out in support of the troops ashore. Rear Admiral Carlton Bryant, tactical commander on the *Texas*, was alarmed by the chaos on land. Rounds fell near the *Texas*, as they had the *Arkansas*. From his vantage point on the bridge of the *Texas*, Bryant saw a gully that the American soldiers had to move up in order to get inland. He obtained permission to fire in that sector, and it produced an immediate result. German soldiers began coming out of the gully with their hands up.

On board the *Arkansas* during the first day of the invasion, men didn't have a chance to get regular meals, so they ate K rations at their battle station during that long, long day. The next morning, landing craft began bringing wounded soldiers out from the beach so they could get medical treatment on board the *Arkansas* and other ships offshore. The "Arky" stayed around for a couple more weeks; by then, the Allied soldiers had moved inland and were out of range of her guns. When the invasion of southern France began on 15 August 1944, the *Arkansas*, along with her Normandy compatriots the *Texas* and the *Nevada*, provided fire support for the landings.

As the need for battleships in the Atlantic rapidly decreased after the third week in August 1944, there was still a large need for them in the Pacific. So, after refits in the United States, the *Nevada*, the *Texas*, and the *Arkansas* headed west.

The Pearl Harbor survivor *Nevada*, photographed in September 1944, gave a good account of herself in the Atlantic during the D-Day invasion of Normandy with the *Arkansas* and the *Texas*. All three ships subsequently steamed for the Pacific, the *Arkansas* after seeing action in the Mediterranean. At war's end the only American battleship in the Atlantic area was the training ship *Wyoming*. *U.S. Navy*

# CHAPTER NINE

## WORLD WAR II

### THE ROAD TO VICTORY

In the spring and summer of 1944 the Central Pacific amphibious offensive moved on to the islands of Saipan, Guam, and Tinian in the Marianas. As usual, the fast battleships traveled with the carriers, and the old ones were assigned to shore bombardment.

The Marianas campaign involved dangers and effort beyond any yet met. Before the invasion of Saipan on 15 June 1944, first the seven new battleships under Vice Admiral Willis A. Lee in the *Washington*, then the old ones under Admiral Jesse B. Oldendorf, bombarded that island for two days. Thereafter, the *California*, the *Colorado*, the *Idaho*, the *Maryland*, the *New Mexico*, the *Pennsylvania*, and the *Tennessee* gave close support day after day to the hard-fighting troops, as well as protection to the transports against surprise sea attack.

On June 18, as the Japanese fleet approached to help their brethren dug in on Saipan, recently promoted Vice Admiral Lee in the *Washington* received a message from Vice Admiral Marc A. Mitscher, also recently promoted. Because the fast battleships were integrated in the carrier task groups, Mitscher asked Lee if he wanted to pull them out to form a battle line and take on the Japanese heavy surface combatants that night. After discussing the situation with his staff, Lee decided against it. As his staff gunnery officer later explained, Lee was concerned that the battleships had not rehearsed

**Left:** The first action of the war against Japan was the attack on the U.S. Battle Force at Pearl Harbor. Among the last shots fired in that conflict were from U.S. dreadnoughts bombarding the Japanese home islands on 14 July 1945. Here the *Indiana* fires a 16-inch salvo at Kamaishi, Japan. Beyond the *Indiana* is the *Massachusetts* and a U.S. heavy cruiser. *U.S. Navy*

Admiral William F. (Bill) Halsey Jr.—called "Bull Halsey" by the press—was an outstanding and outspoken U.S. commander. He flew his flag as Commander Third Fleet in the *New Jersey* in the latter part of the war. He continually sought action with Japanese battleships, but in the multiple battles of Leyte Gulf in October 1944, only the United States' old battleships fought Japanese dreadnoughts. *U.S. Navy*

together tactically. He had been in a night melee off Guadalcanal in late 1942 and knew how confusing it could be. Also, the Japanese superiority at night fighting could very well take away the advantages conferred by radar.

The following day, 19 June, the fast battleships were in plenty of action as they steamed with the aircraft carriers fighting off incoming Japanese planes. In a slaughter that came to be known as "the Great Marianas Turkey Shoot," American pilots shot down more than 300 Japanese aircraft, and ships' gunnery added to the total. The *South Dakota* was one of the ships in the screen. She was hit by a 500-pound bomb dropped from one of the Japanese planes that got through both the fighters and the antiaircraft fire. The explosion from the Japanese bomb killed 23 men and injured another 23.

During the battle for the island of Tinian, the *Colorado* was one of the older battleships called upon to provide gunfire support for the marines ashore. The ship moved to within about 2,000 yards of the beach for close-in support and ended up getting blasted herself. The crew did not realize that the Japanese still had active shore batteries on the island, and the *Colorado* was peppered with 22 rounds of 5-inch and 6-inch gunfire. The incoming fire did considerable damage to the ship's topside area and produced heavy casualties. The

only positive aspect was that the subsequent repair period produced an upgrade in the ship's combat capability. When the Japanese attacked Pearl Harbor back in December 1941, the only Pacific Fleet battleship not present was the *Colorado*, which was in the Puget Sound Navy Yard at Bremerton, Washington. As a result, she had not needed repairs or received the modernization packages that went to the more badly damaged old battleships. Consequently, she went through much of the war with antiquated fire-control equipment and the old 5-inch 51-caliber broadside guns. The latter could be fired only against surface targets and only off the ship's beam. When she returned to Bremerton for repairs, she received a Mark 8 radar, new fire-control computers, and modern 5-inch guns that could fire at both air and surface targets.

## "I HAVE RETURNED": THE INVASION OF THE PHILIPPINES

As Allied armies battled their way east and north across Europe, the Pacific Fleets steadily drove on west and north toward Japan. Admiral Nimitz's forces under the shield of carrier aircraft and battleships had swept in long amphibious leaps across the central Pacific. General Douglas MacArthur pushed in short jumps along New Guinea behind the spearhead of the Seventh

Fire! The camera catches six 16-inch projectiles in flight as the *Missouri* fires during her 1944 shakedown cruise. While the fast battleships were employed in shore bombardment and sought battle with Japanese dreadnoughts, after 1942 their most important role was providing antiaircraft defense for aircraft carriers with their massive batteries of 5-inch and 40mm guns. *U.S. Navy*

Fleet. Here, the Japanese had relatively weak shore defenses, except in certain locations that could usually be bypassed with the mobile fleet and the ability of the amphibians to land almost anywhere. Hence, except for the bombardment of Kavieng, New Ireland, in the Southwest Pacific, by the *Idaho*, the *New Mexico*, the *Mississippi*, and the *Tennessee* in March 1944, the heavy guns of the old battleships were employed in smashing the strong fortifications of the atolls and islands in the Central Pacific.

Leyte was different. In the two decades between the world wars, the war plans of both the Japanese and U.S. navies had contemplated a climactic battle-line gunnery duel that would take place in the western Pacific. At Leyte the Japanese concentrated their power. It was here that the climactic battleship duels of the war (and the battleship era) would take place. So, now the Central Pacific Fleet turned south to provide the air and gun power needed. After the fall of Guam, the old battleships blasted away at the caves of Peleliu in September 1944, hurriedly replenished, and prepared for Leyte. On 20 October 1944, carrying out MacArthur's promise, "I will return," the invasion fleet steamed into Leyte Gulf under an air umbrella from escort carriers and behind the great guns of the *California*, the *Maryland*, the *Mississippi*, the *Pennsylvania*, the *Tennessee*, and the *West Virginia*, the latter now back in battle line to even the score for Pearl Harbor.

The Japanese, meanwhile, assembled every available warship to frustrate the Philippine landings. Their effectiveness had been greatly diminished, particularly in airpower after the plane and pilot losses in the Battle of the Philippine Sea. Remaining strength afloat included the two gigantic battleships *Musashi* and *Yamato*, both the largest in the world, each mounting 18.1-inch guns.

On 23 October the Battle of Leyte Gulf began, with ensuing separate naval actions in the Sibuyan Sea, Surigao Strait, off the island of Samar and off Cape Engaño, as the Japanese attacked from widely separate directions. Hardly had the battle begun when two enemy cruisers were sunk and a third damaged by the submarines *Darter* and *Dace*. Land-based Japanese planes attacked part of the fast carrier force attached to Admiral Halsey's Third Fleet. Most were shot down, but one got through and dropped a bomb on the light carrier *Princeton*. Exploding torpedoes stowed below led to her loss and the serious damaging of the light cruiser *Birmingham*, which had come alongside the

The *Pennsylvania* leads a column of old battleships and heavy cruisers en route to Lingayen Gulf preceding the landings on Luzon in January 1945. Earlier, in October 1944, the *Pennsylvania* and five of her contemporaries—all but one a Pearl Harbor survivor—helped to defeat Japanese battleships at Surigao Strait during the invasion of Leyte. *U.S. Navy*

After being rebuilt, the *Tennessee* departs the Puget Sound Navy Yard in 1943 for the war in the Pacific. Like many of her contemporaries, she bears little outward resemblance to her former persona. Her secondary battery consists of sixteen 5-inch dual-purpose guns in twin mounts, supplemented by numerous "40s" and "20s." Note the similarities to the *South Dakota* design. *U.S. Navy*

A fleet of oilers, store ships, and ammunition ships replenished the battle fleet at sea, alleviating the need to return to port to rearm and provision. The goods could be transferred from ship to ship while under way. Here the battleship *Indiana* receives canisters containing powder bags for her 16-inch guns via high-line transfer from the ammunition ship *Wrangell* (AE 12). *U.S. Navy*

*Princeton* helping her to fight her fires. Fighters, torpedo planes, and bombers from six carriers pounded the super-battleship *Musashi*. Without air protection and overwhelmed by numbers, the giant took 17 bombs and 19 torpedoes before she sank, thanks to her commanding officer's incompetence, and sank in the Sibuyan Sea with great loss of life.

The Japanese had planned a three-pronged attack to get at the American transport ships off the invasion beaches of the island of Leyte. One of those prongs, comprising the battleships *Yamashiro* and *Fuso*, the cruiser *Mogami*, and four destroyers, tried to enter Leyte Gulf through Surigao Strait to reach the beachhead. Standing in the way of the Japanese force was a bombardment outfit consisting of six old battleships, as well as eight cruisers, 28 destroyers, and a flock of motor torpedo boats. An additional disadvantage was that the American positions enabled them to "cross the T," that is, to steam perpendicular to the advancing Japanese, enabling the American battleships to shoot all their turrets broadside, while the Japanese could shoot only their forward turrets at the U.S. ships.

This battle took place during the early hours of 25 October. Even as the Japanese steamed through the smaller ships, they suffered considerable damage. The battleship *Fuso*, which was equipped with a towering superstructure, caught destroyer-launched torpedoes,

broke in two, and sank. Others steamed on toward the reception committee of battleships that included the *Maryland*, the *Mississippi*, the *Pennsylvania*, the *West Virginia*, the *California*, and the *Tennessee*, most of which had been equipped with the latest main battery fire-control radar, the Mark 8, during their Pearl Harbor repairs. These ships did the bulk of the shooting, since they were able to acquire and lock onto their targets.

At 3:52 in the morning the *West Virginia* got off the first salvo at a range of 22,400 yards. From their vantage point the *West Virginia*'s commanding officer and personnel saw the explosions on *Yamashiro* as the "Weevee's" projectiles struck home. The darkness was interrupted time and again as the guns of the *West Virginia*, the *Tennessee*, and the *California* erupted in convulsions of fire and sent projectiles arching through the night, tracing red trails across the sky, seeking vengeance.

It was also a night of frustration for the *Mississippi*. She had the older Mark 3 radar, but the plotting room officer was still able to hold a firing solution (range and bearing to the target) on one of the Japanese ships. However, in accordance with doctrine, the *Mississippi*'s skipper directed his ship, the third in the column, to concentrate fire on the third ship in the Japanese line (not the one they had the fire-control solution on). That destroyed the fire-control solution, and the ship's old fire-control radar was not able to recover. As the flagship of the task group, the *Mississippi* should have fired first, but because of the plotting problem, she couldn't. Thus, the other ships began pumping out rounds at the Japanese as fast as they could. When the ships later turned to a new course, the *Mississippi* and the *California* nearly collided. After the ships finally came around, the *Mississippi* got off one salvo of 12 projectiles. Then firing had to cease because the destroyer *Albert W. Grant* was hit, probably by U.S. projectiles, and the admiral understandably didn't want to risk further damage. The Japanese flagship, the battleship *Yamashiro*, was mortally wounded, but the cessation of American gunfire allowed two of her consorts to escape. The deliverance of one of them, the *Mogami*, was short-lived; she soon collided with a Japanese heavy and finally was sunk by air attack after daybreak.

Another facet of the three-pronged Japanese attack on Leyte Gulf was the deployment of a force of battleships and cruisers that intended to steam through San Bernardino Strait in the Philippine

Archipelago and then leap upon the invasion transports that were still near the beachheads. Admiral William F. Halsey Jr., commander, Third Fleet, had prepared for this possibility by designating the fast battleships as Task Force 34 for use in a potential surface engagement. Unfortunately, he was lured off to the north by a Japanese carrier force that proved to be essentially devoid of planes. Halsey believed the Japanese force that was planned for San Bernardino Strait had been sufficiently beaten up by attacks from carrier planes that it was headed home. Vice Admiral Willis A. Lee wanted to stay behind with some of his battleships to guard the strait in the event Japanese battleships came through to attack the U.S. transports still at Leyte. He called Halsey's attention to sighting reports that indicated the Japanese force had turned around and was headed toward San Bernadino Strait and thus still constituted a threat. Nevertheless, the impulsive Halsey elected to take both the carriers and Lee's fast battleships so that he would have maximum striking power. As a result, the Japanese Center Force, an assemblage of battleships, cruisers, and destroyers under Admiral Takeo Kurita, surged through the unguarded strait and fell upon a small force of destroyers, destroyer escorts, and small aircraft carriers. This was Admiral Clifton Sprague's "Taffy 3," a force solely trained for rendering air support to the invading U.S. troops, and the engagement that followed was known as the Battle off Samar. Had the Japanese gotten through that force, there was nothing between them and the transports and the destruction of the invasion.

In response to myriad pleas for help, most of them broadcast in plain language, Halsey reluctantly turned his force south, but didn't arrive until after the Japanese battleships had left the scene to return home. When victory seemed certain for the Japanese, they withdrew. In the end, the fast battleships had steamed hundreds of miles north, then hundreds of miles south, but never got into action. Had the fast battleships of Task Force 34 been left behind, it would have given Vice Admiral Lee the chance he had prepared for all his professional life. He had the ships to do the job and he also had a superior tactical situation: the ability to cross the Japanese "T" as the old battleships had done at Surigao Strait. However, because of Halsey's tactical mistake in not leaving Task Force 34 to guard the strait, Admiral Lee was denied the opportunity.

The commanders of the Seventh and Third Fleets acted to relieve the critical situation Taffy 3 was in. Aircraft diverted from routine and other missions brought much-needed aid to Taffy 3 before it was too late. Admiral Kinkaid (commander, Seventh Fleet) lost no time in notifying Halsey, in a plain-language dispatch sent on 25 October at 7:07 A.M. and received at 8:22 A.M., that enemy battleships and cruisers were firing on Taffy 3. This was followed by another dispatch, originated at 7:25 A.M., in which Kinkaid said that Oldendorf's battleships were low on ammunition; this reached Halsey only at 9:22 A.M. At 7:27 A.M. Admiral Kinkaid radioed in plain English, and Halsey received the message at 9:00 A.M.: "Request Lee proceed top speed to cover Leyte; request immediate strike by fast carriers." Sprague, too, let Halsey know at 7:35 A.M. that he was under attack by battleships and heavy cruisers. More particulars and repeated requests from Kinkaid to Halsey followed at 7:39 A.M.: "Help needed from heavy ships immediately." Another message at 8:29 A.M.: "Situation critical, battleships and fast carrier strike wanted to prevent enemy penetrating Leyte Gulf." Halsey replied at 9:27 A.M. that he was himself engaged with Admiral Ozawa's Northern Force, but had (at 8:48 A.M.) ordered Admiral McCain's carrier group to assist the Seventh Fleet immediately. The problem was that McCain was then refueling hundreds of miles to the east and was unable to get the carriers the new *Hancock*, the new *Hornet*, and the new *Wasp* to a new launching position 335 miles northeast of the Japanese Center Force until 10:30 A.M. After the carriers arrived at that destination, it took another hour and a half for their planes to reach the target. There was some hope of Halsey's turning back Task Force 34, Admiral Lee's battle line, to engage Kurita; and that is what Halsey finally did, but too late, after repeated needling by Kinkaid and even Nimitz, who pointedly asked, "Where is Task Force 34? The world wonders."

Now comes the logical question: Why wasn't Admiral Oldendorf's battle line sent out to help the Taffies after it had disposed of the Japanese Southern Force? The word spread around that these ships were left very short of armor-piercing ammunition (AP) after the battle. That was in some measure true. The light cruisers had been pouring it out liberally, as light cruisers tended to do, so that they only had 50 to 80 rounds apiece of AP left, but an ample supply of high capacity (HC) ammunition, which in that caliber can, in the opinion of some cruiser commanders, be profitably employed against ships. Supply officers went at once in search of replenishment, but found that the two ammunition ships in Leyte Gulf were difficult to locate, and on top of that those ships had no 6-inch AP to offer.

The following table tells the story of the battleships' main-battery ammunition, which would have been crucial had they engaged Kurita:

## BATTLESHIPS' EXPENDITURE OF MAIN-BATTERY AMMUNITION, 18–25 OCTOBER 1944

| | AP | | | HC | | |
| | | Expended | | | Expended | |
| | On Board 17 Oct. | Bombardment 25 Oct | Left 25 Oct. | On Board 17 Oct. | Bombardment 25 Oct. | Left 25 Oct. |
|---|---|---|---|---|---|---|
| *16-inch (8 guns)* | | | | | | |
| WEST VIRGINIA | 200 | 93 | 197 | 616 | 440 | 172 |
| MARYLAND | 240 | 48 | 192 | 856 | 411 | 445 |
| | | | | | | |
| *14-inch (12 guns)* | | | | | | |
| TENNESSEE | 396 | 69 | 327 | 960 | 692 | 262 |
| CALIFORNIA | 240 | 63 | 177 | 960 | 882 | 78 |
| MISSISSIPPI | 201 | 12 | 189 | 1,200 | 657 | 543 |
| PENNSYLVANIA | 360 | 0 | 360 | 960 | 946 | 14 |

* "Left 25 October" means ammunition left after the battle.

It will be observed that the *Maryland*, the *Tennessee*, and the *Pennsylvania* had 24 rounds or better of AP per gun; the *Mississippi*, 15-3/4 rounds; and the *West Virginia* and the *California* a trifle over 13 rounds per gun. Every gunnery officer wants his magazines full, but the shortage here was nothing to be alarmed about.

What help Admiral Oldendorf could have afforded the escort carriers is doubtful, for at 8:00 A.M. he was a good 65 miles (over three hours' steaming) from gunfire range of the position where the Japanese Center Force turned away at 9:25 A.M. The admiral was eager to do his best to help; but his chief of staff insisted that the proper strategy was to keep his ships together inside Leyte Gulf and do battle where "we, not he" chose. If Kurita had overrun Taffy 3 and steamed farther into the gulf, Admiral Oldendorf might have been able to "cross the T" again with his battle line. He had enough ammunition for that kind of battle, but not for a running fight. And a running fight Oldendorf would have had, had he steamed to Taffy 3's aid.

The Battle of Surigao Strait marks the end of an era in naval warfare. It was the last naval battle in which airpower played no part, except in the pursuit. It was the last engagement of a battle line.

The battle line, as a tactical device for naval combat, dates from the reign of James I, when Sir Walter Raleigh ordered the Royal Navy to abandon attempts to board, as the main objective, in favor of "the whole fleet" following "the admiral, vice-admiral, or other leading ship within musket shot of the enemy. Which you shall batter in pieces, or . . . drive them foul one to another to their utter confusion."

The battle line was first successfully employed in 1655 by James, Duke of York, against the Dutch Admiral Opdum in the Battle of Lowestoft. A standard tactic throughout the days of sail, the battle line was used in all great sea battles, such as Beachy Head, Ushant, the Capes of the Chesapeake, the Battle of the Saints, Cape St. Vincent, and Trafalgar. With ever-increasing range, it served equally well in the era of steam and high-powered ordnance, because it enabled ships of a battle line (from which the term *battleship* is derived) to render mutual support, and, if properly deployed against an irresolute enemy or one with an imperfect line, to defeat him piecemeal. Dewey's victory at Manila Bay, Sampson's off Santiago, Togo's at Tsushima, and the Battle of Jutland were classic line-of-battle actions in the nineteenth and twentieth centuries. The death knell of the battle line was sounded by the development of airpower, which made it impossible to maintain line under air attack; and the only line actions in the Pacific war in which airpower played no part were the night actions off Guadalcanal and Empress Augusta Bay, Rear Admiral McMorris' Komandorski fight on 26 March 1943, and the Battle of Surigao Strait. Thus, when the *Mississippi* discharged her twelve 14-inch guns at the *Yamashiro*, at a range of 19,790 yards, at 4:08 A.M. on 25 October 1944 at Surigao Strait, she was not only giving that battleship the *coup de grâce*, but firing a funeral salute to a finished era of naval warfare. One can imagine the ghosts of all great admirals from Raleigh to Jellicoe standing at attention as the battle line went into obsolescence, to join the Greek phalanx, the Spanish wall of pikemen, the English longbow, and the row-galley tactics of Salamis and Lepanto.

A Japanese kamikaze about to strike the battleship *Missouri*, just below a port-side 5-inch gun mount (a quad 40mm mount is in the foreground). Striking the hull, the suicidal pilot inflicted only superficial damage. Other ships—including some old battleships—suffered grievously from the kamikazes. But no U.S. ship larger than destroyer was lost to the "divine wind." *U.S. Navy*

## BIRTH OF THE "DIVINE WIND"

Soon after the Battle of Surigao Strait, the Japanese threw still another weapon at the American ships off Leyte. This was the kamikaze suicide plane. The Japanese had raised self-sacrifice to yet another level and had committed to a program of crashing bomb-laden aircraft into the ships, using an onboard human guidance system.

On 27 November 1944, two days after the *Colorado* was hit by two kamikazes (19 dead, 72 wounded, and moderate damage), resulting in her receiving the ignominious honor of being the first battleship damaged by kamikazes, it became the *Maryland*'s turn. On the evening of 29 November a Japanese plane suddenly emerged from a patch of sky directly overhead and plunged almost straight down, executed a few last maneuvers, then crashed into Turret No. 2. Men stumbled out of the rapidly spreading flames, their faces blackened and their uniforms on fire. They ran down the deck, got the fires put out, then ran back to their battle stations. After the explosion, those who were topside saw a hole where the kamikaze's 550-pound bomb had plunged through the deck, penetrated down several levels, and then exploded when it hit an armored deck below. It wiped out the ship's sick bay, ignited another fire, and killed 31 men.

On 9 January 1945 U.S. forces invaded Lingayen Gulf on the island of Luzon. This had been the invasion site for the Japanese three years earlier when they had conquered the Philippines. On the same day, a suicide plane crashed into a 5-inch gun mount on the *Mississippi*. The airplane's bomb went over the side and exploded just above the ship's waterline. Pieces of shrapnel pierced the ship's side and traveled through the room next to Barnes', then on into the warrant officers' mess, where they injured a few men. Outside, the devastation was far worse. Gasoline burned in pools on the deck, and men frantically threw ammunition over the side so the fire wouldn't set it off. The kamikaze's last flight had come out of the sun, so gunners didn't see him until he smashed into the battleship. Of the *Mississippi*'s crew, 26 were killed and another 63 were either wounded or burned.

## THE FINAL AMPHIBIOUS OPERATIONS

On 24 January 1945 seven U.S. battleships brought their batteries to bear in Japan's home waters; their target was the island of Iwo Jima. Present were the *Colorado*, the *Idaho*, the *Maryland*, and the *Tennessee*, sturdy stalwarts of the Pacific war; the *Nevada*, the *Texas*, and the *Arkansas*, veterans of the Normandy and southern France invasions; and the *New York*.

Their main guns smashed targets previously invulnerable to attempts to destroy them. For example, the *Nevada* knocked out blockhouse after blockhouse threatening the landings. Later she took under fire the heights beyond the beach. Two rounds took care of a gun firing from a cave; they tore a great hole in the cliff, and when the dust settled both cave and gun had disappeared.

It was a desperate campaign that Lieutenant General Holland M. Smith, USMC, called "the most savage and most costly" in Marine Corps history. Admiral Chester W. Nimitz observed that "uncommon valor was a common virtue" at Iwo Jima. Yet, the cost would have been far greater without the punishing fire of the old battleships and other fire-support ships that day after day served the marines well. Furthermore, the

A trio of old battleships—the *New Mexico* is closest to the camera and a sister ship is next closest—steams toward an amphibious landing operation in early 1945. Beyond the dreadnoughts is an amphibious command ship, a World War II innovation for carrying an amphibious force commander and the landing force commander and their staffs. They direct all aspects of the landing, including assignment of shore targets to the battleships. *U.S. Navy*

Amphibious tractors ("amtracs") packed with marines pass the battleship *Tennessee* as the dreadnought bombards the landing beaches at Okinawa on 1 April 1945—the final amphibious landing of the Pacific war. According to marine commanders, there was never enough gunfire support for the Pacific landings; this was caused, in part, by the fast battleships being needed to screen aircraft carriers. *U.S. Navy*

capture of Iwo Jima, with its air field, contributed much to final victory by providing emergency landing facilities for the B-29s that were attacking Japan. All of the many B-29 pilots who landed safely on Iwo instead of having to ditch into the sea echoed the words of one of them, "whenever I land on this island, I thank God and the marines who fought for it."

Battleships old and new continued their victorious roles in the last giant amphibious assault, the invasion of Okinawa, the door to Japan. On 24 March 1945, following five days of attack by carrier aircraft on the Japanese mainland, the fast battleships *Alabama, Iowa, Indiana, Massachusetts, Missouri, New Jersey, North Carolina, South Dakota, Washington,* and *Wisconsin* were temporarily diverted from protecting the carriers so they could bombard the strong Okinawa defenses. Then, 10 old battleships, masters of shore bombardment, took over the bombardment under the command of a noted master of gunnery, Rear Admiral W.H.P. Blandy. The ships were the *Arkansas,* the *Colorado,* the *Idaho,* the *Maryland,* the *New Mexico,* the *New York,* the *Nevada,* the *Tennessee,* the *Texas,* and the *West Virginia.* Under his command, in a day-after-day unhurried precision bombardment, they knocked out enemy batteries and strong points. Although close to Japan, and open to a swarm of kamikaze attacks, the battleships cruised offshore, methodically blasting targets. Their effective preparatory fire, and the Japanese' bitter experience in trying to resist previous landings on the beach against the hail of gunfire from support ships of all sizes, led the enemy to draw back its main forces so that the marines and soldiers went ashore standing up on 1 April. The planners had considered that it might take a week to capture Yontan air field, yet so much had the foe pulled back that the marines swarmed over the field by noon of the day they landed.

The Japanese attempted a final naval effort to stem the American advance. On 7 April, after they had spent six days bombarding Okinawa, the crew of the *Maryland* was at morning quarters when they received news that the Japanese battleship *Yamato,* accompanied by the light cruiser *Yahagi* and destroyers, were headed their way. The Japanese task force had only enough fuel for a one-way trip. The *Yamato,* with her 18.1-inch guns, had been reduced to what was essentially a suicide mission to fight for the honor of what little remained of Japan's heavy surface combatants. American warships set out to intercept the incoming ship, but carrier planes got to her first and sank her with heavy loss of life.

## BOMBARDING THE JAPANESE HOME ISLANDS

As the summer of 1945 approached, American carrier forces, supported as always by fast battleships, launched air strikes against the Japanese home islands, augmenting those already coming from bombers based in the Marianas. The fast battleships were also peeled off from time to time to bombard the Japanese Islands, something they could do with impunity since Japanese airpower no longer existed.

Victory: Sailors and marines crowd the superstructure of the *Missouri* as Allied and Japanese officials sign the "instruments of surrender" aboard the dreadnought on 2 September 1945. The *Missouri* was selected as being named for the home state of President Harry S. Truman, and having been christened by his daughter, Margaret, less than two years earlier.
*U.S. Army Signal Corps*

On 14 July a force under Rear Admiral John F. Shafroth delivered the first major shore bombardment of the Japanese home islands. The force consisted of the battleships *South Dakota*, *Indiana*, and *Massachusetts*, along with the heavy cruisers *Chicago* and *Quincy* and nine destroyers. The target, the Japan Iron Company Steel Mill at Kamaishi, Honshu, was left in ruins.

The following day, three of the newest battleships, the *Iowa*, the *Wisconsin*, and the *Missouri*, bombarded the steel-production facilities at Muroran, Hokkaido, Japan's northernmost island. They used full powder charges for their 16-inch rounds, because they were firing from ranges of around 30,000 yards. The ships' spotting planes came under fire from anti-

aircraft batteries. Once the ships started firing, "urban renewal" began. Chimneys fell over and the American projectiles generally made a shambles of the facility.

On 9 August Admiral Shafroth's bombardment force, consisting of the *South Dakota*, the *Indiana*, the *Massachusetts*, cruisers, and destroyers, returned once again to Kamaishi to inflict further damage. The three dreadnoughts fired more than 800 rounds of 16-inch projectiles in more than an hour and a half of shooting. The gunnery officer on the *Massachusetts* had to call a temporary halt near the end of the operation because of a problem in Turret No. 2. When it was solved and the turret was ready to fire, the other two battleships had completed their bombardments. The captain

then gave him permission to shoot the remainder of the rounds allotted for the operation. As a result, the *Massachusetts* fired the first and last battleship main-battery rounds in combat during the war. She had opened hostilities with her 16-inch guns in North Africa in November 1942, less than a week before Admiral Lee's savage night battle of Guadalcanal.

## VICTORY

In early August the *North Carolina*, the *Missouri*, and many other ships received a radio directive to remain some 150 miles away from the southern islands of Japan on certain dates. The order engendered all sorts of speculation about what their fellow Americans might do next. They soon found out. On 6 and 9 August two Army Air Forces B-29s dropped atomic bombs on the cities of Hiroshima and Nagasaki. In less than a week, on 14 August, the Japanese government agreed to surrender. The war was over. Admiral Halsey, embarked on the *Missouri*, joined in the celebration. He also learned that his flagship was to be the site of the formal surrender ceremony to mark the end of hostilities.

A large number of Allied warships made their way into Tokyo Bay in late August to attend the proceedings. The ceremony itself was held on 2 September. The British battleship *Duke of York* sent a beautiful mahogany table for the signing, but it wasn't big enough to accommodate the surrender documents, so a working party rustled up a mess table from the crew's eating area and carried it to the captain's promenade deck. A green tablecloth from the officers' wardroom completed the decor. General of the Army Douglas MacArthur, the master of ceremonies for the event, made an opening speech that struck an English-speaking Japanese diplomat as remarkably magnanimous. Then Japan's foreign minister, Mamoru Shigemitsu, came forward to sign on behalf of his nation, as did General Yoshijiro Umezo, Chief of the Imperial General Staff. After that, General MacArthur signed to accept the surrender, followed by representatives of the various Allied nations.

At the conclusion of this discussion of World War II, it is appropriate to spotlight the *Arkansas*, the oldest battleship to see service during that conflict. By the end of the war, she had been in commission 34 years, traveled some 13,000 miles of ocean using machinery that was allegedly too aged to function, and fired nearly 2.5 tons of ammunition from turrets

Scores of photographers and cameramen share the *Missouri*'s bridge and conning tower during the surrender ceremony. The encased flag at the lower right was flown from the flagship of Commodore Matthew C. Perry when he arrived in Yedo (Tokyo) Bay on 14 July 1853 to negotiate the opening of Japan to Western trade. It was sent to Japan from the U.S. Naval Academy in Annapolis, Maryland. *U.S. Army Signal Corps*

As the surrender ceremony came to a conclusion, about a thousand U.S. carrier planes—from the fast carrier force, which had remained at sea—and hundreds of B-29 Superfortress bombers overflew the *Missouri* and other Allied ships in Tokyo Bay. The ship seen between the *Missouri*'s guns is the amphibious command ship *Ancon*. Barrett Gallagher/U.S. Navy

and mounts once considered ready to be scrapped. In early May 1946 the battleship steamed beneath the Golden Gate Bridge and headed for Pearl Harbor, arriving on 8 May 1946. She departed on 20 May 1946, sailing southwest heading toward Bikini Atoll. On 25 July 1946, at the atoll, the *Arkansas* was anchored for use as a target in Operation Crossroads' Test Baker, the underwater blast. On that date Atomic Bomb Number

5 was set off by radio signals. A few seconds before 8:30 A.M. an atomic explosion took place, and 20 minutes later, the *Arkansas* was gone beneath the waters. She was formally decommissioned 29 July 1946 and her name stricken from the Navy List on 15 August 1946.

In 1921 airpower-minded propagandists, as we have seen, had predicted the end of battleships, and indeed of surface navies. Now again in 1945 new military

prophets were sure that the day of the battleship was at last over, and with it that of the new "ship of the line," the far-ranging aircraft carrier that had spearheaded and played a major role in victory. Nuclear power and long-range missiles, along with long-range heavy bombers, they claimed, had made both the battleship and the carrier and most other surface warships a thing of the past. Many men were deluded and put their faith in a single weapon, the atomic bomb, transported in a high-flying plane. Hence, battleships that had been indispensable to victory were rapidly decommissioned. Shortsighted men even forced the retirement of most of the navy's carriers and envisioned the disposition of all of them in a short time. Hence, the navy began to lose at the same time the authoritative power of the battleship's big guns and the far-reaching precise attack capabilities of its aircraft carriers. In five years they would be needed again.

The *West Virginia* anchored in Sagami Wan, outside of Tokyo Bay, with Mount Fuji in the background. In late August the *West Virginia* and other ships of the U.S. and British Pacific Fleets moved into Japanese waters, their guns at last silent. Admiral Nimitz ordered Admiral Raymond A. Spruance in his flagship *New Jersey* off Okinawa to be ready to take command of the fast carrier force "just in case" the Japanese intention was treachery rather than surrender. *U.S. Navy*

# CHAPTER TEN

# THE COLD WAR AND VIETNAM

**W**ith peace obtained, the United States no longer needed a navy as large as the one it had fielded during World War II. The last mission of many of the battleships was to serve in Operation Magic Carpet as well-armed transport ships for the bringing of sailors and soldiers home from battlefields overseas.

The contrast between old prewar ships and the new ones was well symbolized at the Navy Day celebration in New York City on 27 October 1945. Several dozen warships moored in the Hudson River, on the western edge of Manhattan. The newest battleship, the 887-foot, 57,000-ton *Missouri*, was moored just astern of the next-to-oldest battleship in the fleet, the *New York*, which was 573 feet long and displaced 32,000 tons. President Truman ate lunch on board the ship named for his home state, sat at the table where the surrender documents had been signed the previous month, and proclaimed, "This is the happiest day of my life." Then he transferred to the destroyer *Renshaw* for a trip up and down the Hudson, receiving 21-gun salutes along the way. The *Missouri*, just over a year old, was assured a place in the postwar fleet. The *New York*, more than 30 years old by then, was running out of time.

During the spring of 1946 the Soviet Union took advantage of unrest to try to spread the empire of communism. That ideology was gaining in popularity among the

**Left:** Battleships were active during part of the Cold War, seeing combat in the Korean War (1950–53), Vietnam (1967), and during operations in the Middle East-Persian Gulf (1983–91). Here the recently reactivated *New Jersey* loads munitions at Hampton Roads, Virginia, before undertaking her single operational deployment to Vietnam. *Norman Polmar*

From the bridge of the destroyer *Renshaw* President Harry S. Truman waves at crowds on the New York shoreline as the nation celebrates Navy Day on 27 October 1945. At right, smoke from a 21-gun salute lingers over the battleship *Missouri*; in the distance is the dreadnought *New York*. A navy patrol airship lingers overhead. Next to the president is Admiral Royal H. Ingram, Commander in Chief Atlantic Fleet. *U.S. Navy*

governments on the rim of the Mediterranean. The eastern Mediterranean in general, and Greece and Turkey in particular, became communist targets. The United States, as leader of the democratic world, made a counter-move. The battleship *Missouri*, fresh from the victories of Iwo Jima and Okinawa, and the scene of the Japanese surrender, was selected to show the flag around the eastern Mediterranean. A symbol and visible evidence of American power, her imposing presence would significantly influence events 5,000 miles away without firing a shot. This can also be defined as "gunboat diplomacy."

Taking on board the remains of the late Turkish Ambassador Mehmet Munir Ertegun—who died at his post in Washington, D.C., in 1944—on 21 March 1946, the *Missouri* steamed to Istanbul to deliver the diplomat's body, and there fired a 19-gun salute in honor of the dead statesman. She then proceeded to

Piraeus, Greece, to receive another enthusiastic welcome. The visit had far-reaching effects. Greek newspapers observed:

> Russia knocks threateningly at the land gates of Turkey. America knocks at the sea gates . . . in a friendly way and pays a visit, saying, "Don't be afraid, I'm here." The Russian shadow is cast over the Balkans. So America comes and tells us "Sit tight and don't worry. I'm with you." The arrival of *Missouri* is a gesture of good will . . . a symbol of freedom and justice for the whole world.

From Greece, the *Missouri* sailed to Italy, North Africa, and Gibraltar, showing the flag over much the same area as the sailing ships *Independence*, *Washington*, *Franklin*, *North Carolina*, and *Columbus* had done over a hundred years before. The famous journalist Walter Lippmann succinctly stated the key importance of U.S. sea power in the Mediterranean, which the *Missouri* had so dramatically highlighted. He noted, "The Red Army which dominates eastern Europe and could not be removed by a diplomatic frontal attack, can be out-flanked in the eastern Mediterranean."

U.S. sea power had steamed thousands of miles to influence events great and small in the cause of stability and peace. The trip to Turkey and Greece served this cause well. Soon afterward, the U.S. Navy began the regular deployment of warships to the Mediterranean, a pattern that continues to this day.

## OPERATION "CROSSROADS" AND THE OLD BATTLEWAGONS

Now that the atomic age had dawned, the navy planned to turn several old battleships into targets for atomic bomb tests at Bikini Atoll in July 1946. By April of that year, the *New York*, now operating on a skeleton crew, had returned to the Pacific in preparation for the journey to Bikini Atoll in the Marshall Islands. Upon her arrival the *New York* was anchored in her assigned spot among dozens of other target ships, including the *Nevada*; the *Pennsylvania*; the former Japanese fleet flagship, the battleship *Nagato*; and the former German heavy cruiser *Prinz Eugen*, which had accompanied the ill-fated *Bismarck* on her famous sortie into the Atlantic in May 1941. On 1 July the first of three scheduled tests, an airburst, was conducted. The *Nevada*, painted pink for the purpose, was used as the aiming point for the B-29's bombardier. She survived

this and the next test. On 25 July came a second explosion, this one under water. The *Arkansas* sank as a result. Her seagoing journey, which had begun in 1912, had finally ended. The third test, a deeper underwater explosion, was canceled.

After conducting radiological and other tests, the following three ships were sunk: the *Nevada* was sunk as a target 65 miles southwest of Pearl Harbor on 31 July 1948, the *Pennsylvania* was scuttled off the coast of Kwajalein Atoll on 10 February 1948, and the *New York* was sunk 40 miles southwest of Pearl Harbor on 8 July 1948.

## BATTLESHIP DEMOBILIZATION
The U.S. Navy, which had reached its peak in manpower and size at the end of the war, had been rapidly reduced in size. After nearly four years of fighting, the American public wanted to "bring the boys home."

Atomic bomb test Baker at Bikini Atoll on 25 July 1946. Four U.S. battleships were among the target ships for the two atomic detonations at Bikini—the *Arkansas*, the *Nevada* , the *New York*, and the *Pennsylvania*—as was one Japanese dreadnought, the *Nagato*. The *Nagato* had been Admiral Isoroku Yamamoto's flagship on 7 December 1941. Test Able at Bikini was an air-dropped bomb, test Baker a shallow-water detonation of an atomic bomb suspended under the landing ship LSM-60.
*U.S. Army Air Forces*

A Bikini survivor: The hulk of the battleship *Nevada* is towed from Bikini Atoll to Kwajalein for examination and study of the effects of nuclear weapons on ships. Like the battleship bombing tests of the 1920s, the navy had initiated the Bikini tests to determine protective features that should be incorporated in future warship construction.
*U.S. Navy*

The *Mississippi* launches a Terrier surface-to-air missile on 28 March 1955. She was the first battleship to launch a missile. Two Terrier twin-arm launchers, magazines, and fire-control systems were installed. The Terrier, the U.S. Navy's first antiaircraft missile, was subsequently installed in aircraft carriers, cruisers, and destroyers. *U.S. Navy*

Demobilization was quickly enacted, and hundreds of thousands of servicemen who had enlisted for the duration of the war went home. As a result, many ships just couldn't operate because they didn't have sufficient manpower.

Following the atomic tests at Bikini, only the *Texas* of the pre–World War I generation of battleships was saved. She was preserved as a memorial near Galveston, Texas. The *Mississippi* was converted to an ordnance test ship and reclassified as a miscellaneous auxiliary. Her sisters, the *Idaho* and the *New Mexico*, were cut up and scrapped in November and December 1947. The remainder, namely, the "Big 5" battleships *Tennessee*, *California*, *Colorado*, *Maryland*, and *West Virginia*, and the two-ship *North Carolina*- and four-ship *South Dakota* classes, were decommissioned and put into mothballs for possible future service. They were laid up in reserve fleets with precautions taken to minimize the aging process; dehumidification systems were set up to reduce internal corrosion, and cathodic protection systems that limited electrolysis of the external hull were added. Cocoons were put over gun mounts to protect them from the elements, and welders attached steel plates over openings to seal them.

## THE *IOWA* CLASS BETWEEN THE WARS

By the summer of 1947 only the four ships of the *Iowa* class remained in active service. That year, the *Wisconsin* and the *New Jersey*, accompanied by two aircraft carriers and a number of smaller ships, made the first overseas midshipman-training cruise since before World War II. They traveled to Great Britain and Norway. Even though the British Isles were still on desperately short rations after the privations of World War II, they eagerly shared what little they had with their American visitors.

This trip was, by and large, the battleship's last hurrah. The *Wisconsin* and the *New Jersey* were decommissioned on 30 June and 1 July 1948, respectively, and the *Iowa* followed on 24 March 1949. In all likelihood, the *Missouri* would have also been decommissioned if not for one thing: this was the ship that President Truman's daughter had christened, and so the *Missouri* remained in commission as long as he remained president. He was reelected in the fall of 1948 and began his first full term in 1949. This ensured the ship four more years of service, but she was to come to very public grief before Truman's term had gone very far.

On 20 December 1949 the *Missouri* got a new skipper in the person of Captain William D. Brown. He had served in World War II as a destroyer captain and had been chief of staff for a cruiser division commander. When he took command of the "Mighty Mo," it was almost four years since he had been on active sea duty. When he took command, the ship was undergoing a shipyard maintenance period, but the *Missouri* was due to leave in mid-January for training in Guantánamo Bay. As she left her home port of Norfolk, she was scheduled to run through an acoustic range that would measure the acoustic signature emitted by her propellers as part of a navy effort to identify ships by the sounds they emitted into the water.

On the morning of 17 January 1950 the ship got under way and headed out to the channel, following the guidance of a harbor pilot. Captain Brown and his navigator, Lieutenant Commander Frank Morris, were on the 08 level, high in the *Missouri*'s superstructure, so they could have a good perspective. The officer of the deck, Lieutenant Ed Arnold, reported to the captain that he spotted a small orange-and-white buoy. It marked the left edge of the acoustic range that the ship was supposed to run through, and so the ship should have stayed to the right. However, there was a good deal of confusion on the bridge, and both the navigator

On the fourth anniversary of the Japanese surrender—2 September 1949—the USS *Missouri* was the only U.S. battleship in active service (except for the test ship *Mississippi*). Here the officers and men of the *Missouri* mass around the deck marker where the surrender ceremonies occurred. There is a quad 40mm gun mount atop the No. 2 main-battery turret and another to the left of the marker. *U.S. Navy*

and operations officer advised Brown to steam left of the buoy. In doing so, they headed the *Missouri* straight for shoal water. In addition, the skipper increased the speed to 15 knots, adding to the ship's momentum as she headed in the wrong direction. Down in the Combat Information Center (CIC), the men watching radar scopes saw that the ship was going the wrong way, but concluded something must be wrong with the equipment.

The quartermaster steering the ship, Bevan Travis, had been in and out of Norfolk many times during his years on board. He tried to advise Captain Brown that he was going the wrong way, as did the executive officer, Commander George Peckham. Brown was used to running his own show and kept the ship on course. The inevitable disaster occurred when she slid onto the underwater shoal and just kept going until she was 2,500 feet inland—nearly three ship lengths. An unusually high tide at the time of the incident made the result even worse. She was hard aground in very public view. Men at the nearby army and air force bases made sport of the considerable embarrassment of seeing the

navy's foremost battleship aground and literally stuck in the mud. The *Missouri* was immobile on Thimble Shoals and would remain so for two weeks until salvage crews could free her. A combination of removing fuel and ammunition, adding pontoons for buoyancy, and pulling with powerful tugboats was, at last, successful. On 1 February the ship was finally moved from her involuntary berth into a dry dock, which recently held the uncompleted hull of her sistership, the *Kentucky*, for inspection and needed repairs. Captain Brown and his navigator were relieved of their posts two days later and subsequently court-martialed. Captain Brown was found guilty of negligence and was lowered 50 numbers in rank seniority, which in effect killed his once-promising naval career. He retired shortly thereafter.

## THE KOREAN WAR
In late June 1950 North Korea invaded its neighbor to the south, and the U.S. moved quickly to respond. For the next three years the navy was once again involved in a war.

The *Missouri* was beginning a midshipman-training cruise at New York City when she was ordered to leave for Norfolk to resupply and then immediately head to the war zone in Korea.

The *Missouri* would hit storms at sea in both the Atlantic and the Pacific and was late in arriving. While her original purpose was to support General Douglas MacArthur's invasion of Inchon on Korea's west coast on 15 September 1951, the strategy changed just before her arrival; by then, North Korea had already overrun much of South Korea.

When the conflict erupted, the *Missouri* was the only battleship in commission. Her sister ships—the *Iowa*, the *New Jersey*, and the *Wisconsin*—would all see action in the Korea Combat Zone before the war ended.

All four ships operated on both Korean coasts. For example, in February 1952, the *Missouri* bombarded the multiple bridges that span the double rivers to Tanchen. The *Iowa*, which had already softened up many shore targets, shattered heavy gun positions south of Wonsan in June 1952. In September the *New Jersey* covered the U.S. Army's X Corps in a night barrage that pulverized enemy gun positions.

On 27 July 1953, two days after the *New Jersey* shot 191 rounds off of Wonsan, the North Korean and United Nations negotiators came to an agreement, and the war was over. The line of demarcation between North and South Korea was not far from where it had been when hostilities began in June 1950. But South Korea was still free and has remained so ever since. The *New Jersey* alone fired 3,600 rounds of 16-inch projectiles during the Korean War.

**Above:** The Korean War saw the rapid reactivation of the three mothballed battleships of the *Iowa* class. All participated in the conflict, usually bombarding enemy roads, rail tracks, and coastal facilities. Here the *Iowa* (left) and *Missouri* meet in a Far Eastern port in 1952. There are stacks of powder canisters near the *Iowa*'s No. 3 main-battery turret. *U.S. Navy*

**Upper right:** The *Iowa* fires her No. 3 main-battery guns off the coast of Korea during a joint amphibious exercise in 1952. The close operation of air force aircraft led to distinctive recognition markings on U.S. ships: The *Iowa* has the American flag on Turret No. 2 and the number *61* on Turret No. 1. The quad 40mm mount atop her No. 2 turret had been removed. *U.S. Navy*

**Below:** Replenishment at sea: The ammunition ship *Rainer* pulls away from the battleship *Wisconsin* and the aircraft carrier *Antietam* after a simultaneous transfer of munitions to the warships. In this photo and the opening photo of this chapter the battleships' No. 2 turret is trained abeam to uncover the forward 16-inch ammunition loading hatch. *U.S. Navy*

## PEACETIME AND BACK TO THE RESERVE FLEET

With President Truman out of the White House, the *Missouri* was decommissioned at Bremerton, Washington, on 26 February 1955, where she remained in the reserve fleet for the next 30 years. Her three sisters continued in service, primarily to train midshipmen in the summertime, and also to make deployments and conduct maneuvers with other naval units. On 6 May 1956, while operating with a group of ships off the Virginia Capes in a heavy fog, the *Wisconsin* plowed into the destroyer *Eaton*. The battleship was hustled into dry dock at the Norfolk Naval Shipyard for surgery. To save time and expense, she received a graft in the form of a 68-foot section of the bow of her canceled sister ship, the *Kentucky*. An *Iowa*-class battleship, the *Kentucky*'s construction was resumed in December 1944 and was nearly three-quarters complete when work was stopped in 1947. A quick, 16-day repair job got the *Wisconsin* back into action for that summer's midshipman cruise.

By the mid-1950s the navy was undergoing a technological transformation that would make it much different than it had been even a decade and a half earlier, on the eve of World War II. The big gun had been predominant then, but now the navy was commissioning super-carriers, such as the USS *Forrestal*, and they had become the preeminent warships in the fleet.

To help pave the way for this transformation, Admiral Arleigh Burke, Chief of Naval Operations, ordered the remaining three *Iowa*-class battleships to be decommissioned. The *New Jersey* was thus decom-

missioned on 21 August 1957, followed by the *Iowa* on 24 February 1958, and the *Wisconsin* on 8 March 1958. Meanwhile, the proud old battleships still in reserve, such as the *Tennessee* and the *Colorado* class, went to the scrappers in the early 1960s. The earlier fast battleships of the *North Carolina* and the *South Dakota* classes were also scrapped, but the *North Carolina*, the *Massachusetts*, and the *Alabama* were saved and joined the *Texas* as state memorials/museums.

Even as they were being taken out of service, plans were being considered to modify them for future service. Their relatively short active life, high speed, large size, good protection, and great range all made them

The only time that the four *Iowa*-class battleships steamed together occurred on 7 June, off the Virginia Capes, forming Battleship Division 2. From foreground they are the *Iowa*, the *Wisconsin*, the *Missouri*, and the *New Jersey*. The *Iowa*'s main-battery turrets are trained off the port beam; the other ships appear to have their guns fore and aft. *U.S. Navy*

The battleship *Wisconsin* at anchor in Guantánamo Bay, Cuba, in 1956, fully dressed to honor George Washington's birthday. She still has a quad "40" atop the No. 2 main-battery turret; note the complex mast attached to her second funnel that holds an AN/SPS-8 radar. She was the last of the class to be mothballed; when she left the fleet two years later there were no active battleships in the world. *U.S. Navy*

Three of the four *Iowa*-class battleships were mothballed at the Philadelphia Naval Shipyard in 1957 and 1958: from left, the *Wisconsin*, the *New Jersey*, and the *Iowa*. The fourth ship of the class, the *Missouri*, had been mothballed in 1955 at the Puget Sound Naval Shipyard. All four ships were carefully preserved for future use.
*Ruth Bradshaw/U.S. Navy*

very attractive for alternate missions. Proposals spanned the gamut from relatively minor upgrading to almost total reconstruction. The uncompleted hull of the *Kentucky* seemed a prime candidate. Her construction had continued fitfully for several years after World War II. Some thought was given to turning her into a prototype antiaircraft battleship. Under the plan, her armament would have included antiaircraft missiles launched from turrets and 8-inch 55-caliber antiaircraft guns in triple or quadruple mountings. The *Kentucky* was 73 percent complete at that time. In 1955 the Ship Characteristics Board (SCB) decided that the vessel would be finished as a missile battleship retaining two 16-inch turrets and mounting the new 5-inch .54-caliber and 3-inch .50-caliber guns. Her antiaircraft defense would be bolstered by Terrier, Talos, or Tartar missiles, and the Regulus II winged missile would give the ship long-range punch. The SCB projected costs at $130 million. A similar, but more expensive plan in 1956 called for the Polaris ballistic missile in place of the Regulus II. By this time, however, the costs hovered around $200 million. Moreover, the *Kentucky* had been disfigured to fix the *Wisconsin*, and thus plans to use her were dropped and she was sold for scrapping.

The four remaining *Iowas*, however, continued to attract interest as missile ships. One 1958 SCB

scheme proposed ripping out all the guns but four 5-inch 38-caliber; another kept the two forward 16-inch turrets. Polaris appeared in some sketches, Regulus in others. Also floated was a proposal to turn one of the battleships into a specialized satellite-launching ship. Other officers argued that the *Iowas* could be converted into perfect support ships for the fast carrier task forces. Strangely, this idea eventually became the Fast Replenishment Oiler (AOE) concept, and the propulsion systems for the first two ships of the class were obtained from the scrapped *Kentucky*. The Second Fleet initiated the idea of rebuilding an *Iowa* as a combination fleet flagship and combat oiler. Receiving more detailed consideration was the suggestion by the Amphibious Warfare Board in 1961 that an *Iowa* be remade into a commando ship. The project, designed to beef up the navy's declining amphibious capabilities, envisioned the substitution of Turret No. 3 with a helicopter hangar and troop quarters.

All of these radical conversion projects foundered on the rocks of fiscal realities. Thus, the four battleships languished through the first part of the 1960s in the mothball fleet.

## VIETNAM

As the struggle in Southeast Asia intensified during the mid-1960s, some policymakers seriously proposed returning the *Iowas* to active duty. There was intense opposition to battleship reactivation, particularly by the naval aviation community. After an austere reactivation overhaul, she went to Vietnam, where her missions, as in Korea 15 years earlier, were to interdict enemy supplies and troop movements from the north in addition to supporting friendly forces in the south. She did these jobs well—indeed, too well. As her crew was preparing for a second tour of duty in 1969, top officials in the Nixon administration, viewing her as a liability for future peace talks with North Vietnam, sent her back to mothballs rather than to war. For the third time, the *New Jersey* was decommissioned.

The beginning of her Vietnam deployment can be traced to the peculiar military realities of that war. The sinuous coastal land that was North and South Vietnam was divided along the 17th parallel by a supposedly neutral piece of land called the Demilitarized Zone (DMZ). It was through and around this DMZ that the communist North Vietnamese sent forces to assist the Viet Cong, Vietnamese rebels opposed to the

After extensive debate and discussion, in June 1967 the *New Jersey* is moved by tugs from the mothball group to Pier 4 at the Philadelphia Naval Shipyard for the start of her rehabilitation. Proposals to arm the ship with antiaircraft missiles and other updates were rejected in an effort to speed her rejoining the fleet. *J. P. Garfinkel/U.S. Navy*

American-backed government. Because the successive Saigon regimes had shown themselves incapable of dealing with the insurgency, the Kennedy and Johnson administrations committed increasingly substantial American forces.

With this expanding commitment in which the U.S. Navy played an increasingly significant role, some officers became seriously concerned about the decline of their gunfire capabilities. The only new gun deployed in the decade after Korea was the 5-inch 54-caliber, which possessed a good rate of fire but little weight and penetrating power. The four heavy cruisers still in commission carried the largest guns at sea, the 8-inch 55-caliber firing a 355-pound shell.

In November 1964 Vice Admiral Edwin B. Hooper, one of the navy's top gunnery experts, headed a commission to remedy this problem. The group recommended the activation of two *Iowas* and two heavy cruisers. Had the proposal been promptly implemented, the U.S. Navy would have almost certainly saved many planes and pilots lost to North Vietnamese antiaircraft fire over the next four years. Ironically, it was the aviators who blocked the Hooper panel recommendations. Admiral Roy L. Johnson, commander of the Pacific Fleet from 1965 to 1967, opposed battleship reactivation. He defended his stand with erroneous assertions on the range and effectiveness of the 8-inch guns and that the reserve stocks of battleship projectiles had been exhausted.

The Chief of Naval Operations, Admiral David L. MacDonald, also an aviator, and his opposition helped stymie the project until 1967.

Despite this resistance at the top, battleship advocates within both the Defense Department and Congress studied the matter with increasing urgency. The United States by 1967 was losing an average of one aircraft per day in Vietnam. Putting aside all but fiscal considerations, the air campaign was most expensive. Aircraft cost about $2 million each, and pilots cost $1 million to train for a total of $3 million per lost aircraft. One of the *Iowas* could be returned to service with a reduced complement and austere updating for perhaps $25 million. This sum represented little more than one week's loss of aircraft, or 25 B-52 strikes. Given figures like these, Senator Richard Russell pushed strongly for a battleship reactivation, as did General Wallace M. Greene Jr., the Marine Corps Commandant.

These big-gun advocates won out. One day after MacDonald retired on 31 July 1967, the Defense Department announced that the *New Jersey* would be returned to service. Of the four *Iowas*, she was chosen in part because she had been regunned shortly before leaving service in 1957, and also because her deactivation had been performed with unusual care. The plan attracted nationwide attention. Critics derided the expense as outlandish; they claimed that the ship was terribly vulnerable to enemy attack.

Recommissioned and ready for battle, the *New Jersey* steams down the Delaware River for sea trials on the open sea. She will stop at Hampton Roads to load munitions for her 16-inch and 5-inch guns; all lighter antiaircraft guns have been removed. Still, her crew will number some 1,600 officers and enlisted men. She retains an aircraft crane aft, but will operate only helicopters. (Harold Wise/ *U.S. Navy*

En route to war, the *New Jersey* transits the Pedro Miguel lock of the Panama Canal on 4 June 1968. The 108-foot beam of the *Iowa*-class battleships allows *one foot* of space on each side when passing through the canal locks. (Some of the old battleships rebuilt after being damaged at Pearl Harbor were too large to pass through the 110-foot locks.) *U.S. Navy*

More menacing in actuality were the budget trimmers. The reactivation, ruled the Defense Department, would be paid for out of the navy's operating and maintenance funds. Accordingly, one navy proposal called for the reactivation of the ship's 16-inch battery only. She would be towed along the Vietnamese coast as an artillery hulk. A more generous plan would have brought to life two shafts, two firerooms, and two engines, but no 5-inchers. The Philadelphia Naval Shipyard estimated that for $2.4 million it could deliver in nine months the *New Jersey* with the full power plant and all main and secondary turrets operational. The navy selected this configuration. The ship's sole mission was to be shore bombardment; there would be no missiles, no height-finding radar, and only limited upgrading of electronics and communications equipment. This austere conversion—the term *austere* was never really defined and thus was the subject of much bickering—was intended to provide the *New Jersey* with a useful service life of three years.

On 20 September the *New Jersey* entered dry dock. Yard workers found her to be in generally fine condition. Her boilers, for example, required relatively little attention. However, a number of unanticipated problems came to light. Records showed that the timing on one set of reduction gears was suspect; on closer inspection, all four needed retiming, an expensive and lengthy proposition. A number of bearings in pumps, turbines, and generators required replacement, as did all four propellers, which had developed cracks. The packing for both 5-inch and 16-inch recoil mechanisms had to be renewed. An inspection of Turret No. 1 revealed an especially serious and totally unexpected flaw: its port 16-inch gun had locked with Turret No. 2, thus springing the outboard deck lug and cracking the trunnion bearing of the gun. This took two weeks of strenuous work to correct.

Work also started on assuring the *New Jersey* a first-class main battery. Beginning in August, the 16-inch guns were cleaned and reworked at the rate of three monthly. Projectiles were also refurbished at a rate of 1,200 per month. For the first time, spare 16-inch barrels were stocked west of Pearl Harbor, at Subic Bay.

In the interest of economy, planners ordered the crew size to be 1,400 men and 70 officers. Nonetheless, this crew size proved to be inadequate to work the ship safely, and the Defense Department reluctantly increased the crew size to 1,556 men.

Right on time, on 26 March 1968, the *New Jersey* headed down the Delaware River for her engineering trials. The next day she began a full-power run off the Virginia Capes. The ship's pitometer log indicated a speed of 35.2 knots at 207 rpm. At the end of this six-hour high-speed run, Captain J. Edward Snyder, the ship's commanding officer, went to emergency power astern. This radical maneuver showed the ship's plant to be in top working order. The battleship returned to Philadelphia with a broom run up the halyard, indicating a clean sweep of her trials. On 6 April 1968 the *New Jersey* was recommissioned on time and under budget ($21.5 million). On 5 September she left Philadelphia and headed for her third war, with a brief stop at Pearl Harbor.

The huge ship performed well her first day on the gun line, 30 September 1968, expending 29 main-battery rounds on four targets in and around the DMZ. A fortified storage area was destroyed, with the access road cut in two places and 300 meters of trench line torn up. An enemy artillery site was totally destroyed. Another storage area, with five fortified bunkers, was destroyed.

On Tuesday, 1 October the ship took station to the north of Tiger Island and fired at targets seven to 12 miles north of the DMZ. The ship again moved south in the afternoon to fire into the buffer zone. A marine TA-4 aircraft, assigned to the *New Jersey* for spotting, was hit by ground fire while en route to one of the afternoon's targets. The pilot reported that he was fast losing fuel and that he would have to ditch. Vectored to the *New Jersey*'s position by Chief Radarman Macdonald Shand, the *New Jersey*'s air controller, both crewmen of the TA-4 ejected safely and were rescued within minutes. Six bunkers, a supply truck, and an antiaircraft site were destroyed by the big guns that day.

During the afternoon of 14 October, with a Corsair-II (A-7) from the carrier *America* doing the spotting, the *New Jersey* fired for 30 minutes at coastal artillery sites on Hon Matt Island. The spotter noted one secondary explosion and one battery obliterated. As the debris settled, the spotter reported, "You've blown away a large slice of the island—it's down in the ocean."

After departing II Corps, the *New Jersey* received a Chinese-made machine gun captured at the battle of Kinh Mon. The presentation was made to Captain Snyder on behalf of the officers and men of the First Battalion, 61st Infantry, and First Brigade, 5th Infantry in appreciation for the *New Jersey*'s preparation fire just before the battle, which lasted from 23 to 27 October. The area had long been a Communist stronghold, and the army had made two previous attempts to sweep it. The first try resulted in 30 U.S. killed and 60 enemy dead. The second attempt, after a B-52 strike, resulted in 61 Americans dead versus zero enemy. Then the *New Jersey* came on the scene to soften the area for a third try. Results of the third sweep were seven Americans lost and 301 enemy confirmed killed.

During the daytime of 25 October, the *New Jersey* fired two main and two secondary spotted missions, with 12 confirmed enemy killed. The aerial spotter discovered a Communist troop movement, and the *New Jersey* rapidly responded to his call for fire with 16-inch high-capacity projectiles fitted with mechanical time fuses. The observer reported the projectiles burst at optimum height directly over the enemy, who had taken cover in open trenches.

Staff Sergeant Robert Gauthier told the *New Jersey*'s crew, in an interview over the ship's TV system, how he had been leading a platoon in the area where the *New Jersey* was firing in support of the Third Marine Division. "We were ordered to pull back about 200 yards so that somebody, we didn't know who at the time, could start shooting at some Communist bunkers and emplacements that had been giving us a lot of trouble. When we finally moved back about 500 yards, we heard what at first sounded like a subway

The amidships section of the *New Jersey* after her reactivation. The twin and quad 40mm gun "tubs" are empty; two of them on each side of the funnel hold chaff rockets, to be used to deter incoming missiles. The navy feared that North Vietnam might have received Soviet-produced Styx antiship missiles; Egyptian-launched Styx missiles sank the Israeli destroyer *Eliat* in October 1967. *U.S. Navy*

The *New Jersey* fires on a target in South Vietnam with her No. 2 main-battery turret during her single deployment to Vietnam in 1968. The large "ears" atop her conning tower house electric countermeasures equipment to warn of approaching aircraft or missiles. She proved a very effective floating gun platform during the war, complementing the smaller guns of other U.S. warships. *Monty Tipton/ U.S. Navy*

train moving through a tunnel—a big rushing noise— then BANG. Later on when we went back into the area, there was nothing . . . just nothing. It was like something had come along with a big eraser and wiped everything clean. And they were big, heavily fortified bunkers, targets our own artillery couldn't touch."

On Tuesday, 29 October the *New Jersey* destroyed 30 structures, three underground bunkers, and 1,148 feet of trench line. That afternoon an aerial observer located an active enemy artillery position on a hilltop, which recently had been harassing allied ground forces in northern I Corps. After the *New Jersey* sent in four 16-inch rounds, the spotter radioed back, "excellent coverage . . . keep them coming." Two rounds later, the spotter reported, "You've just lowered the mountain by 20 feet. Artillery site destroyed."

During the ensuing month, the *New Jersey* continued to provide critical fire support to friendly ground forces along the South Vietnamese coast. On 25 November she achieved the greatest single day's damage score of the year. During eight main-battery missions, 117 structures and 32 bunkers were destroyed, and eight secondary explosions ripped through two storage areas near Quang Ngai. High-capacity projectiles killed an estimated 40 Communist troops. The battleship also caused heavy damage to 93 structures and destroyed 361 feet of trench line and several tunnel complexes. Several of the targets were widely dispersed and the battleship fired what Chief Gunner's Mate Billie G. Baker

called "spreading fire." The spotter got the ship on target, then walked the shots around until the whole area had been decimated. Observers reported smoke and debris rising 1,000 feet in the air over the targets.

The *New Jersey* moved off the DMZ on Sunday, 29 December, where she would operate into the new year. In one mission into the southern half of the zone that afternoon, the battleship destroyed eight 2,500-square-foot bunkers and demolished six structures in the buffer zone. The spotter reported one large secondary explosion. At 4:12 P.M. that day Turret No. 1 became the first one on the ship to have fired 1,000 combat rounds since arriving on station in September. The other two turrets reached this mark a few days later.

The *New Jersey* demonstrated her all-weather capability during the monsoons of January 1969. On 8 January spotters onshore reported visibility of about 4,920 feet, while the battleship, about four miles off shore, was totally enveloped in fog. Just south of the DMZ, an army observer located a bunker complex containing some enemy troops. "The soup was so thick we couldn't even see the beach," recalled Lieutenant Commander Leroy A. Short Jr., the *New Jersey*'s weapons officer. "But our fire control radar was locked onto the reference point, and the spotter could see well enough to adjust our fire." The ship fired simultaneous 5- and 16-inch salvos and destroyed four bunkers. The observer also reported four enemy troops killed in the action.

On the night of 13 February while on station off Da Nang, three of the *New Jersey*'s fire-control-technicians were on watch in the ship's forward Mark 37 director when the ship responded to an emergency call from a downed pilot in the vicinity of Tiger Island. The trio began a radar search and soon found their tiny objective floating in the South China Sea. Thanks to their alertness, the pilot was rescued by helicopter.

On 15 February the *New Jersey* was firing her main and secondary batteries in support of the Third Marines. Just before dusk, troops ashore reported that the communists were constructing a rocket site for night firing, in the southern half of the DMZ near Con Thien. The *New Jersey* immediately opened up with her main battery and fired until well after dark. The ground observer reported 25 secondary explosions and seven fireballs rising 500 feet in the air and completely lighting up the night sky.

Just after 1:00 A.M. on 22 February 1969, while the *New Jersey* was conducting prearranged, unobserved fire, she received an urgent call for fire from outpost

Oceanview, just south of the DMZ, which was under attack. The post, manned by about 20 marines and a Naval Gunfire Liaison team, was attacked by a force later estimated to be about 130 North Vietnamese regulars. The following is a chronological record of the night's action taken from the ship's operation report:

*"0106—Emergency call for fire from forward observation post, Third Marine Division. Unknown number of enemy troops attacking. Commenced secondary battery fire, two mounts, increasing to four mounts and adding main battery as attack intensified.*

*"0400—Continued high explosive fire, multiple targets, main and secondary batteries, while providing spotter illumination.*

*"0530—Attack intensity diminishing, continued responding to calls for fire, spotter reports enemy withdrawing carrying casualties.*

*"0633—Ceased all fire; attack repulsed."*

That night the *New Jersey* fired 1,710 5-inch rounds in nearly six hours of continuous fire. One spotter on shore, Lance Corporal Roger Clouse of Lincoln, Nebraska, controlled all of the fire of the *New Jersey* as well as several artillery batteries that night.

The *New Jersey*'s last observed fire mission was on the evening of 30 March against an enemy bunker complex near Con Thien. The aerial observer reported seven bunkers destroyed. The ship concluded her six-month deployment off the South Vietnamese coast at 6:00 A.M. on 1 April 1969. During her 120 days on the gunline, she had expended nearly 12 million pounds of ordnance; total rounds expended were 5,866 16-inch and 14,891 5-inch. Main-battery rounds expended during the *New Jersey*'s deployment to Vietnam were only 1,500 rounds short of the total she fired in World War II, two cruises to Korea, and several midshipmen cruises combined.

---

## GUN DAMAGE ASSESSMENT, USS *NEW JERSEY*, 1968–69

### MAIN BATTERY

| | |
|---|---:|
| Structures destroyed | 439 |
| Structures damaged | 259 |
| Bunkers destroyed | 596 |
| Bunkers damaged | 250 |
|     Artillery sites neutralized | 19 |
|     Automatic weapons, AA, and mortar sites silenced | 35 |
|     Secondary explosions | 130 |
|     Roads interdicted | 26 |
|         Feet of trench line rendered unusable | 6,315? |
|         Cave and tunnel complexes destroyed | 75 |
|         Enemy killed in action (confirmed) | 136 |
|         Enemy killed in action (probable) | 17 |
|         Troop movements stopped | 12 |

### SECONDARY BATTERY

| | |
|---|---:|
| Structures destroyed | 56 |
| Structures damaged | 92 |
| Bunkers destroyed | 59 |
| Bunkers damaged | 73 |
|     Artillery sites neutralized | 2 |
|     Mortar sites silenced | 6 |
|     Waterborne Logistic Craft destroyed (Op "Sea Dragon") | 9 |
|     Secondary explosions | 46 |
|         Enemy killed in action (confirmed) | 10 |
|         Enemy killed in action (probable) | 7 |
|         Troop movements stopped | 7 |

In early April the *New Jersey* headed for Long Beach, California, to exchange personnel and refurbish equipment. Within 1,800 miles of the port, she received orders to reverse course and report for action at Yokosuka, Japan, in response to an incident in which North Koreans shot down an unarmed U.S. EC-121 reconnaissance plane over international waters. Steaming at 22 knots, the *New Jersey* arrived off Japan on 22 April 1969. En route to Japan, she took aboard 837 tons of ammunition from the USS *Paricutin*, the largest underway replenishment of her cruise. Thirty minutes after reaching her holding station, she was ordered to return to the United States. She finally docked at Long Beach on 5 May, more than two weeks late.

The *New Jersey*'s schedule called for her to leave for her second Vietnam tour early in September. In the meantime, she undertook a cruise to train both midshipmen and the replacements who had come aboard at Long Beach. For that cruise, the *New Jersey* became the flagship of Rear Admiral Lloyd Vasey, who commanded a flotilla of 15 ships. One of the highlights for the midshipmen cruise was a main-battery practice shoot that sank the obsolete fleet minesweeper *Raven* (MSF-55). The *New Jersey* hit the target ship on the second round. On 12 August the battleship received the well-deserved Navy Unit Commendation "for exceptionally meritorious service."

During the first three weeks of August, as the *New Jersey*'s crew prepared for the next tour, she was to get a new commanding officer, Captain Robert C. Peniston, who would take over from Captain Snyder on 27 August. Her departure from Long Beach for Vietnam was scheduled for 5 September. With the *New Jersey*'s pre-deployment ordnance review completed on 20 August, the crew was startled to hear the announcement the next day from the Defense Department that the *New Jersey* would be one of a hundred naval ships deactivated during the fall. Secretary of Defense Melvin Laird cited budget tightening by Congress as the reason. Captain Snyder's angry remarks reflected the reaction of most of the crew:

> War is hell, and it is also expensive, and the American people have tired of the expense of defending freedom. And so this year when the winter monsoon comes to Vietnam and prevents the planes from accurately supporting Allied ground forces, *New Jersey* will not be there. The ship that made the motto "Firepower for Freedom" a reality will be abandoned in Bremerton and the American boys who looked to the "Big J" for their very lives must look elsewhere.

The bitterness of the captain's tone was understandable precisely because the reason given for decommissioning the ship was so incomprehensible. Dollar for dollar, the *New Jersey* had shown herself to be the best bargain of any warship operating in Southeast Asia. Substantial funding had gone into preparing her for another tour, and now, just before departure, she was to be mothballed. It all made little sense until the truth emerged in a quite dramatic way during a Senate debate on 7 April 1981 over the Reagan administration proposal to reactivate the *New Jersey*.

On opposite sides of the debate stood two former secretaries of the navy, Senator John Chafee from Rhode Island, who opposed reactivation, and Senator John Warner of Virginia, who supported it. Their debate reached a climax over the ship's performance in Vietnam:

**Mr. Warner:** Would the Senator from Rhode Island care to comment on the distinguished record of that ship during the time it was on active duty?

**Mr. Chafee:** I certainly will. It was a very fine ship but we did not keep it.

**Mr. Warner:** Does the Senator . . . ?

**Mr. Chafee:** Let me answer the question. You have opened the floodgate, and you will get the flood. The ship proved ineffective in the mission for which it was designed—ineffective in the Vietnam war. It was tremendously costly to operate. It required a very substantial number of crew. I would say over 1,500 men, and we deactivated it. It was not worth it. It was a fiasco, truly.

**Mr. Warner:** Will the Senator yield?

**Mr. Chafee:** And the Senator knows this well. We sent it back to mothballs.

**Mr. Warner:** Mr. President, if the Senator would yield, does he recall which watch it was sent back into mothballs under? Was it his or mine? It happened to have been my watch after he departed. And I will never forget the circumstances under which this ship was deactivated.

I respectfully contest the statements made by the distinguished Senator from Rhode Island. The ship was very effective. As a matter of fact, it was so effective that we were ordered to take it out of active service because its belligerency and its antagonism was [sic] impeding the progress of the peace talks at that time.

**Mr. Chafee:** It was so effective, you sent it to Bremerton.

**Mr. Warner:** I beg the Senator's pardon.

**Mr. Chafee:** It was so effective, you sent it to Bremerton.

**Mr. Warner:** Against my recommendations. I went down and personally saw the Secretary of Defense and was ordered from the White House that the ship should be deactivated because it was impeding the peace negotiations.

If the *New Jersey* had been deactivated "by the book," the process should have taken four months to complete. Captain Peniston and his crew managed the feat in 100 days. When her ammunition was unloaded at Long Beach, it filled a 26-car train. Ultimately, the *New Jersey* was retired with only one defect unrepaired: a problem on one boiler. So, on 17 December 1969 the *New Jersey* was decommissioned in the most dignified ceremony possible, despite the boycott of the Navy Department.

In certain respects, it could be argued that the *New Jersey* operated off the coast of Vietnam at the worst possible time in terms of fulfilling her potential there. Almost 85 percent of Vietnam, both North and South, lay within range of her 16-inch guns. Had the battleship gone out prior to April 1968 (when President Johnson restricted operations above the 19th parallel), she could have saved valuable aircraft and aircrew by taking out crucial objectives in North Vietnam that were heavily defended against bombing raids. For example, the United States lost 50 aircraft trying to destroy the Thanh Hoa bridge. The *New Jersey* undoubtedly could have wrecked that structure in one hour.

Alternatively, had the battleship been in commission in 1972 when President Richard M. Nixon ordered attacks against previously untouchable targets in North Vietnam, the *New Jersey* could have performed the same sort of surgical strike on the port city of Haiphong that she carried out against Wonsan at the close of the Korean War. As it was, the retirement of the *New Jersey* in the last days of 1969 seemed to sound the final knell for her and for her type. But did it? The four *Iowas* would sleep through the 1970s, only to be reborn once more under President Ronald Reagan's military buildup.

The *New Jersey* passes the battleship *Arizona* memorial at Pearl Harbor during her 1968 deployment to Vietnam. Only the top of the 14-inch barbette of No. 2 turret remains above water (next to the memorial); at right are the mooring structures that lined Battleship Row on the eastern side of Ford Island. The hulk of the *Utah* remains on the western side of the island. *U.S. Navy*

CHAPTER ELEVEN

# REAGAN'S
# 600-SHIP NAVY

**Left:** The *New Jersey*, the first battleship to be reactivated under President Ronald Reagan's buildup to a 600-ship navy, launches a Tomahawk land-attack cruise missile. The long-range Tomahawk and the shorter-range Harpoon greatly enhanced the combat capabilities of the *Iowa*-class battleships. *U.S. Navy*

Following several close escapes from the scrapper's torch in the 1970s, the *Iowas* became the center of controversy again when, late in the term of President Jimmy Carter, an aviator and defense consultant began a single-handed crusade to reactivate the battleships. Despite the most vigorous opposition, the arguments for the ships proved convincing to the incoming Reagan administration. For a relatively modest investment, the battleships began to emerge from the yards with updated equipment and impressive new capabilities. By the end of 1983, the *New Jersey* was back in combat, this time in Mediterranean waters.

The survival of U.S. battleships to that point, however, was by the narrowest of margins. In 1972 some top officers proposed that only the *New Jersey* be retained and the rest be disposed of. Had the navy gone ahead with this scheme, the *Missouri* would certainly have been preserved as a museum ship, but the *Iowa* and the *Wisconsin* would have gone to the breakers. Fortunately, the Marine Corps pressed strongly for the retention of the ships; in fact, the late Colonel Robert Heinl, in a September 1972 article in the *Proceedings of the U.S. Naval Institute*, called for their reactivation as "Instant Sea-Control Ships."

Secretary of the Navy John F. Lehman Jr., who held that position from 1981 to 1987, was the political force behind the reactivation of the four *Iowa*-class battleships. An astute politician and "navalist," Lehman argued for a 600-ship navy centered on four dreadnoughts and 15 large aircraft carriers. However, he was unable to reach his carrier goal. Lehman was controversial but effective. *Helene Stikkel/Department of Defense*

Her superstructure covered with scaffolding, the *New Jersey* is moved by tugs in the Long Beach Naval Shipyard in California, where she was rehabilitated after 12 years in mothballs. During their reactivation, the battleships' 5-inch gun battery was reduced to six twin mounts, that is, the removal of four twin mounts as space and weight were allocated to missiles. *Gary Ballard/U.S. Navy*

Indeed, over the next couple of years, the navy conducted feasibility studies to see if the ships could accept the Aegis air defense system, Sea Sparrow and Harpoon missile launchers, and the CIWS 20mm Gatling gun. All of these weapons represented the latest technology of the time, and planners were especially concerned about the effects of blast overpressure on them. The navy contracted a study by Gibbs and Cox, the respected naval engineering firm, who concluded that all the systems could be accommodated with few problems.

Despite these promising studies, the Naval Ship System Command sent out a precept for survey of the *Iowa* and the *Wisconsin* on 6 June 1973. The *Missouri* was later added to the list. This is the first step taken for the disposal of a ship. The command argued that it seemed most unlikely the battleships would ever go to sea again, and therefore the money spent on their upkeep was being wasted. On 17 November 1973 Admiral Elmo R. Zumwalt, then Chief of Naval Operations (CNO), personally canceled any further actions to dispose of the *Iowa*. Whenever the scrapping of the *Iowas* was suggested—and the idea was advanced numerous times—Zumwalt always favored retention of the battleships on the grounds that their big guns were an irreplaceable asset for amphibious operations.

Narrowly saved, the *Iowas* still faced an uncertain future. In late 1976 talk started about appropriate sites for the *New Jersey* and the *Missouri* as museum ships. A December 1976 *New York Times* article reported that the navy was offering the *New Jersey* to her name state if Trenton officials would raise the funds to maintain her.

Another survey of the ships' condition was conducted in 1977. The inspection teams found all four battleships fit in hull, engineering plant, and main battery, but ruled them unfit in habitability, command, and control. The report concluded that the ships should be stricken for disposal. Once again, the Marine Corps saved them. The marines ably put forward their fears in the Weller Report, issued in 1977, which drew pointed attention to the pathetic state of the fleet's gun-power. A handful of 6-inch guns remained aboard light cruisers, which were shortly to leave active service. The largest guns afloat would soon be the 5-inch 54-caliber if the lightweight 8-inch gun failed to materialize—as indeed it did, despite its successful testing. Seconding these marine concerns was the commander of the Pacific Fleet, who recommended to the then CNO, Admiral James L. Holloway III, that the battleships be retained as mobilization assets. Holloway, who was a former skipper of the *Iowa*, agreed.

The decade closed with alarming developments for the United States. The fall of the Shah of Iran and the Soviet invasion of Afghanistan both boded ill for American interests. Moreover, the Soviet navy was commissioning a number of potent ships, among which was the *Kirov* class, a nuclear-powered battle cruiser armed with cruise missiles. Indeed, the *Kirov* was the largest warship, aside from aircraft carriers, built by any power since the end of World War II.

In early 1979 some congressman began considering a plan to bolster American strength quickly by updating the *Iowas*. The author of this proposal was Charles E. Myers Jr., a defense consultant and, of all things, a former B-25 pilot for the Army Air Force. He had also flown jet fighters for the navy. Myers, with firsthand experience in the strengths and weaknesses of tactical airpower, worried especially about the problem of supporting an amphibious assault. In the spring of 1978 he began to read about battleships. Increasingly enthusiastic about the capabilities of the *Iowas,* Myers contacted Snyder and Peniston, the last COs of the *New Jersey*. From his research, Myers assembled a 40-page brief arguing the need for battleship reactivation. Realizing that no natural congressional constituency existed for the *Iowas*—that is, no legislator stood to gain a great deal from the reactivation of the ships—Myers particularly approached senators such as Daniel Inouye and Strom Thurmond, men who had taken part in assaults like Salerno, Anzio, and Normandy. Myers also condensed his arguments for publication in the Naval

Institute *Proceedings*. This article, headed by a dramatic photo of a *Missouri* broadside, appeared in the November 1979 issue just days after the seizure by Iranian radicals of the American embassy in Tehran. Myers proposed that the *Iowas* be reactivated specifically to support land operations, and his arguments seemed compelling: The ships combined the best protection in existence with high speed, ample space, and big guns. He pointed especially to the Thanh Hoa bridge, that North Vietnamese target that cost 50 American aircraft to destroy. Myers claimed that the battleships offered a unique combination of virtues at a minimal cost compared to other weapons systems.

In the meantime, the new CNO, Admiral Thomas B. Hayward, had become interested in the *Iowas* as a quick fix for the increasing imbalance between the U.S. and Soviet fleets. Accordingly, he instructed his subordinates, shortly after Myers' article appeared, to brief congressmen on the project. Two bills, one introduced by Senator Thurmond, added money to the

then-current Defense Department budget to start the reactivation of the battleships. Hayward testified in favor of the bills, although he clearly regarded increased funding for the carrier groups as a higher priority. Naturally, Marine Corps spokesmen were more enthusiastic. With this support, the plan edged closer to realization. The House Armed Services Committee approved it by a comfortable margin. At this point, President Carter stepped into the argument. Reactivation of the battleships, he maintained, would merely "resurrect 1940s technology," and he ordered top naval officers to cease lobbying for the project. When passage of the necessary legislation looked probable in spite of the presidential opposition, Carter offered at a 25 July 1980 cabinet meeting to involve himself personally in the lobbying process. The presidential initiative proved decisive—for the moment. The funding bill went down to a narrow defeat on the Senate floor.

However, Carter's victory was short-lived indeed. In November 1980 Ronald Reagan won the presidency, in part by promising a dramatic upgrading of America's defenses. To head the Navy Department, Reagan picked John Lehman, a former naval aviator who had chaired the Republican party's committee on defense. Myers knew Lehman and was well aware that he had been an early advocate of the Tomahawk cruise missile. Consequently, Myers' arguments for Tomahawk-armed *Iowas* fell on receptive ears. Lehman approached the president-elect in December about the matter and found Reagan to be "very enthusiastic."

Winning the necessary funding for the project was another matter and involved tumultuous debates in

**Above:** Back in the fleet, the *New Jersey* was an imposing warship. New radars and electronic countermeasures equipment were provided during her 1981–82 reactivation. The white "domes" above her bridge—outboard of the Mark 38 5-inch gun director—are 20mm Phalanx Gatling guns; four of the domes comprise the ship's Close-In Weapons System (CIWS) intended to destroy attacking cruise missiles. *John Bouvia/U.S. Navy*

The *Iowa* was the second battleship to be recommissioned. Although armed with Tomahawk and Harpoon missiles that far outranged the 27-mile 16-inch guns, it was the big guns that symbolized the battleships. Here the *Iowa* unleashes a nine-gun 16-inch and 12-gun 5-inch salvo during a Caribbean exercise on 1 July 1984. The eight box launchers for Tomahawks are visible atop her superstructure. *J. Alan Elliott*

Congress. The very term *battleship* elicited hoots of derision. Senator William Proxmire jeered, "I doubt if the navy could find anything else as wasteful as reviving the battleship. The *battleship*. They have to be kidding." Senator Dale Bumpers attacked the *New Jersey* as " an expensive, highly vulnerable vessel of questionable military utility which would simply siphon off very scarce Navy manpower. . . ." He added that the *Arkansas*, a totally unarmored ship, was "perhaps" more survivable than the *New Jersey*, and concluded one of his numerous diatribes against the battleships by claiming that they were "too slow to keep up with a carrier task force." These inaccurate statements only went to show Senator Bumpers' ignorance of the subject. Senator John Chafee criticized the reactivation plans on the legitimate grounds of manpower shortage, and then added a most absurd statement: "All the Russians have to do is lob a missile into one of those battleships, and they'd knock it out of commission." A late 1970s naval intelligence study concluded that it would take at least six Styx missile hits, all in the superstructure, just to slow an *Iowa* down. The hull was invulnerable to cruise missile technology of the time.

Other critics cited the age of the ships, the uncertain costs involved, or their supposedly unfit condition. The Thimble Shoals grounding weighed against the *Missouri* again with a supposed speed restriction on her, a minor electrical fire suffered by the *Wisconsin* during her deactivation somehow became a major conflagration, and the *Iowa* was reported as stripped virtually bare to support the *New*

***Above:*** Vice President George H. W. Bush reviews the marine honor guard as he visits the battleship *Iowa* prior to the ship's recommissioning ceremony at Pascagoula, Mississippi, on 28 April 1984. The last of the four battleships would be decommissioned in 1992, during Bush's presidency. Beyond the honor guard is the No. 2 16-inch turret. *U.S. Navy*

***Opposite:*** One of the *New Jersey*'s No. 2 main-battery turret guns fires during trials after her reactivation. The ship's silhouette is familiar, but many changes have been made during her career. Particularly evident is the absence of a stern crane, long a feature of U.S. battleships. There is a large radio antenna on her bow. *Terry C. Mitchell/U.S. Navy*

The navy tug *Saco*, near the bow, and commercial tugs help move the *Missouri* in the Long Beach Naval Shipyard. The 40mm gun mounts will be removed during her rehabilitation. Note the absence of radar antennas on her masts.

*Jersey*'s 1968 recommissioning. The *Iowa* had been cannibalized, as had the *Wisconsin*, for that purpose, but all parts that had been removed had been replaced by the mid-1970s.

As a counterweight to these arguments, the Marine Corps strongly supported the ships, as expected. Vice Admiral Robert Walters, a surface warfare expert, fully endorsed the *Iowa* before the House Subcommittee on Defense on 24 June 1981. Senator John Warner's testimony as to the effectiveness of the *New Jersey* in Vietnam (see previous chapter) proved telling. Senator Jeremiah Denton pled for the ships as well. Denton, while a navy aviator, was one of the aviators shot down during the Thanh Hoa bridge strikes.

Most persuasive of all, however, was John Lehman. He fought vigorously for the ships by taking his case to both the Congress and the public. Appearing on the respected PBS program, the *MacNeil/Lehrer Report*, the secretary debunked the contention of the former head of the Central Intelligence Agency, Admiral Stansfield Turner, that the bigger the ship, the easier it was to spot. Arguments used by those against the *Iowa* were getting to be absurd and downright desperate. Lehman

explained that with modern electronic surveillance, a battleship was no more and no less visible to enemy sensors than a frigate one-tenth its tonnage. To congressmen worried about uncontrollable costs, Lehman personally pledged that the *New Jersey* could be reactivated and modernized for no more than $326 million. He summed up his assessment of the *Iowa*s by saying, "the only real disadvantage to the battleships is that there are only four of them."

Lehman and other supporters of the ships argued that battleships could fulfill a variety of tasks, as versatile as they were. By 1982 the navy had officially charged the ships with the following missions: (1) to operate offensively with carrier task forces in the highest threat areas, (2) to operate, backed by appropriate escorts, without carrier air cover in areas of lesser threat, (3) to support amphibious groups, (4) to conduct offensive operations against surface and shore targets, (5) to provide their own close-in defense against aircraft and antiship missiles, (6) to concoct naval gunfire strikes against hostile shores, (7) to control aircraft, (8) to operate and refuel all types of navy helicopters, (9) to refuel escorts, (10) to establish a naval presence, and (11) to ease the severe pressure on carrier deployment cycles and thus to improve retention of personnel. Indeed, the Congressional Budget Office (CBO) eventually decided that the *Iowa*s, modified to carry V/STOL aircraft, could replace two projected nuclear-powered carriers on the navy roster. The CBO claimed that potential savings to the government added up to $37 billion. CNO Hayward opposed the swap, and he ended with battleships plus both carriers.

Congress voted money to start work on the *New Jersey* in the spring of 1981. In a pre-activation meeting in the wardroom of the *New Jersey*, Mr. Ray Schull, the Naval Sea Systems Command program manager for the reactivation of all four *Iowa*s, stated, among other things, "By January of 1983, the Battleship *New Jersey* will be reactivated, modernized and in commission. By January of 1984, the Battleship *Iowa* will be reactivated, modernized and in commission. By January of 1985, the Battleship *Missouri* will be reactivated, modernized and in commission. And by January of 1986, the Battleship *Wisconsin* will be reactivated, modernized and in commission." There was then dead silence in the wardroom. A few seconds later, someone said, "We are going to have a real Navy again."

Since the *New Jersey* had been used in the Vietnam War, she was the most modern of the four ships still in

Back in the fleet, the *Wisconsin*, the last battleship to be recommissioned, is under way for the first time on 30 August 1988. A helicopter landing area is marked on the fantail; the derrick arm on the starboard side, forward of the No. 3 main battery turret, is part of the underway refueling rig. The *Wisconsin* has served on active duty less than any of her sister ships. *Lynn Howell/U.S. Navy*

mothballs, and the first chosen for return to active duty. The ship left Bremerton under tow for Long Beach on 27 July 1981. She had awakened from her long slumber to answer the call once again. In the months to come, the shipyard put into effect a modernization package that would be pretty much standard, as the battleships, one by one, rejoined the fleet during the remainder of the decade. The big guns remained the same, but four of the ten 5-inch 38-caliber twin mounts were removed to make way for armored box launchers capable of firing long-range Tomahawk cruise missiles. Elsewhere in the superstructure came canister-enclosed Harpoon anti-ship missiles and 20mm CIWS Vulcan/Phalanx Gatling guns for use against close-in missile threats. Electronics were improved and upgraded, particularly radars and a computerized fire control system for the new missile systems. Work on the *New Jersey* was completed under budget, as Lehman had promised. Attending her recommissioning ceremony, her fourth commissioning, on 28 December 1982 was President Reagan himself.

Soon the *New Jersey* was involved in various training operations off the West Coast. In June 1983 the *New Jersey* set off on what was intended as a three-month shakedown cruise to the western Pacific. It would be a chance to provide still more training for the crew, and also afforded a chance for the men to hit some enjoyable liberty ports as a payoff for all the time they had spent going through a vast variety of drills and preparing the ship for commissioning. In Pearl Harbor, the ship rendered honors to the crew of the *Arizona*. Then it was on to the Philippines, Singapore, and Thailand. In late July the western Pacific portion of the cruise was abruptly aborted, and the ship was ordered to take station off Central America to support the regime in El Salvador. It was a throwback to the old days of gunboat diplomacy, when a naval presence was used to aid the situation ashore. The *New Jersey* was quite a gunboat. In fact, it was that very attribute that brought on still another change of schedule. She received orders to pass through the Panama Canal into the Atlantic. Men called home to tell their fami-

The battleship *Wisconsin* fires her 16-inch guns to port in a dramatic demonstration of firepower in the Gulf of Mexico in 1988. The reactivated *Iowas* would be in action off the coasts of Lebanon and Iraq as part of the 600-ship navy. Three of the ship's Phalanx CIWS mounts are evident in this photo.
*Lynn Howell/U.S. Navy*

lies they were headed to an undisclosed location and didn't know when they would be back. The ship proceeded to the eastern Mediterranean at high speed in order to be of possible aid in defusing hostilities in Lebanon. The chief petty officers' mess was well aft in the ship, near the propellers, and the vibration at 25 knots was such that it made normal life difficult. No one could set his coffee cup down on a table because it was shaking so much.

Once off Beirut, the ship went into a period of watchful waiting. From their vantage point offshore, the crew of the *New Jersey* observed the shooting that went on night after night in the urban battleground. The ship's mission was to provide gunfire support, if needed, to protect marines who were hunkered down at the Beirut airport. In late October a terrorist killed hundreds of the marines with a suicide bomb. In December Syrians shot down U.S. Navy planes involved in an air strike. In mid-December the *New Jersey* was finally able to fire her guns. The marines were still vulnerable, so the ship had to remain on station. The deployment, originally intended for three months, had stretched to six, with no end in sight. Naval reservists were flown in to replace some of the crewmen and allow them to go on leave. In early February the ship again went into action. On 8 February she fired 288 16-inch rounds in one day against Syrian gun positions

that were shelling Beirut. It was physically exhausting work, and it also shook up the ship.

Still more time passed on station, because the *New Jersey* had to remain as long as the marines did. At the time a well-known U.S. television commercial asked how one spelled relief. The answer was "R-O-L-A-I-D-S." When that same question was posed to the men of the *New Jersey*, the answer was "I-O-W-A," because her sister ship was then undergoing reactivation back in the States. In order to provide a relief for the *New Jersey*, Secretary Lehman ordered the *Iowa*'s originally scheduled recommissioning date of early 1985 to be advanced to 30 June 1984, and then to 28 April. The ship's company and shipyard workers met this deadline by around-the-clock work. Ironically, all this effort proved to be for nothing, because the Reagan administration drastically lowered the U.S. presence in the Middle East. This included releasing the marines from their beleaguered outpost in Beirut, so the *New Jersey* was finally going to go home. After several stops in the Mediterranean, she started across the Atlantic on her long journey to her home port, Long Beach, California. When she finally arrived home on 5 May 1984, 5,000 people welcomed her. The intended three-month cruise had lasted nearly 11 months.

On 28 April 1984 Vice President George Bush was on hand when the *Iowa* was recommissioned. This marked another success for Secretary Lehman's salesmanship to Congress, and the first time more than one battleship had been in commission at the same time since the late 1950s. The men of the *Iowa* harked back to the Teddy Roosevelt era in adopting the nickname "The Big Stick" for their ship. Initially, the *Iowa* deployed to Central America and began working up the concept of the battleship battle group, an idea modeled on the aircraft carrier battle group, but intended for areas in which a lower threat was expected and thus less protection required against air and missile threats.

Two years later, on 10 May 1986, the *Missouri* was recommissioned and joined her sisters in active service. San Francisco was the setting on a brilliant sunny day with deep blue sky above for the recommissioning ceremony. Also on hand for the ceremony was Margaret Truman Daniel. In January 1944, as the daughter of then Senator Harry Truman, she had smashed a bottle of champagne across the ship's bow to christen her on the occasion of launching.

The next year, the *Missouri* went on an around-the-world shakedown cruise that included a stop in

Operating in the Persian Gulf during Operation Desert Storm in January 1991, the *Wisconsin* (foreground) and the *Missouri* simultaneously replenish from the USS *Sacramento*. Ironically, the *Sacramento*'s propulsion machinery is from the never-finished *Iowa*-class battleship *Kentucky*. The *Wisconsin*'s forward 16-inch turrets are trained to starboard, indicating that she is taking ammunition on board. *Brad Dillon/U.S. Navy*

Australia to observe the 75th anniversary of that nation's navy. Still later, she went through the Suez Canal and into the Mediterranean. She then returned to Istanbul, Turkey, where she had made quite a hit in 1946.

As the 1980s progressed, the battleship program continued to sell in Congress. The navy was aiming to build up its fleet to 600 ships, and the battleships symbolized that growing strength. On 22 October 1988 the *Wisconsin* became the fourth and final ship of her class to return to active duty. Like the *Iowa*, she was based in Norfolk and operated with the Atlantic Fleet. She also deployed to the Mediterranean. With two ships now active on each coast, it was possible to set up a regular rotation of deployments. The battleships were no longer the novelty they had been at the beginning of the decade, when it was necessary for the *New Jersey* to remain on station off Lebanon for months because no other ship was available to relieve her.

## BATTLESHIPS IN THE PERSIAN GULF

In 1987 another mission arose for the battleships in the Persian Gulf. For years, Iran and Iraq had been fighting each other, and their conflict had spilled into the gulf in the form of an increasingly dangerous war in which each side was attacking tankers containing the other's oil. The United States sought to keep the oil flowing by transferring a number of Kuwaiti tankers to the U.S. flag and manning them with American crews. U.S. Navy ships were called into action to escort the tankers while they were in the Persian Gulf, and larger ships operated in the Gulf of Oman in support of the mission, which was dubbed Operation Earnest Will. One of those ships was the *Missouri*. In October of that year she began her first support mission. As the tankers and their escorts steamed to the Strait of Hormuz at the mouth of the gulf, the *Missouri* went with them. The smaller ships could be attacked by Iranian Silkworm missiles. The battleship's guns were in position to retaliate if necessary; their ability to do so could serve as an effective deterrent to prevent the firing of the missiles. The Iranians chose not to attack the ship that night or any other. The deterrence was effective, though one of the tankers escorted by the battleship was hit by a Silkworm after she had made her way to the northern part of the Persian Gulf.

On 4 July 1986 the *Iowa*'s skipper, Captain Larry Seaquist, hosted President and Mrs. Reagan on board the ship in New York Harbor to celebrate the 100th anniversary of the Statue of Liberty. The following year, Seaquist and the *Iowa* were half a world away to take

A Tomahawk land-attack missile (TLAM) emerges from its box launcher on Missouri during Operation Desert Storm. A 20mm Phalanx CIWS mount is adjacent to the launcher. *Brad Dillon/U.S. Navy*

The TLAM has fully emerged from the Missouri's box launcher. The stub wings, tail surfaces, and air scoop have not yet deployed as the missile clears the ship. *Brad Dillon/U.S. Navy*

The TLAM transitions from its launch profile to its flight trajectory. There are Phalanx CIWS mounts on both sides of Missouri's conning tower. *Brad Dillon/U.S. Navy*

the *Missouri*'s place in support of Operation Earnest Will. Mobility is obviously an asset for warships, as the *Iowa* demonstrated. As with the *Missouri*, the convoys got through safely on the *Iowa*'s watch. The ship carried a crew of more than 1,500, and a number of them had previous battleship service, because men moved from ship to ship during the battleship renaissance. One individual had a particularly unusual pedigree in that he was a third-generation *Iowa* man. Captain Jeffrey Bolander was the commanding officer of the ship's marine detachment. His father had served as a junior naval officer in the crew during the 1950s, and had married the daughter of the ship's skipper, Captain Wayne Loud. It is a testament to the longevity of the ship that such an achievement was possible.

## TRAGEDY IN THE *IOWA'S* TURRET NO. 2
In the spring of 1989 the *Iowa* participated in a Second Fleet training exercise in the Caribbean. During the morning of 19 April the ship was steaming through light seas 330 miles northeast of Puerto Rico, taking part in a firing exercise with her 16-inch guns. The

The TLAM transitions from its launch profile to its flight trajectory. There are Phalanx CIWS mounts on both sides of Missouri's conning tower. *Brad Dillon/U.S. NavyHere* is a TLAM in flight with tail surfaces, wings, and air scoop deployed. The missile has a subsonic speed, a range in excess of 750 miles, and would have either a 1,000-pound high-explosive warhead or a payload of carbon fiber devices to disrupt electrical power stations. Other Tomahawk variants were fitted with nuclear warheads and conventional warheads with anti-ship guidance. *Brad Dillon/U.S. Navy*

commander of the Second Fleet, Vice Admiral Jerry Johnson, was on the bridge to observe along with the ship's skipper, Captain Fred Moosally. When the crew of Turret No. 1 attempted to fire the left gun, it didn't go off. It was a misfire in the primer, which had failed to set off a charge of black powder at the rear of a large powder bag. The center and right guns of the turret fired without any problem. Two further attempts to shoot the left gun resulted in two more misfires. Though the problem with Turret No. 1 was still unresolved, it was then the turn of Turret No. 2 to shoot.

Boatswain's Mate Gary Fisk operated the hoist that brought up bags of powder from the handling room below for use in the turret's center gun. Gunner's Mate Clayton Hartwig, the gun captain for that gun, was responsible for loading the powder bags into position behind the projectile. Gunner's Mate Robert Backherms, who had never before done so in a live firing, had the job of ramming the bags of powder into the breech. A hitch developed, so Gunner's Mate Richard Lawrence, who was operating the cradle over which the powder went on its way to the gun, reported by sound-powered telephone, "I have a problem here. I'm not ready yet." Shortly afterward came a second report on the telephone, this one from Senior Chief Gunner's Mate Reginald Ziegler in the turret officer's booth behind the three gun rooms. He said the left gun

The "punch" of battleships was their projectiles, like these 16-inch projectiles that were just loaded aboard the *Iowa* at the Naval Weapons Station in Yorktown, Virginia, in March 1985. They will be struck below, into the ship's forward magazines, before she goes back to sea. *Jeff Hilton/U.S. Navy*

The *Missouri* steams out of Pearl Harbor with her crew manning the rail. She was steaming from the Persian Gulf to her home port of Long Beach after seeing action in Desert Storm. She has a communications dome mounted on her second funnel. The *Missouri* and the *Wisconsin* both operated Pioneer Unmanned Aerial Vehicles (UAVs) during Desert Storm. *John Bouvia/U.S. Navy*

Artwork on a bulkhead of the *Missouri* records the ship's firing record in Desert Storm. The battleship fired 289 rounds from her 16-inch main-battery guns. Above the record is a map of Iraq and a Palm Tree symbol. *John Bouvia/U.S. Navy*

was loaded and ready, but there was still some difficulty with the center gun. Then came still another report from Lawrence, this one in an excited voice, "I'm not ready yet. I'm not ready yet."

Up on the bridge, Captain Moosally said to Admiral Johnson, "Turret two is my best crew and—." At that moment, 9:55 in the morning, an explosion erupted inside that turret. A video camera on the bridge captured the force from the center gun as its 500 pounds of powder went off. Before firing, the gun's breech should have been closed and sealed so that the force would exit through the muzzle. But in this case something set it off prematurely, so that much of the force went aft, into the gun room, where it killed the crew instantly. The high-pressure gases generated by the blast then spread into the rest of the turret and down the powder train that led up from below. The result was a fireball, and the ship's crew soon went to general quarters to deal with the fire. Fortunately, the design of the turrets was such that steel bulkheads separated the powder train from the magazine spaces nearby, which prevented the disaster from being even worse. As it was, 47 men from the crew of Turret No. 2 were killed virtually instantly.

The aftermath of the explosion was acrimonious, as the navy instituted an investigation into the cause of the blast. Rear Admiral Richard Milligan, who had commanded the *New Jersey* off Lebanon, conducted the investigation. After taking testimony from witnesses and conducting a physical examination of the scene, Milligan issued a report that concluded the explosion was the result of a suicidal act on the part of Gunner's Mate Hartwig. It argued that he had placed an explosive charge between powder lags, causing them to go off when they were rammed into the breech of the gun. The explanation was treated with skepticism by Congress and the media. The Senate Armed Services Committee held hearings into the matter and then arranged for the Sandia National Laboratories in New Mexico to conduct an independent investigation. In tests, the laboratories dropped powder bags onto a steel plate as a means of simulating the ramming of the bags in the gun's breech. Finally, one exploded. This investigation concluded that the explosion occurred as the result of high-speed over-ramming of the bags, complicated by the number of grains of powder in the layer nearest the end of the bag. The navy changed its own findings and issued an apology to the family of Gunner's Mate Hartwig.

## END OF THE COLD WAR

While these events were taking place, the Cold War was coming to an end. Mikhail Gorbachev, general secretary of the Communist Party, instituted economic and social reforms to open up the regime in the Soviet Union, and worked to develop better relations with other countries. The Berlin Wall, which had been constructed in 1961 and served as a symbol of the Cold War division of Germany, came down in November 1989. For decades, the United States had built its defense budgets on countering the Soviet Union and other threats. Now the Soviet Union was fading away. That led to pressure in 1990 for a reduction in American defense expenditures. Among the high-profile targets were, of course, the battleships. The *Iowa's* turret explosion made them more vulnerable than they might otherwise have been. In any event, battleships were manpower-intensive and expensive to operate. In the summer of 1990, after a final deployment, the *Iowa* and the *New Jersey* again began the inactivation process, and the navy announced that the other two ships would follow suit the following year. After careful inactivation, the *Iowa* was decommissioned on 26 October 1990 and the *New Jersey* on 8 September 1991. They were to be retained as mobilization assets.

On 19 April 1989, as the *Iowa* was conducting a firing exercise in the Caribbean, the center gun of her No. 2 16-inch turret exploded, killing 47 men. It was the worst battleship disaster since World War II. This photo, taken moments after the explosion, shows the center gun depressed. The tragedy was compounded by the actions of the ship's commanding officer and the board of inquiry. *U.S. Navy*

Damage-control/firefighting teams on the *Iowa* responded quickly and efficiently to the No. 2 turret disaster. The tragedy was compounded by the actions of the ship's commanding officer and the navy's board of inquiry. The damage to the turret was about to be fully repaired, with all the material needed, when the *Iowa* was again decommissioned and laid up in reserve in 1990. *U.S. Navy*

## OPERATIONS DESERT SHIELD/ DESERT STORM

But then came an event that changed plans considerably—another war. On 2 August 1990 three Iraqi army divisions invaded neighboring Kuwait in the Persian Gulf. Because of a concern that the Iraqis might move on to nearby Saudi Arabia and endanger supplies of oil from the region, the United States formed a coalition with other nations and mounted a defensive effort named Operation Desert Shield. While Iraq's President Saddam Hussein failed to consolidate his gains and move on, the U.S. Navy quickly shelved its plans to decommission the two remaining battleships, the *Wisconsin* and the *Missouri*. It also took careful precautions concerning ammunition for the battleships' 16-inch guns to ensure there would be no repeat of the *Iowa*'s turret explosion. The *Wisconsin* was the first to arrive in the Persian Gulf, and the *Missouri* joined her on 3 January 1991.

President George Bush gave Iraq an ultimatum: Either its forces leave Kuwait by 15 January, or the international coalition would take steps to liberate Kuwait by force. Operation Desert Shield, the gathering of coalition military forces in Saudi Arabia, failed to cause the Iraqis to back off. The buildup was over; now it was time for combat. Known as Operation Desert Storm, this war would be the first time that the long-range Tomahawk land-attack missiles were used in combat. On board the *Wisconsin*, in the early morning of 17 January, the countdown to war was nearing its end. The armored box launchers in the ship's superstructures were elevated, and men in the combat engagement centers handled the electronic equipment that controlled the firing. One by one, the box launchers erupted in fountains of flame, and the missiles roared off into the dark night and headed for Baghdad, Iraq's capital. Meanwhile, on the *Missouri* virtually the same series of events was occurring. Once the Tomahawks had been fired, there was no way the missiles could be recalled. Iraq was so overwhelmed by the ferocity of the attack that it was unable to launch any forces against the coalition and the battleships, especially since the coalition forces had such effective control of the surrounding airspace.

In early February the two battleships fired their 16-inch guns in anger for the first time since the Korean War. On 3 February the *Missouri* shelled enemy positions at Khafji in northern Saudi Arabia. The *Missouri* had a new piece of equipment for spotting the fall of shells ashore. In previous wars, the spotting had been done by floatplanes or helicopters launched from the battleships. These aircraft were vulnerable to enemy fire. In this war, the battleships were using unmanned remotely piloted vehicles (RPVs), which are drone aircraft fitted with television cameras and infrared sensing devices. In control rooms on board the battleships, men could measure the miss distance from a target ashore, then provide corrections to on-board plotting rooms so that subsequent rounds would be aimed to hit. The TV pictures were piped to sets throughout the giant *Missouri* and *Wisconsin*, so members of her crew were able to see the results of their ship's big runs. These RPVs proved to be unusually versatile. One night, Master Chief Fire Control-man Mark Snedeker was in the *Missouri*'s main battery plot and decided to have the RPV follow a truck that was on the Iraq–Kuwait highway. The in-frared pictures showed the truck going from place to

When the *Iowa*-class dreadnoughts were reactivated in 1980 , quite a number of major modifications were made. The most significant was the installation of 32TLAMs and 16 Harpoon antiship missiles, plus the Phalanx close-in weapon systems (CIWs) and upgraded electronics. There were proposals to remove the No. 3 main-battery turret and fit the ship to carry Harrier "jump-jet" aircraft or a battalion of marines and their helicopters in Phase II of her reactivation, but this was later canceled.

The battleship *Wisconsin* was under way again in May 2000, powered by a bevy of tugs, as the warship was being moved from the Naval Station Norfolk, Virginia, to the Norfolk Naval Shipyard. Subsequently, she was moved to Norfolk's Nauticus Museum and Learning Center as a permanent display, although officially the *Wisconsin* remained on the Naval Vessel Register. *Tina M. Ackerman/U.S. Navy*

A majestic era: the *Iowa*-class battleships were the world's last dreadnoughts in naval service. When the *Missouri* was laid up in 1992, it marked the end of an era for the U.S. Navy.

place, evidently handing out food to troops that materialized from the darkness. During the RPVs two-hour trip, Snedeker recorded the places where it had stopped and thus where enemy troops were located. Then the ship systematically fired at the positions that had been noted, no doubt causing great surprise to the victims of the nocturnal gunfire. After some time had passed, the Iraqis came to realize the connection between the appearance of the drone aircraft and the huge projectiles that followed. So, in one case a group of Iraqi soldiers actually surrendered to the *Wisconsin*'s RPV and were duly observed via television to be doing so. The RPV circled overhead, keeping watch until a helicopter with U.S. troops could be sent to take charge of the prisoners.

In late February the *Missouri* fired a shore bombardment mission at southern Kuwait to create the impression that amphibious landings were about to take place there. Actually, this was a ruse to distract the enemy from the overland force of soldiers coming to make an attack. The ground war to recapture Kuwait began on 14 February, and with it came a sustained period of shore bombardment. Early the next morning, the ship carried out another bombardment. Captain Lee Kiss, once again skipper after recovering from heart trouble, saw an orange glow that grew larger and larger as it neared the ship. He realized it was a Silkworm missile heading toward the *Missouri* and ordered members of the crew to hit the deck. Fortunately, his fears were for nought. The British

guided-missile destroyer *Gloucester* shot down the missile, though its trajectory was such that it probably would not have hit the battleship. The moment of intercept by the Sea Dart missile from the *Gloucester* appeared to those on board the *Missouri* like a huge white flashbulb going off.

After the bombardment had gone on for several days, the *Missouri* was relieved by the *Wisconsin*, which fired a number of 16-inch rounds to cover the occupation of Faylakah Island, off the shore of Kuwait. On 28 February Operation Desert Storm ended in victory for the coalition forces. The *Wisconsin* had become the last battleship ever to fire her guns in anger. Both ships delivered over 2.1 million tons of ordnance, the equivalent

of 542 A-6 Intruder bombing missions. Of the 68 targets that received battle-damage assessments, 68 percent of them were determined to have received damage ranging from heavy to totally destroyed.

Many thought that the *Missouri*'s and the *Wisconsin*'s excellent showing had saved them from the decommissioning list. The Sultan of Oman was so impressed with the ships that he offered to pay the entire bill to keep both active and fully fit for duty as long as one of them was kept in the Persian Gulf for nine months each year. However, none of this was to be. Then-Secretary of Defense Richard Cheney, when queried about keeping the battleships active, said, "We don't have the money."

The word *battleship* and the naval base at Pearl Harbor have been indelibly linked in America's memory since 7 December 1941. More than 50 years later, on 22 June 1998, what will probably be the last battleship to enter Pearl Harbor arrived, the USS *Missouri*. She has been permanently moored near the *Arizona* memorial in Battleship Row. *Kerry Baker/U.S. Navy*

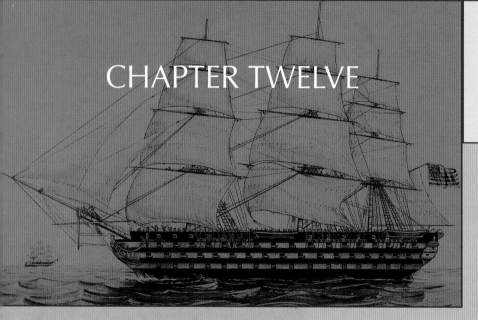

# CHAPTER TWELVE

# THE END OF AN ERA?

After the war, the *Wisconsin* and the *Missouri* were promptly decommissioned. The *Wisconsin* returned to her home port of Norfolk, Virginia. In the summer of 1991 she made a final East Coast cruise and then underwent the mothballing process. She was decommissioned on 30 September 1991. Her sister ship was granted a longer lease on life because of the upcoming 50th anniversary of the attack on Pearl Harbor. In late November the *Missouri* steamed from Long Beach to Hawaii for the celebrations.

The ship arrived off southern Oahu just before morning twilight on 5 December. As the crew looked ashore, thousands of people were watching and waving and aiming their cameras and camcorders at her to record the last official arrival of a battleship at Pearl Harbor.

After the anniversary ceremony on 7 December, which included a visit by President and Mrs. Bush, the *Missouri* headed back to California. She stopped at Seal Beach to off-load her ammunition. Though she hadn't fired her guns during the final voyage, she was armed and ready. Now it was time for the next phase. Once the magazines and projectile decks were empty, the *Missouri* pulled into Long Beach, California, on 20 December; it was the last time a battleship of any nation steamed under her own power. As she approached her berth, she was greeted by a chorus of whistles and horns from

# GLOSSARY OF TERMS

The meanings of terms frequently change, to a greater or lesser extent, with the passage of time. The terms included here are defined in the sense in which they were used during the period covered in this book. Cross-references to glossary entries appear in boldface type.

**Antiaircraft battery:** See **Battery**.

**Armor:** Two types of armor were used: Class A, also known as face-hardened armor, and Class B, also called Special Treatment Steel (STS) armor.

**Automatic gun:** Any gun using the explosive force of its firing to successively and continuously operate its mechanism, loading and firing cartridges in quick succession as long as the trigger is held back and the feed system provides ammunition. Until about 1900, this term was applied to all such guns, while continuous-firing guns operated by an external force, as with the Gatling or the Hotchkiss revolving cannon, were called machine guns. By the early 1900s, rifle-caliber guns were termed machine guns, while heavier-caliber weapons like the 1-pounder Maxim-Nordenfeldt were classed as automatic guns.

**Barbette:** A fixed cylinder of heavy armor extending from a ship's magazines up to weather-deck level and upon which a heavy-gun turret revolves. It supports the weight of the turret and protects its operating machinery and the hoists that supply ammunition to the guns.

**Battery:** A ship's guns of the same caliber (in the case of heavier guns) or used for the same general purpose. Variations exist in contemporary terminology; in this book these definitions are used throughout:

> **Offensive battery:**
>> **Main battery:** The heaviest-caliber turret guns.
>> **Intermediate battery:** Medium-caliber turret guns. In American pre-dreadnoughts these were 8-inch.
>> **Secondary battery:** Lighter-caliber guns mounted in broadside positions. In American ships these were 4- to 7-inch in size.
>
> **Defensive battery:**
>> **Torpedo-defense battery:** Light-caliber rapid-fire guns for use against torpedo boats and destroyers.
>> **Antiaircraft battery:** Guns for use against aircraft. Such guns were installed in pre-dreadnoughts during World War I.

(The unmodified term *battery* also describes a ship's entire gun armament.)

**Battlewagon:** Colloquial term for the battleship, used mainly in the United States. The term was originally applied to the horse-drawn wagons modified for military use by the Bohemian Hussite leader Jan Zizka in 1419. Used defensively at first, through drill and practice these were later used offensively, moving in formation and manned by crossbowmen and gunmen. Modern armored warships, maneuvering in formation, seem to have suggested the evolutions of ZiZka's gun wagons.

**Beam:** The breadth of a ship. Extreme beam is its maximum breadth at the outside of the hull, including armor, at or below the main deck. Waterline beam is the maximum breadth at the waterline.

**Belt:** A band, or strake, of heavy armor extending along a ship's sides for some distance above and below the waterline.

**Berth deck:** The first complete deck below the main deck, used principally for berthing, and on which no guns, or light guns only, are mounted. See **Gun deck**. From 1913 the berth deck was called the third deck.

**Bloomer:** See **Buckler**.

**Boat boom:** See **Boom**.

**Boiler room:** Also called fire room. A compartment in the mid section of a ship's hold in which the boilers are located. Pre-dreadnoughts had from two to six boiler rooms, divided by watertight bulkheads.

**Boom:** A heavy spar or derrick, attached to the base of a mast or kingpost and worked by tackle to handle boats or to lift other loads. A boat boom is pivoted to a ship's side and used as a mooring for small boats when the ship is at anchor.

**Break:** The point where an upper deck, particularly a forecastle deck, is discontinued. Fore castle-deck ships are sometimes referred to as *brokendeck ships*, or *broken-deckers*.

**Breech-loading rifle (BLR):** A single-shot gun using bagged powder charges, later designated bag gun.

**Bridge:** The high forward structure from which a ship is navigated and commanded. The term is also applied to the similar structure fitted to some battleships at the after end of their superstructure for signaling or for the use of a fleet or force commander, as well as to narrow fore-and-aft walkways connecting forward and after bridges. A battleship's bridge structure might consist of several levels, their uses indicated by their names, such as signal bridge, flag bridge, and navigation bridge. An open navigating bridge or bridge wing is also called a flying bridge.

**Buckler:** A flexible cover fastened around the gunport of a turret and to the barrel of the turret gun in such a way as to keep water from entering the port, while allowing the gun to recoil and elevate freely. Sometimes called a bloomer.

**Bureau:** A permanent segment of the organization of the Navy Department, charged with executing a specified portion of its technical or administrative business. The chief of each bureau, a naval officer, reported directly to the secretary of the navy. Bureaus mentioned in this book include the Bureaus of Construction and Repair (design, construction, and maintenance of ships); Engineering (ships' propulsion and auxiliary machinery); Ordnance (weapons, ammunition, and armor); and Navigation (personnel and ships' movements).

**Cage mast:** A type of mast formed of steel tubing interwoven to form a tapering cylindrical tower, reinforced at intervals by horizontal steel rings. Originally referred to as fire-control towers since their purpose was to support early fire-control equipment, they were also described as basket or lattice masts. Fitted to pre-dreadnoughts during refits, before World War I they were included in new-construction dreadnoughts through the *Colorado* class. For some years cage masts were a trademark of the American battleship. The only foreign ships to have them were the U.S.-built Argentine *Rivadavia* and *Moreno* and the Russian *Andrei Pervosvanni* and *Imperator Pavel I.*

**Caliber:** A naval gun's caliber is calculated by dividing the barrel length in inches by the gun's diameter in inches. The larger the caliber, the longer the gun.

**Capital ship:** A warship, such as a battleship or aircraft carrier of the largest class; a general term applied to seagoing heavy-gun warships. With the appearance of the battle cruiser in the early 1900s, *capital ship* was coined as a generic reference to both types. It was given a specific legal meaning by the Washington Treaty after World War I.

**Case gun:** See **Rapid-firing gun (RFG).**

**Casemate:** A broadside gun compartment in a ship's hull or superstructure, protected by side armor. Casemates could be individual or multiple (containing two or more guns). Later multiple casemates in U.S. battleships were subdivided by internal bulkheads of light armor. Some casemate guns had shields attached to their mounts.

**Characteristics:** Also called military characteristics. The operational qualities and physical features (dimensions, power, endurance, armament, protection, etc.) that define the force of a ship and enable it to perform its mission. The definition of characteristics was first step in the development of a ship's design.

**Citadel:** The central portion of a battleship, protected by side and deck armor, multiple bottoms, cofferdams, and coal bunkers. It contained the machinery, magazines, and other portions of the ship essential for flotation, handling, and fighting.

**Class:** One or more ships of the same type, built to the same general design. Ships of the same class, referred to as sister ships, may be built by several builders and differ in details. U.S. Navy practice has been to identify a class by the name and/or the **hull number** of the first ship of that class in hull-number order. Thus, for example, BB 13-17 would be identified as the *Virginia* class or as the BB-13 class.

**Commissioning:** The act of formally placing a man-of-war in active service, as the prospective commanding officer reads his orders and assumes command. Once an American naval ship is commissioned, it becomes an administrative entity in its own right. It has an assigned commanding officer and crew, keeps a daily deck log that is a legal record of its activities, and flies a commissioning pennant as an outward indicator of its status as an active national ship. Today, the term *commissioning* has branched out into several sub-types as a result of administrative whim.

**Compartmentation:** The subdivision of a ship's hull by means of longitudinal and transverse bulkheads. Bulkheads may be watertight or non-watertight; the latter type are not counted in calculating the ability of a ship to withstand underwater damage. Watertight bulkheads either have no openings or are provided with doors that can be closed and dogged shut to form a watertight closure.

**Conning tower:** A heavily armored structure, in or near the forward bridge of an armored warship, from which the ship was controlled in battle and its gunfire directed. Service opinion as to the value of the conning tower in action differed. Some officers felt the protection essential, while others thought the conning officer should be on an open bridge for better visibility.

**Cowl:** A right-angled curve at the top of a ventilation pipe, designed to permit entrance or exhaust of air without admitting water; the curved upper portion could be turned into the wind to scoop in fresh air, or away from the wind to draw exhaust air out. Cowl ventilators are a prominent feature of American pre-dreadnoughts and armored cruisers; some of them were eventually replaced, in some ships, by mushroom ventilators.

**Deck:** Two systems of deck nomenclature were used with pre-dreadnought battleships. The first, based on sailing-ship terminology, was used until 1913, when it was replaced by a new system, which continues in use today. Definitions of decks related to battleship construction are listed as individual entries.

**Decommissioning:** The act of placing a naval ship on inactive status. The ensign is hauled down and the crew detached; the ship is, thereafter, in custody of a navy yard or station. A ship may be decommissioned for disposal, or simply for overhaul or for inactive preservation, to be kept in reserve for an emergency.

**Director:** An instrument used to control a ship's gunfire. Directors installed in pre-dreadnoughts during their later years were simple instruments that transmitted the bearing of a surface target to a plotting room below decks, where train and elevation orders were calculated and sent to the guns. These early directors were mounted in fire-control tops on cage masts and in conning towers. *Director fire* is a method of collective fire of guns in which they are aimed under control of a director and fired from a central position.

**Displacement:** The weight of water displaced by a ship, thus, the weight of the ship. *Full-load displacement*, also called *load displacement*, is that of a ship ready for sea with crew and effects on board, full allowance of ammunition, provisions, and stores, and with coal bunkers and feed-water tanks full. *Normal displacement* was the calculated fighting weight on which hull characteristics and armor layout were based. In the battleships *Maine* and *Texas*, and in the *Indiana, Iowa, Kearsarge,* and *Maine* classes, normal displacement was based on full ammunition and stores and a coal tonnage individually determined for each class. In the *Illinois, Virginia, Connecticut,* and *Mississippi* classes, normal displacement was set at two-thirds, full capacity of coal, ammunition, and stores. *Light displacement* represents the ship with its armament and equipment, but without crew, coal, ammunition, water, or stores.

**Double bottom:** A system of hull construction in which the underwater hull is formed of two layers of plating, with a space between the two layers, or skins, subdivided into watertight compartments. The inner skin is called the *inner bottom,* the outer is the *shell.* In warships, the inner bottom was usually carried around the turn of the bilge and up to the armor belt.

**Draft:** The depth of a ship below the waterline, measured vertically to the lowest part of the ship. This term may be qualified as necessary (draft forward, draft aft, extreme or maximum draft, trial draft, etc.). *Normal draft* is the draft at normal displacement, the design draft at which hull calculations were made.

**Dreadnought:** A battleship whose offensive armament consists entirely of guns of the maximum caliber for its time. The name was given to the type by the HMS *Dreadnought,* the first such ship completed.

**Engine room:** A below-decks compartment, abaft the boiler rooms, in which a ship's propulsion engines are located.

Pre-dreadnoughts after the first *Maine* had two engine rooms, separated by a longitudinal watertight bulkhead.

**Equipment:** A term used in calculating weights, referring to shipboard items under the jurisdiction of the Bureau of Equipment. It included a ship's electrical generating plant, interior communication system, ground tackle, rigging, canvas (i.e., awnings and wind sails), and bunting.

**Extreme beam:** See **Beam**.

**Field gun:** See **Landing-force gun**.

**Fire control:** The organized procedures and systems by which a warship's gun and torpedo fire are directed. Early pre-dreadnought fire control consisted of target designation by oral command, turrets firing in local control. Around 1900, telephones were introduced, and handheld Fiske stadimeters made range estimation somewhat better. Visual battle-order receivers were installed in turrets and at broadside gun positions to indicate commence and cease firing, range and bearing of target, and type of projectile to be used. Similar instruments told handling-room crews the kind of projectile to be sent up to the guns. These battle orders came from the fire-control officer from his station in the conning tower, under the general direction of the commanding officer. During World War I, simple director installations were gradually added, first to newer pre-dreadnoughts and later to older ones. Transmitters in the fire-control tops sent the target bearing to a plotting room below decks, where it was combined with the range, as calculated by the range finder, and ship's heading and speed to plot the range and deflection orders for the guns.

**Fire-control tower:**

1. The portion of a warship's **conning tower** used as a central control station for the ship's armament under the commanding officer's direction. Where conning and fire-control towers are parts of the same structure, the whole is normally referred to as the conning tower.

2. Early term applied to the **cage mast,** designed specifically to carry elevated platforms for fire-control instruments.

**Fire room:** See **Boiler room**.

**Freeboard:** The vertical distance from a ship's waterline to the main deck. In ships with a raised forecastle, freeboard forward is measured to that deck.

**Fuel capacity:** The measured capacity of bunkers designed to carry coal for the operation of a ship. Bunker capacities were measured to the bottoms of the overhead beams.

**Full-load displacement:** Also called *load displacement*; see **Displacement**.

**Great White Fleet:** The popular nickname given by journalists to the four battleship divisions of the Atlantic Fleet during their round-the-world voyage of 1907–9. This is sometimes incorrectly thought of as an official designation. Another misconception is that the white hulls which gave the fleet its nickname were specially painted for this voyage to demonstrate peaceful intent. This was simply part of the normal peacetime color scheme for the battleships of this period.

**Ground tackle:** A collective term for a ship's anchors, anchor chains, and the gear used to handle them.

**Gun:** A metal tube from which projectiles are thrown by the explosive force of gunpowder. In military use the term is restricted to crew-served firearms. Naval guns of the late nineteenth century used brown powder, a modified form of black powder. Beginning with the *Maine*-class, battleship guns were designed for smokeless powder, and smokeless powder was issued to earlier ships. Projectiles included common (explosive); armor-piercing (originally solid shot, designed strictly for ballistic effect, later made with a small explosive charge and a delayed-action impact fuse); and target (inert, and like service projectiles in form and weight, but made of less-expensive materials). Shrapnel projectiles were manufactured for guns up to 12-inch, but by the early 1900s these projectiles were thought unsatisfactory for shore bombardment or defense against torpedo craft and came to be used only in **landingforce guns**.

**Gun deck:** A complete deck, below the main deck, on which guns were mounted in broadside positions. In battleships, the next deck below this was the **berth deck**. After 1913 the gun deck was called the second deck.

**Gun mount:** A system that supports a gun and provides for its train, elevation, recoil, and counterrecoil, interposed between the gun itself and the ship's structure. Heavy guns were carried in turret mounts, with the guns and their armored gunhouse revolving on a circular roller path. Most smaller guns used pedestal mounts, so-called from the fixed pedestal on which the gun was emplaced.

**Gun port:** The opening, in the front armor plate of a gun turret or in the side plating of hull or superstructure, through which a gun projects.

**Gun shield:** A protective armor plating mounted on or around a gun, but not completely enclosing it.

**Handling room:** A compartment at the base of an ammunition hoist, adjacent to magazines and shell rooms. Projectiles and powder charges were brought here from stowage spaces for loading into the hoists.

**Hull number:** A consecutive number assigned to each new American battleship beginning with *Indiana*, which was Battleship No. 1, although she was the third steel battle-ship constructed. This type identification was spelled out, or abbreviated (B.S. No.—), until 1920, when the letter-type symbol *BB* was introduced.

**Initial velocity:** The velocity at which a projectile is moving when it leaves the muzzle of a gun; in small arms this is called the muzzle velocity.

**Intermediate battery:** See **Battery**.

**Knot:** A measure of speed, one nautical mile (6,080.2 feet) per hour. A ship's speed is correctly measured in knots, though some earlier works occasionally use the expression knots per hour.

**Landing-force gun:** A three-inch artillery piece, issued to battleships and other warships for use by ships' landing parties as organic light artillery. Various marks of these weapons were carried by battleships from the 1890s through World War I. Earlier guns were designed for direct fire only; later ones had light shields and panoramic sights for indirect fire. Early, lower-velocity guns were officially described as field guns. Later guns, using higher-velocity ammunition, were called landing guns.

**Length between perpendiculars:** The length of a ship, measured from stem to stern at the normal (design) waterline.

**Length overall:** The length of a ship, measured from the foremost part of the stem to the aftermost part of the stern. The overall length of a pre-dreadnought was considerably more than its **length between perpendiculars**, due largely to the length of the prominent underwater ram bow.

**Light displacement:** See **Displacement**.

**Machine gun:** Originally, a continuous-fire gun operated by an external force (motor or hand crank). Later, a rifle-caliber **automatic gun**.

**Magazine:** The below-decks compartment in which a ship's powder charges are stowed. The term *magazines*, or *magazine spaces*, is also used to refer generally to a ship's ammunition stowage. See **shell room**.

**Main battery:** See **Battery**.

**Main deck:** The highest deck extending the entire length of the ship. This term was used both before and after 1913.

**Mast:** An upright pole-like structure of steel or wood, usually located on the centerline of a ship to support rigging, lookout and fire-control stations, radio antennas, light guns, and flags. Early American battleships had military masts, tubular steel masts carrying platforms called military tops for lookouts, searchlights, and light guns. These were succeeded by **cage masts**, supporting masthead fire-control stations as well as searchlights and gun-control positions; these masts were not used to mount guns. Both types of mast had lighter pole topmasts for flags and antennas.

**Metacentric height:** Abbreviated GM, this is the distance between a ship's center of gravity (G) and the metacenter (M), the latter being the point of intersection of a vertical line drawn through the center of buoyancy and the ship's vertical centerline when the ship is inclined at a small angle. Metacentric height, expressed in feet, is an indication of a ship's initial stability. Designed values of GM were compromises, suited to the type of ship in question, between stiffness and steadiness in a seaway. Excessive GM prevented accurate gunnery—of prime importance in a battleship—since this made a ship roll in a jerky fashion. RHM. Robinson, in *Naval Construction: Prepared for the Use of the Midshipmen of the United States Naval Academy* (Annapolis, Md.: The United States Naval Institute, 1906), cites ordinary values of GM for battleships at 3.5 to 5.5 feet.

**Mushroom:** A circular cover fitted to the top of a ventilation pipe, shaped somewhat like the cap of a mushroom. Air was drawn in or exhausted under the overhang of the mushroom to keep water from entering the ventilation system. Some pre-dreadnoughts had some of their earlier-pattern **cowl** ventilators replaced by mushrooms in their later years.

**Normal displacement:** See **Displacement**.

**Ordinary:** Ships were said to be *in ordinary* when they were placed out of commission and laid up in the custody of a navy yard. Unlike ships in **reserve**, ships in ordinary had no assigned crews and were maintained, as necessary, by shore personnel.

**Outfit:** A term used in calculating weights, covering such items as ships' boats, furniture, ladders, stores, potable water, and crew and effects.

**Pedestal mount:** See **Gun mount**.

**Platform:** A partial deck, located below the **protective deck** (to 1913); a partial deck, located below the lowest complete deck (1913–present).

**Port:**
1. The left-hand side of a ship.
2. An opening in hull or superstructure, as, **gun port**. Air ports (also called portholes) were usually round, though some in earlier ships were rectangular. Fitted with a hinged frame holding a thick pane of glass, they provided light and ventilation. Some air ports also had a second, metal cover for protection in heavy weather and to keep light from showing when the ship was darkened.

**Pre-dreadnought:** An early form of steel battleship, with a mixed-caliber offensive armament consisting of two to four heavy-caliber (10-inch to 13-inch) guns and a lighter-caliber secondary battery (4-inch to 7-inch). Some pre-dreadnoughts also had an intermediate battery of 8-inch guns in turrets.

**Protective deck:** A ballistic deck, of extra strength and thickness, intended for the protection of a ship's vitals. When this deck was stepped a complete deck height toward the bow or stern, the respective portions were called the middle protective deck and forward (after) protective deck. From 1913 on, these specific segments were called protective sections. When two ballistic decks were fitted, the thinner of the two was called the **splinter deck**.

**Rapid-firing gun (R.F.G.):** A single-shot gun with a quick-acting breech mechanism, using metallic powder cases. These were redesignated **case guns** before World War 1.

**Reciprocating engine:** A steam-driven piston engine, as distinguished from a turbine. Pre-dreadnoughts were all propelled by triple-expansion reciprocating engines, the earlier ones having three cylinders and the later ones four.

**Redoubt:** An armored enclosure like the one built into the *Texas* above her main armor belt to protect turret ammunition hoists. This fulfilled the purpose served by **barbettes** in later battleships. During the early design process of the *Indiana* class, the barbettes of these ships were sometimes referred to as redoubts.

**Reserve:** Ships in reserve were berthed at a navy yard in an inactive status, but remained in commission with reduced crews. This was intended to allow ships not needed for immediate operations to be laid up in such a way that they could be recalled to the fleet on short notice. See also **Ordinary**.

**Second deck:** The first complete deck below the **main deck**. Formerly **gun deck**.

**Secondary battery:** See **Battery**.

**Semiautomatic gun:** A single-shot gun in which the force of explosion of the powder charge ejects the fired cartridge case, leaving the breech open so that it closes automatically when a fresh cartridge is correctly inserted. Some rapid-firing guns were semiautomatic, while in others the breech was opened and closed by hand. One-, 3-, and 6-pounder guns were built with semiautomatic Maxim-Nordenfeldt, Hotchkiss, and Driggs-Seabury mechanisms; the later 3-inch 50-caliber single-purpose gun was also semiautomatic.

**Shell room:** A below-decks compartment in which projectiles and fixed ammunition are stowed (see also **Magazine**). Projectiles were stowed in shell rooms in pre-dreadnoughts; later, in dreadnoughts, they came to be stowed inside the **barbette** itself.

**Splinter deck:** A separate ballistic deck situated below a heavier **protective deck**. As its name indicates, it was intended to keep fragments of projectiles that exploded beneath the protective deck from reaching magazines or machinery spaces.

**Sponson:** A projection from the side of hull or superstructure, usually used to contain or support boadside gun positions.

**Strike:** To remove the name of a ship from the Navy Register, a legal formality done after a ship is lost in battle or through natural causes, or before the disposal of an old or obsolete ship. An Act of Congress dated 5 August 1882 provided that ships were to be inspected periodically by "competent boards of officers." If such a board found a ship unfit for service, they were to report this to the secretary of the navy, who, if he agreed, was to "strike the name of such vessel . . . from the Navy Register and report the same to Congress." A later form of this provision is still found in 10 U.S.C. 7304.

**Superfiring turrets:** An arrangement of gun turrets in pairs on the centerline, with one turret higher than, and firing over the top of, the other. Superfiring turrets did not appear in American battleships until the *South Carolina* class, the first U.S. dreadnoughts, which featured two superfiring pairs of 12-inch twin-gun turrets.

**Superposed turrets:** An arrangement of gun turrets in which an intermediate-battery turret is mounted directly on top of a main-battery one; the two turrets form one structure and train together, though guns in each turret elevate independently. This arrangement was used only in the U.S. battleships of the *Kearsarge* and *Virginia* classes. Compare **Superfiring** turrets.

**Superstructure deck:** A partial deck above the main or upper deck, not extending to the sides of a ship.

**Tactical diameter:** Diameter of the track turned by a ship when making a full 360-degree turn with her helm hard over. This measurement furnishes evidence of her maneuverability.

**Third deck:** A second complete deck below the **main deck**. Formerly **berth deck**.

**Torpedo-defense battery:** See **Battery**.

**Torpedo tubes:** Tubes for launching torpedoes. In American battleships these were originally mounted behind armored doors in the hull, above the waterline, and could be trained. Later tubes were fixed and carried below the waterline.

**Turning circle:** The path taken by a ship making a complete 360-degree turn with constant rudder angle. Its diameter depends on speed and amount of rudder carried; like the **tactical diameter**, it is an indicator of maneuverability.

**Turret:** The armored, rotating structure in which a warship's heavy guns are mounted. It rotates on a system of roller bearings, called the roller path. Beneath it are the ammunition hoists that supply its guns, protected by the armored **barbette**. Machinery within the turret and barbette rotates the turret, elevates and depresses the guns, and rams projectiles and powder charges into the guns. The guns can be aimed from within the turret, using telescopic sights.

**Upper deck:** A partial deck extending from the waist of a ship to the bow, above the **main deck**. The *Iowa*, *Illinois*, *Maine*, and *Mississippi* classes were built with such decks, while other American pre-dreadnoughts were flush-decked.

**Upperworks:** Superstructures or other fittings located on or above the **weather deck**. Sometimes this term applied to everything above the waterline; it also can refer to a ship's masts and bridges.

**Uptakes:** A ducting leading from boilers upward, through the decks above, to conduct combustion gases to the stacks and thence to the open air.

**Velocity:** The speed of a projectile, measured in feet per second (f.p.s) or foot-seconds (f.s.). The **initial velocity** is projectile speed at the muzzle. Terminal velocity, the projectile's speed at the time of impact, is combined with projectile weight to determine hitting power.

**Waterline:** The line of intersection between a ship's hull and the water's surface. The designer's waterline is the line at which the ship is intended to float when the design is drawn, calculated at normal displacement in American pre-dreadnoughts. This is important in the calculation of armor distribution. Other terms, such as *load waterline*, refer to the waterline at certain specified conditions of loading.

**Waterline beam:** See **Beam**.

**Weather deck:** A general term for any uncovered or exposed deck.

**Welin breech mechanism:** An interrupted-screw breech mechanism for larger-caliber bag guns in which the breechblock screw threads were arranged in three sets of stepped segments. This gave the breechblock improved holding power with a shorter length and lighter weight. Introduced to the U.S. Navy in the 12-inch guns of the *Maine* class, the Welin system's quicker action allowed heavy guns an improved rate of fire, one of the number of factors that ultimately led to the development of the all-big-gun dreadnought.

**Windsail:** A canvas tube rigged above an open hatch, with wings at the top to catch air and deflect it down the tube into the space below. These are often seen in use in pre-dreadnoughts, in which ventilation seems to have been a continuing problem.

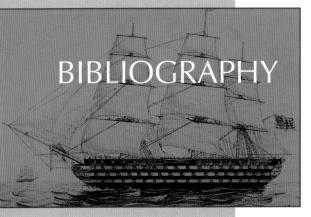

# BIBLIOGRAPHY

Babcock & Wilcox. Steam-Its Generation and Use, 37th ed. New York: Babcock & Wilcox, Co., 1963.

Breyer, Siegfried. Battleships and Battle Cruisers, 1905-1970. Garden City, N.Y.: Doubleday, 1973.

Bryan, Joseph III. Aircraft Carrier. New York: Ballantine Books, 1954.

Bureau of Naval Personnel, Principles of Naval Ordnance and Gunnery. Washington, D.C.: GPO, 1971.

Clagat, John. The United States Navy in Action. Derby, Conn.: Monarch, 1963.

Cole, Robert H. Underwater Explosions. Princeton: Princeton University Press, 1948.

Field, James A. A History of United States Naval Operations, Korea Washington, D.C.: GPO, 1962.

Frank, Richard B. Guadalcanal: The Definitive Account of the Battle. New York: Random House, 1990.

Friedman, Norman. U.S. Battleships: An Illustrated Design History. Annapolis, Md.: Naval Institute Press, 1985.

Garzke, William H. Jr., and Robert O. Dulin Jr. Battleships: United States Battleships, 1935-1992. Annapolis, Md.: Naval Institute Press, 1995.

Hovgaard, William. Structural Design of Warships. Annapolis, Md.: U.S. Naval Institute, 1940.

Jane's Fighting Ships, London: Sampson Low, 1939, 1944–45, 1950–51, 1956, 1968–69, 1981–90.

Jane's Weapon Systems, New York: Jane's Publishing, Inc., 1984–85, 1989.

Kafka, Roger, and Roy L. Pepperburg. Warships of the World. New York: Cornell Maritime Press, 1946.

Korotkin, I. M. Battle Damage to Surface Ships During World War II. Leningrad: Sudpromgiz, 1960.

Lee, Robert Edward. Victory at Guadalcanal. Navato, Calif.: Presidio Press, 1981.
Lord, Walter. Day of Infamy. New York: Harper and Row, 1957.

Manning, G. C., and T. L. Schumacher. Principles of Naval Architecture and Warship Construction. Annapolis, Md.: U.S. Naval Institute, 1928.

Morison, Samuel Eliot. History of U.S. Naval Operations in World War II, vols. 1–14. Boston, Mass.: Atlantic Little Brown, 1947–60.

Muir, Malcolm. The Iowa Class Battleship: Iowa, New Jersey, Missouri, and Wisconsin. Dorset: Blandford Press, 1987.

Muir, Malcolm. The Iowa Class Battleships. New York: Sterling Publishing Company, 1988.

Bureau of Naval Personnel. Principles of Naval Ordnance and Gunnery. Washington, D.C.: GPO, 1971.

Polmar, Norman. Aircraft Carriers. Garden City, N.J.: Doubleday & Company Inc., 1969.

Potter, E. B., and Chester W. Nimitz. Sea Power: A Naval History. Englewood Cliffs, N.J.: Prentice-Hall, 1960.

Reilly, John C. Jr. and Robert L. Scheina. American Battleships 1886-1923: Predreadnought Design and Construction. Annapolis, Md.: Naval Institute Press, 1980.

Reilly, John C. Jr. Operational Experience of Fast Battleships: World War 11, Korea, Vietnam. Washington, D.C.: Naval Historical Center, Department of the Navy, 1989.

Rowe, John S., and Samuel Loring Morison, editors. Ships and Aircraft of the U.S. Fleet, 9th ed. Annapolis, Md.: Naval Institute Press, 1972.

Rowe, John S., and Samuel Loring Morison, editors. Ships and Aircraft of the U.S. Fleet, 10th ed. Annapolis, Md.: Naval Institute Press, 1975.

Rowland, Buford, and William Boyd. U. S. Navy Bureau of Ordnance in World War II. Washington, D.C.: GPO, 1953.

Sumrall, Robert F. Iowa Class Battleships: Their Design, Weapons & Equipment. Annapolis, Md.: Naval Institute Press, 1988.

U.S. Naval Historical Center. Dictionary of American Naval Fighting Ships, vols. 1–8. Washington, D.C.: GPO, 1959–81.

Articles

Anderson, Richard M. "The Midway Class Carriers." Warship International, no. 2 (1975): 166–75.

Bell, G. R. "The New Jersey-Tomahawk Story: From Retirement to Renaissance-A New Strike Warfare Capability." Naval Engineer's Journal, vol. 96, no. 3 (May 1984).

Cary, Peter. "Death at Sea." U.S. News and World Report 108, 16 (23 April 1990): 20–30.

Egan, Robert S. "The Lexington Class Battlecruisers." Warship International 3 (1966): 4–6.

Heinl, Colonel Robert D., USMC. "Welcome to the War." U.S. Naval Institute Proceedings (March 1969): 53–62.

Holtzworth, E. C. "U.S. Navy Battle Damage Pictures from World War II." Journal of the American Society of Naval Engineers, vols. 57, no. 4, part 1, and 58, no. 1, parts 2 and 3 and no. 3, part 4.

Jurens, W. J. "The Evolution of Battleship Gunnery in the U.S. Navy, 1920-1945." Warship International, no. 3 (1991): 240–71.

Lewis, E. R. "American Battleship Main Battery Armament: The Final Generation." Warship International XIII, 4 (1976).

Muir, Dr. Malcolm Jr. "Gun Calibers and Battle Zones." Warship International, no. 1 (1980): 24–28, 35.

Nelson, Ray. "What Really Happened on the Iowa." Popular Science (December 1990): 84–87, 120–21.

Robinson, Lt. Scott A. "Handling a Battleship." U.S. Naval Institute Proceedings (April 1988): 110–13.

Serig, Howard W. Jr. "The Iowa Class: Needed Once Again." U.S. Naval Institute Proceedings (Naval Review 1982).

Sims, P. J. et al. "Design for New Jersey, Iowa, and Des Moines Modernization." Naval Engineers Journal (May 1984).

Terzibaschitsch, Stefan. "The U.S. Navy's Iowa Class Battleships: Value for Money?" International Defense Review (April 1987): 283–87.

## WEBSITES

www.history.navy.mil     Official U.S. Naval Historical Center

www.nvr.navy.mil/nvrships/s_BB.htm     Detailed data on the characteristics of battleship classes

www.maritime.org/hnsa-guide.htm     Historic naval ships listed by location, name, and type

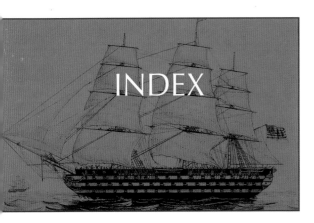

# INDEX